# Industrial Organization
## Contemporary Theory & Practice

**Third Edition**

**Lynne Pepall**
Tufts University

**Daniel J. Richards**
Tufts University

**George Norman**
Tufts University

THOMSON
SOUTH-WESTERN

Australia · Canada · Mexico · Singapore · Spain · United Kingdom · United States

**THOMSON**

**SOUTH-WESTERN**

**Industrial Organization: Contemporary Theory and Practice, 3e**
Lynne Pepall, Daniel J. Richards, and George Norman

**VP/Editorial Director:**
Jack W. Calhoun

**VP/Editor-in-Chief:**
Dave Shaut

**Acquisitions Editor:**
Michael Worls

**Developmental Editor:**
Jennifer Baker

**Marketing Manager:**
Jenny Garamy

**Senior Production Editor:**
Kara ZumBahlen

**Technology Project Editor:**
Peggy Buskey

**Senior Media Editor:**
Pam Wallace

**Senior Manufacturing Coordinator:**
Sandee Milewski

**Production House:**
Cover to Cover Publishing, Inc.

**Printer:**
Transcontinental, Louiseville Canada

**Internal Designer:**
Bethany Casey

**Cover Designer:**
Bethany Casey

**Cover Images:**
© Digital Vision

# Brief Contents

# Contents

# Part Five      Contractual Relations between Firms

# Part Seven     New Developments in Industrial Organization

## Chapter 24   Network Issues  615

## Chapter 25   Auctions and Auction Markets  637

## Answers to Practice Problems  654

## Glossary  664

## Index  668

# About the Authors

**Lynne Pepall** is Professor of Economics at Tufts University. Professor Pepall received her undergraduate degree in mathematics and economics from Trinity College, University of Toronto, and her Ph.D. in economics from Cambridge University in England. She has written numerous papers in industrial organization, appearing in the *Economic Journal, Journal of Industrial Economics, International Journal of Industrial Organization, Journal of Economics and Management Strategy, Review of Industrial Organization, Canadian Journal of Economics,* and *Economica*. She has taught industrial organization and microeconomics at both the graduate and undergraduate levels at Tufts University since 1987. She is also a former director of the University's *Writing Across the Curriculum* program, in which she worked with faculty from all disciplines to develop teaching methods based on the use of writing as a tool for thinking and learning. Professor Pepall lives in Newton, Massachusetts, with her two sons, a dog, a rabbit, and her husband, a coauthor of this book.

**Dan Richards** is Professor of Economics at Tufts University. Professor Richards received his A.B. in economics and history from Oberlin College and his Ph.D. in economics from Yale University. Professor Richards has written numerous articles in both macroeconomics and industrial organization, appearing in the *American Economic Review, Quarterly Journal of Economics, Journal of Industrial Economics, Economica,* the *B. E. Journals in Economic Analysis and Policy, Canadian Journal of Economics,* and the *Journal of Money, Credit, and Banking*. He came to Tufts in 1985 and has taught at both the graduate and undergraduate levels. He served as Director of the Graduate Program in Economics from 1989 through 1998. He has also served as a consultant to the Federal Trade Commission and, since 1996, taught Applied Economics in the Sloan Fellows Program at MIT's Sloan School of Management. Professor Richards lives in Newton, Massachusetts, with his two sons, a dog, a rabbit, and his wife, a coauthor of this book.

**George Norman** holds the William and Joyce Cummings Family Chair of Entrepreneurship and Business Economics at Tufts University. He came to Tufts in 1995 from Edinburgh University, where he had served as head of department. Prior to that, Professor Norman was the Tyler Professor of Economics at the University of Leicester (England). Professor Norman attended the University of Dundee (Scotland) where he was awarded an MA in economics with first class honors. He received his Ph.D. in economics from Cambridge University. His more than 60 published articles have appeared in such professional journals as the *American Economic Review, Review of Economic Studies, Quarterly Journal of Economics, Journal of Industrial Economics,* and *International Journal of Industrial Organization*. He is currently an Associate Editor for two journals, the *Bulletin of Economic Research* and *Regional Science and Urban Economics*. He is also on the editorial board of the *BE Journals in Economic Analysis and Policy*. In addition to *Industrial Organization: Contemporary Theory and Practice*, Professor Norman has written and edited, either alone or in collaboration with others, fifteen other books. Professor Norman has taught courses in industrial organization and microeconomic theory at both the graduate and undergraduate levels. He has also taught introductory economics, corporate strategy, international economics, and business economics. Professor Norman lives in Newbury, Massachusetts with his wife, Margaret, who is *not* a coauthor of this book.

# Preface

There are many reasons why we are happy to bring out the third edition of *Industrial Organization: Contemporary Theory and Practice*. Principal among these is that it confirms our original view that there is a real need for a text that (a) makes available to students the essentials of modern industrial organization; and (b) also educates students about the economic way of thinking in general, and in particular, the process of modeling. We remain convinced that many of the most important lessons of industrial organization start with the recognition that good analysis involves the construction of a rational argument whose implications are, at least in principle, susceptible to empirical testing. Based on the many encouraging comments that we have received to date, we think that we have made this point successfully as well as presented clearly the many insights into corporate strategy, market outcomes, and public policy that industrial organization reveals. At the same time, we have taken the opportunity of preparing this new edition to make some important changes in the text.

The biggest change is organizational. In an effort to make the book leaner while not losing intellectual muscle, we have broken down the longer chapters of the previous editions into about twice as many shorter chapters. Many commentators have urged us to do so as a means of giving students an obvious break spot at which to stop and digest what has been read. More importantly, perhaps, we hope that in going from twelve to twenty-five chapters we now make it easier for instructors to pick and choose exactly those topics that they most prefer to cover. A rough guide to the new chapter organization and its correspondence with that of the first two editions is shown below.

| 1st and 2nd Edition | 3rd Edition |
| --- | --- |
| Chapters 1 and 2 | Chapters 1–4 |
| Chapters 3 and 4 | Chapters 5–8 |
| Chapter 5 | Chapters 9–11 |
| Chapter 6 | Chapters 12–13 |
| Chapter 7 | Chapters 14–15 |
| Chapter 8 | Chapters 16–17 |
| Chapter 9 | Chapters 18–19 |
| Chapter 10 | Chapters 20–21 |
| Chapter 11 | Chapters 22–23 |
| Chapter 12 | Chapters 24–25 |

The organizational change has been accompanied by both some streamlining and the inclusion of new material. To begin with, we have updated our Reality Checkpoints so that they remain contemporary illustrations of the underlying analysis. More importantly, we have also added new information throughout the text. Sometimes, this has simply meant the inclusion of new data such as data on aggregate concentration (Chapter 3) or on Canadian versus U.S. drug prices (Chapter 5). More fundamentally, however, it has meant the introduction of new ideas. Thus, our analysis of vertical product differentiation in Chapter 7 now includes a simple model explaining the monopolist's selection and pricing of two products that differ vertically in quality. Similarly, in Chapter 11 on sequential entry and the Stackelberg model, we briefly present a model of sequential entry with learning by doing and use it to explain the evolution of the cable TV and satellite dish markets. Then, in Chapter 12, we present the basic analytics of Gibrat's Law as a way to motivate the discussion surrounding the empirical tendency toward market dominance by a few initial incumbents. In Chapter 14, we now give a more complete presentation of the role of multimarket contact in facilitating collusion and present supportive empirical evidence from the airline industry. The fear that vertical integration may permit predatory bundling is now analyzed in a simple model and applied to an analysis of the European Commission's denial of the proposed GE/Honeywell merger in Chapter 17. Chapter 18, which focuses exclusively on the issue of resale price maintenance (RPM), now adds a discussion of the use of such contracts by a manufacturer as a means of dealing with price discriminating retailers. Finally, our discussion of patent policy in Chapter 23 has significantly expanded the examination of business method patents, and our presentation of auction theory in Chapter 25 now includes a section on "almost" common value auctions.

For the most part, we have made the above additions by becoming more efficient and without cutting other topics. The two small exceptions to this are that our analysis of multiproduct cost functions has been somewhat shortened and we no longer discuss strategic trade policy. While we were reluctant to make such cuts, we believe that they do not undermine the pedagogical mission of the book. Indeed, we think that, on balance, the book's coverage has been expanded and updated so that it truly reflects the contemporary theory and practice of industrial organization.

## ACKNOWLEDGMENTS

We have noted before that authors are only one source of a text like this. Our students at Tufts and MIT/Sloan have been extremely helpful and we owe each of them a great deal of thanks. In addition, the comments of formal reviewers and many who taught from the book have been both very gratifying and very insightful. They have offered considerable encouragement regarding what we have tried to do and valuable suggestions about how we might do it better. This group includes:

Sheri Aggarwal, *University of Virginia*

Simon Anderson, *University of Virginia*

David Audretsch, *Indiana University*

Gary Biglaiser, *University of North Carolina, Chapel Hill*

Giacomo Bonanno, *University of California at Davis*

Stacey Brook, *University of Sioux Falls*

Erik Brynjolfsson, *MIT*

Henry W. Chappell, Jr., *University of South Carolina*

Yongmin Chen, *University of Colorado, Boulder*

Darlene Chisholm, *Suffolk University*

Coldwell Daniel III, *University of Memphis*

Larry DeBrock, *University of Illinois*

Greg Ellis, *University of Washington*

Glenn Ellison, *MIT*

Stephen Erfle, *Dickinson College*

Robert M. Feinberg, *American University*

Anne Harper Fender, *Gettysburg College*

Sara Ellison Fisher, *MIT*

Mark R. Frascatore, *Clarkson University*

S. N. Gajanan, *University of Pittsburgh*

Ian Gale, *Georgetown University*

Paolo Garella, *University of Bologna*

Gerald Granderson, *Miami University of Ohio*

Arne Hallam, *Iowa State University*

Mehdi Haririan, *Bloomsburg University*

Barry Haworth, *University of Louisville*

Hugo A. Hopenhayn, *University of Rochester*

Peter Huang, *University of Pennsylvania*

Stanley Kardasz, *University of Waterloo*

Phillip King, *San Francisco State University*

Robert Lawrence, *Harvard University, Kennedy School*

John Logan, *Rutgers University*

Nancy Lutz, *Virginia Polytechnic Institute*

Howard Marvel, *Ohio State University*

Catherine Matraves, *Albion College*

Eugenio J. Miravete, *University of Pennsylvania*

Jon Nelson, *Pennsylvania State University*

Craig Newmark, *North Carolina State University*

Debashis Pal, *University of Cincinnati*

Nicola Persico, *University of Pennsylvania*

Raymond Raab, *University of Minnesota*

Steve Rubb, *Bentley College*

Danny Shapiro, *Simon Fraser University*

Nicholas Schmitt, *University of Geneva*

Sarah Stafford, *William and Mary*

Jacques Thisse, *CORE*

William C. Wood, *James Madison University*

James Zinser, *Oberlin College*

Zenon Zyginont, *Reed College*

Among this group, Arne Hallam, Sheri Aggarwal, and Debashis Pal deserve special thanks for their work on successive editions of the Instructor's Manual. Here at Tufts, Lidia Bonaventura gave us, as always, outstanding secretarial assistance. The editorial staff at Thomson Business and Professional Publishing, especially Jennifer Baker and Michael Worls, provided excellent and much-needed editorial guidance. Kara ZumBahlen's production editing was Olympic.

Of course, we owe the greatest debts to our family members. Lynne and Dan wish to thank their sons, Benjamin and William, for their humor, patience, and the independence that they have increasingly shown. The fact that they also occasionally clean their rooms as well as help take care of the family dog (Churchill) and our rabbit (Peter) is more than we ever dared to hope. George would like to thank his wife Margaret for her loving support. Her patience, help, humor, and inspiration are indispensable to his work.

So, for these and countless other reasons, we affectionately dedicate this book to our loved ones.

# Part one

## Foundations

# one
## Foundations

We begin our study of industrial organization by reviewing the basic building blocks of market analysis. The first chapter provides a road map for the entire enterprise. Here, we lay out the essential aim of our analysis, namely, the investigation of firm behavior and industrial outcomes in markets that are imperfectly competitive. We describe how the framework for this analysis has evolved over time and the lens through which such markets are viewed today. The current framework is one that emphasizes strategic interaction as the most salient feature of imperfect competition and it is the framework adopted throughout this book.

In Chapter 2 we review the basic microeconomics of those markets in which strategic interaction plays little or no role. These are the polar cases of perfect competition, in which each firm is so small that its actions have no impact on any rival, and pure monopoly, in which there is only one firm and therefore no rival that the firm's actions could affect. A study of these two cases permits us to introduce the basics of market analysis, for example, demand curves, cost relationships, and so forth. It also identifies a chief concern of both economists and policy makers, namely, the exploitation of monopoly power and the efficiency or deadweight loss that this can impose on society.

Because we are concerned with the exploitation of market power, Chapter 3 focuses on how we might identify those markets in which such power is likely to be a problem. For this purpose, we need some way to measure market structure or monopoly power. Accordingly, Chapter 3 explores the nature of different measures of industrial structure and the insights and cautionary notes that attend each of these.

Finally, in Chapter 4, we turn to the supply side and, specifically, a consideration of costs. Some productive processes enjoy such extensive scale economies that in these markets monopoly is a natural outcome. Similarly, some production techniques are such that it is less costly for a firm to produce many different but related products rather than focusing on just one commodity as is assumed in the basic textbook case. We need to understand these cost concepts and their implications for firm behavior before we explore the strategic interaction of firms because that interaction will, in part, reflect the underlying cost structure.

# Industrial Organization: What, How, and Why?

## Chapter 1

A sample of business news stories from the late 1990s and early 21st century includes the following items. Coke and Pepsi found themselves in the middle of a severe price war. Large drug companies such as Bayer and Aventis were found to be paying smaller firms not to produce generic substitutes. Companies from all industries, but especially those in the finance and telecommunications sector, for example, AOL and Time-Warner, had embarked on a huge merger spree in which two or more firms consolidated into one.

Students often feel that there is a considerable gap between stories like those just described and the economics they study in formal classes. This is so despite the fact that most modern texts include real-world applications. Indeed, it is difficult to think of a contemporary economics textbook that does not include examples drawn from practical business experience. Nevertheless, it is not unusual to hear remarks such as "economics is too abstract" or "this wasn't covered in the microeconomics that I studied."

This book is very much in keeping with the modern practice of illustrating the application of the theory. However, our aim is more ambitious than just showing that formal economics can illuminate the everyday events of the business world. Instead, our goal is to develop a way of thinking about such experiences—a mental framework that permits students to understand the underlying mechanism behind such events even when those events are different from those presented explicitly in a text and long after the students have left the classroom. Of course, we cannot offer a framework for analyzing all economic phenomena. However, we can develop one that applies to a large class of events including the ones described above. That framework rests solidly on modern game theory and the class of events to which it most readily applies falls under the heading of industrial organization.

## 1.1 WHAT IS INDUSTRIAL ORGANIZATION?

What is industrial organization? For a large number of people, the answer to that question is far from clear. Indeed, on a recent, long, cross-Pacific flight the question elicited a wide set of responses when put to several of our fellow passengers. Most supposed that the field had something to do with business. A few thought it was rooted in psychology and possibly applied to human resource management. One thought it dealt with the pattern of international trade. Each of these answers has a grain of truth, yet each is also wide of the mark. While the field of industrial organization does touch on many aspects of business life, it has come to have a fairly precise meaning in economics. Simply put, industrial organization is that branch of economics that is concerned with the study of imperfect competition.

If you are reading this book, the chances are very good that you already have taken some economics classes, especially microeconomics classes. As a result, you have probably been exposed to the concept of perfect competition—that somewhat utopian vision of markets populated by numerous small firms and characterized by economic efficiency. You are also likely to have read about the most obvious counter example, a pure monopoly. The case of a market dominated by one firm alone offers a clear contrast to the ideal of perfect competition. But what happens when the truth lies, as it almost always does, between these two polar extremes? What happens where there are two, three, or several firms? How do competitive forces play out when each firm faces only a limited number of rivals? Will prices be cut to (marginal) costs, or will firms compete instead with advertising and other promotional devices? Or will research and development of new products be the major source of competitive pressure? Alternatively, how do monopolies come about? Once a monopoly establishes itself in a market, what can the monopolist do to maintain such power? Is it possible to keep new competitors from coming into the market?

Industrial organization forms the analytical core that economists use to answer these and many other related questions. Economists long ago worked out the analytics of perfect competition. What happens under the more common setting of imperfect competition—how far the outcomes in this environment lie from those of the perfectly competitive market—is much less settled. This less settled domain is the field of industrial organization.

There is a good reason why industrial organization does not yield clear and simple answers regarding what happens in imperfectly competitive markets. A market described as less than perfectly competitive leaves open a wide range of possibilities. It could be a duopoly market with only two firms, or perhaps a market dominated by one large firm competing with many very small ones. The products of the different firms may be identical, as in the case of cement manufacturers, or highly differentiated, as in the case of cosmetics. Entry by new firms may be easy, as in the restaurant business, or difficult, as in the automobile industry. This variety of possible market characterizations makes it difficult to make broad, unambiguous statements about imperfectly competitive markets.

Matters are further complicated when we consider the decisions that the management of an imperfectly competitive firm must make. Start with a simple case such as a florist setting the price for a dozen roses. Should the price rise on Valentine's Day? Should the price for a dozen roses be exactly 12 times the price of a single rose? Or should the buyer of a dozen roses get a break for buying so many? Or consider Jody Adams, a well-known chef at one of the Boston area's top restaurants, *Rialto*. Jody must choose the complete menu of entrees and appetizers that the restaurant will serve at the start of each season as well as set the price of each menu entry. In making this choice, she must evaluate the cost and availability of different ingredients. For example, what seafood and vegetables are in season and can be served fresh? Should she make available special dishes for those with food allergies? How large a wine list should she maintain? What price should she set for a la carte items and for the fixed price meal? These decisions make clear that product design decisions are certainly as important as pricing decisions. A critical design choice by Microsoft to package its Web browser, Internet Explorer, with its Windows operating system and to sell the two as one product was perhaps the primary reason for Internet Explorer's success against Netscape. It also played a major role in the government's later decision to pursue antitrust charges against Microsoft.

Price and product design choices are not the only decisions that firms make, however. Another choice concerns promotional effort. For example, in 2002 Pepsi paid over $200 million to outbid Coca-Cola for the rights to be the official soft drink of the National Football League.[1] By winning this contract, Pepsi gained the right to use the logos of the Super Bowl and other league properties in ads, signs, and banners. However, for this right it paid more than double the amount Coca-Cola had been paying. Was this a wise decision? Another decision is what markets to enter. Southwest Airlines decided in the late 1990s that the time was right to begin service to points in the Northeast. Neither Pepsi's decision nor Southwest's choice were easy ones for the management of these firms.

Firms make all sorts of decisions and few of them are easy. Industrial organization economists analyze these decisions, and this can be an even more difficult task. But as we hope this book shows, industrial organization has gained considerable insight into how markets work in between the poles of perfect competition and monopoly.

## 1.2  HOW WE STUDY INDUSTRIAL ORGANIZATION

One reason that analyzing imperfect competition is difficult is because of the interdependence that characterizes the firms' decisions in their markets. When Southwest Airlines considers offering service to Boston, it has to recognize that this will have an effect on the other airlines that serve the Boston market. These airlines may react by cutting fares, by changing their flight times, or perhaps by cutting back on Boston service so as to avoid a glut on the market. Similarly, when Pepsi thinks about putting in a high bid to become the National Football League's official soft drink, it has to wonder how Coke will respond. Will it bid even higher? If it does, should Pepsi raise its bid still further? Or what if Coke decides to respond to the advertising advantage that Pepsi gains by launching a price war in the soft drink market?

Imperfect competition then is played out against a background of interdependence, or what economists call a setting of strategic interaction. This means that determining a firm's optimal behavior is also difficult. Because the firms are likely to be aware of the interdependency of their actions, each firm will wish to take into account its rivals' response to its action. Yet that response will also depend on how the rivals think the first firm will react to their reaction, and so on. A firm in this situation needs to "put itself in its rival's shoes" to see how the rival will respond to different actions that the firm could take. The firm must do this in order to understand its best course of action. To understand the logic of strategic interaction we use game theory. Game theory provides us with the necessary framework for an analysis of settings in which the participants or players recognize that what they do affects other players and, in turn, what other players do affects them. It is for this reason that much of the recent work in industrial organization uses game theory to understand market outcomes under imperfect competition. While not all of the analysis in this book relies on game theory, a good bit of our discussion is aimed at developing and applying the logic of game theory in market settings.

Game theory permits one to analyze strategic interaction in both a clear and logically consistent manner. For this reason, it has become an indispensable tool in industrial organization. It is equally important, however, to recognize that game theory

---

1  McKay and Fatsis (2002).

and, more generally, the understanding of strategic interaction also serves a broader goal of illustrating what industrial organization is about. This perhaps is best expressed by reference to a quote from John Maynard Keynes, who wrote insightfully, "the theory of economics does not furnish a body of settled conclusions immediately applicable to policy. It is a method rather than a doctrine, an apparatus of the mind, a technique of thinking which helps its possessor to draw correct conclusions."[2] The same can be said for modern industrial organization. It is a technique of thinking. To be precise, it is a means of thinking strategically and applying the insights of such analysis to model imperfect competition.

Of course, no model is a complete description of reality. A full recounting of each aspect of the actual marketplace would be far too lengthy and unwieldy to be of much use. Instead, any market model is like a road map. It is a deliberate simplification of a very complicated terrain, omitting some features and thereby emphasizing others. The aim of the model is to capture and make transparent the essential features of the interaction among firms. In this light, to say that the real world is more complicated than the model is no criticism. Indeed, if the modeling achieves its aim of making clear the underlying structure and the principles governing the market outcome, then its abbreviated portrait of the real world is a strength. Whether this is the case depends, obviously, on what happens when the predictions of the model are tested against actual data or evidence. Even if a model fails this test, however, it does not mean that the procedure of formal modeling is invalid. All that is implied is that we need to go back to that process—back to the "drawing board"—and build a better model.

As you read this book, you will encounter a number of models, each designed to illuminate the strategic interaction in a specific market setting and the outcome that interaction will produce. We think that these models are insightful in this regard and it will be tempting to interpret this material as saying "this is what happens in an imperfectly competitive market when. . . ." However, we have no doubt that the passage of time will reveal that some of these models need improvement. So, it is better to interpret the various readings as "this is how we think about what happens in an imperfectly competitive market when. . . ." This is how we do industrial organization.

## 1.3  WHY: ANTITRUST AND INDUSTRIAL ORGANIZATION THEORY

The text of the principal U.S. antitrust statutes is given in the Appendix to this chapter. Such legislation came early to the United States with the passage of the first major antitrust law—the Sherman Act—in 1890. This predates much of the formal modeling of imperfect competition and the widespread dissemination of that modeling. However, economists had had an intuitive grasp of the potential problems of monopoly as far back as Adam Smith. In his classic, *The Wealth of Nations*, Smith (1776) had written on both collusion among ostensibly rival firms and on the raw exercise of monopoly power:

> People of the same trade seldom meet together, even for merriment or diversion, but the conversation ends in a conspiracy against the public, or in some contrivance to raise prices.

2  Keynes (1935).

> The monopolists, by keeping the market constantly understocked, by never fully supplying the effectual demand, sell their commodities much above the natural price. . . .

By the late 19th century, many Americans had become convinced that a few very large firms and trusts, such as Standard Oil and American Tobacco, had exploited their market power in just the ways Smith had forecast. There then emerged a consensus—one that has endured throughout the history of antitrust legislation—that some form of legal framework was needed to maintain competition. Moreover, while few people had any understanding of formal economics, there was a reasonably wide familiarity with the sentiments of Adam Smith.

Thus it was that popular sentiment, reinforced by shrewd Smithian insight, led to the enactment of the first U.S. antitrust law, the 1890 Sherman Act. Indeed, it is somewhat remarkable just how directly the concerns of Adam Smith are reflected in the two primary sections of the Sherman Act. Section 1 prohibits contracts, combinations, and conspiracies "in restraint of trade." Section 2 makes illegal any attempt to monopolize a market. The view that government institutions were necessary to achieve these aims was also later reflected in the Clayton and Federal Trade Commission Acts.

Initially, antitrust policy focused primarily on prosecuting and preventing collusive agreements to raise prices under the authority of Section 1. Early cases such as the *Trans-Missouri Freight Association* and the *Addyston Pipes* cases of 1897 and 1898, respectively, established this tradition, and it remains a centerpiece of antitrust policy to this day.[3] Thus, the agricultural products firm, Archer Daniels Midland, the world's two largest auction houses, Sotheby's and Christie's, and the international pharmaceutical giant, Hoffman-LaRoche, have all been successfully prosecuted for price-fixing in recent years.

Unlike the Section 1 statute, the enforcement of Section 2 on monopolization was initially limited by a rather timid and narrow judicial interpretation. Despite wide public perception that many giant firms emerging from the Industrial Revolution had abused and exploited their monopoly power, it was twelve years before one of the trusts, the Standard Oil Company of New Jersey, was prosecuted under Section 2.[4] Eventually that case came before the Supreme Court, and in 1911 the Court issued its now famous finding. It found that Standard Oil had illegally monopolized the petroleum refining industry—first, by acquiring 120 small rival companies and second, by intending to exclude rivals by means of discriminatory freight rates to restrict competitors' access to pipelines and to undercut competitors' prices. The government then won additional cases against a number of trusts, most notably the Tobacco Trust,[5] immediately on the heels of Standard Oil.

An important feature of the *Standard Oil* and *Tobacco* cases is that, unlike the price-fixing cases, the Court's decision left unclear precisely what actions were illegal. In particular, the court established a "rule of reason" framework for monopolization cases that permitted the courts to examine not only whether monopolization of an industry had occurred but, if so, what the market context surrounding the formation

---

3　*United States v. Trans-Missouri Freight Association* 166 U.S. 290 (1897) and *United States v. Addyston Pipe & Steel Co.*, 85 F. 271 (6 Cir. 1898).

4　*Standard Oil Co. of New Jersey v. United States*, 221 U.S. 1 (1911). See also Posner (1970).

5　*United States v. American Tobacco Co.*, U.S. 221 U.S. 106 (1911).

of that monopoly was and the business practices used to achieve it. Only if this additional inquiry found that the firm had had intent to monopolize or had exploited its monopoly power was there a true violation. Practically speaking, this meant that there was a lot of ambiguity in exactly what actions would be found to be violations.

The success against Standard Oil encouraged the belief that antitrust legislation was useful. Simultaneously, those who feared that the rule of reason argument might weaken further antitrust enforcement were motivated to pursue additional reforms so that Section 2 of the Sherman Act would not become a "paper-toothed tiger."[6] The result was that in 1914, the Clayton Act was passed to cover practices that were not included in the Sherman Act. In particular, the Clayton Act was designed to prevent monopoly "in its incipiency" by making explicitly illegal a number of business practices used by John D. Rockefeller, Standard Oil's chairman. Thus, Section 3 of the Clayton Act limits the use of tying and exclusive contracts that oblige a purchaser of a manufacturer's product not to deal in products of competitors. Section 4 allows private parties injured by violations of both the Sherman Act and the Clayton Act the right to sue violators for treble damages. Section 5 eases the burden of proof required by plaintiffs for proving such violations. It permits an adverse judgment in a case brought by the Department of Justice to be used as prima facie evidence against the defendant.[7] Section 7, which was later amended in the 1950s, was passed to prevent anticompetitive mergers.

The Federal Trade Commission Act was also passed in 1914. It established an administrative agency, the Federal Trade Commission, endowed with powers of investigation and adjudication to handle Clayton Act violations. As later amended it also outlaws "unfair methods of competition" and "unfair and deceptive acts or practices." This gave antitrust policy a second arm of law enforcement in addition to that provided by the Justice Department.

Yet the flurry of legal activity and institution building that came on the heels of the Standard Oil case did not succeed in establishing a clear and unchanging course in antitrust policy. Instead, that policy has gone through a number of cycles over the last 90 years. The first of these turns came with the *U.S. Steel* case of 1920. In that case, the Court made clear that in its view "the law does not make mere size an offense or the existence of unexerted power an offense—it does not compel competition nor require all that is possible."[8] As a result, the Court found U.S. Steel—a firm that had through a series of mergers grown to control over 70 percent of U.S. steel-making capacity—innocent of any antitrust violations. This case ushered in a 25-year period in which enforcement of Section 2 (but not Section 1) was rather lenient.

The *U.S. Steel* decision had a major impact on both the steel industry and the U.S. legal framework. But perhaps its most important consequence was an intellectual one. For the conclusion to which many analysts were led by the 1920 decision was that without a good economic road map by which to understand imperfect competition, the making of antitrust policy was a difficult proposition at best. It was this need that motivated the first consistent studies in the field that we now call industrial organization.

---

6   Berki (1966), p. ix.
7   Treble damages are not awarded in a private suit if the Department of Justice case is settled by a consent decree. Not surprisingly, this creates a strong incentive for firms to settle an antitrust case amicably through a consent decree. Otherwise, they face the possibility of losing a court battle and subsequently being sued privately for treble damages.
8   *United States v. United States Steel Corporation*, 251 U.S. 417 (1920).

Economists such as Edward Chamberlin (1933) and Edward Mason (1939), both at Harvard, led the way. In their view the microeconomics of the time offered little guidance either to policy makers or the legal system as to what evidence might be useful in determining the likely outcome that a market would produce. Thus, the Supreme Court's dismissal of the government charges of monopolization in the *U.S. Steel* case was based on an argument that no exploitation of monopoly power or intent to monopolize had been shown. Only U.S. Steel's large market share had been documented and, "*the law does not make mere size an offense*" [emphasis added]. Unless there was good reason to believe that a large market share offered strong evidence of abusive monopolization, or until there was a coherent argument that identified other observable characteristics that in turn implied illegal behavior, the court's decision had a fair bit of justification.

More generally, these scholars realized that any informed legal judgment would require some practical way to determine from observable evidence whether the industry in question was closer to perfect competition or closer to monopoly. Accordingly, they viewed the highest priority of industrial economics to be the determination of whether and how one could infer illegal behavior from either firm size or other structural features. It was precisely to provide this policy guide that the field of industrial organization began to emerge. The very name of the field—industrial organization—dates from this time.

Early work was focused on the key question: how is the production of the industry organized? How is the market structured? How many firms are there and how large are they relative to each other? Are there clear barriers to entry? It was recognized from the outset, however, that answering these questions would not be enough to provide the legal framework needed by legislators and courts to determine whether the antitrust laws had been violated. Achieving this goal required not only that an industry's structural features be revealed but that clear links between structure and market outcomes also be identified. That is, industrial economists needed to obtain data on prices, profits, and market structure, and then use these data to identify statistical relationships between various market structures on the one hand, and industrial performance on the other.

This agenda was explicitly announced by Edward Mason, who in 1939 wrote, "The problem, as I see it, is to reduce the voluminous data concerning industrial organization to some sort of order through a classification of market structures. Differences in market structure are ultimately explicable in terms of technological factors. The economic problem, however, is to explain, through an examination of the structure of markets and the organization of firms, differences in competitive practices including price, production and investment policies."[9] In sum, the early industrial organization economists viewed their goal as one of establishing links between market structure on the one hand, and the conduct of firms in the market on the other. In turn, that conduct would determine the likely outcome or performance of the market in terms of economic efficiency or general social welfare. For this reason, this early approach is typically referred to as the structure-conduct-performance, or SCP, approach. Presumably, if the outcome for a particular industry given its structure was sufficiently bad, legal action was justified either to alter the conduct that structure would otherwise generate or, if necessary, to change the structure itself.

---

9  Mason (1939), 61–74.

The basic principle behind the SCP paradigm was that perfect competition and monopoly are usefully viewed as opposite ends of a spectrum of market structures along which all markets lie. One natural measure of market structure is the degree of concentration, or the percentage of market output produced by the largest firms in that industry. Accordingly, the practice of industrial economics at that time became one of (1) accurately describing the structure of different markets and (2) deriving empirical relations between structures and outcomes in terms of price–cost margins, innovative efforts, and other performance measures. It thus became an effort to examine statistically the broad hypotheses on market structure and performance implied by the SCP paradigm. Here, structure was often identified with the degree of concentration or the percentage of total market output accounted for by the few largest firms. Finding a road map for policy was interpreted to mean providing numerical answers to questions such as how much would a bit more concentration or a bit higher entry barriers raise price above cost.

In pursuit of the SCP quest, the 1940s and 1950s witnessed a vast array of studies attempting to document and to measure the link between industrial performance, say profitability, and an industry's structural features, such as concentration. Moreover, the results of these studies also seemed fairly clear. The bulk of the research established a positive link between a measure of industrial concentration and industry profit and a similarly positive link between advertising and profitability. The first stylized fact gave support to the view that an industry in which there was more than one but still just a few large firms was indeed close to the monopoly pole. The second finding was interpreted as evidence that firms used advertising to build customer loyalty and, thus, to deter other firms from entering the market, so that the incumbent firms could enjoy monopoly power and profit. Together, these and other findings and interpretations increasingly seemed to suggest that perhaps a firm's "mere size" *could* suggest a legal offense if it is sufficiently large.

At about the same time, policy makers seemed to be growing increasingly concerned about the market dominance of large firms. In 1936, Congress passed the Robinson-Patman Act to prohibit price discrimination that allegedly lessened competition. Price discrimination occurs when different buyers of the same good pay a different unit price. In the 1930s, there was increasing awareness and concern that large firms, such as the big supermarket chains, were able to buy from wholesalers in bulk and therefore at a lower unit price than smaller stores, such as street-corner outlets. In turn, this led Congress to fear that large firms could use this buying advantage to drive out their smaller competitors who could not buy in such large quantities.[10]

As the United States moved into the 1940s both intellectual and legislative developments expressed a heightened concern that large firms in concentrated industries constituted a serious threat to economic welfare. The practical question then became whether these developments would also herald a similar change towards a more activist role by the judiciary. The 1945 *Alcoa* case suggested that indeed such a change had occurred.

---

10 In many respects, the Robinson-Patman Act is an odd companion to the antitrust laws because it is primarily designed to limit price-cutting. The view among its supporters was and continues to be that the law is meant to prevent predatory price reductions aimed at preserving monopoly power by driving rivals out of business. Note that passage of the Robinson-Patman Act did not weaken the Court's stance against collusive price agreements as demonstrated in its decisive rejection of such an agreement in *United States v. Socony-Vacuum Oil Co., Inc.*, 310 U.S. 150 (1940).

### 1.3.1 The "New" Sherman Act and the Dominance of Structure-Based Analysis

Alcoa was by far the largest aluminum manufacturer in North America. It had been prosecuted for antitrust violations a number of times prior to the 1945 case. In fact, so many Supreme Court justices in 1945 had had previous litigation experience with Alcoa that they could not participate in this proceeding, with the result that the Supreme Court lacked a quorum to hear the case. Hence, the 1945 decision was issued by a special panel of three circuit court judges. In a key decision, this panel overturned the finding of innocence by the lower district court and found Alcoa guilty of monopolization under Section 2 of the Sherman Act. An explicit consideration for the Court was the issue of size.[11] Alcoa's market share depended critically on how one measured the market, and much attention was given to this issue. Ultimately, the Court defined Alcoa's relevant market to be primary aluminum ingot production. Using this definition, the Court found that Alcoa supplied 90 percent of the market. In effect, this decision was a major policy validation of the SCP approach.

Other cases also reflecting a newly found concern over market domination by large firms soon followed. In 1946, the Supreme Court found the big three tobacco companies, American Tobacco, Ligget & Myers, and R. J. Reynolds, which controlled 75 percent of domestic cigarette production, guilty of monopolization.[12] A number of similar cases continued over the next 20 years, culminating with such well-known ones as the 1962 *Brown Shoe* case and the 1964 case against the Grinnell Corporation. All of these cases gave increasing weight to market structure as an indictment of proposed or past actions.[13] The (in)famous price discrimination case of *Utah Pie* (1967) may also be read as an indictment of any outcome in which a few large firms come to dominate the market.[14] In that case, the Court viewed the pricing strategies of the bigger nationwide companies to be evidence of predatory intent against a smaller firm primarily because the shares of the larger firms grew over a four-year period. In short, the period from 1945 into the late 1960s reflects the growing dominance of the SCP framework as the major intellectual influence on antitrust policy.[15]

### 1.3.2 The Tide Changes Again— the Chicago School and Beyond

Matters began to change in the 1970s. In part, this reflected a growing awareness among academic scholars that the SCP paradigm had important failings. One of these was that the vast array of empirical findings that the SCP scholars had amassed was actually subject to different interpretations. For example, consider the frequent finding that firms with large market shares tend to earn greater profit. This could be taken as a verification of the basic SCP view that the larger a firm's market share, the greater the monopoly power and the higher its profit. However, a more benign interpretation of this evidence is also possible. It could be that the most efficient, or the

---

11　*United States v. Aluminum Co. of America (ALCOA)*, 148 F.2d 416 (2 Cir. 1945).
12　*American Tobacco Company v. United States*, 328 U.S. 781 (1946).
13　*Brown Shoe Co. v. United States*, 370 U.S. 294 (1962) and *United States v. Grinnell Corp.*, 236 F.Supp. 244 (D.R.I. 1964).
14　*Utah Pie Co. v. Continental Baking Co., et al.*, 386 U.S. 685 (1967).
15　For an excellent survey of antitrust history see Mueller (1996).

lowest cost, firms gain a large share of the market, so that both their large size and their healthy profit are simply reflections of their superior technology or talent.[16]

What was really unsatisfactory about the SCP approach, however, was that in considering its middle link—firm conduct—little or no attention was paid to strategic interaction. Something of an exception in this regard was the work of Joseph Bain (1956), a former student of Edward Mason, who made many important contributions to the field. A skilled scholar with a keen eye for actual business practice, Bain was among the first to realize that an industry could not be completely defined by its concentration. In particular, Bain understood that beyond the configuration of the industry's existing firms one also needed to understand the ability of new firms to enter the market. Even a highly concentrated industry might be forced to price competitively if there were new firms ready and able to enter and compete away the profit of any firm pricing above the competitive level. This was an important insight. Indeed, this idea played a central role in the "contestability" theory developed much later by Baumol, Panzar, and Willig (1982). (It also was an important part of Microsoft's defense. The software company argued that its monopoly power was substantially constrained by the potential for makers of personal computers and other companies to enter the operating systems market.) Unfortunately, what went unappreciated for some time was that Bain's point was really a two-edged sword. The ease with which new firms can enter is at least partially the result of actions taken by the firms already in the market. That is, incumbent firms can pursue strategic actions meant to influence the entry decisions of potential rivals. Within the SCP paradigm one could not address this issue.

The weaknesses in the SCP paradigm were accompanied by a discomfort that many felt concerning the more aggressive antitrust enforcements mentioned above. In the *Brown Shoe* case, for example, the Court disallowed the merger of two firms (Brown and Kinney) even though they only controlled about 5 percent of the national market (though a greater percent of individual local markets). Similarly, the *Utah Pie* case seemed to be a decision that did more to protect a specific competitor (Utah Pie) than to protect competitive forces.

The rising concern over flaws in both the SCP approach and the public policy it had fostered made possible a counter movement led by lawyers and economists from the Chicago School such as Richard Posner, Robert Bork, and Sam Peltzman. These and other scholars began to point out that many of the practices that the courts had been viewing as harmful to competition and economic welfare could, when viewed through the lens of corporate strategy and tactics, be seen as actually improving economic efficiency and bringing benefits to consumers. This work initially focused on the vertical relationships between a firm and its suppliers or between a firm and its distributors. Many such contracts include restrictions such as those that grant franchisees exclusive territories, or that require distributors to sell at some minimum price. Chicago School economists argued that there were good economic reasons for these practices and that these restrictions actually brought benefits to consumers.

---

16 As we will show later, this is a standard result in a Cournot model in which costs differ across firms. Specifically, if $P$ is market price, $\eta$ is the market demand elasticity at that price, and $c_i$ and $m_i$ are the unit cost and market share, respectively, of the $i$th firm, then in such a model, it must be the case that: $\dfrac{P - c_i}{P} = \dfrac{m_i}{\eta}$ . Lower cost firms will have larger market shares, larger profit margins, and larger total profit.

Gradually, these arguments were successful and many practices that previously had been found per se or outright illegal the court now began to review for their "reasonability" on a case-by-case method.[17]

The Chicago School influence on vertical relationships soon spread to all of antitrust policy. In 1974, the U.S. Supreme Court rejected the government's efforts to block a large merger in a case involving the General Dynamics Corporation.[18] Many mergers that previously would have been prevented soon followed, justified on both grounds of cost savings and the potential for new entrants to constrain any attempt by the newly merged firm to exercise monopoly power. The government also lost several key cases accusing large firms such as Kodak and IBM of monopolization in violation of the Sherman Act. In addition, the precedent of the Utah Pie case was firmly rejected during these subsequent years. It became increasingly clear—most notably in the case involving a complaint by Zenith Corporation charging that seven Japanese television manufacturers had attempted to drive out competitors—that in the courts' view, efforts to eliminate rivals by pricing below cost rarely made sense.[19]

The Chicago School's contributions are difficult to overestimate and its legal influence is felt to this day. These scholars were right to point out the need to examine the logic and reasonability of a firm's conduct. However, they were hampered by the fact that, as of that time, no language or medium in which to view such strategic behavior on a consistent basis had been developed. Yet such a framework was emerging. Building on the work of Von Neumann and Morgenstern (1944) and Nash (1951), economists such as Thomas Schelling and, in more formal work, Richard Selten and John Harsanyi (both of whom later shared the Nobel Prize with Nash in 1995), made a number of crucial contributions that permitted game theory to become the language for modeling strategic interaction. As we noted earlier, the past two decades have witnessed the rapid spread of game theory to analyze virtually every aspect of imperfect competition. As a result, the field of industrial organization has again been transformed and now reflects, at least in part, what some call a post-Chicago view and what others simply refer to as the "new IO."[20] Moreover, modern empirical work, e.g., Bresnahan (1989) has documented the validity of the new IO approach.

We have already noted that there is much to be said for pursuing a game theoretic understanding of the strategic interaction of firms. What is important at this point is simply to note that game theory has enriched our understanding of firm behavior considerably. Moreover, as game theoretic analysis has spread through modern industrial organization its insights have, to some extent, led to a diminishment of the Chicago School's impact. However, it would be wrong to identify the advent of game theory models and the associated new post-Chicago approach as a total rejection of the Chicago School's work. For example, the Merger Guidelines adopted jointly by the Federal Trade Commission and the Justice Department have deep roots in the Cournot–Nash game theoretic model that we describe more fully in Chapter 15. While these guidelines are far from permissive, they inevitably allow for many more

---

17 See *Continental T.V. Inc. v. GTE Sylvania, Inc.*, 433 U.S. 36 (1977) and, more recently, *State Oil v. Khan, et al.*, 522 U.S. 3 (1997).

18 *United States v. General Dynamics Corp.*, 415 U.S. (1974).

19 *Matsuhita Electric Industrial Co. v. Zenith Radio Corp.*, 475 U.S. 574 (1986).

20 Schmalensee (1988) provides a survey of the "new IO" that is still quite relevant. A good brief view of the influence of game theory on modern antitrust policy can be found in Kovacic and Shapiro (2000). Kwoka and White (1999) offer an excellent and modern discussion of selected antitrust cases.

# Reality **Checkpoint**

## Show Time!

The nature of strategic interaction is illustrated by the behavior of Hollywood studios during the ten week summer season. This is a crucial time in Hollywood because the studios release a number of major "blockbusters." A blockbuster hit is worth hundreds of millions of dollars in box office and merchandising revenues, as well as subsequent sales of home videos and sequel films, but these revenues are very dependent on the success of the opening weekend. A bad opening can quickly lead to a financial flop and, given the staggering costs of these films, one or two flops can bankrupt a studio. The exact opening date for each film is therefore a critical strategic variable to which studio executives devote considerable attention in the hope that their movie can be the only one to open on a key weekend. This is not always possible. In the summer of 2002, for example, more than ten big films were released—including *Spiderman, Star Wars II—Attack of the Clones, Men In Black II, Minority Report, Windtalkers, The Road to Perdition, Insomnia,* and *The Rookie,* among others. The opening dates of several films were reset many times, but conflicts were unavoidable. Thus, *Minority Report* and *The Bourne Identity* both opened on the same weekend, leaving the producers of each film wondering whether they would be able to establish an audience.

**Sources:** D. Chisholm, "The War of Attrition and Optimal Timing of Motion-Picture Releases." Working Paper, Economics Department, Suffolk University (2003), and R. Lyman, "A Box-Office Photo Finish, and Questions of Methodology." *The New York Times*, June 25, 2002, p. E1.

mergers than would ever have legally occurred in the "New Sherman Act" years of the 1950s and 1960s.

The major point of this brief review is that since its inception, through the emergence of the SCP approach to the present, post-Chicago view, a major motivation for industrial economists has been the concerns of antitrust policy. We want to know how firms get market power, what happens when they do, and what the role of public policy might be in helping imperfectly competitive markets achieve outcomes close to the competitive ideal. This is why we study industrial organization.

## SUMMARY

Industrial organization is the study of imperfect competition. Industrial economists are interested in markets that one actually encounters in the real world. However, these real-world markets come in many shapes and flavors. For example, some are comprised of a few large firms; some have one large firm and many smaller ones. In some, the products are greatly differentiated, in some they are nearly identical. Some firms compete largely by trying to keep prices as low as possible. In other markets, advertising and other forms of nonprice competition dominate. Given this variety, developing a careful understanding of each case has meant that, over time, industrial organization has become a field rich with practical insights regarding real business behavior and public policy. This book is all about these developments.

Firms in imperfectly competitive industries need to make strategic decisions—that is, decisions that will have significant effects on other participants in the market, be they rival firms, suppliers, or distributors. As a result, making any such choice must inevitably involve an explicit consideration of how these other players in the game will react. Examples of such strategic choice variables include price, product design, decisions to expand capacity, and whether to invest heavily in research and development of a new product or process.

This book presents the modern analysis of market situations involving such strategic interaction—one that is rooted in noncooperative game theory. We use this analysis to examine such issues as why there are so many varieties of cereals, or how firms maintain a price-fixing agreement, or how advertising and product innovation affect the nature of competition. Our interest is more than just determining the profit-maximizing strategies that firms in a particular market context should adopt. As economists we are interested in the market outcomes that result when firms adopt such strategies, and whether those outcomes are close to those of the competitive ideal. If not, we then need to ask whether and how public policy can improve matters.

We survey the main findings of modern industrial economics. More importantly, we show how the modeling approach employed by economists can enhance our understanding of actual market events. We draw on both statistical evidence and particular cases to document the insights provided by modern scholarship—insights that may then be used to evaluate and design public policy. Our hope is to convey the value of such research and the gains from learning "to think like an economist." More generally, we hope to demonstrate the vitality and relevance of industrial organization, both in theory and in practice.

## PROBLEMS

1. List three markets that you think are imperfectly competitive. Explain your reasoning.

2. Explain why a perfectly competitive market does not reflect a setting of strategic interaction.

3. The Appendix to this chapter lists the current, major antitrust laws of the United States Review Sections 2 and 7 of the Clayton Act. What potential threats to competition do these sections address?

4. Suppose that sophisticated statistical research provides clear evidence that, all else equal, worker productivity increases as industrial concentration increases. How would you interpret this finding?

5. Why do you think that the U.S. courts have consistently disallowed any form of price-fixing agreement among different firms but have been more tolerant of market dominance by one firm?

## REFERENCES

Bain, Joseph. 1956. *Barriers to New Competition*. Cambridge: Harvard University Press.

Baumol, W. J., J. C. Panzar, and R. D. Willig. 1982. *Contestable Markets and the Theory of Market Structure*. New York: Harcourt Brace Jovanovich.

Berki, Sylvester, ed. 1996. *Antitrust Policy: Economics and Law*. Boston: D.C. Heath and Company.

Bresnahan, T. 1989. "Studies of Individual Industries." In R. Schmalensee and R. Willig, eds., *Handbook of Industrial Organization*, Vol. 1. Amsterdam: North-Holland.

Chamberlin, E. H. 1933. *The Theory of Monopolistic Competition*. Cambridge: Harvard University Press.

Keynes, J. M. 1935. *The General Theory of Employment, Interest and Money*. New York: Harcourt Brace and Company.

Kovacic, W. E., and C. Shapiro. 2000. "Antitrust Policy: A Century of Legal and Economic Thinking." *Journal of Economic Perspectives*, 14:43–60.

Kwoka, J. E., and L. J. White. 1999. *The Antitrust Revolution: Economics, Competition, and Policy*. 3rd Edition. Oxford: Oxford University Press.

Mason, E. S., 1939. "Price and Production Policies of Large Scale Enterprise." *American Economic Review* 29:61–74.

McKay, B., and S. Fatsis. 2002. "Pepsi Scores One on Coke, Gaining Sponsorship Rights to the NFL." *The Wall Street Journal* (March 29): B5.

Mueller, Dennis C. 1996. "Lessons from the United State's Antitrust History." *International Journal of Industrial Organization* 14:415–45.

Nash, J. 1951. "Noncooperative Games." *Annals of Mathematics* 54:286–95.

Posner, Richard. 1970. "A Statistical Study of Antitrust Enforcement." *Journal of Law and Economics* 13 (October).

Schmalensee, R. 1988. "Industrial Economics: An Overview." *Economic Journal* 98:643–81.

Smith, Adam. 1776. *An Inquiry into the Nature and Causes of the Wealth of Nations*. New York: Bantam Classics, 2003.

Von Neumann, J., and O. Morgenstern. 1944. *Theory of Games and Economic Behavior*. Princeton: Princeton University Press.

# Appendix | Excerpts from Key Antitrust Statutes

## THE SHERMAN ACT

Sec. 1 Every contract, combination in the form of trust or otherwise, or conspiracy, in restraint of trade or commerce among the several States, or with foreign nations, is declared to be illegal. Every person who shall make any contract or engage in any combination or conspiracy hereby declared to be illegal shall be deemed guilty of a felony, and, on conviction thereof, shall be punished by fine not exceeding $10,000,000,000 if a corporation, or, if any other person, $350,000, or by imprisonment not exceeding three years, or by both said punishments, in the discretion of the court.

Sec. 2. Every person who shall monopolize, or attempt to monopolize, or combine or conspire with any other person or persons, to monopolize any part of the trade or commerce among the several States, or with foreign nations, shall be deemed guilty of a felony, and, on conviction thereof, shall be punished by fine not exceeding $10,000,000,000 if a corporation, or, if any other person, $350,000, or by imprisonment not exceeding three years, or by both said punishments, in the discretion of the court.

## THE CLAYTON ACT, INCLUDING KEY AMENDMENTS OF THE ROBINSON-PATMAN ACT AND CELLER-KEFAUVER ACT

### Sec. 2

(a) Price; selection of customers

It shall be unlawful for any person engaged in commerce, in the course of such commerce, either directly or indirectly, to discriminate in price between different purchasers of commodities of like grade and quality, where either or any of the purchases involved in such discrimination are in commerce, where such commodities are sold for use, consumption, or resale within the United States or any Territory thereof or the District of Columbia or any insular possession or other place under the jurisdiction of the United States, and where the effect of such discrimination may be substantially to lessen competition or tend to create a monopoly in any line of commerce, or to injure, destroy, or prevent competition with any person who either grants or knowingly receives the benefit of such discrimination, or with customers of either of them: Provided, That nothing herein contained shall prevent differentials which make only due allowance for differences in the cost of manufacture, sale, or delivery resulting from the differing methods or quantities in which such commodities are to such purchasers sold or delivered: Provided, however, That the Federal Trade Commission may, after due investigation and hearing to all interested parties, fix and establish quantity limits, and revise the same as it finds necessary, as to particular commodities or classes of commodities, where it finds that available purchasers in greater quantities are so few as to render differentials on account thereof unjustly discriminatory or promotive of monopoly in any line of commerce; and the foregoing shall then not be construed to permit differentials based on differences in quantities greater than those so fixed and established: And provided further, That nothing herein contained shall prevent persons engaged in selling goods, wares, or merchandise in commerce from selecting their own customers in bona fide transactions and not in restraint of trade: And provided further, That nothing herein contained shall prevent price changes from time to time where in response to changing conditions affecting the market for or the marketability of the goods concerned, such as but not limited to actual or imminent deterioration of perishable goods, obsolescence of seasonal goods, distress sales under court process, or sales in good faith in discontinuance of business in the goods concerned.

**(b)** Burden of rebutting prima-facie case of discrimination

Upon proof being made, at any hearing on a complaint under this section, that there has been discrimination in price or services or facilities furnished, the burden of rebutting the prima-facie case thus made by showing justification shall be upon the person charged with a violation of this section, and unless justification shall be affirmatively shown, the Commission is authorized to issue an order terminating the discrimination: Provided, however, That nothing herein contained shall prevent a seller rebutting the prima-facie case thus made by showing that his lower price or the furnishing of services or facilities to any purchaser or purchasers was made in good faith to meet an equally low price of a competitor, or the services or facilities furnished by a competitor.

**(c)** Payment or acceptance of commission, brokerage, or other compensation

It shall be unlawful for any person engaged in commerce, in the course of such commerce, to pay or grant, or to receive or accept, anything of value as a commission, brokerage, or other compensation, or any allowance or discount in lieu thereof, except for services rendered in connection with the sale or purchase of goods, wares, or merchandise, either to the other party to such transaction or to an agent, representative, or other intermediary therein where such intermediary is acting in fact for or in behalf, or is subject to the direct or indirect control, of any party to such transaction other than the person by whom such compensation is so granted or paid.

**(d)** Payment for services or facilities for processing or sale

It shall be unlawful for any person engaged in commerce to pay or contract for the payment of anything of value to or for the benefit of a customer of such person in the course of such commerce as compensation or in consideration for any services or facilities furnished by or through such customer in connection with the processing, handling, sale, or offering for sale of any products or commodities manufactured, sold, or offered for sale by such person, unless such payment or consideration is available on proportionally equal terms to all other customers competing in the distribution of such products or commodities.

(e) Furnishing services or facilities for processing, handling, etc.

It shall be unlawful for any person to discriminate in favor of one purchaser against another purchaser or purchasers of a commodity bought for resale, with or without processing, by contracting to furnish or furnishing, or by contributing to the furnishing of, any services or facilities connected with the processing, handling, sale, or offering for sale of such commodity so purchased upon terms not accorded to all purchasers on proportionally equal terms.

(f) Knowingly inducing or receiving discriminatory price

It shall be unlawful for any person engaged in commerce, in the course of such commerce, to be a party to, or assist in, any transaction of sale, or contract to sell, which discriminates to his knowledge against competitors of the purchaser, in that, any discount, rebate, allowance, or advertising service charge is granted to the purchaser over and above any discount, rebate, allowance, or advertising service charge available at the time of such transaction to said competitors in respect of a sale of goods of like grade, quality, and quantity; to sell, or contract to sell, goods in any part of the United States at prices lower than those exacted by said person elsewhere in the United States for the purpose of destroying competition, or eliminating a competitor in such part of the United States; or, to sell, or contract to sell, goods at unreasonably low prices for the purpose of destroying competition or eliminating a competitor.

## Sec. 3.

Sale, etc., on agreement not to use goods of competitor

It shall be unlawful for any person engaged in commerce, in the course of such commerce, to lease or make a sale or contract for sale of goods, wares, merchandise, machinery, supplies, or other commodities, whether patented or unpatented, for use, consumption, or resale within the United States or any Territory thereof or the District of Columbia or any insular possession or other place under the jurisdiction of the United States, or fix a price charged therefor, or discount from, or rebate upon, such price, on the condition, agreement, or understanding that the lessee or purchaser thereof shall not use or deal in the goods, wares, merchandise, machinery, supplies, or other commodity of a competitor or competitors of the lessor seller, where the effect of such lease, sale, or contract for sale or such condition, agreement, or understanding may be to substantially lessen competition or tend to create a monopoly in any line of commerce.

## Sec. 7.

No person engaged in commerce or in any activity affecting commerce shall acquire, directly or indirectly, the whole or any part of the stock or other share capital and no person subject to the jurisdiction of the Federal Trade Commission shall acquire the whole or any part of the assets of another person engaged also in commerce or in any activity affecting commerce, where in any line of commerce or in any activity affecting commerce in any section of the country, the effect of such acquisition may be substantially to lessen competition, or to tend to create a monopoly.

# Chapter 2

## Some Basic Microeconomic Tools

The principal antitrust statutes in America were put into place over 100 years ago. At that time economic theory offered little understanding of market outcomes beyond Adam Smith's original and intuitive insights. The formal modeling of those insights and of the benefits of competition versus monopoly were just then beginning to appear in professional academic works, most notably, Alfred Marshall's *Principles of Economics, Vol. 1* (1890). A similarly rigorous understanding of what happens in that gray area between competition and monopoly would take time to be developed and then more time to be worked into the economics curriculum. Yet a sound understanding of the perfectly competitive and pure monopolized markets is, even by itself, quite insightful. Indeed, these models continue to provide useful starting points for interpreting much of what one reads about in the daily business press. Such analysis also reveals the primary intellectual force behind public policies designed to limit monopoly power. For all these reasons, we undertake in this chapter a review of the basic analysis of perfect competition and monopoly.

## 2.1 COMPETITION VERSUS MONOPOLY: THE POLES OF MARKET PERFORMANCE

Our review of the perfect competition and monopoly models is necessarily brief. We focus on firm profit-maximizing behavior and the resultant market outcome that such behavior implies. We take as given the derivation of an aggregate consumer demand for the product that defines the market of interest. This market demand curve describes the relationship between how much money consumers are willing to pay per unit of the good and the aggregate quantity of the good consumed. Figure 2-1 shows an example of a market demand curve—more specifically, a linear market demand curve described by the equation $P = A - BQ$. When we write the demand curve in this fashion with price on the left-hand side it is often called an inverse demand curve.[1] The vertical intercept $A$ is the maximum willingness to pay, or maximum reservation demand price that any consumer is willing to pay to have this good. At market prices greater than $A$, no one in this market wants to buy the product. As the market price falls below $A$, demand for the product increases. For example, if the market price of the good is $P_1$, then consumers will desire to purchase a quantity $Q_1$ of the good. The price $P_1$ is the most any consumer would pay to consume the last or the $Q_1$th unit of the good. The price $P_1$ describes consumer willingness to pay at the margin.

---

1   The reason for this terminology is that traditionally in microeconomics, we think of quantity demanded as being the dependent variable, (left-hand side of the equation) and price, the independent variable, (right-hand side of the equation). However, when firms choose quantities and price adjusts to clear the market, it is preferable to put market price on the left-hand side, hence, the inverse demand function.

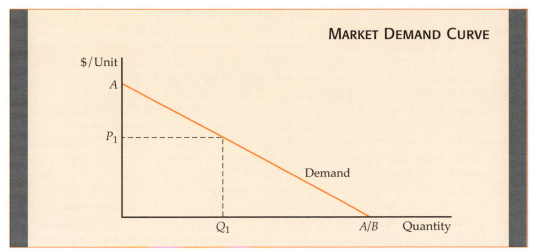

**MARKET DEMAND CURVE**

FIGURE

**2-1**

The price $P_1$ is the marginal consumer valuation of an additional unit of output when current output is $Q_1$.

When we draw a demand curve we are implicitly thinking of some period of time over which the good is consumed. For example, we may want to look at consumer demand for the product per week, per quarter, or per year. Similarly, when we talk about firms producing the good, we want to consider their corresponding weekly, quarterly, or annual production of the good. The temporal period over which we define consumer demand and firm production typically affects what production technologies are available to the firm for producing the good. The shorter the time period, the fewer options a firm has for acquiring or hiring more inputs for use in production. Following the tradition in microeconomics, we distinguish between two time periods: short-run and long-run production periods. The short run is a sufficiently short time period for the industry so that no new production facilities—no new plant and equipment—can be brought on line. In the short run, neither the number of firms nor the fixed capital at each firm can be changed. By contrast, the long run is a production period sufficiently long so that firms can build new production facilities to meet market demand.

For either the short-run or the long-run scenario we are interested in determining when a market is in equilibrium. By this we mean finding an outcome at which the market is "at rest." A useful interpretation of a market equilibrium is a situation in which no consumer and no firm in the market has an incentive to change its decision on how much to buy or how much to sell. Again, the precise meaning of this definition may vary depending on whether we consider the short run or the long run. In either case, the essential element is the same. Equilibrium requires that no one has an incentive to change his or her trading decision.

## 2.1.1 Perfect Competition

A perfectly competitive firm is a "price taker." The price of its product is not something that the perfectly competitive firm chooses. Instead, that price is determined by the interaction of all the firms and consumers in the market for this good, and it is beyond the influence of any one of the perfectly competitive firms. This characterization only makes sense if each firm's potential supply of the product is "small" relative to market demand for the product. If a firm's supply of a good is large relative to the market, we would expect that the firm could influence the price at which the good is sold. An example of a "small" firm would be a wheat farmer in Kansas or a broker on the New York Stock Exchange trading IBM stock. Each is so small that any imaginable change in behavior leaves the prices of wheat and IBM stock, respectively, unchanged.

Because a perfectly competitive firm cannot influence the market price at which the good trades, the firm perceives that it can sell as much or as little as it wants to at that price. If the firm cannot sell as much as it wants to at the market price, then the implication is that selling more would require a fall in the price. But this would imply that the firm has some power over the market price, and such a firm would not be a perfect competitor. If the firm can affect the price received by other producers, its actions have consequences that will affect other participants, leading the firm to engage in strategic behavior. Hence, to be a true perfectly competitive firm, the firm's output must not alter the going price. This feature may be illustrated in a graph by drawing the demand curve for a perfectly competitive firm as a horizontal line at the current market price. Thus, a perfectly competitive firm faces a horizontal demand curve even though the demand curve confronting the industry is downward sloping.[2]

Like all firms, the perfectly competitive ones will each choose that output level which maximizes their individual profit. Profit is defined as the difference between the firm's revenue and its total costs. Revenue is just the product of the industry price, $P$, and the firm's output, $q$. The firm's total cost is assumed to rise with the level of the firm's production according to some function, $C(q)$. It is important to understand that the firm's costs include the amount necessary to pay the owners of the firm's capital (that is, its stockholders) a normal or competitive return. This is a way of saying that input costs are properly measured as opportunity costs. That is, each input must be paid at least what that input could earn in its next best alternative employment. This is true for the capital employed by the firm as much as for the labor and raw materials that the firm uses. Generally speaking, the opportunity cost for the firm's capital is measured as the rate of return that that capital could earn if invested in other industries. This cost is then included in our measure of total cost, $C(q)$. In other words, the concept of profit we are using is that of economic profit, and it reflects net revenue above that necessary to pay all of the firm's inputs at least what they could earn in alternative employment. The reason that this is important is because it makes clear that the fact that a firm earns no economic profit does not mean that its stockholders go away empty-handed. It simply means that those stockholders do not earn more than a normal return on their investment.

A necessary condition for such profit maximization is that the firm chooses an output level such that the revenue received for the last unit produced, or the marginal revenue, just equals the cost incurred to produce that last unit, or the marginal cost. This requirement for profit maximization holds for the output choice of any firm, be

---

2  This follows from the definition of a perfect competitor. One may wonder how each firm can face a horizontal demand curve while industry demand is downward sloped. The answer is that the demand curve facing the industry reflects the summation of the individual demand presented by each consumer—not the individual demand facing each firm.

it a perfectly competitive firm or a monopoly. Since total revenue depends on the amount produced, marginal revenue is also dependent on $q$ as described by the marginal revenue function, $MR(q)$. Because the perfectly competitive firm can sell as much as it likes at the going market price, each additional unit of output produced and sold generates additional revenue exactly equal to the current market price. That is, the marginal revenue function for a competitive firm is just $MR(q) = P$. Similarly, because total cost is a function of total output, $q$, so the marginal cost function also depends on $q$, according to the function $MC(q)$. This function describes the cost incurred by the firm for each successive unit of output produced.

Diagrams like those shown in Figure 2-2. are often used to illustrate the standard textbook model of the perfectly competitive firm and the perfectly competitive market in which the firm sells. For any market to be in equilibrium, the first order condition mentioned earlier must hold for each firm. For a competitive market, this means that for each firm the price received for a unit of output exactly equals the cost of producing that output at the margin. This condition is illustrated in Figure 2-2. The initial industry demand curve is $D_1$ and the market price is $P_C$. A firm producing output $q_C$ incurs a marginal cost of production $MC(q_C)$ just equal to that price. Producing one more unit would incur an extra cost, as indicated by the marginal cost curve $MC$, that exceeds the price at which that unit would sell. Conversely, producing less than $q_C$ would save less in cost than it would sacrifice in revenue. When the firm produces $q_C$ and sells it at market price $P_C$, it is maximizing profit. It therefore has no incentive to change its choice of output. Hence, in a competitive equilibrium each firm must produce at a point where its marginal cost is just equal to the price.

Total market supply, $Q_C$, is the sum of each firm's output, $q_C$. Hence, with each firm maximizing profit, the condition $P = MC(q_C)$ will hold for each firm. If demand

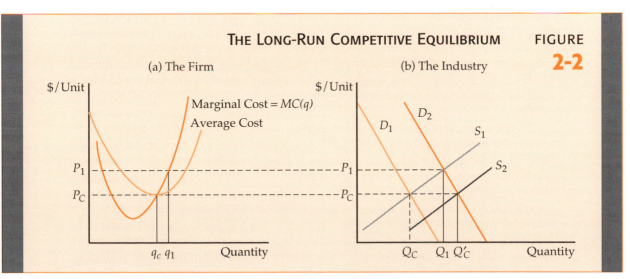

**THE LONG-RUN COMPETITIVE EQUILIBRIUM**    FIGURE **2-2**

(a) The Firm    (b) The Industry

Price $P_1$ is consistent with a short-run equilibrium in which each firm produces at a point where its marginal cost is equal to $P_1$. However, at $P_1$, price exceeds average cost and each firm earns a positive economic profit. This will encourage the entry of new firms, shifting out the supply curve as shown in (b). The long-run competitive equilibrium occurs at price $P_C$, with each firm producing at $q_C$, an output level at which the price equals both average and marginal cost.

rises and the market price increases to $P_1$, each firm would revise its production decision and increase output to $q_1$, where $P_1 = MC(q_1)$. This would increase total production to $Q_1$. Indeed, because the firms' production decisions are governed by costs at the margin, the marginal cost curve of each firm provides the basis for determining the total supply at any given market price. As the price rises, we work out how each firm adjusts its profit-maximizing output by moving up its marginal cost function to a point where $P = MC(q)$ at this new price. Then we add all the firms' revised decisions and compute the total output now supplied. Repeating this exercise for various prices reveals the industry supply function indicating the total output supplied at any given market price. It is illustrated by the curve $S_1$ in Figure 2-2(b). Since for each firm price is equal to its marginal cost, it must be the case that at each point on the supply function for every firm the incremental cost of the last unit produced is just equal to that price.

As a simple linear example [so that the marginal cost curve will be straight instead of curved as shown in Figure 2-2(a)] let the marginal cost of each firm be $MC(q) = 4q + 8$. Given a market price $P$, the optimal output for any one competitive firm is then a choice of $q$ such that $4q + 8 = P$, implying that the optimal output choice for each such firm satisfies

$$q = \frac{P}{4} - 2 .$$

If there are 80 such firms, total industry production, $Q$, at price $P$ is 80 times $q$ or $Q^S = 20P - 160$. Solving for $P$ writes the resultant supply curve in the form implied by Figure 2-2 in which price appears on the vertical axis. This yields $P = 0.05Q^S + 8$. At a price of 8, each firm will produce zero output. Industry output will also be zero. A rise in $P$ to 12 would induce each firm to raise its output to 1 unit, increasing industry output to 80. A further rise to $P = 16$ would lead every firm to raise its output to 2 units, implying a total supply of 160. We could repeat this exercise many times over, each time choosing a different price. Plotting the industry output against each such price yields the industry supply curve. The important point to understand is that the derivation of that supply curve reflects the underlying first order condition that each competitive firm choose a profit-maximizing level of output such that $P = MC(q)$.

In the example shown in Figure 2-2, the market initially clears at the price, $P_C$. Given the demand curve $D_1$, this equilibrium is consistent with the first order condition that each firm produce an output such that $P = MC(q)$. The requirement that each firm produces where marginal cost equals the market price is almost all that is required for a competitive equilibrium in the short run.[3] However, there is an additional condition that must be met in order for this to be a long-run competitive equilibrium. This second requirement is that each firm earns zero economic profit. This requirement is also met in the initial equilibrium illustrated in Figure 2-2(a). At output $q_C$, each firm is just covering its cost of production, including the cost of hiring capital as well as labor and other inputs. In other words, a competitive equilibrium, in the long run, requires that firms just "break even" in the sense that they do not

---

3   We say *almost* because there may be a distinction between average variable cost and marginal cost. No production will occur at all in the short run if the firm cannot produce at a level that will cover its average variable cost.

earn any economic profit—revenue that exceeds the amount required to attract the productive inputs into the industry. This requirement can be stated differently. In the long run, the price of the good must just equal the average or per-unit cost of producing the good. Again, both this zero profit condition and the further requirement that price equal marginal cost are satisfied in the initial equilibrium in which the industry demand curve is $D_1$ and the price is $P_C$.

If demand suddenly shifted to the level shown by the demand curve $D_2$, the existing industry firms would respond by increasing output. In so doing, these firms would maximize profit by again satisfying the first requirement that they each produce where $P = MC(q)$. This would lead each firm to expand its production from $q_C$ to $q_1$, thereby raising the market output to $Q_1$. However, this short-run response does not satisfy the zero profit condition required for a long-run competitive equilibrium. At price $P_1$, the market price equals each firm's marginal cost but exceeds each firm's average cost. Hence, each firm earns a positive economic profit of $P_1 - AC(q_1)$ on each of the $q_1$ units it sells.

Such profit would either induce new firms to enter the industry or existing firms to expand production. This expansion would shift the industry supply curve outward until the equilibrium price again just covered average cost. Figure 2-2(b) illustrates this by the shift in the industry supply curve to $S_2$. As drawn, this shift reestablishes the initial price, $P_C$. Each firm now produces output $q_C$ at which the industry price equals both the firm's marginal cost and its average cost. Of course, total industry output is now higher at $Q_C$. While each firm is producing the output $q_C$, there are now more firms. The point is that the market equilibrium requirement that there be no incentive for a firm to change its production plan must, in the long run, include the notion that no firm wishes either to leave or to enter the market.

## Practice Problem 2.1

Assume that the manufacturing of cellular phones is a perfectly competitive industry. The market demand for cellular phones is described by a linear demand function $Q^D = \dfrac{6000 - 50P}{9}$. The inverse demand can easily be worked out, therefore, to be $P = 120 - \dfrac{9}{50} Q^D$. Assume that there are fifty manufacturers of cellular phones and that each manufacturer has the same production costs. These are described by long-run total and marginal cost functions of $TC(q) = 100 + q^2 + 10q$, and $MC(q) = 2q + 10$.

a. Show that a firm in this industry maximizes profit by producing $q = \dfrac{P - 10}{2}$.
b. Derive the industry supply curve and show that it is $Q^S = 25P - 250$.
c. Find the market price and aggregate quantity traded in equilibrium.
d. How much output does each firm produce? Show that each firm earns zero profit in equilibrium.

### 2.1.2 Monopoly

Under perfect competition each firm's production of the good is small relative to the market. Now suppose that all these sellers become consolidated into one firm that is, by definition, a monopoly. Figure 2-3 describes what happens if the competitive

FIGURE

2-3

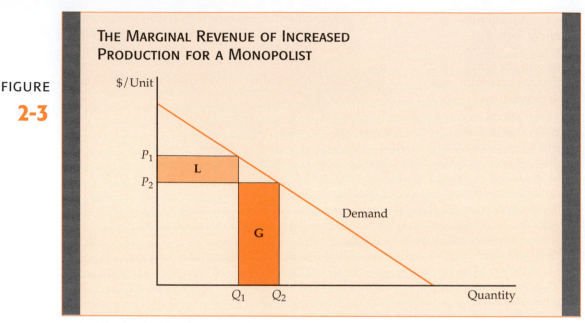

### THE MARGINAL REVENUE OF INCREASED PRODUCTION FOR A MONOPOLIST

A reduction in price from $P_1$ to $P_2$ causes a gain in revenues given by area G and a loss in revenues given by area L. The net change in revenue is G − L.

market suddenly became monopolized and production now takes place in a single firm. Since the monopolist is the only supplier of the good, the monopoly is likely to be large relative to market demand. Specifically, the monopolist's demand curve is identical with the market demand curve. In complete contrast to the competitive firm, the monopoly firm is able to influence the price it receives for selling in this market. The monopolist's output decision will play a decisive role in determining the market-clearing price.

Since the monopolist's demand curve slopes downward, any increased production by the monopolist will lead to a price reduction. For instance, a monopolist who is selling $Q_1$ units at price $P_1$ will find that increasing production to $Q_2$ units will cause the market price to fall from $P_1$ to $P_2$. The good news is that by selling the additional output, the monopolist earns additional revenue. However, the bad news is that the original $Q_1$ units no longer sell at a price of $P_1$. These units now sell for only $P_2$ each. The monopolist cannot charge the first $Q_1$ customers a high price and the next $Q_2 − Q_1$ customers a lower price for the same commodity. The fact that such price discrimination is ruled out means that the monopolist must sell at the market-clearing price to all consumers and, therefore, that increases in the monopolist's total output will reduce the equilibrium market price.

Accordingly, the monopolist firm is very different from the competitive firm in which every additional unit sold will bring in revenue equal to the current market price. Instead, the monopolist knows that every unit sold will bring in a net revenue less than the existing price. Because the additional output can be sold only if the price declines, the marginal revenue from an additional unit sold is not market price but something less.

Marginal revenue for a monopolist is illustrated by the shaded areas G and L in Figure 2-3. These areas reflect the two forces affecting the monopolist's revenue when the monopolist increases output from $Q_1$ to $Q_2$, and thereby causes the price to fall from $P_1$ to $P_2$. Area G is equal to the new price $P_2$ times the rise in output, $Q_2 - Q_1$. It is the revenue gain that comes from selling more units. Area L equals the amount by which the price falls, $P_1 - P_2$, times the original output level, $Q_1$. This reflects the revenue lost on the initial $Q_1$ units as a result of cutting the price to $P_2$. The net change in the monopolist's revenue is the difference between the gain and the loss, or G − L.

We can be more precise about this. Let $\Delta Q = Q_2 - Q_1$ and $\Delta P = P_1 - P_2$. The slope of the monopolist's (inverse) demand curve may then be expressed $\dfrac{\Delta P}{\Delta Q}$. If we describe this demand curve (which is also the market demand curve) as a linear relation, $P = A - BQ$, that slope is also equal to the term $-B$, that is, $\dfrac{\Delta P}{\Delta Q} = -B$. In other words an increase in output, $\Delta Q$,[4] leads to a decline in price, $\Delta P$, equal to $-B\Delta Q$. Since total revenue is defined as price per unit times the number of units sold, we can write total revenue as a function of the firm's output decision, or $R(Q) = P(Q)Q = (A - BQ)Q$. As shown in Figure 2-3, the change in revenue, $\Delta R(Q)$, due to the increase in output, $\Delta Q$, is the sum of two effects. The first is the revenue gain, $P_2\Delta Q$. The second is the revenue loss, $Q_1\Delta P$. Hence,

$$\Delta R(Q) = P_2\Delta Q - Q_1\Delta P = (A - BQ_2)\Delta Q - Q_1(B\Delta Q), \qquad \textbf{(2.1)}$$

where we have used the demand curve to substitute $A - BQ_2$ for $P_2$ in the first term on the right-hand side. $MR(Q)$ is measured on a per-unit basis. Hence, we must divide the change in revenue shown in equation (2.1) by the change in output, $\Delta Q$, to obtain marginal revenue. This yields

$$MR(Q) = \frac{\Delta R(Q)}{\Delta Q} = A - BQ_2 - BQ_1 \approx A - 2BQ. \qquad \textbf{(2.2)}$$

Here we have used the approximation $B(Q_1 + Q_2) \approx 2BQ$. This will be legitimate so long as we are talking about small changes in output, that is, so long as $Q_2$ is fairly close to $Q_1$.

Equation (2.2)—sometimes referred to as the "twice as steep rule"—is quite important, and we will make frequent reference to it throughout the text. It not only illustrates that the monopolist's marginal revenue is less than the current price but, for the case of linear demand, it also demonstrates the precise relationship between price and marginal revenue. The equation for the monopolist's marginal revenue function, $MR(Q) = A - 2BQ$, has the same price intercept $A$ as the monopolist's demand curve but twice the slope, $-2B$ versus just $-B$. In other words, when the market demand curve is linear, the marginal revenue curve facing a monopolist starts from the same vertical intercept as that demand curve, but is everywhere twice as steeply sloped. The monopolist's marginal revenue curve must then lie everywhere below the inverse demand curve.

---

4    Under perfect competition, firm output is different from industry output, so we use a lowercase $q$ to refer to firm output and an uppercase $Q$ for industry output. Under monopoly, firm output is the market output and so we use $Q$ to describe both.

**Derivation Checkpoint**

### The Calculus of Competition

For those familiar with calculus, the competitive firm's problem may be solved by first writing the firm's profit $\pi$ as a function of its output $q$, or as $\pi(q)$ which, in turn, is defined as the difference between revenue $R(q)$ and cost $C(q)$. If we then recognize that revenue is just price times quantity or $R(q) = Pq$, we obtain:

$$\pi(q) = R(q) - C(q) = Pq - C(q).$$

Maximization of the firm's profit requires taking the derivative of the profit function with respect to $q$ and setting it equal to zero. Recall, however, that the competitive firm takes $P$ as given. Hence, the standard maximization procedure yields:

$$\frac{d\pi}{dq} = P - C'(q) = 0.$$

Since $C'(q)$ is the change in cost as one more unit is produced it is precisely what we call marginal cost. Hence the profit-maximizing condition for the competitive firm is to choose the output $q$ for which marginal cost $C'(q)$ equals price $P$.

For the monopoly firm, its output is the same as industry output $Q$ and so its price

is not given but instead declines with output as the firm moves down its demand curve. That is, the monopolist does not face a single price but instead a price function $P(Q)$, which is really the inverse demand curve. Hence, the monopolist's profit maximization problem is to choose output $Q$ so as to maximize:

$$\pi(Q) = R(Q) - C(Q) = P(Q)Q - C(Q).$$

Again, standard maximization techniques yield:

$$\frac{d\pi}{dQ} = P(Q) + QP'(Q) - C'(Q) = 0.$$

The sum, $P(Q) + QP'(Q)$, is the firm's marginal revenue. The monopolist will maximize profit by producing where marginal cost equals marginal revenue. Note that for a linear demand curve the form is $P(Q) = A - BQ$ and $P'(Q) = -B$. Hence, in this case, the firm's marginal revenue is $A - BQ - BQ$, or $A - 2BQ$. The monopolist's marginal revenue curve has the same intercept as its demand curve but is twice as steeply sloped.

In Figure 2-4, we show both the market demand curve and the corresponding marginal revenue curve facing the monopolist. Again profit maximization requires that a firm produce up to the point where the marginal revenue associated with the last unit of output just covers the marginal cost of producing that unit. This is true for the monopoly firm as well as for the perfectly competitive firm. The key and important difference here is that for the monopoly firm, marginal revenue is less than price. For the monopoly firm, the profit-maximizing rule of marginal revenue equal to marginal cost, or $MR(Q) = MC(Q)$, holds at the output $Q_M$. The profit-maximizing monopolist produces at this level and sells each unit at the price $P_M$. Observe that, at this output level, the revenue received from selling the last unit of output, $MR$, is less than the

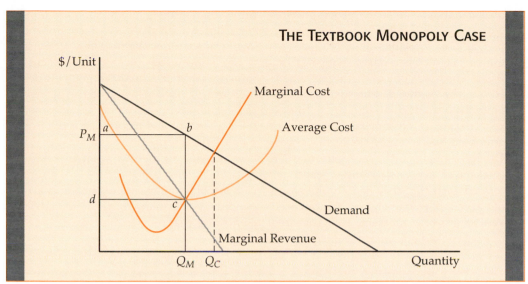

**THE TEXTBOOK MONOPOLY CASE**

FIGURE

**2-4**

The monopolist maximizes profit by choosing the output $Q_M$ at which marginal revenue equals marginal cost. The price at which this output can be sold is identified from the demand curve as $P_M$, which is greater than marginal cost. Profit is *abcd*. The competitive industry chooses the output $Q_C$ at which price equals marginal cost.

price at which that output is sold, $MR(Q_M) < P_M$. It is this fact that leads the monopolist to produce an output below the (short-run) equilibrium output of a competitive industry, $Q_C$.

We have also drawn the average cost function for the monopoly firm in Figure 2-4. The per-unit or average cost of producing the output level $Q_M$, described on the average cost curve by $AC(Q_M)$, is less than the price $P_M$ at which the monopolist sells the good. This means, of course, that total revenue exceeds total cost, and the monopolist earns a positive economic profit. The monopoly profit is shown as the rectangle *abcd*. Furthermore, because the monopolist is the only firm in this market, and because we assume that no other firm can enter and supply this good, this market outcome is a long-run equilibrium. Each consumer buys as much as he or she wants to at price $P_M$ and, given these cost conditions, the monopolist has no incentive to sell more or to sell less. Even in the long run, there is no tendency under monopoly for the market price to equal the unit cost of production.

 **Reality Checkpoint**

### Hung Up on Monopoly

It is not always easy to find examples of the classic monopoly behavior described in economics textbooks. However, Tyco International's control of the plastic hangar market may come close. Retail firms such as J. C. Penney and Kmart use only plastic hangers to display their clothing goods. At the end of the 1990s, Tyco used mergers and acquisitions of rival firms to gain control of 70 to 80 percent of the market for plastic hangars. In many geographic regions, Tyco became the only plastic hangar firm available. In 1996, Tyco acquired a Michigan-based hangar firm, Batts, which was one of the largest suppliers to the Midwest. Immediately thereafter, Tyco tried to raise prices by 10 percent to all its customers. Some clients grumbled but accepted the higher prices. Others though, such as Kmart and VF (makers of Lee and Wrangler jeans) informed Tyco that they had an alternative hangar supplier, namely, a company called WAF. For a brief moment, Tyco appeared to have backed off raising the price. Yet the firm's underlying strategy soon became clear. In the fall of 1999, Tyco bought WAF Corporation. Within a few months, it not only raised prices to all its customers again but also added in a new delivery charge. Tyco also pursued an aggressive repurchase program so as to corner the market on used hangars. If it did not control the supply of this alternative to new hangars, Tyco could again face difficulty in charging a high price. Tyco's success in obtaining monopoly power is evidenced by the many, bitter, and public complaints that retailers have made.

---

**Source:** M. Maremont, "Lion's Share: For Plastic Hangars You Almost Need To Go To Tyco International." *The Wall Street Journal*, February 15, 2000, p. A1.

---

## Practice Problem 2.2

Now suppose that the manufacturing of cellular phones, as described in Practice Problem 2.1, is monopolized. The monopolist has 50 identical plants to run. Each plant has the same cost function as described in Practice Problem 2.1. The overall marginal cost function for the multiplant monopolist[5] is described by $MC(Q) = 10 + Q/25$. The market demand is also assumed to be the same as in Practice Problem 2.1. Recall

$$Q^D = \frac{6000 - 50P}{9}.$$

a. Show that the monopolist's marginal revenue function is $MR(Q) = 120 - 18Q/50$.
b. Show that the monopolist's profit-maximizing output level is $Q_M = 275$. What price does the monopolist set to sell this level of output?
c. What is the profit earned at each one of the monopolist's plants?

---

## 2.2  PROFIT TODAY VERSUS PROFIT TOMORROW: FIRM DECISION MAKING OVER TIME

Both the competition and the monopoly models described in the previous section exhibit only a vague concern with time. While some distinction is made between the short run and the long run, neither concept explicitly confronts the notion of a unit

---

5   Strictly speaking, the monopolist is a multiplant one because there are now 50 plants to run. The profit-maximizing monopolist will want to allocate total production across the 50 plants in such a way that the marginal cost of producing the last unit of output is the same in each plant. Therefore, the monopolist derives the overall marginal cost function in a manner similar to how we constructed the supply function for the competitive industry.

of time such as a day, a week, a month, or a year, or of how many such units constitute say, the long run. To maximize profit in the long run requires, for example, only that the firm make all necessary adjustments to its inputs in order to produce at the optimum level, and then repeatedly choose this input–output combination in every individual period thereafter. From the standpoint of decision making, the long run is envisioned as a single market period and the assumption that the firm will seek to maximize profit is unambiguous in its meaning.

However, the recognition that the long run is a series of individual, finite time periods extending far into the future also raises the possibility that each such period will not be the same. Here, the choice may be between taking an action that yields profit immediately versus taking an action that yields greater profit but not until many periods later. In such a setting, the meaning of maximizing profit is less clear. Is it better or worse to have more profit later and less profit now? How does one compare profit in one period with profit in another? Such questions must be answered if we are to provide a useful analysis of the strategic interaction among firms over time.

Sacrificing profit today means incurring a cost. Hence, the problem just described arises anytime that a cost is incurred in the present in return for benefits to be realized much later. Firms often face such a trade-off. A classic example is the decision to build a new manufacturing plant. If the plant is constructed now, the firm will immediately incur the expense of hiring architects and construction workers and the buying of building materials, machinery, and equipment. It will only be sometime later—after the plant is built and running smoothly—that the firm will actually begin to earn some profit or return on this investment.

In order to understand how firms make decisions in which the costs and benefits are experienced not just in one period but instead over time, we borrow some insight from financial markets. After all, the comparison of income received (or foregone) at different points in time is really what financial markets are all about. Think for a moment. If one buys stock, say in AT&T, one has to give up some funds today—namely, the price of a share in AT&T times the number of shares bought. Of course, investors do this every day. Thousands of AT&T shares are bought each day of the week. These investors are sacrificing some of their current income—which could alternatively be used to purchase a new computer, wardrobe, or other consumer goods—to buy these shares. Why do they do this? The answer is that they do so in the expectation that those shares will pay dividends and also appreciate in value over time. That is, stockholders buy shares of stock and incur the associated investment expense now, in the hope that the ownership of those shares will generate income as dividends and capital gains later.

In short, the financial markets are explicitly involved in trading current for future income. Accordingly, we can use the techniques of those markets to evaluate similar trades of current versus future profit that a firm might make. The key insight that we borrow from financial markets is the notion of present value or discounting. To understand the concept of discounting, imagine that a friend (a trustworthy friend) has asked to borrow $1,000 for twelve months. Suppose further that for you to lend her money requires that you withdraw $1,000 from your checking account, an account that pays 3 percent interest per year. In other words, you will lose about $30 of interest income by making this withdrawal. Although you like your friend very much, you may not see just precisely why you should make her a gift of $30. Therefore, you agree to lend her the $1,000 today if, a year from now, she pays you not only the

$1,000 of principal but also an additional $30 in interest. Your friend will likely agree. After all, if she borrowed from the bank directly she would have to pay at least as much. The bank cannot afford to pay you 3 percent per year if it does not charge an interest rate at least as high when it loans those funds out. In fact, the bank will probably charge an interest rate a bit higher to cover its expenses. So, it pays for your friend to sign a contract (or perhaps just shake hands on the deal) requiring that you give her $1,000 today and that she give you $1,030 in twelve months.

Quite explicitly, you and your friend have just negotiated a trade of present funds for future funds. In fact, you have established the exact terms at which such a trade can take place. One thousand dollars today may be exchanged for $1,030 one year from now. Of course, matters would have been a bit different if the interest rate that your bank paid on deposits had been 5 percent. In that case, you would have asked your friend for $50 (5 percent of $1,000) in repayment beyond the $1,000 originally borrowed. That would have been the only repayment that would truly compensate you for your loss of the interest on your bank deposit. In general, if we denote the interest rate as $r$, then we have that $1,000 today exchanges for $(1 + r)$ times $1,000 in one year. If we now become even more general and consider an initial loan amount different from $1,000, say of $\Upsilon$, we will quickly see that the same logic implies that $\Upsilon$ today trades for $(1 + r)\Upsilon$ paid in twelve months.

There is, however, an alternative way to view the transactions just described. Instead of asking how much money one will receive in a year for giving up $1,000 or $\Upsilon$ now, one can reverse the question. That is, one can ask instead how much one has to pay today in order to get a particular payment one year from the present. For example, we could ask how much does it cost right now to buy a contract requiring that the other party to the deal pay us $1,030 in a year. If the interest rate is 3 percent, the answer is easy. It is simply $1,000. In fact, this is the contract with your friend that we just considered. You essentially paid $1,000 to purchase a promise from your friend to pay you $1,030 in one year. The intuition is that, at an interest rate of 3 percent, the banks and the financial markets are saying that in return for a deposit of $1,000 they promise to pay $1,030 in one year. In other words, we can buy the contract we are thinking about for exactly $1,000 from the banks. There's no sense in paying more for it from anyone else, and no one else is going to accept less. Therefore, when the interest rate is 3 percent, the market is saying that the current price of a contract promising to pay $1,030 in one year is exactly $1,030/1.03$, or $1,000. Since price is just the economist's term for value, we call this the present value or, more completely, the present discounted value of $1,030 due in twelve months.

More generally, the present value of a piece of paper (e.g., a loan contract or share of stock) promising its owner a payment of $Z$ in one period is just $Z/(1 + r)$. The term $1/(1 + r)$ is typically referred to as the discount factor and is often presented just as $R$. In other words, $R = 1/(1 + r)$. Hence, the present value of $Z$ dollars one year from now is often written as $RZ$. The source of the adjective discount should be clear. Income that does not arrive until a year from now is not as valuable as income received today. Instead, the value of such future income is discounted. This has nothing to do with inflation and any possible cheapening of the currency over time. It simply reflects the fact that individuals prefer to have their consumption now and have to be paid a premium—an interest rate return—in order to be persuaded to wait.

What if the term of the loan had been for two years? Let us return again to our original example of a $1,000 loan at 3 percent interest. If your friend had initially asked to borrow the funds for two years, your reasoning might have gone as follows.

Making a two-year loan to my friend requires that I take $1,000 out of my checking account today. Not making the loan means that the $1,000 stays in the bank. In this case, I will earn 3 percent over the next twelve months and, accordingly, start the next year with $1,030 in the bank. I will then earn 3 percent on this amount over the next, or second, year. Accordingly, by refusing my friend and keeping the funds in the bank, I will have on deposit $1,030(1.03) = $1,060.90 in two years. Therefore, I will only lend my friend the funds for two years if she in turn promises to pay me $1,060.90—the same as I could have earned at the bank—when the loan expires two years from now. Note that the amount $1,060.90 can be alternatively expressed as $1,000(1.03)(1.03) = $1,000(1.03)^2$. In general, a loan today of amount $Y$ will yield $Y(1 + r)^2 = YR^{-2}$ in two years. By extension, a loan of $Y$ dollars for $t$ years will yield an amount of $YR^{-t}$ when it matures $t$ years from now.

As before, we can turn the question around and ask how much one needs to pay currently in order to receive an amount of $Z$ dollars at some date $t$ periods into the future. The answer follows immediately from our work above. It is $R^t Z$. How do we know this? If one puts $R^t Z$ dollars in an interest-bearing account today, then the amount that can be withdrawn in $t$ periods is, by our previous logic, $(R^t Z)R^{-t} = Z$. Clearly, the present discounted value of an amount $Z$ to be received in the future is just $R^t Z$.

The only remaining question is how to value a claim that provides different amounts at different dates in the future. For example, consider the construction of a plant that will, after completion in one year, generate $Z_1$ in net revenues, a net revenue of $Z_2$ two years from now, a net revenue of $Z_3$ three years from now, and so on. What is the present value of this stream of future profits? The present value of $Z_1$ in one period is, as we know, $RZ_1$. Similarly, the present value of $Z_2$ to be received in two periods is $R^2 Z_2$. If we continue in this manner we will work out the present value of the income received at each particular date. The present value of this entire stream will simply be the sum of all these individual present values. In general, the present value, $PV$, of a stream of income receipts to be received at different dates extending $T$ periods into the future is

$$PV = RZ_1 + R^2 Z_2 + R^3 Z_3 + \ldots + R^T Z_T = \sum_{t=1}^{T} R^t Z_t \qquad (2.3)$$

A special case of equation (2.3) occurs when the income received in each period $Z_t$ is the same, that is, when $Z_1 = Z_2 = \ldots = Z_T = \bar{Z}$. In this case the present value of the total stream is

$$PV = \frac{\bar{Z}}{(1 - R)} (R - R^{T+1}). \qquad (2.4)$$

An even more special case occurs when not only is the income receipt constant at $Z = \bar{Z}$, but the stream persists into the indefinite future so that the terminal period, $T$, approaches infinity. In that case, since the discount factor $R$ is less than one, the term $R^{T+1}$ in equation (2.4) goes to zero. Hence, when the stream is both constant and perpetual, the present value formula becomes

$$PV = \bar{Z} \left( \frac{R}{1 - R} \right) = \frac{\bar{Z}}{r} . \qquad (2.5)$$

Thus, if the interest rate $r$ is 3 percent, a promise to pay a constant \$30 forever would have a present value of $PV = \$30/0.03 = \$1,000$. Note that for all our present value formulas, an increase in the real interest rate $r$ implies a decrease in the discount factor $R$. In turn, this means that an increase in the interest rate implies a decrease in the present value of any given future income stream.

Again, it is important to remember the context in which these equations have been developed. Often firm decision making has a temporal dimension. Indeed, our focus on long-run equilibria implies that we are considering just such decisions. Hence, we need to consider trade-offs that are made over time. An expense may need to be incurred now in order to reap additional profit at some future date or dates. The simple dictum *maximize profit* does not have a clear meaning in such cases. The only means of evaluating the desirability of such a trade is to discount, that is, translate the future dollar inflows into a current or present value that may then be compared with the current expense necessary to secure those future receipts. If the present value of the future income is not at least as great as the value of the necessary expense, then the trade-off is not favorable. If, for instance, a plant costs \$3 million to build but will generate future profit with a discounted present value of only \$2 million, it is not a desirable investment, and we would not expect a rational firm to undertake it.[6] In short, our usual assumption that firms maximize profit must now be qualified to be that firms maximize the present value of all current and future profit. Of course, for one-period problems, this is identical to the assumption that firms simply maximize profit. However, we will need to be familiar with the idea of discounting and the present value of future profits in the second half of the book when we take up such issues as collusion and research and development, which frequently have a multiperiod dimension.

## Practice Problem 2.3

Suite Enterprises is a large restaurant supply firm that dominates the local market. It does, however, have one rival, Loew Supplies. Because of this competition, Suite earns a profit of \$100,000 per year. It could, however, cut its prices to cost and drive out Loew. To do this, Suite would have to forego all profit for one year during which it earns zero. After that year, Loew would be gone forever and Suite could earn \$110,000 per year. The interest rate Suite confronts is 12 percent per year, hence the discount factor is $R = 0.8929$.

a. Is driving Loew out of the market a good "investment" for Suite?

b. Consider the alternative strategy in which Suite buys Loew for \$80,000 today and then operates the new combined firm, Suite & Loew, as a monopoly earning \$110,000 in all subsequent periods. Is this a good investment?

## 2.3  EFFICIENCY, SURPLUS, AND SIZE RELATIVE TO THE MARKET

Now that we have described the perfectly competitive and pure monopoly market outcomes, it is time to try to understand why perfect competition is extolled and

---

6   We have treated the problem as one of current expenses versus future income receipts. Of course, future costs should be discounted as well.

Reality Checkpoint

## Piracy on the High (Air)waves:
## Discounting, Monopoly Power, and Public Policy

The cost of cable television ranges from $20 to $45 per month and higher, depending on the package bought. In return for this fee, subscribers obtain access to numerous channels and television shows. Nonsubscribers cannot receive such programming because they do not have a "cable box" capable of unscrambling the cable signals that carry the cable company's transmissions.

However, for the right price, one can (or at least could) obtain an unscrambler on the black market. What is the right price? Well, imagine that individuals can borrow at 18 percent per year or about 1.5 percent per month—a rate charged on many credit cards. Hence, the monthly discount factor R is 0.985. Imagine further that a typical customer expects to stay in his or her current residence for three years. Buying an illicit cable box permits this customer to receive cable without having to pay the monthly fee of say, $33, on average. If indeed the customer expects to be in her current residence for three years, then the formula in equation (2.4) implies that the present value of the consumer's savings comes from avoiding the $33 payment each month, for thirty-six months, of approximately $912. This amount proba-

bly overstates the value of an illicit cable box because those using such boxes face sizable fines and penalties if caught. They will therefore buy illegal boxes only if the price is lower than the $912 value in order to compensate them for such risk. As it is, illicit cable boxes sell for about $400. This probably is more than enough of a reduction below the $912 value to provide fair insurance against the risk of getting caught. Even in a black market, consumers earn some surplus.

A huge "bust" on the black market for cable boxes led to the shutdown of the biggest pirate or distributor of the illicit devices, a firm called Leasing Ventures, whose owner pleaded guilty to the charges. What may be most interesting is that Leasing Ventures got caught when it tried to join forces with another pirate firm, Novaplex, in an effort to corner the market in illegal cable boxes. That is, the two firms attempted to form a price-fixing cartel that could earn monopoly profit in this "industry." It is an interesting public policy question as to which offense—the piracy of cable transmissions or the efforts to monopolize the illegal industry—is worse, especially when judged from the viewpoint of economic efficiency!

**Source:** M. Robichaux, "Cable Pirates Sought Plunder, but Blundered Into a Major FBI Sting." *The Wall Street Journal*, May 12, 1997, p. A1.

pure monopoly is guarded against by law. In both cases firms are driven by profit maximization. Also, in both cases the firms sell to consumers who decide how much they want to buy at any given price. What makes one market good and the other not? The answer to this question does not reflect any concern about too much profit or firms "ripping off" consumers. The answer instead lies in the economic concept of efficiency. In economics, efficiency has a very precise meaning. Briefly speaking, a market outcome is said to be efficient when it is impossible to find some small change in the allocation of capital, labor, goods, or services that would improve the well-being of one individual in the market without hurting any others.[7] If the only way we can make someone better off is by making someone else worse off, then there is no slack or inefficiency in how the market is working. If, on the other hand, we can imagine changes that would somehow allow one person to have more goods and services while no one else has less, then the current market outcome is not efficient. As it turns out, that is precisely the case for a monopolized market. One can think of changes to the monopoly outcome that would yield more for at least one individual and no less for any other. However, as we'll see, market forces alone will not get us there in the case of the textbook monopolist.

It is apparent that to implement our efficiency criterion we need some measure of how well-off consumers and firms are in any market outcome. For this purpose, we use the notions of consumer surplus and producer surplus. The consumer surplus obtained from consuming one unit of the good is defined as the difference between the maximum amount a consumer is willing to pay for that unit and the amount the consumer actually pays. Total consumer surplus in a market is then measured by summing this difference over each unit of the good bought in the market. Analogously, the producer surplus obtained from producing a single unit of the good is the difference between the amount the seller receives for that unit of the good and the cost of producing it. Total producer surplus in a market is then measured by summing up this difference over each unit of the good sold.

We illustrate these concepts in Figure 2-5. In the competitive outcome, $Q_C$ units of the good are bought and sold. The maximum amount a consumer is willing to pay for the last unit, the $Q_C$th unit, is just the equilibrium price $P_C$. However, the maximum amount a consumer is willing to pay for the first, second, third, and so on, up to the $Q_C$th unit, is greater than $P_C$. We know this because, at a given sales volume, the demand curve is a precise measure of the maximum amount any consumer is willing to pay for one more unit. Hence, the area under the demand curve but above the market equilibrium price $P_C$ is surplus to consumers. It is a measure of how much they were willing to pay less what they actually did pay in the competitive outcome. This is shown in Figure 2-5 as area *abc*.

For competitive producers, the supply curve tells us the marginal cost of producing each unit.[8] Similar to consumer surplus, we can construct a measure of producer surplus. For each unit of the good sold, producer surplus is measured by the difference between market price, $P_C$, and the corresponding reservation supply price on the supply curve. By adding this difference for each value of output up to the competitive output, we obtain total producer surplus. This is illustrated by the area *cbd* in Figure 2-5.

Note that when the equilibrium quantity, $Q_C$, of the good is produced and sold at price $P_C$, the total surplus or welfare to consumers and producers is given by the area *abd*.[9]

---

7   This notion of efficiency is often referred to as Pareto Optimality after the great Italian social thinker of the late nineteenth and early twentieth centuries, Vilfredo Pareto.

8   Remember that the market supply curve is the horizontal summation of each competitive firm's marginal cost curve; thus the supply curve tells us exactly the opportunity cost to the firm of producing and selling each unit of the good.

9   Observe that the unit of measurement of the areas of consumer and producer surplus is the dollar. To work out the areas you must take $/unit as measured on the vertical axis times units on the horizontal axis. This gives you a measure in dollars, which is a money measure of the welfare created by having this good produced at output level $Q_C$ and sold at price $P_C$.

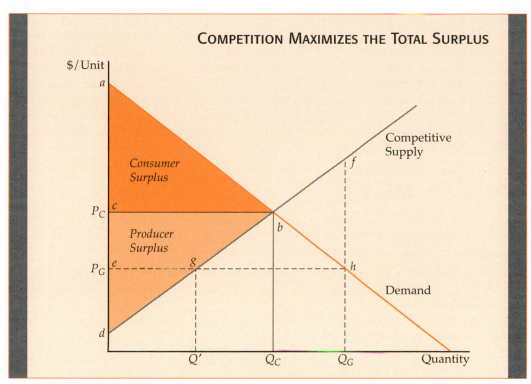

FIGURE

**2-5**

**COMPETITION MAXIMIZES THE TOTAL SURPLUS**

At the competitive price $P_C$ and output $Q_C$, consumers enjoy a surplus equal to triangle *abc*. Producers enjoy a surplus equal to triangle *cbd*. Subsidizing production to output $Q_G$ reduces the price to $P_G$. The required subsidy is triangle *gfh*. Consumers gain additional surplus *cbge*. However, this amount represents a transfer of surplus from producers to consumers and, hence, no net gain in total surplus. Consumers also gain the triangle *gbh*. But this is offset by the need to raise such funds from others to provide the subsidy. Finally, the remaining part of the subsidy, equal to triangle *bfh*, is a deadweight loss as resources valued more highly in alternative uses are transferred to the industry in question where the marginal value of output is only $P_G$.

Suppose that an output greater than $Q_C$, say $Q_G$, was produced in this market. For consumers to buy this quantity of the good, the price must fall to $P_G$. This rise in production and sales results in an increase in consumer surplus. Specifically, consumer surplus increases to *aeh*. Producer surplus, however, falls. Moreover, it falls by more than the increase in consumer surplus. Much of the increase in consumer surplus that results from moving to output $Q_G$—in particular, the shaded area *cbge*—is not an increase in total surplus. It simply reflects a transfer of surplus from producers to consumers. As for the additional increase in consumer surplus—the triangle *gbh*—this is clearly less than the additional decrease in producer surplus—the triangle *gfh*. Producers now receive a positive surplus only on the first $Q'$ units produced. Because the gain in consumer surplus is less than the loss in producer surplus, the overall surplus at output $Q_G$ is less than that at output $Q_C$. It is easy to repeat this analysis for any output greater than $Q_C$. In short, we cannot increase total surplus by raising output beyond the competitive level; we can only decrease it.

A similar thought experiment can be performed to show that output levels below $Q_C$ also reduce the total surplus (see Practice Problem 2.4). This is because restricting output to less than $Q_C$ reduces consumer surplus by more than it raises producer surplus. Accordingly, the overall surplus at an output below $Q_C$ must be smaller than the surplus under perfect competition. Note that saying that neither an increase nor a decrease in output from $Q_C$ can increase the total surplus but only decrease it is equivalent to saying that the surplus is maximized at $Q_C$. Yet if we cannot increase the total surplus then we cannot make anyone better off without making someone worse off. That is, if we cannot make the size of the pie bigger, we can only give more to some individuals by giving less to others. Since this is the case under perfect competition, the perfectly competitive output level is efficient.[10]

## Practice Problem 2.4

Let's return to the cellular phone industry when it was organized as a perfectly competitive industry. We will use the information in Practice Problem 2.1 to work out consumer surplus and producer surplus in a competitive equilibrium.

a.  Show that when $Q^C$ = 500 units and $P^C$ = \$30 per unit then consumer surplus is equal to \$22,500 and producer surplus is equal to \$5,000. This results in a total surplus equal to \$27,500.
b.  Show that when an output of 275 units is produced in this industry the sum of consumer and producer surplus falls to \$21,931.25.

### 2.3.1  The Monopolist and Producer Surplus

Now consider the monopoly outcome. We have suggested that this is inefficient. If this is the case, then it must be possible to show that by producing at an output level different from the monopoly output $Q_M$, one individual can be made better off and no one else worse off. The way to show this is similar to the solution to Practice Problem 2.4 and is shown in Figure 2-6. This figure shows the competitive output and price, $Q_C$ and $P_C$, respectively, much as in Figure 2-5. However, in Figure 2-6 we also show what happens when the industry is monopolized. The monopolist produces output $Q_M$ and sets price $P_M$. Consumer surplus is then the triangle *jax*. The monopolist's profit at $Q_M$ is measured by area *jxzk*. The sum of these two surpluses is area *axzk*. This is clearly smaller than the area *ayk*, which measures the total surplus obtained in the perfectly competitive outcome.

It is worth noting that while the total surplus is greater under perfect competition than it is under monopoly, the opposite holds true for producer surplus. A move from monopoly to competition does gain the producer surplus *wyz*, but to achieve this gain requires setting the competitive price $P_C$ and the consequent loss of the firm's surplus, *hjxw*. The loss is obviously greater than the gain.

Note that the reduction in consumer surplus that monopoly causes is not purely the result of an increase in the monopolist's surplus. Quite to the contrary, the decline in total surplus alerts us to the fact that the monopolist's gain is less than the consumer's loss. In other words, as a result of moving from a competitive industry to one of monopoly, consumers lose more than the profit that the monopolist earns.

---

10 We focus here on the concept of allocational or static efficiency in which we examine the best way to allocate resources for the production of a given set of goods and services with a given technology. Dynamic efficiency, which considers the allocation of resources so as to promote the development of new goods and new production techniques, is addressed explicitly in Chapter 22.

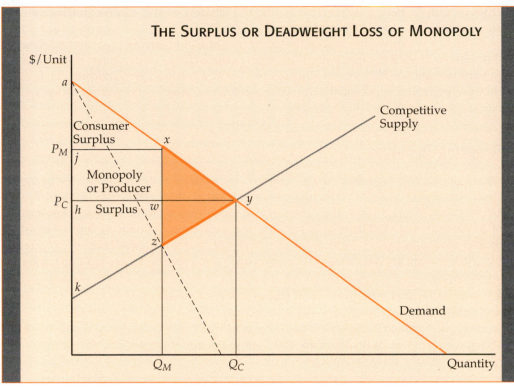

FIGURE

2-6

**THE SURPLUS OR DEADWEIGHT LOSS OF MONOPOLY**

The monopolist prices at $P_M$ and sells $Q_M$ while a competitive industry prices at $P_C$ and sells $Q_C$. The deadweight loss imposed by monopoly is given by the area $xyz$.

Specifically, they also lose an additional amount—the area $xwy$ in Figure 2-6—beyond that part of their surplus that is transferred to the monopolist.

The area of the shaded triangle $xyz$ is an exact measure of inefficiency under monopoly. The upper boundary of this triangle is comprised of points that lie on the consumers' demand curve. Every point on this boundary indicates the marginal value that consumers place on successive increases in output beyond $Q_M$. The lower boundary of this triangle traces the marginal cost of producing this additional output. The triangle $xyz$ thus reflects all the trades that generate a surplus which do not take place under monopoly. Within this triangle, the price consumers would willingly pay exceeds the cost of producing extra units and this difference is the surplus lost—that is, earned by no one—due to monopolization of the industry. If this additional output were produced, there would be a way to distribute it and make one person better off without lowering the profit of the monopolist or the welfare of any other individual. The triangle $xyz$ is often referred to as the deadweight loss of monopoly. It is also a good approximation of the gains to be had by restructuring the industry to make it a competitive one.

The deadweight loss in Figure 2-6 is not due to the excess profit of the monopolist. From the viewpoint of economic efficiency, we do not care whether the surplus generated in a market goes to consumers—as it does under perfect competition—or to producers. The welfare triangle in Figure 2-6 is a loss because it reflects the potential surplus that would have gone to someone—consumers or producers—had the efficient output been produced. It is not the division of the surplus but its total amount that is addressed by economic efficiency.

Efficiency is a powerful concept both because of its underlying logic and because it is open to explicit computation. With appropriate statistical techniques, economists can try to calculate the deadweight loss of Figure 2-6 for a given industry. Hence, they can estimate the potential gains from moving to a more competitively structured market.

## Practice Problem 2.5

Water is produced and sold by the government. Demand for water is represented by the linear function $Q = 50 - 2P$. The total cost function for water production is also a linear function: $TC(Q) = 100 + 10Q$. You will also need to work out both the average cost of production, denoted by $AC(Q)$, equal to the total cost of producing a quantity of output divided by that quantity of output, $TC(Q)/Q$, and the marginal cost of production, denoted by $MC(Q)$, which is the additional cost incurred to produce one more unit.

a. How much should the government charge per unit of water in order to reach the efficient allocation?
b. How much should it charge if it wishes to maximize profit from the sale of water?
c. What is the value of the efficiency loss that results from charging the price in part b rather than the price determined in part a?

### 2.3.2 The Nonsurplus Approach to Economic Efficiency[11]

In considering the deadweight loss of monopoly, it is useful to pursue the question as to why the monopolist fails to earn that lost triangle of surplus. If it is there for the taking, why doesn't the monopolist go out and get it? After all, the monopolist firm is the only seller in the market. Shouldn't it be able to use its power to extract this additional profit?

Our concept of surplus provides a useful tool with which to consider this question. Suppose that the monopolist expands output from $Q_M$ to the competitive level of $Q_C$. By doing so, the monopolist will generate an increase in the total surplus exactly equal to the deadweight loss. That's the good news. The bad news is that the monopolist firm cannot appropriate all of this gain for itself. To begin with, some of the surplus generated by selling an additional $Q_C - Q_M$ units at price $P_C$ will flow to those consumers lucky enough to buy these goods at this lower price. Yet many of these consumers were willing to pay more than $P_C$ for this additional consumption. The surplus that these individuals enjoy as a result of acquiring the good while paying only $P_C$ is surplus that the monopolist cannot claim. Moreover, the monopolist must also confront a second problem. The monopolist cannot sell the same good at two different prices. The monopolist would find it very difficult to get anyone to buy at the higher price, $P_M$. Those who buy the product at the lower price, $P_C$, can make an easy economic profit by reselling the good to anyone to whom the monop-

---

11 This section and the previous one make extensive use of the nonsurplus approach developed in Makowski and Ostroy (1995). It has had an important influence on our understanding of market participation.

olist tries to charge $P_M$. What this means is that selling the additional $Q_C - Q_M$ units requires that the price fall to $P_C$ on every unit sold and not just on the extra $Q_C - Q_M$ units. Yet this price cut lowers the monopolist's profit on the initial $Q_M$ units. It thereby further reduces the surplus that flows to the monopolist as a result of selling the extra $Q_M - Q_C$ units.

Indeed, even in our original equilibrium with output at $Q_M$, the monopolist firm was generating more total surplus than it was actually taking home in profit. To see this, observe what would happen if the monopolist closed shop and left the market entirely. Not only would the monopolist profit be lost, but—and this is the crucial point—consumer surplus would vanish as well. Viewed in this light, we see that the monopolist always creates surplus that it does not get. If the monopolist firm could appropriate the entire surplus created in the market, then it would have an incentive to produce the output that maximizes that surplus—the efficient production level. It is a monopolist firm's inability to appropriate the surplus its production creates that leads it to choose an inefficient output level.

It may seem strange to say that a monopolist firm, which earns some surplus, underproduces just because it does not get the entire surplus when, by comparison, a competitive industry, in which each firm gets no surplus, achieves the efficient higher level of output. Remember, though, that we are making our comparisons at the firm level, not the industry level. The monopolist is a large producer relative to the market. Its choice of output materially alters the market supply and hence the market price. It thereby alters the surplus of consumers as well. This is not the case for the competitive firm. A perfectly competitive firm's supply is tiny relative to the market. Indeed, it is so small that its output decision has no effect on market price. Drop any one competitive firm from the market and nothing happens to either the market price or the industry's total output. That is what we mean in calling a competitive firm a "price taker." But if the competitive firm cannot change the market price it also cannot change anyone's surplus. Again, this is not the case for the competitive industry overall. Taken together, all the firms in that industry do affect the total surplus. If we drop them all from the market, total surplus will decline.

However, decisions are made at the level of the individual firm, thus we must look at the incentives facing a single competitive producer. Here we see that such a firm captures the entire surplus its actions generate. It earns zero profit from its market participation and, as we have just seen, this is an exact measure of the contribution the firm makes to the total surplus. So, the perfectly competitive firm gets out of the market exactly what it puts in.

In contrast, the monopolist firm does not get the entire surplus that its participation in the market generates, even though it earns a positive profit. As shown earlier, that profit is less than the surplus the monopolist generates. Since the monopolist firm gets less than what it puts in, it should not be surprising that its output choice is inefficiently small. We hasten to add that this approach to monopoly is not presented to garner sympathy for the monopolist firm. Rather, our aim is to clarify the source of inefficiency under monopoly. If the monopolist could collect as profit the entire surplus its production generates, it would have every incentive to produce the efficient level of output.

Indeed, the real source of the monopoly problem is not the fact that only one firm is active in the market. The true cause of the inefficiency is that that firm is large relative to the market size. To see this, consider a simple example in which the monopolist is a reproducer of classic cars. Suppose that the monopolist in question is the only maker of reproductions of the classic 1939 Rolls-Royce Wraith. Suppose further that because of limited supplies of parts and materials, the reproduction artist can produce only two such cars—each at a cost of $80,000. Demand, however, is not so limited. There are 50,000 classic car collectors in the world. Of these, the 200 who value the cars the most are each willing to pay a price of $150,000—but not a penny more—to own precisely one of these autos. The next 40,000 are each willing to pay $130,000 to own one car. The remaining 9,800 will willingly pay $100,000 to own a reproduced Rolls-Royce Wraith. In short, the market is characterized by some variety in consumer tastes.

The key point to note is that monopoly does not result in inefficiency. This is because whether the monopolist produces and sells none, one, or the maximum of two cars, the market price of the reproductions will remain at $150,000 apiece. If the monopolist sells both cars, they will be sold to two different buyers, each of whom is among the 200 collectors willing to pay $150,000. If the monopolist decides to sell just one car, it again sells it for $150,000, this time dealing with only one buyer. Finally, if the monopolist sells no reproduced autos, no price will be recorded, but there will be an implicit opportunity cost of $150,000 incurred for each car not produced and sold. In short, the antique car producer cannot move the market price for one car away from $150,000 even though it is a monopolist firm.

Note that any buyer who pays $150,000 for one of the cars enjoys a zero surplus from the deal. The fact that $150,000 is exactly the maximum price that such a buyer is willing to pay indicates that the buyer is essentially indifferent between purchasing the car at that price and not buying it at all. In other words, such a buyer gets no surplus, implying that the car builder appropriates the entire surplus that building and selling a reproduced Rolls generates. Alternatively, if the monopolist were to leave—or, equivalently, not sell any cars—the surplus enjoyed by all other market participants would be unchanged. So, whether the monopolist sells both cars at the market-clearing price of $150,000, or does not participate in the market at all, the monopolist's actions leave unchanged the surplus of each and every other antique car market participant.

Obviously, the above story is a little contrived. Still, it serves to make the point that monopoly, per se, is not the source of market inefficiency. The car firm owner has a monopoly, but its supply of cars is small relative to the potential market. This situation is therefore similar to the one facing a perfectly competitive firm and not the standard monopolist. Just like the perfect competitor, the car firm's decision on how many cars to sell has no effect on the price. Matters would have been different had we assumed that there was only one collector willing to pay $150,000 to own a classic Rolls-Royce, while all other collectors were willing to pay only $20,000 apiece for such an automobile. In this second case, the example is more like the standard monopoly case. The car owner's choice of how many cars to sell affects the equilibrium price and the surplus of others as well.

The foregoing analysis, which focuses on market actions and the surplus that they generate, is called the nonsurplus approach to understanding economic efficiency. It makes the important connection between the incentive to trade in a market and the efficiency of market trading. Firms are motivated by profit to trade. Under perfect competition, a single firm's (zero) profit is equal to that firm's contribution to the surplus or welfare created by market trading. So, profit-maximizing behavior leads to an efficient market outcome. By contrast, the (large) monopolist firm's profit is less than the surplus created by market trading. Consequently, profit maximization under monopoly does not lead to an efficient market outcome.

## SUMMARY

We have formally presented the basic microeconomic analysis of markets characterized by either perfect competition or perfect monopoly. In both cases, the goal of any firm is assumed to be to maximize profit. The necessary condition for this is that the firm produce where marginal revenue and marginal cost are the same. Because firms in competitive markets take the price as given, price equals marginal revenue for the competitive firm. As a result, the competitive market equilibrium is one in which price is set equal to marginal cost. In turn, this implies that the competitive market equilibrium is efficient in that it maximizes the sum of producer and consumer surplus.

The pure monopoly case does not yield an efficient outcome. The monopoly firm understands that it can affect the market price and this implies that marginal revenue is always less than the price for a monopoly firm. If the market demand curve is linear, this difference is reflected in the fact that the monopolist's marginal revenue curve has the same price intercept but is twice as steeply sloped as the demand curve. For the monopolist firm it follows that equating marginal revenue with marginal cost, as required for profit maximization, yields an output inefficiently below that of the competitive equilibrium. Resources are misallocated because too few resources are employed in the production of the monopolized commodity. The inefficiency that results is often called the deadweight or welfare loss of monopoly.

Pure competition and pure monopoly are useful market concepts. Whether they are also useful as a description of actual industries is another question. To answer that question we need some way to determine if a market is monopolized or if it is competitive. That is, we need to develop some way to identify or to measure monopoly power. It is that issue that we address in the next chapter.

## PROBLEMS

1. Suppose that the annual demand for prescription antidepressants such as Prozac, Paxil, and Zoloft is, in inverse form, given by $P = 1000 - 0.025Q$. Suppose that the competitive supply curve is given by $P = 150 + 0.033Q$.

   a. Calculate the equilibrium price and annual quantity of antidepressants.

   b. Calculate producer surplus and consumer surplus in this competitive equilibrium.

2. Assume that the dairy industry is initially in a perfectly competitive equilibrium. Assume that, in the long run, the technology is such that average cost is constant at all levels of output. Suppose that producers agree to form an association and behave as a profit-maximizing monopolist. Explain clearly in a diagram the effects on (a) market price, (b) equilibrium output, (c) economic profit, (d) consumer surplus, and (e) efficiency.

3. Suppose that the total cost of producing pizzas for the typical firm in a local town is given by $C(q) = 2q + 2q^2$. In turn, marginal cost is given by $MC = 2 + 4q$. (If you know calculus, you should be able to derive this expression for marginal cost.)

   a. Show that the competitive supply behavior of the typical pizza firm is described by $q = \dfrac{P}{4} - \dfrac{1}{2}$.

**b.** If there are 100 firms in the industry each acting as a perfect competitor, show that the market supply curve is, in inverse form, given by $P = 2 + Q/25$.

4. Let the market demand for widgets be described by $Q = 1000 - 50P$. Suppose further that widgets can be produced at a constant average and marginal cost of $10 per unit.

   **a.** Calculate the market output and price under perfect competition and under monopoly.

   **b.** Define the point elasticity of demand $\varepsilon_D$ at a particular price and quantity combination as the ratio of price to quantity times the slope of the demand curve, $\Delta Q/\Delta P$, all multiplied by $-1$. That is, $\varepsilon_D = -\dfrac{P}{Q}\dfrac{\Delta Q}{\Delta P}$. What is the elasticity of demand in the competitive equilibrium? What is the elasticity of demand in the monopoly equilibrium?

   **c.** Denote marginal cost as $MC$. Show that in the monopoly equilibrium, the following condition is satisfied: $\dfrac{P - MC}{P} = -\dfrac{1}{\varepsilon_D}$.

5. We mentioned Tyco International and its control of the plastic hangar market in the chapter. Suppose that the inverse demand for hangars is given by $P = 3 - Q/16,000$. Suppose further that the marginal cost of producing hangars is constant at $1.

   **a.** What is the equilibrium price and quantity of hangars if the market is competitive?

   **b.** What is the equilibrium price and quantity of hangars if the market is monopolized?

   **c.** What is the deadweight or welfare loss of monopoly in this market?

6. A single firm monopolizes the entire market for single-lever, ball-type faucets, which it can produce at a constant average and marginal cost of $AC = MC = 10$. Originally, the firm faces a market demand curve given by $Q = 60 - P$.

   **a.** Calculate the profit-maximizing price and quantity combination for the firm. What is the firm's profit?

   **b.** Suppose that the market demand curve shifts outward and becomes steeper. Market demand is now described as $Q = 45 - 0.5P$. What is the firm's profit-maximizing price and quantity combination now? What is the firm's profit?

   **c.** Instead of the demand function assumed in part b, assume instead that market demand shifts outward and becomes flatter. It is described by $Q = 100 - 2P$. Now what is the firm's profit-maximizing price and quantity combination? What is the firm's profit?

   **d.** Graph the three different situations in parts a, b, and c. Based on what you observe, explain why there is no supply curve for a firm with monopoly power.

# REFERENCES

Baumol, W. J., J. C. Panzar, and R. D. Willig. 1982. *Contestable Markets and the Theory of Market Structure*. New York: Harcourt, Brace, Jovanovich.

Hotelling, H. 1929. "Stability in Competition." *Economic Journal* 39:41–57.

Makowski, L., and J. Ostroy. 1995. "Appropriation and Efficiency: A Revision of the First Theorem of Welfare Economics." *American Economic Review* 85:808–27.

Marshall, A. 1890. *Principles of Economics, Volume 1*. New York: Macmillan, 1961.

Schmalensee, R. 1988. "Industrial Economics: An Overview." *Economic Journal* 98:643–81.

# Chapter 3

# Market Structure and Market Power

The structure-conduct-performance paradigm, the old IO, starts with a given market structure and then investigates how firms behave in that kind of market. By contrast, the new IO has in some ways reversed the logic to investigate how the firms' strategic behavior can affect the structure of the market. Yet despite these differences, the two approaches agree that market structure, or the way the industry's producers are organized, affects what happens in the market place. A natural question that arises is how we can characterize a market's structure in a meaningful way.

In our review of basic microeconomics we saw that markets work well when firms are small relative to the size of the market. The idealized competitive market is one with numerous firms, each with a minimal market share. Yet such markets are relatively rare in the real world. Some markets have just two or three firms. Some have ten or twelve of unequal size. In what ways is this difference important? If there are twenty firms, does it matter if one firm has 60 percent of the market and the other nineteen have just over 2 percent each? Alternatively, can we measure market structure in such a way that enables us to make some inference of market power? Can we create an index that allows us to say how close or how far we are from the competitive ideal? Because such a roadmap could be of great use to policy makers it is worthwhile to explore the question at length.

## 3.1 MEASURING MARKET STRUCTURE

One way to think about an industry's structure is to undertake the following, simple procedure. First, take all the firms in the industry and rank them by some measure of size from largest to smallest—one, denoting largest; two, the next largest; etc. Suppose that we use market share as a measure of size. We can then calculate the fraction of the industry's total production that is accounted for by the largest firm, then the two largest firms combined, then the three largest firms combined, and so on. This gives us the cumulative fraction of the industry's total output as we include progressively smaller firms. Plotting this relationship yields a concentration curve. It is called a concentration curve because it gives a sense of the extent to which output is concentrated in the hands of just a few firms.

Figure 3-1 displays concentration curves for each of three representative industries, A, B, and C. The firms' ranked sizes are measured along the horizontal axis, with the first firm being the largest. The cumulative market share is measured on the vertical axis. For example, Industry A has ten firms, each with a 10 percent market share. Industry B has twenty-one firms, the largest of which has a 55 percent market share. The remaining twenty firms each have a 2.25 percent market share. Finally, Industry C has three firms each with a market share of 25 percent and five firms each with a market share of 5 percent. For Industry B the vertical coordinates corresponding to the horizontal values 1 and 2 on this industry's concentration curve are 55 and 57.25, respectively. This reflects the fact that the largest firm has 55 percent of the market and the largest two firms have 57.25 percent between them.

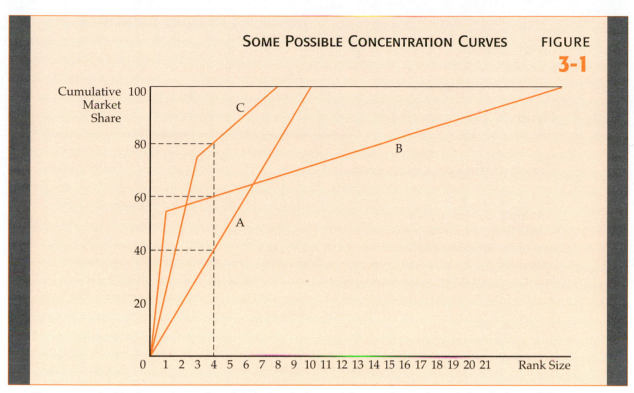

**SOME POSSIBLE CONCENTRATION CURVES**          **FIGURE 3-1**

Firms are ranked in decreasing order of their size. Industry A has ten firms of equal size, Industry B has one large firm and twenty, equal-sized smaller firms. Industry C has three large firms and five smaller firms. The dotted lines identify the four-firm concentration ratios, $CR_4$, for each industry.

Concentration curves are a useful illustrative device.[1] They permit one to get a sense of how industry production is allocated across firms from a quick visual inspection. However, often we need to summarize industrial structure with just a single number or index. One such popular index that focuses on the size of firms (relative to the industry) is the concentration ratio, $CR_n$, defined as the market share of the top $n$ firms. In the United States, the most frequent choice is the four-firm concentration ratio, $CR_4$, or the percent of industry sales accounted for by the top four firms. For the three hypothetical industries described above, we easily can identify the $CR_4$ concentration. All we need to do is draw a vertical line from the value 4 on the horizontal axis to the relevant concentration curve and from that point read horizontally to the vertical axis coordinate. As can be seen, $CR_4$ is 40, 61.75, and 80, for A, B, and C, respectively. A similar exercise yields the eight-firm ratio, $CR_8$, which also is often reported. Its value for markets A, B, and C is 80, 70.75, and 100, respectively.

---

1  Those familiar with the GINI Coefficient typically used to measure income inequality will recognize the concentration curve as the industrial structure analog of the Lorenz Curve from which the GINI Coefficient is derived. For further details, see C. Damguard, "The Lorenz Curve," available on the Internet at http://www.mathworld.wolfram.com/LorenzCurve.html.

An *n*-firm concentration ratio, then, corresponds to a particular point on the industry's concentration curve. It follows that the principal drawback to such a measure is that it omits the other information in the curve. Compare, for example, the four-firm and eight-firm concentration ratios just given for Industries A, B, and C.

 # Reality Checkpoint

## Concentrating on Concentration

Just as we can measure the fraction of an industry's output accounted for by its largest firms, so we can measure the fraction of the economy's entire output, GDP, accounted for by its largest corporations. However, while it may make sense to speak of a concentration index based on just the top four or top eight firms when speaking of a single industry, such a small number of firms would account for much too little of GDP to think seriously about. So, in the case of aggregate economic activity, we consider concentration ratios such as $CR_{50}$ or $CR_{200}$. Such measures can be constructed using data from the Census Bureau's Census of Manufactures. Economist Lawrence White has presented such data for the United States. Some of his results are shown below.

Aggregate Concentration for
Manufacturing (Value-Added Basis);
Selected Years, 1947–1997

| Year | $CR_{50}$ | $CR_{100}$ | $CR_{200}$ |
|------|-----------|------------|------------|
| 1947 | 17% | 23% | 30% |
| 1958 | 23 | 30 | 38 |
| 1967 | 25 | 33 | 42 |
| 1977 | 24 | 33 | 44 |
| 1987 | 25 | 33 | 43 |
| 1992 | 24 | 32 | 42 |
| 1997 | 24 | 32 | 40 |

These data suggest that, at least since the 1950s, aggregate concentration in manufacturing has shown no increasing or decreasing trend. It is approximately the same in 1997 as it was in 1958 whether one looks at the top 50, 100, or 200 largest firms. White shows that somewhat similar results are obtained if one looks at all nonfinancial corporations, or focuses on shares of employment or profit. This does not mean that firms are not getting bigger. If each firm grows at the same rate as the economy, each of us will find ourselves employed in larger and larger organizations over time even though concentration is stable. White shows that this, too, has been happening and that the size of the average firm has, correspondingly, grown.

**Source:** L. White, "Trends in Aggregate Concentration in the United States." *Journal of Economic Perspectives*, Fall 2002, pp. 137–60.

Industry A appears more concentrated than does Industry B using the $CR_8$ measure but less concentrated when evaluated with the $CR_4$ index.

An alternative to $CR_n$ that attempts to reflect more fully the information in the concentration curve is the Herfindahl-Hirschman Index, or HHI. For an industry with $N$ firms, this is defined as follows:

$$\text{HHI} = \sum_{i=1}^{N} s_i^2 , \qquad (3.1)$$

where $s_i$ is the market share of the $i$th firm. In other words, HHI is the sum of the squares of the market shares of all of the firms in the industry. Table 3-1 illustrates the calculation of HHI for Industry C in our example. If we measure market share in decimal terms so that a firm with 25 percent of the market has a share $s_i = 0.25$, the HHI for Industry C is 0.20. This corresponds to a maximum value of HHI = 1.0, which would be the HHI for this case if the industry were a pure monopoly with one firm accounting for all the output. However, it is somewhat more common to measure the shares in percentage terms, in which case the HHI for Industry C is 2000, which compares with a maximum, pure monopoly value of HHI = 10,000 when shares are measured in this way. For Industries A and B, similar calculations yield HHI = 1,000 and HHI = 3,126.25, respectively.

## CALCULATION OF THE HHI FOR INDUSTRY C

| Firm Rank | Market Share (%) $s_i$ | Squared Market Share $s_i^2$ |
|-----------|------------------------|------------------------------|
| 1 | 25 | 625 |
| 2 | 25 | 625 |
| 3 | 25 | 625 |
| 4 | 5 | 25 |
| 5 | 5 | 25 |
| 6 | 5 | 25 |
| 7 | 5 | 25 |
| 8 | 5 | 25 |

TABLE 3-1

Like a concentration ratio, the HHI measure has its drawbacks. However, it does have one strong advantage over a measure such as $CR_4$ or $CR_8$. This is that HHI reflects the combined influence of both unequal firm sizes and the concentration of activity in a few large firms. That is, rather than just reflect a single point on the concentration curve, HHI provides, in a single number, a more complete sense of the shape of the curve. It is this ability to reflect both average firm size and inequality of size between firms that leads economists to prefer HHI to simple concentration ratios such as $CR_4$. In our example, Industry B gets the highest HHI value because it is the one with the greatest disparity in firm sizes.

## Practice Problem 3.1

Consider two industries, each comprising ten firms. In Industry A, the largest firm has a market share of 49 percent. The next three firms have market shares of 7 percent each, and the remaining six firms have equal shares of 5 percent each. In Industry B, the top four firms share the bulk of the market with 19 percent apiece. The next largest firm accounts for 14 percent, and the smallest five firms equally split the remaining 10 percent of the industry.

a. Compute the four-firm concentration ratio and HHI for each industry. Compare these measures across the two industries. Which industry do you think truly exhibits a more competitive structure? Which measure do you think gives a better indication of this? Explain.

b. Now let the three second-largest firms in Industry A merge their operations while holding on to their combined 21 percent market share. Recalculate the HHI for Industry A.

### 3.1.1   Measurement Problems: What Is a Market?

Whether one uses a $CR_4$ or HHI as an overall measure of a market's structure, it should be clear that the ability to make such measurements at all is predicated upon our ability to identify a well-defined market in the first place. In truth, this is not often easy to do. Consider, for example, the automobile industry. Is the relevant market one for passenger cars? Or are specialized vehicles, such as motorcycles, vans, and pickup trucks, also part of the picture? Or think of the beverage industry. Does Pepsi compete only against other carbonated beverages, or should beverages such as fruit juices, iced tea, and flavored milk also be viewed as substitute products? Unless we have a clear procedure for answering such questions, any summary measure of market structure such as HHI will become an arbitrary statistic capable of being manipulated either upward or downward at the whim of the researcher. An analyst can then make $CR_4$ or HHI arbitrarily small or large by defining the market either broadly or narrowly.

In the United States, the Census Bureau is the custodian of the market definitions most frequently used. These definitions have recently changed somewhat in connection with the North American Free Trade Agreement. However, the logic underlying the earlier Standard Industrial Classifications (SIC) definitions and the current North American Industry Classification System (NAICS) is essentially the same. The Census Bureau first categorizes the output of business units in the United States into broad sectors of the economy, such as manufacturing, primary metals, agriculture, and forestry products, each of which receives a numeric code. These sectors are then subdivided further, and each is given a two-digit code. The manufacturing sector, for example, is covered by codes 31–33. These are each divided further into the three-digit, four-digit, five-digit, and six-digit levels. Each additional digit represents a further subdivision of the initial classification. Primarily because of the method by which the data are collected—through surveys of companies—the basis of all such subdivisions is according to the similarity of production processes rather than substitutability in consumption. The results permit the construction of concentration data. Before compiling these data, however, the Census Bureau must determine how to categorize pro-

☑ **Reality Checkpoint**

## Industries Aren't What They Used to Be!

In a press release issued on April 8, 1997, the Executive Office of the President of the United States announced the introduction of a new industry classification system. It stated that the new system enables the North American Free Trade Agreement (NAFTA) partners—the United States, Canada, and Mexico—to better compare economic and financial statistics and ensure that such statistics keep pace with the changing economy.

The new system—the North American Industry Classification System (NAICS)—replaced the countries' separate classification systems with one uniform system for classifying industries. In the United States, NAICS replaced the Standard Industrial Classification.

NAICS, a flexible system that takes into account changes in the global economy, helps to support more informed economic and trade policies, more profitable business decisions, and more cogent public discussion and debate.

The NAICS became effective as of the 1997 Economic Census. One can review this data as well as the translation of the data from the older SIC classification system at the Census Bureau's Web site, http://www.census.gov.

**Source:** Executive Office of the President, Office of Management and Budget, Washington, DC April 8, 1997. Available on the Internet at http://www.census.gov/epcd/naics/pressrel.html.

duction plants that produce more than one product. Its basic procedure is to assign any plant on the basis of that plant's primary product, as measured by sales. Once all the establishments are so assigned, total sales are computed for each market. Market shares and concentration indices are then calculated. These data are published regularly by the Census Bureau. Table 3-2 shows both $CR_4$ and HHI for a sample of well-known industries.[2]

The two measures of industrial concentration, $CR_4$ and HHI, are highly correlated, implying that each gives roughly the same description of an industry's structure. Yet while the $CR_4$ and HHI measures often tell the same story, the crucial question is whether it is the right story.[3] That is, to what extent do the four-digit industry classification codes and the associated measures of market concentration conform to an economist's idea of a market?

Generally speaking, we would like to include production establishments as part of a market if the products produced by the establishments are closely substitutable in consumption. Economists measure substitutability in consumption by the cross-price elasticity of demand $\eta_{ij}$. This is defined as the percentage change in demand for good

---

2   Further details are available on the Internet at http://www.census.gov/epcd/www/naics.html.
3   A quite readable discussion of the advantages and disadvantages of each ratio is available in Sleuwaegen and Dehandschutter (1986) and Sleuwaegen, Dehandschutter, and DeBondt (1989).

## CONCENTRATION MEASURES FOR SELECTED INDUSTRIES

| Industry | $CR_4$ | HHI |
|---|---|---|
| Breakfast Cereals | 82.9 | 2445.9 |
| Soft Drink Manufacturing | 47.2 | 800.4 |
| Automobiles | 79.5 | 2862.8 |
| Textile Mills | 13.8 | 94.4 |
| Paper Manufacturing | 18.5 | 173.3 |
| Petroleum Refineries | 28.5 | 422.1 |
| Petrochemical Manufacturing | 59.8 | 1187.0 |
| Pharmaceuticals | 32.3 | 446.3 |
| Cement Manufacturing | 33.5 | 466.6 |
| Aluminum Sheet/Plate/Foil | 65.0 | 1447.0 |
| Computers & Peripherals | 37.0 | 464.9 |
| Electric Light Bulbs | 88.9 | 2849.0 |
| Dolls, Toys, and Games | 40.0 | 495.9 |
| Aircraft | 80.9 | 2562.2 |
| Semiconductors | 41.7 | 688.7 |
| Telephone Equipment | 55.3 | 1061.1 |
| Plastic Pipes/Fittings | 24.8 | 241.3 |
| Toiletries | 38.6 | 564.2 |
| Women's Footwear | 49.5 | 794.8 |
| Household Refrigerators | 82.8 | 2161.6 |

**Source:** "Concentration Ratios in Manufacturing." Bureau of the Census, 1997 Census of Manufacturing, June 2001.

$i$ that occurs when there is a one percent change in the price of another good $j$. The mathematical definition of this elasticity is

$$\eta_{ij} = \frac{\partial q_i}{\partial p_j} \frac{p_j}{q_i}. \tag{3.2}$$

If this measure is large and positive, then goods $i$ and $j$ are considered reasonably close substitutes.[4] Because the Census Bureau approach groups establishments more on the basis of similarity in production techniques than on the basis of substitutability in consumption its markets definitions do not always satisfy this criterion. For example, wood, ceramic tile, and linoleum are all used as flooring materials and therefore may be viewed as substitutes in consumption. Yet each is listed under a different three-digit NAICS code.

Other problems with the NAICS and similar classifications arise in connection with geographic considerations. The geographic boundaries of a market are just as

---

4    However, the presence of a high monopoly price may inflate the cross-elasticity measure—a point originally emphasized by Stocking and Mueller (1955). That is, at the high price set by a monopolist, the cross-price elasticity may be large and indicate that other goods are substitutes when this would not be the finding had the monopolized industry been pricing competitively.

vital to market definition as are the product boundaries. For example, virtually all newspapers operate in local markets where typically we find one or two other competitors at most. The fact that, taken as a nationwide industry, newspapers exhibit very low concentration measures may not be terribly relevant in terms of indicating the extent of choice available to consumers who purchase newspapers in a particular town or city.[5]

Another issue related to geography is foreign trade. When the volume of such trade is large, the relevant market may well be global instead of domestic. In addition, even if one looks at only the domestic market, the presence of foreign imports can mean that the measurement of market share will depend critically on whether one uses a production total or a sales total. Thus, General Motors, Ford, and Daimler-Chrysler account for roughly 80 percent of all domestic production, but closer to 60 percent of domestic sales as a result of automobile imports.

Finally, structural measures such as HHI and $CR_4$ have trouble reflecting the relationships between firms operating at different stages of the production process. The delivery of a final good or service to the customer often represents the last of many steps. These include the acquisition of the raw materials, their transformation into a semifinished good, the refinement of the semifinished good into a final consumer product and, thereafter, the retailing. In economics jargon, the initial raw materials phase is typically described as the upstream phase after which the product flows "downstream" through the various stages toward its final sale to the consumer. The relationship between the upstream and downstream phases is therefore a vertical one, and there are several forms that this relationship can take. An upstream producer may own all the subsequent phases, in which case we say the firm is vertically integrated. Alternatively, an upstream producer may offer franchising agreements or long-term contracts to downstream sellers. The existence and variability of such relationships can cause difficulty in measuring the structure of the market at any one stage of production. For instance, there are many bottling companies, so conventional measures of concentration in the bottled tin and soft drink industry are typically low. In turn, this suggests a fairly competitive market. However, the reality is that most bottling companies do not compete with each other, but instead are usually tied through strict franchise agreements to one of the national upstream suppliers, such as Coca-Cola or Pepsi.[6]

In sum, interpreting the structural measures such as $CR_4$ and HHI is greatly complicated by a variety of factors such as regional markets, international trade, and vertical relationships. In addition, the standard approach of establishing categories on the basis of similarity in production techniques, rather than the degree to which they serve as substitutes in the eyes of consumers, means that most structural measures are far from ideal in terms of indicating the extent of market competition. Yet while it is good to recognize such limitations, it is equally important to recognize that some measures of industrial structure are probably better than none at all. Moreover, categorizing industries on the basis of closeness of shared production techniques does

---

5  This issue becomes even more complicated for an industry where large, national firms operate in many local markets. For example, *The New York Times* owns a controlling interest in *The Boston Globe* as well as in other newspapers. The Gannett group controls the newspapers in more than two dozen markets. The banking industry outside the United States reveals a similar pattern of national ownership of local branches.

6  Some authors, for example, Gort (1962) and, more recently, Davies and Morris (1995) have tried to obtain a precise, quantitative measure of the extent of vertical integration.

have its advantages. The most explicit theories of industrial structure link the configuration of an industry to the behavior of its production costs. Such a relationship makes sense only if the production technologies are sufficiently similar that we can make general, industry-wide statements about a typical firm's cost structure.

## 3.2  MEASURING MARKET POWER

Throughout this chapter, we have been thinking about market structure in the literal sense of how the industry's production of output is allocated across different firms. We have seen how summary statistics such as $CR_4$ or HHI attempt to describe this configuration of firms in an industry, much as a census taker might use similar statistics to describe the number and size of families in a geographic region. A large part of the motivation for these measures is the desire to summarize succinctly just where an industry might lie relative to the ideal of perfect competition. There is nothing wrong with this structural approach so long as one clear caveat is kept in mind. This is that a particular structure does not necessarily imply a particular outcome.

When we say that an industry is highly concentrated we are saying that it is not comprised of numerous small firms as in the competitive model, but, instead, that a few firms account for much of its production. Does this necessarily mean that prices charged in this industry are above what would prevail in a perfectly competitive market? The answer is not so straightforward. As we shall see in subsequent chapters, markets with just two or three firms may, under certain conditions, come quite close to duplicating the competitive outcome.

The Lerner Index, or LI, is one way to measure how well a market performs from an efficiency point of view. The LI measures how far the outcome is from the competitive ideal in the following way:

$$\text{LI} = \frac{P - MC}{P}.$$
(3.3)

Because LI directly reflects the discrepancy between price and marginal cost it captures much of what we are interested in when it comes to the *exercise* of market power. For a competitive firm, LI would be zero since such a firm prices at marginal cost. For a pure monopolist, on the other hand, the LI can be shown to be the inverse of the elasticity of demand—the less elastic the demand the greater is the price–marginal cost distortion. To see this, recall that for a monopolist the marginal revenue of selling an additional unit of output can be written as $MR = P + \frac{\Delta P}{\Delta Q} Q$. For profit maximization we set marginal revenue equal to marginal cost, or $P + \frac{\Delta P}{\Delta Q} Q = MC$. Rearranging and dividing by price $P$ we obtain

$$\frac{P - MC}{P} = -\frac{\Delta P}{\Delta Q} \frac{Q}{P} = \frac{1}{\eta},$$
(3.4)

where $1/\eta$ is the inverse of the elasticity of demand. The less elastic is demand, or the smaller is $\eta$, the greater is the difference between market price and marginal cost of production in the monopoly outcome. To drive the point home just a bit more deeply, recall that the perfectly competitive firm faces an infinitely elastic or horizontal demand curve. When such a large value is substituted for the elasticity term in equation (3.4) it implies an LI of 0. Again, the perfectly competitive firm sells at a price equal to marginal cost. Note, too, that the LI can never exceed 1 and that it can only achieve this maximum value if marginal cost is 0.

## Practice Problem 3.2

Show that the Lerner Index has a maximum value of 1. What does this imply about the elasticity of demand facing a firm with monopoly power?

For an industry of more than one but not a large number of firms, measuring LI is more complicated and requires obtaining some average index. A particularly easy case in this regard is that in which the commodity in question is homogenous so that all firms must sell at exactly the same price. If this is so, then we can measure a market-wide LI as

$$LI = \frac{P - \sum_{i=1}^{N} s_i MC_i}{P} .$$

(3.5)

Here, as before, $s_i$ is the market share of the $i$th firm and $N$ is the total number of firms.

LI is a useful conceptual tool and we will make reference to it often in the remainder of this book. Like $CR_4$ or HHI, LI is a summary measure. The difference again is that LI is not so much a measure of how an industry's production is structured as it is a measure of the market outcome. The greater the LI, the farther the market outcome lies from the competitive case—and the more market power is being exploited. In this sense, LI is a direct gauge of the extent of market competition.

Robert Hall (1988) uses a production theory approach to derive estimates of LI for 20 broad manufacturing sectors in the United States. These are shown in Table 3.3. Domowitz, Hubbard, and Petersen (1988) obtained similar but generally lower estimates of the index using Hall's (1988) approach corrected for changes in raw material usage. Whereas Hall found an average price-cost margin of 0.577, Domowitz, Hubbard, and Petersen estimate the average to be only 0.37. Even this lower value, however, indicates a substantial degree of nonprice-taking behavior.

However, much like the structural indices, LI also has its problems. To begin, calculating the LI for an industry once again runs into the problem of market definition. In this respect, the relevant industry-wide estimate of LI can be just as difficult to obtain as are good estimates of $CR_4$ and HHI.

Even when the market definition is reasonably clear, use of LI is still complicated. One issue is measurement. It is one thing to count the number and estimate sizes of the various firms in an industry. Measuring marginal cost or even the elasticity of demand is a good deal trickier. Seemingly small changes in the assumptions one makes about the data can lead to sizable differences in estimated price-cost margins as illustrated by the differences between the Hall (1988) and Domowitz, Hubbard, and Petersen (1988) estimates.

TABLE
**3-3**

### ESTIMATED LERNER INDEX FOR SELECTED INDUSTRIES

| Industry | LI |
|---|---|
| Food & Kindred Products | 0.811 |
| Tobacco | 0.638 |
| Textile Mill Products | 0.214 |
| Apparel | 0.444 |
| Lumber and Wood | 0.494 |
| Furniture and Fixtures | 0.731 |
| Paper and Allied Products | 0.930 |
| Printing | 0.950 |
| Rubber & Plastic | 0.337 |
| Leather Products | 0.524 |
| Stone, Clay, and Glass | 0.606 |
| Primary Metals | 0.540 |
| Fabricated Metals | 0.394 |
| Machinery | 0.300 |
| Electric Equipment | 0.676 |
| Instruments | 0.284 |
| Miscellaneous Manufacturing | 0.777 |
| Communication | 0.972 |
| Electric, Gas, and Sanitary Services | 0.921 |
| Motor Vehicles | 0.433 |
| **Average** | **0.57** |

Moreover, even when LI is accurately measured its interpretation can remain ambiguous. For example, suppose that each firm in an industry has to incur a one-time sunk cost, $F$, associated with setting up its establishment. Assume further that each firm's marginal cost is constant. Because each firm needs to earn enough operating profit to cover its sunk cost, the equilibrium price level will need to rise above marginal cost. That is, LI will need to be positive. However, the more positive that difference is—the greater is the price-cost margin—the greater the number of firms that can cover the one-time sunk cost. As a result, we might observe a high LI precisely in a setting in which there are numerous firms, none of which is very large. In such a case, the high LI might erroneously indicate little competition even though no firm has any significant market power.[7]

Conversely, LI might underestimate market power in settings in which cost-reducing innovations are important. Suppose, for example, that an industry has an old and not very efficient incumbent firm with high marginal cost. As long as demand is somewhat elastic, such a firm may have no choice but to price relatively close to marginal cost. At the same time, the incumbent has a great incentive to take whatever actions it can that will keep a low-cost rival from entering the market. In this

---

7  See, for example, Elzinga (1989).

case, LI deceptively indicates a fair bit of competition because price is low relative to the incumbent's marginal cost, when the relevant but unavailable comparison is the price with the potential rival's lower marginal cost.[8]

## SUMMARY

This chapter has focused on the measurement of market structure and market power. We are often interested in summarizing the extent to which an industry departs from the competitive ideal in a single number or index. The issue then becomes whether and how we can construct such a summary measure.

Concentration indices, such as $CR_4$ or HHI, are explicit measures of a market's structure. Both look at firm shares as a fraction of the industry's total output. Both encounter important problems, such as the difficulty of accurately defining the relevant market. HHI, however, is generally preferred by economists since it not only reflects the number of firms but also the discrepancy in their relative sizes.

An explicit measure of market power is LI. Since it is based on a comparison of price and marginal cost, this index directly addresses the extent to which the market outcome deviates from the competitive ideal. However, the need to measure marginal cost accurately, along with other measurement issues, makes LI as difficult to employ as the structural indices.

As long as the foregoing problems are recognized, the $CR_4$, HHI, and LI measures are useful starting points to characterize an industry's competitive posture. However, an industry's degree of concentration and price-cost margin do not materialize out of thin air. Instead, these indices all derive from the interaction of a number of factors. One of those factors is the nature of production costs. The role that technology and cost play in shaping the industrial outcome is examined in the next chapter.

## PROBLEMS

1. The following table gives U.S. market share data in percentages for three paper product markets in 1994.

| FACIAL TISSUE | | TOILET PAPER | | PAPER TOWELS | |
|---|---|---|---|---|---|
| *Company* | *% Share* | *Company* | *% Share* | *Company* | *% Share* |
| Kimberly-Clark | 48 | Procter & Gamble | 30 | Procter & Gamble | 37 |
| Procter & Gamble | 30 | Scott | 20 | Scott | 18 |
| Scott | 7 | James River | 16 | James River | 12 |
| Georgia Pacific | 6 | Georgia Pacific | 12 | Georgia Pacific | 11 |
| Other | 9 | Kimberly-Clark | 5 | Scott | 4 |
| | | Other | 16 | Other | 18 |

a. Calculate the four-firm concentration ratio for each industry.

b. Calculate each industry's HHI.

c. Which industry do you think exhibits the most concentration?

---

8   Hovenkamp (1994), among others, has made this argument.

**2.** Monopoly Air is the sole provider of passenger air service between Eldorado and Erewhon. It flies two flights per day in either direction with the typical flight being about 85 percent booked. A new entrant, Upstart Airways, has announced plans to offer additional service in the Eldorado–Erewhon market. However, Monopoly Air has filed a complaint with the local transportation authority arguing that it is a natural monopoly and that additional air service will only cause losses for both parties. As evidence, Monopoly Air cites the fact that, even now, its planes are not fully booked. Hence, it argues that the market is not large enough to sustain two, efficient-sized air carriers.

Evaluate the argument put forth by Monopoly Air. What problems do you see in its logic? What information would you ideally like to have in order to determine whether this market is a natural monopoly?

**3.** We defined the Lerner Index as LI = $1/\eta$ where $\eta$ is the absolute value of the elasticity of demand. We also showed that LI can be alternatively expressed as $(P - MC)/P$. Use these relationships to show that LI can never exceed 1. What does this imply is the minimum demand elasticity we should ever observe for a monopolist?

# REFERENCES

Davies, S. W., and C. Morris. 1995. "A New Index of Vertical Integration: Some Estimates for UK Manufacturing." *International Journal of Industrial Organization* 13:151–78.

Domowitz, I., R. G. Hubbard, and B. Petersen. 1988. "Market Structure and Cyclical Fluctuations in Manufacturing." *Review of Economics and Statistics* 70 (February): 55–66.

Elzinga, K. 1989. "Unmasking Monopoly Power: Four Types of Economic Evidence." In R. Larner and J. Meehan, Jr., eds., *Economics and Antitrust Policy*. Westport, CT: Greenwood Press.

Hall, R. 1988. "The Relation Between Price and Marginal Cost in U.S. Industry." *Journal of Political Economy* 96 (October): 921–47.

Gort, M. 1962. *Diversification and Integration in American Industry*. Princeton: Princeton University Press.

Hovenkamp, H. J. 1994. *Federal Antitrust Law Policy: The Law of Competition and Its Practice*. St. Paul: West Publishing.

Sleuwaegen, L., and W. V. Dehandschutter. 1986. "The Critical Choice Between the Concentration Ratio and the H-Index in Assessing Industry Performance." *Journal of Industrial Economics* 35 (December): 193–208.

Sleuwaegen, L., W. V. Dehandschutter, and R. DeBondt. 1989. "The Herfindahl Index and Concentration Ratios Revisited." *Antitrust Bulletin* 34 (Fall): 625–40.

Stocking, G., and W. Mueller. 1955. "The Cellophane Case and the New Competition." *American Economic Review* 45 (March): 29–63.

# Technology and Cost

# Chapter 4

Anyone who has observed the extensive growth of electronic commerce in recent years cannot fail to have noticed the low prices charged by many Internet firms. Egreetings Network, Inc., an Internet firm selling e-mail greeting cards, offers a case in point. In just one year, 1998, the firm lowered its price per card from $2.50 to just $0.50. A year later the company reduced its fees still further. Currently the firm charges less than 10 cents for some cards and gives others away for free. Such minimal pricing strategies are not uncommon in digital commerce. Many e-sellers permit customers to download their products for free or for a very modest charge. The question that naturally arises then is how can such behavior be profitable? Surely these firms incur costs in producing their goods and services. How can they cover their costs while selling at such low prices?

Production costs are not only an important factor explaining firm behavior. Costs are also an important determinant of the industry's structure. Four firms—General Mills, Kelloggs, General Foods (Post), and Quaker Oats—currently account for about 80 percent of sales in the U.S. ready-to-eat breakfast cereal industry. By contrast, the largest four manufacturers of games and toys account for 35 to 45 percent of these products—less if video games are included. To understand why market structures differ across industries we need to consider the production technology and associated cost behavior that underlies such structures.[1] In this chapter we introduce the key cost concepts.

## 4.1 PRODUCTION TECHNOLOGY AND COST FUNCTIONS FOR THE SINGLE-PRODUCT FIRM

What is a firm's technology? For our purposes, the firm's technology is a production relationship that describes how a given quantity of inputs is transformed into the firm's output. It is in this sense that we adopt the traditional neoclassical approach in which a firm is solely envisioned as a production unit. The goal of this production unit is profit maximization, which in turn implies minimizing the cost of making any given level of output.

The neoclassical approach is not without its weaknesses. While it does indicate how the firm's production plan changes in response to changes in input and output prices, it says little about how that plan is actually devised. In other words, it says little about what happens inside the firm and, more specifically, about how the various competing interests of management, workers, and shareholders are reconciled in the design and implementation of a production plan.[2]

---

1   Panzar (1989) presents a more extended review of this topic.
2   See Milgrom and Roberts (1992) for a classic discussion of these issues.

Moreover, whatever happens within a firm it is clear that these internal relationships are different from the external ones between the firm itself and those outside such as customers and suppliers. These external relationships are typically mediated by a market. Customers and suppliers buy from and sell to the firm at market prices. Inside the firm, however, relationships are organized by nonmarket methods, such as hierarchical control. Thus, as eloquently argued by Nobel laureate Ronald Coase (1937), the boundary of the firm is really the boundary between the use of nonmarket business transactions and market ones. The question Coase then raised is what determines this boundary. Why is it that production is conducted by many different firms instead of a few large ones? Indeed, what limits are there to having all production organized by one or a few giant, multidivisional and multiplant firms?

These are questions that the neoclassical view of the firm cannot fully answer because its focus on production costs narrowly defined leads it to ignore another important cost—the cost of transacting business. Coase (1937) was the first to raise the issue in his classic paper, "The Nature of the Firm." Hart and Moore (1990), Williamson (1995), and Hart (1995) are some of the more recent contributions to a long series of papers that have explored these issues subsequently. Yet while the neoclassical approach to firm size and market structure is not without its limitations, it does remain insightful. For our purposes, it is useful to be aware of the issues raised by the agency and transactions cost literature, but to explore those concerns satisfactorily would take us beyond the boundaries of this book! As long as its limitations are recognized, the neoclassical view of the firm will permit us to accomplish our objectives. What this means in practice is that throughout the following discussion one should always keep in mind that a firm is interpreted as simply a profit-maximizing production unit.

## 4.1.1  Key Cost Concepts

Standard microeconomic theory describes a firm in terms of its production technology. A firm producing the quantity $q$ of a single product is characterized by its production function $q = f(x_1, x_2, \ldots, x_k)$. This function specifies that the quantity $q$ that the firm produces is obtained from use of $k$ different inputs at levels $x_1$ for the first input, $x_2$ for the second input, and so on through the $k$th input of which $x_k$ is used. The technology is reflected in the precise form of the function, $f(\ )$. In turn, the nature of this technology will be a central determinant of the firm's costs.

The firm is regarded as a single decision-making unit that chooses output $q$ and the associated inputs $x_1, x_2, \ldots, x_n$ to maximize profits. It is convenient to approach this choice by first identifying the relationship between a firm's output choice and its resulting production costs—which is simply the firm's cost function. That is, for any specific output $\bar{q}$ and given the prices $w_1, w_2, \ldots, w_k$ of the $k$ inputs, there is a unique way to choose the level of each input $x_1, x_2, \ldots, x_n$ so as to minimize the total cost of producing $\bar{q}$. The firm is imagined to obtain this solution by choosing that input combination which solves the problem

$$\text{Minimize}_{x_i} \sum_{i=1}^{k} w_i x_i , \qquad (4.1)$$

subject to the constraint $f(x_1, x_2, \ldots, x_n) = \bar{q}$.

If we solve this problem for different levels of output $\bar{q}$, we will obtain the minimum cost of each possible production level per unit of time. This relationship between costs and output is what is described by the cost function for the firm. We denote the firm's cost function by $C(q) + F$, from which we can then derive three key cost concepts: fixed cost, average or unit cost, and marginal cost.

**Fixed cost:** The fixed cost concept is reflected in the term $F$. It describes a set amount of expenditure that the firm must incur each period that is unrelated to how much output it produces. That is, it must incur $F$ whether it produces zero or a thousand units, hence the term *fixed*. This is distinct from the variable cost $C(q)$, which varies as output changes. Costs that may be fixed include interest costs associated with financing a particular size of plant and advertising costs. Note, however, that these costs may be fixed only in the short run. Over a longer period of time, the firm can adjust what plant size it wants to operate and more closely calibrate its promotional efforts to its sales. If this is true, then these costs are not fixed over a longer period of time.

**Average cost:** The firm's average cost is simply a measure of the expenditure per unit of production and is given by total cost divided by total output. This cost measure depends on output, hence its algebraic representation is $AC(q)$. Formally, $AC(q) = [C(q) + F]/q$. We may also decompose average cost into its fixed and variable components. Average fixed cost is simply total fixed cost per unit of output or $F/q$. Average variable cost $AVC(q)$ is similarly just the total variable cost per unit of output, $C(q)/q$. Alternatively, average variable cost is just average cost less average fixed cost, $AVC(q) = AC(q) - F/q$.

**Marginal cost:** The firm's marginal cost, $MC(q)$, is calculated as the addition to total cost that is incurred in increasing output by one unit. Alternatively, marginal cost can be defined as the saving in total cost that is realized as the firm decreases output by one unit. More precisely, marginal cost is the slope of the total cost function and so is defined by the derivative term $MC(q) = dC(q)/dq$.

We now add a fourth key cost concept—one that cannot be inferred from Figure 4-1. This concept is **sunk cost**. Like fixed cost, sunk cost is a cost that is unrelated to output. However, unlike fixed costs, which are incurred every period, a sunk cost is a cost that is incurred just once—typically as a prerequisite for entry. For example, a doctor or a taxi service will need to acquire a license to operate. Alternatively, a firm may need to do market or product research before it enters a market. Yet once the doctor or taxi firm makes the expenditure necessary to obtain licensing, and once the firm completes its research, these costs never have to be incurred again. From that point on, they are sunk and cannot be recovered.

## 4.1.2 Cost Variables and Output Decisions

Figure 4-1 depicts a standard textbook average cost function, $AC(q)$, and its corresponding marginal cost function, $MC(q)$. As discussed in Chapter 2, profit maximization over any period of time requires that the firm produce where marginal revenue is equal to marginal cost. Thus, with one important caveat, marginal cost is the relevant cost concept to determine how much the firm should produce. That caveat is that marginal cost is important for determining how much to produce *given* that the firm is going to produce any output at all.

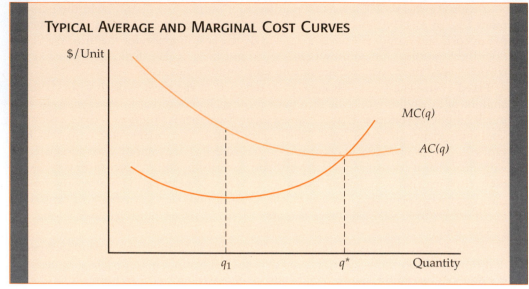

**TYPICAL AVERAGE AND MARGINAL COST CURVES**

Suppose, for example, that demand is very weak. In such a case, equating marginal cost to marginal revenue may result in price falling below average cost. If price is below average cost, the firm loses money on every unit that it sells. It cannot continue to do this in the long run; the firm will eventually shut down if price stays below average cost. Whether this shutdown happens sooner or later will depend on the relation between price and average variable cost, $AVC(q)$. If price exceeds average variable cost, the firm will continue to operate in the short run. If price is above average variable cost, the firm makes some operating profit on each unit that it sells and this provides some funds to cover at least some of its fixed cost. However, if price is below average variable cost, then the firm will shut down immediately.

Consideration of price and average cost also allows us to identify the role played by sunk cost in the firm's decision making. Again, profit per unit in any period is simply price less average cost, $P - AC(q)$. Total profit in any period is just the profit per unit times the number of units, $[P - AC(q)]q$. Before entering an industry, a firm must expect at least to break even. If entry incurs a sunk cost such as a licensing fee or research expense, then the firm will have to believe that it will earn enough profit in subsequent periods to cover that initial sunk cost. Otherwise, it will not enter the market. (Formally, the discounted present value of the expected future profits must be at least as great as the sunk cost.) Note, though, that once it has entered, the sunk cost is no longer relevant. Once the entry decision has been made and the sunk cost incurred, the best that the firm can do is to follow the prescription above—produce where marginal revenue equals marginal cost so long as price is equal to average cost, otherwise shut down. That is, sunk cost affects the entry decision—not the decision on how much to produce after entry has occurred.

In sum, the concept of average cost is relevant to whether the firm will produce positive output. The concept of marginal cost is relevant to how much output the firm will produce given that it opts to produce a positive amount. Sunk cost is relevant to the decision to enter the market in the first place.

## 4.1.3 Costs and Market Structure

Let's take a second, closer look at Figure 4-1. This figure illustrates an important relationship between average and marginal costs. Note that when marginal cost is less than average cost, as at output $q_1$, an expansion of output will lead to a reduction in average cost. Conversely, when marginal cost is greater than average cost, an expansion of output will lead to an increase in average cost. In the figure, marginal cost is less than average cost for all outputs less than $q^*$, and average cost falls throughout this range of output. Marginal cost is greater than average cost for outputs greater than $q^*$, and average cost rises over this range of output. This feature is true for all cost functions. Average cost falls whenever marginal cost is less than average cost and rises whenever marginal cost exceeds average cost. A corollary of this relationship between marginal cost and average cost is that the two are equal at the minimum point on the average cost function.

The basic cost relationships are illustrated in Table 4-1 (the parameter $S$ in this table will be explained later). This table provides measures of total, average, and marginal cost data for a firm.[3] As the table documents, average cost falls when it is above marginal cost, rises when it is below marginal cost, and (because the numbers are an approximation) is essentially equal to marginal cost at the minimum average cost value. Intuitively, if the marginal cost is below average cost when average cost falls but crosses above average cost when average cost starts to rise, then the crossing point at which the two are equal must be at the minimum average cost.

### AVERAGE AND MARGINAL COST

| Output | Total Cost ($) | Average Cost ($) | Marginal Cost ($) | Scale Economy Index (S) |
|---|---|---|---|---|
| 5 | 725 | 145 | — | — |
| 6 | 816 | 136 | 96 | 1.42 |
| 7 | 917 | 131 | 104 | 1.26 |
| 8 | 1024 | 128 | 113 | 1.13 |
| 9 | 1143 | 127 | 123 | 1.03 |
| 10 | 1270 | 127 | 132 | 0.96 |
| 11 | 1408 | 128 | 151 | 0.85 |
| 12 | 1572 | 131 | — | — |

**TABLE 4-1**

As noted earlier, firms have to expect to break even in order for production to be profitable. This means that both average cost and sunk cost play a role in determining market structure. We consider average cost first.

---

3  Note: In Table 4-1, marginal cost is calculated as the average of the increase in cost associated with producing one unit more and the decrease in cost associated with producing one unit less.

**Derivation Checkpoint**

## Relationship between Average and Marginal Cost

Average cost is defined to be $AC(q) = C(q)/q$. Differentiate this with respect to output to give

$$\frac{dAC(q)}{dq} = \frac{q\,\dfrac{dC(q)}{dq} - C(q)}{q^2}$$

using the rule for differentiation of a quotient. This can be simplified to

$$\frac{dAC(q)}{dq} = \frac{q\left(MC(q) - \dfrac{C(q)}{q}\right)}{q^2} = \frac{[MC(q) - AC(q)]}{q}.$$

The denominator is positive, so the slope of the average cost curve depends on the relation between marginal cost and average cost. If marginal cost exceeds average cost, the slope is positive. Raising output raises average cost. If average cost exceeds marginal cost, the slope is negative. Raising output lowers average cost. Minimum average cost is found where the slope is zero, which occurs when average cost equals marginal cost.

The fact that average cost falls as output increases amounts to saying that the cost per unit of output declines as the scale of operations rises. It is natural to describe this state of affairs as one in which there are economies of scale. However, if unit costs rise as production increases we say that there are diseconomies of scale. Fundamentally, the presence of scale economies or scale diseconomies reflects the underlying technology. Some factors of production simply cannot be scaled down to small levels of production. For example, provision of passenger rail service between Omaha and Lincoln, Nebraska, will require approximately sixty miles of track whether the number of trains per day is one or twenty. As a result, a passenger train firm renting the track from the freight company that currently owns it will have to pay the same rent whether it has many passengers or just a few.

Yet it is not just the presence of large fixed costs that give rise to scale economies. For many productive processes, there are efficiencies that come about just as a result of being larger. To begin with, size permits a greater division of labor, as Adam Smith noted over 200 years ago.[4] This in turn permits specialization and more efficient production. Sometimes the simple mathematics of the activity give rise to important scale effects. It is well known, for example, that the cost of a container will rise roughly in proportion to its surface area (essentially, the radius squared), whereas its capacity

---

4  Smith's classic, *The Wealth of Nations*, includes a famous chapter on the division of labor and the productivity enhancement that this yielded at a pin factory.

## ✔ Derivation Checkpoint

### Cost Minimization: Some Comments

Derivation of a cost function assumes that firms produce each output level at minimum cost. A necessary requirement for such minimization is that the following equation be satisfied for any pair of inputs $i$ and $j$:

$$\frac{MP_i}{MP_j} = \frac{w_i}{w_j}, \text{ which is equivalent to } \frac{MP_i}{w_i} = \frac{MP_j}{w_j}.$$

In other words, inputs should be used up to the point where the marginal product of the last dollar spent on input $i$ equals the marginal product of the last dollar spent on input $j$.

---

rises roughly in proportion to its volume (essentially, the radius cubed). Thus, while a 10×10×10 cube will hold 1000 cubic feet, a 20×20×20 cube holds 8000 cubic feet. Since the cost in terms of materials and labor depends on surface area but output depends on volume, it follows that as container size increases there is a less than proportional rise in the cost. In turn, this implies that unit cost declines as output increases. Specifically, unit cost will fall by about 3 percent for every 10 percent increase in output.[5] For a variety of processes, such as distributing natural gas via a pipeline or manufacturing glass products in which molten glass is kept in large ovens, this relationship suggests that it will be less expensive per unit to operate at a large volume.[6]

Whatever the source of the scale economies, the fact that it is defined as a falling average cost gives us a precise way to measure such effects. We know that a declining average cost will be observed only if marginal cost is below average cost. Likewise, the presence of scale diseconomies or rising average cost requires that marginal cost be above average cost. Hence, we can construct a precise index of the extent of scale economies by taking the ratio $S$ defined as $S = AC(q)/MC(q)$. That is, $S$ is the ratio of average to marginal cost. $S$ can also be shown to be the inverse of the elasticity of cost with respect to output. (See the Derivation Checkpoint on Scale Economies.) In other words, $S$ measures the proportionate increase in output one obtains for a given proportionate increase in costs.

The more that $S$ exceeds 1, the greater is the extent of scale economies. In such a setting, a one percent increase in output is associated with a less than one percent increase in costs. Conversely, when $S < 1$, diseconomies of scale are present. Increasing output by one percent now leads to more than a one percent increase in costs. Finally,

---

5  The classic study by Chenery (1949) on natural-gas pipelines is an example of this technical relationship.
6  Note that the technical explanations given here reflect the shortcomings of the neoclassical approach in that they do not make clear why the scale economies associated with a specific production technology must be exploited within a single firm. For example, two or more firms can jointly own pipelines. Indeed, there is growing support for the use of co-ownership or cotenancy, as an alternative to direct regulation in the case of natural monopoly. See Gale (1994).

# Derivation Checkpoint

## The Scale Economy Index and the Elasticity of Total Cost

Using standard definitions, the output elasticity of costs is defined to be the proportionate increase in costs that arises from a given proportionate increase in output, which can be written

$$\eta_C = \frac{dC(q)}{C(q)} \bigg/ \frac{dq}{q}, \text{ which gives } \eta_C = \frac{dC(q)}{dq} \bigg/ \frac{q}{C(q)}.$$

This in turn simplifies to

$$\eta_C = \frac{MC(q)}{AC(q)},$$

from which it follows that $S = 1/\eta_C$.

when $S = 1$, neither economies nor diseconomies of scale are present. In this case, we say that the production technology exhibits constant returns to scale.

In Table 4-1, we can approximate the value of $S$ at $q = 6$ as follows. The addition to total cost of increasing output from 6 to 7 is \$101. The reduction in total cost of decreasing $q$ by one unit is \$91. So, an approximate measure of marginal cost at exactly $q = 6$ is the mean of these two numbers, or \$96. Average cost at $q = 6$ is \$136. Accordingly, $S = 136/96 = 1.42$. $S$ can also be estimated by dividing the percentage increase in total output by the percentage increase in total cost. For example, when output is increased from 6 to 7 the percentage increase is given by

$$\frac{1}{6} \times 100\% = 16.67\%.$$

Meanwhile, this output rise induces a percentage increase in total cost of

$$\frac{917 - 816}{816} \times 100\% = 12.38\%.$$

The ratio of these two percentages is then $16.67\%/12.38\% = 1.35$. This is not far from the measure of $S = 1.42$ that we obtained using the ratio of average to marginal cost. Indeed, if we could vary production more continuously and so consider the cost of producing $6 \frac{1}{4}$ units, or $6 \frac{1}{2}$ units, and so on, the two measures would be virtually equal.

The ratio of the percentage change in total cost with respect to the percentage change in output is called the elasticity of cost with respect to output. What we have just shown is that the inverse of this ratio—the percentage change in output divided by the percentage change in cost—is a good indicator of scale economies. In other words, the inverse of the elasticity of cost with respect to output is a very good measure of $S$.

---

## Practice Problem 4.1

Confirm that at an output of $q = 11$, the scale economy index in Table 4-1 is indeed 0.85.

---

How is the behavior of average cost or the extent of scale economies related to industry structure? Going back to Figure 4-1, we see that $S > 1$ for any level of output less than $q^*$. Scale economies are present at every output level in this range. By contrast, $S < 1$ for all outputs greater than $q^*$. Now suppose that we have other information indicating that demand conditions are such that the maximum extent of the market is less than $q^*$ even if the price falls to zero. We can then state that scale economies are present throughout the relevant range of production. Put another way, economies of scale are global in such a market.

If scale economies are global then the market is a natural monopoly. The term "natural" is meant to reflect the implication that monopoly is an (almost) inevitable outcome for this market because it is cheaper in such cases for a single firm to supply the entire market than for two or more firms to do so. For example, the least expensive way to produce the quantity $q^*$ in Figure 4-1 is to have one firm produce the entire amount. If, instead, two firms divided this production equally, so that each produced an output $q_1 = q^*/2$, each of these two firms would have higher average costs than would the single firm producing $q^*$.

The role of scale economies in determining market structure should now be clear. If scale economies are global, there should be no more than one firm in the market. Even if they are not global but simply quite large, efficiency may still require that all the production be done in one firm. More generally, the greater the extent of scale economies—the larger the output at which average cost is minimized—the fewer firms that can operate efficiently in the market. Thus, large scale economies tend to result in concentrated markets.

---

## Practice Problem 4.2

Consider the following cost relationship: $C = 50 + 2q + 0.5q^2$.

a. Derive an expression for average cost. Plot the value of average cost for $q = 4$, $q = 8$, $q = 10$, $q = 12$, and $q = 15$.

b. Marginal cost can be approximated by a rise in cost, $\Delta C$, that occurs when output increases by one unit, $\Delta q = 1$. However, it can also be approximated by the fall in cost that occurs when output is decreased by one unit, $\Delta q = -1$. Since these two measures will not be quite the same we often use their average. Show that for the above cost relation, this procedure produces an estimate of marginal cost equal to $MC = 2 + q$.

c. Now compute the index of scale economies, $S$. For what values of $q$ is it the case that $S > 1$, $S = 1$, and $S < 1$?

---

Sunk costs also play a role in influencing market structure. It is conceptually similar to the role of scale economies. Again, firms enter a market only if they believe

**Reality** **Checkpoint**

## Fixed Costs in the Shopping Mall

Walk into the typical shopping mall these days, and you will find the main concourse filled with modest boutiques that, unlike regular mall establishments, can be rolled away in minutes. Such shopping mall pushcarts are much like the peddlers' carts of earlier times. Their owners sell specific items such as key chains, specialty foods, artwork, and flowers. By operating out of pushcarts, these vendors cut their fixed costs considerably. Cart owners in the Mall of America, which opened in 1992 and covers the size of seven New York Yankee stadiums, pay rent of $2,200 per month plus 15 percent of any monthly revenues over $14,666. In contrast, the standard store in the Mall of America pays monthly rent of $300,000. Moreover, the market for pushcart items is large. The Mall of America draws 600,000 visitors a week and 900,000 during the Christmas holidays. Many carts earn $30,000 to $40,000 a month in sales. The combination of low fixed costs and large market size implies that the pushcart business should be populated by a large number of firms. In fact, between 1992 and 1996, the number of pushcarts in the Mall of America grew from less than 10 to over 420.

**Source:** B. J. Feder, "The Little Pushcarts that Could." *The New York Times*, May 13, 1999, pp. 33–34.

that they can at least break even. This means that if there are positive sunk costs associated with entry, then firms must earn positive profits in each subsequent period of actual operation to cover those entry costs. If this is the case, entry will occur. Indeed, this view leads naturally to a definition of long-run equilibrium. Firms will stop entering the industry—and therefore the number of firms will be at its equilibrium level—when the profit from operating each period just covers the initial sunk cost that entry requires. Of course, the more firms that enter an industry, the more competitive pricing will be and the less profit a firm will make in any period of actual operation.

The foregoing logic permits us to see clearly the role of sunk cost in determining market structure. The higher the sunk cost, the fewer firms there will be in equilibrium. A high sunk entry cost requires that each firm that enters subsequently earns a fair bit of profit from its operations to repay the initial entry expense. This can happen only if the number of firms that enters is small so that price competition is weak and price can rise above marginal (and average) cost.

To take a fairly simple example, imagine a market in which each firm produces an identical good and in which the elasticity of demand is exactly one, or $\eta = 1$, throughout the demand curve. This means that the total consumer expenditure for the product is constant. A one percent decrease in price is balanced by a one percent increase in quantity sold. Denote this constant total expenditure as $E$. If $P$ is the market price and $Q$ is total market output, we then have $E = PQ$. However, total output $Q$ is also equal to the output of each firm, $q_i$, times the number of firms, $N$, that is, $Q = Nq_i$. Putting these two relationships together we then obtain

$$q_i = E/NP. \qquad (4.2)$$

Now recall the Lerner Index that was discussed in Chapter 3. If we assume that all firms are identical and that each has a constant marginal (and average) production cost $c$, then LI is given by $(P - c)/P$. Since this index is a measure of the extent of monopoly power in the industry, it is natural to assume that it declines as the number of firms $N$ gets larger. We formalize this idea by assuming that the industry LI is negatively related to the number of firms $N$ as follows:

$$(P - c)/P = A/N^\alpha, \qquad (4.3)$$

where $A$ and $\alpha$ are both arbitrary positive constants. Finally, let's assume that firms only operate one period so that to break even requires that $(P - c)q_i = K$, where $K$ is the sunk entry cost. Substituting this break-even requirement into equation (4.2) and then combining that equation with equation (4.3) yields the equilibrium number of firms $N^e$ at which each entrant just covers its sunk entry cost $K$, given by

$$N^e = \left[ \frac{AE}{K} \right]^{\frac{1}{1+\alpha}}. \qquad (4.4)$$

Equation (4.4) says that as the sunk cost $K$ increases, the equilibrium number of firms decreases. That is, higher sunk costs imply, all else being equal, a more concentrated industry.

We have seen that sunk costs arise from licensing and other setup costs. They also arise from the use of inputs that are highly specialized to a particular activity and have little value in other uses. The airplanes used to open a new air service, say between Miami and Houston, can be used elsewhere. Hence, these expenditures are not sunk. However, the market research expenditures incurred in investigating the feasibility of the market in the first place have little value for other markets and so cannot be recovered. Similarly, kilns installed to manufacture cement have almost no alternative uses other than as scrap metal.

## 4.2 COSTS AND MULTIPRODUCT FIRMS

Since scale economies are a description of the behavior of costs as output increases, investigating their existence in any industry requires that we measure the output of the firms in that industry. This is not always easy. Consider, for instance, the case of a railroad. One possible measure of output is the rail ton-mile, defined as the number of tons transported times the average number of miles each ton travels. However, not all railroads carry the same type of freight. Some carry mainly mining and forestry products, some carry manufactured goods, and some carry agricultural products. In addition, through the first half of this century, many private U.S. railroads carried passengers as well as freight. This is still the case elsewhere in the world. Since all of these different kinds of services have different carrying costs, aggregating each railroad's

**Reality Checkpoint**

### High Sunk Costs Can Sink a Profession

Sunk costs affect many professions from medicine to plumbing. A good example of such a profession is veterinary services. Veterinary school is expensive. While annual tuition at such schools varies, the full fee in 2002 was as much as $30,000 at some institutions. Beyond the tuition and other fees, the would-be veterinarian must also consider the opportunity cost of not being part of the regular labor force and not earning income for the four years of required schooling. The result is that a new veterinarian must devote 10 percent or more of her salary to paying off debts incurred in financing her education.

Most of these costs are sunk. Licensing and other restrictions make it difficult to apply the skills learned in vet school to other fields. One cannot, for example, shift from treating animals to treating people. Nor can one go back and undo the investment of four years' time.

These considerations, along with the fact that the anticipated income of a veterinarian is not that large, have led to a recent decline of 12 percent in veterinary school applications.

**Source:** B. M. Kuehn, "Veterinary Students Bearing the Brunt of State Budget Cuts at Universities." *Journal of the American Veterinary Medical Association*, November 15, 2002, pp. 1364–71.

output into a simple measure such as total ton-miles will confuse any cost analysis. Such aggregation does not allow us to identify whether cost differences between railroads are due to differences in scale or to differences in the kinds of service being offered.

The railroad example points to a gap in our analysis of the firm. In particular, it implies the need to extend the analysis to cover firms producing more than one type of good, that is, to investigate costs for multiproduct firms. This need is perhaps more important today than ever before. Evidence provided by Dunne, Roberts, and Samuelson (1988) and others indicates that the great majority of business establishments produce more than one product—often many more. The major automobile firms also produce trucks and buses. Microsoft produces both the Windows operating system and several applications written for that system. Consumer electronics firms produce televisions, stereos, CD players, and so on. Measuring the output of these firms is clearly less than straightforward.

Even when firms produce what might be considered a single basic product, they typically offer several varieties of that good. Thus, in the ready-to-eat breakfast cereal industry, the top four firms market over eighty brands of cereal. If we are to use the technological approach to the firm to gain some understanding of industry structure, we clearly need to extend that approach to handle multiproduct companies. In other words, we need to develop an analysis of costs for the multiproduct firm. The question then becomes whether we can derive average cost and scale economy measures for multiproduct firms that are as precise and clear as the analogous concepts developed for the single-product firm.

The answer to the foregoing question is yes, subject to some constraints. This is the major contribution of Baumol, Panzar, and Willig (1982). These authors show that the principal restriction is simply that we measure average cost for a given mix of products, say two units of freight service for every one unit of passenger service in the railroad case. We can then measure average cost at any production level so long as we keep these proportions constant. This is what Baumol, Panzar, and Willig call ray average cost (RAC). They further show that we can derive a measure of scale economies based on the RAC measure that is conceptually similar to the scale economies measure for the single-product firm. (See Derivation Checkpoint: Ray Average Cost and Multiproduct Scale Economies.)

Perhaps the most important insight of Baumol, Panzar, and Willig (1982), however, is their introduction of the concept of *economies of scope*. Economies of scope are said to be present whenever it is less costly to produce a set of goods in one firm than it is to produce that set in two or more firms. Let the total cost of producing two goods, $q_1$ and $q_2$, be given by $C(q_1, q_2)$. Then, for the two-product case, scope economies exist if $C(q_1, 0) + C(0, q_2) - C(q_1, q_2) > 0$. The first two terms in this equation are the total costs of producing product 1, say passenger services, in one firm and product 2, say freight services, in another. The third term is the total cost of having these products produced by the same firm. If this difference is positive, then scope economies exist. If it is negative, then diseconomies of scope exist. If it is 0, then neither economies nor diseconomies of scope exist. The degree of such economies, $S_C$, is defined by the ratio

$$S_C = \frac{C(q_1, 0) + C(0, q_2) - C(q_1, q_2)}{C(q_1, q_2)} . \tag{4.5}$$

The concept of scope economies is a crucial one that provides the central reason for the existence of multiproduct firms. Perhaps what is most important about scope economies, however, is that they give rise to multiproduct scale economies where we might not have expected any to exist. Considering the production of only one product may not indicate any scale economy effects. However, if producing more of one product lowers the cost of producing another, then the firm may be able to lower its ray average cost as it increases the production of both products.

Economies of scope can arise for two main reasons. The first is that particular outputs share common inputs. This is the source of economies of scope in the railroad example. There, the common factor is the track necessary to offer either passenger or freight rail service. Many other examples can be identified. For instance, a firm's advertising expenditures benefit all of its products to the extent that such advertising is intended to establish the firm's brand name. Similarly, where different products are manufactured with identical components—computer chips, for example—the manufacture of a whole range of such products allows the firm to take advantage of economies of scale in the manufacture of the components.

An alternative source of scope economies is the presence of cost complementarities. Cost complementarities occur when producing more of one good lowers the cost of producing a second good. For example, consider the cost function $C(q_1, q_2) = 25q_1 + 30q_2 - 3q_1q_2/2$. If it were not for the negative sign in the last interactive term, this cost function would exhibit no scope economies. Absent this last term, the total cost of producing both goods at the same firm would be exactly the same as producing each at separate firms: $25 for every unit of $q_1$ and $30 for every unit of $q_2$.

**Derivation Checkpoint**

## Ray Average Cost and Multiproduct Scale Economies

Scale economies are always indicated by declining average cost. The relevant concept of average cost for a multiproduct firm is ray average cost (RAC). If a firm has two products so that its cost function is $C(q_1, q_2)$ we may implicitly define total output $q$ by the equations $q_1 = \lambda_1 q$ and $q_2 = \lambda_2 q$, where $\lambda_1$ and $\lambda_2$ sum to unity. Then ray average cost is

$$RAC(q) = \frac{C(\lambda_1 q,\ \lambda_2 q)}{q}.$$

In the single-product case, the scale economy measure reflects the behavior of average cost as output expands. Similarly, for the two-product case, the issue is the behavior of RAC as output expands. Formally, this is given by derivative of RAC with respect to $q$. This is

$$\frac{dRAC(q)}{dq} = \frac{(\lambda_1 MC_1 + \lambda_2 MC_2)q - C(\lambda_1 q,\ \lambda_2 q)}{q^2} = \frac{q_1 MC_1 + q_2 MC_2 - C(q_1,\ q_2)}{q^2},$$

where $MC_i$ is the marginal cost of producing good $i$. It follows immediately that the sign of $dRAC(q)/dq$ is determined by the sign of the numerator of this expression. In other words, if $q_1 MC_1 + q_2 MC_2 > C(q_1, q_2)$ then $dRAC(q)/dq > 0$, while if $q_1 MC_1 + q_2 MC_2 < C(q_1, q_2)$ then $dRAC(q)/dq < 0$. Now define the ratio

$$S = \frac{C(q_1, q_2)}{q_1 MC_1 + q_2 MC_2}.$$

The sign of the derivative above is then fully described by the value of $S$. If $S > 1$, this is equivalent to saying that ray average cost decreases with output and so exhibits multiproduct increasing returns to scale. If $S < 1$, ray average cost is increasing, and so exhibits multiproduct decreasing returns to scale. If $S = 1$, neither scale economies nor diseconomies exist for the multiproduct firm. Note the similarity of this measure with our single-product scale economy index. In the single-product case, we measured scale economies by the ratio of average to marginal cost. This is more or less what we are doing here except that average cost is now measured by total cost divided by a weighted average of marginal cost. This is why we continue to use $S$ to indicate scale economies. Moreover, while we have worked out this case for just the two-product firm, it easily generalizes to the case in which there are more than two products.

However, the negative interaction term, $-3q_1 q_2/2$ implies that the more $q_1$ that a firm produces, the lower is the cost of producing $q_2$ and vice-versa. There are numerous ways in which such complementarities arise. The exploration and drilling of an oil well often yields not just oil but also natural gas. Hence, engaging in crude oil pro-

## ✓ Reality Checkpoint

### Talk about Scope Economies, Holy Cow!

Economies of scope arise in many situations—including, as noted in the text below, agricultural production. There is ample evidence that farms producing multiple crops and those mixing livestock production with crop production are more cost efficient than farms specializing in just one or two crops. For farms that specialize in livestock, the gains from adding crop production seem less clear. However, this may be because livestock production itself already embodies many scope economies.

Consider a cattle ranch. Raising cattle not only produces beef, but also leather. So clearly it is cheaper for one farm to pro-duce both products rather than for two farms to do each separately. Moreover, beef and leather are far from the only uses of cattle products. Cattle carcasses are in fact used in hundreds of products. Glycerin and collagen are both cattle by-products. Other cattle body parts find their way into vaccines, animal feed, gelatin capsules, engine lubricants, asphalt, paper coatings, and fabric softeners, to name just a few. Imagine how much additional cost would be incurred if separate cattle stocks were maintained for the production of each of these products.

**Sources:** V. Klinkenborg, "The Whole Cow and Nothing but the Whole Cow." *The New York Times*, January 20, 2004, p. 18 and C. Morrison Paul and R. Nehring, "Product Diversification, Production Systems, and Economic Performance in U.S. Agricultural Production." *Journal of Econometrics*, forthcoming.

duction will likely lower the cost of gas exploration. Similarly, a firm that manufactures computer software may also find it easy to provide computer consulting services, or producing graduate education may be easier if one also provides undergraduate education.

## Practice Problem 4.3

The Lauren Ralph company produces a number of products including men's shirts, $q_1$, and cologne, $q_2$. Let the cost functions associated with these products be

$$C(q_1, 0) = 2 + \sqrt{q_1}$$
$$C(0, q_2) = 2 + q_2^2$$
$$C(q_1, q_2) = 3 + \sqrt{q_1} + q_2^2$$

a. Show that production of shirts enjoys substantial product-specific scale economies but that production of cologne does not. What does this suggest about the likely structure of the cologne market?

b. Show that despite the absence of significant product-specific scale economies, the scope economies between shirt and cologne production, along with the significant scale economies in shirts, imply that the cologne market will likely be quite concentrated.

---

In our discussion of a multiproduct cost function such as $C(q_1, q_2)$, we did not distinguish between situations in which the two outputs are somewhat related, as is the case with passenger and freight rail service, and those where the two goods are substantially different products, say cologne and shirts. In the latter case, the two products use different production processes and the presence of scope economies seems less compelling. It seems more likely that scope economies will be found when the goods being produced use similar production techniques since then we are more likely to find shared inputs and cost complementarities.

We expect scope economies to be most prevalent in the joint production of different varieties of the same good, because in that case production similarities are strongest. For instance, the possibilities for cost savings due to sharing a common factor or due to cost complementarities seem clear in the case of a ready-to-eat cereal manufacturer producing many varieties of essentially the same wheat-based cereal product. It is probably also true for a firm such as Campbell Soup Company that produces a wide variety of prepared foods, most notably, soups. To consider these issues, we need to conceptualize more clearly the meaning of different varieties of the same good. For this purpose, we now introduce a model of product differentiation that will be used extensively in later chapters.

To speak about differentiated products in a rigorous way requires that we have some way to measure just how differentiated they are. One way to do this is to imagine that some particular characteristic is the critical distinguishing feature between different versions of the good. In the case of cars, this characteristic could be speed or acceleration. In the case of soft drinks, it could be sugar content. We can then construct an index to measure this feature. Each point on the index, ranging from low to high acceleration capacity, low to high sugar content, etc. represents a different product variety. Some consumers will prefer a car that accelerates rapidly or a very sweet beverage, while others will favor cars capable of less acceleration or beverages with very low sugar content.

As an example, imagine a soft drink company considering the marketing of three versions of its basic cola: (1) Diet or sugar free; (2) Super, with full sugar content; and (3) LX, an intermediate cola with just half the sugar content of Super. In this case, the distinctive feature separating each product type is sugar content. As a result, we first need to construct an index of sugar content. It is customary to normalize such an index so that it ranges from 0 to 1. The spectrum of products for our imaginary company, therefore, ranges from Diet, located at point 0 on our index, to Super, located at point 1, with LX positioned squarely in the middle at point 0.5. This is illustrated in Figure 4-2.

**FIGURE 4-2**

### LOCATION OF COLA PRODUCTS ALONG THE SUGAR CONTENT LINE

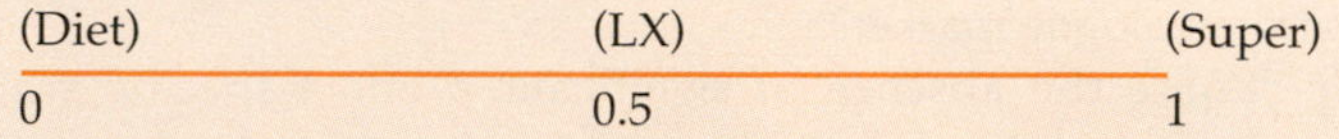

| (Diet) | (LX) | (Super) |
|--------|------|---------|
| 0 | 0.5 | 1 |

The spectrum shown in Figure 4-2 alternatively may be regarded as a street. In turn, we may regard consumers as being located at different addresses on this street. Consumers who really like sugar will have addresses close to the Super product line. In contrast, consumers who need to watch their calorie intake will have addresses near the Diet product line. Similarly, consumers who favor more than a medium amount of sugar but not quite so much as that contained in the Super variety will have addresses somewhere between the LX and Super points.

We suspect that scope economies will exist for a firm producing different varieties of a common good, such as the various soft drink products just described. Indeed, such scope economies have become increasingly likely in recent years as the result of the introduction of new manufacturing techniques, referred to as flexible manufacturing systems. They can be defined as "production unit(s) capable of producing a range of discrete products with a minimum of manual intervention" (U.S. Office of Technology Assessment, 1984, p. 60). The idea here is that production processes should be capable of switching easily from one variant of a product to another without a significant cost penalty.

A common example of a flexible manufacturing system is found in the popular clothing manufacturer Benetton. Almost everyone is familiar with Benetton's advertisements and its array of brightly colored sweaters, T-shirts, and jeans. In fact, the coloring process is a distinctive feature of Benetton's manufacturing technology. The dyeing of the goods is done at the last moment just before shipment to the stores. Using computer-programmable equipment, Benetton is able to shift from one color-specific order to another with minimal adjustment costs. In other words, Benetton's extensive use of computer-assisted-design/computer-assisted-manufacturing (CAD/CAM) technology allows it to produce a wide array of differentiated (by color) products. In recent years, other firms have been similarly aided by CAD/CAM technology. Benjamin Moore paints and Toyota cars are just two of many companies that have used this technology to offer a wide range of choices within the same basic product line.

If scope economies exist, firms have a strong incentive to exploit them. This will lower the firm's costs, possibly permit it to exploit multiproduct scale economies, and allow it to obtain a closer match between the products it offers and those desired by specific customers. Eaton and Schmitt (1994) show that this is exactly what happens in a formal model of flexible manufacturing in which there are $k$ possible versions of the good. They show that when scope economies are very strong, it will be natural for each firm in the industry to produce the entire range of $k$ products. In addition, the presence of such strong scope economies also tends to give rise to important multiproduct scale economies that imply that the industry will tend to be concentrated. Moreover, even weak scope economies are sufficient to imply that it is less costly to organize production in a smaller number of firms. That is, it will be less costly to have fewer firms producing a range of products rather than to have one firm producing each product separately. In short, the presence of scope economies in the production of differentiated products tends to increase industrial concentration in such industries.[7]

---

7  See Evans and Heckman (1986) and Roller (1990) for evidence of scope economies in the telephone industry; Cohn, Rhine, and Santos (1989) and DeGroot, McMahon, and Volkwein (1991) for evidence of scope economies in higher education; and Gilligan, Smirlock, and Marshall (1984) and Pulley and Braunstein (1992) for evidence of scope economies in finance.

**Reality Checkpoint**

### Flexible Manufacturing at Lands' End

In October of 2000, Lands' End started to offer custom-made pants on its website. Customers interested in buying chinos or jeans can simply go to the firm's website, type in measurements like weight and height, and characterize the proportions of thighs, hips, and other variables. A computer program then analyzes the information, calculates the ideal dimensions of the pants, and sends the information to a manufacturing plant in Mexico. At the plant, a computerized cutting machine creates the fabric pattern, and the pants are sewn and shipped to customers two to four weeks later, depending on the volume of orders.

The price in 2000 for a typical pair of customized pants was about $55, plus $6 for shipping. This was noticeably above the $40 to $47 cost of noncustomized pants. Lands' End can charge these higher prices without fear of losing customers because consumers are willing to pay more for customized products. Indeed, within a year, forty percent of the pants sold on the Lands' End website were customized ones. The custom service also helps Lands' End to reduce the amount of unwanted merchandise in its warehouse at the end of the season. In turn, this reduces carrying costs and further increases the average profit margin per item because fewer clothes are sold at clearance prices. It is only a matter of time before this mass customization that flexible manufacturing makes possible spreads to other on-line clothing retailers.

**Source:** B. Tedeschi, "E-Commerce Report; A Lands' End Experiment In Selling Custom-Made Pants Is A Success, Leaving Its Rivals To Play Catch-Up." *The New York Times*, September 30, 2002, p. C3.

## 4.3  NONCOST DETERMINANTS OF INDUSTRY STRUCTURE

So far, we have focused on the role of cost relationships, especially scale and scope economies, as being the main determinants of firm size and industry structure. There are, however, other factors that play an important role. In this section we cover three such factors: (1) the size of the market, (2) the presence of any network externalities on the demand side, and (3) the role of government policy.

### 4.3.1  Market Size

The influence of market size on industry structure has been extensively investigated by Sutton (1991, 2001). The fact that a firm must be large to reach the minimum efficient scale of operations does not necessarily imply a highly concentrated structure if the market in question is large enough to accommodate many such firms. Similarly, the fact that it is cheaper to produce many different products (or many versions of the same product) in one firm rather than in several does not necessarily imply a market dominated by a few firms. Most farms produce more than one crop. Yet farming is a very competitively structured industry, in part because the market for agricultural products is so extensive.

Just how big does a market have to be in order to avoid domination by a few firms? It depends. When scale economies are extensive, for example, when sunk or fixed costs associated with indivisible inputs are considerable, the market will need to be larger than when such factors are less pronounced. Thus, the relationship between market structure and market size will vary according to the specific market being examined.

If scale economies are exhausted at some point and if sunk entry costs do not rise, we should see that concentration declines as market size grows sufficiently large. Some direct evidence of this effect is provided by Bresnahan and Reiss (1991). They gathered data on a number of professions and services from over 200 towns scattered across the western United States. They found that a town of about 800 or 900 will support just one doctor. As the town grows to a population of roughly 3,500, a second doctor will typically enter. It takes a town of over 9,000 people to generate an industry of five doctors. The same positive relationship between market size and the number of firms is also found in other professions. For tire dealers, for example, Bresnahan and Reiss find that a town of only 500 people is needed to support one tire dealer and that five tire dealers will emerge when the town reaches a population of 6,000. The smaller market requirements needed to support a given number of tire dealers instead of doctors probably reflects, among other things, the fact that doctors have higher fixed/sunk costs than do tire dealers.

Sutton (1991, 2001) does, however, provide an important qualification to the idea that concentration will decline with the size of the market. The key issue here is the behavior of sunk cost. In equation (4.4), we took sunk cost as given and equal to some amount $K$ incurred with entry. In many ways, however, advertising and other promotional efforts for a given product are also sunk costs. Sutton shows that for many industries, such costs grow along with market size. As a result, the de-concentrating effects of a larger market are offset by higher concentration induced by rising sunk cost. When this is the case, concentration will not decline as the market grows larger.[8]

## 4.3.2  Network Externalities and Market Structure

It's not news to anyone reading the recent press that there is basically only one firm producing operating systems for personal computers, and that firm is Microsoft. For more than a decade Microsoft Corporation has supplied about 95 percent of the market for operating systems for the personal computer market. Similarly, Microsoft *Word* and Microsoft *Excel* have nearly as great a share of the word-processing and spreadsheet software business. Scale and scope economies are undoubtedly part of the explanation for the highly concentrated nature of these markets. After all, once the costs have been sunk to design the basic program for the operating systems or application software, the cost of reproducing the product many times over is quite trivial. It is also highly likely that there will be a large common component to these design costs.

However, as many witnesses testified at the *Microsoft* antitrust case of 1999–2000, scale and scope economies are not the only reasons behind the dominance of this high-technology firm. A particularly important factor explaining the high concentration in this market is the presence of a demand factor known as *network externalities*. Network externalities refer to the phenomenon by which a consumer's willingness to pay for a good or service increases as the number of other consumers buying the product rises.

---

8  See Baldwin (1995) for some evidence on this point.

Telecommunications is an area in which network externalities are particularly strong. Consider the telephone, for example. The usefulness or value of a single consumer connecting to a telephone system is essentially nil. If no one else is connected, the telephone cannot be used to make even one call. However, as more people sign on to the system, the number of potential calls and hence the utility of owning a phone increases. That is, each customer's individual decision to join the system confers benefits to the other customers—benefits that are external to the consumer who is signing on. This is what we mean by a network externality. When market demand exhibits such an externality, there is a strong incentive for a firm to try to get a large number of consumers signed on to its system. To put it another way, any telephone system without a large number of customers would not be able to survive because it would not be very valuable to the few customers it does have.

We address the topic of network externalities more extensively in Chapter 24. However, from the brief discussion above, it should be easy to see that markets with important network externalities are likely to be ones populated by a few very large firms. In other words, they are likely to have a highly concentrated structure—even if scale economies are not present on the cost side. Indeed, many analysts view network externalities as a case of scale economies on the demand side.

### 4.3.3 The Role of Government Policy

From 1934 to 1988—a period of fifty-four years—the number of medallions authorizing legal ownership of a taxicab in Boston was fixed at 1,525. Not a single additional medallion was issued in all that time despite the fact that the regional population increased by over 50 percent and the level of income and economic activity doubled several times over.

Costs and technology were not the source of this fixed industrial structure. The primary reason for the limited entry into the Boston taxi industry was government policy. City and state officials deliberately limited the number of taxi medallions, largely at the request of those lucky taxi owners who obtained the first batch of medallions. Indeed, even in recent years with a court order to issue 300 new medallions, only a few additional ones have actually been issued as officials have again tried to slow the creation of additional legal taxi operators.

A similar phenomenon prevailed from the 1930s through the 1970s, when the number of so-called trunk airlines flying interstate routes never exceeded sixteen and fell to ten by the end of the period. Not only was the total number of airlines small on a national scale, it was even smaller for individual city-pair markets. Many of these were served by only one or two carriers. Here again, the primary cause was government policy. In this case, that policy was implemented by the Civil Aeronautics Board (CAB), the federal agency established in 1938 as the economic regulator of the airline industry. Throughout its existence, the CAB deliberately limited entry and sustained concentration in the U.S. domestic airline industry. Indeed, this forty-year period witnessed numerous applications by freight and charter airlines to be granted the right to offer scheduled passenger services, as well as frequent applications of existing passenger carriers to enter new city-pair markets. Virtually all of these requests were turned down. The CAB argued that this policy was necessary to promote the stability and healthy development of the airline industry. Whether it achieved its perceived goals, or whether such goals were appropriate, is a question to be answered elsewhere. The central point illustrated by both the taxicab and airline example is that explicit government policies often play an important role in determining market structure.

More often than not, the role of government policy has been to increase market concentration, as both of the previous examples illustrate. However, some government policies do work to increase the number of firms in an industry. The Robinson-Patman Act, which prohibits price discounts to large firms if such discounts are deemed to be anticompetitive, reflects a conscious effort to keep independent retailers in business. These are typically small firms who otherwise would have been driven out of the market by the large retail chains. Similarly, the decision of the U.S. government after World War II to force the Alcoa company to sell some of its wartime aluminum plants to the Kaiser and Reynolds corporations was clearly an effort to promote a more competitive structure.

## SUMMARY

This chapter has focused on key cost concepts and their implications for industrial structure. Scale economies tend to increase market concentration. Economies of scope have a similar effect of concentrating the production of different products within a single firm. Scope economies also give rise to important multiproduct scale economies. This is particularly the case when the various products are not truly different goods but, instead, different versions of the same goods. In such product-differentiated markets, the presence of scope and scale economies will again imply a more concentrated structure.

Other factors influence market structure as well. One of these is market size. Because a large market has room for a number of firms even if each is of considerable size, larger markets tend to be less concentrated than small ones. However, increasing market size does not lead to less concentration in markets in which sunk costs also increase with size. These are typically markets in which advertising plays a major role.

Another important determinant of market structure comes from the demand side of the market in the form of network externalities. Network externalities imply that the value of a product to any one consumer increases as other consumers use it. Such externalities act much like scale economies to foster industrial concentration.

Finally, government policy is also an important determinant of market structure. Regulations such as those long applied to local taxi markets and the airline industry have an important effect upon the size and number of firms. These regulations also affect the ability of new firms to enter the market.

## PROBLEMS

**1.** Let the cost function be $C = 100 + 4q + 4q^2$. Derive an expression for average cost. Derive an expression for marginal cost. Is there any range of production characterized by scale economies? At what production level are scale economies exhausted?

**2.** An urban rapid-transit line runs crowded trains (200 passengers per car) at rush hours, but nearly empty trains (10 passengers per car) at off-peak hours. A management consultant argues as follows: "The cost of running a car for one trip on this line is about $50 regardless of the number of passengers. So, the per-passenger cost is about 25 cents at rush hour but rises to $5 in off-peak hours. Consequently, we had better discourage the off-peak business." Is the consultant a good economist? Why or why not?

3. Consider the following cost relationships for a single-product firm:

$$C(q) = 50 + 0.5q \text{ for } q \le 7$$
$$C(q) = 7q \text{ for } q > 7$$

  a. Derive average and marginal cost for all integer outputs less than or equal to 7.

  b. What are average and marginal cost for all outputs above 7?

  c. Is there a minimum efficient scale of plant implied by these cost relationships? If so, what is it?

  d. Let $P$ be industry price and $Q$ be total industry output. If the industry demand curve is $P = 84 - 0.5Q$, what is the maximum number of efficient-sized firms that the industry can sustain?

4. How would your answer to 3d change if industry demand were instead $P = 14 - 0.5Q$? Explain.

5. Some estimates for the cement industry suggest the following relationship between capacity and average cost:

| Capacity (thousands of tons) | Average Cost |
|---|---|
| 250 | $28.78 |
| 500 | 25.73 |
| 750 | 23.63 |
| 1,000 | 21.63 |
| 1,250 | 21.00 |
| 1,500 | 20.75 |
| 1,750 | 20.95 |
| 2,000 | 21.50 |

  a. At what production level are scale economies exhausted?

  b. Calculate the scale economy index for the production levels 500, 750, 1,000, 1,500, and 1,750.

6. An article (J. Peder Zane, "It Ain't for the Meat; It's for Lotion," *The New York Times,* May 5, 1996, p. E5) presented the following data for a cow brought to market:

| Part | Use | Price/lb ($) |
|---|---|---|
| Horns | Gelatin Collagen | 0.42 |
| Cheek | Sausage Baloney | 0.55 |
| Adrenal Gland | Steroids | 2.85 |
| Meat | Beef | 1.05 |
| Lips | Taco Filling | 0.19 |
| Hide | Footwear Clothing | 0.75 |

Comment on the scope economies illustrated by this example. What is the source of such economies? What does the existence of such economies imply about the supply of such products as leather skins, beef, and gelatin powder?

# REFERENCES

Baldwin, John R. 1995. *The Dynamics of Industrial Competition: A North American Perspective*. Cambridge: Cambridge University Press.

Baumol, W. J., J. C. Panzar, and R. D. Willig. 1982. *Contestable Markets and the Theory of Industry Structure*. New York: Harcourt, Brace, Jovanovich.

Bresnahan, T., and P. Reiss. 1991. "Entry and Competition in Concentrated Markets." *Journal of Political Economy* 99 (October): 977–1009.

Chenery, H. 1949. "The Engineering Production Function." *Quarterly Journal of Economics* 63 (May): 507–31.

Coase, R. H. 1937. "The Nature of the Firm." *Economica* 4 (March): 386–405.

Cohn, E., S. L. Rhine, and M. C. Santos. 1989. "Institutions of Higher Education as Multi-Product Firms: Economies of Scale and Scope." *Review of Economics and Statistics* 71 (May): 284–90.

De Groot, H., W. McMahon, and J. F. Volkwein. 1991. "The Cost Structure of American Research Universities." *Review of Economics and Statistics* 73 (August): 424–31.

Dunne, T., M. J. Roberts, and L. Samuelson. 1988. "Patterns of Firm Entry in U.S. Manufacturing Industries." *Rand Journal of Economics* 19 (Winter): 495–515.

Eaton, B. C., and N. Schmitt. 1994. "Flexible Manufacturing and Market Structure." *American Economic Review* 84 (September): 875–88.

Evans, D., and J. Heckman. 1986. "A Test for Subadditivity of the Cost Function with Application to the Bell System." *American Economic Review* 74 (September): 615–623.

Gale, I. 1994. "Price Competition in Noncooperative Joint Ventures." *International Journal of Industrial Organization* 12: 53–69.

Gilligan, T., M. Smirlock, and W. Marshall. 1984. "Scale and Scope Economies in the Multi-Product Banking Firm." *Journal of Monetary Economics* 13 (May): 393–405.

Hart, O. 1995. *Firms, Contracts, and Financial Structure*. New York: Oxford University Press.

———, and J. Moore. 1990. "Property Rights and the Nature of the Firm." *Journal of Political Economy* 98 (December): 1119–58.

Milgrom, P., and J. Roberts. 1992. *Economics, Organization, and Management*. Upper Saddle River, NJ: Prentice Hall.

Panzar, J. C. 1989. "Technological Determinants of Firm and Industry Structure." In R. Schmalensee and R. Willig, eds., *Handbook of Industrial Organization*. Vol. 1. Amsterdam: North-Holland, 3–60.

Pulley, L. B., and Y. M. Braunstein. 1992. "A Composite Cost Function for Multiproduct Firms with an Application to Economies of Scope in Banking." *Review of Economics and Statistics* 74 (May): 221–30.

Roller, L. 1990. "Proper Quadratic Cost Functions with Application to the Bell System." *Review of Economics and Statistics* 72 (May): 202–10.

Sutton, John. 1991. *Sunk Costs and Market Structure*. Cambridge, MA: The MIT Press.

———. 2001. *Technology and Market Structure*. Cambridge, MA: The MIT Press.

Williamson, O. E. 1995. *Markets and Hierarchies: Analysis and Antitrust Implications*. New York: Free Press.

# Part two

## Monopoly Power and Practice

# Monopoly Power and Practice

In Part Two, we consider a range of price and nonprice tactics that can be employed by firms that have monopoly power. An understanding of such tactics is useful for at least two reasons. First, some firms probably do have monopoly power. Once one has flown to a ski area or an amusement theme park, it is unlikely that one will turn back and shop for an alternative. At that point, the ski lift operator and the amusement park become the only game in town—at least for a while—and therefore enjoy some monopoly power. Similarly, firms such as Microsoft, which control 90 to 95 percent of the operating systems market for personal computers, are also close enough to the monopoly case to make analysis of that case interesting. The second reason for studying the tactics of a monopolist is that those same tactics will be employed in the context of more competitive markets where strategic interaction is the case. Studying the logic of these tactics in the monopoly case thus serves as a useful preparation for considering their role in this later framework.

We consider four basic techniques that a firm with a downward-sloping demand curve can use to improve its profit. All of these tactics share one common feature. They each enable a firm to lower the price to those consumers who are not willing to pay very much but whom it can serve at a small profit, while continuing to charge a high price to customers who are willing to pay more and from whom it can extract a large profit. That is, each technique effectively permits firms to charge different prices to different customers. This practice is typically referred to as price discrimination.

Price discrimination can be achieved in a number of ways. Some techniques reflect a simple or what we might call a linear approach. Here, the firm simply separates its customers into different groups and charges each a different price based on the willingness to pay of each group. The trick, of course, is to identify the group to which a consumer belongs and then to make sure that there is no trading, or what economists call arbitrage, between the groups. Chapter 5 explores a number of linear price discrimination techniques. There are, however, some rather more sophisticated, nonlinear price discrimination tactics as well. These are examined in Chapter 6.

The monopoly firm also has other tactics at its disposal besides pricing to help it increase its profit. Some of these involve the product design or choice of product quality. By choosing the right design or by offering different versions of its product the firm can enhance consumers' willingness to pay. These tactics are explored in Chapter 7.

Finally, in Chapter 8 we consider various strategies in which the firm relates the sale of one product to the purchase of another. For example, Microsoft bundles its Excel and Word programs together, along with a number of other programs in its Office package. Similarly, the purchase of a Hewlett-Packard inkjet printer requires that the consumer also purchase Hewlett-Packard inkjet cartridges. These bundling and tying techniques are common and have been the source of considerable controversy in antitrust cases.

# Price Discrimination and Monopoly: Linear Pricing

**Chapter** 5

During the past few years there has been much debate about whether Americans should be allowed to import cheaper prescription drugs from Canada and Europe. Legislation to allow such imports was passed by Congress in 2000—during the Clinton administration. However, this legislation contained an important proviso. For a drug to be eligible to be imported, the Secretary of Health and Human Services must certify that the drug "pose no additional risk" to consumers. No such certifications have been issued. Hence, no prescription drugs are officially eligible to be imported.

Whatever the risk of Canadian prescriptions, it is indisputable that there are significant differences in prescription drug prices between the United States and Canada. Graham and Robson (2000) collected detailed 1999 price information for 45 prescription drugs, collectively covering approximately 25 percent of the total prescriptions written in the United States. From this sample they calculated that Canadian retail prices were far less than American prices, with the median discount approximately 46 percent. Indeed, for one drug in their sample, this discount was 95 percent. In a related study Graham and Tabler (2001) analyzed the retail prices charged in 2001 by a randomly selected set of pharmacies for three patented drugs in three Canadian and three neighboring American areas. Table 5.1 provides summary information on the prices of drugs that they examined. This evidence further confirms that drug prices are generally lower in Canada than in the United States. Once again, discounts in the range of 50 percent are the norm.[1]

In July 2003, the U.S. House of Representatives passed the Gutknecht-Emerson bill, which differs from the existing legislation at that time in a vital respect: it does not include the certification requirement. This legislation was passed despite an aggressive lobbying campaign by the Pharmaceutical Research and Manufacturers Association (Phrma), the U.S. Chamber of Commerce, and many other organizations. However, even at the time the House legislation was passed, 53 senators were already publicly opposed to the legislation, making it unlikely that the bill would pass into law. Indeed, it is widely believed that Phrma coordinated this signature campaign.[2]

Drugs sold in Canada and those sold in the United States are typically made by the same pharmaceutical companies. The question arises as to why these companies have so vigorously pursued a practice of selling their products at different prices on different sides of the border. Why would the drug companies oppose so strongly the passage of the Gutknecht-Emerson bill that merely permits Americans to buy drugs at the same prices that the companies are already charging Canadians?

One explanation is that blocking the legislation is good for drug company profits. This idea is investigated in this chapter and the next. Specifically, we show that whenever a monopolist is able to keep the various markets it serves separate, the monopolist will be more profitable by setting different prices in the different markets than by setting a common price across all these markets. Simply put, *price discrimination*, or charging different prices to different consumers for the same product, is more

---

1   It is also interesting to note that there is significant price dispersion in the United States.
2   "Drug Lobbyist Pushed Letter by Senators on Medicare." *The New York Times*, July 28, 2003, p. 15.

| TABLE 5-1 | COMPARISON OF PRESCRIPTION DRUG PRICES (U.S. DOLLARS) | | | | | |
|---|---|---|---|---|---|---|
| | CELEBREX® 200 MG | | LIPITOR® 40 MG | | PAXIL® 20 MG | |
| | *Mean* | *Standard Deviation* | *Mean* | *Standard Deviation* | *Mean* | *Standard Deviation* |
| Washington | $86.26 | $5.66 | $110.01 | $8.97 | $82.47 | $3.86 |
| British Columbia | $33.17 | $2.37 | $52.83 | $3.50 | $40.75 | $2.54 |
| North Dakota and Minnesota | $78.08 | $5.70 | $107.75 | $7.03 | $78.63 | $6.08 |
| Manitoba | $32.36 | $1.60 | $52.43 | $1.52 | $39.80 | $2.00 |
| New York | $88.57 | $7.59 | $117.69 | $5.44 | $85.06 | $4.39 |
| Ontario | $34.82 | $1.96 | $55.52 | $2.09 | $42.62 | $2.03 |

**Source:** John R. Graham and Tanya Taylor, "Prescription Drug Prices in Canada and the United States—Part 3: Retail Price Distribution." *Public Policy Sources Number 50*, The Fraser Institute, 2001.

profitable than no price discrimination. Of course, this raises other important issues. The increased profit must come from somewhere—either from consumer surplus or from improved market efficiency. From a policy perspective, it matters a great deal as to which of these is the case. In addition, discriminatory prices can affect market competition. This occurs when the buyers, such as the drugstores, are charged different wholesale prices for the goods, in this case pharmaceutical drugs, and then must compete with each other at the retail level. All of these issues are addressed in turn.

## 5.1 FEASIBILITY OF PRICE DISCRIMINATION

A firm with market power faces a downward-sloping demand curve, so if the firm charges the same price to each consumer—the standard case of nondiscriminatory pricing—the revenue it gets from selling an additional unit of output is less than the price charged. In order to sell the additional unit the firm must lower its price not only to the consumer who buys the additional unit but to all other consumers as well. Having to lower price to all its customers in order to gain an additional consumer limits the monopolist's incentive to serve more consumers. As a result, the textbook monopoly undersupplies its product relative to the efficient outcome.

However, nondiscriminatory pricing is not just a source of potential inefficiency. It is also a constraint on the monopolist's ability to extract consumer surplus, particularly from those consumers who are willing to pay a lot for its product. What happens if we allow the monopolist to charge different prices to different customers? We shall see that this is a powerful technique that permits the firm to appropriate more of the consumer surplus that its product creates and thereby earn more profit. In addition, price discrimination may induce the monopolist to sell more output and so come closer to the competitive market outcome. That is, price discrimination can sometimes make a monopolized market more efficient.

While a monopolist can increase profit through price discrimination, it is important to realize that price discrimination is not always easily accomplished. In other words, there is a reason that the standard textbook case assumes that each customer pays the same price. To discriminate successfully the monopolist must overcome two main obstacles. The first of these is identifying who is who on the demand curve. The second is the problem of arbitrage.

In considering the identification problem it is useful to recall a common assumption in the textbook monopoly model. This model assumes that the monopolist has somehow learned the amount demanded at each price—otherwise it would not know its marginal revenue curve and, hence, would not be able to determine the profit-maximizing output. Let's examine what this assumption means in practice.

For some products such as bicycles, CD players, or haircuts a single consumer will purchase at most one unit of the good over a given period of time. The firm's demand curve is an explicit ordering of consumers by their reservation prices—the top price each is willing to pay. For these goods, knowledge of the demand curve means that the firm knows that the top part of the demand curve is made up of those consumers willing to pay a lot for the one unit they will purchase, while the bottom part of the demand curve is made up of those willing to pay only a little. For other products, however, such as movies, CDs, refreshments, and tennis lessons, the practical translation of the demand curve is more complex. This is because each individual consumer can be induced to purchase more than one unit of such goods if the price is sufficiently low. Hence, for these goods the demand curve reflects not only differences in the willingness to pay across consumers but also differences in the willingness to pay as any one consumer buys more of the product. If the monopolist practices uniform pricing, by choice or as a result of regulation, these distinctions are not relevant. The assumption that the firm knows its demand curve means only that it knows how willingness to pay for the good *in the overall market* varies with the quantity of the good sold.

To be able to practice price discrimination the monopolist must learn or know more information about consumers than is assumed in the standard model. The monopolist must know how the market demand curve has been constructed from the individual consumer demand curves. In other words, the monopolist must know how consumers differ in their demands for its good. This is easier for some sellers than for others. For example, tax accountants effectively sell one unit of their services to each client in any given year. Further, they know exactly how much their clients earn and, more importantly, how much they save their clients by way of reduced tax liabilities. They can use this information to identify the customer's willingness to pay. Similarly, a car dealer sells at most one unit to a customer. The dealer may be able to identify those with the greatest or least willingness to pay by asking potential buyers where they live or work or shop. The same is often true for realtors, dentists, and lawyers.

Sellers of retail merchandise, however, face a more anonymous market. Various schemes such as varying the price depending on time of purchase, offering "early-bird" specials or Saturday morning sales, or offering coupons that take time to collect can help retailers identify "who's who" on their demand curve. Nevertheless, the identification problem is still difficult to overcome. Moreover, even if weekend sales or coupon schemes successfully identify the firm's different consumers, such schemes may be too costly to implement.

Even when a monopolist can solve the identification problem, there is still a second obstacle to price discrimination, arbitrage. To discriminate successfully, the monopolist must be able to prevent those consumers who are offered a low price from reselling their purchases to other consumers to whom the monopolist wants to offer a high price. Again, this will be more easily accomplished for some goods and services than for others. Medical, legal, and educational services are not easily resold. One consumer can't sell her appendectomy to another! Similarly, a senior citizen cannot easily resell a discounted movie theater ticket to a teenager. For other markets, though, for example, bicycles and automobiles, resale—or sale across different markets—is difficult to prevent. This is an important part of the drug pricing story noted at the start of this chapter. Pharmaceutical companies can only price discriminate successfully if they can keep the American and Canadian markets separate, that is, if they can prevent arbitrage.

To summarize, we expect firms with monopoly power to try to price discriminate. In turn, this implies that we should expect such firms to attempt both to identify the different types of consumers who buy their goods and to prevent resale or consumer arbitrage among them. The ability to do this and the best strategy for achieving price discrimination will vary from firm to firm and from market to market. We now turn to the practice of price discrimination and investigate some of the more popular techniques. The tradition in economics has been to classify these techniques into three

 **Reality Checkpoint**

### You Can Taste It but You Can't Buy It

Anyone who visits the vineyards in the wine-growing districts of California and tastes the local produce will find something strange. Suppose (not unreasonably) that you find wines that you like. Unless you happen to live in selected states you will also find that the vineyard is prohibited from shipping the wine to you. Indeed, in some states such direct shipment would constitute a Federal offense. Similar regulations are in place if you return home and try to order wine from the vineyard over the Internet. These regulations are coming under attack. In July 2002, a U.S. District Court in Texas declared such prohibition on direct shipments unconstitu-

tional. Similar findings have been made in Virginia and South Carolina. The impact of such regulations is easy to predict. Their effect is to prevent consumer arbitrage from high-price locations to low-price locations. The result should be higher prices and a narrower selection. That this is, indeed, the case is confirmed by the results of a Federal Trade Commission study published in July 2003. According to this report, "states could significantly enhance consumer welfare by allowing direct shipment of wine to consumers. Through direct shipping, online sales offer consumers lower prices and greater selection." (p. 3)

**Source:** Ben Lieberman, "Internet Wine Sales: Old Monopolies Fight Against New Bottles." Competitive Enterprise Institute, August 14, 2002, available on the Internet at http://www.cei.org/gencom/; "Possible Anticompetitive Barriers to E-Commerce: Wine." Federal Trade Commission Report, June 2003, available on the Internet at http://www.ftc.gov/os/2003/07/winereport2.pdf.

broad classes: first-degree, second-degree, and third-degree price discrimination.[3] More recently, these types of pricing schemes have been referred to respectively as personalized pricing, menu pricing, and group pricing.[4] In this chapter we focus on third-degree price discrimination, or group pricing.

## 5.2 THIRD-DEGREE PRICE DISCRIMINATION OR GROUP PRICING

Third-degree price discrimination, or group pricing, is defined by three characteristics. First, there is some easily observable characteristic such as age, income, geographic location, or education status by which the monopolist can group consumers in terms of their willingness to pay for the monopolist's product. Second, the monopolist can prevent arbitrage across the different groups. In the prescription drug case with which we started this chapter, for example, it must be possible to prevent re-import of prescription drugs initially exported from the United States to Canada. Finally, third-degree price discrimination requires that the monopolist quotes the same price per unit to all consumers within a particular group and consumers in each group then decide how much to purchase at the quoted price.

Group pricing reflects price discrimination because the price quoted to one group of consumers is not the same as the price quoted to another group. This type of pricing policy is the one most commonly found in economics textbooks and is referred to in the industrial organization literature as *linear pricing*—hence the title of this chapter. Consumers within a group are free to buy as much as they like at the quoted price, so that the average price per unit paid by each consumer is the same as the marginal price for the last unit bought.

The world is full of examples of third-degree price discrimination, such as senior discounts and "kids are free" programs. An interesting case that is particularly familiar to economists is the fee schedule for membership in the American Economic Association (AEA), the major professional organization for economists in the United States. Payment of the fee entitles a member to receive professional announcements, newsletters, and three very important professional journals, *The American Economic Review*, *The Journal of Economic Perspectives*, and *The Journal of Economic Literature*, each of which is published quarterly.

The 2003 fee schedule is shown in Table 5.2. As can be seen, the aim is to price discriminate on the basis of income. A particularly interesting feature of this scheme is that the AEA makes no attempt to check the veracity of the income declared by a prospective member. What they appear to rely upon is that economists will be either honest or even boastful in reporting their income. In addition, the AEA must also hope to avoid the arbitrage problem whereby junior faculty members who pay a low subscription fee resell to senior faculty members who pay a high one. Here again, we can only report on casual observation. On this basis, such reselling appears to be rare, so the arbitrage problem seems to be effectively nonexistent.

---

3 Price discrimination is a fascinating topic and its interest to economists goes well beyond the field of industrial organization. The distinction between first-, second-, and third-degree discrimination follows the work of Pigou (1920). A more modern treatment appears in Phlips (1983).

4 These terms were first coined by Shapiro and Varian (1998).

| TABLE 5-2 | SCHEDULE OF ANNUAL MEMBERSHIP FEES FOR THE AMERICAN ECONOMIC ASSOCIATION | |
|---|---|---|
| Regular Members with annual incomes of $42,000 or less | | $64 |
| Regular Members with annual incomes above $42,000 but no more than $56,000 | | $77 |
| Regular Members with annual incomes above $56,000 | | $90 |
| Junior Members (available to registered students—student status must be certified) | | $32 |
| Family Member (persons living at the same address as a regular member, additional membership without a subscription to AEA publications) | | $13 |

The practice of the AEA is not unique. Many academic journals charge a different price to institutions such as university libraries than to individuals. The subscription rate to the *Journal of Economics and Management Strategy*, for example, is $45 for an individual but $115 for an institution.

Airlines are particularly adept at applying third-degree price discrimination. Indeed, it has sometimes been suggested that the number of different fares charged to economy-class passengers on a particular flight is approximately equal to the number of passengers! A common feature of this type of price discrimination is that it is implemented by restrictions on the characteristics of the ticket. These include constraints upon the time in advance by which the flight must be booked, whether flights can be changed, the number of days between departure and return, whether the trip involves staying over a Saturday night, and so on. We return to the airline case later in this chapter.

Other examples of third-degree price discrimination are restaurant "early-bird specials" and supermarket discounts to shoppers who clip coupons. Similarly, department stores that lower their apparel prices at the end of the season are attempting to charge a different price based on the observable characteristic of the time of purchase.[5] Segmenting consumers by time of purchase is also evident in other markets. Consumers typically pay more to see a film at a first-run theater when the film is newly released than to see it at a later date at a second-run cinema or, still later, as a rented video at home.

As previously stated, an essential feature of all third-degree price discrimination schemes is that the monopolist has some easily observed characteristic that serves as a good proxy for differences in consumer willingness to pay. This characteristic can be used to divide the market into two or more groups, each of which will be charged a different price. The monopolist must next be able to ensure that resale of the product by those who are offered a low price to those who are offered a high one is not feasible. Consider the airlines again. The requirement to stay over a Saturday night that is typical of many discounted fares effectively discriminates between those who are traveling on business and those who are not.

---

5  Discounting over time in a systematic fashion runs the risk that if consumers know prices will fall in the future, they will delay their purchases. If the number of customers that postpones purchases is "too" large, seasonal discounts will not be a good strategy.

Once the different consumer groups have been identified and separated, the general rule that characterizes third-degree price discrimination is easily stated. *Consumers for whom the elasticity of demand is low should be charged a higher price than consumers for whom the elasticity of demand is relatively high.*

## 5.3 IMPLEMENTING THIRD-DEGREE PRICE DISCRIMINATION OR GROUP PRICING

The logic underlying our rule can be illustrated with a simple example. The Derivation Checkpoint, Discriminatory and Nondiscriminatory Pricing that follows later provides a more general treatment. Suppose that the publishers of J.K Rowling's fifth volume in the Harry Potter series, *Harry Potter and the Order of the Phoenix,* estimate that demand for this book in the United States is $P_U = 36 - 4Q_U$ and in Europe is $P_E = 24 - 4Q_E$. In each case prices are measured in dollars and quantities in millions of books sold at publication of the first edition of the book. Marginal cost is taken to be the same in each market, which is not unreasonable in these days of electronic publishing. For convenience, we assume this common marginal cost to be $4 per book. The publisher also incurs a set of other costs associated with the publication—typesetting, marketing, and so on—but we treat these costs as fixed, independent of sales volume and thus can ignore them in the analysis.

Assume first that the publisher decides to set the same price for the book in the two markets. What is the profit-maximizing price? Recall the rule that governs monopoly pricing. Profit is maximized when marginal revenue equals marginal cost. So we need to identify the marginal revenue curve. Given that the monopolist is setting the same price in both markets, the firm is actually treating these two markets as a single, integrated market. So we need to calculate aggregate market demand at any price $P$. This means that we need to add the two market demand curves *horizontally.*

In the United States we have $P = 36 - 4Q_U$, which can be inverted to give $Q_U = 9 - P/4$, provided, of course, that $P \leq \$36$. In Europe we have $P = 24 - 4Q_E$ so that $Q_E = 6 - P/4$, in this case provided that $P \leq \$24$. This gives us the following aggregate demand equation:

$$Q = Q_U + Q_E = 9 - P/4 \quad \text{for} \quad \$36 \geq P \geq \$24 \qquad (5.1)$$
$$Q = Q_U + Q_E = 15 - P/2 \quad \text{for} \quad P < \$24$$

We can write this in the more normal inverse form as

$$P = 36 - 4Q \quad \text{for} \quad \$36 \geq P \geq \$24 \qquad (5.2)$$
$$P = 30 - 2Q \quad \text{for} \quad P < \$24$$

This demand relationship is illustrated in Figure 5-1. The kink in the aggregate demand function at a price of $24 and a quantity of 3 million arises because at any price above $24 books will be sold only in the United States whereas once the price drops below $24 both markets are active. The marginal revenue function associated with this demand function satisfies the usual "twice as steep" rule:

$$MR = 36 - 8Q \quad \text{for} \quad Q \leq 3 \qquad (5.3)$$
$$MR = 30 - 4Q \quad \text{for} \quad Q > 3$$

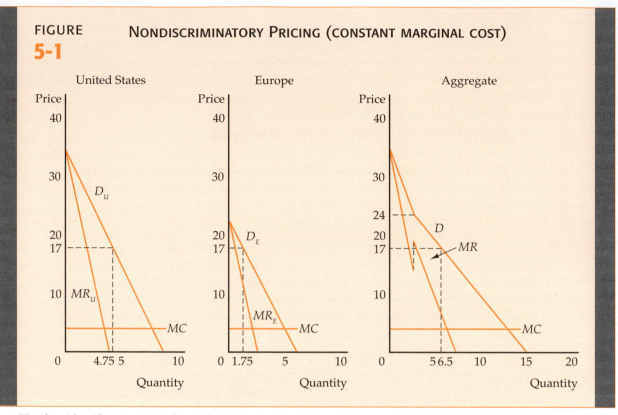

**FIGURE 5-1    NONDISCRIMINATORY PRICING (CONSTANT MARGINAL COST)**

The firm identifies aggregate demand and the associated marginal revenue. It chooses total output where marginal revenue equals marginal cost and the nondiscriminatory price from the aggregate demand function. Output in each market is the market-clearing output.

This is also illustrated in Figure 5-1. The jump in the marginal revenue function at a quantity of 3 million arises because when price falls from just above $24 to just below $24 the inactive European market becomes active. That is, when the price falls to just below $24, it brings in a new set of consumers.

We are now in a position to calculate the profit-maximizing price, aggregate quantity, and quantity in each market. Equating marginal revenue with marginal cost assuming that both markets are active we have $30 - 4Q = 4$, so that $Q^* = 6.5$ million. From the aggregate demand curve this gives a price of $P^* = \$17$. It follows that 4.75 million books will be sold in the United States and 1.75 million books in Europe. Aggregate profit (ignoring all fixed and setup costs) is $(17 - 4) \times 6.5 = \$84.5$ million.

That this pricing strategy is not the best that the monopolist can adopt is clear from Figure 5-1. At the equilibrium we have just calculated, the marginal revenue on the last book sold in Europe is greater than marginal cost, whereas marginal revenue on the last book sold in the United States is less than marginal cost. Transferring some of the books sold in the United States to the European market will, therefore, lead to an increase in profit.

Let us be more explicit. A necessary condition for profit maximization under third-degree price discrimination is that marginal revenue must equal marginal cost in *each* market that the monopolist serves. If this were not the case in a particular market, the last unit sold in that market is generating either more or less in cost than it is earning in revenue. Cutting back or increasing total production in that market would therefore raise profits. If marginal cost in serving each market is identical, as in our case, then the rule also implies that marginal revenue will be the same on the last unit sold in each market. If this condition does not hold, the monopolist can raise revenue and profit with no increase in production (and hence, no increase in costs) simply by shifting sales from the low marginal revenue market to the high one.

The application of these rules to our example is illustrated in Figure 5-2. Recall that demand in the United States market is $P_U = 36 - 4Q_U$ and in Europe is $P_E = 24 - 4Q_E$. This means that marginal revenue in the United States is $MR_U = 36 - 8Q_U$ and in Europe is $MR_E = 24 - 8Q_E$. Now apply the rule that marginal revenue equals marginal cost in each market. This gives a profit-maximizing output in the United States of $Q_U^* = 4$ million books at a price of $P_U^* = \$20$, and a profit-maximizing output in Europe of $Q_E^* = 2.5$ million books at a price of $P_E^* = \$14$. Profit from sales in the Unites States is $64 million and in Europe is $25 million, giving aggregate profit (again ignoring all fixed and setup costs) of $89 million, an increase of $4.5 million over the nondiscriminatory profit.

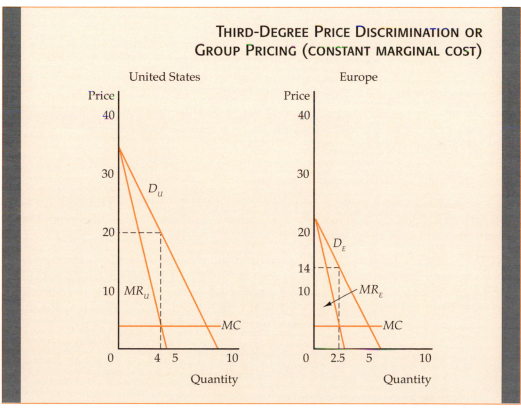

**THIRD-DEGREE PRICE DISCRIMINATION OR GROUP PRICING (CONSTANT MARGINAL COST)**

FIGURE

**5-2**

The firm sets output where marginal revenue equals marginal cost in each market and sets the market-clearing price in each market.

How does this relate to the elasticity rule that we presented above? An important property of linear demand curves is that the elasticity of demand falls smoothly from infinity to zero as we move down the demand curve.[6] This means that for any price less than \$24 (and greater than zero), the elasticity of demand in the U.S. market is lower than in the European market. (You can check this by evaluating the demand elasticity in the two markets at this or any other price.) Our rule then states that we should find a higher price in the United States than in Europe. This, of course, is precisely the result that our example gave.

How is our analysis affected if marginal cost is not constant? Very simply, the same basic principles apply with one slight change. If marginal production costs are not constant, we cannot treat the two markets independently since whatever output the monopolist chooses to supply to the United States, for example, affects the marginal cost of supplying Europe. Thus the different markets have to be looked at together. Nevertheless, we still have simple rules that guide the monopolist's pricing decisions in these markets.

To illustrate this, suppose that the publisher of *Harry Potter and the Order of the Phoenix* has a single printing facility that produces books for both the U.S. and European markets and that marginal cost is given by $MC = 0.75 + Q/2$, where $Q$ is the total number of books printed.

Figure 5-3 illustrates the profit-maximizing behavior if the monopolist chooses not to price discriminate. The basic analytical steps in this process are as follows.

1. Calculate aggregate market demand as above.
2. Identify the marginal revenue function for this aggregate demand function. From our example, if $Q > 3$ so that both markets are active, this is $MR = 30 - 4Q$.
3. Equate marginal revenue with marginal cost to determined aggregate output. In our example we have $0.75 + Q/2 = 30 - 4Q$, giving $Q^* = 6.5$ million books.
4. Identify the equilibrium price from the aggregate demand function. Since both markets are active, the relevant part of the aggregate demand function is $P = 30 - 2Q$, giving an equilibrium price of $P^* = \$17$.
5. Calculate demand in each market at this price: 4.75 million books in the United States and 1.75 million books in Europe.

Now assume that the monopolist chooses to price discriminate. This outcome is illustrated in Figure 5-4 on page 96. The underlying process is clearly different. The steps in this process are as follows.

1. Derive marginal revenue in each market and add these horizontally to give aggregate marginal revenue. Marginal revenue in the United States is $MR = 36 - 8Q_U$ for any price less than \$36, and in Europe is $MR = 24 - 8Q_E$ for any price below \$24. Inverting these gives $Q_U = 4.5 - MR/8$, respectively and $Q_E = 3 - MR/8$, respectively. Summing these gives the aggregate marginal revenue

$$Q = Q_U + Q_E = 4.5 - MR/8 \quad \text{for} \quad Q \leq 3 \qquad \text{(5.4)}$$
$$Q = Q_U + Q_E = 7.5 - MR/4 \quad \text{for} \quad Q > 3$$

This can be inverted to give aggregate marginal revenue its more usual form

$$MR = 36 - 8Q \quad \text{for} \quad Q \leq 3 \qquad \text{(5.5)}$$
$$MR = 30 - 4Q \quad \text{for} \quad Q > 3$$

---

6  The elasticity of demand at any given price is also independent of the slope of the demand curve when demand is linear.

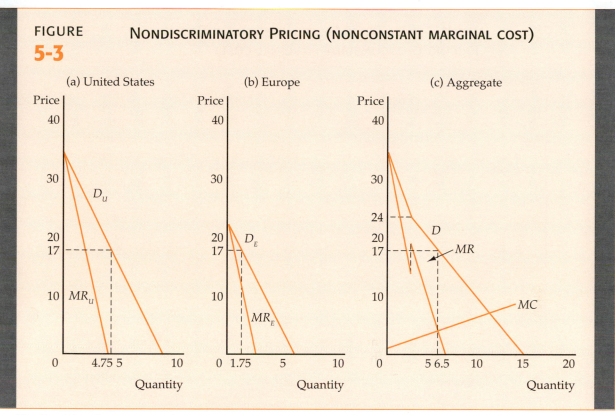

FIGURE
**5-3**

NONDISCRIMINATORY PRICING (NONCONSTANT MARGINAL COST)

(a) United States    (b) Europe    (c) Aggregate

The firm identifies aggregate demand and the associated marginal revenue. It chooses total output where marginal revenue equals marginal cost and the nondiscriminatory price from the aggregate demand function. Output in each market is the market-clearing output.

You might think that this is a redundant step since the aggregate marginal revenue function we have just calculated is the same as the marginal revenue function derived from the aggregate demand function. It is important to note, however, that this equivalency of the two marginal revenue functions applies *only* when demands are linear in the two markets because then the marginal revenue curves are linear as well. Our procedures as stated apply to *any* demand functions, not just linear ones.

2. Equate aggregate marginal revenue with marginal cost to identify the equilibrium aggregate quantity *and* marginal revenue. In our example we have $30 - 4Q = 0.75 + 2Q$, giving $Q^* = 6.5$. As a result, the equilibrium marginal revenue (and marginal cost) is $4.

3. Identify the equilibrium quantities in each market by equating individual market marginal revenue with the equilibrium marginal revenue (and marginal cost). In the United States this gives $36 - 8Q_U = 4$ or $Q_U^* = 4$ million books, and in Europe $24 - 8Q_U = 4$ or $Q_E^* = 2.5$ million books.

4. Identify the equilibrium price in each market from the individual market demand functions, giving a price of $20 in the United States and $14 in Europe.

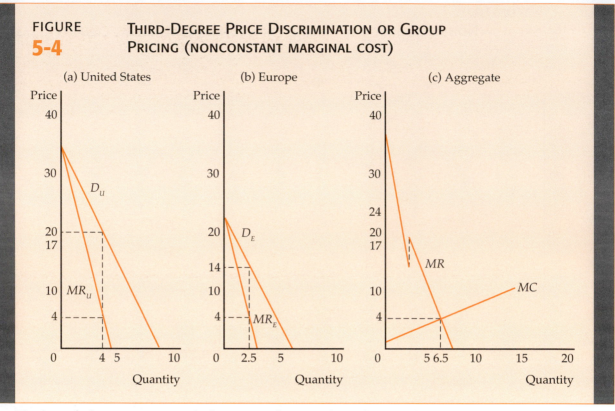

FIGURE
**5-4**

**THIRD-DEGREE PRICE DISCRIMINATION OR GROUP PRICING (NONCONSTANT MARGINAL COST)**

(a) United States
(b) Europe
(c) Aggregate

The firm calculates aggregate marginal revenue and equates this with marginal cost. Output in each market equates marginal revenue with aggregate marginal cost. Price in each market is the market-clearing price.

The foregoing procedure is derived from two simple rules that guide the monopolist's pricing decisions with third-degree price discrimination. These rules apply no matter the shape of the monopolist's marginal cost function. The rules are

1. Marginal revenue must be equalized in each market.
2. Marginal revenue must equal marginal cost, where marginal cost is measured at the *aggregate* output level.

We complete our discussion of third-degree price discrimination in this section by making explicit the relationship between the price set and the elasticity of demand in any specific market segment. Our review of monopoly and market power in Chapters 2 and 3 showed that we could express the firm's marginal revenue in any market in terms of price and the point elasticity of demand at that price. Specifically, marginal revenue in market $i$ is given by $MR_i = P_i\left(1 - \dfrac{1}{\eta_i}\right)$, where $\eta_i$ is (the negative of) the elasticity of demand. The larger is $\eta_i$, the more elastic is demand in this market. Now recall that third-degree price discrimination requires that at the profit-maximizing output marginal revenue in each market must be equalized (and, of course, equal to marginal cost). This tells us that if there are two markets that $MR_1 = MR_2$. Substitut-

# ✓ Derivation Checkpoint

## Discriminatory and Nondiscriminatory Pricing

Suppose that a monopolist supplies two groups of consumers with inverse demand for each group given by

$$P_1 = A_1 - B_1 Q_1$$
$$P_2 = A_2 - B_2 Q_2$$

(d.1)

In these demand functions we assume that $A_1 > A_2$ so that group 1 is the "high demand" group whose demand is the less elastic at any given price. Inverting the inverse demands gives the direct demands at some price $P$:

$$Q_1 = (A_1 - P)/B_1; \, Q_2 = (A_2 - P)/B_2,$$

so aggregate demand is

$$Q = Q_1 + Q_2 = \frac{A_1 B_2 + A_2 B_1}{B_1 B_2} - \frac{B_1 + B_2}{B_1 B_2} P.$$

(d.2)

Of course, this holds only for any price less than $A_2$. Invert this to get the aggregate inverse demand for the two groups, again for any price less than $A_2$ yields

$$P = \frac{A_1 B_2 + A_2 B_1}{B_1 + B_2} - \frac{B_1 B_2}{B_1 + B_2} Q.$$

(d.3)

The marginal revenue associated with this aggregate demand is

$$MR = \frac{A_1 B_2 + A_2 B_1}{B_1 + B_2} - 2 \frac{B_1 B_2}{B_1 + B_2} Q.$$

(d.4)

We can simplify matters a bit by assuming, without loss of generality, that marginal cost is zero. Solving $MR = 0$ for $Q$ gives the equilibrium aggregate output with uniform pricing

$$Q^U = \frac{A_1 B_2 + A_2 B_1}{2 B_1 B_2}.$$

(d.5)

Substituting $Q^*$ into (d.3) gives the equilibrium uniform price

$$P^U = \frac{A_1 B_2 + A_2 B_1}{2(B_1 + B_2)}.$$

(d.6)

Substituting this price into the individual demands of equation (d.1) gives the equilibrium output in each market

$$Q_1^U = \frac{(2A_1 - A_2)B_1 + A_1 B_2}{2 B_1 (B_1 + B_2)}; \, Q_2^U = \frac{(2A_2 - A_1)B_2 + A_2 B_1}{2 B_2 (B_1 + B_2)}.$$

(d.7)

With third-degree price discrimination the firm sets marginal revenue equal to marginal cost for each group. From equation (d.1) we know that the marginal revenues are

$$MR_1 = A_1 - 2B_1Q_1; \quad MR_2 = A_1 - 2B_2Q_2. \qquad \textbf{(d.8)}$$

It follows immediately that the equilibrium outputs for each group are

$$Q_1^D = \frac{A_1}{2B_1}; \quad Q_2^D = \frac{A_2}{2B_2}. \qquad \textbf{(d.9)}$$

Comparison with equation (d.7) confirms that $Q_1^D < Q_1^U$ and $Q_2^D > Q_2^U$. In other words, third-degree price discrimination diverts output from the high-demand market to the low-demand market, increasing price in the former and lowering price in the latter. You can also confirm that $Q_1^D + Q_2^D = Q^U$. In other words, when demands are linear *aggregate output is identical with uniform pricing and with third-degree price discrimination or group pricing.*

---

ing from the equations above, we then know that $= MR_1 = P_1\left(1 - \dfrac{1}{\eta_1}\right) = MR_2 = P_2\left(1 - \dfrac{1}{\eta_2}\right)$. We can solve this for the ratio of the two prices to give

$$\frac{P_1}{P_2} = \frac{(1 - 1/\eta_2)}{(1 - 1/\eta_1)} = \frac{\eta_1\eta_2 - \eta_1}{\eta_1\eta_2 - \eta_2}. \qquad \textbf{(5.6)}$$

From this it is clear that price will indeed be lower in the market with the higher elasticity of demand. The intuition is that prices must be lower in those markets in which consumers are sensitive to price. Such sensitivity implies that raising the price will lose sufficient customers to negate any gain in the surplus per customer. To put it differently, when consumers are very sensitive to price the strategy of lowering the price a bit actually raises the monopolist's total surplus because it brings in many additional customers. We encourage you to reinterpret the various examples with which we motivated our analysis in terms of demand elasticities. For example, is it reasonable to think that business travelers will have a lower elasticity of demand for air travel at a particular time than vacation travelers?

## Practice Problem 5.1

The manager of a local movie theater believes that demand for a film depends on when the movie is shown. Early moviegoers who go to films before 5 PM are more sensitive to price than are evening moviegoers. With some market research the manager discovers that the demand curves for daytime (D) and evening (E) moviegoers are $Q_D = 100 - 10P_D$ and $Q_E = 140 - 10P_E$, respectively. The marginal cost of showing a movie is constant and equal to $3 per customer no matter when it is shown. This includes the costs of ticketing and cleaning.

a. What is the profit-maximizing pricing policy if the manager charges the same price for daytime and evening attendance? What is attendance in each showing and what is aggregate profit per day?

b. Now suppose that the manager adopts a third-degree price discrimination scheme, setting a different day and evening price. What are the profit-maximizing prices? What is attendance at each session? Confirm that aggregate attendance is as in part a. What is aggregate profit per day?

# 5.4 PRODUCT VARIETY AND THIRD-DEGREE PRICE DISCRIMINATION OR GROUP PRICING

We have thus far defined price discrimination as occurring whenever a firm sells an identical product to two or more buyers at different prices. But what if the products are not identical? Ford, for example, offers several hundred (perhaps even several thousand) varieties of the Ford Taurus with slightly different features. Procter & Gamble offers a wide range of toothpastes in different tastes, colors, and claimed medicinal qualities. Kellogg offers dozens of breakfast cereals that vary in terms of grain, taste, consistency, and color.

Many examples of what looks like third-degree price discrimination or group pricing arise when the seller offers such *differentiated* products. For example, books are first released as expensive hardcover editions and only later as cheap paperbacks. Hotels in a ski area are more expensive in winter than in summer. First-class air travel costs more than coach. The common theme of these examples is that they all involve variations of a basic product. This is a phenomenon that we meet every day in buying restaurant meals, refrigerators, haircuts, and many other goods and services. In each of these situations, what we observe is a firm selling different varieties of the same good—distinguished by color, material, or design. As a brief reflection on the typical restaurant menu will reveal, what we also usually observe is that the different varieties are aimed at different groups and sell at different prices.

In considering these as applications of price discrimination we have to be careful. After all, the cost incurred in producing goods of different types, such as hardback and paperback books, or first-class versus coach flights, is different. Phlips (1983) provides perhaps the best definition of third-degree price discrimination or group pricing once we allow for product differentiation:

> Price discrimination should be defined as implying that two varieties of a commodity are sold (by the same seller) to two buyers at different *net* prices, the net price being the price (paid by the buyer) corrected for the cost associated with the product differentiation. (Phlips, 1983, p. 6)

Using this definition, it would not be discriminatory to charge $750 extra for a car with antilock brakes if it costs $750 extra to assemble a car with such brakes. By contrast, the difference in price between a coach-class fare of $450 and a first-class fare of more than $8,000 for service between Boston and London must be seen as almost entirely reflecting price discrimination because the additional cost of providing first-class service is well below the $7,500 difference in price. In other words, price discrimination among different versions of the same good exists only if the difference in the price is not justified by the difference in the underlying costs, which is what Phlips means by the *net price*.

Consideration of product variety leads to an important question. Does offering different varieties of a product enhance the monopolist's ability to charge different net prices? That is, does a firm with market power increase its ability to price discriminate by offering different versions of its product? As we shall see, the general answer is yes.

We can obtain at least some insight into this issue by recalling the two problems that successful discrimination must overcome, namely, identification and arbitrage. In order to price discriminate, the firm must determine who is who on its demand curve and then be able to prevent resale between separate consumers. By offering different versions or models of its product the monopolist may be able to solve these problems. Different consumer types may buy different versions of product and therefore reveal who they are through their purchase decision. Moreover, since different customers are purchasing different varieties, the problem of resale is considerably reduced.

As an example of the potential for product differentiation to enhance profit, consider an airline, Northwest Airlines (NA), operating direct passenger flights between Boston and Amsterdam. NA knows that there are three types of customers for these flights: those who prefer to travel first class, those who wish to travel business class, and those who are reconciled to having to travel coach. One part of the arbitrage

 **Reality** **Checkpoint**

### Driving Miss Crazy: Price Discrimination in the European Car Market

In 1992, the price of Renault Company's Clio RT Hatchback in Britain was $7,519. This was more than 30 percent higher than the $5,750 charged for the car in Belgium. The two cars were identical in most respects, but they differed in one critical dimension. The one marketed in Britain had its steering wheel on the right-hand side—the proper placement for a country in which cars are driven on the left-hand side of the street. When charged with discrimination by an irate journalist, Renault replied that the two cars were really not the same because the more expensive car also had fuel injection, tinted windows, and a sunroof.

The validity of Renault's defense rests heavily on how much these "extras" cost to install. If the cost of including such features as a standard option were large enough, then the price differential of 30 percent would be justifiable and no charge of discrimination would be valid. In other words, Renault was arguing that the two goods did not differ in terms of their "net" price.

However, the journalist did some research and then made some rough calculations as to how much it would cost Renault to add all the extras to the Belgium car that the company said were standard on the U.K. car. His results suggested that substantial discrimination was going on, as cost differences appeared to account for only a very small fraction of the quoted price differential.

**Source:** "Europe's Car Market—Carved Up." *The Economist*, October 31, 1992, p. 73.

problem is easily solved: In order to sit in a first-class seat you need a first-class ticket. However, there is another aspect to this problem. If the difference in price is great enough relative to the valuation a consumer places on a higher class of travel, a business-class traveler, for example, might choose to fly coach. For simplicity, we assume that this arbitrage, or self-selection, problem does not arise. That is, we assume that first-class passengers prefer not to travel rather than sit in business or coach and business-class passengers similarly will not consider coach travel—they place sufficiently high values on the differences in quality between the types of seat that they will not trade down.[7]

Suppose that NA's market research indicates that daily demand for first-class travel on this route is $P_F = 18{,}500 - 1{,}000Q_F i$, for business-class travel is $P_B = 9{,}200 - 250Q_B$, and for coach travel is $P_C = 1{,}500 - 5Q_C$. The marginal cost is estimated to be \$100 for a coach passenger, \$200 for a business-class passenger, and \$500 for a first-class passenger.

The profit-maximizing third-degree price discrimination scheme for differentiated products of this type satisfies essentially the same rules as for homogeneous products. Simply put, NA should identify the quantity that equates marginal revenue with marginal cost for each class of seat and then identify the equilibrium price from the relevant demand function. For first-class passengers this requires $MR_F = 18{,}500 - 2{,}000Q_F = 500$, or $Q_F^* = 9$. The resulting first-class fare is $P_F^* = \$9{,}000$. In business class we have $MR_B = 9{,}200 - 500Q_B = 200$, or $Q_B^* = 18$ and $P_B^* = \$4{,}700$. Finally, in coach we have $1{,}500 - 10Q_C = 100$, giving $Q_C^* = 150$ and $P_C^* = \$750$.

The example we have just presented resolved the arbitrage problem by assuming that different types of travelers are committed to particular classes of travel. Of course, this may not always be the case. For example, the downturn in economic activity through 2003 has encouraged firms to seek ways to cut costs. In particular, business travelers increasingly are required by their companies to fly coach. However, it remains the case that these types of travelers are willing to pay more (though not as much more as before) for air travel than casual or vacation travelers. Now, however, the airline's ability to exploit the difference in willingness to pay faces a potentially severe arbitrage problem.

To see this more clearly, suppose that the airline has two types of customers, businesspeople and vacationers. Businesspeople are known to have a high reservation price, or willingness to pay, for a return ticket, which we will denote as $V^B$. Vacationers, by contrast, have a low reservation price, denoted as $V^V$. By assumption, $V^B > V^V$, and the airline would obviously like to exploit this difference by charging business customers a high price and vacationers a low one. However, the airline cannot simply impose this distinction. A policy of explicitly charging business customers more than vacationers would quickly lead to every customer claiming to be on holiday and not on business. The airline could try to identify which passengers really are on holiday, but this would be costly and likely to alienate customers.

If this were the end of our story, it would appear that the airline has no choice but to sell its tickets at a single, uniform price. It would then face the usual textbook monopoly dilemma. A high price will earn a large surplus from every customer that still flies but clearly lead to a smaller, mostly business set of passengers. In contrast, a low

---

7　There is also the possibility that coach or business travelers would want to trade up. The equilibrium prices that we derive in the example preclude such a possibility.

price will encourage more people to fly but, unfortunately, leave the company with little surplus from any one consumer.

Suppose, however, that business and holiday travelers differ in another respect as well as in their motives for flying. To be specific, suppose that business travelers want to complete their trip and return home within three days, whereas vacationers want to be away for at least one week. Suppose also that the airline learns (through surveys and other market research) that business travelers would pay a premium beyond a normal ticket price if they could be guaranteed a return flight within their preferred three-day span. In this case, product differentiation by means of offering two differentiated tickets—one with a minimum time away of one week and another with no minimum stay—will enable the airline to extract considerable surplus from each type of consumer.

The complete strategy would be as follows: First, set a low price of $V^V$ for tickets requiring a minimum of one week before returning. Since holiday travelers do not mind staying away seven days, and since the ticket price does not exceed their reservation price, they will willingly purchase this ticket. Since such travelers are paying their reservation price, the airline has extracted their entire consumer surplus and converted it into profit for itself.[8]

Second, the airline should set a price as close to $V^B$ as possible for flights with no minimum stay. The limit on its ability to do this will be such factors as the cost of

 # Reality Checkpoint

## Unfair Fares

Facilitated by computer and Internet technology, and motivated by an increasingly lean market, airlines have become perhaps the leading practitioners of price discrimination. On a single flight, passengers often will have paid as many as a dozen different prices for essentially the same service. Frequent flyers cashing in for a free trip will pay zero. Those who purchased well ahead of time and plan to stay over a Saturday night will get a very large discount. A different discount will be offered to senior citizens and those on group plans or to those who have purchased a lodging and air travel package. The resulting range in airfares can be phenomenal. In 1999, a coach ticket for a flight from New York to Seattle was free to frequent flyers cashing in; $239 for those who bought over the Internet; $307 for those who purchased through an agent 14 days in advance; and $1,828 for those who bought the full-price, same day coach ticket. One might say this is unfair, but it would be more accurate to say that it is discriminatory—price discriminatory.

**Source:**  E. McDowell, "Winging It, With Internet Fares." *The New York Times*, March 7, 1999, p. D1.

---

8   An alternative and frequently used distinction is to require that the traveler stay over a Saturday night in order to qualify for a cheap fare. Presumably a corporation will not want to finance the lodgings of its employees when they are not on company business. Further, business travelers typically want to spend weekends with family and loved ones. On both counts, the Saturday night requirement works as a self-separating device.

paying for a hotel for extra nights, the price of alternative transportation capable of returning individuals in three days, and related considerations. Denote the dollar value of these other factors as $M$. Businesspeople wanting to return quickly will gladly pay a premium over the one-week price, $V^V$, up to the value of $M$, so long as their total fare is less than $V^B$. (The precise condition is $V^V + M < V^B$.) Using such a scheme enables the airline to extract considerable surplus from business customers, while simultaneously extracting the entire surplus from vacationers.

In short, even if the airline cannot squeeze out the entire consumer surplus from the market, it can nevertheless improve its profits greatly by offering two kinds of tickets. This is undoubtedly the reason that the practice just described is so common among airlines and other transportation companies. (See Reality Checkpoint: Unfair Fares.) Such companies offer different varieties of their product as a means of having their customers self-select into different groups. Automobile and appliance manufacturers utilize a similar strategy—offering different product lines meant to appeal to consumers of different incomes or otherwise different willingness to pay. Stiglitz (1977) labels such mechanisms as *screening devices* because they screen or separate customers precisely along the relevant dimension of willingness to pay.

A rather curious kind of screening is illustrated by Wolfram Research, manufacturers of the Mathematica® software package. In making their student version of the software, Wolfram disables a number of functions that are available in the full academic or commercial versions. In 2000, Wolfram offered the full version of Mathematica® at around $1500, the academic version at around $400, and the student version at around $140. There is little doubt that this is a case involving substantial differences in net prices.

The motivation behind this screening by means of product differentiation seems equally clear. Wolfram realizes that some customers do not need—or at least do not

 ## Reality Checkpoint

### You Can't Go Before You've Come Back

It is not uncommon to find that a coach fare to fly out on Tuesday and return quickly on Thursday costs well over twice the coach fare to fly out on Tuesday and return the next Tuesday. So one possible strategy is to buy two round-trip tickets, the first from departure airport A to arrival airport B leaving on Tuesday and returning the following Tuesday, and the second from B to A, departing on Thursday and returning the following Thursday. The traveler uses only the outward half of each ticket, throwing away the unused portions—or giving them to impoverished students.

Airlines have caught on to this type of arbitrage, however, and have designed systems to check whether a passenger has an unused portion of a return flight when checking in on what appears to be the first leg of a flight. The airlines want to make sure that those who are really willing to pay a substantial premium to return in two days actually do pay it.

**Source:** "Why It Doesn't Pay to Change Planes or Plans." *London Daily Telegraph*, March 11, 2000, p. 27.

want to pay very much for—the full version of their software. Wolfram markets the low-priced version of Mathematica® for these consumers, and then sells the extended version to customers with a high willingness to pay for the improved product. Note that the two products must differ in some important respect (to consumers at least). If Wolfram did not reduce the capabilities of the student version it would have to worry about arbitrage between the two customer groups, with students buying for their parents!

The Wolfram example just described is a type of screening referred to by marketing experts as "crimping the product." Deneckere and McAffee (1996) argue that crimping, or deliberately damaging a product to enhance the ability to price discriminate, has been a frequent practice of manufacturers throughout history. Among the examples that they cite are (1) IBM's Laser Printer E, an intentionally slower version of the company's higher priced top-of-the-line laser printer and (2) cooking wine, which is ordinary table wine with so much salt added that it is undrinkable. Some people have even argued that the U.S. Post Office deliberately reduces the quality of its standard, first-class service so as to raise demand for its two-day priority and overnight mail services.

Each of these examples is a clear case of a difference in net prices. The lower quality product sells for a lower price, yet—because it starts as a high-quality product and then requires the further cost of crimping—the lower quality product is actually more expensive to make. Why do firms crimp a high-quality product to produce a low-quality one instead of simply producing a low-quality one in the first place? The most obvious answer relates to costs of production. Given that a firm with monopoly power such as Wolfram knows that there are consumers of different types willing to buy different varieties of its product, the firm must decide how these consumer types can be supplied with products "close" to those that they most want at the least cost. It may well be cheaper to produce the student version of Mathematica® by crimping the full version rather than to set up a separate production line dedicated to manufacturing different versions of the software package.

The final type of product differentiation that we consider in this chapter is differentiation by *location of sale*.[9] In many cases a product for sale in one location is not the same as the otherwise identical product for sale in another location. A prescription drug such as Lipitor® for sale in Wisconsin, for example, is not identical to the same prescription drug for sale in New York State. Even with the advent of sophisticated Internet search engines, a new automobile for sale in one state is not identical to the same new automobile for sale in another state.

To illustrate why this type of product differentiation can lead to price discrimination, suppose that there is a company, Boston Sea Foods (BSF), which sells a proprietary brand of clam chowder. BSF knows that demand for its chowder in Boston is $P_B = A - BQ_B$ and in Manhattan is $P_M = A - BQ_M$, where quantities are measured in thousands of pints. In other words, the firm believes that these two markets have identical demands. BSF has constant marginal costs of $c$ per thousand pints of chowder. Transportation costs to reach the Boston market are negligible but it costs BSF $t$ to transport a thousand pints of chowder to Manhattan.

How does BSF maximize its profits from these two markets, given that BSF employs linear pricing? BSF should apply the rules that we have already developed. It

---

9   We return to spatial differentiation in more detail in Chapter 7.

should equate marginal revenue with marginal cost in each market. In the Boston market this requires that $A - 2BQ_B = c$, so that $Q_B^* = (A - c)/2B$ and the Boston price is $P_B^* = (A + c)/2$. In the Manhattan market we have, by contrast, $A - 2BQ_M = c + t$, so that $Q_M^* = (A - c - t)/2B$ and the Manhattan price is $P_M^* = (A + c + t)/2$.

Why is this an example of price discrimination through third-degree price discrimination? Recall our definition of price discrimination with differentiated products. For there to be *no* such discrimination any difference in price should be equal to the difference in the costs of product differentiation. In our BSF example it costs BSF $t$ per thousand pints to send chowder from Boston to Manhattan but the difference in price in the two markets is only $t/2$. In other words, BSF is price discriminating by absorbing 50 percent of the transportation costs of sending its chowder to Manhattan.

What about the arbitrage problem in the BSF example? Manhattanites might want to buy their chowder directly in the Boston market but it is economic for them to do so only if they have access to a transport technology that is at least 50 percent cheaper than that employed by BSF, a very tall order other than for those who choose to vacation in Boston.

Returning to our prescription drug example in Table 5.1, one possible explanation for the difference in prices in the three United States regions might be differences in costs of supplying these three regions. Another, of course, would be differences in demands in the three regions arising, for example, from differences in these regions' demographics or incomes.

## Practice Problem 5.2

NonLegal Seafoods (NS) sells its excellent clam chowder in Boston, New York, and Washington. NS has estimated that the demands in these three markets are respectively $Q_B = 10,000 - 1,000P_B$, $Q_{NY} = 20,000 - 2,000P_{NY}$ and $Q_W = 15,000 - 1,500P_W$, where quantities are pints of clam chowder per day. The marginal cost of making a pint of clam chowder in its Boston facility is $1. In addition, it costs $1 per pint to ship the chowder to New York and $2 per pint to ship to Washington.

a. What are the profit-maximizing prices that NS should set in these three markets? How much chowder is sold per day in each market?
b. What profit does NS make in each market?

## 5.5 THIRD-DEGREE PRICE DISCRIMINATION OR GROUP PRICING AND SOCIAL WELFARE

The term "price discrimination" suggests inequity and, from a social perspective, sounds like a "bad thing." Is it? To answer this question we must recall the economist's approach to social welfare and the problem raised by the standard monopoly model. Economists view arrangements as less than socially optimal whenever there are potential trades that could make both parties better off. This is the reason that a standard monopoly is suboptimal. The textbook monopolist practicing uniform pricing restricts output. At the margin, consumers value the product *more* than it costs the monopolist to produce it. A potentially mutually beneficial trade exists but under uniform pricing such a trade will not occur.

The question that arises with third-degree price discrimination is whether such discrimination worsens or reduces this monopoly distortion. The intuitive reason why third-degree discrimination may reduce efficiency relative to the uniform pricing case is essentially that such a policy amounts to uniform pricing within two or more separate markets. It thus runs the risks of compounding the output-reducing effects of monopoly power.

We can be more specific regarding the welfare effects of third-degree price discrimination by drawing on the work of Schmalensee (1981). This is illustrated for the case of two markets in Figure 5-5. In this Figure, $P_1$ and $P_2$ are the profit-maximizing discriminatory prices—obtained by equating marginal revenue with marginal cost in each market—while $P_U$ is the optimal nondiscriminatory price. Market 2 is referred to as the strong market since the discriminatory price is higher than the uniform price, while market 1 is the weak market. $\Delta Q_1$ and $\Delta Q_2$ are respectively the difference between the discriminatory output and the nondiscriminatory output in the weak and the strong market. It follows, of course, that $\Delta Q_1 > 0$ and $\Delta Q_2 < 0$.

**FIGURE**

**5-5**

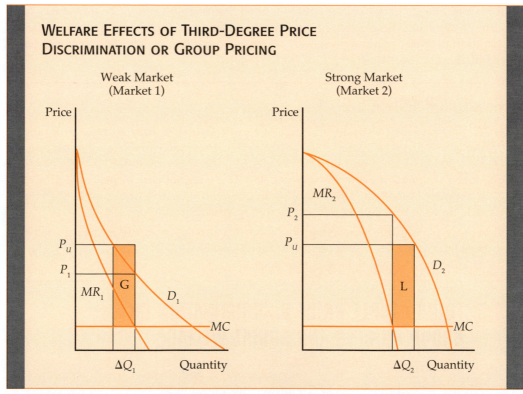

**WELFARE EFFECTS OF THIRD-DEGREE PRICE DISCRIMINATION OR GROUP PRICING**

The upper limit on the welfare gain is area G and the lower limit on welfare loss is area L. The upper limit of the net welfare impact is G – L and is positive only if aggregate output is greater with discriminatory pricing than with nondiscriminatory pricing.

Our normal definition of welfare is the sum of consumer plus producer surplus. Using this definition, an upper limit on the increase in surplus that follows from third-degree price discrimination in Figure 5-5 is the area G minus the area L. This gives us the following equation. (In writing equation (5.7) we have used the property that $\Delta Q_2 < 0$.)

$$\Delta W \le G - L = (P_U - MC)\Delta Q_1 + (P_U - MC)\Delta Q_2 = (P_U - MC)(\Delta Q_1 + \Delta Q_2). \quad \textbf{(5.7)}$$

Extending this analysis to $n$ markets, we have

$$\Delta W \le (P_U - MC)\sum_{i=1}^{n}\Delta Q_i . \qquad\qquad \textbf{(5.8)}$$

It follows from equation (5.8) that for $\Delta W \ge 0$ it is necessary that $\sum_{i=1}^{n}\Delta Q_i \ge 0$. In other words, a necessary condition for third-degree price discrimination to increase welfare is that it increases total output.

We know from the Harry Potter example and from the more general Derivation Checkpoint on pages 97–98 that when demands in the various markets are linear, total output is identical with discriminatory and nondiscriminatory pricing. It follows that with linear demands third-degree price discrimination reduces total welfare. The increase in profit is more than offset by the reduction in consumer surplus. Schmalensee states:

> If one thinks that demand curves are about as likely to be concave as convex . . .
> (this) . . . might lead one to the conclusion that monopolistic third-degree price
> discrimination should be outlawed. (1981, p. 246)

However, before jumping to the suggested conclusion, we need to note an important *caveat* to this analysis. The qualification is that while our analysis implicitly assumes that the same markets are served with and without price discrimination this may not be the case. In particular, one property of price discrimination is that it can make it profitable to serve markets that would not be served with nondiscriminatory prices. If this is the case, then the additional welfare from the new markets that third-degree price discrimination introduces more than offsets any loss of welfare in the markets that were previously being served.

A simple example serves to make this point. Suppose that monthly demand for a patented AIDS drug treatment in North America is $P_N = 100 - Q_N$ and in Sub-Saharan Africa is $P_S = \alpha 100 - Q_S$, with $\alpha < 1$ reflecting the assumption that African consumers have a lower demand because their income is so much smaller. Further assume that the marginal cost of producing each month's treatment is constant at $c$ per unit and that transportation costs to the African market are negligible. Now assume that the patent holder either does not or cannot price discriminate across the two markets, and let marginal cost be $c = 20$.

As before, we start by inverting the demand functions to give $Q_N = 100 - P$ and $Q_S = \alpha 100 - P$. If the price is low enough to attract buyers in both markets then aggregate demand is $Q = (1 + \alpha)100 - 2P$ or $P = (1 + \alpha)50 - Q/2$, and marginal revenue is $MR = (1 + \alpha)50 - Q$. Equating marginal revenue with marginal cost $c = 20$ gives the equilibrium output $Q = (1 + \alpha)50 - 20$, and price $P = 35 + 25\alpha$.

Now recall our assumption that both markets are active without price discrimination. For this assumption to hold it must be that the equilibrium price when there is no discrimination is less than the maximum price—$\alpha 100$—that Sub-Saharan African consumers are willing and able to pay. That is, for our assumption to hold it must be the case that $35 + 25\alpha < \alpha100$. In turn, this implies that for both markets to be active with no price discrimination it is necessary that $\alpha > 35/75$ or $\alpha > 0.466$. In other words, for the Sub-Saharan African market to be served it is necessary that the maximum willingness to pay for AIDS drugs in that market be about 47 percent of the maximum willingness to pay in North America.

Moreover, even if $\alpha > 0.466$ the Sub-Saharan African market may not be served. From the patent-holding firm's perspective, it is not quite enough that the maximum willingness to pay exceeds the price charged if it serves both markets. This is because the monopolist always has the option of choosing a higher price and serving only the North American market. In Problem 5 at the end of the chapter, you are asked to show that $\alpha > 0.531$ for it to be profitable for the firm to serve both markets when price discrimination is for some reason prohibited.

What about the welfare impact of price discrimination in this case? Suppose that in the absence of the ability to price discriminate, only the North American market is served. Then consumers in that market will be charged the monopoly price. Now allow for price discrimination across the two markets. The price in North America will be unchanged so that consumers in that market will be no worse off. The firm will, in addition, now open up supplies to the Sub-Saharan market provided only that the maximum willingness to pay in Sub-Saharan Africa is greater than marginal cost. Given that this condition is satisfied, the ability to price discriminate leads to the African market being served and to an increase in welfare.

## Practice Problem 5.3

Return to Practice Problem 5.1 and confirm that total welfare is greater with nondiscriminatory pricing than with third-degree price discrimination.

## SUMMARY

We started this chapter with a discussion of prescription drug prices and of proposals to remove the barriers that exist to prevent re-import of such drugs to the United States. At the heart of this discussion lies a simple proposition. If a firm with monopoly power knows that consumers of different types and with different demands buy its products, then the firm has a profit incentive to charge different prices to the different types of consumers. Our analysis has concentrated on third-degree price discrimination or group pricing, in which the firm offers different prices to different groups of consumers but leaves it up to the consumers to determine how much they will purchase at the quoted prices; this is termed linear pricing.

In order to price discriminate in this way the firm has to solve two problems. First, it needs some observable characteristic by which it can identify the different groups of consumers: the identification problem. Second, the firm must be able to prevent consumers who pay a low price from selling to consumers offered a high price: the arbitrage problem. Provided that both problems can be overcome, there is a simple principle that guides the monopolist in setting prices. Set a high price in markets in which elasticity of demand is low and a low price in markets in which elasticity of demand is high. When the firm makes a single homogeneous product this implies that different groups of consumers will be paying different prices for the same good. If the firm sells differentiated products, it implies that the prices of different varieties will vary by something other than the difference in their marginal production costs.

While third-degree price discrimination or group pricing when feasible is undoubtedly profitable, it is less clear that it is socially desirable. Again there is a simple principle that can guide us. For third-degree price discrimination to increase social welfare it is necessary, but not sufficient, that it lead to an increase in output. This makes intuitive sense. After all, we know that a monopolist makes profit by restricting output. If price discrimination leads to increased output it might reduce the monopoly distortion. This is, however, a tall order, usually requiring restrictive conditions regarding the shapes of the demand functions in the different markets. For example, it is a condition that is never satisfied when demands are linear and the same markets are served with and without price discrimination.

The qualification regarding the same markets being served is, however, quite important. In particular, group price discrimination has the beneficial effect of encouraging the monopolist to serve markets that would otherwise have been left unserved. For example, markets populated by low-income groups might not be supplied if the monopolist were not able to set discriminatory prices. When price discrimination leads the monopolist to serve additional markets, the likelihood that it increases social welfare is greatly increased.

We conclude by noting one limitation of third-degree price discrimination. Restricting the monopolist to simple, linear forms of price discrimination is qualitatively the same as allowing it to charge a monopoly price in each of its separable markets. Yet we know that, in any given market, charging a monopoly price reduces the surplus. The monopolist also knows this and, therefore, cannot help but wonder if a more complicated, that is, a nonlinear pricing strategy, might permit it to achieve more of the potential surplus as profit. It is to this question that we turn in the next chapter.

# PROBLEMS

1. True or False: Price discrimination always increases economic efficiency, relative to what would be achieved by a single, uniform monopoly price.

2. A nearby pizza parlor offers pizzas in three sizes: small, medium, and large. Its price schedule is $6, $8, and $10, respectively. Do these data indicate that the firm is price discriminating? Why or why not?

3. A monopolist has two sets of customers. The inverse demand for one set may be described by $P = 200 - X$. For the other set, the inverse demand is $P = 100 - 2X$. The monopolist faces constant marginal cost of 40.

   a. Show that the monopolist's total demand, if the two markets are treated as one is

   $$
   \begin{aligned}
   &X = 0; &&P \geq 200 \\
   &X = 200 - P; &&100 < P \leq 200 \\
   &X = 300 - (3/2)P; &&0 \leq P \leq 100
   \end{aligned}
   $$

   b. Show that the monopolist's profit-maximizing price is $P = 120$ if both groups are to be charged the same price. At this price, how much is sold to members of Group 1 and how much to members of Group 2? What is the consumer surplus of each group? What are total profits?

**c.** Suppose the monopolist can separate the two groups and charge separate, profit-maximizing prices to each. What will these prices be? What is consumer surplus? What are total profits?

**d.** If total surplus is defined as consumer surplus plus profits, how has price discrimination affected total surplus?

**4.** Suppose that Coca-Cola uses a new type of vending machine that charges a price according to the outside temperature. On "hot" days—defined as days in which the outside temperature is 77° Fahrenheit (25° Celsius) or higher—demand for vending machine soft drinks is $Q = 300 - 2P$. On "cool" days—when the outside temperature is below 77° Fahrenheit (25° Celsius)—demand is $Q = 200 - 2P$. The marginal cost of a soft drink is 20 cents.

**a.** What price should the machine charge for a soft drink on "hot" days? What price should it charge on "cool" days?

**b.** Suppose that half of the days are "hot" and the other half are "cool." If Coca-Cola uses a traditional machine that is simply programmed to charge the same price regardless of the weather, what price should it set?

**c.** Compare Coca-Cola's profit from a weather-sensitive machine to the traditional, uniform pricing machine.

**5.** Return to the final example of section 5.4, in which the demand for AIDS drugs was $Q_N = 100 - P$ in North America and $Q_S = \alpha 100 - P$ in Sub-Saharan Africa. Show that with marginal cost = 20 for such drugs, it must be the case that $\alpha > 0.531$ if the drug manufacturer is to serve both markets while charging the same price in each market. (*Hint*: Calculate the total profit if it serves only North America and then calculate the total profit if it serves both markets. Then determine the value of $\alpha$ for which the profit from serving both markets is at least as large.)

# REFERENCES

Deneckere, R., and R. P. McAffee. 1996. "Damaged Goods." *Journal of Economics and Management Strategy* 5 (Summer): 149–74.

Graham, John R., and Beverly A. Robson. 2000. "Prescription Drug Prices in Canada and the United States—Part 1: A Comparative Survey." Fraser Institute, *Public Policy Sources, Number 42.*

Graham, John R., and Tanya Taylor. 2001. "Prescription Drug Prices in Canada and the United States—Part 3: Retail Price Distribution." Fraser Institute, *Public Policy Sources, Number 43.*

Phlips, L. 1983. *The Economics of Price Discrimination.* Cambridge: Cambridge University Press.

Pigou, A. C. 1920. *The Economics of Welfare.* London: Macmillan Publishing.

Schmalensee, R. 1981 "Output and Welfare Implications of Monopolistic Third-Degree Price Discrimination." *American Economic Review* 71 (March): 242–47.

Shapiro, Carl, and Hal Varian. 1998. *Information Rules.* Cambridge: Harvard Business School Press.

Shih, J., C. Mai, and J. Liu. 1988. "A General Analysis of the Output Effect Under Third-Degree Price Discrimination." *Economic Journal* (March): 149–58.

Smith, W. J., and J. Fornby. 1981. "Output Changes Under Third-Degree Price Discrimination." *Southern Economic Journal* (July): 164–71.

Stiglitz, J. 1977. "Monopoly, Non-Linear Pricing, and Imperfect Information: The Insurance Market." *Review of Economic Studies* 44 (July): 407–30.

Varian, H. 1989. "Price Discrimination." In R. Schmalensee and R. Willig, eds., *The Handbook of Industrial Organization, Vol. 1*. Amsterdam: North-Holland, 597–654.

# Chapter  6
# Price Discrimination and Monopoly: Nonlinear Pricing

If you buy the *New Yorker* magazine at the newsstand you will pay $3.95; if you buy all 46 issues this year at the newsstand you will end up spending $181.70. If instead you had an annual subscription to the magazine you would have paid $46 for 46 issues—a savings of 74 percent over the newsstand price. Or if you are a baseball fan you will find that the price per ticket on a season pass is much less than the price per ticket on a game-by-game basis. Likewise, when you go grocery shopping you will discover that a 24-pack of Coca-Cola costs less per can than does a six-pack or a single can. These are all examples of price discrimination that reflect quantity discounts—the more you buy the cheaper it is on a per-unit basis. This kind of pricing is nonlinear. This is because in these examples, the price is not simply set at a different value for each group but instead varies across many different customers depending on the consumer's income, value of time, the quantity bought, and many other characteristics. Such tactics are of course employed for one purpose: to convert as much as possible of the individual consumer's willingness to pay into the seller's revenues and profits. As we shall see, such techniques are generally more profitable than the third-degree price discrimination or linear pricing discussed in Chapter 5, precisely because they permit the seller to set a price closer to willingness to pay *of each consumer*. As a result, nonlinear pricing can help the monopolist to extract more of the consumer surplus and convert it into profit.

The design and implementation of nonlinear pricing systems are the focus of this chapter. We shall explore how a firm with monopoly power can implement such tactics to a greater or lesser extent along with the welfare implications of such pricing. Traditionally, nonlinear pricing is divided into two general categories: first-degree price discrimination and second-degree price discrimination. These have recently been renamed by Shapiro and Varian (1999) as, respectively, personalized pricing and menu pricing.[1]

## 6.1 FIRST-DEGREE PRICE DISCRIMINATION OR PERSONALIZED PRICING

First-degree, or perfect, price discrimination is practiced when the monopolist is able to charge the maximum price each consumer is willing to pay for each unit of the product sold. Suppose, for example, that you have inherited five antique cars, each a classic Ford Model T, and you want to sell them to finance your college education. Your research tells you that there are several collectors interested in buying a Model T. When you rank these collectors in terms of their willingness to pay for a car, you estimate that the keenest collector is willing to pay up to $10,000, the second keen-

---

1  Pigou (1920) is the classic piece on price discrimination. Good modern summaries of price discrimination in both theory and practice are provided by Phlips (1983) and Varian (1999).

est up to $8,000, the third keenest up to $6,000, the fourth up to $4,000, and the fifth up to $2,000. First-degree price discrimination means that you are able sell the first car for $10,000, the second for $8,000, the third for $6,000, the fourth for $4,000, and the fifth for $2,000. The revenue from such a discriminatory pricing policy will be $30,000. Not surprisingly, this strategy is also called personalized pricing.

What if, on the other hand, you chose to sell all your cars at the same, uniform price? It is easy to calculate that the best you can do is to set a price of $6,000 at which you will sell three cars for a total revenue (and profit) of $18,000. Any higher or lower price generates lower revenues. In short, under uniform pricing your highest possible revenue is $18,000, while successful first-degree price discrimination yields much higher revenue of $30,000. Simply put, first-degree price discrimination enables you to extract the entire surplus that selling your car generates. No consumer surplus remains if you can successfully discriminate to this extent, whereas with a uniform price the keenest buyer has consumer surplus of $4,000 and the second keenest buyer has consumer surplus of $2,000.

Since first-degree price discrimination or personalized pricing redirects surplus from consumers to the producer it should be expected to raise the incentive for the monopolist to produce. In fact, under first-degree price discrimination, the monopolist chooses the same socially efficient amount that would be achieved under perfect competition. In our Model T example no mutually beneficial trades are left unmade: all five cars are sold. By contrast, with uniform pricing only three cars are sold, leaving two of the cars in the "wrong" hands.

The same is true in more general cases. For a monopolist able to practice first-degree price discrimination, selling an additional unit never requires lowering the price on other units. Each additional unit sold generates revenue exactly equal to the price at which it is bought. Hence, with first-degree price discrimination marginal revenue is equal to price. Accordingly, for such a monopolist, the profit-maximizing rule that marginal revenue equals marginal cost yields an output level at which price equals marginal cost as well. As we know, this is the output level that would be generated by a competitive industry.

## Practice Problem 6.1

Suppose that a monopoly seller knows that his demand curve is linear, and knows that at a price of $40, he sells five units, while at a price of $25, he sells 10 units.

a. Find the equation for the monopolist's demand curve. Now find the equation for his marginal revenue curve.
b. If each potential consumer buys only one unit, what is the reservation price of the consumer with the greatest willingness to pay?
c. Suppose that each consumer will buy a second unit at a price $8 below the price at which they purchase just one. How many units will be sold at a price of $34? (Use whole dollar amounts.)

At first glance it might seem that first-degree discrimination is little more than a theoretical curiosity. How could a monopolist ever have sufficient information about potential buyers and the ability to prevent arbitrage so as to implement effectively a pricing scheme in which a different, personalized price is charged to each buyer and for each unit bought? The problems of identification and arbitrage prevention seem insurmountable. However, in some cases the monopolist seller may have the ability to achieve the personalized pricing outcome. Think, for example, of the tax accountant who knows the financial situation of his or her clients. Or another example, perhaps closer to home, are the students who apply to private universities in the United States. When they apply for financial aid they are required to complete a detailed statement of financial means. The universities can use this information, as well as SAT scores and other data, to determine the aid that will be granted and thus the net tuition that each prospective student will be required to pay. Look around you. If one breaks down the total tuition on a per-class basis, chances are that many of your classmates are paying a different fee for this class than you are!

Of course, the accountant or university example may be somewhat special because often the fee is set *after* the customer has contracted to purchase the service. What we now want to consider is whether there are pricing strategies that will permit the seller to achieve the same effect even when fees are announced in advance. The answer, to a greater or lesser extent, is yes. One such strategy is a *two-part* pricing scheme and another is *block pricing*. We discuss each in turn.

## 6.1.1 Two-Part Pricing

A two-part pricing scheme is a pricing strategy that consists of (1) a fee, such as a membership fee, that entitles the consumer to buy the good; and (2) a price or usage fee charged for each unit the consumer actually buys. Many clubs use such two-part tariffs. They charge a flat annual fee for membership in the club (which is sometimes differentiated by age or some other member characteristic), and additional user fees to use particular facilities or buy particular goods. Country clubs, athletic clubs, and discount shopping clubs are all good examples of clubs that use this kind of pricing. A related example of two-part pricing is that used by theme parks under which a flat

 **Reality Checkpoint**

### The More You Shop the More They Know about You

Internet shopping has undoubtedly brought with it considerable convenience in shopping for books, DVDs, wine, and gourmet foods. At the same time, however, it has provided e-commerce retailers such as Amazon.com and Wine.com the ability to track your purchases. The result is that companies such as these are able to tailor special offers to each individual consumer based on their predictions of the books, wines, condiments, and so on that the consumer is most likely to find attractive. In other words, the Internet has made possible a kind of personalized marketing that is not feasible through more traditional media.

**Source:** C. Shapiro and H. Varian, *Information Rules: A Strategic Guide to the Internet Economy.* Boston: Harvard Business School Press, 1999.

# Reality Checkpoint

---

## Call Options

Nonlinear pricing is an increasingly common feature of everyday life. Consider the packages available for cell phone service. All of the plans offered by the six major providers, T-Mobile, Verizon, Sprint, Nextel, AT&T, and Cingular, involve some variant of a two-part tariff. There is a basic fee that is independent of the number of minutes used, and also a number of free minutes that may be unlimited for off-peak hours, but that is limited to, say, 300 minutes per month during peak hours. When the limit is exceeded, there is an extra minute charge ranging between 35 and 50 cents per minute. Yet while these features are common to all plans, there is also a quantity discount feature built into the different plans targeted at different customers. For example, T-Mobile currently offers a casual user plan that has an upfront fee of $30 and a limit of 300 free minutes in peak hours. In contrast, its frequent user plan doubles the upfront fee to $60 but more than triples the number of free minutes in peak hours to 1000. There is also a family plan that charges a lower price for extra peak minutes because families typically make so many calls during these hours.

---

**Source:** "The Bottom Line on Calling Plans." *Consumer Reports*, February 2004, pp. 11–18.

fee is charged to enter the park and additional fees (sometimes set to zero) are charged on a per-ride basis.[2]

To see how a two-part tariff can work to achieve first-degree price discrimination, let us consider a jazz club where people meet for drinks and music. Assume that the club's customers are of two types: old and young (but both above the legal drinking age), and there are just as many old customers as young ones. The inverse demand curve for the club's services given by a typical old customer is

$$P = V_o - Q_o, \tag{6.1}$$

while each young customer has the inverse demand curve

$$P = V_y - Q_y, \tag{6.2}$$

where $Q_i$ is the number of drinks consumed in an evening by a customer of type $i$ ($o$ or $y$), $P$ is the price per drink, and $V_i$ is the maximum amount a customer of type $i$ will pay for just one drink. We shall assume that old customers are willing to pay more for a given number of drinks than young customers, that is, $V_o > V_y$. We

---

2 Versions of such a pricing scheme have been used, for example, at Disney World and Disneyland. See Oi (1971) for the seminal discussion of two-part pricing.

further assume that the jazz club owner incurs a cost of $c$ dollars per drink served plus a fixed cost $F$ of operating the club each night. That is, the cost function for the club is

$$C(Q) = F + cQ. \qquad (6.3)$$

This example is illustrated in Figure 6-1. The demand curve for a typical customer starts at $V_i$ and declines with slope $-1$ until it hits the quantity axis. The constant marginal cost curve is a horizontal line through the value $c$.

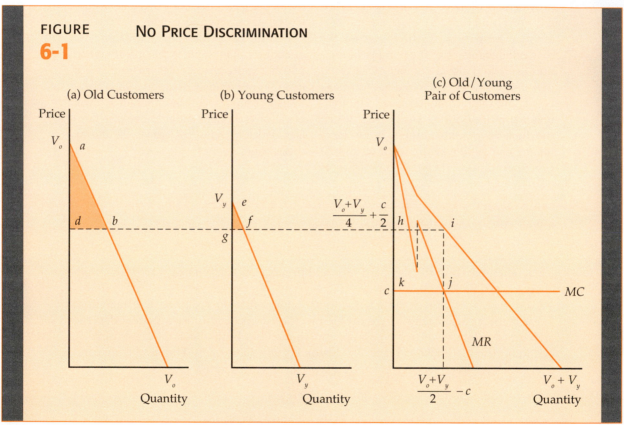

**FIGURE 6-1        NO PRICE DISCRIMINATION**

No price discrimination leaves both types of consumers with consumer surplus that the monopolist would like to convert to profit.

Suppose that the jazz club owner is a "traditional" monopolist who employs simple linear pricing. Entry to the club is free. The club owner sets a simple price per drink and customers decide how many drinks to buy at that price. The jazz club owner would like to employ third-degree price discrimination, charging old customers more per drink than young customers. While the identification problem is easily resolved by carding the customers, the arbitrage problem is not. Each old customer could ask (or bribe) a young customer to buy his drinks. So most likely the best that the traditional linear pricing monopolist can do is to set a uniform price for drinks to customers of both types.

Inverting equations (6.1) and (6.2) and adding gives the aggregate demand for each pair of customers consisting of one old and one young customer:[3]

$$Q = Q_o + Q_y = (V_o + V_y) - 2P. \tag{6.4}$$

Solving this demand curve for the price variable $P$ to get the aggregate inverse demand for each old/young pair, assuming that both types of customer are allowed into the club, gives

$$P = (V_o + V_y)/2 - Q/2. \tag{6.5}$$

The jazz club monopolist maximizes profit by identifying the quantity, in this case the number of drinks, at which marginal cost equals marginal revenue and then identifying the price at which this quantity can be sold. Given the straight-line demand curve of equation (6.5) it is clear that the marginal revenue curve for each old/young pair is

$$MR = (V_o + V_y)/2 - Q. \tag{6.6}$$

Setting marginal revenue equal to marginal cost $c$ requires that $(V_o + V_y)/2 - Q = c$, which gives the profit-maximizing output – number of drinks sold to each old/young pair as

$$Q_U = (V_o + V_y)/2 - c, \tag{6.7}$$

where the subscript $U$ denotes uniform pricing. Substituting this into the demand function gives the profit-maximizing price per drink of

$$P_U = (V_o + V_y)/4 + c/2. \tag{6.8}$$

Each old customer buys $Q_o = V_o - P_U = (3V_o - V_y)/4 - c/2$ drinks and each young customer buys $Q_y = V_y - P_U = (3V_y - V_o)/4 - c/2$ drinks. The monopolist earns a surplus $\pi_U$ from each pair of old and young customers of

$$\pi_U = (P_U - c)Q_U = \frac{1}{8}(V_o + V_y - 2c)^2, \tag{6.9}$$

which is the area *hijk* in Figure 6-1(c). If there are $n$ customers of each type per evening, the jazz club owner's profit, $\Pi_U$, is

$$\Pi_U = n\pi_U - F = \frac{1}{8}(V_o + V_y - 2c)^2 - F. \tag{6.10}$$

For example, if $V_o$ is $16, $V_y$ is $12, and $c$ is $4, then the optimal uniform price is $9 per drink. Old customers each buy 7 drinks and young customers each buy 3 drinks. Under this strategy, the club owner earns a profit of ($9 – $4) × 10 = $50 for serving an old and a young customer. [Note that this is what we obtain when substituting the values for $V_o$, $V_y$, and $c$, respectively, in equation (6.10).] If there were 100 old and 100 young customers per evening, the jazz club owner would earn a profit of $5,000 each night less any fixed costs $F$ that are incurred.

---

3 We can do this because we have assumed that there are equal numbers of each type of customer. With different numbers of each type we need a slightly different approach. See the end-of-chapter problems.

To see that the jazz club owner can improve on this outcome, first note that at the uniform price $P_U$ = \$9 every customer of the jazz club enjoys some consumer surplus. Each old customer has consumer surplus given by the shaded triangle *abd* in Figure 6-1(a) and each young customer has consumer surplus given by area *efg* in Figure 6-1(b). This area is, by standard geometric techniques, $CS_o^U = \frac{1}{2}(V_o - P_U) \cdot$

$$Q_o = \frac{1}{2}(Q_o)^2 = \frac{1}{2}\left(\frac{3V_o - V_y}{4} - \frac{c}{2}\right)^2 \text{ for each old customer and } CS_y^U = \frac{1}{2}(V_y - $$

$$P_U) \cdot Q_y = \frac{1}{2}(Q_y)^2 = \frac{1}{2}\left(\frac{3V_y - V_o}{4} - \frac{c}{2}\right)^2 \text{ for each young customer. In our nu-}$$

merical example, each old customer has consumer surplus of \$24.50 and each young customer has consumer surplus of \$4.50. This is a measure of the surplus that the club owner has failed to extract. The owner will clearly prefer any pricing scheme that appropriates at least some and perhaps even all of this surplus.

One possibility is for the jazz club owner to switch to a nonlinear pricing scheme that has two parts—a cover charge to enter the club and an additional charge for every drink consumed. It is for this reason that this pricing design is often referred to as a two-part tariff. In this case, the tactic would be implemented by charging an

entry fee of just under $E_o = \frac{1}{2}\left(\frac{3V_o - V_y}{4} - \frac{c}{2}\right)^2$ to each old customer and just

under $E_y = \frac{1}{2}\left(\frac{3V_y - V_o}{4} - \frac{c}{2}\right)^2$ to each young customer, while continuing to

charge a price per drink of $P_U$. In our example, each old customer is charged (just under) \$24.50 and each young customer (just under) \$4.50 for entry while drinks are priced at \$9 each. Checking IDs at the door easily solves both arbitrage and identification problems.[4] Moreover, the customers will still be willing to patronize the club. Paying the entry fee reduces their surplus to (nearly) zero but does not make it negative. Finally, since the entry fee is independent of the amount the customer actually drinks, each customer will also continue to buy the same number of drinks as before. Because the entry fee is equal to the consumer surplus each customer previously enjoyed under the uniform pricing policy, the immediate effect of this two-part tariff is to extract (almost) the entire consumer surplus and to convert it into profit for the club owner. This implies a profit increase of $E_o$ per old customer and $E_y$ per young customer. Again, in our example, this yields a profit increase of \$24.50 per old customer and \$4.50 per young one, to a total of \$79 for each old and young pair.

However, the club owner can do better still. By reducing the price per drink the club owner can increase the consumer surplus each consumer earns. In turn, this permits the owner to increase the entry fees, which extracts that additional surplus and

---

4   We assume that the expense of serious facelifts, hair coloring, and falsifying IDs is more than the surplus older consumers lose by paying the higher price.

further increases profit. The profit-maximizing two-part pricing scheme is illustrated in Figure 6-2. It has the following properties:[5]

**1.** Set the price per unit (drink) equal to marginal cost $c$.

**2.** Set the entry fee for each type of customer equal to that customer's consumer surplus.

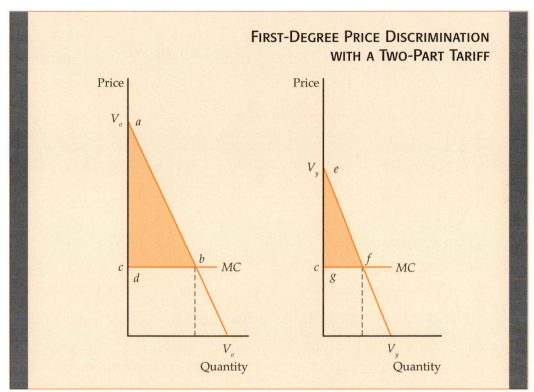

### FIRST-DEGREE PRICE DISCRIMINATION WITH A TWO-PART TARIFF

FIGURE

**6-2**

The monopolist sets a unit price to each type of consumer equal to marginal cost. It then charges each consumer an entry or membership fee equal to the resulting consumer surplus.

In our jazz club case the price per drink is set at $c$. The area of the triangles $abd$ and $efg$ give consumer surplus at this price for old customers and for young customers, respectively. These areas are $CS_o = \frac{1}{2}(V_o - c)^2$ and $CS_y = \frac{1}{2}(V_y - c)^2$. As a result, the jazz club owner can now increase the entry fee to just under $CS_o$ for old customers and just under $CS_y$ for young customers.

---

5   To see why these properties hold, denote the fixed portion of the two-part tariff for a particular type of consumer as $T$ and the user charge as $p$. Express the demand curve for this type of consumer in inverse form, $p = D(q)$, and assume that the firm's total cost function is $C(q)$. The monopolist's problem is to choose the production level for this type of consumer, $q^*$, implying a price $p^* = D(q^*)$ that maximizes profits, $\Pi(q)$, where $\Pi(q)$ is given by $\Pi(q) = \int_0^q D(x)dx - C(q)$. Standard calculus then reveals that maximizing this profit always requires setting a price or user charge equal to marginal cost, and a fixed charge $T$ equal to the consumer surplus generated at that price.

Under this optimal pricing scheme, the profit per drink from each consumer is zero, since drinks are sold at cost. As noted, though, this has the effect of encouraging consumers to purchase many drinks, resulting in a considerable surplus. In turn, the jazz club owner can claim that surplus by imposing the appropriate cover charge. Since the funds claimed by the entry fees are profit, total profit has, therefore, been increased to

$$\Pi_f = \frac{n}{2}\left((V_o - c)^2 + (V_y - c)^2\right) - F. \tag{6.11}$$

In our example, profit per old customer is now \$72 and profit per young customer is now \$32, instead of the \$59.50 and \$19.50 earned from each when the cover charge was associated with a \$9 drink price. This is a hefty profit increase.[6]

Yet while the increase in profit is sizable and important, the two-part tariff has had another result that is equally significant. Note that each customer is now buying the quantity of drinks, $V_o - c$ for the typical old customer and $V_y - c$ for the typical young one, that each would have bought if the drinks had been priced competitively. The ability to practice first-degree price discrimination leads the monopolist to expand output to the competitive level. That is, the market outcome is now efficient. The total surplus is maximized—and that surplus is claimed entirely by the monopolist.

## Practice Problem 6.2

Consider an amusement park operating as a monopoly. Figure 6-3 shows the demand curve of a typical consumer at the park. There are no fixed costs. The marginal cost associated with each ride is constant. It is comprised of two parts, each also a constant. There is the cost per ride of labor and equipment, $k$, and there is the cost per ride of printing and collecting tickets, $c$. A management consultant has suggested two alternative pricing policies for the park. Policy A: Charge a fixed admission fee, $T$, and a fee per ride of $r$. Policy B: Simply charge a fixed admission fee, $T'$, and a zero fee per ride.

a. For pricing policy A, show on the graph the admission fee, $T$, and the per-ride price, $p$, that will maximize profits.
b. For pricing policy B, show on the graph the single admission fee, $T'$, that will maximize profits.
c. Compare the two policies. What are the relative advantages of each policy? What determines which policy leads to higher profits?

## 6.1.2 Block Pricing

There is a second nonlinear pricing method by which the jazz club owner can achieve the same level of profit. This can be done by using block pricing. With this type of pricing scheme a firm *bundles* the quantity that it is willing to sell with the total charge that it wishes to levy for that quantity. In our jazz club example, the owner sets a pricing policy of the form "Entry plus X drinks for Y dollars." In order to earn

---

6   It is also easy to show that the jazz club owner's profit would be smaller than that achieved by the two-part tariff if the owner could engage in third-degree price discrimination by somehow charging a different drink price for each group. We invite you to work this out for yourselves.

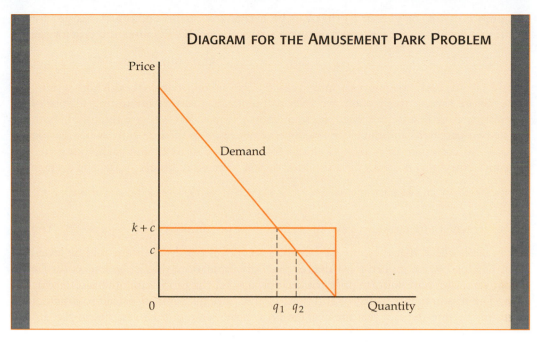

**DIAGRAM FOR THE AMUSEMENT PARK PROBLEM**

FIGURE

**6-3**

maximum profit and appropriate all consumer surplus, that is, achieve first-degree price discrimination, two simple rules determine the optimal block-pricing strategy:

**1.** Set the quantity offered to each consumer type equal to the amount that type of consumer would buy at competitive pricing, that is, the quantity bought at a price equal to marginal cost.

**2.** Set the fixed charge for each consumer type at the total willingness to pay for the quantity identified above.

Let's examine how this would work in our jazz club example. Applying rule 1, we know that each old customer will buy $V_o - c$ drinks and each young customer will buy $V_y - c$ drinks if the drinks are priced at marginal cost. The total willingness to pay for these quantities by old and young customers, respectively, is again the area under the relevant demand curve at these quantities. In the case of old and young customers, respectively, this is:

$$WTP_o = \frac{1}{2}(V_o - c)^2 + (V_o - c)c = \frac{1}{2}(V_o^2 - c^2)$$

$$WTP_y = \frac{1}{2}(V_y - c)^2 + (V_y - c)c = \frac{1}{2}(V_y^2 - c^2)$$

**(6.12)**

Applying rule 2 we then have the following pricing policy. Offer each old customer entry plus $V_o - c$ drinks for a total charge of $\frac{1}{2}(V_o^2 - c^2)$ dollars and each young customer entry plus $V_y - c$ drinks for a total charge of $\frac{1}{2}(V_y^2 - c^2)$ dollars.

How would we implement this strategy in our jazz club example? One way would be to card the customers at the door and then give each customer the appropriate number of tokens (12 or 8) that can be exchanged (at no additional charge) for drinks. Profit from a customer of type $i$ is the charge $WTP_i$ minus the cost of the drinks, $c(V_i - c)$, or $\frac{1}{2}(V_o - c)^2$ or \$72 from each old customer and $\frac{1}{2}(V_y - c)^2$ or \$32 from each young customer, exactly as in the two-part pricing system.

Before leaving this section, we wish to point out a further interesting feature of both types of first-degree price discrimination schemes that we have discussed. Both the two-part tariff and the block pricing schemes result in the jazz club owner serving each old customer entry plus 12 drinks for a total fee of \$120 and each young customer entry plus 8 drinks for a total fee of \$64. Therefore, in each case, the average price paid by an old customer is $\frac{1}{2}(V_o^2 - c^2) / (V_o - c) = \frac{1}{2}(V_o + c)$, or \$10. Similarly, each young customer pays an average price per drink of $\frac{1}{2}(V_y + c) = \$8$. You can easily check that these are exactly the same prices per drink that would be levied if the club owner applied third-degree price discrimination; that is, had no cover fee but set a different uniform price for each group. Yet the profit outcome is different.

The reason that first-degree and third-degree price discrimination lead to different profits despite the fact that the average price is the same in each case lies in the different nature of the two pricing schemes. Recall that a demand function measures the marginal benefit that a consumer obtains from the last unit consumed. The quantity demanded equates marginal benefit with the marginal cost to the consumer of buying the last unit where, of course, marginal cost to the consumer is just the price for that last unit. With third-degree price discrimination or linear pricing, there is no difference between the price paid for the first unit and the price paid for the last unit. Hence, average price and marginal price are the same. By contrast, the nonlinear pricing scheme permits the club owner effectively to charge an old customer \$16 for the first drink, \$15 for the second, and so on, while charging a young customer \$12 for the first drink, then \$11, etc. With the linear pricing scheme, the old customer would pay \$10 for each drink, from the first to the last, while a young customer would pay \$8. As noted, the average price to each type of customer is the same under either regime. Yet nonlinear pricing so lowers the price of the last unit purchased that consumers are willing to buy more units. This permits the owner to charge very high prices on the first few drinks purchased. As a result, the average price under first-degree discrimination is just as high as it is under third-degree discrimination. However, since first-degree discrimination so greatly increases sales at that average price, and since that average price is greater than the firm's marginal cost, nonlinear pricing generates considerably more profit.

## 6.2 SECOND-DEGREE PRICE DISCRIMINATION OR MENU PRICING

First-degree price discrimination, or personalized pricing, is possible for the jazz club owner for two reasons. First, the club's different types of customers are distinguishable by means of a simple, observable characteristic. Secondly, the club has the ability to deny access to those not paying the entry charge that was designed for them.

Not all services can be marketed in this way. For example, if instead of a jazz club the monopoly seller is a refreshment stand located in a campus center, then limiting access by means of a cover charge is not feasible.

Even in the jazz club case, first-degree discrimination by means of a two-part tariff would not be possible if the difference in consumer willingness to pay was attributable to some characteristic that the jazz club owner could not observe. For example, suppose that what differentiates high-demand and low-demand customers is not age but income. The club will now find that any attempt to implement the first-degree price discrimination scheme of charging high-income patrons an entry fee of $72 and low-income patrons an entry fee of $32 is doomed to failure. Every customer would claim to have low income in order to pay the lower entry charge and there is no obvious (or legal) method by which the club owner can enforce the higher fee.

What about the block pricing strategy of offering entry plus 12 drinks for $120 and entry plus 8 drinks for $64? Will that work? Again, the answer is no. It is easy to show that high-income customers are willing to pay up to $96 for entry plus 8 drinks. So they derive $32 of consumer surplus from the 8 drinks, $64 package but no consumer surplus from the 12 drinks, $120 package. They will prefer to pretend to be low-income customers in order to pay the lower charge and enjoy some surplus rather than confess to being high-income customers.

The monopolist could, of course, decide to limit entry only to high-income customers by setting the entry charge at $72 or offering only the 12 drinks, $120 package but this loses business (and profit) from low-income customers. Suppose, for instance, that there are $N_o$ older customers and $N_y$ younger customers. The profit from selling to only the older customers is $72N_o$. Setting the lower entry fee or offering only the 8 drinks, $64 package in order to attract both types of customer gives profit of $32(N_y + N_o)$. Clearly, the latter strategy is more profitable if $32N_y > 40N_o$. In other words, if the ratio of low-income to high-income customers is more than 1.25:1 (the ratio of the difference in the entry fees to the low entry fee) the restrictive policy of setting the higher entry fee or offering only the 12 drinks, $120 package will generate less profit than offering just the lower entry fee or the 8 drinks, $64 package to all customers.

The point is that once we reduce either the seller's ability to identify different customers or to prevent arbitrage among them (or both), the complete surplus extraction achieved by perfect price discrimination is no longer possible. Both the two-part and block pricing mechanisms can still be used to raise profit above that earned by uniform pricing, but they cannot earn as much as they did previously. Solving the identification and arbitrage problem has now become costly. It is still possible that the monopolist can design a pricing scheme that will induce customers to reveal who they are and keep them separated, but now the only way to do this is to incur some cost—a cost that is reflected in less surplus extraction. Such a pricing scheme is called second-degree price discrimination or menu pricing.

Second-degree price discrimination is usually implemented by offering quantity discounts targeted to different consumer types. To see how it works, let's continue with our jazz club example illustrated in Figure 6-4. Again, the high-demand customers have (inverse) demand $P_h = 16 - Q_h$, and the low-demand customers have (inverse) demand $P_l = 12 - Q_l$. Now, however, the jazz club owner has no means of distinguishing who is who because the source of the difference between consumers is inherently unobservable. All the owner knows is that two such different types of consumer frequent the club.

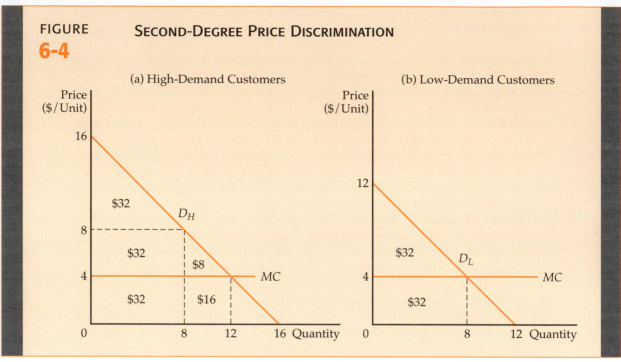

FIGURE
**6-4**

**SECOND-DEGREE PRICE DISCRIMINATION**

Low-demand customers are willing to pay $64 for entry plus 8 drinks. High-demand customers are willing to pay up to $96 for entry plus 8 drinks and so get $32 consumer surplus from the 8 drinks, $64 package. They will therefore be willing to buy a 12 drinks, $88 package, which also gives them a $32 surplus.

Any attempt to implement a differentiated two-part tariff will not work in this case. Both types of customer will claim to be low-demand types when entering the club in order to pay the lower entry fee of $32. Only *after* they are in the club will the different consumers reveal who they are. Since the price per drink is set at marginal cost of $4, the high-demand customers will buy 12 drinks and reveal themselves to be high demanders, whereas the low-demand customers will buy 8 drinks and reveal themselves as low demanders.

You might be tempted to think that the club owner could implement first-degree price discrimination using the following strategy. When entering the club, patrons are given tickets that allow them to buy drinks. If they pay an entry charge of $32 they will be given 8 tickets while if they pay $72 they will be given 12 tickets. Yet this approach will not work either, and for the same reason that the block pricing strategy of offering 12 drink, $120 and 8 drink, $64 packages failed. High-demand customers again have every reason to pretend to be low-demand customers and pay an entry charge of only $32, thereby getting 8 tickets and buying 8 drinks at $4 each for a total expenditure of $64. Because, as can be seen from Figure 6-4(a), their total willingness to pay for the 8 drinks is $96, high-demand consumers will enjoy a surplus of $32 from this deception. By contrast, they will enjoy no surplus if they pay the entry charge of $72 and get 12 tickets because their total expenditure will be $120, which exactly equals their willingness to pay for 12 drinks. So, setting cover charges of $32 and $72 and tying these to 8 and 12 drink tickets, respectively, will not lead the high- and low-demand consumers to separate.

Yet, while unsuccessful, the idea of offering different price and drink combinations as different packages does contain the hint of a strategy that the jazz club owner can use to increase profit. The trick is to employ a variant on the block pricing strategy described earlier. The difference now is that, since there is no easy way to identify and separate the different types of customers, the block pricing itself must be designed to achieve this purpose. As noted above, this imposes a new constraint or cost on the owner, thus, this approach will not yield as much profit as first-degree price discrimination. However, it will substantially improve on simply offering all customers the 8 drink, $64 package that yields a profit of $32 from each.

To see how one might use block pricing to achieve the identification and separation necessary for price discrimination let us start with the low-demand customers. The jazz club owner knows that these customers are willing to pay a total of $64 for 8 drinks. We know that the jazz club owner can offer entry to the club plus the right to consume 8 drinks as a package at a set charge of $64 and still attract these low-demand customers, effectively extracting all the $32 surplus from each such consumer as profit. The problem as we have seen is that high-demand customers will also be willing to buy this package because their willingness to pay for 8 drinks is $96. Note, though, that this implies that while the club owner also gets $32 in profit from the high-demand customers, those customers still enjoy a surplus of $96 – $64 = $32.

The club owner's optimal strategy at this point is to offer a well-designed second package. The owner knows that the high-demand customers are willing to pay a total of $120 for 12 drinks. Yet the owner also knows that this price cannot be charged because the high-demand customers will not be willing to pay this much, given that they can buy the 8 drinks, $64 package and enjoy consumer surplus of $32. For an alternative package to be attractive to high-demand consumers it has to be what economists call *incentive compatible* with the 8 drinks, $64 package. This means that any alternative package must also offer the high-demand customers a surplus of at least $32.

A package that meets this requirement but that also generates some additional profit for the club owner is a package of entry plus 12 drinks for a total charge of $88. We know that the high-demand customers value entry plus 12 drinks at $120. By offering this deal at a price of $88, the club owner permits these customers to get $32 of surplus when they buy this package, just enough to get them to switch from the 8 drinks, $64 package.[7] Note, though, that while the high-demand customers get a $32 surplus on this package, the club owner's profit is also higher than it is on the 8 drinks, $64 package. On the latter, the owner earns $32, but on the new package, the owner earns $88 – ($4 × 12) = $40. Of course, the low-demand customers will not buy the 12 drinks, $88 package since their maximum willingness to pay for 12 drinks is only $72. Nevertheless, the club owner still earns $32 from these consumers by continuing to sell them the 8 drinks, $64 package. So, the club owner's total profit is increased.

The two menu options have been carefully designed to solve the identification and arbitrage problems by inducing the customers themselves to reveal who they are by the purchases they make. The club owner now offers a menu of options, 8 drinks for $64 or 12 drinks for $88, geared to separate the different types of customers the club

---

7   We are working in round numbers to keep things neat. What the jazz club owner might actually do is price the package of entry plus 12 drinks at $87.99 to ensure that the high-demand customers will strictly prefer this to the 8 drinks, $64 package.

attracts. This is the reason that this strategy is often referred to as *menu pricing*. There is, moreover, a further important feature of menu pricing. Note that as before, the average price per drink of the 8 drinks, $64 package is $8. However, the average price per drink of the 12 drinks, $88 package is $7.33. The second package thus offers a *quantity discount* relative to the first.

Quantity discounts are common. Movie theaters, restaurants, concert halls, sports teams, and supermarkets all make use of them. It is cheaper to buy one huge container of popcorn than many small ones. Wine sold by the glass is more expensive per unit than wine sold by the bottle. A 24-pack of Coca-Cola is cheaper than 24 individual cans. It is cheaper per ticket to buy a season's subscription to your favorite football team's home games than to buy tickets to each game individually. A full-day pass at a ski resort will reflect a lower price per run than will a half-day lift ticket. In these and many other cases, the sellers are using a quantity discount to woo the high-demand consumers.

There is an additional twist to consider. What if the club owner decides that the package offered to attract low-demand customers will allow the consumption of only 7 drinks? The maximum willingness to pay for entry plus this number of drinks by a low-demand customer is $59.50, so this new package will be 7 drinks, $59.50. The profit it generates from each customer is $31.50, which is 50 cents less than the 8 drinks, $64 package. Now consider the high-demand customers. Their maximum willingness to pay for 7 drinks is $87.50, so buying this new package gives them consumer surplus of $28. As a result, the jazz club owner can increase the price of the 12-drink package. Rather than pricing it so that it gives the high-demand customers $32 of consumer surplus, the owner can now price it so that it gives them only $28 of surplus. In other words, the second package of entry plus 12 drinks can be priced at $120 − 28 = $92, increasing profit from each such package to $44, up by $4 from the 12 drinks, $88 package.

The example illustrates the importance of the incentive compatibility constraint. Any package designed to attract low-demand customers constrains the ability of the monopolist to extract surplus from high-demand customers. Again, this is because the high-demand customers cannot be prevented from buying the package designed for low-demand customers and will always enjoy some consumer surplus from doing so. As a result, the monopolist may find it more profitable to reduce the number of units offered to low-demand customers since this will allow an increase in the price charged for the package aimed at high-demand customers. In fact, there may even be circumstances in which the monopolist would prefer to push this to the extreme and not serve low-demand customers at all in view of the constraint this imposes on the prices that can be charged to other customers. Whether it does so will depend on the number of low-demand customers relative to high-demand ones. The fewer low-demand customers there are relative to high-demand ones, the less it becomes desirable to serve low-demand customers, since any effort to do so imposes an incentive compatibility constraint on the extraction of surplus from high-demand ones.

For the more general case of more than two types of consumers the profit-maximizing second-degree price discrimination or menu pricing scheme will exhibit some key characteristics. In particular, if consumer willingness to pay can be unambiguously ranked, then any optimal second-degree price discrimination scheme will:

1. Extract all of the consumer surplus of the lowest-demand types but leave some consumer surplus for all other types.

**2.** Contain a quantity that is less than the socially optimal quantity for all consumer types other than the highest-demand type.

**3.** Exhibit quantity discounting.

In sum, second-degree discrimination enhances the ability of the monopolist to convert consumer surplus into profit, but does so less effectively than first-degree discrimination. With no costless way to distinguish the different types of consumers, the monopolist must rely on some sort of block pricing scheme to solve the identification and arbitrage problems. However, the incentive compatibility constraints that such a scheme must satisfy restrict the firm's ability to extract all surplus. Instead, the firm is forced to make a compromise between setting a high charge that loses sales to low-demand buyers and a low charge that foregoes the significant surplus that can be earned from the high-demand buyers. Finally, it is also important to note that, contrary to what many consumers may think, the lower price charged for a larger quantity is entirely unrelated to scale economies. If in our example the jazz club owner had no fixed costs and thus no economies of scale the owner would still find it profitable to offer a quantity discount to high-demand customers.

## Practice Problem 6.3

Assume as in the text that a monopolist knows that customers are of two types, low-demand customers whose inverse demand is $P_l = 12 - Q_l$, and high-demand customers whose demand is $P_h = 16 - Q_h$. However, the monopolist does not know which type of customer is which. Production costs are $4 per unit.

a. Complete the following table for this example.

| LOW-DEMAND CUSTOMERS | | | HIGH-DEMAND CUSTOMERS | | | |
|---|---|---|---|---|---|---|
| Number of Units in the Package | Charge for the Package* | Profit per Package | Consumer Surplus from Low-Demand Package | Maximum Willingness to Pay for 12 Units | Charge for Package of 12 Units | Profit from Each Package of 12 Units |
| 0 | 0 | 0 | 0 | $120.00 | | $72.00 |
| 1 | $11.50 | | $4.00 | $120.00 | $116.00 | |
| 2 | | $14.00 | $8.00 | $120.00 | | $64.00 |
| 3 | | | | | | |
| 4 | $40.00 | $24.00 | | $120.00 | | |
| 5 | $47.50 | $27.50 | $20.00 | $120.00 | $100.00 | $52.00 |
| 6 | $54.00 | | | $120.00 | | $48.00 |
| 7 | $59.50 | $31.50 | $28.00 | $120.00 | $92.00 | $44.00 |
| 8 | $64.00 | $32.00 | $32.00 | $120.00 | $88.00 | $40.00 |
| 9 | | | | | | |
| 10 | $70.00 | $30.00 | $40.00 | $120.00 | | |
| 11 | | | | | | |
| 12 | $72.00 | | $48.00 | $120.00 | $72.00 | |

* This is the low-demand customer's maximum willingness to pay for the number of units in the package.

b. Assume that there are the same numbers of high-demand and low-demand customers. What is the profit-maximizing number of units that should be offered in the package aimed at the low-demand customers?

c. Now assume that there are twice as many low-demand customers as high-demand customers. What is the profit-maximizing pair of packages for the monopolist?

d. The monopolist is considering offering two packages, one containing 6 units and the other 12 units. What are the charges at which these packages will be offered? What is the ratio of high-demand to low-demand customers above which it will be better for the monopolist to supply only the high-demand customers?

## 6.3 SOCIAL WELFARE WITH FIRST- AND SECOND-DEGREE PRICE DISCRIMINATION

Price discrimination clearly raises the profit of the monopoly firm. Does it also raise social welfare more generally, that is, does it raise the total surplus of producers and consumers? The easiest way to understand the welfare implications of price discrimination is to consider a particular consumer group $i$. Suppose each consumer in this group has the inverse demand

$$P = P_i(Q). \tag{6.13}$$

Assume also that the monopolist has constant marginal costs of $c$ per unit. Now let the quantity that each consumer in group $i$ is offered with a particular pricing policy be $Q_i$. Then the total surplus—consumer surplus plus profit—generated for each consumer under this pricing policy is just the area between the inverse demand function and the marginal cost function up to the quantity $Q_i$, as illustrated in Figure 6-5. The pricing policy chosen by the firm affects the quantity offered to each type

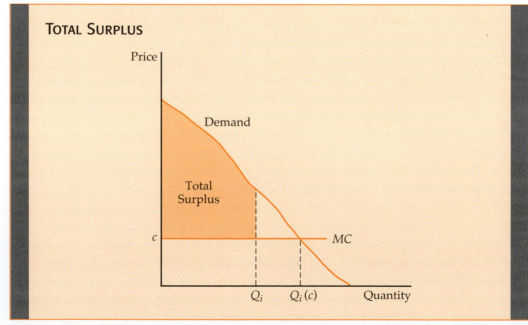

**FIGURE 6-5**

TOTAL SURPLUS

When the total quantity consumed is $Q_i$, total surplus is given by the shaded area. Total surplus is maximized at quantity $Q_i(c)$.

of consumer and alters the distribution of total surplus between profit and consumer surplus.[8]

The first effect implies some change in social welfare due either to raising or lowering output relative to the level chosen by the uniform pricing monopolist. However, the second effect does not imply a change in total welfare. It simply reflects a transfer of surplus between consumers and producers. As a result, *price discrimination increases (decreases) the social welfare of consumer group* i *if it increases (decreases) the quantity offered to that group.*

It follows immediately that first-degree price discrimination always increases social welfare even though it extracts all consumer surplus. With this pricing policy we have seen that the monopoly seller supplies each consumer group with the socially efficient quantity (the quantity that would be chosen if price were set to marginal cost). Hence first-degree discrimination always increases the total quantity to a level $[Q_i(c)$ in Figure 6-5] that exceeds that which would have been sold under uniform pricing.

With second-degree price discrimination matters are not as straightforward. As we have seen, this type of price discrimination leads to high-demand groups being supplied with quantities "near to" the socially efficient level. However, we have also seen that the seller will want to restrict the quantity supplied to lower demand groups and, in some cases, not supply these groups at all. The net effect on output is therefore not clear a priori.

The impact on social welfare of second-degree price discrimination can nevertheless be derived using much the same techniques that we used in Chapter 5. By way of illustration, suppose that there are two consumer groups with demands as illustrated in Figure 6-6 (i.e., group 2 is the high-demand group). In this figure $P^U$ is the nondiscriminatory uniform price, and $Q_1^U$ and $Q_2^U$ are the quantities sold to each consumer in the relevant group at this price. By contrast, $Q_1^s$ and $Q_2^s$ are the quantities supplied to the two groups with second-degree price discrimination.[9] We define the terms

$$\Delta Q_1 = Q_1^s - Q_1^U; \ \Delta Q_2 = Q_2^s - Q_1^U. \tag{6.14}$$

In the case illustrated we have $\Delta Q_1 < 0$ and $\Delta Q_2 > 0$. This tells us that an upper limit on the increase in total surplus that follows from second-degree price discrimination is the area G minus the area L. This gives us the equation

$$\Delta W \le \text{G} - \text{L} = (P^U - MC)\Delta Q_1 + (P^U - MC)\Delta Q_2$$
$$= (P^U - MC)(\Delta Q_1 + \Delta Q_2). \tag{6.15}$$

Extending the analysis to *n* markets, we then have

$$\Delta W < (P^U - MC)\sum_{i=1}^{n} \Delta Q_i. \tag{6.16}$$

It follows that for $\Delta W \ge 0$ it is necessary that $\sum_{i=1}^{n} \Delta Q_i \ge 0$. In other words, *a necessary condition for second-degree price discrimination to increase welfare is that it increases total output.*

---

8   See Schmalensee (1981) for a welfare analysis of third-degree price discrimination.
9   Since group 2 is the high-demand group, we know that $Q_2^s = Q_2(c)$.

FIGURE

**6-6**

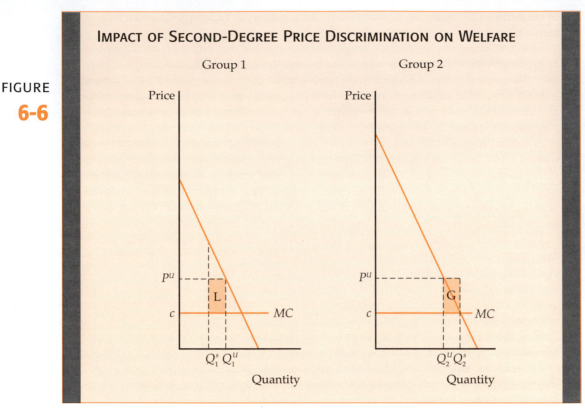

IMPACT OF SECOND-DEGREE PRICE DISCRIMINATION ON WELFARE

An upper limit on the change in total surplus that arises from second-degree price discrimination is the upper limit on the gain, G, minus the lower limit on the loss, L.

We know from the last chapter that this requirement is generally not met in the case of third-degree price discrimination and linear demands because then the monopolist supplies the same total quantity as with uniform pricing, so third-degree price discrimination must reduce welfare. By contrast, it is often the case that second-degree price discrimination leads to an increase in the quantity supplied to both markets and so must increase social welfare. In the jazz club owner case, for example, this will be the case if there are equal numbers of high-demand and low-demand customers. (You are asked to show this in problem 5 at the end of the chapter.)

# SUMMARY

In this chapter we have extended our analysis of price discrimination to cases in which firms employ more sophisticated, nonlinear pricing schemes. Our focus has been on commonly observed examples of nonlinear pricing schemes. These are (1) two-part pricing, in which the firm charges a fixed fee plus a price per unit; and (2) block pricing, in which the firm bundles the quantity being offered with the total charge for that quantity. Both schemes have the same objective, to increase the monopolist's profit either by increasing the surplus on existing sales or by extending sales to new markets (or both).

The most perfect form of price discrimination, first-degree price discrimination or personalized pricing, can only be practiced when the firm can costlessly solve the identification and arbitrage problems. The firm needs to be able to identify the different types of consumers and must also be able to keep them apart. If this is possible, then two-part tariffs and block pricing can, in principle, convert *all* consumer surplus into revenues for the firm. The positive side to this is that the firm supplies the socially efficient level of output to each consumer type. The negative side is that there are potentially severe distributional inequities in that all social surplus takes the form of profit.

If the requirements necessary to practice perfect price discrimination are not met, then the monopoly seller cannot achieve as large a profit. The monopolist may then rely on second-degree price discrimination or menu pricing. This type of pricing shares the property with first-degree price discrimination in so far as the monopolist employs nonlinear pricing. It differs from both first- and third-degree price discrimination, however, in that it relies on the pricing mechanism itself—usually some form of quantity discount—to induce consumers to *self-select* into groups that reveal their true identity. Yet the use of a quantity discount or similar technique to achieve such sorting must always satisfy an *incentive compatibility* constraint. This constraint affects in a negative way the monopolist's ability to extract consumer surplus. Because the incentive compatibility constraint adversely affects profits, the monopolist may choose to avoid this restriction and not serve the low-demand market. In this case, the consumers in that market are clearly worse off. As a result, the net output effects of second-degree price discrimination are not clear. Yet unlike the case of third-degree discrimination (with linear demand curves at least), second-degree pricing strategies do have some positive probability of making things better.

## PROBLEMS

1. Many universities allocate financial aid to undergraduate students on the basis of some measure of need. Does this practice reflect pure charity or price discrimination? If it reflects price discrimination, do you think it lies closer to first-degree discrimination or third-degree discrimination?

2. A food co-op sells a homogenous good, called groceries, with the quantity sold denoted by $g$. The co-op's cost function is described by $C(g) = F + cg$; where $F$ denotes fixed cost and $c$ is the constant per-unit variable cost. At a meeting of the co-op board, a young economist proposes the following marketing strategy for the co-op: Set a fixed membership fee, $M$, and a price per unit of groceries, $p_M$, that members pay. In addition, set a price per unit of groceries, $p_N$, higher than $p_M$, at which the co-op will sell groceries to nonmembers.

    a. What must be true about the demand of different customers for this strategy to work?

    b. What kinds of price discrimination does this strategy employ?

3. In the United States, the top three providers of wireless or cell phone service are Cingular, Verizon, and Sprint. All three offer consumers a variety of service plans. Typical of these are Sprint's "Free and Clear" plans. Consider the two main

options that Sprint offers in this category, Free and Clear 1 and Free and Clear 2. The key features of each plan are as follows:

|  | | Free and Clear 1 | Free and Clear 2 |
| --- | --- | --- | --- |
| Monthly Fee | | $34.99 | $39.99 |
| Quantity of Free Minutes: | Weekdays | 200 | 350 |
| | Nights/Weekends | 3300 | 3650 |

Comment on these two plans. What type of price tactic do you think they reflect?

4. A nightclub owner has both student and adult customers. The demand for drinks by a typical student is $Q^S = 18 - 3P$. The demand for drinks by a typical adult is $Q^A = 10 - 2P$. There are equal numbers of students and adults. The marginal cost of each drink is $2.

   a. What price will the club owner set if she cannot discriminate between the two groups? What will her total profit be at this price?

   b. If the club owner could separate the groups and practice third-degree price discrimination what price per drink would be charged to members of each group? What would be the club owner's profit?

   c. If the club owner can "card" patrons and determine who among them is a student and who is not and, in turn, can serve each group by offering a cover charge and a number of drink tokens to each group, what will the cover charge and number of tokens given to students be? What will be the cover charge and number of tokens given to adults? What is the club owner's profit under this regime?

5. Now return to our club owner in the text in which low-demand consumers have an inverse demand of $P = 12 - Q$; while high-demand consumers have an inverse demand of $P = 16 - Q$. Marginal cost per drink is again $4. Assume that there are $N_h$ high-demand customers and $N_l$ low-demand customers. Show that under these circumstances the firm will only serve low-demand customers, that is, will only offer both packages if there are at least as many low-demand consumers as high-demand ones. In other words, $\dfrac{N_h}{N_l} \geq 1$ in order for low-demand consumers to be served.

# REFERENCES

Oi, W. 1971. "A Disneyland Dilemma: Two-part Tariffs for a Mickey Mouse Monopoly." *Quarterly Journal of Economics* 85 (February): 77–96.

Phlips, L. 1983. *The Economics of Price Discrimination*. Cambridge, MA: Cambridge University Press.

Pigou, A. C. 1920. *The Economics of Welfare*. London: Macmillan Publishing.

Shapiro, C., and H. Varian. 1999. *Information Rules: A Strategic Guide to the Internet Economy*. Boston: Harvard Business School Press.

Schmalensee, R. 1981. "Output and Welfare Implications of Monopolistic Third-Degree Price Discrimination." *American Economic Review* 71 (March): 242–47.

Varian, H. 1989. "Price Discrimination." In R. Schmalensee and R. Willig, eds., *The Handbook of Industrial Organization, Vol. 1*. Amsterdam: North-Holland: 597–654.

# Product Variety and Quality under Monopoly

# Chapter 7

Most firms sell more than one product. Microsoft offers not only an operating system and an Internet browser but a number of other products, including the word-processing package Word, the spreadsheet software Excel, and the presentation package PowerPoint. Photographic firms such as Eastman Kodak sell both cameras and film, and in each case in a wide range of varieties. The telecommunications giant Comcast now offers telephone service, high-speed Internet service, and cable TV. A newer giant in the same field, AOL-Time Warner offers a combination of Internet access and entertainment programming. Fashion designers such as Ralph Lauren offer a broad range of apparel from sportswear to haute couture, for both women and men.

In short, the multiproduct firm is likely to be the norm. This leads us to raise the question as to how great a variety of goods a firm should offer. The breakfast cereal firm, Kellogg's, offers cereals in dozens of combinations of grains, color, sweetness, and extra ingredients, such as marshmallow bits. The consumer goods giant, Procter & Gamble, offers 12 different versions of its Head and Shoulders shampoo and another 12 varieties of its Crest toothpaste.

As a question of corporate strategy, Procter & Gamble needs to know if this is too little or too much variety. Because we are interested in the outcome of a firm's strategic planning, we need to know the answer to that question as well. Fortunately, economic analysis can help find the answer.

The firm's motivation to offer many varieties of what is essentially the same product—breakfast foods, hair care, or tooth care—is simple enough to see. It is a way for the firm to reach consumers with different tastes. Because consumers often differ regarding their most preferred color, flavor, or combination of features, selling successfully to many consumers requires offering something a little different to each of them. Specifically, to induce consumers to make a purchase they must find a product that is reasonably close to the version that they prefer. When a firm offers a variety of products in response to different consumer tastes, it is called *horizontal product differentiation*.

Often, however, consumers do agree on what features make for a good product. For example, all consumers may agree that a car with antilock brakes is better than one without such a stopping mechanism. Similarly, all probably agree that while the X-type Jaguar is an attractive car, it pales in comparison to the XJ. Everyone is likely to agree that flying from Boston to San Francisco first class is a better experience than flying coach. Consumers differ in these instances, not in what features they consider desirable, but how much a desired feature is worth—that is, how much they are willing to pay for antilock brakes, a better Jaguar, or first-class airfare. When a firm responds to differing willingness to pay among consumers by offering different qualities of the same product it is called *vertical product differentiation*.

In this chapter we analyze the horizontal and vertical product differentiation strategies of a monopoly firm. We examine how product differentiation may be used by a firm to increase profitability. We also consider whether these strategies increase consumer welfare as well.

# 7.1    A SPATIAL APPROACH TO HORIZONTAL PRODUCT DIFFERENTIATION

There are many situations in which individual consumers have their own preferred brand or variety of product, whether this is breakfast cereal, hair treatment, or an automobile. We begin, then, by considering a market in which consumers differ regarding the features that make the product attractive to them. However, they are more or less alike in terms of their basic willingness to pay for one of these products. For example, all consumers might be willing to pay the same price for a meal if it is sold at a restaurant or shop close to their home. However, not all consumers will be equidistant from the shop. Some will be close and some will be far away. Given the time and effort required to travel, the willingness to pay of those who live far from the shop will be lower. Alternatively, those who live close—and who therefore do not have to incur travel expenses—will be willing to pay a higher price. The fact that a product sold close to home is different from one that is sold far away is a good example of what is referred to as horizontal product differentiation. Such differentiation is characterized by the property that each consumer has a preferred location of the shop or product, namely, one close to the consumer's own address.

When the consumer market is differentiated by geographic location, a firm can vary its product strategy through its choice of where the product is sold. The firm may choose to sell its product only in one central location to which all shoppers must come; Giorgio Armani, for example, does this. Alternatively, it may decide to offer the product at many locations spaced throughout the city; McDonald's, Dunkin' Donuts, and Subway are examples of this. Customers are not indifferent between these alternative strategies. If the firm sells at only one central location, those who do not live in the middle of town have to incur travel costs to come to the store. These costs are greatest for those living farthest from the center. The alternative strategy of selling at many different locations allows more consumers to purchase the good without going too far out of their way.

When geography is taken into account and traveling is costly, consumers are willing to pay more for a product marketed close to their own geographic location. This is a setting in which there is an inherent demand for products to be differentiated, in this case, by the location of their sale. This setting is known as the spatial model of product differentiation, pioneered by Hotelling (1929).[1] Before presenting the model formally, there is an additional point worth emphasizing. The point is that while the model is easiest to present in terms of a geographic representation, it can easily be more broadly interpreted. With just a little imagination, geographic space can be transformed into a "product" or, more properly, "characteristics space." There, each consumer's "location" reflects his or her most preferred set of product characteristics such as color, style, or other features. Recall our discussion in Chapter 4 of a soft drink firm offering a product line differing in terms of sugar content. This example made use of precisely this type of horizontal or spatial differentiation.

Likewise, the travel cost of the geographic model can be understood as a psychic or utility cost that the consumer incurs if the consumer must purchase a good whose characteristics are "distant" from the most preferred type. Just as consumers prefer to

---

1    Hotelling (1929) was concerned with analyzing competition between two stores, whereas we consider here the case in which the stores are owned by the same firm and so act cooperatively.

go to video stores close to their home, so they prefer to buy clothes that are "close" to their individual preferred style, or soft drinks close to their preferred amount of sugar content. In fact, Hotelling suggested just this interpretation in his seminal article. As he wrote:

> Distance, as we have used it for illustration, is only a figurative term for a great congeries of qualities. Instead of sellers of an identical commodity separated geographically we might have considered two . . . cider merchants . . . one selling a sweeter liquid than the other. If consumers of cider be thought of as varying by infinitesimal degrees in the sourness they desire, we have much the same situation as before. The measure of sourness now represents distance, while instead of transportation costs there are degrees of disutility resulting from the consumer getting cider more or less different from what he wants. (1929, p. 54)

## 7.2   MONOPOLY AND HORIZONTAL DIFFERENTIATION

Assume that there is a town spread out along a single road, called Main Street, of one mile in length. There are $N$ consumers spaced evenly along this road from one end of town to the other. A firm that has a monopoly in, for example, fast food must decide how to serve these consumers at the greatest profit. What this means is that the monopolist must choose the number of retail outlets, or shops, that it will operate, where these should be located on Main Street, and what prices it should charge. In the product differentiation analogy to drinks of different sweetness, the monopolist has to decide how many different drinks it should offer, what their precise degrees of sweetness should be, and what their prices should be. More generally, what range of products should the monopolist bring to the market and how should they be priced? In what follows we use the specific geographic interpretation of the model in order to make the analysis clear, but we again emphasize that you should always bear in mind its much wider interpretation.

In this section we consider cases in which the monopolist does not price discriminate among consumers. Consumers travel to a retail outlet in order to buy the product, incurring transport costs. On a per unit of distance there-and-back basis, we assume that this transportation cost is $t$. Except for their addresses, that is, their locations, consumers are identical to each other. We assume that in each period each consumer is willing to buy exactly one unit of the product sold by the monopolist provided that the price paid, including transportation costs, which we shall call the *full price*, is less than the reservation price, which we denote by $V$.

Suppose that the monopolist decides to operate only a single retail outlet. Then it seems reasonable to suggest that this will be located at the center of Main Street. Now consider the monopolist's pricing decision. The essentials of the analysis are illustrated in Figure 7-1. The westernmost resident (residing at the left end of the diagram) has an address of $z = 0$. The easternmost resident has an address of $z = 1$. The shop is located at $z = 1/2$.

The vertical axis in Figure 7-1 is, as usual, a measure of price. The value $V$ in this diagram is the reservation price for each consumer. The full price that each consumer pays is comprised of two parts. First, there is the price $p_1$ actually set by the monopolist. Second, there is the additional cost consumers incur in getting to the shop (and back home with the food). Measured per unit of distance there and back, the *full price* actually paid by a consumer who lives a distance $x$ from the center of town is the

FIGURE

**7-1**

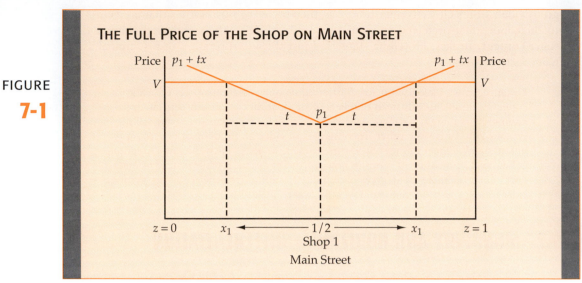

**THE FULL PRICE OF THE SHOP ON MAIN STREET**

The full price, including transport cost, rises as consumers live farther from the shop.

monopolist's price plus the transportation cost, or $p_1 + tx$. This full price is indicated by the Y-shaped set of lines in Figure 7-1. It indicates that the full price paid by a consumer at the center of town—one who incurs no transportation cost—is just $p_1$. However, as the branches of the Y indicate, the full price rises steadily beyond $p_1$ for consumers both east and west of the town center. So long as distance from the shop is less than $x_1$, the consumer's reservation price $V$ exceeds the full price, $p_1 + tx$, and such a consumer buys the monopolist's product. However, for distances beyond $x_1$ the full price exceeds $V$ and these consumers do not buy the product. In other words, the monopolist serves all those who live within $x_1$ units of the town center. How is the distance $x_1$ determined? Consumers who reside distance $x_1$ from the shop are just indifferent between buying the product and not buying it at all. For them, the full price, $p_1 + tx_1$, just equals $V$, so we have

$$p_1 + tx_1 = V \text{ which implies that } x_1 = \frac{V - p_1}{t}. \tag{7.1}$$

Now $x_1$ is really just a fraction. Since the town is one mile long, $x_1$ is a fraction of a mile and the retail outlet sells to a fraction $2x_1$ of the whole town—since it sells to consumers to the left and to the right of the market center so long as they live no further than $x_1$ from the shop. Moreover, there are $N$ consumers evenly distributed over Main Street. Accordingly, there are $2x_1 N$ consumers who each are willing to buy one unit of the product if it is priced at $p_1$. By substituting the expression for $x_1$ from equation (7.1) into the number of customers served by the monopolist, $2x_1 N$ at price $p_1$, we find that the total demand for the monopolist's product given that it operates just one shop is

$$Q(p_1, 1) = 2x_1 N = \frac{2N}{t}(V - p_1). \tag{7.2}$$

Equation (7.2) says something interesting. Despite our assumption that each consumer buys exactly one unit or none of the monopolist's product, the demand function in the equation shows that aggregate demand increases as the monopolist lowers the price. The reason is illustrated in Figure 7-2. When the shop price is reduced from $p_1$ to $p_2$, demand increases because *more consumers are willing to buy the product at the lower price*. Now all consumers within distance $x_2$ of the shop buy the product.

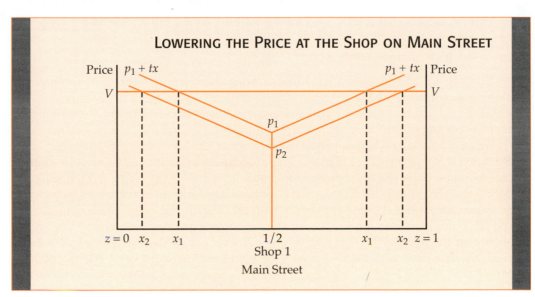

**LOWERING THE PRICE AT THE SHOP ON MAIN STREET**

FIGURE

**7-2**

A fall in the shop price brings additional customers from both east and west.

Suppose that the monopolist wants to sell to every customer in town. What is the *highest* price that the monopolist can set and still be able to sell to all $N$ consumers? The answer must be the price at which the consumers who live furthest from the shop, that is, those who are half a mile away, are just willing to buy. At a shop price $p$ these consumers pay a full price of $p + t/2$, and so will buy only if $p + t/2 \leq V$. What this tells us is that with a single retail outlet at the market center the maximum price that the monopolist can charge and still supply the entire market of $N$ consumers with its one store is $p(N, 1)$, given by

$$p(N, 1) = V - \frac{t}{2} . \tag{7.3}$$

Let the monopolist's costs be $c$ per unit sold and assume that there are setup costs of $F$ for each retail outlet. These setup costs could be associated with the cost of buying a site, commissioning the building, and so on. In the product differentiation analogy, the setup costs might be the costs of designing and marketing the new product. Whatever the framework, the monopolist's profit with a single retail outlet that supplies the entire market is

$$\pi(N, 1) = N(p(N, 1) - c) - F = N\left(V - \frac{t}{2} - c\right) - F. \tag{7.4}$$

We are now ready to investigate why this single shop should be located in the center of town. The reason that this is the best location is because this location makes it easiest to reach all the customers. At the price $p = V - \dfrac{t}{2}$, a move a little to the east will not gain any new customers on the east end of town (there are no more to gain) and it will lose some of those at the extreme west end of town. In other words, if the firm moves from the center, the only way it can continue to serve the entire town is by cutting its price below $V - \dfrac{t}{2}$. Only by keeping its single location at the center can it reach all customers with a price as high as $V - \dfrac{t}{2}$.

Now we wish to consider what happens when there are two, three, or $n$ outlets along Main Street. As before, we continue to assume that unit cost at each shop is $c$ per unit sold and that the setup cost for each outlet is $F$. In other words, there are no scope economies from operating multiple outlets.

We start by asking what happens if the number of retail outlets is increased to two. Because each segment of the market along Main Street looks the same and each shop has the same costs the monopolist will choose to set the same price at each shop. Moreover, the monopolist will want to coordinate the location of these two shops so as to maximize price charged at a shop while still reaching the entire market. In fact, the same intuition that justifies a central location with just one firm can be used to show that the optimal location plan now is to locate one of the two shops 1/4 mile from the left-hand end and the other 1/4 mile from the right-hand end of Main Street as in Figure 7-3.[2]

**FIGURE 7-3**

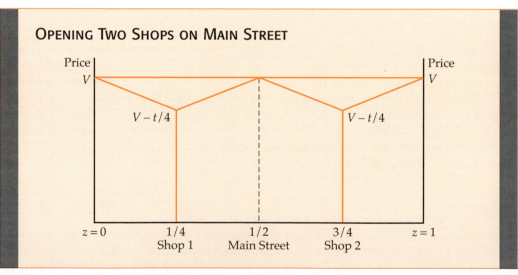

**OPENING TWO SHOPS ON MAIN STREET**

The maximum shop price is higher with two shops than it is with one.

Consider the maximum price that the monopolist can now charge while still supplying the entire market. The maximum distance that any consumer has to travel to a shop is 1/4 mile—much less than the 1/2 mile when there is only one retail out-

---

2   For the interested reader a formal proof of this result is given in Appendix A to this chapter. Appendix B extends the analysis to include the possibility that the two shops have different costs.

let. As a result, the highest price that the monopolist can charge and supply the entire market is

$$p(N, 2) = V - \frac{t}{4},$$ (7.5)

which is higher than the price with a single retail outlet. The monopolist's profit is now

$$\pi(N, 2) = N\left(V - \frac{t}{4} - c\right) - 2F.$$ (7.6)

What happens if the monopolist decides to operate three shops? By exactly the same argument as above, these shops should be located symmetrically at 1/6, 1/2, and 5/6 miles from the left-hand end of the market so that each supplies 1/3 of the market, as illustrated in Figure 7-4. The maximum distance that any consumer has to travel now is 1/6 mile, so the price at each shop (again assuming that all consumers are to be served) is

$$p(N, 3) = V - \frac{t}{6},$$ (7.7)

while profit is now

$$\pi(N, 3) = N\left(V - \frac{t}{6} - c\right) - 3F.$$ (7.8)

**OPENING THREE SHOPS ON MAIN STREET**

FIGURE **7-4**

There is, in fact, a general rule emerging. If the monopolist has $n$ shops to serve the entire market, they will be located symmetrically at distances $1/2n$, $3/2n$, $5/2n$, . . . , $(2i - 1)/2n$, . . . , $(2n - 1)/2n$ from the left-hand end of the market. The maximum distance that any consumer has to travel to a shop is $1/2n$ miles, so the price that the monopolist can charge at each shop while supplying the entire market is

$$p(N, n) = V - \frac{t}{2n}. \tag{7.9}$$

At this price, its profit is

$$\pi(N, n) = N\left(V - \frac{t}{2n} - c\right) - nF. \tag{7.10}$$

The important feature that emerges from this analysis is that as the number of retail outlets, $n$, increases, the monopolist's price at each shop gets closer to the consumer's reservation price, $V$. In other words, by increasing the number of shops the monopolist is able to charge each consumer a price much closer to the maximum willingness to pay, $V$, and thereby appropriate a much greater proportion of consumer surplus.

The moral of the foregoing analysis is clear—especially when we remember to interpret the geographic space of Main Street as a more general product space. Even if no scope economies are present, a monopolist has an incentive to offer many varieties of a good. Doing so allows the monopolist to exploit the wide variety of consumer tastes, charging each consumer a high price because each is being offered a variety that is very close to the most preferred type. It is not surprising, therefore, that we see such extensive product proliferation in real-world markets such as those for cars, soft drinks, toothpastes, hair shampoos, cameras, and so on.[3]

However, there must be some factor limiting this proliferation of varieties or outlets. We do not observe a McDonald's on every street corner, individually made Nike shoes, and custom-designed breakfast cereals or soft drinks! We therefore need to think about what constrains the monopolist from adding more retail outlets or product variants. Equation (7.10) gives the clue. Admittedly, adding additional retail outlets allows the monopolist to increase its prices. However, the establishment of each new shop or new product variant also incurs the setup cost. If, for example, the monopolist decides to operate $n + 1$ retail outlets its profit is

$$\pi(N, n + 1) = N\left(V - \frac{t}{2(n + 1)} - c\right) - (n + 1)F. \tag{7.11}$$

This additional shop, variety of drink, or new product variant increases profit only if $\pi(N, n + 1) > \pi(N, n)$, which requires that

$$\frac{t}{2n}N - \frac{t}{2(n + 1)}N - F > 0.$$

This simplifies to

$$n(n + 1) < \frac{tN}{2F}. \tag{7.12}$$

Suppose, for example, that there are 5 million consumers in the market so that $N$ = 5,000,000, and that there is a fixed cost of $F = \$50,000$ associated with each shop.

---

3   See Shapiro and Varian (1999) for a similar argument regarding product variety in e-commerce.

Suppose further that the transportation cost is $t = \$1$. Hence, $tN/2F = 50$. Then if $n$ is less than or equal to 6, equation (7.12) indicates that it is profitable to add another shop. However, once the monopolist sets up $n = 7$ shops, equation (7.12) indicates that it is not worthwhile to add any more. (You can easily check that the monopolist should operate exactly 7 shops for any value of $tN/2F$ greater than 42 but less than 56.)

While it may look complicated, equation (7.12) actually has a simple and appealing intuition. The monopolist has to balance the increase in price and revenues that results from increased product variety against the additional setup costs that offering increased variety entails. What this tells us is that we would expect to find greater product variety in markets where there are many consumers ($N$ is large), where the setup costs of increasing product variety are low ($F$ is small), and where consumers have strong and distinct preferences regarding product characteristics ($t$ is large).

The first two conditions should be obvious. It tells us why there are many more retail outlets in Manhattan than in Austin, Texas; why we see many franchise outlets of the same fast-food chain but not of a gourmet restaurant; and why we see many more Subway outlets in a city than Marriott hotels. What does the third condition mean? For a given number of $n$ shops, equation (7.12) tells us that an additional ($n + 1$) shop will be increasingly desirable as the transportation cost $t$ becomes greater. Thus, as $t$ increases so will the monopolist's optimal number of outlets or degree of product variety.

The sense of this is that when $t$ is high consumers incur large costs if they are not being offered their most preferred brand. That is, a large value of $t$ implies that consumers are strongly attached to their preferred product type and are unwilling to purchase products that deviate significantly from this type—or travel very far to buy the product. If the monopolist is to continue to attract consumers it must tailor its products more closely to each consumer's unique demands, which requires that it offer a wider range of product variants or operate more retail outlets.

In this kind of market, adding a new shop does not necessarily mean increasing the total supply of the good. Instead, it means replacing some of an existing variety with an alternative variety that more closely matches the specific tastes of some customers. As we have seen, this also allows the firm to charge a higher price. Yet this advantage does not come free. The firm must incur the setup cost, $F$, for each new shop. However, we have not actually checked whether it makes sense and profit for the monopolist to serve the entire market. That is, we need to identify the condition that determines whether the monopolist will prefer to supply only part of the market rather than the whole market. If only part of the market is served then each retail outlet is effectively a "stand-alone" shop whose market area does not touch that of the remaining outlets as in Figure 7-5. We show in the Derivation Checkpoint: Optimal Market Price that the profit-maximizing price if only part of the market is to be served is $p^* = (V + c)/2$, which does not depend on the number of shops the monopolist has. This leads to a simple rule that determines whether the entire market is to be served. Suppose that there are $n$ retail outlets. Then we know from equation (7.9) that the price at which the entire market can be served is $p(N, n) = V - t/2n$. Serving the entire market is therefore better than supplying only part of the market, provided

$$p(N, n) > p^*, \text{ which implies } V - \frac{t}{2n} > \frac{V + c}{2}, \text{ which implies } V > c + \frac{t}{n}. \quad \textbf{(7.13)}$$

FIGURE

**7-5**

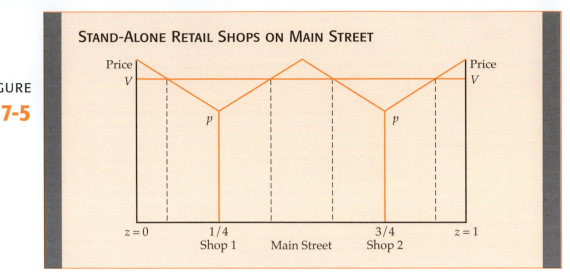

STAND-ALONE RETAIL SHOPS ON MAIN STREET

We can put this another way. What equation (7.13) tells us is that the monopolist's optimal pricing policy can be described as follows:

1. If marginal production cost plus per-unit transportation cost divided by the number of retail outlets, $c + t/n$, is greater than the consumers' reservation price, $V$, the monopolist should set a price at each shop of $p^* = (V + c)/2$ and supply only part of the market.

2. If marginal production plus per-unit transportation cost divided by the number of retail outlets, $c + t/n$, is less than the consumers' reservation price, $V$, the mo-

 **Derivation Checkpoint**

### Optimal Partial Market Price

Assume that the left-hand shop is located at 1/4 mile. At a price $p$, this shop sells to consumers distance $r$ on each side such that $p + tr = V$, or $r = (V - p)/t$.

Total demand to this shop is $2r$. Profit to this shop is, therefore, $\pi = 2N(p - c)(V - p)/t$.

Differentiating with respect to $p$ gives the first-order condition

$$\frac{d\pi}{dp} = \frac{2N}{t}(V - 2p + c) = 0,$$

which gives $p^* = (V + c)/2$. Profit to this shop is, therefore,

$$\pi^* = \frac{N}{2t}(V - c)^2.$$

nopolist should set a price at each shop of $p(n) = V - t/2n$ and supply the entire market.

The intuition behind this rule is relatively straightforward. When the consumer reservation price is low relative to production and transportation costs and when there are few outlets, trying to supply the entire market gives the monopolist a very low margin over operating costs and might even entail selling at a loss. By contrast, when the consumer reservation price is high relative to the cost of production and transportation and there are many outlets, a price that allows the monopolist to supply the entire market offers a reasonable margin over costs. In these latter circumstances, the monopolist will not wish to set a high price that sacrifices any sales. Since the marginal revenue of every unit sold significantly exceeds the production cost, the monopolist will wish to sell all the units it can.

## 7.3  IS THERE TOO MUCH PRODUCT VARIETY?

The profit-maximizing firm with market power has an incentive to create a large number of outlets or product varieties so as to provide each consumer with something close to the most preferred location and thereby extract a high price. It is easy to think of real-world firms that, while not pure monopolists, have substantial market power and employ this strategy. For instance, automobile manufacturers market many varieties of compact, midsize, and large, luxury cars. Franchise operations such as McDonald's or Subway grant exclusive geographic rights so as to space their outlets

 **Reality Checkpoint**

### You Will Soon Be Able to Buy a Sandwich Anywhere

McDonald's has for many years been the model of a successful franchise operation. Approximately 85 percent of McDonald's outlets are operated by franchisees who have also been responsible for more than 60 percent of its annual revenues. Despite some recent problems that have led McDonald's to close more than 700 underperforming restaurants, the company still has some 30,000 outlets worldwide, making it one of the largest owners of retail property in the world. There is, however, a threat looming on the horizon. An increased demand for healthier fast-food options has diverted demand to newer restaurant chains offering an alternative to the fat-rich traditional hamburger and fries. For the eleventh time in 15 years *Entrepreneur* magazine has named Subway as the number one franchise opportunity. Subway now has more than 18,000 locations in 72 countries and has more restaurants than McDonald's in the United States and Canada. Subway aims to open a further 2,000 outlets in the United States this year as well as expanding in the United Kingdom, Eastern Europe, and India.

**Source:** "Healthier Options are in Demand," "Landmark 18,000th Subway Restaurant Opens," *Financial Times*, June 4, 2003, available on the Internet at http://www.prnewswire.com.

evenly over an area and avoid competition between neighboring franchises. Telephones come in an increasingly wide variety of styles and colors. Soft drink and cereal companies purvey a wide array of minimally differentiated goods.

The sometimes overwhelming degree of product variety that we frequently observe raises the question of whether the incentive to offer a variety of product types could be too strong. Simply put, does the monopolist provide the degree of product variety consistent with maximizing social welfare? Or are the incentives so strong that the monopolist provides too much product variety? To answer this question, we first need to describe the socially optimal degree of product variety. Although the argument can be made in general terms, it is easiest to see it for the case in which the entire market is served.

As usual, we use the efficiency criterion to determine the optimality of the market outcome. This requires that we maximize the total net surplus of value minus cost. In this light, note that once the entire market is served, the total value to consumers of the output is unchanged no matter how many shops the monopolist operates. That is, once all $N$ consumers are buying the product, the total value placed on this production is $NV$ no matter how many shops or product variants there are. Similarly, once all $N$ consumers are served, the total variable production cost is constant at $cN$, again regardless of the number of outlets.

Once all $N$ consumers are served, only two factors change as more stores or product varieties are added. One of these is the transportation cost incurred by a typical or average consumer. Clearly, as more shops are added more consumers find themselves closer to a store and this cost falls. That's the good news. The bad news is that adding more shops also incurs the additional setup cost of $F$ per shop. Our question about whether the monopolist provides too many (or too few) shops thus comes down to determining whether it is the good news or the bad news that dominates. More formally, when all consumers are served, the total surplus is the total value, $NV$, minus the total production cost, $cN$, minus the total transportation and setup costs. Since the first two terms are fixed independent of the number of shops, maximizing the net social surplus is equivalent to minimizing the sum of transportation and setup costs. Does the monopolist's strategy achieve this result?

One feature of the monopoly outcome makes answering this question a little easier. It is the fact that the monopolist always spaces its shops evenly along Main Street no matter how many it operates. That is, a single shop is located at the center; two shops are located at 1/4 and 3/4, and so on. This feature greatly facilitates the calculation of total transportation cost that consumers incur for any number of shops, $n$.

Consider Figure 7-6, which shows both the full price and the transportation cost paid by those consumers buying from a particular outlet, shop $i$. As before, the top Y-shaped figure shows that a consumer located right next to the store has no transportation cost and pays a full price of just $p = V - \dfrac{t}{2n}$. As we consider consumers farther from the shop, the branches of the Y show that the full price rises because these consumers incur greater transportation costs. The lower branches in the figure provide a direct measure of this transportation cost for each such consumer. Again, the transportation cost for a consumer located right next to the store is zero. It rises gradually to $t/2n$—the transportation cost paid by a consumer who lives the maximum distance from the shop. Total transportation cost for the consumers of shop $i$ is the sum of the individual transportation costs of each consumer.

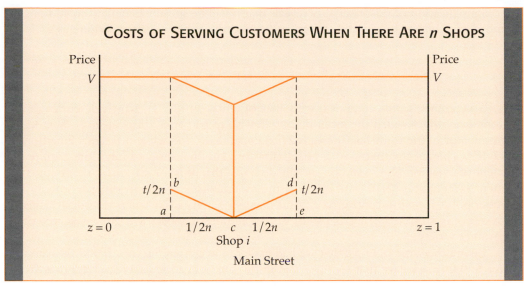

**COSTS OF SERVING CUSTOMERS WHEN THERE ARE $n$ SHOPS**

FIGURE

**7-6**

The transportation costs for consumers of any one shop are *abc* plus *cde* times consumer density, $Nt/4n^2$.

This is indicated by the areas of the symmetric triangles *abc* and *cde* in Figure 7-6. Each of these triangles extends to a height of $t/2n$. Each also has a base $1/2n$. Hence, the area of each is $t/8n^2$. Remember that the base reflects the fraction of the total $N$ consumers that shop $i$ serves in either direction. This means that to translate this area into actual dollars of transportation costs that the consumers of shop $i$ pay we have to multiply by $N$. The result is that the customers who patronize shop $i$ from the east pay a total transportation cost of $tN/8n^2$, as do those who patronize it from the west. The total transportation costs incurred by all consumers of shop $i$ is therefore the sum of these two amounts, or $tN/4n^2$. If we now multiply this by the number of shops $n$, we find that the total transportation costs associated with all $n$ shops is simply $tN/4n$. The same exercise tells us that the total setup costs for all $n$ shops is $nF$. Accordingly, the transportation plus setup costs associated with serving all $N$ customers and operating $n$ shops are

$$C(N, n) = \frac{tN}{4n} + nF. \tag{7.14}$$

By the same argument, total transportation plus setup costs with $(n + 1)$ shops are

$$C(N, n + 1) = \frac{tN}{4(n + 1)} + (n + 1)F. \tag{7.15}$$

Recall that our goal is to minimize this total cost. Therefore, we will always wish to add an additional shop so long as total costs fall. Comparison of equations (7.15) and (7.14) indicates that this will be the case, that is, $C(n + 1) < C(n)$, if

$$\frac{tN}{4n} - \frac{tN}{4(n + 1)} > F. \tag{7.16}$$

Simplification of this inequality reveals that it will be socially beneficial to add one more shop or one more product variant beyond the $n$ existing ones so long as

$$n(n + 1) < \frac{tN}{4F}. \tag{7.17}$$

Now compare this condition with that of equation (7.12), which describes the condition under which the monopolist will wish to add an additional shop. The denominator of the right-hand term is $2F$ in equation (7.12) while it is $4F$ in equation (7.17). This means that it is less likely for an additional shop to meet the requirement of equation (7.17) and be socially desirable than it is for it to meet the requirement of equation (7.12) and enhance the monopolist's profit. In other words, the monopolist has an incentive to expand product variety even when the social gains from doing so have been exhausted. The monopolist chooses too great a degree of product variety.

Taking the same example that we had earlier in which $t = \$1$, $N = 5,000,000$, and $F = \$50,000$, we have that $tN/4F = 25$. In this case, equation (7.17) implies that the socially optimal number of shops is four. However, we have already shown that the monopolist would like to operate seven shops or offer seven product varieties in this market. In short, the monopolist offers too much product variety.

The casual evidence cited at the beginning of this chapter supports the "too much variety" hypothesis. The myriad of ready-to-eat breakfast cereals, shampoos, and cosmetics; the multitude of options available on automobiles; and the variety of mobile phone service plans all give evidence of the strong incentive to offer multiple versions of one's product. Admittedly, the producers of these goods are not pure monopolists, but they do exercise considerable market power and so are subject to many of the same influences that we have just been considering.

The basic reason why a monopolist offers too much variety is because the firm maximizes profit, not total surplus. When deciding to add another shop, the monopolist balances the additional setup cost against the additional revenues that it can earn from being able to increase prices. However, from the viewpoint of efficiency this additional revenue is not a net gain. It is just a transfer of surplus from consumers to the monopolist. The true social optimum would balance the setup cost of an extra shop against the reduction in transportation costs that results. Clearly, this criterion will lead to the establishment of fewer shops.

Operating additional shops is attractive to a monopolist because this is the easiest way to reach what would otherwise be distant consumers. The monopolist operating just one shop at the center of Main Street can sell to customers at the eastern and western ends of town only by greatly reducing the price *to all customers*. The incentive to operate additional shops is that it permits reaching these distant consumers without such a general price reduction.

This raises another issue that takes us back to the discussion in Chapters 5 and 6. If somehow the firm could charge a price to distant consumers that they are willing to pay *without* lowering the price to nearby ones, then reaching these distant consumers from just a few shops or with just a few varieties would not be so expensive. That is, if the monopolist could price discriminate the tendency to oversupply variety might be much less strong. We now examine this possibility.

## 7.4 MONOPOLY AND HORIZONTAL DIFFERENTIATION WITH PRICE DISCRIMINATION

In our discussion to date we have been assuming that the monopolist does not price discriminate between its customers. This makes sense when customers travel to the shop to purchase the good and so do not reveal their addresses or who they are to the monopolist. Suppose instead that the monopolist controls delivery of the product, and so will know who is who in the market. What pricing policy might we expect the firm to adopt?

First, it should be clear that the monopoly will charge every consumer the consumer's reservation price, $V$. This is a pricing policy known as *uniform delivered pricing*. A firm adopting such a pricing policy charges all consumers the same prices and absorbs the transportation costs in delivering the product to them. This is discriminatory pricing because, even though consumers pay the same price, this price does not reflect the true costs of supplying consumers in different locations. By way of analogy, charging a consumer in San Francisco the same price as a consumer in New York for a product manufactured in New York is just as much discriminatory pricing as charging a different price for this product to two different New York residents.

As in the no price discrimination case, we should check whether the firm actually wants to supply every consumer. Suppose that, as before, the firm operates $n$ retail outlets evenly spaced along Main Street. Then the transportation and production costs that the firm incurs in supplying the consumers located furthest away from a retail outlet are $c + t/2n$. There is profit to be made from such sales provided that

$$V > c + t/2n. \tag{7.18}$$

Notice that this is a weaker condition than equation (7.13) without price discrimination. This is another example of a typical property of price discrimination. It allows the monopolist to serve consumers who might otherwise be left unserved; that is, it expands the market.

Now consider how many shops (or product varieties) the price-discriminating monopolist should operate. Given that the firm is supplying the entire market and is charging every consumer the consumer's reservation price of $V$, total revenue is fixed at $NV$. Total costs are variable production costs, which are fixed at $cN$, plus the transportation costs that the firm absorbs and the setup costs, $nF$. These latter costs are just the costs $C(N, n)$ from equation (7.14). So the profit of the price-discriminating monopolist is

$$\pi(N, n) = NV - cN - \left( \frac{tN}{4n} + nF \right). \tag{7.19}$$

How does the monopolist maximize profit in this case? Here, profit maximization is simply achieved by minimizing the costs $C(N, n)$, since total revenue and production costs are fixed. But this means that *the discriminating monopolist offers the socially efficient degree of product variety.*

If you recall our discussion of price discrimination in Chapter 6, you should not find this too surprising. We saw in that chapter that a monopolist who engages in first-degree price discrimination will extract all consumer surplus and therefore will want to produce the efficient amount of output. The result just obtained extends that finding to the case of a product-differentiated market. In such a market, a firm that can achieve first-degree price discrimination will not only produce the right output but also the right degree of variety. With price discrimination the firm can reach far-away customers by means of a price designed specifically for those customers rather than by adding extra variety. Hence, the incentive to go beyond the socially optimal amount of variety does not exist.

The one point that remains to be considered is how the price discrimination case might be interpreted as a model of product differentiation in a product characteristics space rather than a geographic one. The core of this interpretation lies in the change we made in our analysis that allowed the monopolist to adopt discriminatory prices. In the no price discrimination case we assumed that consumers travel to the shops to purchase the product and so do not have to reveal their addresses. By contrast, in the price discrimination case we assumed that the monopolist controls delivery and so can adopt uniform delivered pricing by providing and paying for the delivery service.

How can a monopolist control "delivery" of products that are differentiated by characteristics rather than by location? MacLeod, Norman, and Thisse (1988) provide the analogy:

> In the context of product differentiation, price discrimination arises when the producer begins with a "base product" and then redesigns this product to the customers' specifications. This means that the firm now produces a *band* of horizontally differentiated products . . . instead of a single product. . . . Transport cost is no longer interpreted as a utility loss, but as an additional cost incurred by the firm in adapting its product to the customers' requirements. . . . (So) long as product design is under the control of the producer—equivalent to the producer controlling transportation—he need not charge the full cost of design change. (1988, pp. 442–43)

Consider, for example, buying a Ford Taurus. On the one hand you might choose one of the standard variants. Alternatively, the salesperson might persuade you into taking a different sound system, different wheels, an attractive stripe along the side that makes the car sportier, and so on. Effectively, what the salesperson is doing is making you reveal your actual "address" through the options you choose with the intention, of course, of separating you from more of your money.

How easy is it, though, for firms to offer such mass customization? The multitude of product variety mentioned above suggests that it is relatively easy. Indeed, as we discussed in Chapter 3, modern techniques of flexible manufacturing provide the scope economies that increasingly make it easy for firms such as Levi Strauss, Mitsubishi, Hitachi, and Italian ceramic makers to produce in small batches at little extra cost. Internet firms such as Amazon.com change the initial page a customer sees based on the customer's recent purchases. In principle, each consumer can have her own customized page—and customized prices.[4] In short, product variation is here to stay.

---

4    A clear if brief expression of the view that e-commerce firms greatly facilitate price discrimination may be found in Krugman (2000).

## Practice Problem 7.1

Henry Shortchap is the only blacksmith in the small village of Chestnut Tree. The village is comprised of twenty-one households evenly distributed one-tenth of a mile apart along the main street of the town. Each household uses at most one unit of smithing services per month. In addition, each household incurs a there-and-back-again transportation cost of $.50 for every tenth of a mile it lives from Shortchap's smithy. The reservation price of each household for such services is $10. Henry's cost of providing smithing services is $2 per unit. However, he can operate only one shop. Where should Henry locate his shop and what price should he charge? Suppose instead that Henry could operate a mobile smithy that allowed him to offer his services at his customers' homes. However, it would cost him $.75 there-and-back-again transportation costs for every tenth of a mile he has to move his smithy. Should he switch to this mobile service?

# 7.5 VERTICAL PRODUCT DIFFERENTIATION

The distinguishing feature of horizontal product differentiation is that consumers disagree on what is the preferred variety of product. Thus, if two different varieties are offered at the same price some consumers are likely to buy one and other consumers the other. Vertical differentiation is different. In this case all consumers agree what is the preferred or best product, the next to best product, and so on. Consumers rank products in the same way, and the best is considered to be the highest quality product and the least-preferred good is the lowest quality product. Consumers differ, though, in their willingness to pay for quality. This may be because consumers have different incomes or simply because they have different attitudes regarding what quality is worth. If a high- and low-quality good are offered at the same price all consumers will buy the high-quality good, so lower quality goods will find a market only if they are offered at sufficiently lower prices. A Chevrolet costs much less than a Cadillac. No-frills airlines such as JetBlue and SouthWest attract customers because their flights are offered at large discounts relative to the larger carriers such as United and American. The Peninsula Hotel in New York charges much less than the Waldorf Astoria.

We would like to be a bit more specific regarding the qualities of products that a firm might offer and the prices that it will charge for them. The analysis we use for this purpose is a simplified one. Nevertheless, it captures much of the flavor of more general treatments.[5]

## 7.5.1 Price and Quality Choice with Just One Product

As a start, we consider how changes in quality might affect a firm's demand when it offers just one product. This will give us some idea of how quality or product design can be used to enhance a firm's profit. Then we will examine how the firm might increase its profit still further by offering more than one quality of a product. Let's begin with a monopoly firm selling one product. The firm knows that there is some feature, or set of features, that measures the product quality valued by consumers.

---

5  The first and classic treatment of this problem is Mussa and Rosen (1978). Unfortunately, this is also a rather complex analysis.

The firm's ability to choose these features also means that it can choose the quality of product as well as its price.

The firm also knows that while each consumer is willing to pay something extra to get a high-quality product, the precise amount extra that would be willingly paid varies across consumers. Some consumers place a high value on quality and will gladly pay a considerable premium for even a modest quality improvement. Others are less concerned with quality and, unless the accompanying price increase is minimal, such consumers would not buy a better quality good. To simplify further, we will assume that each consumer buys at most one unit of the good. That is, each consumer examines the price and quality of the product and the utility obtained from consuming it. If the consumer places a value on the product of the particular quality offered greater than the price being charged, the good is purchased. If not, the consumer simply refrains from buying altogether.

The demand curve facing the monopolist will now depend on the quality of the product marketed. This is reflected in the inverse demand function, $P = P(Q, z)$. This function implies that the market-clearing price will depend not only on how much the firm produces, $Q$, but also on the quality of these units, $z$. To put it somewhat differently, a rise in quality $z$ will raise the market-clearing price for any given quantity, $Q$. The demand curve shifts out (or up) as product quality $z$ increases.

It is useful to distinguish between two different ways an increase in quality can shift the inverse demand curve, $P(Q, z)$. Each is illustrated in Figure 7-7. To better understand this diagram note that, since consumers vary in terms of their willingness to pay for a good of any given quality, $z$, and since each buys at most one unit of the good, the demand curve really reflects a ranking of consumers in terms of their reservation price for a good of a specific quality, $z$. The reservation price of the consumer most willing to pay for the good is the intercept term. The reservation price of the consumer next most willing to pay is the next point on the demand curve as we move to the right, and so on. In both Figures 7-7(a) and 7-7(b), the initial quantity produced is $Q_1$ and the initial quality is $z_1$. The market-clearing price for this quantity–quality combination is $P_1$. From what we have just said, this price must be the willingness to pay, or reservation price, of the $Q_1$th consumer. At price $P_1$, this consumer is just indifferent between buying the good and not buying it at all given that it is of quality $z_1$. This consumer is called the marginal consumer. Consumers to the left— those consumers who also buy the product—are called *infra*marginal consumers.

Figure 7-7(a) shows how the inverse demand curve shifts when the increase in quality raises the willingness to pay of the inframarginal consumers by more than it raises the willingness to pay of the marginal consumer. An increase in quality from $z_1$ to $z_2$ raises the price at which the quantity $Q_1$ sells from $P_1$ to $P_2$. However, the increase in the reservation price is greatest for consumers who were already purchasing the product, so the demand curve shifts by "sliding along" the price axis. Figure 7-7(b) illustrates the alternative case. Here, the increase in quality from $z_1$ to $z_2$ increases the willingness to pay of the $Q_1$th or marginal consumer by more than it raises the reservation price of the inframarginal consumers. Once again, this quality increase will raise the market price of quantity $Q_1$ from $P_1$ to $P_2$. However, the demand curve now shifts by "sliding along" the quantity axis.[6]

---

6   For models based on the case illustrated in Figure 7-7(b), some care must be taken to limit the ultimate size of the market. That is, quality increases cannot indefinitely expand the quantity demanded at a given price.

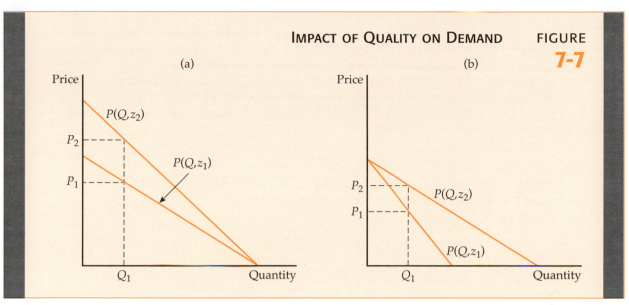

**IMPACT OF QUALITY ON DEMAND** FIGURE **7-7**

In case (a) an increase in quality raises the consumer reservation price but not the maximum size of the market. In case (b) an increase in quality raises the consumer reservation price and the maximum market size.

Whether demand is described by Figure 7-7(a) or 7-7(b), we can see that for the monopolist the choice of quality amounts to a decision as to where its demand curve will be. Increases in quality are attractive because they rotate the demand curve and so increase the firm's revenue at any given price. However, it is normally costly to increase product quality. What the monopolist has to do is balance the benefits in increased revenue that improved quality generates against the increased costs that increased quality imposes. More precisely, the monopolist choosing quality should go through an analysis qualitatively similar to that which is done when choosing output or price. For any given choice of output, the monopolist should choose the level of quality at which the marginal revenue from increasing quality equals the marginal cost of increasing quality. In other words, the monopolist who controls both quality and quantity of product has two profit-maximizing conditions to satisfy:

1. For a given choice of quality, the marginal revenue from the last unit sold should equal the marginal cost of making that unit at that quality.

2. For a given choice of quantity, the marginal revenue from increasing quality of each unit of output should equal the additional (marginal) cost of increasing the quality of that quantity of output.

Let us illustrate the quality or product design choice by assuming demand is of the type shown in Figure 7-7(a). More specifically, assume that the demand function is given by the equation

$$P = z(50 - Q). \tag{7.20}$$

Equation (7.20) says that no matter the quality of the product, at a price of zero a total of 50 units will be sold but increased quality causes the demand function to rotate clockwise about the point $Q = 50$.

Let us also keep matters simple case by assuming that the cost of improving quality is incurred as a sunk design cost so that marginal production cost is independent of the quality of the product. A better film or software package may require more expensive script or programming, respectively, but the actual costs of showing the film or printing the CD are independent of how good it is. To make matters even simpler, let us add the further assumption that production costs are not only constant but zero. Design costs, however, rise with the quality level chosen. Specifically, we shall assume that

$$F(z) = 5z^2, \tag{7.21}$$

which implies that the marginal cost of increasing product quality is $10z$ (see Derivation Checkpoint: Optimal Choice of Output and Quality). We can now write the firm's profit, which is

$$\pi(Q, z) = P(Q, z)Q - F(z) = z(50 - Q)Q - 5z^2. \tag{7.22}$$

 # Derivation **Checkpoint**

## Optimal Choice of Output and Quality

Demand and costs are given respectively by

$$P = z(\theta - Q) \text{ and } C(Q, z) = \alpha z^2.$$

Hence, the profit function is

$$\pi(Q, z) = PQ - D(z) = z(\theta - Q)Q - \alpha z^2.$$

Differentiate this with respect to $Q$ to give the profit-maximizing output choice

$$\frac{\partial \pi(Q, z)}{\partial Q} = z(\theta - 2Q) = 0,$$

which gives $Q^* = \theta/2$.

Differentiate profit with respect to $z$ to give the profit-maximizing quality choice

$$\frac{\partial \pi(Q, z)}{\partial z} = (\theta - Q)Q - 2\alpha z = 0.$$

Substitute for $Q^*$ to give

$$2\alpha z^* = \theta^2/4,$$

which implies $z^* = \theta^2/8\alpha$. In the text example, $\theta = 50$ and $\alpha = 5$ so that $Q^* = 25$ and $z^* = 62.5$.

Consider first the profit-maximizing choice of output. This turns out to be very simple in this case. As usual, marginal revenue has the same intercept as the demand function but twice the slope. So with the demand function $P = 50z - zQ$ we know that marginal revenue is $MR = 50z - 2zQ = z(50 - 2Q)$. Equating this with marginal cost gives the profit-maximizing output condition $z(50 - 2Q) = 0$. Hence, the profit-maximizing output is $Q^* = 50/2 = 25$.

In other words, in this case the monopolist's choice regarding the quantity is independent of the choice of quality. The profit-maximizing output remains constant at $Q^* = 25$ no matter the choice of quality. Going back to the demand function, the profit-maximizing price is given by $P^* = z(50 - Q^*)$, so that the optimal price is $P^* = 50z/2$. Unlike output, the profit-maximizing price is affected by the choice of quality. Moreover, the quality choice will also affect the firm's design costs. A higher quality design permits the monopolist to raise price and earn more revenue but it also raises the firm's costs. This is the trade-off that the monopolist must evaluate.

To make the quality decision the monopolist must compare the additional revenue resulting from an increase in $z$ with the increase in design cost that the higher quality requires. Because the quantity sold is constant at $Q^* = 25$, the additional revenue of an increase in quality is just this output level times the difference in price that can be charged following the rise in quality. In our example, we can see from equation (7.20) that the firm's revenue, $PQ$, at product quality $z$ when it charges the profit-maximizing price $P^* = 50z/2$ is

$$P^*Q^* = \frac{50z}{2} \cdot \frac{50}{2} = z\frac{2{,}500}{4} = 625z. \tag{7.23}$$

So, increasing product quality by one "unit" increases revenue by \$625, which is, therefore, the marginal revenue from increased quality. We know also from equation (7.21) that the marginal cost of increased quality is $10z$. Equating marginal revenue with marginal cost then gives the profit-maximizing quality choice

$$z^* = 625/10 = 62.5. \tag{7.24}$$

An interesting question that arises in connection with the monopoly firm's choice of quality is how that choice compares with the socially optimal one. Does the monopolist produce too high or too low a quality of good? A little thought should convince you that the monopolist's quality choice will, in this setting, be too low. The reason is straightforward. An increase in $z$ rotates the demand curve upward and increases the total surplus earned from the 25 units that are always sold. The social optimum requires that quality be increased so long as this gain in the total surplus exceeds the extra design cost. However, the monopolist only gets to keep the producer surplus that a quality increase generates, not the consumer surplus that it creates. As a result, profit maximization will lead the firm to increase quality only so long as the extra producer surplus covers the additional design cost. Since the producer surplus is less than the total surplus, the monopolist will stop short of producing the socially optimal quality. Of course, the monopolist holds quantity below the optimal amount, too.[7]

---

7  Our results regarding the monopolist's quality choice might have been different had we instead assumed that quality affects demand as in Figure 7-7(b).

Our primary objective, however, is not to determine whether firms with monopoly power choose to market products of either insufficient or excessive quality. The main point is that for such firms the quality choice matters. By carefully choosing product quality jointly with product price, the monopolist can again extract further surplus from the market.

## Practice Problem 7.2

Will Barret is the only lawyer in the small country town of Percyville. The weekly demand for his legal services depends on the quality of service he provides as reflected by his inverse demand curve $P = 4 - Q/z$. Here, $P$ is the price per case, $Q$ is the number of cases or clients, and $z$ is the quality of service Will provides. Will's costs are independent of how many cases he actually takes, but they do rise with quality. More specifically, Will's costs are given by $C = z^2$.

a. Draw Will's demand curve for a given quality, $z$. How do increases in $z$ affect the demand curve?
b. Consider the three options: $z = 1$, $z = 2$, and $z = 3$. Derive the profit-maximizing output for each of these choices.
c. Compute the market price and profit—net of quality costs—for each of the three choices above. Which quality choice leads to the highest profits?

## 7.5.2  Offering More Than One Product in a Vertically Differentiated Market

Having worked through the basics of how product quality can affect market demand, we now consider a multiproduct strategy that the monopolist can use to earn even greater profit. To make it simple, suppose the monopolist knows that there are only two types of consumer. Each of these consumers will buy exactly one unit of the firm's product per period provided that the consumer's surplus is nonnegative. If more than one of the firm's products satisfies this criterion then the consumer will, as usual, buy the product offering the greatest surplus. Once again, the different types of consumer are distinguished by their willingness to pay for quality. For consumer type $i$ the indirect utility obtained from consuming a product of quality $z$ at price $p$ is

$$V_i = \theta_i(z - \underline{z}_i) - p \quad (i = 1, 2). \tag{7.25}$$

In this equation, $\theta_i$ is a measure of the value that consumer type $i$ places on quality, and $\underline{z}_i$ is the lower bound on quality below which a consumer type $i$ would not buy a product. We assume that $\theta_1 > \theta_2$. That is, type 1 consumers place a higher value on quality than type 2 consumers, perhaps because type 1 consumers have higher incomes than type 2 consumers or more generally because they have more intense preferences for quality. We also assume that $\underline{z}_1 > \underline{z}_2 = 0$. In other words, type 1 consumers will not buy the monopolist's product unless it is at least of quality $\underline{z}_1$. These are consumers who "wouldn't be seen dead" flying in coach, eating in fast-food outlets, or shopping in discount stores. By contrast, type 2 consumers are willing to buy the monopolist's product of any quality provided, of course, that consumer surplus is nonnegative.

Unfortunately for the firm, while it knows that these different consumer types exist it has no objective measure by which it can distinguish the different types.

## ✔ Reality Checkpoint

### I'll Have the 1999 Bordeaux and an Appendectomy . . . Medium Rare

Most hospitals serve a very large area. There are rarely more than a few hospitals serving the same population center. Hence, the hospital care market appears to be one in which firms do have market power. Of course, various factors may constrain the exercise of such power. Indeed, a common perception in the current era of managed care and cuts in Medicare and Medicaid is that U.S. hospitals are cutting services to the bone. However, evidence suggests that as these developments have strapped hospitals for cash, they have begun to gamble on a new strategy to raise revenue and profits. They have begun to offer patients the option of private,

deluxe suites to lure wealthy customers. In such suites, the fare is prepared by top chefs trained at world-class culinary institutes and served at any time of day the patient requests. The staff is recruited from nearby fancy hotels. Linens are made of the finest cotton. International patients can receive television programming from their home countries. While the profitability of this strategy remains unclear, Mount Sinai Hospital in New York has estimated that it earns a net profit of $1 million on such suites. Perhaps it is not surprising, then, that in the past few years, over a dozen hospitals have opened pavilions housing ten or more such suites.

**Source:** L. Lagnado, "Stylish Operations: Hospitals Add Deluxe Suites." *The Wall Street Journal*, September 16, 1996, p. B1.

Hence, just as in our analysis of second-degree price discrimination in the previous chapter, the monopolist must implement a strategy that identifies and separates customers of different types. To be specific, what the monopolist would like to do is somehow persuade type 1 consumers to buy a product of high quality, $z_1$, at a very high price while simultaneously persuading type 2 consumers to purchase a low quality, $z_2$, product at a price equal to their maximum willingness to pay. The firm is able to produce any quality in the quality range $[\underline{z}, \overline{z}]$. In addition, we also continue with our assumption of the previous section that marginal costs of production are identical across all qualities of product and are equal to zero.[8]

Let's look first at a consumer of type 2, the one with a low willingness to pay for quality. What the firm will do is charge this consumer a price that is just low enough for the consumer to be willing to purchase the low-quality product. From equation (7.25), and given that $\underline{z}_2 = 0$, consumer type 2 will buy $z_2$ if

$$p_2 = \theta_2 z_2. \tag{7.26}$$

---

[8]  It might be, for example, that the majority of the firm's costs are setup costs and that crimping higher quality products makes lower quality products. Relaxing this assumption doesn't change much. Having it makes the analysis a bit easier.

Now consider a consumer of type 1 with a stronger preference for quality. This consumer can, of course, buy the low-quality product. So, in pricing the high-quality product the firm faces the same type of *incentive compatibility constraint* that we met when discussing second-degree price discrimination. (There is also the incentive compatibility constraint, of course, that the type 2 consumers do indeed buy the low-quality rather than the high-quality product. We return to this below.) For a type 1 consumer to buy the high-quality product it is necessary that

$$\theta_1(z_1 - \underline{z}_1) - p_1 \geq \theta_1(z_2 - \underline{z}_1) - p_2$$
$$\theta_1(z_1 - \underline{z}_1) - p_1 \geq 0 \tag{7.27}$$

The expressions in equation (7.27) say that the consumer surplus that a type 1 consumer obtains from buying the high-quality product must be nonnegative and greater than or equal to the consumer surplus that could be obtained if the type 1 consumer bought the low-quality good. Substituting $p_2 = \theta_2 z_2$ from equation (7.26) into the first expression in equation (7.27), we find that

$$p_1 \leq \theta_1 z_1 - (\theta_1 - \theta_2)z_2. \tag{7.28}$$

Equation (7.28) says that the maximum price, $p_1$, that can be charged for the high-quality product is $p_1 = \theta_1 z_1 - (\theta_1 - \theta_2)z_2$. It is greater the higher are the values $\theta_1$ and $\theta_2$ that the two types of consumers place on quality, and the higher is the quality difference between the quality, $z_1$, of the high-quality good and the quality, $z_2$, of the low-quality good. That is, quality can be priced more highly when it is valued more highly by all consumers. And because the monopolist is effectively competing with itself by offering two products of different qualities, increasing the quality differential between the products is useful because it makes the two goods more different. The monopolist thereby weakens the competition between its two products, which allows the firm to increase the price of its high-quality good.

Note that when $p_1 = \theta_1 z_1 - (\theta_1 - \theta_2)z_2$, the condition that consumers type 1 receive nonnegative surplus when they buy the high-quality good can now be written as $\theta_1(z_1 - \underline{z}_1) - p_1 \geq 0 \Rightarrow (\theta_1 - \theta_2)z_2 - \theta_1\underline{z}_1 \geq 0$.

It is easy to check that the incentive compatibility constraint is always satisfied for type 2 consumers. For this type of consumer *not* to want to buy the high-quality product it must be the case that $\theta_2 z_1 - p_1 < 0$, which given that $p_1 = \theta_1 z_1 - (\theta_1 - \theta_2)z_2$ implies $-(\theta_1 - \theta_2)z_1 + (\theta_1 - \theta_2)z_2 < 0$. Since $z_1 > z_2$ and $\theta_1 > \theta_2$, this must be true. In other words, the prices given by equations (7.26) and (7.28) guarantee that type 1 consumers buy the high-quality product and type 2 consumers buy the low-quality product.

Now assume that there are $N_i$ consumers of each type. Furthermore, suppose that variable costs of production do not depend on quality and so for simplicity we set the unit production costs of each good as $c_1 = c_2 = 0$. Again for simplicity assume that there are no fixed costs. Given that $p_1 = \theta_1 z_1 - (\theta_1 - \theta_2)z_2$ and $p_2 = \theta_2 z_2$, the firm's total profit is

$$\Pi = N_1 p_1 + N_2 p_2 = N_1 \theta_1 z_1 - (N_1 \theta_1 - (N_1 + N_2)\theta_2)z_2. \tag{7.29}$$

The issue that we want to address now is what quality of goods, $z_1$ and $z_2$, will maximize the firm's profit. In this respect, it is clear from equation (7.29) that the coefficient on $z_1$ is the positive term $N_1\theta_1$. That is, profit rises as $z_1$ rises, so the firm should set $z_1$ as high as possible; that is

$$z_1 = \bar{z}. \tag{7.30}$$

The firm should set the quality of its highest quality product at the maximum quality level possible.

For $z_2$ matters are not quite as straightforward. The impact of $z_2$ upon the monopolist's profit depends upon the sign of the coefficient, $N_1\theta_1 - (N_1 + N_2)\theta_2$. When this term is positive, the monopolist's profit decreases as $z_2$ increases. When it is negative, profit increases as $z_2$ increases. We need to examine these two possibilities separately.

**i) Case 1: $N_1\theta_1 > (N_1 + N_2)\theta_2$ so that $N_1\theta_1 - (N_1 + N_2)\theta_2 > 0$**

From equation (7.29) it is clear that in this case profit is decreasing in $z_2$. As a result, if this condition is satisfied then the firm should offer both a high- and a low-quality product. It will set $z_1$ as high as possible at $z_1 = \bar{z}$, and set $z_2$ as low as it needs. This does not mean, however, that $z_2$ needs to be reduced to its minimum of $\underline{z}$. Recall the condition that consumer type 1 receives nonnegative consumer surplus from buying the high-quality good. That is, $\theta_1(z_1 - \underline{z}_1) - p_1 \geq 0 \Rightarrow (\theta_1 - \theta_2)z_2 - \theta_1\underline{z}_1 \geq 0 \Rightarrow z_2 \geq \frac{\theta_1\underline{z}_1}{\theta_1 - \theta_2}$. The monopolist in this case will want to choose $z_2$ as low as possible. This means that

$$z_2 = \frac{\theta_1\underline{z}_1}{\theta_1 - \theta_2}. \tag{7.31}$$

Given equation (7.31) and the fact that $z_1$ is set at its maximum, we can now work out the profit-maximizing prices for the two goods. Substituting equation (7.31) in equation (7.26), we find that the price of the low-quality product is $p_2 = \frac{\theta_2\theta_1\underline{z}_1}{\theta_1 - \theta_2}$.

Similarly, substituting equation (7.31) and $z_1 = \bar{z}$ into $p_1 = \theta_1 z_1 - (\theta_1 - \theta_2)z_2$ we find that $p_1 = \theta_1(\bar{z} - \underline{z}_1)$. In other words, type 1 consumers are charged their maximum willingness to pay for the high-quality product, which is, in fact, designed to be the highest quality possible. Meanwhile, type 2 customers are sold a good of lesser quality as given by equation (7.31), and charged the highest price for this quality that is possible given the firm's need to satisfy the incentive compatibility constraint. Aggregate profit is then

$$\Pi = N_1(\bar{z} - \underline{z}_1)\theta_1 + N_2 \frac{\underline{z}_1\theta_2\theta_1}{\theta_1 - \theta_2}. \tag{7.32}$$

**ii) Case 2: $N_1\theta_1 < (N_1 + N_2)\theta_2$ so that $N_1\theta_1 - (N_1 + N_2)\theta_2 < 0$**

If $N_1\theta_1 < (N_1 + N_2)\theta_2$, then it follows from equation (7.29) that profit is increasing in $z_2$. In this case the firm should set $z_2 = z_1 = \bar{z}$. In other words, the firm should offer only one product and that product should be of the highest possible quality.

It is, perhaps, easier to see the intuition behind this result by rewriting the inequality $N_1\theta_1 < (N_1 + N_2)\theta_2$ as

$$\frac{N_1}{N_1 + N_2} < \frac{\theta_2}{\theta_1} < 1. \tag{7.33}$$

Thus, what we are saying is that if there are not too many type 1 consumers, those who really like quality, or if their willingness to pay for quality is very high relative to that of type 2 consumers, then the firm should offer only one type of good. The intuition is that whenever the monopolist offers two products, the low-quality product tends to cannibalize sales from the high-quality product.

To be precise, we can see from equation (7.28) that offering both a high-quality and a low-quality product costs the firm $(\theta_1 - \theta_2)z_2$ in foregone revenue from each type 1 consumer. Accordingly, when there are many type 1 consumers and/or when the difference between $\theta_1$ and $\theta_2$ is large, the firm will want to minimize this cost by offering a second good that is very low in quality so that it does not compete too vigorously with the high-quality product. On the other hand, when there are roughly equal numbers of consumers of the two types and/or when preferences do not differ greatly across different consumer types the monopolist should offer a single high-quality good. Of course, this leaves the question of whether the firm in this case should price the high-quality product to sell to both types of consumer or price it to sell only to type 1 consumers.

Selling to both types of consumer raises total sales but requires that the product be priced low at $\theta_2\bar{z}$, giving the firm a total profit of $N\theta_2\bar{z} = (N_1 + N_2)\theta_2\bar{z}$. Selling to only type 1 consumers means that the product can be priced at $\theta_1(\bar{z} - \underline{z}_1)$, giving the firm a total profit of $N_1\theta_1(\bar{z} - \underline{z}_1)$. Comparing these two profit levels reveals that selling to both types of consumer is more profitable if

$$N_1\theta_1(\bar{z} - \underline{z}_1) < (N_1 + N_2)\theta_2\bar{z} \Rightarrow N_1\theta_1 < (N_1 + N_2)\theta_2 \frac{\bar{z}}{(\bar{z} - \underline{z}_1)} . \quad \textbf{(7.33)}$$

A close look at equation (7.33) reveals that for this second case in which we have assumed that $N_1\theta_1 < (N_1 + N_2)\theta_2$, the condition in the equation must hold true. Therefore, the monopolist will price the product to sell to both consumer types.[9]

## Practice Problem 7.3

General Foods is a monopolist and knows that its market for Bran Flakes contains two types of consumer. Type A consumers have indirect utility functions $V_a = 20(z - \underline{z}_1)$ while type B consumers have indirect utility functions $V_b = 10z$. In each case $z$ is a measure of product quality, which can be chosen from the interval $[0,2]$. There are $N$ consumers in the market, of which General Foods knows that a fraction $\eta$ is of type A and the remainder is of type B. For simplicity, assume all costs are zero.

a.  Suppose that General Foods can tell the different consumer types apart and so can charge them different prices for the same quality of breakfast cereal. What is the profit-maximizing strategy for General Foods?

Now suppose that General Foods does not know what type of consumer is which.

b.  Show how its profit-maximizing strategy is determined by $\eta$.

c.  What is the profit-maximizing strategy when $\underline{z}_1 = 0$?

## SUMMARY

This chapter has investigated product-differentiated strategies that a monopolist may use when it sells to consumers with diverse tastes. By offering a line of products the

---

9   Unlike the result in Section 7.5.1, the monopolist here chooses the highest quality because there is no cost to increasing $z$.

firm can better appropriate consumer surplus and increase profit. First we considered horizontal product differentiation. In this scenario, consumers differ in their preferences for specific product characteristics. Some prefer yellow, some black, some soft, some hard, some sweet, and some sour. By selling different varieties of the product, the monopolist expands its market and simultaneously enhances its ability to charge customers higher prices in return for selling a variety of product that is close to their specific, most preferred flavor, color, or design. A feature of this kind of market is that the monopolist tends to offer too much variety—a prediction for which there is a good bit of supportive casual evidence. However, the monopolist's incentive to oversupply variety is mitigated if the firm is able to price discriminate. Indeed, perfect or first-degree price discrimination encourages the firm to offer the socially efficient degree of product variety.

In the second case, we examined vertical differentiation. Here, all consumers agree that more quality is better, where quality is measured by some feature or set of features of the product. Consumers, however, differ in their willingness to pay for quality. In the case where the monopolist offers only one type of product and quality is costly we found that the monopolist may choose too low a quality. We also found that there is an incentive for the monopolist to offer a range of goods of different qualities in order to exploit the differences in consumers' preferences. In doing so, however, the firm faces an incentive compatibility constraint. Its quality and price choices must be such that different types of consumers actively choose to purchase the quality aimed at them. The result is that the monopolist will try to maintain a significant differential in the varying qualities of products that it offers.

## PROBLEMS

1. A monopolist faces the following inverse demand curve: $P = (36 - 2Q)z$, where $P$ is price; $Q$ is total output; and $z$ is the quality of product sold. $z$ can take on only one of two values. The monopolist can choose to market a low-quality product for which $z = 1$. Alternatively, the monopolist can choose to market a high-quality product for which $z = 2$. Marginal cost is independent of quality and is constant at zero. Fixed cost, however, depends on the product design and increases with the quality chosen. Specifically, fixed cost is equal to $65z^2$.

   a. Find the monopolist's profits if it maximizes profits *and* chooses a low-quality design.

   b. Find the monopolist's profits when it maximizes profits *and* chooses a high-quality design.

   c. Comparing your answers to a and b, what quality choice should the monopolist make?

2. In the early 1970s, the six largest manufacturers of ready-to-eat breakfast cereals had 95 percent of the market. Over the preceding twenty years, these same manufacturers introduced over eighty new varieties of cereals. How would you evaluate this strategy from the standpoint of the Hotelling spatial model described earlier in this chapter?

3. Crepe Creations is considering franchising its unique brand of crepes to stall-holders on Hermoza Beach, which is five miles long. CC estimates that on an average day there are 1,000 sunbathers evenly spread along the beach and that each sunbather will buy one crepe per day provided that they are priced at no more than $5. The

effort of getting up from the sand to get a crepe and return to the sunbed is estimated at 25 cents for every 1/4 mile the sunbather is from a stall. Each crepe costs 50 cents to make and it costs $40 per day to operate a stall no matter how many crepes are made.

**a.** How many franchises should Crepe Creations award given that it determines the prices the stall-holders can charge and that it will have a profit-sharing royalty scheme with the stall-holders? What will be the price of a crepe at each stall?

**b.** Suppose instead that each stall-holder delivers the crepes in its designated territory. How many franchises should now be awarded, given that the travel costs of the stall-holders are the same as the sunbathers? What if the stall-holders' transportation costs are only 12.5 cents per 1/4 mile from a sunbather?

4. Sony is considering manufacturing two new types of laptop: one with high performance and the other with medium performance. To do so, it crimps the high performance machine, with the result that the marginal costs of production of the two machines are identical at $500. Sony knows that there are two types of consumers for these new machines. "Techies" have indirect utility function $V_t = 2000(z-1)$ and "Normals" have indirect utility function $V_n = 1000z$. In each case, $z$ is a measure of product quality, which can be chosen from the interval $[1, 3]$. Sony also knows that there are $N_t$ techies and $N_n$ normals in the target market.

**a.** Suppose that Sony can identify the two consumer types and sell to them separately. What is its profit-maximizing strategy?

**b.** Now suppose that Sony does not know the type of each consumer. Show how Sony's profit-maximizing strategy is determined by the relative numbers of each type of consumer.

5. Assume a monopolist faces an inverse demand curve given by: $P = 22 - Q/100z$, where $z$ is an index of quality. Cost per unit is $2 + z^2$.

**a.** How do increases in product quality $z$ affect demand?

**b.** Imagine that the firm must choose one of three possible quality levels: $z = 1$; $z = 2$; and $z = 3$. Which quality choice will maximize the firm's profit? What will be the profit-maximizing output and price if the firm chooses the optimal quality level?

# REFERENCES

Hotelling, H. 1929. "Stability in Competition." *Economic Journal* 39 (January): 41–57.

Krugman, P. 2000. "Reckonings: What Price Fairness?" *The New York Times* (October 4): A16.

Macleod, W. B., G. Norman, and J. F. Thisse. 1988. "Price Discrimination and Equilibrium in Monopolistic Competition." *International Journal of Industrial Organization* 6: 429–46.

Mussa, M., and S. Rosen. 1978. "Monopoly and Product Quality." *Journal of Economic Theory* 18: 301–17.

Shapiro, C., and H. R. Varian. 1999. *Information Rules*. Boston: Harvard Business School Press.

# Appendix A   Location Choice with Two Shops

Since the shops have identical costs, the monopolist locates them symmetrically, perhaps some distance $d$ from each end of the market.

1. $d \leq 1/4$: Suppose that $d$ is less than $1/4$. Then the maximum full price that can be charged if all consumers are to be served is determined by the consumers at the market center. These consumers can be charged a price, $p$, such that, when transportation costs are added, they pay a full price equal to their reservation price, $V$. In other words, since a consumer located at $x = 1/2$ dictates the highest price that can be charged for any value of $d \leq 1/4$, the maximum price the firm can charge is $p(d)$ such that

$$p(d) + t\left(\frac{1}{2} - d\right) = V, \text{ which implies that } p(d) = V - t\left(\frac{1}{2} - d\right).$$

Aggregate profit at this price is also a function of $d$ and is given by

$$\pi(d) = \left[\,p(d) - c\,\right]N = \left(V + td - \frac{t}{2} - c\right)N.$$

This profit increases as $d$ gets larger. Thus, if $d$ is less than $1/4$, the firm can increase its profit by making $d$ larger until $d = 1/4$. Thus $d$ should never be less than $1/4$.

2. $d \geq 1/4$: Suppose now that $d$ is greater than $1/4$. Then the maximum price that can be charged if all consumers are to be served is determined by consumers at the endpoints of the market. They will pay a full price equal to their reservation price, so that the maximum price the monopolist can charge is now determined by

$$p(d) + td = V, \text{ which implies that } p(d) = V - td.$$

Aggregate profit as a function of $d$ is now

$$\pi(d) = [p(d) - c]N = (V - td - c)N.$$

This is decreasing in $d$. If $d$ is greater than $1/4$, the firm can increase its profit by making $d$ smaller until $d = 1/4$. Thus $d$ should never be greater than $1/4$.

If $d$ should not be less than $1/4$ and if it should also not be more than $1/4$, then it must be the case that optimization requires that $d$ should be exactly equal to $1/4$. The shops should be located with shop 1 a distance of $1/4$ mile from the left-hand end of the market and shop 2 a distance of $1/4$ mile from the right-hand end of the market.

# Appendix B | The Monopolist's Choice of Price When Its Shops Have Different Costs

Assume that shop 1 has marginal cost $c_1$ and shop 2 has marginal cost $c_2$. Once again, we have to consider cases in which the monopolist chooses to supply only part of the market and cases in which it chooses to supply the entire market.

**1.** Supply only part of the market:

Consider shop 1. At a price $p_1$ this shop will supply a fraction $x_1$ of the market, where $x_1$ is given by $p_1 + tx_1 = V$, which implies $x_1 = (V - p_1)/t$. Profit to this shop is then

$$\pi_1 = (p_1 - c_1)x_1 N = (p_1 - c_1)(V - p_1)N/t.$$

Differentiating with respect to $p_1$ gives the first-order condition

$$(V - 2p_1 + c_1)N/t = 0.$$

The profit-maximizing price for shop 1 is

$$p_1^* = (V + c_1)/2.$$

This simply replicates the equation we derived in "Derivation Checkpoint: Optimal Partial Market Price." It follows immediately, of course, that the profit-maximizing price for shop 2 is

$$p_2^* = (V + c_2)/2.$$

**2.** Supply the entire market:

Consider the marginal consumer—the consumer who is indifferent between buying from shop 1 and shop 2. If the entire market is to be served, then this marginal consumer will be charged a full price just equal to his reservation price. If prices are set any lower, profits can always be increased by increasing the price at both shops since there will be no loss of sales. So we know that if the marginal consumer is distance $x'$ from shop 1, $p_1 + tx' = V$, which implies that $x' = (V - p_1)/t$. Also, $p_2 + t(1 - x') = V$. Substituting for $x'$ gives

$$p_2 = V - t(1 - x') = V - t[1 - (V - p_1)/t] = 2V - t - p_1.$$

In other words, the prices at the two shops are connected. Increasing the price at shop 1 requires that the price at shop 2 be reduced if the entire market is to be served and the price charged to the marginal consumer is to be as high as possible. Profit to the monopolist is

$$\pi = (p_1 - c_1)x' N + (p_2 - c_2)(1 - x')N.$$

Substituting for $x'$ and $p_2$ gives

$$\pi(p_1) = N\left[(p_1 - c_1)\frac{(V - p_1)}{t} + (2V - p_1 - t - c_2)\left(1 - \frac{(V - p_1)}{t}\right)\right].$$

Since the monopolist must coordinate the prices at the two shops, profits are fully determined by the price at shop 1. (Of course, we could also write the profits of the monopolist as a function of the price at shop 2.)

Differentiating profit with respect to $p_1$ gives

$$\frac{\partial \pi(p_1)}{\partial p_1} = N\left[\frac{1}{t}(V - 2p_1 + c_1) - \left(1 - \frac{(V - p_1)}{t}\right) + \frac{1}{t}(2V - p_1 - t - c_2)\right].$$

Collecting terms gives the first-order condition

$$\frac{N}{t}(4V - 4p_1 + c_1 - c_2 - 2t) = 0,$$

which gives the optimal price at shop 1

$$p_L^1 = V + \frac{(c_1 - c_2 - 2t)}{4}.$$

You can confirm that this is equal to $p_L$ when $c_1 = c_2$. Substituting into the equation for $p_2$ gives the price at shop 2

$$p_L^2 = V - \frac{(c_2 - c_1 - 2t)}{4}.$$

The final question is under what circumstances is it better for the monopolist to serve only part of the market? For this to hold, it must be the case that, for example, $p_1^* > p_L^1$. This requires that

$$\frac{(V + c_1)}{2} < V + \frac{(c_1 - c_2 - 2t)}{4}, \text{ or } V < \frac{c_1 + c_2}{2} + t = \bar{c} + t,$$

where $\bar{c}$ is the mean of the marginal production costs of the two shops. So we have a rule that is nearly identical to that in the text:

1. Serve the entire market if the consumer reservation price is greater than the sum of transportation costs plus the mean of the shops' marginal costs.
2. Serve only part of the market if the consumer reservation price is less than the sum of transportation costs plus the mean of the shops' marginal costs.

The intuition behind this result is exactly the same as that presented in the main body of the chapter.

# Commodity Bundling and Tie-In Sales

# Chapter 8

On November 5, 1999, Judge Thomas Penfield Jackson issued his "Findings of Fact" in the Microsoft antitrust trial. These findings, which later served as the basis for Judge Jackson's guilty verdict (April 3, 2000), included two key conclusions that are of interest to us in this chapter. Judge Jackson argued that Microsoft's Windows operating system and its Internet Explorer Web browser constituted separate but related products. The judge then found that Microsoft's bundling or selling these two products as one package constituted an illegal effort to tie the purchase of the browser to the purchase of Windows in an effort to extend Microsoft's operating systems monopoly to the browser market. This finding raises a number of issues because, as seen in the last chapter, most firms with monopoly power do sell more than one good. What are the possible gains to the firm from linking the sale of its products? Are there gains because such a strategy stifles competition?[1] Or, are there other profit or efficiency-enhancing reasons to tie together the purchase of products? Finally, do consumers necessarily lose out from these bundling strategies?

That consumers might actually gain from bundling is easily seen when we examine the prices that Microsoft charges, not for its Windows operating system but for its software applications. The Microsoft Office suite is one of the most popular applications packages. Office XP Professional contains the Word, Excel, Outlook, Power-Point, and Access programs. In September 2003 this package was priced at $499. You could also buy the individual components separately, Word, Excel, PowerPoint, and Access selling for $229 each and Outlook for $109, a total of $1,025. Thus, it costs much less to buy the bundle of applications in Office than it does to purchase each application individually.

The concern for antitrust policy is that this type of bundling might allow a firm to extend its market power. For example, this argument was used by the European Commission when they blocked the proposed $42 billion merger between General Electric and Honeywell.[2] The action taken by the Commission was controversial since this same merger had already been approved by the U.S. Department of Justice. Nevertheless, the Commission argued that the merger would combine GE's dominant position in aircraft engine manufacture with Honeywell's dominant position in avionics and that this would allow the merged firm to bundle these complementary products, leading to substantial price discounts. Nonmerged rivals in both sectors would be unable to match these discounted prices and so would exit the market, leading to strengthened dominance of the market by GE-Honeywell. There are clear parallels here with the Microsoft case, although these were not cited by the European Commission. A sharp difference between the two cases is that in the Microsoft case Judge Jackson was commenting on actual actions whereas in the GE-Honeywell case the Commission referred to the *potential* for harm.

---

1  This is discussed in a speech by Joel Klein when Assistant Attorney General at the Antitrust Division; see http://www.usdoj.gov:80/atr/public/speeches/4707.pdf.

2  More details can be found in Geotsakis (2001) and Nalebuff (2004).

An important feature of commodity bundling is that the bundled package contains fixed proportions of the individual components: one unit of each software product in the Office suite, one operating system and Web browser in the Microsoft antitrust case, and fixed proportions of aircraft engines and avionics equipment in the GE-Honeywell case. Similarly, a fixed-price menu, whether at McDonald's or at a fancy French restaurant, will typically specify *one* appetizer, *one* entree, and *one* dessert—all sold at one price. A holiday travel package might consist of *one* return flight to London, *five* nights' accommodation, and *three* West End plays.

A related type of strategy is one in which a firm *ties* the sale of one product to the purchase of another but does not control the proportions in which the two products are consumed. Under a tying strategy the purchase of some amount of one good is conditional upon the purchase of some amount of a second, tied product. One of the classic examples of a tie-in sale was the practice adopted by IBM in the early days of business machines and computing. At that time, IBM was the dominant producer of tabulating or punch-card machines. More importantly, it sold these machines with the condition that the buyer use only IBM-produced tabulating cards. In other words, the purchase of the machine was tied to the additional purchase of IBM cards.[3] Note that this is not commodity bundling because IBM did not specify the number of cards that the consumer had to purchase.

IBM's tying arrangement was found to be a violation of the antitrust laws, but this did not stop other companies from using similar strategies. American Can and Continental Can had a policy of tying the purchase of their cans to the leasing of their can-sealing equipment. They were able to do so because the technological superiority of this equipment gave them considerable market power in that sector. These tying agreements were found to be illegal.[4] In the mid-1980s, Kodak adopted a policy of not selling parts for its large-scale photocopiers and its micrographics equipment to independent service organizations. The result was to make it difficult, if not impossible, for these operations to offer maintenance contracts to owners of the relevant Kodak equipment. A number of the independent service organizations filed suit against Kodak in 1987, alleging that the result of Kodak's policy was to allow the company to extend its monopoly in the production of parts for its equipment into a monopoly in the provision of maintenance services and that it had tied its parts to its service labor. This case dragged on for ten years. The tying claims were dropped at trial but the monopolization argument was not. Kodak lost at trial and on appeal.[5]

More recent examples of tie-in sales are not difficult to find. Whenever you buy a computer printer, you are also committing yourself to buying the ink cartridges that fit into that printer. Hewlett-Packard cartridges do not fit Canon printers and vice versa. Sony's PlayStation 2 games do not work on either a Nintendo GameCube or a Microsoft Xbox system. Note that what is tied in all these cases is just the brand of the associated product, not its quantity. You can always reduce your reliance on Hewlett-Packard ink cartridges, for example, by being very strict with yourself regarding how many drafts of a term paper you actually print! Note also that these modern examples of tie-in sales are *technology*-based rather than *contractual* as in the IBM case, a point that has emerged as having very important antitrust implications.

---

3　See *International Business Machines v. U.S.*, 298 U.S. 131 (1936). Similar charges arose repeatedly in the many private antitrust suits against IBM in the following decades.

4　*United States v. American Can Company*, 87, F. Supp. 18 (1949).

5　See McKie-Mason and Metzler (2004) for a detailed discussion of this case and its implications. We discuss this case in greater detail in Chapter 17.

With this background we now turn to a more formal analysis of a monopolist's incentive to bundle together products or to have tie-in sales.

# 8.1  COMMODITY BUNDLING AND PRICE DISCRIMINATION

We begin with a story told almost thirty years ago by Nobel Laureate George Stigler, who was one of the first to understand bundling as a mechanism for price discrimination.[6] At the time that he published his brief analysis he was responding to a recent Supreme Court case involving the movie industry. Throughout the 1950s and 1960s, airing older Hollywood films provided a good part of television fare. Film distributors who owned the rights to the films would sell presentation rights for a fee to local television stations. However, they rarely sold films individually. Instead, they sold them in packages typically combining screen gems such as *Casablanca* and *Treasure of the Sierra Madre* with such "grade B" losers as *Gorilla Man* and *Tear Gas Squad*.[7] Stigler's insight was to recognize that while every television station would value the first two films (or others of similar quality) more than the last two films, the relative valuation of the two types of movies would vary from station to station. Such differences provided a motive for the observed bundling.

A modified version of Stigler's example is as follows. Suppose that there are two films, X and Y, and two stations (located in different cities), A and B. Each station's reservation prices for the two films are as follows:

|  | *Maximum Willingness to Pay for Film X* | *Maximum Willingness to Pay for Film Y* |
| --- | --- | --- |
| Station A | $8,000 | $2,500 |
| Station B | $7,000 | $3,000 |

As we saw in Chapter 5, successful price discrimination must surmount the twin problems of identifying which station is which and then avoiding arbitrage between stations. If this is not possible and the distributor is forced to charge a uniform price for each film, its best bet is to charge $7,000 for film X and $2,500 for film Y. At these prices, both stations will buy both films, and the distributor's total revenue will be $19,000.

Bundling, however, permits further revenues to be earned. Instead of selling the two films separately, suppose that the distributor offers the two films only as a bundle for a combined price of $10,000. Since both stations value the bundle at least this highly, the distributor will sell both films to both stations, but now its revenue rises to $20,000.

The reason that bundling raises revenue is straightforward. Offering the films unbundled means that, if both stations are to be sold both films, the highest price that can be charged for any specific film is the minimum reservation price either station would pay for that film—$7,000 for film X and $2,500 for film Y. When the products are bundled, the highest bundle price that can be charged is the minimum of the sums of each station's reservation prices. This permits additional surplus extraction

6  Stigler (1968).
7  See *United States v. Loew's Inc.*, 371 U.S. 38 (1962).

from both stations. Bundling extracts more from station A because it permits the distributor to circumvent the low value that station A places on film Y and to exploit its relatively high valuation of film X. Similarly, bundling avoids the need to charge a low price for film X in order to induce station B to buy it by exploiting that station's relatively high willingness to pay for film Y.

Stigler's insight into bundling as a way to price discriminate was surely valid. However, his analysis was incomplete on two fronts. First, his model included no discussion of production costs. The movie seller and television station example treats the distributor's costs as either sunk or nonexistent. The second limitation of Stigler's model was that it failed to consider the strategy of *mixed bundling*, that is, selling both products individually as well as in a bundle. Adams and Yellen (1976) address these issues and their paper has become the standard piece on commodity bundling. We now turn to a presentation of their analysis.

Assume that there are two goods, labeled 1 and 2. Each of these goods is produced with constant marginal (and average) cost, denoted by $c_1$ and $c_2$, respectively. In other words, we assume that there are no cost advantages of multiproduct production. In particular, there are no scope economies of the type discussed in Chapter 4. Accordingly, the cost of producing a bundle or a package consisting of one unit of each good is $c_B = c_1 + c_2$.

We will also assume that a consumer buys exactly one unit of each good per unit of time provided that the price charged is less than his or her reservation price for that good. The consumer's reservation price or maximum willingness to pay for good 1 is $R_1$, and the reservation price for good 2 is $R_2$. Finally, we assume that the consumer's reservation price for a commodity bundle consisting of one unit of each good is $R_B = R_1 + R_2$. This final assumption, that the reservation price for the bundle is the sum of the reservation prices for the individual goods, is a common one (and one made by Stigler as well). Yet the assumption is, at least in some circumstances, restrictive. If the two goods are complementary goods, such as nuts and bolts, the assumption is almost certainly false. One would expect that the willingness to pay for bolts would be quite low in the absence of any nuts and vice versa. To put it differently, for complementary goods, the reservation price for the bundle would likely be higher than the sum of the separate reservation prices for each good. Yet while the assumption that $R_B = R_1 + R_2$ is restrictive, it is also useful. It permits us to focus explicitly on the price discrimination motive for bundling. We return to the case of complementary goods in Section 8.3.

Suppose that consumers differ in their separate valuations of the two goods—that is, the values of $R_1$, $R_2$, and $R_B$ vary across consumers. Some consumers have a high $R_1$ and a low $R_2$; for others just the reverse is true. Some place a high value on both goods. For others, $R_1$ and $R_2$ are both quite low. If we draw a diagram with $R_1$ on the horizontal axis and $R_2$ on the vertical axis as in Figure 8-1, then our assumptions allow us to describe each consumer's reservation prices by a point in the $(R_1, R_2)$ quadrant.

It might be helpful to use a specific example, such as a restaurant menu. We are all familiar with restaurants that offer an à la carte menu from which we can pick individual items, and a set menu that contains perhaps an appetizer and an entrée or an entrée and a dessert sold as a bundle.

Figure 8-1 illustrates the simplest pricing strategy for the monopolist offering two goods. Sell the two products separately at their monopoly prices, $p_1^M$ and $p_2^M$. (We leave aside for the moment just how these monopoly prices might be identified.) In

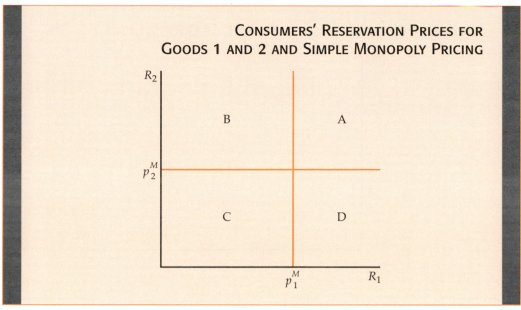

CONSUMERS' RESERVATION PRICES FOR
GOODS 1 AND 2 AND SIMPLE MONOPOLY PRICING

FIGURE

**8-1**

At monopoly prices $p_1^M$ and $p_2^M$, group A buys both goods, group B buys good 2, and group D buys good 1.

our example, this might be a restaurant that sells soup at price $p_1^M$ and a sandwich at price $p_2^M$. Buying both goods costs $p_1^M + p_2^M$. With these prices, consumers are partitioned into four groups. Consumers in group A have reservation prices for both goods that are greater than the price being charged and therefore purchase one unit of each product. Consumers in group B have reservation prices for good 2 that are higher than its price, $p_2^M$, and so buy good 2. However, their reservation prices for good 1 are lower than the price $p_1^M$, so they do not buy good 1. Similarly, consumers in group D have reservation prices for good 1 that are higher than its price, so they buy good 1. However, they do not buy good 2. Consumers in group C have reservation prices for both goods that are lower than the prices being charged and so do not purchase either product.

Now suppose that the monopolist adopts a *pure bundling* strategy in which the two goods can be purchased only as a bundle at a fixed price of $p_B$. In our restaurant setting, this would mean that the only deal on offer is soup plus a sandwich at a fixed price of $p_B$. An important feature of such pure bundling is that the price of the bundle will be less than or equal to the sum of the two monopoly prices, that is, $p_B \le p_1^M + p_2^M$. Since the individual monopoly prices maximize the firm's profit in each market individually, setting a bundle price that exceeds the sum of the two individual prices cannot possibly be optimal.

The bundle price is illustrated in Figure 8-2 as a straight line with intercept on each axis of $p_B$ and so with slope of minus one. Now consumers are partitioned into two groups. Each consumer in group E has reservation prices for the two goods the sum of which is greater than $p_B$, and so will buy the package. By contrast, each consumer in group F has reservation prices for the two goods the sum of which is less than $p_B$, and so will not buy the package.

FIGURE

**8-2**

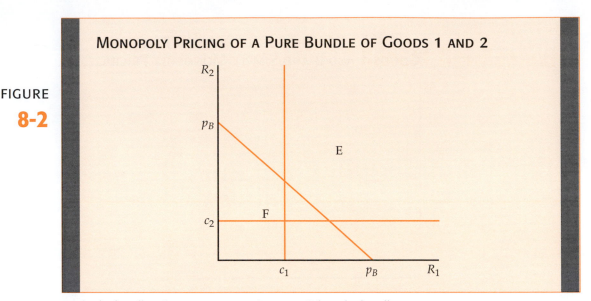

MONOPOLY PRICING OF A PURE BUNDLE OF GOODS 1 AND 2

At the bundle price $p_B$, consumers in group E buy the bundle.

Figure 8-2 illustrates an interesting feature of the pure bundling strategy. There are consumers who, as a result of the two goods being offered as a bundle, are able to buy one of the goods even though their reservation prices for that good are less than its marginal production cost. This is true in the case of good 1 for all consumers in group E whose reservation price for good 1 is less than $c_1$, and in the case of good 2 for all consumers in group E whose reservation prices for good 2 are less than $c_2$.

Now consider the hybrid case of *mixed bundling*. Here, the monopolist offers to sell the two goods separately at specified prices, respectively, of $p_1$ and $p_2$ (which are not necessarily the monopoly prices), and also sells them as a bundle at price $p_B$ (not necessarily the pure bundle price). Of course, for this to make sense it must again be the case that $p_B < p_1 + p_2$. Figure 8-3 illustrates such a strategy. The restaurant offers the possibility of buying either soup or a sandwich individually at the stated prices or buying them as a set meal at price $p_B$.

Once again, we find that consumers are partitioned by this strategy into four groups. The determinants of these groups are, however, slightly different from those considered previously. What we need to do is to determine whether a consumer will prefer to buy only one of the two goods, the bundle, or nothing.

Clearly, anyone who values good 1 at more than $p_1$ and good 2 at more than $p_2$, that is, anyone who is willing to buy both goods at the individual prices, will buy the bundle since its price is less than the sum of the individual prices. Consider now a consumer whose reservation price for good 2 is less than $p_2$. If this consumer buys anything, he or she will buy either the bundle or only good 1. Of course, the consumer will make the choice that gives the greatest consumer surplus. Suppose then that the reservation prices are $R_1$ for good 1 and $R_2$ for good 2. If the bundle is purchased, then the consumer pays $p_B$ and gets consumer surplus of $CS_B = R_1 + R_2 - p_B$. If only good 1 is purchased, consumer surplus of $CS_1 = R_1 - p_1$ is obtained.

This type of consumer will buy only good 1 if two conditions are satisfied. First, $CS_1 > CS_B$, which requires that $R_2 < p_B - p_1$. Second, $CS_1 > 0$, which requires that $R_1 > p_1$.

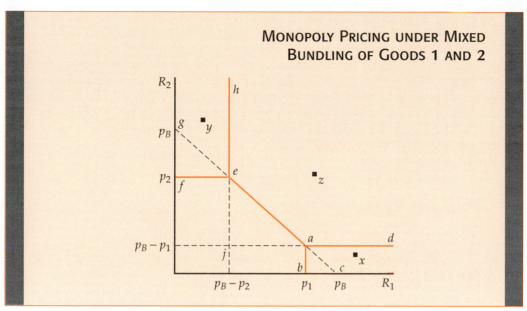

MONOPOLY PRICING UNDER MIXED
BUNDLING OF GOODS 1 AND 2

FIGURE

8-3

The firm sets prices $p_1$ for good 1, $p_2$ for good 2, and $p_B < p_1 p_2$ for the bundle.

The difference $p_B - p_1$ is easily illustrated in Figure 8-3. Since the line $p_B p_B$ has a slope of minus one, the distance $ab$ is equal to the distance $bc$, which is equal to $p_B - p_1$. So all points below the line $jad$ represent consumers whose reservation prices for good 2 are such that $R_2 < p_B - p_1$ and, of course, all points to the right of $ab$ represent consumers for whom $R_1 > p_1$. So all consumers with reservation prices in the region $dab$, such as consumer $x$, buy only good 1.

By exactly the same argument a consumer will buy only good 2 if two conditions are satisfied: first, $R_1 < p_B - p_2$, and second, $R_2 > p_2$. The difference $p_B - p_2$ is illustrated in Figure 8-3 by the line $jeh$ and all points above $fe$ represent consumers for whom $R_2 > p_2$. Therefore, all consumers with reservation prices in the region $feh$, such as consumer $y$, will buy only good 2.

Now consider a consumer for whom $R_2 > p_B - p_1$ and $R_1 > p_B - p_2$. This is a consumer whose reservation price for good 1 is to the right of $jeh$ and for good 2 is above $jad$. If such a consumer buys anything at all he or she will buy the bundle since this gives more consumer surplus than either only good 1 or only good 2. For this consumer actually to buy the bundle it is then necessary that $R_1 + R_2 > p_B$, which means that the reservation prices must put the consumer above the line $caeg$ in Figure 8-3. In other words, all consumers in the region $daeh$, such as consumer $z$, will buy the bundle.

This leaves only the region $feab$. What will be the choice of these types of consumers? Their reservation prices are less than the individual prices of the two goods, so they will not buy either good individually. In addition, the sums of their reservation prices are less than the bundle price, so they will not buy the bundle. Consumers in $feab$ do not buy anything.

When we compare either pure or mixed bundling with simple monopoly pricing, it is clear that mixed bundling always increases the monopolist's sales. What is less clear is whether bundling will increase the monopolist's profits. What we should expect is that the profit impact of commodity bundling will depend upon the distribution of consumer preferences for the goods on offer and the costs of making those goods. An example will serve to illustrate this and some of the other ideas introduced so far.

Assume that the monopolist knows that it has four consumers, A, B, C, and D, each interested in buying the two goods, 1 and 2. The marginal cost of good 1 is $c_1$ = \$100 and of good 2 is $c_2$ = \$150. Each consumer has reservation prices for these two goods as given in Table 8-1 and buys exactly one unit of either good in any period so long as its price is less than the reservation price for that good. Each consumer will consider buying the goods as a bundle provided that the bundle price is less than the sum of the reservation prices.

**TABLE 8-1**

### CONSUMER RESERVATION PRICES

| Consumer | Reservation Price for Good 1 ($) | Reservation Price for Good 2 ($) | Sum of Reservation Prices |
|---|---|---|---|
| A | 50 | 450 | 500 |
| B | 250 | 275 | 525 |
| C | 300 | 220 | 520 |
| D | 450 | 50 | 500 |

Suppose that the monopolist decides to adopt simple monopoly pricing. Table 8-2 allows us to identify the profit-maximizing monopoly prices for the two goods. Profit from good 1 is maximized at \$450 by setting a price of \$250 and selling to consumers B, C, and D. Profit from good 2 is maximized at \$300 by setting a price of \$450 and selling only to consumer A. Total profit from simple monopoly pricing is, therefore, \$750.

Now consider the pure bundling strategy. The firm can choose a bundle price of (1) \$525, which will attract only consumer B; (2) \$520, which will attract consumers B and C; or (3) \$500, which will attract all four consumers. The third strategy is

**TABLE 8-2**

### DETERMINATION OF SIMPLE MONOPOLY PRICES

| | GOOD 1: MARGINAL COST $100 | | | | GOOD 2: MARGINAL COST $150 | | |
|---|---|---|---|---|---|---|---|
| Price | Quantity Demanded | Total Revenue ($) | Profit ($) | Price | Quantity Demanded | Total Revenue ($) | Profit ($) |
| 450 | 1 | 450 | 350 | 450 | 1 | 450 | 300 |
| 300 | 2 | 600 | 400 | 275 | 2 | 550 | 250 |
| 250 | 3 | 750 | 450 | 220 | 3 | 660 | 210 |
| 50 | 4 | 200 | −200 | 50 | 4 | 200 | −400 |

preferable because it yields a total profit of 4($500 − $100 − $150), or $1,000. Pure bundling is, in this case, preferable to simple monopoly pricing. Notice, however, that consumer A is able to obtain good 1 and consumer D is able to obtain good 2 even though they each value the relevant good at less than its marginal production costs.

Can a mixed bundling strategy do better? Suppose that the monopolist merely combines the simple monopoly and pure bundling strategies. It sets a price of $250 for good 1, $450 for good 2, and $500 for the bundle. Consumer A is indifferent between buying the bundle or only good 2. However, the seller is definitely not indifferent. The seller makes a profit of $300 if consumer A buys just good 2 but only $250 if consumer A buys the bundle, thus the seller would like to find a way to encourage consumer A to opt only for good 2. Consumer D is willing to consider either the bundle or buying only good 1. If consumer D buys the bundle, there is no consumer surplus; while if consumer D buys only good 1, there is consumer surplus of $200. Therefore, consumer D will buy only good 1 with profit to the monopolist of $150. In this case, the monopolist would actually prefer that consumer D buy the bundle but is unable to induce the consumer to do so without adversely affecting overall profits. Finally, consumers B and C are each willing to buy the bundle with profit to the monopolist of $500. So this mixed bundling strategy gives the monopolist a total profit of $900 or $950, depending upon whether consumer A buys the bundle or only good 2. This is certainly better than simple monopoly pricing but not as good as pure bundling.

The monopolist can, however, do better than this. Once mixed bundling is considered, the seller can change the prices of both the bundle and the individual goods. Suppose, for example, that the seller sets the price of good 1 at $450, the price of good 2 at $450, and the price of the bundle at $520. Now consumer A will buy good 2 but will not consider the bundle, consumer D will buy good 1 but not the bundle, and consumers B and C will buy the bundle. Total profit is $300 + $270 + $270 + $350 = $1,190.

This is actually the best that the monopolist can do in this case. The monopolist has extracted the entire consumer surplus of consumers A, C, and D and all but $5 of the consumer surplus of consumer B. In other words, the monopolist has done nearly as well as it would have done if it had been able to adopt first-degree price discrimination.

Mixed bundling (in which the bundle price is less than the price of buying each component separately) is always at least as profitable as pure bundling. The reason is simple enough to see. The worst that a mixed bundling strategy can do is to replicate the pure bundling strategy—by setting arbitrarily high individual prices and a bundle price equal to the pure bundle price—but it will usually be possible to improve on this. However, it is not always the case that some sort of bundling is more profitable than no bundling at all. A drawback to bundling—one illustrated in the previous example—is that it can lead to an outcome in which some of the consumers buying the bundle actually have a reservation price for one of the goods that is less than marginal production cost. Clearly, the firm would prefer that these consumers not be able to buy the good in question. Our example also demonstrates that any bundling is likely to be profitable only when the variation in consumer valuations of the goods is significant. In our example, consumers A and D—who buy a single good—have very different valuations of the individual goods. In contrast, consumers B and C—who buy the bundled good—have very similar valuations. Adams and Yellen (1976) make clear that the gains from bundling arise from the differences in consumer valuations.

Some people may value an appetizer relatively highly (soup on a cold day), others may value dessert relatively higher (Baked Alaska, unavailable at home), but all may wish to pay roughly the same amount for a complete dinner. The à la carte menu is designed to capture consumer surplus from those gastronomes with extremely high valuations of particular dishes, while the complete dinner is designed to retain those with lower variance. (p. 488)

We can see the same basic point in the context of the Stigler example above. If station A valued both movies at $8,000, and station B valued both at $3,500, the differences in the relative valuation of the products would vanish. In that case, bundling is no longer a profitable strategy.

It is because the bundle price, $p_B$, is less than the sum of the individual prices, $p_1 + p_2$, that commodity bundling may be viewed as discriminatory pricing. The lower bundle price serves to attract consumers who place a relatively low value on either of the two goods but are willing to pay a reasonable sum for the bundle. The two separate prices serve to extract surplus from those customers who have a great willingness to pay for only one of the products. We would therefore expect most multiproduct firms with monopoly power to engage in some sort of mixed bundling.

Mixed bundling is in fact a common practice. As noted at the start of this chapter, Microsoft sells its Office applications both individually and as a package. Similarly, restaurants serve combination platters and also offer items à la carte. Resorts often offer both food and lodging or just lodging. These common practices reflect the fact that bundling is an effective way to implement price discrimination. However, it also may be a tool to limit competition. We address this issue further in Section 8.4.

## Practice Problem 8.1

A cable company has two services. One service is the Basic Service channel. The other is the Walt Disney Movie channel. The potential subscribers for the services—students, families, hotels, schools, young adults, and pensioners—regard the two services as separate alternatives, that is, not as complementary products. Thus, the demands for the two services are completely unrelated for each and every consumer. Each buyer is characterized by a pair of reservation prices as shown in the following table.

**RESERVATION PRICES FOR EACH CABLE SERVICE BY TYPE OF SUBSCRIBER**

|  | Basic Service ($) | Disney Channel ($) |
| --- | --- | --- |
| Students | 5 | 15 |
| Families | 11 | 9 |
| Hotels | 14 | 6 |
| Schools | 4 | 16 |
| Young Adults | 0 | 17 |
| Pensioners | 17 | 0 |

The marginal cost of each service is $3. Assume there are equal numbers of consumers in each category.

a. If the services are sold separately and not offered as a bundle, what price should the cable operator set for each service? What profits will it earn? Which consumers will subscribe to which service?

b. Suppose that the operator decides to pursue a mixed bundling strategy. What price should be set for the bundled service? What price should be set for each service if purchased individually? Which consumers buy which options, and what are the cable operator's profits?

c. How would your answers to the first two questions change if the marginal cost of producing each service had been $10 instead of $3?

# 8.2 REQUIRED TIE-IN SALES

Tie-in sales arrangements differ from bundling in two respects. First, they tie together the purchase of two or more products without prescribing the amount of at least one of them that must be bought. Second, the tied goods typically exhibit a complementary relationship with each other whereas bundled goods need not. We can use an example to illustrate why this is an effective marketing strategy.

Consider an imaginary product called a Magicam that is produced by only one firm, Rowling Corp. A Magicam is much like an ordinary camera with one exception—the figures in a Magicam photograph can actually move and even wave back at the picture viewer because of Rowling's patented, magical method of placing the images on film. In all other respects, however, the Magicam is essentially identical to a typical camera. In particular, both a Magicam and a regular camera can be used to produce anywhere from one to a large number of pictures per day or per month. That is, neither product imposes any serious limitation on how many pictures an owner will take per period of time.

This fact does not mean that every consumer who has a Magicam will take a large number of snapshots. After all, they have to pay for the film and spend time in taking pictures rather than doing other things. Presumably, consumers differ in this regard. Suppose that there are one thousand low-demand consumers each with a monthly demand for pictures described by $Q = 12 - P$, and one thousand high-demand consumers each with a monthly demand for pictures given by $Q = 16 - P$. In other words, if cartridges of film were free the first group of consumers would each take 12 pictures per month and the second group 16 pictures. Unfortunately, Rowling Corp. has no way, magical or otherwise, of identifying these different types.

Because of the sensitive nature of the technology incorporated in Magicams we assume that Rowling Corp. does not sell the cameras but rather uses its monopoly power to offer them on monthly lease agreements that include servicing the camera to maintain its magical properties.[8] Given that the lease fee is set such that each of the two thousand consumers leases a Magicam we can ignore the manufacturing costs of the cameras—these are effectively fixed costs for Rowling Corp. The same is not true for the camera film. Suppose that film production takes place under competitive conditions and that the marginal cost of producing film is $2 per photograph that the film can take. This means, of course, that film will be priced at the competitive price of $2 per picture. Now consider Rowling Corp.'s potential strategies for leasing its cameras.

If a Magicam and camera film are all that is necessary for producing the wonderful pictures, Rowling Corp. might find the situation somewhat frustrating. Because it

---

8 This is actually the strategy that IBM, Kodak, and Xerox used initially with their machines.

cannot tell one type of consumer from another, it cannot easily lease its Magicams at different prices to each type. About the best that Rowling Corp. can do is to charge a monthly rental rate of $50. Why? Because this is the consumer surplus earned by a low-demand consumer faced with a film price of $2 per picture and Rowling Corp. cannot price discriminate across the two consumer types. (You should check that this is indeed the consumer surplus for a low-demand consumer when film is priced at $2 per picture.)

Both types of consumer will lease the camera. High-demand consumers will use it to take 14 pictures per month while the low-demand consumers will take 10 pictures per month. Rowling earns a monthly profit of $50 on each of the two thousand cameras leased—one thousand to the low-demand and one thousand to the high-demand types—or $100,000 per month.

The situation is not desperate, but like any good profit-maximizer Rowling wonders if somehow it can do better. After thinking a bit, Rowling management realizes that with a bit of redesign of the camera and some clever marketing it can tie the lease of a Magicam to the use of its own Magifilm. This gives Rowling an idea. Assuming that it, too, can produce film for $2, why not implement a tying strategy by a redesign that makes it impossible to use a Magicam unless one uses Magifilm and then price the film at $4 per exposure?

Both low- and high-demand consumers now pay $4 at the margin for a picture. The low-demand consumers will therefore reduce their monthly demand for Magicam photos to just 8. Note, though, that if low-demand consumers pay only the $4 per picture price of Magifilm, they will enjoy a surplus of $32. This surplus is the rental rate at which Rowling can lease the Magicam. (Notice the connection between this and our discussion of two-part pricing in Chapter 6.) As a result, Rowling earns $32 from each of the one thousand low-demand consumers in camera rentals and $16 from each in cartridge sales, giving a total profit of $48,000 from the low-demand customers.

High-demand consumers will also lease the Magicam at $32. However, at $4 per picture in film costs, these consumers will shoot 12 photos per month. Hence, Rowling earns a profit of $32 on cameras and $24 on film cartridges from each of the one thousand high-demand customers, giving a total profit from this group of $56,000. In total, Rowling now earns a combined profit of $104,000—greater than the $100,000 it earned without the tie-in. It has achieved this profit increase by exploiting its ability to *tie* the use of its camera to the use of its film.

To understand the way that tying helps Rowling, first note that high-demand consumers receive a quantity discount under either of the two strategies. When the Magicam is leased for $50 and the film is purchased competitively at $2 per photo, high-demand consumers take 14 photos and pay only $5.57 per photo, while low-demand consumers take 10 photos and pay $7 for each. Under the tied film arrangement, high-demand consumers pay a total charge of $80 for 12 photos, or $6.67 per photo. By contrast, low-demand consumers pay a total of $64 and take only 8 photos per month, or $8 per photo. Thus, the tied sale is not attractive solely because it permits a quantity discount.

What tying does accomplish is to permit Rowling to solve the identification and arbitrage problems by exploiting its post-lease monopoly in the supply of Magifilm. Now the high-demand consumers are revealed by their film purchases and the quantity discount is put to work in a profit-increasing way. Nor is arbitrage capable of undoing the discrimination. After all, both the camera and the film are readily available to all consumers at the same prices. Given that a single Magicam can serve either a low-demand or a high-demand consumer equally well, solving the identification and arbitrage problems can only be achieved by tying its use to another product whose volume does change depending on the consumer's type. No consumer will ever lease more than one Magicam, but they will differ in terms of how much Magifilm they purchase.

Now let's take Rowling one step further. The low- and high-demand functions we have used may look familiar to you. They are the same ones we used in Chapter 6 in our discussion of quantity discounts with second-degree price discrimination. In fact, if you look back at that earlier example you may get an idea of how Rowling can package the camera to do even better. For example, suppose that Rowling redesigns the Magicam so that the cartridge of Magifilm becomes an integral part of the camera that only Rowling's film developers can take out without destroying the camera.

Rowling can then design two varieties of its new, integrated product, one of which has a 10-picture capacity and the other a 14-picture capacity.[9] Rowling offers to lease the 10-picture Magicam for $70 per month and the 14-picture Magicam for $88 per month. In both cases, the lease agreement also offers free developing as well as free replacement of the cartridge. Our analysis in this chapter makes it clear what will happen. Low-demand consumers will lease the 10-picture Magicam while high-demand consumers will lease the 14-picture Magicam. Rowling now earns an even greater profit of $50,000 + $58,000 = $108,000. This technological integration plus the monthly leasing agreement has enabled Rowling to identify and separate the different customers even more effectively.

## Practice Problem 8.2

Consider the Magicam story in the text. Again, let there be one thousand high-demand and one thousand low-demand consumers and let them have inverse demand functions of $P = 16 - Q$ and $P = 12 - Q$, respectively. Show that the price of $4 per photo is, indeed, the profit-maximizing price for Magifilm when the film is sold separately from the camera. Now suppose that Rowling Corp. produces the integrated camera plus film cartridge in 8-picture and 14-picture varieties. What rental rates will be charged for the two varieties? What are Rowling Corp.'s profits? Finally, suppose that there are one thousand low-demand consumers and $N_h$ high-demand consumers. How many high-demand consumers would there have to be for Rowling to wish to manufacture only the 14-picture variety of integrated Magicam given that the other variety is

a. 10-picture
b. 8-picture

We have seen that, like bundling, sales tie-ins can be used to implement price discrimination schemes. This is no doubt one reason that such tie-ins are frequently used, especially in situations where one of the components is, like our fictitious Magicam, capable of different intensities of use covering a very large range. Thus, as noted earlier, IBM tied the use of its punch card machines to its own punch cards in the early days of computing. Similarly, Xerox initially tied the sale of its copying machines to the use of paper that Xerox sold. However, these and other early tie-ins were typically the

---

9  With marginal film costs of $2, these are the socially efficient quantities to offer.

result of contractual requirements. Other punch cards and other paper would work in the IBM and Xerox machines. It was the lease contract offered by the companies that prevented customers from using these alternatives. More modern tie-ins are typically a technological tie-in of the Magicam and Magifilm type. Polaroid instant picture cameras use only Polaroid film. Nintendo 64 players and Game Boys use only Nintendo or Nintendo-licensed games. The leading maker of computer printers, Hewlett-Packard, designs its printers so that they use only Hewlett-Packard cartridges.

However, as we cautioned above, both bundling and tie-in sales can reduce the degree of competition in at least one of the markets. For example, Rowling may face stiff competition from other, admittedly less magical, cameras, but once a consumer has signed the lease agreement on a Magicam Rowling is able to leverage its technological monopoly in camera-making to create a monopoly in the camera film market. Thus, as with bundling, tied sales may have potentially anticompetitive effects, which is undoubtedly why they have been the source of numerous antitrust cases.

We defer this issue for the moment. Instead we turn more explicitly to another aspect that often characterizes both bundling and tie-in sales: that the bundled or tied goods typically exhibit a complementary demand relationship. As we shall see, this feature has important implications for the monopolist's profit-maximizing strategy.

## 8.3 COMPLEMENTARY GOODS, NETWORK EXTERNALITIES, AND MONOPOLY PRICING

The Magicam and Magifilm are, like real-life cameras and film, complementary goods. There is no point in buying a camera—magical or otherwise—unless one also buys film. Likewise, there is little point in owning a CD player without also purchasing CDs, in owning a PC without also buying some software applications, or in buying bolts without buying nuts. In passenger airline manufacture it is necessary to have both engines and avionics equipment.

Sometimes the market for at least one of the complementary goods is reasonably competitive. Other times, the same firm may control both goods. However, there is a third possibility. This is that each of the complementary goods is produced by a different monopolist. Thus, there might be just one camera corporation and one, separate, film company. As the French mathematical economist Augustin Cournot recognized over 150 years ago, this last situation may have particularly bad implications for both profit and efficiency.

Cournot's basic argument can be demonstrated fairly simply. For this purpose, let us assume that the two complementary goods in question are nuts and bolts. A separate monopoly firm produces each and, to keep things simple, marginal production cost for each firm is zero. (We provide in the Derivation Checkpoint: Firms with Complementary Goods and Nonzero Marginal Cost an alternative solution in which we allow the two firms to have different marginal costs.) The two goods are perfect complements. A consumer who wants to purchase 100 bolts also wishes to buy 100 nuts. In other words, the two goods are always consumed in the fixed proportion of one-to-one.[10] For this reason, consumers care only about the combined price, $P_B + P_N$, in

---

10 This makes our example one of bundling rather than tie-in sales. The connection to the Microsoft and GE-Honeywell cases should be clear.

determining their demand. As you can see, the demands for the two products are clearly interrelated. The price of bolts will affect the demand for nuts and vice versa.

Suppose that the demand for nut and bolt pairs is given by the demand function

$$Q = 12 - (P_B + P_N). \tag{8.1}$$

Since consumers always buy the two goods together—one nut for every bolt— equation (8.1) also describes the separate demand facing each monopolist. That is, the bolt producer and the nut producer each face demand curves

$$\begin{aligned} Q_B &= 12 - (P_B + P_N) & \text{Bolt Demand Curve} \\ Q_N &= 12 - (P_B + P_N) & \text{Nut Demand Curve} \end{aligned} \tag{8.2}$$

 # Derivation Checkpoint

## Firms with Complementary Goods and Nonzero Marginal Costs

Assume that demand for nuts and for bolts are given respectively by $Q_N = Q_B = A - P_B - P_N$. Suppose also that the marginal cost of the nut producer is $c_N$ and that of the bolt producer is $c_B$. The profit of the nut producer is $\pi_N = (P_N - c_N)Q_N = (P_N - c_N)(A - P_B - P_N)$. Differentiate with respect to $P_N$ to give the first-order condition

$$\frac{\partial \pi_N}{\partial p_N} = (A - P_B - 2P_N + c_N) = 0.$$

This gives the nut price rule

$$P_N = (A + c_N - P_B)/2.$$

It follows immediately that the bolt price rule is

$$P_B = (A + c_B - P_N)/2.$$

Solving these two equations for $P_N$ gives

$$P_N = \frac{1}{2}\left(A + c_N - \frac{1}{2}(A + c_B - P_N)\right),$$

which simplifies to $P_N = \dfrac{A + 2c_N - c_B}{3}$. So we have also that $P_B = \dfrac{A + 2c_B - c_N}{3}$.

If the two firms merge and set a price of $P$ for a nut and bolt product pair, profit of the merged firm is

$$\pi_M = (P - c_B - c_N)(A - P).$$

The first-order condition is

$$\frac{\partial \pi_M}{\partial P} = A - 2P + c_B + c_N = 0,$$

which gives the combined price

$$P = \frac{A + c_B + c_N}{2}.$$

The merger reduces the combined price of nuts and bolts, benefiting both producers and consumers.

---

The problem with separate production is easy to see. The nut producer's pricing decision affects the bolt producer's demand curve, and vice versa. A change in the price of nuts not only changes the quantity demanded in the nut market but also in the bolt market. This implies that any one firm's pricing decision has profit implications not just for itself but for the other firm as well. In other words, the pricing policy of either of the two firms imposes an externality on the other firm. In this situation, we might reasonably expect that a merger or creation of a business network to coordinate the pricing decisions of the two firms will offer significant advantages for them by at least partially correcting the market failure associated with the externality. Less obvious but, as we shall see, nonetheless true, it is also possible that consumers will gain from such coordination.

To see the problem that this can cause, we need to calculate the profit-maximizing decisions of the two firms both without and with coordination between them. We begin with the situation in which the firms act independently. We can rewrite the demand curves of equation (8.2) in inverse form.

$$P_B = (12 - P_N) - Q_B \quad \text{Inverse Demand Curve for Bolts}$$
$$P_N = (12 - P_B) - Q_N \quad \text{Inverse Demand Curve for Nuts}$$

(8.3)

From this we know that the marginal revenue curve facing each firm is

$$MR_B = (12 - P_N) - 2Q_B \quad \text{Bolt Marginal Revenue}$$
$$MR_N = (12 - P_B) - 2Q_N \quad \text{Nut Marginal Revenue}$$

(8.4)

Notice that, just as each firm's demand curve depends on the other firm's price, so each firm's marginal revenue is affected by the other firm's price decision.

We know that profit maximization requires that each firm operates where marginal revenue equals marginal cost, here assumed to be zero. So, setting each of the equations in (8.4) to zero and solving for $Q_B$ and $Q_N$ gives

$$Q_B = (12 - P_N)/2 \quad \text{Bolt Production}$$
$$Q_N = (12 - P_B)/2 \quad \text{Nut Production}$$

(8.5)

If we now substitute these outputs into the individual demand curves we obtain each firm's optimal price as a function of the other firm's price, as follows

$$P_B = (12 - P_N)/2 \quad \text{Bolt Price Rule}$$
$$P_N = (12 - P_B)/2 \quad \text{Nut Price Rule}$$

(8.6)

These equations show that each producer's profit-maximizing price depends on the price chosen by the other firm. More specifically, the equations identify the firm's best or profit-maximizing choice of price given the price chosen by the other firm. Whatever price is being charged by the nut firm is communicated to the bolt firm through the effect on the demand curve facing the bolt producer. If nut prices are high, the demand curve will be low. Alternatively, if nut prices are low, bolt demand will be strong. Taking the demand curve as given, the bolt producer simply selects the price–quantity combination that maximizes profits using the familiar $MR = MC$ rule.

We can identify the price equilibrium in the two markets by graphing equations (8.6) in a diagram with the two prices $P_B$ and $P_N$ on the axes. This is done in Figure 8-4. The more gently sloped line gives the bolt company's best choice of $P_B$ for every alternative value of the nut price, $P_N$. For example, if the nut price is zero, the profit-maximizing bolt price is $6. If the nut price rises to somewhere near $12, the profit-maximizing bolt price falls to near zero. Higher nut prices reduce bolt demand and lower the bolt firm's profit-maximizing price. The more steeply sloped line describes the same strategic choices from the perspective of the nut company. This line gives the best choice of $P_N$ for every choice of $P_B$.

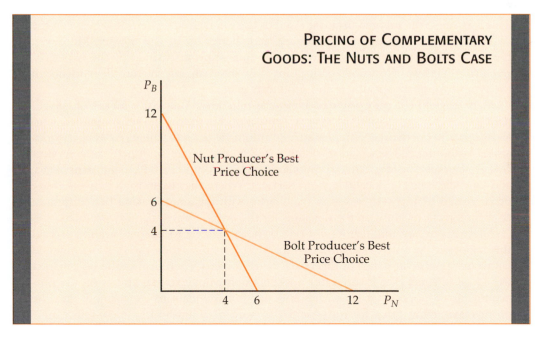

**PRICING OF COMPLEMENTARY GOODS: THE NUTS AND BOLTS CASE**

FIGURE

**8-4**

Equilibrium occurs at the intersection. At this point, each firm has selected a price that is best given the price choice of the other firm. Accordingly, neither has an incentive to change. In order to identify this equilibrium, we substitute the equation for the nut price, for example, into the equation for the bolt price. This gives

$$P_B = \frac{1}{2}(12 - P_N) = \frac{1}{2}\left(12 - \frac{1}{2}(12 - P_B)\right) = \frac{12}{4} + \frac{P_B}{4} \text{ so that } \frac{3P_B}{4} = 3, \text{ or } P_B = 4.$$

(8.7)

This tells us that the profit-maximizing bolt price is $P_B$ = \$4. Substituting into equation (8.6) also gives the profit-maximizing nut price as $P_N$ = \$4. As a result, the combined nut/bolt price is $P_B + P_N$ = \$8, and from the demand equation (8.1), the number of bolt and nut pairs sold is 4. The bolt firm makes profits of $P_B Q_B$ = \$16, as does the nut producer.

Now consider the outcome if the two firms merge and the newly combined firm provides a single, bundled "nut-and-bolt" product. Such a firm faces the joint demand curve of equation (8.1) and so recognizes that the price of relevance to its customers is the sum of individual bolt and nut prices, or the total price paid for the bundled nut-and-bolt product. The marginal revenue curve associated with the demand curve of equation (8.1) is $MR = 12 - 2Q$, where $Q$ is the number of nut-and-bolt pairs sold. Equating marginal revenue with marginal cost identifies the optimal quantity of nut-and-bolt pairs to sell. Since we have assumed that marginal cost is zero, it is easy to see that the optimal quantity of nut-and-bolt pairs that the merged monopolist should offer for sale is $Q^* = 6$. The demand function then tells us that each pair can be sold at a combined price of $P^* = \$6$ (or separate prices of \$3 each). The merged firm's total profit is $P^* Q^* = \$36$.

Comparing these values with those obtained earlier shows that a merger of the two firms leads to lower prices and more output than when the two firms act separately. This is because the merged firm understands the interaction of demands between the two products. As a result, consumers are made better off by this merger. Moreover, the profit of the combined firm exceeds the sum of profits earned by the two separate firms. This was Cournot's basic point.[11] By internalizing the interdependence of the two firms, both consumers and producers gain.

Merger is not the only way to achieve this outcome. Alternative means of coordinating the separate decisions of the two firms exist. For example, they might decide to form a product network. Examples include automatic teller machine (ATM) networks, airline computerized reservation systems (CRS), real estate multiple-listing services (MLS), markets for interactive components such as computer CPUs and peripherals, and long-distance and local telephone services. Where they exist, such networks have been created by the joint action of many firms with the aim of taking better account of the interactions between the demands for the firms' complementary products.

Alternatively, we might hope for one or both markets to become competitive. If this happened in only one of the two markets, say bolts, then the bolt price would fall to marginal cost, which in this case is equal to zero. Each firm in the bolt market would be so small that it could not possibly impose any external effects on the nut-producing monopoly. Given a zero price for bolts, equations (8.6) imply that the profit-maximizing price for nuts—and therefore of a nut-and-bolt combination—would be \$6. Accordingly, this outcome would duplicate that which occurs under merger. Of course, if both markets were to become competitive, then bolt price and the nut price would each fall to marginal cost. This would yield the maximum total surplus and all of that surplus would accrue to consumers.

Unfortunately, there is a factor that can work against the emergence of competition in markets for certain complementary goods. This is the presence of network ex-

---

11 Allen (1938) made the same point with regard to the price-reducing effects of merging two complementary goods monopolies. A calculus-based presentation of our analysis is provided in the Appendix to this chapter.

ternalities. For some goods and services, there is a scale economy effect that operates on the demand side of the market. For example, the more consumers there are connected to a phone system, the more valuable the phone system is to existing and new consumers. Each consumer who connects to the phone system generates an external benefit to all those already connected and makes the system more attractive to potential consumers. Sometimes this feature is described as a positive feedback.

Product complementarities of the sort we have been discussing here can also give rise to a positive feedback. Consider again the Microsoft case. Microsoft's operating system Windows serves as the platform from which software applications such as word processing packages, computer games, and graphic arts programs can be launched. A technical aspect of this relationship is that the code for a particular application must include an applications program interface (API) in order to work with the operating system. Typically, the API that works with one operating system will not work with another. In other words, applications such as Harvard Graphics or Mathematica are usually written to work on a specific operating system such as Windows. The two products, the applications and the operating system, are therefore complements.

Two additional features of the design and production of applications programs are also important. First, such production exhibits substantial scale economies. The cost is almost entirely in the design phase. Once the underlying source code is written, the program can be put on CD-ROMs (or Web sites) and sold (or downloaded) to millions of consumers almost costlessly. Second, there is a network externality in that the more people who use the application, the more consumers who want to use it. It is convenient to know that I can put my presentation graphics on a floppy disk or in an e-mail attachment and have it read by a colleague miles away because we both use the same graphics software. For both of these reasons, firms that make applications naturally want to design them to work with the most widely used operating system because this permits them to exploit these supply-side and demand-side scale economies more effectively.

By exactly the same reasoning, the operating system that consumers want is the one for which there are the most applications. Thus, the complementary relationship between applications and operating systems has resulted in a very favorable positive feedback for Microsoft's Windows. As Windows has become the dominant operating system, applications are increasingly written to run on it. In turn, this ever-expanding menu of applications has greatly fortified the position of Windows as the dominant system. This interaction is sometimes called the *applications barrier to entry*. The idea is that any would-be rival operating system will have a great deal of difficulty entering the market. Applications producers will not design their products to run on the alternative system until it has a significant market share. Yet the system will never get any sizable market share unless applications are written for it.

We now have a countervailing force to the benefits from closer coordination in the production and marketing of complementary products. It is generally true that such coordination is profitable and our nut-and-bolt example indicates that coordination is also beneficial for consumers when there is monopoly power in the production of each of the complementary goods. The complicating factor introduced by network effects, and the positive feedback that they generate, is that monopoly power can be enhanced. It is then further possible that monopoly power in one product line might be extended to others.

# 8.4 ANTITRUST, BUNDLING, AND TIE-IN SALES

We are now in a better position to consider the antitrust issues that bundling and tie-ins raise. The main question is whether such practices may be used by firms with entrenched market power either to sustain or to extend that power against competitors or potential competitors. We illustrate these issues primarily by reviewing the Microsoft case with which we opened this chapter. We then briefly discuss other cases and legal developments in this area.

## 8.4.1 Bundling and the Microsoft Case

A central issue in the Microsoft case was the government's claim that Microsoft had integrated or bundled its browser, Internet Explorer, directly into its operating system, Windows, as a means to eliminate the rival browser, Netscape's Navigator, from the market. The argument was that since Microsoft had monopoly power in the operating systems market, every consumer of Windows would now find Internet Explorer as the default browser, thereby eliminating or greatly reducing Netscape's market share. To prove its claim and demonstrate a violation of the antitrust laws, the government would have to show that (1) Microsoft did possess monopoly power, (2) an operating system and a browser were two related but distinct products that did not need to be tightly bundled, and (3) Microsoft's practices constituted an abuse of its power motivated by the firm's desire to maintain or extend its dominant position.

In light of the foregoing, let us recall Judge Jackson's three key findings of fact. First, the judge found that Microsoft is indeed a monopoly power in the sense of the Sherman Act. The evidence for this finding appears strong. To begin with, Windows has had 90 percent or more of the operating systems market for well over a decade. Moreover, Microsoft practices mixed bundling on a wide scale and such clear price discrimination provides further evidence of something less than a competitive market. Thus, both the structural and behavioral evidence seems to be consistent with Judge Jackson's finding that Microsoft possesses monopoly power.

Now consider the judge's second finding that an operating system and an Internet browser are two separate, albeit complementary, products. This finding was a rejection of Microsoft's claim that a browser was really just an integrated part of a modern operating system. The firm had used this argument to justify its practice of selling Internet Explorer as an increasingly integrated bundle with Windows. An analogy might be photographic flash bulbs. Originally, flash bulbs were a separate and exterior component of a camera that was sold separately. Over time, however, the flash mechanism became more and more an internal part of the camera itself. Today, virtually all cameras have an internal flash that cannot be separated from the camera without seriously damaging the product.

Microsoft argued that a similar technological development had led it to make its browser a part of its operating system and claimed that separation of the two could not be achieved without damaging at least one of them. However, the fact remained that Netscape still marketed its Navigator browser independently, suggesting that there was no real need or even a consumer demand for an integrated operating system and browsing experience. In addition, evidence was presented at the trial showing that it was relatively easy to separate Internet Explorer from the operating system with which Microsoft had bundled it, without harming either product. So, Judge

Jackson's finding that Windows and Internet Explorer are separate products can also be justified.

In light of these first two findings, Microsoft's only remaining defense is that although it possesses monopoly power, its practice of bundling its distinct operating system and browser products did not amount to "acting badly." In other words, Microsoft might still avoid a finding that it had violated the antitrust laws by arguing that its integration of Windows and Internet Explorer was not done with a view to hurt competition but instead to help consumers. One way to make such a defense would be to pursue the coordination argument we discussed above. That is, Microsoft might argue that the complementarity between an operating system and a browser requires centralized coordination of the marketing of the two products in order to ensure that consumers receive both goods at low prices. Microsoft could then make a case that its behavior was, in fact, pro consumer.

As we saw in the previous section, the existence of a complementary relationship between two products can lead to serious inefficiencies if each product is produced by a separate monopoly. This was arguably the case in the software industry. Microsoft's Windows controlled the lion's share of the operating systems market and Netscape's Navigator dominated the complementary browser market. As just mentioned, there was also a good case to be made that some mechanism for coordinating the marketing of these two products was desirable. One way to achieve this coordination is by means of a merger of the two firms.[12] What happens, however, if one of the firms does not want to merge?

For example, suppose that Netscape feels that, as a much smaller company, any merger would amount to its being swallowed up by Microsoft and losing all its managerial independence. Its management might then decide to reject a merger proposal and to continue the separate marketing of its browser. In these circumstances we can imagine that Microsoft might decide to create its own browser and bundle it with its operating system.

We can illustrate how the market outcome might evolve, again using our simple nut-and-bolt example. Suppose that the demand by consumers who want both an operating system and a Web browser is given by

$$Q = 12 - (P_O + P_B), \tag{8.8}$$

where the subscripts $O$ and $B$ now indicate operating system and browser, respectively. Again, let us also simplify by assuming that marginal costs for both products are zero. (We noted earlier that for software, this assumption is reasonably realistic.)

Our nut-and-bolt example tells us that, when operating independently, Microsoft will sell its operating systems at $P_O = \$4$ and Netscape will sell its browser at $P_B = \$4$, so that the price of a combined operating system and browser service is $8. We also know that this is an inefficient outcome. If the two firms coordinate or become one firm, the price of a combined system falls to $6. Total profit of the two firms would simultaneously rise.

Now suppose that in recognition of this inefficiency, Microsoft proposes a merger to Netscape but is rejected. Microsoft might then develop its own browser, which we also assume can be produced at a marginal cost of zero. It would then appear that

---

12 In June 1995, Microsoft did in fact offer to work cooperatively with Netscape in the browser market and, allegedly, even suggested a merger—a proposal that was rejected by Netscape.

Microsoft could offer the operating system at $3 and the browser at $3, or a package price of $6. However, this ignores the competition from Netscape. If Microsoft proceeds with this plan, Netscape can no longer offer its browser at a price of $4. It could, however, offer to sell its browser at a price of $2. After all, this is still well above marginal cost. Moreover, this price is sufficiently low that consumers would then be attracted to the Netscape browser while still buying Microsoft's operating system at the price of $3. Of course, Microsoft would then want to reduce the price of its browser, perhaps to $1.95. Netscape would respond by selling its browser at perhaps $1.80, and so on.

What we have just described is an outbreak of price competition in the browser market. The ultimate effect of this price competition will be to drive the browser price to marginal cost—in this case to zero. This is certainly bad news for Netscape. What about Microsoft? A review of its optimal pricing strategy as given by equations (8.6) implies that when the browser price falls to zero, Microsoft's optimal price for operating systems rises to $6. Further, a browser price of 0 implies that $6 is also the best price for a combined operating system and browser package—exactly as would occur if the two firms merged. Moreover, the profit increase that a merger would bring is also realized, although it now goes entirely to Microsoft. In other words, a merger is not the only way to solve the coordination problem. Competition in one of the markets will remove the inefficiency that would otherwise result when each market is monopolized and the monopolists fail to coordinate their pricing. Prices are lower and both consumer and producer surplus have increased.

It is insightful to note that the outcome of the "browser war" just described involves a final browser price of zero. That is, in equilibrium Microsoft sells its operating system for $6 and then throws in its browser for free. This looks very much like bundling, the only complicating factor being that Netscape is also offering a free browser and so can be expected to retain a share of the browser market.

The foregoing should make clear that the view that Microsoft bundled its browser with its operating system to exploit its monopoly power and harm competition can be challenged. Microsoft could legitimately argue that it has simply acted in a way that promotes price competition. As evidence, it can point to the fact that consumer prices are now lower. Browser prices are zero and a combined browser and operating system now costs only $6. Microsoft can (and did) argue that the antitrust laws are about protecting competition, not specific competitors. The fact that the browser competition made Netscape less profitable is not properly a concern of the antitrust authorities. This is precisely the result that we hope and expect competition will bring to a market that has previously been monopolized. Accordingly, Microsoft could forcefully argue that rather than be tried as a villain, the Justice Department should be singing the firm's praises for the pro-competitive role it has played.

There is, however, an additional aspect to the case that we have not yet considered. This involves the interaction between complementary products and network externalities. The complementarity between operating systems and the applications written for them has created a substantial positive feedback loop for Microsoft. Because Windows has a monopoly in operating systems, the majority of applications are written to run on Windows. In turn, because most applications are written for Windows, no other operating system can challenge the Windows dominance. Internet browsers, however, offer a potential way around this problem. Particularly with the advent of the JAVA programming language developed by Sun Microsystems, applications can also be made to run on an Internet browser. That is, the browser itself can serve as a platform from which to launch applications.

Thus, even after the development of Internet Explorer, Netscape's Navigator might be expected to retain a reasonable share of the browser market because it too would be an attractive outlet for applications firms. If this was indeed the case, then firms would begin to write their applications to run on the browser alternative to the Windows platform. As this happened, Navigator would benefit from the same positive feedback that Windows enjoyed. As more applications could be run from the browser, the browser would become more popular and still more applications would be written for it. Clearly, such a development would strike at the core of Microsoft's success by leading to fierce competition in the platform market. Testimony at the trial revealed that Microsoft management was both aware and fearful of this development.

In light of the foregoing, Microsoft's explicit bundling of Internet Explorer with its Windows operating system may take on a somewhat different light. Instead of a competitive act that reduces a coordination inefficiency between complementary products, Microsoft's bundling can be viewed as a deliberate effort to reduce Netscape's share of the browser market by an amount sufficient to render the Netscape browser unattractive to applications designers. In turn, this would eliminate Netscape as a threat to Microsoft's operating system monopoly. Indeed, Microsoft initially required that PC manufacturers such as Compaq and Dell, who installed Windows as their operating system, also install Internet Explorer as the default browser appearing on the Windows desktop. They did this presumably on the supposition that most consumers want only one browser, even if a second can be obtained for free. The subsequent integration of Internet Explorer into the Windows software can then be interpreted as an attempt to replace contractual bundling with technological bundling.

Note that this alternative interpretation of Microsoft's behavior does imply a violation of the antitrust laws. It says that Microsoft abused its power primarily to sustain its monopoly, that is, to hurt competition. In this connection, the Justice Department offered much suggestive evidence, only a bit of which we can summarize here.

First, there were internal Microsoft documents revealing management's concern over the potential threat that Netscape might pose to the dominance of Windows as the applications platform. Second, some additional evidence of malicious intent was the fact that in addition to its bundling that effectively required Windows users to acquire Internet Explorer as their default browser, Microsoft also pressured Macintosh to support Internet Explorer as its default browser. It did so by refusing to develop applications, such as its Office products, for the Macintosh computers unless Macintosh complied. Since Macintosh computers do not use the Windows operating system, this action was hard to justify as reflecting a technical improvement to Windows in the way that an internal flash device was an improvement to cameras. Finally, and perhaps equally damaging, was the fact that Microsoft actually paid Internet service providers such as AmericaOnline (AOL) to adopt its browser, and even gave AOL a space on the Windows desktop. Since AOL competes directly with Microsoft's own Internet service, this action is again hard to understand except as a way to close the AOL market to Netscape. These stories and others were enough to convince Judge Jackson of Microsoft's guilt. Accordingly, he ruled that the firm had bundled its browser and operating system not with a view of promoting competition but with the goal of crushing it.

In sum, the finding that Microsoft has monopoly power does not, by itself, constitute a violation of the Sherman Act. Nor does the additional finding that Microsoft exploits that power through various bundling and product tie-in schemes. These strategies facilitate price discrimination and coordinate the marketing of complementary products, and are not per se illegal activities. The importance of these findings lies rather in the fact that they are necessary conditions for Judge Jackson's third conclusion. This is that, in the case of bundling Windows and Internet Explorer, Microsoft exercised its power in a manner designed to prevent the emergence of competition to its operating systems monopoly. If this is true, then we have a violation of the antitrust laws. This is what Judge Jackson found. It is also, by and large, what the appellate court to which Microsoft appealed its original verdict found, although that court was particularly skeptical of the claim that bundling Internet Explorer with Windows was a violation. Where the appellate court differed most strongly with Judge Jackson was on the issue of remedy. Judge Jackson had argued that the only way to prevent further violation was to break up Microsoft into separate companies much as John D. Rockefeller's Standard Oil was broken up 90 years earlier. Instead, the court remanded the case to Judge Colleen Kollar-Kotelly to work out a less drastic remedy that would be based on restrictions on Microsoft's actions and monitoring to ensure that those restrictions are enforced. These arrangements appear to have been worked out and the case is now essentially resolved as a legal matter. However, the economic issues are quite complex and their resolution will take a good bit longer. Indeed, the European Commission has recently found Microsoft guilty of similar anticompetitive charges. The Commission ruled that Microsoft has used its "near monopoly" to eliminate rivals in related software applications—most currently, rivals offering alternatives to Microsoft's audio and visual software, Media Player—by bundling Media Player in its standard package. The Commission has ordered Microsoft to alter this practice and has fined the company €497 million ($610 million).[13]

## 8.4.2  Antitrust Policy and Product Tying: Additional Developments

The issues raised in the Microsoft case are not new. They have been at the heart of all antitrust policy on tying for many years. The central concern has always been the impact of tying and bundling on competition. Again, both Section 1 of the Sherman Act and, even more explicitly, Section 3 of the Clayton Act focus on proscribing monopoly power whenever its exercise weakens competition. The language of the Clayton Act, for example, is that, "It shall be unlawful . . . to lease (or sell) goods . . . on the condition, agreement, or understanding that the lessee or purchaser thereof shall not use or deal in the goods . . . of a competitor or competitors of the lessor or seller, where the effect . . . may be *to substantially lessen competition or tend to create a monopoly in any line of commerce* [emphasis added]." The question that the Justice Department and the courts have always had to address then is whether the tying or bundling practice under investigation serves to "substantially lessen competition." As

---

13  For the legal record, see *U.S. v. Microsoft*, 253 F.3d 34 (D.C. Cir., 2001) and *U.S. v. Microsoft*, 231 F. Supp. 2d 144 (D.D.C. 2002). For a discussion of the economics of the U.S. case and related material, see Rubinfeld (2004), Economides and Salop (1991), and Shapiro and Varian (1999). The more recent European case is reported in P. Miller, "Microsoft Sanctions: The Overview; Europeans Rule Against Microsoft; Appeal Is Promised." *The New York Times*, March 25, 2004, p. C1.

the Microsoft case implies, this is often far from easy. For the same reason, antitrust policy on tying has evolved slowly as the complexities of these practices have come to be recognized.

The first clear statement on the general practice of requirement tie-ins was issued in 1947 by the Supreme Court in the case involving International Salt Company. The company had refused to lease its salt-processing machines unless the lessee also agreed to purchase all its salt from International Salt. The requirement was justified, International Salt argued, as a means of safeguarding the quality and care of its machines. However, the court rejected that argument. In a strongly worded statement, the Supreme Court instead made clear its view that tie-ins fundamentally reflected an attempt to "close . . . the market . . . against competition." It viewed the tie-in requirement of International Salt as no different in this regard. Further, because the salt sales affected by the tie-in requirement were valued at $500,000,000, the assault on competition was deemed substantial.[14] In short, the 1947 ruling suggested that any required tie-in sale or bundling scheme that involved substantial dollar sums would be regarded as a per se violation of the antitrust laws. This ruling reinforced and strengthened a similar decision made earlier against IBM when that company had required users of its card-punch machines to use only IBM-produced cards. In both cases, the Court argued that if quality control were the goal, contracts could specify the standards that salt, punch cards, or whatever had to meet without explicitly requiring a tie-in. Hence, the Court's early posture approached the view that the only purpose of a tied-sale requirement was to limit competition.

Over the years, the Court's views mellowed. To begin with, it became clear that tying would only be profitable in the case of related goods. That is, a monopolist in cameras would have no reason to tie its good to laundry detergent as a means of extending its monopoly to that market. If the detergent market is competitive, those who use detergent can still get it at the competitive price. Those who want both can buy the monopolist's camera and detergent bundle. However, because the products are unrelated, the profit-maximizing bundle price cannot exceed the monopoly price for cameras alone plus the competitive price of detergent. This is just the price of both goods before the monopolist starts bundling. The only outcome that bundling would achieve would be to lose sales to those consumers who only want to buy cameras. In short, it became widely recognized that a monopolist would not leverage its power into an unrelated competitive product line.

In the case of related products, such as Microsoft presents, the fear of monopoly extension remained. However, here too the courts began to appreciate the price discrimination and market coordinating roles of tying and bundling. In 1960, the Court accepted the use of a tied-sales clause in a case involving Jerrold Electronics Corporation. This company was a pioneer in the development and installation of cable television systems used in the community antenna television (CATV) industry. Jerrold tied its basic subscription to the CATV service to the purchase of various connecting wires and also to a five-year service contract. While this may appear no different from the earlier International Salt and IBM cases, the Court this time upheld the tie-in on the grounds that the industry in this instance was new and "taking root." The Court

---

14 *International Salt Co. v. United States*, 332 U.S. 392 (1947). However, Peterman (1979) notes that firms were allowed to use salt from producers other than International Salt if they showed International Salt's prices were not competitive. This suggests that the real purpose of the contract was to induce customers to reveal to International Salt the pricing practices of its rivals.

concluded that the tie-in was a legitimate way of guaranteeing quality performance in this early, developmental stage of an industry.[15]

The issue of tied sales and bundled goods remained one of active litigation but with a variety of confusing rulings for many years after the Jerrold case. Then, in 1984, the Supreme Court attempted to articulate a clear set of guidelines under which any such arrangement would be per se illegal. In its decision in that year, the Court stated three conditions, all of which would have to be met for the tie-in to violate antitrust laws. These are

1. the existence of two distinct products, the tying product and the tied one;
2. the firm tying the products must have sufficient monopoly power in the tying market to force the purchase of the tied good; and
3. the tying arrangement must foreclose, or have the potential to foreclose, a substantial volume of trade.[16]

The first two requirements are necessary conditions for the third. But it is the third finding that is the heart of the matter. Again though, the difficulty remains that tying and bundling have beneficial effects as well and it is not easy either to disentangle these or weigh them against any harm they may do to competition. Notice how closely Judge Jackson's findings parallel these requirements. Clearly the judge was trying to fashion his analysis along the standards required by established law.

# SUMMARY

In this chapter we have shown that a firm with monopoly power in more than one product line may have additional opportunities to price discriminate. By bundling its two goods together as a package or, more generally, by tying the sale of one good to the purchase of the other, the firm can induce customers to sort themselves out, that is, identify who is who. This permits charging a higher net price to those consumers with a greater willingness to pay.

In the case of two complementary products for which a fall in the price of one good raises the quantity demanded of both, sales coordination may occur for reasons other than price discrimination. In the absence of such coordination through merger or business networks, for example, the separate production and marketing of two complementary products will typically raise prices, reduce output, and reduce profits. By taking account of the interrelationship between the demand for each product, coordination potentially offers benefits to both consumers and firms alike.

We have also shown, however, that there can be a downside to both bundling and tie-in sales. In some cases, bundling or tying two complementary products together allows a firm with monopoly power in one market to extend its monopoly into other markets or otherwise limit competition. This was the charge against Microsoft. It was also the charge against Kodak in the United States and the proposed GE-Honeywell merger in Europe. These and other cases, and the general case history of litigation involving tying and bundling, reveals just how complicated these issues are.

So far, our analysis has focused primarily on the tactical choices of a monopoly firm either acting alone or interacting in a second market that is also monopolized. The

---

15 *United States v. Jerrold Corporation*, 187 F. Supp. 545 (1960), affirmed *per curiam* at 363 U.S. 567 (1961).
16 *Hyde v. Jefferson Parish Hospital District No. 2, et al.*, 466 U.S. 2, 15–18(1984).

next step is to consider firms' strategies in the context of imperfect competition where neither one nor many firms but just a few firms interact. In such a setting, a firm can no longer simply address the issue of how to extract greater surplus from consumers. Each firm must now also consider how its production and pricing strategies affect not just consumers but the other, rival firms. This is the stuff of game theory and it is to this topic that we turn next.

# PROBLEMS

1. A university has determined that its students fall into two categories when it comes to room and board demand. University planners call these two types Sleepers and Eaters. The reservation prices for a dormitory room and the basic meal plan of the two types are as follows:

|  | Sleepers | Eaters |
|---|---|---|
| Dorm Room | $5,500 | $3,000 |
| Meal Plan | $2,500 | $6,000 |

Currently, the university offers students the option of selecting just the dorm room at $3,000, just the meal plan at $2,500, or both for a total price of $5,500. An economic consultant advises the university to stop offering the two goods separately and, instead, to sell them only as a single, combined room and board package. Explain the consultant's strategy and determine what price the university should set for the combined product.

2. Bundling is not always superior to nonbundling. To see this, consider a telecommunications firm that offers both phone service and a high-speed modem service. It has two types of consumers who differ in their willingness to pay a monthly rental fee for either service.

|  | Talkers | Hackers |
|---|---|---|
| Phone Service | $30 | $a |
| High-Speed Connection | $16 | $24 |

Determine for what values of $a$ bundling would be more profitable than not bundling.

3. Many years ago, the major alternative to xerography in copying was the Electrofax copying process. Electrofax machines used a special paper coated with a heavy wax film. Like Xerox, the Electrofax companies charged a low price for the use of the machine but set a paper price per page of 4 cents. The actual and marginal cost of manufacturing the paper was, in fact, only 1 cent per page.

   a. Explain the pricing policy of the Electrofax producers.

   b. The high markup on Electrofax paper soon attracted new firms offering to supply the paper at a much lower price than the Electrofax producers. How do you think Electrofax will respond to this competition?

4. Computer software, $S$, and hardware, $H$, are complementary products used to produce computer services. Customers make a one-time purchase of hardware, but buy various amounts of software. That is, once the hardware is purchased, the price of additional computer services is $P_S$, the price of a unit of software. The

software market is competitive. However, the hardware market is monopolized by the firm HAL, Inc. The cost of producing software and hardware is $c_S$ and $c_H$, respectively:

**a.** Assume that all users of computer services are alike, that is, have the same demand curve for computer services. Use a graph to describe the profit-maximizing price HAL can charge.

**b.** Would HAL gain anything by buying software at the competitive price, branding it as its own, and then selling its hardware only to customers who use the HAL-brand software?

# REFERENCES

Adams, W. J., and J. Yellen. 1976. "Commodity Bundling and the Burden of Monopoly." *Quarterly Journal of Economics* 475 (May): 475–98.

Allen, R. G. D. 1938. *Mathematical Analysis for Economists.* New York: St. Martin's Press.

Economides, N., and S. Salop. 1992. "Competition and Integration among Complements, and Network Market Structure." *Journal of Industrial Economics* 40 (March): 105–23.

Giotakos, D., L. Petit, G. Garnier, and P. DeLuyck. 2001. "General Electric/Honeywell—An Insight into the Commission's Investigation and Decision." *Competition and Policy Newsletter* 3 (October): 5–13.

McKie-Mason, J., and J. Metzler. 2004. "Links Between Markets and Aftermarkets: Kodak." In J. E. Kwoka and L. J. White, eds., *The Antitrust Revolution: Competition and Policy.* 4th Edition. Oxford: Oxford University Press: 428–52.

Nalebuff, Barry. 2004. "Bundling: GE-Honeywell (2001)." In J. E. Kwoka and L. J. White, eds., *The Antitrust Revolution: Competition and Policy.* 4th Edition. Oxford: Oxford University Press: 388–412.

Peterman, J. 1979. "The International Salt Case." *Journal of Law and Economics* 22: 351–64.

Rubinfeld, Daniel. 2003. "Maintenance of Monopoly: *U.S. v. Microsoft* (2001)." In J. E. Kwoka, and L. J. White, eds., *The Antitrust Revolution: Economics, Competition, and Policy.* 4th Edition. Oxford: Oxford University Press.

Stigler, G. 1968. "A Note on Block Booking." *The Organization of Industry.* Homewood, IL: Irwin.

Shapiro, C., and H. R. Varian. 1999. *Information Rules.* Boston: Harvard Business School Press.

# Appendix | Formal Proof of the Inefficiency Induced by the Marketing of Complementary Goods by Separate Monopolists

Assume that the products of two monopolists, A and B, are complementary goods. Consumers require one unit of B for every unit of A consumed. The price charged by each firm will be denoted as $P_A$ and $P_B$, respectively. However, since consumers only buy the two goods in equal proportions, the price of concern to either firm's customers is the sum of $P_A$ and $P_B$, denoted here as $S$.

Total demand, $Q$, for the composite product, or $AB$ pair, may be expressed as

$$Q = D(S), \text{ where } D' = \partial Q / \partial S < 0, \text{ and } S = P_A + P_B. \qquad \text{(A.1)}$$

To simplify still further, we will assume that each firm has a constant marginal cost of production of zero. Hence, revenue maximization and profit maximization are the same thing. Firm A's profits, $\Pi(A)$, and Firm B's profits, $\Pi(B)$, are therefore given by

$$\Pi(A) = P_A D(S)$$
$$\Pi(B) = P_B D(S). \qquad \text{(A.2)}$$

Individual profit maximization at each firm implies choosing a price such that the derivative of $\Pi(A)$ with respect to $P_A$, or $\Pi(B)$ with respect to $P_B$, is zero. That is, individual profit maximization implies

$$\partial \Pi(A) / \partial P_A = P_A D'(S) + D(S) = 0$$
$$\partial \Pi(B) / \partial P_B = P_B D'(S) + D(S) = 0. \qquad \text{(A.3)}$$

Since each firm will always set its price so as to maximize profits, equation (A.3) must always hold. This will certainly be true in equilibrium. Denote the equilibrium value of $S$ when both firms act individually as $S^1$. By definition, $S^1$ is the sum of the equilibrium choices of $P_A$ and $P_B$. We obtain some insight into the value of $S^1$ by first summing the two equations in (A.3) to obtain

$$S^1 D'(S^1) + 2D(S^1) = 0, \qquad \text{(A.4)}$$

where we have made use of the fact that $S^1 = P_A + P_B$. Subtracting from each side of equation (A.4) the term $D(S^1)$, which is simply the total demand for the composite $AB$ product in the decentralized equilibrium, yields the inequality

$$S^1 D'(S^1) + D(S^1) = -D(S^1) < 0. \qquad \text{(A.5)}$$

In a market outcome in which each firm sets its price independently of the other, the price for the composite good, $S^1$, must satisfy equation (A.5).

Now consider the strategy of a firm, $M$, that markets both goods as a single, composite product at the single price $S^M$. Its profits are given by

$$\Pi(M) = S^M D(S^M).\qquad\text{(A.6)}$$

In turn, profit maximization for this firm requires that

$$\partial\Pi(M)/\partial S^M = S^M D'(S^M) + D(S^M) = 0.\qquad\text{(A.7)}$$

If instead of choosing the price $S^M$, the merged firm chose the price implicitly selected by the two individual firms, $S^1$, it would not be at the zero derivative point indicated by equation (A.7). In fact, we can determine the precise sign of the derivative of the merged firm's profit function at the price $S^1$ simply by replacing $S^M$ in equation (A.7) with $S^1$, yielding

$$\partial\Pi(M)/\partial S^1 = S^1 D'(S^1) + D(S^1).\qquad\text{(A.8)}$$

But from equation (A.5), we know that this expression is less than zero. In other words, if the merged firm selected the combination price, $S^1$, implicitly chosen by the two independent firms, a *reduction* in that price would *increase* its profits. Since $S^M$ is the merged firm's best price from which no improvement is possible, this means that $S^M$ must be less than $S^1$. That is, the two independent monopolists set a higher price and consequently sell fewer pairs of the complementary goods than does the centralized or merged firm. Since the merged firm's profits at price $S^M$ exceed what it earns at price $S^1$, and since the latter amount equals the sum of profits earned by the two individual firms, merging also produces higher overall profits.

# Part three

## Game Theory and Oligopoly Markets

# three
# Game Theory and Oligopoly Markets

This part formally starts our analysis of strategic interaction. Today, the analytic framework for such analysis is what is formally known as game theory. Game theory provides the language and the logic of understanding strategic play. Accordingly, this section presents the essential ingredients of game theoretic analysis when applied in the setting of imperfect competition. The central solution concept to all such games is the Nash equilibrium concept named after the Nobel Laureate, John Nash.

Perhaps the most common market setting in which strategic interaction arises is one that economists call oligopoly. These are markets with more than one but still just a few large firms. This is the setting we adopt here. Indeed, for illustration purposes, it is often convenient to focus on the strategic interaction between just two firms. Hence, much of our work in the next several chapters focuses on the rivalry or game between just two firms. The results from this duopoly analysis can then be generalized as the number of firms or players increases.

An important insight of game theory is that the rules of the game are crucial. In an oligopoly setting, this means that it is important to know, for example, whether the firms compete by choosing production levels and then letting whatever output results determine the industry price or, whether they compete by choosing prices and then matching their production to meet the industry demand. The first of these cases in which firms compete in production quantities is called Cournot competition and it is the focus of Chapter 9. The second case of price competition or, as it is often called, Bertrand competition is the subject of Chapter 10.

Another important rule in any game is the order of play. In some games, including the Cournot and Bertrand games described above, firms are assumed to choose simultaneously, just as the players do in the children's game of "rock-scissors-paper." However, many games, for example, "tic-tac-toe," are characterized by sequential play in which one player moves first. Only then can the other player move. These games then have a dynamic or intertemporal feature and this has important implications for the outcome or equilibrium of the game. Often, as in "tic-tac-toe," the first mover has an advantage. We consider the basic dynamic oligopoly game known as the Stackelberg game in Chapter 11. As we will see, this game does indeed have an important first mover advantage.

Our analysis in this part is central to all that follows in the rest of the text and, indeed, to all modern industrial economics. Each of the chapters beyond Chapter 11 will build on the game theoretic concepts developed in Part Three to analyze additional, sometimes more complicated settings of strategic interaction. Understanding the models developed in Chapters 9, 10, and 11 is essential therefore to proceeding further in industrial organization.

# Static Games and Cournot Competition

## Chapter 9

One of the most successful companies in the history of business is Coca-Cola. "Coca-Cola" is said to be the second most well-known phrase in the world, the first being "okay."[1] But despite its icon status in American popular culture, Coca-Cola is not a monopoly. Coca-Cola shares the carbonated soft drink market share with its archrival PepsiCo. An ongoing battle for market share has engaged these two companies for almost 100 years. The cola wars have been fought with a number of strategies, one of which is the frequent introduction of new soft drink products. Vanilla is the latest flavor to enter this part of the battleground. Pepsi marketed Pepsi Vanilla in the summer of 2003, about one year and 90 million cases after Vanilla Coke was introduced.

In fighting this cola war, each company must identify and implement the strategy it believes is best suited to gaining a competitive advantage in the soft drink industry. If Coca-Cola were a monopoly, it would not have to worry about the entry of Pepsi Vanilla. Life is much simpler when a firm does not have to worry about how rivals will react to its price or its output decisions. The simpler life is a feature common to both monopoly and perfect competition. When either a monopoly or a competitive firm chooses how much output to produce, neither has to worry at all about how that decision affects other firms. In a pure monopoly, there *are* no other firms in the market. In a perfectly competitive market, there are other firms, but no one firm needs to be concerned with the effect its output decision will have on the others. Each firm is so small that its output decision will cause not even a ripple in the industry.

The truth is, however, that Coke, Pepsi, and many other firms are neither monopolists nor perfect competitors. These firms, perhaps the majority of corporations, live in the middle ground of *oligopoly* where firms have visible rivals with whom strategic interaction is a fact of life. Each firm is aware that its actions affect others, thus prompting reactions. Each firm must, therefore, take these interactions into account when making a decision about prices, output, or other business actions. Decisions in such an interactive setting are called *strategic* decisions, and *game theory* is the branch of social science that formally analyzes and models strategic interaction. As a result, it is not surprising that game theory and the study of oligopoly are closely intertwined. A central goal of this chapter is to introduce some basic game theoretic analysis and to show how it may be used to understand oligopoly markets.

Game theory itself is divided into two branches: *noncooperative* and *cooperative* game theory.[2] The essential difference between these two branches is that in noncooperative games, the unit of analysis is the individual decision maker or player, that is, the firm. By contrast, in cooperative game theory the unit of analysis is a group or a coalition of players, for example, a group of firms. We will focus almost exclusively on noncooperative game theory. The individual player will be the firm. The *rules of the game* will define how competition between the different players, that is, firms,

---

1 Richard Tetlow, author of *The Great Cola Wars*, makes these claims and further adds the sentence "Coca-Cola is okay." It is understood in more places by more people than any other sentence.

2 A good textbook that offers a more formal treatment of game theory and its applications to economics is Rasmusen (2001).

takes place. The noncooperative setting means that each player is concerned only with doing as well as possible for herself, subject to the rules of the game. She is not interested in advancing a more general group interest. As we shall see, though, such noncooperative behavior can sometimes look very much like cooperative behavior because cooperation sometimes turns out to maximize the well-being of each individual player as well.

Two basic assumptions underlie the application of noncooperative game theory to oligopoly. The first is that *firms are rational*. They pursue well-defined goals, principally profit maximization. The second basic assumption is that firms apply their rationality to the process of *reasoning strategically*. In making its decisions, each firm uses all the knowledge it has to form expectations regarding how other firms will behave. The motivation behind these assumptions is that our ultimate goal is to understand and predict how real firms will act. We assume that firms are rational and reason strategically because we suspect that real firms do precisely this or will be forced to do so by market pressures. Hence, understanding what rational and strategic behavior implies ought to be useful for understanding and predicting real-world outcomes.

There is one caution that any introduction to the study of oligopoly must include. It is that, unlike the textbook competition and monopoly cases, there is no single, standard oligopoly model. Differences in the rules of the game, the information available to the various players, and the timing of each player's actions all conspire to yield a number of possible scenarios. Yet while there is not a single theory or model of oligopoly, common themes and insights from the various models of oligopoly do emerge. Understanding these broad concepts is our goal for the next three chapters. In this chapter we introduce the Cournot model of oligopoly, the next chapter studies the Bertrand model, and Chapter 11 focuses on the Stackelberg model. In this connection we should add that the lack of one single oligopoly model is not entirely a disadvantage. Rather, it means that one has a rich assortment of models from which to choose for any particular investigation. One model will be appropriate for some settings and a different model for other settings. Because the real business world environment is quite diverse, it is useful to have a variety of analyses on which to draw for the purpose of investigating real business behavior.

## 9.1  STRATEGIC INTERACTION: INTRODUCTION TO GAME THEORY

In game theory, each player's decision or plan of action is called a *strategy*. In turn, a list of strategies showing one particular strategy choice for each player is called a *strategy combination*. For any given strategy combination, the game will produce an *outcome* describing the payoffs or final net gains earned by each player. In the context of oligopoly theory, these payoffs are naturally interpreted as each firm's profit.

For a game to be interesting, at least one player must be able to choose from more than one strategy so that there will be more than one possible strategy combination. If so, there will be more than one possible outcome to the game. Yet while there may be many possible outcomes, not all of these will be *equilibrium* outcomes. By equilibrium we mean a strategy combination such that no firm has an incentive to *change* the strategy it is currently using given that no other firm changes its current strategy. If this is the case, then the combination of strategies across firms will remain unaltered since no one is changing his behavior. The market or game will come to rest. Nobel Laureate John Nash developed this notion of an equilibrium strategy combination for a noncooperative game. In his honor, it is commonly referred to as the Nash equilibrium concept.[3]

In the oligopoly models studied in the next three chapters, a firm's strategy focuses on either its price choice or its output choice. That is, each firm is assumed to be choosing either the price it will set for its product or how much of that product to produce. A corresponding Nash equilibrium will, therefore, be either a set of prices—one for each firm—or a set of production levels—again one for each firm—for which no firm wishes to change its price (quantity) decision given the decisions of all the other firms.

We note parenthetically here that, unlike the monopoly case, the price strategy outcome differs from the quantity strategy outcome in oligopoly models. For a monopolist, the choice of price implies—through the market demand curve—a unique output. In other words, the monopolist will achieve the same results whether he picks the profit-maximizing price or the profit-maximizing output.[4] Matters are different in an oligopoly setting. When firms interact strategically, the outcome obtained when they each focus on selecting a price will usually differ from the outcome obtained when each firm focuses on choosing the best output level. The fact that the outcome depends on whether the rules of the game specify a price or quantity strategy is just one of the reasons that, as previously noted, the study of oligopoly does not yield a unique set of theoretical predictions.

Since interaction is the central fact of life for an oligopolist, rational strategic action requires that such interaction be recognized. For example, when one firm in an oligopoly lowers its price, the effect will be noticeable to its rivals as they lose customers to the price-cutter. If these firms then lower their price too, they may win back their original customers. Indeed, because prices have fallen throughout the industry, the quantity demanded at each firm may well increase. However, each firm will now be meeting that demand at a lower price that earns a lower mark-up. Our assumption that the oligopolist is a rational strategic actor means that she will understand and expect this chain of events *and* that she will include this information in making the decision whether to lower her price in the first place. Our opening story about Coca-Cola serves as an example except that instead of cutting its price, Coca-Cola introduced its new Vanilla Coke. Before doing so, it must have formed some idea as to how its rival Pepsi would react. It would have been *irrational* to anticipate no reaction from Pepsi, when, in fact, Coke understands that not reacting is not in Pepsi's interest. Similarly if Coke lowers the price of its soft drinks, it doesn't make sense for Coke to hope that Pepsi will continue to charge a high price if Coke knows that Pepsi would do better to match its price reduction.

But how can an oligopolist know what the response of his rivals will be to any specific action? The only way to make such a prediction is to have information—information regarding the structure of the market and the strategy choices available to

---

3  Nash shared the 1994 prize with two other game theorists, R. Selten and J. Harsanyi. The award to the three game theorists served as widely publicized recognition of the importance game theory has achieved as a way of thinking in economic analysis.

4  Competitive firms have no option as to which choice variable—price or quantity—to select. Competitive firms by definition cannot make a price choice. They are price-takers and can only choose the quantity of output they sell.

other firms. In a symmetric situation where all firms are identical, such information is readily available. Any one firm can proceed by asking itself, "What would I do if I were the other player?" Sometimes, even when firms are not symmetric, they will still have enough experience, business "savvy," or other information to be fairly confident regarding their rivals' behavior. As we shall see later, however, precisely what information firms have about each other is a crucial element determining the final outcome of the game. For the moment, we proceed assuming that each firm has a good idea of the strategy choices available to its rivals.

Another crucial element in determining the outcome of the game is the time-dimension of the strategic interaction. In a two-firm oligopoly (like Coca-Cola and Pepsi), which is referred to as a *duopoly*, we can imagine that one firm, say Coca-Cola, makes its choice—to introduce Vanilla Coke first. Then in the next period, the other firm, Pepsi, follows with its choice. Here, the strategic interaction is *sequential*. Each firm moves in order and each, when its turn comes, must think strategically about how the course of action it is about to choose will affect the future action of the other firm and how those *re*actions will then feed back on its own future choices. Chess and Checkers are each classic examples of two-person, sequential games.

Alternatively, both players might make their choices *simultaneously*, thereby acting without knowledge as to what the other player has actually done.[5] Yet even though the other player's choice is unknown, knowledge of the strategy choices available to one's rival still permits a rational strategic choice for one's own actions to be made. The childhood game, "rock-scissors-paper" is an example of a simultaneous two-person game.

Whether the game is sequential or simultaneous, the requirement that the rational strategic firm sensibly predicts the choices of its rivals is the same. Once it has done this, the firm may then choose what action is in its own best interest. In other words, being rational means that the firm's choice of strategy is the optimal (profit-maximizing) choice against the anticipated actions of its rivals. When each firm does this, and when each has, as a result of rational strategizing, correctly predicted the choice of the others, we will obtain a Nash equilibrium. In this chapter we will focus on solving for Nash equilibria in simultaneous or static games.

## 9.2 DOMINANT AND DOMINATED STRATEGIES

Sometimes, Nash equilibria are rather easy to determine. This is because some of a firm's possible strategies may be *dominated*. Suppose that two firms, A and B, are involved. Suppose further that one of A's strategies is such that it is *never* a profit-maximizing strategy regardless of the choice made by B. That is, there is always an alternative strategy for firm A that yields higher profits than does the strategy in question. We say, then, that the strategy in question is dominated—meaning that it will never be chosen. Player A would never choose a dominated strategy since to do so would be to guarantee that A's profit was not maximized. No matter what B does, the dominated strategy by definition does worse for A than one of A's alternatives. In turn, this means that in determining the game's equilibrium, we do not have to worry

---

5   The important aspect of simultaneous games is not that the firms involved actually make their decisions at the same time. Rather, it is that no firm can *observe* any other firm's choice before making its own. This lack of information makes the actions of each firm effectively simultaneous.

about any strategy combinations that include the dominated strategy. Since these will never occur, they cannot possibly be part of the equilibrium outcome.

Dominated strategies can be eliminated one by one. Once the dominated strategies for one firm have been eliminated, we turn to the other firms to see if any of their strategies have the same feature *in light of the strategies still remaining for the first firm examined*. We then proceed firm-by-firm, eliminating all dominated strategies until only nondominated ones remain available to each player. Often, but not always, this iterative procedure of eliminating dominated strategies leaves one or more players with only one strategy choice remaining.[6] It is then a simple matter to determine the game's outcome since, for such firms, their course of action is clear.

An example should help to clarify the foregoing remarks. To this end, consider the case of two airlines, Delta and American, each offering a daily flight from Boston to Budapest. We will assume that each firm has already set a price for the flight, but that the departure time is still undecided. That is, departure time is the strategy choice in this game. We will also assume that the two firms choose simultaneously. Neither can observe the departure time selected by the other before it makes its own departure time selection. Managers for each airline do realize, however, that at the very time American's managers are meeting to make their choice, Delta's managers are too. The two firms are engaged in a strategic game of simultaneous moves.

In part, the choice of departure time will reflect consumer preferences. Suppose that market research has shown that 70 percent of the potential clientele for the flight would prefer to leave Boston in the evening and arrive in Budapest the next morning. The remaining 30 percent prefer a morning Boston departure and arrival in Budapest late in the evening of the same day. Both firms know this distribution of consumer preferences. Both also know that, if the two airlines choose the same flight time, they split the market. Profits at each carrier are directly proportional to the number of passengers carried so that each wishes to maximize its share of the market.

If they are rational and strategic, Delta's managers will reason as follows: If American flies in the morning, then we at Delta can either fly at night and serve 70 percent of the market (compared with American's 30 percent), or, like American, depart in the morning in which case we (Delta) will serve 15 percent of the market (half of the 30 percent served by the two carriers in total). On the other hand, if American chooses an evening flight time, then we at Delta may choose either a night departure as well, and thereby serve 35 percent (half of 70 percent) of the market or, instead, offer a morning flight and fly 30 percent of the market while American flies the remaining 70 percent at night.

As a bit of reflection will reveal, the implication of these numbers is that Delta does better by scheduling an evening flight *no matter which departure time American chooses*. In other words, choosing a *morning* departure time is a dominated strategy. If Delta is interested in maximizing profits, it will never select the morning flight option. But of course, American's managers will reason similarly. They will recognize that flying at night is their best choice regardless of Delta's selection. Thus, it seems clear that the only equilibrium outcome for this game is to have both airlines choose an evening departure time.

The formal analysis that underlies the foregoing intuition and that demonstrates rigorously that both carriers choosing an evening flight is, in fact, this game's Nash

---

6    If the process continues until only one strategy remains for each player, then we have found an iterated dominance equilibrium.

equilibrium and can be illustrated by reference to Table 9-1. The table shows four entries, each consisting of a pair of values. These entries reflect the four feasible strategy combinations that the game has corresponding to whether each airline chooses a morning flight, each chooses an evening flight, or one chooses a morning flight, and the other chooses an evening flight. American's choices are shown as the columns, while Delta's choices are shown as the rows. The pair of values at each row-column intersection gives the payoffs to each carrier if that particular strategy combination occurs. The first (left-hand) value of each pair is the payoff—the percent of the total potential passenger market—that goes to Delta. The second (right-hand) value is the payoff to American.

**TABLE 9-1**

### STRATEGY COMBINATIONS AND FIRM PAYOFFS IN THE FLIGHT DEPARTURE GAME

|  |  | American | |
|---|---|---|---|
|  |  | Morning | Evening |
| Delta | Morning | (15, 15) | (30, 70) |
|  | Evening | (70, 30) | (35, 35) |

Now we put ourselves in the shoes of Delta's managers and ask first what Delta should do if American chooses a morning flight. The answer is obvious. If Delta also chooses a morning flight, then Delta's market share will be 15 percent; whereas, if Delta chooses an evening flight, its market share will be 70 percent. The evening flight is clearly the better choice. Now consider Delta's response should American choose an evening flight. If Delta opts for a morning departure, its market share is 30 percent; whereas, if it goes for an evening departure, its market share is 35 percent. Once again, the evening departure is the better choice. In other words, no matter what American does, Delta will never choose to depart in the morning. Whatever the equilibrium outcome is, it must involve Delta choosing an evening flight.

If we now place ourselves in American's shoes, a similar result occurs. Here, we start by considering American's best response should Delta choose a morning flight. The answer is that American should choose an evening flight to gain 70 percent of the market as compared to the 15 percent that a morning departure would generate. Similarly, should Delta choose an evening departure, American should do likewise since this will give it 35 percent of the market compared to the 30 percent share that a morning departure would give. As in Delta's case, we discover that flying in the morning is a dominated strategy for American since it never does as well as flying in the evening no matter what Delta does. Hence, just like Delta, American will always choose the evening departure time.

The outcome of the game is now fully determined. Both carriers will choose an evening departure and share equally the 70 percent of the potential Boston-to-

Budapest flyers who prefer that time. That this is a Nash equilibrium is easy to see by virtue of the dominated strategy argument. Clearly, neither carrier has an incentive to change its choice from evening to morning since neither would ever choose a morning flight time in any case.

Solving the flight departure game was easy because each carrier had only two strategies, and for each player one of the strategies—the morning flight—was dominated. To put it another way, we might refer to the evening departure strategy as *dominant*. A dominant strategy is one that outperforms all of a firm's other strategies *no matter what its rivals do*. That is, it leads to higher profits (or sales, or growth, or whatever the objective is) than any other strategy the firm might pursue regardless of the strategies selected by the firm's rivals. This does not imply that a dominant strategy will lead a firm to earn higher profits than its competitors. It only means that the firm will do the best it possibly can if it chooses such a strategy. Whether this is as good as or better than the outcome obtained by its rivals depends on the structure of the game.

Except when the number of strategy choices is two, a firm may have some dominated strategies (or choices that are never good ones because better ones are available) but not have any dominant strategy (or a choice that consistently yields better results than all others). Sometimes, a firm will have neither a dominant nor a dominated strategy. But for a firm that has a dominant strategy, the choice is clear. Use it! Such a firm really does not have to think very much about what other firms do.

Let us rework the departure time game in a case where at least one firm has no dominated strategies (and so, since the number of strategies is just two, it has no dominant strategy). To do this, we will now suppose that because of a frequent flyer program, some of the potential Boston-to-Budapest flyers prefer Delta even if the two carriers fly at the same time. To be specific, assume now that flying at the same time does not yield an even split of customers between the two carriers. Instead, whenever the two carriers schedule identical departure times, Delta gets 60 percent of the market and American gets only 40 percent. Table 9-2 depicts the new payoffs for each strategy combination.

### STRATEGY COMBINATIONS AND FIRM PAYOFFS IN THE MODIFIED FLIGHT DEPARTURE GAME

TABLE

9-2

|  |  | American | |
|---|---|---|---|
|  |  | Morning | Evening |
| Delta | Morning | (18, 12) | (30, 70) |
|  | Evening | (70, 30) | (42, 28) |

As can be seen from the table, a morning flight is still a dominated strategy for Delta. It always carries more passengers by choosing an evening flight than it would by choosing a morning flight, regardless of what American does. However, American's strategy choices are no longer so clear. If Delta chooses a morning flight, American should fly at night. But if Delta chooses an evening departure time, American does better by flying in the morning.

It may appear that American cannot easily determine its own best course without actually observing Delta's choice. Yet this is not the case. There is a self-evident way for American to make a selection even without waiting to see what Delta does. This is because we assume that each carrier knows the payoff structure shown in Table 9-2. If this is the case, then American can readily determine that its rival, Delta, is never going to select a morning flight. Since a morning flight is a dominated strategy for Delta, there is no question of this strategy ever being that carrier's choice. Knowing that Delta will never choose the morning departure, it is then an easy matter for American to select a morning departure as its best response to Delta's action since it knows that Delta will choose an evening departure. The equilibrium outcome for this modified departure time game is therefore just as clear as that for the earlier version. In this case, the equilibrium involves Delta choosing an evening flight and American opting to fly in the morning. Again, it is easily verified that this equilibrium satisfies the Nash criteria.

In solving both our previous games, we made extensive use of the ability to rule out dominated strategies and, when possible, to focus on dominant ones.[7] We also showed that the outcomes obtained by this process were Nash equilibrium outcomes. Sometimes though, no dominated or dominant strategies can be found. In such cases, the Nash equilibrium concept becomes more than just a criterion to check our analysis. It becomes part of the solution procedure itself. This is because rational, strategic firms can use the Nash concept to determine the reactions of their rivals to their own strategic choice. In the modified departure time game just described, for instance, Delta can work out that if it selects an evening departure, its rival, American, will choose a morning flight. Delta, and also we as outside observers, can infer that the strategy combination of both carriers flying at night can never be an equilibrium—in the Nash sense—because if that outcome occurred, American would have a clear incentive to change its choice.

## 9.3  NASH EQUILIBRIUM AS A SOLUTION CONCEPT

In order to see further the use of the Nash equilibrium concept, let us now change the Boston-to-Budapest game more substantively. In particular, we will change the decision variable for each carrier from one of the choice of flight time to one regarding the ticket price. We will now assume that consumers are indifferent about the time of departure and, instead, care only about the price they pay for the flight. Specifically, we will suppose that there are 60 consumers with a reservation price of $500 for the flight, and another 120 with the lower reservation price of $220. If the two carriers set a common price, they share equally all those customers willing to pay that fare. On

---

7   It is worth emphasizing that some care needs to be taken in the process of ruling out dominated strategies. In particular, while one can eliminate *strictly* dominated strategies as a rational choice, so-called *weakly* dominated strategies cannot be so ruled out. A strategy is *weakly* dominated if there exists some other strategy, which is possibly better but never worse, yielding a higher payoff in some strategy combinations and never yielding a lower payoff. The Nash equilibrium may be affected by the order of exclusion of *weakly* dominated strategies. See Mas-Colell, *et al.* (1995).

the cost side, we will suppose that the unit cost of serving a single passenger for either airline is $200, whether the flight leaves in the morning or the evening. Let us also assume that each airline is flying a plane with a 200-seat capacity.

Although many price strategies are available to each firm, let's limit ourselves to just two. One is to set a high price of $500. Another is to set a low price of $220. So, as before, each firm has two options and there are four possible strategy combinations. Each such strategy combination will have associated with it a set of profits. If both Delta and American set the high price of $500, then each airline will serve half of the 60 passengers willing to pay that fare, or 30 passengers. Because each such passenger involves a cost of $200, each airline will earn profits of $30x(\$500) - 30x(\$200) = \$9,000$. On the other hand, if each sets a price of $220, they will each share equally in a market of 180 customers and therefore carry 90 passengers apiece. Profits in this case are only $90x(\$220) - 90x(\$200) = \$1,800$ for each airline, because the margin per passenger is now much smaller ($20).

What happens if one airline sets a high price and the other a low one? If, say, Delta sets a fare of $500 and American sets a fare of $220, Delta will carry *no* passengers. All 180 consumers willing to pay the fare of $220 or higher will choose American. Delta's profits will be zero. American's profits will be given by $(\$220 - \$200) \times 180 = \$3,600$. Obviously, just the reverse will occur if instead American sets the high price and Delta sets the low one.

The payoff matrix for the new airfare game is shown in Table 9-3. As before, the entries in each row-column intersection show the profit to each firm associated with that strategy combination, with Delta's profit listed as the first entry in each case.

## PAYOFF MATRIX FOR THE AIRFARE GAME

|  |  | American | |
|---|---|---|---|
|  |  | $P_H$ = $500 | $P_L$ = $220 |
| Delta | $P_H$ = $500 | ($9,000, $9,000) | ($0, $3,600) |
|  | $P_L$ = $220 | ($3,600, $0) | ($1,800, $1,800) |

TABLE 9-3

The first thing to notice is that there is no dominant or dominated strategy for either firm. If American selects a high price, Delta should also select a high price. But if American selects a low price, Delta's best bet is to match this price reduction. So we cannot rely on eliminating dominated strategies to identify the outcome of the game.

What can we do? Again, we can place ourselves in the shoes of each company's managers. We'll start with Delta. The managers of Delta will look at the payoff matrix of Table 9-3 and reason, as we just did, that their best bet is to choose the same fare as American does. The issue then becomes one of predicting what American will do. Let us suppose that Delta's managers expect American to set a low fare. Then their best choice is to also set the low fare of $220. But when would this expectation

# Derivation Checkpoint

## Mathematical Presentation of the Nash Equilibrium

The examples in Section 9.3 suggest a more formal description of what we mean by a Nash equilibrium. Suppose that there are two firms, 1 and 2.[a] The profit of each firm $\Pi_i$ is a function of the strategies chosen by the two firms. That is, $\Pi^i = \Pi^i(s_i, s_j)$, $i = 1,2$, $j \neq i$. Let $S_i$, $i = 1,2$, be the set of all feasible strategies from which firm $i$ can choose. Then a feasible strategy combination or a pair of feasible strategies, $(s_i^*, s_j^*)$ is a Nash equilibrium if, for each firm $i$:

$$\Pi^i(s_i^*, s_j^*) \geq \Pi^i(s_i, s_j^*), \text{ for every feasible strategy } s_i \; \varepsilon \; S^i, \; i = 1,2, \; j \neq i.$$

For a strategy combination to be a Nash equilibrium, the strategy $s_i^*$ must be firm $i$'s *best* feasible response to firm $j$'s strategy, $s_j^*$, and conversely, $s_j^*$ must be firm $j$'s best feasible response to strategy $s_i^*$.

Often, the strategy set $S^i$ is a subset of the set of real numbers, and the profit function $\Pi^i$ is continuous and smooth, that is, has no corners, and therefore has nice differentiability properties, and is concave or quasi-concave. In such cases, if a pure strategy Nash equilibrium exists, it can be found by differentiating each firm's profit function with respect to its own strategy. In other words, the strategy $s_i^*$ is found by solving the maximization problem: choose $s_i$ to maximize $\Pi^i(s_i, s_j^*)$.

Therefore, firm $i$'s best response, $s_i^*$ to firm $j$'s choice of $s_j^*$ can be found by solving the first-order necessary condition for the maximization problem:

$$\Pi_i^i(s_i^*, s_j^*) = 0$$

where $\Pi_i^i = \partial\Pi^i/\partial s_i$, the partial derivative of firm $i$'s profits with respect to its own strategy.

The first-order conditions for each firm may be combined to form a system of two equations in the two unknowns, $s_i^*$, $s_j^*$. If a solution to this system exists, and assuming the second-order condition for profit maximization[b] for each firm is also satisfied, then we have found a Nash equilibrium.

---

a   The following exposition easily generalizes to the case of $n$ firms.
b   The second order condition for the strategy $s_i^*$ to maximize firm $i$'s profit is $\partial\Pi_i^i(s_i^*, s_j^*)/\partial s_i^2 \leq 0$. This condition will be satisfied if the profit function is quasi-concave in $s_i$.

---

make sense? It will only do so if Delta also believes that American's management team is likewise persuaded that it, that is, Delta, is going to set a low fare. Indeed, Delta can go a small step further and reason that if this is in fact the expectation of American, then it may as well go ahead and set the low fare, because that is exactly what American is going to do. In other words, Delta's expectation that American will set a low fare because American, in turn, expects Delta to do so will in fact induce Delta to set a low fare. The low fare strategy is Delta's *best response* to its prediction of

American's strategy, and that predicted strategy is also the *best response* to Delta's *best response* to that predicted strategy.

In the language of game theory, the strategy combination (*low fare, low fare*) is a Nash equilibrium. If each firm chooses the low fare strategy, then neither will have any incentive to change its behavior. Each will be pursuing its best course of action given what the other is doing. However, in the airfare game of Table 9-3, there are *two* such equilibria. Following precisely the same reasoning, we can work out that the strategy combination (*high fare, high fare*) is also a Nash equilibrium. This game does not have a unique Nash equilibrium.

As we shall see, the existence of more than one Nash equilibrium for a game is not uncommon. But the fact that a unique Nash equilibrium does not always exist does not diminish the usefulness of the concept. To begin with, even if focusing on Nash equilibria does not completely solve the game, it certainly narrows the list of potential outcomes. In the airfare game just described, the requirement that the solution be a Nash equilibrium has permitted us to eliminate two, that is, half, of the possible strategy combinations from consideration. Moreover, there are often good, largely intuitive means for determining *which* Nash equilibrium is most likely. Schelling's (1960) book, *The Strategy of Conflict*, offers much guidance in this respect.

Consider the airfare game once more. We want to know which Nash equilibrium (*low fare, low fare*) or (*high fare, high fare*) is more likely to be the outcome. As Schelling observed, taking account of other factors, such as the past experience and learning of each firm's managers, may be helpful. If the managers of both sides are "old pros" who have dealt with each other for many years, they may be able to avoid the "price war" outcome and coordinate to achieve the more profitable (*high fare, high fare*) outcome. But if management of either or both sides is new and inexperienced, it will be harder to determine which Nash equilibrium will occur.[8]

We should note that the foregoing presentation refers to *pure* strategy equilibria. In game theory, a strategy choice is *pure* if a player picks it with certainty, for example, always calls "heads" in a coin toss. Such pure strategies should be distinguished from *mixed* strategies in which the player uses a probabilistically weighted mixture of two or more strategies, for example, calling "heads" half the time and "tails" the other half. In some games, mixed strategies or randomizing among strategies makes the most sense. However, in this text we focus primarily on market games in which the only sensible Nash equilibria are those involving pure strategies.

## Practice Problem 9.1

Firm 1 and firm 2 are movie producers. Each has the option of producing a blockbuster romance or a blockbuster suspense film. The payoff matrix displaying the payoffs for

---

8   Alternatively, we might think about the "regret" either player would feel if he or she plays the wrong strategy. If, for example, Delta chooses $P_H$ expecting American to do the same only to discover that American actually chooses $P_L$, it will find that it actually earns zero. But if it chooses $P_L$ expecting American also to set a low price and then discovers that American chooses the high price, $P_H$, Delta will find that this mistake actually increases its profit from \$1,800 to \$3,600. In other words, Delta will have much less regret when it assumes the Nash equilibrium will be $(P_L, P_L)$ than when it assumes it will be $(P_H, P_H)$. The same is of course true for American. This thinking suggests that the low price Nash equilibrium will prevail.

each of the four possible strategy combinations (in thousands) follows. Each firm must make its choice without knowing the choice of its rival.

|  |  | Firm 2 | |
|---|---|---|---|
|  |  | **Romance** | **Suspense** |
| **Firm 1** | **Romance** | $\Pi_1 = 300$  $\Pi_2 = 300$ | $\Pi_1 = 400$  $\Pi_2 = 1,000$ |
|  | **Suspense** | $\Pi_1 = 1,000$  $\Pi_2 = 400$ | $\Pi_1 = 750$  $\Pi_2 = 750$ |

Identify the Nash equilibrium or equilibria for this problem. Explain your answer.

## 9.4  STATIC MODELS OF OLIGOPOLY: THE COURNOT MODEL

All the games of the previous section are single period or static. Delta and American, for example, are assumed to choose either their departure times or their airfares without regard to the possibility that, at some later date, they might play the game again. This is also a feature of the early work on modeling oligopoly markets. Firms in these models "meet only once." The market then clears once-and-for-all. No repetition occurs of the interaction and, hence, no opportunity for firms to learn about each other over time. This of course is an obvious limitation. Yet it does not render such analyses useless. Far from it. Important insights can be gained from single period models of oligopoly behavior. Moreover, studying such static models is a good preparation for later examining more dynamic analyses.

Perhaps the most well-known static oligopoly models are the Cournot and Bertrand models, each named after its respective author whose work was done in the late nineteenth century. Interestingly enough, these models incorporate modern game theoretic elements. Indeed, the solution proposed by each author implies the concept of a Nash equilibrium, even though the two models were developed well before the formal development of game theory. In the Cournot model the choice or strategic variable firms choose when they compete is the quantity of output, whereas in the Bertrand model, the strategic variable chosen is price. In this chapter we present the Cournot model, and in the next chapter the Bertrand model.

The work of Augustin Cournot, a French mathematician in the mid-nineteenth century, has come to be understood as part of the cornerstone of modern industrial organization theory despite the fact that it went largely unrecognized for more than the first 100 years following its publication in 1836. Indeed, the Cournot duopoly model, which we are about to study, also anticipates Nash's concept of an equilibrium. For that reason, Cournot's work is regarded as a classic in game theory.

The story that Cournot told to motivate his analysis went as follows. Assume a single firm wishes to enter a market currently supplied by a monopoly. The entrant is able to offer a product that is identical in all respects to that of the incumbent monopolist and to produce it at the same cost. Entry will be attractive, therefore, because, under the assumption of constant and identical costs, we know that the monopolist is producing where price is greater than marginal cost, which means that the price also exceeds the marginal cost of the would-be entrant. Hence, the entrant firm will see that the current price exceeds its marginal cost and that it can profitably sell some amount in this market. However, the new entrant will, Cournot reasoned, choose an output level that maximizes profit *taking account of the output being sold by the monopolist.*

Of course, if entry occurred and the new firm produced its chosen output, the monopolist would react. Before entry, the monopolist chose a profit-maximizing output assuming no other rivals. Now, the former monopolist will have to re-optimize and choose a new level. In so doing, the monopolist will (as did the new entrant previously) choose an output level that maximizes profits *given the output sold by the new rival firm.*

This process of each firm choosing an output conditional on the other's output choice is to be repeated—at least as a mental exercise. For every output choice by the incumbent, firm 1, the entrant, firm 2, is shown to have a unique, profit-maximizing response and vice versa. Cournot called the graph representations of these responses the Reaction Curves. Each firm has its own Reaction Curve that can be graphed in the $q_1 q_2$ quadrant. That Cournot anticipated Nash is evidenced by the fact that he then described the equilibrium outcome of this process as that pair of output levels at which each firm's choice is the profit-maximizing response to the other's quantity. Otherwise, Cournot reasoned, at least one firm would wish to change its production level. A further appealing aspect of Cournot's two-firm or duopoly model is that the equilibrium price resulting from the output choices of the two firms is below that of the pure monopoly outcome. Yet it is also greater than that which would occur if there were not two firms but many and pure competition prevailed.

To present Cournot's analysis more formally we assume that the industry *inverse* demand curve[9] is linear, and can be described by

$$P = A - BQ = A - B(q_1 + q_2), \tag{9.1}$$

where $Q$ is the sum of each firm's production, that is, the total amount sold on the market, $q_1$ is the amount of output chosen by firm 1, the incumbent firm, and $q_2$ is the amount of output chosen by firm 2, the new competitor. As noted earlier, we also shall assume that each firm faces the same, constant marginal cost of production, $c$.

If we now consider firm 2, alone, and take firm 1's output, $q_1$, as given, the inverse demand curve facing firm 2 is

$$P = A - Bq_1 - Bq_2, \tag{9.2}$$

which is formally identical to (9.1). However, from firm 2's perspective, the notable point about equation (9.2) is that the first two terms on the right-hand side are to be considered given. In other words, those two terms together form the intercept of firm 2's perceived demand curve so that firm 2 understands that the only impact *its* output choice has on price is given by the last term of the equation, namely, $-Bq_2$. Note though, that any change in firm 1's output will be communicated to firm 2 by means of a shift in firm 2's perceived demand curve. Figure 9-1 illustrates this point.

As we can see from Figure 9-1, a different choice of output by firm 1 will imply a different demand curve for firm 2 and, correspondingly, a different profit-maximizing output for firm 2. Thus, for each choice of $q_1$ there will be a different optimal level of

---

9   Recall that by an inverse demand curve we mean a demand curve in which price is expressed as a function of quantity rather than quantity being expressed as a function of price.

FIGURE

**9-1**

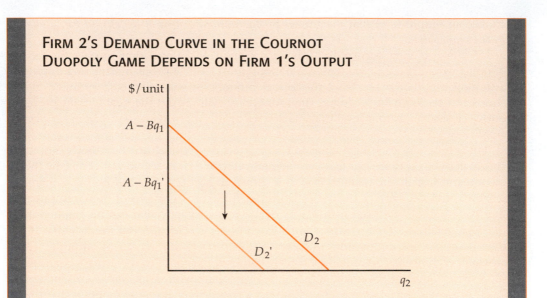

**FIRM 2'S DEMAND CURVE IN THE COURNOT DUOPOLY GAME DEPENDS ON FIRM 1'S OUTPUT**

An increase in $q_1$ to $q_1'$ shifts $D_2$, the demand curve facing Firm 2, downwards.

$q_2$. We can solve for this relationship algebraically, as follows. Associated with each demand curve illustrated in Figure 9-1 there is a marginal revenue curve that is twice as steeply sloped: this was discussed in Chapter 2, and is adapted to the present model in the inset. That is, firm 2's marginal revenue curve is also a function of $q_1$ given by

$$MR_2 = (A - Bq_1) - 2Bq_2. \qquad (9.3)$$

 **Derivation Checkpoint**

### Review of Marginal Revenue and Demand

Assume that the inverse demand curve facing firm 2 is:

$$P = A - Bq_1 - Bq_2$$

Then total revenue is:

$$TR_2 = (A - Bq_1 - Bq_2)q_2 = Aq_2 - Bq_1q_2 - Bq_2^2.$$

Marginal revenue is the differential of total revenue with respect to output, so that:

$$MR_2 = \partial TR_2 / \partial q_2 = A - Bq_1 - 2Bq_2$$

This has the same price intercept as the inverse demand function but twice the slope.

Marginal cost for each firm, we know, is constant at $c$. Setting marginal revenue $MR_2$ equal to marginal cost $c$, as required for profit maximization, and solving for $q_2^*$ yields firm 2's Reaction Curve. So we have $MR_2 = c$, which implies that $A - Bq_1 - 2Bq_2 = c$ or $2Bq_2 = A - c - Bq_1$. Further simplification then gives the Reaction Function for firm 2

$$q_2^* = \frac{(A - c)}{2B} - \frac{q_1}{2}. \qquad (9.4)$$

Equation (9.4) describes firm 2's best output choice, $q_2^*$, for every choice of $q_1$. Note that the relationship is a negative one. Every increase in firm 1's output lowers firm 2's demand and marginal revenue curves and, with a constant marginal cost, also lowers firm 2's profit-maximizing output.

Of course, matters work both ways. We may rework symmetrically the industry demand curve to show that firm 1's individual demand depends similarly on firm 2's choice of output, so that as $q_2$ changes, so does the profit-maximizing choice of $q_1$. Then, we may analogously derive firm 1's Reaction Curve giving its best choice of $q_1$ for each alternative possible value of $q_2$. By symmetry with firm 2, this is given by

$$q_1^* = \frac{(A - c)}{2B} - \frac{q_2}{2}. \qquad (9.5)$$

As was the case for firm 2, firm 1's profit-maximizing output level $q_1^*$ falls as $q_2$ increases.[10] The Reaction Curve for each firm is shown in Figure 9-2 in which the strategic variables for each firm, outputs, are on the axes.

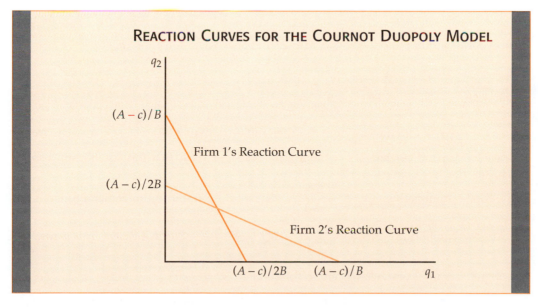

**REACTION CURVES FOR THE COURNOT DUOPOLY MODEL**

FIGURE **9-2**

---

10 We could alternatively solve for $q_2^*$ by writing firm 2's profit function, $\Pi^2$, as revenue less cost, or: $\Pi^2(q_1, q_2) = (A - Bq_1 - Bq_2)q_2 - cq_2 = (A - Bq_1 - c)q_2 - Bq_2^2$. When we differentiate this expression with respect to $q_2$ and set the result equal to 0, (first order condition for maximization), and then solve for $q_2^*$ we get the same result as equation (9.4). A similar procedure may be used to obtain $q_1^*$.

Consider first the Reaction Curve of firm 1, the initial monopolist. This shows that if firm 2 produces nothing, then firm 1 should optimally produce quantity $\dfrac{(A-c)}{2B}$, which is, in fact, the pure monopoly level at which we assumed firm 1 to be producing in the first place. Now consider the Reaction Curve for firm 2. That curve shows that if firm 1 were producing at the assumed level of $\dfrac{(A-c)}{2B}$, then firm 2's best bet would *not* be to produce no output, but instead, to produce at level $\dfrac{(A-c)}{4B}$. However, if firm 2 chooses that level, firm 1 will no longer do best by producing the monopoly level. Instead, firm 1 will maximize profits by selecting quantity $q_1 = \dfrac{3(A-c)}{8B}$.

As Cournot understood, none of the output or strategy combinations just described corresponds to an equilibrium outcome. In each case, the *Reaction* of one firm is based upon a choice of output for the other firm that is not, itself, that other firm's *Reaction*. For the outcome to be an equilibrium, it must be the case that each firm is responding optimally to the (optimal) choice of its rival. We want each firm to choose a Reaction based upon a prediction about what the other firm will produce and, in equilibrium, we want each firm's prediction to be correct. Put more simply, equilibrium requires that *both* firms be on their respective Reaction Curves. This happens at only one point in Figure 9-2, namely, the intersection of the two Reaction Curves. To see how this works, recall the Reaction Function for firm 2: $q_2^* = \dfrac{(A-c)}{2B} - \dfrac{q_1}{2}$. We know and firm 2 knows that in an equilibrium, firm 1 also must be on its Reaction Function, or that $q_1^* = \dfrac{(A-c)}{2B} - \dfrac{q_2}{2}$. Substituting this into firm 2's Reaction Function allows firm 2 (and also us) to solve for: $q_2^* = \dfrac{(A-c)}{2B} - \dfrac{1}{2}\left(\dfrac{A-c}{2B} - \dfrac{q_2^*}{2}\right) = \dfrac{A-c}{4B} - \dfrac{q_2^*}{4}$ so that $\dfrac{3q_2^*}{4} = \dfrac{A-c}{4B}$. In turn, this implies: $q_2^* = \dfrac{(A-c)}{3B}$. Of course, symmetry then indicates that $q_1^* = \dfrac{(A-c)}{3B}$ as well. We leave it as an end-of-chapter exercise for the reader to verify that this equilibrium also satisfies the Nash criterion.

Total output is then $Q^* = \dfrac{2(A-c)}{3B}$. Substituting this into the demand function gives the equilibrium price as $P = A - BQ = \dfrac{A+2c}{3}$. Profit for each firm is total revenue less total cost, which can be solved as $\pi_i = \dfrac{(A-c)^2}{9B}$.

As Figure 9-2 makes clear, the Cournot duopoly model just presented has a unique Nash equilibrium. Hence, in terms of our earlier discussion regarding the strategy of solving games, we can solve the Cournot duopoly game simply by focusing on its Nash equilibrium. Since there is only one of these, this must be the outcome of the game. The importance of this insight is difficult to overstate.

To see the power of the Nash concept, let us briefly reflect on the initial Cournot setup. We had two firms, each choosing quantity as its strategic variable. If, as also postulated, each knows the industry demand curve and the fact that each has an identical constant marginal cost, how should each firm act? Our discussion of Reaction or Reaction Curves borrowed from Cournot suggests a sequential, trial-by-learning process by which the two firms act and react until the equilibrium is achieved. But the power of the Nash equilibrium is that it makes such an iterative procedure unnecessary. Recall the basic game theory assumptions that firms are rational and strategic. In choosing its own production level, firm 1 *must anticipate* that firm 2 will do whatever maximizes firm 2's profits. An expectation, for instance, by firm 1 that firm 2 will produce 0 and that therefore firm 1 ought to choose the monopoly output would *not* be rational because the reaction curve tells us that 0 is not firm 2's Reaction to that situation. Hence firm 1 would never predict 0 as firm 2's output choice. Similarly, firm 1 also ought never to predict $q_2 = \dfrac{(A - c)}{4B}$. Here, such a prediction would lead to an inconsistency because it would imply a Reaction output for firm 1 of $q_1^\star = \dfrac{3(A - c)}{8B}$, for which the predicted value of $q_2 = \dfrac{(A - c)}{4B}$ is again not optimal. In short, firm 1 can make only one prediction for $q_2$ if it is to act rationally. This is that $q_2 = \dfrac{(A - c)}{3B}$ the value of $q_2$ in the Nash equilibrium. This is the only prediction, which, if made, will actually induce the behavior consistent with that expectation being fulfilled. If firm 1 expects $q_2$ to be equal to $\dfrac{(A - c)}{3B}$, then firm 1 will *optimally* choose that output level, too. In turn, this choice by firm 1 is such that firm 2 should indeed produce at the level of $\dfrac{(A - c)}{3B}$ if it wishes to maximize its profits.

To put it another way, what we are saying is that rational and strategic firms can work through the Cournot model as a pure thought experiment, without any time-consuming real-world trials and errors. When they do, such firms will quickly realize that the only sensible prediction is that each will produce the unique Nash equilibrium output value, $q_i^\star = \dfrac{(A - c)}{3B}$. It is only when each makes and then acts on that particular expectation that each firm will find its prediction comes true.

Many economists including ourselves prefer to use the term "*best response function*" instead of "Reaction Curve." The point is to emphasize that the correct interpretation of the Cournot model is one of simultaneous and *not sequential* output choice. The Cournot equilibrium is one in which each seller's predictions are consistent both with profit maximization and with the actual market outcome.[11]

As a numeric example, suppose that only two firms, Untel and Cyrox, supply the market for computer chips for toaster ovens. Untel's chips are perfect substitutes for Cyrox's chips and vice versa. Market demand for chips is estimated to be $P = 120 - 20Q$, where $Q$ is the total quantity (in millions) of chips bought. Both firms have a

---

11 Friedman (1977) includes a brief discussion of these issues, particularly valuable to those interested in the history of economic thought. He notes that Cournot's fate was not quite one of total obscurity owing to his friendship with the father of the French economist Walras. The English economist Marshall apparently also was well aware of and influenced by Cournot's work.

constant marginal cost equal to $20 per unit of output. Untel and Cyrox independently choose what quantity of output to produce. The price then adjusts to clear the market of the total quantity of chips produced. What quantity of output will Untel produce? What quantity of output will Cyrox produce? What will be the price of computer chips and how much profit will each firm make?

Let's put ourselves on the management team at Untel to see the problem from its perspective. The demand curve that Untel faces can be written as $P = 120 - 20q_c - 20q_u$, where $q_c$ is the output of Cyrox and $q_u$ is the output of Untel. As a result, Untel's marginal revenue curve is $MR_u = 120 - 20q_c - 40q_u$. To maximize profit Untel chooses a quantity of output $q_u^*$ such that its marginal revenue is equal to marginal cost. That is, $120 - 20q_c - 40q_u^* = 20$. This condition for profit maximization implies that

$$q_u^* = \frac{120 - 20}{40} - \frac{20}{40}q_c \text{ or } q_u^* = \frac{5}{2} - \frac{1}{2}q_c. \tag{9.6}$$

This is, in fact, Untel's Reaction Function for any given level of output by Cyrox. In other words, Untel knows that its profit-maximizing choice of output depends on what its rival, Cyrox, chooses to produce. Untel wants to predict what Cyrox is going to do, and then respond to it in a way that maximizes Untel's profit. Of course Untel knows that Cyrox is also a profit maximizer, and so Untel anticipates that Cyrox will want to produce $q_c^*$ to satisfy the condition for profit maximization at Cyrox. By precisely the same argument that we have just gone through, Untel knows that Cyrox's Reaction Function is $q_c^* = \frac{120 - 20}{40} - \frac{20}{40}q_u$ or $q_c^* = \frac{5}{2} - \frac{1}{2}q_u$. Untel can recognize that Cyrox's choice of output depends on Untel's. Untel also knows that Cyrox knows that Untel is a profit maximizer, and that Cyrox will anticipate that Untel will choose a profit-maximizing level of output $q_u^*$. Therefore, Untel predicts that Cyrox will choose $q_c^* = \frac{5}{2} - \frac{1}{2}q_u^*$. Substituting this prediction into Untel's Reaction Curve, equation (9.6), leads Untel to produce $q_u^* = \frac{5}{2} - \frac{1}{2}q_c^* = \frac{5}{2} - \frac{1}{2}\left(\frac{5}{2} - \frac{1}{2}q_u^*\right)$

$$\Rightarrow q_u^* = \frac{5}{3} .$$

Now let's put ourselves on the management team at Cyrox and repeat the exercise. Because the two firms are *identical* there is no reason why Cyrox would do anything different from Untel, and so we quickly can jump to the conclusion that Cyrox also will produce $q_c^* = \frac{5}{3}$. Note that when Untel produces $\frac{5}{3}$, Cyrox's best response is to produce $q_c^* = \frac{5}{3}$, and similarly when Cyrox produces $\frac{5}{3}$, Untel's best response is to produce $q_u^* = \frac{5}{3}$.

Aggregate market output is $Q^* = \frac{10}{3}$, and so the price that clears the market is

$P^* = 120 - 20\left(\frac{10}{3}\right) = \$53.33$. For each firm the margin of price over unit cost is

$33.33 so that each firm makes a profit of $53.33.

## Practice Problem 9.2

Assume that two identical firms are serving a market in which the inverse demand function is given by $P = 100 - 2Q$. The marginal costs of each firm are $10 per unit. Calculate the Cournot equilibrium outputs for each firm, the product price and the profits of each firm.

Cournot's model is insightful in its treatment of the interaction among firms and remarkably modern in its approach. Yet these are not its only strengths. Cournot's analysis has the further advantage that the results also blend well with economic intuition. In the standard Cournot duopoly model previously described each firm produces its Nash equilibrium output of $\dfrac{(A - c)}{3B}$, total industry output is $\dfrac{2(A - c)}{3B}$. This is clearly greater than the monopoly output for the industry, which would be $Q^M = \dfrac{(A - c)}{2B}$. Yet it is also less than the perfectly competitive output, $Q^C = \dfrac{(A - c)}{B}$, where price equals marginal cost. Accordingly, the market-clearing price in Cournot's model, $P = \dfrac{(A + 2c)}{3}$ is less than the monopoly price, $\dfrac{(A + c)}{2}$ but it is higher than the competitive price, $c$, which is equal to marginal cost. That is, Cournot's duopoly model has the intuitively plausible result that the interaction of two firms yields more industry output at a lower price than would occur under a monopoly, but not as much as the output produced under perfect competition.

## 9.5  VARIATIONS ON THE COURNOT THEME: MANY FIRMS AND DIFFERENT COSTS

Cournot's model can be enriched in several ways. For example, we have just seen that an attractive feature of the analysis is its prediction that the addition of a second firm moves the industry outcome away from the monopoly result and toward that which is obtained under perfect competition. A natural question then arises. Does introducing a third firm bring the industry still closer to the competitive ideal? What about a fourth? or a fifth? Is the Cournot analysis consistent with the notion that when there are numerous firms the price converges to marginal cost?

To explore the Cournot model's implications for various numbers of competitors, let us work with the general case of $N$ firms. These firms are, as before, assumed to be identical. Each produces the same homogenous good and each has the same, constant marginal cost $c$. Industry demand is again given by $P = A - BQ$ where $Q$ is aggregate output. But now we have that $Q = q_1 + q_2 + \ldots + q_N = \sum_{i=1}^{N} q_i$ so that

$P = A - B \sum_{i=1}^{N} q_i$, where $q_i$ is the output of the $i$th firm. In turn, this means that we can write the demand curve facing just a single firm, say firm 1, as: $P = (A - Bq_2 - Bq_3 - \ldots - Bq_N) - Bq_1$. The parenthetical expression reflects the fact that for firm 1, this term is totally beyond its control and merely appears as the intercept in firm 1's demand curve. It is conventional to use the notation $Q_{-1}$ as a shorthand method of denoting the sum of all industry output *except* that of firm 1's. Using this notation, we can write firm 1's demand curve even more simply as: $P = A - BQ_{-1} - Bq_1$. Clearly, firm 1's profits depend on both $Q_{-1}$, over which it has no control, and its own production level, $q_1$, which it is free to choose. Given its constant unit cost of $c$, firm 1's profits $\Pi^1$ can be written as: $\Pi^1(Q_{-1}, q_1) = (A - BQ_{-1} - Bq_1)q_1 - cq_1$.

Profit maximization requires that firm 1 chooses its output level where marginal revenue equals marginal cost. Since marginal revenue is given by a curve with the same intercept but twice as steeply sloped as firm 1's demand curve, the condition for profit maximization at firm 1 is

$$(A - BQ_{-1}) - 2Bq_1^* = c. \tag{9.7}$$

Solving this equation for $q_1^*$ gives us the Reaction Curve or what we will now call the *best response function* for firm 1 of

$$q_1^* = \frac{(A - c)}{2B} - \frac{Q_{-1}}{2}. \tag{9.8}$$

Since all firms are identical, we can extend this same logic to develop the best response function for any firm. Using the same shorthand notation, we can use $Q_{-i}$ to mean the total industry production *excluding that of firm i*. This means that the demand function for firm $i$, taking the output of all other firms as given, is

$$P = (A - BQ_{-i}) - Bq_i.$$

The associated marginal revenue function of firm $i$ is

$$MR_i = (A - BQ_{-i}) - 2Bq_i.$$

Equating marginal revenue with marginal cost gives the *best response function* for firm $i$

$$q_i^* = \frac{(A - c)}{2B} - \frac{Q_{-i}}{2}. \tag{9.9}$$

In a Nash equilibrium, each firm $i$ chooses a best response, $q_i^*$ that reflects a correct prediction for the other $N - 1$ firms. Denote by $Q_{-i}^*$ the sum of all the outputs excluding $q_i^*$ when each element in that sum is *each firm's best output response decision*. Then an algebraic representation of the Nash equilibrium is

$$q_i^* = \frac{(A - c)}{2B} - \frac{Q_{-i}^*}{2}; \text{ for } i = 1, 2, \ldots N. \tag{9.10}$$

Recall however that the $N$ firms are identical. They each produce the *same* good at the *same* unit marginal cost, $c$. From this it follows that, in equilibrium, each will produce the *same* output, that is, $q_1^* = q_2^* = \ldots = q_N^*$, or just $q^*$ for short. So, noting that $Q_{-i}^* = (N - 1)q^*$, we can rewrite equation (9.10) as

$$q^* = \frac{(A - c)}{2B} - \frac{(N - 1)q^*}{2}, \tag{9.11}$$

from which it follows that the equilibrium output for each firm, what we refer to as the *Cournot-Nash* equilibrium output, is

$$q^* = \frac{(A - c)}{(N + 1)B}. \qquad \textbf{(9.12)}$$

$N$ firms are each producing $q^*$ as given by equation (9.12). From this we may derive both the Cournot-Nash equilibrium industry output, $Q^* = Nq^*$, and the Cournot-Nash equilibrium industry price, $P^* = A - BQ^*$, as

$$Q^* = \frac{N(A - c)}{(N + 1)B}; \quad P^* = \frac{A}{(N + 1)} + \frac{N}{(N + 1)}c. \qquad \textbf{(9.13)}$$

Examine the two equations in (9.13) carefully. When $N = 1$, industry output is $\frac{(A - c)}{2B}$ and the price is $\frac{(A + c)}{2}$. But this is just the monopoly outcome, as of course, it should be. When $N$ increases to two we obtain the duopoly output and price levels derived in our earlier analysis. What happens when the number of firms rises above two? In particular, what happens when $N$ gets very large?

Consider first the Cournot-Nash equilibrium price, $P^*$. As $N$ gets larger and larger, the term $\frac{A}{(N + 1)}$ gets closer and closer to zero and, in the limit, vanishes. Similarly, as $N$ increases the term $\frac{N}{(N + 1)}$ becomes arbitrarily close to 1. Thus, equation (9.13) says that when the number of industry firms gets very large, the industry equilibrium price, $P^*$, converges to the level of marginal cost, $c$. But this is just the perfectly competitive result. Confirmation of this result is further obtained by noting that total industry output [the first part of equation (9.13)] is similarly close to the competitive output of $\frac{(A - c)}{B}$ when $N$ is large.

For example, if the inverse demand curve is: $P = 100 - 2Q$, so that $A = 100$, and $B = 2$; and if the unit cost $c = 4$, then the monopoly output $Q^M$ and price $P^M$ are: $Q^M = 24$ and $P^M = 52$. Moving from a monopoly to a duopoly raises the equilibrium output, $Q^D = 32$, and lowers the price to $P^D = 36$. If the number of firms increases to 99 then the price falls to $P^{99} = \frac{100}{100} + \frac{99}{100} \times 4 = \$4.96$. As we increase the number of firms selling in the market the Cournot equilibrium market output continues to rise and the price continues to fall until, with many, many firms, we approximate the competitive equilibrium with $Q = 48$ and $P = 4$.

In short, the Cournot model implies that as the number of *identical* firms in the market grows, the industry equilibrium gets closer and closer to that prevailing under perfect competition. Of course, this result seems quite natural since, as $N$ increases, each Cournot firm becomes smaller relative to the market. It is though an obviously appealing feature of Cournot's analysis that it predicts a plausible relationship between market structure and market performance. Market outcomes improve, and the competitive standard is approached, as market concentration falls.

What if the firms are not identical? Specifically, what if each firm has a different marginal cost? We first handle this question for the case of two firms, as usual, numbered

1 and 2. Assume that the marginal costs of firm 1 are $c_1$ and of firm 2 are $c_2$. We use the same approach as before with the duopoly model, starting with the demand function for firm 1, which we can write as

$$P = (A - Bq_2) - Bq_1.$$

The associated marginal revenue function is

$$MR_1 = (A - Bq_2) - 2Bq_1.$$

As before, firm 1 maximizes profit by equating marginal revenue with marginal cost. So setting $MR_1 = c_1$ and solving for $q_1$ gives the best response function for firm 1 as

$$q_1^* = \frac{(A - c_1)}{2B} - \frac{q_2}{2}. \tag{9.14a}$$

By an exactly symmetric argument, the best response function for firm 2 is

$$q_2^* = \frac{(A - c_2)}{2B} - \frac{q_1}{2}. \tag{9.14b}$$

Notice that the only difference from our initial analysis of the Cournot model is that now each firm's best response function reflects its own specific marginal cost.

An important feature of these best response functions that is obscured when the firms are identical is that the *position* of each firm's best response function is affected by its marginal cost. For example, if the marginal cost of firm 2 increases from say, $c_2$ to $c'_2$, its best response curve will shift inwards.

Figure 9-3 illustrates this point. It shows the best response function for each firm assuming initially that each firm has identical costs as in Figure 9-2. It then shows what happens when firm 2's unit cost rises. As equation (9.14) makes clear, this cost increase *lowers* firm 2's best output response for any given level of $q_1$. That is, it shifts firm 2's best response curve inward. This change in firm 2's best response function affects the equilibrium outputs that the two firms will choose. As you can see from the diagram, an increase in firm 2's marginal cost leads to a new equilibrium in which firm 1 produces more than it did in the initial equilibrium and firm 2 produces less. This makes intuitive sense. We should expect that low-cost firms will generally produce more than high-cost firms. The changes are not offsetting, however. Firm 2's output falls by more than firm 1's production rises so that the new equilibrium is characterized by less output in total than was the original equilibrium. (Can you say why?)

The Cournot-Nash equilibrium can be obtained as before by substituting the expression for $q_2^*$ into firm 1's best response to solve for $q_1^*$. Then we may use this value to solve for $q_2^*$. In other words, we have

$$q_1^* = \frac{(A - c_1)}{2B} - \frac{1}{2}\left(\frac{(A - c_2)}{2B} - \frac{q_1^*}{2}\right),$$

which can be solved for $q_1$ to give the equilibrium

$$q_1^* = \frac{(A + c_2 - 2c_1)}{3B}. \tag{9.15a}$$

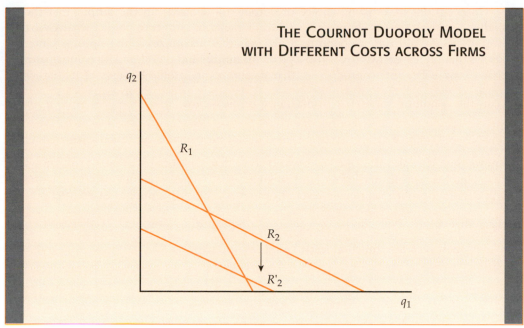

THE COURNOT DUOPOLY MODEL
WITH DIFFERENT COSTS ACROSS FIRMS

FIGURE

**9-3**

A rise in Firm 2's unit cost shifts the Firm 2 Response Function downward from $R_2$ to $R'_2$. In the new equilibrium, Firm 1 produces more and Firm 2 produces less.

By an exactly symmetric argument, the equilibrium output for firm 2 is

$$q_2^* = \frac{(A + c_1 - 2c_2)}{3B}.$$  (9.15b)

It is easy to check that the relative outputs of these two firms are determined by the relative magnitudes of their marginal costs. The firm with the lower marginal costs will have the higher output.

Let us return to our Untel and Cyrox example of the two firms who produce computer chips for toaster ovens but now change this story a bit. While we still assume that Untel's chips are perfect substitutes for Cyrox's chips and vice versa, we no longer assume that they have identical costs. Instead, we now assume that Untel is the low-cost firm with a constant unit cost of 20, and Cyrox is the high-cost producer with a constant unit cost of 40. Market demand for chips is still estimated to be $P = 120 - 20Q$, where $Q$ is the total quantity (in millions) of chips bought. What now happens when Untel and Cyrox independently choose the quantity of output to produce? What quantity of output will Untel produce? What quantity of output will Cyrox produce?

Again we put ourselves on the management team at Untel to see the problem from Untel's perspective. The demand curve that Untel faces is still $P = 120 - 20q_c - 20q_u$, where $q_c$ is the output of Cyrox and $q_u$ is the output of Untel. Untel's marginal revenue is again $MR_u = 120 - 20q_c - 40q_u$. To maximize profit Untel should sell a quantity of output $q_u^*$ such that at that quantity marginal revenue is equal to marginal cost. That is, $120 - 20q_c - 40q_u^* = 20$, and so the condition for profit maximization implies that

$$q_u^* = \frac{5}{2} - \frac{1}{2}q_c.$$  (9.16)

Untel's profit-maximizing choice of output still depends on the output that the higher cost rival, Cyrox, chooses to produce. Untel again wants to predict what Cyrox is going to do and then respond to it in a way that maximizes Untel's profit. Untel knows that higher cost Cyrox is also a profit maximizer and therefore Untel anticipates that Cyrox will want to produce $q_c^*$ that maximizes its profit. Because of its higher cost, the condition for Cyrox to maximize profit is now: $q_c^* = \dfrac{120-40}{40} - \dfrac{20}{40} q_u$ or $q_c^* = 2 - \dfrac{1}{2} q_u$. Once again, Cyrox's choice of output depends on Untel's, and Untel knows this. It is also the case, as it was before, that Untel knows that Cyrox knows that Untel is a profit maximizer, and so knows that Cyrox will anticipate that Untel will choose a profit-maximizing level of output $q_u^*$. All of this implies that Untel predicts that Cyrox will choose $q_c^* = 2 - \dfrac{1}{2} q_u^*$. Substituting this new prediction into Untel's best response function leads Untel to produce

$$q_u^* = \frac{5}{2} - \frac{1}{2} q_c^* = \frac{5}{2} - \frac{1}{2}\left(2 - \frac{1}{2} q_u^*\right) \Rightarrow q_u^* = 2 \,.$$

Now we put ourselves on the management team at Cyrox and repeat the exercise. To cut to the chase, we know that Cyrox's best response is $q_c^* = 2 - \dfrac{1}{2} q_u^*$. Moreover we know that Cyrox will predict that Untel will produce a best response that is based on a prediction that Cyrox also will produce a best response. That is, Cyrox predicts that Untel will produce $q_u^* = \dfrac{5}{2} - \dfrac{1}{2} q_c^*$. Substituting this prediction into Cyrox's best response function leads to: $q_c^* = 2 - \dfrac{1}{2} q_u^* = 2 - \dfrac{1}{2}\left(\dfrac{5}{2} - \dfrac{1}{2} q_c^*\right) \Rightarrow q_c^* = 1$. Again note that when Untel produces 2, Cyrox's best response is to produce $q_c^* = 1$, and similarly when Cyrox produces 1, Untel's best response is to produce $q_u^* = 2$.

Although the foregoing analysis is limited to just two firms, it still yields important insights. One of these is that in the Cournot model, firms with higher costs have smaller market shares and smaller profits. This means that a Cournot firm benefits when its rival's costs go up, as in our previous example. Moreover, when costs vary across firms, the equilibrium Cournot output $Q^*$ is not only too low (that is, less than the competitive level), it also is produced inefficiently. As we know from Chapter 4, efficient production among two or more firms would allocate output such that, in the final configuration, each firm's marginal cost is the same. This would be the outcome, for example, if the industry were comprised of a single, profit-maximizing, multiplant monopolist. It also will obtain under perfect competition. However, as we have just seen, the Cournot-Nash equilibrium does not require that firms' marginal costs be equalized.[12] Hence, the Cournot equilibrium with different costs between firms is not an efficient one.

---

12 Our example assumed constant but different marginal costs across firms. The same insight could be easily obtained for the more general presentation in which the marginal cost of firm $i$, $c_i$, is a general function of its output, $q_i$, as in $c_i = c_i(q_i)$.

## Practice Problem 9.3

What is aggregate output, market price, and Untel's profit and Cyrox's profit for the previous case in which Untel is the low-cost producer and Cyrox the high-cost one? Compare your answers to the ones you work out when the two firms are identical and have a constant unit cost of 20.

# 9.6  CONCENTRATION AND PROFITABILITY IN THE COURNOT MODEL

Let us now try to combine the case with many firms with the assumption of *non*identical costs. That is, let us evaluate the Cournot model for the case of $N$ firms, each with its own (constant) marginal cost such that the marginal cost of firm $i$ is $c_i$. A little reflection tells us that we can use the first order condition of equation (9.7) and identify the profit-maximizing condition for each firm $i$ merely by substituting $c_i$ for $c$ in this equation. This gives us the following

$$A - BQ_{-i} - 2Bq_i^* - c_i = 0, \tag{9.17}$$

where $Q_{-i}$ again is shorthand for the industry production accounted for by all firms other than the $i$th one.

In a Nash equilibrium though, the equilibrium output $q_i^*$ *for each firm i* must satisfy the first-order profit-maximizing condition. Hence, in the Nash equilibrium, the term $Q_{-i}$ must be the sum of the *optimal* outputs $q_j^*$ for each of the "not $i$" firms. Denote this equilibrium sum as $Q_{-i}^*$. Then we can rewrite (9.17) as

$$A - BQ_{-i}^* - 2Bq_i^* - c_i = 0. \tag{9.18}$$

By definition, the total equilibrium output, $Q^*$, equals the sum of $Q_{-i}^*$ and $q_i^*$. Hence, (9.18) implies that

$$A - B(Q_{-i}^* + q_i^*) - Bq_i^* - c_i = 0,$$

which can be reorganized to give

$$A - BQ^* - c_i = Bq_i^*. \tag{9.19}$$

We also know that the Nash equilibrium price, $P^*$, is obtained by substituting the Nash equilibrium output into the industry demand curve yielding, $P^* = A - BQ^*$. Substitution into equation (9.19) then yields

$$P^* - c_i = Bq_i^*. \tag{9.20}$$

Dividing both sides of equation (9.20) by $P^*$, and multiplying the *right-hand side* by $\dfrac{Q^*}{Q^*}$, we obtain

$$\frac{P^* - c_i}{P^*} = \frac{BQ^*}{P^*}\, s_i^*, \tag{9.21}$$

where $s_i^* = \dfrac{q_i^*}{Q^*}$ is the $i$th firm's market share in equilibrium.

# Reality Checkpoint

## Cournot Theory and Public Policy: The 1982 Merger Guidelines

In our review of antitrust policy in Chapter 1, we noted the dramatic change in policy regarding the treatment of mergers that occurred in 1982. In that year, the Department of Justice issued a new version of its *Horizontal Merger Guidelines*. This version replaced the original guidelines issued in 1968. Like the first set of guidelines, the 1982 document specified the conditions under which the government would challenge horizontal mergers. Unlike their predecessor, however, the new guidelines were based explicitly on the Herfindahl Index. Specifically, they stated that a merger would not be challenged if the industry Herfindahl Index was less than 1,000 (0.1 if shares are expressed in deci-

mals). A merger also would not be challenged if the index was over 1,000 but less than 1,800 *and* if the merger did not raise the Herfindahl Index by over 100 points. If the Herfindahl Index exceeded 1,800 points, then any merger that raised the index by over 50 points would cause concern and likely be challenged.

We will discuss these guidelines and their more recent modifications again in Chapter 16. For now, the point to note is that the explicit use of the Herfindahl Index may be viewed as a bow to the Cournot model, which, as shown in the text, directly connects that index to the price-cost margin measure of monopoly power.

**Source:** Department of Justice, *Horizontal Merger Guidelines* (1982, 1984, 1992, 1997), http://www.usdoj.gov/atr/public/guidelines/horiz_book/hmg1.html.

A close look at equation (9.21) reveals that the left-hand side is simply firm $i$'s Lerner Index, the measure of market power that we introduced in Chapter 3. This measure focuses on the ability of a firm to keep price above marginal cost. The lowest value of the Lerner Index is 0, which occurs when the firm is a perfect competitor and $P = MC$. The maximum value is 1, which indicates the maximum price-cost margin that a monopoly could charge.

Now consider equation (9.21) more closely. The right-hand side has two terms. The first is the slope of the industry demand curve times the ratio of output to price. But the slope is just $B = dP/dQ$ so that we have $\dfrac{BP^*}{Q^*} = \dfrac{dP}{dQ}\dfrac{P^*}{Q^*}$ . Now recall the definition of the price elasticity of demand: $\eta = \dfrac{dQ}{dP}\dfrac{P}{Q}$ . From this, it is clear that the first term on the right-hand side of equation (9.21) is just the inverse of the price elasticity of demand. The second term is, of course, the market share of the $i$th firm. So, we may write equation (9.21) alternatively as

$$\frac{P^* - c_i}{P^*} = \frac{s_i^*}{\eta},$$ 
(9.22)

where $\eta$ is the price elasticity of industry demand.

Equation (9.22) is a further implication of the Cournot model, now extended to allow for many firms with differing costs. What it says is this. Firms that operate in an industry where demand is relatively inelastic and where firms have relatively large market shares, also will be firms with a substantial degree of market power as measured by the Lerner Index or the firm's price-marginal cost distortion.

The relationship described in equation (9.22) tells us about market power at the level of the firm. In Chapter 3, we discussed the structure-conduct-performance (SCP) paradigm in industrial organization that linked market power, as measured by the Lerner Index, to the structure of the *industry*. The question that remains is whether we can extend our theoretical results at the firm level to the level of the entire industry.

To see that we can, first multiply each side of equation (9.22) by the firm's market share, $s_i^*$. Then add together the result that this yields for firm 1 with the result that it yields for firm 2 and the result that it yields for firm 3 and so on until we add together all $N$ equations. The left-hand side of this sum of $N$ equations is

$$\sum_{i=1}^{N} s_i^* \left( \frac{P^* - c_i}{P^*} \right) = \frac{\left( \sum_{i=1}^{N} s_i^* P^* - \sum_{i=1}^{N} s_i^* c_i \right)}{P^*} = \frac{P^* - \bar{c}}{P^*},$$

where $\bar{c}$ is the weighted average unit cost of production, the weights being the market shares of the firms in the industry. The right-hand side of the summed $N$ equations is

$$\frac{\sum_{i=1}^{N} (s_i^*)^2}{\eta} = \frac{H}{\eta},$$

where $H$ is the Herfindahl Index that we defined as a measure of concentration in Chapter 3 (here expressed using fractional shares, for example, a 10 percent share is recorded as $s_i = 0.10$). Therefore equation (9.22) aggregated at the level of the industry implies that

$$\frac{(P^* - \bar{c})}{P^*} = \frac{H}{\eta}. \tag{9.23}$$

Our generalized Cournot model thus gives theoretical support for the view that as concentration (here measured by the industry's Herfindahl Index) rises, prices also rise farther and farther above marginal cost. A variant of this relationship was tested in Marion *et al.* (1979) for food products. They collected price data for a basket of 94 grocery products, and market share data for 36 firms operating in 32 U.S. Standard Metropolitan Statistical Areas, and found that price is significantly higher in markets with a higher Herfindahl Index. Likewise Marvel (1989) found that for 22 U.S. cities, concentration in the retail market for gasoline, as measured by the Herfindahl Index, had a significant impact on the average price of gasoline.

# SUMMARY

For industries populated by few firms, strategic interaction is a fact of life. Each firm is and must be aware of the fact that its decisions will have significant impact on its rivals. Each firm will wish to take account of the anticipated response of its rivals when determining its course of action. We think that is reasonable to believe that firms' anticipations or expectations are rational.

Game theory is the modern formal technique for studying rational strategic interaction. Each player in a game has a set of strategies from which to choose. A strategy combination is a set of strategies—one for each player. Each such strategy combination implies a particular payoff or final outcome for each player. A Nash equilibrium is a strategy combination such that each player is maximizing his or her payoff *given* the strategies chosen by all other players. In a Nash equilibrium, no player has an incentive to change his or her behavior unilaterally.

In this chapter we presented the well-known Cournot model of competition. It is a static or single market period model of oligopoly. Although this model was developed prior to the formal development of game theory, the outcome proposed by Cournot embodies some basic game theoretic principles. The Cournot equilibrium also satisfies the Nash criterion.

The Cournot model makes clear the importance of firms recognizing and understanding their interdependence. The model also has the nice intuitive implication that the degree of departure from competitive pricing may be directly linked to the structure of the industry as measured by the Herfindahl Index. However, as pointed out before in Chapters 1 and 3, a market's structure is endogenous. Strategies that generate above-normal profits for existing firms will induce new firms to enter. At the same time, incumbent firms may be able to take actions that deter such entry. We need to develop an analysis that can examine these issues.

The Cournot model studied in this chapter has firms interacting only once. The reality, of course, is that firms are involved in strategic interactions repeatedly. In such a setting, issues such as learning, establishing a reputation, and gaining credibility become quite important. We turn to a consideration of strategic effects on market structure and the nature of strategic interaction over time in Chapters 11–13.

# PROBLEMS

1. Harrison and Tyler are two students who met by chance the last day of exams before the end of the spring semester and the beginning of summer. Both students had a lot in common and liked each other very much. Unfortunately, they forgot to exchange addresses. Fortunately, each remembered that they spoke of attending a campus party that night. Unfortunately, two such parties were being held. One party is small. If each attends this party, they will certainly meet. The other party is huge. If each attends this one, there is a chance they will not meet because of the crowd. Of course, they will certainly not meet if they attend separate parties. Payoffs to each depending on the combined choice of parties follow, with Tyler's payoffs listed first.

|  |  | Harrison | |
|---|---|---|---|
|  |  | Go To Small Party | Go To Large Party |
| Tyler | Go To Small Party | 1,000, 1,000 | 0, 0 |
|  | Go To Large Party | 0, 0 | 500, 500 |

**a.** Identify the Nash equilibria for this problem.

**b.** Identify the Pareto optimal outcome for this "two party" system.

2. Suppose that the small party of Problem 1 is hosted by the "Outcasts," 20 men and women students trying to organize alternatives to the existing campus party establishment. All 20 Outcasts will attend the party. But many other students—not unlike Harrison and Tyler—only go to a party to which others (no one in particular, just people in general) are expected to come. As a result, total attendance, $A$, at the small party depends on just how many people, $X$, everyone *expects* to show up. Let the relationship between $A$ and $X$ be given by: $A = 20 + 0.6X$.

**a.** Explain this equation. Why is the intercept 20? Why is the relation between $A$ and $X$ positive?

**b.** If the equilibrium requires that partygoers' expectations be correct, what is the equilibrium attendance at the Outcasts' party?

3. A game known well to both academics and teenage boys is "Chicken." Two players each drive their car down the center of a road in opposite directions. Each chooses either STAY or SWERVE. Staying wins adolescent admiration and a big payoff *if* the other player chooses SWERVE. Swerving loses face and has a low payoff when the other player stays. Bad as that is, it is still better than the payoff when both players choose STAY in which case they each die. These outcomes follow.

|          |        | Player A |          |
|----------|--------|----------|----------|
|          |        | STAY     | SWERVE   |
| Player B | STAY   | –6, –6   | 2, –2    |
|          | SWERVE | –2, 2    | 1, 1     |

**a.** Find the Nash equilibria in this game.

**b.** This is a good game to introduce mixed strategies. If Player A adopts the strategy, STAY one-fifth of the time, and SWERVE four-fifths of the time, show that Player B will be indifferent between the strategies, STAY and SWERVE.

**c.** If *both* players use this probability mix, what is the chance that they will both die?

4. You are a manager of a small "widget"-producing firm. There are only 2 firms including yours that produce "widgets." Moreover your company and your competitor's are identical. You produce the same good and face the same costs of production described by the following total cost function: Total cost = $1,500 + 8q$ where $q$ is the output of an individual firm. The market-clearing price, at which you can sell your widgets to the public, depends on how many widgets both you and your rival choose to produce. A market research company has found that market demand for widgets can be described as: $P = 200 - 2Q$ where $Q = q_1 + q_2$, where $q_1$ is your output and $q_2$ is your rival's. The board of directors has directed you to choose an output level that will *maximize* the firm's profit. How many widgets should your firm produce in order to achieve the profit-maximizing goal? Moreover you must present your strategy to the board of directors and explain to them why producing this amount of widgets is the profit-maximizing strategy.

5. You are a manager of a small widget-producing firm. Now, however, there are 14 such firms (including yours) in the industry. Each firm is identical; each one

produces the same product and has the same costs of production. Your firm, as well as each one of the other firms, has the same total cost function, namely: Total cost = $200 + 50q$ where $q$ is the output of an individual firm. The price at which you can sell your widgets is determined by market demand, which has been estimated as: $P = 290 - \frac{1}{3} Q$ where $Q$ is the sum of all the individual firms producing in this industry. So, for example, if 120 widgets are produced in the industry, then the market-clearing price will be 250 whereas if 300 widgets are produced, then the market-clearing price will be 190. The board of directors has directed you to choose an output level that maximizes the firm's profit. You have an incentive to maximize profits because your job and salary depend upon the profit performance of this company. Moreover, you also should be able to present your profit-maximizing strategy to the board of directors and explain to them why producing this amount maximizes the firm's profit.

6. The inverse market demand for fax paper is given by $P = 400 - 2Q$. There are two firms who produce fax paper. Each firm has a unit cost of production equal to 40, and they compete in the market in quantities. That is, they can choose any quantity to produce, and they make their quantity choices simultaneously.

   a. Show how to derive the Cournot-Nash equilibrium to this game. What are the firms' profits in equilibrium?

   b. What is the monopoly output, that is, the one that maximizes total industry profit? Why isn't producing one-half the monopoly output a Nash equilibrium outcome?

   c. Suppose now that firm 1 has a cost advantage. Its unit cost is constant and equal to 25 whereas firm 2 has the higher unit cost of 40. What is the Cournot outcome now? What are the firms' profits?

## REFERENCES

Cournot, Augustin. 1897. *Researches into the Mathematical Principles of the Theory of Wealth*. Translated by N. T. Bacon. New York: Macmillan.

Friedman, J. 1977. *Oligopoly Theory*. Amsterdam: North Holland Press.

Marion, B. W., W. F. Mueller, R. W. Cotterill, F. E. Geithman, and J. R. Schmelzer. 1979. *The Food Retailing Industry Market Structure, Profits and Prices*. New York: Praeger.

Marvel, H. 1989. "Concentration and Price in Gasoline Retailing." In Leonard Weiss ed., *Concentration and Price*. Cambridge, MA: The MIT Press.

Mas-Colell, A., M. D. Whinston, and J. Green. 1995. *Microeconomic Theory*. New York: Oxford University Press.

Rasmusen, E. 1994. *Games and Information*. Cambridge, MA: Blackwell Publishers Inc.

Schelling, T. 1960. *The Strategy of Conflict*. Cambridge, MA: Harvard University Press.

# Price Competition

The access to and use of high-speed Internet connections is spreading rapidly. According to the Federal Communications Commission (FCC), such access grew in America at a rate of over 80 percent in 2001 and over 150 percent in 2000. So far, most of this growth has been service provided by cable companies such as Comcast. At the beginning of 2003, cable companies had more than twice as many American subscribers as did telephone companies, but this could be changing. In the early spring of 2003, two major phone companies, Verizon and SBC, reduced their prices for Internet connection from $50 per month to about $35 per month. This fee undercut the typical cable company's rate, which was then $45 per month. Not surprisingly, both phone companies added many new subscribers and closed in on the cable companies lead in this fast-growing market.

Consumers of high-speed Internet connection often buy their service from the lowest priced provider. The providers post their prices, consumers decide from whom to buy, and then the consumer's line is hooked up. In other words, the firm does not produce the service or output until the consumer makes the purchase at the firm's posted price. This is the way competition works in many markets, including restaurants, electricians, moving companies, consulting firms, and numerous financial services. Note, though, that this is quite different from the way competition works in the Cournot model. There each competing firm independently produces an amount of output so that production occurs before the consumer makes a purchase. It is only afterwards that the price adjusts so that consumers will buy the total output that firms produced. This is what is meant by the phrase "the price adjusts so that the market clears," and it is perhaps an apt description of how automobile, aircraft, and other manufacturing firms compete.

In a monopolized market, it would make no difference whether the firm initially set a price and then produced whatever amount consumers demanded at that price or first chose its production and let the price settle at whatever level was necessary to sell that output. If the monopolist is truly profit maximizing, the optimal choice if it first selects a price will imply, via the demand curve, an output level which is precisely that amount of production that the monopolist would choose if it instead initially chose how much to produce. For a monopolized market, the equilibrium outcome is the same whether the firm regards price or output as its major decision variable.

However, once we leave the world of monopoly the equivalence of price and output strategies vanishes. As we shall see, once we move into a setting of oligopoly it matters very much whether firms compete in terms of quantities, as do perhaps aircraft manufacturers and other Cournot-type competitors, or in terms of price, as do the high-speed Internet providers. The nature of the competition is markedly different. To understand these differences we begin by turning the Cournot model on its head and looking at a market in which firms again produce identical products but now compete by first setting prices instead of production levels. This is known as the Bertrand model. Later, we retain the assumption of competition but allow the products to be less than perfect substitutes, that is, to be differentiated. As in Chapter 9, we also focus on static or simultaneous models of price competition limited to a single market period.

## 10.1 THE BERTRAND DUOPOLY MODEL

The standard Cournot duopoly model, recast in terms of price strategies rather than quantity strategies, is typically referred to as the Bertrand model. Joseph Bertrand was a French mathematician who in 1883 reviewed and critiqued Cournot's work nearly fifty years after its publication in an article in the *Journal des Savants*. Bertrand saw the absence of price competition as a weakness in Cournot's analysis and, indeed, in the general notion of mathematical modeling in economics altogether. The legacy of Bertrand is not, however, his criticism of what he termed "pseudo-mathematics" in economics. Instead, Bertrand's contribution was the recognition that using price as a strategic variable is different from using quantity as the strategic variable, and that this difference is worth investigating.

Let us now rework the Cournot duopoly model with each firm choosing the price it will charge rather than the quantity it will produce. Otherwise, the model and the assumptions are exactly the same as before. There are two firms who choose their strategies simultaneously. Each produces the identical good at the same, constant marginal cost, $c$. Each firm knows the structure of market demand. Before we described demand by a linear inverse demand function, $P = A - BQ$. When firms choose prices rather than quantities it is more convenient to rewrite the demand function and have total output as the dependent variable.[1] Therefore, we have

$$Q = a - bP, \text{ where } a = \frac{A}{B} \text{ and } b = \frac{1}{B}. \qquad \textbf{(10.1)}$$

Consider the pricing problem first from firm 2's perspective. In order to determine its best price response to its rival firm 1, firm 2 must first work out the demand for its product *conditional* on both its own price, denoted by $p_2$, and firm 1's price, denoted by $p_1$. Rationally speaking, firm 2's reasoning should be as follows. If $p_2 > p_1$, firm 2 will sell no output. The product is homogenous so that consumers always buy from the cheapest source. Setting a price above that of firm 1 therefore means that firm 2 will serve no customers. The opposite is true if $p_2 < p_1$. When firm 2 sets the lower price, it will supply the entire market, and firm 1 will sell nothing. Finally, we will assume that if $p_2 = p_1$, the two firms evenly split the market. When both firms charge identical prices the same number of customers patronize both producers.

The foregoing implies that the demand for firm 2's output, $q_2$, may be described as follows:

$$
\begin{aligned}
q_2 &= 0 & \text{if } p_2 > p_1 \\
q_2 &= \frac{a - bp_2}{2} & \text{if } p_2 = p_1 \\
q_2 &= a - bp_2 & \text{if } p_2 < p_1
\end{aligned}
\qquad \textbf{(10.2)}
$$

---

1　When firms choose quantities (as in Cournot's model), it is best to work with the inverse demand curve and treat price as the dependent variable. When firms select prices, as in Bertrand's analysis, it is usually best to let quantity be the dependent variable.

As Figure 10-1 shows, this demand structure is *not* continuous. For any $p_2$ greater than $p_1$, demand for $q_2$ is zero. But when $p_2$ falls and becomes equal to $p_1$, demand jumps from zero to $\dfrac{a - bp_2}{2}$. When $p_2$ then falls still further so that it is below $p_1$, demand again jumps to $a - bp_2$.

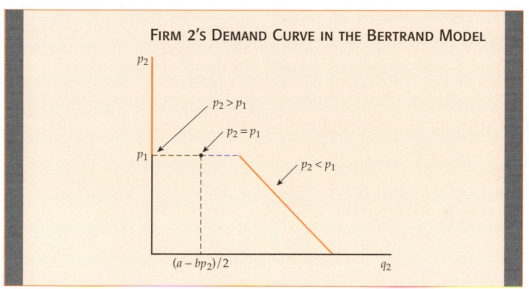

### FIRM 2'S DEMAND CURVE IN THE BERTRAND MODEL

**FIGURE**

**10-1**

Industry demand equal to $a - bp_2$ is the same as firm 2's demand for all $p_2$ less than $p_1$. If $p_2 = p_1$, then the two firms share equally the total demand. For $p_2 > p_1$, firm 2's demand falls to zero.

This discontinuity in firm 2's demand curve was not present in the quantity version of the Cournot model. It turns out to make a crucial difference in terms of firms' strategies. This is because the discontinuity in demand carries over into a discontinuity in profits. Firm 2's profit, $\Pi_2$, as a function of $p_1$ and $p_2$ is

$$\Pi_2(p_1, p_2) = 0 \qquad\qquad\qquad \text{if } p_2 > p_1$$

$$\Pi_2(p_1, p_2) = (p_2 - c)\frac{a - bp_2}{2} \quad \text{if } p_2 = p_1 \qquad\qquad \textbf{(10.3)}$$

$$\Pi_2(p_1, p_2) = (p_2 - c)(a - bp_2) \quad \text{if } p_2 < p_1$$

To find firm 2's *best response* function, we need to find the price, $p_2$, that maximizes firm 2's profits, $\Pi_2(p_1, p_2)$, for any given choice of $p_1$. For example, suppose firm 1 chooses a very high price—higher even than the pure monopoly price, which is $p^M = \dfrac{a + c}{2b}$.[2] Since firm 2 can capture the entire market by selecting any price lower than $p_1$, its best response would be to choose the pure monopoly price, $p^M$, and thereby earn the pure monopoly profits.

----

2   This is, of course, the same monopoly price as we showed in Chapter 8 for the quantity version of the model with the notational change that $a = A/B$, and $b = 1/B$.

Conversely, what if firm 1 set a very low price, one below its unit cost, $c$? This would be an unusual choice, of course. However, if we wish to construct a complete *best response* function for firm 2, we must determine its value for *all* the possible values $p_1$ can take. Continuing then, if $p_1 < c$, firm 2 is best setting its price at some level above $p_1$. This will mean that firm 2 will sell nothing and earn zero profits. But any other choice will lead to *negative* profits. For if $p_2$ is less than or equal to $p_1$, firm 2 will sell a positive amount of output. Since such a price will be below its unit cost, firm 2 will lose money on each unit sold.

So much for firm 2's best response to the extreme choices of $p_1$. What about the more likely case in which firm 1 sets its price above marginal cost, $c$, but either equal to or below the pure monopoly price, $p^M$? How should firm 2 optimally respond in these circumstances? The simple answer is that it should set a price *just a bit less than* $p_1$. The intuition behind this strategy is illustrated in Figure 10-2, which shows firm 2's profit given a price, $p_1$, satisfying the relationship $\frac{a+c}{2b} \geq p_1 > c$.

**FIGURE 10-2**

**FIRM 2'S PROFITS AS A FUNCTION OF $p_2$ WHEN FIRM 1 PRICES ABOVE COST BUT BELOW THE PURE MONOPOLY PRICE**

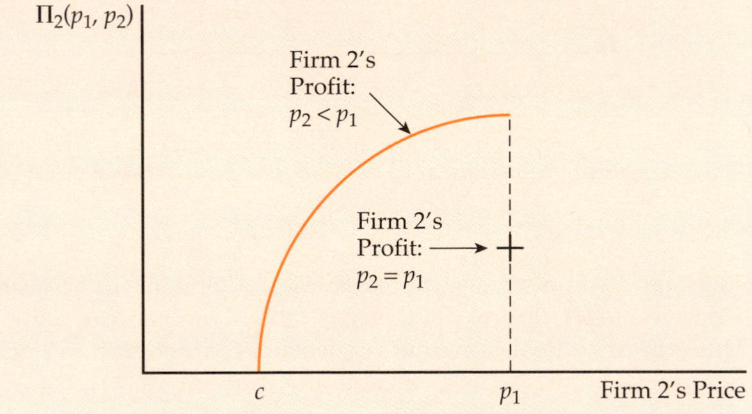

Firm 2's profits rise continuously as its price rises from the level of marginal cost, $c$, to just below firm 1's price. When $p_2$ equals $p_1$, firm 2's profits fall relative to those earned when $p_2$ is just below $p_1$. For $p_2$ greater than $p_1$, firm 2 earns zero profits.

Note that firm 2's profits rise continuously as $p_2$ rises from $c$ to just below $p_1$. Whenever $p_2$ is less than $p_1$, firm 2 is the only company that any consumer buys from. However, in the case where $p_1$ is less than or equal to $p^M$, the monopoly position that firm 2 obtains from undercutting $p_1$ is constrained. In particular, it cannot achieve the pure monopoly price, $p^M$, and associated profit because, at that price, firm 2 would lose all its customers. Still, the firm will wish to get as close to that result as possible. It could, of course, just match firm 1's price exactly. But whenever it does so it shares the market equally with its rival. If instead of setting $p_2 = p_1$, firm 2 just *slightly* reduces its price below the $p_1$ level, it will double its sales while incurring only an infinitesimal decline in its profit margin per unit sold. This is a trade well worth the making as Figure 10-2 makes clear. In turn, the implication is that for any $p_1$ such that

$p^M \geq p_1 > c$, firm 2's best response is to set $p_2^* = p_1 - \varepsilon$, where $\varepsilon$ is an arbitrarily small amount.

The last case to consider is the case in which firm 1 prices at cost so that $p_1 = c$. Clearly, firm 2 has no incentive to undercut this value of $p_1$. To do so would only lead to losses for firm 2. Instead, firm 2 will do best to set $p_2$ either equal to or above $p_1$. If it prices above $p_1$, firm 2 will sell nothing and earn zero profits. If it matches $p_1$, it will enjoy positive sales but break even on every unit sold. Accordingly, firm 2 will earn zero profits in this latter case, too. Thus, when $p_1 = c$, firm 2's best response is to set $p_2$ either greater than or equal to $p_1$.

Our preceding discussion may be summarized with the following description of firm 2's best price response:

$$
\begin{aligned}
p_2^* &= \frac{a + c}{2b} &&\text{if} && p_1 > \frac{a + c}{2b} \\
p_2^* &= p_1 - \varepsilon &&\text{if} && c < p_1 \leq \frac{a + c}{2b} \\
p_2^* &\geq p_1 &&\text{if} && c = p_1 \\
p_2^* &> p_1 &&\text{if} && c > p_1 \geq 0
\end{aligned}
\tag{10.4}
$$

By similar reasoning, firm 1's best response, $p_1^*$, for any given value of $p_2$, would be given by

$$
\begin{aligned}
p_1^* &= \frac{a + c}{2b} &&\text{if} && p_2 > \frac{a + c}{2b} \\
p_1^* &= p_2 - \varepsilon &&\text{if} && c < p_2 \leq \frac{a + c}{2b} \\
p_1^* &\geq p_2 &&\text{if} && c = p_2 \\
p_1^* &> p_2 &&\text{if} && c > p_2 \geq 0
\end{aligned}
\tag{10.5}
$$

We may now determine the Nash equilibrium for the duopoly game when played in prices. We know that a Nash equilibrium is one in which neither firm has an incentive to change its strategy. For example, the strategy combination $\left( p_1 = \dfrac{a+c}{2b}, \right.$ $\left. p_2 = \dfrac{a+c}{2b} - \varepsilon \right)$ *cannot* be an equilibrium. This is because in this combination, firm 2 undercuts firm 1's price and sells at a price just below the monopoly level. However, in such a case, firm 1 would have no customers and earn zero profit. Since firm 1 could earn substantial profit by lowering its price to just below that set by firm 2, it would wish to do so. Accordingly, this strategy cannot be a Nash equilibrium. To put it another way, firm 2 could never expect firm 1 to set the monopoly price of $p_1 = (a + c)/2b$ precisely because firm 1 would know that so doing would lead to zero profit as firm 2 undercut that price by a small amount $\varepsilon$ and stole all of firm 1's customers.

As it turns out, there is only one Nash equilibrium for the Bertrand duopoly game we have described. It is the price pair $(p_1^* = c, p_2^* = c)$.[3] If firm 1 sets this price in the

---

3   If prices cannot be set continuously but are restricted to whole dollar amounts, then there are two Nash equilibria. One is where both firms set price equal to marginal cost, $p_1 = p_2 = c$. The other is where each firm sets a price equal to $1 above marginal cost, $p_1 = p_2 = c + 1$.

# Reality Checkpoint

## Bertrand Competition—The Eyes Have It

Perhaps one of the most dramatic examples of Bertrand competition comes from the market for laser eye surgery. Such surgery uses a specialized laser machine to reshape the cornea, which acts like a second lens to focus light on the retina. Age and other factors can change the cornea's shape so that the focal point moves either to the front or the back of the retina wall. Laser machines originally designed for etching computer chips can correct this problem. Under the direction of a doctor, laser slices are made in the patient's eyeball, allowing the curvature to be reshaped so as to produce the proper focal point. The entire procedure takes about 15 minutes per eye. In 1997, the price for such surgery was close to $3,000 per eye. Cur-rently, it is not uncommon to find prices as low as $499 per eye—a dramatic price reduction of 83 percent in just six years. It reflects two factors. First, the two initial makers of the laser machines, Visx and Summit Technologies (now owned by Nestle), were subsequently joined by other manufacturers, including Bausch & Lomb, Lasik, and Nidek. Each of these firms offers a virtually identical product to the eye surgery clinics. The second factor was the rapid discounting of eye surgery prices by the clinics themselves. Virtually every major city has at least two such clinics. Faced with a competitor offering a nearly identical service, each clinic can do little to attract customers except offer a lower price.

**Source:** M. Freudenhiem, "Turning Surgery Into a Commodity: Laser Eye Centers Wage an All-Out Price War." *The New York Times*, December 9, 2000.

expectation that firm 2 will do so, and if firm 2 acts in precisely the same manner, neither will have an incentive to change. Hence, the outcome of the Bertrand duopoly game is that the market price equals marginal cost. This is, of course, exactly what occurs under perfect competition. The only difference is that here, instead of many small firms, we have just two large ones.

It is no wonder that Bertrand noted the different outcome obtained when price replaces quantity as the strategic variable. Far from being a cosmetic or minor change, this alternative specification has dramatic impact. It is useful, therefore, to explore the nature and the source of this powerful effect more closely.

# Practice Problem 10.1

Let the market demand for carbonated water be given by $Q^D = 100 - 5P$. Let there be two firms producing carbonated water, each with a constant marginal cost of 2.

a. What is the market equilibrium price and quantity when each firm behaves as a Cournot duopolist choosing quantities? What are the firms' profits?
b. What is the market equilibrium price and quantity when each firm behaves as a Bertrand duopolist choosing price? What are the firms' profits?

## 10.2 BERTRAND RECONSIDERED

Like its Cournot cousin, the Bertrand analysis of a duopoly market is not without its critics. The chief source of criticism with the Bertrand model is its assumption that *any* price deviation between the two firms leads to an immediate and complete loss of demand for the firm charging the higher price. It is this assumption that gives rise to the discontinuity in both firms' demand and profit functions. It is also this assumption that underlies our derivation of each firm's best response function.

Such a consumer response to minor price differences seems extreme. More importantly, there are two reasons why a firm's decision to charge a price higher than its rival would not result in the loss of all its customers. One is that because of a capacity constraint the rival firm will not be able to serve all of the customers demanding the product or service at the low price.[4] The second is that the two products may not be perfect substitutes.

As an example of the importance of capacity constraints, consider a small New England area with two ski resorts, Pepall Ridge and Snow Richards, each located on different sides of Mount Norman. Skiers regard the services at these resorts to be the same and will choose whenever possible to ski at the resort that quotes the lowest lift ticket price. Pepall Ridge is a small resort that can accommodate 1,000 skiers per day. Snow Richards is slightly bigger and can handle 1,400 skiers a day. Skiing on Mount Norman has become extremely popular. The demand for skiing services on Mount Norman is estimated to be $Q = 6,000 - 60P$, where $P$ is the price of a daily lift ticket and $Q$ is the number of skiers per day.

The two resorts compete in price. Suppose that the marginal cost of providing lift services is the same at each resort and is equal to $10 per skier. As a little thought will reveal, the outcome where each resort sets a price equal to marginal cost *cannot* be a Nash equilibrium. Demand when the price of a lift ticket is equal to $10 would be equal to 5,400, far exceeding the total capacity of the two resorts. If each resort had understood the extent of demand, each might have built additional lifts, ski runs, and parking facilities such that each would have had much greater capacity. Nevertheless, it is not likely that the Nash equilibrium will end up with each resort setting a price equal to the marginal cost of $10 per skier. Why? Think of it this way. If Pepall Ridge sets a price of $11, Snow Richards could set a price of $10.02, in which case it would steal all of Pepall Ridge's customers and, in fact, serve just about all 5,400 skiers. However, this is only a credible threat—one that will inhibit Pepall Ridge from pricing at $11 in the first place—if Snow Richards really can serve that many customers. However, to build that much capacity would be fairly short-sighted behavior for Snow Richards. For if Pepall Ridge is serving no skiers at a price of $11 while Snow Richards is serving all the skiers at a price of $10.02, Pepall Ridge will retaliate with a price of $10.01 and steal all the market demand for itself. Again, however, for this to be a credible threat Pepall Ridge must also have capacity of nearly 5,400.

The logical extension of this analysis is that the pressure for each resort to cut price to marginal cost rests implicitly on each having sufficient capacity to serve the entire competitive market supply of 5,400. However, when each charges a price of $10, the market is split and each serves only 2,700. It seems unlikely that each will

---

4   Edgeworth (1897) was one of the first economists to investigate the impact of capacity constraints on the Bertrand analysis.

build capacity of 5,400 if each will serve only 2,700 skiers in equilibrium. Yet unless each does so, there is little pressure on price to fall to the marginal cost of $10.

More generally, denote as $Q^C$ the competitive output or the total demand when price is equal to marginal cost, that is, $Q^C = a - bc$. If neither firm has the capacity to produce $Q^C$ (neither could individually meet the total market demand generated by competitive prices), but instead can each produce only a smaller amount, then the Bertrand outcome with $p_1 = p_2 = c$ will *not* be the Nash equilibrium. The reason for this should be clear from our previous work. In the Nash equilibrium, it must be the case that each firm's choice is a best response to the strategy of the other. Consider the original Bertrand solution with prices chosen to be equal to marginal cost, $c$, and profit at each firm equal to zero. Because we have now imposed a capacity constraint, a firm such as firm 2 can contemplate *raising* its price. If firm 2 sets $p_2$ above marginal cost, and hence above $p_1$, it would surely lose some of its customers. But it would not lose all of them. Firm 1 *does not have the capacity* to serve them. Some customers would remain with firm 2. Yet firm 2 is now earning some profit from each such customer $(p_2 > c)$, implying that its total profit is now positive whereas before it was zero. It is evident, therefore, that $p_2 = c$ is not a best response to $p_1 = c$. Accordingly, the strategy combination $(p_1 = c, p_2 = c)$ cannot be a Nash equilibrium if there are binding capacity constraints.

Once we bring a consideration of capacity constraints into the analysis, the game becomes a two-stage one. In the first stage, firms determine capacity. In the second, they then compete in price. Formal analysis of such games is tricky. However, as previously noted, neither firm is likely to acquire enough capacity to serve the entire market when pricing at marginal cost. Again, though, if neither acquires that large amount of capacity, then the Bertrand solution of each charging a price equal to marginal cost *cannot* be a Nash equilibrium. We will return to the issue of capacity choice in Chapter 12. It is worth noting, however, that the equilibrium in a model of price competition *with* capacity constraints takes us away from the efficient outcome, and closer towards the outcome in the Cournot model.[5]

Let us now return to the ski resort competition between Pepall Ridge and Snow Richards, and let's also make a special additional assumption. Let's assume that at any price at which a resort has demand beyond its maximum capacity, the skiers that it actually serves are those who are the most eager, that is, those who have the highest willingness to pay. For example, at a price of $50 at each resort, total market demand is 3,000. This is beyond the total market capacity of 2,400 and, therefore, each resort will need somehow to ration or choose which skiers will actually ski. Our assumption, sometimes called the efficient rationing assumption, is that they will do this by serving customers in order of their willingness to pay. For example, Pepall Ridge will choose those 1,000 potential skiers with the top willingness to pay. If we proceed in this way, then we can derive the residual demand curve facing Snow Richards at any price.

A price of particular interest is $60. Suppose that both resorts have set $p_1 = p_2 = $60$. At these prices, total demand is equal to 2,400, which is just equal to the total capacity of the two resorts. Is this a Nash equilibrium? We can answer this question by using the above logic to determine the demand function facing Snow Richards when Pepall Ridge sets a price equal to $60. Under our assumption of efficient rationing, this is shown in Figure 10-3. It is the original demand curve shifted to the

---

5   This result is formally modeled in a two-stage game in Kreps and Scheinkman (1983).

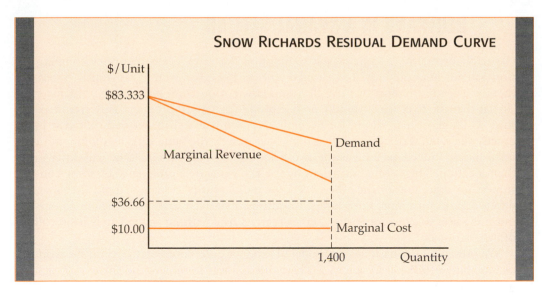

SNOW RICHARDS RESIDUAL DEMAND CURVE

FIGURE

**10-3**

left by 1,000 units, that is, it is $Q = 5,000 - 60P$ (or, in inverse form, $P = 83.333 - Q/60$). The marginal revenue curve facing Snow Richards when Pepall Ridge charges a price of $60 is also shown.

Note that while changes in its price also change the demand facing Snow Richards, it is always constrained to serve no more than its capacity of 1,400. In this light, consider again the situation in which Snow Richards sets a price just equal to the $60 that Pepall Ridge is charging. Is this a best response? We check this by asking whether Snow Richards has an incentive to change its price. The answer is no. Lowering its price will not lead to any more customers since Snow Richards is at capacity. Yet raising its price is not an attractive option, either. This will lower its demand below capacity of 1,400. Since marginal revenue exceeds marginal cost, losing customers also loses profit. Accordingly, Snow Richards has no incentive to lower or to raise its price from $60, assuming that Pepall Ridge is also setting that price. By a similar logic, we can show that Pepall Ridge has no incentive to change its price from $60 given that Snow Richards is charging that amount. Therefore, $p_1 = p_2 = \$60$ is the Nash equilibrium for this game.

As noted earlier, the logic of the above example is quite general. Firms competing in prices selling identical products will rarely choose the capacity necessary to serve the total market demand forthcoming at competitive prices. As a result, both output and capacity will be less than the competitive level. In turn, this implies that prices must rise to a level at which demand equals the total industry capacity—a level that is necessarily above marginal cost. Thus, the efficiency property of the Bertrand solution can break down when firms are capacity constrained.

## Practice Problem 10.2

Suppose now market demand for skiing increases to $Q^D = 9,000 - 60P$. However, because of environmental regulation the two resorts cannot increase their capacities and serve more skiers. What is the Nash equilibrium outcome for this case? That is, what are the profit-maximizing prices set by Pepall Ridge and Snow Richards?

## 10.3 BERTRAND IN A SPATIAL SETTING

Capacity constraints are one reason to question Bertrand's view that price competition will automatically lead to marginal cost pricing. However, as previously noted, there is a second reason that the Bertrand efficient outcome may not be obtained. This is that the two firms typically do not produce identical products as Bertrand assumed. Think of hair salons, for example. No two hair stylists cut and style hair in exactly the same way. Nor will the salons have exactly the same sort of equipment or furnishings. Indeed, as long as the two firms are not side by side, they will differ in their location. This is often sufficient by itself to generate a preference by some consumers for one salon or the other, even when different prices are charged. In short, differences in locations, furnishings, or cutting styles can each be sufficient to permit one salon to price somewhat higher than its rival without immediately losing all of its customers.

We presented the basic spatial model of product differentiation based on the work of Hotelling (1929) in Chapter 7.[6] There our aim was to understand the use of such differentiation by a monopoly firm to extract additional surplus. The same model of demand, however, may also be used to understand the nature of price competition when there is more than one firm marketing differentiated products. Let's review the basic setup presented earlier. There is a line of unit (say, one mile) length along which consumers are uniformly distributed. This market is supplied by two stores. This time, however, the same company does not operate the two stores. Rival firms operate them. One firm—located at the west end of town—has the address $x = 0$. The other—located at the east end of town—has the location $x = 1$. Each of the firms has the same constant unit cost of production, $c$.

Each point on the line is associated with a value of $x$ measuring the location of that point relative to the west or left end of town. A consumer who's most preferred style or location is $x'$ is called consumer $x'$. While consumers differ about which variant or location of the good is best, they are the same insofar as each has the same reservation demand price, $V$, for their most preferred good. Naturally we assume that $V$ is substantially greater than the unit cost of production, $c$. Each consumer will also buy at most one unit of the product. If consumers purchase a good located "far away" from their most preferred location, they incur a utility cost. In particular, consumer $x'$ incurs the cost $tx'$ if he or she consumes good 1 (located at $x = 0$), and the cost $t(1 - x')$ if he or she consumes good 2 (located at $x = 1$). Figure 10-4 describes this market setting.

Again, it bears repeating that the location difference that we have introduced serves as a metaphor for other qualitative differences. Thus, instead of having two

FIGURE
10-4

**THE "MAIN STREET" SPATIAL MODEL ONCE AGAIN**

| Firm 1 | | Firm 2 |
|---|---|---|
| 0 | $x'$ | 1 |

---

6   Friedman (1977), pp. 50–76, is a very readable discussion. See also our discussion in Chapter 4.

stores geographically separated we could think of two products marketed by two different firms that are differentiated by some characteristic, such as sugar content in the case of soft drinks, or an index of fuel efficiency and ride comfort in the case of automobiles. Our unit line in each case would represent the spectrum of products differentiated by this characteristic and each consumer would have a most preferred product specification on this line. For the case of soft drinks our two firms could be Pepsi and Coca-Cola. For the case of automobiles, our two firms could be Ford and GM.

As Bertrand assumed, the two firms compete for customers by setting prices, $p_1$ and $p_2$, respectively. These are chosen simultaneously. As always, we look for a Nash equilibrium as the solution to the game. One requirement for such an equilibrium is that both firms have a positive market share as long as both prices are greater than or equal to $c$. If this condition is not satisfied it would mean that at least one firm's price is set so high that it has zero market share and, therefore, zero profits. Since in our case the two firms have the same unit cost, $c < V$, a firm could always obtain positive profits by cutting its price, and hence a zero market share situation cannot be part of a Nash equilibrium.

We will make the further assumption that the Nash equilibrium outcome is one in which the entire market is served. That is, we will assume the outcome involves a market configuration in which every consumer buys the product from either firm 1 or firm 2.[7] This assumption will be true so long as each consumer's reservation price, $V$, is sufficiently large. When $V$ is large, firms will have an incentive to sell to as many customers as possible because such a high willingness to pay will imply that each customer can be charged a price sufficiently high to make each such sale profitable.

As we saw in Chapter 7, an important implication of the assumption that the entire market is served is that there will be some consumer, whom we call the marginal consumer, $x^m$, who is indifferent between buying from either firm 1 or firm 2. That is, that consumer enjoys the same surplus either way. Algebraically, this means that for consumer $x^m$

$$V - p_1 - tx^m = V - p_2 - t(1 - x^m). \tag{10.6}$$

Equation (10.6) may be solved to find the address of the marginal consumer, $x^m$. This is

$$x^m(p_1, p_2) = \frac{(p_2 - p_1 + t)}{2t}. \tag{10.7}$$

At any set of prices, $p_1$ and $p_2$, all consumers to the west or left of $x^m$ buy from firm 1. All those to the east or right of $x^m$ buy from firm 2. In other words, $x^m$ is the fraction of the market buying from firm 1 and $(1 - x^m)$ is the fraction buying from firm 2. If the total number of consumers is denoted by $N$, the demand function facing firm 1 at any price combination $(p_1, p_2)$ in which the entire market is served is[8]

$$D^1(p_1, p_2) = x^m(p_1, p_2)N = \frac{(p_2 - p_1 + t)}{2t}N. \tag{10.8}$$

---

7   Refer to Figure 7-3 in Chapter 7 for a discussion of this point.
8   We are using $N$ here to refer to the number of consumers in the market.

Similarly, firm 2's demand function is

$$D^2(p_1, p_2) = [1 - x^m(p_1, p_2)]N = \frac{(p_1 - p_2 + t)}{2t}N. \qquad (10.9)$$

Notice that unlike the original Bertrand duopoly model shown earlier, the model presented here is one in which the demand function facing either firm *is* continuous in both $p_1$ and $p_2$. This is because when goods are differentiated, a decision by firm 1 to set $p_1$ a little higher than its rival's price $p_2$ does not cause firm 1 to lose all of its customers. Some of its customers will still prefer to buy good 1 even at the higher price simply because they prefer that version of the good to the style (or location) marketed by firm 2.[9]

The continuity in demand functions carries over into the profit functions. Firm 1's profit function is

$$\Pi^1(p_1, p_2) = (p_1 - c)\frac{(p_2 - p_1 + t)}{2t}N. \qquad (10.10)$$

Similarly, firm 2's profits are given by

$$\Pi^2(p_1, p_2) = (p_2 - c)\frac{(p_1 - p_2 + t)}{2t}N. \qquad (10.11)$$

In order to work out firm 1's best response pricing strategy, we need to work out how firm 1's profit changes as the firm varies price $p_1$ in response to a given price $p_2$ set by firm 2. The most straightforward way to do this is to take the derivative of the profit function in equation (10.10) with respect to $p_1$. We can then solve for the firm's best response price $p_1^*$ to a given price $p_2$ where we set the derivative equal to zero.[10] However, careful application of our standard alternative of converting firm 1's demand curve into its inverse form and solving for the point at which marginal revenue equals marginal cost will also work.

From equation (10.8), we can write firm 1's inverse demand curve for a given value of firm 2's price, $p_2$, as $p_1 = p_2 + t - \frac{q_1}{N}2t$. Hence, firm 1's marginal revenue is $MR_1 = p_2 + t - \frac{q_1}{N}4t$. This may be equated with firm 1's marginal cost to yield the first-order condition for profit maximization, $p_2 + t - \frac{q_1^*}{N}4t = c$. Solving for the optimal value of firm 1's output, again given the price chosen by firm 2, we then obtain

$$q_1^* = \frac{p_2 + t - c}{4t}N. \qquad (10.12)$$

When we substitute the value for $q_1^*$ in equation (10.12) into firm 1's inverse demand curve, we find the optimal price for firm 1 to set given the value of the price set by firm 2. This is by definition firm 1's best response function. It is

---

9   Our assumption that the equilibrium is one in which the entire market is served is critical to the continuity result.

10   Setting $\Pi_1^1(p_1, p_2)/p_1 = 0$ in equation (10.10) yields immediately $p_1^* = (p_2 + c + t)/2$.

$$p_1^* = \frac{p_2 + c + t}{2},$$ (10.13)

where $t$ is the per-unit distance transportation or utility cost incurred by a consumer. Of course, we can replicate this procedure for firm 2. Because the firms are symmetric, the best response function of each firm is the mirror image of that of its rival. Hence, firm 2's best price response function is

$$p_2^* = \frac{p_1 + c + t}{2}.$$ (10.14)

The Nash equilibrium is a pair of best response prices, $p_1^*$, $p_2^*$, such that $p_1^*$ is firm 1's best response to $p_2^*$, and $p_2^*$ is firm 2's best response to $p_1^*$. Thus, we may replace $p_1$ and $p_2$ on the right-hand side of equations (10.14) and (10.15) with $p_1^*$ and $p_2^*$, respectively. Then, solving jointly for the Nash equilibrium pair, $p_1^*$, $p_2^*$, yields

$$p_1^* = p_2^* = c + t.$$ (10.15)

The best response functions for the two firms are shown in Figure 10-5. They are upward sloping. The Nash equilibrium set of prices is shown as well. In equilibrium, each firm charges a price that is equal to the unit cost *plus* an amount, $t$, the utility cost per unit of distance a consumer incurs in buying a good that is at some distance from the preferred good. At these prices, the firms split the market. The marginal consumer is located at the address $x' = \frac{1}{2}$. The profit earned by each firm is the same and equal to $\frac{Nt}{2}$.

Consider again, for example, the two hair salons located one mile apart on Main Street. All their potential customers live along this stretch of Main Street and they are

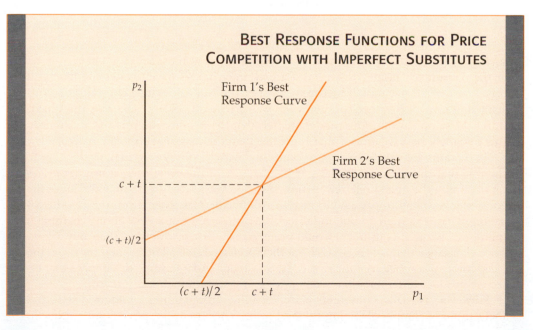

**BEST RESPONSE FUNCTIONS FOR PRICE COMPETITION WITH IMPERFECT SUBSTITUTES**

Firm 1's Best Response Curve

Firm 2's Best Response Curve

$p_2$

$c + t$

$(c + t)/2$

$(c + t)/2$    $c + t$    $p_1$

FIGURE

**10-5**

# Reality Checkpoint

## Unfriendly Skies: Price Wars in Airline Markets

Following general deregulation in 1977, the profitability of the airline industry has generally deteriorated and become much more volatile. An important source of these developments has been the continued outbreak of price wars. Morrison and Winston (1996) define such conflicts as any city-pair route market in which the average airfare declines by 20 percent or more within a single quarter. Based on this definition, they estimate that over 81 percent of airline city-pair routes experienced such wars in the 1979–95 time period. In the wars so identified, the average fare in fact typically falls by over 37 percent and sometimes by as much as 79 percent. These wars appear to be triggered by unexpected movements in demand and the entrance of new airlines on a route, espe-

cially low-cost airlines like Southwest. Morrison and Winston also find that the effect of such fare wars on industry profits is important. On average, they estimate that the intense price competition costs airlines $300 million in foregone profits in each of the first 16 years following deregulation. This amounts to over 20 percent of total net income over these same years. Of course, to the extent that this profit loss simply reflects movement toward the Bertrand outcome of marginal cost pricing it shows up as a gain to consumers and a net improvement in efficiency. Judging from the comments in the press, however—especially since September 11, 2001—airline executives take little comfort in such gains.

**Sources:** S. Morrison and C. Winston, "Causes and Consequences of Airline Fare Wars." *Brookings Papers on Economic Activity, Microeconomics, 1996*, 1996, pp. 85–124; M. Maynard, "Yes, It Was a Dismal Year for Airline; Now for the Bad News." *The New York Times*, December 16, 2002, p. C2.

uniformly spread out. Each consumer is willing to pay at most $50 for a haircut done at the consumer's home. However, if a consumer has to travel to get the haircut a travel cost of $5 per mile is incurred. Each of the hair salons can cut hair at a constant unit cost of $10 per cut, and each wants to set a price per haircut that maximizes the salon's profit. Our model predicts that the equilibrium price of a haircut in this town will be $15, a price that is greater than the marginal cost of a haircut.

Two points are worth making in connection with the foregoing analysis. First, note the role that the parameter $t$ plays. It is a measure of the value each consumer places on obtaining the most preferred version of the product. The greater is $t$, the more the consumer is willing to pay a high price to avoid being "far away" from the favorite location. That is, a high $t$ value indicates that firms need not worry about charging a high price because consumers would prefer to pay that price rather than buy a low-price alternative that is "far away" from their preferred style. Thus, when $t$ is large, the price competition between the two firms is softened. A large value of $t$ implies that effective product differentiation makes price competition much less intense.

However, as $t$ falls, consumers place less value on obtaining a preferred style and focus more on simply obtaining the best price. This intensifies price competition. In the limit, when $t = 0$, differentiation is of no value to consumers. They treat all goods as essentially identical. Price competition becomes fierce and, in the limit, forces prices to be set at marginal cost just as in the original Bertrand model.

The second point to be made in connection with this analysis concerns the location of the firms. We simply assumed that the two firms were located at either end of town. However, as we discussed in Chapter 7, the location or product design of the firm is also an object of choice. Unfortunately, allowing the firms in the model to choose *both* their price and their location strategies makes the problem too complicated to work out here. Still, the intuition behind this indeterminacy is instructive. Two opposing forces make the combined choice of price and location difficult. On the one hand, the two firms will wish to avoid locating at the same point because to do so eliminates all differences between the two products. Price competition in this case will be fierce as in the original Bertrand model. On the other hand, each firm also has some incentive to locate near the center of town. This enables a firm to reach as large a market as possible. Evaluating the balance of these two forces is what makes determination of the ultimate equilibrium so difficult.[11]

## Practice Problem 10.3

Imagine that the two hair salons located on Main Street no longer have the same unit cost. In particular, one salon has a constant unit cost of $10, whereas the other salon has a constant unit cost of $20. The low-cost salon, Cheap-Cuts, is located at the east end of town, $x = 0$. The high-cost salon, The Ritz, is located at the west end of town, $x = 1$. There are 100 potential customers who live along the one-mile stretch, and they are uniformly spread out along the mile. Consumers are willing to pay $50 for a haircut done at their home. If a consumer has to travel to get a haircut then a travel cost of $5 per mile is incurred. Each salon wants to set a price for a haircut that maximizes the salon's profit.

a. The demand functions facing the two salons are not affected by the fact that now one salon is high-cost and the other is low-cost. However, the salons' best response functions are affected. Compute the best response function for each salon. How does an increase in the unit cost of one salon affect the other salon's best response?

b. Work out the Nash equilibrium in prices for this model. Compare these prices to the ones derived in the text for the case when the two salons had the same unit cost equal to $10. Explain why prices changed in the way they did. It may be helpful in your explanation to draw the best response functions when the salons are identical and compare them to those when the salons have different costs.

## 10.4 STRATEGIC COMPLEMENTS AND SUBSTITUTES

Best response functions in simultaneous-move games are extremely useful tools for understanding what we mean by a Nash equilibrium outcome. But an analysis of such functions also serves other useful purposes. In particular, examining the properties of

---

11 There is a wealth of literature on this topic, with the outcome often depending on the precise functional forms assumed. See, for example, Eaton (1976); D'Aspremont, Gabszewicz, and Thisse (1979); Novshek (1980); and Economides (1989).

best response functions can aid our understanding of how strategic interaction works and how that interaction can be made "more" or "less" competitive.

Figure 10-6 shows both the best response functions for the standard Cournot duopoly model and the best response functions for the Bertrand duopoly model with differentiated products. One feature in the diagram is immediately apparent. The best response functions for the Cournot quantity model are *negatively* sloped—firm 1's best response to an increase in $q_2$ is to *decrease* $q_1$. But the best response functions in the Bertrand price model are *positively* sloped. Firm 1's best response to an increase in $p_2$ is to increase $p_1$ as well.

**FIGURE**
**10-6**

**BEST RESPONSE FUNCTIONS FOR THE COURNOT (QUANTITY) CASE AND THE BERTRAND (PRICE) CASE**

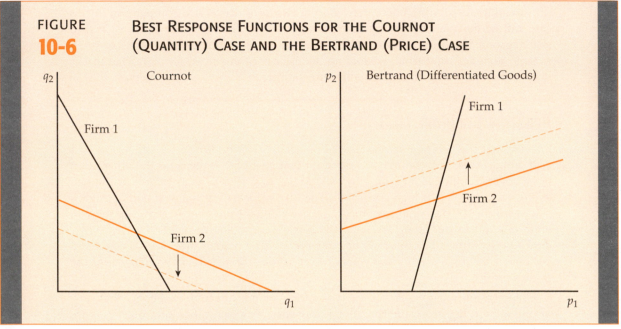

A rise in firm 2's cost shifts its response function inwards in the Cournot model but outwards in the Bertrand model. Firm 1 reacts aggressively to increase its market share in the Cournot case. It reacts mildly in the Bertrand price by *raising* its price.

Whether the best response functions are negatively or positively sloped is quite important. The slope reveals much about the nature of competition in the product market. To see this, consider the impact of an increase in firm 2's unit cost, $c_2$. Our analysis of the Cournot model indicated that the effect of a rise in $c_2$ would be to shift *inward* firm 2's best response curve. As Figure 10-6 indicates, this leads to a new Nash equilibrium in which firm 2 produces less and firm 1 produces more than each did before $c_2$ rose. That is, in the Cournot quantity model, firm 1's response to firm 2's bad luck is a rather aggressive one in which it seizes the opportunity to expand its market share at the expense of firm 2.

Consider now the impact of a rise in $c_2$ in the context of the differentiated goods Bertrand model. The rise in this case shifts *out* firm 2's best response function. Given the rise in its cost, firm 2 now finds it better to set a higher $p_2$ than it did previously in response to any given value of $p_1$. How does firm 1 respond? Unlike the Cournot case, firm 1's reaction is not aggressive. Quite to the contrary, firm 1—seeing that firm 2 is now less able to set a low price—realizes that the price competition from firm 2 is now less intense. Hence, firm 1 now reacts by raising $p_1$.

When the best response functions are upward sloping, we say that the strategies (prices in the Bertrand case) are *strategic complements*. When we have the alternative case of downward-sloping response functions, we say that the strategies (quantities in the Cournot case) are *strategic substitutes*. This terminology comes from Bulow, Geanakopolos, and Klemperer (1985) and reflects similar terminology in consumer demand theory. When a consumer reacts to a change in the price of one good by buying either more or less of *both* that good and another product, we say that the two goods are complements. When a consumer reacts to a change in the price of one product by buying more (less) of it and less (more) of another, we say that the two goods are substitutes. This is the source of the similarity. Prices in the spatial Bertrand model are called strategic complements because a change (the rise in $c_2$) inducing an increase in $p_2$ also induces an increase in $p_1$. Similarly, quantities in Cournot analysis are strategic substitutes because such a change in $c_2$ induces a fall in $q_2$ but a rise in $q_1$.

Clearly, the choice of whether to use price or quantity as the strategic variable to model competition in a market is an important one. What factors influence the choice? In those industries in which firms set their production schedules far in advance of putting the goods on the market for sale, there is a good case to assume that firms compete in quantities. Examples include the world energy market, coffee growers, automobile producers, and the cement industry. In many service industries, such as banking, insurance, and air travel, it is more natural to think in terms of price competition. In certain manufacturing industries, such as cereal and detergents, the price competition for customers is a stronger factor than the setting of production schedules, and so Bertrand price competition may be the more appropriate model.

## SUMMARY

The Bertrand model makes clear that price competition is quite different from quantity competition. Under quantity or Cournot competition, prices remain substantially above marginal cost so long as the number of firms is not large and high-cost firms can survive in equilibrium. Under Bertrand competition, prices are pushed to marginal cost even if there are just two firms. Moreover, high-cost firms cannot survive Bertrand competition against a firm with lower costs. In short, the simplest Bertrand model predicts competitive and efficient market outcomes even when the number of firms is quite small.

However, the efficient outcomes predicted by the pure Bertrand model are predicated on two key assumptions. One of these is that firms have extensive capacity so that it is possible to serve all a rival's customers after undercutting the rival's price. The other key assumption is that the firms in question produce identical products so that relative price is all that consumers use in choosing between brands. If either of these assumptions is relaxed, the efficiency outcomes of the simplest Bertrand model are no longer obtained. If firms must choose production capacities in advance, the outcome with Bertrand price competition approaches that of the Cournot model. If products are differentiated, prices are again likely to remain above marginal cost. Indeed, given the fierceness of price competition, firms have a real incentive to differentiate their products.

A useful model of product differentiation is the Hotelling spatial model explored in Chapter 7. This model uses geographic location as a metaphor for more general distinctions between different versions of the same product. It thereby makes it possible to consider price competition between firms selling differentiated products. As noted, the model demonstrates that Bertrand competition with differentiated products does not result in efficient marginal cost pricing. It also makes clear that the deviation from such pricing depends on how much consumers value variety. The greater value that the typical consumer places on getting the most preferred brand or version of the product, the more prices will rise above marginal cost even with Bertrand competition.

Ultimately, the differences between Cournot and Bertrand competition reflect an underlying difference between quantities and prices as strategic variables. The quantities chosen by Cournot firms are strategic substitutes—increases in one firm's production lead to decreases in the rival's output. In contrast, the prices chosen by Bertrand competitors are strategic complements. A rise in one firm's price permits its rival to raise price, too.

## PROBLEMS

1. Suppose firm 1 and firm 2 each produce the same product and face a market demand curve described by $Q = 5{,}000 - 200P$. Firm 1 has a unit cost of production, $c_1$, equal to 6, whereas firm 2 has a higher unit cost of production, $c_2$, equal to 10.

   **a.** What is the Bertrand Nash equilibrium outcome?

   **b.** What are the profits of each firm?

   **c.** Is this outcome efficient?

2. Suppose that market demand for golf balls is described by $Q = 90 - 3P$, where $Q$ is measured in kilos of balls. There are two firms that supply the market. Firm 1 can produce a kilo of balls at a constant unit cost of $15 whereas firm 2 has a constant unit cost equal to $10.

   **a.** Suppose firms compete in quantities. How much does each firm sell in a Cournot equilibrium? What is the market price and what are the firms' profits?

   **b.** Suppose firms compete in price. How much does each firm sell in a Bertrand equilibrium? What is market price and what are the firms' profits?

   **c.** Would your answer in (b) change if there were three firms, one with unit cost = $20 and two with unit cost = $10? Explain why or why not.

   **d.** Would your answer in (b) change if firm 1's golf balls were green and endorsed by Tiger Woods, whereas firm 2' s are plain and white? Explain why or why not.

3. In Tuftsville everyone lives along Main Street, which is 10 miles long. There are 1,000 people uniformly spread up and down Main Street, and each day they each buy one fruit smoothie from one of the two stores located at either end of Main Street. Customers ride their motor scooters to and from the store and the motor scooters use $0.50 worth of gas per mile. Customers buy their smoothies from the store offering the lowest price, which is the store's price plus the customer's travel expenses getting to and from the store. Ben owns the store at the west end of Main Street and Will owns the store at the east end of Main Street.

**a.** If both Ben and Will charge $1 per smoothie, how many will each of them sell in a day? If Ben charges $1 per smoothie and Will charges $1.40, how many smoothies will each sell in a day?

**b.** If Ben charges $3 per smoothie what price would enable Will to sell 250 smoothies per day? 500 smoothies per day? 750 smoothies per day? 1,000 smoothies per day?

**c.** If Ben charges $p_1$ and Will charges $p_2$, what is the location of the customer who is indifferent between going to Ben's and going to Will's? How many customers go to Will's store and how many go to Ben's store? What are the demand functions that face Ben and Will?

**d.** Rewrite Ben's demand function with $p_1$ on the left-hand side. What is Ben's marginal revenue function?

**e.** Assume that the marginal cost of a smoothie is constant and equal to $1 for both Ben and Will. In addition, each of them pays Tuftsville $250 per day for the right to sell smoothies. Find the equilibrium prices, quantities sold, and profits.

4. Return to Main Street in Tuftsville. Now suppose that George would like to open another store at the midpoint of Main Street. He, too, is willing to pay Tuftsville $250 a day for the right to sell smoothies.

**a.** If Ben and Will do not change their prices, what is the best price for George to charge? How much profit would he earn?

**b.** What do you think will happen if George opens another store in the middle of Main Street? Will Ben and Will have an incentive to change their prices? Their locations? Would one or both leave the market?

5. Suppose that two firms, firm B and firm N, produce complementary goods, say bolts and nuts. The demand curve for each firm is described as follows:

$$Q_B = Z - P_B - P_N \text{ and } Q_N = Z - P_N - P_B.$$

For simplicity, assume further that each firm faces a constant unit cost of production, $c = 0$.

**a.** Show that the profits of each firm may be expressed as $\Pi^B = (P_B)(Z - P_B - P_N)$ and $\Pi^N = P_N(Z - P_B - P_N)$.

**b.** Show that each firm's optimal price depends on the price chosen by the other as given by the optimal response functions $P_B^* = (Z - P_N)/2$ and $P_N^* = (Z - P_B)/2$.

**c.** Graph these functions. Show that the Nash equilibrium prices are $P_B = P_N = Z/3$.

**d.** Describe the interaction between two monopolists selling separate but complementary goods.

# REFERENCES

Bertrand, Joseph. 1883. "Review." *Journal des Savants* 68: 499–508. Reprinted in English translation by James Friedman in A. F. Daughety, ed., *Cournot Oligopoly*, Cambridge, MA: Cambridge University Press (1988).

Bulow, J., J. Geanakopolos, and P. Klemperer. 1985. "Multimarket Oligopoly: Strategic Substitutes and Complements." *Journal of Political Economy* 93(3): 488–511.

D'Aspremont, C., J. Gabszewicz, and J. Thisse. 1979. "On Hotelling's Stability in Competition." *Econometrica* 47 (September): 1145–50.

Eaton, B. C. 1976. "Free Entry in One-Dimensional Models: Pure Profits and Multiple Equilibrium." *Journal of Regional Science* 16 (January): 21–33.

Economides, N. 1989. "Symmetric Equilibrium Existence and Optimality in Differentiated Products Markets." *Journal of Economic Theory* 27 (February): 178–94.

Edgeworth, Francis Y. 1897. "The Pure Theory of Monopoly." *Giornale degli Economisti*: 111–42.

Friedman, J. 1977. *Oligopoly Theory*. Amsterdam: North Holland Press.

Hotelling, H. 1929. "Stability in Competition." *Economic Journal* 39 (January): 41–57.

Kreps, D., and J. Scheinkman. 1983. "Quantity Precommitment and Bertrand Competition Yield Cournot Outcomes." *Bell Journal of Economics* 14 (Autumn): 326–37.

Novshek, W. 1980. "Equilibrium in Simple Spatial (or Differentiated Products) Models." *Journal of Economic Theory* 22 (June): 313–26.

# Dynamic Games and First and Second Movers

## Chapter 11

Airbus has been thinking for years about producing an airliner to rival Boeing's 747, the 416-seat jumbo jet that has enjoyed a monopoly for over 30 years. Now it seems that the time is at hand. At the end of 2004 Airbus will market the new A380, a 555-seat super jumbo jet that is set to go head to head with Boeing's 747. Airbus has been in business since 1970. Clearly, the decision to follow the market leader Boeing into this segment of the market took Airbus some time. And while production of the A380 is underway, Boeing is planning its production schedule for its tried and true 747.

The strategic interaction just described between the production decisions of the world's two principal manufacturers of commercial aircraft is sequential. First, Boeing takes an action. Then, after that action has been taken and observed, Airbus chooses its action. Subsequently, it becomes Boeing's turn to respond, and so on. This is quite different from the static or simultaneous games that we studied in the previous two chapters. Games in which the players take their actions sequentially are called dynamic games, and dynamic games are the focus of this chapter. In general, these games have many rounds of play or stages. Here, we concentrate mostly on games with just two stages and, for convenience, just two firms. Thus one firm will get to play in the first round, the first mover, and the other will play in the second round, the second mover.

Popular business literature is replete with stories about first-mover advantages and often gives advice as to how firms can establish a leadership position by moving first.[1] A classic example of first-mover advantage can be found in the prepared soup industry. In the late nineteenth century, Campbell was the first entrant into the prepared soup market in the United States. Later, in the early twentieth century, Heinz was the first entrant in the U.K. market. Campbell did subsequently try to enter the U.K. market after Heinz, and similarly Heinz entered the U.S. market. However, the first mover in each market dominates. Campbell has roughly 63 percent of the U.S. market and only 9 percent of the U.K. market, whereas Heinz has a 41 percent share in the U.K. market and a relatively minor share in the U.S. market.[2]

The observation that early entry into a market sometimes confers substantial advantages relative to later entrants raises a further possibility of great interest to industrial economists. This is that the initial entrant's advantages could be so great that it would be impossible for any subsequent firm to enter at all. Remember, entry is a key part of the market's success story as an allocative mechanism. Entry is the policing mechanism that ensures a market will return to marginal cost pricing whenever an industry is earning substantial economic profits. If entry does not occur then the market may not be working very well. In the next two chapters, we will explore in detail the strategic interaction between an incumbent firm and a potential or actual entrant. Again, this is an important issue in industrial organization because it examines the validity of the simple microeconomic view that entry is a means by which competitive

---

1  See, for example, Lieberman and Montgomery (1998).
2  See Sutton (1991).

pressure is enforced. At this juncture the point to realize is that entry is a sequential process—there are firms that enter early and those that enter late. Developing an understanding of dynamic games is good groundwork for our later investigation of entry and entry deterrence in oligopoly markets.

We first examine quantity and price competition when firms move sequentially rather than simultaneously. We will discover again that price and quantity competition are different and, depending on the kind of competition, there can be first-mover and second-mover advantages. This raises the interesting question of whether and how a firm can become either a first or second mover. As we shall see, the key to achieving the desired outcome and the associated higher profits is the ability of the firm to make a credible commitment to its strategy when the market opens for trade. We examine what credibility means in game theory and how it affects our solution concept or equilibrium concept in dynamic models.

Simultaneous games, such as the traditional Cournot or Bertrand model, describe a once-and-only market interaction between the rival firms. In some sequential games as well there is only one market period where trade takes place. However, the more likely scenario is that rival firms that interact and trade today in the market are likely to interact again in the future. Moreover, the competing firms understand the likelihood of future interaction today. When a game proceeds over time through a sequence of moves, it becomes a dynamic game. The conflicts between an incumbent and an entrant that we examine in this and the next chapter typically exhibit such a dynamic quality. However, a dynamic element also can be introduced when the rivals move simultaneously in any one period, but the game is repeated many times in a number of subsequent periods. We defer the discussion of repeated games until Chapter 14, when we begin to investigate price-fixing.

## 11.1  THE STACKELBERG MODEL OF QUANTITY COMPETITION

The duopoly model of Stackelberg (1934) is similar to the Cournot model except for one critically important difference. While both firms choose quantities, they now do so *sequentially* rather than *simultaneously*. The firm that moves first and chooses its output level first is called the leader firm. The firm that moves second is called the follower firm. The sequential choosing of output is what makes the game dynamic. However, the firms meet only once and their interaction yields a "once-and-for-all" market-clearing outcome.

Let market demand again be represented by a linear inverse demand function $P = A - BQ$. Let firm 1 be the leader that moves first, and let firm 2 be the follower that chooses its output *after* the choice of the leader is made. Each firm has again the same constant unit cost of production, $c$. Total industry output, $Q$, equals the sum of the outputs of each firm, $Q = q_1 + q_2$.

Firm 1 acts first and chooses $q_1$. How should it make this choice? Again, we rely on the fact that both firms are rational and strategic and both firms know this, and know that each other knows this. As a result, firm 1 will make its choice taking into account its best guess as to firm 2's rational response to the observed choice of $q_1$. In other words, firm 1 will work out firm 2's best response to each value of $q_1$, and then choose that $q_1$ option which, given firm 2's best response to that output, turns out to maximize firm 1's profit.

We can solve for firm 2's *best response function*, $q_2^*$, exactly as we did in the Cournot model in Chapter 9. For any choice of output $q_1$, firm 2 faces the inverse demand and marginal revenue curves

$$P = (A - Bq_1) - Bq_2 \tag{11.1}$$
$$MR_2 = (A - Bq_1) - 2Bq_2.$$

Setting marginal revenue equal to marginal cost yields firm 2's best response, $q_2^*$, as the solution to the first-order condition

$$A - Bq_1 - 2Bq_2^* = c, \tag{11.2}$$

from which we obtain

$$q_2^* = \frac{(A - c)}{2B} - \frac{q_1}{2}. \tag{11.3}$$

If firm 1 is rational, firm 1 will understand that equation (11.3) describes what firm 2 will do in response to each alternative value of $q_1$ that firm 1 chooses. We can summarize equation (11.3) by $q_2^*(q_1)$. Knowing this, firm 1 can substitute $q_2^*(q_1)$ for $q_2$ in its demand function so that its inverse demand function may be written as

$$P = A - Bq_2^*(q_1) - Bq_1 = \frac{A + c}{2} - \frac{B}{2}q_1. \tag{11.4}$$

In turn, this implies that its profit function is

$$\Pi_1\left[q_1, q_2^*(q_1)\right] = \left[\frac{A + c}{2} - \frac{B}{2}q_1 - c\right]q_1 = \left(\frac{A - c}{2} - \frac{B}{2}q_1\right)q_1. \tag{11.5}$$

Note we have expressed firm 1's demand and profits as dependent only on its own output choice, $q_1$. This is because firm 1 effectively sets $q_2$ as well, by virtue of the fact that $q_2$ is chosen in response to $q_1$ according to firm 2's best response function. In short, by moving first, firm 1 gains the ability to manipulate its rival's output choice.

To solve for firm 1's profit-maximizing output, $q_1^*$, we can find the marginal revenue curve associated with firm 1's demand curve in equation (11.4), that is, $MR_1 = \frac{A + c}{2} - Bq_1$, and find that output $q_1^*$ at which marginal revenue is equal to marginal cost. Alternatively, we could solve for the first-order condition for profit maximization in equation (11.5), using the calculus technique of differentiation and setting, $\frac{d\Pi(q_1^*, q_2^*(q_1^*))}{dq_1} = 0$, and solve for $q_1^*$. Either way we find that

$$q_1^* = \frac{(A - c)}{2B}. \tag{11.6}$$

Because of this choice, firm 2 selects its best response as given by equation (11.3), which yields

$$q_2^* = \frac{(A - c)}{4B}.$$    (11.7)

Together, equations (11.6) and (11.7) give the Stackelberg–Nash equilibrium production levels of each firm. Note that the leader's output is exactly equal to the level of output chosen by a uniform-pricing monopolist. This is a well-known feature of the Stackelberg model when demand and costs are linear.

The total industry production is the sum of the two outputs shown in equations (11.6) and (11.7). This sum is $Q^s = \frac{3(A - c)}{4B}$. We may compare this with the earlier Cournot–Nash equilibrium industry output $Q^C = \frac{2(A - c)}{3B}$. Clearly, the Stackelberg model yields a greater industry output. Accordingly, the equilibrium price is lower in the Stackelberg analysis than it is in the Cournot analysis. The price and output results are illustrated in Figure 11-1.

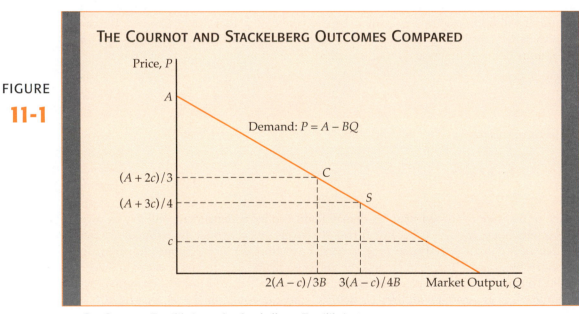

FIGURE

**11-1**

**THE COURNOT AND STACKELBERG OUTCOMES COMPARED**

$C$ = Cournot Equilibrium; $S$ = Stackelberg Equilibrium

A central result of the Stackelberg model is the difference in the relative outcome of the two firms. Recall that from the standpoint of both consumer preferences and production techniques, the firms are identical. They produce identical goods and do so at the same constant unit cost. Yet because one firm moves first, the outcome for the two firms is different. Comparing $q_1^*$ and $q_2^*$ reveals that the leader gets a far larger market share and earns a much larger profit than does the follower. Moving first clearly has advantages. Alternatively, entering the market late has its disadvantages.

An interesting additional aspect of the relatively poor outcome for firm 2 in the Stackelberg model is that this result occurs even though firm 2 has full information regarding the output choice of $q_1$. Indeed, the assumption is that firm 2 actually observes that choice before selecting $q_2$. In the Cournot duopoly model, firm 2 did not have such concrete information. Because the Cournot analysis was predicated upon simultaneous moves, each firm could only make a (rational) guess as to its rival's output choice. Paradoxically, firm 2 does worse when it has complete information about firm 1's choice (the Stackelberg case) than it does when its information is less than perfect (the Cournot case). This is because saying the information is concrete amounts to saying that firm 1's choice—at the time that firm 2 observes it—is irreversible. In the Stackelberg model, by the time firm 2 moves, firm 1 is already fully committed to $q_1 = \dfrac{(A-c)}{2B}$. In the Cournot context, $q_1 = \dfrac{(A-c)}{2B}$ is not a best response to the choice $q_2 = \dfrac{(A-c)}{4B}$, and so firm 2 would not anticipate that firm 1 would produce that quantity. In contrast, in the Stackelberg model we do not derive firm 1's choice as a best response to $q_2 = \dfrac{(A-c)}{4B}$. Instead, we derive firm 1's output choice as the profit-maximizing output when firm 2's decision rule is to choose its best value of $q_2$ conditional upon the output choice of firm 1. It is this fact, which reflects the underlying assumption of sequential moves, that distinguishes the Stackelberg approach.

Stackelberg's modification to the basic Cournot model is, as noted, quite important. It is a useful way to capture the feature that often one firm in the market has a dominant or leadership position. The Stackelberg model reveals that moving first can have its advantages and can therefore be a crucial element of strategic interaction.

## Practice Problem 11.1

Consider the following game. Firm 1, the leader, selects an output, $q_1$, after which firm 2, the follower, observes the choice of $q_1$ and then selects its own output, $q_2$. The resulting price is one satisfying the industry demand curve $P = 200 - q_1 - q_2$. Both firms have zero fixed costs and a constant marginal cost of 60.

a. Derive the equation for the follower firm's best response function. Draw this equation on a graph with $q_2$ on the vertical axis and $q_1$ on the horizontal axis. Indicate the vertical intercept, horizontal intercept, and slope of the best response function.

b. Determine the equilibrium output of each firm in the leader-follower game. Show that this equilibrium lies on firm 2's best response function. What are firm 1's profits in the equilibrium?

c. Now let the two firms choose their outputs simultaneously. Compute the Cournot equilibrium outputs and industry price. Who loses and who gains when the firms play a Cournot game instead of the Stackelberg one?

## 11.2 SEQUENTIAL PRICE COMPETITION

What if the two firms, the leader and follower, in this dynamic game competed in price instead of quantity? If we continue to assume that the firms are identical, that is, they produce the same product at the same costs, then the outcome to the sequential price-setting game is no different from the simultaneous price game of the previous chapter. Prices again fall to marginal cost!

To see this, let us rework the Stackelberg quantity-setting model with each firm choosing the price it will charge. Firm 1 will again be the leader and set its price first; firm 2 will be the follower and set its price second. Otherwise, the model and the assumptions are the same as before. Each firm produces an identical good at the same, constant marginal and, in this case, unit cost, $c$, and consumers will purchase the good from the lower priced firm. If they set the same prices then each firm will serve half the market.

In setting its price, firm 1 must anticipate firm 2's best response. Clearly firm 2 will have an incentive to slightly undercut firm 1's price when firm 1 sets a price greater than unit cost $c$. In that case, firm 2 will serve the entire market and earn all the potential profits. On the other hand, if firm 1 sets a price less than unit cost $c$, firm 2 will not match or undercut firm 1's price because firm 2 has no interest in making any sales when each unit sold loses money. Finally, if firm 1 sets a price equal to unit cost $c$ firm 2's best response is to match it. The anticipated behavior of firm 2 in stage 2 puts firm 1 in a tight bind. Any price greater than marginal cost $c$ will get underbid and there is no sense in setting a price less than $c$. The best firm 1 can do is to set a price equal to unit cost $c$. Firm 2's best response is to match.

Matters are very different, however, if the two firms are not selling identical products. In this case, not all consumers buy from the lower priced firm. As we saw in Chapter 10, product differentiation changes the outcome of price competition quite a bit.

In fact, to illustrate the nature of price competition with differentiated products, let's recall the spatial model of product differentiation that we developed previously. The setup is the following. There is a product spectrum of unit length along which consumers are uniformly distributed. Two firms supply this market. One firm has the address $x = 0$, whereas the other has the address $x = 1$. Each of the firms continues, however, to have the same constant unit cost of production, $c$.

Each point on the line is associated with a value of $x$ measuring the location of that point relative to the two products being marketed. A consumer who's most preferred style or location is $x'$ is called consumer $x'$. That is, consumers differ about which good is best. However, consumers have the same reservation demand price, $V > c$, for their most preferred good. Each consumer will also buy at most one unit of the product. If consumers purchase a good located "far away" from their most preferred location, they incur a utility cost. In particular, consumer $x'$ incurs the cost $tx'$ if purchasing good 1 (located at $x = 0$), and the cost $t(1 - x')$ if purchasing good 2 (located at $x = 1$).

The two firms compete for customers by setting prices $p_1$ and $p_2$, respectively. However, unlike the simple Bertrand model, it is now the case that firm 1 sets its price, $p_1$, first, and firm 2 follows by setting $p_2$. In order to find the demand facing the firms at prices $p_1$, $p_2$, we will assume that in any market outcome the entire market is served. This means there will be some consumer that we call the marginal consumer, $x^m$, who is indifferent between buying from either firm 1 or firm 2. Indifference means that the consumer $x^m$ gets the same consumer surplus from either product and so satisfies

$$V - p_1 - tx^m = V - p_2 - t(1 - x^m). \tag{11.8}$$

From equation (11.8) we find that the address of the marginal consumer, $x^m$, is

$$x^m(p_1, p_2) = \frac{(p_2 - p_1 + t)}{2t}. \tag{11.9}$$

At any set of prices, $p_1$ and $p_2$, all consumers to the left of $x^m$ buy from firm 1, and all those to the right of $x^m$ buy from firm 2. In other words, $x^m$ is the fraction of the market buying from firm 1 and $(1 - x^m)$ is the fraction buying from firm 2. If the total number of consumers is denoted by $N$ the demand function facing firm 1 at any price combination, $(p_1, p_2)$, is

$$D^1(p_1, p_2) = x^m(p_1, p_2)N = \frac{(p_2 - p_1 + t)}{2t}N. \tag{11.10}$$

Similarly, firm 2's demand function is

$$D^2(p_1, p_2) = [1 - x^m(p_1, p_2)]N = \frac{(p_1 - p_2 + t)}{2t}N. \tag{11.11}$$

Firm 1 acts first and sets its price, $p_1$. Firm 1 will set its price taking into account firm 2's rational response to its choice of price, $p_1$. In other words, firm 1 will work out firm 2's best response to each possible price $p_1$, and then set its profit-maximizing price $p_1$ given firm 2's best response to that price. We can solve for firm 2's best response function $p_2^*$ exactly as we did in Section 3 of Chapter 10. It is

$$p_2^* = \frac{p_1 + c + t}{2}. \tag{11.12}$$

If firm 1 is rational, firm 1 will understand that equation (11.12) describes what firm 2 will do in response to each alternative value of price, $p_1$, that firm 1 could set. We can summarize equation (11.12) by $p_2^*(p_1)$. Firm 1 knows that if it sets first a price, $p_1$, then firm 2 will set a price, $p_2^*(p_1)$, and then firm 1 will face

$$D^1(p_1, p_2^*(p_1)) = x^m(p_1, p_2^*(p_1))N = \frac{(p_2^*(p_1) - p_1 + t)}{2t}N = \frac{c + 3t - p_1}{4t}N. \tag{11.13}$$

In turn, this implies that its profit function is

$$\Pi_1\left[p_1, p_2^*(p_1)\right] = (p_1 - c)\left(\frac{c + 3t - p_1}{4t}\right)N. \tag{11.14}$$

In order to work out firm 1's optimal pricing strategy we need to work out how firm 1's profit changes as the firm varies price $p_1$ in response to a given price $p_2$, set by firm 2. The most straightforward way to do this is to take the derivative of the profit function in equation (11.14) with respect to $p_1$ and set the derivative equal to zero. That is, solving $\dfrac{d\Pi(p_1^*, p_2^*(p_1^*))}{dp_1} = 0$ leads us to

$$p_1^* = c + \frac{3t}{2}. \tag{11.15}$$

As a result of this choice, firm 2 selects its best response as given by equation (11.12), which yields

$$p_2^* = c + \frac{5t}{4}. \tag{11.16}$$

The profit-maximizing prices in equations (11.15) and (11.16) for the sequential price game differ in important ways from the prices that we found for the simultaneous price game in Section 10.3 from the last chapter. One difference is that prices now are generally higher. In the simultaneous price game the two firms set the same prices, $p_1^* = p^* = c + t$, whereas in the sequential game firm 1 sets a price in stage 1 that is greater than $c + t$, and firm 2 responds by setting a slightly lower price, but still higher than $c + t$. A second difference is that the two firms in the sequential price game have different market shares and earn different profits. In the simultaneous price-setting game each firm served one half the market and earned the same profit equal to $\frac{Nt}{2}$. In the sequential game, on the other hand, firm 1 serves $\frac{3}{8}$ of the market, and earns a profit equal to $\frac{18Nt}{32}$, whereas firm 2 serves $\frac{5}{8}$ of the market and earns a profit equal to $\frac{25Nt}{32}$. This outcome is described in Figure 11-2.

FIGURE **11-2**

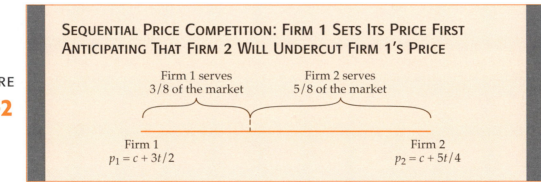

**SEQUENTIAL PRICE COMPETITION: FIRM 1 SETS ITS PRICE FIRST ANTICIPATING THAT FIRM 2 WILL UNDERCUT FIRM 1'S PRICE**

Firm 1 serves 3/8 of the market — Firm 2 serves 5/8 of the market

Firm 1 $p_1 = c + 3t/2$ — Firm 2 $p_2 = c + 5t/4$

Finally, note that unlike the Stackelberg output game, the sequential price game just described presents a clear second-mover advantage. Firm 2 enjoys a larger market share and higher profit than firm 1. Both are better off than in the simultaneous game but firm 2, the second mover, does particularly well.

## Practice Problem 11.2

Let there be two hair salons located on Main Street, which is one mile long. One is located at the West End of town, $x = 0$, and the other is located at the East End, $x = 1$. There are 100 potential customers who live along the one-mile stretch, and they are uniformly spread out along the mile. Consumers are willing to pay $50 for a haircut done at their home. If a consumer has to travel to the salon and back to get a haircut then a travel cost of $5 per mile is incurred. Each salon has the same unit cost equal to $15 per haircut.

a. Suppose the East End Salon posts its price for a haircut first and then the West End Salon posts its price for a haircut. What prices will the two salons set? How many customers does each salon serve? What are the profits?

b. Compare the prices to the ones we found when the two salons set their prices simultaneously (see p. 240 in Chapter 10). Explain why prices changed in the way they did.

---

Firms generally seem to do better when they compete sequentially in prices than when they compete sequentially in output. The average price is higher and both firms earn higher profits when price competition is sequential rather than simultaneous. In contrast, the industry price falls and only one firm earns higher profit when quantity competition becomes sequential rather than simultaneous. This is related to a further distinction. Whereas it is the first mover who has the clear advantage in the quantity game, in the price game it is the firm who moves last that does best.

The fact that one firm has an advantage over the other in the sequential version of either the quantity or the price game is due largely to the fact that we have taken the first mover's initial play as given and irrevocable by the time the second player moves. This may make some sense in the output game if the first mover actually has completed its production and incurred its costs before firm 2 selects its output. For the price game, though, it seems to be less plausible. Rather than settle for a second best profit, what is to stop firm 1 from taking an additional move and trying to undercut the price of firm 2? Yet if it is possible that when the market opens firm 1 can still undercut firm 2's price, then it is also clear that firm 2 will anticipate that price cut by firm 1 and cut its price still further. Yet if firm 1 anticipates that behavior, it will wish to reduce its price all the more. Very quickly, this reasoning brings us back to the simultaneous price-setting game. In other words, the sequential aspect of the price game requires that firm 1 *not* be able to change its price after it is set. Instead, firm 1 must be committed to that price. In turn, this raises the question as to how firm 1 can commit to its initial price setting in a manner that is *credible* to firm 2.

The issue of making a credible commitment is also crucial in the quantity-setting Stackelberg game. As noted, if the first mover actually incurs the cost and produces the output before the follower moves, then its production decision is irreversible and the credibility question is resolved. However, talk is cheap. If the leader simply announced an intention to produce the monopoly output, the follower would have good reason to doubt this threat since that output is not a best response to the firm 2 output that it would induce.

 # Reality Checkpoint

## First-Mover Advantage in the TV Market: More Dishes and Higher Prices

When a firm markets a new good or service its consumers are likely to be aware of the fact that it may not work that well. In particular, it may take time to learn how to use the good properly or to use it in such a way that one gets full use of all the features that the product or service contains. Think, for example, of such goods and services as personal computers, personal digital assistants, cellular phones, DVD players, and online auctions. It takes experience using a Palm Pilot or an Apple computer or purchasing a product on e-Bay before one really can get the most out of these goods or services. Gabszewicz, Pepall, and Thisse (1992) build on this idea to show how it may confer a first-mover advantage to the first firm to market a new product. Imagine then a simple two-stage model. Firm 1 introduces its version of the new product and a rival enters in the second stage with its own, differentiated version of the same good. Gabszewicz, Pepall, and Thisse argue that those consumers who bought firm 1's product in stage 1 will know how it works but they won't know that for firm 2's new product. As a result, they will tend to prefer firm 1's good even if firm 2 sells at a lower price.

Indeed, Gabszewicz, Pepall, and Thisse show that the pricing implications of their analysis can be quite novel. Assume that when firm 1 introduces its product in stage 1, it foresees the later entry of firm 2. Then firm 1 will have an incentive to price very low in the first stage so as to induce a lot of consumers to buy and to become experienced with its product before firm 2 enters. This will create a large group of captive consumers for firm 1 who will be willing to pay a higher price for its product in stage 2 now that they know how the product works. Thus, when firm 2 finally enters, firm 1 can actually raise its price and still retain a larger number of con-

sumers because they simply have not learned how to work with firm 2's imperfect substitute. In other words, the first mover may not only have a large market share but we may actually see that firm raise its prices at the very time that new competition emerges—exactly the opposite of what simple textbook analysis often implies.

Evidence of the first-mover advantage suggested by Gabszewicz, Pepall, and Thisse may come from the television market. Here, the initial new product was cable TV, which has rapidly spread so that now 70 percent of American homes receive cable service. The Telecommunications Act of 1996 essentially deregulated the cable TV industry hoping that new firms, especially telephone companies, would provide competition to the local cable franchises. By and large, however, competition from alternative cable providers has remained weak. Instead, the major competition to cable that has emerged is from direct broadcast satellite (DBS) TV, which consumers receive through a satellite dish. Textbook analysis would suggest that DBS competition would lead to lower cable prices. However, Goolsbee and Petrin (2003) find that, to the contrary, penetration of the market by DBS has led, on average, to an increase in the annual cable fee of about $34.68. The ability of cable firms to raise price as new rivals appear may reflect precisely the first-mover advantage noted by Gabszewicz, Pepall, and Thisse.

**Source:** J. Gabszewicz, L. Pepall, and J-F. Thisse, "Sequential Entry with Brand Loyalty Caused by Consumer Learning-By-Doing." *Journal of Industrial Economics* 60 (December 1992): 397–416; and: A. Goolsbee and A. Petrin, "The Consumer Gains from Direct Broadcast Satellite and Competition with Cable TV." forthcoming, *Econometrica* (2003).

The bottom line is that while dynamic games yield different results than those played simultaneously, those results depend crucially on the credibility of the firms' strategies. Further, since credibility is so important, we should expect that the firms playing such games will also distinguish between credible strategies and noncredible ones. Thus, we need to understand what makes strategies credible in dynamic games. We need to investigate dynamic games and ways to solve them.

In the next section we explore what credibility means in a dynamic game. We do so in the context of a dynamic game that has been of great interest to industrial organization economists. It is a market entry game. The firm to move first is a potential entrant to a monopolized market. The firm that moves second is the incumbent firm and the interest here is whether the incumbent can choose a strategy that deters the entrant from entering its profitable market. Before making its initial move, the entrant anticipates the incumbent's subsequent reaction. The question is what reactions are credible ones.

## 11.3 CREDIBILITY OF THREATS AND NASH EQUILIBRIA FOR DYNAMIC GAMES

We begin first by introducing a notion critical to all dynamic games, namely, that of a subgame. A subgame is a part of an entire game that can stand alone as a game in itself. A subgame is a game within a game. Simultaneous games cannot have subgames, but dynamic games can. An example of a subgame in a two-period model can be the competition in the second period, which is a one-shot game within the larger two-period game. Closely related to the notion of subgame is the concept of subgame perfection, first introduced by Nobel Prize winner Reinhard Selten (1978). It is the concept of subgame perfection that permits us to understand whether a firm's strategy is credible in a dynamic game. The term sounds very technical but it is actually quite simple. Subgame perfection means that if a strategy chosen at the start of a game is truly optimal, it must continue to be optimal to stick with that strategy at every later juncture in the game as play progresses. However, it may be easier to understand the concept of subgame perfection by seeing its application in practice. We now consider a market entry game in which we need that understanding.

Imagine a dynamic game between two software firms, one a giant called Microhard, which is the incumbent firm in the market, and the other an upstart firm, Newvel, which wishes to enter the market. In this game the potential entrant, Newvel, moves first, choosing either to enter Microhard's market or stay out. If Newvel stays out it earns a normal profit from being somewhere else in the economy, say $\Pi = 1$, and Microhard continues to earn a monopoly profit in the software market, say $\Pi = 5$. If Newvel enters the market, then Microhard can choose either to accommodate the new entrant and share the market or to fight the new entrant by slashing prices. If Microhard accommodates Newvel's entry, then each firm earns a profit $\Pi = 2$. If, on the other hand, Microhard fights, then neither firm makes any profit and each firm earns $\Pi^d = 0$.

This game can be described by a payoff matrix of the type introduced in Chapter 9. Each firm has two actions. Their choice of actions leads to an outcome, all of which are described by the following payoff matrix.

|  |  | Microhard | |
|---|---|---|---|
|  |  | Fight | Accommodate |
| Newvel | Enter | (0,0) | (2,2) |
|  | Stay Out | (1,5) | (1,5) |

Dynamic games with moves in sequence require more care in presentation than single-period, simultaneous games. In a one-period simultaneous game, a firm's action is the same as its strategy and we can use the action payoff matrix to work out a Nash equilibrium in strategies. For a dynamic game, a firm's strategy is a complete set of instructions that tell the firm what actions to choose at every conceivable situation in the game. The difference between a strategy and an action can be illustrated in the case of Microhard's strategy to fight. The fight strategy does not always specify the action, Fight. Instead, it should be viewed as specifying two different actions depending on whether Newvel enters. If Newvel doesn't enter, then the strategy says that Microhard should continue to price high and enjoy the associated high profits. But if Newvel does enter, then the strategy says that Microhard should respond with aggressive price cuts that lower the profit of each firm. Similarly, Microhard's strategy to accommodate will also yield different actions depending on Newvel's decision to enter (Microhard accepts lower profits, perhaps accepting some market price reduction so as to absorb Newvel's output) or not to enter (Microhard continues to price like a monopoly and earn the associated monopoly profit).

Yet despite the fact that the options now facing the firms are strategies and not merely actions, we can still use the payoff matrix to gain some insight into which strategy pairs yield a Nash equilibrium to this game. Start with the combination (Enter, Fight). This *cannot* correspond to an equilibrium. Enter will lead Newvel to come into the market. If Microhard has adopted the fight strategy, it must respond to such entry very aggressively. Yet, as the payoff matrix makes clear, such an aggressive action is not Microhard's best response to entry by Newvel. Now try (Enter, Accommodate). This *is* a Nash equilibrium in strategies. If Newvel chooses to enter, and if Microhard has adopted the accommodate strategy, this will produce an action and an associated outcome that is a best response for Microhard. Similarly, if Microhard has adopted a strategy to accommodate, then an enter strategy is the best response for Newvel. So, the combination (Enter, Accommodate) satisfies our notion of a Nash equilibrium.

What about the combination (Stay Out, Fight)? It also satisfies the Nash definition. If Newvel chooses to stay out, then the fight strategy gives a best response for Microhard, while if Microhard has chosen its fight strategy, then the stay out strategy is a best response for Newvel. Therefore, (Stay Out, Fight) is also a Nash equilibrium in strategies. Fighting is aggressive conduct that is keeping or deterring the entrant from entering the market. We leave it for the reader to show that the strategy combination (Stay Out, Accommodate) is not a Nash equilibrium.

Again, it is important to understand that a Nash equilibrium is defined in terms of strategies that are best responses to each other. In the second Nash equilibrium, (Stay Out, Fight), Microhard never actually takes fighting action. Instead, it relies fully on the *threat* to do so as a device to deter Newvel. The Nash equilibrium concept is not based on what actions are observed in the marketplace, but rather upon what thinking or strategizing underlies what we observe. This is what is meant when we say we need to define a Nash equilibrium not in terms of firms' actions but in terms of firms' strategies.

As we have just seen, there appear to be two Nash equilibria to this game. On reflection, though, there is something troubling about one of these, namely, the Nash equilibrium (Stay Out, Fight). It is true that if Microhard has fully committed itself to the fight strategy, then Newvel's best strategy is to stay out. But Newvel might question whether such a commitment is really possible. By adopting the fight strategy, Microhard essentially says to Newvel, "I am going to price high so long as you stay out but, if you enter my market, I will cut my price and smash you." The problem is that this threat suffers a serious credibility problem. We already know that once Newvel has entered the market, taking action to fight back is not in Microhard's best interest. It does much better by accommodating such entry. Consequently, Microhard does not have an incentive to carry out its threat. So, why should Newvel believe that threat in the first place?

What we have just discovered is that any Nash equilibrium strategy combination based on noncredible threats is not very satisfactory. This means that we need to strengthen our definition of Nash equilibrium to rule out such strategy combinations. This is where the notion of subgame perfection, or a subgame perfect Nash equilibrium, becomes important. If Microhard starts the game by adopting a strategy that includes the threat of a fight, then it must be optimal to fight in the event that Microhard reaches the point in the game where Newvel enters. However, this is not the case for the predatory fight strategy. Accordingly, it is not subgame perfect.

A Nash equilibrium is said to be perfect if, given everything that could happen *before* it becomes time for a player to make good on a promise or a threat, doing what is claimed would be done is still the optimal choice. In other words, if any promises or threats are made in one period, carrying them out is still part of a Nash equilibrium later should the occasion arise to do so.

The reason we originally found two Nash equilibria in the game above is that we ignored this notion of subgame perfection. This is particularly easy to do when, as here, all one is viewing is the outcome matrix because that matrix does not make clear that the game is a dynamic one with a particular sequence of moves. Strategies that employ threats over future actions hinge critically upon the timing of the moves, and this is lost in the matrix representation of the game. It is for this reason that analysis of dynamic games often relies on an extensive or tree representation of the game.

The extensive form of a game is comprised of dots, lines, and vectors of payoffs. The dots are called nodes and describe where we are in the game. They are labeled by which firm makes the move at that position—*N* for Newvel and *M* for Microhard, in our case. The lines that are drawn from a node represent the choice of actions available to the player at that node. Each line points either to another node, where further action takes place, or to a vector of payoffs (Newvel's payoff shown first), which means that this particular choice of action has ended the game. Finally, at any node it is assumed that the players are perfectly informed about the course of play that has led to that node. The extensive form of the Microhard–Newvel game is shown in Figure 11-3.

When we represent a sequential game in extensive form it is easy to identify a subgame. A subgame is defined as a single node and all the actions that flow from that node. In the extensive game illustrated in Figure 11-3, there are two subgames. There is the full game starting from node *N*1 (the full game is always a subgame). Then there is the subgame starting at node *M*2, and including all subsequent actions that flow from this node. A strategy combination is subgame perfect if the behavioral strategy it contains for each player is a best response against the behavioral strategies of the other players in every subgame. In the case at hand, it is readily apparent that for the subgame beginning at node 2, the Nash equilibrium strategy for Microhard is Accommodate, not Fight. Hence, the strategy combination (Stay Out, Fight) cannot correspond to a subgame perfect equilibrium. The only such equilibrium in this case is that of (Enter, Accommodate).

FIGURE

**11-3**

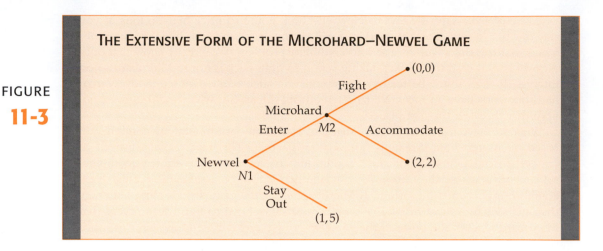

THE EXTENSIVE FORM OF THE MICROHARD–NEWVEL GAME

There is an important technique for solving games with a finite number of nodes. In such games, the simplest way to identify the subgame perfect equilibria is to work backwards. This takes advantage of the property that a subgame perfect equilibrium strategy combination must be an equilibrium in each subgame. In our example, we first calculate the equilibrium for the subgames starting at node *M2*. This gives the unique strategy combination (Enter, Accommodate) and the associated payoff (2,2). We then use these payoffs to determine Newvel's payoffs *if* the game proceeds either to *N1* or *M2*, effectively creating a shorter game. In our example, this is the full game starting at node *N1*, at which Newvel moves. Obviously, it will choose Enter. In other words, this procedure has eliminated the combination (Stay Out, Fight) as a perfect Nash equilibrium.

## Practice Problem 11.3

Centipede is a well-known variant of games involving a chance to "grab a dollar." The game is played between two players, as follows. A neutral third party, called Nature, puts $1 on the table. Player 1 can either "grab" this dollar or "wait." If Player 1 takes the dollar, the game is over. Player 1 gets $1 and Player 2 obviously gets nothing. However, it is completely understood that, if Player 1 waits, Nature will triple the amount on the table to $3. At that point, it becomes Player 2's turn to move. Player 2 can either take the entire $3 or share the money equally with Player 1.

a. Construct the 2 × 2 payoff matrix for this game taking Player 1's actions to be either Grab or Wait, and Player 2's actions to be either Grab (the whole $3) or Share. Assume the payoffs are equal to the amount of money the player receives.
b. Draw the game in its extensive form.
c. Suppose that Player 2 promises Player 1 that he or she will take the action Share if Player 1 waits. Is this promise credible? Why or why not?

## 11.4  THE CHAIN STORE PARADOX

In the Microhard and Newvel game there is just one market and one potential entrant, and fighting the entrant was not an optimal response to entry. However, what if Microhard faced more than one entrant? Perhaps fighting one entrant builds a reputation for aggressive behavior that will scare off later entrants. Consideration of the reputational effects of fighting may alter our conclusion about what is Microhard's optimal strategy. Taking predatory action against a rival—costly though it is—may be useful if it serves to make the threat credible against other rivals, either those in other markets or those who may appear later in time. If we introduce this possibility into the previous setting, then Microhard's threat to fight could become credible because the subsequent gains in other markets from establishing a reputation as a fighter are sufficiently large. In other words, reputation could make the strategy combination (Stay Out, Fight) subgame perfect.

The fact that extension of the previous game to many markets (distributed over time or space) and other rivals may not lead to a different outcome is a famous result dubbed by Selten as *the chain store paradox.*[3] To see the logic of this puzzling result, consider now a situation in which Microhard has established operating units in each of twenty markets, perhaps twenty different cities. In each such market, we will suppose that Microhard faces potential entry by a single, small competitor. At the moment, none of these potential competitors has the capital to start operations. However, as time goes on, one after the other will raise the necessary funds. To make matters simple, assume that the payoffs in each of the twenty markets are just as in the payoff matrix of the previous section. The question facing Microhard is how to react to this sequence of potential entrants. In particular, should Microhard adopt an aggressive response to the first entrant and drive it out of business? Will this tactic earn Microhard a reputation for ruthlessness such that subsequent entrants in its other markets will get the message and choose not to enter?

Again, working backwards will help us to sort matters out. Let's start with one possible scenario in which Microhard hopes only to persuade the potential entrant in the final, twentieth market. To this end, Microhard has followed through on its threat to cut price and drive out any entrant not just in the first market, but in all previous nineteen markets. One would think that such an extreme policy must surely convince the last potential entrant to stay out, and that Microhard would at least be spared a fight in this final case.

However, consider the viewpoint of the entrant to the twentieth market. Upon reflection, this firm will realize that because there are no subsequent entrants, it is involved in exactly the limited one-period game we previously discussed. So, using the argument of the previous section, this last entrant will understand that Microhard should in fact accommodate its entry. Microhard's profit is greater if it follows a "live and let live" strategy in this last case because it cannot gain from any further demonstration of its ruthlessness.[4] There are no other entrants left to impress. Since Microhard's only possible reason to respond to entry with aggressive price-cutting is to establish a reputation for toughness, and because, after the twentieth market battle having such a reputation does it absolutely no good, Microhard has to accommodate the entrant in this last market. The entrant will understand this and of course enter. Note that the threat to fight in the twentieth market is not credible even though Microhard has already done so in nineteen prior cases! Obviously, the threat to fight will be made no more credible by Microhard fighting only in eighteen markets, or

---

3  Selten (1978). We have, obviously, limited ourselves here to consideration of finitely repeated games only. Infinitely repeated games are considered in the next chapter.

4  Implicit here is the presumption that accommodating an entrant is, in the short run, more profitable than engaging in a price war.

seventeen, or just one. If a record of nineteen previous rounds of aggressive price-cutting does not convince the final entrant, nothing will.

One might think that the foregoing simply implies that Microhard cannot credibly threaten the potential entrant in its final market, but that there is still hope to deter the entry of earlier rivals by means of a threat. To see why this is not possible, let us now turn to a consideration of the potential entrant in the nineteenth rather than the twentieth market. Once again, let's take the extreme case in which Microhard has taken predatory action in the prior eighteen markets.

Now the potential entrant in the nineteenth market can reason as well as we can. As a result, this firm will work out the logic of the preceding case and rightfully conclude that Microhard will not fight in the twentieth market. Having realized that, however, the entrant in the nineteenth or next-to-last market will go on and reason as follows: "Microhard will let the last rival firm survive because it is pointless to cut price at that point to gain a tough reputation. Since I know that the entry of the last rival will not be challenged, there is, in fact, no reason for Microhard to act tough on me. Its only reason to do so would be to convince the entrant in the next market. Since this is not possible in any case, the only justification of fighting in market nineteen has been removed." Once again, Microhard's promise to fight if entry occurs is not credible. It gains Microhard nothing by way of a demonstration to the next rival. Absent such a reputation effect, Microhard's best response to entry in the nineteenth market is again to accommodate. Knowing this, the potential entrant in market nineteen will enter.

We may continue in this fashion repeatedly, bringing us back all the way to the initial market. At every stage, we will find that a strategy to fight after entry occurs is not subgame perfect and accordingly not credible. This will be just as true in the first market as in the last. There is no way for the incumbent to threaten credibly an aggressive low-price response to entry.

So far the only perfect Nash strategy equilibrium is one in which entry occurs and fighting never happens. If this were the end of the story, our interest in the predatory conduct described in this game would certainly be very low. Why should we worry about an event that presumably never occurs? The answer is that there may be ways to make the threat to fight credible other than actual fighting itself. A firm's predatory efforts, no matter what form they take, will work only if they are credible to actual and potential rivals and so influences their beliefs about competing in the market.[5] Predatory conduct that is credible is what we will investigate in the next two chapters.

# SUMMARY

Sequential market games are different from simultaneous ones. Moreover, the effect of changing from simultaneous to sequential play differs depending on whether the strategic variable of choice is quantity or price. The basic sequential quantity game, typically referred to as the Stackelberg model, confers a large advantage to the firm that chooses production first. In the linear demand and cost case, the first mover in

---

5   Schelling (1960) defines a strategic move as "one that influences the other person's choice in a manner favorable to oneself by affecting the other person's expectations of how oneself will behave." This definition is important in understanding what is meant by a credible strategy. Schelling had an important influence in developing equilibrium notions for dynamic games.

a Stackelberg game produces the monopoly output. The follower produces only half this much. Prices are lower than in the basic Cournot model but the large market share of the first mover gives that firm an increase in profit over what it would earn in the simultaneous production game.

In contrast, a sequential price game with differentiated products yields higher profits for both firms than either would earn if prices were set simultaneously. Moreover, in this case, it is the firm that sets price last that does best. Sequential price games therefore confer a second-mover as opposed to a first-mover advantage.

Crucial to any sequential game is the issue of commitment. How do firms establish themselves as leaders or followers? How can a firm commit to its initial choice of output or price in a way that a rival finds credible? This issue can only be explored by considering the game in its extended form and looking for strategy combinations that are subgame perfect, that is, strategies that call for actions at later dates in which those actions continue to be optimal when the time comes to take them given the history of play up to that date.

Threats and promises of later punishments and rewards are particularly important in games in which one firm is trying to prevent another from entering its market (or perhaps trying to induce it to leave). The question again is whether such threats and promises can be made credible. If they can, then incumbent firms may be able to maintain their dominant position in an industry and not fear competitive entry. This is the subject of our next chapter.

## PROBLEMS

1. Consider a Stackelberg game of quantity competition between two firms. Firm 1 is the leader and firm 2 the follower. Market demand is described by the inverse demand function $P = 1,000 - 4Q$. Each firm has a constant unit cost of production equal to 20.

   a. Solve for Nash equilibrium outcome.

   b. Suppose firm 2's unit cost of production is $c < 20$. What value would $c$ have so that in the Nash equilibrium the two firms, leader and follower, had the same market share?

2. Let's return to Tuftsville (Chapter 10) where everyone lives along Main Street, which is ten miles long. There are 1,000 people uniformly spread up and down Main Street, and each day they each buy a fruit smoothie from one of the two stores located at either end of Main Street. Customers ride their motor scooters to and from the store and the motor scooters use $0.50 worth of gas per mile. Customers buy their smoothies from the store offering the lowest price, which is the store's price plus the customer's travel expenses getting to and from the store. Ben owns the store at the west end of Main Street and Will owns the store at the east end of Main Street. The marginal cost of a smoothie is constant and equal to $1 for both Ben and Will. In addition each of them pays Tuftsville $250 per day for the right to sell smoothies.

   a. Ben sets his price $p_1$ first and then Will sets his price $p_2$. After the prices are posted consumers get on their scooters and buy from the store with the lowest price including travel expenses. What prices will Ben and Will set?

   b. How many customers does each store serve and what are their profits?

3. In Centipede[6] there are two players. Player 1 moves first, Player 2 moves second. After at most two moves, the game ends. The game begins with $1 sitting on a table. Player 1 can either take the $1 or wait. If Player 1 takes the $1 the game is over, and Player 1 gets to keep the $1. If Player 1 waits the $1 quadruples to $4. Now it is Player 2's turn. Player 2 can either take the entire $4 or split the $4 evenly with Player 1.

   a. Draw the extensive form for the game of Centipede.

   b. What is the equilibrium to this game? Can Player 2's strategy of splitting the money ever be a part of an equilibrium outcome to the game?

   c. Now suppose Centipede has three moves. If Player 2 waits then the money on the table quadruples again and Player 1 can either take it all or split it. Draw the extensive form for the new game and solve for the equilibrium outcome.

4. Dry Gulch has two water suppliers. One is Northern Springs, whose water is crystal clear but not carbonated. The other is Southern Pelligrino, whose water is naturally carbonated but also somewhat "hard." The marketing department of each firm has worked out the following profit matrix depending on the price per 2-gallon container charged by each firm. Southern Pelligrino's profits are shown as the first entry in each pair.

|  |  | Northern Springs' Price | | | |
|---|---|---|---|---|---|
|  |  | 3 | 4 | 5 | 6 |
| Southern Pelligrino's Price | 3 | 24,24 | 30,25 | 36,20 | 42,12 |
|  | 4 | 25,30 | 32,32 | 41,30 | 48,24 |
|  | 5 | 20,36 | 30,41 | 40,40 | 50,36 |
|  | 6 | 12,42 | 24,48 | 36,50 | 48,48 |

   a. What is the Nash equilibrium if the two firms set prices simultaneously?

   b. What is the Nash equilibrium if Northern Springs must set its price first and stick with it, and Southern Pelligrino is free to respond as best it can to Northern Springs' price?

   c. Show that choosing price first is a disadvantage for Northern Springs. Why is this the case?

5. Suppose that Firm 1 can choose to produce either good A, good B, both goods, or nothing. Firm 2, on the other hand, can produce only good C or nothing. Firms' profits corresponding to each possible scenario of goods for sale are described in the following table.

| Product Selection | Firm 1's Profit | Firm 2's Profit |
|---|---|---|
| A | 20 | 0 |
| A, B | 18 | 0 |
| A, B, C | 2 | -2 |
| B, C | -3 | -3 |
| C | 0 | 10 |
| A, C | 8 | 8 |
| B | 11 | 0 |

---

6  This game was first introduced by Rosenthal (1981).

**a.** Set up the normal form game for when the two firms simultaneously choose their product sets. What is the Nash equilibrium (or equilibria)?

**b.** Now suppose that Firm 1 can commit to its product choice before Firm 2. Draw the extensive form of this game and identify its subgame perfect Nash equilibrium. Compare your answer to (a) and explain.

**c.** The game is like the one in (b) only now suppose that Firm 1 can reverse its decision after observing Firm 2's choice and this possibility is common knowledge. Does this affect the game? If so, explain the new outcome. If not, explain why not.

6. Find three examples of different ways individual firms or industries can make the strategy "This offer is good for a limited time only" a credible strategy.

7. The Gizmo Company has a monopoly on the production of gizmos. Market demand is described as follows: at a price of $1,000 per gizmo 25,000 units will be sold whereas at a price of $600 per gizmo 30,000 units will be sold. The only costs of production are the initial sunk costs of building a plant. Gizmo Company has already invested in capacity to produce up to 25,000 units.

**a.** Suppose an entrant to this industry could capture 50 percent of the market if it invested in $10 million to construct a plant. Would the firm enter? Why or why not?

**b.** Suppose Gizmo could invest $5 million to expand its capacity to produce 40,000 gizmos. Would this strategy be a profitable way to deter entry?

# REFERENCES

Lieberman, Marvin B., and David B. Montgomery. 1998. "First Mover (Dis)Advantages: Retrospective and Link with Resource-Based Views." *Strategic Management Journal* 19: 1111–25.

Rosenthal, R. W. 1981. "Games of Perfect Information, Predatory Pricing and the Chain Store Paradox." *Journal of Economic Theory* 25: 92–100.

Schelling, T. 1960. *The Strategy of Conflict.* Cambridge, MA: Harvard University Press.

Selten, R. 1978. "The Chain Store Paradox." *Theory and Decision* 9 (April): 127–59.

Stackelberg, H. von. 1934. *Marktform and Gleichgewicht.* Translated by A. T. Peacock as *The Theory of the Market Economy.* London: William Hodge (1952).

Sutton, J. 1991. *Sunk Cost and Market Structure.* Cambridge, MA: The MIT Press.

# Part four

## Anticompetitive Strategies

# Anticompetitive Strategies

Part Four builds on our game theoretic analysis of Part Three to explore the tactics that firms can employ to increase their profits above those that they would earn in the standard oligopoly models of the previous three chapters. In the Stackelberg setting, the first mover or original incumbent has to worry about later entry. In the Cournot model and even more so in the Bertrand case, the firms find themselves earning less profit than would a monopolist. Accordingly, it is natural to consider the tactics that an incumbent firm might use to deter a potential entrant or perhaps to drive out an existing rival. Likewise, it is natural to explore ways in which rival firms might coordinate to come closer to achieving jointly the profits of a single monopoly firm.

Chapters 12 and 13 focus on the use of market power by a dominant firm to keep out or to drive out rivals from its market. This is typically referred to as predation in the antitrust literature and it has been a major point of contention in court cases since the antitrust laws were passed. Standard Oil, Alcoa, and Microsoft are just some of the many larger firms that have been alleged to have engaged in predatory practices. In order to consider the validity of such charges, we need to have a formal model to explore the logic of predation. Chapter 12 focuses on what are sometimes called limit pricing models. Here, the incumbent firm commits to such a low price (alternatively, such a large output) that no entrant can enter. A closely related practice is for the incumbent to set such a low price that smaller rivals are driven out. In either case, a central issue is the ability of the dominant firm to commit to the low price or high output in the face of rival entry and to do so in such a way that is credible to the entrant.

In Chapter 13, we refine the notion of predation by permitting the firm to employ a variety of nonprice tactics to deter entry. These include exploiting inside information about the nature of the market and using long-term contracts to preclude the entrant from winning any customers. These tactics also include the use of the bundling and tying arrangements discussed in Chapter 8.

Chapters 14 and 15 then turn to a consideration of the ability of firms to suppress competition by cooperating with each other. This practice is formally called collusion and usually is referred to in the media as price-fixing. Like predation, price-fixing cases have had a central role in the history of antitrust litigation. Indeed, the last decade has seen the prosecution of a record number of international price-fixing cartels involving products as diverse as vitamins and auctioned art. In Chapter 14 we develop the famous folk theorem outlining the game theoretic requirements for firms to collude successfully. In Chapter 15, we turn to a consideration of historical price-fixing cases and what they tell us about how such instances can be detected by the authorities.

# Limit Pricing and Entry Deterrence

# Chapter 12

For most of the past fifty years, Campbell has accounted for 60 percent or more of the volume of canned soup sales in the United States. For at least two decades, the American firm Sotheby's and the British firm Christie's have shared control of 90 percent of the world auction market. Each firm has more than half of its domestic auction market. For ten years Intel, maker of the Pentium chip, has controlled over 90 percent of the market for PC processors. Over that same period, Microsoft has maintained control of over 90 percent of the market for operating systems software.[1] There can be little doubt that each of these firms has substantial market power. Indeed, some appear almost to be pure monopolies. Accordingly, we must expect that such dominant firms exercise their market power and earn supracompetitive profits.

The Microsoft, Intel, and other examples of sustained market power just described are not isolated cases. Work by Baldwin (1995) and Geroski and Toker (1996) finds that, on average, the number one firm in an industry retains that rank for somewhere between 17 and 28 years. The fact that continued market power is so common does, however, raise the question as to how such firms can sustain this profit-winning position. Surely the profitability enjoyed by these firms is an invitation to other firms to enter the market. Yet additional production by such new entrants would erode the incumbent firm's market power and supranormal returns. In other words, just as oligopoly firms have to worry about the actions and reactions of existing rivals, monopoly or near-monopoly firms must be concerned with the actions and reactions of entrants and potential rivals.

The focus of this and the next chapter is on the strategic interaction between an existing dominant firm and potential or actual new entrants. We emphasize at the outset that this issue is of much more than mere academic interest. The question of whether large incumbent firms can eliminate rivals goes to the heart of many concerns that inspired the creation of the antitrust laws and that have remained central in subsequent antitrust cases ever since. Indeed, this concern lay at the crux of the Microsoft antitrust case.[2] Section 2 of the Sherman Act deems it illegal to "monopolize or attempt to monopolize . . . any part of the trade or commerce." Enforcement of this provision requires an understanding of what a firm can do in order to "monopolize" the market.

How is it that a firm can come to dominate a market? How does it displace and drive out existing rivals, or alternatively, how does it prevent new entrants from emerging? Strategies that are designed to deter rival firms from competing in a market are what economists call *predatory* conduct.[3] A firm engaging in predatory conduct wants to influence the behavior of its rivals—either those currently in the market or those thinking of entering it. Predatory conduct often involves the making of threats and, if necessary, actually implementing the threats in a way that ensures such

---

1   See "Squeeze Gently." *The Economist*, November 30, 1996, pp. 65–66.
2   Indeed, each of the firms mentioned has been accused of unfair practices by its respective rivals. Each has also been the subject of antitrust scrutiny.
3   See, e.g., Fisher (1991).

threats are credible. Credibility is absolutely essential for predatory conduct to be successful. After all, as we learned from the chain store paradox in Chapter 11, "talk is cheap." A threat aimed at dissuading a rival from entering one's market will have the desired effect only if it is credible. Such threats will work only if the rival or prey believes that the predator really "means business" and will pursue the predatory conduct even when the rival chooses to ignore the threat.

In this chapter we investigate predatory conduct that is designed to deter rivals from entering an incumbent's market. Moreover, we limit ourselves to cases of no uncertainty, that is, complete information. We defer the examination of tactics aimed at actually eliminating existing rivals and consideration of uncertainty to Chapter 13. Considerable care is needed to pursue our objectives. In particular, we must be careful not to characterize efforts by a firm either to improve its cost efficiency or to promote its product as predatory, even if such efforts have the side effect of enhancing the firm's market position. For a firm's conduct to be predatory or anticompetitive it must be the case that the firm's action is profitable *only if* it causes a rival firm to exit, or deters a potential rival from entering the market in the first place. This is in keeping with the spirit of the antitrust provisions themselves, which focus on efforts "to monopolize . . . any part of the trade or commerce" and to "materially reduce competition."[4] The basis for this legislative concern is, of course, the fear that with existing rivals and the threat of entry removed, a dominant firm will pursue monopoly practices that reduce efficiency.

## 12.1  MONOPOLY POWER AND MARKET STRUCTURE OVER TIME: SOME BASIC FACTS

The evolution of an industry's structure, whether into one of persistent monopoly, concentrated oligopoly, or more competitive configurations, depends on a number of factors. One of these is the relationship between a firm's size and its growth rate. An early finding in this respect is known as the Law of Proportionate Effect or, more commonly, Gibrat's Law, after its originator Robert Gibrat (1931). Gibrat asked what would happen if, starting with a population of 100 equally sized firms, each firm in each period was randomly assigned a growth rate drawn from a distribution with a constant average growth rate and variance of growth rates over time. The answer is perhaps surprising. Even though the industry firms all start at the same size and even though each has the chance for growth in every period thereafter, it is still the case that over time the industry becomes more and more concentrated. In particular, the distribution of firm sizes approaches a log normal one in which the logarithm of firm sizes approaches a normal distribution. Gibrat produced some data that was supportive of this natural concentrating tendency. Beginning with Kalecki (1945), economists have steadily provided additional supporting evidence.

The Gibrat hypothesis serves as a useful catalyst to thinking about the forces behind the evolution of industrial structure. However, as that investigation proceeds, what is most striking about the Gibrat analysis is what it leaves out rather than what it keeps in. This is because as originally presented, Gibrat's process is very mechanistic. There is no talk of research and cost-saving innovations. There is no considera-

---

4   Our definition is also similar to that of Ordover and Willig (1981).

# ✔ Derivation Checkpoint

## The Gibrat Logic

Let $x_t$ denote a firm's size at time $t$, where size might be measured in sales or assets or employees. Similarly, denote the firm's size in period $t-1$ as $x_{t-1}$. Now let $\varepsilon_t$ be the rate of growth of the firm from time $t-1$ to time $t$, where growth is measured as the rate of proportional change, that is, a growth rate of 4 percent is expressed as $\varepsilon_t = 0.04$. This growth factor is a random variable drawn each period from a normal distribution with constant mean and variance, and that distribution is the same for all firms. It then follows that the firm's size from time $t-1$ to time $t$ evolves according to the equation

$$x_t = (1 + \varepsilon_t)x_{t-1}.$$

Next, take the log of both sides. If the time interval between $t$ and $t-1$ is short, then the random growth term $\varepsilon_t$ is small. This permits us to use the approximation that $\log(1 + \varepsilon_t) \approx \varepsilon_t$. With this approximation we may now write

$$\log x_t = \log x_{t-1} + \varepsilon_t.$$

In turn, this implies that we may also write

$$\log x_{t-1} = \log x_{t-2} + \varepsilon_{t-1}.$$

By repeated substitution, we then obtain

$$\log x_t = \log x_0 + \varepsilon_t + \varepsilon_{t-1} + \varepsilon_{t-2} + \varepsilon_{t-3} + \ldots + \varepsilon_1.$$

This last equation says that the logarithm of the firm's size at time $t$ will just be a random variable reflecting the accumulation of all the random growth shocks it has experienced up to that time. Since each shock is assumed to be a random variable drawn from the normal distribution, the sum over time of all those accumulated shocks is also a normal random variable. Recall, however, that logarithms reflect exponential power. As the log of a firm's assets doubles the actual volume of those assets is squared. So, although the log of firm size may be normally distributed, the distribution of actual firm sizes will be skewed. Those firms with above average values for the log of firm size will have way above average values when size is measured without logs. Thus, if firm sizes evolve so that each firm is generated by the process described above, the industry will eventually become quite heavily concentrated and ultimately dominated by one firm.

tion of mergers and firm combinations over time. Perhaps most relevant for our present purpose, there is no discussion of new firms entering an industry or older firms leaving, or what strategic interaction may lie behind such entry and exit. Subsequent research has tried to remedy these omissions and to develop theoretical models of industry evolution that build in such features. [See, for example, Jovanovic (1982), Nelson and Winter (1982), Sutton (1997), and Klepper (2002).]

Of course, any theoretical model must ultimately confront the facts. On this front, too, however, there has been much work. Forty or fifty years ago, we knew precious little regarding the life cycle of firms, their births (entry), and their deaths (exit). In recent years, though, there have been substantial efforts in this field. As a result, a number of stylized facts about firm entry and exit—facts that any valid theory must be able to explain—emerged.

The first stylized fact is that *entry is common*. Dunne *et al.* (1988), using U.S. census data between 1963 and 1982, computed rates of entry in a wide cross-section of two-digit SIC manufacturing industries. The entry rate, which is defined as the number of new firms in an industry divided by the total number of incumbent firms in the previous census five years earlier, ranged between 41.4 and 51.8 percent for the industries studied in their sample (about 8 to 10 percent on an annual basis). For the United Kingdom, Geroski (1995) estimated somewhat smaller but still significant rates of entry for a sample of 87 three-digit manufacturing industries. These ranged between 2.5 and 14.5 percent over the period 1974 to 1979. Cable and Schwalbach (1991) show similar rates of entry across a wide range of developed countries.[5]

The second stylized fact is that when entry occurs it is, by and large, *small-scale entry*. The study by Dunne *et al.* showed that the collective market share of entrants in an industry ranged between 13.9 and 18.8 percent again between census years.[6] Similarly, in Geroski's U.K. study, the market share of entrants was found to be quite modest, ranging from 1.45 to 6.35 percent. In the United States, Cable and Schwalbach found that while new entrants typically constitute 7.7 percent of an industry's firms in any year, they account for only 3.2 percent of its output. Together these first two stylized facts indicate that small-scale entry is relatively easy and is frequently observed.

The third stylized fact is that the *survival rate is relatively low*. Dunne *et al.* found that roughly 61.5 percent of all entrant firms exited within five years of entry and 79.6 percent exited within ten years. Similarly, Birch (1987) used Dun and Bradstreet data for all sectors in the United States including, but not limited to, manufacturing and found that about 50 percent of all new entrant firms fail within the first five years.

The fourth stylized fact is a twofold one. The first part is that within an industry, *the rate of entry is highly correlated with the rate of exit*. For example, Cable and Schwalbach found that corresponding to an entry rate of 7.7 percent accounting for 3.2 percent of industry output, the exit rate is 7.0 percent accounting for 3.3 percent of industry output. The second part is that, across industries, *rates of both entry and exit vary considerably*. In industries such as clothing, furniture, and metal-working, for example, we frequently observe new firms coming and other firms leaving. In contrast, industries such as chemicals, petroleum, and paper have had very little entrance by new firms and correspondingly little exit of old ones. As mentioned, new entrants are, in general, noticeably smaller than are the incumbent firms. Firms that exit the market are also smaller than long-standing industry leaders. Exiting firms produce roughly 20 percent of the output of all firms in the relevant industry sectors.

The fact that entry and exit go hand-in-hand is not consistent with the hypothesis that entry occurs in response to above-normal profit or that exit reflects a below-

---

5   The Dunne *et al.* (1988) entry (and exit) estimates are generally higher than those obtained by other researchers owing to the fact that Dunne *et al.* explicitly recognize the multiproduct and multiplant nature of firms.

6   Dunne, *et al.* (1988, 1989) do find that existing firms who enter a new market through diversification typically enter at a larger scale than new, or *de novo*, entrants do.

normal profit. If profit is high, and therefore entry attractive, there is no reason for firms to leave. Similarly, if profit is so low that firms are induced to leave the industry, there should be little incentive for new entrants to emerge. So, the oft-told story that high (low) industry profit is what induces entry (exit) appears to be at odds with the fact that we typically observe both entry and exit simultaneously.

Taken together, the stylized facts can be read as suggesting a sort of revolving-door setting in which mostly small firms enter, eventually fail and exit, only to be replaced by a new cohort of small-scale entrants. In this view, the major difference across industries would be the pace at which this entry-fail-exit cycle proceeds. One interpretation of this evidence is that it reflects repeated attempts and, just as often, repeated failures of small firms to penetrate the markets dominated by large incumbents. This interpretation is further buttressed by the work of Urban, Carter, Gaskin, and Mucha (1984) on the benefits of incumbency. They studied 129 frequently purchased brands of consumer products in twelve U.S. markets and found that market shares were a decreasing function of the order of entry of the brand. Earlier entrants enjoyed larger market shares, all else equal.[7]

Perhaps the most obvious question is whether the foregoing evidence on entry and survival can be related to explicit predatory conduct by the incumbent firms. One potential clue is provided by a second finding of Urban, Carter, Gaskin, and Mucha. They found that long-standing incumbent firms earn persistently greater profits than do more recent entrants. However, this finding is not conclusive because we could also observe this outcome in cases where predation is not involved. For example, factors such as superior cost efficiency, longer market experience, or acquiring the most favorable location (either in geographic or product space) could also be part of the explanation behind the persistent dominance and profitability of established firms. To the extent that this is true, it implies that such dominance is not the result of predation.

In short, entry and exit are common, especially among small firms. Whether such evidence also indicates widespread predatory conduct in which small entrants are consistently driven out by aggressive and large incumbents seems unlikely. If predation were the primary force underlying these data, one would wonder why small firms continue to challenge established companies that are determined to drive them out of existence. Yet the findings do suggest an important advantage to incumbency in which predation may play an important, if not a dominant, part. Indeed, the relative infrequency of entry by medium- and large-scale firms may suggest that incumbents' entry-deterring tactics have focused on these larger and perhaps more threatening potential rivals. While we cannot resolve this issue here, we can determine what economic theory has to say on the possibility of incumbent firm advantages and the possibility of predation. These are the issues to which we now turn.

## 12.2 PREDATORY CONDUCT AND LIMIT PRICING

Economists interpret predatory conduct to be actions taken by a firm that are profitable *only* if they drive existing rivals out of the market or deter potential rivals from

---

7   As Caves (1998) notes, though, there is regression toward the mean in firm growth rates. That is, large firms tend to grow more slowly than do small ones. This feature blunts the ever-increasing concentration tendency implied by Gibrat's Law.

coming into the market. Predatory conduct is some costly action for which the only justification is the reduction in competition that such action is designed to achieve. If there is no cost to the firm to engage in some conduct, then that behavior is simply part of a profit-maximizing strategy and, hence, not explicitly anticompetitive. To put it somewhat loosely, predatory conduct must appear on the surface to reduce the predator firm's profit and seem to be "irrational." Its only rationality can be the additional profit the predator earns if the conduct is successful.

When a firm charges such an "irrationally" low price such that other rival firms cannot compete it is called *predatory pricing*. Historically, predatory pricing refers to cases where rival firms are driven out of the market. However, setting a low price that deters firms from entering the market is also predatory. The low price in this case is called the *limit price*. However, actual litigation rarely involves limit pricing. Instead, the courts and policy makers have focused on cases in which existing firms are forced to leave the market.

It is not difficult to understand how and why there is this legal bias in predatory pricing. Predatory pricing cases in which existing firms are driven from the market have no *habeas corpus* problem. There is an actual victim or victims. As a result, there is a supply of plaintiffs ready to press charges against the alleged predator. Moreover, the existence of a "body" can serve as powerful evidence to persuade a judge or a jury that a crime has been committed. In contrast, the victims of limit pricing are typically *potential* competitors. Here, no firm actually dies, some are just prevented from ever being born. Such cases are difficult to prosecute.

However, economic theory can proceed even where lawyers fear to tread. Accordingly, we start the important work of this chapter by reviewing two approaches to limit pricing. The first is an earlier approach predating the advent of a game theoretic treatment of the subject. The second approach takes the insight of the first and investigates the entry deterrent effect in a dynamic game between the incumbent and the entrant.

## 12.2.1  An Informal Model of Entry Deterrence

The traditional limit pricing story of entry deterrence is told in the work of Bain (1956) and later modeled in Sylos-Labini (1962). These earlier industrial organization economists were shrewd observers of everyday business practices and had reasons to believe that predatory pricing and entry-deterring behavior occurred. We can illustrate the essence of the limit pricing strategy using a simple variant of the Stackelberg model. Recall from Chapter 11 that the strategic variable in the Stackelberg model is quantity. So, the analysis we will present might more properly be labeled a limit output model rather than a limit price model. Yet the basic idea of setting the strategic variable so as to deter entry is the same in either case—especially since the dominant firm's output choice will greatly influence the industry price. That is, we might regard the resulting price in our model as the limit price in the sense that it reflects the incumbent's commitment to produce an output great enough that the price will never rise above this level.

Figure 12-1 illustrates the essential features of the model.[8] The incumbent firm is the Stackelberg leader and it is allowed to choose its output first. For now, we will simply assume that whatever this choice is, the entrant believes that its own entry into

---

8   This presentation borrows heavily from that of Gilbert (1989).

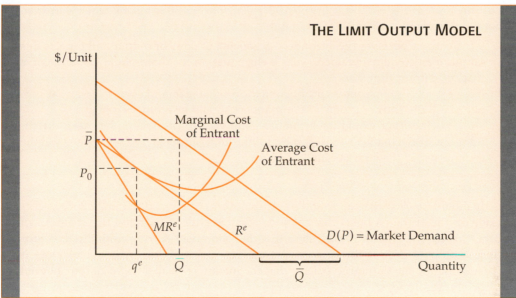

FIGURE

**12-1**

By producing at $\bar{Q}$, the incumbent can preclude any profitable entry.

the market will not alter the leader's choice of output. That is, the entrant regards the incumbent as irrevocably committed to its output choice. A further crucial assumption is that the entrant's average cost declines over at least the initial range of low levels of production. When both of these assumptions hold then, by the right choice of its pre-entry output level, the incumbent can manipulate the entrant's profit calculation and discourage entry.

In Figure 12-1, the appropriate production level to which the incumbent must commit to deter any entry is $\bar{Q}$. If the entrant stays out, this implies a market price $\bar{P}$. What would happen to market price if the entrant now produced any positive output? The answer is shown in Figure 12-1. Because the entrant believes that the incumbent will maintain $\bar{Q}$, the quantity of demand it will face at any price $P$ is the quantity that would be demanded in total at that price $D(P)$ less $\bar{Q}$. That is, the entrant faces a *residual demand curve*, $R^e$, which in this case is simply the market demand curve $D(P)$ shifted inward along the horizontal axis by the amount $\bar{Q}$. Corresponding to this residual demand curve is the entrant's marginal revenue curve $MR^e$. The entrant will maximize its profit by selecting output $q^e$ at which its marginal revenue just equals its marginal cost. As shown in Figure 12-1, this output is such that when it is added to the output $\bar{Q}$ of the incumbent firm market price becomes $P_0$, and this price just covers the entrant's average cost. In other words, by committing to the output $\bar{Q}$, the incumbent firm removes any and all profit incentive for the entrant to actually participate in the market.

## Practice Problem 12.1

Suppose that market demand is described by $P = 100 - (Q + q)$, where $P$ is the market price, $Q$ is the output of the incumbent firm, and $q$ is the output of a potential entrant to the market. The incumbent firm's total cost function is $TC(Q) = 40Q$, whereas the cost function of the entrant is $C(q) = 100 + 40q$, where 100 is a sunk cost incurred to enter the market.

a. If the entrant observes the incumbent producing $\overline{Q}$ units of output and expects this output level to be maintained, what is the equation for the residual demand curve that the entrant firm faces?

b. If the entrant firm maximizes profit given the residual demand curve in (a), what output $q^e$ will the entrant produce? (Your answer should be a function of $\overline{Q}$.)

c. How much output would the incumbent firm have to produce to just keep the entrant out of the market? That is, solve for the limit output $\overline{Q}_L$. At what price will the incumbent sell the limit output?

---

It should be clear that successful predation of the type just described depends crucially on the entrant's belief that the incumbent is truly committed to its action. In other words, the entrant must believe that the incumbent is truly committed to produce output $\overline{Q}$ even if the entrant entered the market. Is this reasonable? Does it make sense for the entrant to believe that the incumbent will stick to output $\overline{Q}$ even if the entrant invades?

Earlier scholars such as Bain (1956) and Sylos-Labini (1962) did not make use of the formal model just described. Nevertheless, they appear to have understood that in order to deter entry the incumbent firm had to commit or "lock in" to the predatory behavior. They assumed that such commitment was achieved by further supposing that the incumbent's output $\overline{Q}$ was costly to adjust. Hence, the potential entrant was right to assume output would remain at $\overline{Q}$ because it was too costly to change. In other words, the presence of adjustment costs once the incumbent is already producing at a particular level acted as a mechanism to commit the incumbent to the output $\overline{Q}$ even in the face of entry.

The idea sounds plausible and may well be true. Unfortunately, as stated, it is a little ad hoc. Without a full specification of how such costs are generated and how they fit into a complete analysis of strategic interaction between the two firms, the adjustment cost story amounts to little more than a statement that the incumbent's output is given because it is given. Producing $\overline{Q}$ is a credible action only if $\overline{Q}$ is the incumbent's best response to the entrant coming into the market and choosing an output level to produce. In other words, at the heart of the limit pricing story is the question of whether the incumbent firm can commit to producing the limit output even if entry occurs.

## 12.2.2 Capacity Expansion as a Credible Entry-Deterring Commitment

In a classic article, Spence (1977) recognized that what may make limit pricing a credible deterrent strategy is the incumbent firm's ability to make a prior and irrevocable investment in production capacity, and specifically an investment in the *capacity* to produce the limit output $\overline{Q}$. Spence did not work out the underlying logic of this approach in a complete manner. He did, however, make it clear that if the entrant believes that the incumbent will, after entry, produce at its pre-entry capacity, then the incumbent firm has an incentive to invest in a capacity level that keeps the potential entrant at bay. What was still required, however, was an analysis demonstrating that the post-entry game between the incumbent and the new entrant could in fact justify the entrant's belief that the incumbent's post-entry output is equal to its pre-entry capacity, that is, a model that is subgame perfect. This was Dixit's (1980) contribution. Dixit's model of the post-entry game between the two firms formally captured Spence's insight. We present the essentials of his analysis below. We warn the reader in advance that this model is hard work. While no one piece of the analysis is terribly difficult, considerable care is required in putting all the pieces together.

The game Dixit posits between the two firms is a dynamic, two-stage one. In the first stage, the incumbent firm moves first and chooses a capacity level $\overline{K}_1$ at a cost $r\overline{K}_1$. This capacity is measured in terms of output, and the cost $r$ is the constant cost of one unit of capacity. By investing in capacity $\overline{K}_1$ in the first stage of the game, the incumbent firm gains the capability of producing any output less than or equal to $\overline{K}_1$ when the second stage of the game begins. The incumbent's capacity can be further increased in stage two of the game. However, it cannot be reduced. One may think of the capacity investment as the construction of say, a uranium processing plant, a plant for which any other industry has little use. If so, the plant cannot be resold if the firm decides it no longer needs it. In this sense, the $r\overline{K}_1$ spent on capacity investment in stage one is an irrevocable or sunk cost.

The potential entrant is assumed to observe the incumbent's choice of capacity in stage one. It is only after that observation that the potential entrant makes its entry decision in stage two. If entry does occur then, in the second stage of the game the two firms play a Cournot game in output. Market demand for the product in stage two is described by $P = A - B(q_1 + q_2)$. It is important to note that the two firms simultaneously choose both their outputs $(q_1, q_2)$ and their ultimate capacity levels $(K_1, K_2)$ in stage two. However, for the incumbent, this choice is, as noted, constrained such that its capacity in the second stage must be no less than the capacity chosen in the first stage, that is, $K_2 \geq \overline{K}_1$. Again, the incumbent firm can increase its capacity in stage two but not decrease it.

We will denote any sunk costs incurred by the incumbent other than those associated with its capacity choice $\overline{K}_1$ as $F_1$. For simplicity, we will further assume that every unit produced requires the input of one unit of labor as well as a unit of capacity. If labor can be hired at the wage $w$, then the incumbent's marginal cost of production for output less than $q_1$ is just $wq_1$. However, if the incumbent wishes to produce an output greater than $q_1$ then it must hire additional capacity, again at the price of $r$ per unit. That is, for every unit of output above $q_1$, the incumbent must hire one unit of labor at price $w$ and one unit of capital at price $r$. Hence, the marginal cost of production for output greater than $q_1$ is $w + r$. These relationships are reflected in the following description of the incumbent's cost function in stage two of the game:

$$C_1(q_1, q_2; \overline{K}_1) = F_1 + wq_1 + r\overline{K}_1, \text{ for } q_1 \leq \overline{K}_1; \text{ Marginal cost } = w \qquad \textbf{(12.1)}$$
$$= F_1 + (w + r)q_1, \text{ for } q_1 > \overline{K}_1; \text{ Marginal cost } = w + r.$$

The only difference between the entrant and the incumbent is that the entrant cannot invest in any capacity in stage one. Instead, the entrant must hire both labor and capital as they are needed to produce whatever output it selects during the second stage. Thus, the entrant's marginal cost is always $w + r$ no matter what output it chooses. If we denote any sunk cost the entrant incurs as a result of participating in the market as $F_2$, its cost function in stage two is

$$C_2(q_2) = F_2 + (w + r)q_2; \text{ Marginal cost } = w + r. \qquad \textbf{(12.2)}$$

It is important to note that the two firms face different marginal costs of production in stage two of the game. For the incumbent firm, the marginal cost of producing any output $q_1$ is equal to $w$ so long as it is within its initial capacity, or so long as $q_1 \leq \overline{K}_1$. However, because the entrant does not enjoy the first-mover advantage of having already invested in capacity in stage one, it faces a marginal cost of production equal to $(w + r)$ for all output levels. This difference is reflected in Figure 12-2 where we draw the marginal cost curve for both firms. The diagram suggests why investment in capacity can have a commitment value. The incumbent's commitment to produce at least as much as $\overline{K}_1$ is made more believable by the fact that up to that production level, its marginal cost is relatively low.

FIGURE

**12-2**

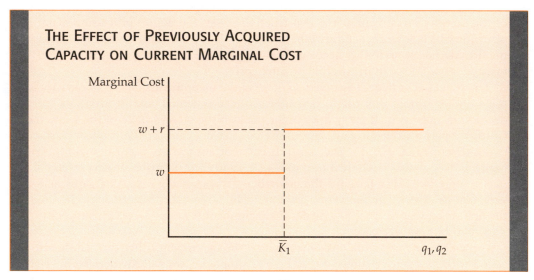

### THE EFFECT OF PREVIOUSLY ACQUIRED CAPACITY ON CURRENT MARGINAL COST

The incumbent has previously acquired capacity $\overline{K}_1$ and therefore incurs a marginal cost of only $w$ up to this level of production. For greater levels, its marginal cost is $w + r$. The entrant has no previously acquired capacity. Its marginal cost is $w + r$ for all production levels.

We noted previously that in a sequential game such as we have here, we begin by working out what happens in the last stage in order to work out the incumbent firm's optimal move in the first stage. To solve for a perfect equilibrium strategy for the incumbent firm, we need to determine how the incumbent's choice of capacity in stage one affects the market outcome when the two firms compete in stage two. We start by working out what happens in stage two for any particular level of capacity chosen in stage one. We then determine what happens in stage one by choosing that capacity that maximizes the incumbent's profits in stage two.

In stage two the firms are playing a Cournot game in quantities. The incumbent firm's profit will be

$$\pi_1(q_1, q_2, \overline{K}_1) = \text{Revenue} - \text{Cost} = [A - B(q_1 + q_2)]q_1 - [wq_1 + F_1] \text{ for } q_1 \leq \overline{K}_1$$
$$\pi_1(q_1, q_2, \overline{K}_1) = \text{Revenue} - \text{Cost} = [A - B(q_1 + q_2)]q_1 - [(w + r)q_1 + F_1] \text{ for } q_1 > \overline{K}_1.$$

$$(12.3)$$

From equation (12.3), we can see that the marginal revenue to the incumbent associated with an incremental unit of $q_1$ is always given by $MR_1 = A - 2Bq_1 - Bq_2$.

However, its marginal cost will change depending on whether the firm decides to add capacity. When the incumbent firm's best response, $q_1^*$, to the entrant's choice of output, $q_2$, is such that it does not need to add capacity, that is, when $q_1^* \leq \overline{K}_1$, the incumbent's marginal cost is just $w$. But if the incumbent's best response, $q_1^*$, is such that it needs additional capacity, $q_1^* > \overline{K}_1$, its marginal cost becomes $w + r$. Accordingly, equating the incumbent's marginal revenue and marginal cost and solving for its optimal output in stage two leads to a best response function with two parts. These are

$$q_1^* = \frac{(A - w)}{2B} - \frac{q_2}{2} \text{ when } q_1^* \leq \overline{K}_1; \text{ and}$$

$$q_1^* = \frac{(A - w - r)}{2B} - \frac{q_2}{2} \text{ when } q_1^* > \overline{K}_1.$$

(12.4)

This means that the incumbent firm's best response function jumps at the output level $q_1^* = \overline{K}_1$. We can see the jump more clearly when we draw the reaction function for the incumbent firm in the second stage of the game. We do this in Figure 12-3. Again, $\overline{K}_1$ is the capacity that that the incumbent firm chose in stage one of the game.

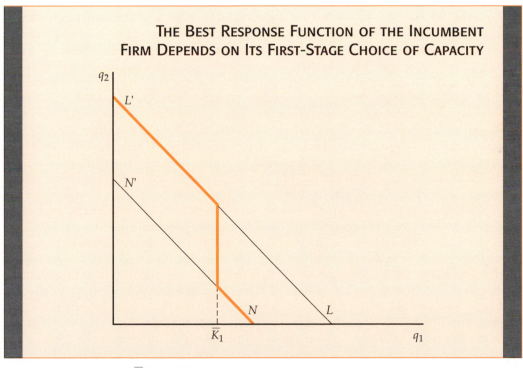

## THE BEST RESPONSE FUNCTION OF THE INCUMBENT FIRM DEPENDS ON ITS FIRST-STAGE CHOICE OF CAPACITY

FIGURE

**12-3**

For output less than $\overline{K}_1$, the incumbent will have low marginal cost and operates on the higher response function, $L'L$. For output greater than $\overline{K}_1$, the incumbent has higher marginal cost and operates on the lower best response function, $N'N$.

For output levels $q_1^* \leq \overline{K}_1$, the incumbent firm's reaction function is the solid line described by $L'L$, whereas for output levels $q_1^* > \overline{K}_1$ the reaction function jumps to the lower solid line described by $N'N$.

Now consider the situation facing the entrant in stage two. Profits for the entrant firm are, as always, the difference between its revenue and its cost, which implies

$$\pi_2(q_1, q_2, \overline{K}_1) = \text{Revenue} - \text{Cost} = [A - B(q_1 + q_2)]q_2 - [(w + r)q_2 + F_2]. \quad \textbf{(12.5)}$$

The requirement that marginal revenue equals marginal cost implies that the entrant firm's best response function is

$$q_2^\star = \frac{(A - w - r)}{2B} - \frac{q_1}{2}. \quad \textbf{(12.6)}$$

One point is worth stressing before going further. It is that equation (12.6) is the entrant's best response function *given* that it chooses to produce a positive level of output at all, that is, so long as it is the case that the entrant's profit at that output will be nonnegative. The best response function is derived using the marginal conditions and therefore does not take account of the sunk cost $F_2$ that the potential entrant incurs should it actually decide to enter. The intercept of equation (12.6) with the $q_2$ axis, $(A - w - r)/2B$, is the entrant's optimal output if the incumbent somehow decided to produce nothing. That would correspond to the entrant being a monopoly and would almost certainly imply positive profits (otherwise we could rule out entry from the start). However, as one moves from left to right along the response function, the entrant's output becomes successively smaller as it adjusts to larger and larger production by the incumbent. This decline limits the volume over which the entrant's fixed cost may be spread. As a result, firm 2's average total cost rises as its output falls. It is quite possible that, at some point where the incumbent's production $q_1$ is sufficiently large, the market price implied by the combined output of both firms will not cover the entrant's average cost *at the production level implied by its best response curve.* Accordingly, the entrant will lose money if it actually produces that output once the fixed cost $F_2$ is taken into account. Recall, however, that the entrant always has the option of not producing at all and, instead, to stay out and thereby earn a zero profit. If, at the output implied by equation (12.6), the entrant's profit would in fact be negative, it will not produce at that level but simply refrain from entering the market. We will return to this point later.

We know that the Nash equilibrium in stage two will occur at the intersection of the incumbent's best response function and that of the potential entrant's providing, as just noted, that the latter earns a nonnegative profit. This brings us back to the first stage. Seeing how matters work out in stage two, the incumbent firm can manipulate this intersection by its choice of $\overline{K}_1$ in stage one. Naturally, the incumbent firm will choose $\overline{K}_1$ in the first stage to give itself the maximum profit possible in stage two. Let us now investigate this choice and whether it implies the possibility that the incumbent firm will choose $\overline{K}_1$ to deter the second firm from entering.

We begin by drawing a diagram that describes all the possible equilibria for stage two of the game. In Figure 12-4 we draw the two reaction functions for firm 1, one corresponding to the low marginal cost of production $W$, labeled $L'L$, and the other reaction function corresponding to the higher marginal cost of production $w + r$, labeled $N'N$. We then add the reaction function for firm 2, labeled $R'R$. We denote the point where firm 2's reaction function meets $N'N$ by $T$. This point corresponds to stage two outputs for the incumbent and entrant of $T_1$ and $T_2$, respectively. Similarly, the point where $R'R$ meets $L'L$ is labeled $V$ and corresponds to respective outputs of $V_1$ and $V_2$.

## ✔ Derivation Checkpoint

### The Calculus of Predation: Limit Output/Price and Capacity Commitment

In the Stackelberg limit output model, inverse market demand is given by $P = A - BQ$. Once the dominant firm commits to a specific output $q^F$, the entrant's residual demand is $P = A - B(q^F + q)$, where $q$ is the amount produced by the entrant. The entrant's marginal revenue curve is then described by $MR = A - Bq^F - 2Bq$. Setting this equal to the entrant's marginal cost then yields the entrant's optimal output, $q^*$. The incumbent's limit output is that choice of $Q^F$ such that the entrant's residual demand curve is just tangent to its average cost curve at the output choice, $q^*$.

The Dixit model of capacity commitment to deter entry relies on the fact that while the capacity can be installed in varying amounts it is, once made, a sunk cost. Because the incumbent firm will never let installed capacity stand idle, its ability to build capacity prior to any entrant allows it to transform the structure—but not the total amount—of its costs. The incumbent's marginal cost will be $w$ for output less than or equal to its capacity choice $\overline{K}$, but $w + r$ for all outputs greater than that amount. In contrast, the entrant's marginal cost is always $w + r$. Competition is of the Cournot or quantity type. The industry inverse demand function is $P = A - BQ = A - B(q_1 + q_2)$, where $q_1$ and $q_2$ are the outputs of the incumbent and entrant firm, respectively. This implies a profit function of $\pi_1 = [A - B(q_1 + q_2)]q_1 - wq_1 - r\overline{K} - F_1$ if output is less than $\overline{K}$, and $\pi_1 = [A - B(q_1 + q_2)]q_1 - (w + r)q_1 - F_1$ if output is greater than $\overline{K}$. Setting the derivative with respect to $q_1$ equal to zero in each case then yields the incumbent's two possible reaction functions. For output less

than or equal to $\overline{K}$, the incumbent's optimal response curve is $q_1 = \dfrac{A - w}{2B} - \dfrac{q_2}{2}$. For output above $\overline{K}$, its optimal response is $q_1 = \dfrac{A - (w + r)}{2B} - \dfrac{q_2}{2}$.

We may simultaneously solve for $q_1$ and $q_2$ using the best response curve of each firm. If both firms follow the response function, $q_i = \dfrac{A - (w + r)}{2B} - \dfrac{q_j}{2}$, each firm will produce $q_i = \dfrac{A - (w + r)}{3B}$. This corresponds to the outputs at point $T$ in Figure 12-5. If the entrant has the response function $q_2 = \dfrac{A - (w + r)}{2B} - \dfrac{q_1}{2}$, but the incumbent has the response function, $q_1 = \dfrac{A - w}{2B} - \dfrac{q_2}{2}$, the incumbent will produce at level $q_1 = \dfrac{A - w}{3B} + \dfrac{r}{3B}$. In this case, the entrant will produce at level $q_2 = \dfrac{A - w}{3B} - \dfrac{2r}{3B}$. This combination corresponds to point $V$ in Figure 12-5. The monopoly or Stackelberg leader output is $q_1 = \dfrac{A - (w + r)}{2B}$.

As explained in the text, the equilibrium must be one in which firm 1 produces between the monopoly output and $V_1$. In the example in the text, $A = 120$, $B = 1$, and $w = r = 30$. The incumbent's output as a Stackelberg leader is therefore $q_1 = 30$. The intersection of the best response functions corresponding to point $V$ is one at which $q_1 = 40$ and $q_2 = 10$. The final outcome must lie between these two points.

FIGURE

**12-4**

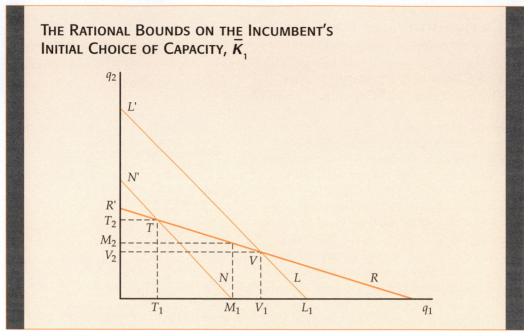

## THE RATIONAL BOUNDS ON THE INCUMBENT'S INITIAL CHOICE OF CAPACITY, $\bar{K}_1$

The incumbent firm will choose an initial capacity investment somewhere between $T_1$ and $V_1$.

In the second stage, firm 2 is either going to enter or stay out. Consider what happens if firm 2 does enter. In this case, the Nash equilibrium must lie somewhere between points $T$ and $V$ on firm 2's response function $R'R$. The actual point will depend on the capacity choice of the incumbent and, in particular, on the output level at which it shifts from response function $L'L$ to $N'N$. The minimum amount that firm 1 will produce if its rival enters is $T_1$ and the maximum amount it will produce is $V_1$. Accordingly, firm 1 would never wish to choose a capacity level less than $T_1$ or larger than $V_1$ if it foresaw that firm 2 was definitely going to enter.

What if firm 2 does not enter? First, think of what this means. If firm 2 does not enter it must be because entry is not profitable. This will happen if firm 2 is unable to make a positive profit even in its most favorable Nash equilibrium, namely, the one at $T$. At $T$, firm 2 produces its highest equilibrium output $T_2$. If it cannot break even at this volume then it surely cannot break even at any smaller level such as $V_2$. However, if this is the case, and if firm 1 understands this fact, then it must recognize that it will be a monopolist in stage two. A monopoly firm in this market would of course produce at production level $M_1$. The marginal cost of producing any output that fully utilizes capacity is $w + r$. Equating this amount with its marginal revenue gives the pure monopolist's profit-maximizing output, which is the production level $M_1$, corresponding to firm 1's optimal output when firm 2 produces zero and firm 1 is on its lower response function.

Even at this early stage of our analysis we have obtained some useful results. First, the incumbent's choice of capacity in stage one must lie in the interval ranging from $T_1$ to $V_1$. Second, if the entrant cannot break even at output $T_2$, the incumbent's best choice within this interval is $M_1$, namely, the output chosen by a pure monopolist with marginal cost $w + r$, which is precisely what the incumbent will be.

What we need to do now is to determine the incumbent's best initial choice of capacity when the entrant *can* break even at an output as low as $T_2$. In this regard, the capacity level of $M_1$ is again relevant because it is not only the monopoly output but, as just noted, also the output of a Stackelberg leader. Because only the incumbent gets to choose capacity in stage one, we might expect that even if the entrant can operate at levels of output below $T_2$, the incumbent still ought to be able to achieve the market share and profit of a Stackelberg leader. In other words, we should expect that the incumbent will never choose an initial capacity less than $M_1$. Note, though, that if this presumption is true, we have then reduced the set of sensible initial capacity choices from the broad range of $T_1$ to $V_1$, to the much narrower range of $M_1$ to $V_1$. In fact, we will soon see that this conjecture is correct. The incumbent's profit-maximizing initial capacity choice will always lie within the $M_1$ to $V_1$ range.

To see why the incumbent will do best by choosing initial capacity in the $M_1$ to $V_1$ range, and also to determine precisely what point within that range is best, we proceed as follows. We denote by the point $B$ the output level at which the entrant, firm 2, ceases to make a profit, that is, when the revenue from the entrant's best output response just covers both its variable and its fixed cost so that $\pi_2 = 0$. By definition, the relevant range of $B$ lies somewhere on the entrant's response function, $RR'$. Indeed, $B$ must lie on $RR'$ somewhere to the left of where that response curve intersects the $q_1$ axis, since with a sunk cost of $F_2$ the entrant cannot break even if it enters but produces nothing ($q_2 = 0$).

The incumbent firm's best choice of its initial capacity $\overline{K}_1$, which again determines both where the jump occurs in its reaction function and the location of the stage two equilibrium, depends on just where the point $B$ lies. Figure 12-5 shows four possibilities. For example, suppose that because of a relatively high sunk cost $F_2$, firm 2's

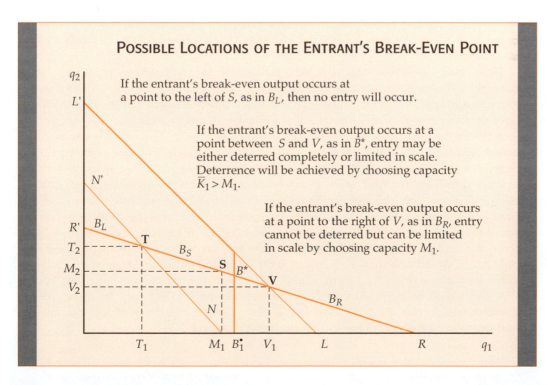

**POSSIBLE LOCATIONS OF THE ENTRANT'S BREAK-EVEN POINT**

If the entrant's break-even output occurs at a point to the left of $S$, as in $B_L$, then no entry will occur.

If the entrant's break-even output occurs at a point between $S$ and $V$, as in $B^*$, entry may be either deterred completely or limited in scale. Deterrence will be achieved by choosing capacity $\overline{K}_1 > M_1$.

If the entrant's break-even output occurs at a point to the right of $V$, as in $B_R$, entry cannot be deterred but can be limited in scale by choosing capacity $M_1$.

FIGURE

**12-5**

profit is negative when it produces $T_2$ and firm 1 produces $T_1$, or $\pi_2(T_1, T_2) < 0$. In other words, $B$ is at a point like $B_L$ to the left of $T$. This is the case that we have already discussed. Here, entry by firm 2 is not profitable under any condition and will not occur. The incumbent firm will understand at the time of its first stage investment that it will be a monopoly in stage two, and therefore will choose the pure monopoly capacity level $M_1$. It will then produce at output $q_1 = M_1$ in stage two.

What if $B$ is at a point such as $B_S$? This means that the entrant can break even at a production level below $T_2$ so long as it does not fall so low as $M_2$. What is the incumbent's best choice now?

In Figure 12-5 we have designated the output combination $(M_1, M_2)$ by $S$. The reason for this notation is that as previously noted, $M_1$ is not only the incumbent's pure monopoly output but also the output chosen by the Stackelberg leader. For the moment, this fact is not of great relevance. Instead, the key point here is that even if the entrant can break even at output levels less than $T_2$, so long as it cannot cover its costs at output levels below $M_2$, then $M_1$ remains the optimal capacity choice by the incumbent.[9] If the entrant cannot profitably enter when the incumbent produces the pure monopoly output $M_1$, then by selecting that capacity the incumbent guarantees that entry will not occur. In turn, this will justify the incumbent's decision to build capacity $M_1$ in the first place. Using Bain's (1956) terminology, this is a case of blockaded entry. It is not really predatory conduct, however. The firm is producing and pricing like the monopolist that it is. It is not engaging in any action that is solely profitable by virtue of its entry-deterring effect.

We now consider a third possibility at the other end of firm 2's reaction function. Here we consider a break-even point $B$ that lies to the right of $V$ as is the case at $B_R$. This means that firm 2's costs are such that its profit is still positive at $(V_1, V_2)$, where it produces the relatively small amount $V_2$ and firm 1 produces the much larger quantity $V_1$. As previously noted, this implies that firm 2 will definitely find it profitable to enter the market. Not only is entry not blockaded in the sense of Bain, it is in fact an inevitability.

Now think a bit about what this really means. The incumbent knows that entry is inevitable. It simply cannot maintain its monopoly position. Yet if entry cannot be prevented it may at least be limited. That is, since the incumbent can see that it will have an active rival in stage two, it may as well take actions in stage one that give the incumbent the best possible profit in the presence of firm 2. The obvious choice in this regard is to play the Stackelberg leader. This is where the equality between the output of the pure monopolist and that of the Stackelberg leader becomes relevant because it implies that here again, the incumbent will install an initial capacity equal to $M_1$. True enough, this will no longer lead to an equilibrium in which the incumbent is a monopoly. Entry will occur and output will rise above the monopoly case while the market price will decline. Yet the installation of capacity equal to $M_1$ will force the entrant to enter on the limited scale of a Stackelberg follower producing only $M_2$. To install less than $M_1$ foregoes some of the incumbent's first-mover advantage. To install more would further limit the scale of the entrant's production, but this gain would be more than offset by the negative price effect that the extra production would exert. $M_1$ is then the best choice. Entry is not deterred but it is limited or, to use Bain's terminology, is "ineffectively impeded."

---

9   Strictly speaking, when the entrant's break-even output lies between $T_2$ and $M_2$, the incumbent would be indifferent between choosing $M_1$ or a smaller capacity just sufficient to preclude entry and then expanding output in stage two to the level of $M_1$.

What we have just shown is that so long as point $B$ lies to the left of $S$, such as in the cases of $B_L$ or $B_S$, or to the right of $V$, as in the case of $B_R$, the incumbent's optimal choice of initial capacity $\overline{K}_1$ is to set $\overline{K}_1 = M_1$. These possibilities cover the case in which when entry is blockaded and the entrant cannot break even at any output less than $M_2$, and the case in which entry is certain and the best that the incumbent can do is to limit the entrant's scale.

The remaining and perhaps the most interesting case to consider is what happens when firm 2's costs of production are such that firm 2's profit, as we move down its reaction function, switches to negative at an output level somewhere between $M_2$ and $V_2$. This corresponds to a point $B$ lying between $S$ and $V$, such as $B^*$. In this case, firm 1 has a choice to make. On the one hand, it can continue to play the Stackelberg leader by initially installing capacity $M_1$ and producing at that level in stage two. Firm 2 will then choose its optimal response of producing $M_2$. On the other hand, firm 1 can expand its initial capacity choice to the level $B_1^*$. This will require that it produce more output, which lowers the industry price, but it is also enough to drive firm 2 out altogether, which raises the industry price. The latter strategy may well prove the more profitable one. It is in this case then that entry deterrence is a real possibility. If the incumbent earns less profit at $S$ than it earns when it deters entry by initially choosing capacity $B_1^*$, it will act so as to preclude entry altogether. This outcome corresponds to what Bain describes as the case in which entry is effectively impeded. We emphasize that this will not always be the case. Even if $B$ lies at $B^*$ so that the output at which the entrant just breaks even lies between $M_2$ and $V_2$, the incumbent may still better exploit its first-mover advantage by acting as a Stackelberg leader. Yet credible deterrence by a capacity choice greater than $M_1$ is now a real possibility. Moreover, even when absolute deterrence does not occur, the incumbent can still limit the scale of entry by playing the Stackelberg leader. Practice Problem 12.2 provides a numerical example of these calculations.

## Practice Problem 12.2

Suppose that the inverse demand function is described by $P = 120 - (q_1 + q_2)$, where $q_1$ is the output of the incumbent firm and $q_2$ is the output of the entrant. Let both the labor cost and capital cost per unit be 30, that is, $w = r = 30$. In addition, let each firm have a fixed cost of $F_1 = F_2 = 200$.

a. Suppose that in stage one the incumbent invests in capacity $\overline{K}_1$. Show that in stage two the incumbent's best response function is $q_1 = 45 - \frac{1}{2}q_2$ when $q_1 < \overline{K}_1$, and $q_1 = 30 - \frac{1}{2}q_2$ when $q_1 > \overline{K}_1$.

b. Show that the entrant's best response function in stage two is $q_2 = 30 - \frac{1}{2}q_1$.

c. Draw the best response functions in a well-labeled diagram.

d. Show that the monopoly or Stackelberg leader's output is equal to 30. If the incumbent commits to a production capacity of $\overline{K}_1 = 30$, show that in stage two the entrant will come in and produce an output equal to 15. Show that in this case firm 2, the entrant, earns a profit equal to $25, whereas the incumbent earns a profit of $250.

e. Show that if the incumbent instead commits in stage one to a production capacity $\overline{K}_1 = 40$, then in stage two the entrant's best response to this choice is to produce $q_2$

= 10. However, in this case the entrant does not earn sufficient revenue to cover its total cost. Specifically, the entrant earns –100.

f.  Now show that if the incumbent chooses $\overline{K}_1$ = 32 in stage one then the entrant in stage two cannot earn a positive profit if it enters the market. In this case the incumbent produces slightly more output than the monopolist and earns a profit equal to $696, which is far greater than the profit earned in (d).

g.  Complete your diagram with the information in (d)–(f) and compare it to Figure 12-6.

FIGURE

12-6

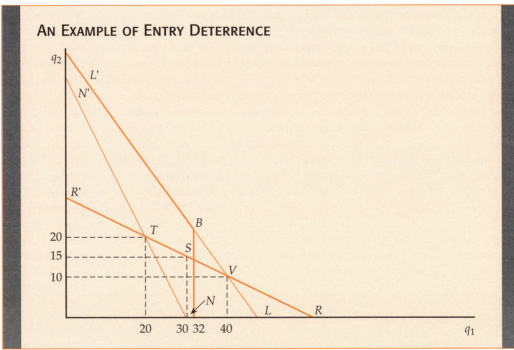

**AN EXAMPLE OF ENTRY DETERRENCE**

By initially investing in capacity of 32 in stage one, the incumbent firm insures that it will operate on the response function, $L'L$, up to this output level. This signals the potential entrant that the incumbent will produce an output $q_1$ = 32 in stage two. The entrant's best response to this production level is to set $q_2$ = 14. However, the entrant will not cover its costs even with this best response. Therefore, by committing to an output of $q_1$ = 32, the incumbent deters any actual entry.

In sum, entry may well not occur. This can happen because the entrant's costs are so high that it cannot profitably enter even if the incumbent produces and prices as a pure monopolist. It can also happen when entry might otherwise be profitable except that the incumbent, foreseeing this, deters entry by investing in enough capacity to produce beyond the output of a pure monopoly. A second result is that when entry does occur the incumbent still retains the lion's share of the market because it acts as a Stackelberg leader.

The Dixit model makes clear that the incumbent firm has an advantage. More importantly, the model reveals precisely the source of that advantage. It is the incumbent's

# ✓ Reality Checkpoint

## Take-or-Pay . . . and Win!

Firms typically have contracts with their key suppliers stipulating the amount of the input to be bought and the price to be paid per unit, say, for the coming year. A common additional feature of such contracts, especially for supplies of natural gas, electricity, and commodity raw materials, is a "take-or-pay" clause. A contract that includes a take-or-pay clause requires that the purchasing firm either uses all the amount of the input initially contracted or, that if it orders less than that amount, it still pays some amount, usually less than the full contract price, for the additional amount remaining.

Take-or-pay contracts stabilize both the production schedule and the revenues of supplier firms. However, as you should recognize, they also serve another purpose. They are a straightforward way to implement the Dixit entry deterrence strategy.

For example, Corning is one of the leading manufacturers of fiber optic cables. One of its key suppliers is Praxair, a major producer of specialty gases. Suppose that Corning signs a contract with Praxair that calls for Corning to purchase 1,000,000 cubic feet of helium (which is used as a coolant in the production of fiber optic cable) at $400 per 1,000 cubic feet. The contract also includes a take-or-pay contract such that Corning has to pay $300 per cubic feet for any amount of the 1,000,000 that it does not use. What this does is effectively transform the structure of Corning's costs. If Corning orders all of the 1,000,000 cubic feet its helium bill will be ($400/1,000) × 1,000,000 = $400,000. Suppose, though, that Corning uses only 900,000 cubic feet of helium (perhaps because a new rival steals some Corning customers). Because of the take-or-pay clause, it will still pay $300 per thousand cubic feet for the 100,000 cubic feet that it did not order. Hence, Corning's total helium cost in this case will be ($400/1,000) × 900,000 + ($300/1,000) × 100,000 = $390,000. In other words, using the last 100,000 cubic feet of helium only raises Corning's total helium bill by $10,000. Effectively, the contract has changed the marginal cost of helium for Corning from $400 to $100 per thousand cubic feet. Note that it has not changed the total cost of using one million cubic feet of helium. The contract has simply transformed some of those costs into fixed costs so that up to the one million volume, Corning has a very low marginal cost.

There is a downside to the take-or-pay contract. This is that if another large rival, for example, the British fiber optic producer Marconi, already exists and both firms sign take-or-pay contracts with their helium suppliers, the industry could find itself in a nasty price war in which prices fall to the low levels of marginal cost via Bertrand competition. Some believe that this is part of what happened in the fiber optic market following the burst of the telecommunications bubble.

**Sources:** A. M. Brandenburger and B. J. Nalebuff, *Co-opetition*. New York: Doubleday, 1996; and F. Norris, "Disaster at Corning: At Least the Balance Sheet is Strong." *The New York Times*, July 13, 2001, p. C2.

ability to commit credibly to a particular output level in stage two by means of its choice of capacity in stage one. Effectively, the incumbent commits to producing at least as much as whatever initial capacity it installs because to produce any less amounts to throwing away some of that investment, which is costly. In this respect, two further aspects of the model are worth noting. First, when the incumbent deters entry it does so by deliberately overinvesting in initial capacity. That is, installing an initial capacity greater than $M_1$ would not be profitable were it not for the fact that doing so eliminates the competition. Therefore, such capacity expansion is predatory in the usual sense of the word. Such a choice is illustrated in Practice Problem 12.2, where the incumbent's strategy to increase capacity to $\overline{K}_1 = 32$ is predatory. If the entrant could break even at low levels of output, the incumbent would not choose the initial capacity level $\overline{K}_1 = 32$ to deter entry. In other words, this investment is profitable only because it keeps the entrant from the market altogether so that the incumbent can sell its 32 units at a very high price.

Second, note that capacity expansion is credible as a deterrent strategy only to the extent that capacity, once in place, is a sunk cost. If unused plant capacity can be sold off for a fee, $r$, then capacity is truly flexible and acquiring it does not reflect any real commitment on the part of the firm. Indeed, it is the assumption that such flexibility is not possible that makes capacity investment a much more effective way to deter entry than simply a promise to set a low price. A price commitment is much less credible precisely because it may easily be changed.

Now think back to the empirical evidence on entry that we reviewed at the beginning of the chapter. Two of the stylized facts are (1) entry is commonly observed in a wide cross-section of industries, and (2) market penetration as measured by market share is relatively low for the entrants. These stylized facts are consistent with this model. The incumbent has a strategic advantage in being the first to invest in capacity, and can use this advantage to strategically limit the impact of entry into its market—perhaps eliminating it altogether.

## Practice Problem 12.3

A model similar to Dixit's in which the incumbent incurs costs now to deter a rival's entry later is described by the extensive form game in Figure 12-7. The incumbent moves first and chooses whether to spend C to enhance its fighting ability. The entrant moves next and decides whether to enter the market. If the entrant enters then the incumbent decides whether to accommodate its new rival or to fight. If the entrant does not enter, the incumbent earns 8 minus C if it has made that expenditure, and 8 if it has not. If the entrant does enter, the incumbent's payoffs depend on whether it fights or accommodates. Fighting when the expenditure C has been sunk yields a payoff of 3. Fighting is more bloody when the incumbent has not spent C to increase its ability to wage war. Accommodation when C has been spent wastes that investment. The final payoffs are described in parentheses, the first being the incumbent's payoff and the second the entrant's.

a. Show that for C greater than or equal to 1, the incumbent will always fight if it has invested in the capacity to do so, that is, if it has initially made the expenditure C.

b. Show that for C greater than or equal to 3.5, the incumbent will not make the initial investment C.

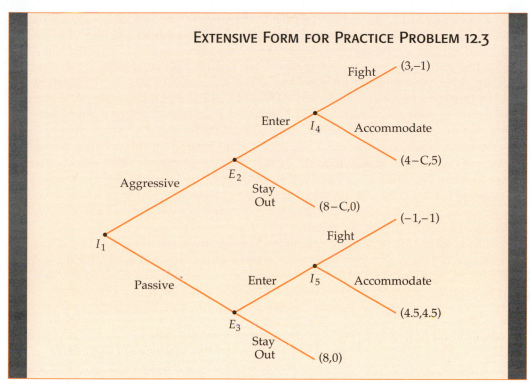

EXTENSIVE FORM FOR PRACTICE PROBLEM 12.3

FIGURE

**12-7**

Nodes labeled *I* indicate that it is the incumbent's turn to move. Nodes labeled *E* indicate that it is the entrant's turn to move.

## 12.3 PREEMPTION AND THE PERSISTENCE OF MONOPOLY

The scale of a plant or plant capacity is rarely a continuous variable. Instead, it comes in discrete sizes, say one efficient scale corresponding to the U-shaped average cost curve. This means, for example, that one plant may be the most efficient way to supply an industry even if that plant is operating at a volume beyond the point of minimum average cost. Because a second plant cannot be built to operate at an arbitrarily small scale but must, instead, be of the same size as the first, it pays to operate just one plant at a high volume and somewhat high average cost rather than to build an additional establishment. Only when market demand has expanded sufficiently to operate a second plant at close to the minimum average cost will building that plant be worthwhile.

In this setting, the possibility arises for an incumbent firm to take actions that are similar to but logically distinct from the predatory investment of the Spence and Dixit models. In particular, the first-mover advantage of the incumbent may now permit it to *preempt* the entry of a rival firm by investing before that entry is on the horizon. The distinction between this and the investment stories told earlier is subtle. Here, we are essentially talking about *timing*, with the issue being who will build the next plant first. Will it be the entrant as the expanding market offers the entrant an opportunity to participate, or will it be the incumbent rushing ahead of the entrant and thereby eliminating the entrant's opportunity?

Rather than work out a formal model in its entirety,[10] we will simply sketch out the intuition behind the basic notion. Imagine a market in which one firm is operating and earning a monopoly profit, $\pi^M$. Everyone knows, however, that demand is about to grow. In particular, everyone can see that next period the market demand at any price will double. It will then stay at this higher level for every period thereafter. If entry was not a problem, the monopolist would expand its plant at the start of the next period, pay the cost of such expansion $F$, and earn $2\pi^M$, thereafter assuming that the profit increment $\pi^M$ of doing so exceeds the cost $F$.

Recall, though, that there is a potential entrant lurking on the sidelines. Should this entrant come in, it will share the market with the incumbent and each will earn the Cournot profit. This is $\pi^C$ in the first period and $2\pi^C$ for every period afterwards when the market is twice as big. For the second firm to enter, however, it must build a new plant just as the monopolist does when it expands. So the entrant will also incur a cost of $F$ if it builds the next plant.

The point to note is that the entrant has a choice about *when* it enters as well as *if* it enters. That is, the entrant can come into the market now, or wait until the next period when the market is bigger. Consider then, the consequences of each choice. If the entrant builds its plant in the first period, it will earn $\pi^C$ for one period and $2\pi^C$ thereafter. Using the discount techniques described in Chapter 2, the present value of this profit stream is $\pi^C + \dfrac{2\pi^C}{1-R}$, where $R$ is the discount factor equal to 1 plus the interest rate, $r$. So, the net present value of entering the market now is $\pi^C + \dfrac{2\pi^C}{1-R} - F$. If, on the other hand, the entrant delays entering until the start of next period, and if the incumbent does not build a second plant before then, the entrant may look forward to a net income stream whose present value is $\dfrac{2\pi^C}{1-R} - RF$. We will assume that the sunk cost of building a plant $F$ is less than $2\pi^C$. This ensures that the entrant would like to enter at some point, again assuming no action by the incumbent. Let us now also assume that it is more profitable for the second firm to enter the next period rather than today. In other words, we assume that the second of the two net present value streams is the larger one.[11]

Of course, the incumbent can work this all out, too. When it does, the incumbent will understand that unless it does something right now, firm 2 will enter at the start of the next period and take away its monopoly position. The only way that the incumbent can stop this from happening is if it decides to build a second plant today. Yes, this means that it incurs the cost $F$ right away instead of being able to put it off. However, it also means that when the next period arrives, there is no room for a new entrant. The incumbent is ready to meet the market growth fully with supply from its own factories.

Will this strategy be in the incumbent's best interest? Quite possibly, yes. If the incumbent waits and lets the entry occur it will only earn $2\pi^C$ in every subsequent period. The present value of this is $\dfrac{2\pi^C}{1-R}$. If, however, the incumbent invests now,

---

10 See Gilbert and Harris (1984).

11 The necessary condition is that $rF > (1 + r)\pi^C$. Roughly speaking, the interest payments on the fixed sum invested in the plant are not covered by the first-period Cournot profit.

## ✓ Reality Checkpoint

### The Alcoa Case: Do It First, Do It Right, . . . and Keep On Doing It

In 1945, a U.S. Court of Appeals for the Second Circuit, under the direction of Judge Learned Hand, rendered one of the most famous decisions in U.S. antitrust history. The case involved the charge against the Aluminum Co. of America (Alcoa) that it had unlawfully monopolized the domestic market for aluminum and aluminum products. Alcoa had previously been involved in an antitrust case in 1912. At that time it was found guilty of restrictive and anticompetitive practices, including (1) signing contracts with electric power companies to obtain the large amount of electricity needed to process raw alumina and including in those contracts covenants that prohibited the power companies from selling electricity to any other aluminum manufacturer, and (2) forming a cartel with foreign manufacturers to divide the world aluminum market into regions and restrict sales in any one region to primarily one member of the cartel. In part, the 1945 case was based on the allegation that these practices had continued despite the 1912 settlement.

However, the court's decision against Alcoa this time was predicated primarily on the view that Alcoa expanded capacity to keep out competitors. The court noted that Alcoa increased its capacity eight-fold between 1912 and 1934. It noted that there had been "one or two abortive attempts to enter the industry, but Alcoa effectively anticipated and forestalled all competition." The court continued, saying that "we can think of no more effective exclusion than . . . to face every newcomer with new capacity already geared into a great organization."

Of course, much as the Microsoft case revealed 55 years later, the finding that a firm has illegally abused its market power does not make clear what the remedy to such abuse should be. Even a serious fine may seem too weak a penalty because it leaves the firm intact and able perhaps to resume its illegal practices. Yet breaking up a successful organization as was done in the Standard Oil case may seem overly harsh. In the Alcoa case, the government was fortunate to have an alternative remedy. The case was decided in the immediate aftermath of World War II. During that war, the government had operated a number of aluminum plants. The decision was made to sell these plants to two new firms, Kaiser and Reynolds, and thereby create a more competitive market structure.

**Source:** *U.S. v. Aluminum Co. of America*, 148 F. 2d 416 (1945).

it precludes later entry and so will earn $2\pi^M$ indefinitely into the future. The present value of investing this period then is $\dfrac{2\pi^M}{1-R} - F$. So long as $2\pi^M - rF > 2\pi^C$, the incumbent will invest today, and thereby preclude subsequent entry.

Why is it that that investing in a new plant right away is more likely to be profitable for the incumbent than it is for the entrant? The reason is that the incumbent's gain is the maintenance of its monopoly position and the monopoly income, $\pi^M$. By contrast, the best that the incumbent can do is to get a share of a Cournot duopoly and earn $\pi^C$. Since $\pi^M$ exceeds $\pi^C$, the incumbent's incentive to invest right now exceeds the entrant's incentive.

## 12.4 EVIDENCE ON PREDATORY CAPACITY EXPANSION

Both the Dixit–Spence and the preemption models discussed in the preceding sections suggest that we may observe dominant firms expanding capacity rapidly as a means to deter entry. Is this a serious concern? Is there any evidence that such capacity investment actually occurs?

To begin, there is the stylized fact noted at the start of this chapter that the same firms continue to dominate their industries and earn superior profit for long periods of time. However, this could happen for many reasons, including superior management or cost efficiency at such firms. The specific question is whether we have evidence of the maintenance of such market power explicitly by means of capacity expansion or preemptive investment.

We will not answer this question with a complete review of all empirical evidence. Instead, we will simply add to the case of Alcoa (see Reality Checkpoint) two additional cases, each of which suggests that sustained dominance through capacity expansion does happen. The first is set in the town of Edmonton, Alberta, during the 1960s and early 1970s. The major retail grocer in Edmonton at that time was Safeway. However, in the early 1960s a number of other grocery stores from other regions began to enter the Edmonton market, including two Ontario firms, Loblaws and Dominion, and one Western Canadian firm, Tom Boy. Between 1960 and 1963, these three firms opened 12 new stores in the Edmonton area. By 1964, they were operating a total of 21 stores—not far behind Safeway's then total of 25. Safeway could clearly see that continued entry by these and other firms was a real possibility, and it rapidly responded. It opened four new stores in 1963–64, another four new stores in 1965–66, and then added five new stores in 1968. Moreover, Safeway chose the locations of these new stores quite carefully. Some were sites of potential entry, located in areas of increasing population and with no competition. To drive home the seriousness of its intentions, Safeway located other new stores next to locations where its rivals also had a store. The strategy worked. By 1973, Safeway was operating 35 stores in the Edmonton area whereas, due to closings, its three major rivals were operating just 10. Indeed, Safeway had so effectively established its credibility as a fierce competitor that whenever its major rivals or even fringe firms opened up a new store, they typically located near each other rather than in neighborhoods already served by Safeway but sufficiently densely populated to permit room for a second store.[12]

Our second anecdote comes from the market for titanium dioxide. This is a chemical additive used as a whitener in such products as paint, paper, and plastics. It can be produced by three processes. One of these is a sulfate procedure that uses ilmenite ore. Another technique is a chloride process that uses rutile ore. Both of these processes are known and available to all producers. The third process, however, is a special chloride process that because of legal restrictions is known and available for

---

12 Safeway was charged with monopolizing the Edmonton market in 1972 and, in late 1973, signed a consent decree that, among other things, prohibited it from expanding its total square footage in Edmonton for three-and-a-half years. See West and Von Hohenbalken (1986).

use only by DuPont. Like the sulfate process, DuPont's procedure uses ilmenite ore. Yet like the generic chloride process, DuPont's method emits little pollution. This is not the case with the sulfate procedure, which has bad pollution affects.

Seven domestic firms were active in the titanium dioxide market during the 1970s. DuPont was the largest of these with about 34 percent of the market, but NL Industries—which used the sulfate procedure—was a close second. Then, two events happened in the early 1970s that gave DuPont a decided advantage. First, rutile ore became more expensive, implying that other producers using the generic chloride technique might have to cut back. Second, strict pollution controls were imposed that made the sulfate process very expensive, too. Suddenly, DuPont's proprietary chloride technique based on ilmenite ore gave the company an edge with respect to costs. A strategic firm would lose no time in exploiting that edge. It would know that those producers using sulfate were not likely to expand. It might also recognize that rutile could someday become cheap again (it did). If in addition the firm expected, as did all participants in the titanium oxide market, that demand would grow, a firm in DuPont's position might wish to expand capacity immediately. This would preclude those rivals using the rutile-based technique from expanding production when and if rutile prices dropped, and thus permit the firm to capture the gap caused by market growth and the declining sulfate-based production entirely for itself.

In point of fact, DuPont increased its capacity by over 60 percent in the next five years while the industry, in general, stagnated. By 1977, DuPont's market share had risen to 46 percent. Moreover, when rival Kerr-McGee began to construct a new plant in 1974, just before DuPont got its planned expansion going, DuPont reacted by trumpeting its plans to the whole industry. This likely precluded any further entry beyond that of Kerr-McGee's.[13]

In short, there is much anecdotal evidence that supports the use of capacity expansion to overcome the chain store paradox and thereby maintain market power. We should note that such evidence may be even greater when we use a spatial interpretation of expansion along the lines of the Hotelling "Main Street" model that we discussed in Chapter 10. Indeed, it is often claimed that General Motors' strategy of offering many different automobile varieties and the ready-to-eat breakfast cereal manufacturers' strategy of selling a wide assortment of cereals both reflect attempts to "crowd out" any would-be rival by leaving it no market niche in which it can profitably operate.

## SUMMARY

This chapter investigated the ability of firms to maintain a dominant market position in their industry for a prolonged period of time. Both anecdotal and formal evidence indicate that such sustained market power is a widespread feature. In turn, this implies that the entry of new rivals who can compete away an incumbent firm's profits is not as powerful in the real world as it is in basic microeconomic texts. Something permits an incumbent to preserve its market position and successfully defend itself against rival entry.

---

13 See Ghemawat (1984). See also Hall (1990) for evidence that DuPont's action was consistent with the Dixit model.

There are good theoretical reasons to believe that market structures may evolve toward increasing concentration over time. The Law of Proportionate Effects or Gibrat's Law is a random growth process that generates such an outcome. Richer theoretical models such as Klepper's (2002), in which innovation becomes easier as firms get larger and more experienced, also yield oligopoly as their equilibrium outcome. Thus, the fact that many industries are long-dominated by one or two firms does not necessarily imply that those firms have obtained and kept that dominance by predatory means. Yet the clear concerns that motivated the antitrust laws, as well as numerous court cases, also imply that predatory entry deterrence is a common concern. An important question in this respect is whether economic theory can shed light on such concern.

The proper analytical framework for studying entry deterrence is a dynamic game of sequential moves. Here, the key issue is credibility. Broadly speaking, the question is whether the incumbent dominant firm can persuade a would-be rival that it is committed to a price or output level that, if maintained, would make entry unprofitable. Capacity expansion and preemption may be ways to achieve such a commitment. There is some reason to believe that such tactics are used by real-world firms.

In both theory and practice, there is an analytical distinction between preventing entry of new firms and driving existing ones out of business. It is also important to recognize that firms may not have complete information about each other and so are only able to guess at a rival's likely response to any action. In this chapter we have focused on the issue of entry deterrence and limited the analysis to a setting of complete certainty. We explore predation aimed at existing rivals and set in a world of uncertainty in the next chapter.

# PROBLEMS

1. Suppose that the domestic market for small specialized calculators and similar office equipment is currently served by firm I. The firm has the following cost schedules: $TC(q_I) = 0.025q_I^2$ and $MC(q_I) = 0.05q_I$. Market demand is $P = 50 - 0.1Q$, and right now $q$ is equal to $q_I$ because the only firm in the market is the incumbent firm I.

   a. If the incumbent acts as a simple monopolist, what price will it charge and at what level of output will it produce?

   b. Suppose now that a foreign producer of calculators is considering exporting to the U.S. market. Because of transportation costs and tariffs this foreign firm faces some cost disadvantage vis-à-vis the domestic incumbent. Specifically, the foreign firm's cost schedules are $TC(q_E) = 10q_E + 0.025q_E^2$ and $MC(q_E) = 10 + 0.05q_E$. Suppose that the incumbent firm is committed to the monopoly level of output. What is the demand curve faced by the potential entrant? Facing this demand what level of output will the foreign firm actually export to the domestic market? What will be the new industry price?

   c. To what level of output would the incumbent firm have to commit in order to deter the foreign firm from entering the market? (*Hint:* You must solve for output level $q$ with the property that if the entrant believes that the incumbent will produce $q$ then the entrant's profit-maximizing response will be to produce $q_E^*$ such that $\Pi^E(q_E^*, \underline{q}) = 0$.) What is the incumbent firm's profit?

    d. Suppose that the incumbent and the entrant instead will play a Cournot game if and when the entrant enters. What are firms' profits in this case? Is it reasonable to believe that the incumbent will try and commit to $q$ in order to deter entry? Why?

2. Suppose that the inverse demand function is described by $P = 100 - 2(q_1 + q_2)$, where $q_1$ is the output of the incumbent firm and $q_2$ is the output of the entrant. Let the labor cost per unit be $w = 20$ and capital cost per unit be $r = 20$. In addition, let each firm have a fixed cost of $F_1 = F_2 = \$100$.

    a. Suppose that in stage one the incumbent invests in capacity $\overline{K}_1$. Show that in stage two the incumbent's best response function is $q_1 = 15 - \dfrac{1}{2}q_2$ when $q_1 \leq \overline{K}_1$ and $q_1 = 20 - \dfrac{1}{2}q_2$ when $q_1 > \overline{K}_1$.

    b. Show that the entrant's best response function in stage two is $q_2 = 15 - \dfrac{1}{2}q_1$.

    c. Show that if the incumbent commits to a production capacity of $\overline{K}_1 = 15$, the entrant will do best by producing 7.5 and earn a profit of \$12.5, while the incumbent earns a profit of \$125.

    d. Show that if the incumbent instead commits in stage one to a production capacity of $\overline{K}_1 = 16$, then in stage two the entrant's best response to this choice is to produce $q_2 = 7$, but at this output level, the entrant does not earn a positive profit.

    e. In light of your answer to (d), show that committing to a production capacity of $\overline{K}_1 = 16$, gives the incumbent a profit of \$348.

3. Two firms, firm 1 and firm 2, must decide whether to enter a new industry. The industry demand is described by $P = 900 - Q$, where $Q = q_1 + q_2$, $q_j \geq 0$. To enter the new industry a firm must build a production facility. Two types of facility can be built: small and large. A small facility requires an investment of \$50,000 and it allows the firm to produce as many as 100 units of the good at a unit production cost of $c = 0$. Alternatively, the firm can pay \$175,000 to construct a large facility that will allow the firm to produce any number of units of output at zero unit cost. A firm with a small production facility is capacity constrained whereas a firm with a large facility is not. Firm 1 makes the entry decision first. It must choose whether to enter, and if it enters what kind of production facility to build. Then, after observing firm 1's action, firm 2 chooses from the same set of alternatives. If only one firm enters the industry, then it selects a quantity of output and sells it at the corresponding price. If both firms are in the industry, then they compete as Cournot firms. All output decisions in this stage are subject to the capacity constraints of the production facilities.

    a. Draw the extensive tree that represents the entry game being played between firms 1 and 2.

    b. What is the outcome? Does firm 1 enter and at what size? Does firm 2 enter and at what size?

4. Suppose that the demand for hand-blown glass vases is given by $q = 70,000 - 2,000P$, where $q$ is the quantity of glass vases consumed per year and $P$ is the dollar price of a vase. Suppose that there are 1,000 identical small sellers of hand-blown

glass vases. The marginal cost function of such a seller is $MC(q) = q + 5$, where $q$ is the firm's output.

**a.** Assuming that each small seller acts as a price taker in this market, derive the market supply curve and the equilibrium price and quantity traded.

**b.** Suppose that a new mechanized technique of producing vases is discovered and monopolized by firm B. Using this technique vases can be produced at a constant average and marginal cost of $15 per vase. Consumers cannot tell the difference between vases produced by the old and the new technique. Given the existence of the fringe of small sellers, what is the demand curve facing firm B?

**c.** Facing this demand curve what is the profit-maximizing quantity produced by firm B? What is the price that it sets and the overall amount of vases traded in the market?

# REFERENCES

Bain, J. 1956. *Barriers to New Competition: Their Character and Consequences in Manufacturing Industries.* Cambridge, MA: Harvard University Press.

Baldwin, J. 1995. *The Dynamics of Industrial Competition.* Cambridge, MA: Cambridge University Press.

Birch, D. 1987. *Job Creation in America: How Our Smallest Companies Put the Most People to Work.* New York: MacMillan, Free Press.

Cable, J., and J. Schwalbach. 1991. "International Comparisons of Entry and Exit." In P. Geroski and J. Schwalbach, eds., *Entry and Market Contestability.* Oxford: Blackwell Publishers.

Caves, R. E. 1988. "Industrial Organization and New Finding on the Turnover and Mobility of Firms." *Journal of Economic Literature* 36 (December): 1947–82.

Dixit, A. 1980. "The Role of Investment in Entry Deterrence." *The Economic Journal* 90 (January): 95–106.

Dunne, T., M. J. Roberts, and L. Samuelson. 1988. "Patterns of Firm Entry and Exit in U.S. Manufacturing Industries." *Rand Journal of Economics* 19 (Winter): 495–515.

————. 1989. "The Growth and Failure of U.S. Manufacturing Plants." *Quarterly Journal of Economics* 104 (November): 671–98.

Fisher, F. 1991. *Industrial Organization, Economics and the Law.* Cambridge, MA: The MIT Press.

Geroski, P. A. 1995. "What do we know about entry?" *International Journal of Industrial Organization* 13 (December): 421–40.

————, and S. Toker. 1996. "The Turnover of Market Leaders in UK Manufacturing Industries, 1979–86." *International Journal of Industrial Organization* 14: 141–58.

Ghemawat, P. 1984. "Capacity Expansion in the Titanium Dioxide Industry." *Journal of Industrial Economics* 33 (December): 145–63.

Gibrat, P. 1931. *Les inegalities economiques; applications: aux inegalities des richesses, a la concentration des enterprises, aux populations des villes, aux statistiques des familles, etc., d'une loi nouvelle, la loi de l'effet proportionnel.* Paris: Librairie du Recueill Sirey.

Gilbert, R. 1989. "Mobility Barriers and the Value of Incumbency." In R. Schmalensee and R. Willig, eds., *Handbook of Industrial Organization*, Vol. 1. Amsterdam: North-Holland: 476–535.

————, and R. Harris. 1984. "Competition with Lumpy Investment." *Rand Journal of Economics* 15 (Summer): 197–212.

Hall, E. A. 1990. "An Analysis of Preemptive Behavior in the Titanium Dioxide Industry." *International Journal of Industrial Organization* 8 (September): 469–84.

Jovanovic, B. 1982. "Selection and the Evolution of Industry." *Econometrica* 50 (May): 649–70.

Kalecki, M. 1945. "On the Gibrat Distribution." *Econometrica* 13 (April): 161–70.

Klepper, S. 2002. "Firms Survival and the Evolution of Oligopoly." *Rand Journal of Economics* 33 (Summer): 37–61.

Nelson, R., and S. G. Winter. 1982. *An Evolutionary Theory of Economic Change*. Cambridge, MA: Harvard University Press.

Ordover, J., and R. Willig. 1981. "An Economic Definition of Predation: Pricing and Product Innovation." *Yale Law Journal* 91: 8–53.

Spence, A. M. 1977. "Entry, Investment, and Oligopolistic Pricing." *Bell Journal of Economics* 8: 534–44.

Sylos-Labini, P. 1962. *Oligopoly and Technical Progress*. Cambridge, MA: Harvard University Press.

Sutton, J. 1997. "Gibrat's Legacy." *Journal of Economic Literature* 35 (March): 40–59.

Urban, G., T. Carter, S. Gaskin, and Z. Mucha. 1984. "Market Share Rewards to Pioneering Brands." *Management Science* 32 (June): 645–59.

Von Hohenbalken, B., and D. West. 1986. "Empirical Tests for Predatory Reputation." *The Canadian Journal of Economics* 19: 160–78.

# Chapter 13

## Predatory Conduct: Recent Developments

The most prominent antitrust case of recent years, indeed, what some have even called the trial of the century, was the antitrust suit against Microsoft. The heart of the government's contention—a charge that was eventually validated by both a district and appellate court—was that Microsoft had abused its market power in a manner that substantially weakened competition. Of particular concern to many was the charge that Microsoft had engaged in unfair tactics to benefit its Web browser, Internet Explorer, and to drive Netscape's Navigator out of the market.

Such fears are not new. To the contrary, they lie at the heart at the foundation of the antitrust laws. Indeed, it was precisely such a fear that led to the first major "trust-busting" in the *Standard Oil* case. The belief that large firms could drive out competitors by pricing low today with a view tomorrow to raising prices to monopoly level was given forceful expression by Supreme Court Justice Louis Brandeis, a member of the *Standard Oil* court. Brandeis warned in 1913 that "Americans should be under no illusion as to the value of price-cutting. It is the most potent weapon of monopoly—a means of killing the small rival to which the great trusts have resorted most frequently. Far-seeing organized capital secures by this means the cooperation of the shortsighted consumer to his own undoing. Thoughtless or weak, he yields to the temptation of trifling immediate gain; and selling his birthright for a mess of pottage, becomes himself an instrument of monopoly."[1]

Charges of predatory pricing to drive out existing rivals are historically much more frequent than allegations of limit pricing to deter entry. An early example of such alleged behavior is the *U.S. Sugar Trust* case (see Reality Checkpoint: Sweet (Sugar) and Low (Price): Predation in the Sugar Refining Industry). Another famous example is the *Mogul Steamship* case.[2] In order to monopolize the China trade the Mogul Steamship Company allegedly drove out rivals by quoting shipping rates so low that trade at that rate was unprofitable. Over the years, many other companies have been similarly charged with such behavior. In recent years this has included Wal-Mart, which is facing several predatory pricing damage suits filed by smaller retailers;[3] AT&T, which has been accused of pricing unfairly to stop local phone companies from entering the long distance market;[4] Toyota and Mazda, which were found by the U.S. Department of Commerce in 1991 to be pricing minivans in the United States below cost;[5] and American Airlines, which is currently in litigation for allegedly attempting to drive out a number of small, discount airlines in the south Midwest.

What makes predatory pricing profitable is the market power eventually gained from eliminating a rival from the market. But if the prey can recognize that the predator does not have an incentive to price low and sustain losses forever then why should the prey be scared and leave what is in fact a profitable market? And even if

---

1  Brandeis (1913).
2  This case is discussed in Yamey (1972) and more recently in Morton (1997).
3  "Slinging Pebbles at Wal-Mart." *The Economist*, October 23, 1993.
4  "AT&T Discounts Signal a National Price War." *The Wall Street Journal*, May 8, 1996, p. B1.
5  Note, though, that the International Trade Commission subsequently ruled that U.S. automakers were not in fact harmed by the pricing policies of Toyota and Mazda.

# ✓ Reality Checkpoint

## Sweet (Sugar) and Low (Price): Predation in the Sugar Refining Industry

In the late 19th and early 20th centuries, the American Sugar Refining Company (ASRC), originally the U.S. Sugar Trust, dominated U.S. sugar refining. The company was first formed in 1887 as a consolidation of 18 firms that then controlled 80 percent of the domestic market for refined sugar. The consolidation was quickly followed by a rationalization in which the 20 plants brought together by the merger were reduced to only 10, and the price of refined sugar rose by 16 percent. However, many owners of the plants that were bought and also other entrepreneurs each then began to operate a new plant, so that a growing number of small sugar refineries emerged. Consistent with our earlier observations on entry, these new firms were small—each about 1/50 the size of ASRC. Some succeeded but most failed, though not as a result of any obvious predation by ASRC.

The first attempt at large-scale entry was made by Claus Spreckels, Senior, a West Coast refiner. Spreckels opened a new refinery on the East Coast with a capacity twice that of the largest of the small refiners and with an announcement of plans to double capacity shortly. This threat did invoke an aggressive ASRC response. A price war soon erupted in which the difference between the prices of refined and raw sugar—which had been about 70 cents per 100 pounds before the Spreckels plant opened—quickly fell to between 19 and 31 cents. Given the costs of other inputs besides raw sugar, this price decline implied prices well below marginal cost. Industry trade publications of that time estimated that ASRC and its rivals were losing about 10 cents per 100 pounds of refined sugar, which implied substantial losses in total. The price war ended when Spreckels exited the market by selling his plants to ASRC.

Several years later, two new large entrants emerged. Arbuckle Brothers, who also controlled a large segment of the U.S. coffee roasting market, operated one. The other was the Doschler Company. Each firm opened a plant of roughly the same size as the earlier Spreckels plant so that together the two possessed the capacity that Spreckels had claimed as his short-run goal. Once again a price war emerged in which it is again generally agreed that prices fell below a short-run marginal cost and all firms were losing money. The war came to an end when Doschler merged with two other small firms in a deal arranged by ASRC. One possible motive for this action was that ASRC feared that with the end of the war, Doschler would start to use its profits to expand capacity. When this was added to the existing industry capacity, it would exert downward pressure on prices. However, if Doschler expanded by purchasing existing plants, no net increase in industrial capacity would arise. Of course, the price war also worked to limit such expansion by eliminating the profits of both Arbuckle and Doschler. Genesove and Mullin (1998) find that ASRC's profit from limiting entry was probably sufficient to justify the losses incurred in the price wars.

**Source:** D. Genesove and W. Mullin, "Testing Static Oligopoly Models: Conduct and Cost in the Sugar Industry, 1890–1914." *Rand Journal of Economics* 14 (Summer 1998), pp. 355–77.

the predator could induce the prey to leave the market then what? Wouldn't any attempt by the predator to raise price attract new rivals to enter the market? The logic of predatory pricing seems to break down in a world of rational business behavior. The reason for the breakdown can be found in the logic of the chain store paradox that we introduced in Chapter 12. We revisit that scenario in the first section of this chapter and explain why an incumbent firm, or predator, is simply unable to make predatory conduct credible.

We then investigate more deeply the logic of predation. We are interested in understanding whether the chain store paradox and its relevance to predation depends in an important way on what information the incumbent or predator and prey have about each other and about the market. As it turns out, information and specifically "who knows what" does play a key role in predatory behavior. To understand predation we need to examine very carefully the information that each player has about each other and about the market.

The logic of predation requires at least two periods—one period to get or keep the rival out and another to reap the benefit. Usually we assume, typically implicitly, that the transactions an incumbent firm has with its customers are simple ones. The incumbent sets the price for its product in each period and consumers buy at that price in that period. But what if instead the incumbent firm had a longer term contract with its customers? That is, what if the incumbent firm could offer consumers a contract to buy its product in both periods? Could such long-term contracts lock out rivals from the market, and if they did would consumers willingly agree to and accept such long-term contracts? We also examine in this chapter exactly how long-term contracts between a firm and its customers can preserve market dominance and keep rivals out. Lastly, we examine alleged cases of predatory behavior and the role of public policy.

## 13.1  PREDATORY PRICING: MYTH OR REALITY?

For many economists, the term *predatory pricing* conjures up the image of John Rockefeller and Standard Oil. The famed antitrust case against Standard Oil occurred at the turn of the century. Between the years 1870 and 1899 Standard Oil built a dominant 90 percent market share in the U.S. petroleum refining industry. It did this by acquiring more than 120 rival companies. The conventional story is that Rockefeller would first make an offer to acquire a rival refiner and, when rebuffed, would cut prices until the rival exited the market.[6] After achieving its market dominance in oil refining capacity and distribution, Standard raised prices to oil producers. This eventually led to its federal prosecution and dissolution in 1911 under the Sherman Antitrust Act of 1890.

On the face of it there seems little doubt that Standard Oil did engage in fierce price competition with its rivals and that rival firms in the refining business did leave the market. There is some doubt, however, whether this is in fact evidence of predatory pricing. Such doubt has foundations in both theory and evidence.

---

6  There is an extensive literature on the varied business practices used by Standard Oil during this period. Other practices include securing discriminatory rail freight rates and rebates, foreclosing crude oil supplies to competitors by buying up local pipelines, and allegedly blowing up competing pipelines. See Yergin (1991).

There are two theoretical arguments that imply predatory pricing is not an optimal strategy and therefore we should not expect a firm to practice it. The first argument is basically that predatory pricing as in the chain store paradox is not subgame perfect.

To understand the power of this argument we will review the Microhard–Newvel game that we introduced in Chapter 12. However, we will add some new twists that make the game more like the real-world setting facing a dominant incumbent firm, such as Standard Oil, and a smaller rival. The game is again a two-period one, and in the first period, Newvel, the new firm, has already entered the market. Microhard is the long-established incumbent who has the first move and must decide whether to engage in predatory practices. One important new twist is that we assume that each firm incurs a fixed cost of $115 million in each market period. This amount must be paid at the start of each period. Unlike Microhard, which has internal retained earnings from its long track record in the market, Newvel has no internal funds. Therefore, Newvel must borrow such funds from a (competitive) banking sector. Next we introduce some uncertainty into the market. Independent of Microhard's actions, there is a 50 percent chance in any period that Newvel will be successful and enjoy a high operating profit of $200 million. There is also a 50 percent chance that it will not be successful and earn a lower profit of $100 million. In the former case, Newvel's net profit for the period is $200 million less what it must pay back to the bank for its loan. In the second case, Newvel does not earn enough to repay even the principal, equal to $115 million, of the loan. As a result, Newvel will simply default and turn over the $100 million it earned to the bank.

If we assume a competitive banking sector, then the bank should expect to earn roughly zero profit on the loan that it makes to Newvel. For simplicity, let us also assume that the discount factor $R$ between periods is equal to 1 (the interest rate $r = 0$). To earn zero profit the bank, or more generally the investor, must ask for a repayment of $130 million when Newvel's operating profit is high and $100 million when it is low. With such a contract, the bank will be paid $130 million half the time and $100 million the other half of the time when Newvel defaults. Hence, on average, such a contract would result in the bank just earning $115 million and covering its loan. Perhaps, to be more realistic, we should give the bank some incentive to take on the risk by allowing it to do just a bit better than this. In particular, we could assume that it can demand a repayment of $132.5 million in the event that Newvel's operating profit is high. This gives the bank an expected net return of 0.5($132.5 + $100) − $115 = $1.25 million each period. In contrast, Newvel will either net $200 − $132.5 = $67.5 million with probability 0.5 or else nothing, also with probability 0.5. Hence, Newvel's expected net income in any period is $33.75 million.

Now consider Microhard. Suppose that in any period that Newvel is in the market Microhard earns an operating profit of $150 million, but that it would earn an expected monopoly profit of $325 million if Newvel exits. Suppose further that by cutting prices and sacrificing $100 million of profit in any period, Microhard could raise the probability to 70 percent that Newvel is not successful and earns only $100 million in that same period. Will Microhard have an incentive to cut prices and worsen Newvel's chances?

Let's begin by analyzing the second period of the game. First, Microhard will not engage in predation and cut prices in period two. As there is no "next period" this would only sacrifice profit with no prospect of recovering the loss at a later date. Hence, if Newvel stays after the first round, the outcome in the last period has to be a duopoly in which each earns an expected $150 million in operating or gross profit. Thus, regardless of what happened in the first period, Newvel will be able to get a loan for its fixed cost at the start of the second period. For even if Newvel defaulted in the first period, and the bank lost $15 million, Newvel and the bank would still have an incentive to renegotiate another loan for the second period. Because Microhard will not engage in predation the bank has an expectation of earning $1.25 million, which will at least help in covering its first-period loss. Similarly, Newvel can expect to earn $33.75 million.

Now consider the first period of the game. Will Microhard engage in predation and try to drive Newvel out of the market in this period? Again, the answer is no. No matter what happens in the first period, we know that Newvel will want to stay for the second period. Hence, no amount of predation by Microhard in the first period can prevent Newvel from operating in the second. Microhard will therefore recognize that Newvel is here to stay, in which case there is no reason to pursue predatory pricing and lose revenue in the first period. The feared predation will not occur.

## Practice Problem 13.1

Suppose that Newvel's chance of success worsens and the probability that it will earn a high operating profit of $200 million falls to 40 percent. For a loan of $115 million, what would be the contingent contract demanded by a bank in a competitive banking sector? In other words, how much repayment would the bank demand when operating profits are high and when they are low? Does the worsening of Newvel's prospects affect Microhard's incentive to price low in the first period? Explain why or why not.

If the foregoing scenario is close to capturing the reality of the corporate battlefield, then predatory tactics such as selling below cost just don't seem to make sense and so should not be observed in practice. Indeed, the argument is even stronger than the one just presented because we have assumed that if Microhard were somehow successful in driving out Newvel that it would then enjoy monopoly power. Yet there is no reason to believe that a new rival would not emerge at that time. If such later entry is a possibility, then there is even less for Microhard to gain by means of predation.

Beyond the reasoning that predation is not a subgame perfect strategy, there is also a second argument implying that predatory tactics should not be used. This argument is due to the economist John McGee who reviewed the *Standard Oil* case extensively and argued that the firm was not engaged in predation. In his classic 1958 article, "*Predatory Price Cutting: The Standard Oil Case*," McGee argued that predatory pricing only makes sense if two conditions are met. The first is that the increase in post-predatory profit (in present value terms) is sufficient to compensate the predator for the loss incurred during the predatory price war. This amounts to a requirement that the predation be subgame perfect. However, if this requirement were met, McGee also noted that there was a second requirement that a predation strategy would have to meet. This is that there is *no more profitable strategy* to achieve the same outcome. It was this second point that drew McGee's attention. He argued that a merger is always more profitable than predatory pricing. Hence, the latter should not occur.

McGee's reasoning is straightforward and can again be illustrated with reference to game theory. Basically the point is that predatory pricing is a dominated strategy and, hence, one that will never be used. Consider again our Microhard and Newvel example. Whatever happens in the first period, it seems clearly irrational for Microhard to engage in predation and thereby sacrifice, say, $100 million of profit in the second period in order to weaken the chances of Newvel's success. Note though that in any period that Newvel does operate, Microhard suffers a profit loss of $325 million – $150 million = $175 million. Now suppose that if Microhard acts in a really crazy manner—say by sacrificing an equivalent $175 million in the first period—it not only significantly raises Newvel's probability of first-period failure but also establishes the fact that Microhard is "crazy" and might actually engage in further predation in the second period even though that is irrational. On the face of it, it may look as if this strategy might work. With "crazy" predation a real threat in both periods, Newvel might be dissuaded from entering altogether.

However, McGee (1958) pointed out that such thinking still does not provide a logical foundation for predation because there is a better strategy that could accomplish the same outcome. The reason for this is that while Microhard loses $175 million in keeping Newvel out, Newvel only gains $150 million if it comes in. Hence, rather than engage in irrational predation that costs $175 million, Microhard would do better to buy out or merge with Newvel at a price of, say, $160 million. That is, the predatory strategy is dominated by the buying out strategy.

McGee's point is quite general and easily extends to other game theoretic settings. Consider for example the case of a Stackelberg leader confronting a follower firm. Suppose that each firm has a constant average and marginal cost $c$, and that the inverse market demand curve is $P = A - BQ = A - B(q_L + q_F)$. Here, $q_L$ is the output of the Stackelberg leader and $q_F$ is the output of the follower. In Chapter 12, we found that the Nash equilibrium outcome is $q_L = (A - c)/2B$, and $q_F = (A - c)/4B$, leading to an industry price of $(A + 3c)/4$. At this price, the leader earns the profit $(A - c)^2/8B$, while the follower earns half this amount. Large as it may be, however, the leader's profit is still less than that earned by a pure monopolist—namely, $(A - c)^2/4B$.

The leader would obviously prefer to be alone in the market. Let us again extend the model to two market periods, thus giving scope to the leader to engage in predatory behavior. Now imagine that for the first market period, the leader is fully committed to producing an output so large that it can only be sold at a price just equal to its average cost of $c$. Since the follower can only sell additional units by driving the market price below $c$, and therefore losing money, the follower will exit or not enter. Suppose further that this is enough to keep the follower out forever, so that in the second market period, the leader is a monopolist and earns the monopoly profit, $(A^2 - c^2)/4B$.

Under the predatory strategy just described, the leader or predator earns a stream of profit of 0 in the first market period and then $(A - c)^2/4B$ in the second. The follower or victim can look forward to a stream of 0 profit in both periods. Here again, as McGee pointed out, it would be more profitable for the leader to buy out or merge with the follower at the start of the first period. The merged firms can then act as a monopoly and earn the monopoly profit $(A - c)^2/4B$ in both market periods. Even if the leader has to share this first period profit with the follower, say on a 50/50 basis, *both* firms still do better than they did under predation when both the predator and prey earned a zero profit in period one. The merger strategy again dominates the predatory one.

To be sure, there are weaknesses in McGee's (1958) argument that merging is a preferred strategy to predatory pricing. To begin with, a merger between rivals is a public event, and the antitrust authorities may prohibit the merger. Indeed, the authorities may be more concerned about such a merger than they would be about predatory pricing, since the merger would eliminate the short, predatory period in which prices are low. Second, and more importantly, the logic of the merging strategy weakens when extended to include additional potential entrants. Once a dominant firm is seen as willing to buy out any rival, it will likely face a stream of entrants who enter just for the profit of being purchased.[7] That is, the merger tactic may actually encourage entry—the last thing the dominant firm wants to do. In this light, predatory pricing may be more attractive because it not only encourages existing rivals to exit but can deter subsequent entrants as well. Still, McGee's basic point is surely valid. A credible claim of predation must demonstrate that predation was not a dominated strategy.[8]

## Practice Problem 13.2

Suppose that there are two firms in a market. One firm is a dominant firm and behaves like a Stackelberg leader. The other rival firm is the follower. The firms compete in quantities and face market demand described by $P = 100 - Q$. Assume that marginal production cost is constant and equal to 10.

a. Solve for the single-period equilibrium outcome, that is, the quantity produced by each firm and the firms' respective profits.
b. Now consider a two-period game. One possibility is that the two firms play the Stackelberg game twice, once in each period. The other possibility is that the dominant firm chooses an output level so great in the first period that the rival firm exits the market or sells zero output. In the second period the dominant firm is alone in the market and acts like a monopoly. Solve for the dominant firm's first- and second-period output choices under this scenario, and the firm's overall profit.
c. Suppose that we allow the dominant firm the option of making an offer at the beginning of the first period to the rival firm to buy it out. What is the maximum amount the dominant firm will have to pay the rival firm to buy it out? Show that the dominant firm is better off buying out its rival in the first period and monopolizing the market through merging than through predation.

In short, there may be good reasons to be wary of predatory pricing allegations. Business is tough and it will inevitably be the case that some firms lose market share or even go out of business entirely. Yet such outcomes may simply reflect vigorous competition and not "cutthroat" pricing. For example, consider the famous *Utah Pie* case decided by the U.S. Supreme Court in 1967. Utah Pie was a producer of frozen dessert pies operating out of Salt Lake City and selling to supermarkets in Utah and the surrounding states. In 1957, it had over two-thirds of the Salt Lake City market. However, three national firms—Continental Bakeries, Pet, and Carnation—all began

---

7   Rasmusen (1993) explores this possibility.
8   This point was made by Yamey (1972): "The aggressor will, moreover, be looking beyond the immediate problem of dealing with its current rival. Alternative strategies for dealing with that rival may have different effects on the flow of future rivals."

## ✓ Reality Checkpoint

### Getting to the Heart of the Matter—McGee on Drugs

Millions of Americans, including Vice-President Dick Cheney, suffer from hypertension (high blood pressure) and coronary heart disease or angina. Two major prescription drugs used to treat these conditions are Cardizem CD, produced by Aventis (formerly Hoechst Marion Roussel) and Hytrin, produced by Abbott Laboratories. These drugs are protected by patents and therefore protected from competition by generic or unbranded substitutes. However, the Hatch-Waxman Act of 1984 does provide some conditions under which a firm is permitted to market a generic substitute to a patented drug even before the patent expires. The generic producer must claim either that the new substitute does not really infringe on the patent or that the patent was not really valid in the first place. If the patent holder challenges this claim, then entry of the generic drug is automatically delayed for 30 months to decide the issues. Such delay clearly makes life more difficult for the generics. As partial compensation aimed at promoting generic entry, the Hatch-Waxman Act has another provision. The first generic to enter obtains, after entry, a 180-day immunity against all other generics. That is, once one firm is granted the right to sell a generic substitute to the patented product, no other firm is allowed to do so for at least 180 days.

In the mid 1990s, the pharmaceutical firm Andrx applied for permission to market a generic substitute for Cardizem CD. Another firm, Geneva (a division of Novartis), requested authorization to market a generic substitute for Hytrin. Both Aventis and Abbott challenged these applications and the automatic 30-month delay began. As the end of the 30 months drew near and with the cases still not resolved, each incumbent was faced with the imminent entry of a rival. Presumably, each firm could have pursued predatory pricing to deter such entry. But each instead went the route proposed by McGee. They bought out the potential competitor.

Aventis forged an agreement to pay Andrx $10 million per quarter in return for not entering the Cardizem market starting in July 1998, when Andrx gained FDA approval. Aventis also agreed to pay an additional $60 million per year from 1998 until the end of the ongoing patent trial if Andrx eventually won that litigation. A similar agreement between Abbott and Geneva required that Abbott pay $4.5 million per month in return for Geneva agreeing to stay out of the Hytrin market. A common feature of both agreements was that Andrx and Geneva each also agreed not to transfer their 180-day immunity to any other firm. Since no other generic could enter the relevant market until 180 days after Andrx or Geneva entered, and since each of these two firms had agreed not to enter at all, these agreements had the effect of blocking all generic entry in these markets. Thus, neither Aventis nor Andrx had to face the prospect of paying off an endless stream of entrants.

A somewhat related case involves Mylan laboratories, the maker of two major anti-anxiety drugs, lorazepam and clorazepate. Both drugs use a key ingredient produced by a European firm, Cambrex. Starting in 1998, Mylan paid Cambrex not to sell this ingredient to any other firm. As a result, no other firm could compete with Mylan. Once in effect, Mylan raised the price of its drugs on the order of 2,000 to 3,000 percent.

Pursuant to a complaint filed by the FTC, Abbott agreed to terminate its agreement with Geneva. Mylan also settled with the FTC and agreed to pay $100 million into a fund designed to reimburse those who paid the exorbitant prices. Aventis pursued the matter in the courts but both a federal district court and an appellate court found its agreement with Andrx to be a violation of the antitrust laws. It has so far paid out over $200 million in settlements with drug wholesalers and individual states.

---

**Sources:** J. Guidera and R. T. King, Jr., "Abbott Labs, Novartis Unit Near Pact with FTC Over Agreement on Hytrin." *The Wall Street Journal*, March 14, 2000, p. B6; M. Schroeder, "Mylan to Pay $100 Million to Settle Price-Fix Case." *The Wall Street Journal*, July 13, 2000, p. A4. See also various press releases at the FTC Web site, http://www.ftc.gov.

a vigorous competition in the Salt Lake City area. Over the next three years, this resulted in prices falling by over a third and Utah Pie's market share declining to as low as 33 percent, though it later climbed to nearly 45 percent. Utah Pie filed suit arguing that the three national firms were selling at prices below those that they charged in other cities and that the three were therefore engaged in illegal price discrimination with a predatory objective.

However, Utah Pie's sales grew steadily throughout the period of alleged predation as did its net worth. Moreover, except for the first year of the intensified competition, Utah Pie also continued to earn a positive net income. To many economists, it appeared that Utah Pie's real complaint was more about preserving the initial near monopoly position that the company had and the high prices that permitted it than it was about real predatory tactics. In the end, the Supreme Court found in favor of Utah Pie in a decision that was widely decried, and since largely repudiated. The lesson should be clear. Company officials will inevitably wish to claim that the source of their profit and market share decline is illegal activity by rivals who are "not playing fairly" rather than confess to their own incompetence. For that reason, charges of predatory pricing must be taken with at least a few grains of salt.

The foregoing suggests both theoretical and practical reasons for skepticism that predation, especially predatory pricing, ever occurs. This highly skeptical view is closely associated with the Chicago School. It has had a profound effect on both public policy and court judgments regarding predatory pricing cases. However, over the last 15 years or so, a new view—sometimes called the post-Chicago School—has emerged. In this alternative view, predatory tactics are not a theoretical impossibility and real-world predation is not an idle threat.

## 13.2 PREDATION AND IMPERFECT INFORMATION

Much of the post-Chicago literature on the topic of predation is based on two-period games in which one firm knows something and the other firm does not, and both firms understand that there is asymmetry in information.[9] In this section, we

---

9   Early important papers in this vein included Milgrom and Roberts (1982), Benoit (1984), and Fudenberg and Tirole (1986).

present two important models that build on this feature of asymmetric information. The first is due to Bolton and Scharfstein (1990), and focuses on the informational asymmetry between the new rival, such as Newvel, and the bank from which it borrows. The second is due to Milgrom and Roberts (1982), and focuses on the information asymmetry between the new rival, in our case Newvel, and the dominant incumbent rival, Microhard.

## 13.2.1 Predatory Pricing and Financial Constraints

Recall the two-period model in which Microhard is the incumbent and Newvel is the new firm that must borrow $115 million at the start of each period in order to operate. Following Bolton and Scharfstein (1990) we make one fundamentally important change. We now assume that at the end of any period only Newvel, and not its bank or lender, knows whether Newvel's operating profit is $100 million or $200 million. To make clear how this informational asymmetry affects both Newvel's incentives in its dealing with the bank and the bank's incentive to lend to Newvel we introduce the bank as an explicit player in the game. Figure 13-1 illustrates the interaction between the Bank (B) and Newvel (R) for just a single market period. The Bank first makes a loan. Then Nature (N) chooses whether Newvel's profit is high or low. Subsequently, Newvel chooses whether to report high or low operating profit. For each outcome, both the net profit to the Bank and to Newvel are shown, and since the Bank moved first its payoff is shown first.

Focusing on the game for just one period is insightful because, as Figure 13-1 makes clear, the Bank would never lend Newvel the required $115 million if the game were only one period long. The reason is straightforward. At the end of the period, only Newvel knows what its profit is. Accordingly, it has every incentive to say that it was only $100 million, pay that amount to the bank, and default on any remaining amount. Obviously, if operating profit really was $100 million this is all Newvel can do. However, if actual profit was $200 million, lying by reporting that profit was only $100 million allows Newvel to walk away with $100 million for itself. In other words, because only Newvel knows the truth it has an incentive to exploit this informational asymmetry to its own advantage. Anticipating this, however, the Bank would realize that in a one-period setting it would never get more than $100 million in return for the $115 million that it lent. Therefore, it would never agree to the loan.

The one-period analysis carries two immediate insights for a two-period model. The first is that whatever repayment R the Bank gets at the end of the first period, it can never get more than $100 million at the end of the second period. When the second period comes about, it will simply be a replay of the one-period game just described. The other and related insight is that if the Bank is actually to make a loan, it will have to write a contract that extends over both periods. Two one-period contracts will just run into the same problem twice. Somehow, the Bank and Newvel will have to agree on a contract that links the repayment over both market periods.

Bolton and Scharfstein show that the optimal contract has the following terms. First, recognizing that it will never get paid more than $100 million at the end of period two, the Bank will contract for a high repayment at the end of period one. Second, to give Newvel an incentive to report a high income at the end of the first period, the Bank will cut funding, that is, refuse to make a loan for the second period if Newvel reports low first-period income. Since Newvel only ever pays $100 million to the Bank at the end of the second period, and therefore can expect to earn $150

FIGURE

**13-1**

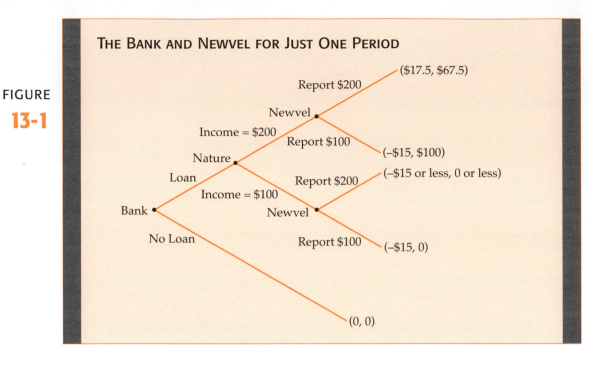

THE BANK AND NEWVEL FOR JUST ONE PERIOD

- Report $200 → ($17.5, $67.5)
- Newvel
- Income = $200
- Report $100 → (–$15, $100)
- Nature
- Report $200 → (–$15 or less, 0 or less)
- Loan
- Income = $100
- Newvel
- Bank
- Report $100 → (–$15, 0)
- No Loan
- → (0, 0)

– $100 = $50 million at that time, this contractual feature gives Newvel a real interest in making sure that the second period happens.

In our example the lending contract might look as follows. The Bank loans the required $115 million at the start of the first period. At the end of that period, if Newvel reports the higher profit of $200 million, then it is required to repay $150 million—its average profit. When it does so the Bank will lend the $115 million necessary to operate in the second period. At the end of that second period, the Bank is paid $100 million whatever happens by virtue of our earlier argument about a one-period loan. Alternatively, if at the end of the first period Newvel reports only the lower profit of $100 million, the Bank is paid that amount but no further loans are made. Newvel, in this case, does not survive into the second period.

Figure 13-2 describes the nature of the loan contract. After the Bank makes an initial loan Nature's choice of profit outcome occurs. This is not shown in the diagram because at the end of the first period Newvel's incentive is to report Nature's draw accurately, and the Bank understands this. If it is low, the loan is terminated and Newvel exits. If it is high, the loan is extended for a second period, after which Nature again draws a profit outcome. As we know, at the end of the second period Newvel always has an incentive to report a low profit. The payoff pair shows the total payoff for the Bank and Newvel over the two periods, with the Bank's shown first.

Note that both parties do well with this contract. Consider the Bank. If first-period profits are low, Newvel is liquidated and the Bank walks away with only $100 million, for a loss of $15 million. If, on the other hand, first-period profits are high, the Bank is paid $150 million, thereby netting $35 million. However, it is then obligated to lend out $115 million for a second time. At the end of the second period the Bank receives only $100 million, because at that point Newvel never reports a high income. Because good luck and bad luck happen with equal probability, the Bank's expected profit from the two-period contract is 0.5($100 – $115) +

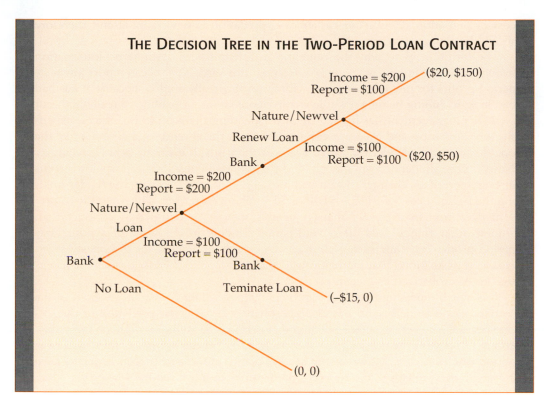

FIGURE

**13-2**

THE DECISION TREE IN THE TWO-PERIOD LOAN CONTRACT

$0.5[(\$150 - \$115) + (\$100 - \$115)] = \$2.5$ million. Note that this is exactly the profit the Bank earned with two, one-period contracts when it was fully informed of Newvel's income.

Newvel also earns a positive expected profit. With probability 0.5, it receives a net payment of $200 – $150 million at the end of the first period, and with equal probability it receives nothing. Similarly, at the end of the second period, Newvel receives a net payment of either $200 – $100 million or again zero, each with probability 0.5. Thus, the firm's expected profit under the contract is $50 million.

Yet while both players earn profit under the contract, there is a flaw. Half the time, Newvel fails after the first period and no second-period loan is made. This is inefficient because that investment does have an expected profit of $35 million. Again, such inefficiency is the result of the asymmetric information that characterizes the relationship between the Bank and Newvel. The only way to prevent Newvel from exploiting its informational advantage is to include a promise to stop funding Newvel should it perform badly in the first period.

Now think about adding some game competition from Microhard. Suppose again that Microhard's duopoly profit is $150 million, its monopoly profit is $325 million, and by preying and cutting prices its profit is reduced by $50 million. But when it prices low, Microhard raises the probability that Newvel fails from 50 to 70 percent. Since now Newvel must exit whenever it fails to earn a first-period profit of $200 million, cutting prices results in increasing Microhard's chance of being a monopolist in the second period by 20 percent. As a result, the expected payoff from this predatory strategy is $0.2 \times \$325 = \$65$ million—more than enough to cover the $50 million cost of predation. Unlike our earlier case, predation is now rational and therefore should be expected to occur.[10]

The intuition as to why the outcome is different with asymmetric information from what it was in our earlier analysis is straightforward. Newvel can report low first-period profits for one of two reasons. Either profits really are low because it has had bad luck, including being a possible victim of predation, or profits are really high but Newvel's management has hidden them by spending them on lavish offices, expensive business trips, and excessive compensation. In the absence of a contract like the one described, the lender cannot easily know the truth. If it simply believes whatever Newvel says, the lender will quickly find that Newvel constantly reports low profits in every period and blames this on bad luck and predation—leaving the lender holding the bag at a cost of $115 − $100 or $15 million each time. The only way to prevent deception by Newvel's management is to write a two-period contract that, among other things, cuts off second-period funding in the wake of a poor first-period profit. Yet while such a contract removes the potential for dishonesty, it increases the likelihood that predation will be successful and therefore raises the incentive for Microhard to engage in predatory tactics.

It is worth repeating that "pulling the plug" and killing Newvel at the start of the second period is inefficient. Because Microhard will never use predation in the second period, Newvel's expected profit in that period is $150 million. This is more than enough to pay off the needed loan of $115 million. Yet the optimal contract is a two-period one that cannot look at the second period alone and that in order to keep Newvel honest must call for Newvel's premature death if it reports low profit.[11]

## Practice Problem 13.3

In the above example it is worthwhile for Microhard to engage in predatory behavior because such behavior increase the odds of Newvel failing in the market from 50 to 70 percent, an increase of 20 percent. What is the lowest increase in unfavorable odds that will induce Microhard to engage in predatory behavior?

### 13.2.2 Asymmetric Information and Limit Pricing

In the Bolton and Scharfstein (1990) model, the upstart rival firm, Newvel, knows a lot about the market. Newvel knows not only its own profitability but it understands the profits and incentives facing Microhard as well. In reality, this is unlikely to be the case. A new firm typically can only guess at the profits and costs of the rival incumbent. In their classic paper, Milgrom and Roberts (1982) present a model in which the assumption that the rival entrant is perfectly informed is relaxed. Specifically, they assume that the rival entrant does not know the incumbent firm's cost of production. In this context charging a low price to keep the entrant out may no longer be an empty bluff. We now present the basic Milgrom and Roberts limit pricing model based on the above information asymmetry.

---

10  The predation story told here is closely related to "long purse" or "deep pockets" models. See, for example, Phlips (1995).

11  Strictly speaking, the contract described is only optimal if it is unobserved by Microhard. If Microhard can observe the details of the loan, the contract may be written in a way that deters predation.

The setting is again a two-period game in which there is a long-standing incumbent and a potential entrant. At the risk of repetition, let's again call the incumbent Microhard and the potential entrant, Newvel. There is no lender or other player. Microhard is alone in the market in the first period. During that time, Newvel observes Microhard's behavior, specifically the price that Microhard chooses to set for that period, and then Newvel decides whether to enter the market in the second period. As before, we assume the interest rate is zero so that we do not have to worry about discounting future profits.

Newvel knows its own unit cost and the market demand in each period, but Newvel does not know Microhard's unit cost. Microhard, on the other hand, knows its unit cost, Newvel's unit cost, as well as market demand in each period. Also, who knows what is understood by both firms. From Newvel's perspective Microhard's unit cost could be either high or low, depending on factors such as the expertise of management, the quality of equipment, or the input advantages of location. These are all features of production costs that are in fact not easily ascertained by outsiders. But while Newvel does not know Microhard's unit cost, it does know something about how likely it is that Microhard is a high-cost or low-cost type. Specifically Newvel knows that there is a probability $\rho$ that Microhard has a low cost and a probability $(1 - \rho)$ that it has a high cost.

In the interest of making matters concrete, let's work through a specific numeric example. Let's assume that when Microhard has low costs and acts like a profit-maximizing monopoly in the first period, it sets a relatively low price but, because of its low costs, earns a profit equal to $100 million. In contrast, if it is a less efficient high-cost monopoly, Microhard's profit-maximizing price will be higher but, again due to its cost inefficiency, it will earn less profit at that price, namely, $60 million. Finally, we assume that if Microhard is a high-cost firm but, nevertheless, chooses the price that is optimal for a low-cost incumbent, its profit will fall still further to $40 million.

Microhard's second-period profits depend both on its unit cost and whether Newvel comes into the market. We will assume that if Microhard is alone in the second period, it simply sets the monopoly price appropriate for its cost structure since entry is no longer a worry. It then earns either $100 million or $60 million in the second period when no entry occurs. We also assume that the potential entrant, Newvel, earns a profit of 0 whenever it stays out of the market.

If, however, entry occurs in the second period, Microhard's profit suffers. If it is a low-cost firm, it earns only $50 million in the second period when Newvel is present. If Microhard is a high-cost firm, it is less able to compete and earns only $20 million. If Newvel enters and competes against an inefficient, high-cost incumbent, it earns a positive profit of $20 million. But if the incumbent turns out to be a low-cost type, then entry results in a loss of $20 million for Newvel.

The extensive form for this version of the entry game is shown in Figure 13-3. Newvel's uncertainty about Microhard's cost is modeled by introducing the player Nature who moves first and chooses the cost of the incumbent firm. With probability $\rho$, Nature chooses a low-cost incumbent and with probability $(1 - \rho)$, Nature chooses a high-cost incumbent. Microhard moves next and sets either a high or low price when it sells output in the first period. Then Newvel decides whether to enter and to compete in period two or to stay out. At the end of each path, we show the total payoffs for each firm over the two periods depending on the choices about prices and entering. Microhard's total profit is the sum of its profit in each period. Newvel's profit is just that which it earns in the market for the final period.

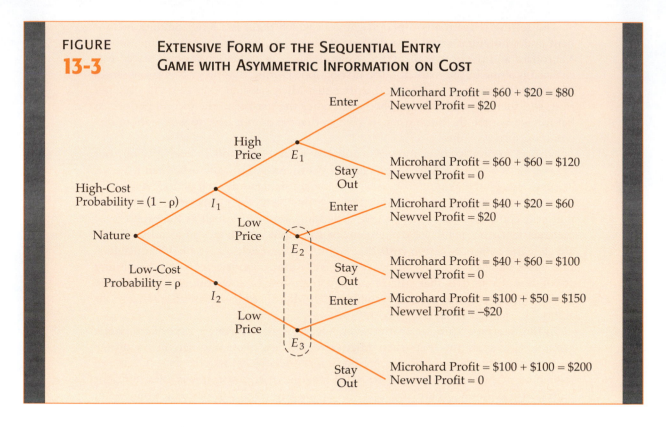

**FIGURE 13-3**  EXTENSIVE FORM OF THE SEQUENTIAL ENTRY GAME WITH ASYMMETRIC INFORMATION ON COST

Figure 13-3 shows three possibilities for Microhard. The first is that it is a high-cost firm and sets a first-period monopoly price that is appropriate for this kind of firm. The second possibility is that it is again a high-cost firm but now chooses to set the lower price appropriate for a more cost-efficient firm. Finally, the third possibility is that Microhard is truly is a low-cost firm and sets the low monopoly price appropriate for this case. Note that we have ruled out the possibility of a low-cost Microhard charging the high-cost monopoly price. We will see in a moment that it has no incentive to do so. One important point to understand is that we capture the asymmetry of information or who knows what by circling together the nodes $E_2$ and $E_3$. This is meant to indicate that when the entrant Newvel observes a low price in the first period it does not know whether it is at $E_2$ or at $E_3$, and Microhard, the incumbent, knows that the entrant firm does not know at which node it is.

You may ask at this point why a high-cost incumbent firm would ever set a suboptimally low price that would lead to a lower level of profit. The answer is that this may influence the entrant's decision to enter in period two. For example, Newvel might reason as follows: "If Microhard charges a high price during the first period, it must be an inefficient, high-cost firm and I will enter. However, if Microhard charges a low price, it must be a cost-efficient firm and I am best to stay out of the market." In this setting, there is a considerable incentive for a high-cost incumbent initially to play against type and set the low monopoly price in period one. True, this will mean that it earns only a profit of $40 million instead of the $60 million during the first period. Yet given the entrant firm's reasoning, this sacrifice pays off in the second period because it deters entry and thereby permits Microhard to earn a profit of $60 million rather than the $20 million it would have earned had it initially set a high price that would have encouraged entry.

This same reasoning helps explain our assertion that a low-cost incumbent firm will never initially set the high-cost monopoly price. Such a choice is not profit-maximizing in the short run and, in addition, serves to attract entry.

Our analysis so far makes clear that the outcome to this game is very sensitive to the nature of the beliefs Newvel holds based on the behavior of Microhard observed in the first period. What we have just said is that if Newvel believes "low price means low-cost, high price means high-cost," its entry decision will be easily manipulated by Microhard. Accordingly, this may not be a reasonable sort of belief for Newvel to hold. We should therefore expect Newvel to realize this problem and, hence, to adopt some alternative means to interpret the evidence observed in the first period.

The important issue here is what beliefs are reasonable. Suppose that Newvel—recognizing the foregoing argument—thinks in a different way. Since Newvel understands that it is possible for both a high-cost and a low-cost firm to play a low-price strategy, it reasons that observing a low first-period price really gives no useful information as to the type of incumbent it is facing. Instead, when Newvel observes a low initial price it simply draws upon its knowledge of the probabilities associated with different cost types. Specifically, when it observes a low price it simply concludes that Microhard is a low-cost firm with probability $\rho$ and a high-cost one with probability $(1 - \rho)$. However, because a low-cost firm never has an incentive to charge a high price, Newvel continues to believe that a high price in the first period means that Microhard has high costs. In other words, Newvel's conditional inferences are as follows:

> If Microhard sets a low price in period one, it has a low unit cost with probability $\rho$ and a high unit cost with probability $1 - \rho$. Accordingly, second-period entry will yield an expected profit of $[(1 - \rho)\$20 - \rho\$20]$ million.

> If Microhard sets a high price in period one, it has a high unit cost. Second-period entry will yield a certain profit of $20 million.

As it turns out, the foregoing beliefs are rational. Note, though, that they imply that if Newvel observes a low first-period price and then enters, its expected profit when it enters is $-\$20\rho + \$20(1 - \rho) = 20 - 40\rho$ (in millions). If the Nature's draw or the probability that Microhard is a low-cost firm is high enough, in our example, if $\rho > 1/2$, then Newvel's expected profit from entering is negative. Consequently, it will not enter if it observes a low price. Yet Microhard can work this out, too. It will therefore recognize that if the probability of being a low-cost firm is $\rho > 1/2$, it will do better by pretending to be a low-cost firm and setting a low price in the first period even if, in reality, it is a high-cost firm. Once again, this will lead to a profit of $40 million initially and then, in the second period when the firm is a secure monopoly, a profit of $60 million, for a total profit of $100 million. This is better than the alternative strategy of initially charging a high price, which would reveal its type to the potential entrant, invite entry, and lead to the lower total profit of $80 million ($60 million in period one and $20 million in period two). That is, when $\rho > 1/2$, a high-cost Microhard will set a limit price—one lower than its true profit-maximizing price—in order to deter an imperfectly informed entrant from entering the market. This is, of course, predatory conduct.[12]

In sum, both the Bolton and Scharfstein (1990) and the Milgrom and Roberts (1982) model show how predatory pricing can be rational or, more formally, part of a subgame perfect strategy in a dynamic game. When new players face informational issues either vis-à-vis their investors or vis-à-vis their established rivals, those incumbents may find that predation can be an effective tool to eliminate the upstarts. This incentive for strategic low pricing to improve the terms of a takeover is explored in Saloner (1987) in a premerger game that is somewhat similar to the Bolton and Scharfstein model.

A study of the business practices of American Tobacco from 1891 to 1906 by Burns (1986) supports this idea that predatory pricing can be used to improve the terms of a takeover. During the period of study, American Tobacco acquired some 43 rival firms. American Tobacco would identify the rival that it wished to buy and offer a new, low-price brand in the target's market. The drop in the rival's profit would then lead it to sell out for less money. Burns estimates that this tactic lowered takeover costs by about 25 percent.[13] Note that it suggests, contrary to McGee (1958), that mergers and predation are not substitute tactics but complementary ones.

## 13.3 CONTRACTS AS A BARRIER TO ENTRY

We discussed the Microsoft antitrust trial extensively in Chapter 9. However, that discussion focused mainly on Microsoft's practice of bundling its Windows operating system with its Internet Explorer Web browser as a means of pushing Netscape out of the browser market. While such behavior might well be and indeed was deemed predatory by the federal court, this was not the only predatory practice of which Microsoft was accused. An additional crucial question in the case was whether Microsoft was able through its contracts with PC makers to foreclose other rivals from entering the operating systems market in which Microsoft had a virtual monopoly.

---

12 We can complicate the story by introducing uncertainty on both sides of the game. Suppose, for instance, that Newvel does not know what Microhard's payoff is from fighting an entrant, and Microhard does not know exactly what is a potential entrant's payoff from entering. Specifically, from an entrant's point of view, Microhard can be one of two types: with probability $\rho^0$ Microhard is believed to be "tough" (that is, low cost), which means that its payoffs are such that it will always fight in every market; and with probability $1 - \rho^0$ Microhard is believed to be "weak" (high cost), and perhaps more accommodating of entry. Similarly, each potential entrant is believed by Microhard to be "tough" with probability $q^0$, in which case the entrant's payoffs are such that it will always enter no matter what Microhard does, and to be "weak" with probability $1 - q^0$, in which case its payoffs are those we have already met. The "tough" version of Microhard always fights and so is of no interest to us. What *is* of interest is that a Microhard that knows itself to be "weak" will, as before, still have an incentive to fight entry in order to develop a reputation in the minds of potential entrants that it might, in fact, be "tough." The willingness of a "weak" incumbent to fight is an increasing function of $\rho^0$ and a decreasing function of $q^0$. More importantly, the greater the number of markets there are, say more than 20, the lower is the probability $\rho^0$ that is necessary for entry to be deterred. Simply put, a "weak" incumbent is more likely to fight entry if there are "many" of its markets remaining in which entry has not taken place than if there are "few."

13 In 1911, immediately following the Standard Oil decision, the Supreme Court found American Tobacco guilty of monopolizing the cigarette and tobacco product market, and cited predation to induce rivals to sell out as evidence of illegal monopolistic intent. A district court ordered that American Tobacco be dissolved and reconstituted as separate firms, the big three being American Tobacco, Ligget and Myers, and Lorillard.

The idea that formal agreements that impose penalties for breach of contract between a monopoly firm and its buyers can be a predatory instrument to deter other firms from competing with the monopolist has an important place in antitrust history. It underlies the reasoning of Judge Wyzanksi in the famous *United Shoe Machinery Corporation* antitrust case in the early 1950s. At that time, United Shoe controlled about 85 percent of the shoe-making equipment market, and it leased its machinery to shoe manufacturers. These leasing contracts were binding and were viewed by the court as a way to foreclose the market for shoe machinery.

Perhaps not surprisingly, the Chicago School has traditionally been skeptical of the use of contracts as a predatory device. The simple logic of this counterargument is well expressed by prominent antitrust scholars Bork (1978) and Posner (1976). It is that buyers do not have an incentive to sign contracts that disadvantage them with respect to a monopolist. Any contract signed must give not just the supplier but also the buyer some benefit—say by way of increased service or repair—and therefore a step toward greater efficiency. These proponents of the Chicago School thus emphasize the efficiency grounds for observed contracts rather than the predatory motive. Again, however, more recent theory has provided consistent arguments supporting the view that predation can be rational.

## 13.3.1 Long-Term Exclusive Contracts as Predatory Instruments

Two basic analyses have been advanced to show that buyers may voluntarily sign contracts with suppliers that are, in fact, predatory and inefficient. The first is due to Aghion and Bolton (1987). The second is due to Rasmussen, Rasmeyer, and Wiley (1991). We briefly present each model in turn.

Aghion and Bolton assume a market setting for some essential intermediate good that extends over two periods. In the first period, there is an incumbent monopoly seller of the good whose unit cost is $50. In the second period, each buyer of this good uses exactly one unit of it as an input and is willing to pay up to $100 for the product. The second period also brings the arrival of a new entrant. This is recognized by all parties at the start of the first period. However, neither a buyer nor the monopoly seller initially in the market knows the unit cost $c$ of this second-period potential entrant. All that these initial participants know is that $c$ is distributed randomly but uniformly on the interval between $0 and $100.

We begin by considering matters from the viewpoint of a buyer looking forward to the second period. We assume that if the entrant actually enters the market at that time, Bertrand or price competition will emerge between the initial monopoly supplier and the new rival. If the entrant's unit cost $c$ exceeds $50, however, it will lose this competition. With $c > \$50$, the incumbent can always underbid the entrant. The entrant obviously knows this. Hence, if $c > \$50$, no entry will occur. In this case, which by our assumption happens with probability $1/2$, the incumbent remains a monopolist and can charge a buyer its full reservation price of $100 for the good.

However, if $c \leq \$50$, then entry will occur. In this case, the competition between the entrant and the incumbent will bid the price down to $50, at which point the incumbent will drop out. Once this happens, however, the entrant is under no additional pressure to lower its price, so a buyer will end up paying $50 for the good for any case in which $c \leq \$50$. This too happens with probability $1/2$. Notice that once again, there is an element of uncertainty as well as some asymmetry. For $0 \leq c \leq 50$, only the entrant will know its true cost as the buyer will be charged $50 whatever that cost is.

Now one of the two scenarios just outlined must happen. Therefore, in the absence of any contract obligating a buyer to purchase from the initial incumbent, the buyer's expected price for the intermediate good next period is

$$1/2 \times \$50 + 1/2 \times \$100 = \$75. \tag{13.1}$$

Note that equation (13.1) also implies that since a buyer values the product at $100, it should expect a surplus of $25 in the absence of any contract with the initial monopolist supplier. To put it another way, any contract that the incumbent offers to the buyer must promise the buyer an expected surplus of at least $25, or the buyer will not sign it. The question then is whether the monopolist can and will offer such a contract. If it will, we would also like to know the efficiency aspects of such an arrangement.

One long-term contract that a buyer might find attractive is the following. In the first period, the buyer agrees to make its second-period purchase of the good from the incumbent at a price of $75 with only one possible exception. The exception is that the buyer can instead make its second-period purchase from the new entrant so long as it pays the initial incumbent a $50 breach-of-contract fee.

There are several features of this proposed contract that deserve emphasis. First, note that the entrant will now enter the market only if its cost $c \leq \$25$. The reason is that in the second period, a buyer can either buy from the incumbent for $75 or from the entrant at some price $p$ plus the breach-of-contract fee of $50. Hence, a buyer will prefer to fulfill the contract rather than switch to the alternative supplier unless that supplier charges a price of $25 or less. However, the only way that the entrant can do this is if its cost $c \leq \$25$. Accordingly, the entrant will only enter the market when $c \leq \$25$. Notice that this also implies that the contract restricts entry. Without the contract, entry occurred with probability $1/2$. With the contract, entry will only occur when $c \leq \$25$, which happens only with probability $1/4$.

Will the buyer actually sign the proposed contract? This is where the second noteworthy feature of the agreement becomes relevant. The contract is such that no matter what happens, the buyer will pay $75 for the good. Three-fourths of the time, the potential rival will not enter and the buyer will pay the stipulated $75 to the initial incumbent. One-fourth of the time, the rival will have a cost $c \leq \$25$. In this case, it will enter and charge the buyer the highest price it can while still making a sale, namely, $25 (or just a penny less). A buyer will then switch and purchase the good from the new entrant at $25 but, in addition, pay a $50 breach-of-contract fee to the initial incumbent. Again, the buyer's total payment is $75, leaving it a surplus of $25. Thus, a buyer's expected (in fact, guaranteed) surplus with this contract is $25. Since this is also its expected profit or surplus without the contract, a buyer will be willing to sign the agreement.

The next question is whether the incumbent monopoly seller will actually find it worthwhile to offer the agreement. Here again, the answer is yes. To see this, we now need to consider the monopoly seller's expected profit both without and with the contract.

In the absence of any agreement, the incumbent monopolist will sell to a buyer at a price of $100 half the time. The other half it will be underbid by the new entrant. When it does sell at $100, the incumbent makes a profit of $50. Since this happens with probability $1/2$, the monopoly seller's expected profit without the contract is $1/2 \times \$50 = \$25$ per customer.

# ☑ Reality Checkpoint

## Coke Takes Out a Contract on Texas Rivals

Dangerfield, Texas, gets awfully hot. The summertime temperature can regularly top 100 degrees Fahrenheit and shade is hard to find. That's probably one reason that Dangerfield residents and their neighbors drink a lot of soft drinks every year. Indeed, for convenience stores in the area, it is estimated that as much as half of their sales are from beverages. In the years just before 1992, the stores received their soft-drink supplies from a number of small, soft-drink firms and bottlers, as well as from Coca-Cola and Pepsi. However, that all began to change after 1992.

Bruce Hackett, a former Coke employee and owner of Hackett Beverages, supplied ice-filled barrels to a number of stores that were also stoked with his soft-drink bottles. The barrels were usually displayed just outside the cash register line so that customers could easily grab a cold beverage and pay for it on the way out. However, starting in 1992, Hackett found more and more of his barrels turned upside down and left at the side of the road. In four years, he went from having barrels in 52 stores to barrels in just 2 stores. Other independent bottlers and small beverage firms had similar experiences. They found stores abandoning the refrigerator units they gave them to display their products, dumping their fresh soda dispensing and vending machines, and even refusing them any shelf space.

The reason for these changes was easy to find. Coca-Cola had started an aggressive marketing campaign in which it paid store owners to display its products exclusively and refused to give them access even to non-Coke drinks handled by Coca-Cola bottlers if they did not. Thus, one contract offered a bonus of $2 million to a regional supermarket chain, Brookshire's, in return for just selling Coke products alone. Another contract required that "Coca-Cola products will occupy a minimum of 100 percent of total soft-drink space" in the store.

The case went to trial before a Texas court in 2003. Coke's defense was that the stores wanted the contract deals it was offering. They argued that the stores felt they had little to offer in the soft-drink category unless they offered the national Coke brand at the best terms possible. Coke argued that the contracts it offered allowed the stores to do just that. However, it was indisputable that as the smaller firms were driven from the market, Coke prices went up. At Nu-Way, a popular Dangerfield convenience store that still offers Royal Crown Cola, a 20-ounce container of the Royal Crown product sells for 69 cents while the same size container of Coke sells for 92 cents. However, at another convenience store, E Z Mart, a short distance away, there is no Royal Crown alternative and Coke sells for $1.09. Whether this was a case of predation or not is a question of judgment. However, a comment by Coca-Cola spokesperson Polly Howes probably did not help Coke's cause. In a widely distributed statement, Ms. Howes said that far from "a lack of competition. There was too much competition." The Texas jury found Coca-Cola guilty of violating the antitrust laws.

**Source:** C. Hays, "How Coke Pushed Rivals Off the Shelf." *The New York Times*, August 6, 2003, Section 3, p. 1.

With the contract, the calculation of the incumbent's profit is just slightly more complicated. With probability 3/4, the monopolist will still sell to the buyer at the specified price of $75. Since the monopolist has a unit cost of $50, such a sale generates a profit of $25. With probability 1/4, however, the monopolist makes no sale because the buyer breaks the contract and switches to the new entrant. This is not bad news, however. The switch means that the monopolist no longer has to incur the $25 unit production cost. Moreover, the buyer's breach of contract entitles the seller to a $50 fee in the one-fourth of the time that the contract is broken. In short, the contract offers the initial incumbent seller an expected surplus per customer of

$$3/4 \times (\$75 - \$50) + 1/4 \times \$50 = \$31.25 > \$25. \qquad \textbf{(13.2)}$$

As equation (13.2) makes clear, the monopoly seller's expected profit with the contract is $31.25, an amount that definitely exceeds its expected profit of $25 without the contract. Moreover, we have already shown that a typical buyer's expected surplus is the same whether the agreement is in force or not. In other words, the incumbent monopolist is made better off and the buyer is made no worse off by the contract. Accordingly, with one party desiring the contract and the other indifferent, we expect that the contract will be offered and signed.

From a social viewpoint, however, the contract is inefficient. To be sure, it increases the expected surplus of the buyer and seller together from $50 (= $25 + $25) to $56.25 (= $25 + $31.25) for a net gain of $6.25. However, it reduces the entrant's expected surplus by more than this amount. Why?

Without the contract, the entrant will stay out of the market half the time and enter the other half. When it does enter, the entrant will sell at a price of $50 per unit. In such cases, the entrant's unit cost $c$ will range from 0 to $50, or $25 on average. This implies that the entrant has an expected profit of $1/2 \times (\$50 - \$25) = \$12.50$ when there is no contract. When the incumbent binds the buyer with a contract, however, the potential rival only enters the market with probability 1/4 and sells at a price of only $25. Its unit cost in such cases will range from 0 to $25, or $12.50 on average. So, once the contract is signed, the potential rival's expected profit is only $1/4 \times (\$25 - \$12.50) = \$3.13$. From this, we can see that the issuance of a contract reduces the potential entrant's expected surplus per customer from $12.50 to $3.13, or by $9.37. As noted, this reduction exceeds the joint gains to the buyer and seller ($6.25), so the total social surplus is less with the contract than without it.

The intuition behind the foregoing result, however, is subtle. From the buyer's perspective, the problem is that without the contract, the new entrant will never sell at a price less than $50—even if it has a cost of $0—because that is the next best price alternative that the buyer has. Ideally, the buyer would like to benefit more in such cases where the entrant has such a particularly low cost. Yet in the absence of the contract, nothing compels the new entrant to engage in such sharing. Once the price falls to $50, the initial incumbent drops out of the market and the entrant faces no further pressure to reduce its price. By offering the contract, the incumbent monopolist effectively enables the buyer to force the seller never to charge a price above $25. The buyer is, as just noted, willing to pay for this service.

The point is that even though a contract may bring benefits to a monopoly supplier and its buyers, the contract is still inefficient if it achieves these gains only by reducing the surplus of the new entrant by an even greater amount. The inefficiency reflects the fact that under the contract regime some desirable entry is prevented.

Specifically, entry does not occur when the new rival has a cost $c$ satisfying $\$25 < c \le \$50$ despite the fact that, within this range, the entrant is more efficient than the initial monopoly seller. Because of the long-term contract including its breach-of-contract clause, the entrant finds it difficult to enter the market.

The Rasmusen, Ramseyer, and Wiley (1991) model differs from the above insofar as it focuses on an externality in the contract rather than an uncertainty. Suppose again that there is one supplier and, say, three buyers. As before, each buyer will pay $100 for one unit of the input and the incumbent has a unit cost of $60. There is also an entrant with a unit cost of $40 waiting to enter the market next period. However, the entrant also has a sunk cost—say due to market research or promotional activities—of $60. Hence, to underbid the incumbent and cover its sunk cost, the entrant has to serve at least two customers. For example, if the new entrant serves three customers, it can charge each a price as low as $60. The $20 in operating profit that it makes on all three customers combined will then give it enough extra to cover its overhead. If it serves two customers, the entrant can still underbid the incumbent but it must now charge a price no lower than $70. If it serves only one customer, the entrant must charge a price of $100 to acquire the $60 needed to cover its sunk cost. In this case, of course, the entrant will not enter.

The incumbent can, of course, match any of the entrant's price offers in the second period. Still, the incumbent has to recognize that if the entrant comes in at a price of $70 and the incumbent has to match that price, the incumbent's profit falls from $120 to $30 even if it keeps all three customers. The incumbent therefore has some incentive to stop the entrant from acquiring two or more clients with a long-term contract. To sell this contract, the incumbent engages in the following tactic. It tells two customers that each will be able to buy the input at $70 if, and only if, they sign an exclusive contract promising not to buy from any other supplier. Why might this work?

Each buyer who is offered an exclusive contract with a purchase price of $70 has to worry about what the other buyers will do. Once two sign the contract, no offer needs to be made to the third because once two buyers are bound to the incumbent, the entrant cannot profitably underbid the incumbent's price. Therefore, the third buyer may well face a price of $100 once the other two have signed. In an effort to avoid such an outcome, each buyer will rush to sign the contract. In fact, by playing buyers off against each other in this way, the incumbent may be able to sign exclusive deals even if it offers a small price reduction to only $90.

Here again the contract inefficiently blocks entry. The potential entrant is a more efficient producer. The problem is that each buyer looks only to the effect that the contract has on that buyer's profit. Each ignores the impact that signing the contract has on overall competition and the profitability of other buyers (perhaps some of whom are rivals to the buyer in the downstream market).

## 13.3.2 Tying as a Predatory Contract

In the contracting scenarios previously described, the mechanism that blocks entry is a contract that extends over two periods, that is, a long-term contract. The contract is written in the first period, before a potential second entrant arrives, and then it extends into the next period. When the rival does arrive in period two, it finds that potential customers are hard to come by because they have already been contractually bound to the initial monopolist.

Rather than extending a contract over two or more periods, one might instead consider extending a contract to two or more markets. That is, an incumbent seller in one market might be able to contract with its customers in a manner that effectively binds them to that same seller in a second market. This is what generally happens with a tying arrangement. As we saw in the Magicam and Magifilm parable of Chapter 9, a primary motivation for tying is the implementation of effective price discrimination—not predation. In that story, the Rowling Corp. markets a Magicam camera that only works with its own Magifilm. Tying can enable Rowling to price discriminate among its consumers.

If the Magicam worked equally well with film cartridges made by any firm, Rowling would still enjoy a monopoly in the Magicam, but its ability to extract additional surplus by means of price discrimination would be limited. Tying the two goods together is therefore good for Rowling Corp. Indeed, it may even be good for consumers because, as we know, price discrimination often works to expand the market and increase the social surplus. This price discrimination motive was not part of the long-term contract model described above and, in this respect, the two contractual arrangements are not equivalent.

Yet it remains the case that while the tying of Magicam and Magifilm is primarily a means to help Rowling Corp. price discriminate more effectively, other makers of film cartridges will nonetheless find that this practice causes them to lose customers. Once again, this raises the fear that the tie-in may permit Rowling Corp. to extend its Magicam monopoly into the film market. This will be particularly true if, for instance, there are significant scale economies in film production so that loss of part of the market makes it more difficult for a rival maker of film to produce at minimum average cost.

Whether Rowling or any other firm has an incentive to extend its monopoly in the manner just described is, however, far from clear. After all, consumers are ultimately interested in Magicam pictures—not the Magicam or the Magifilm itself. From this perspective, a higher price for say, Magifilm, requires a lower price for the Magicam. To put it another way, Rowling has little incentive to monopolize the Magifilm market solely as a means to raise the price of Magifilm since this will reduce the demand for its Magicam product.

Yet such an analysis is perhaps too limited. Suppose, for instance, that there are economies of scope between film and camera production. Then by extending its monopoly from the Magicam market to that of Magifilm, Rowling may prevent other manufacturers from realizing such scope economies. In turn, this may prevent other firms from developing their own Magicam product. That is, the extension of the Rowling monopoly from one product line to another may be a means of protecting its core monopoly.

It is for this reason that whenever a firm possesses substantial market power in a tying product, and coerces the buyer to take the tied product as a condition to obtaining the desired good, the arrangement is almost always found to be a violation of the antitrust laws. (See Reality Checkpoint: Tied Up on the Rock.)

## 13.4  PREDATORY CONDUCT AND PUBLIC POLICY

Should there be public policies that restrain the conduct of firms who have acquired or are likely to acquire a dominant position in the marketplace? The answer to this

## ✓ Reality Checkpoint

### Tied Up on the Rock

Roughly 1,500 inmates were incarcerated in Alcatraz, or "the Rock" as it was sometimes called, during the 30 years of its use as a federal penitentiary from 1934 to 1963. Born in the Depression Era, the prison was envisioned as a necessary response to the violence that first, Prohibition, and later, severe economic dislocation, brought to America. Law enforcement officials including J. Edgar Hoover sought to build a special institution in which the most violent and hardened criminals, such as George "Machine Gun" Kelly, would be kept securely. The prison's location on an island in the middle of San Francisco harbor also made it ideal as a place to hold gang leaders such as Al Capone in a manner that made it difficult for such criminals to maintain any control of their still-active criminal organizations. The prospect of imprisonment with such a hardened crew of inmates and in such an isolated place led many if not every prisoner to dream of escape. Indeed, many risked life and limb in such attempts. Yet no successful breakout has ever been documented. Escape was impossible.

These days getting to the island, which is now operated as a tourist attraction, is almost as difficult as escape used to be. The National Park Service issues 4,200 daily tickets to visit the tiny island and all are typically bought. Pursuant to an exclusive contract, these tickets are issued to Blue and Gold Fleet cruise lines, the only tour boat company operator permitted to transport visitors to the island. The contract also permits Blue and Gold, if it so desires, to sell 1,800 of the Alcatraz tickets to travel agents and others who put together vacation and excursion packages. Because of the strong demand for such tickets, those operators who receive them find that they are very popular with vacationers. In turn, this gives Blue and Gold considerable leverage with the tour operators. Indeed, soon after it first received the exclusive rights, the cruise company exploited this leverage by requiring that any tour operator receiving Alcatraz tickets must also use Blue and Gold for its harbor cruises and other boating excursions. In other words, Blue and Gold tied the sale of Alcatraz tickets to the mandatory use of its other services. Of course, the other boating companies who lost customers to Blue and Gold were unhappy. Several complaints were filed with the California Attorney General's Office. In a settlement with these officials, Blue and Gold agreed to terminate its tying practices.

**Source:** A. Chiu, "San Francisco Tourboat Antitrust Case is Settled." *San Jose Mercury News*, September 13, 2000, p. A1.

question rests largely on three issues. The first of these is whether predation is or can be a rational strategy. The second is the empirical issue as to whether there is any actual evidence of predatory behavior. The third is whether any such policy can actually be made workable. It is not too much of an exaggeration to say that little attention was paid to either of the first two issues (and possibly the third) in the years immediately following the passage of the Robinson-Patman Act in 1936. For a number of years thereafter, price cuts by large firms that had the effect of severely reducing or eliminating the market share of small firms were almost routinely regarded as predatory if the prices reflected any degree of discrimination, that is, if the large firm sold at a lower price in more competitive markets. The culmination of this period of stringent prosecution of even vague charges of predatory pricing came with the *Utah Pie* case previously discussed.[14]

Against a history of cases such as *Utah Pie,* the work of McGee (1958, 1980), Koller (1971), Posner (1976), Bork (1978), Easterbrook (1984), and others of the Chicago School reflected something of a necessary corrective. Many firms achieve dominance not because of predation but because of their superior competitive skill. Hence, policies that constrain "bigness" would have adverse incentive effects on competitive behavior. A corollary to this view is that market dominance will not persist if it is due to any factor not related to superior skill or efficiency. Indeed, these very arguments were made by Microsoft during its 1999–2000 trial. As a result of the force of these arguments, the Chicago School perspective on predatory behavior became increasingly influential. It received an official blessing in the *Matsushita* case in which the Supreme Court wrote "For this reason, there is a consensus among commentators that predatory pricing schemes are rarely tried, and even more rarely successful."[15] A few years later, in the *Brooke* case of 1993, the Court went even further and outlined stringent evidentiary standards that had to be met before a predation claim would be supported.[16]

The Brooke Group (also known as Ligget) was a small cigarette manufacturer that began selling a generic brand in 1980 at prices well below those of the major brands. When consumers responded favorably to the introduction of these cheap cigarettes, Brown & Williamson and other large tobacco companies responded with vigorous price cuts. Indeed, in its effort to undersell Brooke, it seems clear that Brown cut prices so low that it sustained millions of dollars of losses over a period as long as a year or more. Ultimately, however, Brooke could not keep pace. It raised the price on its cigarettes. Almost immediately thereafter, Brown & Williamson and other cigarette manufacturers did the same.

The Supreme Court did not find the foregoing evidence conclusive. As noted, the Court had moved to a view that believed there was an economic consensus that predatory pricing was irrational. The court then established two broad requirements for a successful prosecution of a predatory pricing case. The first was evidence of selling below some measure of cost. The second, and really new element introduced by the court, was evidence that the predator had a reasonable expectation of recouping the losses endured during the predatory period. Just how strong the new requirements were can be seen in the fact that there was not one successful prosecution of predatory action in the first forty cases that followed the *Brooke* decision. It was not until the important case of Microsoft that a finding of guilty was made.

It should be clear that our view is that the consensus to which the Supreme Court referred in *Matsushita* no longer exists—if it ever did. Commitment via capacity expansion, asymmetric information, and contractual exclusions are all features that can be combined to make a coherent argument for the rationality of predatory actions.

---

14 *Utah Pie Co. v. Continental Baking Co. et al.*, 386 U.S. 685 (1967).

15 *Matsushita Electronic Industrial Co., Ltd. v. Zenith Radio Corporation, et al.*, 475 U.S. 574 (1986).

16 *Brooke Group v. Brown & Williamson Tobacco*, 509 U.S. 209 (1993). Interestingly enough, Brooke actually won the initial jury trial but lost in subsequent appeals to the federal courts.

Moreover, with respect to recoupment, it is important to recognize that successful predation has important reputation effects. Once a firm is successful in eliminating one rival, it sends a message to all other potential competitors. Thus, in measuring the ability of a firm to recover its losses, one has to include in the calculations all the profits secured by the deterrent effect that the firm's reputation has on other would-be entrants.

However, the Court's statement of necessary evidence does speak to an important issue. For the recognition that predation can be rational and does happen does not carry any clear policy implications unless one has a clear standard by which predatory actions can be identified and distinguished from conduct that is truly pro-competitive. Any entry will generally evoke some reaction from the incumbent(s). Typically, this may come in the form of lower prices or other expanded consumer benefits. Yet not all or even most such responses are predatory in nature. To the contrary, they are exactly the conduct that we expect and hope that markets will promote. Similarly, when any firm, large or small, first comes into a market as a new entrant, it may set a low initial price—lower than the short-term, profit-maximizing one, in fact—as a means to get consumers to forego their usual brand and try the entrant's relatively unknown product. Once established the firm may then raise price. Clearly, the intent of this kind of promotional pricing is not to drive a rival from the market. Yet it may be difficult empirically to distinguish this pricing strategy from predatory pricing.

In other words, to the extent that antitrust enforcement seeks to prevent predatory practices, policy makers need to create workable legal standards that are able to distinguish pro-competitive from anticompetitive conduct. Ideally, one would like such policy to be governed by a simple rule that would be used to detect the presence of predation. This would permit all parties to understand just what is and what is not legal. Yet what one finds in the area of predation is that simple rules rarely work.

Of the various rules that have been proposed, the most famous is that of Areeda and Turner (1975), which essentially finds any price to be predatory if it is below the firm's short-run average variable cost standing in as a proxy for marginal cost. Unfortunately, it is not a very good proxy. In actual practice, average variable cost can be significantly less than short-run marginal cost so that a firm could set a price below its current marginal cost yet still above its average cost. In so doing, the firm would be acting within the legal range permitted by the Areeda and Turner rule even though a price below short-run marginal cost would likely be judged as predatory by many economists. Hence, as Scherer (1976) was quick to point out, the use of the average cost standard could still permit serious predation.[17] Moreover, if there are important learning curve effects so that average cost falls with a firm's cumulative production over time (as opposed to scale economies in which average cost falls with the volume of production per unit of time), predation can occur by means of a vigorous output expansion without prices ever falling below cost.[18]

Another problem is that the rule ignores the strategic component of predatory pricing. To take a simple example, consider a market in which there is one firm operating as a monopoly. Suppose that if a new firm enters it will produce an identical good to that of the monopolist and that the game is one of Bertrand or price competition. As we saw in Chapter 11 the equilibrium of this game is price equal to unit

---

**17** See Scherer's (1976) exchange with Areeda and Turner (1976) on this and other points.
**18** See Cabral and Riordan (1997) for an elaboration of this point.

cost. Prices fall immediately to their marginal cost. By Areeda and Turner's rule, this would not be predatory. Yet if the entrant foresees this outcome, the existence of any sunk entry cost will be enough to induce it to stay out. Here again, the Areeda and Turner rule might permit entry-deterring behavior. Indeed, whenever the threat of "cutthroat pricing" is sufficiently effective that it never is actually used, the evidence Areeda and Turner look for will not be found.

Despite its shortcomings, the Areeda and Turner rule has been applied in many U.S. antitrust cases. It has, for example, been frequently relied upon by Supreme Court Justice Stephen Breyer.[19] It was also used to exonerate IBM against predatory price-cutting charges in *California Computer Products, Inc., et al. v. International Business Machines* [613 F. 2d 727 (9th Cir. 1979)]. Perhaps the clearest statement is that of Judge Kaufman who, in *Northeastern Telephone Company v. American Telephone and Telegraph Company et al.* [651 F. 2d 76 (2nd Cir. 1981)], wrote: "We agree with Areeda and Turner that in the general case, at least, the relationship between a firm's prices and its marginal costs provides the best single determinant of predatory pricing."

Yet despite its frequent use, the weaknesses in the Areeda and Turner rule have led many economists to propose modified alternatives. Some of these are like the Areeda and Turner approach in that they focus essentially on the behavior of a single variable. Baumol (1979), for example, focuses primarily on the behavior of the incumbent's price before entry and after exit of a rival. Essentially, this rule requires that any price reduction by a dominant firm in the face of entry be required to be "quasi-permanent," say for a period of five years. In particular, if the price reduction that entry induced is quickly reversed following the entrant's exit, Baumol's rule would find the pricing behavior predatory. In a recent updating of this work, Baumol (1996) also suggests comparing the predator's price with a measure of average avoidable cost (AAC). AAC is a measure of the cost that the alleged predator could have avoided had it not engaged in the predatory increase in output. Thus, if the predatory action lasted for a year, AAC would be the total amount of extra costs produced in that year divided by the extra quantity produced.

In contrast, Williamson (1977) suggests looking at the incumbent's output before and after entry. The idea is that a rapid expansion of output after entry would be a sign of possible predation. This rule has two advantages. First, because of the prohibition against expansion after entry, the incumbent might well expand output earlier. In turn, this eliminates some of the monopoly distortion that would otherwise occur when the incumbent is alone in the market. Second, Williamson's rule may also prevent capacity expansion as an entry-deterring strategy by making the threat to expand after entry no longer credible.

While both the Baumol (1979) and Williamson rules are insightful, both are also limited by focusing on a single variable to indicate predation. As we have emphasized, predatory conduct is part of an often complicated corporate strategy. As a result, it is unlikely to be reflected accurately in the behavior of a single variable. The Dixit (1980) model of capacity deterrence does not involve pricing at all and so would go undetected by both the Areeda-Turner and the Baumol tests. Similarly, Williamson's test would not prevent deterrence by preemption. None of these tests involve any consideration as to whether the strategic environment actually permits predation.

---

19 See, for example, his decision in *Barry Wright Corporation v. ITT Grinnell Corporation, et al.*, 724F. 2d 227 (1st Cir. 1983).

**Reality Checkpoint**

## Cut-Rate or Cutthroat Fares?

In 1994, Sun Jet Airlines began offering service between Dallas-Fort Worth airport and a select few other cities including Tampa, Florida, and Long Beach, California. Its entry was subsequently followed by that of Vanguard Airlines flying between Dallas and Kansas City, and Western Pacific offering flights between Dallas and Colorado Springs. All three airlines are small startup carriers whose operating costs are widely recognized to be well below those of the major, established airlines. Indeed, it was this cost advantage that gave these small startups their only hope of surviving in the Dallas-Fort Worth market. This is because the Dallas-Fort Worth airport is a central hub for American Airlines. American carries 70 percent of all the passengers who travel from any city nonstop to Dallas and 77 percent of all those nonstop passengers originating in Dallas. It has concessions from local businesses and has already sunk the costs necessary to operate its gates, ticketing desks, and so on. Internal documents obtained from American by the Justice Department reveal that these and other advantages made the firm confident that its dominance would not be challenged by another major airline. However, those same documents suggest that American was concerned about the entry of low-cost startups, especially after observing how much market share such firms had taken from other major carriers at their hub airports.

American responded aggressively to the three startups. It greatly expanded its flight offerings in the challenged markets and lowered its fares. In each of the three markets shown, this strategy ultimately led the startup to exit the market. Immediately thereafter, American cut its flights and raised fares back to or above earlier levels. This is shown for the case of three markets in the following table.

| | BEFORE ENTRY | | DURING CONFLICT | | AFTER EXIT | |
| | # Daily Flights | Price | # Daily Flights | Price | # Daily Flights | Price |
|---|---|---|---|---|---|---|
| Kansas City | 8 | $108 | 14 | $80 | 11 | $147 |
| Long Beach | 0 | — | 3 | $86 | 0 | — |
| Colorado Springs | 5 | $150 | 7 | $81 | 6 | $137 |

Was this a case of predatory pricing? The Justice Department thinks so. It claims that during the battle with the startups, American lost money on each flight. The actual losses are claimed to be even greater because to offer the additional flights, aircraft were diverted from profitable routes to these unprofitable ones. American won an initial decision in district court. An appellate court later upheld the decision. [*United States of America v. AMR Corp.*, 335 F.3d 1109 (10th Cir. 2003)].

**Source:** D. Carney and W. Zellner, "Caveat Predator: The Justice Department is Cracking Down on Predatory Pricing." *Business Week*, May 22, 2000, p. 116.

Joskow and Klevoric (1979) were among the first to suggest a more complete assessment of alleged predation within a strategic framework. Their rule combines the separate criteria previously mentioned—below-cost pricing, output expansion, and price reversal—but requires as well that there be evidence that such actions were or at least could have been conceived as part of an overall strategy. In particular, Joskow and Klevoric would examine company documents to determine whether a firm was intentionally pursuing the aggressive policies. These authors would also examine the industry's structural features to see whether the conditions for predatory pricing exist.

Ordover and Willig (1981) and Bolton, Brodley, and Riordan (2000) reflect attempts to present a comprehensive framework for evaluating predatory accusations. The Ordover and Willig paper is important for its clear and modern definition of predatory conduct as any action for which the profitability is dependent on driving the rival out or preventing it from entering in the first place. In this view, predatory pricing is but one of a number of predation tactics. Both papers argue that an important first step is to check the market structure for the preconditions necessary to make predation worthwhile. The structural conditions so identified are that the accused predator really has significant market power and that entry be difficult so that if a rival is forced to exit it is not subsequently replaced. Bolton, Brodley, and Riordan also argue that recoupment can be shown by relating the predator's actions to a clear and evidence-supported strategy of predation. In the case of predatory pricing, these authors would rely on an AAC measure as a benchmark.

Again, none of the proposed predatory standards is simple or easily translated into a courtroom proceeding. The difficulty of distinguishing between good, fierce competition on the one hand, and predatory efforts on the other, is substantial. Moreover, as tough as this distinction is to make in the case of pricing, it is even more difficult to achieve in considering other actions.

Consider, for example, the possibility of predatory product innovation illustrated by two well-known cases, *Telex v. IBM* and *Berkey v. Kodak*. In the former, the issue at hand was the claim by Telex (and others) that IBM, which at the time admittedly controlled the market for mainframe computers but faced serious competition in markets for peripheral equipment, began to develop new equipment designs such that only new IBM peripherals were compatible with IBM mainframes (a tying arrangement). In the *Berkey* case, Berkey was a photo-finisher and camera manufacturer who claimed that Kodak should have given it advance notice of Kodak's introduction of a new 110 camera so as to permit Berkey to redesign its cameras and remain viable in the market. In both cases, the courts eventually ruled against the plaintiffs and in favor of IBM and Kodak, respectively. There is perhaps good reason to believe that the technological alterations reflected in these two cases truly were motivated by predatory considerations. However, there is also a legitimate fear that punishing such actions could have a chilling effect on all innovation.[20]

# SUMMARY

Charges of predatory pricing or pricing below cost to drive out a competitor and other similar activities have typically been met with considerable skepticism by the

---

20 See Ordover and Saloner (1989) for a discussion of technological predation.

courts. This reflects the Chicago School view that predation is irrational; that is, in the language of game theory predation is neither a subgame perfect strategy nor a dominant strategy. Accordingly, few charges of predatory activity have been successfully prosecuted in the last twenty years or so. The *Microsoft* case is a notable exception in this regard.

Contemporary industrial organization theory does, however, suggest that predatory actions can be rational. Numerous economic models have been developed that overturn the logic of the chain store paradox. An important common feature in these models is asymmetric information. Asymmetries between a lender and a firm regarding the firm's true profitability, or between an established firm and an upstart regarding the incumbent's cost, can make predation a feasible and attractive strategy. Historically, there seem to be many cases of predation. Long-term contracts that lock in buyers can also now be better understood as a strategy to lock out new entrants as well.

Yet while the viability of predation in both theory and practice seems clear, the proper role of public policy remains clouded. The principal problem is one of distinguishing aggressive pricing and other tactics from ones that are truly predatory—profitable only if they succeed in driving a rival out of business. Some antitrust enforcement—especially those cases prosecuted under the Robinson-Patman Act in the first 35 years after it was passed—appear to have been misguided efforts to protect competitors and not competition. Both economists and the courts continue to struggle with the implementation of a workable definition of predation.

## PROBLEMS

1. Return to the Microhard–Newvel game as discussed in Section 13.1. Suppose now that Newvel's fixed costs are only $80 million per period. What would be the loan contract that a bank in a competitive banking industry would accept to loan Newvel $80 million in each period? Now suppose that the worst-case scenario facing Newvel worsens. Specifically, there is a 50 percent chance of earning $200 million and a 50 percent chance of earning only $40 million. Fixed costs are $80 million per period. Now what would be the loan contract that a bank in a competitive banking industry would accept to loan Newvel $80 million in each period?

2. An incumbent firm operates in a local computer market, which is a natural monopoly. That is, there is room for only one firm to sell profitably in this market. Market demand for the good is estimated to be $Q^D = 100 - P$. Another firm would like to enter this market, but only if the incumbent firm has a higher unit cost than it does. Specifically, there is a 25 percent chance that the incumbent is a low-cost firm with a unit cost equal to 20, and there is a 75 percent chance that the incumbent is a high-cost firm with a unit cost of 30. The entrant's unit cost is 25. The entrant knows its costs but not that of the incumbent. The incumbent does know its unit cost. Market demand is common knowledge to both firms. The entrant, however, does get to observe the current or pre-entry market price at which the incumbent sells its good. If the entrant decides to enter the market it incurs a setup cost of $1,000. Does the high-cost firm have an incentive to set a low price in order to masquerade as a low-cost firm?

3. Suppose a buyer is willing to pay up to $200 for one unit of some good. There is currently only one supplier of the good and the cost of supplying one unit of the

good is $100. Next period a rival supplier may appear in the market. The rival's cost of supplying the good is not known. It is assumed to be uniformly distributed on the interval [$50, $150]. Describe a long-term contract that the current supplier can offer the buyer that will be attractive to the buyer and that at the same time will strengthen the monopoly power of the current supplier.

4. An incumbent firm has a cost function $C_I = 100 + 1.5q_I^2$. Hence, its marginal cost is given by $MC_I = 3q_I$. Recently, an upstart firm has entered the market. The upstart has the cost function $C_U = 100 + 110q_U$. Suppose the incumbent sets a price of 74 and meets all the demand at that price.

   **a.** Does the incumbent's behavior violate the Areeda-Turner rule of selling below marginal cost?

   **b.** Does the incumbent's behavior violate the Areeda-Turner rule when average variable cost is used as a proxy for marginal cost?

# REFERENCES

Aghion, P., and P. Bolton. 1987. "Contracts as a Barrier to Entry." *American Economic Review* 77: 388–401.

Areeda, P. E., and D. F. Turner. 1975. "Predatory pricing and related practices under section 2 of the Sherman Act." *Harvard Law Review* 88 (February): 697–733.

———. 1976. "Scherer on Predatory Pricing: A Reply." *Harvard Law Review* 89 (March): 891–900.

Baumol, W. J. 1979. "Quasi-Permanence of Price Reductions: A Policy for Prevention of Predatory Pricing." *Yale Law Journal* 89: 1–26.

———. 1996. "Predation and the Logic of the Average Variable Cost Test." *Journal of Law & Economics* 39 (April): 49–72.

Benoit, J. P. 1984. "Financially Constrained Entry in a Game with Incomplete Information." *Rand Journal of Economics* 15: 490–9.

Bolton, P., J. Brodley, and M. Riordan. 2000. "Predatory Pricing: Strategic Theory and Legal Policy." *Georgetown Law Review* 88 (August).

Bolton, P., and D. Scharfstein. 1990. "A Theory of Predation Based on Agency Problems in Financial Contracting." *American Economic Review* 80 (March): 93–106.

Bork, R. 1978. *The Antitrust Paradox*. New York: Basic Books.

Brandeis, Louis. 1913. "Cutthroat prices—the competition that kills." *Harpers Weekly* (November 15): 10–12.

Burns, M. R. 1986. "Predatory pricing and the acquisition cost of competitors." *Journal of Political Economy* 94 (April): 266–96.

Cabral, L. M. B., and M. J. Riordan. 1997. "The Learning Curve, Predation, Antitrust, and Welfare." *Journal of Industrial Economics* 45 (June): 155–69.

Dixit, A. 1980. "The Role of Investment in Entry Deterrence." *The Economic Journal* 90: 95–106.

Easterbrook, F. H. 1984. "The Limits of Antitrust." *The Texas Law Review* 63 (January): 1–40.

Fudenberg, D., and J. Tirole. 1986. "A Signal-Jamming Theory of Predation." *Rand Journal of Economics* 17: 366–76.

Joskow, P. L., and A. K. Klevoric. 1979. "A Framework for Analyzing Predatory Pricing Policy." *Yale Law Journal* 89: 213–70.

Koller, R. H., II. 1971. "The Myth of Predatory Pricing: An Empirical Study." *Antitrust Law & Economics Review* 4: 105–43.

McGee, J. S. 1958. "Predatory Price Cutting: The Standard Oil (N.J.) Case." *Journal of Law and Economics* 1 (April): 137–69.

———. 1980. "Predatory pricing revisited." *Journal of Law and Economics* 23 (October): 289–330.

Milgrom, P., and J. Roberts. 1982. "Limit pricing and entry under incomplete information: an equilibrium analysis." *Econometrica* 50 (March): 443–60.

Morton, F. Scott. 1997. "Entry and Predation: British Shipping Cartels 1879–1929." *Journal of Economics and Management Strategy* 6: 679–724.

Ordover, J. A., and G. Saloner. 1989. "Predation monopolization an antitrust." In R. Schmalensee and R. Willig, eds., *Handbook of Industrial Organization*, Vol. 1. Amsterdam: North-Holland: 537–95.

———, and R. Willig. 1981. "An Economic Definition of Predation: Pricing and Product Innovation." *Yale Law Journal* 91: 8–53.

Phlips, L. 1995. *Competition Policy: A Game Theoretic Analysis*. Cambridge, MA: Cambridge University Press.

Posner, R. 1976. *Antitrust Law: An Economic Perspective*. Chicago: University of Chicago Press.

Rasmusen, E. 1993. *Games and Information*. Oxford: Basil Blackwell.

Rasmusen, E., J. M. Ramseyer, and J. Wiley. 1991. "Naked Exclusion." *American Economic Review* 81 (December): 1137–45.

Saloner, G. 1987. "Predation, mergers and incomplete information." *Rand Journal of Economics* 18 (Summer): 165–86.

Schelling, T. 1960. *The Strategy of Conflict*. Cambridge, MA: Harvard University Press.

Scherer, F. M. 1976. "Predatory Pricing and the Sherman Act: A Comment." *Harvard Law Review* 89 (March): 869–90.

Williamson, O. E. 1977. "Predatory Pricing: A Strategic and Welfare Analysis." *Yale Law Journal* 87: 284–340.

Yamey, Basil S. 1972. "Predatory price cutting: notes and comments." *Journal of Law and Economics* 15: 129–42.

Yergin, D. 1991. *The Prize*. New York: Simon and Schuster.

# Chapter 14

# Price-Fixing and Repeated Games

The 1990s are a landmark period in the history of U.S. antitrust policy. Prior to 1993, the record fine for price-fixing in the United States was $2 million. Many cases resulted in fines much less than that amount. Yet by the end of the decade just seven years later, well over a billion dollars of price-fixing fines had been levied. How did this change come about and what can the process tell us about the theory and practice of industrial organization?

A major development in the application of policy toward price-fixing conspiracies came in the wake of the Archer Daniels Midland (ADM) company, which in 1996 pleaded guilty and agreed to pay a fine of $100 million in response to charges of criminal price-fixing in the markets for lysine, a livestock feed additive, and citric acid, a flavored beverage ingredient. The record $100 million in penalties (which came on top of $90 million paid in civil suits) reflected a view that the ADM case revealed a dark side in American corporate practice that had been given too little attention for too long, and that a major effort was necessary to thwart collusive practices. This change in attitude was confirmed when, two years later in 1998, the record ADM fine was surpassed when UCAR International pleaded guilty and agreed to pay a fine of $110 million for its part in an international conspiracy to fix prices and volumes of electrodes. Even this record did not last long, however. In 1999, the German company SGL Carbon AG was fined $135 million for its part in the same conspiracy. Later in that same year the Swiss pharmaceutical company Hoffman-LaRoche Ltd. agreed to pay a massive $500 million penalty and BASF of Germany agreed to pay a penalty of $225 million for their role in running a decade-long conspiracy to restrict competition and fix vitamin prices worldwide. The century closed with Sotheby's auction house admitting that it had spent most of the 1990s colluding with rival Christie's to strong-arm money from elite art and antiques dealers and agreeing to pay a fine of $45 million. Moreover, because many of these large conspiracies were international in scope, European and Canadian prosecutors got into the act as well. Between 1996 and 2002, the fines imposed by all three regions on just five cartels (lysine, citric acid, vitamins, sodium gluconate, and graphite electrodes) totaled $2.89 billion.

Of course, many more than just the five cartels were prosecuted. As the data in Table 14-1 and the display in Figure 14-1 quickly verify, the last decade has witnessed an unprecedented rise in the enforcement of competition. As a result, price-fixing conspiracies have also been found and prosecuted in the copper concentrate, cement, hydrogen peroxide, creosote, naphthalene, polyethylene film, and many other industries. As noted, this vigorous enforcement has spread beyond North America to Europe, as evidenced by the fact that in just the three years leading up to 2002, the European Commission alone levied fines totaling $1.6 billion.[1]

Two points follow from this discussion. First, it is clear that cartels happen. Firms do enter into collusive agreements to fix prices and avoid competition. Second, it is equally clear that such conspiracies are generally illegal. Both the antitrust laws of the

---

1 "Fixing for a fight." *The Economist*, April 20, 2002, p. 63.

## ANTITRUST DIVISION: SHERMAN ACT VIOLATIONS WITH A FINE OF $10 MILLION OR MORE

TABLE
14-1

| Defendant | Product | Year | Fine ($ million) | Geographic Scope |
|-----------|---------|------|------------------|------------------|
| F. Hoffman-LaRoche Ltd. | Vitamins | 1999 | $500 | International |
| BASF AG (1999) | Vitamins | 1999 | $225 | International |
| SGL Carbon AG | Graphite Electrodes | 1999 | $135 | International |
| UCAR International Inc. | Graphite Electrodes | 1998 | $110 | International |
| Archer Daniels Midland Co. | Lysine and Citric Acid | 1997 | $100 | International |
| Haarman & Reimer Corp. | Citric Acid | 1997 | $50 | International |
| HeereMac v.o.f. | Marine Construction | 1998 | $49 | International |
| Hoechst AG | Sorbates | 1998 | $36 | International |
| Showa Denko Carbon Inc. | Graphite Electrodes | 1998 | $32.5 | International |
| Fujisawa Pharmaceuticals Co. | Sodium Gluconate | 1998 | $20 | International |
| Dockwise N.V. | Marine Transportation | 1998 | $15 | International |
| Dyno Nobel | Explosives | 1996 | $15 | Domestic |
| F. Hoffman-LaRoche Ltd. | Citric Acid | 1997 | $14 | International |
| Eastman Chemical Co. | Sorbates | 1998 | $11 | International |
| Jungblunzlauer International | Citric Acid | 1997 | $11 | International |
| Lonza AG | Vitamins | 1998 | $10.5 | International |
| Akzo Nobel Chemicals BV & Glucona BV | Sodium Gluconate | 1997 | $10 | International |
| ICI Explosives | Explosives | 1996 | $10 | Domestic |
| Mrs. Bairds' Bakeries | Bread | 1996 | $10 | Domestic |
| Ajinomoto | Lysine | 1996 | $10 | International |
| Kyowa Hakko Kogyo Co. | Lysine | 1996 | $10 | International |

**Source:** U.S. Department of Justice, http://www.usdoj.gov/atr/public/press_releases/1999/2456.htm.

United States and the legal framework established in Articles 85 and 86 of Europe's Treaty of Rome makes explicit collusion illegal.[2] More importantly, government agencies can and sometimes do catch the culprits.

There must be some reason that firms choose to break the law and enter into collusive price-fixing arrangements, risking fines and, in some cases, even imprisonment. The motivation obviously is profit. Competing firms recognize that by limiting competition they may be able to replicate the monopoly outcome and together jointly earn the greatest possible profit in the industry. However, the record suggests that prior to the early 1990s, governments were not terribly concerned about such conspiracies. What possible arguments might be made that would justify such a view? Are there reasons to suspect that despite the profit incentive to collude the market also

2   Article 85 also makes implicit or *tacit* collusion illegal in that the Article prohibits "concerted practices" based upon a "concordance of wills." In this respect, European law would appear to go further than that in the United States but as we shall see when we consider problems of cartel detection, this difference is probably more apparent than real.

**FIGURE**

**14-1**

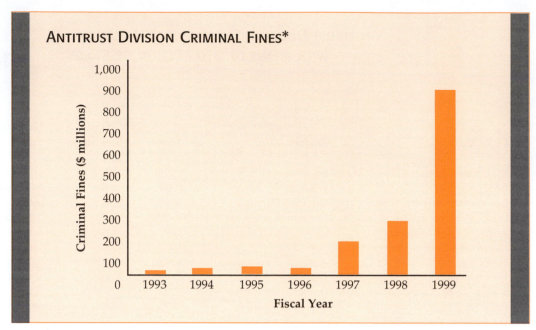

**ANTITRUST DIVISION CRIMINAL FINES\***

*Criminal Fines ($ millions)*

*Fiscal Year*

\* Data cover only part of 1999.
**Source:** U.S. Department of Justice, http://www.usdoj.gov/atr/public/press_releases/
1999/2456.htm.

provides a counter incentive that will block such collusion and maintain competition?
The answer is, at least in part, yes.

Collusive agreements cannot be enforced by written, legal contracts. As a result,
there is a real question as to how firms effectively enforce and execute any collusive
agreement that they make. If there is an incentive for any firm to cheat on the agreement, say to produce more than was agreed, or to offer customers a lower price than
the cartel price, there is no legal way to prevent such cheating. As we shall see, the
incentive to cheat may well be very strong. If it is, then the fact that the cartel agreement is not an enforceable, written agreement may make the collusion untenable. At
the same time, the absence of any written agreement also makes life a bit difficult for
the antitrust authorities. In the absence of such a document, existence of the crime is
harder to prove. In this chapter and the next we explore the balance between these
various forces—the incentive to form cartels, the temptation of cartel members to
cheat on the price-fixing agreement, and the ability of the antitrust authorities to detect and prosecute such collusion.

## 14.1 THE CHALLENGES FACING CARTELS

The motivation to form a cartel or collusive agreement to increase price is straightforward. The profit of a monopolist is the maximum profit the industry can earn. By
acting as one firm, the cartel members hope to achieve that profit as a group. Since
that is the maximum industry profit, it follows that there is some way to share that
profit so that all firms (though not consumers) are better off with the cartel than

# ✓ Reality Checkpoint

## School for Scandal—Bid Rigging by Suppliers to New York City Schools

On June 1, 2000, almost all of the companies that supply food to New York City's schoolchildren were charged in a bid-rigging scheme that overcharged the city at least $21 million for frozen goods and fresh produce. Twelve of the officials and six of the companies involved immediately pled guilty. Some of these defendants were also charged with rigging the bidding to supply schools in Newark as well. The defendants reportedly designated which of the companies would be the low bidder on several contracts with the New York Board of Education. The system of schools supervised by the Board services a student population of nearly 1.1 million and serves about 640,000 lunches and 150,000 breakfasts every day. The school board buys more food than any other single U.S. customer except the Defense Department. The conspirators allegedly agreed on prices to bid for supplying such standard items as french fries, meat, and fish sticks. One firm would be designated as the low bidder and all others would either refrain from bidding or submit intentionally high or complementary bids on the contracts. The cartel also allegedly paid potential suppliers not to bid competitively, including a payment of $100,000 to one produce company.

**Source:** A. Smith, "N.Y. Schools' Food Suppliers Accused of Bid-Rigging." *The Washington Post*, June 2, 2000, p. A8.

without it. However, the challenge firms face in forming a cartel and sustaining the price increase is equally clear. At the price set by the cartel, the price-cost margin facing each firm is especially large. In turn, this gives each individual firm a strong profit incentive to sell a little more output—to cheat on the agreement. Yet if every firm acts on this incentive and chisels on the agreement by selling a little more, the amount of extra output on the market will not be a little but a lot. Market price will fall and the price-fixing agreement breaks down.

Another factor that complicates price-fixing is the fear of discovery and legal prosecution. As previously noted, most antitrust law makes collusive behavior illegal. Indeed, in the United States, the courts have consistently refused to consider any mitigating circumstances that might justify collusion. That is, there is no defense. Such agreements are treated as a per se violation of the law,[3] and the firms that are party to the agreement face potentially heavy legal penalties.[4] As a result, any cartel-like agreements that firms make will necessarily have to be secret—covert as opposed to overt—so as to reduce the likelihood of being caught. Yet the more secretive the agreement is—the more hidden the firms' actions are—the more opportunities arise

---

3   See Chapter 1, pp. 7–14 for a brief history of earlier antitrust cases and a discussion of how price-fixing agreements have been viewed by the courts as per se violations of Section 1 of the Sherman Act and hence have been uniformly condemned.

4   Posner (1970) found that cartels were more active when the regulatory authorities were relatively lax in their enforcement of antitrust legislation.

for firms to cheat on the agreement and sell more output without being caught. This, of course, undermines the cartel still further.

Some international cartels such as OPEC are overt. Here, the members come from different countries, at least some of which have governments that support the cartel. The diamond cartel De Beers is another example in this regard. While such cartels violate the antitrust laws of the United States and other nations, prosecution of these international cartels is difficult because it requires that one country reach into the sovereign affairs of others. Nevertheless, even overt international cartels have to worry about members cheating or breaking the agreement. This is because there is no supranational authority to enforce the agreement. Here, too, the cartel is faced with the problem about how to implement its output restrictions. Indeed, stories of cheating and agreement breakdown have accompanied virtually all of the major cartels such as the electrical conspiracy of the 1950s, OPEC, and the NASDAQ pricing agreement (see Reality Checkpoint: Diamonds Are Forever, But What About a Diamond Cartel?). In order to understand how cartels might work, we need also to understand why they might not. That is, we need to know the source of any conflict between cartel members.[5]

A good place to begin is with the simple Cournot duopoly model that we introduced in Chapter 9. There we had two identical firms, each producing the same good and facing the same costs of production. To make matters concrete, let us suppose that the inverse market demand curve for this duopoly market is described by a specific linear function, $P = 150 - Q$, where $Q$ is total industry output and $Q = q_1 + q_2$, the sum of outputs produced by firms 1 and 2, respectively. We will assume as well that the marginal cost of production is the same for each firm and assumed to be constant at \$30.

When the firms act noncooperatively, each firm maximizes profit by choosing an output on its best response function. Given this demand function, we know that firm 1's best response function is $q_1^* = 60 - q_2/2$, and firm 2's best response function is $q_2^* = 60 - q_1/2$. From these best response functions it is easy to confirm that in a Nash equilibrium each firm chooses to produce an output level $q_1^* = q_2^* = 40$, which leads to an aggregate market output of $Q^C = 80$ and to a market-clearing price of $P^C = \$70$. In this Cournot–Nash equilibrium, each firm earns profit of $\pi_i^C = \$1,600$.

How would matters change if instead the firms cooperated with each other and formed a cartel? Ideally, the cartel would act like a pure monopolist. In this case, this means that the cartel would produce a joint output of $Q^M = 60$, with each firm producing a share $q_i^M = 30$. As a result, the market-clearing price would rise to $P^M = \$90$, from which it follows that the aggregate cartel or industry profit is $\pi^M = \$3,600$. Dividing this equally between the two firms gives each a profit of $\pi_i^M = \$1,800$, which is greater than the profit earned in the Cournot–Nash noncooperative outcome.

Cooperation obviously pays. Yet the cartel solution has one problem: cheating. We know this for one very simple reason. The cooperative output levels of $q_1 = q_2 = 30$ do not constitute a pair of best responses. That is, 30 is not firm 1's best response to firm 2's production of 30 and 30 is not firm 2's best response to firm 1's decision to produce this amount. If firm 1, for example, believed that firm 2 was going to stick to this agreement, then firm 1's best course of action would be to produce an output $q_1^d$ (where the superscript $d$ denotes defecting from the agreement) that is a best

---

5   A terrific guide to the intuition underlying the cartel problem and, indeed, behind all of game theory is
    Schelling (1960).

## ✓ Reality Checkpoint

### Diamonds Are Forever, but What About a Diamond Cartel?

In a seismic strategy shift announced in July 2000, the De Beers Consolidated Mines company decided to retreat from its 70-year-old practice of manipulating diamond prices by hoarding excess diamonds and keeping them off the market. Ever since the 1930s, De Beers has followed a simple rule that wherever excess diamonds existed, it would buy them. At one point, De Beers controlled 90 percent of the global diamond supply, sustaining an empire worth $20 billion. But during the 1990s new suppliers emerged, reducing De Beers share to 40 percent. First, the Russians dumped a vast amount on the market in order to raise money for their fledg-ling transition economy. Then the Australian firm BHP and the London-based firm Rio Tinto emerged as powerful competitors with newly discovered mines that pushed prices down further. De Beers found that keeping excess diamonds off the market required that it keep an expensive and ever-increasing inventory. As a result, the firm's profits and stock price sagged. The firm's new strategy is to sell off its excess inventory at a rate of about $1.5 billion per year, and to use the proceeds to fund a new advertising campaign that will be focused on luxury, processed diamond products.

**Source:** R. Ratnesar and P. Hawthorne, "A Gem of a New Strategy." *Time Magazine*, September 25, 2000, p. B18.

response to $q_2^M = 30$. From firm 1's best response function we can see that $q_1^d = 60 - q_2^M/2 = 45$. With firm 1 producing 45 and firm 2 producing 30, total output will then be $Q^d = 75$, which leads to a price of $P^d = \$75$. As a result, profit to firm 1 is now $\pi_1 = \$2,025$, noticeably higher than the $1,800 it earned by acting cooperatively. Thus, firm 1 has a real incentive to break the agreement. Of course, when it does, it drives down the profit at firm 2 to $\pi_2 = \$1,350$. But firm 1 did not go into business to make firm 2 rich. Firm 1's management cares only about firm 1's profit and if firm 2 is really going to produce 30 units, then firm 1's profit is maximized by firm 1 producing at 45.

Note that our initial, noncooperative Cournot–Nash solution $q_1^* = q_2^* = 40$ is a pair of best responses. Indeed, this is how we determined that equilibrium in the first place. In fact, for this case, the Cournot outcome is the only Nash equilibrium. This is made clear by the payoff matrix of Table 14-2. The unfortunate fact of life for the would-be colluding firms is that the collusive outcome $q_1 = q_2 = 30$ cannot be supported by any equilibrium strategies available to these firms. Each firm has a stronger profit incentive to defect or to cheat upon the cooperative agreement than to stick with it.[6]

---

6 Throughout this and succeeding chapters, we restrict our analysis to pure strategies. The reader should be aware, however, that the analysis can be extended, with qualifications, to include mixed strategies. See, for example, Harsanyi (1973).

## PAYOFFS TO COOPERATION (*M*) AND DEFECTION (*D*) IN THE DUOPOLY GAME ($ THOUSAND)

|  |  | Strategy for Firm 2 | |
|---|---|---|---|
|  |  | Cooperate (*M*) | Defect (*D*) |
| Strategy for Firm 1 | Cooperate (*M*) | ($1.8, $1.8) | ($1.35, $2.025) |
|  | Defect (*D*) | ($2.025, $1.35) | ($1.6, $1.6) |

The game we have just described and illustrated in Table 14-2 is a specific example of many games in which players share possibilities for mutual gain as well as for conflict of interest. Such games are often referred to as "prisoners' dilemma" games because one of the earliest illustrations of this case involved dealings between a prosecutor and two suspects. (See Practice Problem 14.1.) Each firm has a mutual interest in cooperating and achieving the monopoly outcome. However, there is also a conflict in that if one firm cooperates and sticks to the agreement, then the other firm can do much better for itself (in terms of profit) by deviating from the cooperative agreement and producing more output. In deciding whether to cooperate, each of our two firms must take this conflict of interest into account. In so doing, each may reason as follows: "If I cooperate and the other firm cooperates, then we share monopoly profit. However, if the other firm does not cooperate, then I lose a lot of profit, and in fact I am worse off than if we played Cournot–Nash. If, on the other hand, I don't cooperate and the other firm does, then I make a lot of money, more than one-half the monopoly profit; if the other firm does not cooperate, then it's as if we were playing Cournot. No matter what the other firm does, I am better off not cooperating."

If both firms follow the logic just described, we will not observe cooperation. Such is the prisoners' dilemma. Together, both firms are worse off not cooperating than if they cooperate. Individually, however, each firm gains by not cooperating. Unless there is some way to overcome this conflict, antitrust policy need not be terribly worried about cartels because they will not happen.

## Practice Problem 14.1

Jacoby and Myers are two attorneys suspected of mail fraud in the small principality of Zenda. In an effort to obtain a confession, Detective Chief Inspector Morse has had the two suspects brought in and subjected to separate questioning. Each is given the following options: (1) Confess (and implicate the other), or (2) Do Not Confess. Morse indicates to each suspect that if only one suspect confesses, that one will be released in return for providing evidence against the other and will spend no time in jail. The one not confessing in this case will "have the book thrown at them" and do ten years. If both confess, Morse indicates that he will be a bit more lenient and each will spend six years behind bars. When asked what will happen if neither confesses, Morse responds that he will find some small charge that he knows will stick, so that, in this case, each will do at least one year.

Using Confess and Do Not Confess as the possible actions of either Jacoby or Myers, derive the payoff matrix and Nash equilibrium for the game between these prisoners of Zenda.

As the introduction to this chapter makes abundantly clear, cartels do happen. The evidence is compelling that collusive agreements are not uncommon and firms do pursue cooperative strategies. This implies that the prisoners' dilemma argument must not be the full story. There must be some way that firms can escape that logic and create incentives that will sustain cartel agreements among them.

In the last twenty years, economists have come to understand that there is a way around the logic of the prisoners' dilemma. As it turns out, though, surmounting that conflict requires that firms look at their strategic interaction from a somewhat different perspective than that postulated in the static Cournot-type model. In particular, what we need to do is to move from a single-period framework in which the colluding firms interact only once to a dynamic one in which the strategic interaction is repeated over time. This, of course, is a quite reasonable change. The firms considering the formation of a cartel are very likely to have been competing with each other for some time—otherwise how did they meet in the first place? More importantly, they are likely to believe that their market interactions will continue or repeat for some time into the future. However, the change from one period of interaction to many is more than just plausible. It fundamentally alters the incentives firms have to defect on collusive agreements. As we shall see, when market interaction is repeated over and over again it is possible for the firms that are party to a collusive agreement to reward "good" behavior by sticking with the agreement, and to punish "bad" behavior by guaranteeing a breakdown of the cartel.

In order to work out a strategy for games that are played over time, we need to analyze what economists call a repeated game. Repeated games are dynamic games in which a simultaneous market interaction is repeated in each stage of the dynamic game. By moving from one period to many, we are changing the rules of the game. Thus the appropriate strategies also change. How and why the firms' strategic choices change in the dynamic setting of repeated games is the subject matter of the next section.

## 14.2 FINITELY REPEATED GAMES

Let's return to the game of Table 14-2. As we showed, collusion between the two firms to produce the monopoly output is unsustainable in that it is not a Nash equilibrium. Now, though, suppose that firm 2 thinks forward a bit, knowing that its interactions with firm 1 are going to occur several, perhaps many, times. Then firm 2's calculations may go very differently. Firm 2 might calculate as follows: "If I cheat on the cartel my profits go up to $2,025 and I gain a one-time increase in profits of

$225. However, firm 1 will then punish me for cheating by reverting to the noncooperative, Cournot equilibrium in which I earn only $1,600 in profits per period. So, after the one-period gain, I will earn $200 less per period than if I had not cheated in the first place. Is it worth my while to cheat?"

The foregoing reasoning suggests that if firm 2's horizon is sufficiently long and if firm 2 does not discount the future too heavily, then contrary to our earlier analysis, firm 2 may decide not to leave the cartel. The short, one-period gain of $225 may be offset by the subsequent loss of $200 every period thereafter. Whether this is in fact the case—whether firm 2's calculations are fully reasonable—remains to be seen. Nevertheless, one can see that moving our setting from that of a static one-period game to that of a repeated game may alter a firm's thinking in a manner that dramatically raises the profitability of cooperative, cartel behavior.

The reason that a repeated game framework makes successful collusion more likely is that when the market interaction among firms extends over a number of periods, there is the real possibility that cartel members are able to retaliate against defectors. Because potential defectors will rationally anticipate such retaliation, that punishment can act as a deterrent—stopping the noncooperative behavior before it starts.

The formal description of a strategy for a repeated game is quite complicated. The main source of the increased complexity is that current and future actions are now conditional on past actions. That is, a firm's actions today depend critically on what has happened in previous plays of the game. To get some idea of how rapidly the complexity grows, consider the simple Cournot game that we described in Table 14-2. Suppose that this game, which we will call the stage game, is played three times in succession. At the end of the first round there are four possible outcomes, that is, four possible histories after one play of the game. At the end of the second round, we have sixteen possible historic sequences—four second-round outcomes for each of the first-round results. By the third round, sixty-four sequences of play, or game histories, are possible—and this assumes that there are only two players with two possible actions to take in each round. Since, formally speaking, a strategy must define how a player acts at each round of play depending on the precise history of the game to that point, the complexity introduced by considering repeated games is formidable.

There are, fortunately, a few mental shortcuts available to us. The critical concept in this regard is a familiar one, that of Nash equilibrium. From our work in previous chapters, we know that resolving the outcome of any game requires identifying the game's Nash equilibrium (or equilibria). The same holds true in repeated games. It is possible to identify the Nash equilibrium or equilibria for a repeated game relatively quickly if one keeps a few key principles clearly in mind. We can best illustrate these principles by working through some examples. We first develop two examples that demonstrate what we hinted at in the foregoing discussion—that the equilibrium of a repeated game can be very different from that of the same game played only once. Later we will show how the principles we develop can be used to understand how price-fixing could be arranged in the NASDAQ market.

## EXAMPLE 1: THE SIMPLE COURNOT GAME

This is just the example of Table 14-2, but now with the possibility that the interaction between the two firms is going to be repeated. The payoff matrix is repeated for convenience as Table 14-3.

### PAYOFFS TO COOPERATION (*M*) AND DEFECTION (*D*) IN THE DUOPOLY GAME ($ THOUSAND)

TABLE
**14-3**

| | | Strategy for Firm 2 | |
|---|---|---|---|
| | | Cooperate (*M*) | Defect (*D*) |
| Strategy for Firm 1 | Cooperate (*M*) | ($1.8, $1.8) | ($1.35, $2.025) |
| | Defect (*D*) | ($2.025, $1.35) | ($1.6, $1.6) |

## EXAMPLE 2: A BERTRAND DUOPOLY GAME

Suppose that there are two vitamin producers who sell differentiated products. They compete in prices and, for marketing reasons, know that they can each set a price per unit of $105, $130, or $160. The resulting payoffs are given in Table 14-4.

### PAYOFFS IN A DIFFERENTIATED PRODUCT BERTRAND GAME ($ THOUSAND)

TABLE
**14-4**

| | | Strategy for Firm 2 | | |
|---|---|---|---|---|
| | | $105 | $130 | $160 |
| Strategy for Firm 1 | $105 | ($7.3125, $7.3125) | ($8.25, $7.25) | ($9.375, $5.525) |
| | $130 | ($7.25, $8.25) | ($8.5, $8.5) | ($10, $7.15) |
| | $160 | ($5.525, $9.375) | ($7.15, $10) | ($9.1, $9.1) |

Tables 14-3 and 14-4 are all that we need to find the Nash equilibrium to each game if it is played only once. In each payoff matrix a shaded box indicates an equilibrium outcome. This is often referred to as the "one-shot" equilibrium. Example 1 has a unique one-shot equilibrium. In example 2, by contrast, there are two one-shot Nash equilibria. You may wish to check Example 2 to see that the actions of each firm corresponding to a shaded box do indeed constitute a pair of best responses for the one-shot game.

Our interest is to see what happens in each of these examples when the firms interact with each other over and over again. We shall show that the number of times they interact is of critical importance. In fact, the key factor is whether the interaction is repeated over a finite (though perhaps large) number of periods or whether it goes on indefinitely. We call the latter an infinitely repeated game. Therefore, we will separate repeated games into two classes: (1) those in which the number of repetitions is finite and known to the potentially colluding firms, and (2) those in which the number of repetitions is infinite. In the next section, we focus on infinitely repeated games. Here we examine games with a known finite horizon.

When is it reasonable to assume that the number of times that the firms interact is finite and known to both firms? At least three situations come to mind. First, it may be that the firms exploit an exhaustible and nonrenewable resource such as oil or natural gas. Clearly, this interaction will end (and be foreseen to end) as the reserves dwindle. Secondly, the firms might operate in a market with proprietary knowledge protected by patents, such as the pharmaceutical market. All patents are awarded for a finite period—in the United States, the duration is twenty years dated from the filing of the application. Once the patent expires the product or process to which it applies can be copied without penalty. As a result, a market protected from entry suddenly becomes competitive. For example, as the patents on serotonin-based antidepressants Prozac, Zoloft, and Paxil have expired, the manufacturers of these drugs have foreseen a potentially large increase in the number of competitors in this market. If this threat materializes, it will end the market interaction of the original three firms as it had prevailed for the previous fifteen years. Finally, while we conventionally equate the players in the game with firms, the truth is that it is ultimately individuals who make the output or price decisions. The same management teams can be expected to be around for only a finite number of years. When there is a major change in management at one or more of the firms the game ends. Often, say as in the case of an upcoming retirement, this end can again be foreseen.

It turns out that what happens in a one-shot or single stage game gives us a good clue to what is likely to happen in a repeated game when the number of repetitions is finite. After all, a one-period game is just one that is very finite. So, in this spirit, let us make a simple experiment. Let us consider a simple extension of the Cournot game in Example 1 from one period to two and determine what the equilibrium will be in this limited but nonetheless repeated setting.[7] When we do this we find that the two-period repeated game will have the same outcome in each round as the one-shot game. To see why, consider the following alternative strategy for firm 1:

First play:    Cooperate

Second play:  Cooperate if firm 2 cooperated in the first play, otherwise choose noncooperation.

The idea behind this strategy is clear enough. Start off on a friendly footing by giving firm 2 a chance to show its willingness to cooperate. If firm 2 does indeed cooperate, then in the second round firm 1 promises to continue to take the cooperative action. However, should firm 2 fail to reciprocate firm 1's initial cooperation then in the second round firm 1 will "take the gloves off" and fight back.

---

7  Even though the game lasts for two market periods we will keep things simple and assume that profits in the second period are not discounted. In other words we will assume that the discount factor $R = 1$ or, equivalently, the interest rate $r = 0\%$. See the discussion of discounting in Chapter 2.

The problem with this strategy is that it suffers from the same basic credibility problem that afflicted many of the predatory threats that we discussed in Chapters 12 and 13. To see why this strategy lacks credibility suppose that firm 2 does choose to cooperate in the first round. Now think of firm 2's position at the start of its second and last interaction with firm 1. The history of play to that point is one in which both firms adopted cooperative behavior in the first round and both earned a profit of $1,800. Further, firm 2 has a promise from firm 1 that, because firm 2 cooperated in the first round, firm 1 will continue to do so in the second. However, this promise is worthless. When firm 2 looks over the payoff matrix for the last round, it cannot fail to note that—regardless of firm 1's promise—the dominant strategy for firm 1 in the last round is not to cooperate. True, this would violate the cooperation promised in firm 1's strategy. But there is nothing firm 2 can subsequently do to punish firm 1 for breaking its promise. There is no third round in which to implement such punishment. Firm 2 should anticipate then that firm 1 will adopt the noncooperative behavior in the last round.

Firm 2 has just discovered that any strategy for firm 1 that involves playing the cooperative strategy in the second and final round is not credible, that is, it is not subgame perfect. Again, the wording derives from the fact that we may isolate part of the complete game and focus on that part as a smaller version, or subgame, of the complete one. In the case at hand, the second or last period of the two-period game is the subgame, and, as we have just seen, a strategy that calls for firm 1 to cooperate in this last period cannot be part of a Nash equilibrium in that period. Hence, cooperation in the second round is not subgame perfect. However, the jargon is less important than the idea. What you should understand at this point is that, from firm 2's perspective, no promise from firm 1 to cooperate in the final round is believable. No matter what has transpired in the first round, firm 1 can be counted upon to adopt noncooperative behavior in the final period of play. Of course, the same is true viewed from firm 1's perspective. Firm 2's dominant strategy in the last round is likewise not to cooperate. In short, both firms realize that the only rational outcome in the second round is the noncooperative equilibrium in which each earns a profit of $1,600.

The fact that we have identified the equilibrium in the final round may seem like only a small part of the solution that we were originally seeking—especially if the game has 10 or 100 rounds instead of just 2. However, as you may recall from the chain store paradox in Chapter 11, the outcome for the terminal round can directly lead to a solution for the entire game. Consider again our two-period repeated game. Ignoring for the moment the second round, firm 1 reasons that firm 2's dominant first-round strategy is not to cooperate. The only hope that firm 1 has of dissuading firm 2 from such noncooperative action is to promise cooperation in the future if firm 2 cooperates today. Yet such a promise is not credible. No matter how passionately firm 1 promises to cooperate tomorrow in return for cooperation today, firm 2 will recognize that when tomorrow actually comes, firm 1 will not cooperate. It follows that the only hope firm 1 had of dissuading firm 2 from noncooperative action in the first round is gone.

As always, symmetry implies the same holds true for any hope firm 2 had of inducing cooperation from firm 1. Hence, we have identified the complete equilibrium for the entire game. Both firms adopt strategies that call for noncooperative behavior in both period one and period two. In other words, running the game for two periods produces outcomes identical to that observed by playing it as a one-period game.

# Practice Problem 14.2

Consider our first example but now assume that the interaction between the firms extends to three periods. What will be the outcome in the final period? What does this imply about the incentive to cooperate in period two? If both firms believe that there will be no cooperation in either period two or period three, will either cooperate in period one?

We have identified the equilibrium for our first example when the game is played for two periods. However, as Practice Problem 14.2 illustrates, our analysis also points to a solution for the game whether it is played two, three, or any finite number of periods, $T$. In all such cases, no strategy that calls for cooperation in the final period is subgame perfect. Therefore, no such strategy can be part of the final equilibrium. In the last period, each firm always chooses not to cooperate regardless of the history of the game to that point. But this means that the same noncooperative behavior must also characterize the penultimate, or $T-1$, period. The only possible gain that might induce either firm 1 or firm 2 to cooperate in period $T-1$ is the credible promise of continued cooperation from its rival in the future. Since such a promise is not credible, both firms adopt noncooperative behavior in both period $T-1$ and period $T$. In other words, any strategy that calls for cooperative behavior in either of the last two periods can also be ruled out as part of the final equilibrium. An immediate implication is that a three-period game must be one in which the players simply repeat the one-shot Nash equilibrium three times.

We can reiterate this logic for larger and larger values of $T$. The outcome will always be the same Nash equilibrium as in our first example no matter how many times it is played, so long as that number is finite and known. The one-shot Nash equilibrium is just repeated $T$ times, as each firm takes noncooperative action in every period.

This is by no means a special case. Rather, the foregoing analysis is an example of a general theorem first proved by Nobel prize winner Reinhard Selten (1973).

> **Selten's Theorem:** If a game with a unique equilibrium is played finitely many times, its solution is that equilibrium played each and every time. Finitely repeated play of a unique Nash equilibrium is the Nash equilibrium of the repeated game.[8]

We suggested earlier that introducing repetition into our game theoretic framework adds history as an element of the analysis. When players face each other over and over again, they can adopt strategies that base today's action on the behavior of their rivals in previous periods. This is what rewards and punishments are all about. What Selten's theorem demonstrates is that history really does not play a role in a finitely repeated game whose one-shot or single stage game has a unique Nash equilibrium. In that setting, history and rewards and punishments still play no role.

An obvious implication of Selten's theorem is that cooperative or cartel-like behavior is difficult for firms to achieve in a finitely repeated number of interactions. No collusive agreement can be enforced by law because it is not a legal contract. Yet if

---

8    A formal proof can be found in Eichberger (1993).

the game is finite and has a unique one-period equilibrium, no promise of coopera-tion or threat of punishment will work to enforce the agreement, either.

Again, however, we know that effective collusion does occur in the real world. So, there must be some way to escape the logic of Selten's theorem. In fact, the way out is suggested by the two qualifications stated in the theorem itself. First, the theorem applies only when the one-shot or single stage game has a unique Nash equilibrium. Second, and perhaps more importantly, we have so far limited our analysis to finitely repeated games in which the firms understand exactly when their interaction together will end. If firms think that their interactions might be repeated over and over, indef-initely, the outcome could be quite different.

To illustrate what happens if the game has more than one Nash equilibrium con-sider now our second example (Table 14-4). This game has three important features. First, there are two equilibria to the one-shot game, ($105, $105) and ($130, $130). Second, both firms agree that the second equilibrium is "good" and the first is "bad," or at least not as good. Third, the firms would each do much better than they do in either equilibrium if they could each agree to set a price of $160. The problem is, of course, that any such agreement is likely to break down since ($160, $160) is not a Nash equilibrium if this game is played once.

Suppose, however, that once again the firms expect to interact twice.[9] We can show that repeated play over two periods will, in this case, permit a new equilibrium outcome not found in the one-shot version of the game. In the new equilibrium each firm agrees to charge a price of $160 in the first period and $130 in the second pe-riod. In other words, the firms cooperate in the first period and then move to the su-perior of the two one-shot Nash equilibria in the second or final period. One strat-egy that supports this outcome goes as follows:

First period:      Set price equal to $160.

Second period:   If the history from the first period is ($160, $160), then set price of $130; otherwise set price of $105.

Note that this strategy reflects historical dependence. A firm's second-period choice of price is directly dependent on the history of play up to that point in time. With each firm playing this strategy, the equilibrium path is ($160, $160), then ($130, $130).

To show that this is indeed a Nash subgame perfect equilibrium, we need to show that the strategy illustrated for each firm is the best response to the strategy of the other firm. This is easy for the final period, which is a subgame that is just a one-shot game. Each firm sets a price of $130 and we know that this is a Nash equilibrium of the one-shot game. Hence, neither firm has an action that will improve its fortunes in the last period. But what about the firms' actions in the first period? Why doesn't one firm, say firm 2, set a price of $130 in period one and raise its profit from $9.1 million to $10 million? After all, firm 2 anticipates that firm 1 will set a price of $160 in that period and $130 is firm 2's best response to a price of $160 set by firm 1.

The answer to this question lies in the fact that firm 2 knows that the strategy firm 1 has adopted is the one that we have laid out above, namely, one that has a credible second-period punishment for bad first-period behavior. If firm 2 sets a price of $130 in period one, the history going into period 2 will be ($160, $130), and this will lead

---

9   Again, we will keep things simple and assume that profits in the second period are not discounted, or that the discount factor $R = 1$ or, equivalently, the interest rate $r = 0\%$.

firm 1 to set a price of $105 in period two. If that happens, the best response for firm 2 in the last period is also to set a price of $105. Moreover, firm 1's promise to charge the price $105 is credible because ($105, $105) is a Nash equilibrium to the final period game.

In short, if firm 2 undercuts the cooperative price in period 1 it can expect to suffer a loss of profit in period 2 because cheating in period 1 leads to the "bad" Nash equilibrium in period 2. The increase in profit in period 1 from cheating is $0.9 million, which is less than the decrease in profit, equal to $1.1875 million, that firm 2 suffers in the punishment strategy. In other words, the total profit from cheating is equal to $10 + $7.3125 = $17.3125, which is less than the total profit from cooperating, $9.1 + $8.5 = $17.6.[10] Undercutting the cartel's agreed price in period 1 does not pay. Once again, we can use the symmetry argument to show that firm 1 likewise has an incentive to cooperate in the first round. Hence, the strategies we have outlined do indeed constitute a pair of best responses. Moreover, because they are based upon threats or promises that are Nash equilibria of the one-shot game, these strategies also constitute a subgame perfect equilibrium.

We can extend this analysis in two ways. First, we can consider what happens when the number of repetitions is greater than 2. The game or market interaction could be repeated three or four or even $T$ times, again we will assume with no discounting. In the final period both firms will play the "good" Nash equilibrium so long as the cartel has held together up to that point. We know that the "good" Nash outcome in the last period can support cooperation in the second-last period. Thus, when we add a third period of play, or a fourth, on up to a $T$th, there will always be an incentive to cooperate and achieve the ($160, $160) outcome in every period except the last. The credible threat of collapsing to the "bad" Nash equilibrium in any of these periods and every period thereafter if anyone cheats on the cartel agreement works to maintain this outcome. Whatever the finite number of repetitions, cooperation can be sustained in each period until the last one, at which point the two firms revert to the "good" Nash equilibrium.

## Practice Problem 14.3

Confirm that the following strategy is a Nash subgame perfect equilibrium strategy to the game in example 2 when the firms interact 5 times, or $T = 5$.

| | |
|---|---|
| For period $T = 1$: | Set price of $160. |
| For any period $1 < t < T$: | Set price of $160 if the history through period $t − 1$ has been ($160, $160), otherwise set price of $105 in this and all subsequent periods. |
| For period $T$: | Set price of $130 if the history through period $T − 1$ has been ($160, $160), otherwise set price of $105. |

There is, however, a second modification to our Bertrand game that could undo the achievement of the cooperative outcome just described. This modification involves discounting future profits as discussed in Chapter 2. If the interest rate is

---

10 Recall that we are assuming here that second-period profits are not discounted.

nonzero then the discount factor $R$ is less than one. Hence, the future rewards to co-operation will be discounted by firms. Let's see how this affects the game when it is repeated twice. Now the reward to firm 2, for example, of setting a price of $160 in the first period is somewhat diminished in present value terms. Yes, pricing at $160 in the first period guarantees the "good" Nash equilibrium in the second period, but the present value of firm 2's profits from sticking to the cartel agreement in period 1 is now

$$PV_2^c (\pi_2) = \$9.1 + \$8.5R,$$

whereas the present value of firm 2's profits from undercutting the agreed price in the first period is

$$PV_2^d (\pi_2) = \$10 + \$7.3125R.$$

For the cartel agreement to hold in period 1 it is necessary that $PV_2^c (\pi_2) > PV_2^d (\pi_2)$, which requires that the discount factor $R$ be greater than 0.756, equivalent to an interest rate $r$ of less than 32 percent. In other words, with a sufficiently high interest rate $r$ (or, alternatively, a sufficiently low discount factor $R$), defecting from the cartel agreement in period one becomes attractive.

The foregoing is in fact a general point. As the interest rate rises above zero (as the discount factor falls below 1), limits to the sustainability of cooperative behavior emerge. However, in the Bertrand game above, these limits become weaker as we lengthen the number of repetitions. Suppose, for example, that the firms discount the future sufficiently heavily such that $R < 0.756$. However, let us also suppose that the interaction takes place over three periods rather than just two. Now consider the following strategy for each firm:

First period: Set price of $160.

Second period: Set price of $160 if the history from the first period is ($160, $160), otherwise set price of $105 in this and all subsequent periods.

Third period: Set price of $130 if the history through periods 1 and 2 has been ($160, $160), otherwise set price of $105.

The present value of firm 2's profits from sticking to the cooperative strategy in period 1 is now

$$PV_3^c (\pi_2) = \$9.1 + \$9.1R + \$8.5R^2,$$

while the present value of firm 2's profits from undercutting the cartel agreement in period 1 is[11]

$$PV_3^d (\pi_2) = \$10 + \$7.3125R + \$7.3125R^2.$$

It is straightforward to show that $PV_3^c (\pi_2) > PV_3^d (\pi_2)$, provided that the discount factor $R$ is greater than 0.398, that is, for any interest rate less than 150 percent. So, this is a sustainable equilibrium strategy.

---

11 Note that since the strategy we have outlined requires that a Nash equilibrium be played in the second and third periods, there is no incentive for firm 2 to deviate from the announced strategy in period 2.

Let's take a moment away from the math to clarify the main lesson of our recent examples. When the one-shot Nash equilibrium is not unique, repetition of the game may permit the firms to formulate a credible strategy that leads to a stable cartel for at least part of the time even when the number of repetitions is finite. In fact, Benoit and Krishna (1985) have shown that this outcome becomes a certainty provided the number of times $T$ that the game is played is "sufficiently high" and the discount factor $R$ is "sufficiently close to unity." Multiplicity of Nash equilibria sets up the possibility of rewarding cooperation and punishing defection in a way that is not possible when the Nash equilibrium is unique. It does so because the punishments and rewards are now credible. It is the presence of just such a credible threat that is essential to the maintenance of any successful cartel. Without a credible threat of retaliation, there is no way to deter cheating behavior. This insight will also be crucial in the analysis of infinitely repeated games—the topic of the next section.

## 14.3 REPEATED GAMES WITH AN INFINITE HORIZON

We have shown that collusion can be sustained for part of the time in a finitely repeated setting but not right through to the very end. At the end there is no next period, and everyone knows it. In that period there is no credible promise of future punishment or reward that can induce firms to cooperate because, at that point, all the players understand that there is no future.

For certain situations the assumption of finite repetition makes a great deal of sense. However, for others it does not. Generally speaking, firms should be regarded as having an infinite or, more precisely, an indefinite life. General Motors may not last forever but nobody inside or outside the giant automaker works on the assumption that there is some known date $T$ periods from now at which it will cease to exist. We do best if we treat General Motors and other firms as if they will continue indefinitely. Moreover, even when a game is finite, our assumption that everyone knows the final period with certainty is probably far too strong. The more likely situation is that after any given period, the players see some positive probability that the game will continue one more round. So, while firms may understand that the game will not last forever, they cannot look ahead to any particular period as the last.

So long as the probability of continuing into another round of play is positive, there is, probabilistically speaking, some reason to hope that the next round will be played cooperatively and, therefore, some reason to cooperate in the present. Whether that motivation is sufficiently strong to overcome the short-run gains of defection (or can be made to be so by means of some reward-and-punishment strategy) will depend on certain key factors that we discuss below. We may anticipate our results, however, by stating that once we permit the possibility that the strategic interaction will continue indefinitely, the possibility of successful collusion becomes a good bit more real.

Before turning to the formal analysis of infinitely repeated periods we must first consider how a firm might discount a profit stream of indefinite duration. The answer is simply that it will apply the discount factor $R$ to the expected cash flow in any period. Suppose, for example, that a firm knows that its profits are going to be $\pi_0$ this period and, if the game continues to period 1, $\pi_1$ in that period, if it reaches period 2, it will earn $\pi_2$ in that period, and so on. Suppose that the firm also knows that in each period there is a probability $\rho$ that the market interaction will continue into the next period. Then the probability of reaching period 1 is $\rho$, the probability of reaching period 2 is $\rho^2$, of reaching period 3 is $\rho^3$, . . . of reaching period $t$ is $\rho^t$, and so on. Accordingly, the profit stream that the firm actually expects to receive in period $t$ is $\rho^t \pi_t$.

Now assume that the firm's discount factor is $R$. Then the expected present value of this profit stream is given by

$$PV(\pi_t) = \pi_0 + R\rho\pi_1 + R^2\rho^2\pi_2 + R^3\rho^3\pi_3 + \ldots + R^t\rho^t\pi_t + \ldots . \quad \textbf{(14.1)}$$

You should notice that this equation is very similar to those we presented in Chapter 2 when discussing the concept of discounting. The factor $R$ is now simply replaced by the factor $\rho R$ raised to the appropriate power. We might think of it as a "probability-adjusted" discount factor $\rho R$. It is the product of the discount factor reflecting the interest rate and the belief the firm holds regarding the probability that the market will continue to operate from period to period.

At first sight, consideration of games that are infinite or indefinitely repeated (often referred to as supergames) may seem hopeless. Repetition allows history to figure in strategy making, and with infinitely repeated play the number of possible histories also becomes infinite. Once again, however, we have a shortcut available to us. It turns out that the actual strategies on which firms rely to secure compliance with cartel policy can be made remarkably simple. The type of strategy that will work is called a *trigger strategy*. The idea is similar to the approach used in the Bertrand game of the previous section. A player will play the cooperative action upon which the players have agreed as long as the other players have always stuck to the agreement. However, if another player should deviate from the agreement then the player will play the punishment action.

To see how this might work, consider Example 1 and suppose that both firms expect in each period that there is a probability $\rho$ that their interaction will continue into the next period. A trigger strategy for firm 1 could be as follows:

Period 1:   Produce the cooperative output of 30.

Period $t$:   Produce the output of 30 in period $t$ provided that firm 2 has also produced an output of 30 in every previous period. If firm 2 produces more than 30 in any period then produce 40 in the period immediately following firm 2's violation AND in every subsequent period.

It should be clear why strategies of this type are called trigger strategies. Firm 1's move to increase its output is triggered by a deviation from the agreement by firm 2. The promise or threat to make this move, that is, to punish firm 2, is credible because it simply requires that firm 1 move to the noncooperative Nash equilibrium.

To see that the adoption of this trigger strategy by both firms can work to achieve an equilibrium that is different from the one-shot noncooperative Nash equilibrium, consider again Example 1. Assume that at the beginning of the game both firms announce the trigger strategy just described. Now consider a possible deviation from the agreement by firm 2 in any given period $t$. We already understand the temptation to do so. If firm 1 continues to produce 30, then firm 2 can raise its profit to $2,025 by increasing its output to 45.

However, that gain lasts for only one period, given that firm 1 has adopted the trigger strategy. In the next period following firm 2's aggression, firm 1 retaliates and produces an output of 40 for every period thereafter. Since firm 2's best response is to match that production, the result of its initial defection is that the one period profit of \$2,025 is followed by an endless number of periods in which its profit is only \$1,600. This represents a real cost to firm 2 since, had it not broken the agreement, it could have enjoyed its share of the cartel profit, \$1,800 indefinitely. In short, firm 1's adoption of the trigger strategy means that firm 2 realizes both a gain and a loss if it breaks the cartel agreement. The gain is an immediate, but only one-period, rise in profit from \$1,800 to \$2,025. The loss is a delayed, but permanent, fall in profit from \$1,800 to \$1,600 in every period that the game continues thereafter.

The only way to compare the gain with the loss is in terms of present values. The present value of profits from sticking to the agreement is[12]

$$PV_\infty^M(1.8) = 1.8 + 1.8\rho R + 1.8\rho^2 R^2 + 1.8\rho^3 R^3 + \frac{1.8}{(1 - \rho R)}. \qquad (14.2)$$

The present value of firm 2's profit if it deviates is

$$PV_\infty^D = 2.025 + 1.6\rho R + 1.6\rho^2 R^2 + 1.6\rho^3 R^3 + \ldots$$

$$= 2.025 + 1.6\rho R(1 + \rho R + \rho^2 R^2 + \rho^3 R^3 + \ldots) \qquad (14.3)$$

$$= 2.025 + \frac{1.6\rho R}{(1 - \rho R)}.$$

Sticking to the cartel agreement pays if $PV_\infty^M > PV_\infty^D$. From the last two equations, this requires

$$\frac{1.8}{(1 - \rho R)} > 2.025 + \frac{1.6\rho R}{(1 - \rho R)}. \qquad (14.4)$$

If we multiply both sides by $(1 - \rho R)$ and then solve for the value of $\rho R$ that is required so that deviation does not pay, we obtain a value of

$$1.8 > 2.025(1 - \rho R) + 1.6\rho R \Rightarrow (2.025 - 1.6)\rho R > 2.025 - 1.8$$

$$\Rightarrow \rho R > \frac{2.025 - 1.8}{2.025 - 1.6} = 0.529. \qquad (14.5)$$

In other words, so long as the probability-adjusted discount factor is greater than or equal to 0.529, firm 2 recognizes that it does not pay to deviate from the cartel agreement. Of course, the same is true for firm 1. Hence, for $\rho R > 0.529$, the cartel is sustainable indefinitely. Note that we never observe firms "pulling the trigger." Each firm produces 30, one-half the monopoly output ad infinitum.

To get some feel for the numerical magnitudes involved, suppose that both firms believe that their interaction will always be repeated with certainty, so that $\rho = 1$. Then this probability-adjusted discount factor corresponds to a pure discount factor of $R = 0.529$. That is, if $\rho = 1$, firm 2 will not deviate so long as the money rate of interest $r$ does not exceed 89 percent. Now suppose instead that both firms attribute only a 60 percent probability that their interaction lasts from one period to the next,

---

12 We are using the equation for the sum of an infinite series: $1 + \rho R + \rho^2 R^2 + \rho^3 R^3 + \ldots = 1/(1 - \rho R)$.

that is, $\rho = 0.6$. For the trigger strategy to sustain the cartel agreement now, it is necessary that the pure discount factor $R > 0.529/0.6 = 0.882$. That is, successful collusion now requires that the interest rate $r$ does not exceed 14.4 percent, which is a much more restrictive requirement. This example points to a general result. If a cartel is more sustainable over an indefinite horizon, the greater is the probability that the firms will continue to be in the market together and the lower is the interest rate.

Indeed, the example just worked out is a particular case of a more general result, which goes as follows. Suppose we have a group of firms that wish to form a cartel. If each firm cooperates and produces in a market period the cartel share of output then each firm $i$ earns profit $\pi_i^M$. If in a period firm $i$ alone cheats on the agreement then the highest profit it can earn is $\pi_i^D$. Finally, call the profit that each firm $i$ makes in the noncooperative Nash equilibrium $\pi_i^N$. A little reflection will make clear that $\pi_i^D > \pi_i^M > \pi_i^N$. (In Example 1 we have $\pi_i^D = \$2,025$, $\pi_i^M = \$1,800$ and $\pi_i^N = \$1,600$.) The general result is that cheating on the cartel does not pay provided that the probability-adjusted discount factor $\rho R$ is such that

$$\rho R > \frac{\pi_i^D - \pi_i^M}{\pi_i^D - \pi_i^N}. \tag{14.6}$$

Of course, we have so far cast our discussion of infinitely repeated games in the context of Example 1 in which there is a unique Nash equilibrium to the one-shot game. You may be wondering what happens in an infinitely repeated game to cases such as Example 2 in which there is more than one Nash equilibrium to the one-shot game. The answer is that the same basic principle applies but that now we can describe at least two trigger strategies. Firm 2, for example, could adopt either the strategy:

Period 1:   Set price of $160.

Period $t$:   Set price of $160 in period $t$ provided that firm 1 has also priced at $160 in all previous periods. If firm 1 has ever deviated from the price $160 then in the period following firm 1's deviation set price of $130 and set price of $130 in all subsequent periods.

or:

Period 1:   Set price of $160.

Period $t$:   Set price of $160 in period $t$ provided that firm 1 has also priced at $160 in all previous periods. If firm 1 has ever deviated from the price $160 then in the period following firm 1's deviation set price of $105 and set price of $105 in all subsequent periods.

The difference between these two trigger strategies is that the second imposes a much harsher penalty for cheating than does the first. Is there any guide that will help us determine whether the firms will wish to adopt this tougher stance? The answer is yes, at least in part. When the probability-adjusted discount factor $\rho R$ is sufficiently small—either because the probability $\rho$ of continued interaction is small or the interest rate $r$ is sufficiently large—only the tough strategy will work to sustain the cartel. In general, the more severe the punishment that reversion to the Nash equilibrium imposes, the more likely it is that the cartel is sustainable. Again, when the cartel is sustainable we do not observe the trigger being pulled. The two firms set the monopoly price of $160 today and tomorrow and so on.

## Practice Problem 14.4

Assume that the game of Example 2 is infinitely repeated. Show that there is a range of probability-adjusted discount factors such that both firms stay in the cartel when the trigger strategy leads to a price of $105 forever but cheat on the cartel if the trigger strategy leads to a price of $130 forever.

Our investigation of the above two examples suggests that once we move to a setting of infinitely repeated games, the use of trigger strategies can produce equilibria in which cooperative arrangements can be self-sustaining. As it turns out, this insight generalizes well beyond these two examples. It easily extends to cases where the number of firms is more than two.

However, there are two objections to trigger strategies. One of these is that such strategies are based on the assumption that cheating on the cartel agreement is detected quickly and that punishment is swift. What if, as seems likely, it takes time for cartel members to discover a firm that is cheating and additional time to retaliate?

The fact that detection and punishment of cheaters takes time certainly makes sustaining the cartel more difficult. Such delay allows the culprit to enjoy the gains for more periods and this raises the incentive to engage in cheating behavior. Nevertheless, this does not necessarily make collusion impossible. Trigger strategies can still work even if detection of cheating on the agreement takes more than one period, and even if it takes the remaining cartel members some time to agree on the proper punishment. So long as the probability-adjusted discount factor $\rho R$ is high enough, the trigger strategy will be effective.

A second and related objection to the trigger strategy is that it is harsh and unforgiving because it does not permit mistakes. For example, suppose that market demand fluctuates within known, but nonzero bounds, as shown in Figure 14-2, and that the cartel has agreed to set a price $P^C$ or has agreed to production quotas that lead to that market price. In this setting, a cartel firm that observes a decline in its sales cannot know whether this reduction is due to cheating by one of its partners or to an unanticipated reduction in demand. Yet under the simple trigger strategies we have been discussing, the firm is required quickly and permanently to move to the retaliatory behavior. Clearly, this will lead to some regret if the firm later discovers that its partners were innocent and that it has needlessly unleashed a damaging price war.[13]

However, this objection can be overcome. The trick here is to adopt a modified trigger strategy. For instance, the firm might take retaliatory action only if sales or price fall outside some agreed range. That is, the firm refrains from retaliation against minor infractions. A different modification would impose punishment swiftly after any deviation from the cartel agreement is observed but limit the period of punishment to a finite period of time. Thus, we can envision a trigger strategy of the form "I will switch to the Nash equilibrium for $\tau \geq 1$ periods if you deviate from our agreement but will then revert to our agreed cooperative strategies." This approach may mistakenly punish innocent cartel members, but by limiting the period of such punishment, it permits reestablishment of the cartel at a later date.

---

13 Two different views of oligopolistic behavior in the face of uncertain demand that makes detection difficult may be found in Green and Porter (1984) and Rotemberg and Saloner (1986).

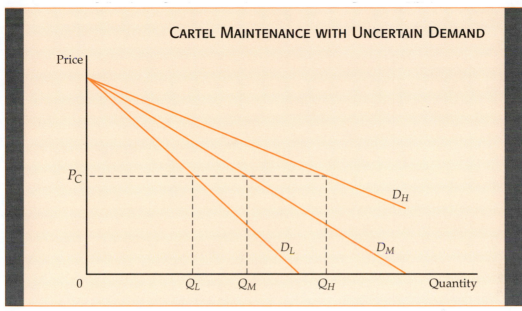

**CARTEL MAINTENANCE WITH UNCERTAIN DEMAND**

FIGURE

**14-2**

If demand is uncertain and varies between $D_L$ and $D_H$ with a mean of $D_M$, cartel members will not be able to tell whether a variation in their output is the result of normal variations in the market or cheating by other members of the cartel.

The point is that in an infinitely repeated game there are many trigger strategies that allow a cartel agreement to be sustained. Indeed, in some ways, there are almost too many. This point is made clear by what is called the *folk theorem* for infinitely repeated games (Friedman 1971):[14]

> **Folk Theorem:**  Suppose that an infinitely repeated game has a set of payoffs that exceed the one-shot Nash equilibrium payoffs for each and every firm. Then any set of feasible payoffs that are preferred by all firms to the Nash equilibrium payoffs can be supported as subgame perfect equilibria for the repeated game for some discount rate sufficiently close to unity.

We can illustrate the folk theorem by means of our Example 1. If the two firms collude to maximize their joint profits, they share aggregate profits of $3,600. If they act noncooperatively they each earn $1,600. The folk theorem says that any cartel agreement in which each firm earns more than $1,600 and in which total profit does not exceed $3,600 can, at least in principle, be sustained as a subgame perfect equilibrium of the infinitely repeated game. The shaded region of Figure 14-3 shows the range of profit for Example 1 that can be earned by each firm in a sustainable cartel.

---

14 The term "folk theorem" derives from the fact that this theorem was part of the "folklore" or oral tradition in game theory for years before Friedman wrote down a formal proof. While we present the cooperation as if each firm charges the same price, in a repeated bidding game where, for instance, firms compete for government contracts by submitting the lowest bid, cooperation may take the form of an agreement to have one firm offer the cooperative price and all other firms offer somewhat higher bids. The privilege of being the low bidder could then be rotated among the cartel members. See Comanor and Schankerman (1976).

FIGURE

**14-3**

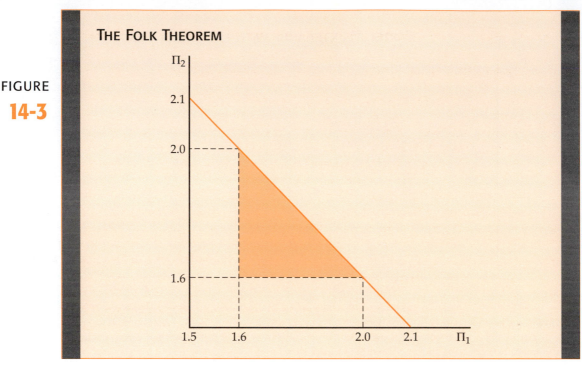

Any distribution of profits in the shaded area can be supported by a trigger strategy for some discount factor sufficiently close to unity.

A qualifying note should be added here. The folk theorem does not say that firms can always achieve a total industry profit equal to that earned by a monopoly. It simply says that firms can do better than the noncooperative, Cournot–Nash (or Bertrand–Nash) equilibrium. The reason that exact duplication of monopoly may not be possible is that the monopoly outcome always results in the highest possible price relative to marginal cost. At such a high price, any cartel member can earn substantial short-term profit with even a small deviation from the cartel agreement. Consequently, duplicating the monopoly outcome gives members a tremendous incentive to cheat unless the probability-adjusted discount factor is fairly large. Yet this does not mean that no cartel can be sustained. Firms still can earn profits higher than the noncooperative equilibrium by means of a sustainable cartel agreement, even if they cannot earn the highest possible profits that the industry could yield. This is what the folk theorem says.

## Practice Problem 14.5

Take Example 1 but now assume that the two firms agree on a cartel output of 35 thousand units each and that they expect to interact indefinitely. What is the probability-adjusted discount factor above which this cartel is sustainable? (*Hint:* Recalculate Table 14-3 by calculating each firm's best response to an output of 35 by its cartel partner.)

In sum, once we consider a framework of infinitely or indefinitely repeated interaction between firms, there is a real possibility for sustainable collusive behavior among

# ✓ Reality Checkpoint

## The Sky's the Limit—Multimarket Contact and Air Travel Prices

Firms that meet repeatedly through time may be able to solve the prisoners' dilemma and establish a more cooperative equilibrium because the many subsequent rounds permit punishment for noncooperative behavior today. Somewhat analogously, firms that meet again and again not over time but across different markets may also find it easier to sustain collusion. The rough equivalent of the trigger strategy is to revert to the Nash equilibrium in all markets where the firms compete any time a rival reneges on the collusive agreement in one market. This intuition, first presented by Edwards (1955) was later refined by Bernheim and Whinston (1990) who show that there are indeed conditions in which multimarket contact can lead to successful collusion in all the markets in which rivals meet even though the necessary conditions for such collusion in any one market do not appear to be met.

Empirical evidence in support of the view that multimarket contact helps to sustain collusion is provided by Evans and Kessides (1994) in their investigation of airline prices. In air travel, each city-pair, for example, New York to San Francisco, is considered a market. In any one such market there are typically four airlines competing. However, these airlines will also serve and compete in other city-pair markets as well. Evans and Kessides try to construct a measure of how large is this outside contact for each market. Suppose, for example, that a route is served by American, Delta, United, and Northwest. Suppose further that American and Delta competed in 312 routes in total, that American and United competed in 340 routes in total, and that American and Northwest competed in 180 routes. Imagine as well that Delta and United appeared jointly in 240 routes, Delta and Northwest were together in 190 routes, and that United and Northwest appeared together in 220 routes. Evans and Kessides (1994) would then say that the multimarket contact among the airlines on this route is given by the average route contact equal to (312 + 340 + 180 + 240 + 190 + 220)/6 = 247. They measure this variable for all of the top 100 city-pair airline markets and use it in statistical analysis designed to explain airline ticket prices in each market. If multimarket contact works to make collusion more sustainable, then ticket prices should be higher in markets with higher average route contact. This is exactly what Evans and Kessides find. While the average route contact value is 180, they find that as it increases from, say 115 to 250 and higher, ticket prices rise by about 5 to 7 percent, even after accounting for all the other effects operating on ticket prices.

**Sources:** B. D. Bernheim and M. D. Whinston, "Multimarket Contact and Collusive Behavior." *Rand Journal of Economics* 31 (1990), pp. 1–26; C. D. Edwards, "Conglomerate Bigness as a Source of Market Power." *Business Concentration and Price Policy*, Princeton: Princeton University Press, 1955; and W. N. Evans and I. N. Kessides, "Living by the Golden Rule: Multimarket Contact in the U.S. Airline Industry." *Quarterly Journal of Economics* 109 (1994), pp. 341–66.

these firms so long as the discount rate is not too high and the probability of their continued interaction is not too low. Indeed, the cases noted at the start of this chapter offer ample evidence that this is the case. There are good reasons for the Justice

Department and other antitrust authorities to worry about collusion. Yet these agencies have limited resources. Since they cannot patrol every industry and every market, they must focus on those settings where collusion is most likely to occur. Furthermore, they must develop methods to detect such collusion if and when it occurs. This is the subject to which we turn in the next chapter.

# SUMMARY

At least since the time of Adam Smith, there has been the fear that firms in the same industry may try to collude and set a price close to the monopoly price rather than vigorously compete. The good news over the last dozen years or so is that a large number of such collusive cartels have been caught and successfully prosecuted in the courts both in Europe and North America. The bad news is that this same evidence also reveals that such collusion is a real possibility. Somehow firms are occasionally able to work out and implement cooperative strategies rather than noncooperative ones. So, while the competition authorities can feel good about the cartels that have been broken, they must also worry that there may be many other price-fixing agreements that they have not uncovered.

The primary feature of corporate interaction that makes cartels possible is repetition. The firms rarely meet on the corporate battlefield just once. Instead, they can expect to meet many times (and perhaps in many other markets as well). When a game is played only once, each firm has a very strong incentive to cheat on the collusive agreement. Since the agreement is not legally enforceable, there is little any firm can do to deter others from cheating. However, when the game is played repeatedly over a number of periods, the scope for cooperation widens considerably. This is because a firm can threaten to "punish" any cheating on the collusive agreement in one period by being more aggressive in the remaining subsequent periods.

While repetition of the game over time is necessary for firms to collude successfully, it is not by itself sufficient. In addition to the game being repeated over more than one period, at least one of two conditions must be met. Either the one-period version of the game must have more than one Nash equilibrium, or the game must have an indefinite ending, that is, in any given period, there is always a positive probability that the game will be played one more time. Absent these conditions, Selten's theorem makes clear that a finitely repeated game with a unique Nash equilibrium will simply result in that Nash equilibrium being the outcome in each period. However, for repeated games that go on indefinitely, the folk theorem makes clear that collusion in which both firms gain relative to that one-shot Nash equilibrium is possible. As noted, such collusion is also possible if the one-period Nash equilibrium is not unique. Based on the recent historical experience, it appears that these conditions for successful collusion are often met. Antitrust concern with price-fixing agreements is then justified.

# PROBLEMS

**1.** Suppose that two firms compete in quantities (Cournot) in a market in which demand is described by $P = 260 - 2Q$. Each firm incurs no fixed cost but has a marginal cost of 20.

a. What is the one-period Nash equilibrium market price? What is the output and profit of each firm in this equilibrium?

b. What is the output of each firm if they collude to produce the monopoly output? What profit does each firm earn with such collusion?

c. If one firm decides to cheat on the collusion, assuming that the other firm will continue to produce its half of the monopoly output, how much will the cheating firm produce? What will be the industry price and the deviating firm's profit in this case?

d. Suppose that the market game described above is now repeated indefinitely. Show that the collusive agreement can be maintained so long as the probability-adjusted discount factor is $\rho R > 0.53$.

2. Suppose that, just as in Problem 1, market demand is given by $P = 260 - 2Q$ and that firms again have a constant marginal cost of 20, while incurring no fixed cost. Now, however, assume that firms compete in prices (Bertrand) and have unlimited capacity.

a. What is the one-period Nash equilibrium price? Assuming that firms share the market evenly any time they charge the same price, what is the output and profit of each firm in this market equilibrium?

b. What will be the equilibrium output and profit of each firm if each agrees to charge the monopoly price?

c. If one firm charges the monopoly price, what price will maximize the profit of the other firm? How much will the profit of this cheating firm be?

d. Now suppose that the market game is repeated indefinitely. What probability-adjusted discount factor is necessary now in order to maintain the collusive agreement?

3. Compare your answers in 1(d) and 2(d). Based on this comparison, which market setting do you think is more amenable to cartel formation, one of Cournot competition or one of Bertrand competition?

4. Once again, assume Cournot competition in an industry in which market demand is described by $P = 260 - 2Q$ and in which each firm has a marginal cost of 20. However, instead of two firms there are now four.

a. What is the one-period Nash equilibrium market price? What is the output and profit of each firm in this equilibrium?

b. What is the output of each firm if they collude to produce the monopoly output? What profit does each firm earn with such collusion?

c. If one firm decides to cheat on the collusion, assuming that the other firms will continue to produce their monopoly output, how much will the cheating firm produce? What will be the industry price and the deviating firm's profit in this case?

d. Suppose that the market game described above is now repeated indefinitely. Show that the collusive agreement can be maintained so long as the probability-adjusted discount factor is $\rho R > 0.610$.

5. Compare your answers in 1(d) and 4(d). Based on this comparison, what do you infer about the ability of firms to sustain a collusive agreement as the number of firms in the industry expands?

**6.** In the 1990s, the market for the food additive, lysine, was comprised of six firms. Their market share and marginal cost per pound are shown below.

| Firm | Market Share | Marginal Cost |
|------|--------------|---------------|
| Ajinomoto | 32% | $0.70 |
| Archer Daniels Midland | 32% | $0.70 |
| Kiyowa Hakko | 14% | $0.80 |
| Sewon/Miwon | 14% | $0.80 |
| Cheil Sugar | 4% | $0.85 |
| Cargill | 4% | $0.85 |

A rough estimate of the demand elasticity in this market is $\eta = 1.55$. Use this estimate and the given data to determine the weighted-average industry equilibrium price if the firms are competing in quantities. During the 1990s, the lysine producers formed a (now famous) cartel that maintained the shares shown in the table. Under the cartel, the world price of lysine rose to an average of $1.12 per pound. Total world production at this time was about 100 thousand tons per year. One metric ton = 2,200 pounds. Focusing on Archer Daniels Midland (ADM), and assuming market shares are the same in the Cournot and collusive settings, use the data and what you know about the Cournot price equilibrium from Chapter 9 (equation 9.25) to determine:

**a.** ADM's profits in the Cournot equilibrium, and

**b.** ADM's profits under the cartel.

**7.** Return to Problem 6. If the relevant interest rate was 16% ($r = 0.16$) and if ADM thought that the probability that the cartel will continue from any one period to the next was 0.5, what does this suggest would have been ADM's profit if it cheated on the cartel?

# REFERENCES

Benoit, J. P., and V. Krishna. 1985. "Finitely Repeated Games." *Econometrica* 53: 890–904.

Comanor, W. S., and M. A. Schankerman. 1976. "Identical Bids and Cartel Behavior." *Bell Journal of Economics* 7: 281–86.

Eichberger, J. 1993. *Game Theory for Economics*. New York: Academic Press.

Friedman, J. 1971. "A Non-Cooperative Equilibrium for Supergames." *Review of Economic Studies* 78: 1–12.

Green, E. J., and R. Porter. 1984. "Noncooperative Collusion Under Imperfect Price Information." *Econometrica* LII: 87-100.

Harsanyi, J. C. 1973. "Games with Randomly Distributed Payoffs: A New Rationale for Mixed Strategy Equilibrium Points." *International Journal of Game Theory* 2: 1–23.

Posener, R. 1970. "A Statistical Study of Cartel Enforcement." *Journal of Law and Economics* 13: 365–419.

Rotemberg, J., and G. Saloner. 1986. "A Supergame Theoretic Model of Price Wars During Booms." *American Economic Review* 76: 390–407.

357

Schelling, T. 1960. *The Strategy of Conflict.* Cambridge, MA: Harvard University Press.

Selten, R. 1973. "A Simple Model of Imperfect Competition Where 4 Are Few and 6 Are Many." *International Journal of Game Theory* 2: 141–201. Reprinted in R. Selten, *Models of Strategic Rationality*, Amsterdam: Kluwer Academic Publishers (1988).

# Chapter 15

# Collusion in Practice

Policy concerns about possible collusion have a long history in antitrust legislation, beginning with Section 2 of the Sherman Act. Yet even though explicit price-fixing is illegal in the United States, we learned in the last chapter that tacit collusion to keep prices high can be achieved in a noncooperative setting through repeated interaction. Often in real-world settings we observe that a firm in an industry will announce a price increase that is then quickly matched by the other rival firms in the industry. One of the best examples of this behavior is found in the cigarette industry in the earlier part of the twentieth century, where several price increases that were announced by Reynolds were followed the next day by Liggett and Meyers and American Tobacco. Is this tacit collusion or, alternatively, were all firms raising price to cover rising costs or to meet increased demand?

We will not directly answer the foregoing question here. The point is that both overt collusion and tacit price cooperation are difficult to detect. Without detailed information on the costs facing each firm and on industry demand, all one can do is try to develop a sense as to where such illegal behavior is most likely to occur, and then police those areas heavily. In this respect, being a good industrial economist is like being a good detective. One has to look at clues regarding which firms have the motive, the means, and the opportunity to commit the crime.

## 15.1 WHERE IS COLLUSION MOST LIKELY TO OCCUR?

In principle, collusive behavior could occur in almost any market. However, one suspects that it is more likely to occur in some markets rather than others. In order to identify precisely those market features that facilitate collusion we first review the central problem that colluding firms have to surmount.

Figure 15-1 presents the basic problem facing any cartel, here illustrated in the case of a duopoly. To help make the point as clearly as possible, the figure is drawn under the assumption that marginal cost is not constant but rises for each firm and that it rises somewhat faster for firm 2 than for firm 1. The curve $\pi_1^* \pi_2^*$ describes the *profit-possibility frontier* for these two firms. This frontier defines the maximum profit firm 2 can achieve for any specific profit level assigned to firm 1. In turn, the profit levels at $M$ and other points on the frontier are achieved by an appropriate choice of output at each firm. Thus, if firm 2 is assigned zero profit (zero output), the maximum profit possible for firm 1 is $\pi_1^*$. Similarly, if firm 1 is assigned zero profit or zero output, the maximum amount of profit firm 2 can earn is $\pi_2^*$. Our assumption that firm 2's costs rise somewhat more rapidly than do firm 1's is reflected by the fact that $\pi_2^*$ is a bit smaller than $\pi_1^*$.

There is one point on the profit frontier that generates the highest total profit for both firms. This is point $M$. It is identified by the fact that a straight line with slope $-1$, that is, the line $\pi_m \pi_m$, is just tangent to the frontier at this point. This implies that at $M$, a small change in the allocation of production would not affect the industry total profit. Production has been allocated such that marginal cost is equal at both

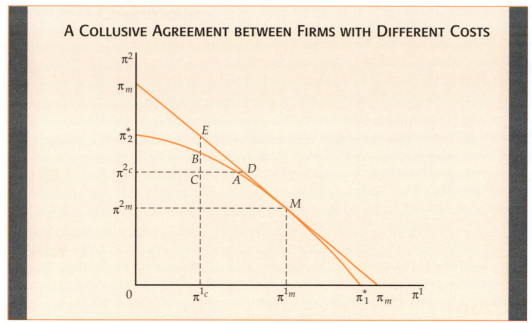

**A COLLUSIVE AGREEMENT BETWEEN FIRMS WITH DIFFERENT COSTS**

FIGURE

**15-1**

The maximum joint profits that the two firms can generate is $\pi_m$, and this would give the distribution of profits at point $M$. The Cournot–Nash equilibrium is point $C$. Hence, point $M$ is unattainable but a side payment from firm 1 to firm 2 could get the cartel somewhere on $DE$. In the absence of side payments the best the two firms can do is attain some point on $AB$.

firms and this common marginal cost is equal to industry marginal revenue. At $M$, firm 1 enjoys profit $\pi_1^m$, and firm 2 earns $\pi_2^m$, which is the most that it can earn given that firm 1 earns $\pi_1^m$. The sum of these two profit levels is just $\pi_m$.

Because it has a slope of $-1$, all points on the line $\pi_m\pi_m$ are such that they add up to the same total profit level $\pi_m$. Note that neither firm can earn this profit level by itself. That is, both $\pi_1^*$ and $\pi_2^*$ are less than $\pi_m$. This is because of our assumption of rising marginal cost. For firm 1 to do all the production by itself, marginal cost would rise to a sufficiently high level that it could not earn $\pi_m$. The same is true for firm 2. The two firms need each other if they are to achieve the joint maximum at $M$.

The point $C$ gives the profit to each firm in the Cournot–Nash equilibrium. Notice that it does not lie on the curve $\pi_1^*\pi_2^*$. Remember, the Cournot outcome is a noncooperative one. Each firm tries to maximize its own profit, not the combined profit of the industry. As a result, each ignores the fact that increases in its own production lowers the rival's profit and too much output is produced.

Suppose, as illustrated, that $C$ lies above and to the left of $M$. What this means is that firm 2 earns more profit in the Cournot–Nash equilibrium than it does producing the output it would produce at $M$ and earning the profit associated with that output, $\pi^{2m}$. This creates a real conflict in achieving the cartel goal of $M$. Potentially, though, this conflict can be overcome. To do so, however, requires that firm 2 be persuaded to act cooperatively and produce the output associated with $M$. The most obvious way to do this is by means of side payments from firm 1 to firm 2. Under such arrangement, both firms produce the outputs necessary to achieve the industry maximum at $M$. Then, to make this acceptable to firm 2, firm 1 gives up some of the large profit it makes at $M$ and pays it to firm 2. This transfer allows the firms to move along the $\pi_m \pi_m$ line and to end up somewhere on the interval $DE$.

If side payments are not possible, the best that the cartel can do is to reach some point on the arc $AB$. Total industry profit is not maximized, but at least both firm 2 and firm 1 earn a level of profit as least as great as their respective Cournot–Nash levels. However, while side payments are not necessary to achieve this outcome, some cooperation is. We know this because we know that the noncooperative Cournot solution lies inside the frontier.

Figure 15-1 thus illustrates the central dilemma—essentially the prisoners' dilemma—facing all oligopolists. Maximization of individual profit by each firm does not yield an outcome on the profit frontier. Some cooperation is necessary to achieve such a result. Achieving the point on the frontier that actually maximizes industry profit not only requires cooperation but also typically requires side payments in order for this to be profitable for both firms.

We know from Chapter 14 that firms can sometimes achieve at least some degree of cooperation, and realize a point on the profit frontier, perhaps even point $M$. The question that remains is when is such cooperation most likely? That is, what industry characteristics are most conducive to firms achieving a cooperative outcome? This question has been the focus of considerable theoretical and empirical research.[1] The broad findings of that research now seem clear. Successful collusion is more likely when there is a sufficiently strong profit motive and when there are easily understood methods by which firms can reach and enforce a collusive agreement. We discuss in turn each of the market features necessary for collusive behavior to occur.

## 1. Potential for Monopoly Profit

The incentive for firms to collude depends upon their potential to earn monopoly profit, that is, on the size of the total profit at $M$. This potential depends on two factors. First, the demand curve facing the cartel members should be relatively inelastic. This means that the products of the cartel have few close substitutes and that the cartel controls a relatively high proportion of the total market. A study of international commodity cartels by Eckbo (1976), for example, indicates that of nine successful cartels for which reasonably detailed information is available, seven had inelastic industry demand and eight had no short-term substitutes. Second, firms in the market must be able to restrict entry. No matter how successful colluding firms are at hiding their cartel agreement, concealing their increased profitability is much more difficult. Higher profit will attract new entrants. So, for the cartel to be sustained, it must be able to limit entry. (See Reality Checkpoint: Snap, Crackle, Pop Goes the Cartel.)

One way for cartel members to deter the entry of nonmember firms is to form a *common marketing agency* through which all output must be channeled. For this to be effective, the cartel must prevent nonmembers from gaining access to consumers of the cartel's product. This could happen, for example, when consumers are persuaded of the advantages of the marketing agency, such as lower search costs, or wider access to sellers, or security of supply. Moreover, consumers buying from a common marketing agency are likely to worry about being denied access to the products of cartel members if they decide to purchase outside the cartel.[2]

---

1   Stigler (1964) is a classic in this field.
2   See Bernheim and Whinston (1985) for discussion of this type of policy.

## ✔ Reality Checkpoint

### Snap, Crackle, Pop Goes the Cartel

In the breakfast cereal industry they call it "Grape-Nuts Monday." That's the unofficial name for April 15, 1996. On that date, Post Cereal, the nation's third-largest manufacturer of ready-to-eat breakfast cereals, announced an across-the-board cut of about 20 percent in the prices it charged retailers of its cereal products. The move sent shock waves through the industry. For decades, the cereal market had been viewed as a stable oligopoly in which manufacturers had worked out a means of maintaining high prices and deterring entry by offering multiple varieties that foreclosed the chance for any new entrant to find a niche (see Chapter 6). Indeed, the industry had been the subject of a major antitrust investigation in the 1970s. In 1996, however, whatever collusive equilibrium had existed clearly broke down. Kellogg, the nation's largest cereal maker, initially refrained from matching Post's price reductions. This led to huge gains for Post as Kellogg's market share fell from 35 to 32 percent in a very short time.

Eventually, Kellogg (like the number two cereal maker, General Mills, before it) was forced to respond with similar price reductions. Two factors appear to have led to the emergence of more competitive pricing in the breakfast cereal market. One is the marketing by supermarkets of generic versions of the cereals sold by the leading manufacturers. Unless such entry can be prevented, any collusive pricing in the breakfast cereal cannot be sustained. The other factor was a change in consumers' breakfast habits. There was an increasing tendency to eat bagels and muffins rather than cereal. In other words, these products became closer substitutes for breakfast cereals.

**Source:** R. Gibson, "Cereal Prices Are Cut by Post" and "Kellogg Cutting Prices of Some Cereals in Bid to Check Loss of Market Share." *The Wall Street Journal*, April 16 and June 1, 1996.

A cartel may also use a *trade association* to control access to the market. Often trade associations engage in activities to persuade consumers that buying from nonmembers is risky. Regionally based agricultural commodity associations of this type are common. Witness the marketing campaigns to persuade consumers to buy juice only made from "Florida oranges," or to eat only "California raisins." Doctors, accountants, and lawyers all limit access to their markets through exams designed and administered by their professional associations, and they do so in the name of protecting quality.

### 2. The Costs of Reaching a Cooperative Agreement

Even when there is significant potential monopoly profit to be earned in an industry, this profit will not be realized if reaching a cooperative agreement among the member firms is too time-consuming and costly. Serious transaction costs can be incurred when searching for potential partners, in negotiating an agreement, and, ultimately, in enforcing it. This is especially the case when the agreement is illegal and covert, as it must be with a cartel. Accordingly, we should expect cartels to be most successful in those industries in which the transaction costs of cooperation are low. This is most likely when there is (1) a small number of firms, (2) high industry concentration, (3) similar production costs across firms, and (4) lack of significant product differentiation.

The intuition behind the first two factors should be clear from the logic of Figure 15-1. As tough as it may be to reach an agreement when there are just two firms, it will be that much more difficult when the number of firms increases to three or more. Similarly, one only has to negotiate with a few firms rather than many if a small number of these firms account for the bulk of industry output. Remember, too, that a cartel agreement is illegal. As with any inherently illegal activity, the fewer the parties involved, the less likely it is to be discovered. Finally, for the trigger strategies that we described in the previous chapter to be effective, cartel members have to be able to detect and punish deviations with some speed. The greater the number of firms involved, the more difficult it will be for them to detect cheating and to identify correctly the firm that has cheated.

The third factor, similar production costs, may also be illustrated by Figure 15-1. When firms have identical costs, the profit frontier becomes symmetric. As a result, each firm's output and profit is the same at the jointly maximizing point $M$. Moreover, each firm's profit at that point exceeds its profit in the Cournot–Nash equilibrium. Accordingly, agreeing that $M$ should be the common goal is easy. In contrast, when the cartel firms have different marginal costs, as in Figure 15-1, the cartel's profit-maximizing agreement would, as we saw, have the member firms produce different levels of output and earn different levels of profit—possibly less than the Cournot profit for some of them. This, of course, makes cooperation difficult. Indeed, it may only be achieved by the use of side payments.

There are at least two factors that make the implementation of such side payments difficult. First, the payments will require detailed negotiations among the firms. However, firms have a strong incentive not to reveal their true production costs and to claim that they should be allocated a large output quota so that these negotiations become difficult. Second, side payments have the added disadvantage that they are difficult to hide in company accounts and, therefore, noticeably increase the risk that the cartel will be detected by the antitrust authorities.[3]

The fourth factor, product heterogeneity, makes collusion more difficult to achieve for reasons similar to cost heterogeneity. When the cartel firms' products are heterogeneous, or highly differentiated, the cartel must do more than simply agree on a single price or market share. Any agreement, to be complete, must set a whole range of prices and outputs for each of the different products. This increases the costs of the negotiations and the potential sources of disagreement among the firms.[4]

### 3. The Costs of Maintaining a Cooperative Agreement

Monitoring the cartel agreement to detect cheating, where cheating often takes the form of price-cutting, is more difficult when products are highly differentiated. In some markets a cartel may be able to use one product as a benchmark and tie all the

---

3  See Cramton and Palfrey (1990) for a discussion of the difficulties that arise when costs are not only different but uncertain and known only to each firm itself, as well as how such difficulties may be overcome.

4  In effect, McGee's (1958) merger argument, discussed in Chapter 12, amounts to a suggestion that the incumbent firm make a side payment to the entrant to stay out of the industry.

# ✓ Reality Checkpoint

## The Guild Trip

European guilds first appeared in the eleventh century as a result of growing commercial activity and urbanization. Merchants from the same city traveling to distant markets protected themselves by banding together in a caravan, called a Gilde or Hansa in the Germanic countries and a caritas or fraternitas in Latin-speaking ones. Caravan members had specific duties for defense if the caravan were attacked, and were also required to support each other in any legal disputes. Since the members of a hansa or fraternitas remained in touch with each other when they returned to their home city, they also began to assume rights and privileges in regard to trade within their local community—rights often supported by the authorities. This led in time to the merchant guilds monopolizing all of the industry and commerce of the city. Nonguild members were only permitted to sell goods at wholesale.

Guilds based on specialized crafts replaced the earlier merchant guilds by the fourteenth century. The members of the craft guilds were all those engaged in any particular craft. They monopolized the making and selling of a particular commodity within the cities in which they were organized.

They did this in two ways: (1) by preventing goods from other cities being imported, and (2) by controlling local entry to membership in the craft guild. All those fortunate enough to be accepted as members were required to establish both uniform hours for all shops making the same commodity and uniform wages for workers in the same industry. Similarly, the number of people to be employed in each shop, the tools to be used, and the prices to be charged were all strictly regulated and enforced by close supervision. No advertising was allowed and improvements in techniques of production, which might give one artisan a cost advantage, were also prohibited. Note that both the merchant and craft guilds were based in the cities of their day. These were small by our standards. This size coupled with the "everyone knows everyone else's business" aspect of medieval life meant that the setting was one of frequent, repeated encounters extending over an indefinite future.

Indeed, the decline of the crafts guilds came in the sixteenth century with the emergence of capitalist methods of production. This made possible the manufacture of goods on a very large scale at one point and shipping them to many others. Hence, competition came now not from one's fellow local craftsmen but from anonymous sources abroad. Policing and enforcement became impossible and the new, more efficient production methods gradually forced the craft guilds out of existence.

**Source:** M. Weber, *General Economic History*. New York: Collier, 1961.

other product prices to this benchmark. This facilitates the task of monitoring prices and detecting price cuts. Indeed this is the reason often cited for *basing-point pricing*, a somewhat unusual method of pricing products that are going to be transported at some cost to the consumer. The common way to account for the cost of delivery is for the firm to charge a uniform price at the plant, called a mill price, and then vary the price paid by each customer depending on how much it costs to deliver the product to the customer's doorstep. This scheme is usually referred to as *free-on-board* or *FOB* pricing. The alternative is basing-point pricing. Here, one or, at most, a few plant locations are picked as a basing point. Then all delivered prices are quoted as the mill or factory price plus the delivery cost from the basing point. For example, for the first twenty years or so of this century, Pittsburgh was the basing point used in pricing domestic steel. A consumer in Columbus, for example, paid the same price for delivered steel—the mill price plus the transportation cost from Pittsburgh—whether the delivery actually came from Pittsburgh or from Birmingham, Alabama.

The advantages of basing-point pricing in sustaining collusion are twofold. First, it ensures that all customers at any specific location are quoted the same delivered price by every producer, regardless of the producer's location. This is not the case with FOB pricing, in which the delivered price to a given spot depends on the location of the producer. Thus, basing-point pricing considerably simplifies collusion by streamlining the price structure. This also makes for easier monitoring to detect cheaters.

The basing-point system also enjoys an advantage in terms of its implications for the incentive to cheat. To stick with our earlier example, suppose that there are just two steel plants—one in Pittsburgh and one in Birmingham—and that the two firms aim to set a cooperative monopoly price. Under FOB pricing, prices are set at the mill. If one firm cheats, retaliation by the other firm requires a reduction in that firm's mill price. This reduces its surplus on sales to all customers and so imposes a considerable cost, making the threat of retaliation less credible. With basing-point pricing, however, a price cut can be made by shading the delivered price to just the area or areas in which the noncooperative firm violated the agreement. As a result, the retaliation can be more surgically precise and, most importantly, less costly. This considerably enhances the threat of retaliation, discouraging cheating in the first place. It is little surprise, then, that basing-point pricing schemes have now been declared illegal in the United States.

Some additional factors that facilitate a cartel's task of monitoring its members and responding to transgressions swiftly are also worth mentioning. Detection of noncooperative behavior is easiest when all prices and/or market shares are easily observed. Cartels that intend to rig bids are considerably assisted, for example, when government agencies are required by law to publish the bids they have received. If, on the other hand, the bids are submitted to private sector companies, a trade association among the companies could help in that case to facilitate collusive behavior in bidding for contracts.

In many consumer product markets most-favored-customer and meet-the-competition clauses can be used to help maintain a price-fixing agreement among firms.[5] *Most-favored-customer clauses* guarantee that if the seller offers the same product to another buyer at a lower price, the first buyer will receive a rebate equal to the difference in the two prices, whereas *meet-the-competition clauses* guarantee that a firm will match any lower price offered by another seller. It might seem surprising to think of these clauses as being anti- rather than pro-competitive. But a moment's thought should indicate how they each work to maintain cartel discipline. The most-

---

5   See Salop (1986) for more details on these competition clauses.

# ✓ Reality Checkpoint

## Most-Favored-Customer Policy Was a Bad Prescription for Medicaid

The Omnibus Budget Reconciliation Act of 1990 (OBRA 90) contained a most-favored-customer clause that applied to reimbursement for pharmaceuticals purchased under Medicaid. Medicaid is a very large program that accounts for nearly 15 percent of the prescription drug market sales in the United States. The drug companies routinely offered other large buyers of drugs, such as HMOs and drug store chains, quantity discounts of the type discussed in Chapter 5. However, because Medicaid did not purchase the drugs directly in bulk itself but, instead, reimbursed hospitals and pharmacies on an individual basis, it never received these discounts.

OBRA 90 included a number of steps that Congress hoped would alleviate this problem. On the one hand, it required that the drug price charged Medicaid had to be no more than 12.5 percent *less* than the average price charged all customers. Moreover, a most-favored-customer clause further required that if a firm charged any customer a price that was below the average by more than 12.5 percent, it would have to offer that same low price to all Medicaid customers.

The theory outlined in this and the preceding chapter implies that these well-intentioned regulations may well have backfired. The most-favored-customer clause tends to soften price competition. If a firm tries to cut its price in one market to gain competitive advantage there, the most-favored-customer clause requires that it will have to cut its price in all other markets, too. This acts as a disincentive to aggressive price competition. Indeed, the legislation also required that the Office of Inspector General monitor all firms so that there would be no secret price discounts that were not passed on to Medicaid. Of course, this meant no secret price discounts at all and, as a result, a further weakening of price competition.

Economist Fiona Scott Morton (1997) studied the impact of OBRA 90 on cardiovascular drug prices in the two years starting with January 1, 1991—the date that the regulations went into effect. She found that prices for well-know brand drugs that had been facing tough price competition from generic substitutes actually rose by over 4 percent. This finding supports the view that most-favored-customer clauses, like meet-the-competition clauses, facilitate collusive behavior aimed at reducing price competition.

**Source:** Fiona Scott Morton, "The Strategic Response by Pharmaceutical Firms to the Medicaid Most Favored Customer Rules." *Rand Journal of Economics* 28 (Summer, 1997), pp. 269–90.

favored-customer clause severely restricts the temptation of any seller to reduce its price since the price reduction has to be offered to all previous buyers as well. Similarly, meet-the-competition clauses make the process of detecting cheating particularly effective, since now the firms offering these guarantees have vast numbers of unpaid market watchers in the person of every consumer who has bought the product. At the same time, such clauses effectively bind the hands of the firms that offer them.

Given that meet-the-competition clauses have anticompetitive effects it might seem surprising that consumers would be lured by such guarantees. Note, however, that a price-matching clause may be valuable to any one buyer, who is assured of getting the very best deal possible. However, because that buyer then becomes implicitly a monitor of prices on behalf of the colluding firms, there is an externality to the buyer's purchase of which he or she may be unaware. Such monitoring will lead to prices being set higher (albeit identical) for all consumers. So the equilibrium will be one in which buyers, as a group, are all made worse off.

Meet-the-competition clauses also strengthen the trigger strategies that support collusive behavior among firms. To get some idea as to just how powerful these clauses can be, consider a simple one-shot pricing game between two firms. The payoff matrix shown in Table 15-1 describes a prisoners' dilemma game. The one-shot nature of the game leads the firms inevitably to the only Nash equilibrium in which both firms price low. But now consider what happens when we retain the assumption of one-shot play but permit both of the firms to publish meet-the-competition guarantees that are legally and instantaneously binding.[6] These guarantees render the off-diagonal price pairs in Table 15-1 unattainable. There is no opportunity to undercut one's cartel partner when each firm has announced a meet-the-competition policy that goes into effect immediately. Because the combinations of one firm pricing low and the other firm pricing high are unattainable, neither firm has any incentive to deviate from the Price High policy. The cartel works even in this simple one-period setting.

**TABLE**
**15-1**

### Payoff Matrix for a 2 × 2 Pricing Game

|  |  | Strategy for Firm 2 | |
|---|---|---|---|
|  |  | Price High (*H*) | Price Low (*L*) |
| **Strategy for Firm 1** | **Price High (*H*)** | (12, 12) | (5, 14) |
|  | **Price Low (*L*)** | (14, 5) | (6, 6) |

Finally, a cartel is better able to enforce an agreement when there is frequent market interaction among its members. Frequency may relate to time—the interactions among the firms occur on a daily, weekly, or perhaps monthly basis—or may instead be related to space in cases where the firms interact in many product markets simultaneously. An example might be the case of two airlines, each of which offers flights between many of the same city-pair markets. Each city-pair market can be looked upon as one play of the competitive game between these firms.

The reason why frequent market interaction makes collusion easier stems directly from our analysis of repeated games in the previous chapter. To see this, consider the

---

6  This is perfectly legal since the price-matching guarantees are offered to buyers rather than communicated to other sellers.

alternative scenario in which market interactions are infrequent. Spreading interactions out over time is equivalent to the interest rate being very high, or the discount factor being very low. Also, when interactions are infrequent, there is considerable time between detecting cheating on the agreement and implementing any punishment. Hence, if interactions are repeated but only infrequently, the cartel may no longer be sustainable.

### 4. Stable Market Conditions

Stable market conditions, such as relatively small changes in demand and costs, are important because they facilitate the detection and punishment of cheating on the cooperative agreement. The simple trigger strategy of punishing a defector forever may need to be amended when demand or production costs are uncertain and subject to random shocks. A modified trigger strategy is one that punishes the defector for a number of periods and not forever. However, it would not be as potent a deterrent as a trigger strategy that retaliates forever. Moreover, with uncertain demand, the kinds of strategies that work to sustain collusion often do so only by establishing a market price well below that of a pure monopoly.

The best hope for a cartel in an unstable market is to add to the trigger strategy the auxiliary tactic of establishing a centralized sales agency, as is the case in the De Beers diamond cartel, or a trade association. Either institutional arrangement can monitor and report upon both market conditions and individual firm performance. Monitoring may be further facilitated by agreements to divide the market explicitly, say by percentage of total sales or by geographic territory.

In brief, cooperative price-fixing agreements are facilitated when an industry exhibits characteristics that make the detection and the deterrence of cheating easier. Such factors include the presence of only a few firms, and selling homogeneous products on a reasonably frequent basis and under relatively stable market conditions. Indeed, all of these factors were present in the numerous recent international cartels.[7] In addition, agreements on market division, whether by geography or sales, also make it easier to monitor the behavior of cartel members. The potential for punishment, in some cases, violence, is greatly enhanced by such features.[8]

## 15.2 AN ILLUSTRATION: COLLUSION ON THE NASDAQ EXCHANGE

The NASDAQ stock market is the largest stock market in the United States. In June 2000 share volume was 33.8 billion shares with a dollar volume of $1,612 billion, compared with a share volume on the New York Stock Exchange (NYSE) of 21.7 billion shares and a dollar volume of $918.7 billion and considerably greater than the AMEX market.[9] NASDAQ trading is made online and for any given stock there are multiple traders.

The traders post two quotes for each stock in which they deal—an "ask" price at which they will sell the stock and a "bid" price at which they will buy the stock. In

---

7   See Connor (2001) for a detailed and readable analysis of these cartels.
8   A number of cartels in New York City have used violence to enforce their market power; see footnote 15 on page 374.
9   For further details visit the NASDAQ Web site at http://www.nasd.com.

those days, such prices were quoted in increments of eighths of a dollar and the trader made profits by quoting ask prices that were greater than bid prices. Traders competed with each other through the ask and bid prices that they quoted. Market prices were determined by the lowest ask price and the highest bid price—called the *inside prices*—with the difference between the lowest ask and highest bid price being referred to as the *inside spread*.

The NASDAQ market would seem to be close to satisfying the competitive market ideal. But the work of two economists, Christie and Schultz, suggest otherwise. They found that in the 1990s NASDAQ was not the competitive market it seemed.[10] The evidence came to light when Christie and Schultz constructed a matched sample of securities on the NASDAQ and on the NYSE/AMEX exchanges and compared the distribution of inside spreads. Figure 15-2 reports their results. They concluded that a much higher proportion of NASDAQ stocks had inside spreads of even eighths—2/8 or 4/8—than did similar stocks on NYSE/AMEX.

FIGURE

**15-2**

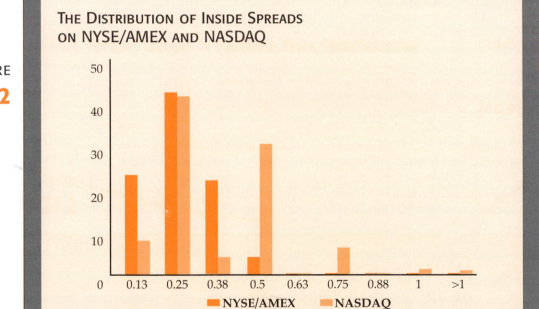

**Source:** W. G. Christie and P. Schultz, "Why do NASDAQ market makers avoid odd-eighth quotes?" *Journal of Finance*, December 1994, pp. 1813–49.

You might wonder why this should matter. After all, what is an eighth of a dollar between friends? However, given a share volume of around 1 billion shares per day, an additional spread of 1/8 is equivalent to additional profits of $125 million *per day*, a gift that most friends would be delighted to receive. Christie and Schultz suggested that collusion among NASDAQ dealers could explain the higher proportion of even eighths. The argument goes as follows: Essentially the NASDAQ dealers are engaged

10 "Why do NASDAQ market makers avoid odd-eighth quotes?" *Journal of Finance*, December 1994, pp. 1813–49.

☑ **Reality Checkpoint**

### "I Am the Broker, You Are the Brokee!"

Once upon a time, two economists named Paul Schultz (of Ohio State) and William Christie (of Vanderbilt) were talking about stock prices for trades in the over-the-counter market quoted by the National Association of Securities Dealers Automated Quotation (NASDAQ) system. As described in the text, this is a computerized market in which dealers list the prices at which they will buy (the "bid" price) and sell (the "ask" price) various stocks. The difference between the bid and ask prices is the "spread," and it is a major source of dealer profits. Over time, the two economists noticed something odd. The spread was rarely less than seventy-five cents and always expressed as a multiplier of twenty-five cents, even though stock themselves are priced in odd eighths (e.g., 20 and 3/8, or 24 and 5/8). The two economists subsequently published a research paper suggesting that NASDAQ prices could only come about as a result of a price-fixing agreement.

The paper caused an immediate stir and, ultimately, led to an investigation by the antitrust division of the Justice Depart-

ment. Some time later, the Justice Department filed a civil complaint against two dozen securities dealers. The complaint documented the earlier findings of Schultz and Christie. It also showed that cheating was a potential problem that the dealers dealt with by harassment and verbal assault of the culprit. For example, consider this recorded conversation of one dealer complaining to a second dealer that the latter employed a trader who was not maintaining a spread divisible by twenty-five:

> (First trader): "He's trading it at one-eighths and embarrassing your firm."
>
> (Second trader): "I understand."
>
> (First trader): "You know, I would tell him to straighten up his act, stop being a (expletive deleted) moron!"

The agreement did not require the two dozen dealers involved to admit guilt or pay a fine. But it did require the dealers to cease and desist the practice and to tape randomly 3.5 percent of all trader conversations to ensure compliance.

**Source:** D. Lohse and A. Raghavan, "Will NASDAQ Accord Lead to Better Prices." *The Wall Street Journal*, July 18, 1996, p. C1.

in an infinitely repeated game. Current and past quotes of all dealers are available to all of the dealers, thus making it a game of complete and perfect information. When the dealers collude in the bid and ask prices they quote, then under certain conditions a dealer will earn a higher stream of profit sticking to the collusive agreement then would be earned if the dealer defected from the agreement and undercut the other traders' inside spreads.

Let's investigate under what conditions this could be so. Suppose that there are $N$ dealers in a particular stock.[11] Dealer $i$ quotes an ask price of $a_i$ and a bid price of $b_i$,

---

11 For a more complete analysis, see Dhutta (1999), and Dhutta and Madhavan (1997).

both measured by convention in eighths of a dollar. The inside ask is defined as $a = \min_i a_i$, the lowest ask price, and the inside bid is defined as $b = \max_i b_i$, the highest bid price. The inside spread is, of course, $a - b$. The demand for shares of this stock by members of the public who wish to purchase at price $a$ is denoted $D(a)$, while the supply of shares by members of the public who wish to sell at price $b$ is denoted $S(b)$. Specifically, we will assume that

$$D(a) = 200 - 10a \text{ and} \tag{15.1}$$
$$S(b) = -120 + 10b, \tag{15.2}$$

where, again by convention, quantities are measured in blocks of 10,000 shares.

We make two further simplifying assumptions. First, we assume that dealers set their bid and ask prices to equate expected demand with expected supply. That is, they do not buy for inventory. What this means is that dealer $i$ quotes ask price $a_i$ and bid price $b_i$ such that $200 - 10a_i = -120 + 10b_i$, which implies that $b_i = 32 - a_i$. As Figure 15-3 shows, this assumption means that the only combinations of ask and bid prices that we need consider are [(20, 12), (19, 13), (18, 14), (17, 15), (16, 16)]. Secondly, we assume that any dealer who does not quote the inside spread gets no business while all market makers who quote the inside spread share the orders equally.

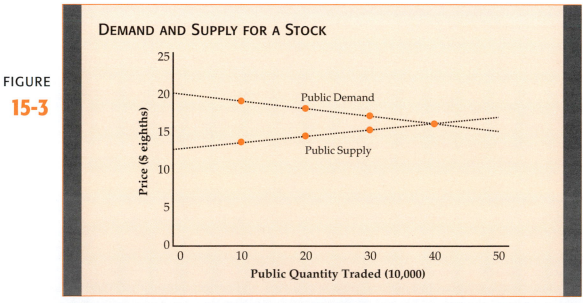

**DEMAND AND SUPPLY FOR A STOCK**

The stock is traded in units of 10,000 shares and priced in increments of one-eighth of a dollar. Ask (demand) and bid (supply) prices are quoted to equate demand and supply.

We define the value of this stock, $v$, as the price that equates public demand with public supply. You can easily confirm that, given our demand and supply functions, $v = 16$. In other words, the value of this stock is 16 (or $2.00) and at that price a quantity of 400,000 shares would be traded. Aggregate profit from trading in this stock is made up of two components: revenues from selling at greater than $v$ and revenues from buying at less than $v$. In other words,

$$\pi(a, b) = (a - v)D(a) + (v - b)S(b). \qquad \textbf{(15.3)}$$

Given our specific demand and supply functions and the "no inventory" assumption, so that $b = 32 - a$ and $D(a) = S(b)$, this simplifies to

$$\pi(a) = (a - b)(200 - 10a) = (2a - 32)(200 - 10a) = 20(a - 16)(20 - a). \qquad \textbf{(15.4)}$$

Table 15-2 gives these profits at the five possible bid and ask prices.

| Ask Price a | Bid Price b + 32 − a | Volume of Shares (10,000) | Aggregate Profit ($000) |
|---|---|---|---|
| 20 | 12 | 0 | 0 |
| 19 | 13 | 10 | 75 |
| 18 | 14 | 20 | 100 |
| 17 | 15 | 30 | 75 |
| 16 | 16 | 40 | 0 |

**PROFITS IN THE NASDAQ EXAMPLE**

TABLE **15-2**

Aggregate profit is maximized at an ask price of 18 (or $2.25) and a bid price of 14 (or $1.75) with a spread of 4 (or 50 cents) and a volume of 200,000 shares. The question is can dealers sustain an agreement to quote these prices, or will some dealer have an incentive to defect and quote a lower ask and a higher bid price? Consider a particular dealer, Millennial Securities Inc. Table 15-3 gives the payoff matrix given that it quotes prices $(a_m, b_m)$ while all other dealers quote prices $(a_j, b_j)$.[12]

It would appear that there are two Nash equilibria to this game—(17, 15) and (16, 16). But this ignores one of the beauties of a convention to set prices in increments of eighths of a dollar. The strategy (16, 16) is (weakly) dominated for Millennial Securities. It never does any worse and usually does better by quoting (17, 15). So we can eliminate the (16, 16) strategy. As a result, we are left with yet another prisoners' dilemma game. If this game were to be played between these market makers only once, the collusive agreement (18, 14) could not be sustained. It is not a Nash equilibrium. Millennial Securities, among others, has the incentive to undercut the agreed prices by quoting (17, 15).

What happens, however, if this game is repeated indefinitely? Does Millennial Securities now have the incentive to stick with the collusive prices or will it still wish to undercut them? Recall from the previous chapter that $\rho$ is the probability that Millennial Securities will be competing with these dealers in the next period and $R$ is

---

12 We can confine ourselves to the three sets of prices (18, 14), (17, 15), and (16, 16) since no trader would wish to charge (19, 13) given an agreement to charge (18, 14).

TABLE

**15-3**

**PAYOFF MATRIX FOR THE NASDAQ CARTEL GAME ($000)**

| | | Strategy for Millennial Securities (ask, bid) Quotes | | |
|---|---|---|---|---|
| | | **(18, 14)** | **(17, 15)** | **(16, 16)** |
| **Strategy for All Other Market Makers (ask, bid) Quotes** | **(18, 14)** | $\left(\dfrac{100(N-1)}{N},\dfrac{100}{N}\right)$ | $(0, 75)$ | $(0, 0)$ |
| | **(17, 15)** | $(75, 0)$ | $\left(\dfrac{75(N-1)}{N},\dfrac{75}{N}\right)$ | $(0, 0)$ |
| | **(16, 16)** | $(0, 0)$ | $(0, 0)$ | $(0, 0)$ |

the discount factor. We can work out that Millennial's stream of discounted profits from sticking to the collusive agreement would be

$$PV_{\infty}^{M} = \frac{100}{N} + \frac{100}{N}\rho R + \frac{100}{N}\rho^{2}R^{2} + \frac{100}{N}\rho^{3}R^{3} + \dots = \frac{100}{N(1-\rho R)}. \quad \text{(15.5)}$$

If, instead, Millennial undercuts the agreed spread it can expect rapid reaction. After all, as Christie and Schultz noted, all asks and bids are public knowledge with screen trading. So let us assume that the other dealers react to Millennial's undercutting in one period and that the collusive agreement breaks down forever. Then Millennial Securities' expected profit from cheating on the agreement is

$$PV_{\infty}^{D} = 75 + \frac{75}{N}\rho R + \frac{75}{N}\rho^{2}R^{2} + \frac{75}{N}\rho^{3}R^{3} + \dots = 75 + \frac{75\rho R}{N(1-\rho R)}. \quad \text{(15.6)}$$

Cheating on the collusive agreement does not pay if $PV_{\infty}^{M} > PV_{\infty}^{D}$. Simple manipulation shows that for this to be the case the probability-adjusted discount factor must satisfy

$$\rho R > \frac{3N-4}{3N-3}. \quad \text{(15.7)}$$

At the time Christie and Schultz were writing, NASDAQ indicated that there were about 11 market makers for each stock (currently they report an average of around 13 market makers per stock). If $N = 11$, the necessary value of $\rho R$ then is $\rho R > 0.966$. If $N = 13$, then $\rho R$ must be as high as 0.972. Since $\rho R = \dfrac{\rho}{1+r}$, the necessary value

of $\rho R$ appears to require both very high probability $\rho$ of continued play and a very low interest rate. Note, however, that the relevant time period between trades is probably not much more than an hour in any given trading day and that market makers' memories carry over from day to day (if they ever go to sleep and stop trading!). So the probability in any given period that a particular market maker will continue making a market in this specific stock one hour from then is near unity, that is, $\rho \approx 1$. Moreover, since the relevant period is only an hour long, the interest rate that we use must also be measured on a per-hour basis. A rate of 10 percent per year, for instance, implies a very small value for $r$ per hour—less than 0.01 percent, in fact. Hence, values for $\rho R$ on the order of 0.99 are not at all unreasonable.

In short, the Christie and Schultz suggestion of NASDAQ dealer collusion is consistent with the conditions that economic theory says are necessary for such behavior. Indeed, NASDAQ's Preference Trade Rule acts very much like a "no price undercutting" guarantee. It specifies that a dealer who does not post the inside spread can nevertheless receive preferred orders provided he or she matches the best intermarket prices. Thus, not only does NASDAQ meet the basic conditions for successful collusion but the dealers also appear to have implemented an effective enforcement mechanism. A firm like Millennial Securities knows that deviating from the cartel price (18, 14) and pricing at (17, 15) will not win the market even for one period since all the other brokers are committed to match it.

Of course, the proof of any pudding is in the eating of it. The paper by Christie and Schultz served as a catalyst to an investigation of NASDAQ pricing by the Department of Justice and the Securities and Exchange Commission. The eventual outcome suggests that this is one of the few times that academic research has led directly to the detection of a cartel.[13] As we noted in the inset on page 369, the investigation produced convincing evidence of collusion. Eventually, the case was settled with an agreement by NASDAQ to change its practices. Dealers were required to record at least 3.5 percent of their traders' telephone conversations with other traders and to report any violations. In addition, NASDAQ introduced a *limit order display*. This allows investors to compete directly with dealers by specifying a price and quantity at which they are willing to buy or sell a stock. If the current inside bid on a particular stock is $20 $\frac{7}{8}$ and a private investor specifies a limit order, for example, to buy 10,000 shares of this stock at $21, then the market makers must raise their bids to $21. The result appears to have been a considerable narrowing in spreads. For example, the weighted-average inside spread per stock quoted on NASDAQ in June 2000 was 15 cents, just above 1/8.

Finally, for a variety of reasons including the above analysis, the SEC required NASDAQ and other markets to change their pricing practices by moving to decimal quotations in dollars (SEC order in June 2000) beginning "on or before September 5, 2000."[14] Interestingly enough, NASDAQ accompanied this move by a press release on the NASDAQ Web site citing the "increased savings potential for investors if decimal pricing leads to smaller price increments and narrower bid-ask spreads."

## 15.3 DETECTING COLLUSION AMONG FIRMS

When the conditions are right, firms in an industry will have an incentive to organize and sustain collusive behavior. The goal of antitrust policy is to limit the abuse of

---

13 For details, see the Department of Justice press release at http://www.usdoj.gov/atr/public/press_releases/1996/343.html.

14 To view this order go to http://www.sec.gov/rules/other/34-42914.htm.

such monopoly power. In the preceding sections we have offered some guiding principles that suggest where the authorities should watch most closely for collusive arrangements. Just watching, however, can never be enough. Even if the authorities are looking in the right place they may not detect price-fixing behavior. What tactics can officials use if they truly want to uncover and prosecute cartels?

Some idea as to how difficult it is for the government to detect collusive behavior may be gleaned from the fact that the vast majority of cartels that have been uncovered, at least until recently, have been disclosed through "finking." Sometimes the disclosure has been made by firms in the industry who have been unhappy either with the shares that they have been allocated in the cartel or because they have been excluded altogether. Sometimes it has been former employees of cartel members who have blown the whistle after losing their jobs.[15]

Despite the finking, legally proving the existence of the cartel to the satisfaction of the courts has not been easy in many of these cases. Where successful, such prosecution has almost always been the result of the cartel members being careless. For example, they have spoken on telephones that have been tapped, or have kept permanent records of their agreements—on paper, or hard drives on computers, and in one spectacular case inadvertently sending a copy of the agreement to a buyer along with the bid documents!

Without such evidence it is remarkably difficult for the authorities to prove, legally, the existence of a cartel. If the colluding firms are sufficiently sophisticated, they can also create the illusion of competition and fool the regulatory authorities. Consider firms bidding for a series of government contracts, for example. LaCasse (1995) shows that an equilibrium collusive strategy for such firms will imply that on some occasions the firms do not collude. That is, in order to disguise the cartel, the firms will sometimes act competitively. This mitigates the damage done by the cartel. However, as LaCasse also shows, it makes it almost impossible for a government agency to detect the underlying cooperative agreement, even when the firms routinely submit a number of identical bids.[16]

Moreover, even if uncovering a cartel is possible, there is a large difference between such detection and successful legal prosecution. The conspiring firms are entitled to their "day in court" and they have both the incentive and the ability to put up a strong defense. This is primarily because the cartel members have an informational advantage over any government agency, namely, the fact that they are the ones that know the nature of market demand as well as the cost of production and transportation. The best the authorities can do is to infer this information from data provided by the very same firms who are being investigated. In these circumstances, counsel for the defense can make the proof of collusion extremely difficult by making a collusive outcome appear to be competitive. This problem has been termed the *indistinguishability theorem* by Harstad and Phlips (1991).[17]

---

15 For years, the garbage-hauling business in New York was controlled by a cartel of firms who carved up the city between them. If one cartel firm took business from another, the association forced that company to pay compensation of "up to forty times the monthly pickup charge." Any firm attempting to enter the industry was met by arson and physical violence. Ex-mobsters who had been victims of the financial penalties and the violence provided some of the evidence necessary to break the cartel. (S. Raab, "To Prosecutors, Breakthrough After 5 Years of Scrutiny," *The New York Times*, June 23, 1995, p. 3.)

16 LaCasse's (1995) analysis also applies to the analysis by Comanor and Schankerman (1976) of firms that had been successfully prosecuted for collusive bidding, which found that rotating bids is a cumbersome strategy when the cartel involves many firms. It is much easier to implement when there are few conspirators since then bidding is easier to coordinate.

17 For a more detailed exposition of the indistinguishability theorem, see Phlips (1995a).

To show the indistinguishability theorem in action, we consider a case in which the European Commission ultimately rendered a verdict against ICI and Solvay, the two firms that control the European market for soda ash, a raw material used in glass manufacture. ICI and Solvay had operated a number of cartel agreements for many years, which led to Solvay supplying continental Europe while ICI supplied the United Kingdom, Ireland, and the British Commonwealth. These explicit agreements finally terminated in 1972, but there was no subsequent market interpenetration by the two producers. In the 1980s, prices in the United Kingdom rose some 15 to 20 percent above those in continental Europe, which the Commission argued was greater than the transport costs across the English Channel. The Commission judged that the lack of market invasion by either firm into the other's historic regional market—especially in the face of such price differentials—was strong evidence of continued tacit collusion by the two firms.

Yet while the Commission's judgment may appear to be sound there is a counterargument. If each firm has the same marginal cost schedule and if each sets its price equal to marginal cost plus the cost of transportation across the Channel, no cross-market penetration will ever occur. Such pricing behavior would reflect true rivalry, would lead to prices well below the collusive level, and yet there would be no market invasion of one firm by the other. Unless the regulatory agency has independent data on transportation costs, the nature of demand on each side of the Channel, and also on production costs, it cannot make a definitive case that the continued market segmentation is the result of collusive action.

Effectively, Solvay and ICI tried to avoid the charge of collusion by arguing that Solvay's marginal cost was higher. Perhaps the Commission was correct to reject this defense. However, without detailed information on (marginal) cost—information that can only be provided by Solvay and ICI—it is difficult to know.

Similar considerations apply when defending companies who are being charged with collusion because of evidence that they changed their prices in parallel. MacLeod (1985) shows that when the firms' profit functions are not known to each other then there is no systematic difference in the way that collusive and noncollusive equilibrium prices change in response to exogenous shocks. This is relevant to a 1984 judgment by the European Commission against a number of North American, Finnish, and Swedish companies who exported wood pulp to Europe for use by paper manufacturers. The Commission determined that these companies had to pay fines of between 50,000 and 500,000 ECU because they had announced and enforced parallel seasonal price changes. The judgment was thrown out on appeal in 1993 to the European Court of Justice for lack of proof.

The situation facing government authorities is not hopeless. Sometimes a bit of good detective work can find the necessary evidence. The studies by Porter and Zona (1993) and Hendricks and Porter (1988) are good illustrations of the kind of hard and thoughtful work that is necessary.

Porter and Zona reviewed the bidding on highway paving projects on Long Island in the early 1980s. They noted that since the Department of Transportation specified exactly what was to be built, the product of each firm was effectively identical. They also noted that while not all firms bid on any given contract, each firm that was bidding knew precisely who the others were. In addition, the winning firm and its bid were publicly announced. Hence, detection of any cheating on a cartel agreement would be easy. The market was concentrated. Of the 76 largest contracts, half went to one of just four firms. Finally, there were active trade associations and union groups through which the firm could and did communicate. In short, the highway

**Reality Checkpoint**

---

### Percolating Prices

On February 21, 1997, Procter & Gamble, maker of the world's most popular coffee, announced its intention to raise the price of its leading brand, Folgers, by more than previously intended. The company said that it now would raise the price of a 130-ounce tin of Folgers by 20 percent as of March 3.

Procter & Gamble's announcement drew an immediate response from the Kraft food unit of Philip Morris, Inc. This rival coffee maker announced that the price increase on its own leading brands, Maxwell House and Yuban, would exactly match the Folgers price rise as of March 31.

Do such parallel price hikes indicate collusion? It is difficult to know, especially in this case. The price of raw coffee had been rising for months prior to the Procter & Gamble announcement following a frost that destroyed the Brazilian coffee crop. Yet whether there was a conspiracy or not, coffee drinkers were in for a different kind of jolt from imbibing their favorite beverage.

---

**Source:**  "Procter & Gamble, Rival to Increase Coffee Prices." *Boston Globe*, February 22, 1997, p. E1.

---

construction industry on Long Island exhibited many of the characteristics necessary for successful collusion. Perhaps it is not surprising then that, in 1984, one of the largest firms in this industry was convicted of price-fixing along with four other unindicted co-conspirators. (The other four later faced charges in other suits.) The conviction came as the result of a "confession" by one executive.

Porter and Zona then examined the record for any clear behavioral evidence that could have been used independently to verify the existence of the cartel. They found that the cartel members regularly bid against themselves and that the bids were not, on their face, obviously different from the bids of the non-cartel firms. However, deeper analysis revealed that there were important differences between the bids submitted by the two groups. First, the cartel firm bids were distributed over a much narrower range than those of the non-cartel firms. This makes sense. On any given contract, the cartel members have already identified which of them will submit the lowest bid and what that bid will be. Hence, the others simply need to submit phantom bids that are just a bit higher than what they know will be a lower one. Non-cartel members, however, do not know what others are bidding. Accordingly, they face a wider range of possibilities and their bids correspondingly show a greater variance.

The same basic logic then led Porter and Zona to take a second step. For each contract, they ranked separately the cartel firms and the non-cartel firms by order of their unit cost. They then compared this ranking with the ranking of the submitted bids. They found that for the non-cartel firms, the ranking of bids and costs was similar. The lower a firm's cost, the lower its bid. This was not the case, though, for the cartel firms. For these firms, there was little relationship between their cost and bid ranks. Again, this makes intuitive sense. The choice by the cartel firms as to who among them will be the low bidder had little to do with cost and the bid was designed to generate profit. Once that firm and that bid was chosen, all the others needed to do was to bid a bit higher, whether their costs were a little higher or not.

Porter and Zona's paper is insightful. However, it has the advantage of working backwards. As noted, members of the cartel had already been convicted by the time that Porter and Zona began their work. That is, they knew that a cartel was there and the only remaining question was what kind of evidence forensic economics might uncover that would further verify the collusive arrangement. While such analysis is helpful for prosecuting alleged price-fixing conspirators, the question from a policy perspective is whether this sort of work is also helpful in uncovering collusion in the first place. The paper by Hendricks and Porter (1988) shows that similarly careful application of economic analysis can also be productive in this regard.

Hendricks and Porter analyzed collusive bidding in drainage auctions for offshore oil and gas leases. In a drainage sale, the government auctions off tracts of land that are adjacent to tracts on which deposits have already been discovered. Typically, a tract sold at a drainage auction neighbors many different tracts that have already been explored. Moreover, these neighboring tracts are usually owned by more than one firm. Because these firms own land adjacent to that being auctioned, one would expect that these neighboring firms would have better information regarding the prospects for the tract being sold than do nonneighboring firms that own tracts farther away. Competitive bidding by the neighboring firms should lead them to bid close to the true value of the land. Being less well-informed, the nonneighboring firms should be more cautious and submit lower bids. That is, competitive bidding by neighboring firms should result in few drainage tracts being sold to nonneighbor firms and, when this does happen, nonneighboring firms should not earn significant profit on the tract since the auction price should be close to the land's true value. Hendricks and Porter found, however, that nonneighbor firms frequently won the bidding and earned their greatest profit on tracts for which neighboring firms also bid. The obvious conclusion is that the neighboring firms (that are allowed to unite to pump oil and gas from their tracts by means of common facilities) were coordinating their bids and keeping them quite low.

A more general test of collusion comes from Osborne and Pitchik (1987). Recall our discussion of the Spence (1977) and Dixit (1980) models in which a large firm invests in extra capacity as a means to discipline a new rival (Chapter 12). Osborne and Pitchik show that extra capacity may play a similar disciplinary role in cartels.[18] To see this, recall from Chapter 9 that Bertrand price competition cannot yield the competitive outcome unless each firm has the capacity to serve the entire market. In the case of a cartel, however, this also means that by acquiring such large capacity, each firm obtains the means to threaten the other with the competitive outcome if either one should cheat on the collusive agreement. Thus, Osborne and Pitchik argue that cartel members have an incentive to acquire a large amount of capacity.

However, it is likely that the firms have to choose their capacities before the collusive agreement is implemented, with the result that the agreement covers only their pricing behavior. Because the capacity choice is made noncooperatively, each will acquire more capacity than may truly be needed to discipline the rival. However, it is

---

18 Davidson and Deneckere (1990) offer a similar analysis.

unlikely that each will choose exactly the same amount of capacity. Accordingly, when collusion subsequently begins, the price-marginal cost distinction may be the same for each firm but the profit per unit of capacity will then necessarily be greater for the firm with the smaller amount of capacity. Indeed, not only will the smaller firm have a higher profit per unit of capacity, but Osborne and Pitchik also show that this difference will increase as the total amount of excess capacity grows as it will, for example, in a general business downturn. By contrast, if there is no collusion the unit profits would be identical across firms.

Phlips (1995b) illustrates how this analysis can be applied to examine the behavior of the two British producers of white salt, British Salt and ICI Weston Point. Many analysts have suspected these two firms of collusion even after abandoning an earlier explicit price agreement when the United Kingdom adopted its Restrictive Practices Act in 1956. Phlips claims that:

> Throughout the period under investigation, both British Salt (BS) and ICI Weston Point (WP) had excess capacity. BS had a given capacity of 824 kilotons, WP had a given capacity of 1095 kilotons. All I had to do was to divide the yearly profits by the capacities and to divide the sum of the capacities by total sales, to find the . . . numbers (shown in Table 15-4). Not only was BS's profit per unit of capacity larger than WP's: it also increased relative to WP's as their joint capacity increased relative to market demand. None of these numbers is disputable. . . . This beats the indistinguishability theorem: I wish more such tests were available. (Phlips, 1995b, p. 15)

TABLE 15-4

### THE GREAT SALT DUOPOLY

|  | 1980 | 1981 | 1982 | 1983 | 1984 |
|---|---|---|---|---|---|
| BS Profit | 7065 | 7622 | 10489 | 10150 | 10882 |
| WP Profit | 7273 | 7527 | 6841 | 6297 | 6204 |
| BS Profit per Unit of Capacity | 8.6 | 9.3 | 12.7 | 12.3 | 13.2 |
| WP Profit per Unit of Capacity | 6.6 | 6.9 | 6.3 | 5.8 | 5.7 |
| Industry Capacity/Total UK Sales | 1.5 | 1.7 | 1.7 | 1.9 | 1.9 |

The common theme to all of the foregoing studies is that careful economic reasoning and hard work can help to detect and prosecute price-fixing conspiracies. Yet the job is not an easy one and the resources necessary for its completion are not trivial. To date, luck and dissension among the conspiracy members have probably played a larger role in the battle against cartels than has pure economic analysis.

However, there is one insight from economic theory that has acted as a quite powerful weapon in the antitrust arsenal. This insight is reflected in the important procedural change that the U.S. Department of Justice instituted in 1993. At that time, the department revised its Leniency Policy (also referred to as their Amnesty Program) so as now to offer complete amnesty to the first firm that comes forward with information on the cartel, provided that no investigation is currently under way. Even if an investigation has been started, total amnesty might still be offered to the first firm coming forward with evidence if this evidence proves central to successful prosecution of the cartel.[19] As the evidence reviewed at the start of the previous chapter makes clear, this new program has been wildly successful. As the Antitrust Division itself has said:

> Today, the Amnesty Program is the Division's most effective generator of large cases, and it is the Department's most successful leniency program. Amnesty applications over the past year have been coming in at the rate of approximately two per month—a more than *twenty-fold increase* as compared to the rate of applications under the old Amnesty Program. Given this remarkable rate of amnesty applications, it certainly appears that the message has been communicated. (http://www.usdoj.gov/atr/public/speeches/2247.htm)

Or as an article in *Forbes* magazine put it:

> If someone in your company has been conspiring with competitors to fix prices, here's some sound advice. Get to the Justice Department before your co-conspirators do. Confess and the U.S. Department of Justice will let you off the hook. But hurry! Only one conspirator per cartel. (Janet Novack, "Fix and tell," *Forbes*, May 4, 1998).

In effect, the Justice Department's new Amnesty Program really puts the prisoners' dilemma to work!

## SUMMARY

Collusion, both explicit and tacit, is a topic of great interest to both industrial economists and antitrust authorities. Indeed, uncovering and prosecuting cartels is a major policy goal for these officials. To pursue this goal efficiently, the authorities need to use economic theory so as to focus on those markets in which collusion is the greatest threat.

Theory suggests that markets in which collusive agreements are likely to succeed are ones with just a few firms in total or at least where just a few firms account for most of the output. Such markets will also typically exhibit a low elasticity of demand, substantial obstacles to new entry, relatively homogeneous products, similar cost functions across firms, and relatively stable market conditions. Virtually all cartels that have been uncovered have occurred in industries that met these conditions.

Just knowing where to look for cartel arrangements, however, is not enough. Authorities must have the additional ability to identify collusion accurately and to prosecute it successfully. Yet obtaining compelling evidence of price-fixing is difficult, particularly since the authorities often have to rely on the very same firms it is investigating to obtain the incriminating information. This is no doubt why so many cartels have been uncovered only as a result of revelations by rivals, suppliers, employees, or customers of the firms involved. In this light, Phlips' call for the development

---

19 For further details of the precise conditions under which amnesty might be granted, see the speech by the Deputy Assistant Attorney General at http://www.usdoj.gov/atr/public/speeches/2247.htm.

of more tests to discriminate between collusion and non-collusion is well noted. Whether economists will be able to answer that call remains to be seen. In the meantime, the Antitrust Division has probably done the best it can by using its revised Amnesty Program. Since the executives of the firm that is first to confess go free while those at other firms may end up in jail, this policy brings cartel members face-to-face with a very real prisoners' dilemma.

# PROBLEMS

1. Explain why collusion is more likely to occur in industries with higher concentration.

2. Suppose that fence companies submit sealed bids for government contracts to install guardrails on highways. Devise a method for submitting bids that spreads the work evenly among the companies.

3. When highway departments receive bids from guardrail and other construction firms, they regularly open the sealed bid tenders and announce the identity and the bid of the winning bidder. Do you think that this practice facilitates or hinders collusion among the construction firms?

4. List the features of the NASDAQ market that facilitate collusion. What features would make collusion in this market difficult? How should this affect policy?

5. The government-sponsored OPEC oil cartel controls about 2/3 of the world's oil reserves and just a bit less of world oil production. In contrast, another government-sponsored cartel, CIPEC or the International Council of Copper Exporting Countries, controls a bit over 1/3 of world copper reserves and production. While there is little substitute for oil in terms of gasoline and diesel fuel, aluminum substitutes for copper in various products—such as electrical power cables, electrical equipment, automobile radiators, and cooling and polyvinyl chloride (pvc) pipes. One country, Saudi Arabia, controls over 70 percent of all OPEC production. The largest member of CIPEC, Chile, controls about 40 percent of CIPEC production. Use these facts to predict the relative success of the OPEC and CIPEC cartels. Briefly explain your answer.

6. Suppose that a cartel has just been created and it includes both large and small firms, each having different average and marginal cost curves. The cartel agreement is for each member to reduce its output by 20 percent from the current level. Suppose that the current level of industry output approximates the competitive output level. Will this 20 percent reduction rule maximize the cartel's profit? Explain why or why not.

7. It has been noted that cartel firms often maintain excessive capacity. This is true, for example, in the case of OPEC (especially for Saudi Arabia). It was also true in the electric turbine conspiracy of the 1950s and, more recently, the international lysine conspiracy of the 1990s, among others. One explanation of this is that the success of the cartel inevitably leads the members to reinvest their profits in new capacity. In this view, the cartel sews the seeds of its own destruction. Based on the analysis of this chapter, can you give an alternative explanation? What implications does your explanation have for the long-run viability of the cartel?

# REFERENCES

Bernheim, B. D., and M. D. Whinston. 1985. "Common Marketing Agency as a Device for Facilitating Collusion." *Rand Journal of Economics* 16 (Summer): 269–81.

Comanor, W. S., and M. A. Schankerman. 1976. "Identical Bids and Cartel Behavior." *Bell Journal of Economics* 7 (Summer): 281–86.

Connor, J. M. 2001. *Global Price Fixing: Our Customers Are the Enemy.* Boston: Kluwer Academic Publishers.

Davidson, C., and R. Deneckere. 1990. "Excess Capacity and Collusion." *International Economic Review* 31 (August): 521–42.

Dhutta, P. K. 1999. *Strategies and Games: Theory and Practice.* Cambridge, MA: The MIT Press.

————, and A. Madhavan. 1997. "Competition and Collusion in Dealer Markets." *Journal of Finance* 25 (May): 245–76.

Dixit, A. 1980. "The Role of Investment in Entry Deterrence." *The Economic Journal* 90 (January): 95–106.

Eckbo, P. 1976. *The Future of World Oil.* Cambridge, MA: Ballinger.

Harstad, R. M., and L. Phlips. 1991. "Interaction Between Resource Extraction and Futures Markets: A Game Theoretic Analysis." In R. Selten, ed., *Game Equilibrium Analysis*, Vol. II. Berlin: Springer: 289–307.

Hendricks, K., and R. H. Porter. 1988. "An Empirical Study of an Auction with Asymmetric Information." *American Economic Review* 78 (December): 865–83.

LaCasse, C. 1995. "Bid Rigging and the Threat of Government Prosecution." *Rand Journal of Economics* 26 (Autumn): 398–417.

MacLeod, W. B. 1985. "A Theory of Conscious Parallelism." *European Economic Review* 27 (February): 25–44.

McGee, J. S. 1958. "Predatory Price Cutting: the Standard Oil (N.J.) Case." *Journal of Law & Economics* 1 (April): 137–69.

Osborne, M. J., and C. Pitchik. 1987. "Cartels, Profits, and Excess Capacity." *International Economic Review* 28 (June): 413–28.

Phlips, L. 1995a. *Competition Policy: A Game-Theoretic Perspective.* Cambridge, England: Cambridge University Press.

————. 1995b. "On the Detection of Collusion and Predation." EUI Working Papers in Economics, no. 95/35. Florence, Italy: European University Institute.

Porter, R. H., and J. D. Zona. 1993. "Detection of Bid Rigging in Procurement Auctions." *Journal of Political Economy* 101 (June): 518–38.

Salop, S. 1986. "Practices that (Credibly) Facilitate Oligopoly Coordination." In J. Stiglitz and F. G. Mathewson, eds., *New Developments in the Analysis of Market Structure.* Cambridge, MA: The MIT Press: 265–90.

Spence, A. M. 1977. "Entry, Investment, and Oligopolistic Pricing." *Bell Journal of Economics* 8 (Spring): 1–19.

Stigler, G. 1964. "A Theory of Oligopoly." *Journal of Political Economy* 72 (February): 44–61.

# Part five

## Contractual Relations between Firms

# Contractual Relations between Firms

Part Five examines the various ways in which firms may interact that involve formal and legally enforceable contracts. Such formal interactions employ strategic considerations just as much as did the pricing and production decisions discussed in Part Four. However, the manifestation of those tactical issues is more subtle largely because, by its very nature, a formal contract involves some element of cooperation as well as the usual ingredient of self-interest.

Chapters 16 and 17 explore the implications of the most binding of all contracts, the marriage contract. The corporate term for marriage, however, is merger (or acquisition). Chapter 16 explores the issues surrounding the merger of two firms that previously competed against each other—a horizontal merger. Here, a principal challenge is to understand the "merger paradox." This paradox refers to the fact that while we observe numerous mergers in actuality, standard theory suggests that such corporate combinations should not be profitable. We explore this issue along with many other aspects of horizontal mergers.

Chapter 17 then turns to a consideration of a union between an upstream supplier such as a manufacturer and a downstream firm such as a retailer. Here the principle issue is the mechanism(s) explaining why and how such vertically connected firms would wish to combine in this fashion. Possible reasons include the ability of a merger to resolve important contractual issues between the two firms and the ability of the merger to advantage the downstream retailer in its competition with other retailers.

Mergers are perhaps the most dramatic of the formal mechanisms that firms may use to harmonize their interests. Other mechanisms take the form of contracts such as those between a firm and its supplier or between a manufacturer and a retailer. These types of contractual relations are explored in Chapters 18 and 19. Chapter 18 explores the strategic implications of vertical contracts that focus exclusively on the issue of price. Chapter 19 then analyzes similar contracts that are designed to ensure cooperation on nonprice issues, such as the level of retail services or the amount of advertising that a retailer might do. These are critical decisions not just for the retailer but for the firm supplying the retailer as well. The strategic considerations that come into play in the nature of the vertical contract will be influenced by the nature of competition in the industry. Moreover, the reverse is also true. The extent of industrial competition will likely be affected by the nature of the vertical relations between firms.

# Horizontal Mergers

**Chapter** 16

The merger mania that transformed much of corporate America through the 1990s largely disappeared in the wake of the terrorist attack of September 11, 2001; the corporate scandals at companies such as Enron, Tyco, HealthSouth, and WorldCom; and the general turndown in the market as a result of the bursting of the dot.com bubble. This does not mean, however, that mergers are things of the past. Around twenty major deals were announced in the summer of 2003, including Oracle's $6.2 billion hostile bid for PeopleSoft Inc.; Alcan Inc.'s $3.9 billion bid for Pechinet SA, a deal that has received approval from the European Commission; Liberty Media Corp.'s $7.9 billion purchase of QVC Inc.; and the proposed merger of Air France and KLM. October 2003 saw further resurgence, with merger activity in the United States in that month alone amounting to $103.1 billion.

Of course, this latest mini-wave could be reversed if there were further bad news on the economy or on corporate governance. However, there is a view among some analysts that the past three years of reduced merger deals has created a pent-up demand that is just waiting to be released, particularly since acquisitions are seen by senior executives as levers of growth. Moreover, there is the view that merger deals create more merger deals, with senior executives closely watching how their competitors are behaving and seeking to emulate them.

The organization and reorganization of firms brought about by mergers and acquisitions raises several issues. Perhaps the most central of these is the question, why? What is the motivation behind the marriage of two (or more) firms? One rationale is that the merger creates cost savings, perhaps by eliminating wasteful duplication or by improving information flows within the merged organization. Similarly, the merger may lead to more efficient pricing and/or improved services to customers because it is between two firms producing complementary goods such as nuts and bolts, as we discussed in Chapter 8.

To the extent that reducing cost or rationalizing complementary production is the primary motivation behind most mergers, such combinations are likely to be beneficial to society as well as to the merging firms and ought not to be discouraged. However, mergers also can be an attempt to create legal cartels. The merged firms come under common ownership and control. Hence, the new corporate entity will coordinate what were formerly separate actions with a view to achieving the joint profit-maximizing outcome. Such coordination is legal precisely because it takes place within the boundaries of the firm rather than across different firms. Viewed in this light, mergers are seen as an undesirable attempt to create and exploit monopoly power in a market. This brings us to a second and closely related issue in the analysis of mergers, namely, the public policy implications raised whenever two or more firms merge. The Antitrust Division of the Justice Department has issued (jointly with the Federal Trade Commission) a set of merger guidelines. The agencies make clear that their focus is "on the one potential source of gain that is of concern under the antitrust laws: market power." In other words, the ever-present danger that serves as a unifying theme for the guidelines is the possibility that a merger will enhance either market power or the ability to facilitate its exercise, in which case the merger might not be in the public interest.[1]

An important question is whether this fear of market power via mergers is justified. Can we distinguish between mergers that enhance monopoly power and those that do not? To some extent, this distinction is the motivation behind the guidelines in the first place. The tension inherent in distinguishing between anticompetitive mergers and those that are not injurious to competition is openly admitted in the Overview to the Merger Guidelines. "While challenging competitively harmful mergers, the Agency seeks to avoid unnecessary interference within the larger universe of mergers that are either competitively beneficial or neutral."

Our aim in this chapter and the next is to explore these issues. We examine what economic theory can tell us about the rationale for mergers. In particular, we investigate the threat of monopoly power that mergers may create, and the public policy toward merger activity that this implies. These are topics that have been the subject of debate among economists and others for a long time. The merger wave of the 1990s in the United States occurred under a regulatory environment that was much more relaxed than in previous decades. This has caused some to worry that the enforcement of antitrust policy with respect to mergers has been too lenient. Our goal in these chapters is to examine the motives for mergers and the consequences of mergers for firms and consumers, and to use the results of this analysis to discuss public policy with respect to mergers.

Before going further, it is perhaps appropriate that we point out that the material in this chapter—especially in Section 16.3—is some of the most challenging in the entire book. The basic models are not new but they are more complicated. We believe that this complication is necessary if we are to come anywhere close to capturing the real issues raised by mergers. Our recommendation is to be patient and to work through the material carefully. Keep in mind that the analysis we use is simply an extension of that presented in Chapter 9. If you are able to follow the models presented there, then you certainly can understand the analysis we do here.

We begin our study by providing a classification of merger types. All mergers are not alike. An important source of distinction is the nature of the relationship that existed between the merging firms prior to their combination. This gives rise to three different kinds of mergers.

First, there are horizontal mergers. These occur when the firms joining together in the merger were formerly competitors in the same product market. That is, a horizontal merger involves two or more firms that, so far as their buyers are concerned, market substitute products. The merger of Alcan and Pechinet is one example of a horizontal merger.

Vertical mergers are the second type. These typically involve firms at different stages in the vertical production chain. A typical example is the oil producers' ownership of petroleum refining operations. A more recent example is the acquisition by the Disney Company of Capital Cities/ABC. Here, a major producer of films and television programs acquired a major distributor and network that airs this material. The focus on such hierarchical links is, however, a bit restrictive. The analysis of vertical mergers can be applied to any combination of firms that, prior to the merger, pro-

---

1   The Justice Department and Federal Trade Commission Horizontal Merger Guidelines can be read at http://www.ftc.gov/bc/docs/horizmer.htm. Section Two on the potential adverse effects of mergers is particularly relevant. We return to some of these policy issues more directly in the next chapter.

duced complementary goods. Oil producers and refiners may be seen in this light. As noted, they are a typical example of a vertical combination. But the union of other firms with a less hierarchical yet nonetheless complementary relationship also falls under this category of analysis. The merger that was proposed between British Telecommunications and MCI offers an example. These two firms operate in different geographical markets for many of their customers but provide potentially complementary services to any caller originating a call in the United Kingdom and terminating it in the United States or vice-versa. The merger of CSX and Conrail, two large freight rail companies in the eastern United States, provides another example. An important rationale for this merger was that the two firms provided complementary services to customers who wish to transport goods from the southeast of the United States to the northeast.

Finally, conglomerate mergers involve the combination of firms without either a clear substitute or a clear complementary relationship. Examples include (1) the purchase of Duracell Batteries by Gillette, (2) the purchase of Snapple (iced tea) and Gatorade (a sports drink) by Quaker Oats, and (3) the series of acquisitions in 1986 by Daimler-Benz, a luxury car and truck manufacturer, which turned it into Germany's largest industrial concern, producing aerospace to household goods.

In this chapter we focus on horizontal mergers. Since these reflect combinations of two or more firms in the same industry, they raise the most obvious antitrust concerns. Vertical and conglomerate mergers are discussed in Chapter 17.

## 16.1 HORIZONTAL MERGERS AND THE MERGER PARADOX

Horizontal mergers replace two or more former competitors with a single firm. The merger of two firms in a three-firm market changes the industry to a duopoly. The merger of two duopolists creates a monopolist. The potential for a merger to create monopoly power is clearly an issue in the horizontal case. Our first order of business is therefore rather surprising. It is to discuss a phenomenon known as the *merger paradox*. The paradox is that it is, in fact, quite difficult to construct a simple economic model in which there are sizable gains for firms participating in a horizontal merger *that is not a merger to monopoly*.[2] We illustrate this paradox using the Cournot model developed in earlier chapters.[3]

Let's start with a simple example. Suppose we have three firms, each with a constant marginal cost of $c = \$30$ and jointly facing an industry demand curve described by $P = 150 - Q$. As we know from Chapter 9, the Cournot equilibrium results in each firm producing one-fourth of the competitive output, or 30, so that total output is 90. The price, therefore, is $P = \$60$ and each firm earns a profit of $30(\$60 - \$30) = \$900$.

What happens if two of these firms merge? In the wake of a two-firm merger, the industry will become one with two firms, each of which will produce one-third of the competitive output, or 40, so that total output now falls to 80. The price will then rise to $70 and each of the two remaining firms will earn a profit of $1,600.

We may now evaluate the impact of the merger. First, note that the merger is bad for consumers. Output falls and the price rises. Second, observe that the merger is

---

2   A merger to monopoly is when all the firms in an industry combine into a single monopoly producer.
3   The paradox was first formalized in a slightly different form by Salant, Switzer, and Reynolds (1983).

good news for the firm that did not merge. It now expands its output to 40 units and sells these at a higher price than previously so that it enjoys a profit increase of $1,600 – $900 = $700. Finally, we come to the central element in the merger paradox. For the two firms that merged, the merger did not pay off. Previously, each produced 30 units and earned a profit of $900 for a combined pre-merger output and profit of 60 units and $1,800, respectively. In the post-merger market, however, these two firms have a combined output of only 40 and a total profit of $1,600. The merger has hurt the firms that merged and brought benefits to their rival. If this example is reflective of a more general result, then we ought not to observe many mergers. Of course, the paradox is that we do observe mergers all the time.

The fact of the matter is that the foregoing example is not a special case. It is, in fact, easy to show that a merger will almost certainly be unprofitable in the basic Cournot model whether it is between two firms or even more so long as the merger does not create a monopoly. To see this more general result, start by assuming a market of $N > 2$ firms, each of which produces a homogeneous product and acts as a Cournot competitor. The firms have identical costs given by the total cost function

$$C(q_i) = cq_i \text{ for } i = 1, \ldots, N, \tag{16.1}$$

where $q_i$ is output of firm $i$. Market demand is linear and, in inverse form, is given by the equation

$$P = A - BQ = A - B(q_i + Q_{-i}), \tag{16.2}$$

where $Q$ is aggregate output produced by the $N$ firms and $Q_{-i}$ is the aggregate output of all firms except firm $i$; that is,

$$Q_{-i} = Q - q_i.$$

The profit function for firm $i$ can then be written as

$$\pi_i(q_i, Q_{-i}) = q_i[A - B(q_i + Q_{-i}) - c]. \tag{16.3}$$

In a Cournot game, firms choose their output levels simultaneously to maximize profit. Recall from our analysis in Chapter 9 that the resulting profit to each firm in a Cournot equilibrium is

$$\pi_i^C = \frac{(A - c)^2}{B(N + 1)^2}. \tag{16.4}$$

Suppose now that $M \geq 2$ of these firms decide to merge. In order to exclude the case of merger to monopoly we assume that $M < N$. Such a merger leads to an industry in which there are now $N - M + 1$ firms competing in the industry. Since all firms are the same, we can think of the merged firm as comprised of firms 1 through $M$.

The newly merged firm picks its output $q_m$ to maximize profit, which is given by

$$\pi_m(q_m, Q_{-m}) = q_m[A - B(q_m + Q_{-m}) - c], \tag{16.5}$$

where $Q_{-m} = q_{m+1} + q_{m+2} + \ldots + q_N$ denotes the aggregate output of the $N - M$ firms that have not merged. Each of the nonmerged firms chooses its output to maximize profit given, as before, by

$$\pi_i(q_i, Q_{-i}) = q_i[A - B(q_i + Q_{-i}) - c]. \tag{16.6}$$

In this case the term $Q_{-i}$ denotes the sum of the outputs $q_j$ of each of the $N - M$ non-merging firms excluding firm $i$, plus the output of the merged firm $q_m$.

The only difference between equations (16.5) and (16.6) is that in the former we have a subscript $m$ while in the latter we have a subscript $i$. In other words, a crucial implication of equations (16.5) and (16.6) is that, after the merger, *the merged firm becomes just like any one of the other firms in the industry.* This means that all of these $N - M + 1$ firms, each having identical costs and producing the same product, must in equilibrium produce the same amount of output and therefore earn the same profit. In other words, in the post-merger Cournot equilibrium, it must be the case that the output and profit of the merged firm, $q_m^C$ and $\pi_m^C$, are the same as the output and profit of each nonmerged firm. For a market with $N - M + 1$ firms, these are, respectively

$$q_m^C = q_{nm}^C = \frac{A - c}{B(N - M + 2)} \text{ and } \pi_m^C = \pi_{nm}^C = \frac{(A - c)^2}{B(N - M + 2)^2}, \quad \textbf{(16.7)}$$

where the subscript $m$ denotes the merged firm and $nm$ a nonmerged firm.

Equations (16.4) and (16.7) allow us to compare the profit of the nonmerging firms before and after the merger. In this context, the first point to note is the free riding that nonmerging firms can do when other firms merge. We know from the Cournot presentation in Chapter 9 that industry output falls (and price rises) as the number of firms fall. Of course, a merger does just that. It reduces the number of firms. So, price rises for all firms, including those that did not merge. The merger allows these firms to gain market share while also benefiting from an increase in the market price.

What about the merging firms? There are $M$ of these and, prior to the merger, each one earned the profit shown in equation (16.4). Hence, the aggregate profit of these firms taken together is $M$ times that amount. After the merger, the profit of the merged firm is the profit shown in equation (16.7). Is the profit of the merged firm greater than the aggregate profit earned by the $M$ firms before the merger? In order for the answer to be yes, it must be the case that

$$\frac{(A - c)^2}{B(N - M + 2)^2} \geq M \frac{(A - c)^2}{B(N + 1)^2}. \quad \textbf{(16.8)}$$

This requires

$$(N + 1)^2 \geq M(N - M + 2)^2. \quad \textbf{(16.9)}$$

Note that equation (16.9) does not include any of the demand parameters or the firms' marginal costs. In other words, equation (16.9) tells us about the profitability of *any M* firm merger. All that is required is that demand is linear and that the firms each have the same, constant marginal costs.

Let's take the case of our example in which the number of firms is $N = 3$, and the number of firms merging is $M = 2$. It's easy to see that the inequality in (16.9) is not satisfied. The left-hand side is 16 while the right-hand side is 18. That is, we have now shown for the general case what our special example already suggested: in a three-firm market satisfying our demand and cost assumptions, *no two-firm merger is profitable.*

Indeed, condition (16.9) turns out to be very difficult to satisfy even when more than two firms merge as long as the merger does not result in a monopoly. To see this, suppose that we substitute $M = aN$ in equation (16.9), with $0 < a < 1$. That is, $a$ is the fraction of firms that merge. We can then work out how large $a$ has to be for the merger to be profitable. A little manipulation of condition (16.9) shows that for this to be the case, we must have $a > a(N)$ where[4]

$$a(N) = \frac{3 + 2N - \sqrt{5 + 4N}}{2N} .$$   **(16.10)**

Table 16-1 gives $a(N)$ and the associated minimum number of firms $M$ that have to merge for the merger to be profitable for a range of values of $N$.

TABLE
**16-1**

### NECESSARY CONDITION FOR PROFITABLE MERGER

| $N$ | 5 | 10 | 15 | 20 | 25 |
|-----|-----|-----|-----|-----|-----|
| $a(N)$ | 80% | 81.5% | 83.1% | 84.5% | 85.5% |
| $M$ | 4 | 9 | 13 | 17 | 22 |

Equation (16.10) and Table 16-1 illustrate what has come to be termed the 80 percent rule. For a merger to be profitable in our simple Cournot world of linear demand and identical linear costs, it is necessary that at least 80 percent of the firms in the market merge. The problem is that this is a merger of a magnitude that would almost never be allowed by the antitrust authorities.

## Practice Problem 16.1

Suppose that demand for carpet-cleaning services in Dirtville is described by $P = 130 - Q$. There are currently twenty identical firms that clean carpets in the area. The unit cost of cleaning a carpet is constant and equal to \$30. Firms in this industry compete in quantities.

a. Show that in a Cournot–Nash equilibrium the profit of each firm is $\pi = 22.67$.
b. Now suppose that six firms in the industry merge. Show that the profit of each firm in the post-merger Cournot game is $\pi = 39.06$. Show that the profit earned by the merged firm is insufficient to compensate all the shareholders/owners who owned the six original firms and earned profit from them in the pre-merger market game.
c. Show that if fewer than seventeen firms merge, the profit of the merged firm is not great enough to buy out the shareholders/owners of the firms who merge.

The merger paradox is that many, if not most, horizontal mergers are unprofitable when viewed through the lens of our standard Cournot–Nash model. Yet as the events of the 1990s and more recent years tell us, horizontal mergers such as that of Alcan and Pechiney happen all the time. What aspect of real-world mergers has our

4   You can check this equation by direct substitution of $a(N)$ in equation (16.9).

simple Cournot model failed to capture? Alternatively, what aspect of the Cournot model is responsible for this prediction that seems at odds with reality?

The critical aspect of the Cournot model that gives rise to the merger paradox is not difficult to find. When firms merge in the Cournot model, the new combined firm behaves after the merger just like any of the remaining firms that did not merge. Thus, if two firms in a three-firm industry merge, the new firm competes as a duopolist. The nonmerging firm in this case has, after the merger, equal status to the merged firm even though it now faces the combined strength of both of its previous rivals.

One cannot help but suspect that, for a merger of any substantial size, the resulting new firm must, in some sense, be larger or stronger or something more than its old rivals that did not merge. What is missing from the simple Cournot model is some credible means by which the merged firm can take advantage of its potential size.[5] The question then is whether any mechanisms exist that permit the merged firm to use its size in a manner that makes the merger profitable.[6] To consider such strategies, however, requires that we depart from the simple Cournot model to at least some extent. In the following sections we consider three such deviations: asymmetric costs, timing, and product differentiation.

## 16.2 MERGER AND COST SYNERGIES

In developing the merger paradox we assumed that all firms in the market have identical costs and that there are no fixed costs. What happens if we relax these assumptions? It seems reasonable to suppose that if a merger creates sufficiently large cost savings it should be profitable. In this section we develop an example to show that this can indeed be the case.[7]

Suppose that the market contains three Cournot firms. Consumer demand is given by

$$P = 150 - Q, \tag{16.11}$$

where $Q$ is aggregate output, which pre-merger is $q_1 + q_2 + q_3$. Two of these firms are low-cost firms with a marginal cost of 30 so that total costs at each are given by

$$C_1(q_1) = f + 30q_1; \ C_2(q_2) = f + 30q_2. \tag{16.12}$$

The third firm is a potentially high-cost firm with total costs given by

$$C_3(q_3) = f + 30bq_3, \tag{16.13}$$

where $b \geq 1$ is a measure of the cost disadvantage from which firm 3 suffers. In these cost functions $f$ represents fixed costs associated with overhead expenses such as those

---

5   Credibility is used here in the sense we have developed in earlier chapters. As things stand, the merged firm cannot credibly commit to any output other than that given by equation (16.7).
6   There are other approaches. Perry and Porter (1985), for example, assume that each firm's cost function depends upon the amount of capital it owns and that capital is in fixed supply. When firms merge they combine their capital and so form a firm that is larger than the firms outside the merger.
7   This is a special case of a more sophisticated analysis by Farrell and Shapiro (1990), who show in a general setting that for consumers to benefit from a profitable horizontal merger of Cournot firms the merger has to create substantial cost synergies.

for marketing or for maintaining corporate headquarters. We now consider the effect of a merger of firms 2 and 3.

## 16.2.1  Case A: The Merger Reduces Fixed Costs

Consider first the case in which $b = 1$ so that all firms have the same marginal cost of 30. Suppose, however, that after the merger the merged firm has fixed costs $af$ with $1 \leq a \leq 2$. What this means is that the merger allows the merged firms to economize on overhead costs, for example, by combining the headquarters of the two firms, eliminating unnecessary overlap, combining R&D functions, and economizing on duplicated marketing efforts. These are, in fact, typical cost savings that most firms state that they expect to result from a merger.

Because the merger leaves marginal costs unaffected, this is just a case of our initial example when firms also have fixed costs. Accordingly, we know that in the pre-merger market each firm earns a profit of $900 - f$. In the post-merger market with just two firms, one earns a profit of $1,600 - f$ while the merged firm earns $1,600 - af$. Hence, for this merger to be profitable, it must be the case that $1,600 - af > 1,800 - 2f$, which requires that $a < 2 - 200/f$. What this says is that a merger is more likely to be profitable when fixed costs are relatively high and the merger gives the merged firm the ability to make "substantial" savings in these costs. Note, however, that even if the merger is profitable for the merging firms, consumers are actually worse off as a result of the higher equilibrium price. That same higher price also raises the profit of the nonmerged firm. Indeed, for any $a$ value strictly greater than one, the nonmerged firms enjoy a greater profit increase than do the merged ones. This leaves the paradox somewhat unexplained since it would appear to be more profitable to wait for other firms to merge rather than for a firm to seek a merger itself.

## 16.2.2  Case B: The Merger Reduces Variable Costs

Now consider the case in which the source of the cost savings is not a reduction in fixed costs but instead a reduction in variable costs, which we capture by assuming that $b > 1$. In other words, firm 3 is a high variable cost firm. It follows that after a merger of firms 2 and 3, production will be rationalized and the high-cost operations will be shut down. To make matters as simple as possible we will assume that there are no fixed costs ($f = 0$).

Once again we assume a Cournot framework. The outputs and profits of the three firms prior to the merger are

$$q_1^C = q_2^C = \frac{90 + 30b}{4}; \quad q_3^C = \frac{210 - 90b}{4} \quad \text{and}$$

$$\pi_1^C = \pi_2^C = \frac{(90 + 30b)^2}{16}; \quad \pi_3^C = \frac{(210 - 90b)^2}{16}. \tag{16.14}$$

The equilibrium pre-merger price is $P^C = \dfrac{210 + 30b}{4}$.[8] Total output is $Q = \dfrac{390 - 30b}{4}$ with each of the low-cost firms, 1 and 2, producing a greater amount than their high-cost rival, firm 3.

---

8  Note that this equilibrium will exist only if there is an upper limit on the cost disadvantage $b$ that firm 3 suffers. To be specific, firm 3's pre-merger output will be positive only if $b < 210/90 = 7/3$. If this were not the case then firm 3 would not be able to operate in this market in the first place.

Now, as before, suppose that firms 2 and 3 merge. Since for any $b > 1$ it is always more expensive to produce a unit of output at firm 3 than it is at firm 2, all production will be transferred to firm 2. The result is that the market now contains two identical firms, 1 and 2, each with marginal costs of $30. Accordingly, in the post-merger industry, each firm produces 40 units, the product price is $70, and each firm earns $1,600.

Is this a profitable merger? For the merger to increase aggregate profit of the merged firms it must be the case that

$$1{,}600 - \left( \frac{(90 + 30b)^2}{16} + \frac{(210 - 90b)^2}{16} \right) > 0. \qquad \text{(16.15)}$$

You can check that this simplifies to

$$\frac{25}{2}(7 - 3b)(15b - 19) > 0. \qquad \text{(16.16)}$$

The first parenthetical term in equation (16.16) has to be positive for firm 3 to have been in the market in the first place. (See footnote 8). So the merger is profitable provided that the second parenthetical term is also positive, which requires that $b > 19/15$. In other words, *a merger between a high-cost and a low-cost firm will be profitable provided that the cost disadvantage of the high-cost firm prior to the merger is large enough*. In the case at hand, "large enough" means that firm 3's unit cost is about 27 percent greater than firm 2's unit cost. However, as we have already demonstrated, whether the merger is profitable or not, the price rises and consumers are made worse off.

Together, our analysis of a merger that generates fixed cost savings and one that generates variable cost savings makes clear that mergers can be profitable when the cost savings are great enough. However, there is no guarantee that consumers gain from such a merger. Admittedly, the merger removes a relatively inefficient firm but it also reduces competitive pressures between the remaining firms. Farrell and Shapiro (1990) demonstrate that in the Cournot setting used here, the cost savings necessary to generate a gain for consumers are much larger than those needed simply to make the merger profitable. In turn, this suggests that we should be skeptical of cost savings as a justification of the benefits to consumers of horizontal mergers. Beyond all this it is also worth noting that part of our initial paradox still remains since the biggest profit gains accrue to the firms that do not merge.

## Practice Problem 16.2

Return to the market for carpet-cleaning services in Dirtville, now described by the demand function $P = 180 - Q$. Suppose that there are currently three firms that clean carpets in the area. The unit cost of cleaning a carpet is constant and equal to $30 for two of them and is $30b for the third firm, where $b \geq 1$. In addition, all firms have fixed overhead costs of $900. Firms in this industry compete in quantities.

a. What is the Cournot–Nash equilibrium price and what are the outputs and profits of each firm? What is the upper limit on $b$ for the third firm to be able to survive?

b. Now suppose that a low-cost firm merges with the high-cost firm. In doing so, the fixed costs of the merged firm become $900a with $1 \leq a \leq 2$. What is the post-merger equilibrium price? What are the outputs of the nonmerged and the merged firms?

c. Derive a relationship between *a* and *b* that is necessary to guarantee that the profit earned by the merged firm is sufficient to compensate all the shareholders/owners who owned the two original firms and earned profit from them in the pre-merger market game. Graph this relationship and comment on it.

# 16.3 THE MERGED FIRMS AS STACKELBERG LEADERS—PARADOX LOST

The merger paradox arises because the merged firms are unable to make a credible commitment that allows them to take advantage of their potentially greater post-merger size. We have just shown that cost synergies arising from the merger may resolve this paradox, but only if they are large. Another possibility is to introduce a mechanism that enables the merged firms to make a credible commitment to operate on a large scale after the merger. One possibility is that merged firms become Stackelberg leaders in the post-merger market.[9] Recall from our discussion in Chapter 11 that the source of a Stackelberg leader firm's advantage is its ability to commit to an output before output decisions are taken by the follower firms. This permits a leader to choose an output that takes into account the reactions of the followers.

Let us assume that a merged firm does acquire a leadership role and see whether this assumption can help resolve the merger paradox. Certainly, such a role seems plausible. After all, the new firm has a combined capacity twice that of any of its non-merged rivals, and so might well be able to act as a Stackelberg leader. Yet if this is the case, what about the reaction of the nonmerging firms to firms that merge to become an industry leader? Will these firms passively sit back and watch their profits be eroded? Or will these firms respond by seeking their own merger partners?

The idea that one merger in an industry could spawn subsequent ones is not only a theoretical possibility worth exploring, but also a common, real-world phenomenon. Frequently, a merger generates a "domino effect" in which soon after two firms merge, two others merge and then two more, and so on. Indeed, this is the essence of a merger wave. We would like our model of horizontal mergers to be consistent with this empirical observation.

If merging to become a large leader firm is profitable for more than one pair of firms we should envisage a series of two-firm mergers that leads to some group *L* of industry leaders. But what does it mean to have more than one leader? How do such leading firms compete? What stops all firms from merging so as to become part of the leader group?

Let us begin by supposing that a chain of two-firm mergers has already occurred in the industry and that there is currently a set of *L* leader firms. There are also *F* follower firms so that there are $N = F + L$ firms in total. As usual, we assume a linear model in which demand is given by $P = A - BQ$, and each firm has total costs $C(q_i) = cq_i$. What it means to be a Stackelberg leader is to be able to choose one's output first. Thus, we have a two-stage game. In stage one, each of the previously merged firms (the set of leaders) independently chooses its output $q_l$, yielding aggregate out-

---

9  This analysis draws on Daughety (1990), who was the first to suggest this type of role for the merged firms.

put for these firms of $Q^L = \sum_{l=1}^{L} q_l$. In the second stage, the firms in the follower group independently choose their outputs in response to the aggregate output chosen by the leaders. As we know from Chapter 11, going first is an advantage in this sort of game because choosing outputs first allows the leaders to anticipate the responses of the follower, nonmerged, firms.

To find the equilibrium, we work through the game backwards. Accordingly, we consider the second stage of the game in which the follower nonmerged firms make their output decisions in response to the *aggregate* output choice, $Q^L$, of the leader or merged firms. As usual, we start by identifying the residual (inverse) demand function for a representative firm $f$ in the follower group. We have already defined the aggregate output of the leader group as $Q^L$. We use the notation $Q_{F-f}$ to denote the aggregate output of the follower firms *other than $f$*. Suppose that the output of follower firm $f$ is $q_f$. Then aggregate output of all firms is $Q = Q^L + Q_{F-f} + q_f$. The residual demand for firm $f$, which is the demand left after taking into account the outputs of the leader group and the followers other than firm $f$, is

$$P = [A - B(Q^L + Q_{F-f})] - Bq_f. \qquad (16.17)$$

Marginal revenue for firm $f$ is, therefore,

$$MR_f = [A - B(Q^L + Q_{F-f})] - 2Bq_f. \qquad (16.18)$$

Equating this with marginal cost gives the best response function for firm $f$:

$$A - 2Bq_f - BQ^L - BQ_{F-f} = c \Rightarrow q_f^* = \frac{A - c}{2B} - \frac{Q^L}{2} - \frac{Q_{F-f}}{2}. \qquad (16.19)$$

Equation (16.19) is the best response of a typical follower firm to both the output of the leaders and the output of all the other follower firms. It says that the typical follower firm reduces its output by one-half unit for every one-unit increase by either the leaders or the other followers. If you review our work on the Cournot and Stackelberg models in Chapters 9 and 11, you will find essentially the same response function behavior there.

Now note that, since all follower firms are identical, symmetry demands that in equilibrium the output of each of the follower firms must be identical. The group of followers excluding firm $f$ contains $F - 1 = (N - L - 1)$ firms. Therefore, $Q_{F-f}^* = (N - L - 1)q_f^*$. Substituting this into equation (16.19) and simplifying gives the optimal output for each nonmerged follower firm as a function of the aggregate output of the leader group of merged firms:

$$q_f^* = \frac{A - c}{B(N - L + 1)} - \frac{Q^L}{(N - L + 1)}. \qquad (16.20)$$

The aggregate output of all followers as a function of the output of the leaders is then

$$Q^F = (N - L)q_f^* = \frac{(N - L)(A - c)}{B(N - L + 1)} - \frac{(N - L)Q^L}{(N - L + 1)}. \qquad (16.21)$$

We can use the same basic technique to determine the output for a typical leader firm in stage one of the game. The residual inverse demand function for a leader firm $l$ is dependent upon the output of all the other firms. This output contains two elements, the total output of the followers, $Q^F$, and the output of all the leaders other than firm $l$, which we denote $Q_{L-l}$. This gives the residual demand function for firm $l$:

$$P = [A - B(Q^F + Q_{L-l})] - Bq_l. \tag{16.22}$$

There is, however, a vital difference between the leader firms and the followers. Each leader firm knows that $Q^F$ is going to be given by equation (16.21). In other words, the typical leader firm correctly anticipates the output reaction of the group of followers. This means that we can substitute equation (16.21) into equation (16.22) before we find the best response function for firm $l$. This substitution gives

$$P = A - B\left[\frac{(N - L)(A - c)}{B(N - L + 1)} - \frac{(N - L)Q^L}{(N - L + 1)} + Q_{L-l}\right] - Bq_l. \tag{16.23}$$

We know that, by definition, $Q^L = Q_{L-l} + q_l$. Substituting this into equation (16.23) and collecting terms gives the residual inverse demand function for leader firm $l$:

$$P = \frac{A + (N - L)c - BQ_{L-l}}{(N - L + 1)} - \frac{B}{(N - L + 1)}q_l. \tag{16.24}$$

Its associated marginal revenue function is

$$MR_l = \frac{A + (N - L)c - BQ_{L-l}}{(N - L + 1)} - \frac{2B}{(N - L + 1)}q_l. \tag{16.25}$$

Equating this marginal revenue with marginal cost gives the leader firm $l$'s best output response to the output produced by all the other leader firms, $Q_{L-l}$:

$$MR_l = \frac{A + (N - L)c - BQ_{L-l}}{(N - L + 1)} - \frac{2B}{(N - L + 1)}q_l = c \Rightarrow q_l^* = \frac{A - c}{2B} - \frac{Q_{L-l}}{2}. \tag{16.26}$$

Once again, we can take advantage of the fact that since all of the leader firms have the same costs they will each produce the same level of output in equilibrium. Because there are $L - 1$ leaders other than firm $l$, this gives the symmetry condition $Q_{L-l}^* = (L - 1)q_l^*$, which when substituted into equation (16.26) allows us to solve for the output chosen in stage one by each merged firm in the leader group:

$$q_l^* = \frac{A - c}{2B} - \frac{(L - 1)}{2}q_l^* \Rightarrow q_l^* = \frac{A - c}{B(L + 1)}. \tag{16.27}$$

Note that if there were just one merged firm, so that $L = 1$, there would be a single Stackelberg leader and equation (16.27) with $L = 1$ is identical to equation (11.6) for the output of a Stackelberg leader. More generally, as the number of leader or merged firms increases the output of each merged firm falls.

Since there are $L$ leaders, the aggregate leader output is, from equation (16.27), $Q^L = L(A - c)/B(L + 1)$. Substituting this into equations (16.20) and (16.21), we can then find the individual output for each follower and the aggregate output of all followers. These are, respectively,

$$q_f^* = \frac{A - c}{B(L + 1)(N - L + 1)} \quad \text{and} \quad Q^F = \frac{(N - L)(A - c)}{B(L + 1)(N - L + 1)}. \quad \text{(16.28)}$$

It has taken a bit of work, but now we can investigate the incentive to merge in this model. Let us start by comparing the output of a typical leader and a typical follower firm as given by equations (16.27) and (16.28). It is clear that the leader firms are larger than the followers. This means that a merger that confers a leadership role does, indeed, create a credible commitment to greater size for the merged firm. The incentive to merge, however, depends on whether merging two firms to become a leader raises profit.

To work out the profitability of a merger it is necessary to compute the profit of a typical leader and the profit of a typical follower. Note though that the profitability of any firm is just the industry price-cost margin, $P - c$, times that firm's total output. To get total output we just add the total leader output and the total follower output together to obtain the aggregate industry output. This is

$$Q^T = Q^L + Q^F = \frac{(N + NL - L^2)(A - c)}{B(L + 1)(N - L + 1)}. \quad \text{(16.29)}$$

We can solve for the price-cost margin by substituting the total output given in equation (16.29) into the demand curve. Simple manipulation yields

$$P - c = \frac{A - c}{(L + 1)(N - L + 1)}. \quad \text{(16.30)}$$

Multiplying the margin in equation (16.30) by the outputs shown in equations (16.27) and (16.28) yields a profit for each firm type of

$$\pi^L(N, L) = \frac{(A - c)^2}{B(L + 1)^2(N - L + 1)} \quad \text{and} \quad \pi^F(N, L) = \frac{(A - c)^2}{B(L + 1)^2(N - L + 1)^2}. \quad \text{(16.31)}$$

It is clear from the profit equations in (16.31) that the leader firms are more profitable than the nonmerged followers. Yet that is not the real issue facing two firms that are contemplating merger. The question is whether *one more merger* is profitable, given that there will then be one more leader, two fewer followers, and one less firm in total. This is why we have written the profit expressions as functions of $N$ and $L$. The point is that an additional merger creates two countervailing forces. On the one hand there are fewer firms in total, which ought to increase profits, but there are also more leaders, which ought to decrease the profits of the leaders. Which force is greater?

Suppose there is an additional merger of two followers, so that the newly merged firm and all other leaders earn profit given by equation (16.31) with $N$ replaced by $N - 1$ and $L$ replaced by $L + 1$ to give $\pi_l^L(N - 1, L + 1)$. For there to be an incentive to merge, this profit must exceed the combined profit earned by the two follower firms prior to the merger. This latter profit is, from equation (16.22), $2\pi_f^F(N, L)$. So, the merger will be profitable if the following condition is satisfied:

$$\pi^L(N-1, L+1) = \frac{(A-c)^2}{B(L+2)^2(N-L-1)} > 2\pi^F(N, L) = \frac{2(A-c)^2}{B(L+1)^2(N-L+1)^2}.$$

(16.32)

This simplifies to the condition

$$(L+1)^2(N-L+1)^2 - 2(L+2)^2(N-L-1) > 0.$$  (16.33)

Note that this condition does not include the demand parameters $A$ and $B$ or the marginal cost $c$. In other words, the profitability or otherwise of this type of merger depends only on the number of leaders and followers, not on the precise demand and cost conditions.

Even though equation (16.33) is not very elegant, it does turn out that it is always positive. This is shown in Table 16-2 where we have calculated the left-hand side of equation (16.33) for any two-firm merger for a range of values of $N$ and $L$. In other words, starting from any configuration of leaders and followers, *an additional two follower firms always wish to merge.*

---

**TABLE**

**16-2**

**PROFIT EFFECT OF TWO FOLLOWER FIRMS MERGING TO BECOME A LEADER: PRIOR TO THE MERGER THERE ARE *N* FIRMS AND *L* LEADERS**

| *Original Number of Leaders* *L* | *Original Number of Firms N* | | | | | | | | | |
|---|---|---|---|---|---|---|---|---|---|---|
| | 5 | 10 | 15 | 20 | 25 | 30 | 35 | 40 | 45 | 50 |
| 2 | 80 | 505 | 1380 | 2705 | 4480 | 6705 | 9380 | 12505 | 16080 | 20105 |
| 4 | | 865 | 2880 | 6145 | 10660 | 16425 | 23440 | 31705 | 41220 | 51985 |
| 6 | | 841 | 3876 | 9361 | 17296 | 27681 | 40516 | 55801 | 73536 | 93721 |
| 8 | | 529 | 3984 | 11489 | 23044 | 38649 | 58304 | 82009 | 109764 | 141569 |
| 10 | | | 3204 | 12049 | 26944 | 47889 | 74884 | 107929 | 147024 | 192169 |
| 12 | | | 1920 | 10945 | 28420 | 54345 | 88720 | 131545 | 182820 | 242545 |
| 14 | | | | 8465 | 27280 | 57345 | 98660 | 151225 | 215040 | 290105 |
| 16 | | | | 5281 | 23716 | 56601 | 103936 | 165721 | 241956 | 332641 |
| 18 | | | | 2449 | 18304 | 52209 | 104164 | 174169 | 262224 | 368329 |
| 20 | | | | | 12004 | 44649 | 99344 | 176089 | 274884 | 395729 |
| 22 | | | | | 6160 | 34785 | 89860 | 171385 | 279360 | 413785 |
| 24 | | | | | | 23865 | 76480 | 160345 | 275460 | 421825 |

Note: The entries in Table 16-2 are derived from equation (16.33).

---

This result is encouraging. It says that our model offers one way to resolve the merger paradox. A merger raises the profit of the two merging firms by allowing them to take a position as one of perhaps several industry leaders. Moreover, the fact that such a merger is always profitable also helps us to understand better the domino effect so often observed within an industry. Once one firm merges and becomes a leader, the remaining firms will wish to do the same rather than watch their output and their profits be squeezed.

## Practice Problem 16.3

Return again to the town of Dirtville where the inverse demand for carpet-cleaning services is described by $P = 130 - Q$. Once again assume that there are twenty identical firms that clean carpets in the area, and the unit cost of cleaning a carpet is constant and equal to $30. Firms in this industry compete in quantities.

a. Show that in a Cournot equilibrium the aggregate number of carpets cleaned is $Q = 95.24$. What is the equilibrium price?
b. Suppose that five two-firm mergers occur, that these five merged firms become leader firms, and the remaining ten nonmerged firms are followers. Now there are fifteen firms in the industry. Work through the model just described and show that in the two-stage game a leader firm cleans 16.67 carpets and each follower firm cleans 1.51 carpets. Leadership certainly has its benefits! Show that the total industry output in this case will be $Q = 98.48$. What is the equilibrium price now?
c. If after the five two-firm mergers took place there were no leadership advantage conferred to the merged firms, then we would have fifteen firms competing like Cournot firms in the market. Show that in this case aggregate output is $Q = 93.75$.

While our analysis can resolve the merger paradox it does leave unanswered the question as to whether such mergers are in the public interest. Is there some point at which further mergers are harmful to consumers? The answer to this question can be derived from the price-cost margin of equation (16.30). Since marginal costs are constant, any merger that reduces the price-cost margin benefits consumers by reducing the equilibrium price. We know from equation (16.30) that with $L$ leader merged firms and $N - L$ follower nonmerged firms the price-cost margin is given by $\dfrac{A - c}{(L+1)(N-L+1)}$. An additional two-firm merger increases $L$ to $L + 1$ and decreases $N$ to $N - 1$, so that the price-cost margin is now $\dfrac{A - c}{(L+2)(N-L-1)}$. So for this additional merger to benefit consumers it must be the case that

$$\frac{A - c}{(L + 2)(N - L - 1)} > \frac{A - c}{(L + 1)(N - L + 1)} \Rightarrow (L + 1)(N - L + 1) >$$

$$(L + 2)(N - L - 1) \Rightarrow N - 3(L + 1) > 0.$$

What this tells us is that an additional two-firm merger benefits consumers only if $N > 3(L + 1)$ or, equivalently, $L < N/3 - 1$. In other words, *a two-firm merger that increases the number of leaders benefits consumers only if the current group of leaders contains fewer than a third of the total number of firms in the industry.*

For example, return to Practice Problem 16.3 in which we had five leader firms and ten follower firms cleaning carpets in Dirtville. In that scenario we know that the

**Reality Checkpoint**

## Merger Take-Over Premiums . . . You Signal What You Pay for

While mergers take place in different industries and involve a variety of firm sizes and types, a few key patterns common to the merger phenomenon do emerge. One of these is the distribution of any merger gains. Shareholders in the acquired firms do far better than those in the acquiring firms. Andrade, Mitchell, and Stafford (2001), for example, provide just one of many studies confirming that the acquiring firms typically pay a premium price for shares of the acquired firms that is far above the market price of that stock at the time that the merger is announced, on the order of 20 percent or higher. As a result, the shareholders in such firms enjoy substantial gains. However, the returns to the shareholders in the acquiring firms are on average little different from zero and frequently negative.

A second observation is that mergers are especially common following some sort of technical or regulatory shock. Thus, Mitchell and Mulherin (1996) provide evidence that major changes in an industry's technology are typically followed by a wave of mergers. Similarly, Winston (1998) summarizes the evidence as indicating that "substantial merger activity has generally occurred within a decade of deregulation."

Richards (2003) links these phenomena together in a strategic view of the merger process. His argument is that in the wake of a shock, new entrants may appear and/or old rivals may expand unless they fear reprisal from a strong incumbent. By merging, two firms may create a strong firm. However, only the two merging firms will really know the inside details of their two companies and hence whether their creation is a strong firm or a weak one. Paying a high takeover premium may be a means to signal to would-be entrants or expanding rivals that the new firm is indeed a strong one capable of exacting a severe punishment on such aggression. Although paying a high share price is expensive for the acquiring firm, it may turn out to be worthwhile if it works to deter rival expansion before that expansion gets started. Thus, even mergers that produce very weak firms and that would not be profitable if rivals were aggressive may be made profitable if rivals can be fooled into believing that the merger is a strong one by means of paying a high acquisition price for the acquired firm's shares.

Richards shows how this rush to signal strength will lead to an upward bias in takeover prices. Moreover, because both weak and strong mergers now occur, this strategic manipulation of the takeover price will lead to many more mergers taking place than one may have expected. Hence, this argument also helps resolve the merger paradox.

**Sources:** G. Andrade, M. Mitchell, and E. Stafford, "New Evidence and Perspectives on Mergers." *Journal of Economic Perspectives* 15, Spring 2001, pp. 103–20; M. L. Mitchell and J. H. Mulherin, "The Impact of Industry Shocks on Takeover and Restructuring Activity." *Journal of Financial Economics* 41, June 1996, pp. 193–229; C. Winston, "U.S. Industry Adjustment to Economic Deregulation." *Journal of Economic Perspectives* 12, Summer 1998, pp. 89–110; and D. Richards, "Mergers and Deterrence." *B.E. Journals in Economic Analysis and Policy*, http://www.bepress.com/bejeap.

equilibrium price for cleaning a carpet is $31.55. Now suppose that two additional firms merge to join the leadership group. We then have a market structure of six leaders and eight followers. In this case, the equilibrium price for cleaning a carpet is $31.60. This merger harms the consumers in Dirtville.

In other words, some mergers are bad—at least for consumers. Once the number of leaders equals or exceeds one-third of the number of industry firms, additional mergers raise price and reduce output. Yet our results also show that firms will find it profitable to merge even when such levels of concentration are reached. This suggests that the antitrust authorities are, indeed, justified in their policy of restricting mergers in any industry with significant concentration.

The model just developed is only suggestive. In the real world, it is rather unlikely that we will find industries divided so sharply into groups of followers and leaders, each comprised of equal-sized firms. Moreover, it remains the case that the precise mechanism by which any firm acquires the leadership mantle is not fully specified. Recall, though, that we started this section by showing that it is not easy to detect the motivation for and the ill effects of mergers in a simple oligopoly model. Yet actual mergers occur in great numbers, and the antitrust authorities, among others, are concerned whether such mergers have anticompetitive effects. In this light, the model just analyzed does yield qualitatively useful answers.

## 16.4 HORIZONTAL MERGERS AND PRODUCT DIFFERENTIATION

Our discussion thus far has assumed that firms competing in the same industry produce the same product. Yet everyday observations suggest that this is frequently not the case. Firms expend considerable effort differentiating the products that they sell from the products of their competitors. As a result, we should consider the incentives for and the impact of mergers in industries in which firms produce and market differentiated products.

Indeed, it may be especially important to explore the merger phenomenon in the context of differentiated products because the setting of quantity competition that we have so far used may tend to understate the potential gains from merger. The idea here derives from the property that in quantity competition best response functions are downward sloping, that is, quantities are strategic substitutes as discussed in Chapter 10. Because the merging firms have an incentive to reduce output in order to drive up the market price, the nonmerged firms are encouraged to increase their outputs, undermining the effectiveness of the merger. By contrast, with price competition best response functions are upward sloping as prices are strategic complements. In this setting, a merger can be expected to encourage the merged firms to coordinate their prices, weakening competition between them. The result is likely to be an increase in prices that will encourage the nonmerged firms also to increase their prices, potentially strengthening the effectiveness of the merger.

We develop this intuition more explicitly using two different approaches to product differentiation. The first approach is to extend our standard linear demand system to incorporate product differentiation. The second is to consider the impact of a merger in the spatial model of horizontal differentiation, which we first introduced in Chapter 4, and then revisited in Chapter 10.[10]

## 16.4.1 Bertrand Competition and Merger with Linear Demand Systems

Rather than provide a general analysis we consider a simple case that serves to make the point.[11] Suppose that there are three firms in the market, each producing a single differentiated product. Inverse demand for each of the three products is assumed to be given by

$$
\begin{aligned}
p_1 &= A - Bq_1 - s(q_2 + q_3) \\
p_2 &= A - Bq_2 - s(q_1 + q_3) \qquad (s \in [0, B]). \\
p_3 &= A - Bq_3 - s(q_1 + q_2)
\end{aligned}
\tag{16.34}
$$

In these inverse demands the parameter $s$, which can take values between zero and $B$, measures how similar the three products are to each other. If $s = 0$ the products are totally differentiated. In this case, each firm is effectively a monopolist. By contrast, as $s$ approaches $B$ the three products become increasingly identical, moving us closer to the homogeneous product case. We will also assume that the three firms have identical marginal costs of $c$ per unit. Finally, assume that the three firms are Bertrand competitors, that is, they compete in prices and set their prices simultaneously.

We show in Appendix A to this chapter that when these firms compete they each set a price of $p_{nm}^* = \dfrac{A(B-s) + c(B+s)}{2B}$ and each sell quantity $q_{nm}^* = \dfrac{(A-c)(B+s)}{2B(B+2s)}$. Profit of each firm is then

$$
\pi_{nm}^* = \frac{(A - c)^2 (B - s)(B + s)}{4B^2(B + 2s)}.
\tag{16.35}
$$

Now suppose that firms 1 and 2 merge but that the merged and nonmerged firms continue to set their prices simultaneously. That is, the merged firms do not become market leaders. Rather, the two previously independent, single-product firms now become divisions of a two-product merged firm, coordinating their prices to maximize the joint profits of the two divisions. The result of the merger is that each division of the merged firm sets its product price to $p_1^m = p_2^m = \dfrac{A(2B + 3s)(B - s) + c(2B + s)(B + s)}{2(2B^2 + 2Bs - s^2)}$, while the remaining nonmerged firm 3 sets its product price as $p_3^{nm} = \dfrac{A(B+s)(B-s) + cB(B+2s)}{(2B^2 + 2Bs - s^2)}$.

It is straightforward to confirm that the merger increases the prices of all three products, as we might have expected since the merger reduces competitive pressures

---

10  The spatial model was first formulated in Hotelling (1929), and subsequently extended in Schmalensee (1978) and Salop (1979). We saw in Chapters 4, 7, and 10 that this sort of spatial model has proven insightful in analyzing a variety of topics in industrial organization, including brand proliferation in the ready-to-eat breakfast cereal industry, Schmalensee (1978); and the effects of deregulation of transport services such as airlines or passenger buses, Greenhut, Norman, and Greenhut (1991). It is not surprising that the spatial model is also useful in analyzing mergers of firms selling differentiated products.

11  An excellent example of the full analysis can be found in Deneckere and Davidson (1985).

in the market. As before, however, the important question is whether the merger is profitable. The profits of each division of the merged firm, and of the independent nonmerged firm, are

$$\pi_1^m = \pi_2^m = \frac{(A-c)^2 B(B-s)(2B+3s)^2}{4(B+2s)(2B^2+2Bs-s^2)^2} \; ; \; \pi_3^m = \frac{(A-c)^2(B-s)(B+s)^3}{(B+2s)(2B^2+2Bs-s^2)^2}. \tag{16.36}$$

In comparing equations (16.35) and (16.36) we can simplify matters by normalizing $A - c = 1$ and $B = 1$, so that profits are functions solely of the degree of product differentiation $s$. It is then easy to confirm that this two-firm merger is profitable for the merged firm *and* for the nonmerged firm. More generally, Deneckere and Davidson (1985) show that in a market containing $N$ firms any merger of $M \geq 2$ firms is profitable for the merged firms and for the nonmerged firms.

## 16.4.2 Mergers in a Spatial Market

In the spatial model, a merger between two firms may bring increased profit for reasons similar to those in the previous section. Although merging means that the firms lose their separate identity, they do not lose the ownership or control of the product varieties they can offer. For example, the merger of two major banks, Bank of America and Fleet Bank, results in a single new corporate entity. Yet it does not require that the new firm give up any of the locations at which either Bank of America or Fleet currently operate—or that it lose control over the choice of moving some of those locations. Similarly, the acquisition some years ago of American Motors by Chrysler did not mean that the Jeep product line immediately disappeared.

Indeed, when we consider product lines, there is a second source of potential profit increase. The merged firms can now coordinate not just the prices but also their product design or location choices. Chrysler can redesign the Jeep line to better fit in its overall range of models. Similarly, Bank of America and Fleet can change the locations of their branches in those areas where each formerly operated an outlet quite close to the other.

To investigate the impact of a merger in the spatial model we begin by recalling the basic setup of the model.[12] There is a group of consumers who are uniformly distributed over a linear market of length $L$. Again, we can think of this as Main Street in Littlesville. However, one problem with the Main Street analogy is that outlets at either end of the market can reach consumers on only one side. This is a bit inconvenient for our present purpose. We avoid this difficulty by bending the ends of the line around until they touch each other. In other words, we replace our straight line of length $L$ with a circle of circumference $L$. Thus, for example, if we use the spatial analogy to represent departure time in the airline market, the circle represents the twenty-four hours of the day about which consumers differ in terms of their most preferred time of departure. In all other respects, the spatial model remains as before.

Each consumer has an "address" indicating his or her location on the circle and, hence, the most preferred product type. Each consumer is also willing to buy at most one unit of a particular good. The consumer's reservation price for the most preferred good is denoted by $V$. Different varieties of the good are offered by the firms

---

12 A more general, but much more complicated version of this analysis, can be found in Brito (2003).

that are also located on Main Street—or, more appropriately, Main Circle.[13] A consumer buys from the firm who offers the product at the lowest price, taking into account the costs of transporting the good from a particular firm to that consumer. We assume that these transportation costs are linear in distance. If the distance between a firm and a consumer is $d$, the transportation costs from the firm to the consumer is $td$, that is, $t$ is the transportation cost per unit of distance. Recall that in the nongeographic interpretation of the model, transportation costs become the consumer's valuation of the loss of utility incurred by consuming a product with characteristics that are not the consumer's most preferred characteristics.

As an example, suppose that there are five firms selling to a group of $N$ consumers who are distributed evenly around the circle of circumference $L$. A firm is differentiated only by its location on the circle. We also assume that the distance between any two neighboring firms is the same and equal to $L/5$. Each firm has identical costs given by $C(q) = F + cq$, where $F$ is fixed cost and $c$ is (constant) marginal cost. One important difference from our earlier merger analysis (in which products were not differentiated) is that, in this setting, we do not set $F$, the fixed cost, equal to zero. Instead, we set unit cost $c = 0$. This simplifies the analysis without losing any generality because it makes it easy to talk about the price-cost margin, which is now just price, denoted by $m$ for mill price.[14]

### 16.4.2.1 No Price Discrimination

We start by considering the case in which firms do not price discriminate. This means that each firm sets a single mill price $m$ that consumers pay at the firm's store or mill location. The consumer then pays the fee for transporting the product back to his or her location. As a result, the full price paid by a consumer who buys from firm $i$ is $m_i + td_i$, where $m_i$ is firm $i$'s mill price and $td_i$ is the consumer's transportation cost (or the utility lost by this consumer in buying a product that is not "ideal"). Since marginal cost is zero, the net revenue or profit margin earned by firm $i$ on every such sale is $m_i$. Consumers buy from the firm offering the product at the lowest full price. As a result, for any set of mill prices across our five hypothetical firms ($m_1$, $m_2$, $m_3$, $m_4$, $m_5$) the market is divided between the firms as illustrated in Figure 16-1. The dotted lines indicate the market division between the firms. Firm 1, for example, supplies all consumers in the region ($r_{15}$, $r_{12}$).

When the firms set their prices noncooperatively and the maximum willingness to pay $V$ is not too small, the market is completely covered. That is, every consumer buys from some firm. Hence, the marginal consumer for any firm is the one who is just indifferent between buying from that firm and buying from one of the firm's neighbors.[15] We show in Appendix B to this chapter that in equilibrium the mill price set by each firm is $m_i^* = tL/5$. At this price, the profit earned by each firm is

$$\pi_i^* = \frac{NtL^2}{25} - F. \tag{16.37}$$

---

13 It bears repeating that the spatial or geographic interpretation of this model is only the most obvious one. See the discussion in Chapters 4 and 10.

14 If the reader is interested in working out the outcome for the case of $c \neq 0$, then we note here for the record that in each case that we examine, the equilibrium price $m^*$ that we derive should be replaced by $c + m^*$.

15 We assume no firm prices so low as to lure buyers from beyond its two immediate neighbors. See Appendix B.

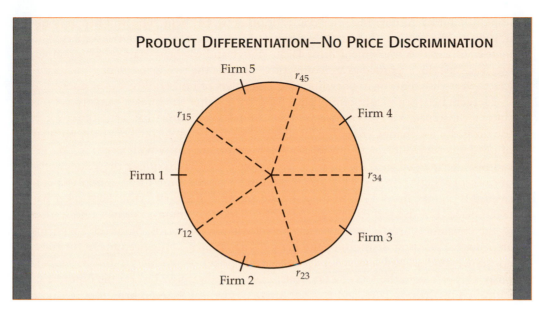

PRODUCT DIFFERENTIATION—NO PRICE DISCRIMINATION

FIGURE

**16-1**

The market outcome is illustrated in Figure 16-2 in which we have "flattened out" the market to simplify the geometry. Thus, you should imagine that firm 1 is to the right of firm 5 and firm 5 is to the left of firm 1. In Figure 16-2, the vertical distance is the effective price—mill price plus transportation cost—that each buyer pays. The sloped lines show that this price rises as one lives farther from a firm.

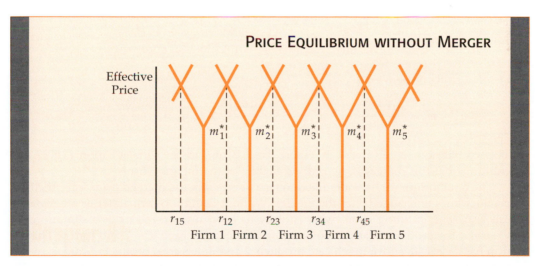

PRICE EQUILIBRIUM WITHOUT MERGER

FIGURE

**16-2**

Now consider a merger between some subset of these firms. The first point to note is that, taking store locations or product choice as given, *such a merger has no effect unless it is made between neighboring firms.* A merger, for example, between firms 2 and 4 leaves prices and market shares unaffected. More generally, this suggests that a merger has no effect on the market outcome unless the market areas of the merging firms have a common boundary. The reason is straightforward. The merging firms hope to gain by eliminating price competition between them. This will happen only if, prior to the merger, they actually competed for some of the same consumers. The merger of the two investment firms Dean Witter and Morgan Stanley, for example, was not generally regarded as anticompetitive because the two firms market their services to very different, or nonneighboring, customers of households and businesses.

Mergers between neighboring firms, however, *do* alter the market outcome. Consider, for instance, a merger between firms 2 and 3. We assume that, after the merger, the firms do not change either the locations of their existing products or the number of products they offer. Acting now as a single corporate entity with stores in two locations, the merged firm has an incentive to set prices to maximize the joint profits of both products 2 and 3, while the remaining firms continue to price noncooperatively. Of course, firms 1, 4, and 5 also take account of the fact that the merger has taken place. But the real change concerns the market common to firms 2 and 3, that is, the consumers arrayed on the circle between these two firms. Since the two firms are now cooperating divisions of the merged firm they no longer compete for these consumers and so have an incentive to raise the prices of products 2 and 3.[16] Obviously, this results in the loss of a few consumers, namely, those just on the boundaries identified by the points $r_{12}$ and $r_{34}$. But provided that the merged firm does not raise prices too much the loss of market share will be more than offset by the increased profit margins on their "captive" consumers—the consumers between the two merging firms. Moreover, the increased prices set by the merged firm will induce a similar increase in prices set by firms 1, 4, and 5. (Recall, prices are strategic complements.) Such a response reduces the loss of market share that the merged firm actually suffers, making the price increase all the more profitable.

We show in Appendix B to this chapter that the merger leads to a new equilibrium with the following prices:

$$m_2^* = m_3^* = \frac{19tL}{60}; \quad m_1^* = m_4^* = \frac{14tL}{60}; \quad m_5^* = \frac{13tL}{60}. \tag{16.38}$$

Profits to each product are

$$\pi_2^* = \pi_3^* = \frac{361\,NtL^2}{7{,}200} - F; \quad \pi_1^* = \pi_4^* = \frac{49\,NtL^2}{900} - F; \quad \pi_5^* = \frac{169\,NtL^2}{3{,}600}. \tag{16.39}$$

This equilibrium is illustrated in Figure 16-3. Comparison with equation (16.37) confirms that this merger is, indeed, profitable for the merging firms.

The equilibrium we have identified so far assumes that the merged firms leave their product lines unchanged after the merger. Without being too formal, let us see if we can get some intuition about what is likely to happen if we relax this assumption. Consider the product location choice facing the newly merged firm 2 and firm 3. This firm has a clear incentive to relocate products 2 and 3 nearer to products 1 and 4, respectively. Doing so gives it two advantages. First, it softens the competition between the combined firm's own two product lines. This means that it can try to reach out to customers near the boundary with a slightly lower price without fear of simply

---

16  If the merger leaves products 2 and 3 under the control of separate, competing product divisions, prices will not change. It is important, in other words, that the merged firms take advantage of the opportunity they now have to coordinate their prices.

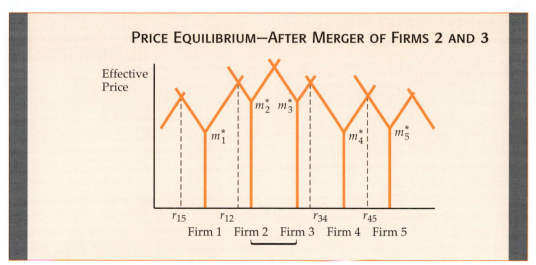

**PRICE EQUILIBRIUM—AFTER MERGER OF FIRMS 2 AND 3**

Effective Price

$m_1^*$  $m_2^*$  $m_3^*$  $m_4^*$  $m_5^*$

$r_{15}$    $r_{12}$    $r_{34}$    $r_{45}$

Firm 1   Firm 2   Firm 3   Firm 4   Firm 5

FIGURE

**16-3**

"robbing Peter to pay Paul." Second, the move also makes it easier for the firm to steal some customers away from its true rivals, firms 1 and 4.[17]

As in the linear demand case of the previous section, a merger between two neighboring firms in our spatial market is clearly advantageous to the merging firms but is disadvantageous to consumers because a merger tends to raise prices throughout the industry. Both merged and unmerged firms enjoy greater profit and consumers obtain less surplus from a given product. There is, though, one ray of hope for consumers that we have not yet considered. This is that the merger may lead to cost savings that permit lower prices. Remember that the two products, while not identical, are close substitutes. They might be, for example, low-sugar and high-sugar versions of a soft drink. We might expect there to be some cost complementarities in the production of these products. If so, then production of both goods by one firm will be cheaper than production of both by two separate firms. In short, we should not be surprised if in a product-differentiated market, production of many closely related product lines exhibits economies of scope of the type that we discussed in Chapter 4.

When scope economies are present, they give a strong incentive to merge. The merger allows the new firm to operate as a multiproduct company and thereby exploit the cost-savings opportunities this generates. These savings may be reflected in a reduction in fixed costs. For example, the firms can combine their headquarters,

---

17 There is one complication that we have ignored in this discussion. Judd (1985) argues that a merger that creates a multiproduct firm, as for example a merger of firms 2 and 3, may not be sustainable. The intuition is as follows: Assume that an entrant comes in exactly at firm 3's location after the merger of firms 2 and 3. Price competition will drive the price for this product down to marginal cost, in which case the entrant and the incumbent earn zero profits at this location (ignoring fixed costs). But the merged firm also loses money at the neighboring location 2 since the price war with the new entrant forces it to reduce the price there as well. If the merged firm were to close down its location 3 product, the entrant will raise price above marginal cost, and so the merged firm can raise the price at location 2. There is, in other words, a stronger incentive for the merged firm to exit location 3 than for the entrant to do so. Hence, this kind of multiproduct merger may not be sustainable because it is not credible. This argument turns, however, on two important assumptions: that entry costs are not recovered on exit and that the merged firm has no incentive to try to develop a reputation for toughness. If only part of the entry costs are sunk (unrecoverable costs), or if reputation is important, the merged firm can sustain the multiproduct configuration.

**Reality** Checkpoint

## Love Thy Neighbor . . . Then Marry Them!

The spatial model generates insight into many real-world mergers. An example is the 1997 proposal of Staples, the largest retail office supply company, to buy one of its competitors, Office Depot, for $3.4 billion. This merger would have created an office supply colossus with 1,110 stores and annual sales of $10.7 billion. The only remaining operator of retail office supply supermarkets would have been OfficeMax, with about 500 stores and $3.3 billion in annual sales. These figures were sufficiently large to warrant an investigation by the FTC, which ultimately disallowed the merger. Staples and Office Depot defended the proposal, arguing it would not really reduce competition since much of the demand for office supplies is also met by catalogues, warehouse clubs, stationery stores, and large discount retailers such as Wal-Mart so that, overall, this product market is quite fragmented.

However, there was also evidence that a motive for the merger was a desire to coordinate pricing and location decisions with a view to increase the combined companies' total profit. As our analysis suggests, a merger of two neighboring firms provides an incentive to move farther apart in their locations, allowing them also to raise their prices to local customers. The natural translation of this phenomenon in the case of the proposed Staples and Office Depot merger is for the new, combined firm to close down outlets of one of the two formerly separate companies in areas where they both used to operate. It may then raise prices at the one remaining store in such locations. A study by a group affiliated with consumer advocate Ralph Nader—the Consumer Project on Technology—found that prices were much lower in markets where Staples and Office Depot operated neighboring stores than they were in markets where only one operated. For example, the group found that the average price for fax paper was $13.99 where the two companies competed, but $26.99 when only one was present. The FTC found similar price discrepancies in its own investigation and decided in early April 1997 to block the merger despite the fact that Staples and Office Depot agreed to sell 63 stores to the remaining competitor, OfficeMax. The FTC's decision was upheld in Federal Court in June of that year.

**Source:** J. M. Broder, "Compromise May Be in Works on Acquisition by Staples," and "F.T.C. Rejects Deal to Join Two Giants of Office Supplies." *The New York Times*, March 1, 1997, p. 29, and April 5, 1997, p. 1.

research and development, marketing, accounting, and distribution operations. If in addition the merger leads to a reduction in variable costs of production, then this will be reflected in lower prices. Moreover, even if scope economies are not present, it is still possible that one of the merging firms has a more effective purchasing division or a superior production technology that, following the merger, will be extended to its new partners. The greater are such cost synergies, the more likely it is that consumers will benefit from the merger.

### 16.4.2.2 Price Discrimination

The foregoing analysis leaves out one aspect of spatial competition that is potentially quite critical. Firms that operate in a spatial or product-differentiated setting clearly have some monopoly power. A firm does not instantaneously lose all its customers when it raises price above that of other firms. Yet if firms have monopoly power, we might expect them to use pricing strategies that exploit monopoly power. In particular, we might expect firms with monopoly power to pursue some of the price discrimination strategies outlined in Chapters 5 and 6. If this is the case, then we need to modify our analysis. Indeed, we ought to do this in any case just to ensure that we have covered all the possible features that might influence the impact of mergers on consumer welfare.

With this in mind then, consider the possibility that the firms adopt (perfect or first-degree) discriminatory pricing policies (see Chapter 5) but maintain at the same time all the remaining assumptions of our spatial model in the no price discrimination case. The noncooperative price equilibrium is then easy to identify. Remember that firms compete in price for customers. Accordingly, they set the price as low as need be—at the margin—to attract customers, so long as that price covers their marginal cost. As a result, the equilibrium must be characterized by the following condition. Suppose that firm $i$ is the firm that can supply consumer location $s$ at the lowest unit cost, say $c + ts$ (the marginal production cost plus transportation fee), and that firm $j$ is the firm that can supply this location at the next cheapest unit cost, $c + ts + e$, where $e$ is a measure of precisely how much closer the consumer is to firm $i$ than it is to firm $j$. Then the Bertrand–Nash equilibrium price to consumer $s$ will be for firm $i$ to charge one cent less than the cost of firm $j$, that is, to charge just less than $c + ts + e$.

The heavy shaded line in Figure 16-4 illustrates this equilibrium. Firm 2, for example, is the lowest-cost supplier (including transportation cost) for all consumers in the region ($r_{12}$, $r_{23}$). Therefore, firm 2 supplies all consumers in this market region, charging its consumers on the left one cent less than firm 1's costs of supplying them, and its consumers to the right one cent less than firm 3's marginal costs. By adopting this pricing strategy, each firm earns a gross profit (profits before deducting fixed costs) given by the shaded areas for their market regions in Figure 16-4.

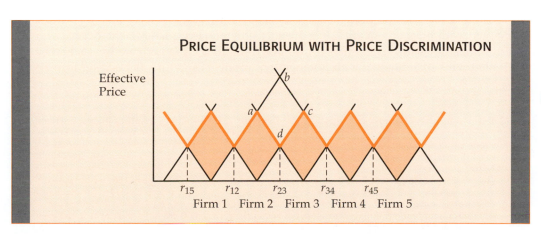

PRICE EQUILIBRIUM WITH PRICE DISCRIMINATION

FIGURE

**16-4**

An interesting feature of the set of discriminatory prices is that the highest pre-delivery price now paid by any consumer is $c + tL/5$. This is the lowest price paid by anyone when firms do not price discriminate. Price discrimination in this oligopolistic market unambiguously benefits consumers. Why is this?[18] With nondiscriminatory pricing, if a firm reduces the price to one consumer, it has to reduce prices to every consumer—an expensive prospect. With discriminatory pricing, by contrast, a firm can lower prices in one location without having to lower its prices elsewhere. But this means that price discrimination weakens each firm's ability to commit to a set of prices, making price competition between the firms much fiercer and so leading to the lower prices that we have just identified.

Now consider the effect on this equilibrium of a merger between two of these firms, say firms 2 and 3, as before. Two points should be clear. First, as in the no price discrimination case, a merger of nonneighboring firms has no effect. Second, the merged firm's ability to coordinate the formerly separate pricing strategies is particularly valuable in this discriminatory setting. This is because firms are engaged in what is nearly cutthroat price competition. By merging, the two firms can avoid this expensive conflict, at least with respect to each other.[19] So far as the merged firm is concerned, for consumers in the region between firm 2's location and $r_{23}$, the nearest competitor is now firm 1. Similarly, for consumers in the region between firm 3's location and $r_{23}$, the nearest competitor is now firm 4. As a result, the merged firm can raise prices to all consumers located between firms 2 and 3, as indicated by the line *abc* in Figure 16-4. Thus, the merger increases the profits of the merging firms by an amount given by the area *abcd*. One further effect of this type of merger, which is not quite so intuitive, is that in this case the merger only benefits the merging firms. Prices and profit increase only for those consumers who were served by the merged firm prior to the merger. All other prices are unaffected, and so the profits of the non-merging firms are unaffected by the merger.

We could, as before, also consider the further issues regarding the merged firm's product location strategies. However, the basic point has now been made. Our conclusions for the no price discrimination case hold all the more strongly when firms engage in discriminatory pricing practices. Prices to consumers rise and the merging firms are more profitable. There is absolutely no paradox about merging in this price discrimination case. From the viewpoint of the partner firms, if not from the viewpoint of public policy, a merger is a very good thing indeed.

There is one final point that should be made in closing this section. Why is it that mergers with price competition in a product-differentiated market, whether with linear demand or with spatial markets, do not run into the merger paradox that so bedeviled our earlier analysis with homogenous products and quantity-setting firms?

---

18  This is discussed in Norman and Thisse (1996). They show that with a given number of firms, discriminatory pricing always benefits consumers. They also show, however, that the much more competitive environment of discriminatory pricing may cause enough firms to want to leave the market that prices actually increase for some consumers. In our example, there is no incentive to exit the market. See also Reitzes and Levy (1995).

19  There is a further important feature of this type of merger. The potential problems that we discussed previously in footnote 15 cannot arise when firms charge discriminatory prices. Consider, for example, an entrant coming in at product 3's location. This would lead to the price equilibrium in Figure 16-4 whether or not the merged firm removes its product at this location. There is, in other words, no benefit to the merged firm in exiting from this market. Since a potential entrant can correctly anticipate this, no such entry will take place.

The first part of the answer was discussed at the beginning of this set of models. Prices are strategic complements whereas quantities are strategic substitutes. With price competition, therefore, the strategic responses of nonmerged firms are potentially beneficial to the merged firms, whereas with quantity competition they are potentially harmful.

The second part of the answer is equally important and reflects our point regarding credible commitment discussed in Chapters 11 and 12. The reason why mergers are profitable in the spatial or differentiated products context is that the merged firms can credibly commit to produce some particular *range* of products—that is, the commitment required in the spatial context is a commitment to particular locations and in the linear demand system it is to continue marketing the products of the previously independent firms. By contrast, the commitment necessary with homogenous products must be in terms of production *levels*. The merging firms must be able to commit to a high volume of output following the merger. Generally, this is not credible because such a high volume of production is not the merged firm's best response to a Cournot output decision by the other firms. Assuming that the merged firm becomes a Stackelberg leader, by contrast, makes the commitment to a high level of post-merger output credible.

## 16.5 PUBLIC POLICY TOWARD HORIZONTAL MERGERS

U.S. public policy with respect to horizontal mergers has changed rather dramatically over the last forty years. To a large extent, this change is reflected in the differences between the first Merger Guidelines issued by the Justice Department in 1968 and the guidelines currently in force. While it is tempting to summarize these differences as a move from a very strict regime to a more permissive one, we think it is more accurate to describe the evolution of merger policy as one that has increasingly become more sophisticated and that gives greater recognition to the complexity of corporate combinations in the real world.

As we noted in Chapter 1, the 1968 Merger Guidelines relied heavily on market structure—particularly concentration ratio data—to determine the legality of a proposed merger. In turn, this reflected many years of academic analysis within the structure-conduct-performance framework. The rigidity of this approach led to increasingly questionable decisions culminating in perhaps one of the most controversial merger cases ever, *U.S. v. Von's Grocery* (1966). In that case, the Supreme Court upheld the government's prohibition of a merger between two grocery store chains in Los Angeles that, in combination, had less than 10 percent of the market. It was this same strong antimerger sentiment that was reflected in the Merger Guidelines issued two years later.

Ironically, courts began to deviate from the rigid, structure-based guidelines of 1968 almost as soon as they were adopted. An early such case was the acquisition by General Dynamics of the outstanding shares of a major coal producer, United Electric. While this merger almost certainly violated the 1968 Guidelines, the truth was that General Dynamics already owned a major interest in United Electric by virtue of General Dynamics' ownership of Material Services, a firm that in turn already owned a large fraction of United Electric's stock. The merger was ultimately allowed by the Supreme Court in 1974. Subsequently, the courts permitted a number of similar mergers that also appeared to violate the guidelines and it soon became clear that the 1968 Guidelines were no longer compelling. This eventually led to the emergence of a new set of merger guidelines in 1982 (see Reality Checkpoint: Mellowing with Age . . . The Evolution of the Merger Guidelines).

 # Reality Checkpoint

## Mellowing with Age . . . The Evolution of the Merger Guidelines

In 1968, the U.S. Department of Justice issued its first formal set of guidelines outlining the standards for acceptable mergers. Yet over the years, these guidelines have evolved considerably. The 1968 document used as its guide to industry structure the four-firm concentration ratio (see Chapter 3). Horizontal mergers would be challenged in any industry in which that ratio exceeded 75 percent if both the acquiring and the acquired firm each had a market share of as little as 4 percent. In industries with a four-firm concentration ratio of less than 75 percent, mergers would be challenged if the two firms each had market shares of as low as 5 percent. Thus, a combined share of 10 percent would, in most cases, be sufficient to challenge the legitimacy of a merger.

In 1982, accumulated legal and economic dissatisfaction with the earlier standards led to major changes in the guidelines. Reliance on the four-firm concentration ratio was abandoned in favor of the Herfindahl-Hirschman Index (HHI) (again, see Chapter 3 for a definition). In addition, both the structural conditions for and the language about intervention were softened. The threshold for intervention now became an HHI of 1,800 (a little more concentrated than an industry of six equal-sized firms). Mergers in less concentrated industries were not likely to be chal-

lenged unless they increased the HHI by well over 100 points, and even then would not typically be challenged if the industry had an HHI of less than 1,000. Further modification—and easing of restrictions on mergers—came in 1984 when the guidelines were amended to permit mergers that might otherwise be challenged if they led to "significant, net efficiencies" that could not otherwise be achieved.

The Merger Guidelines were further amended in April 1992. The revisions made at that time were meant to reflect the lessons and experiences with the 1982–84 standards. Two central points were addressed. First, the government elaborated carefully the potential harmful effects that a merger might create, as well as how it would evaluate this potential for harm. Second, the government offered a much more extensive discussion as to how entry conditions would be considered as an additional factor in judging the impact of a merger.

The most recent amendment to the Merger Guidelines came in April 1997. That change focused on Section 4 of the Guidelines. The thrust of this revision was to make clear both that cost savings could be an important justification for a merger and precisely what sort of documentation was necessary to make such an argument.

**Source:** U.S. Department of Justice, *Merger Guidelines*, Washington, D.C., May 30, 1968, July 14, 1984, April 2, 1992, and April 12, 1997.

Underlying this trend was an increasing awareness of modern industrial organization theory as well as a growing body of empirical data that suggested many mergers did not threaten competition as much as the structure-conduct-performance paradigm implied. If they did, one might expect mergers to be fairly profitable. However, a growing number of studies including Mueller (1982), Ravenscraft and Scherer (1989), Loughran and Vijh (1997), and most recently, Andrade, Mitchell, and Stafford (2001), has found that mergers are not terribly profitable—especially for the acquiring firm. Indeed, many acquisitions are later reversed by "spin-offs."[20]

The change in attitude reflected by the 1982 Guidelines has led to many more mergers being permitted. These have included such major consolidations as Union Pacific and Southern Pacific (railroads), AOL and Time Warner (telecommunications), Chase Manhattan and J.P. Morgan (finance), Exxon and Mobil and also British Petroleum and Amoco (petroleum), Westinghouse and Infinity Broadcasting (radio), Aetna and U.S. Healthcare (health services), and MCI and WorldCom (telecommunications), among others. Many of these mergers were controversial and virtually all raised some competitive concerns. Yet, as noted, these and other mergers were nevertheless approved.

Beyond relying on modern theory and evidence that proposed merger will not harm competition, the government has taken two additional steps that permit horizontal mergers to be approved despite some clear antitrust concerns. First, the government has increasingly used a "fix-it-first" approach regarding proposed mergers. This procedure usually centers on divestiture of some of the assets of the merging parties to another, third firm so as to ensure that competitive pressures are maintained. If, for example, the two firms operate in several towns across the country, but in one town they are the only two such suppliers, then the government may permit the merger so long as one of the firms sells off its operations in the town in question to a new, rival entrant. This principle was applied in both of the petroleum mergers mentioned above and is often used in the case of media mergers where newspaper and broadcasting firms have been required to sell their operations in certain locations before being permitted to conclude a merger.

However, divestiture does have some problems. For example, in 1995 Schnucks Markets, a supermarket chain, acquired National Food Markets, which was the major competitor of Schnucks in the St. Louis area. The merger was approved when Schnucks agreed to divest 24 supermarkets in the St. Louis area over the next year. However, no immediate buyer was named. Schnucks then took the stores to be divested and proceeded to run them into the ground. It closed departments. It kept the stores understaffed, and referred customers to the other Schnucks stores that were not being divested. Soon, sales at the divesting stores had declined by about one-third and, as a result, they posed less of a competitive threat to those stores that the new Schnucks/National firm continued to operate. While the Schnucks case is extreme (and eventually led to further FTC litigation) the general problem it illustrates is real. The usefulness of divestiture as a remedy for a merger's anticompetitive effects depends critically on the buyer of the divested assets being able to offer true competition to the newly merged firm. This is why the FTC now generally requires that the buyer of the divested plants be named in advance and that the firm be one that has the industry knowledge to be an effective competitor.

---

20 Note, though, that these findings also raise doubts about any cost savings that mergers are alleged to generate.

A second, alternative procedure has been to approve mergers subject to behavioral constraints on the uniting firms, and then to follow this agreement with active monitoring by government agents. Typically, these consent agreements require the firms to take specific actions and to avoid engaging in certain practices. Note that in monitoring these agreements, the regulatory agencies can always count on a reliable source of outside help, namely, the competitors of the merged firms and other parties who opposed the merger. These organizations are always quick to report violations of the consent agreement. Since 1992, the number of consent decrees issued by the FTC and the Justice Department has dramatically increased.

In addition to the procedural developments, the FTC and the Justice Department have also continued to adjust the merger guidelines themselves. In this connection, an important recent modification is the 1997 expansion of Section 4 of the Guidelines to permit greater reliance on documented cost savings as a justification of a merger. With this change, the antitrust authorities have indicated an increased willingness to judge a merger to be pro-competitive if it generates cost savings that are likely to translate into lower consumer prices. As we noted previously in this chapter, most analysis finds that the cost savings necessary to generate lower prices are substantial. This may be why the proposed acquisition of Beech-Nut baby food by the Heinz Corporation (see Reality Checkpoint: Baby, Baby Where Did that Brand Go?) was ultimately denied. Hence, the full implication of the 1997 cost efficiencies amendment is yet to be seen.

 # Reality Checkpoint

## Baby, Baby, Where Did that Brand Go?

Cost savings have always been a possible justification for horizontal mergers. Such efficiencies took on increased importance after 1997, however, because the U.S. Federal Trade Commission (FTC) and Department of Justice amended their well-known merger guidelines to give greater weight to such cost efficiencies as a rationale for what otherwise might be a questionable merger. The intuition is that while there may be potential harm to consumers from the monopoly power that the merger creates, this is often offset by the lower prices that result from the lower costs that the merger makes possible.

Evaluation of the cost efficiency defense is therefore important. It is also tricky. Besides the question of how real the cost savings may be, there is the further question as to whether the cost savings will be passed on to consumers in the form of lower prices.

Consider, for example, the proposed acquisition of Beech-Nut Baby Food by Heinz in 2001. Along with Gerber, these two companies controlled the bulk of the jarred or prepared baby food market. Gerber was the industry giant with a market share between 65 and 70 percent. The remaining 30 to 35 percent was split fairly evenly between Heinz and Beech-Nut.

The FTC sought to block the merger, arguing that it would significantly decrease competition in the baby food industry. Heinz and Beech-Nut responded that the merger would actually increase competition. Their analysis relied heavily on cost savings. In brief, the merging parties argued that Beech-Nut has a superior brand image but very old and costly production techniques relative to Heinz. They further argued that the merger would permit the two firms to offer a single product of the higher Beech-Nut quality but at the lower Heinz cost. As a result, this product would enable the merged firm to really put pressure on the industry giant, Gerber. Given Gerber's large size and market share, a fall in its price would bring large gains to consumers.

Heinz and Beech-Nut backed up their claims with statistical evidence. Using a model of the baby food industry that is similar in spirit to the circular spatial model used here, they provided simulations of the post-merger market that implied a fall in baby food prices. These simulations took the assumption of a 15 percent cost savings as given and suggested that between 50 and 100 percent of these savings would be passed through to consumers as lower prices.

The claim that much of the cost savings would be passed on to consumers depends critically on the nature of competition in the post-merger market. As noted, Heinz and Beech-Nut assumed that that market could be described as a spatial one of the type used in this chapter. Recall, however, from Chapter 7 that this sort of horizontal differentiation is not the only type of product differentiation that we observe. An alternative approach is to view the market as vertically differentiated with each brand representing a different level of quality and consumers differing in how much they are willing to pay for quality. Thus, Gerber would be the highest quality, Beech-Nut the next highest, and Heinz (well known as the discount brand) would be the lowest. Note that in this configuration, it is the Beech-Nut quality that directly competes with the Gerber premium brand. If this is the case, then Heinz and Beech-Nut have a strong incentive to discontinue the Beech-Nut brand after the merger. This would allow them to soften price competition in the market by producing the brand that is maximally differentiated (furthest) from Gerber. If so, consumers could be hurt in two ways. Not only would prices rise but consumers would also suffer a loss in choice as one brand was removed from the market. Moreover, removal of a brand in the post-merger market means that the demand estimates made for the pre-merger market (the ones relied on by Heinz and Beech-Nut in their simulations) would no longer be relevant.

Norman, Pepall, and Richards (2002) show that the foregoing concern is very real. Indeed, they show that no matter what the cost savings, a merger of two lower quality brands will always lead to the removal of the higher quality one and a rise in consumer prices on the remaining brands. They show that this is true even when there is potential competition from a later entrant.

---

**Sources:** G. Norman, L. Pepall, and D. Richards, "Product Differentiation, Cost-Reducing Mergers, and Consumer Welfare." Tufts University Economics Department, Working Paper 2002-14. See also J. Baker, "Efficiencies and High Concentration: Heinz Proposes to Acquire Beech-Nut (2001)." In J. Kwoka and L. White, eds., *The Antitrust Revolution*, Oxford: Oxford University Press, 2004, pp. 150–69.

---

# SUMMARY

Horizontal mergers are combinations of firms that are rivals within the same industry. Because they result in the joining of firms that were previously competitors, horizontal mergers raise obvious antitrust concerns. Such mergers may, in fact, be a means to create a legal cartel. However, economic theory does not give a clear endorsement of this view. Indeed, a major puzzle in economic analysis is the merger paradox. This paradox reflects the fact that many commonly used economic models suggest that merger is not profitable for the merging firms and that the true beneficiaries are the nonmerging firms.

The clue to resolving the merger paradox is to find some means of credibly committing the newly merged firm to a profit-enhancing strategy. One way to do this in quantity-setting models is to permit the merged firm to take on the role of Stackelberg leader whose production announcements are taken as credible commitments by assumption. This greatly raises the profitability of mergers and provides a strong motive for such consolidations. It also helps to explain the "domino effect," often observed, by which a merger of two firms in an industry is quickly followed by similar marriages among other firms in the same industry, as firms try to join the leadership group.

The merger paradox can also be resolved by setting the analysis in a context in which firms market differentiated products and compete in price for customers. In this case the merging firms can easily make a convincing commitment to specific locations or product designs—namely, those used by the firms before they merged. The ability to make such a commitment is sufficient to make merger profitable.

The ambiguous effects of mergers found in economic theory are also found in empirical analysis. To date, there is little clear evidence that mergers have resulted in legalized cartels with significant monopoly power. Instead, what is clear is that the combination of theoretical and empirical ambiguity has led the legal authorities to take a much less aggressive and much less rigid stand against proposed mergers, though, as we will see in the next chapter, this relaxed approach has not been universal. Merger cases today are inevitably handled on a case-by-case approach. In the absence of definitive evidence—either from economic theory or economic data—there appears to be little alternative.

---

# PROBLEMS

For problems 1, 2, 3, and 4 consider a market containing four identical firms, each of which makes an identical product. The inverse demand for this product is $P = 100 - Q$, where $P$ is price and $Q$ is aggregate output. The production costs for firms 1, 2, and 3 are identical and given by $C(q_i) = 20q_i$; $(i = 1, 2, 3)$, where $q_i$ is the output of firm $i$. This means that for each of these firms, variable costs are constant at \$20 per unit. The production costs for firm 4 are $C(q_4) = (20 + \gamma)q_4$, where $\gamma$ is some constant. Note that if $\gamma > 0$, then firm 4 is a high-cost firm, while if $\gamma < 0$, firm 4 is a low-cost firm ($|\gamma| < 20$). Note also that $Q = \sum_{i=1}^{4} q_i$.

1. Assume that the firms each choose their outputs to maximize profits given that they each act as Cournot competitors.

   a. Identify the Cournot equilibrium output for each firm, the product price, and the profits of the four firms. For this to be a "true" equilibrium, all of the firms must at least be covering their variable costs. Identify the constraint that $\gamma$ must satisfy for this to be the case.

**b.** Assume that firms 1 and 2 merge and that all firms continue to act as Cournot competitors after the merger. Confirm that this merger is unprofitable.

**c.** Now assume that firms 1 and 4 merge. Can this merger be profitable if $\gamma$ is positive so that firm 4 is a high-cost firm? What has happened to the profits of firm 2 as a result of this merger?

2. Now assume that each firm incurs fixed costs of $F$ in addition to the variable costs noted above. When two firms merge the merged firm has fixed costs of $bF$ where $1 \le b \le 2$.

**a.** Suppose that firms 1 and 2 merge and that $\gamma \ge 0$. Derive a condition on $b$, $F$, and $\gamma$ for this merger to be profitable. Give an intuitive interpretation of this condition.

**b.** Suppose by contrast that firms 1 and 4 merge. Repeat your analysis in (a).

**c.** Compare the conditions derived in (a) and (b). What does this tell you about mergers that create cost savings?

3. Assume that if two firms merge, the merged firm will be able to act as an industry leader, making its output decision before the nonmerged firms make theirs. Further assume that $\gamma = 0$ so that the firms are of equal efficiency.

**a.** Confirm that a merger between firms 1 and 2 will now be profitable. What has happened to the profits of the nonmerged firms and to the product price as a result of this merger?

**b.** Confirm that the two remaining firms will also want to merge and join the leader group given that the leaders act as Cournot competitors with respect to each other. (*Hint:* This merger will create a leader group containing two firms and a follower group containing none.) What does this second merger do to the market price?

4. Continue with the conditions of question 3 but now suppose that for a merger to be undertaken, the merging firms each have to incur a fixed cost, $f$ (this might include costs of identifying a merger partner, negotiating the terms of the merger, legal fees, and so on).

**a.** How high must $f$ be for the merger between firms 1 and 2 to be unprofitable?

**b.** How high must $f$ be for the subsequent merger between firms 3 and 4 to be unprofitable?

5. In the chapter it was shown that for a two-firm merger to be profitable, the following condition must be satisfied:

$$\pi_I^L(N-1, L+1) = \frac{(A-c)^2}{B(L+2)^2(N-L-1)} > 2\pi_f^F(N, L) = 2\frac{(A-c)^2}{B(L+1)^2(N-L+1)^2}.$$

Assume as in questions 1 and 2 that $A = 100$, $B = 1$, $c = 20$. Further assume that $\gamma = 0$.

**a.** Assume that the number of firms in the market is ten, that is, $N = 10$, and that, as in question 4, a two-firm merger requires that each of the merging firms incurs a fixed cost of $f$ prior to the merger. Derive a relationship, $f(L)$, between $f$ and the size of the leader group, $L$, such that if $f > f(L)$, the two-firm merger will be unprofitable. Calculate $f(L)$ for $L = 1, 2, 3, 4$, and 5 to confirm that $f(L)$ is decreasing in $L$. Interpret this result.

**b.** Now assume that there are eight firms in the market, that is, $N = 8$. Repeat your calculations in part (a) to show that the function $f(L)$ rises as $N$ falls. Interpret this result.

**6.** Normansville consists of a single High Street that is 1 mile long and has 100 residents uniformly located along it. There are three independent video rental stores located in the town at distances 1/6, 1/2, and 5/6 of a mile from the left-hand edge of Normansville. Each resident rents one video per day provided that the price charged is no more than $5. If a consumer is located $s$ miles from a store the transportation costs in getting a video from that store is $0.50s$. Suppose first that the two stores do not price discriminate.

    **a.** What rental charge will the three stores set given that they act as price competitors?

    **b.** What profits do they earn?

    **c.** Now suppose that two neighboring stores merge. What does this do to prices and profits?

**7.** Recalculate your answers to 6(a)–(c), assuming that the stores can perfectly price discriminate.

# REFERENCES

Andrade, G., M. Mitchell, and E. Stafford. 2001. "New Evidence and Perspectives on Mergers." *Journal of Economic Perspectives* 15 (Spring): 103–20.

Brito, D. 2003. "Preemptive Mergers Under Spatial Competition." Working Paper, FCT, Universidade Nova de Lisboa.

Daughety, A. F. 1990. "Beneficial Concentration." *American Economic Review* 80: 1,231–7.

Deneckere, R., and C. Davidson. 1985. "Long-Run Competition in Capacity, Short-Run Competition in Price, and the Cournot Model." *Rand Journal of Economics* 17 (Autumn): 404–15.

Farrell, J., and C. S. Shapiro. 1990. "Horizontal Mergers: An Equilibrium Analysis." *American Economic Review* 80: 107–26.

Greenhut, J., G. Norman, and M. L. Greenhut. 1991. "Aspects of Airline Deregulation." *International Journal of Transport Economics* 18: 3–30.

Hotelling, H. 1929. "Stability in Competition." *Economic Journal* 39 (January): 31–47.

Judd, K. 1985. "Credible Spatial Preemption." *Rand Journal of Economics* 16: 153–66.

Loughan, T., and A. Vijh. 1997. "Do Long-Term Shareholders Benefit from Corporate Acquisitions?" *Journal of Finance* 52: 1765–90.

Mueller, D. C. 1982. "A Theory of Conglomerate Mergers." *Quarterly Journal of Economics* 82: 643–59.

Norman, G., and J. F. Thisse. 1996. "Product Variety and Welfare under Soft and Tough Pricing Regimes." *Economic Journal* 106: 76–91.

Perry, M., and R. Porter. 1985. "Oligopoly and the Incentive for Horizontal Merger." *American Economic Review* 75: 219–27.

Ravenscraft, D. J., and F. M. Scherer. 1989. "The Profitability of Mergers." *International Journal of Industrial Organization* Special Issue (March): 101–16.

Reitzes, J. D., and D. T. Levy. 1995. "Price Discrimination and Mergers." *Canadian Journal of Economics* 28: 427–36.

Salant, S., S. Switzer, and R. Reynolds. 1983. "Losses from Horizontal Merger: The Effects of an Exogenous Change in Industry Structure on Cournot–Nash Equilibrium." *Quarterly Journal of Economics* 98: 185–213.

Salop, S. C. 1979. "Monopolistic Competition with Outside Goods." *Bell Journal of Economics* 10 (Spring): 141–56.

Schmalensee, R. 1978. "Entry Deterrence in the Ready-to-Eat Breakfast Cereal Industry." *Bell Journal of Economics* 9 (Autumn): 305–27.

# Appendix A | Bertrand Competition and Merger with Linear Demand Systems

## 16A.1 A SIMPLE LINEAR DEMAND SYSTEM

Start with the inverse demand system of equations (16.34):

$$
\begin{aligned}
p_1 &= A - Bq_1 - s(q_2 + q_3), \\
p_2 &= A - Bq_2 - s(q_1 + q_3), \quad (s \in [0, B]). \\
p_3 &= A - Bq_3 - s(q_1 + q_2),
\end{aligned}
\tag{16A.1}
$$

In order to identify the Bertrand–Nash equilibrium prices we first need to invert this demand system to get the direct demands. Some simple manipulation gives these demands as

$$
q_1 = \frac{A(B - s) - (B + s)p_1 + s(p_2 + p_3)}{(B - s)(B + 2s)},
$$

$$
q_2 = \frac{A(B - s) - (B + s)p_2 + s(p_1 + p_3)}{(B - s)(B + 2s)}, \quad (s \in [0, B]).
\tag{16A.2}
$$

$$
q_3 = \frac{A(B - s) - (B + s)p_3 + s(p_1 + p_2)}{(B - s)(B + 2s)},
$$

Note that these make intuitive sense: demand for each firm is decreasing in the firm's own price and increasing in its rivals' prices.

## 16A.2 THE PRE-MERGER CASE

We begin by identifying the equilibrium when each firm acts independently. Profit to firm 1 is

$$
\pi_1 = (p_1 - c)q_1 = (p_1 - c)\left[ \frac{A(B - s) - (B + s)p_1 + s(p_2 + p_3)}{(B - s)(B + 2s)} \right].
\tag{16A.3}
$$

Differentiating with respect to $p_1$ and simplifying gives the first-order condition for firm 1

$$
\frac{\partial \pi_1}{\partial p_1} = \frac{A(B - s) - 2(B + s)p_1 + s(p_2 + p_3) + c(B + s)}{(B - s)(B + 2s)} = 0.
\tag{16A.4}
$$

There are similar best response functions for firms 2 and 3. Rather than use these to identify the equilibrium, we can take advantage of the knowledge that this equilibrium will be symmetric, that is, in equilibrium $p_1^* = p_2^* = p_3^* = p_{nm}^*$. Substituting this into the best response function (16A.4) gives $\dfrac{A(B-s) - 2Bp_{nm}^* + c(B+s)}{(B-s)(B+2s)} = 0$.

Solving for the equilibrium price gives

$$p_{nm}^* = \frac{A(B-s) + c(B+s)}{2B}. \tag{16A.5}$$

Substituting these prices into the direct demand functions (16A.2) gives the equilibrium output for each firm of $q_{nm}^* = \dfrac{(A-c)(B+s)}{2B(B+2s)}$ and substituting into the profit function (16A.3) gives the no-merger profit for each firm of

$$\pi_{nm}^* = \frac{(A-c)^2(B-s)(B+s)}{4B^2(B+2s)}. \tag{16A.6}$$

## 16A.3 MERGER OF FIRMS 1 AND 2

Now assume that firms 1 and 2 merge. Post-merger, the merged firm chooses its prices $p_1$ and $p_2$ to maximize its aggregate profit $\pi_1 + \pi_2$, while the nonmerged firm chooses $p_3$ to maximize its profit $\pi_3$. This gives the first-order conditions

$$\frac{\partial(\pi_1 + \pi_2)}{\partial p_1} = \frac{A(B-s) - 2(B+s)p_1 + 2sp_2 + sp_3 + cB}{(B-s)(B+2s)} = 0,$$

$$\frac{\partial(\pi_1 + \pi_2)}{\partial p_2} = \frac{A(B-s) - 2(B+s)p_2 + 2sp_1 + sp_3 + cB}{(B-s)(B+2s)} = 0, \tag{16A.7}$$

$$\frac{\partial \pi_3}{\partial p_3} = \frac{A(B-s) - 2(B+s)p_3 + s(p_1 + p_2) + c(B+s)}{(B-s)(B+2s)} = 0.$$

Solving for the equilibrium prices gives $p_1^m = p_2^m = \dfrac{A(2B+3s)(B-s) + c(2B+s)(B+s)}{2(2B^2 + 2Bs - s^2)}$

for the merged firm and $p_3^{nm} = \dfrac{A(B+s)(B-s) + cB(B+2s)}{(2B^2 + 2Bs - s^2)}$ for the nonmerged firm.

Substituting these prices into the profit equation (16A.3) gives the profit of equation (16.36):

$$\pi_1^m = \pi_2^m = \frac{B(A-c)^2(B-s)(2B+3s)^2}{4(B+2s)(2B^2 + 2Bs - s^2)^2}; \pi_3^m = \frac{(A-c)^2(B-s)(B+s)^3}{(B+2s)(2B^2 + 2Bs - s^2)^2}. \tag{16A.8}$$

# 16A.4 COMPARISON OF THE PRE-MERGER AND POST-MERGER CASES

Comparison of the pre- and post-merger profits looks on first sight to be difficult. However, if we define $\sigma = s/B$, where $\sigma$ lies in the interval $(0, 1)$ since we have that $0 \leq s < B$, then we can write the nonmerged profit as

$$\pi_{nm}^{*} = \frac{(A-c)^2 (B-s)(B+s)}{4B^2(B+2s)} = \frac{(A-c)^2 B^2(1-\sigma)(1+\sigma)}{4B^3(1+2\sigma)} = \frac{(A-c)^2(1-\sigma^2)}{4B(1+2\sigma)}, \quad \text{(16A.9)}$$

and we can write profit of each division of the merged firm as

$$\pi_1^m = \pi_2^m = \frac{B(A-c)^2(B-s)(2B+3s)^2}{4(B+2s)(2B^2+2Bs-s^2)^2} = \frac{B^4(A-c)^2(1-\sigma)(2+3\sigma)^2}{4B^5(1+2\sigma)(2+2\sigma-\sigma^2)^2}$$
$$= \frac{(A-c)^2(1-\sigma)(2+3\sigma)^2}{4B(1+2\sigma)(2+2\sigma-\sigma^2)^2}. \quad \text{(16A.10)}$$

Note that both profit equations (and post-merger the profit of firm 3) have the term $(A-c)^2/B$ in common. As a result, in comparing pre- and post-merger profits no generality is lost if we normalize this term to unity. The result is that profits are function solely of $\sigma$ and can be compared by plotting equations (16A.8) and (16A.9) in the interval $\sigma \in (0, 1)$. Doing so confirms that the merger increases the profits of the merged firms and of the nonmerged firm.

# Appendix B | Equilibrium Prices in the Spatial Model

## 16B.1 PROOF OF THE EQUILIBRIUM PRICES IN THE SPATIAL MODEL WITHOUT A MERGER

We can take any one of the five firms as typical of the others. So consider firm 3. Demand for this firm from consumers to its left is $Nr_{23}$, where $r_{23}$ is the marginal consumer given by

$$m_3 + tr_{23} = m_2 + t\left(\frac{L}{5} - r_{23}\right) \Rightarrow r_{23} = \frac{m_2 - m_3}{2t} + \frac{L}{10}. \qquad \text{(16B.1)}$$

Similarly, demand from consumers to the right of firm 3 is $Nr_{34}$, where $r_{34}$ is

$$r_{34} = \frac{m_4 - m_3}{2t} + \frac{L}{10}. \qquad \text{(16B.2)}$$

Firm 3's profit is, therefore,

$$\pi_3 = Nm_3(r_{23} + r_{34}) = Nm_3\left(\frac{m_2 - m_3}{2t} + \frac{m_4 - m_3}{2t} + \frac{L}{5}\right). \qquad \text{(16B.3)}$$

Differentiate this with respect to $m_3$ to give the first-order condition for firm 3:

$$\frac{\partial \pi_3}{\partial m_3} = N\left(\frac{m_2 + m_4}{2t} - \frac{2m_3}{t} + \frac{L}{5}\right) = 0. \qquad \text{(16B.4)}$$

Since the five firms are identical, in equilibrium we must have $m_3 = m_2 = m_4$. Substituting this into equation (16B.4) then gives the Bertrand–Nash equilibrium price:

$$m^* = tL/5. \qquad \text{(16B.5)}$$

## 16B.2 PROOF OF THE EQUILIBRIUM PRICES IN THE SPATIAL MODEL WITH A MERGER OF FIRMS 2 AND 3

Profit for each firm is easily identified by changing the firms' "labels" in equation (16B.3), so that we have

$$\pi_1 = Nm_1 \left( \frac{m_5 - m_1}{2t} + \frac{m_2 - m_1}{2t} + \frac{L}{5} \right),$$

$$\pi_2 = Nm_2 \left( \frac{m_1 - m_2}{2t} + \frac{m_3 - m_2}{2t} + \frac{L}{5} \right),$$

$$\pi_3 = Nm_3 \left( \frac{m_2 - m_3}{2t} + \frac{m_4 - m_3}{2t} + \frac{L}{5} \right),$$ (16B.6)

$$\pi_4 = Nm_4 \left( \frac{m_3 - m_4}{2t} + \frac{m_5 - m_4}{2t} + \frac{L}{5} \right),$$

$$\pi_5 = Nm_5 \left( \frac{m_4 - m_5}{2t} + \frac{m_1 - m_5}{2t} + \frac{L}{5} \right).$$

After the merger, the merged firm chooses $m_2$ and $m_3$ to maximize aggregate profit $\pi_2 + \pi_3$, while the remaining firms choose their prices to maximize their individual profits. This means that we have five first-order conditions to solve:

$$\frac{\partial \pi_1}{\partial m_1} = N \left( \frac{m_5 + m_2}{2t} - \frac{2m_1}{t} + \frac{L}{5} \right) = 0,$$

$$\frac{\partial (\pi_2 + \pi_3)}{\partial m_2} = N \left( \frac{m_1 + m_3}{2t} - \frac{2m_2}{t} + \frac{L}{5} \right) + N \frac{m_3}{2t} = 0,$$

$$\frac{\partial (\pi_2 + \pi_3)}{\partial m_3} = N \left( \frac{m_2 + m_4}{2t} - \frac{2m_3}{t} + \frac{L}{5} \right) + N \frac{m_2}{2t} = 0,$$ (16B.7)

$$\frac{\partial \pi_4}{\partial m_4} = N \left( \frac{m_3 + m_5}{2t} - \frac{2m_4}{t} + \frac{L}{5} \right) = 0,$$

$$\frac{\partial \pi_5}{\partial m_5} = N \left( \frac{m_4 + m_1}{2t} - \frac{2m_5}{t} + \frac{L}{5} \right) = 0.$$

Solving these equations simultaneously gives the prices in the text. In determining this equilibrium, we assume that no firm $i$ ever finds it profitable to price so low that it actually competes with firms beyond $i - 1$ and $i + 1$.

# Vertical and Conglomerate Mergers

**Chapter 17**

In the fall of 2000, General Electric and Honeywell International announced a deal in which the two companies would merge, with GE acquiring Honeywell. GE is a well-known firm with annual revenues well over $100 billion. Its businesses are involved in everything from lighting and appliances to television (it owns NBC) and financial services. It is also a major supplier of jet engines for commercial aircraft for which its chief competitors are Rolls-Royce and Pratt-Whitney. Honeywell was originally a leader in temperature and environmental controls but had, over time, developed into a major aerospace firm whose products included electric lighting, ventilation units, and braking systems for aircraft and also starter motors for aircraft engines. The deal was approved in the United States. However, in July 2001, the European Commission followed the recommendation of Competition Commissioner, Mario Monti, and blocked the merger.

The proposed GE–Honeywell merger was a marriage of complementary products. The more aircraft engines a firm—for example, Boeing—buys, the more starter motors and other related aircraft items it will also want. Such mergers fall under the classification of vertical mergers. In their simplest and most recognizable form, vertical mergers are combinations of firms operating at different levels of the production chain, say, a wholesaler and a retailer. However, the connection between an upstream and a downstream firm is qualitatively the same as the relation between Honeywell and GE, or that between computer hardware and software, nuts and bolts, or zinc and copper (which are combined to make brass). In all of these cases, two or more products are combined to yield the final ultimate good or service. Because an upstream–downstream relationship is just one of the many types of complementary relationships that may exist between firms, the term *vertical merger* has come to have the more general interpretation of a merger between any firms that produce complementary products.

We showed in Chapter 8, Section 8.3, that the separate production of such goods—when each one is in the hands of a firm with monopoly power—reduces the joint profit of the two firms and imposes an efficiency loss on the economy. The intuition behind this result is straightforward. Each firm's pricing decision imposes an externality on the other firm. A high price for computer hardware reduces demand for PCs. It also reduces demand for programs and operating systems. The hardware manufacturer takes the first effect into account. The second is not considered. The same is true, of course, in reverse. The software manufacturer does not take into account the impact its price choice has on the demand for hardware. As a result, in the noncooperative equilibrium, the prices of both goods are too high. If, say, the hardware firm were to cut its price, this would generate additional demand and additional profit for the software firm. However, since the hardware firm does not receive any of this additional profit, it does not reduce its price. This implies that, with cooperation, both firms would lower their prices and be better off. Consumers, too, would gain as a result of lower prices and expanded output.

We also noted in Chapter 8 that one way to achieve the profit and efficiency gains of cooperation is for the two firms to merge. Such a merger creates a single decision-making entity and, therefore, permits the externality to be internalized. The combined hardware and software firm certainly wishes to maximize its total profit, which means that it wishes to price the two individual goods so as to maximize the joint profit from each. Thus, whenever firms with monopoly power produce complementary products, they have a strong incentive either to merge or to devise some other method to ensure cooperative production and pricing of the complementary products.

Precisely the same issues of cooperation are present when the complementary relationships in question arise as a result of the firms occupying different levels in the vertical production chain. This is important in that it sheds light on how vertical mergers affect competition and so consumer welfare. Indeed, in the 1980s the realization of this motivation led to something of a revolution in antitrust policy related to vertical mergers. In the decades prior to 1980, vertical mergers were typically seen as anticompetitive because of the fear that such mergers would facilitate foreclosure. That is, the upstream merger partner would, after the merger, refuse to supply its product to its downstream rivals and thereby either drive them out of the market or create barriers to entry that would facilitate collusion.

Economists primarily associated with the Chicago School challenged this negative view of vertical mergers. They argued that vertical combinations were really attempts to achieve complementary efficiencies and that "vertical integration was most likely procompetitive or competitively neutral." (Riordan, 1998, p. 1232) By the 1980s, the Chicago School approach began to gain in the courts and vertical mergers were treated increasingly favorably by the antitrust authorities. However, by the mid-1990s the pendulum once more began to swing the other way. A post-Chicago approach has now emerged that employs new game theoretic tools to build new, realistic, and logically consistent models of vertical mergers in which once again the potential for consumer harm is real. This counterrevolution has led to a detailed scrutiny of a number of vertical combinations, most notably, those in the telecommunications sector.

We begin this chapter by developing an analysis of vertical mergers based on the proposition that these are procompetitive by correcting market inefficiencies. In Section 2, we consider some of the more recent analysis suggesting that such mergers might adversely affect competition in final product markets. Section 3 presents a simple formal model to highlight this issue.

Section 4 turns to the third and final type of mergers. These are conglomerate mergers involving the combination of firms without either a clear substitute or a clear complementary relationship. Examples include the purchase of Duracell Batteries by Gillette, the purchase of Snapple (iced tea) and Gatorade (a sports drink) by Quaker Oats, and the series of acquisitions in 1986 by Daimler-Benz, a luxury car and truck manufacturer, which turned it into Germany's largest industrial concern, producing aerospace to household goods. Finally, Section 5 presents a brief extension of our analysis to consider the fundamental issues raised by mergers regarding the theory of the firm.

## 17.1  PROCOMPETITIVE VERTICAL MERGERS: RESOLVING A COMPLEMENTARITY

When firms occupy different stages of the production stream the convention is to label those firms farthest from the final consumer of the product as upstream and those closest to that consumer as downstream. Film companies and movie theaters are an example. In this case, the film company is the upstream firm and the theater that shows the film is the downstream firm. Manufacturers and retailers have a similar upstream–downstream relationship. As we noted previously, all such relationships can be viewed through the lens of complementarity. Each firm in the vertical chain provides an essential service to other firms in the chain. The implication is that vertical relationships between two firms—each with monopoly power—leads to a loss of economic efficiency in the absence of some mechanism to coordinate the decisions of the two firms. In the case of vertically related firms, this is referred to as the problem of *double marginalization*. We now give a formal illustration of this problem.

Our setting is as follows. We have a single upstream supplier, the manufacturer, who sells a unique product to a single downstream firm, the retailer. The manufacturer produces the good at constant unit cost, $c$, and sells it to the retailer at a wholesale price, $r$. The retailer resells the product to consumers at the market-clearing price, $P$. For simplicity, we assume that the retailer has no retailing cost. Consumer demand for the good is described by our familiar linear inverse demand function $P = A - BQ$, and we assume that $c < A$.

Given that the retailer purchases $Q$ units from the manufacturer at wholesale price $r$ and resells these $Q$ units to consumers at price $P = A - BQ$, the retailer's profit is

$$\Pi^D(Q, r) = (P - r)Q = (A - BQ)Q - rQ. \tag{17.1}$$

As usual, the retailer maximizes profit by equating marginal revenue with marginal cost. We know from our assumptions that marginal revenue is $MR = A - 2BQ$ and that marginal cost is $r$. Equating these two terms then yields the optimal downstream output,

$$Q^D = (A - r)/2B. \tag{17.2}$$

Substituting this into the demand function gives the market-clearing retail price $P^D = (A + r)/2$. From equation (17.1) the retailer's profit is, therefore, $\Pi^D = (A - r)^2/4B$. Figure 17-1 illustrates these results.

What about the manufacturer? What wholesale price should be charged? It is clear from equation (17.2) that the wholesale price determines the number of units the upstream supplier is able to sell to the retailer. At the wholesale price $r$ the retailer chooses to produce $Q^D = (A - r)/2B$ units. To do so, the retailer must purchase this number of units from the manufacturer. In other words, $Q = (A - r)/2B$ is the demand curve facing the upstream manufacturer: the relationship between the wholesale price $r$ set by the manufacturer and the quantity of its product demanded by the retailer. In other words, *the inverse demand facing the upstream manufacturer at wholesale price* r *is* r = A − 2BQ, *is simply the marginal revenue function of the retailer.*

## Practice Problem 17.1

The inverse market demand curve facing a monopoly retailer of gold bracelets is described by $P = 3{,}000 - Q/2$. The retailer buys gold bracelets at a wholesale price, $r$, set by the manufacturer and has no other costs. Show that the inverse demand curve facing the manufacturer is $r = 3{,}000 - Q$.

FIGURE

**17-1**

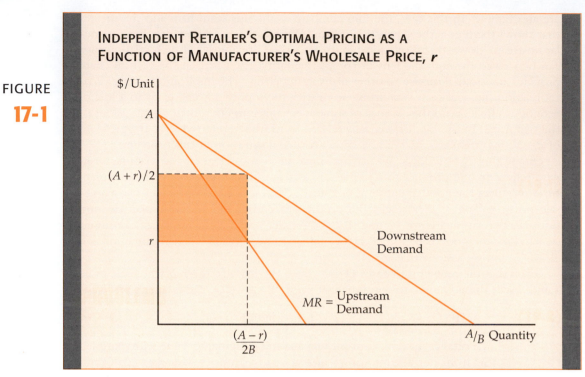

INDEPENDENT RETAILER'S OPTIMAL PRICING AS A
FUNCTION OF MANUFACTURER'S WHOLESALE PRICE, *r*

At wholesale price *r* the retailer will set retail price $P = (A + r)/2$ to maximize profit. Its total profit is indicated by the shaded region.

We can now derive the profit-maximizing price that the manufacturer charges for its product. Very simply, the manufacturer equates marginal cost with marginal revenue. The inverse demand curve for the manufacturer is $r = A - 2BQ$, so the marginal revenue curve for the manufacturer is $MR = A - 4BQ$. Equating this with marginal cost, $c$, yields the profit-maximizing output and wholesale price. These are, respectively,

$$Q^U = \frac{A - c}{4B} \text{ and } r^U = \frac{A + c}{2}. \tag{17.3}$$

This analysis is illustrated in Figure 17-2. When the upstream manufacturer sets the price $r^U = (A + c)/2$, the downstream retailer charges a price $P^D = (A + r^U)/2 = (3A + c)/4$. The retailer sells $Q^D = (A - c)/4B$ units, which is, of course, precisely the amount the upstream manufacturer anticipated it would sell when it set its upstream price $r^U = (A + c)/2$ in the first place. The profit of the manufacturer, shown in Figure 17-2 as the lightly shaded area *wrgv*, is $\Pi^U = (A - c)^2/8B$. The profit of the retailer, shown as the darkly shaded area *refg*, is $\Pi^D = (A - c)^2/16B$. The combined profit of the two firms is, of course, just the sum of these two areas, $3(A - c)^2/16B$.

Suppose now that the two firms merge so that the manufacturer becomes the upstream division of an integrated firm, selling its output through the downstream retail division of the same parent company. The good is still produced at constant marginal cost, $c$. This effectively transforms the integrated firm into a simple monopoly whose goal is to maximize monopoly profit through its choice of retail price $P$. This profit is just total revenue $PQ$ minus total cost $cQ$, which is $\Pi^I = (A - BQ) - cQ$.

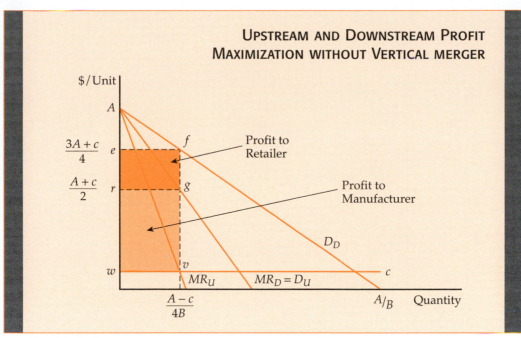

**UPSTREAM AND DOWNSTREAM PROFIT MAXIMIZATION WITHOUT VERTICAL MERGER**

FIGURE

**17-2**

The retailer's marginal revenue curve, $MR_D$, is the manufacturer's demand curve, $D_U$. Double marginalization results when the manufacturer sets its optimal wholesale price of $r = (A + c)/2$ above its marginal and unit cost $c$, and then the retailer adds on a further markup above this wholesale price by setting the profit-maximizing retail price of $P = (3A + c)/4$. The retailer will earn the profit shown as the darkly shaded area *refg*. The manufacturer or wholesaler will earn the profit shown as the lightly shaded area *wrgv*.

The marginal revenue curve of the integrated firm is just the marginal revenue curve of the non-integrated retailer, $MR^I = A - 2BQ$. Equating this with marginal cost $c$ gives the profit-maximizing output of the integrated firm, $Q^I = (A - c)/2B$. Substitution of this into the inverse demand curve then gives the retail price to consumers, $P^I = (A + c)/2$.

The merger of the manufacturer and retailer results in consumers being charged a lower price. As a result, the merged firm sells more of the product than did the two independent firms. But is this merger profitable? Yes! The profit earned by the integrated firm is $\Pi^I = (A - c)^2/4B$. This is 12.5 percent greater than the aggregate pre-merger profit of the manufacturer and the retailer, which we saw was $3(A - c)^2/16B$. From a social welfare point of view, *integrating the two monopoly firms has benefited everyone.* Total profit is increased *and* consumer surplus is increased with more of the good being sold at a lower price.

The gains from this vertical merger are illustrated in Figure 17-3. The retailer's pre-merger profit, area *refg*, is redistributed to consumers as surplus. In addition, consumers gain the area *fgi*. The manufacturer's profit has doubled from area *wrgv* to *wrib* and this more than offsets the loss of the retailer's profit.

A merger of vertically related firms generates an all-round efficiency gain because it allows the separate but related activities to be coordinated and, thereby, to internalize the externality each imposes on the other. In the absence of such a merger, the final price reflects a double marginalization. The independent manufacturer marks up

FIGURE

**17-3**

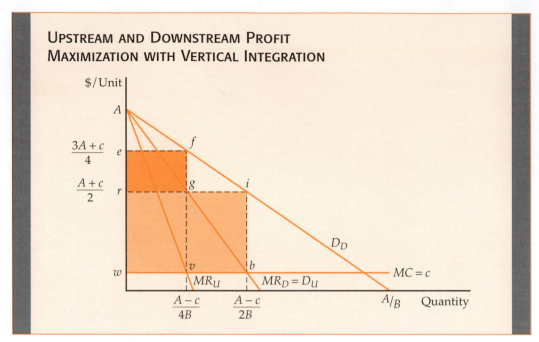

UPSTREAM AND DOWNSTREAM PROFIT
MAXIMIZATION WITH VERTICAL INTEGRATION

An integrated manufacturer–retailer will set price to consumers at $P = (A + c)/2$. The darkly shaded area, *refg*, which is profit that would have been earned by a non-integrated retailer, is now transferred to consumers as consumer surplus. However, the increase in sales volume generates an increase in the firm's profit equal to the second of the two lightly shaded areas, *gibv*. This gain more than offsets the loss of area *refg*.

its price to the retailer, who then compounds that price-cost distortion by adding a further markup in setting a price to the consumer. This is the source of the old saying, "What is worse than a monopoly? A chain of monopolies." It is not surprising that the antitrust authorities have been generally less concerned about vertical mergers than about horizontal ones.

## Practice Problem 17.2

Suppose that the downstream market for widgets is characterized by the inverse demand curve $P = 100 - Q$. Widget retailing is controlled by the monopolist WR Inc., which obtains its widgets from the monopoly wholesaler WW Inc. at a wholesale price of $w_w$ per widget. WW Inc. obtains the widgets in turn from the monopoly manufacturer WM Ltd. at a manufacturing price of $w_m$ per widget. WM Inc. incurs marginal costs of $10 per unit in making widgets. WW and WR each incur marginal costs of $5 in addition to the prices that they have to pay for widgets.

a. What is the equilibrium widget price to consumers $P$, the equilibrium wholesale price $w_w$, and the equilibrium manufacturing price $w_r$? What is the profit earned by each firm at these prices?

b. Show that vertical integration by any two of these firms increases profit and benefits consumers.

c. Show that integration of all three firms is even more beneficial.

☑ **Reality Checkpoint**

## Soft Drinks and Hard Choices . . . Pepsi and Its Bottlers

Pepsico, the well-known manufacturer of Pepsi and other soft drinks, is one of the largest soft-drink makers in the world. It has made particularly large gains in the market for canned and bottled soft drinks where the brand Pepsi now roughly shares the lead with the industry's longtime leader, Coke, in terms of U.S. market share. However, Pepsi has lagged behind Coca-Cola in the market for soft-drink syrup. As a result, Pepsi's overall U.S. market share is 32 percent versus Coca-Cola's share of 44 percent.

Syrup is sold not to household consumers but, instead, to restaurants that then mix the syrup with carbonated water for sale to their customers. This is commonly referred to as the soda fountain market. One reason that Pepsi fell behind Coca-Cola in the fountain market long ago is related to the problem of double marginalization. For many years, Pepsi sold its syrup to regional bottlers that typ-ically possess monopoly power over a given region. It was these bottlers that then sold the syrup to local restaurants. Thus, Pepsi had monopoly power with respect to the bottlers that, in turn, had monopoly power with respect to the local restaurants in their region. This resulted in double marginalization on Pepsi syrup and, as a result, somewhat high prices for this product and a lower Pepsi market share.

Pepsi decided to change the nature of its bottling contracts. In particular, it recently made efforts to eliminate the restrictions in those contracts that prevent Pepsi's direct sale of syrup to local restaurants through its food distribution companies, such as Sysco. Pepsi clearly believes that eliminating the middle persons and offering its syrup to local restaurants through its own integrated subsidiary is its best hope to make inroads into the fountain business.

**Sources:** N. Deogun, "Pepsi Seeks Changes at Bottlers to Speed Attack on Coke's Lock on Soda Fountain Business." *The Wall Street Journal*, January 23, 1997, p. B8; and S. Leith, "Pepsi Adds US Market Share As Coke Dips." *Atlanta Journal-Constitution*, March 5, 2004, p. B1.

There is one qualification to the foregoing analysis that should be noted. The benefits of vertical merger assume that the downstream firm uses a fixed amount of the upstream firm's product for every unit of output that the downstream firm sells. In our example of a producer and a downstream retailer, this assumption makes sense. The retailer has to have one unit of the manufacturer's product for every unit it resells to its customers. But in other situations this assumption is too strong. For example, if the upstream firm is a steel producer and the downstream firm is an automobile manufacturer, the steel firm's decision to charge the car company a price $r$ that includes a high markup may induce the automaker to reduce its use of steel in favor of aluminum or perhaps fiberglass. In such a case, the benefits of the car company integrating backwards into the steel market are less clear-cut. If substitution possibilities are great enough, they may be sufficient to offset the benefits that accrue from removal of double marginalization.

We summarize this part of our discussion as follows. Vertical integration of a chain of producers, each of which has monopoly power, is likely to benefit both firms and consumers by correcting the market failure associated with double marginalization. These benefits are more likely to arise when the technology operated by downstream firms offers limited opportunities for substitution into other inputs.

# 17.2  POSSIBLE ANTICOMPETITIVE EFFECTS OF MERGERS

If the analysis of the previous section were all that we needed to worry about it would, indeed, seem to be the case that the antitrust authorities need not be concerned about the welfare effects of vertical mergers. It should be recognized, however, that this analysis makes important assumptions that drive the results. In particular, we have assumed that there is a single market in which the final output is sold and that there is monopoly at each stage in the vertical chain. Before coming to the general conclusion that "vertical mergers are good for firms and consumers" we should check on the effects of relaxing these assumptions.

## 17.2.1  Vertical Merger to Facilitate Price Discrimination

We know from Chapters 5 and 6 that, while it is nice to be a monopolist, it is even nicer to be a monopolist who price discriminates. This is also true for an upstream monopolist selling to a number of downstream firms. Moreover, there are many cases in which those downstream firms differ in their willingness to pay for the upstream firm's product. Examples include a wholesaler supplying retailers in different cities, a manufacturer of motorcar parts supplying automakers in different countries, a consultant advising different firms in different industries, and so on. In these circumstances, the upstream firm would like to charge a high price for its product to those firms whose demand is inelastic and a low price to those whose demand is elastic.

Our discussion of price discrimination showed, however, that successful price discrimination has two requirements. First, the firm must be able to identify which buyers have elastic and which have inelastic demand. Second, the firm must somehow prevent resale of its product among its buyers. Such arbitrage would clearly undo any price discrimination efforts. We will assume that the firm has somehow solved the identification problem. The question then becomes, what mechanisms can it use to surmount the arbitrage problem?

The simplest approach would be for the upstream firm to write a no-resale contract with its buyers. In many circumstances, however, such contracts are unenforceable—for example, when the client firms are in different legal jurisdictions—in which case some other approach is necessary. One such approach is for the upstream firm to merge with some or all of its downstream customers.

Suppose that the upstream firm supplies a series of downstream firms and that, because of financial constraints, the upstream firm can integrate forwards with only some of the downstream firms. Then, as Practice Problem 17.3 shows, *it should merge first into markets with the highest elasticities of demand*. Because merger allows the firm to prevent resale, it also allows the firm to charge high, profit-maximizing prices in the other, low-demand elasticity markets. Is such a merger pro- or anticompetitive? We noted in Chapter 6 that successful price discrimination often improves economic efficiency. However, when that success is achieved by means of a vertical merger the effect on economic efficiency is ambiguous. The reason is that while the merger increases profits and removes double marginalization in one group of markets, the merger also leads to increased prices in the remaining markets. In other words, some consumers gain and others lose from the vertical merger. The overall effect is uncertain and can be resolved only when we have more information on the precise nature of demand in the various markets.

## Practice Problem 17.3

Assume that Widget International supplies widgets to Gizmo Inc. in Boston, where the demand for gizmos is $P_{gb} = 1 - Q_{gb}$, and TruGizmo Inc. of New York, where demand for gizmos is $P_{gn} = 0.75 - 0.2Q_{gn}$. Assume that WI's marginal costs of supplying both markets is $0.1 per widget and that both Gizmo Inc. and TruGizmo Inc. need exactly one widget for every gizmo they sell. Both gizmo dealers have other costs of production that amount to $0.1 per gizmo.

a. What are the profit-maximizing prices for widgets and gizmos in these two markets if Widget International cannot price discriminate? What are the profits of the three firms?
b. What are the profit-maximizing prices for widgets and gizmos in these two markets if Widget International can price discriminate? What are the profits of the three firms?
c. Show that if WI can merge with either Gizmo Inc. or TruGizmo Inc., it prefers to merge with TruGizmo Inc.
d. What is the effect of the merger on consumer prices and consumer surplus when WI (i) cannot and (ii) can price discriminate pre-merger?

### 17.2.2 Vertical Merger, Oligopoly, and Market Foreclosure

Now consider the second important assumption underlying our analysis in section 1. The gains from the merger hinge crucially on the fact that prior to the merger there was monopoly at both levels of activity, manufacture and retail. Suppose, instead, that we had started with either a competitive manufacturing sector upstream selling to a monopoly downstream, or a monopoly upstream selling to a competitive retail sector. Price competition upstream among manufacturers leads to a wholesale price equal to marginal cost. Similarly, competition among retailers downstream brings the retail price equal to the upstream price $P^U$ plus downstream marginal cost $r$. In either case, no double marginalization can occur, and there is no efficiency gain to vertical integration.

## Practice Problem 17.4

Suppose that the downstream market for widgets is perfectly competitive and characterized by the inverse demand curve $P = 100 - Q$. Retailers have zero production costs, but do incur a fee, $r$, for every unit sold. This fee is the payment that retailers must pay to the only manufacturer of widgets, the monopolist Widget International (WI). WI bears no fixed cost. It does, however, have a constant marginal cost of $10.

a. What is the equilibrium price to consumers, $P$, and fee to retailers, $r$? What is the profit earned by retailers and WI at these prices?
b. Show that vertical integration by which WI becomes the single producer and retailer of widgets does not raise WI's profit and does not lower the price to consumers.
c. What is the price to consumers if both widget manufacturing and retailing are competitive?

---

It could be argued, of course, that assuming perfect competition rather than monopoly in either the upstream or downstream market merely replaces one extreme assumption by another. We now turn, therefore, to the more realistic case in which both upstream and downstream markets are oligopolies. This raises another important issue that needs to be considered explicitly. Beyond the desire to reduce or eliminate double marginalization, there is an additional motive for vertical integration that is more clearly anticompetitive. This is where merger creates the possibility of *market foreclosure*. That is, the merger of vertically related firms might result in an upstream–downstream company that can deny downstream rivals a source of inputs or upstream competitors a market for their products.

Consider, for example, a motorcar manufacturer that merges with its gearbox supplier. This is likely to have two effects. First, other gearbox manufacturers are no longer able to compete for this automaker's business. Second, it is possible that the merged firm prefers not to sell its gearboxes to any other auto company. Alternatively, the merged firm may attempt a "price squeeze" by offering to sell its gearboxes to outside firms but only at exorbitant prices.[1]

Such market foreclosure effects of vertical mergers may reduce competitive forces in both the upstream and downstream markets, offsetting the benefits from eliminating the double marginalization problem. Indeed, this is a primary reason that the regulatory authorities investigate a proposed vertical merger. An early Alcoa case illustrates the point. Alcoa was accused of maintaining a powerful market position by extracting promises from power companies not to supply electricity—vital to the refining of aluminum—to competing aluminum producers. They were also accused of employing a price squeeze by charging very high prices for aluminum ingots that were used by companies that competed with Alcoa in certain downstream markets, such as the aluminum sheet market.

In telecommunications, the regulatory authorities have had similar concerns in both the United States and in Europe. In this industry, the local network has generally been monopolized while the long-distance market has been more competitive. However, any long-distance provider, such as Sprint or MCI, has to gain access to its potential customers by connecting to the local network. This gives the local network provider the potential to price its long-distance competitors out of the market by charging them a very high price for network access or, in an extreme case, denying them access to the network at all. Accordingly, a major concern of the regulatory authorities has been the prices that suppliers of local telephone networks are allowed to charge for access to the local network.

In short, we need to consider the foreclosure possibilities that vertical integration raises. In the remainder of this section we briefly describe two of the most important

---

1   There is, in fact, a whole host of methods by which merged firms can effectively foreclose their competitors. For an illustration of some of these, see Krattenmaker and Salop (1986).

✓ **Reality Checkpoint**

## Soft Drinks and Hard Choices 2 . . .
## The Coca-Cola Empire Strikes Back

The possibility of foreclosure by means of vertical integration is quite real in the minds of many executives and industry analysts. As an example, consider again the struggle between Pepsi and Coca-Cola. From our earlier recounting, we know that the bottlers are an important element in this conflict. The importance of the bottlers was made crystal clear in August 1996 when the Venezuelan bottling enterprise run by the Cisneros Group—the major bottler in Venezuela and also an owner of supermarkets and television/radio stations in Latin America, Europe, and the United States—sold a majority interest in its bottler to Coca-Cola. The Cisneros bottler had been working under contract for Pepsi for over a decade. It had helped propel Pepsi's market share in Venezuela to over 40 percent while Coke languished at 10 percent. Now, overnight, Coca-Cola had acquired the bottling capacity to increase its market share by 40 points. Meanwhile, with no bottler and no distribution, Pepsi's share is zero. One stock market analyst described Coke's purchase of the Venezuelan bottler as "a dagger to Pepsi's heart." Other analysts and investors apparently agreed. A 5 percent drop in Pepsi's stock price followed the announcement while Coca-Cola shares reached a 52-week high.

Pepsi did not take the announcement lying down. It quickly claimed that Cisneros was breaking a contractual arrangement obligating the bottler through 2003. It charged that Coca-Cola paid a price for the bottler that could only be justified if Coca-Cola saw the purchase as a means to obtain monopoly power in Venezuela by eliminating any opportunity for Pepsi to sell its product. It initiated legal action to block the purchase under Venezuela's monopoly law and threatened to do so in the United States.

This was not the end, however, of Coca-Cola's bottling purchases. A few months after the Venezuela purchase, Coca-Cola announced an agreement to purchase, through a subsidiary, all of a British bottler formerly jointly owned with Cadbury Schweppes. Once again, Pepsi (through its affiliate, BritVic Soft Drinks) took legal action to block the deal through the European Union's competition laws. It was joined by another British soft drink firm from the Virgin Group of companies. Fear of foreclosure was the heart of these firms' complaint, which alleged that Coca-Cola was acquiring sufficient power to pressure retailers to stop carrying other brands.

**Sources:** M. Freudenheim, "Pepsi Bottler Goes Over to the Enemy." *The New York Times*, August 21, 1996, p. 1; and N. Deogun and K. Strassel, "Coca-Cola Enterprises Faces EU Snag." *The Wall Street Journal*, November 22, 1996, p. A3.

models of foreclosure through vertical integration. One is due to Salinger (1988) and based on Cournot competition. The other is due to Ordover, Saloner, and Salop (1990) and is rooted in price competition. We develop more formal models of vertical foreclosure in Section 3.

Salinger's (1988) point can be understood as follows. Consider a downstream market with $N^D$ firms competing in quantities. Each of these firms buys exactly one upstream input at price $P^U$ for every unit that it produces downstream. The unit cost for each downstream firm is then $P^U + c^D$, where $c^D$ is the constant marginal cost incurred downstream that reflects the cost of other inputs. So the downstream market is described by a Cournot model in which each downstream firm has a constant marginal cost of $P^U + c^D$. Given the number of firms $N^D$ and the cost of other factors $c^D$, we know from Chapter 9 that the downstream quantity $Q^D$ will rise and the downstream price $P^D$ will fall as the upstream price $P^U$ falls. That is, the downstream equilibrium determines the demand facing the upstream firms. More importantly, because competition is not perfect we know that $P^D > P^U + c^D$. Note that this implicitly puts some constraint on the upstream price. $P^U$ cannot be too large otherwise downstream firms will not be able to break even.

Now consider the upstream market. Assume that it contains $N^U$ firms and that these firms face a constant marginal cost of $c^U$. Given the downstream demand just described, we can work out the upstream Cournot equilibrium. Here again, because upstream competition is not perfect, it must be the case that $P^U > c^U$. In short, we have a Cournot version of the double marginalization problem. The upstream price exceeds cost and that markup is further compounded in the downstream market.

What happens when an upstream and a downstream firm merge? Right away, this integrated firm has an advantage in the downstream market because it can buy the upstream input at cost $c^U$ instead of at $P^U$. The integrated firm will never pay $P^U$ and buy from an upstream firm when it can pay $c^U$ and buy from its own upstream division. It is precisely in this way that it avoids the double marginalization problem. Thus, the vertically integrated firm becomes a low-cost competitor in the downstream market. All firms in that market will earn a positive profit per unit, but the low-cost firm will earn $P^D - c^U - c^D$ per unit of output while its high-cost rivals will earn the smaller but still positive amount $P^D - c^U - P^U > 0$.

Will the integrated firm ever sell the upstream input to a non-integrated downstream rival? The answer is no. To see this, consider the following thought experiment. Suppose that the integrated firm takes one unit of its upstream input and sells it to an independent downstream firm. Such a small reallocation in production will leave both upstream and downstream prices unchanged. Because the upstream price is $P^U$, the integrated firm will gain $P^U - c^U$ from this transaction. However, it will lose the profit $P^D - c^U - c^D$ that it would have made using that input to produce its own downstream output. It is easy to see that this loss exceeds the gain, that is, that

$$P^D - c^U - c^D > P^U - c^U. \qquad \textbf{(17.4)}$$

All this requires is that $P^D - P^U - c^D > 0$, which we know must be true if there are to be any independent downstream firms at all.

We have just shown that foreclosure can happen as a result of a vertical merger. The integrated firm will not buy from independent upstream firms and will not sell to independent downstream ones. However, while foreclosure happens and the vertically integrated firm has an advantage over its competitors, this is not the same as saying that such foreclosure is harmful to consumers. That issue hinges on the balance of two forces. First, vertical integration and market foreclosure reduces the number of independent suppliers and thereby reduces the competitive pressure on price. However, vertical integration also eliminates double marginalization between the two formerly independent firms and, as we know, this makes it more cost effective. The vertically integrated firm is a fiercer competitor in the downstream market and this effect tends to reduce downstream consumer prices. It is difficult to know how this will play out. What is certainly the case is that the anticompetitive effect will be relatively weak if the number of independent competitors upstream remains large. If this is the case, the regulatory authorities can be reasonably assured that a vertical merger and its potential market foreclosure effects will not have detrimental effects on consumers.

Moreover, the Salinger analysis does not take into account the potential strategic reactions of downstream (and upstream) firms whose markets are threatened by vertical mergers. Is it likely that they will stand passively by and see their markets destroyed? One obvious reaction of a downstream firm to the threat of foreclosure by a vertically integrated rival is for this firm itself to seek a merger with an upstream supplier. This will have the effect of significantly increasing competitive pressures in the downstream market since all the downstream firms' costs will then be lower. We return to this point in the next section.

An alternative model that addresses these issues is that of Ordover, Saloner, and Salop (1990). These authors address the foreclosure issue while paying explicit attention to the fact that one vertical merger can lead to a second, with the result that downstream price competition is intensified. Their model differs from Salinger's (1988), however, in that it assumes price rather than quantity competition.

To get a flavor of the Ordover, Saloner, and Salop model, consider an industry in which there are two downstream firms and two upstream firms. The downstream firms make differentiated products, while the upstream firms produce a homogeneous product that is used as input by the downstream firms. Both sets of firms compete in prices in their relevant markets. Suppose that upstream firm $U_1$ and downstream firm $D_1$ merge. Suppose further that the newly merged firm can refuse (credibly) to supply the remaining downstream firm $D_2$. Then upstream firm $U_2$ becomes a monopoly supplier to $D_2$ and these two firms will set prices that reflect the familiar double marginalization problem. Seeing this, $D_2$ and $U_2$ may well choose to merge. In other words, the initial merger of $D_1$ and $U_1$ induces a subsequent merger of $D_2$ and $U_2$. The result is two vertically integrated firms which, because of their lower costs, compete vigorously in the downstream market, reducing profit for all firms. Of course, $D_1$ and $U_1$ can foresee all this and therefore may choose not to merge in the first place.[2]

Note that for this argument to work, it must be the case that there is no alternative input that the independent downstream firm $D_2$ can use. If such a substitute supplier does exist, then it constrains the price upstream firm $U_2$ can charge, potentially making $D_2$ less interested in a vertical merger.

Also, in the absence of an outside supplier there is the question of whether it is credible for the merged firm $D_1U_1$ to refuse to supply $D_2$, particularly if such a

---

2   Pepall and Norman (1997) show in a more complicated version of a similar model that vertical foreclosure is never an equilibrium. In this case, vertical foreclosure forces the exit of foreclosed downstream firms and has the effect of bringing the vertically integrated firms into very strong, direct competition with each other. They would prefer to continue to supply non-integrated firms in order to soften downstream competition by maintaining a greater degree of downstream product variety. However, their analysis assumes constant returns to scale. Whinston (1990) demonstrates how contractual relationships between an upstream and downstream firm may enable a monopolist to extend its marker power to a second market by means of foreclosing contracts.

refusal undermines the merger in the first place. Another scenario presents itself. It is possible that the newly merged firm $D_1U_1$ could offer to supply $D_2$ at a price somewhat below the price that the independent upstream supplier $U_2$ would want to charge in the absence of a merger between $D_2$ and $U_2$. Specifically, $D_1U_1$ could put a squeeze on $U_2$ by offering to supply $D_2$ at a price that is just less than the price that would encourage $D_2$ and $U_2$ to merge. In either case, complete foreclosure is avoided but only by some mechanism that permits the non-integrated downstream firm to enjoy lower cost.

The Ordover, Saloner, Salop analysis also has an implicit assumption on timing. First, $U_1$ and $D_1$ decide whether to merge. If they do not the market continues as it is. If they do, we then have the strategic issues outlined above that might lead to a merger of $U_2$ and $D_2$, undermining the initial merger decision. This ignores an important issue. If $U_1$ and $D_1$ decide not to merge then $U_2$ and $D_2$ have a strong incentive to merge. So we should consider an alternative analysis in which the merger decisions by firms are made simultaneously. As in the Salinger case, it is likely that the fear of vertical merger by one pair of upstream–downstream firms leads to merger of other pairs of upstream–downstream firms, potentially harming the firms but benefiting consumers.

In short, if there are gains that make a vertical merger profitable for one pair of firms, then other upstream and downstream firms will find such mergers profitable as well. If all pairs respond to this incentive by merging, consumer prices will quite likely be lower. Against this backdrop, foreclosure is likely to be ineffective either because the downstream firm has a substitute input or because the integrated firm will tend to supply the independent downstream firms. When no such substitute is available, however, foreclosure is a real possibility. This was certainly Pepsi's concern in the Reality Checkpoint: Soft Drinks and Hard Choices. Yet, if healthy competition prevails in the upstream market, neither the downstream firms nor the antitrust authorities need to worry a great deal about vertical integration.

## 17.3  MODELING OLIGOPOLISTIC VERTICAL MERGERS

An important lesson that should be drawn from the discussion of the previous section is that vertical mergers in oligopolistic markets should not be considered in isolation. There are important strategic issues—particularly on whether there will be more than one merger—that need to be considered in assessing the competitive impacts of such mergers. These in turn are likely to be affected by *how* the relevant firms compete—for example, whether they are Bertrand or Cournot competitors. We investigate these issues in this section using a model inspired by the Salinger analysis.

Assume that there are two upstream and two downstream firms. The upstream firms are Cournot competitors that produce a homogeneous intermediate good that is used by the downstream firms to make a good for final consumption. One unit of downstream output requires exactly one unit of the intermediate product. Each upstream firm has constant marginal costs of $c^U$ per unit and each downstream firm has constant marginal costs, excluding the cost of the intermediate good, of $c^D$ per unit. The downstream firms are Cournot competitors producing an identical final consumption good for which inverse demand is

$$P = A - BQ = A - B(q_1 + q_2).$$     **(17.5)**

Competition takes place in three stages. In the first stage upstream and downstream firms decide simultaneously whether to integrate vertically. If a vertical merger takes place we assume that downstream firm 1 (2) merges with upstream firm 1 (2). In the second stage nonmerged upstream firms compete in quantities, generating a price $P^U$ for the intermediate product. An upstream division of a vertically merged firm supplies its intermediate product to the downstream division at marginal cost $c^U$. Finally, in the third stage the downstream firms compete in quantities. As usual, we solve this game "backwards," starting with competition in the downstream market. There are three cases to consider: no vertical merger, vertical merger by both sets of firms, and vertical merger by only one set of firms. We consider these in turn. Throughout, we will continue to work with the general case; however, it will also be useful to have a specific example in mind. For this purpose, we use the values $A = 100$, $B = 1$, and $c^U = c^D = 23$.

### (i) No Vertical Mergers

Let us first determine the market outcome in the absence of any vertical mergers. For this case, we know that competition in the upstream market results in some intermediate product price of $P^U$ so that each downstream firm faces marginal cost $P^U + c^D$. Standard Cournot analysis (Chapter 9) then yields an output for each downstream firm of

$$q_1^D = q_2^D = \frac{A - P^U - c^D}{3B}, \tag{17.6}$$

and downstream profit of

$$\pi_1^D = \pi_2^D = \frac{(A - P^U - c^D)^2}{9B}. \tag{17.7}$$

We can use equation (17.6) to identify the *derived demand* that the upstream firms face. Aggregate downstream output is $Q^D = 2(A - P^U - c^D)/3B$. Since each unit of final product output requires one unit of the intermediate product, this is also the aggregate demand, $Q^U = Q^D$, for the intermediate product, which we can write in the more familiar inverse form as

$$P^U = (A - c^D) - \frac{3B}{2} Q^U. \tag{17.8}$$

This is in the standard linear form $P = a - bQ$, where $a = A - c^D$ and $b = 3B/2$. As a result, we know that the Cournot equilibrium output of each upstream firm is

$$q_1^U = q_2^U = \frac{a - c^U}{3b} = \frac{(A - c^D) - c^U}{9B/2} = \frac{2(A - c^U - c^D)}{9B}. \tag{17.9}$$

It follows that aggregate output in the upstream market is $Q^U = 4(A - c^U - c^D)/9B$. Substituting this into the upstream demand in equation (17.10) gives the equilibrium upstream price for the intermediate product:

$$P^U = (A - c^D) - \frac{3B}{2} \times \frac{4(A - c^U - c^D)}{9B} = \frac{(A - c^D + 2c^U)}{3}. \tag{17.10}$$

Profit of each upstream supplier is $(P^U - c^U)q^U_i$, which from equations (17.9) and (17.10) gives

$$\pi^U_1 = \pi^U_2 = \frac{2(a - c^U - c^D)^2}{27B}.$$

(17.11)

Finally, substituting the upstream price into equations (17.6) and (17.9) gives the equilibrium output and profit for each downstream firm:

$$q^D_1 = q^D_2 = \frac{2(A - c^U - c^D)}{9B}.$$

(17.12)

$$\pi^D_1 = \pi^D_2 = \frac{4(A - c^U - c^D)^2}{81B}.$$

(17.13)

It is easy to check that, as we would expect, aggregate downstream demand equals aggregate upstream output. Using the numbers from our example, total output is now 24 units. The upstream price is $41 and the retail price to consumers is $76.

## (ii) Two Vertical Mergers

This is a simple case. Both downstream divisions are supplied with the intermediate product at marginal cost $c^U$, meaning that each downstream division has marginal cost $c^U + c^D$. Accordingly, each downstream division sets its Cournot output (see Chapter 9) equal to

$$q^D_1 = q^D_2 = \frac{A - c^U - c^D}{3B}.$$

(17.14)

Profit of each vertically integrated firm is profit of the downstream division:

$$\pi^D_1 = \pi^D_2 = \frac{(A - c^U - c^D)^2}{9B}.$$

(17.15)

Thus, in our example, two vertical mergers would result in each firm producing 18 units and earning a profit of $324. Note that the efficiencies associated with eliminating double marginalization are beneficial to consumers. In our example, the total industry output has risen from 24 units in the no-merger case to a new total of 36 units. Correspondingly, the final consumer price has fallen from $76 to $64.

## (iii) One Vertical Merger

Now suppose that there is only one vertical merger, between upstream firm 1 and downstream firm 1. We know from Salinger's analysis that the merged firm will not supply downstream firm 2, with the result that upstream firm 2 is effectively a monopoly supplier to downstream firm 2. This does not, however, give the upstream firm total power since it must take into account the impact that its pricing of the intermediate product has on the ability of its customer, downstream firm 2, to compete in the downstream market with its vertically integrated rival.

Suppose that upstream firm 2 sets a price $P^U$ for its intermediate product. Then we know that downstream firm 2 has marginal cost $P^U + c^D$ while downstream firm 1 has marginal cost $c^U + c^D$. In other words, downstream firm 1 is a low-cost and downstream firm 2 a high-cost producer in the final product market. Applying the standard Cournot equations we know that the equilibrium outputs of the two firms are

$$q_1^D = \frac{A - 2(c^U + c^D) + (P^U + c^D)}{3B} = \frac{A - 2c^U - c^D + P^U}{3B},$$

$$q_2^D = \frac{A - 2(P^U + c^D) + (c^U + c^D)}{3B} = \frac{A - 2P^U - c^D + c^U}{3B}, \qquad \textbf{(17.16)}$$

and their equilibrium profits are

$$\pi_1^D = \frac{[A - 2(c^U + c^D) + (P^U + c^D)]^2}{9B} = \frac{(A - 2c^U - c^D + P^U)^2}{9B},$$

$$\pi_2^D = \frac{[A - 2(P^U + c^D) + (c^U + c^D)]^2}{9B} = \frac{(A - 2P^U - c^D + c^U)^2}{9B}. \qquad \textbf{(17.17)}$$

The independent upstream firm has monopoly power so we know that $P^U > c^U$. Equation (17.16) then confirms, as we expected, that the downstream division of the integrated firm has a greater output than its non-integrated rival.

As in our analysis of both firms being merged, we can use equation (17.16) to identify the derived demand, $q_2^U = q_2^D$, for the independent upstream firm. Again, writing this in inverse form we have

$$P^U = \frac{A - c^D + c^U}{2} - \frac{3B}{2} q_2^U. \qquad \textbf{(17.18)}$$

This is in the form $P = a - bq$ and we know that with this demand function the monopoly output is $(a - c^U)/2b$.

Substituting $a = (A - c^D + c^U)/2$ and $b = 3B/2$ gives the equilibrium output for upstream firm 2:

$$q_2^U = \frac{A - c^U - c^D}{6B}. \qquad \textbf{(17.19)}$$

The equilibrium price for the intermediate product is, therefore,

$$P^U = \frac{A - c^D + c^U}{2} - \frac{3B}{2} \times \frac{(A - c^U - c^D)}{6B} = \frac{(A + 3c^U - c^D)}{4}. \qquad \textbf{(17.20)}$$

Profit of the independent upstream firm is $(P^U - c^U)q_2^U$, which from equations (17.19) and (17.20) is

$$\pi_2^U = \frac{(A - c^U - c^D)^2}{24B}. \qquad \textbf{(17.21)}$$

Finally, we can substitute the equilibrium intermediate product price into equations (17.16) and (17.17) to identify the equilibrium outputs and profits in the downstream market:

$$q_1^D = \frac{5(A - c^U - c^D)}{12B},$$

$$q_2^D = \frac{(A - c^D - c^U)}{6B}. \qquad \textbf{(17.22)}$$

$$\pi_1^D = \frac{25(A - c^U - c^D)^2}{144B},$$

$$\pi_2^D = \frac{(A - c^D - c^U)^2}{36B}.$$

(17.23)

We noted previously that this vertical merger makes upstream firm 2 a monopoly supplier to downstream firm 2 rather than a Cournot competitor. Nevertheless, comparison of equations (17.21) and (17.11) indicates that the merger reduces upstream firm 2's profit. It has a monopoly, but it supplies a high-cost downstream firm. Again, using our specific numerical example, we find that without any vertical mergers, upstream firm 2 earns a profit of $216. With vertical integration between upstream firm 1 and downstream firm 1, however, upstream firm 1 earns a profit of only $121.50. Its downstream customer earns a profit of $81. So, the independent firms earn a combined profit of $202.50. Their integrated rival, however, earns a total profit of $506.25.

In turn, because downstream firm 2 has a high cost, it reduces its output relative to the no-merger case. However, by virtue of its vertical merger, firm 1 has enjoyed a reduction in cost which, in turn, allows it to expand its output relative to the no-merger case. Using our example, it is then easy to illustrate the general result that the output expansion of firm 1 more than offsets the contraction at firm 2 so that total output rises and the price to consumers falls relative to the no-merger case. Output would now be 31.5 units and the consumer price would be $68.50.

### (iv) Reappraisal and Application: The GE–Honeywell Merger

Let us now briefly review our calculations and use these to consider the GE–Honeywell merger described at the start of this chapter. Table 17-1 shows the combined profit to each set of firms as a result of whether they or their rivals decide to merge. Note that the result is a typical prisoners' dilemma game. Both pairs of upstream and downstream firms would prefer no vertical integration. Yet, the strategy "Integrate" is a dominant strategy for each pair. This means that we should expect each pair eventually to integrate. Moreover, since "Integrate" is a dominant strategy, the timing of the integration decision has no impact on the outcome. Both sets of firms will choose to integrate vertically whether this decision is made simultaneously or sequentially.

Vertical integration, then, has three effects. First, it removes inefficient double marginalization. Second, because it reduces downstream cost for an integrated firm,

**TABLE 17-1**

**PAYOFF MATRIX FOR THE COURNOT VERTICAL MERGER GAME**

|  |  | Firms 1 | |
|---|---|---|---|
|  |  | Do Not Integrate | Integrate |
| Firms 2 | Do Not Integrate | $360; $360 | $202.50; $506.25 |
|  | Integrate | $506.25; $202.50 | $324; $324 |

it makes the downstream market more competitive. Third, it reduces competitive pressures on nonmerged firms in the upstream market. In our example, the first two effects dominate the third. As a result, even if only one firm integrates, the final price to consumers falls.

Note that when one firm integrates, it gains a competitive advantage over its non-integrated rivals. As noted above, this leads the integrated firm to expand while its rivals contract. It is this competitive advantage and its implications for rival firms that appears to have guided the European Commission in its judgment against the GE–Honeywell merger. The fear was that the merger would allow the GE–Honeywell to bundle, that is, to integrate their products in a way that would disadvantage its rivals. You should also now understand why many economists were somewhat surprised by this decision. While the non-integrated rivals would surely suffer, consumers would likely benefit. Moreover, as we have seen, the rivals have a clear strategic response—integrate themselves. If they did, consumers would gain even more.

In reaching its decision, the European Commission appears to have been persuaded that integration by the GE–Honeywell rivals was not possible and that foreclosing the Honeywell products to firms would so hurt rivals that they would be forced to exit, resulting in a monopoly. Hence, it wrote:

> Because of their lack of ability to match the bundle offer, . . . [independent] suppliers will lose market shares to the benefit of the merged entity and experience an immediate damaging profit shrinkage. As a result, the merger is likely to lead to market foreclosure on the existing aircraft platforms and subsequently to the elimination of competition in these areas.

For this argument to be valid, one must show not only that integration by GE–Honeywell rivals was not possible but also that it would never be so. Moreover, even if that were the case and a GE–Honeywell monopoly did emerge, one would have to show still further that that monopoly price would exceed the price that prevails in the absence of any vertical mergers. For our specific example, this is not the case. The integrated monopolist would sell 27 units at a final consumer price of $73, which is $3 less than the price it obtains in the no-merger case. One should, of course, be wary of arguing our analysis is definitive. Nevertheless, the European Commission's ruling in this case does at least seem questionable.[3]

## 17.4 CONGLOMERATE MERGERS

The final type of merger we consider is a conglomerate merger. Such mergers bring under common control firms whose products are neither direct substitutes nor complements. The result is a set of firms producing a diversified range of products with little or nothing in common.

While conglomerate companies have been with us for some time, the U.S. merger wave starting in the 1960s and continuing into the early 1980s is, particularly in the earlier years, generally perceived to be the period when many of the conglomerates that we see today were formed. The question that we address is whether we can

---

3   For a similar analysis of the GE–Honeywell case, but one that is set in a framework of differentiated products, see Nalebuff (2004).

develop a convincing economic rationale for this development. If not, then perhaps we should think of conglomerates as an accident of history that is being gradually corrected through corporate downsizing and the focus on "core businesses" that appear to characterize corporate change as we move into the new millennium. A number of reasons have been advanced to support the emergence of conglomerate firms. We examine these in turn.

## 17.4.1  Possible Economies Associated with Conglomeration

Scope economies and saving on transactions costs are two possible advantages that may accrue to conglomerate firms. Again, by scope economies we mean that a variety of products or services are more cheaply produced by one firm than by two or more firms. By transactions costs we mean the costs that are incurred by firms when they use external markets in order to exchange goods and services.[4] These include, for example, the costs of searching for the desired inputs, negotiating supply contracts, monitoring and enforcing these contracts, and the risk associated with unforeseen changes in supply conditions.

As we noted in Chapter 4, scope economies derive primarily from the ability of the firm to exploit common inputs in the manufacture of a range of products. The same production line can be used for several products, marketing efforts can promote the whole range of goods a firm produces, and the fruits of research and development may extend to many of the firm's products. This line of argument implies that for scope economies to be an important element in conglomerate mergers it is necessary that the firms that merge are related in some respect. Either they sell in similar markets or they have similar production technologies. The data on conglomerates do not appear to be consistent with this hypothesis. A detailed study by Nathanson and Cassano (1982) concludes that there are at least as many conglomerate firms that produce goods with little in common, whether this be technology or the markets at which they are targeted, as there are firms that have relatively low product and market diversity.

The role for transactions costs in yielding scope economies derives mainly from the problem of contracting for the services of specific inputs. Consider first a specialized asset, such as a sophisticated machine that is specifically designed to produce two goods, A and B. Let us also suppose that the markets for A and B are highly concentrated with a small number of producers, and that the machine has spare capacity if the owner uses it only to produce A. This might arise, for example, if demand for A is limited relative to the productive capacity of the machine. If such spare capacity exists, the owner of the machine may wish to use it to also produce B goods. Conglomeration or merging together A and B production is one way that this can happen. However, as Teece (1982) and others have argued, conglomeration is not strictly necessary. The machine owner can instead simply lease the spare capacity to B producers.

There is a problem with the leasing arrangement, however. Because the number of B producers is small, each will have some monopoly power in bargaining over the terms of the lease. As a result, the machine owner may find that the costs and risks associated with the negotiations between the interested parties are large as each side tries to get the best possible deal. Conglomeration may be a means of avoiding such

---

4   For an excellent discussion of transactions costs, see Besanko, Dranove, Shanley, and Schaefer (2004).

## ✓ Reality Checkpoint

### American Can to Primerica or, Who Put Eight, Great Companies in That Itty-Bitty Firm

American Can was for a long time a major manufacturer of various types of metal containers, primarily intended to hold foodstuffs or drinks. This was, however, a highly competitive business through the relative ease of entry into the metal can business and as a result of growing competition from other types of containers such as plastic. As a result, American Can began a process of diversification from the 1950s, with the result that by 1980 it was also involved in paper production, print-ing, record distribution, retailing, and direct mail marketing.

During the 1980s American Can moved heavily into the financial services business, acquiring Associated Madison, Barclays Bank, and Smith Barney. By the late 1980s it had sold off its can business and many of its other businesses, to concentrate upon financial services, changing its name in the process from American Can to Primerica . . . by any name, a true conglomerate.

**Source:** M. Best, *The New Competition: Institutions of Corporate Restructuring.* Cambridge, MA: Harvard University Press, 1990.

costs. By using the machine to produce both A and B within the same firm, the machine owner avoids all the bargaining hassles. There is no longer any conflict over how to divide the gains from using the machine because those gains all go to the same person.

Transactions cost problems are particularly important when the asset involved is knowledge or information intensive. The knowledge of such matters as organizational routines or specialized customer needs is generally embodied in specific individuals or teams employed by the company. It is difficult to envision contracts to "lease" such personnel.

In short, the effort to minimize the transactions costs associated with contracting between firms may explain conglomerate mergers to some extent. Still, this motivation seems unlikely to be the major factor behind such mergers. The reason is that we are talking about some asset that is common to all the lines of production operated by the conglomerate. As we pointed out in our discussion of scope economies, such commonality in productive assets does not seem to be a feature of conglomerate firms.

### 17.4.2 Managerial Motives

The skepticism surrounding the explanations based on scope economies, transaction cost savings, and other arguments that conglomerate mergers improve efficiency has led many to postulate a different, less benign motivation. This is that conglomeration is in the interest of management even if it is not in the interest of shareholders. Because management calls the shots, it is the managerial interest that prevails.

In any reasonably large public company the ownership, which essentially resides with the shareholders, may be separated from the control, which essentially resides with the management team. This separation would not matter much if management performance could be perfectly observed and monitored by shareholders. Yet this is almost never the case. Absent such monitoring, management can pursue its own agenda at least to some extent. Again, this would not matter so long as the best interests of management are served by maximizing shareholder wealth. It is precisely the attempt to secure this harmony of interest that lies behind the use of performance-related clauses and payment in stock options in many executive compensation schemes. Still, the match between the interests of shareholders and management is rarely perfect, leaving management with at least some incentive to pursue goals other than maximization of shareholders' returns.

Suppose, for example, that management compensation is based upon company growth.[5] Growth is far from easy to generate internally. It requires that market share be won from competitors who can hardly be expected to sit passively by when they lose market share. Nor is it easy to buy growth through horizontal merger, since this is the kind of acquisition that is watched by the antitrust authorities. In these circumstances we should not be surprised to find management supporting a conglomerate merger, even if this is not necessarily in the best long-term interests of shareholders. Such a merger offers management the desired growth while avoiding antitrust problems. In this light it is, perhaps, significant that the greatest wave of conglomerate mergers in the United States coincided with a period in which the antitrust authorities were particularly fierce in their examination of mergers between related companies.

Management may also pursue conglomeration as a means to minimize risk. When a firm is involved in many distinct markets it avoids putting "all its eggs in one basket." Such diversification may be important to management.[6] As noted, shareholders often use compensation schemes that closely tie management's pay to the firm's profit performance.[7] Yet while these practices work to tie management's interest more closely to that of the stockholders, they also increase the risk that management faces. As profits can go up and down, management's compensation rises and falls as well, whether the profit results were management's fault or not. To protect against such fluctuations, management may seek to diversify the sources of the firm's income by pursuing conglomeration. This smoothes the firm's income stream because with many product lines operating, positive and negative shocks tend to cancel each other out. As a result, the derived income stream of the firm's executives is also smoother. Indeed, even shareholders might prefer this approach if, in the absence of such diversification, the firm would have to pay its executives higher salaries to compensate them for the greater risk.

In their tests of this proposition, Ahimud and Lev (1981) take as their measure of management control the degree to which the firm's stock lies in a single hand. For example, if more than 30 percent of the stock is held by a single party, they treat this as a company with strong owner control, while if no party owns more than 10 per-

---

5   This analysis is treated in detail in Mueller (1969).
6   For a detailed discussion of these ideas, see Ahimud and Lev (1981).
7   For example, Boeing Corp. linked its annual award of stock options to its 1,500 top executives to the performance of the company's share price over the next five years. See F. M. Biddle, "Boeing Links Managers' Stock Options to Five-Year Performance of Shares." *The Wall Street Journal*, February 26, 1998, p. B12.

cent of the stock, they treat this as a firm under management control. They conclude that the evidence favors this model: "Manager-controlled firms were found to engage in more conglomerate acquisitions than owner-controlled firms. Second, regardless of the means by which a firm achieves diversification, the operations of manager-controlled firms were found to be more diversified than those of owner-controlled firms" (p. 615).

## 17.5 A BRIEF DIGRESSION ON MERGERS AND THE THEORY OF THE FIRM

A merger involves the acquisition of one company by another. As a result of that purchase, the acquiring firm gets the physical capital—buildings, equipment, and land—and perhaps certain intangible assets, such as reputation, that formerly belonged to the acquired company. The ultimate question raised by a merger is, what does this ownership permit the merged firms to do that could not be done before?

In the case of a horizontal merger, the possibility of enhanced market power is clearly part of the motivation. Yet we often see horizontal mergers in which such an increase in market power is not likely. Indeed, the merger paradox discussed in Chapter 16 implies that increases in market power as the result of a merger are rare. In the case of a vertical merger, the market power motivation is even more suspect. If the upstream and downstream firm each had five percent of their respective markets before the merger, little seems changed by moving the ownership of those market shares from two different firms to two different divisions of the same firm.

Similarly, consider the problem of double marginalization. We have suggested merger as a response to that problem. It is not the only response, however. Various contracts between two vertically related firms can be written to surmount the problem of double marginalization, and these contracts fall short of integrating the two firms into one. Indeed, we will examine such contracts in depth in the next chapter. Here we simply want to raise the question as to why firms merge rather than make use of such contracts. Put differently, why don't more firms merge? What in fact limits the size of a firm? What stops firms from merging into bigger and bigger firms?

These questions take us back to the issues raised in Chapter 4 relating to the determination of the boundaries of a firm. What is the difference between organizing the production of a commodity through many independent companies and organizing that production through many units of the same company? Viewing the matter in this way makes transparent the fact that this issue is rightfully regarded as an important one for industrial organization theory.

Many alternative theories of the firm have been developed over the last thirty years. Indeed, there is sufficient work in this area now to comprise a course in itself. Our aim here is not to cover this material in depth. Instead, we wish simply to offer a brief discussion of the limits of a firm. Now seems a particularly appropriate time to raise this topic since a merger, by definition, is a transaction that increases those limits.

Neoclassical theory does not tell us much as to what such a transaction gains for the parties. Nor does it tell us why firms operate internal divisions rather than "spinning them off" into individual companies. However, neoclassical theory is not alone in this regard. Other approaches to the theory of the firm also fall short of a complete answer. Take, for instance, the agency view of the firm. Under this view, a firm is a mechanism designed to generate the proper incentives when the various parties engaged in the production process have different and private information. A supplier of, say, glass may contract with an automobile producer to provide windshields of a particular quantity and quality according to a particular schedule. Obviously, the actual quality of such windshields is beyond the complete control of the glass firm but the glassmaker knows whether it gave its full effort to supplying the specified quality. The automaker, though, is not so well informed. It cannot be sure whether a batch of low-quality glass is due to bad luck or, instead, bad faith on the part of its supplier. Agency theory has generated extremely useful insights into the types of contracts that might be used to surmount such problems and provide the proper incentives for both parties to live up to their contractual obligations. Yet it does not tell us whether such contracts must be between two separate firms, as in the automaker and the glass supplier of our story, or whether the contract could simply be the incentive scheme offered to the windshield division of a giant car company.

Similar problems arise with the transactions cost approach to the firm. Under this approach, the firm is viewed as a mechanism to minimize the costs of negotiating, interpreting, enforcing, and renegotiating contracts. However, the precise mechanism by which this cost reduction is achieved is not typically spelled out. There is no reason, a priori, to assume that haggling is less a problem between two divisions within one firm than between two firms.

In short, the issue of corporate mergers reveals a weakness in economic theory regarding the limits or boundaries of a firm's activities. Why is it that we observe General Motors supplying auto bodies internally rather than purchasing them from an independent supplier? How is this different from a state of affairs in which these divisions are independent?

One answer is provided in the work of Hart (1995) and centers on the issue of ownership. A merger changes the ownership of assets and ownership gives control. The carmaker that owns its own windshield supply unit is in a position to resolve, by itself, any dispute between its assembly line and the glass unit. As noted, this does not necessarily minimize the cost of haggling. However, it may permit investments that increase efficiency. Suppose, for instance, that there is specific machinery that can be used to produce, inexpensively, windshields of a quality and style unique to the automaker in question. An independent glass company might not invest in such equipment because it ties the glassmaker too closely to the particular auto firm. If it did make the investment, its bargaining position in disputes with the automaker would be weak because it has no other buyer for the one product that this machinery permits it to make. From the perspective of the glassmaker, it is less risky to use more general equipment that makes it easy to produce glass products for other firms as well. This is true even though the use of such generic processes requires the firm to incur an extra cost to mold the windshield to the specific dimensions specified by the carmaker.

A merger or acquisition of the glass company by the automaker offers a way out. By operating windshield production as a unit within its own firm, the automaker removes the potential conflict. Now, the specialized machinery can be bought and the windshields produced at lower cost because there is no longer any friction over how the gains from this investment will be shared. They all go to the one, common owner of the assets.

In other words, common ownership is desirable whenever there are complementarities—or synergies—between different assets. As a result, we should expect firms to combine whenever such complementarities are present—and to split apart if such complementarities vanish. Since technological changes are ever present, and since such innovations are constantly altering the extent of production complementarities, we should also expect a constant fluctuation in the size and organization of firms. This approach may help explain the recent wave of mergers in the telecommunications industry where rapid innovations have greatly altered the production technology.

## SUMMARY

We have considered two broad types of merger in this chapter: vertical and conglomerate. A vertical merger involves the union of companies operating at different stages of production in the same product line. A conglomerate merger occurs when two firms unite that have little or no common markets or products.

Vertical mergers raise complicated issues. On the one hand, such mergers can benefit firms and consumers by eliminating the practice of double marginalization. On the other hand, they may be a means to foreclose either upstream or downstream markets to rivals, and to facilitate price discrimination. There is no simple way of determining which of these forces is likely to be the stronger. However, there is at least some reason for believing that the negative impact of potential vertical foreclosure itself sets up a countervailing force. Companies that are negatively affected by foreclosure are likely to react by themselves seeking to integrate vertically. If they do so, this will toughen competition in the final product markets, resulting in the vertical mergers being procompetitive. More generally, the problems that might arise with vertical mergers are more likely to be of relatively minor concern if the upstream market remains somewhat competitive following the merger.

Conglomerate mergers probably raise the fewest problems from an antitrust perspective. However, for this very reason the motivation for such mergers is difficult to see. They may reflect an attempt to minimize risk either for stockholders or managers. But there would seem to be other means to achieve these same ends.

## PROBLEMS

1. Norman International has a monopoly in the manufacture of whatsits. Each whatsit requires exactly one richet as an input and incurs other variable costs of $5 per unit. Richets are made by PepRich Inc., which is also a monopoly. The variable costs of manufacturing richets are $5 per unit. Assume that the inverse demand for whatsits is $p_w = 50 - q_w$, where $p_w$ is the price of whatsits in dollars per unit and $q_w$ is the quantity of whatsits offered for sale by Norman International.

   a. Write the profit function for Norman International assuming that the two monopolists act as independent profit-maximizing companies, with Norman International setting a price $p_w$ for whatsits and PepRich setting a price $p_r$ for richets. Hence, derive the profit-maximizing price for whatsits as a function of the price of richets, and use this function to obtain the derived demand for richets.

   b. Use your answer in (a) to write the profit function for PepRich. Hence, derive the profit-maximizing price of richets. Use this to derive the profit-maximizing price of whatsits. Calculate the sales of whatsits (and also of richets) and calculate the profits of the two firms.

c. Now assume that these two firms merge to form NPR International. Write the profit function for NPR given that it sets a price $p_w$ for whatsits. Hence, calculate the post-merger profit-maximizing price for whatsits, sales of whatsits, and the profits of NPR.

d. Confirm that this merger has increased the joint profits of the two firms while reducing the price charged to consumers. By how much has consumer surplus been increased by the merger in the market for whatsits?

e. Assume that the two firms expect to last forever and that the discount factor $R$ is 0.9. What is the largest sum that PepRich would be willing to pay the owners of Norman International to take over Norman International? What is the lowest sum that the owners of Norman International would be willing to accept? (*Hint:* Calculate the present value of the profit streams of the two firms before and after the merger, and notice that neither firm will want to be worse off with the takeover than without it.)

2. Now assume that PepRich gets the opportunity to sell to an overseas market for whatsits, controlled by a monopolist FC Hu Inc., which has the same operating costs in making whatsits as Norman International. PepRich knows that it will have to pay transportation costs of $2 per richet to supply the overseas market. Inverse demand for whatsits in this market is $p_w = 40 - q_w/2$.

   a. Repeat your calculations for problem 1.

   b. The authorities in the overseas market are contemplating taking an antidumping action, accusing PepRich of dumping richets into its market. They calculate that by doing so, they will induce PepRich to offer to take over FC Hu. Assume that PepRich has limited access to funds, so that it can take over only one of the two firms Norman International and FC Hu. Are the overseas authorities correct in their calculations? (*Hint:* Compare the maximum amounts that PepRich would be willing to pay for Norman International and FC Hu.)

3. Go back to the conditions of problem 1, so that PepRich is supplying only Norman International. But now assume that the manufacture of each whatsit requires exactly one richet and one zabit. Zabits are made by ZabCor, another monopolist, whose variable costs are $2.50 per zabit.

   a. Assume that the three firms act independently to maximize profit. Calculate the resulting prices of richets, zabits, and whatsits and the profits of the three firms.

   b. Assume an infinite life for all three firms and a discount factor $R = 0.9$. PepRich and ZabCor are each contemplating a takeover of Norman International. Which of these two companies would win the bidding for Norman International? What will be the effect of the winning takeover on consumer surplus in the market for whatsits?

4. As an alternative to buying Norman International, the owners of PepRich and ZabCor contemplate merging to form PRZ, which will control the manufacture of both richets and zabits.

   a. Calculate the impact of this merger on (1) the prices of richets, zabits, and whatsits; (2) the profits of these firms; and (3) consumer surplus in the whatsit market.

   b. Which merger will be preferred

      (1) by consumers of whatsits?

**(2)** by the owners of PepRich and ZabCor?

**(3)** by the owners of Norman International?

**5.** (More difficult) Ginvir and Sipep are Bertrand competitors in the market for carbonated drinks. Consumers consider their products to be differentiated with the demands for the products of the two firms being given by the inverse demand functions

$$p_G = 25 - q_G - q_S/2 \text{ for Ginvir and}$$
$$p_S = 25 - q_S - q_G/2 \text{ for Sipep.}$$

To make their drinks, both companies need syrup that is supplied by two competing companies, NorSyr and BenRup. These companies incur costs of $5 per unit in making the syrup. Both Ginvir and Sipep can use the syrup of either supplier.

**a.** Confirm that competition between NorSyr and BenRup leads to the syrup being priced at $5 per unit.

**b.** What are the resulting equilibrium prices for Ginvir and Sipep and what are their profits?

**c.** Now suppose that Ginvir and NorSyr merge and that in doing so NorSyr no longer competes for Sipep's business.

**(1)** What price will BenRup now charge Sipep for the syrup?

**(2)** What are the resulting profits to the three post-merger companies?

**(3)** Do BenRup and Sipep have an incentive also to merge?

# REFERENCES

Ahimud, Y., and Lev, B. 1981. "Risk Reduction as a Managerial Motive for Conglomerate Mergers." *Bell Journal of Economics* 12: 605–17.

Besanko, D., D. Dranove, M. Shanley, and S. Schaefer. 2004. *Economics of Strategy*, 3rd ed., New York: John Wiley and Sons.

Hart, O. 1995. *Firms, Contracts, and Financial Structure*. Oxford: Oxford University Press.

Krattenmaker, T., and S. Salop. 1986. "Anticompetitive Exclusion: Raising Rivals' Costs to Achieve Power Over Price." *Yale Law Journal* 96: 209–95.

Mueller, D. C. 1969. "A Theory of Conglomerate Mergers." *Quarterly Journal of Economics* 82 (November): 643–59.

Nalebuff, B. 2004. "Bundling: GE-Honeywell." In J. Kwoka and L. White, eds., *The Antitrust Revolution*. Oxford: Oxford University Press, 4th ed.: 388–412.

Nathanson, D. A., and J. Cassano. 1982. "What Happens to Profits When a Company Diversifies?" *Wharton Magazine* 24: 19–26.

Ordover, J. A., G. Saloner, and S. Salop. 1990. "Equilibrium Vertical Foreclosure." *American Economic Review* 80: 127–42.

Pepall, L., and G. Norman. 1997. "Product Competition and Upstream Flexible Specialization." Mimeo. Tufts University.

Riordan, M. H. 1998. "Anticompetitive Vertical Integration by a Dominant Firm." *American Economic Review* 88 (December): 1232–48.

Salinger, M. A. 1988. "Vertical Mergers and Market Foreclosure." *Quarterly Journal of Economics* 103: 345–56.

Teece, D. 1982. "Towards an Economic Theory of the Multiproduct Firm." *Journal of Economic Behavior and Organization* 3: 39–63.

Whinston, M. 1990. "Tying, Foreclosure, and Exclusion." *American Economic Review* 80 (September): 837–59.

# Vertical Price Restraints

When the holiday season approaches, you will likely want to make some purchases. These could include asked-for books, apparel, jewelry, or perhaps some toys for your younger siblings or relatives. Let's suppose that buying a toy is your top priority. Once in the market for toys, you must decide what brand of toy, say Lego, Playmobile, or Fisher-Price, is your best buy. You may find that the same Fisher-Price toy is available at both Wal-Mart and Toys "R" Us, but that you can find the customized Lego train set only at the small toy store on your college town's Main Street. The decisions of what toy to buy and where to buy it are affected by two different levels of competition. One level is the competition between the different manufacturers of toys or what we might call brand competition. The other level is competition between the different retailers who sell toys to customers, that is, retail competition.

Now let us take the story a bit further. After deciding what and where to buy your holiday presents, you will then need to get back home. Suppose you want to drive home. This will put you in the market for a new car if you do not already have one. (Remember that this is the holiday season, traditionally a time of big spending.) As you begin to shop for a new automobile, you will quickly discover that you cannot buy one at Sears or at any other large department store. For instance, to buy a Ford Taurus you will need to go to a Ford dealership; to buy a Toyota Corolla requires that you visit a Toyota dealership; and so on.

Even after the purchase of the car, there are still some shopping decisions. On your drive home, you will likely need to purchase some fuel. You will find that one can only get Mobil gasoline at a Mobil station, British Petroleum gasoline at a BP station, and Sunoco gasoline at a Sunoco station. This may or may not strike you as terribly odd. Yet it is certainly different from your experience right before starting for home when you bought some Cheerios to eat as a healthy, low-sugar snack during the drive. For that purchase, it was certainly not the case that you had to worry about finding a General Mills dealership. Almost every grocery store from the corner convenience store to the discount supermarket carries that brand of cereal.

Now the fact that you are reading this book clearly reveals that you are a bright and inquisitive student. So, at some point in your trip home—perhaps as the tedium of driving builds—you will likely ask yourself, "What's going on here? What makes the retailing of cars, toys, gasoline, and cereal so different?" "What is the relationship between manufacturers, on the one hand, and retailers, on the other?" "What sorts of agreements exist between manufacturers and retailers that lead to this wide array of retailing options?"

These questions lie at the heart of the next two chapters. Our goal is to understand what underlies the variety of relationships between manufacturers and retailers. Toy stores and supermarkets sell the products of many different manufacturers. Gasoline stations and auto dealers sell the products of only one or, at most, a few producers. These different arrangements must reflect the various contractual agreements made between manufacturers and retailers, each of whom accepts some restraints on their behavior.

Sometimes the contractual arrangement restricts the price at which the retailer can sell the manufacturer's product. For example, if we go back to the purchase of a car in our opening holiday scenario, then you will likely find that a new car will have a sticker on it indicating the Manufacturer's Suggested Retail Price. This is a price at which the carmaker has "suggested" that the dealer should sell to you. It is a suggested price and not a required one, but it does serve as a reference point for the dealer's price decision and so probably restrains the dealer's behavior in some way. More broadly, it indicates the general nature of the truly binding vertical price restrictions. Replace the word "suggested" with the word "required" and you have what is called resale price maintenance (RPM). Because of the great attention historically given to vertical price agreements, they are the focus of this chapter.

Other aspects of the contractual agreements between manufacturers and retailers may restrict who the manufacturer can sell to or who the retailer can buy from, or set the level of promotional and support services each party is expected to provide, and so on. These are called nonprice vertical restraints and are the topic of the next chapter.

## 18.1 RESALE PRICE MAINTENANCE— SOME HISTORICAL BACKGROUND

In the United States, RPM agreements were initially considered to be a form of price-fixing outlawed under the Sherman antitrust act and therefore considered illegal per se. The view—first enunciated in the 1911 decision of the Supreme Court in the *Miles Medical* case[1]—was that since the Sherman Act clearly outlawed any arrangement for different retailers to collude on a common price, the attempt by a manufacturer to achieve the same outcome by means of an agreement with a retailer should also be prohibited. Moreover, this view was applied to RPM agreements that set retail price ceilings as well as price floors. Thus, such restrictions could not be justified either by arguing that the economic environment in which the agreement was made was special or by arguing that the agreement would actually lower prices to consumers.

Since the *Miles Medical* case the legal framework in which RPM agreements have been evaluated has grown increasingly permissive, although that growth has been sporadic. A very important development was the *Colgate* case of 1919 in which the Supreme Court ruled that a unilateral decision by a producer to stop supplying a specific price-cutting dealer was legitimate, so long as this was not part of an RPM involving many separate dealers.[2] This permissive attitude was expanded in the wake of the Great Depression by the Miller-Tydings Act of 1937, which explicitly exempted RPM agreements from antitrust prosecution. At that time, RPM agreements became legal. Moreover, their use was greatly strengthened by the 1952 McGuire Act, which permitted the enforcement of an RPM agreement even on firms who had not signed on to the arrangement, provided at least one retailer and manufacturer had agreed to it.

The one loophole in the Miller-Tydings and McGuire legislation was that it required participation by state legislatures to make it effective. Some states, however,

---

1   *Dr. Miles Medical Co. v. John D. Park and Sons, Co.*, 220 U.S. 373 (1911).
2   *United States v. Colgate & Co.*, 250 U.S. 300 (1919).

# ✓ Reality Checkpoint

## Yesterday's News

As we will discuss later in the text, resale price maintenance contracts have both a variety of motivations and a variable legal history. As a way to solve the double marginalization problem, however, you should recognize that such contracts are favored by the manufacturer in order to ensure that the downstream dealer does not set a price for the product that is too high. In short, a manufacturer relying on an RPM agreement to avoid double marginalization will wish to constrain the retailer to set a price below which the retailer would otherwise find optimal.

As an example, consider the important legal case of *Albrecht v. The Herald Co.* settled in 1968. The Herald Co. was a newspaper firm publishing, among others, the St. Louis *Globe Democrat*. In turn, the company hired various carriers to deliver the morning paper to subscribers. Each carrier was given an exclusive territory from which all other carriers were excluded. On the newspaper itself, The Herald Co. printed the suggested retail price for the *Globe Democrat*.

Albrecht was one of the carriers hired by the newspaper who served about 1,200 customers. In 1961, Albrecht began charging his customers a newspaper price above that recommended by The Herald Co. The company quickly objected. However, when its several requests to lower the price back to the suggested level were not heeded by Albrecht, The Herald Co. took matters into its own hands. Initially, it contacted Albrecht's customers and offered to deliver the paper to them itself at the lower price. Later, it contracted a second carrier to "invade" Albrecht's territory and deliver the paper there at a lower price. Albrecht's response was thoroughly American. He filed a lawsuit charging The Herald Co. with attempting to fix prices in violation of the Sherman Act.

In 1968, the Supreme Court found in Albrecht's favor, holding that The Herald Co.'s efforts amounted to price-fixing and were therefore per se illegal. However, on November 4, 1997, the Court overturned this finding in the case of *State Oil Co. v. Khan*. This case involved a dispute between an oil company and a gasoline dealer, Barkat Khan. State Oil Co. had required that all dealers who set a markup of more than 3.25 cents per gallon would have to rebate the excess markup to the company itself. Much like Albrecht did earlier, Khan, who operated a Unocal station, filed suit. In a landmark and unanimous decision, the Supreme Court held that RPM agreements involving an *upper* limit on retail prices—such as those in the *Albrecht* and *Khan* cases—were no longer per se illegal but would be judged on a rule of reason basis. However, the Court did not overturn the per se illegality of RPM agreements that set a lower limit on prices.

**Source:** *Albrecht v. The Herald Co.*, 390 U.S. 150 (1968), and *State Oil Co. v. Khan*, 522 U.S. 3 (1997). See also L. Greenhouse, "High Court, in Antitrust Ruling, Says Price Ceilings Are Allowed." *The New York Times*, November 5, 1997, p. A1.

continued to prohibit RPM agreements so that in these states, RPM agreements did not become legal. Over time, this led to considerable discounting of prices in these states relative to those with pro-RPM legislation. Consumers willing to drive across the state line, or just willing to deal with a mail-order firm, were able to gain access to discount stores with their lower prices. Such competition put tremendous pressure on firms participating in RPM agreements. In 1975, in the wake of the substantial inflation induced by OPEC's four-fold increase in the price of crude oil, both the Miller-Tydings and the McGuire Acts were repealed. This reestablished the presumed illegality of RPM agreements, but it did not remove the ability of manufacturers to cut off discount dealers established by the *Colgate* decision.

Indeed, two subsequent legal cases have expanded the ability of manufacturers to impose retail price restrictions. In the *Sharp Electronics* case,[3] the Court expanded its *Colgate* exception by permitting the manufacturer to terminate a discount dealer and not infer any illegal agreement even if the termination came as a result of other dealers' complaints. Then, in the 1997 *State Oil v. Khan* case, the Court moved to explicitly renounce any per se illegality for RPM agreements establishing a maximum price, that is, a price ceiling. In short, despite the initial 1911 ruling, manufacturers now have considerable scope to implement RPM agreements establishing either a maximum or a minimum price.

We want to understand manufacturers' and retailers' incentives to restrict price and the effect of such restrictions on consumer welfare. In this light the historical record can also be helpful. It is noteworthy that most of the political support for legislation such as the Miller-Tydings and McGuire Acts did not come from upstream manufacturers, but rather from downstream retailers. The retail lobby consistently led the fight to legalize and enforce RPM agreements at both the federal and state levels. In addition, as documented by both Overstreet (1983) and Steiner (1985), the vast majority of RPM legal cases have been ones in which the issue was the setting of a minimum retail price, not a maximum price. Similar evidence for the United Kingdom has been presented by Pickering (1966). This record establishes an additional requirement for our analysis. Any theoretical explanation for RPM agreements must be consistent with this evidence.

## 18.2 VERTICAL PRICE RESTRAINTS AS A RESPONSE TO DOUBLE MARGINALIZATION

One reason that a manufacturer may wish to restrict the pricing discretion of a downstream retailer is to remedy the double marginalization problem. Let us review that argument here. For this purpose, we assume the simple case of a monopoly manufacturer selling to a single or monopoly retailer. The manufacturer produces the good at constant unit cost $c$ and sells it to the retailer at a wholesale price $r$. The retailer then resells the product to consumers at price $P$. For simplicity, we will assume that the retailer has no retailing cost. Consumer demand for the good is described by the linear demand function $P = A - BQ$. Hence, marginal revenue in the downstream market is $MR = A - 2BQ$. Equating marginal revenue and marginal cost downstream yields the optimal downstream output, $Q^D = (A - r)/2B$. Substituting this into the demand function then implies that the associated optimal downstream or retail price, $P^D$, is

$$P^D = \frac{A + r}{2}.$$   **(18.1)**

---

3   *Business Electronics Corp. v. Sharp Electronics Corp.*, 488 U.S. 717 (1988).

This will yield a maximum downstream profit, $\Pi^D = (A - r)^2/4B$.

At the downstream price, $P^D = (A + r)/2$, the retailer sells $Q^D = (A - r)/2B$ units of the good, which must also be the amount sold by the upstream supplier. Accordingly, $Q^D = (A - r)/2B$ describes the demand facing the upstream firm given any price it charges $r$. The inverse demand function confronting the upstream firm is thus $r = A - 2BQ$. This implies a marginal revenue curve upstream of $A - 4BQ$. Equating this with the manufacturer's marginal cost $c$ then yields the upstream manufacturer's profit-maximizing output, $Q^U$, and, by implication, its optimal wholesale price, $r^U$. These are

$$Q^U = (A - c)/4B, \text{ and}$$
$$r^U = (A + c)/2. \tag{18.2}$$

As we know, an integrated firm resulting from a merger of the downstream and upstream companies will earn greater profit and set a lower retail price because the merger eliminates the double marginalization inherent in the preceding analysis. Such a merger transforms the two firms into a simple monopoly whose goal is to maximize total profit from manufacturing and retailing. The final price to consumers under integration is $p^I = (A + c)/2$, at which output is $Q^I = (A - c)/2B$.

For example, if final demand is (in inverse form) described by $P = 100 - 2Q$, then the monopoly retailer's marginal revenue is $MR^D = 100 - 4Q$. Profit maximization at the retail level requires that this be equated to whatever wholesale price $r$ the manufacturer sets. In turn, this implies that the manufacturer's demand curve is $r = 100 - 4Q$. Hence, the manufacturer's marginal revenue curve is $MR^U = 100 - 8Q$. Accordingly, if a constant production cost of \$12 per unit is incurred, the manufacturer will produce 11 units. These will be sold to the retailer at a wholesale price of $r = \$56$. The goods will then retail at a price of \$78. Total profit is \$242 for the retailer and \$484 for the manufacturer. By contrast, an integrated firm facing the same demand curve will set the retail price at $p^I = \$56$, at which it will sell $Q = 22$ units. It will earn a total profit of \$968, which clearly exceeds the total combined profit of the separate manufacturer and retailing firms (\$968 > \$242 + \$484). Consumer surplus also increases under integration since consumers now get more of the product at a lower price.

This simple example suggests that there are gains from having the manufacturer restrict the retailer's price decision. Specifically, the manufacturer may impose a retail price agreement that requires that the retailer never charge a price above \$56. With this restriction in place, the manufacturer would then set a wholesale price also equal to \$56. The retailer would then have to charge that price as well. By the terms of the contract, the retailer cannot set a higher price and has no interest to set a lower one. In short, by imposing a maximum price at which the retailer can sell the manufacturer can achieve an outcome in which the total retail price is the one that maximizes the total combined profit and which, moreover, transfers all of that profit to the manufacturer itself.

## Practice Problem 18.1

Tiger-el is an upstream manufacturer of electric trains that sells wholesale to The Great Toy Store, the only such store in the area. Demand for the trains at the retail store level in inverse form is $P = 1,000 - 2Q$, where $Q$ is the total number of trains sold. The Great

Toy Store incurs no service cost in selling the train. Its only cost is the wholesale price it pays for each train. Tiger-el incurs a production cost of $40 per train.

a. What wholesale price should Tiger-el charge for its trains? What price will these trains sell for at retail? How many trains will be sold?
b. What profit will Tiger-el and the toy store earn under the pricing choices found in part (a)?
c. How would the quantity of trains sold and the retail price change if Tiger-el sold the trains to The Great Toy Store at cost but also received a 66.67 percent sales royalty on every train sold? How would your profit calculations in part (b) change?

---

We have shown that one motivation for the manufacturer to restrain the pricing of the retailer is the double marginalization problem. In such a setting, an RPM agreement acts as a ceiling on the price consumers pay. As the *Albrecht* and *Khan* cases (see Reality Checkpoint: Yesterday's News) illustrate, this motivation is clearly one of the forces that leads firms to seek such restraints. However, double marginalization cannot be the sole explanation for vertical price restriction. The issue in double marginalization is that in the absence of an RPM agreement, the retail price will be too high. Yet, as noted earlier, much of the support for vertical price restraints reflects the view that without them retail prices will be too low.

Note that no double marginalization issue will occur if either the upstream market or the downstream market is competitive. If the manufacturer competes with other producers to sell to a single retailer, then the wholesale price will fall to marginal cost $c$, or $12 in our earlier example. Equating marginal revenue with marginal cost, the retailer will then set a price to consumers of $(A + c)/2$, which is the same as the integrated price. Thus, in our example, competition in the upstream market will result in a retail price of $($100 + $12)/2 = $56$. A similar result will occur if the retail market is competitive. In this case, the manufacturer will find that the retail price will be the same as the wholesale price $r$. As a result, all the manufacturer need do is set the wholesale price at $56 to each retailer. With competition at either the wholesale or retail level, only one segment adds a markup. Therefore, no double markup can occur.

If neither the wholesale nor retail sector is competitive, then the double marginalization problem is potentially a real one. However, there are solutions other than the establishment of an RPM agreement. One could be for the upstream manufacturer to adopt a nonlinear pricing strategy. In particular, it can adopt a two-part tariff pricing strategy. The manufacturer might specify that the retailer first pay a lump sum amount $T$ but after that be permitted to buy as much of the product as it wishes at the price $r$ per unit. The optimal pricing strategy in such a two-part scheme calls for the per-unit fee $r$ to be set equal to marginal cost $c$. With a wholesale price of $c$, the retailer maximizes profit by setting a price of $(A + c)/2$, just as in the case in which the manufacturing market is competitive. At this price the retailer will earn the maximum total profit of

$$\pi^D(c, T) = \frac{(A - c)^2}{4B} - T. \tag{18.3}$$

Once again, using the numerical values from our earlier example in which the market inverse demand curve was given by $P = 100 - 2Q$, and $c = $12$, we find that the retailer's profit will be $968 – T$. The role of the fixed fee $T$ is now clear. It is this fee that permits the manufacturer to claim some of the total profit generated by its product. Presumably, the manufacturer would set $T$ no less than $484, since this is the amount that can be earned without the agreement. By the same logic, $T$ could be no greater than $726, since values above this amount would leave the retailer with less than the $242 that could be earned in the absence of the agreement. Accordingly, we would expect $T$ to lie somewhere between $484 and $726, depending on the outcome of negotiations between the two parties. Whatever value is chosen for $T$, the point is that this somewhat more complicated vertical arrangement again solves the double marginalization problem without recourse to an RPM agreement.

We hasten to add that the two-part pricing arrangement just described is not merely a theoretical curiosity. It is precisely the agreement specified in many franchising agreements. Franchising is a vertical relationship under which an upstream company gives a downstream firm, or franchisee, the exclusive right to market and sell its product. Franchise contracts typically involve the franchisee paying a lump sum amount up front to the franchiser for the right to carry the product. In our discussion, $T$ corresponds to this franchising fee.[4]

In sum, double marginalization can be a real problem that reduces the profit at both the manufacturing and retailing levels when both segments possess market power. RPM agreements that put a ceiling on the retail price can solve this issue. Yet there are three reasons why the double marginalization problem cannot be the only reason that we observe such agreements. First, many RPM contracts are motivated by a desire to establish a floor and not a ceiling on the retail price. Second, the double marginalization problem does not arise when either segment is competitive. Finally, even when double marginalization is a legitimate concern, firms can and do use alternative arrangements to remedy the problem. We now consider other possible explanations for the use of RPM agreements.

## 18.3 RPM AGREEMENTS AND RETAIL PRICE DISCRIMINATION

If a retailer can figure out "who is who" on its demand curve and separate consumers into different groups the retailer will find it profitable to charge the different groups different prices for the same good. In particular, the retailer will wish to charge a higher price to those customers with the less elastic demand. Coupons, quantity discounts, variations in quality in which the price difference does not match the cost difference, and market segmentation are all mechanisms by which a retailer may price discriminate. However, while such price discrimination can enhance retail profits, it can make life difficult for the upstream manufacturer.

To see the problem that retail price discrimination can raise for the manufacturer, let's return to our example. However, we now suppose that the retailer actually serves two, separate markets. In each market, retail demand is again characterized by $P = 100 – 2Q$ and, again, the only retail cost is the wholesale price $r$ set by the manufacturer. In one market, the retailer is a monopolist. In the other, the retailer faces

---

4   See Lafontaine (1992, 1993, and 1995) for evidence on this point.

competition from a potential rival who will buy from the manufacturer and sell at cost if the retailer ever charges a price greater than $r$. Thus, in the first market, the retailer can add a markup to the wholesale price $r$. In the second, potential competition forces the retailer to sell at a retail price exactly equal to $r$. Again we assume that the manufacturer's unit cost is $c = \$12$.

Although the retailer sells in two markets, there is just one contract covering all its purchases from the manufacturer. Following our logic from above, we will allow this contract to specify both a wholesale price $r$ and an upfront franchise fee, $T$. The manufacturer's problem is to choose $T$ and $r$ to maximize its total profit. We know that each market is capable of generating \$968 in total profit and that to achieve this it is necessary to set a retail price of $P = \$56$. Again, however, the manufacturer cannot sign a separate contract with the retailer for the goods sold in each market separately. Instead, the manufacturer must sign a single contract that covers the total amount of goods sold by the retailer in both markets.

Without an RPM agreement the manufacturer's dilemma should now be clear. To achieve a retail price of \$56 in the competitive market, it needs to set the wholesale price $r$ also equal to \$56. This will lead to 22 units being sold and ($\$56 - \$12) = \$44$ being earned on each for the desired total of \$968 in this segment. However, if the manufacturer specifies a wholesale price of $r = \$56$, then in the monopolized market, the retailer will set a price of \$78 and sell only 11 units, leading to a total profit in this market of only ($\$78 - \$12) \times 11 = \$616$. Although the manufacturer may be able to capture part or even all of this profit by means of the franchise fee, it is still well below the potential maximum of \$968. Of course, the manufacturer could lower the wholesale price $r$. Yet as we know, to realize the maximum profit of \$968 in the monopolized market requires that the wholesale price fall all the way to cost, that is, to \$12. At this price, the profit in the monopolized segment will be maximized but the profit in the competitive segment will fall to zero because in that segment, competition always forces the retail price to equal $r$.

In short, with a single contract covering all the retailer's wholesale purchases, the manufacturer faces a painful tradeoff if the retailer can price discriminate. In order to capture the maximum profit from the retail establishment facing less elastic demand (the monopolized market), the wholesale price should be close to marginal cost and charge a large franchise fee. However, since no franchise fee is possible in the market where the retail establishments face more elastic demand (the competitive market), the only way to make profit is to charge a wholesale price well above marginal cost. No single contract can satisfy both of these requirements.

In the Appendix to this chapter, we show that, without an RPM agreement, the best that the manufacturer can do in this case is to set a wholesale price of \$47.20, which results in a combined profit from both markets of \$1,742.40. The retail prices in the monopolized and competitive market are then, respectively, \$73.60 and \$47.20. Relative to the profit-maximizing retail price \$56 in each market, the price is too high in the monopolized segment and too low in the competitive segment.

An RPM agreement, however, can solve the manufacturer's problem. One solution is to set a wholesale price of $r = \$56$ and to impose an RPM agreement that the retail price can never exceed this amount. Alternatively, one could set a wholesale price of \$12 and impose an RPM requirement that the retail price never fall below \$56. In the first case, the retailer will sell at cost = \$56 in the competitive segment and, because of the RPM price ceiling, also sell at \$56 in the monopolized segment. In the second case, the retailer will mark up the wholesale cost to a retail price of \$56.

This will also be the price in the competitive market by virtue of the RPM price floor. In either case, the manufacturer will attempt to extract some or all of the downstream profit by means of a franchise fee, $T$.

There are many reasons, of course, that the retailer may engage successfully in price discrimination. Hence, while the two-market story told above is somewhat contrived, it nonetheless serves as a useful illustration of a general principle. Whatever the source of a retailer's ability to discriminate in prices, such discrimination makes it difficult for the upstream manufacturer to establish a wholesale contract that maximizes the total, manufacturing, and retail profit unless that agreement includes an RPM provision. Without an RPM agreement, there will be a tendency for the retail price to be too low to consumers with more elastic demand and too high to those whose demand is less elastic.[5]

We mentioned the *State Oil v. Khan* case in which the Supreme Court removed the per se presumption against RPM agreements specifying a maximum price. In this case, State Oil Co. had imposed a maximum retail price on its distributors, one of whom, Barkat Khan, tried to exceed that price. However, Khan's actual pricing strategy was more complex. He did want to raise the price to premium buyers, but he wanted to lower the price to consumers of regular grade fuel. That is, Khan wanted to price discriminate. The RPM agreement subsequently legitimized by the Supreme Court thus appears to have been motivated in part by State Oil's need to prevent such price discrimination. In turn, this suggests that this motivation may be important in promoting RPM contracts more generally.

## 18.4 RPM AGREEMENTS TO INSURE THE PROVISION OF RETAIL SERVICES

In the preceding two sections, we have treated retailing as simply an extra stage that occurs between production and final consumption. This approach has allowed us to gain some important insights on the downstream pricing issues that the retailing stage raises. However, our approach to retailing to date has failed to incorporate any actual positive role for retailers. In reality, though, retailers such as supermarkets, discount chains, and department stores form the crucial link between those who make goods and those who use them. In particular, retailers provide many services that are valuable to the manufacturers. Not only do they gather information about customer satisfaction and desired changes in the manufacturer's product, but they also provide such valuable services as the provision of desirable shelf space, large displays, advertising, and product demonstration. These services can be crucial to the marketing and sales of the manufacturer's product.

Consider, for example, the magazine industry. Supermarkets and discount chains presently account for over 55 percent of single-copy sales of U.S. magazines. Because such sales are made at the full, nonsubscription price, they are quite profitable and important to publishing firms. Yet the publishers must rely heavily on the efforts of the retailers. A prominent display near the checkout register, for example, can greatly increase sales. So can advertising, say, a promotional visit to the store by a celebrity.

---

5   See Chen (1999).

As a result, publishers have a deep interest in making sure that the retailers undertake such efforts. Indeed, in recent years, publishers of *People* and other magazines, such as *Cosmopolitan* and *Harper's Bazaar*, have had tense negotiations with retailers such as Wal-Mart and Winn Dixie supermarkets over the display and promotion of various issues of these publications.[6]

This example makes clear that any analysis of the relationship between a manufacturer and its retailers must address the upstream manufacturer's interest in the provision of retail services. It must also address the motivation for the retailer to incur the expense of such services. Promotion, product demonstration, and simply providing a pleasant place to shop are costly. Moreover, it is extremely difficult for the manufacturer to monitor the provision of such services. Taken together, these two facts mean that a manufacturer cannot simply specify the level of retail services that it wants for its product and assume that they will be provided. Instead, an enforceable contract is required that specifies the obligations of both the manufacturer and the retailer. It is the nature of this vertical contract—particularly as it pertains to the provision of retail services—that we now wish to examine.

Let us begin by describing how demand is affected by retail services. Denote by $D(p, s)$ the amount of the good demanded at price $p$ with retail service level $s$. Increases in the level of services raise the quantity demanded at any price or, alternatively, raise the willingness to pay of each consumer. For our present purposes, let us assume that this effect takes the form shown in Figure 18-1. In this case, an increase in the service level from $s_1$ to $s_2$ raises the willingness to pay of the marginal consumer. As Figure 18-1 shows, this means that the demand curve rotates about its price level intercept, sliding along the quantity axis. A demand curve that reflects this view is $Q(p, s) = s(A - p)N$, where $N$ is the number of consumers in the market. In inverse form this is $p = A - Q/sN$. The top price anyone is willing to pay for the product is $\$A$, no matter the service level, and more is bought as $s$ rises.

As noted, providing retail services is costly. Let the cost of supplying $s$ retail services per unit of the good be described by a function $\phi(s)$. We will assume that the provision of retail services is subject to diminishing returns so that raising the service level $s$ raises the cost of providing such services and does so at an ever-increasing rate. [In formal calculus terms, this means that both $\phi'(s)$ and $\phi''(s)$ exceed zero.] For a given level of services, $s$, the retailer's marginal cost of selling the manufacturer's product is $r + \phi(s)$. This is the sum of the wholesale price paid to the manufacturer $r$ plus the cost of providing $s$ retail services per unit sold, $\phi(s)$.

We can now consider the provision of retail services under a variety of circumstances. We point out in advance that this material is a little advanced. For those who wish to skip this section, our main result is that, in the absence of vertical price restraints, it is unlikely that a retailer will provide the manufacturer's preferred level of service. The intuition behind this argument is straightforward. The manufacturer wants a high level of service because this will raise the price consumers are willing to pay and, hence, the manufacturer's profit. Yet while the profit gain of better service flows at least in part to the manufacturer, the cost of providing such service falls entirely on the retailer. Accordingly, the retailer's incentive to offer such service is reduced. Vertical restrictions such as a resale price maintenance agreement may be a way to overcome this difficulty, at least in part.

---

6  See Knecht (1997).

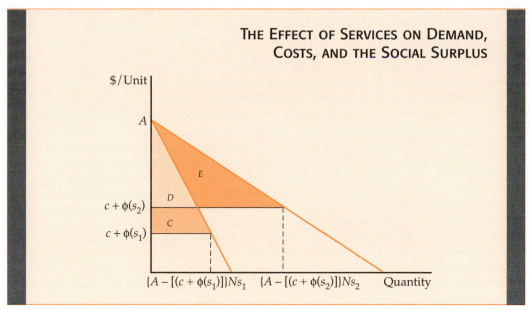

THE EFFECT OF SERVICES ON DEMAND,
COSTS, AND THE SOCIAL SURPLUS

FIGURE

**18-1**

Demand is given by $P = A - Q/sN$. This means that as the level of services rises from $s_1$ to $s_2$, the demand curve rotates up. At service level $s_1$, marginal cost $= c + \phi(s_1)$. If price equals marginal cost, total demand is $[A - (c + \phi(s_1))]Ns_1$, and social surplus is areas $C + D$. At service level $s_2$, marginal cost $= c + \phi(s_2)$. If price is equal to marginal cost then, in this case, total output will be $\{A - [c + \phi(s_2)]\}Ns_2$, and the social surplus will be areas $D + E$.

## 18.4.1  Optimal Provision of Retail Services

Let's start by thinking about the most efficient level of services from the viewpoint of society overall, that is, the level that would maximize the combined consumer and producer surplus. Recall, however, that optimality also requires that price equal marginal cost. Because marginal cost for a given level of services is constant we have that $p = c + \phi(s)$; this means that there is no producer surplus. Hence, as shown in Figure 18-1, the social surplus at any price equal to $c + \phi(s)$ is just the triangular area above the cost line but below the demand curve. Accordingly, the optimal choice of service level $s$ is that level that maximizes the area of this triangle. By definition, this area is given by $\{A - [c + \phi(s)]\}^2(Ns)/2$. To find the surplus-maximizing value of services, denoted by $s^*$, we take the derivative of this expression with respect to $s$, and set it equal to zero. This yields

$$\{A - [c + \phi(s^*)]\}^2 N - 2Ns^*\{A - [c + \phi(s^*)]\}\phi'(s^*) = 0. \qquad \textbf{(18.4)}$$

In turn, this implies that $s^*$ must satisfy

$$(A - c)/2 = \phi(s^*)/2 + \phi'(s^*)s^*. \qquad \textbf{(18.5)}$$

Suppose that $N = 100$, $c = 5$, $A = 10$, and that $\phi(s) = s^2$. Then a small bit of algebra will reveal that the social optimum calls for a service level of $s^* = 1$. (Remember, $s$ is an just an index so it is measured in arbitrary units.) At this level of service, optimality would require that the price be equal to $c + \phi(s^*) = \$6$.

What would be the outcome if the monopolist could operate as a vertically integrated manufacturing and retailing business? Certainly, the price will be higher. The monopolist will not make a profit at a price equal to cost. Yet what about the integrated firm's choice of service level? How will this compare to the optimum described in equation (18.5)?

The profit of the integrated firm conditional upon the price it sets and the service level it provides is

$$\pi(p, s) = p(A - p)Ns - [c + \phi(s)](A - p)Ns. \tag{18.6}$$

To maximize profit, the firm must choose both the right price $p$ and the right service level $s$. Hence, we take the derivative of the profit function with respect to each of these variables and set it equal to zero, yielding

$$\frac{\partial \pi(p, s)}{\partial p} = -pNs + (A - p)Ns + [c + \phi(s)]Ns = 0, \tag{18.7}$$

and

$$\frac{\partial \pi(p, s)}{\partial s} = p(A - p)N - [c + \phi(s)](A - p)N - Ns\phi'(s)(A - p) = 0. \tag{18.8}$$

Equation (18.7) may be simplified to read

$$p^I = [A + c + \phi(s)]/2. \tag{18.9}$$

Here, $p^I$ is the firm's optimal price conditional upon a given service level $s$. Equation (18.9) implies that, as usual, the integrated monopolist will set a price of obtaining a unit of the good along with a given service level that exceeds the marginal cost of providing the good and the associated service cost $c + \phi(s)$. This is shown in Figure 18-2.

FIGURE

**18-2**

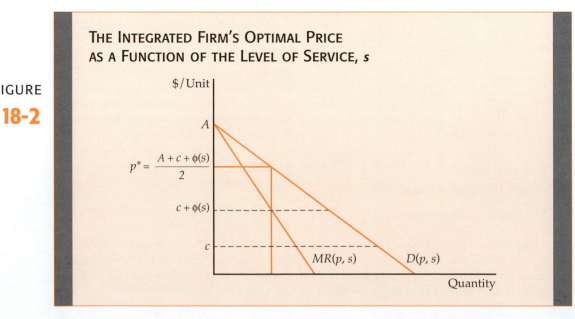

THE INTEGRATED FIRM'S OPTIMAL PRICE
AS A FUNCTION OF THE LEVEL OF SERVICE, s

The next step is straightforward. Substitute the optimal price value from equation (18.9) into the condition for the profit-maximizing service level shown in equation (18.8). Simplification then yields the following necessary condition for the profit-maximizing service level $s^I$:

$$(A - c)/2 = \phi(s^I)/2 + \phi'(s^I)s^I. \tag{18.10}$$

Comparing equations (18.5) and (18.10), it is clear that they are the same. Although the integrated monopoly firm sets too high a price, the service level $s^I$ that it prefers is the same as the socially optimal service level $s^*$. As it turns out, this specific result reflects the particular demand and cost relationships that we assumed and is not fully general. Nevertheless, the result is useful because it helps illuminate the fact that the manufacturer's interest in providing retail services is often in harmony with the public interest as well. As we shall shortly see, this is why vertical price restrictions can play a potentially welfare-enhancing role.

## 18.4.2  The Case of a Monopoly Retailer and a Monopoly Manufacturer

Let us next examine the case where the retailing of the good is done by an independent monopoly downstream retailer. Thus, the manufacturer sells the product to the monopoly retailer at price $r$, after which the retailer sells the good to final consumers at retail price $p^M$ and provides $s^M$ retail services. The retailer's profit downstream is

$$\Pi^D(p^M, s^M, r) = [p^M - r - \phi(s^M)]D(p^M, s^M) = [p^M - r - \phi(s^M)]s^M(A - p^M)N. \tag{18.11}$$

As in the case of the integrated firm, the retailer must choose the two strategic variables, price $p$ and the level of services $s$. Indeed, the retailer in this case has exactly the same profit-maximizing problem as did the integrated firm of the previous discussion, except that the retailer faces a marginal cost $r$ that may differ from the true production cost $c$, depending on the upstream firm's price choice. So, we can work out the monopoly retailer's choices just by replacing $c$ with $r$ in equations (18.9) and (18.10). This yields the choices $p^M$ and $s^M$ satisfying

$$p^M = \frac{A + r + \phi(s^M)}{2}, \tag{18.12}$$

and

$$(A - r)/2 = \phi(s^M)/2 + \phi'(s^M)s^M. \tag{18.13}$$

Because $r > c$, the price implied by equation (18.12) exceeds that implied by equation (18.9). This is simply the double marginalization problem again. At any given service level, the monopoly retailer adds its markup to the markup already reflected in the manufacturer's wholesale price. Yet as a comparison of equations (18.10) and (18.13) also makes clear, having $r > c$ further implies that this double markup is now compounded by a further problem, namely, a suboptimally low level of retail services. A careful examination of these two equations reveals that if $r > c$, then the level of retail services chosen by the retailer $s^M$ is less than the level $s^*$ that is optimal from the viewpoint of both society and the upstream manufacturer. For example, if the manufacturer sets a wholesale price of $r = \$6$ (just \$1 above marginal cost), the service level falls to 0.8—a reduction below the optional service level of 20 percent. As previously mentioned, the intuition behind this outcome is straightforward. Providing retail services is costly and this, along with the fact that the manufacturer charges a wholesale price $r$ above marginal production cost, puts the squeeze on the retailer's profit. In response, the retailer tries to recapture some of its surplus by cutting back on services.

## Practice Problem 18.2

Assume as in the example in the text that $c = 5$ while $\phi(s) = s^2$, so that $\phi'(s) = 2s$. Assume that the manufacturer sells through a monopoly retailer and initially sets a wholesale price, $r$, of \$6. Assume that retail demand is $Q(p, s) = s(10 - p)100$.

a. What will be the retail service level and the retail price? How much output will be sold at this price and service level combination? What will be the manufacturer's profit?

b. Would the manufacturer's profit rise or fall if it raised its wholesale price to \$7? At this price, how does the profit of the manufacturer selling through the retailer compare with the profit of the integrated manufacturer?

Our analysis once again demonstrates how the failure to coordinate the actions of the manufacturer and the retailer leads to a less than desirable outcome—both for the firms and for consumers. Clearly, the manufacturer will not be happy with this situation. From the manufacturer's perspective, the retail firm is charging too high a price and offering too few retail services. Both of these reduce the final consumer demand facing the retailer and, by extension, the ability of the manufacturer to earn profit. A full harmonization of the upstream and downstream operations would result in lower prices and better services, increasing the joint profits of the two firms and making consumers better off. In the absence of vertical integration, what can be done to improve matters?

As with the double marginalization problem, we consider two possible solutions. The first is an RPM agreement. The second is a two-part pricing strategy comprised of a fixed franchise fee $T$ and a constant wholesale price $r$ charged to the monopoly retailer.

In general, resale price maintenance will not solve the upstream manufacturer's problem. It is true that under an RPM agreement, the manufacturer can require the retailer to sell the product at the price $p^*$ and thereby solve the double marginalization problem. However, since there is no franchise fee, the manufacturer will make a profit only by charging a wholesale price $r$ to the retailer that is greater than marginal cost $c$. Thus, referring to our earlier example, the RPM agreement could specify that the retail price be \$8, exactly as the integrated firm would choose. In order to make a profit, though, the manufacturer must set a wholesale price $r > c$, that is, above the \$5 wholesale price charged in the two-part tariff scheme. With the retail price capped at \$8, this means that the retailer now has a smaller margin of price over wholesale cost. Because the contract still leaves the retailer free to choose the level of services $s$, the downstream firm will react to this profit squeeze by cutting its service provision below $s^*$. Of course, this is precisely what the manufacturer wishes to avoid.

What happens if the manufacturer adopts a two-part pricing mechanism? To begin with we know that the manufacturer will set $r$ equal to marginal production cost, or $r = c$. Only when $r$ is equal to $c$ can the retailer's final retail price and level of services be exactly the same as those chosen by the integrated firm. Accordingly, for the manufacturer to induce the retailer to pursue the manufacturer's preferred strategy, it is absolutely essential that the manufacturer set a wholesale price equal to $c$.

Faced with a wholesale price of $r = c$, however, the retailer is in exactly the same position as our integrated firm was earlier. Hence, it will make the identical choices regarding the price to consumers $p^I$ and the service level $s^I$. The retailer's profit $\Pi^R$ prior to paying any franchise fee $T$ will therefore be

$$\Pi^R = [p^I - c - \phi(s^I)]s^I(A - p^I)N, \tag{18.14}$$

where $p^I$ and $s^I$ now take on those values that maximize the joint profit of the manufacturer and retailer together, namely, the values described by equations (18.9) and (18.10). Of course, if $r = c$, the manufacturer earns nothing and all profit goes to the dealer. As usual, this is where the franchise fee $T$ comes in. By setting a fee equal to the integrated firm's profit, the manufacturer can claim that profit for itself. For instance, in our earlier example in which $c =$ \$5 and demand is described by $Q = s(10 - p)100$, the manufacturer should set its wholesale price $r =$ \$5. The dealer will then find it optimal to set a retail price of \$8 and to provide a service level $s = 1$. This will generate the maximum profit of \$400, which the manufacturer can appropriate by means of a franchise fee $T$. We note again that if the retailer is truly a monopoly without which the manufacturer cannot bring its good to market, then the retailer is unlikely to agree to such a scheme. Some profit sharing is likely. Again, however, the point is that this arrangement can yield the optimal service outcome.

The foregoing analysis suggests that franchising agreements are superior to an RPM agreement as a means to achieve the provision of retail services. However, the analysis again assumes that the downstream retail market is monopolized. As we show below, matters change greatly if there is retail competition.

## 18.4.3 The Case of Competitive Retailing

We now wish to examine the case in which our assumption of a single monopoly retailer is replaced with one in which the retailing sector is competitive. This is often the more realistic case. It is also a market structure that should work to the manufacturer's benefit. When there is only one retailer, the manufacturer's reach into the retail market is limited, as is its bargaining power with respect to claiming any of the additional profit that coordination yields. When there are many retailers, both the manufacturer's reach and bargaining power are enhanced. As we saw previously, competition among the retailers downstream will bring the retail price-cost margin to zero, and therefore minimize the problem of double marginalization. However, the issue of the provision of promotional or retail services still remains. Hence, we want to examine the level of services $s^C$ provided by a competitive retail sector and compare that level with the manufacturer's preferred amount, $s^*$.

For simplicity, we will assume that all the downstream retailers are identical. Each buys the manufacturer's product at a wholesale price $r$ and incurs the cost $\phi(s)$ per unit of output for retail service $s$. A little thinking then leads us to two quick results.

First, we know that retail competition will drive the retail price down to marginal cost. In other words, the price to final consumers will have to be $p = r + \phi(s)$. Second, that same competitive pressure will also force every retailer to offer at that price the level of services most preferred by consumers. Any retailer who offers a lower service level will quickly lose all its customers. Accordingly, competitive pressure will lead each and every retailer to offer the same retail price and the same service package. The competitive retail price will be $p^C = r + \phi(s^C)$, and the competitive service level $s^C$ will be that level that maximizes consumer surplus given the price $p^C$. As we showed in our derivation of the socially optimal service level described in equation (18.8), consumer surplus when the price is just equal to its true marginal cost, that is, when $p = c + \phi(s)$, is just $\{A - [c + \phi(s)]\}^2(Ns)/2$. It follows that consumer surplus when the price now satisfies $p = r + \phi(s)$ is then just $\{A - [r + \phi(s)]\}^2(Ns)/2$. Maximizing this with respect to $s$ yields the service level under competitive retailing, $s^C$:

$$(A - r)/2 = \phi(s^C)/2 + \phi'(s^C)s^C. \qquad \textbf{(18.15)}$$

Comparison of the value $s^C$ that satisfies equation (18.15) with the manufacturer's and society's preferred outcome [$s^*$ in equation (18.5) or $s^I$ in (18.10)] reveals that the competitive outcome will again provide too low a level of services so long as the wholesale price $r$ exceeds the production cost $c$. Since the manufacturer only earns a profit if $r > c$, we once again have the problem that from the manufacturer's point of view the retail sector—now organized competitively—will provide too low a level of retail services. As always, the source of the problem is that the profit that flows from providing increased service flows to the upstream manufacturer. As a result, each competitive retailer focuses only on the cost of services and ignores the extra profit that they bring to the upstream manufacturer.

Is there a solution to this problem of suboptimal service provision in the case of a competitive retail sector? If there is, it will not be by means of the two-part tariff strategy that worked before. The reason for this is straightforward. Competition among retailers drives the price-cost margin to zero. Consequently, there is no profit margin in the retail sector from which the manufacturer can extract the lump sum fee $T$. The only way that the manufacturer can earn any profit is to set $r > c$. However, unless it takes some additional steps, this will raise retailing costs and thereby create an incentive to cut services further.

The solution is to impose a carefully designed RPM agreement by working backwards from the desired outcomes. The manufacturer wants a retail price equal to the integrated price of $p^I$. Hence, it should impose an RPM agreement that stipulates $p^I$ at the retail level. The manufacturer also wants a level of services equal to the integrated level of $s^I$. Given that the retail price is $p^I$, this requires a wholesale price of $r$ that is below $p^I$ by just enough to cover the cost of providing the desired service level, $s^I$. In an effort to win consumers, retailers will provide as much service as they can afford given the difference between $p^I$ and $r$. By setting this difference to $p^I - r = \phi(s^I)$, the manufacturer can count on retail competition in services to result in service provision at the desired level $s^I$. Again, continuing with our working example, with $c = \$5$, $A = 10$, and $N = 100$, we have a preferred service level of $s^I = 1$ and an optimal retail price of $p^I = \$8$. The cost of providing this service level is $s^2 = \$1$. Hence, the manufacturer should impose an RPM agreement with each retailer requiring a retail price of \$8 and sell at a wholesale price of \$7. This will give retailers exactly \$1 of revenue above cost, which retailers will then compete away by providing the optimal service level of $s^I = 1$.

## 18.4.4 Free Riding and the Provision of Retail Services

We have just shown that once there is competition in the retail market, an RPM agreement may become a better method to ensure the provision of retail services than is a two-part tariff scheme. There is, in fact, another reason why this may be the case. This is because, contrary to our assumptions thus far, a retailer may not always be able to obtain a higher price by providing more services. Services that are provided by one store, particularly informational services, such as the strengths and weaknesses of different brands of digital cameras, can be consumed freely by consumers and yet they may buy the camera at a different store. In turn, this creates the potential for a serious free-riding problem.

Think about it for a moment. A consumer electronics shop may keep experts on hand to assist a customer in choosing the digital camera that (1) best meets the customer's needs in terms of portability and convenience, (2) works most effectively with the customer's computer and other peripherals, and (3) fits best within the customer's budget. Similarly, wine shops may employ personnel to advise customers regarding the quality of a particular vintage or the food that best accompanies a given wine.

Providing such presale or point of sale services is costly. Unfortunately, there is no obligation for the consumer, once educated by the store's expert staff, to buy from that specific establishment. To the contrary, once fully informed, the consumer has a strong incentive to go to the "no frills" electronics shop down the street or to the discount wine shop around the corner and purchase what he or she now knows to be the proper digital camera and the appropriate wine at a lower price. Even worse, the consumer is free to share this information with friends who can then use this knowledge to bypass the specialty shops altogether and go directly to the low-price, low-service outlets.

The problem is that information is a public good and, therefore, hard to deny even to those who do not pay for it. The low-price discount dealers of our two simple examples are "free riding" on the specialty shops. We call this behavior free riding because the discounter benefits from the activities of the specialty shop but does not pay for it. The scenarios above indicate the likely outcome of this problem. Specialty shops that incur the cost of providing in-store demonstrations and consultations will lose market share to the "no frills" discount stores. As such stores come to dominate the retail market, the outcome will be one in which few retail services are provided.

It is important to emphasize that the source of this underprovision of services is, in this setting, somewhat different from the cause of such underprovision in our earlier examples. In the analysis of the previous sections, retailers tended to overprice and underservice the products of a monopoly manufacturer because the impact on the upstream firm's profit is ignored in setting the downstream price and service level. This was true whether the retail sector was monopolized or competitive. In the current case, though, we are talking about a problem that is explicitly related to the presence of retail competition. If retailing were monopolized, then no free riding would be possible because there would be no potential free riders. While we already had reason to believe that retail services would be underproduced—at least from the viewpoint of the monopoly manufacturer—the argument just presented implies that this result is all the more likely once one acknowledges the public good aspect of presale services and the presence of retail competition. To put it another way, the first externality with which we dealt was a vertical one between the downstream and upstream firms. The externality now introduced is a horizontal one between the different downstream firms.

**Reality Checkpoint**

### Publish or Perish

In January 1995, almost 100 years of resale price maintenance in the British book industry came to end. That's when the publisher Hodder Headline International (HHI) withdrew from the Net Book Agreement. Under that agreement—first established in 1899—British publishers agreed to establish a fixed price for their books, and bookstores were forbidden to reduce that price through sales or discounts for a *minimum* of six months. The price printed on the book jacket or dustcover was always the price paid at the cash register. Several years earlier, Reed International had become the first big publisher to withdraw from the agreement and to permit bookstores to sell its books at a discount. But it was the withdrawal of HHI—vigorously opposed by the Publishers Association, a trade group—that signaled the collapse of the system. In September 1995, three other large firms—Random House, HarperCollins, and Penguin—all announced their withdrawal from the agreement. The retailer, W. H. Smith, which sells 20 percent of Britain's books, also withdrew.

The Publishers Association argued that the agreement helped consumers. It induced bookstores (1) to stock unusual books that catered to specialized tastes, and (2) to offer their books in attractive stores providing personalized services. Evidence from Germany, where the same issue has arisen even more recently, suggests that the association may well be right. With resale price maintenance, Germany regularly publishes between two and three times as many books per capita annually as does the United States. Retailers and some consumer groups have argued that this is because resale price maintenance encourages German retailers to cater to the individualized tastes of a diverse audience. Whether this claim is true, a purely bottom line perspective makes it easy to see why the British publishers felt that they could no longer ignore the advantage of selling through discount stores. In the United States, book sales account for $50 billion each year—more than any other kind of entertainment. Moreover, at the time of HHI's decision, U.S. book sales had been growing at an annual rate of 7 percent while the British book market had been flat. One big British chain, Dillons, actually went bankrupt. To the British publishers, these data seemed to indicate clearly that their best bet was to permit discounts to move their stock of publications even if that meant emphasizing fewer highbrow books in favor of more blockbuster ones and the elimination of many customer services.

**Source:** "Dusting Off the Bookshelves." *Economist*, September 30, 1995, pp. 77–78; and S. Lyall, "Cracks Appear in British Book-Pricing System." *The New York Times*, January 9, 1995, p. D1.

Yet, while the source of the problem is new, the effect from the manufacturer's point of view is the same. When retail competition leads to an undersupply of customer services, the manufacturer suffers because this adversely affects the overall demand for the manufacturer's product and reduces the manufacturer's profit. In the present case, however, we do not need to assume anything specific about demand or cost conditions to obtain the result that the undersupply of services will hurt both the manufacturer and consumers. Competitive markets generally do undersupply goods with beneficial externalities, such as the retail services described above. Accordingly, if the resultant losses are sufficiently severe, the extension of monopoly power by means of some sort of vertical restraint may be in the public interest. One such possible restraint is an RPM agreement.

At this point, the advantage of an RPM agreement should be clear. It prevents one retailer from undercutting another and, hence, stifles the emergence of discount stores. In turn, this implies that consumers will visit the retailer who provides the best services since they will not find a lower price elsewhere. By putting a freeze on price discounting, the effect of an RPM agreement is to foreclose discount outlets, resulting in a possibly higher average retail price. Yet this price effect and the loss it imposes on consumers may be offset by the gains that the provision of retail services generate, not only for consumers but for the manufacturer as well.

The view that RPM contracts enhance efficiency by restoring incentives to provide valued retail services was first articulated by Telser (1960). It is associated with the Chicago School economists (of whom Telser was one) who strongly advocate the efficiency-enhancing role of vertical contracts between firms. Note, though, that this free-riding argument, which endorses the efficiency effect of resale price maintenance, really is limited to presale services, such as advertising or instructional demonstrations. Other services, such as warranty service, can easily be provided and, more importantly, charged for by any retailer. In fact, Telser's argument was frequently criticized because it was applied to many goods for which presale informational services play a limited role.[7] In the case of fashion apparel, for example, consumers can go to the store and examine clothes for style and appropriate fit for themselves with little assistance from store personnel.[8]

Yet even in these cases the Chicago School has a rejoinder. This is that the free-riding justification for RPM might still be valid in this alternative setting because such stores play a screening or certification role. Thus, one of the services provided by top stores such as Bloomingdales, Neiman-Marcus, and Bergdorf Goodman is to identify (and then sell) "what's hot" or in fashion. Here again, providing this service is not cheap. Prestigious retail stores must spend considerable resources to build up their reputation for being on the "cutting edge" of fashion trends. When the store carries a manufacturer's fashion line, the store's reputation stands behind the quality or fashionability of the garment. Hence, proponents of RPM agreements argue that if a consumer can go window shopping at a prestigious store to find out "what's in" this season and then buy the apparel at a discount store, we again have the problem of free riding. The discount store free rides on the market research and quality certification of the prestigious store. This problem could become sufficiently severe that, absent

---

7   See, for example, Steiner (1985).
8   See also Bork (1966), Posner (1981), Marvel and McCafferty (1984) for related analyses in the Chicago School tradition. Matthewson and Winter (1998) present a thorough and very readable survey of various explanations for resale price maintenance efforts, including those that suggest the practice is welfare-reducing as well as those that suggest it is welfare-enhancing.

RPM protection, no store will find it worthwhile to screen and identify the fashion-ability and quality of products.[9]

## 18.5 RETAIL PRICE MAINTENANCE AND UNCERTAIN DEMAND

We have been discussing in the preceding two sections the way in which competitive pressures in the retail market can reduce the profit of the manufacturer and the welfare of consumers by creating disincentives to provide customer services. However, retail competition can be destructive in other ways as well. Consider the case of Nintendo, the dominant player in the video games market. When Nintendo first introduced its video game players and cartridges in the late 1980s, it faced one very serious obstacle. This was the recent history of the video game market. Led by Atari, that market grew from $200 million in 1978 to over $3 billion in 1982. However, the market then crashed even more rapidly, with sales falling to just $100 million in 1983. In that year, retailers found themselves with greatly excessive inventories and cut prices drastically in order to liquidate this stock. Atari itself went bankrupt.

The boom-and-bust cycle of the video game market in the early 1980s, and especially the sizable losses incurred in 1983, made retailing firms highly skeptical about the prospects for any new video game product. Nintendo representatives found that department and toy stores were almost totally unwilling to talk to them about their product. Nobody wanted to buy Nintendo's games and risk getting caught with an inventory that could only be sold at distressed prices as in the previous video game cycle. Eventually, of course, Nintendo prevailed. To this day, it continues to be a leader in the video games market. However, that success was not guaranteed from the outset. Indeed, Nintendo's product—so obviously valued by consumers—might never have survived had it not been for Nintendo's pricing strategy.

The Nintendo story has recently been used by Deneckere *et al.* (1997) to offer another explanation for RPM agreements when retailing is competitive. Their argument is based on the simple fact that retail demand for any product is uncertain. Like many of the analyses of vertical restrictions offered earlier, this analysis also raises the possibility that both producers and consumers will benefit from the imposition of an RPM agreement.

When demand is uncertain, a retailer faces a dilemma in determining how much output to stock for sale to final consumers. On the one hand, the retailer will wish to have the amount on hand necessary for profit maximization during periods when demand is strong. On the other hand, if demand is weak, retailers with a lot of stock will have to do one of two things. Either they must throw away the extra output and thereby keep the price high, or they can sell it, thereby lowering the price and perhaps even driving it to zero.[10] It is in this situation that the behavior of the monopolist and the competitive firm will differ. Faced with weak demand, the monopolist will tend to throw away a good bit of its excess inventory because the monopolist recognizes that every extra unit sold lowers the price on all units. A firm in a com-

---

9  Matthewson and Perry (1983) make a similar argument that resale price maintenance can benefit consumers by economizing on consumer search costs since they no longer will spend time trying to find out which retailer sells at the lowest price. This argument assumes, however, that no other means is available to inform consumers about retail prices.

10  Throughout this section, we assume that inventories cannot be stored beyond the current period. Either they physically perish or become worthless because of the introduction of new products.

petitive retail sector, however, will do the opposite. Under competition, each retailer perceives that its own sales have no effect on the market price. Accordingly, each such competitive retailer will try to sell all of its stock. After all, it has already paid for it and it may as well try to get something for it rather than throw any of it away. The problem is that if all retailers act this way the market price will fall, possibly quite far.

The fact that competition induces sharp price-cutting during periods of weak demand has two implications. First, a manufacturer selling through a competitive retail sector will not earn the profit of an integrated firm. Second, as Nintendo discovered, the manufacturer will also find it difficult to induce retailers to hold any sizable inventory. An RPM agreement that establishes a minimum retail price can solve the manufacturer's problem. The reason is straightforward. Setting a minimum price at which the good can be sold makes sure that, in periods of low demand, retailers will deal with excess inventory exactly the way that an integrated manufacturer would choose. They will throw away the amount that cannot be sold at the specified retail price.

We illustrate the essential insight of the Deneckere *et al.* argument in Figure 18-3. The figure shows the price and profit outcome for an integrated monopolist manufacturer facing variable demand. As usual, we assume a constant unit cost, $c$. With probability one-half, demand is strong and the demand curve is $D_H$. Similarly, with probability one-half, demand is weak and the demand curve is $D_L$. The integrated monopolist then faces a two-stage problem. In stage one, the firm must choose how

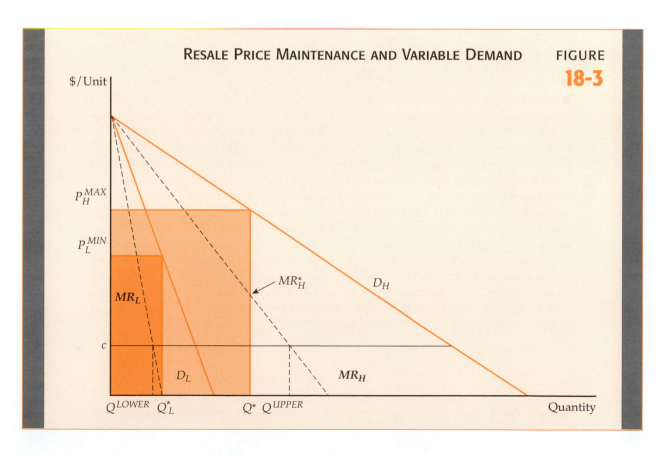

**RESALE PRICE MAINTENANCE AND VARIABLE DEMAND**     FIGURE 18-3

much to produce, $Q$. Once the firm has produced this amount, it will have incurred a sunk cost equal to $cQ$. Afterwards, demand will be either strong or weak, $D_H$ or $D_L$. At that point, the firm will have no additional cost and will simply have to choose how much of the output in its inventory that it actually wants to sell. Of course, the integrated firm can sell no more than it originally produced, $Q$. Subject to this constraint, however, it will simply sell the amount that maximizes its revenue conditional upon demand. Since all its costs are sunk, revenue maximization and profit maximization amount to the same thing in the second stage.

The integrated firm will never initially produce more than the amount that would maximize profit if it knew for sure that demand would be high. This is an amount at which the marginal revenue when demand is $D_H$ equals marginal production cost, $c$. It is shown as $Q^{UPPER}$ in Figure 18-3. To produce more than this level would guarantee that the firm earns a marginal revenue below its production cost even in the best of demand conditions. Similarly, the firm will never produce for inventory an amount less than $Q^{LOWER}$, the amount it would produce if it were certain demand would be low. To do so would be to guarantee too little inventory even in the weakest of markets. The firm must produce somewhere between $Q^{LOWER}$ and $Q^{UPPER}$. Within this interval, optimization requires that it choose an amount whereby its marginal cost $c$ equals its expected marginal revenue, or one-half times the marginal revenue in a high-demand state plus one-half times the marginal revenue in a low-demand state.

As we have drawn Figure 18-3, the optimal amount of initial production is $Q^*$. Note that in this figure, demand is quite variable. As a result, in order to come even close to the true profit-maximizing level in a high-demand state, the amount produced for inventory $Q^*$ is enough to drive the price to zero if it is all sold in a weak-demand state.

If demand is strong, the firm will sell the entire amount $Q^*$ at the price $P_H^{MAX}$. If demand is weak, an inventory of $Q^*$ is excessive. Since the integrated firm has already incurred its production cost, all it can do is maximize its revenue. It will do this by selling the amount $Q_L^*$ at the price $P_L^{MIN}$. This is an output at which marginal revenue is zero. Note, though, that weak demand does not lead the firm to try to liquidate its entire inventory. As noted previously, that would drive the price to zero. Instead, the firm throws away the amount $Q^* - Q_L^*$. When demand is weak, the firm drives its marginal revenue to zero. However, because this occurs where the price is still positive, the firm's total revenue remains greater than zero even in the face of weak demand. Its marginal revenue when demand is strong is the marginal revenue at $Q^*$, shown here as $MR_H^*$. Its expected marginal revenue is therefore $MR_H^*/2$, which is an amount just equal to $c$.

The integrated monopolist firm will expect to earn a positive profit in this story. Its total cost is $cQ$. Its revenue in a low-demand period is $P_L^{MIN} Q_L^*$. This is the darkly shaded rectangle in Figure 18-3. Its revenue in a high-demand period is $P_H^{MAX} Q^*$. This is the sum of the lightly shaded region and the darkly shaded rectangle in the figure. The expected profit for the integrated firm, $\Pi_I^e$, is therefore

$$\Pi_I^e = \frac{1}{2} P_H^{MAX} Q^* + \frac{1}{2} P_L^{MIN} Q_L^* - cQ^*. \qquad (18.16)$$

Now consider the outcome under competitive retailing. If competitive retailers stocked the optimal amount $Q^*$, they would earn less total profit than that shown in equation (18.16). The reason is the nature of competition. In a low-demand period, the integrated firm sells only up to the point where its marginal revenue is zero. However, competitive firms holding a total inventory of $Q^*$ will sell more than this amount. Each such firm perceives price and marginal revenue to be the same. Hence, having already sunk the cost of acquiring its inventory, each such firm will continue to sell its inventory so long as the price is positive. Yet if demand is weak, the amount $Q^*$ can only be sold by driving the retail price—and not just the marginal revenue—to zero. In turn, this means that a competitive retail sector with an inventory equal to $Q^*$ will earn no revenue when demand is low. Of course, when demand is high, retailers will sell the entire stock $Q^*$ for the price $P_H^{MAX}$ and generate exactly the same revenue as would an integrated monopolist. However, because the competitive outcome during a low-demand period is a zero price, competitive retailers will always generate less total profit from the optimal inventory stock, $Q^*$, than would an integrated monopolist whose revenue remains positive even when demand is weak.

In short, unfettered competition during a period of weak demand dramatically reduces the revenue retailers can expect to earn. Accordingly, a manufacturer can only persuade retailers to stock the optimal amount $Q^*$ by selling to them at a sufficiently low wholesale price $P_W$, so that retailers can still expect to break even. Since retailers only earn positive revenue when demand is high, $P_W Q^*$ must equal the revenue earned by retailers in a high-demand period, times the probability that such a period occurs. Therefore, $P_W Q^*$ must equal $P_H^{MAX} Q^*/2$, implying that $P_W = P_H^{MAX}/2$. In turn, this implies an expected profit, $\Pi^e$, for the non-integrated manufacturer without an RPM agreement of

$$\Pi^e = \left( \frac{1}{2} P_H^{MAX} - c \right) Q^*. \tag{18.17}$$

A comparison of equations (18.16) and (18.17) shows that the profit of the non-integrated firm will be less than that earned by its integrated counterpart by an amount equal to $P_L^{MIN} Q_L^*/2$. However, an RPM agreement can save the day. The necessary features of such an agreement are in fact suggested by Figure 18-3. That figure shows that the integrated firm never sells at a price below $P_L^{MIN}$. So, the non-integrated firm should negotiate an RPM agreement that likewise prohibits anyone from selling below this price. In addition, it should charge a wholesale price $P_W^*$, satisfying

$$P_W^* Q^* = \frac{1}{2} P_H^{MAX} Q^* + \frac{1}{2} P_L^{MIN} Q_L^*. \tag{18.18}$$

In turn, this implies that

$$P_W^* = \frac{1}{2} P_H^{MAX} + \frac{1}{2} P_L^{MIN} \frac{Q_L^*}{Q^*}. \tag{18.19}$$

At this wholesale price, the competitive retail sector will in fact buy and inventory the optimal amount, $Q^*$. Why? When they buy this amount, retailers know that their expected revenue, $P_H^{MAX} Q^*/2 + P_L^{MIN} Q_L^*/2$, just equals their expected cost, $P_W^* Q^*$. Hence, the inventory of $Q^*$ is exactly the amount that leads to an expected profit of zero for retailers. This is the requirement for a competitive equilibrium. Moreover, since retailers buy the amount $Q^*$ at this wholesale price, the manufacturer's expected profit, $\Pi^e_{RPM}$, with an RPM is

$$\Pi^e_{RPM} = P_W Q^* - cQ^* = \frac{1}{2} P^{MAX}_H Q^* + \frac{1}{2} P^{MIN}_L Q^*_L - cQ^*. \qquad \textbf{(18.20)}$$

A comparison of equations (18.16) and (18.20) quickly reveals that this RPM agreement permits the manufacturer to earn the same profit as that earned by an integrated firm.

In fact, something like an RPM arrangement seems to have been the source of Nintendo's ultimate victory. It closely monitored inventories and cut off dealers who sold below Nintendo's suggested retail prices. Indeed, Nintendo was forced in 1991 to sign a consent decree with the FTC under which it promised not to engage in any further implicit RPM behavior. By that time, however, Nintendo was well established in the video games market.

As the Nintendo example is meant to illustrate, it is not just the manufacturer who may benefit from the RPM agreement. Absent an RPM agreement, retailers may not be willing to offer the product to consumers at all. More formally, such an agreement can benefit consumers in the sense that it leads to a bigger expected consumer surplus. The intuition behind this result is that, depending on the nature of demand fluctuations, the equilibrium without an RPM agreement will result in retailers buying less than the amount they would purchase for inventory with such an agreement. As a result, the price during a period of strong demand will be higher without an RPM contract than it would be with one. This price increase hurts consumers and may more than offset the gains consumers enjoy from permitting prices to fall quite far when demand is weak. Hence, both producers and consumers can benefit from an RPM agreement.[11]

## Practice Problem 18.3

Suppose that demand is either strong (with probability one-half) and described by $Q = (10 - p)100$, or weak (with probability one-half) and described by $Q = (10 - p)30$. To simplify further, assume that the manufacturer's unit cost is constant at $c = 0$.

a. Show that the revenue-maximizing price is $5 regardless of whether demand is weak or strong.

b. Assume that the firm produces 500 units prior to learning the strength of demand. How much of this will it sell when demand is strong? How much will it sell when demand is weak? What is the firm's expected profit?

c. Suppose now that the firm sells the 500 units through a competitive retail sector. If retailers buy and stock the entire 500 units, what will be the retail price when demand is strong? What will be the retail price when demand is weak?

d. In light of your answer to (c), what wholesale price will induce the retailers to purchase initially an inventory of 500? What will be the manufacturer's profit at this price?

---

11 The manufacturer always gains from the specified RPM agreement. The outcome for consumers depends on just how variable is demand. If demand is highly variable, consumers are probably hurt by the agreement. However, if demand is only moderately variable, consumers may well benefit from the agreement.

## SUMMARY

Consumers buy most of their products from retailers such as department stores, supermarkets, automobile dealers, and gasoline stations. In these and many other cases, the firm from which the consumer buys is not the firm that originally made the product. The manufacturer lies further upstream in the chain of production.

Because a manufacturer relies on retailers to get its goods to the market, the manufacturer must hope that the retailers will share its views about the appropriate price to consumers and the proper amount of promotional and other services to provide. Unfortunately, this is rarely the case. Double marginalization and other problems lead to a divergence of interests between the manufacturer and its agent, that is, the retailer. However, contractual agreements governing this vertical relationship can resolve some of these differences. Yet such agreements can also have the appearance and perhaps the substantive effect of restricting competition. As a result, public policy regarding vertical restraints is complicated.

In this chapter we have focused on one particular type of vertical restraint—a resale price maintenance or RPM agreement. Such agreements may specify a maximum price above which a retailer may not charge, or a minimum price that the retailer cannot discount. For many years, RPM agreements were considered anticompetitive and treated as per se illegal. However, starting as early as 1919, the courts have chipped away at this strict view so that now RPM agreements and behavior that closely duplicates such a contract, even when the contract itself does not formally specify a retail price, are subject to a more flexible rule of reason.

The reason that the courts have moved to a more lenient attitude toward RPM agreements is straightforward. Increasingly, economists have understood that without such agreements, such problems as double marginalization, insuring the provision of services to consumers, and dealing with demand uncertainty work against consumer as well as producer interests. While the concern that vertical price restraints may be anticompetitive is certainly warranted, the potential benefits of such restraints make it undesirable to treat them as per se illegal.

## PROBLEMS

1. Suppose that a car dealer has a local monopoly in selling Volvos. It pays $w$ to Volvo for each car that it sells, and charges each customer $p$. The demand curve that the dealer faces is best described by the linear function $Q = 30 - p$, where the price is in units of thousands of dollars.

   a. What is the profit-maximizing price for the dealer to set? At this price, how many Volvos will the dealer sell and what will the dealer's profit from selling the cars be?

   b. Now let us think about how the situation looks from the car manufacturer's point of view. If Volvo charges $w$ per car to its dealer, calculate how many cars the dealer will buy from Volvo. In other words, what is the demand curve facing Volvo? Suppose that it costs Volvo $5,000 to produce each car. What is the profit-maximizing choice of $w$? What will Volvo's profits be? What price $p$ will the dealer set and what profit will the dealer earn at Volvo's profit-maximizing choice of wholesale price $w$?

    c. Now suppose Volvo operates the dealership and sells directly to its customers. What will be Volvo's profit-maximizing price $p$? What will Volvo's profit be? Compare your answer in (c) to the answer you worked out in (b). Give an intuitive explanation for why the answers differ.

2. ABC, Inc., is a monopolist selling to competitive retailers. It faces a constant marginal cost of 10. Demand at the retail level is described by $P = 50 - Q$.

    a. What wholesale price will maximize ABC's profit? What retail price will this imply?

    b. What will be the value of consumer surplus if ABC sets a profit-maximizing wholesale price?

    c. What will be the value of ABC's maximum profit?

3. ABC is still a monopolist selling to competitive retailers but it now discovers that if retailers supply customer services, demand shifts to $P = 90 - Q$. Each retailer can provide the required services at a total cost of $400.

    a. ABC decides now to implement an RPM agreement with retailers. Under this agreement, what retail price should ABC specify? How many units will retailers sell at this price?

    b. What is consumer surplus under the RPM agreement?

    c. Under the RPM agreement and the price specified in 3(a), what is the maximum wholesale price that ABC can set? What will its profit at this wholesale price be?

4. A significant number of the resale price maintenance cases that have been the subject of antitrust policy involve the pricing of such simple consumer products as Russell Stover candy, Levi's jeans, Arrow shirts, and Colgate toiletries. Who has the incentive for resale price maintenance for these products? Explain why.

5. In the antitrust case *Albrecht v. The Herald Co.*, the successive monopoly problem was created by the publisher granting an exclusive territory to the distributor. Could the problem have been solved by opening up home delivery to competition among several distributors?

# REFERENCES

Bork, Robert. 1966. "The Rule of Reason and the Per Se Concept: Price Fixing and Market Division." *Yale Law Journal* 75 (January): 399–441.

Chen, Yongmin. 1999. "Oligopoly Price Discrimination and Resale Price Maintenance." *Rand Journal of Economics* 30 (Autumn): 441–55.

Deneckere, R., H. P. Marvel, and J. Peck. 1997. "Demand Uncertainty and Price Maintenance: Markdowns as Destructive Competition." *American Economic Review* 87 (September): 619–41.

Knecht, G. B. 1997. "Big Retail Chains Get Special Advance Looks at Magazine Contents." *The Wall Street Journal* (October 27): A1.

Lafontaine, Francine. 1992. "Agency Theory and Franchising: Some Empirical Results." *Rand Journal of Economics* 23 (Summer): 263–83.

———. 1993. "Contractual Arrangements as Signaling Devices: Evidence from Franchising." *Journal of Law, Economics, and Organization* 9 (October): 256–89.

————. 1995. "Pricing Decisions in Franchised Chains: A Look at the Restaurant and Fast-Food Industry." Mimeo, University of Michigan (April).

Marvel, Howard, and S. McCafferty. 1984. "Resale Price Maintenance and Quality Certification." *Rand Journal of Economics* 15 (Autumn): 346–59.

Matthewson, F., and R. Winter. 1998. "The Law and Economics of Resale Price Maintenance." *Review of Industrial Organization* 13 (April): 57–84.

Matthewson, G. F., and R. A. Winter. 1983. "The Incentives for Resale Price Maintenance under Imperfect Information." *Economic Inquiry* (1983): 337–48.

Overstreet, T. 1983. *Resale Price Maintenance: Economic Theories and Empirical Evidence.* Washington, D.C.: Federal Trade Commission Bureau of Economics Staff Report (November).

Pickering, J. F. 1966. *Resale Price Maintenance in Practice.* New York: August M. Kelley Publishers.

Posner, R. 1981. "The Next Step in the Antitrust Treatment of Restricted Distribution: Per se Legality." *University of Chicago Law Review* 48: 6–26.

Steiner, Robert L. 1985. "The Nature of Vertical Restraints." *Antitrust Bulletin* (Spring): 143–97.

Telser, L. 1960. "Why Should Manufacturers Want Free Trade?" *Journal of Law and Economics* 3 (October): 86–105.

# Appendix | Resale Price Maintenance and Retail Price Discrimination

In this appendix, we derive the optimal wholesale price $r$ and fixed fee $T$ that a manufacturer should select to maximize total profit when the retailer sells in two identical markets, one of which is a monopoly but the other of which is constrained by potential entry to sell at a price equal to the wholesale price.

Demand in each market is given by $P = A - BQ$. Manufacturing cost is $c$. No cost is incurred in retailing. In the monopolized market, profit maximization by the retailer will lead to an output of

$$Q_M = \frac{A - r}{2B},$$

$$(18A.1)$$

and a price of

$$P_M = \frac{A + r}{2}.$$

$$(18A.2)$$

The retailer's profit $\Pi_M^R$ in this market will therefore be

$$\Pi_M^R = \frac{(A - r)^2}{4B}.$$

$$(18A.3)$$

Absent any franchise fee $T$, the manufacturer's profit $\Pi_M^M$ derived from sales in the retailer's monopoly market will be

$$\Pi_M^M = \frac{(r - c)(A - r)}{2B}.$$

$$(18A.4)$$

In the entry-constrained market, the price to consumers will be $r$ and the retailer will earn no profit. Output will be given by

$$Q_C = \frac{A - r}{B}.$$

$$(18A.5)$$

The manufacturer's profit $\Pi_C^M$ from the retailer's sales in this competitive market will therefore be

$$\Pi_C^M = \frac{(r - c)(A - r)}{B}.$$

$$(18A.6)$$

For a given $r$ at which the retailer buys goods to be sold in both its markets, total profit to the manufacturer and retailer combined is

$$\Pi = \Pi_C^M + \Pi_M^M + \frac{(A - r)^2}{4B} = \frac{(r - c)(A - r)}{B} + \frac{(r - c)(A - r)}{2B} + \frac{(A - r)^2}{4B} .$$

(18A.7)

Maximizing this with respect to $r$ yields the following necessary condition:

$$r = \frac{4A + 6c}{10} .$$

(18A.8)

With $A = 100$ and $c = 12$, this yields the value of $r = \$47.20$ reported in the text.

# Chapter 19

# Nonprice Vertical Restraints

Bake sales, book fairs, and other events are commonly used as fund-raising devices at hundreds of elementary and secondary schools throughout North America. Just as typically, the event organizers offer beverages at these events, sometimes giving drinks away for free. Yet these well-intentioned citizens may be breaching a contract. This is because many schools have exclusive sales agreements with a soft drink company. Under such a contract, the beverages of only one soft drink firm, for example, Coca-Cola or Pepsi, may be sold on the school's premises. Indeed, most contracts specify that only milk and (at most) a few juices are allowed to be sold at school at all. Other restrictions are also common. For example, the drinks of the permitted company are usually not to be offered at a discount price, let alone for free. School personnel are often required to keep the vending machines stocked, and so on.

Requiring the school to sell no other soft drink is known as an exclusive dealing requirement. Such contracts are common not just between soft drink makers and schools, but also between manufacturers of many products and their dealers. Hence, such contracts reflect a restraint imposed by the vertical contract between upstream and downstream firms. Such vertical restraints take a number of forms and they create many of the same issues raised by the vertical price restrictions studied in Chapter 18. Here again, as was the case with the price restrictions, nonprice agreements may have beneficial effects. Yet these contracts also have obvious potential for weakening competition both between different manufacturers, or what we call *interbrand* competition, and between different retailers selling the same brand, or *intrabrand* competition. In this chapter, we examine such nonprice vertical restraints.

## 19.1 UPSTREAM COMPETITION AND EXCLUSIVE DEALING

As the soft drink and school example illustrates, exclusive dealing is a contractual agreement in which the relevant restrictions apply to the behavior of the dealer. Essentially, the dealer is not allowed to buy (and then resell) brands that may compete with the manufacturer's brand. Justifications for exclusive dealing agreements are typically based on a free-rider problem in the provision of services and promotion. In particular, the concern is that in the absence of such restrictions, the retail firm may free ride on the efforts of the upstream manufacturer.

To understand this concern, we need first to recognize that manufacturers often expend considerable resources promoting their products. Household products companies such as Procter & Gamble, cosmetic manufacturers such as Revlon, and appliance firms such as Maytag are just some of the many manufacturers that extensively advertise their products. Such advertisements may increase demand for the manufacturer's brand. However, they may also increase demand for the product category in general.

Consider advertisements for Tylenol, the well-known nonaspirin pain reliever. Undoubtedly, such advertising helps raise the consuming public's awareness of both Tylenol, in particular, and of the benefits of nonaspirin pain relievers in general. We may be equally assured, however, that such advertising is expensive. To recover the cost of the advertising, Johnson & Johnson, Tylenol's manufacturer, will have to raise Tylenol's price.

In this setting, one can easily imagine the following transaction between a pharmacy and a customer searching for Tylenol. When asked "Why Tylenol?" the customer will say because he or she needs nonaspirin medication for pain and fever. In response, the pharmacist may say that Tylenol will work fine but that a lower-cost, unadvertised brand that is the chemical equivalent of Tylenol is also available. Note that the price of this alternative may not be a lot below the Tylenol price—just enough to persuade the customer to switch to this brand. Indeed, it is precisely because the pharmacist can charge something close to the Tylenol price for a product that costs much less that the pharmacist has an incentive to pursue this strategy. From the perspective of Tylenol, however, the pharmacist's behavior is undesirable because Tylenol now makes no sale even though it was the Tylenol advertising that may have induced the customer to ask for a nonaspirin pain reliever in the first place.

An exclusive dealing agreement offers a solution to this problem because it permits the manufacturer to prevent retailers from making such substitutions.[1] This is particularly important in the case of goods in which the retailer plays a role similar to that of a doctor whose recommendation acts like an informal guarantee of the product's quality. Many intermediate goods sold between firms, for example, chemical products, may have this feature. At the retail consumer level, appliances, electronic goods, pharmaceuticals, and automobiles may also be of this nature.

From an antitrust perspective, however, exclusive dealing can be a means of suppressing competition. We have already shown one way that this can happen in Chapter 13. There we discussed the Rasmussen, Ramseyer, and Wiley (1991) argument illustrating how exclusive dealing requirements can prevent entry when there are important scale economies in upstream production.[2]

However, entry prevention is not the only way that exclusive dealing can limit competition. Such contracts can also be used to limit competition between existing firms. By excluding a rival's product, the remaining firm can enjoy more monopoly power. It will, however, have to share the profit from that power with the retailer. Indeed, in order to get the exclusive contract in the first place, a manufacturer will have to offer as much profit as its rival can offer to the retailer. As Matthewson and Winter (1987) show, this consideration can greatly complicate the analysis of exclusive dealing. In particular, the firm that gets the exclusive contract may only do so by offering to sell to the retailer at a very low wholesale price. In turn, this low wholesale price will translate into a low retail price. Whether the fall in the retail price is sufficient to compensate consumers for the loss of the alternative product will depend on various features such as the elasticity of demand and the behavior of production costs. It is clear, however, that there are plausible parameter values such that consumer welfare improves despite the fact that the exclusive deal eliminates one product line from the market.[3]

---

1  Marvel (1982) in particular has insisted on this role for exclusive dealing.
2  Strictly speaking, the long-term contract model of Aghion and Bolton (1987) in Chapter 13 is not an exclusive dealing contract though, practically speaking, it may have the same effect.
3  The foreclosure argument behind exclusive dealing is a hot topic in current research in industrial organization. Bernheim and Whinston (1990) show that when there are two brands produced by two upstream firms and a single retailer, there are no incentives to adopt exclusive dealing. The retailer will always be a common dealer of both products. In the case of several retailers, O'Brien and Schaffer (1994) and Besanko and Perry (1994) find that exclusive dealing is always adopted. However, in the last two models, foreclosure is explicitly ruled out as an option.

However, exclusive dealing can serve to limit competition among retailers and manufacturers, simultaneously. For example, suppose that there are two manufacturers selling to two retailers who are spatially separated but still within a given territory. Without any exclusive dealing, each retailer may offer both products. As a result, price competition between the two products, that is, interbrand competition, will be fierce at each retail location. However, if each manufacturer signs one of the retailers to sell its product by means of an exclusive contract, then interbrand competition can be softened. Effectively, the exclusive dealing equilibrium injects an element of spatial differentiation between the two goods that did not previously exist.[4]

## 19.2 EXCLUSIVE SELLING AND TERRITORIAL ARRANGEMENTS

We now turn to selling and exclusive territorial arrangements. These cases differ from our soft drink and school example, however, in two important respects. Whereas the restrictions in that example were aimed at limiting *interbrand* competition between rival soft drink companies, exclusive selling and territorial arrangements are aimed at limiting *intrabrand* competition between downstream dealers. In the case of an exclusive selling arrangement, for example, the upstream firm agrees that only one specific retailer will have the right to sell its product, much as the seller of a home agrees to give the selling rights to just one specific real estate agent. Similarly an exclusive territorial agreement grants the right to sell the manufacturer's product to just one firm within a specific region. Thus, Toyota may sign agreements with a number of Lexus dealers that require each dealer to agree that it will not open a new outlet in any region where one of the other dealers already operates. To some extent then, the territorial restraints have a more obvious horizontal element, that is, they can be more easily interpreted as an agreement among dealers not to compete.

We saw in Chapter 18 that retail competition can help manufacturers in that it reduces or even eliminates the double marginalization problem. We may wonder, then, why a manufacturer would ever sign a contract that limits such competition. However, the rationale behind such restrictions is relatively intuitive.

Consider a simple case of a single manufacturer that sells to two downstream retailers. In addition, assume that while the manufactured product is the same, the retailers are differentiated by location. In other words, consumers do not view the purchase of the good at each retailer as perfect substitutes, so retail competition is not perfect.

In this context, two externalities quickly emerge. The first of these is a pricing externality. If one retailer lowers its price, it will attract consumers and thereby reduce the profit of the other retailer. However, in deciding whether to lower its price, the retailer will consider only the impact of that decision on its own profit—not on the profit of its rival. Because each retailer fails to take account of its pricing decisions on its rival's profit, each tends to set its price too low, that is, below the level that would maximize industry profit. This not only reduces retail profit but also lowers the profit that the manufacturer may claim through any two-part tariff or profit-sharing contract.[5]

---

4   See Besanko and Perry (1994) for a model along these lines.
5   This case differs from those considered in Chapter 18, where downstream competition helped solve the double marginalization problem. Here, the retailers are differentiated and so, therefore, are the products they sell. As we saw in Chapter 10, the prices of such retailers are strategic complements and coordination of their price-setting can raise the profit of each firm.

The second externality that plagues intrabrand competition is the service externality that we encountered in Chapter 18. If one retailer incurs the expense of advertising or providing informational services, it benefits the other retailer as well. For example, if one Lexus dealer runs Lexus commercials on local TV, it potentially raises the demand for all Lexus dealers in the area. Similarly, if one camera store provides information to customers of how to get the best pictures with a Kyoscera digital camera, those customers may make their camera purchase from a cheaper, no-frills retailer who does not offer such services. In short, there is a temptation for each retailer of a specific brand to free ride on the services provided by other sellers of that brand. As a result, the level of such services will likely be too low. Moreover, because consumers value such services, this externality not only reduces the profit available to the manufacturer and the retailer, it also reduces consumer surplus.

It should be clear how exclusive selling and territorial agreements may remedy the foregoing externality problems. Effectively, such contracts limit the number of sellers of the manufacturer's good to just one within any given region. As a result, that one seller reaps all the benefits of any price and service decisions that it makes. There is no externality because there is no firm external to the one in question. Hence, exclusive selling and territorial restrictions can serve to raise both the price and the service level associated with the manufacturer's good. This will increase the profit available to the manufacturer and dealer jointly. The impact on consumers, though, is ambiguous. The reduction in intrabrand competition and resultant price increase lowers consumer welfare. The increase in the service level, however, benefits consumers.

Exclusive selling and territorial arrangements have two other potentially important effects. One of these is that because these contracts result in a single dealer being the only seller of a specific product in its area, the dealer's willingness to dump its merchandise on the market when demand is weak is reduced. As we saw in Chapter 18, this effect can be important in getting dealers to stock an appropriate amount of the manufacturer's good in the first place. The second effect is that by creating a local monopoly an exclusive selling or territory agreement makes the setting within each region to be one of a monopoly upstream supplier selling to a monopoly downstream retailer. In turn, this makes the use of a two-part tariff or franchise fee attractive as a tool to prevent the double marginalization and low service problems that we discussed in the previous chapter. Indeed, viewed in this light, it should not be surprising that we usually observe exclusive territories and franchise fees in the same contract.[6]

However, so far we have only considered exclusive selling and territorial arrangements in the context of a single manufacturer. When there is more than one upstream producer, these contracts can be used to reduce interbrand competition—to the detriment of consumers.

Assume that there are two upstream manufacturers producing products that are imperfect substitutes, and that the two manufacturers sell to a competitive retail sector. If the two producers have identical costs, and assuming symmetric demand curves for each, then the competitive equilibrium will result in each setting the same wholesale price $w^C$, which, in turn, will also be the retail price $p^C$ because competition eliminates any retail markup. Hence, all downstream retailers will earn zero profit. More importantly, the fact that $p^C = w^C$ means that every increase in the wholesale price $w$ will be one-for-one translated into an equivalent increase in the retail price $p$.

---

6   See Lafontaine (1993).

Now, following Rey and Stiglitz (1995), let us imagine that the market for these products can be divided into regions or territories. Suppose further that each producer grants an exclusive territory to a retailer in each territory giving that retailer the exclusive right to sell its product in that region. As a result, within any given territory each producer's product will be sold by a retail monopoly.

In the absence of a two-part tariff agreement, we know that selling to a monopoly retailer will give rise to the double marginalization problem. Why, then, should the two producers decide to do this? The answer, in part, is that it softens the intensity of the competition between the two brands. It does this because it weakens the link between the wholesale price $w$ and the retail price $p$. From the perspective of each retailer, $w$ is a cost. Suppose that one producer raises $w$. For the dealer selling this product, costs have risen. To some extent, the dealer will want to pass on this increase by means of a higher retail price $p$. Competition with the other retailer will limit how much the price can be increased. However, prices are strategic complements. As the rival retailer sees the first dealer's price rising, he or she will see an opportunity to raise price without losing customers even though the wholesale cost has not risen. As a result, when a manufacturer raises its wholesale price it will no longer lose as many customers as it did under the competition that prevailed without exclusive territories. Even though the rival producer does not raise its wholesale price, the rival retailer does raise the retail price.

Of course, both producers realize the foregoing logic. By each granting an exclusive territory, they weaken retail competition, which feeds back to weaker wholesale competition. As a result, the granting of exclusive territories will lead to higher prices at both the retail and the wholesale level. Whether the agreement will increase producer profit is another question. It might not because although wholesale prices are higher, the double marginalization problem means that the quantity sold is lower than it would be if retailing remained competitive. However, if the double marginalization problem is not too large (as would be the case if the two goods are fairly close substitutes) the exclusive territorial arrangement will lead to higher upstream profits. Indeed, if the firms can also adopt a two-part tariff arrangement, the double marginalization problem can be overcome altogether.[7]

Indeed, it may even be possible to use exclusive selling arrangements to achieve monopoly profit in what would otherwise be a competitive industry. To see this, suppose that the products of the two producers are perfect substitutes. With a competitive retail sector, neither manufacturers nor retailers will make any profit. However, suppose that the two producers coordinate in that, within any territory, they give the exclusive rights to their products to the same retailer, each agreeing not to sell to other dealers in that region. The lucky retailer in the region is thereby transformed into a monopolist who can set the monopoly retail price. Since monopolies make extra profit, the lucky downstream retailer will be happy with this scheme.

What about the manufacturers? To some extent, their situation is unchanged. Each still produces a good for which there is a very close substitute, so competition between the two may still be expected to be fierce. If this happens, all the monopoly profit will flow to the retailer. Yet, there are some possible contracts, which even in the absence of a two-part tariff, the manufacturers may use to extract some of the profit for themselves. One such technique is to offer the exclusive sales contract only

7    The mechanism by which exclusive territories soften interbrand price competition described in Rey and Stiglitz (1995) is conceptually similar to the argument in Bonanno and Vickers (1988).

if the retailer also agrees to purchase a minimum amount from the producer even if that producer charges a price higher than the rival's price. This technique—known as a quantity-forcing requirement—has an effect similar to that described previously. It softens upstream price competition. (In this extreme case, it falls from infinite to zero.) When each producer does this, each can raise its price above cost without fear of losing sales to its rival. As a result, producers now earn some profit.[8] Of course, the higher wholesale prices will translate into higher retail prices. That is, this arrangement does not enhance efficiency. The profit gain of the producers is more than offset by a reduction in retailer profit and a fall in consumer surplus. Again, while vertical contracts can be socially beneficial there is a downside risk. Indeed, the type of upstream coordination orchestrated by the retailer that we have just described appears to have been an important element in the recent Toys "R" Us case (see the Reality Checkpoint: Trouble in Toyland).

## 19.3 PUBLIC POLICY TOWARD VERTICAL RESTRAINTS

As we have seen, nonprice vertical agreements can have both positive and negative effects. Accordingly, a "rule of reason" approach has dominated the legal cases in this area. The outcome typically reflects the court's balancing of the conflicting pro- and anticompetitive forces. Not all analysts agree on the wisdom of this approach. For some, such as Posner (1981), the potential efficiency gains of exclusive selling and territorial agreements are likely to be sufficiently large that all such vertical restrictions ought to be considered per se legal under the antitrust laws. The argument is essentially that vertical restrictions must at least benefit the upstream and downstream firms that have agreed to such restraints. They may, as we have seen, benefit consumers as well. Attempting to use a rule of reason and judge each situation on a case-by-case method will, in this view, be very difficult and produce a large number of inconsistent and quite possibly wrong decisions. According to this view, the wisest course for antitrust policy is simply to let all vertical restrictions alone. The U.S. Justice Department came close to adopting such a view in its Vertical Restraints Guidelines of 1985, and there was little prosecution of vertical arrangements for the next several years. However, those guidelines were rejected in 1993 and the antitrust authorities have since taken a less generous attitude towards vertical restraints.

It seems clear that the motivation behind many vertical arrangements is benign. The authors of this book are therefore somewhat sympathetic to the argument that public policy regarding vertical agreements should tread carefully. Still, such agreements have the potential to do considerable harm to competitive forces. For this reason, we are reluctant to endorse a total abandonment of enforcement efforts in this area.

For example, both the entry deterrence and price coordination effects that exclusive dealing can generate were found by the FTC in a recent case involving the two principal manufacturers of water pumps used by fire engines. Hale Products, Inc., and Waterous Company, Inc., were the pump-makers in question. Each manufactured a water pump that is installed on fire trucks in the United States. Each sold its pumps directly to the makers of such fire trucks through exclusive dealing contracts. Thus,

---

8   Note that in the final equilibrium, the quantity constraint does not need to be binding.

**Reality Checkpoint**

### Trouble in Toyland: "It's Toys "R" Us or Them!"

On September 31, 1997, an administrative law judge at the FTC ruled against the toy retailing firm, Toys "R" Us, in connection with an exclusive dealing arrangement. Three years later, a U.S. Appeals Court upheld this action. Government prosecutors had claimed that Toys "R" Us reached informal agreements with many of America's leading toy makers, including the two largest, Mattel and Hasbro. Toys "R" Us agreed to sell the manufacturers' products only if the manufacturers refused to sell those products to the large discount firms (e.g., Sam's Club) that had recently gained market share in the retail toy market. As we have seen, this may have helped not only Toys "R" Us but also the toy makers by creating a pool of monopoly profit downstream that the toy makers could then partially claim for themselves. Somewhat prior to the Appeals Court ruling, Toys "R" Us agreed to a settlement with 44 states in which it agreed to stop the practice and paid a settlement fee of $50 million. Hasbro and Mattel also joined in this agreement and paid about an additional $5 million each.

Toys "R" Us did not deny the charges. The company's lawyer, Mr. Michael Feldberg, instead argued that what Toys "R" Us did was "perfectly lawful." [We] "simply posed a choice to manufacturers: It's us or them. If you sell an item to the warehouse clubs, we may not buy it." Feldberg argued that Toys "R" Us screened what toys were hot and did the bulk of the retail promotion for these items, while the discount firms simply picked those items and sold them at deep discount, thereby free riding at the expense of Toys "R" Us.

Toys "R" Us is no stranger to such tactics. The firm's clothing subsidiary, Kids "R" Us, had itself sued Macy's in 1990, alleging that it was being boycotted by the clothing manufacturers at the urging of the department store chain. However, Macy's was found not guilty. An important aspect that may have distinguished the earlier Macy's case from the current Toys "R" Us one is that in the current case, the restraint of trade included a horizontal component as well as a vertical one. The judge found that Mattel agreed to cut off the discount clubs if Hasbro did, and Hasbro agreed to do so if Mattel did. Thus, there appears to have been an element of collusion coordinated by the retailer, Toys "R" Us. As noted in the text, the possibility that a vertical arrangement may facilitate horizontal agreements is a continuing worry; when this appears to be happening it is certain to raise the suspicions of the antitrust authorities.

**Sources:** W. M. Bulkeley and J. R. Wilke, "Toys Loses a Warehouse-Club Ruling with Broad Marketing Implications." *The Wall Street Journal,* October 1, 1997, p. B10; and "Toys "R" Us Loses Ruling." *The New York Times,* August 2, 2000, p. C2. For further details, consult the Federal Trade Commission at http://www.ftc.gov.

those fire truck manufacturers who bought from Hale agreed not to buy from any other pump-maker and likewise for those who agreed to purchase their pumps from Waterous. In determining the effect of these agreements, the FTC noted that together the two firms accounted for 90 percent of the U.S. market for water pumps and had done so for nearly 50 years, with the remainder accounted for by a small third firm, W. S. Darley & Company. During that time, no new entrant had come into the market. This was taken as evidence by the FTC that the exclusive dealing agreements had effectively blocked such entry. In addition, the FTC alleged that the agreements also worked to reduce competition between Hale and Waterous. Documents were presented indicating that each firm realized that as long as it dealt only with its half of the engine manufacturers, it did not need to fear competition from the other. Further, the FTC noted that neither pump-maker would wish to cheat on this tacit agreement because such cheating would be quickly detected. Waterous would know immediately if one of its customers stopped buying the Waterous pump. The same would be true for Hale. Ultimately, the FTC prevailed and the two firms agreed to cease the exclusive dealing arrangements.[9]

The FTC's finding in the water pumps case is consistent with the current treatment of exclusive dealing agreements by the courts. The threshold issue in recent exclusive cases has been the fraction of the market such agreements cover. Unless that fraction is large, the agreements are presumed not to weaken competition in any meaningful way and are therefore deemed legal. However, if the exclusive dealing agreements extend to much of the market, they are then viewed as potentially harmful to competition. Other factors such as the history of entry and the behavior of prices are then examined to determine whether the anticompetitive threat is real. This is the rule of reason in practice.

## 19.4 FRANCHISING AND DIVISIONALIZATION

Our discussion of vertical relations has often included references to franchising. We have seen that franchising contracts can be a way to solve many of the pricing problems associated with upstream–downstream relations. Moreover, exclusive territorial agreements are often granted to franchisees, and exclusive dealing is often the way that franchisees are bound to the upstream franchiser. However we have not emphasized the fact that franchising is an increasingly popular way of doing business in both the United States and elsewhere. There has been a marked and rapid franchise growth both of firms actually supplying a specific line of products, such as Merle Norman cosmetics, and of firms essentially selling just a trademark and a way of doing business, such as McDonald's [Lafontaine (1993)]. In a single year McDonald's has opened between 800 and 1,000 new U.S. restaurants. Such behavior has led leading analysts to suspect that McDonald's and other franchisers believe that "whoever has the most outlets wins."[10]

The growing tolerance by the legal authorities may help explain the recent popularity of franchising as a way to solve vertical incentive problems. Still, the rapid growth of franchising leads to some puzzles. It seems clear, for example, that the expansion of several dominant franchisers, such as McDonald's, Burger King, and Wendy's, is sufficiently rapid that some of these new franchises will compete with existing franchises of these chains, despite the implicit promise of territorial integrity

---

9 See Federal Trade Commission, Decision and Order, In the Matter of Hale Products Inc., Docket No. C-3694, November 22, 1996, and Decision and Order, In the Matter of Waterous Company, Inc., Docket No. C-3694, November 22, 1996.
10 R. Gibson, "A Bit of Heartburn." *The Wall Street Journal*, April 17, 1996, p. A1.

(see the Reality Checkpoint: Big Mac Attacks). A somewhat similar puzzle arises when we consider the automobile industry. While growth here has been less rapid, it is nevertheless the case that, at least in the United States, each of the domestic car manufacturers has set up independent divisions that compete with each other. This intrabrand competition is then further extended to the retail level in which a Chevrolet dealer will compete with Buick and Pontiac dealers even though all three models are ultimately made by General Motors. Similarly, we observe Lincoln-Mercury and Ford dealers competing even though the Ford Motor Company is the parent of each division.

There are many advantages to the upstream firm having a large number of retail franchises or dealers. One of these stems from the now familiar problem of double marginalization. As we saw earlier, this problem is mitigated when the retail sector is competitive because competition reduces the markup at the retail level. Thus, oper-

 # Reality Checkpoint

## Big Mac Attacks . . . and the Franchisees Don't Like It!

The loyalty among owners of the nearly three thousand franchises for fast-food giant McDonald's has been legendary for forty years. These franchisees operate over three-fourths of McDonald's 11,368 restaurants and provided nearly $3 billion in sales in 1995. Over the years, such franchises have earned high profits. McDonald's itself has prospered, too. As a result, relations between the franchisees and the fast-food company have historically been friendly and, indeed, a standard to which other firms have aspired.

However, McDonald's growth dropped 2.5 percent in 1995–96 in the face of intensifying competition. The company reacted by cutting prices and changing its procedures with respect to franchises. These changes quickly led to something of a crisis in relations between McDonald's and its franchisees.

One of the disputes centered on McDonald's attempt to appropriate some of the franchisee's profit by opening up new stores (often close to existing franchises) in which it is a part owner and, therefore, claims part of the profit. McDonald's also implemented a new plan, Franchising 2000, exerting more detailed control over such franchise matters as cleanliness and customer service. Franchisees were graded on such features, and only those receiving As and Bs were eligible to buy more restaurants. In addition, McDonald's used Franchising 2000 to enforce a single pricing strategy, so that a Big Mac, for instance, would cost the same everywhere. In all these instances, McDonald's motivation seems clear. McDonald's feared that its franchisees provided too few services and charged too high a price and were cutting into the restaurant chain's profit. The moves were aimed at reversing the firm's then sluggish growth and grabbing a greater share of the profit for McDonald's.

**Source:** R. Gibson, "Some Franchisees Say Moves by McDonald's Hurt Their Operation." *The Wall Street Journal*, April 17, 1996, p. A1.

ating with many dealers may reflect an effort by upstream firms to lower the retail price of their product so as to penetrate the market more effectively.

From a spatial perspective, operating many dealers may also reflect an attempt to operate at many locations—defined either geographically or in terms of product attributes. By having a large number of dealers—each selling a product that is somewhat differentiated either by location or by various features—the manufacturer may be better able to meet the specific preferences of each individual customer. As we have seen, this enables the manufacturer to extract more surplus by charging customers an amount much closer to their maximum willingness to pay for their most preferred variety. In short, operating many dealerships may enhance the manufacturer's ability to price discriminate.

Finally, the operation of a large number of dealerships may be a means for an upstream firm to overcome the asymmetric information and attendant moral hazard problems that are often a feature of vertical relations between a manufacturer and a dealer. With just one dealer, the manufacturer cannot tell whether a low-profit outcome is due to bad luck—which could happen to anyone—or to the dealer's poor management. With many dealers, it is less likely that they all will have bad luck at the same time. Hence, the average performance of a large number of retailers may serve as a benchmark against which to measure the performance of each franchise individually.

All of the foregoing are perfectly plausible explanations as to why firms should operate many divisions or contract many franchises. It is possible, however, that the extensive use of divisionalization and franchising that we observe reflects instead a noncooperative equilibrium in which each manufacturer attempts to commit to a large output only to find that its rivals have done the same thing, with the result that industry price and profits are lower. This is the approach taken by Baye, Crocker, and Ju (1996), who illustrate the result with a two-stage model. In the first stage, each oligopoly firm chooses its number of competing divisions. Then, in the second stage, all the divisions from both firms compete together in a Cournot quantity-setting game.

Divisionalization is attractive because independent divisions, acting like Cournot firms, will ignore the negative, price-reducing effect that their output has on other divisions from the same firm. While this may seem paradoxical, the advantage that it offers is that, by ignoring this effect, the firm overall is able to commit to a larger amount of output in total than it could if it just operated as a single division. By committing to such a large output, the firm hopes to achieve the same sort of advantage obtained by a Stackelberg leader. As we shall see, however, this is not possible in this setting. Instead, each firm may find itself operating too many divisions but unable to reduce that number unless the other manufacturers do so as well.

We will present the Baye, Crocker, and Ju analysis in the framework of a simple duopoly model. We interpret the parent firms as upstream manufacturers or suppliers who sell to consumers through divisions (or franchises) in their downstream market. For simplicity, we ignore the service aspect of such retailing here so that we may focus on the implications of the model for divisionalization. Accordingly, let there be two identical upstream parent firms that each produce a homogenous product at constant marginal cost, $c$. The divisions of these firms produce at this marginal cost, as well. The inverse demand for the product in the downstream market is described by our usual linear function, $P = A - BQ$, where $Q$ is total market output.

In stage one of the game, each of the two firms chooses the number of divisions to operate in the downstream market. Let $n_1$ and $n_2$ denote the number of downstream divisions chosen by firms 1 and 2, respectively. A firm incurs a sunk cost $K$ in the first stage when it sets up a division. In stage two, all of the divisions act like independent players in a simultaneous-move Cournot game. By that we mean that each franchise acts like an independent profit maximizer.

To solve this game we begin with the stage two competition. Let $q_{ij}$ denote the quantity of output chosen by the $i$th division of firm $j$, where $i$ runs from 1 to $n_j$ and $j$ is equal to 1 or 2. Let $Q_{-ij}$ describe the total output of all divisions except the $i$th division of firm $j$. The profit of this division, $\pi_{ij}$, can then be written as

$$\pi_{ij}(q_{ij}, Q_{-ij}) = [A - (BQ_{-ij} + q_{ij})]q_{ij} - cq_{ij}, \tag{19.1}$$

where total market output, $Q$, is equal to $\displaystyle\sum_{j=1}^{2}\sum_{i=1}^{n_j} q_{ij}$.

The $i$th division of firm $j$ chooses output $q_{ij}$ to maximize its profit. This, of course, requires setting its marginal revenue to its marginal cost. This implies that the optimal output of any division $q_{ij}^*$ satisfies

$$A - BQ_{-ij} - 2Bq_{ij}^* = c. \tag{19.2}$$

Since all divisions are identical, they must all choose the same optimal output in equilibrium—that is, $q_{ij}^* = q^*$ for all $i, j$. This greatly simplifies matters. Since there are $n_1 + n_2$ divisions in total, $Q_{-ij}$ must equal $(n_1 + n_2 - 1)q^*$. Substitution into equation (19.2) then yields

$$q^* = \frac{A - c}{(n_1 + n_2 + 1)B}, \tag{19.3}$$

from which it follows that the total industry output $Q$ and associated market price $P$ in stage two are

$$Q = \left(\frac{n_1 + n_2}{n_1 + n_2 + 1}\right)\left(\frac{A - c}{B}\right) \text{ and } P = \frac{A + (n_1 + n_2)c}{n_1 + n_2 + 1}. \tag{19.4}$$

At this price, each division will earn a stage two profit $\Pi_{ij}$, given by

$$\Pi_{ij} = \frac{(A - c)^2}{B(n_1 + n_2 + 1)^2}. \tag{19.5}$$

The two firms who anticipate competition among divisions in stage two along the lines just described must decide in stage one how many divisions to set up.

Firm 1's profit can be written as $\Pi_1 = \displaystyle\sum_{i=1}^{n_1} \Pi_{i1} - Kn_1$, where $i_1$ is the stage two profit of the $i$th division of firm 1. Since equation (19.5) shows the profit earned by each of firm 1's $n_1$ divisions in stage two, we can rewrite firm 1's overall profit as

$$\Pi_1(n_1, n_2) = n_1\frac{(A - c)^2}{B(n_1 + n_2 + 1)^2} - Kn_1. \tag{19.6}$$

Firm 1 chooses its total number of divisions $n_1^*$ so as to maximize its profit, $\Pi_1(n_1, n_2)$, when firm 2 has $n_2$ divisions of its own. In other words, firm 1 wants to choose a best response $n_1^*$ to the number of divisions, $n_2$, that firm 2 has. It is straightforward to show that this best response function satisfies[11]

$$\frac{(A - c)^2}{B(1 + n_1^* + n_2)^2}\left(1 - \frac{2n_1^*}{(1 + n_1^* + n_2)}\right) - K = 0. \tag{19.7}$$

Since firm 2 is identical to firm 1, we have a symmetric condition for $n_2^*$. So, using the notation that $n_1^* = n_2^* = n^*$, and recognizing that this symmetry implies that $n_1^* + n_2^* = 2n^*$, we can solve for $n^*$. This solution is

$$n^* = \frac{1}{2}\left[\left(\frac{(A - c)^2}{BK}\right)^{1/3} - 1\right]. \tag{19.8}$$

The insight of the model is revealed by equation (19.8). This shows that the greater is $(A - c)$ and/or the smaller is $K$, the greater is the number of divisions chosen by firm 1 and firm 2 in stage one of the game. Recall that the difference between price and cost, $P - c$, is $(A - c)/2$ under a monopoly. One implication of the model then is that firms will create more divisions the greater the maximum potential price-cost differential. However, having more divisions is tantamount to having more Cournot-type units. We know from Chapter 9 that this brings us closer to the competitive equilibrium. Hence, the greater the possible markup under a monopoly, the greater the divisionalization or franchising that takes place under a duopoly, and the more closely the two duopolists will end up approximating the competitive equilibrium. This obviously is not their goal. The problem, though, is the familiar "prisoners' dilemma," in which the best response of each firm acting separately is not optimal from the standpoint of the two firms collectively. Such analysis may help to explain the wave of divisionalization and franchising that we have recently witnessed in U.S. markets. It also suggests once again that the proliferation of such vertical arrangements may not be as harmful to consumer interests as the restrictions embodied in the accompanying contracts might at first seem to imply.

## Practice Problem 19.1

Assume two firms confront each other in an industry in which the inverse demand is $P = 100 - Q$. Let marginal cost be constant at $c = 25$, and let the sunk cost of setting up a division be $K = 45$.

a. According to equation (19.8), how many divisions will each firm operate?
b. According to equation (19.6), what profit will each firm make if each operates the number of divisions derived in part (a)?
c. According to equations (19.4) and (19.5), what will be the industry price, $P$, and output, $Q$?

---

[11] The response function in equation (19.7) is derived by taking the derivative of the profit function (19.6) with respect to $n_1$ and setting it to zero. This technique assumes that we can ignore the constraint that $n_1$ be an integer.

d. Calculate the output chosen by a monopolist and the price at which this output would sell. Compare this with your answers in part (b).

# 19.5 AFTERMARKETS

The vertical restrictions that we have examined so far reflect constraints on the sale of the same product as it moves through the product chain from the upstream producer to the downstream dealer. In recent years, a different kind of vertical restriction has caught the interest of economists—one that is closely related to the tying arrangements that we considered in Chapter 9. This restriction effectively involves an excusive selling arrangement in what are known as aftermarkets.

The key legal case in the aftermarkets debate is the *Kodak* case. The specifics of that case are as follows. Kodak was one of a number of manufacturers of micrographic equipment—used for creating, viewing, and printing microfilm and microfiche—and office copiers. This was the primary or foremarket. However, Kodak also provided repair parts and services to these machines through a nationwide network of technicians. Indeed, Kodak advertised the quality of this network as a means of persuading consumers to buy its machines in the first place. Because no one needs micrographic or copier parts and services if they have not already purchased a micrographic machine or copier, the parts and services market is referred to as the aftermarket.

Of course, just as in the foremarket, Kodak had competition in the aftermarket. There were many independent firms providing parts and services to firms using Kodak's office machines. However, to the extent that these firms needed replacement parts, they relied on Kodak to provide them. Kodak was happy enough to do so until it lost a service contract with Computer Service Corporation (CSC) to an independent firm, Image Technical Services (ITS). After that, Kodak announced a new policy of not providing replacement parts to any independent service provider. Effectively, Kodak agreed to an exclusive selling arrangement with its service network. It would only sell its repair parts to that group. As Kodak enforced the new policy more and more strictly, ITS and other independents filed a lawsuit contesting Kodak's action.

In court, Kodak asked for a summary dismissal of the plaintiffs' case. Kodak's basic argument ran along the following lines. There were many other producers of photographic office equipment. That is, Kodak faced competition in the foremarket. As a result, Kodak argued it could not possibly exert monopoly power in the aftermarket. Before making a purchase in the foremarket, consumers consider the full cost of, say, a copier—both the price at the initial time of purchase and the price of services later in time. If Kodak were to try to charge a high price in the aftermarket for services, it would attract foremarket customers only if it reduced its machine prices by a corresponding amount. Hence, Kodak argued that it could not impose monopoly pricing in the aftermarket. The Supreme Court rejected Kodak's contention. Later, a jury turned in a verdict against Kodak.

The *Kodak* case has been followed by a number of similar cases (see the Reality Checkpoint: Aftermarkets After Kodak). Again, the central issue is whether and how a firm can exercise monopoly power in the aftermarket if it does not have such power in the foremarket. It seems clear that this will not happen if consumers find it easy to switch service providers in the aftermarket in the face of any price increase by one such supplier. That is, there must be some sort of lock-in or switching cost such that once

## ✓ Reality Checkpoint

### Aftermarkets after Kodak

As noted in the text, the controversy over the aftermarkets issue raised in the *Kodak* case has continued to this day. Two cases subsequently decided by different circuit courts amply illustrate the continuing tension.

The case of *Allen-Myland v. IBM*, 33 F.3d 194 (3rd Cir. 1994), involved a suit filed by an independent firm, Allen-Myland, that specialized in the maintenance and upgrading of IBM mainframe computers. The upgrade market was a substantial one—in some years as valuable as the mainframe market itself. At one point, Allen-Myland had half the upgrade market. Then IBM introduced a set of new policies. Specifically, IBM began to offer lower installation prices for firms that committed to using only IBM's upgrade services. Subsequently using an independent like Allen-Myland would then involve a financial penalty for breeching this contract. IBM also started to require customers to return used parts to them, thus drying up a potential alternative source of parts. Although the District Court originally ruled for IBM, the Appeals Court overturned the ruling noting that IBM could have substantial power in the upgrade market.

In *PSI v. Honeywell*, 104 F.3d 811 (6th Cir. 1997), the Court considered the case of PSI Repair Services, Inc., an independent firm engaged in the repair of computer systems. PSI filed suit under the Sherman Act against the computer manufacturer Honeywell, Inc. The basis of the suit was the fact that Honeywell forced computer chip makers to refrain from selling parts unique to Honeywell computers to any independent repair services such as PSI and also to any Honeywell customers. PSI contended that this practice was precisely what was found to be illegal in the *Kodak* case. After losing in the District Court, PSI appealed to the Sixth Circuit U.S. Court of Appeals. That court also rejected PSI's claims, citing two reasons. First, the Court noted that unlike Kodak, Honeywell's refusal to deal was not a change in policy but something that it had always done. Second, the Court rejected the assertion of aftermarket power based on lock-ins. The Court instead said that the relevant market was not the aftermarket for Honeywell parts but rather the equipment market shared by Honeywell and its competitors. Consumers were free to purchase computers from other sources with different servicing policies.

**Sources:** *Antitrust Litigation Reporter*, June 5, 1997; and G. Graham, "IBM Sent Back By Appeals Court To Face Retrial In Anti-Trust Suit." *Financial Times*, August 19, 1994, p. 6.

a firm has, say, a Kodak copier, it cannot easily switch to another copier by selling its Kodak machine in a used-machine market and buying an alternative machine for which no services are excluded from obtaining parts. This seems a reasonable assumption in many cases so long as the used machine market is not very well developed.

However, if consumers are forward looking, the presence of lock-in or switching cost effects may not be enough to permit the exercise of pricing power in an aftermarket. If firms understand that buying a Kodak machine also means later buying expensive Kodak parts and service, Kodak will only sell its machine by cutting its price below that of its rivals for whose machines cheaper service is available. Thus, Kodak (and other companies) since has argued that it has no incentive to raise aftermarket prices because this will simply require that Kodak lower the price in the primary market by an offsetting amount.

We think that there are at least two reasons to suspect that the lock-in effect may translate into the ability to raise price above cost in the aftermarket. The first is simply that consumers may not be so forward looking as to consider the machine and its subsequent service as one integral purchase. To do so would require that they acquire information regarding their future service needs and future service costs many years in the future, and that they do this across all machine brands. This is both difficult and expensive and quite probably not worthwhile. Yet if consumers do not do this, then a firm with a lock-in technology can raise its aftermarket price without lowering its primary market price.

The second reason is more subtle. It is that firms such as Kodak may have no credible way to commit to a low service price far into the future because there are always some locked-in customers who have recently bought the machine and who can be exploited. There are many ways to make this point. To see it in a simple context, consider the following scenario.

Imagine that there are two producers of copying machines. Each machine lasts potentially for two periods. A machine runs without problems the first period but has a 50 percent chance of breaking down in the second period. When it breaks down, the firm can have it repaired but only by using the repair service of the company that manufactured the machine. For simplicity, we will assume that the costs of producing the machine and also of repairing it are each zero.

Consumers are assumed to derive $50 of value from the machine for each period that it runs well. However, once a consumer buys a particular brand and integrates it into their production, the cost of switching to an alternative brand, setting up, and reintegrating it into the firm's operations midway through the machine's expected life is also $50. In any given period, there are equal numbers of consumers who are in the market for new machines and consumers who have already owned a machine for one period.

If consumers are forward looking, they will be willing to pay $75 for a new machine. This is the expected value they will receive over the machine's two-period life. With 50 percent probability, the machine will run fine for two periods and generate $100 worth of value. With an equal probability, it will break down in the second period, at which point switching to an alternative machine is not worthwhile given the switching cost.

Of course, the price of a new machine will be far less than $75. Indeed, competition between the two firms will likely lower this price quite close to cost. However, the price for repairs is another story. Consumers who have bought a machine that has broken down after one period either have to do without a machine and lose $50 of value or get their machine fixed. As long as the cost of fixing the machine is less than $50, these consumers will be willing to pay for the repairs.

There is, in other words, a time inconsistency in the firm–customer relationship in that consumer behavior changes once a machine is bought. By the second period, whatever price consumers paid for the machine initially is an irrelevant sunk cost. As a result, the firm always has some motivation to raise the repair price and extract some surplus from these consumers. Note that even if the repair price rises to close to $50, consumers with a broken machine will still be willing to pay to have it fixed since they get $50 of value from the machine working. In other words, even with that high of a repair price, the expected value of a machine when it is first purchased remains at $75. That is, the willingness to pay of forward-looking consumers will not be changed even if they understand that the price for repairs, should they be needed, is close to $50. However, $50 is well above the cost of repairs. Thus, the equilibrium is one in which the repair price exceeds marginal cost and everyone, including consumers, understands that this will be the case.

The model just used is a simple one. However, its basic point can be generalized in a more sophisticated model as Borenstein, Mackie-Mason, and Netz (2000) have shown. Indeed, recent work by Gabaix and Laibson (2004) suggests that the presence of some unsophisticated consumers can interact with the lock-in effects just described in a way that makes firms unwilling to announce low prices for the aftermarket repairs even if they could and even when competition is strong.

Suppose that while most consumers are rational, there are a few consumers who, if repairs are needed, do not look at the alternative of buying and integrating a new machine but just purchase the repairs as long as these cost $50 or less. Suppose further that, unlike our earlier case, the true cost of switching to a new machine and integrating it with one's operations is only $25. Rational consumers will foresee the possibility of machine failure and the need to switch. Competition may lead to market entry until all profits are exhausted, implying that the price of machine and repairs *together* has to be close to cost. This does not mean, however, that the equilibrium price of both the machine and repairs has to equal zero. Instead, the outcome is likely to be one in which each firm sells its machine below cost but sells repairs well above cost, say at $50. Firms will lose money on rational consumers because these consumers will buy the machine at a price below cost and, if it breaks down, pay $25 in switching costs. The firms will recoup these losses from the unsophisticated consumers who pay $50 for repairs rather than switching. Note that each firm has very little incentive to announce or commit to a low repair price. If it does, this will only affect the demand of the people who are forward looking and consider that repair price in their decision making—the sophisticated consumers. Yet for these consumers, the current arrangement in which they get a subsidy on their initial machine purchase is beneficial. If a firm announced low repair prices, it would lose sophisticated consumers, who would now understand that the lower repair price will force the firm to raise the machine price. Meanwhile, that lower price will reduce the profit earned from the unsophisticated consumers. Think about it. Hotels often charge a very low room price while saying nothing about the fees incurred for making a phone call. Car rental companies set a low price for the car itself, but charge supracompetitive rates for insurance and gasoline. In neither case, do the firms try to compete by announcing low prices for their aftermarket products. They have no incentive to do so. The price of the aftermarket products thus remains inefficiently high and, in this example, the price of the foremarket product is inefficiently low.

## SUMMARY

Contracts between manufacturers and the various retailers that sell the manufactured products directly to consumers include a variety of nonprice restrictions. These may include an exclusive dealing restriction that the retailer not sell the products of any other manufacturer, or exclusive selling and territorial arrangements that restrain the manufacturer from permitting any other retailer from selling the manufacturer's product. Because these restrictions so clearly bear the appearance of a restraint on trade, they cannot hope but fall under suspicion as anticompetitive.

In reality, however, there may be many benign explanations behind such restrictions. Often they may serve to ensure adequate promotional activities and other consumer services. They may also be useful in creating an environment in which retailers can better handle demand shocks.

However, there can be little doubt that many nonprice vertical restraints are motivated by a desire to soften either interbrand competition, intrabrand competition, or both. Indeed, this may occur even when this is not the main objective of the parties to the agreement. Effectively, exclusive dealing and sales agreements are a grant of monopoly power and the potential for harm to consumers is always present. For this reason, there seems to be little alternative to evaluating such restrictions on a case-by-case method, applying some criterion of reasonability as to whether the benefits of the agreement outweigh the costs.

An especially complicated vertical relationship arises in the context of so-called aftermarkets. For a number of technological goods, the firms that supply the initial equipment also compete in an aftermarket to provide repair services to those machines. Frequently, these firms impose vertical restrictions that require that machine owners buy their repair services from the same firm from which they bought the machine. The effects of such lock-in costs are difficult to determine. However, it is plausible that these restrictions give firms the ability to charge supracompetitive prices in the aftermarket even when the primary market has lots of competition. This issue has yet to be resolved fully.

Before concluding we make two further points. First, we note that in many respects, the retailer acts as an agent on behalf of the manufacturer. It learns about consumer tastes; makes display, promotional, and other service decisions; and sets the final consumer price. Consequently, the vertical relationship between the producer and the dealer is a principal–agent relationship akin to the relationship between a client and lawyer, or between shareholders and management. The contractual issues that arise between manufacturer and retailer are part of a broader set of questions that arise in connection with contracts that govern all principal–agent relationships. In turn, this raises important issues in the theory of the firm. For example, what is the difference between a producer connected to its retailer by means of a formal contract and a producer that simply is fully integrated into the retail market or a producer that operates a retail division? Why do firms choose one form of organization over another? We do not answer these questions here. However, we do want to acknowledge that the issue of vertical relationships is part of a larger question regarding the boundaries and limits of the firm.

Our second point is simply that an analysis of vertical relationships can help explain many of the observed features of the retail market such as those noted in our parable of holiday shopping at the start of Chapter 18. Food, such as ready-to-eat cereal, is likely one of those goods about which many consumers feel perfectly able to judge for themselves. For these goods, the retailer provides little information that will directly influence the consumer's purchase decision. Hence, we should expect such products to be widely available through many outlets. This is not the case for automobiles and gasoline (that is, car servicing). It may not even be the case for toys. For such products, consumers may feel much well-informed, so that the retailer takes on more of a physician's role in actually prescribing the product choice. Under such circumstances, a manufacturer will wish to make sure that the retailer's efforts are directed to only one product line. From the viewpoint of Chevrolet, a dealer selling both Chevies and Fords presents real problems.[12] The maker of either Lego or Lionel electric trains may similarly feel concerned about a store selling both its product as well as one of the many HO scale rival models.

Of course, the vertical arrangements that we observe may also be explained as efforts by automakers, oil firms, and electric train companies and others to limit either interbrand or intrabrand competition. Again, only a detailed examination of each case can reveal who gains and who loses from the restriction in question. Whether the nonprice vertical restrictions that we see in practice reflect concerns for consumer services or efforts to soften price competition, one point remains. When we apply the insights of the neoclassical approach regarding cost structures and strategic interaction, we can explain a good bit of what we observe in actual markets. All that is required is that we be willing to explore fully all the logical implications of that analysis.

# PROBLEMS

1. Most beer companies impose an exclusive dealing clause on the supermarkets that sell their products. Discuss whether you think this practice will yield efficient market outcomes.

2. General Motors, Ford, and Daimler-Chrysler all operate many divisions of automobile lines, for example, Chevrolet, Pontiac, Cadillac, and Buick. Discuss the motivation for this practice. Who do you think this practice benefits the most, automakers or consumers?

3. In Europe, automobile dealers have traditionally been granted exclusive territories. Do you think that this practice should be legal?

4. Review the model of Rasmussen, Ramseyer, and Wiley (1991) from Chapter 13. Why are scale economies important for this argument that exclusive dealing can deter entry?

5. Most McDonald's hamburger outlets are owned by individual entrepreneurs who pay franchise fees to McDonald's for the right to use the McDonald's name and recipes. Recipes for food at least as good as McDonald's are easy to find and cost less than the fees these entrepreneurs pay to McDonald's.

   a. Given the lower cost of equally good products, why are franchise holders willing to pay so much money to the franchiser corporation?

   b. Who would be willing to pay more for the right to use the McDonald's name—an outlet located in the center of Centerville, or one that would do the same amount of business at the interstate turnpike?

   c. What are the incentives for McDonald's to require franchisees to buy hamburger buns, meat, napkins, and other supplies from it rather than from other, possibly lower-cost local suppliers, other than the incentive of removing double marginalization?

---

12 Note that both gasoline—which must be stored in large underground tanks—and cars—which must be kept in stock to meet consumer demand—have very large inventory costs at the retail level. This may be another reason that car dealers and gasoline stations typically offer few brand choices.

# REFERENCES

Aghion, P., and P. Bolton. 1987. "Contracts as a Barrier to Entry." *American Economic Review* 77 (June): 388–401.

Bonanno, G., and J. Vickers. 1988. "Vertical Separation." *Journal of Industrial Economics* 36 (March): 257–65.

Borenstein, S., J. Mackie-Mason, and J. Netz. 2000. "Exercising Market Power in Proprietary Aftermarkets." *Journal of Economics and Management Strategy* 9 (Summer): 157–88.

Baye, Michael, K. Crocker, and J. Ju. 1996. "Divisionalization, Franchising, and Divestiture Incentives in Oligopoly." *American Economic Review* 86 (March): 223–36.

Bernheim, B. D., and M. Whinston. 1990. "Multimarket Contact and Collusive Behavior." *Rand Journal of Economics* 21 (Spring): 1–26.

Besanko, David, and M. K. Perry. 1994. "Exclusive Dealing in a Spatial Model of Retail Competition." *International Journal of Industrial Organization* 12 (Fall): 297–329.

Gabaix, X., and D. Laibson. 2004. "Shrouded Attributes and Information Suppression in Competitive Markets." MIT, Department of Economics, Working Paper (March).

Marvel, Howard. 1982. "Exclusive Dealing." *Journal of Law and Economics* 25 (April): 1–25.

Matthewson, G. F., and R. A. Winter. 1987. "The Competitive Effects of Vertical Agreements: Comment." *American Economic Review* 77: 1057–62.

O'Brien, D. P., and G. Schaffer. 1994. "The Welfare Effects of Forbidding Discriminatory Discounts: A Secondary Line Analysis of Robinson-Patman." *Journal of Law, Economics, and Organization* 10 (October): 296–318.

Posner, R. 1981. "The Next Step in the Antitrust Treatment of Restricted Distribution: Per se Legality." *University of Chicago Law Review* 48: 6–26.

Rasmussen, E., J. Ramseyer, and J. Wiley. 1991. "Naked Exclusion." *American Economic Review* 81 (December): 1137–45.

Rey, P., and J. Stiglitz. 1995. "The Role of Exclusive Territories in Producer Competition." *Rand Journal of Economics* 26 (Fall): 431–51.

# Part six

## Nonprice Competition

# Nonprice Competition

Firms compete in many dimensions. So far, we have examined strategic interaction primarily in those cases in which firms compete in either price or quantity. We now consider two other possible arenas of competition, advertising (Chapters 20 and 21) and research and development (Chapters 22 and 23).

The economic function of advertising has long been an issue of interest. Initially, economists focused on the anticompetitive role that advertising might play, principally by building brand loyalty that would both soften price competition between brands and deter entry by new brands. Initial empirical evidence seemed to support precisely this interpretation of advertising's central role.

However, more modern analysis has shown that the effects of advertising are subtle and complex. For example, market power may be more important in causing firms to advertise than is advertising in causing market power. Moreover, advertising may perform a number of functions that benefit consumers. It may indicate the quality of the goods promoted or other useful consumer information. In addition, by letting consumers know which firms are selling which goods and at what prices, advertising may intensify price competition as the recent experience of e-commerce suggests. We examine each of these issues in Chapters 20 and 21. Because the workings of advertising are complicated, this requires careful modeling and evaluation of the evidence. The analysis of advertising as a phenomenon requires a thorough understanding of how advertising works.

We then turn to the analysis of research and development (R&D). Here we begin with a well-known proposition typically referred to as the Schumpeterian hypothesis after the great mid-twentieth century economist, Joseph Schumpeter. In brief, this hypothesis argues that large firms and concentrated industries will be more conducive to technological progress than will the idealized competitive market comprised of numerous small firms with very little concentration. Chapter 22 addresses explicitly the nature of R&D competition and precisely the sort of market structure that will most encourage technical progress. Here, we also explore the possibility of inter-firm cooperation on research projects. Then, in Chapter 23, we consider the design of patent policy. Such policy must walk a thin line between granting wide access to available technologies while simultaneously encouraging the development of new ideas and new goods by conferring monopoly rights to the creators of such new products. This tension lies at the heart of our analysis of optimal patent policy just as it lies at the heart of the actual policy debate.

# Advertising, Market Power, and Information

## Chapter 20

Large retail stores that sell many different kinds of goods and many different brands of each good are a relatively recent phenomenon. A customer buying a pair of shoes in the early twentieth century would have faced a different shopping experience from the one faced today. Our customer would have been restricted to making this purchase in a specialized shoe store carrying only one or at most two brands, or possibly a cobbler's shop that made its own shoes. Moreover, the consumer of 100 years ago would also have to deal directly with the store proprietor and not been able to examine and compare the merchandise directly.

How different the modern shopping experience is from the practices of the not-so-distant past. Today's consumer can go to a shoe or department store and see more than a dozen different brands. Once there, the consumer can personally handle and inspect each different style without any need to deal with a store employee. Only when trying on a specific pair of shoes will the consumer sometimes require assistance from a store employee. Indeed, consumers now may choose directly from perhaps a hundred different brands and never deal with a sales representative at all simply by purchasing shoes over the Web.

What has made this dramatic change in the nature of retailing possible? Our reference to the Web provides a clue. The retailing revolution of the twentieth century owes much to the advent of mass media, specifically, radio and television. This technological change made it possible for manufacturers to reach their consumers en masse and promote their products directly to the public. Using wide-scale advertising, manufacturers themselves were able to promote the important features of their products to a wide target audience. As a result, the task of selling goods at the retail level required much less specialized expertise, and in turn this greatly facilitated the formation of large-scale retail establishments such as department stores and discount stores, selling several varieties of hundreds of different kinds of goods. As mass communication technology continued to evolve, these retailers were joined by large mail-order businesses and, more recently, by e-tailers. The fact is that the advent of large-scale advertising by manufacturers has been the source of a major revolution in the way consumers learn about the products that are out there waiting for them to buy.[1]

Yet while it is clear that the emergence of large-scale advertising has played a crucial role in the development of retailing, the precise role played by advertising is less clear. We do not know exactly how advertising affects the consumer's decision of whether to buy and if so, what brand to buy. Consider, for example, television ads for Nike shoes. These ads often tell little about the nature of the shoes and instead feature a collage of images accompanied by the Nike Company's famous "swoosh" logo. How does this affect a consumer's decision to buy? Or does the fact that Nike is a corporate sponsor and apparel provider for the 2004 U.S. Olympic team affect a consumer's decision of whether to purchase Nike shoes?

---

1 For a good discussion of this revolutionizing effect of modern advertising and other aspects of advertising and promotional activities, see Pope (1983). A classic piece on the role of price versus nonprice (advertising) competition is Stigler (1968).

The question as to how ads like those run by Nike actually work is important for many reasons. To begin with, Nike is not alone. Its promotional efforts are typical of many firms marketing consumer products, and these efforts are costly. Advertising on network television can cost millions of dollars for a single minute of airtime. For Super Bowl 2004, the average price of even a 30-second spot was a record-breaking $2.25 million. Yet Anheuser-Busch, Frito-Lay, Pepsi-Cola, Procter & Gamble, and others all bought spots for that game. We need to have some idea of how advertising works in order to understand the incentives for these firms to bear such costs. Only then can we examine the decisions of firms to incur the costs of advertising to promote their products and why firms in some industries do so much more advertising than firms in other industries. Understanding how advertising works allows us to move on and then investigate how advertising affects the strategic interaction between firms, and what all this means for the consumer.

Our goal in the next two chapters is to understand the role of advertising and the implications that this carries for strategic interaction in the marketplace and consumer welfare. We will focus most of our attention on the advertising that is done by firms that manufacture the product being advertised, rather than the promotional activities of retailers that sell these products. The promotional efforts of large, national or international manufacturing firms differ markedly from the advertising of local retailers. Retailers' promotional efforts are aimed at a local market, and their advertisements are often informative, telling consumers the price, availability or the inventory of specific items, store location, and so on. In contrast, the large-scale advertising campaigns of manufacturers are typically aired or circulated to millions of potential customers over a wide geographic area. We explore these advertising efforts because they loom so large in the overall picture.

The Nike example suggests that much of the advertising done by manufacturers contains little explicit information. This is not, however, a criticism of such promotional efforts. Advertising by manufacturers may not be viewed in the same way by consumers as, say, information found in consumer guidebooks or *Consumer Reports*. Consumers are aware that the firm that manufactures the good is also providing the advertising for the good. Consumers therefore may expect to find a different kind of information—information that is less objective or less factual—when they view a manufacturer's commercial than when they read a review from *Consumer Reports*. In addition, advertising is available to consumers for free. No one has to pay to view a Nike commercial or to read a Nike billboard ad, despite the fact that such advertising is costly to produce. In contrast, consumers typically have to pay for informational sources such as guidebooks, magazines like *Consumer Reports*, and other publications, which are only available to those paying the purchase price. We do not expect firms to give costly items away for free unless they gain some offsetting advantage. The fact that firms expend considerable amounts on advertising suggests that it brings benefits even if advertising earns no direct fee itself. What is this gain and more generally what are the economic consequences of advertising?

One way to view advertising is as an essential element of competition among firms selling different brands of the same good. In this case, high advertising in an industry would be a sign of good health—a way to increase consumer awareness of different brands that intensifies price competition to the benefit of consumers. On the other hand, advertising can also be seen as a way to differentiate one manufacturer's brand from another and thereby weaken competition by making it more difficult for a consumer to switch from one brand to another. High advertising in this case would be a sign of monopoly power. Our analysis will hopefully help us determine which, if either, of these two cases is more likely. We should also note, however, that there is a long-standing policy concern that advertising expenditures overall could be socially wasteful—that is, that firms spend far too much on promotional activities that yield little net gain for anyone and far too little on more important matters such as product development. Our analysis should also help to address this issue. All of these issues are important. However, gaining insight into such matters requires that we learn the underlying economic logic behind advertising. Why do firms do it and how does it work?

## 20.1 THE EXTENT OF ADVERTISING

The phenomenon of advertising is something of a paradox. Promotional efforts such as TV commercials are often barely tolerated by social critics. More often than not, advertising is disparaged as something that is wrong with contemporary society—something that tricks us into wanting and even buying things we don't need. Yet at the same time, advertising is ubiquitous. It airs on our television sets and radios, accounts for many of the pages in magazines and daily newspapers, dots the landscape and cityscape with billboards, and even shows up on our T-shirts and other apparel. However much one might be critical of advertising, it seems that we can hardly live without it.

In fact, the magnitude of the advertising phenomenon as reflected in total dollars of expenditure is staggering. In 2002, for instance, U.S. firms spent about $236.9 billion dollars or approximately 2.3 percent of the gross domestic product on advertising.[2] This is not unusual. From the 1940s on, advertising expenditures in the United States have consistently claimed about 2 percent of the U.S. national income.

Roughly 58 percent of total advertising expenditure is measured media advertising. This includes spending on nationwide broadcast and cable television networks, radio networks, national magazines, newspapers, yellow pages, and the Internet. The other 42 percent is nonmeasured or only indirectly measured media spending. This category includes expenditures on direct mailings, promotions, coupons, catalogs, business publications, and the sponsorship of special events. Retail advertising is often more heavily concentrated in nonmeasured media spending.

The number one advertiser in the United States for the year 2002 was General Motors (GM). In that year, GM spent about $3.65 billion on advertising, about two-thirds of which ($2.45 billion) was allocated to measured media spending. Similarly, the consumer goods giant Procter & Gamble ranked number three and spent $2.67 billion, of which 76 percent was spent on measured media spending. In contrast, the fourth-ranked firm, the pharmaceutical company Pfizer, spent $2.57 billion on advertising, of which only 32 percent was on measured media. Our analysis of advertising will focus on measured media spending. This is because the promotional campaigns in the nonmeasured category include mainly coupons and free samples. As we saw in Chapters 5 through 8, these can be analyzed as price discrimination strategies. It is not surprising, then, that pharmaceutical companies' advertising expenditures are more of the nonmeasured kind.

---

2  The data on advertising expenditures at the aggregate and firm level have been collected from the Web site AdAge.com.

Clearly, whether we look at total spending or just spending on measured media, there are important differences between firms. However, some of these differences are due to size. GM, after all, is gigantic, and giants are likely to spend more. To get a better picture of the importance of advertising efforts by manufacturing firms we instead focus on advertising expenditure as a percentage of sales revenue. This fraction—the advertising-to-sales ratio—also varies enormously across products. For example, the ratio averages about 2.4 percent in the automobile industry but ranges as high as 12 percent in the market for soaps and cleaners. Perhaps even more surprising is the fact that even for firms that sell the same kind of product in essentially the same kind of way there are different advertising-to-sales ratios. For example, in 2002 the advertising-to-sales ratio of Ford was 2.1 percent, whereas for Volkswagen it was 3.8 percent and for Mitsubishi it was 5.8 percent. In the pharmaceutical industry the variations are even more marked. In 2002 the advertising-to-sales ratio at Merck & Co was 2.7 percent, at Wyeth it was 7.8 percent, and at Pfizer it was 12.4 percent. Among firms marketing personal care products, the advertising-to-sales ratio varies from 4.1 percent at Kimberly-Clark to 28 percent at Estee Lauder Co.

In considering both the scale of advertising overall and its variation across firms, economists have made some consistent findings. One of these is that the profitability of a consumer goods industry appears to be positively correlated with the advertising intensity in that same industry.[3] In particular, consumer goods such as cereals, perfumes, soaps, and pharmaceutical drugs have traditionally been characterized by relatively high profit rates and also by high advertising expenditures relative to sales. In contrast, other consumer goods such as hats, carpets, and jewelry have both lower profit rates and lower advertising expenditures. A further and equally interesting finding is that the pattern of advertising across industries has remained relatively constant over time—and even across countries. Industries that had relatively high advertising expenditures in the 1950s continue to have relatively high advertising expenditures in the 2000s, and do so whether they are located in North America or in Europe.

## 20.2 ADVERTISING, PRODUCT DIFFERENTIATION, AND MONOPOLY POWER

Economists have long been interested in understanding the role of advertising in the marketplace. Some of the early writings came in the early 1950s and 1960s. Much of this work concluded with a fairly negative assessment that advertising is a socially wasteful way for firms to compete [Kaldor (1950), Galbraith (1958), Solow (1967)]. Essentially, these studies view advertising as an effort undertaken by the firm to alter consumer tastes and to persuade consumers that there are few if any substitutes for its products. To the extent that this effort is successful with at least some consumers, the firm will enjoy some monopoly power because it will not lose its customers to a rival should the firm raise its price. Yet while beneficial for the firm, these efforts in persuasion are bad for consumers not only because of the monopoly power and re-

---

3    This is one of the nine stylized facts on industry profitability in the United States reported in Schmalensee (1989), and is based on the studies by Comanor and Wilson (1967, 1974), among others. Their findings have been replicated by other studies done on U.S. data as well as on data from other countries. Schmalensee's (1972) early work also remains relevant.

sultant deadweight loss, but also because these advertising efforts are costly in themselves. Since the differentiation achieved by advertising was not considered to be "real" but instead an artificial distinction created in the consumer's mind, the resources expended in creating that differentiation were seen as wasted. Accordingly, they would be better used to produce real goods and services.[4]

Recall that the advent of wide-scale advertising followed closely the advent of mass production technology or economies of scale in production. If it were substantial, the persuasive role of mass advertising would then enable manufacturing firms to expand their market and sell more, and hence exploit economies of scale in production. The fear was that the outcome of this would be a more concentrated industrial structure. Moreover, persuasive advertising could deter potential competition and new entrants from coming into the market. Indeed, the great early industrial organization economist Joe Bain explicitly considered the advertising-to-sales ratio of an industry as a proxy for barriers to entry. Many other economists—particularly those working in the earlier structure-conduct-performance framework—essentially shared this view. The fear was that established firms would have a history of advertising and therefore possess a market identity for their products that any new entrant would find difficult to overcome. As a result, the incumbent firm would be more immune to potential competitors. (See the discussion of the ReaLemon case in Chapter 21.)

It is worth noting that the fear that advertising would confer monopoly power was not without empirical support. In fact, there is both anecdotal and formal evidence to support the hypothesis that wide-scale advertising enhances a firm's market power and its ability to raise price above cost. The casual evidence is readily obtainable from a trip to the local drug store or supermarket. Anyone who compares the price of a nationally advertised brand of pain reliever with that of its generic substitute will find that the national brand sells at a noticeable premium. The same is true for soft drinks, shampoos, laundry bleaches, and a host of other products. In these cases and others, substitutes are available that are chemically identical or nearly identical to the nationally advertised brand. Hence, production costs should be roughly the same. In turn, this implies that the higher price commanded by the national brand reflects an increase in the markup over cost that monopoly power makes possible.

Formal evidence along these same lines has been provided by the many statistical studies that find a significant positive relationship between advertising and industry profitability across a wide range of consumer goods industries. The pioneering work in this regard is that of Comanor and Wilson (1967). Their basic finding that industries with high profitability are associated with a high advertising-to-sales ratio has been replicated many times both for different time periods and different countries.[5] A more specific study is that done by Nichols (1951). He focuses on the American cigarette market and offers statistical evidence that the major brands relied heavily on advertising to differentiate their products and thereby insulate themselves from price competition, especially that of "penny cigarettes."

There are, however, reasons to be wary of the view that advertising strengthens market power and inhibits competition. First, there is a fine line between persuasion and information. After all, persuasion requires more than empty words. Usually to persuade the consumer some information must be given. To the extent that advertising provides information it will play a useful role, and one that could promote

---

4  Viewed in this light, advertising is much like rent-seeking behavior. See, for example, Posner (1975).
5  See, for example, Lambin (1976), Geroski (1982), and Round (1983).

competition. Telser (1964) was one of the earlier studies to challenge the idea that advertising fostered monopoly. There, the relationship between firms' advertising expenditures and market shares in three consumer good industries—food, soap, and cosmetics—were studied. Telser found that market shares are less stable, that is, more likely to change, the greater is the advertising in that industry. This finding contradicts the persuasive view. Persuasive advertising would cause consumers to be less likely to switch among brands and so would promote market share stability. Instead, Telser's findings suggest advertising makes consumers less loyal or makes competition fiercer.

Second, any evidence of a positive link between market power and the extent of advertising must be carefully examined. It may reflect the fact that monopoly power itself leads a firm to advertise more and not that advertising leads a firm to have monopoly power. Finally, if advertising does change consumer tastes then calculating its effects requires that we think carefully about how it does so and what this implies for the benefits that consumers derive from the product. We address all these issues in turn.

## 20.3 THE MONOPOLY FIRM'S PROFIT-MAXIMIZING LEVEL OF ADVERTISING

Advertising is a costly activity. Rational firms will expend considerable resources on advertising only if it is profitable to do so. It is natural in this regard to suppose that the advertising is profitable because of its effect on sales. Remember that a monopoly firm faces a downward-sloping demand curve. If advertising is not too costly, the firm would likely prefer to push its demand curve out and sell more at the same price rather than sell more by lowering its price along a given demand curve. Thus we assume that a monopoly firm's demand depends not only upon the price the firm sets but also upon the amount of advertising that the firm chooses. This can be described by the demand function $Q^D(P, \alpha)$, where $P$ is the product price and $\alpha$ is the amount of advertising messages sent, measured, for example, as seconds of television or radio time, or perhaps as page space in newspapers or magazines. For a given level of advertising, the firm's demand is decreasing in price and for a given price the amount demanded is increasing in advertising. Alternatively, we can write the firm's inverse demand function as $P(Q, \alpha)$, where, for a given level of advertising, the price consumers are willing to pay falls as quantity is increased and, for a given quantity, the price consumers are willing to pay increases with a given level of advertising.

The ability of advertising to increase demand is the "good news" of advertising. The "bad news" is that advertising is costly. Suppose that every unit of advertising costs the firm $T$ dollars.[6] Let us also assume that every unit of output costs $c$ dollars to produce. (We assume no economies of scale in either production or advertising.) We can now characterize fully the problem confronting the firm. It must pick a level of advertising, $\alpha$, and a level of production, $Q$ (or price, $P$), that together lead to a maximum profit. In particular this means that the firm needs to quantify the good

---

6  This assumption may not always hold. Often there is considerable quantity discounting when air time, network time, or magazine space is purchased by a firm for advertising.

news and bad news aspects of advertising, and work out whether the benefit of sending one more ad is greater than the incremental cost incurred $T$.

Let us first work out the profit-maximizing quantity of output to produce for a given number of advertising messages, $\alpha$. Holding $\alpha$ constant, the firm's marginal revenue curve is

$$MR(Q, \alpha) = P(Q, \alpha) + \frac{\partial P(Q, \alpha)}{\partial Q} Q. \qquad \textbf{(20.1)}$$

Profit maximization implies choosing $Q^*$ such that marginal revenue is equal to marginal cost or

$$MR(Q^*, \alpha) = P(Q^*, \alpha) + \frac{\partial P(Q^*, \alpha)}{\partial Q} Q^* = c. \qquad \textbf{(20.2)}$$

We can rewrite the profit-maximizing equation (20.2) and express it in terms of the Lerner Index, which is the firm's price-cost margin as a percentage of price, or $\frac{P^* - c}{P^*}$, where $P^* = P(Q^*, \alpha)$.[7] If at a given level of advertising $\alpha$ the firm chooses to sell the profit-maximizing quantity $Q^*$ at a price $P^*$, the Lerner Index will satisfy

$$\frac{P^* - c}{P^*} = \frac{1}{\eta_P}, \qquad \textbf{(20.3)}$$

where $\eta_p = \dfrac{\partial Q \big/ Q}{\partial P \big/ P} = \dfrac{P}{Q} \dfrac{\partial Q}{\partial P}$ is the price elasticity of demand evaluated at the firm's choice of output $Q^*$ and corresponding price $P^*$.[8]

Now consider the monopoly firm's optimal amount of advertising, or $\alpha^*$. At any output level $Q$ the firm's corresponding price, $P(Q, \alpha)$, will increase in the amount of advertising $\alpha$. To maximize profit the firm should choose an amount of advertising $\alpha^*$ such that the marginal revenue from an additional unit of advertising is equal to its marginal cost $T$. In other words, the firm should choose $\alpha^*$ such that

$$\frac{\partial P(Q, \alpha^*)}{\partial \alpha} Q = T. \qquad \textbf{(20.4)}$$

We can rewrite equation (20.4) by multiplying each side by $\alpha$ and dividing each side by $PQ$ so that we have

$$\frac{\alpha^*}{P^*} \frac{\partial P(Q^*, \alpha^*)}{\partial \alpha} = \frac{\alpha^* T}{P^* Q^*}. \qquad \textbf{(20.5)}$$

---

7  For a derivation of the Lerner Index see Chapter 3, Section 3.3.
8  Actually, $\eta_p$ is the negative of the elasticity of demand as the actual elasticity is formally a negative value.

Note that the right-hand side of equation (20.5) is the optimal or profit-maximizing advertising expenditure to sales ratio for the firm. Next, rewrite the left-hand side of equation (20.5) by defining a new elasticity measure, the elasticity of demand with respect to advertising, or $\eta_\alpha = \dfrac{\partial Q / Q}{\partial \alpha / \alpha} = \dfrac{\alpha}{Q}\dfrac{\partial Q}{\partial \alpha}$. Then use it along with the

elasticity of price, $\eta_p = \dfrac{\partial Q / Q}{\partial P / P} = \dfrac{P}{Q}\dfrac{\partial Q}{\partial P}$, to show that the ratio of these two elastic-

ities, $\dfrac{\eta_\alpha}{\eta_p}$, is equal to the right-hand side of equation (20.5). We now have a key result. The monopoly firm maximizes profits by choosing a level of output (or price) and a level of advertising such that the ratio of advertising expenditure to sales is just equal to the ratio of the advertising elasticity of demand to the price elasticity of demand. That is, profits are maximized when

$$\frac{\text{Advertising Expenditure}}{\text{Sales Revenue}} = \frac{\alpha^* T}{P^* Q^*} = \frac{\eta_\alpha}{\eta_P}. \qquad (20.6)$$

The condition in equation (20.6) is usually referred to as the Dorfman-Steiner condition, after the pioneering paper on advertising written by Dorfman and Steiner in 1954.[9] It states that the monopoly firm maximizes profit by choosing to spend a proportion of its revenue on advertising that is just equal to the ratio of the advertising elasticity of demand to the price elasticity of demand. That is, the firm will advertise until the ratio of dollar advertising to dollar sales equals the ratio of the advertising elasticity of demand to the price elasticity of demand. The *more price inelastic* is demand, or the smaller is $\eta_P$, the *more* the firm should spend on advertising, and the *more advertising elastic* is demand, or the greater $\eta_\alpha$, the *more* the firm should spend on advertising as well.

---

## Practice Problem 20.1

Suppose that a monopoly firm faces an inverse demand curve described by $P(Q, \alpha) = 100 - \dfrac{1}{\sqrt{\alpha}} Q$. The firm has a constant marginal production cost equal to 60. Each advertising message costs the firm $1.

a. What is the slope of the demand curve when $\alpha = 100$? When $\alpha = 1,000$? Illustrate your answers.

b. Suppose that firm decides to send $\alpha = 2,500$ advertising messages.
   1. What is the monopolist's marginal revenue curve?
   2. What will be the monopolist's profit-maximizing price and output values?
   3. What is the price elasticity of demand at this price and output combination?

---

9  See Dorfman and Steiner (1954).

c. The demand function is such that the advertising elasticity of demand is constant at 1/2. Does the price and output combination derived in part (b) satisfy the Dorfman-Steiner condition?

---

The Dorfman-Steiner condition is an extremely useful reference point in the analysis of advertising behavior. The condition helps illuminate the positive relationship typically observed between the firm's profit margin and the extent of advertising. This relationship is often used as evidence in support of the argument that advertising is a way for a firm to differentiate its product in the eyes of the consumer and, thereby, to achieve some market power. That is, advertising enhances a firm's control over price by making a firm's customers less likely to switch brands even when the firm raises its price. The Dorfman-Steiner condition in equation (20.6) makes it clear that advertising will be greater in a market where the demand elasticity is low. The profit margin, as measured by the Lerner Index, is inversely proportional to the elasticity of demand. Therefore, what the Dorfman-Steiner condition says is that, all else equal, advertising will be more intense the more monopoly power there is in the industry. In other words, the Dorfman-Steiner condition suggests a reverse causality. Rather than the heavy advertising causing the market power, it is in fact the market power (really the low price elasticity of demand) that induces the heavy advertising. Think about this for a minute. A perfectly competitive firm faces an infinitely elastic demand curve and, as a result, has a price-cost margin of zero. Clearly, such a firm has little incentive to advertise. It can sell all it wants to at the current price without any additional promotional effort. Moreover, because its price just equals its cost, selling extra units does not bring in any additional profit. In contrast, a firm with monopoly power has a much smaller elasticity of demand and, accordingly, a significantly positive price-cost margin. Therefore, if such a firm can shift out its demand curve it can earn its margin, $P - c$, on every additional unit sold. If not, the firm can only make additional sales by cutting its price. Clearly, it is the firm with market power that has the greater incentive to advertise. In short, the Dorfman-Steiner condition makes clear that the frequent statement that high advertising and low price elasticity go together cannot be used to vindicate the view that advertising is used by the firm to increase its monopoly power. It is rather the monopoly power already there that gives the firm a strong incentive to advertise.

A second insight of the Dorfman-Steiner result is its implication for how a firm's advertising-to-sales ratio changes in response to changes in the cost of advertising. The condition in equation (20.6) shows that unless the change in cost alters the ratio of the two elasticities—the price elasticity of demand and the advertising elasticity of demand—the profit-maximizing advertising-to-sales ratio will be constant. Thus, even if the cost of advertising increases, the firm's advertising-to-sales ratio will not change if these elasticities are unaffected. This result suggests that the ratio of advertising expenditure to sales across industries will not be greatly affected by changes in the cost of advertising.

Table 20-1 reports the advertising-to-sales ratio for a sample of 4-digit industries manufacturing consumer products for the year 2003. The advertising-to-sales ratio for this small sample of industries range from 1.2 percent for dairy products to 11.3 percent for soaps and detergents. The Dorfman-Steiner condition suggests that the differences in advertising-to-sales ratios could be explained by differences in both the advertising and price elasticity of demand. A firm's price elasticity of demand is

| TABLE 20-1 | ADVERTISING-TO-SALES RATIO $\left(\dfrac{\alpha T}{PQ}\right)$ FOR SELECTED INDUSTRIES | | | | |
|---|---|---|---|---|---|

| Industry | SIC | $\dfrac{\alpha T}{PQ}$ | Industry | SIC | $\dfrac{\alpha T}{PQ}$ |
|---|---|---|---|---|---|
| Amusement Parks | 7996 | 10.7 | Mobile Homes | 2451 | 1.4 |
| Bakery Products | 2050 | 1.7 | Motor Vehicles | 3711 | 2.4 |
| Beverages | 2080 | 9.2 | Perfumes, Cosmetics | 2851 | 7.4 |
| Canned Fruit, Veg., Jam | 2033 | 1.5 | Soaps & Detergents | 2844 | 11.3 |
| Dairy Products | 2020 | 1.2 | Tires | 3011 | 2.0 |
| Greeting Cards | 2771 | 2.0 | Household Video & Audio | 3651 | 6.9 |
| Hotels & Motels | 7011 | 2.3 | Wood Furniture | 2511 | 3.6 |

**Source:** Advertising Age, http://www.adage.com.

affected by the availability of substitute products, which in turn is affected by the number of rivals and the degree of product differentiation. Yet what determines a firm's advertising elasticity of demand? The magnitude of this elasticity reflects just how responsive consumer demand is to an increase in advertising. This begs the larger question to which we now turn. Why do consumers respond to advertising?

## 20.4 ADVERTISING AS CONSUMER INFORMATION

The traditional textbook model of consumer choice assumes that consumers are perfectly informed about the kinds of goods and services available. In fact, however, consumers often do not know which brands of products are available, how quality varies across brands, and which stores sell which brands at the lowest prices. Certain consumer goods and services, such as cars, flat-screen televisions, furniture, and medical procedures are relatively expensive items in the consumer's budget and they are products that tend to be rather infrequently purchased. These goods are called *shop goods* because consumers find it worthwhile to "shop around" and become informed about what is available before deciding which brand of good or service to buy. The time and effort spent by the consumer to become informed makes sense for goods that are costly for the consumer to buy.

On the other hand, many consumer goods such as detergent, soda, shampoo, socks, and taxi rides are relatively inexpensive and frequently purchased. These goods are called *convenience goods*. For these goods consumers expend less time doing research on what is available and where. We might expect advertising to be a more influential factor in the purchase of a convenience good than in the purchase of a shop good. Because consumers consider the buying decision for a shop good carefully they will want to seek out reliable information on their own. Advertising sent out by the party interested in selling is likely to be less influential than a trusted friend's endorsement. The opposite holds in the case of convenience goods. For these products, consumers simply want to know such things as what the product does (Is Old Spice a deodorant or a food seasoning?) and where it can be bought. Advertising can provide this information quickly and cheaply. Hence, we would expect the advertising elasticity of demand to be greater for convenience goods than for shop goods. Note that to the extent that advertising plays this informational role it serves an economically useful function for the consumer.

We can also take another step and distinguish within the categories of shop and convenience goods those products whose quality or performance cannot be known by consumers before being tried. With certain goods, such as sweaters, dishes, or foodstuffs like sugar and salt, consumers can more or less ascertain the quality before they decide to buy them. These goods are called *search* goods, indicating that the primary issue confronting the consumer is one of seeking out where the best deals on such goods are to be found. However, for other goods, such as cars, electrical appliances, skin creams, wine, and health care services, consumers can only learn the actual quality or product performance after purchasing them and actually trying them out. As a result these kinds of goods are called *experience* goods.

Some shop goods will also be search goods whose quality or performance can be more or less identified prior to purchase, for example, a dining room table. In contrast, other shop goods will be experience goods (for example, a Palm Pilot) whose quality is not well understood until the good is tried or consumed. A similar division may be imposed on convenience goods where, for example, salt is a search good and hand cream an experience good. We might expect that consumers would be more responsive to advertising for convenience goods that are also experience goods. The ad is an inexpensive way for the consumer to learn whether he or she is likely to enjoy this relatively inexpensive experience good. In other words, we might expect the advertising elasticity of demand to be greatest for goods that are both convenience and experience goods. Following the logic of the Dorfman-Steiner condition and, for the moment holding all else equal, the foregoing logic implies that we should expect a higher advertising expenditure to sales ratio for convenience goods that are also experience goods.

Table 20-2 classifies the sample of industries and their advertising-to-sales ratios that were described in Table 20-1 according to each of the four product categories just identified. These data tend to support our conjectures that products that are both convenience goods and experience goods ought to be among those most heavily advertised. The experience good industries in our sample tend to have higher advertising-to-sales ratios and these ratios are highest for the convenience category. Of course, other factors such as the degree of competition in the market—because it affects the price elasticity of demand—are also important. Overall though, these data support the view that advertising plays, at least in part, a useful role of informing consumers about the function and availability of various goods.

Indeed, to the extent advertising provides consumers with information on price, quality, and retail location advertising would strengthen competition rather than weaken it. Such ads make it difficult for a seller to sell a product at a high price when consumers are aware that a perfect or at least a good substitute is available nearby at a lower price. When viewed in this light, advertising or brand awareness is a highly useful and procompetitive force that works to reduce the type of product differentiation that results because each consumer knows only a local store's offerings but lacks information about what products and prices are available elsewhere.

| TABLE 20-2 | ADVERTISING EXPENDITURES AS A PERCENTAGE OF SALES BY DIFFERENT CATEGORIES OF PRODUCTS |
|---|---|

| Convenience, Search | | Convenience, Experience | | Shop, Search | | Shop, Experience | |
|---|---|---|---|---|---|---|---|
| Bakery Products | 1.7 | Amusement Parks | 10.7 | Tires | 2.0 | Hsehold Video & Audio | 6.9 |
| Can Fruit, Veg., Jam | 1.5 | Soaps & Detergents | 11.3 | Mobile Homes | 1.4 | Hotels & Motels | 2.3 |
| Greeting Cards | 2.0 | Beverages | 9.2 | Wood Furniture | 3.0 | Motor Vehicles | 2.4 |
| Dairy Products | 1.2 | Perfumes, Cosmetics | 7.4 | | | | |

Moreover, there is sound empirical evidence to support the view that advertising prices and retail location intensifies price competition. The classic study is that of Benham (1972), who showed that the average price of eyeglasses was significantly higher in states where advertising the price and retail location of opticians' services was prohibited. Similar price effects when advertising is restricted were found by Cady (1976) in the market for prescription drugs. The view that advertising promotes price competition may also explain why many professional associations, such as those of lawyers, doctors, and dentists, have long argued for legislation to restrict such price advertising in their professions.

It is important to emphasize again, however, that it is typically local retailers and, increasingly, mail-order firms that provide the advertisements that inform consumers of the price and retail location and which play a procompetitive role. While this kind of advertising is important, its quantitative significance in dollar terms is limited in comparison with the image advertising launched by large manufacturers. The real bone of contention in the debate on advertising is the role of the expensive promotional spending done by the car manufacturers, household goods producers, and other makers of consumer products. Unlike the advertising in a local newspaper done by a retailer, or the advertising done by a firm in a specialty magazine such as *Field and Stream*, the image advertising of these large manufacturers carries little or no direct information about the product. Indeed, a recent television commercial for the automaker Mercedes-Benz never shows a car at all. There is simply a giant yellow rubber duck whose pupils shine to reveal the familiar Mercedes-Benz logo. The question then becomes what is the role of this kind of advertising and what are its economic effects?

## 20.5 PERSUASIVE ADVERTISING

The Mercedes-Benz advertisement mentioned above appears devoid of any useful information. Instead, it aims at somehow persuading consumers that a Mercedes-Benz car is special. This kind of advertising raises the same issue as that raised in early analyses of advertising. These ads appear largely persuasive, aimed at differentiating the firm's products so as to soften price competition. Yet even if this view is true some important questions remain. In particular, we need to examine more carefully what it means to say that advertising convinces some consumers that Brand X is superior and worth a higher price.

If advertising messages devoid of any true information can persuade consumers to favor one brand, then what one is really saying is that advertising can effectively *change* consumer preferences. This presents a new and important twist in how we model consumer behavior. Typically, we assume that the consumer preferences that underlie consumer demand are given or are exogenous. The utility function is a formal way to represent the consumer's set of tastes. The conventional textbook model then focuses on how the consumer chooses goods that reflect his or her tastes, that is, that maximize his or her utility given the constraints imposed by income and the set of product prices.

If advertising does change consumer tastes and hence utility, then we must take that into account when we evaluate whether there is too much advertising. For example, suppose that without any advertising, consumers regard one box of Brand X to be worth about $8 at the margin, and without advertising firm X finds that it maximizes profit at a price of $10 per box. Now suppose that if the firm advertises it raises consumers' valuation of Brand X from $8 to $20 per box and that the firm finds it profitable to raise its price from $10 to $15 per box. In this scenario, advertising is purely persuasive but it is not harmful. Consumer surplus on every box sold will rise from $2 to $5 even as the firm has become more profitable.[10]

Moreover, consumer tastes change over time. In some sense, every taste is an acquired one developed in response to what one might call persuasive efforts. The training and experience, for example, to appreciate fully a classical symphony or an abstract painting or, for that matter, a baseball game can also be thought of as persuasive effort. Similarly, children have to be taught (persuaded of) the value of a healthy diet and adults often have to learn the value of regular exercise. We do not generally complain about efforts to persuade or encourage individuals to enjoy such activities, even though such efforts are an attempt to change an individual's tastes. Why then should we be concerned about promotional efforts to change consumer preferences among competing brands? But perhaps the real question here is *how* the Mercedes-Benz ad changes consumers' tastes. That is, how does the image of a giant yellow duck with the Mercedes-Benz eyes persuade a consumer that Mercedes-Benz is a superior product?

## 20.6 ADVERTISING AND SIGNALING

Persuasive advertising challenges the basic tenet of "the invisible hand." According to the persuasive view of advertising, it is not the invisible hand but rather visible advertising that convinces consumers what it is that they want and what they should

---

10 Dixit and Norman (1978) proposed a way to evaluate welfare effects by using both pre-advertising demand and post-advertising consumer tastes. If on the basis of both sets of tastes one gets the same welfare effects then conclusions can be drawn about the effect of persuasive advertising on welfare. This approach was subsequently criticized in Fisher and McGowan (1979) because Dixit and Norman compare welfare before and after advertising using either one set of preferences or the other for both equilibrium outcomes. The comparison that should be made is a comparison of the pre-advertising equilibrium using pre-advertising tastes to the post-advertising equilibrium using post-advertising tastes. But this raises the familiar problem of interpersonal comparison of utility levels.

buy. Perhaps not surprisingly, it was the Chicago School with its long intellectual heritage of defending free markets that took up this challenge to the invisible hand.[11] The important contribution of these economists was to recognize that image advertising may be more informative than first meets the eye. But what sort of information can be inferred from the commercials aired on television that seem almost entirely devoted to building a brand image? This was the question raised by the Chicago School economist Philip Nelson in two seminal articles written in the 1970s (1970 and 1974). Nelson began answering the question by first posing another. "What do consumers *know* about a product *before* they purchase it?" Specifically, can consumers identify the quality or other characteristics of the product before they try it?

For certain goods, such as sweaters, dishes, or foodstuffs like sugar and salt, Nelson argued that the answer is yes. Nelson regarded these to be search goods, in the sense identified earlier. Consumers can more or less ascertain the quality of these goods before they decide to buy them, and the primary issue confronting the consumer was one of seeking out where the best deals on such goods were to be found. However, Nelson also recognized that some goods such as cars, electrical appliances, wine, and health care products are what we earlier referred to as experience goods. For these goods, consumers can only learn the actual quality *after* purchasing them and actually trying them out. Nelson called these goods *experience goods*.

It was in this second category of experience goods that Nelson saw a role for image-based advertising that might otherwise appear to be totally uninformative. His argument is quite straightforward. The manufacturer of an experience good knows whether it is a high-quality or a low-quality product. That is, the producer often knows whether the consumer will be satisfied with the product after purchasing it. The problem is that the consumer does not have this information and can only acquire it by perhaps painful experience. How can the producer—particularly one who knows that the good is a high-quality product—get this information across to potential customers? Advertising, suggested Nelson, is the key.

The manufacturer of, say, an analgesic does not want the customer's business only once but hopes to gain that patronage on a repeated basis. If the good is of high quality and works well then the consumer will probably buy the product again. As long as experience with the pain reliever is satisfactory, the typical consumer will very likely continue to purchase that same product repeatedly rather than start all over searching for an alternative brand. This is not the case, though, for an ineffective pain-relief product. The consumer who buys a low-quality product will, in all probability, switch to an alternative brand the next time. Accordingly, only makers of high-quality analgesics have any hope of earning repeat purchases.

Nelson's model combines the above intuition with the discounting and present value analysis that we first presented in Chapter 2. He argues that a firm's advertising expenditures are incurred up front. They can only be justified if the discounted value of the future stream of revenues generated by the advertising is sufficient to cover this sunk cost. Nelson's idea is that if a consumer tries an experience good and finds it to be a "good deal" then the consumer is likely to continue to buy it. Indeed, the "better the deal" the producer offers, the higher the probability of repeat purchase, and therefore the greater the present value of the profits that the firm can ex-

---

11 It is also important to point out the Chicago school's belief in the stability of consumer preferences. Since this assumption is the starting point of most economic models, there is a lot at stake in taking up this challenge.

pect from an ad that induces or persuades the consumer to try the good in the first place. That is, only the maker of a high-quality product can be sure that an extra customer lured to the store by a successful ad will also come back for a second and third purchase. Hence, only the maker of a high-quality product can be sure that an advertisement will generate the extra income necessary to cover the initial expense. The better the quality of its product, the more customers who will return in the future and the higher the price they will pay. Accordingly, the better the quality of its product, the more advertising the firm will wish to do. Moreover, Nelson argued that consumers can recognize this logic, too. They will rationally conclude that if a firm does a lot of advertising it must be because the firm is offering a high-quality product at a reasonable price. This is true even though the explicit content of the advertising may simply be an image and little else. It is the fact of advertising and not its content that signals to the consumer the good deal that the firm is offering.

Nelson's dual insight was that in a world in which firms know the quality of their products, but consumers do not, the makers of high-quality products would look for some technique to signal that quality, and that advertising might be precisely the signaling device they would use. Moreover, since the argument applies explicitly to experience goods, a natural test of Nelson's idea would be to examine whether the manufacturers of experience goods do more advertising than manufacturers of search goods. In fact, we saw that this is the case with the data shown in Table 20-2. Nelson provided further statistical evidence that this relationship holds.

For the next 15 years Nelson's insight into advertising and signaling set the agenda for most of the theoretical work on advertising. An important early paper in this regard is Schmalensee (1978). That paper makes the point that Nelson's argument that a firm offering a "good deal" has a stronger incentive to advertise than a firm offering a "bad deal" depends quite a bit on the price-cost margin of a "good deal" relative to that of a "bad deal." Suppose, for example, that a high-quality pain reliever can be produced at a cost of ten cents per dose while a worthless pain reliever, made from a commonly available extract of carrot roots, costs only one cent per dose to make. Then a firm offering the carrot root painkiller may find that it can earn a very high markup on each bottle sold. Even if no repeat purchases occur, the firm may earn enough on every first-time purchase to justify considerable advertising expense. Quite possibly, this expense will exceed the amount the maker of the high-quality pain reliever will spend.

Nevertheless, the signaling possibility raised by Nelson remained the subject of investigation despite Schmalensee's cautionary note, and much additional work has been done.[12] Among the more important analyses in this later signaling literature is that offered by Kihlstrom and Riordan (1984) and Milgrom and Roberts (1986). Kihlstrom and Riordan develop a two-period model in which a firm's advertising alone in the first period determines whether consumers believe the good to be a high- or low-quality product. Given consumer beliefs about quality, prices are then determined in a traditional demand and supply manner. The important result of the Kihlstrom and Riordan study is that they too find a strong incentive for high-quality producers to lure "repeat buyers" by advertising heavily in the first period, just as Nelson (1970 and 1974) found in his earlier and much simpler analysis. The contribution of Milgrom and Roberts is to show that pricing can serve as a quality signal

---

12 The interested reader can refer to Bagwell and Riordan (1991) and Schwartz and Wilde (1985).

as well as can advertising. Because both advertising and pricing can indicate product quality, the extent to which either is used is complicated. As a result, while the Milgrom and Roberts paper may be taken as confirming Nelson's fundamental point, it also tends to weaken the tight theoretical link between advertising and product quality. The Milgrom and Roberts signaling model is a monopoly or single-firm model. Fluet and Garella (2001) show instead that when the firm competes in price with other firms it may be necessary to use advertising to signal quality.[13]

The large volume of theoretical investigations into the signaling theory of advertising and prices has generated empirical research as well. In general, this research has tried to provide evidence on the extent to which the quality of a good is linked with the manufacturer's advertising-to-sales ratio. Of course, an obvious qualification to all such scholarship is that the task of measuring quality is far from easy. The truth is that quality has many dimensions and it is not obvious how to combine the many dimensions into a single index. Nevertheless, broad rankings of product quality are regularly published by Consumers Union. An important early study using this data was done by Reisz (1978) on over 10,000 brands of 685 products. He found, however, only a weak correlation between price and quality.

If high prices do not necessarily signal high quality, what about advertising? Kotowitz and Matthewson (1986) examined this relationship for both automobiles and whole-life insurance. They did not, however, find evidence that the higher the advertising the better the deal. Similarly, Archibald, Haulman, and Moody (1983) examined running shoes and again found that neither price nor advertising levels for 187 brands were strongly correlated with the quality rankings, which were published in the magazine *Runner's World*. However, these authors did find that the magazine's quality ratings, once publicized and circulated, were positively correlated with the extent of advertising done *after* those rankings were published. Firms with a high ranking were anxious to let consumers know this fact, while those with a low ranking were less interested in displaying their product's deficiencies.[14]

A study of 196 different industries by Caves and Green (1996) finds few discernible tendencies in the relationship between advertising and brand quality. For many industries, these authors find that the quality–advertising expenditure correlation approaches a negative one—the exact opposite of Nelson's prediction. They do, though, find a positive relationship between advertising and quality in the case of new, innovative goods.[15] They also find a weaker but still positive correlation between advertising and the quality of those goods in their sample that might be called "experience goods." The Caves and Green evidence on Nelson's hypothesis may then best be described as mixed.

As a final but less formal bit of evidence on this issue we offer in Table 20-3 a recent analysis of canned tuna fish reported in *The New York Times*.[16] Five "experts" participated in a blind sample of 14 different brands of canned tuna and then evaluated them on a scale of 1 to 10 (worst to best) in terms of overall quality. The results

---

13  We must keep in mind the fact that we are assuming that firms care about repeat business. If not, and if consumers always inferred that high quality meant high price, every producer would find it in its interest to raise its price whether it made a high-quality or a low-quality product.

14  It is worthwhile noting that the magazine *Runner's World* allows manufacturers to quote their rankings in advertisements, whereas the magazine *Consumer Reports* does not.

15  See Judd and Riordan (1994) for a theoretical analysis of a firm's ability to signal the quality of its new product.

16  S. Gugino, "Canned Tuna: In Search of Flavor and Texture." *The New York Times*, August 6, 1997, p. C1.

<table>
<tr><td colspan="2" align="center">RANKING OF A SAMPLE OF CANNED TUNA<br>PRODUCTS BY QUALITY—BEST PRODUCT IS<br>LISTED FIRST, WORST PRODUCT IS LISTED LAST</td></tr>
</table>

**TABLE 20-3**

| Brand Name | Price per Can ($) |
| --- | --- |
| Progresso Light Tuna in Light Oil | 2.59 |
| Dave's Alderwood Smoked Albacore in Soybean Oil | 4.00 |
| Genova Tuna in Olive Oil | 1.89 |
| Lazio in Olive Oil | 3.16 |
| Dave's Albacore | 4.00 |
| Lazio in Water | 3.16 |
| Master Choice Fancy Albacore Solid Tuna | 1.99 |
| Asti Albacore in Olive Oil | 1.99 |
| Pastene Fancy White Tuna in Olive Oil | 1.99 |
| Bumble Bee Solid White Tuna in Water | 1.55 |
| Star Kist Solid White Tuna in Spring Water | 1.49 |
| Dave's Garlic Albacore | 4.00 |

are quite interesting. While there was a general tendency for the more expensive tunas to earn higher evaluations, this was by no means a uniform result. Dave's Alderwood Smoked Albacore, for example, was the most expensive product but was not ranked first in quality. Instead, first place honors went to Progresso's tuna, which ranked seventh out of fourteen in price. In addition, the most heavily advertised tuna products, sold by Bumble Bee and Star Kist, were ranked almost last in quality.

In sum, Nelson's insight that advertising might serve as a means for producers to signal the quality of their goods remains a valuable one, the theory has not held up to empirical testing as well as one might have wished. Moreover, there are other problems with the signaling theory of advertising. First, the basic idea that the greater the extent of the advertising the higher the quality of the product suggests that a firm that spends a great deal on its advertising has an incentive to let consumers know just how costly that campaign is. However, firms do not announce to consumers how much they spend on advertising.

Further difficulties with the view that advertising signals quality derive from the fact that this analysis applies specifically to experience goods. Some experience goods are sold to consumers while others (producer experience goods) are sold to businesses. The signaling approach would suggest that the type of buyer should not matter and hence, that the extent of advertising should not differ across these two types of experience goods. However, advertising expenditure to sales ratios are markedly higher for experience goods that are marketed to consumers than for those that are marketed to other firms, that is, producer goods. Indeed, even within the consumer goods category advertising expenditures are also relatively high for search goods as well as experience goods. For example, a Ralph Lauren Polo shirt or a pair of Calvin Klein jeans can be tried on and inspected before purchase. Thus these are search goods. Yet Ralph Lauren, Calvin Klein, and the manufacturers of clothing apparel in general do a great deal of advertising. Here again, it is not clear how the signaling approach can explain this observation.

Finally, it should be noted that the signaling theory is only relevant for untried products. Hence, after many or most consumers have tried the good and experienced its quality, the underlying logic of the signaling approach suggests that there is little further role for advertising. Yet if this is the case, that approach cannot tell us why firms who market established and well-known brands, such as Coca-Cola, Miller Lite, Chevrolet, and Rice Krispies, each continue to launch expensive advertising campaigns.[17]

In sum, while the signaling approach to advertising initiated by Nelson (1970 and 1974) is insightful, it cannot provide a complete explanation for all the advertising we observe. In the next chapter we will explore some alternative approaches to how advertising influences consumers' behavior. We will also move beyond the single-firm model and investigate how competition affects the incentive to advertise. Before concluding this chapter, however, it is useful to turn to an old but venerable public policy concern regarding advertising. This is that persuasive advertising may be effective because it is dishonest, that is, fraudulent.

## 20.7 CONSUMER FRAUD AND TRUTH IN ADVERTISING

Fraudulent claims and product scams are at least as old as alchemy. Sometimes, the harm in such activities is relatively minor, such as a claim that a particular toothpaste will leave one's teeth 30 percent whiter. Frequently, however, fraudulent advertising claims have turned trusting consumers into unwilling victims. The main wounds suffered in these episodes are usually financial ones as individuals have parted with large sums of money to pursue "get rich quick" schemes or have fallen for other phony promises. However, in the case of health products and health care services, the victims of the fraudulent claims of both ancient and modern "snake oil" salesmen have suffered pain, physical harm, and even death in addition to any monetary loss. Indeed, it was in part such events that led Congress to include in the Federal Trade Commission Act a prohibition of methods of competition deemed unfair, including the practice of false or deceptive advertising.

Advertising is considered false by the FTC when it includes actual or implied claims about a product that are verifiably untrue. In addition, these claims must have affected the decision of a substantial number of consumers to buy the product before the FTC will take enforcement action. Omitting information about a product does not constitute false advertising unless the product is one for which the advertising is

---

17 A model of advertising content by Anderson and Renault (2004) may be illustrated as follows. Let there be three consumer types, 1, 2, and 3, and three kinds of widgets, red, blue, and yellow. Consumer type 1 values red widgets at $40, blue widgets at $20, and yellow widgets at $15. Type 2 values red widgets at $15, blue widgets at $40, and yellow widgets at $20. For type 3, the respective valuations are $20, $15, and $40. Each consumer incurs a transport cost of $5.01 to visit the store. Once there, that cost is sunk. The store incurs zero cost per widget but has only red widgets. If it advertises red widgets, no one will come to the store. Since the transport cost is sunk, the firm will never charge less than $15 to anyone who visits. Knowing this, only type 1 consumers would respond to an ad for red widgets but then the store would charge $40 to any store visitors following such a commercial. Yet if the firm simply states that it has widgets without revealing their color, then each consumer type will visit. Not knowing who is who, the firm will lower its price to $15 to sell to all consumers. With symmetry, each consumer earns expected surplus of $5 and the firm earns $45. It does not lie, but it does limit the information in its ads.

regulated by the Food and Drug Administration. Subjective claims, such as "this product can change your life," are almost nonverifiable by definition and also are not considered false advertising under current law. Illegal advertising then consists of claims that are demonstrably false and that induce a large number of consumers to buy the product. Firms found guilty of such conduct are frequently required to compensate the customers who were deceived by the false advertisement.

Popular culture is filled with images of dishonest promoters. The used car salesman tirelessly pushing his stock that he knows to be filled with "lemons," the real estate dealer selling the Brooklyn Bridge or some other phony property claim, and the "quack" medical expert promoting the latest miracle cure are all common, even stereotypical images. The widespread currency of such images, coupled with a general suspicion that Madison Avenue can manipulate consumer tastes at will, has focused the attention of both the public and the regulatory agencies on fraudulent or deceptive claims as perhaps the major issue in connection with advertising.

When we review the FTC case files regarding charges of illegal advertising over the past several years, what do we find? Broadly speaking, we find that most cases involve situations in which customers have little ability to pursue any compensation from the firm engaged in such advertising. There may be two reasons for this difficulty. One is that the substance of the advertised claim—while verifiable in a laboratory or by individuals with specialized knowledge—is one that most consumers are ill equipped to monitor and verify. Thus, for example, Pizzeria Uno was asked to stop making the claim that its Thinzetta pizza line is low fat not because it is misleading but because it is virtually impossible for the consumer to evaluate. Similarly, the FTC stopped the frequent claim of weight-loss company Jenny Craig that nine out of ten clients would recommend Jenny Craig to a friend. This claim reflects a statement that can only be judged for accuracy by a formal statistical survey and not by most potential customers of Jenny Craig.

The second and perhaps more important reason the victims of false advertising may have difficulty pursuing their claims is that often the guilty firms are "fly-by-night" operations that disappear into thin air whenever an irate customer tries to track them down. Fly-by-night firms have little concern for repeat business. These firms know that the product or service they sell will be revealed as a failure to the customer, but only after the customer has paid up front. The "snake oil" medical quacks of the American Old West quickly left town after selling their wares. A more modern example of a fly-by-night firm using false advertising might be the New York City–based firm Student Aid Incorporated, which guaranteed each of its customers that in return for a fee of $97 the company would obtain for them a minimum of $1,000 in college scholarship funds. Note that these examples effectively make the cautionary point first raised by Schmalensee (1978) regarding the signaling approach to advertising. Low-quality firms will advertise if the profit from a one-time sale is sufficiently high.

In light of the foregoing, we expect fraudulent advertising to be most prevalent in markets in which two conditions are satisfied. The first is that the firm is selling a product for which an actual purchase is necessary in order to evaluate the product's efficacy, what Nelson (1970 and 1974) called experience goods. The second is that a customer who is dissatisfied with the product's performance cannot easily claim compensation from the firm. While the latter condition is most easily met by "fly-by-night" firms, we should recognize that it may well be difficult for consumers to verify how well many modern products, such as medications, software, and automobile

**Reality Checkpoint**

## Taken for a Ride on the Internet Superhighway

As emphasized in this chapter, the advent of mass media and the associated mass advertising that development has made possible has greatly altered the selling of goods to final consumers. The advent of the Internet and World Wide Web is certainly part of this information revolution. At the same time, because it is easy for virtually anyone to advertise on the Web but difficult for the recipients of those ads to trace the location of the advertisers in real space, this medium has also prompted a wave of fraudulent claims. These deceptive practices have included promotions for products falsely alleged to help one lose weight without exercise or dieting, products to increase the size of sexual organs, and perhaps most commonly, get-rich-quick schemes.

For example, Michael J. Gardner and Rebecca Dahl Gardner operated several businesses that offered buyers the chance to make as much as $900 per week working at home and using the specialized software that the Gardners would provide to operate a billing service for a health care firm whose name would also be provided by the Gardners. In return, the customer had to pay the Gardners an upfront fee ranging from $59 to $150. However, after paying the fee consumers found that they either never received the software or that if they did, it did not work properly. Nor were the customers ever given any health care firms as clients.

Similarly, Gregory P. Roth and Peter W. Stolz operated a company known as 30 Minute Mortgage that promised consumers incredibly low-interest-rate mortgages. Potential customers were asked for all kinds of sensitive private information such as names, addresses, phone numbers, Social Security numbers, employment information, income, first and second mortgage payments, and bank account balances. However, no mortgages were ever actually offered. Instead, the firm sold this sensitive information to other firms who could then better target their own promotions.

Snake oil remedies still sell. For example, David L. Walker maintained a Web site and conducted seminars and personal consultations promoting his purported cancer cure, the "CWAT-Treatment: BioResonance Therapy and Molecular Enhancer." The Web site claimed his treatments, for which he charged between $2,400 and $5,200, made surgery, chemotherapy, and other conventional cancer treatments unnecessary. However, there was no real evidence that Walker's BioResonance Therapy had any therapeutic effects.

All the firms mentioned above and others were caught and prosecuted by the Federal Trade Commission. Yet many other fraudulent promotions undoubtedly persist. As Schmalensee (1978) noted, when advertising is cheap and the gains from one sale are large, it matters little if dissatisfied customers make no repeat purchases and Nelson's (1970 and 1972) hypotheses that advertising itself is a signal of quality breaks down.

**Sources:** Federal Trade Commission, Various News Releases, http://www.ftc.gov.

repair parts, are working and to obtain compensation if they are not performing. More generally, different products will satisfy these two criteria to a greater or lesser extent. In turn, this has implications beyond the narrow issue of fraudulent advertising because consumers are smart, too. Because they understand the settings in which advertising will need to be less honest, consumers' response to advertising will be equally strategic and they will accept such promotional efforts as truthful only to the extent that they can verify the product's quality prior to purchase, and even that criterion will be moderated by whether the consumer will be back in this product market for additional purchases later. Here again we have the implication that the way in which advertising affects consumers' decisions to buy will vary across product markets. As a result, there will be no single role that advertising plays in consumer decision making and, as we noted above, we therefore need to expand our approach to advertising to include additional models.

# SUMMARY

Large-scale advertising has played a pivotal role in shaping the modern shopping experience. The development of large retail outlets offering numerous varieties of each good to which consumers have direct access is largely a result of the rise of mass media and the promotional efforts that have accompanied this rise. Yet from the beginning, advertising has had its critics. In particular, early economic analyses viewed advertising as a way to increase and protect monopoly power. The evidence that firms with relatively high profit and in relatively concentrated industries tended to do relatively more advertising lent support to this view.

The view that advertising strengthens market power and weakens price competition is based, in part, on the empirical finding that advertising is most intense in industries with considerable market power and also on the assumption that advertising is persuasive and changes consumer tastes in favor of the advertised brand. Yet from a purely economic perspective, such arguments must be viewed as, at best, incomplete. To begin with, the observed empirical correlation of market power and advertising may well result from the fact that the more a firm's demand curve slopes downward, the more it will find it worthwhile to use advertising to push that demand curve out rather than to try to sell more units by dropping the price. That is, firms with market power have an incentive to advertise more than perfectly competitive firms.

Moreover, if consumers are rational, they are not likely to be duped by any artificial distinction advertising tries to create. Alternatively, the preference for an advertised good may reflect some real element that the advertising contains. The most obvious such element is the information that advertising provides about product characteristics and prices. Indeed, a sizable amount of advertising—mostly that done by local retailers—is explicitly of this price and location variety. In distributing this information to customers, advertising actually makes the market better informed and more competitive. In fact, several empirical studies have documented cases in which laws that have been changed to permit various professional occupations and stores to advertise have led to lower prices and increased consumer welfare.

Following the work of Philip Nelson (1974), many economists have explored the possibility that advertising may confer information even when it does not explicitly mention price or function. This literature focuses on the fact that a consumer can learn the true value of many goods only by a process of trial and error so that when a particular brand of a good is found to be satisfactory, the consumer will likely continue to purchase that brand in the future. If good products enjoy a high likelihood of repeat business then the firms marketing good products have a strong incentive to advertise to get consumers to make an initial purchase. Rational consumers will recognize this and therefore infer that a product must be of high quality simply because it is widely advertised—regardless of the content of the advertising message. Yet while the theoretical basis of the advertising signaling model is sound, its empirical validity remains questionable. There does not seem to be a close connection between product quality and advertising expense. The prediction that experience goods will be more heavily advertised than search goods also seems to fail.

In sum, advertising is a complex phenomenon. The precise way it works to influence consumer demand is only partly explained by signaling or more explicit informational content. Moreover, our analysis so far has paid little explicit attention to the role of advertising as part of the strategic interaction between firms. In the next chapter, we examine economic theories of advertising that explore both these issues.

## PROBLEMS

**1.** You have been hired to market a new music recording that is expected to have target sales of $20 million for the coming year. The marketing department has estimated that a 1 percent increase in advertising the recording would increase the recordings sold by about 0.5 percent, and that a 1 percent increase in the price of the recording would reduce the number sold by about 2 percent. How much money should you commit to advertising the recording in the coming year?

**2.** Suppose that the demand for a new wrinkle cream is described by a nonlinear demand function $Q(P, A) = P^{-1/2}A^{1/4}$, and so $\partial Q(P, A)/\partial P = -P^{-3/2}A^{1/4}/2$ and $\partial Q(P, A)/\partial A = P^{-1/2}A^{-3/4}/4$. Show that the price elasticity of demand is $\eta_P = 1/2$, and that the advertising elasticity of demand is $\eta_A = 1/4$.

**a.** What do you predict the advertising-to-sales ratio would be in this industry?

**b.** Does it depend on how costly it is to advertise for this product?

**3.** A firm has developed a new product for which it has a registered trademark. The firm's market research department has estimated that the demand for this product is $Q(P, A) = 11,600 - 1,000P + 20A^{1/2}$, where $Q$ is annual output, $P$ is the price, and $A$ the annual expenditure for advertising. The total cost of producing the new good is $C(Q) = .001Q^2 + 4Q$. This implies that the marginal cost of production is $MC(Q) = .002Q + 4$. The unit cost of advertising is constant and equal to one, or $T = 1$.

**a.** Find the inverse demand function $P(Q, A)$, and show that the marginal revenue from an additional dollar of advertising is $MR_A = QA^{-1/2}/100$.

**b.** Calculate the optimal output level $Q^*$, price $P^*$, and advertising level $A^*$ for the firm.

**c.** What is firm profit if it follows this optimal strategy?

**d.** What is consumer surplus if the firm adopts this strategy?

**4.** Consider again the firm in problem 3. Work out the firm's profit-maximizing output, price, and profit if the firm did not advertise. By how much does the use of advertising in this market change the firm's profit and consumer surplus for the customers of the firm?

**5.** Explain the different advertising-to-sales ratios of the following firms.

| Firm | Main Products | Advertising-to-Sales, $\alpha T/PQ(\%)$ |
| --- | --- | --- |
| Philip Morris | Tobacco, food, beer | 7.0 |
| Procter & Gamble | Soaps, paper, food | 5.3 |
| General Motors | Autos | 3.5 |
| Kodak | Photo supplies | 9.0 |
| Johnson & Johnson | Pharmaceuticals | 11.0 |
| Pepsico | Soft drinks, snacks | 5.2 |
| Sears, Roebuck | Retailing | 3.4 |
| American Home Products | Pharmaceuticals | 17.0 |

# REFERENCES

Anderson, S., and R. Renault. 2004. "Advertising Content." Working Paper, Department of Economics, University of Virginia (April).

Archibald, R., C. A. Haulman, and C. E. Moody. 1983. "Quality, Price, Advertising, Published Quality Ratings." *Journal of Consumer Research* 9 (March): 347–53.

Bagwell, K., and M. Riordan. 1991. "High and Declining Prices Signal Product Quality." *American Economic Review* 81: 224–39.

Benham, L. 1972. "The Effects of Advertising on the Price of Eyeglasses." *Journal of Law and Economics* 15 (October): 337–52.

Cady, J. F. 1976. "An Estimate of the Price Effects of Restrictions on Drug Price Advertising." *Economic Inquiry* 14 (July): 493–510.

Caves, R. E., and D. P. Green. 1996. "Brands' Quality Levels, Prices, and Advertising Outlays: Empirical Evidence on Signals and Information Costs." *International Journal of Industrial Organization* 14 (1996): 29–52.

Comanor, W. S., and T. A. Wilson. 1967. "Advertising Market Structure and Performance." *Review of Economics and Statistics* 49 (November): 423–40.

———. 1974. *Advertising and Market Power*. Cambridge, MA: Harvard University Press.

Dixit, A., and V. Norman. 1978. "Advertising and Welfare." *Bell Journal of Economics* 9 (Spring): 1–17.

Dorfman, R., and P. O. Steiner. 1954. "Optimal Advertising and Optimal Quality." *American Economic Review* 44 (December): 826–36.

Fluet, C., and P. Garella. 2002. "Advertising and Prices as Signals of Quality in a Regime of Price Rivalry." *International Journal of Industrial Organization* 20 (September): 907–30.

Fisher, F., and J. J. McGowan. 1979. "Advertising and Welfare: Comment." *Bell Journal of Economics* 10: 726–7.

Galbraith, J. K. 1958. *The Affluent Society*. Boston: Houghton-Mifflin.

Geroski, P. 1982. "Simultaneous Equations Models of the Structure-Performance Paradigm." *European Economic Review* 19 (September): 145–58.

Judd, K. L., and M. Riordan. 1994. "Price and Quality in a New Product Monopoly." *Review of Economic Studies* 61 (October): 773–89.

Kaldor, N. V. 1950. "The Economic Aspects of Advertising." *Review of Economic Studies* 18 (February): 1–27.

Kihlstrom, R., and M. Riordan. 1984. "Advertising as a Signal." *Journal of Political Economy* 92 (June): 427–50.

Kotowitz, Y., and G. F. Matthewson. 1986. "Advertising and Consumer Learning." In P. M. Ippolito and D. T. Schefman, eds., *Empirical Approaches to Consumer Protection Economics.* Federal Trade Commission. Washington, D.C.: U.S. Government Printing Office.

Lambin, J. J. 1976. *Advertising, Competition, and Market Conduct in Oligopoly Over Time.* Amsterdam: North-Holland.

Milgrom, P., and J. Roberts. 1986. "Price and Advertising Signals of Product Quality." *Journal of Political Economy* 94 (August): 796–821.

Nelson, P. 1970. "Information and Consumer Behavior." *Journal of Political Economy* 78 (May): 311–29.

————. 1974. "Advertising as Information." *Journal of Political Economy* 82 (August): 729–54.

Nichols, W. H. 1951. *Price Policy in the Cigarette Industry.* Nashville, TN: Vanderbilt University Press.

Pope, D. 1983. *The Making of Modern Advertising.* New York: Basic Books.

Posner, R. 1975. "The Social Costs of Monopoly and Regulation." *Journal of Political Economy* 83 (June): 807–28.

Reisz, P. 1978. "Price versus Quality in the Marketplace." *Journal of Retailing* 54 (Winter): 15–28.

Round, D. K. 1983. "Intertemporal Profit Margin Variability and Market Structure in Australian Manufacturing." *International Journal of Industrial Organization* 1 (June): 189–209.

Schmalensee, R. 1972. *Economics of Advertising.* Amsterdam: North-Holland.

————. 1978. "A Model of Advertising and Product Quality." *Journal of Political Economy* 86 (June): 485–503.

————. 1989. "Inter-industry Studies of Structure and Performance." In R. Schmalensee and R. D. Willig, eds., *Handbook of Industrial Organization* Vol. 2. Amsterdam: North Holland.

Schwartz, A., and L. Wilde. 1985. "Product Quality and Imperfect Information." *Review of Economic Studies* 52 (April): 251–62.

Solow, R. M. 1967. "The New Industrial State or Son of Affluence." *Public Interest* 9: 100–8.

Stigler, G. 1968. "Price and Non-Price Competition." *Journal of Political Economy* 76 (February): 149–54.

Telser, L. 1964. "Advertising and Competition." *Journal of Political Economy* 72 (December): 537–62.

# Advertising, Competition, and Brand Names

## Chapter 21

Many of the most memorable advertising campaigns have promoted a brand by emphasizing that it is different in some way from other leading brands in the market. The soft drink 7-Up, for example, was long touted as the Uncola Drink. Similarly, Kellogg's Frosted Flakes are uniquely identified with Tony the Tiger and his testimony that this cereal is Grrreat. Perhaps most famous of all is Coca-Cola's claim that "Coke is the real thing." These and other campaigns for countless other products tell consumers that the advertised brand is special and different from all others. Of course, sometimes the differences emphasized by the ads are real. Apple Computer offers a unique product. Likewise, Palm's personal digital assistant is different from most others. When the product differences across the brands are important to consumers, advertising can play an important and useful role in matching consumers to the brand that they prefer.

However, when the different brands of products do not appear to be very different advertising turns into a "capture-the-consumer" game. As such it has the potential to become a form of wasteful competition. The advertising expenditure on product promotions yields little useful information to consumers. This may be the case when it appears that it is the advertising itself that is the chief source of differences among the brands.

In this chapter, we consider the role that advertising can play when, in contrast to the previous chapter, there are many firms competing for customers. Advertising and the creation of brand names are important strategies for a firm. As the foregoing paragraphs make clear, we again have some tension in the role that advertising can play. When consumers have a preference for variety and product differentiation is important to them the creation of brand names can play an important matching role—directing consumers to the products that they prefer. Advertising is a key part of developing and promoting brand names. On the other hand, advertising can yield little additional information and be both wasteful and harmful to consumers. Which outcome occurs will depend on how one thinks advertising works when employed as a tool by rival firms. This issue is the central focus of this chapter.

## 21.1 ADVERTISING AS WASTEFUL COMPETITION

One concern about advertising is that it allows firms a way to differentiate their products in the minds of consumers and thereby soften price competition. In other words, there is the fear that advertising confers or strengthens monopoly power. There is, however, added concern as to why advertising could be socially inefficient in markets with strategic interaction. Under competition, advertising expenditures may simply be a form of wasteful competition that does not increase firm profitability.

This insight can be illustrated by means of a simple game. Suppose that ZIP Studios and Gamma Studios are both in the entertainment industry and they compete for customers through advertising. Thus the profit of each company depends on both its own advertising expenditure as well as that of its rival. To be specific, let the profits of each studio be

$$\text{ZIP profit} = (60 - A_G)A_Z - A_Z^2 \text{ and}$$
$$\text{Gamma profit} = (60 - A_Z)A_G - A_G^2, \tag{21.1}$$

where $A_Z$ and $A_G$ are the advertising expenditures of ZIP and Gamma, respectively. Each studio maximizing its profit by choosing the profit-maximizing advertising expenditure leads to the best response functions

$$R^Z: A_Z = 30 - A_G/2 \text{ and}$$
$$R^G: A_G = 30 - A_Z/2. \tag{21.2}$$

Simple algebra then confirms that the Nash equilibrium, that is, a pair of mutual best responses for this game, is $A_Z^* = A_G^* = \$20$. Total advertising expenditure in the industry is \$40 and each studio earns a profit of \$400. However, it is also easy to show that each studio would be better off if they both advertised less. Specifically, the joint profit of the two firms is maximized when $A_Z = A_G = \$15$. In that case, total advertising in the industry is \$30 and each studio earns a profit of \$450.

The problem is that the two studios are caught in a "prisoners' dilemma" game, spending extra resources on advertising in a futile struggle to steal consumers from each other. If advertising does not bring additional consumers to the market, then the loss in producer surplus that results from this dilemma is not counterbalanced by any gain in consumer surplus. Instead, each studio is led to advertise so as to avoid being the loser whose customers will be lured to the rival. However, the net result of such spending in total is that each studio ends up with basically the same number of customers it would have had if it and its rival had agreed not to advertise.

## 21.2 ADVERTISING AND INFORMATION IN PRODUCT-DIFFERENTIATED MARKETS

When there is little difference among the products marketed, advertising strategies are often used to play a capture the consumer game, and as such can lead to wasteful competition. However, the game changes when the products marketed are different in some key dimension that is important to consumers. In this case advertising can play an important information role—matching consumers to brands. To investigate the role and impact of advertising in this context, we need to work in a setting of differentiated products. For this purpose, we employ the now familiar Hotelling model of spatial competition. Here, the set of different kinds of products potentially available is described by a unit line segment. Each point on the line represents a potential brand or variety of product. The total population of consumers in this market, again denoted by $N$, is uniformly distributed along the line. Each consumer is identified by a point on the line that corresponds to that consumer's most preferred version of the product. A consumer wants to buy at most one unit of the product and is willing to pay $V$ for the most preferred brand.

Of course, if the consumer's most preferred brand is not being offered for sale, then the consumer must decide whether to purchase another brand at some distance

# Reality Checkpoint

---

## The Brush War in Hog Heaven

An example of wasteful advertising resulting from a "prisoners' dilemma" situation is provided by the ongoing battle between Braun and Optiva, the two primary producers of electric toothbrushes. For years the two firms have been engaged in a "no holds barred" public relations battle that has become the stuff of advertising legends. Often these conflicts have become so intense that commercials for each side have attacked the rival's product as well as promoted the firm's own toothbrush. This has led to legal battles that have added tens of millions of dollars to the hundreds of millions already spent directly on advertising.

One of the most recent rounds of this continuing battle involved claims by Optiva that its Sonicare toothbrush was both less abrasive to tooth enamel and better at attacking bacteria below the gumline than was Braun's Oral B Plaque Remover model. The claim was based on trial evidence from brushing the teeth of 3,000 dead pigs. This was quite expensive. It required the purchase of pig heads from slaughterhouses and then arranging for the refrigeration of those heads both in transport and in storage. In addition, further expenses were necessary to ensure that the tests were completed quickly before decay began in the teeth. Not to be outdone, Braun responded by brushing the teeth of *live* pigs. They flew researchers to various farms, anesthetized the pigs, and then cleaned their teeth repeatedly. This effort also incurred significant costs.

No doubt, both sides would like to call a cease-fire in this advertising war. But each one finds it difficult to stop unilaterally. The result is the continuation of mutually offsetting advertisements and economic waste—that is, unless one puts a high value on pigs (whether alive or dead) having very clean teeth.

---

**Source:** M. Maremont, "Braun, Sonicare Brush Up on their Legendary Feud." *The Wall Street Journal*, April 30, 1999, p. A1.

---

$x$ along the line from the most preferred brand. The consumer's willingness to pay for a brand at a distance $x$ from the most preferred brand is $V - tx$, where $t$ is the cost incurred by the consumer per unit of distance traveled from the most preferred brand. As $t$ increases, consumer tastes in this market become more specialized. A high value of $t$ implies that a consumer incurs a large cost when forced to buy a brand even a short distance removed from the most preferred type. In this case, we would consider consumer tastes to be very specialized.

We assume that there are two firms, each located at opposite ends of the line. Firm X markets brand $x$ and is located at point 0, the leftmost or farthest westward location. Firm Y markets brand $y$ and is located at point 1, the rightmost or most eastern end of the line. The unit cost of production of each brand, denoted by $c$, is constant and the same for the two firms. The benchmark model is one in which consumers are *perfectly informed* about the exact locations (that is, characteristics) of the two brands and their prices, $p_x$ and $p_y$. The decision of a consumer in this case is which brand to buy given that the most preferred brand is located at a distance $d$ from brand $x$ and a distance $1 - d$ from brand $y$. That consumer will buy the brand that gives the most consumer surplus, provided that the surplus from buying is positive. In other words, this consumer will buy brand $x$ if such a purchase yields a positive surplus,

$$V - td - p_x \geq 0, \tag{21.3}$$

and if that surplus is greater than the surplus earned from buying the alternative good, $y$,

$$V - td - p_x > V - t(1 - d) - p_y. \tag{21.4}$$

Let us suppose that $V$ is sufficiently high and the prices of the brands, $p_x$ and $p_y$, are sufficiently low so that all consumers find it worthwhile to buy one of the two brands and that both brands have positive market share at these prices. This means that there is a consumer whose preferred brand is located at a distance $\bar{d}$ from brand $x$ and who is indifferent between buying brand $x$ at price $p_x$ and buying brand $y$ at price $p_y$. However, for a consumer to be indifferent to the two brands, it must be the case that the same consumer surplus is obtained from buying one or the other—that is,

$$V - t\bar{d} - p_x = V - t(1 - \bar{d}) - p_y. \tag{21.5}$$

The location of the marginal consumer, $\bar{d}$, the one who is indifferent between buying $x$ and buying $y$, is affected by the prices that the two firms set for their brands. Specifically, we can solve equation (21.5) in terms of $\bar{d}$. Thus,

$$\bar{d} = \frac{1}{2t}(p_y + t - p_x). \tag{21.6}$$

If the price $p_x$ of brand $x$ increases, then the location of consumer $\bar{d}$ moves to the left and the fraction of consumers who buy $x$ falls. In contrast, if the price $p_x$ decreases, then the location of consumer $\bar{d}$ moves to the right and the fraction of consumers who buy $x$ rises. Indeed, $\bar{d}$ and $(1 - \bar{d})$ are the market shares of brands $x$ and $y$, respectively. Recall that $N$ is the total number of consumers evenly distributed from one end of the line to the other. Therefore, at any set of prices, $p_x$ and $p_y$, consumer demand for brand $x$ can be written as

$$q_x(p_x, p_y) = \bar{d}N = \frac{(p_y + t - p_x)}{2t}N. \tag{21.7}$$

Similarly, the demand for brand $y$ is

$$q_y(p_x, p_y) = (1 - \bar{d})N = \frac{(p_x + t - p_y)}{2t}N. \tag{21.8}$$

Accordingly, the profit from selling brand $x$ is $\pi^x(p_x, p_y) = (p_x - c)(p_y - p_x + t)N/2t$, while the profit from selling brand $y$ is $\pi^y(p_x, p_y) = (p_y - c)(p_x - p_y + t)N/2t$.

We can now derive each firm's profit-maximizing best response function in prices and work out the Nash equilibrium in prices when consumers are perfectly informed about brands. The best response function for brand $x$ is $p_x^* = p_y + c + t/2$, and the best response function for brand $y$ is $p_y^* = (p_x + c + t)/2$.[1] Of course, our assumption that each firm has an identical unit cost of $c$ implies that in a symmetric equilibrium each firm also has the same profit-maximizing price. This leads to equilibrium prices in the benchmark case that include a markup over cost equal to the measure of how specialized are consumer tastes, as represented by the parameter $t$. Hence, the equilibrium prices in the benchmark case are

$$p_x^* = p_y^* = c + t. \qquad\qquad (21.9)$$

## Practice Problem 21.1

Consider two firms producing differentiated products and serving a market of 1,000 customers. Each firm has a unit cost, $c$, of \$5. Assume as well that the degree of specialization in consumer tastes is $t = \$4$.

a. What will be the equilibrium price of each firm according to equation (21.9)?
b. What market share will each firm have at these prices? What profit will they each earn?
c. Suppose that one firm lowered its price by \$1 below the equilibrium derived in part (a).
   1. What would happen to this firm's market share?
   2. What would happen to its profit?

It is worth emphasizing that the equilibrium prices in equation (21.9) and the underlying demand functions upon which they are based depend strongly on the assumption that all consumers in the market are perfectly informed about the availability of the two brands. In the absence of an airtight means to distribute that information to each and every potential customer, however, it is more likely that consumers are not well informed about the brands. Obviously, advertising can play an informational role here. Yet it is far from a foolproof technique to "get the word out" about one's product. As we pointed out earlier, some consumers may remain uninformed about how many brands are on the market and the specific features of each brand even after an extensive advertising campaign.

In order to incorporate a realistic role for advertising in the context of this model, we will adopt the following approach based on Grossman and Shapiro (1984).[2] We will assume that a consumer knows the important information about a brand (that is, its location and price) only when the consumer receives an advertisement from the firm selling that brand. We also assume that the probability that each consumer actually receives that message is less than one. In other words, when a firm airs a commercial, it is quite likely that some consumers will not hear it.

Formally, we assume that consumers located along the segment have the same chance of receiving an advertisement about a brand. In particular, we assume that only a proportion, $\theta_x$, of the total population of $N$ consumers receives an advertisement

---

1    The best response function for firm 1 is found by maximizing firm 1's profit with respect to its price $p_1$ given $p_2$. The benchmark model is essentially the differentiated product model of price competition presented in Chapter 10.
2    Our model is similar to that developed in Tirole (1988) as a simplification of the Grossman and Shapiro model.

about brand $x$.[3] Similarly, we assume that only a proportion, $\theta_y$, of all potential consumers receives an advertisement about brand $y$. The fraction $\theta_x$ that receives an advertisement for brand $x$ may be further divided into two groups. One group is the proportion $\theta_x\theta_y$ who also received an advertisement for brand $y$. The remaining group is comprised of that fraction $\theta_x(1-\theta_y)$ who only received the message of firm X and did not hear a commercial for brand $y$. There is also some fraction of consumers, $(1-\theta_x)(1-\theta_y)$, who receive no advertisement from either firm. We will assume that this last group of consumers simply does not participate in the market—that is, consumers who receive no commercial from either firm do not buy either brand $x$ or brand $y$.

The situation is illustrated in Figure 21-1. Here, the top part of the figure shows the two firms and the distribution of the $N$ potential customers along the line segment or "Main Street" between the addresses of 0 and 1. Of course, if each of these customers were perfectly informed as in our earlier example, this entire set of $N$ customers would end up buying either brand $x$ or brand $y$. However, the illustration shows that not all of these individuals are truly potential customers for each firm. From the viewpoint of firm X, for instance, only two subsets of the original $N$ customers may actually purchase the firm's product. The first group is comprised of that fraction of customers, $\theta_x(1-\theta_y)N$, who heard only the commercial of firm X. These consumers are expected to be distributed evenly between the two ends of the town, but less densely than the full population of $N$ consumers. Thus, whereas there is a customer at every vertical mark along the line segment between 0 and 1, those that are also marked with an $x$ are the consumers who received ads only about brand $x$. If we draw a picture of this set of customers by themselves, it will look exactly like the picture of the original $N$ customers except that there will be fewer people living less densely between the two town ends. This is what is shown in the middle illustration of Figure 21-1. We will assume that each of these consumers buys a unit of firm X's product; that is, firm X does not have to compete for their business but, instead, captures all these consumers for itself.

The other set of potential customers for the brand $x$ version of the good are those who have heard the commercials of both firms. These consumers are also distributed randomly between the addresses of 0 and 1, and are each indicated with an asterisk in the top illustration of Figure 21-1. A picture of this group—who are $\theta_x\theta_yN$ in number—is shown in the bottom illustration of the figure. Once again, this subset of customers is scattered along the line between the two ends of town. But again, they are distributed less densely than the total set of $N$ consumers.

There is an important difference between this last group of consumers and those in the subset illustrated in the middle diagram of Figure 21-1. Unlike that earlier group who we assumed would buy only brand $x$, this last group that has received both firms' commercials will potentially buy the product of either firm depending on which deal is more attractive. In other words, these $\theta_x\theta_yN$ consumers are perfectly informed, just as in our earlier benchmark case. Hence, the two firms will compete in price for this subset of $\theta_x\theta_yN$ customers in exactly the same way as they competed for the full range of $N$ customers in that previous case. In turn, this means that we can

---

3   This means that firms do not target their advertising to those most likely to buy their product. Firm X, for example, is assumed not to concentrate its advertising on the leftward or eastern part of town near its own location but, instead, to advertise over the entire market evenly. Television commercials that are aired to all viewers probably come close to this description, although even here we typically observe some targeting. Think of the advertising of kids' cereals and toys that is concentrated on Saturday mornings during the "cartoon hours."

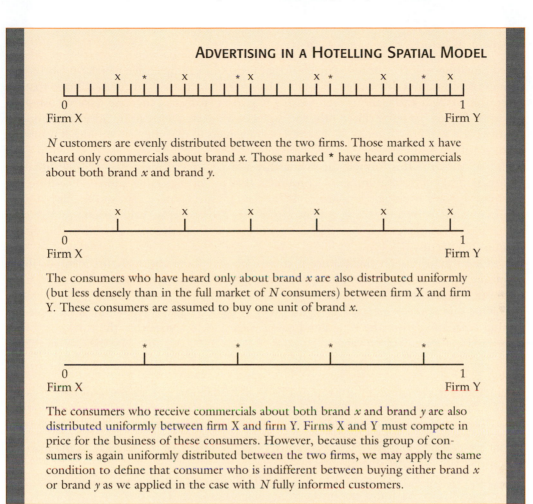

ADVERTISING IN A HOTELLING SPATIAL MODEL

N customers are evenly distributed between the two firms. Those marked x have heard only commercials about brand x. Those marked * have heard commercials about both brand x and brand y.

The consumers who have heard only about brand x are also distributed uniformly (but less densely than in the full market of N consumers) between firm X and firm Y. These consumers are assumed to buy one unit of brand x.

The consumers who receive commercials about both brand x and brand y are also distributed uniformly between firm X and firm Y. Firms X and Y must compete in price for the business of these consumers. However, because this group of consumers is again uniformly distributed between the two firms, we may apply the same condition to define that consumer who is indifferent between buying either brand x or brand y as we applied in the case with N fully informed customers.

FIGURE

**21-1**

once again talk about a critical consumer with an address of $\bar{d} = (p_y + t - p_x)/2t$. The only difference is that this consumer now defines the dividing line between the two parts of the smaller market comprised only of the $\theta_x \theta_y N$ customers who have received the advertisements of both firms rather than the entire market of $N$ consumers as in the perfect information case.

The foregoing analysis implies that the demand for brand $x$ is comprised of two parts. The first part is the $\theta_x(1 - \theta_y)N$ consumers who heard only firm X's commercial and who we assume buy firm X's product. The second part comes from the $\theta_x \theta_y N$ consumers who heard commercials for both products and for whose patronage the two firms compete in price. Using our earlier analysis, we may indicate that the demand for brand $x$, denoted by $q_x$, depends on the advertising efforts of each firm, $\theta_x$ and $\theta_y$, and the prices each charge, $p_x$ and $p_y$, as given by the equation

$$q_x(\theta_x, \theta_y, p_x, p_y) = \theta_x(1 - \theta_y)N + \theta_x \theta_y \bar{d}N = \left( \theta_x(1 - \theta_y) + \theta_x \theta_y \frac{(p_y + t - p_x)}{2t} \right) N,$$

**(21.10)**

where, as before, $\bar{d} = \dfrac{1}{2t}(p_y + t - p_x)$.

Equation (21.10) makes quite clear that firm X has an incentive to raise $\theta_x$ and to increase consumer demand for brand $x$. However, to increase $\theta_x$ or the likelihood that consumers will know about brand $x$ also requires that firm X increase its advertising expenditures. To put it differently, the expenses associated with airing advertisements for brand $x$ will be larger as the fraction of consumers $\theta_x$ that the firm decides it wants to reach becomes greater.

We can write this formally by saying that a firm's advertising costs, $T(\theta_x)N$, are a function of the total number of consumers that the firm tries to inform. The function exhibits a positive relationship. As the firm tries to contact a greater fraction, $\theta_x$, of consumers, its advertising expenses increase. Moreover, we will assume that this happens at an increasing rate. Thus, we will assume that advertising is subject to diminishing returns.

One way to obtain this feature is to assume that the additional cost incurred in raising $\theta_x$—that is, the marginal cost of raising the fraction of consumers that hear about brand $x$, or what we will denote as $T'$—is given by the equation $T' = \alpha\theta_x N$. Such a function is illustrated in Figure 21-2. It is, of course, a simple linear relationship emanating from the origin and rising with slope $\alpha$. Note that the total cost of advertising for any given value of $\theta_x$, such as $\hat{\theta}_x$, is $T(\hat{\theta}_x)N$ and is just the sum of the marginal cost of each increment in $\theta_x$ up to the value $\hat{\theta}_x$. This is the area of the triangle under the curve, which is equal to $\dfrac{\alpha}{2}\hat{\theta}_x^2 N$. Hence, our assumption that $T' = \alpha\theta_x N$ is equivalent to assuming that $T(\theta_x)N = \dfrac{\alpha}{2}\theta_x^2 N$. In other words, we have implicitly assumed that advertising costs rise with the square of the fraction of the market that the firm attempts to inform.[4]

Given its demand curve, firm X wants to choose a price, $p_x$, and an advertising strategy, $\theta_x$, to maximize the profit from selling brand X. This profit is equal to the firm's revenue less its costs. Its revenue is equal to the price it sets times the amount demanded at that price. Its cost is the sum of its production cost—the unit cost, $c$, times the amount it sells—and its advertising cost, $T(\theta_x)$. Formally, the firm wants to maximize its profit, $\Pi_x$:

$$\Pi_x(\theta_x, \theta_y, p_x, p_y) = [p_x - c_x]\,[\theta_x(1 - \theta_y)N + \theta_x\theta_y\bar{d}N] - \frac{1}{2}\alpha\theta_x^2 N. \qquad \textbf{(21.11)}$$

It turns out that maximization of this profit function requires that the firm's price and advertising choices jointly satisfy two conditions. The first of these conditions is the familiar one that, given its advertising level and the price and advertising level of its rival, the firm sets its price to just balance the gain in revenue net of cost from a further price cut against the loss in revenue on existing sales. This condition can be solved to find the best response function in price for firm X:

---

4   Recall that the area of a triangle is given by $bh/2$, where $b$ is the length of the triangle's base and $h$ is the triangle's height. In Figure 21-2, the base or $b$ is $\theta_x$, and the height is $\alpha\theta_x N$. Hence, the area of the triangle, or total cost of reaching the fraction $\theta_x$ of all $N$ consumers, is $\alpha\theta_x^2 N/2$.

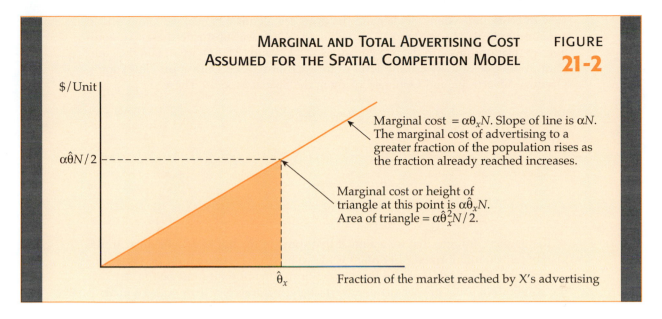

MARGINAL AND TOTAL ADVERTISING COST
ASSUMED FOR THE SPATIAL COMPETITION MODEL

FIGURE
**21-2**

$/Unit

Marginal cost $= \alpha\theta_x N$. Slope of line is $\alpha N$. The marginal cost of advertising to a greater fraction of the population rises as the fraction already reached increases.

$\alpha\hat{\theta}N/2$

Marginal cost or height of triangle at this point is $\alpha\hat{\theta}_x N$. Area of triangle $= \alpha\hat{\theta}_x^2 N/2$.

$\hat{\theta}_x$

Fraction of the market reached by X's advertising

$$p_x^* = \frac{p_y + t + c}{2} + \frac{(1 - \theta_y)}{\theta_y} t. \quad (21.12)$$

Equation (21.12) is firm X's best price response function given the price and advertising effort of firm Y. Note that it is made up of two terms. The first term is the best price response function for firm X when all consumers are perfectly informed about both brands as in our benchmark case.[5] The second term describes the additional markup when consumers do not know about the competing brand $y$. The smaller the fraction of consumers who receive advertising about brand $y$, the higher is the profit-maximizing price for brand $x$.

The second necessary condition is also one that is familiar to us. This is the requirement that the marginal benefit of reaching additional consumers just equal the marginal cost of such advertising, again given the firm's price level and the actions of its rival. The marginal benefit of additional advertising is the increased number of customers it brings in times the price-cost margin that the firm earns on each of these additional sales. Since we have assumed that the marginal cost of such additional advertising is $\alpha\theta_x N$, this condition can be written as

$$(p_x - c)\left[(1 - \theta_y) + \theta_y\left(\frac{p_y - p_x + t}{2t}\right)\right] N = \alpha\theta_x^* N. \quad (21.13)$$

We can then work out the corresponding profit-maximizing conditions for firm Y. To find the equilibrium outcome we can take a shortcut because from the point of

---

5   You can easily confirm this. Since the two firms are identical, the equilibrium must involve $p_x^* = p_y^*$. When the second term in equation (21.12) is omitted, imposing this condition then yields our initial, fully informed equilibrium, $p_x^* = p_y^* = c + t$.

view of costs and symmetric demand the firms are identical. Thus, we know that in equilibrium both $p_x^* = p_y^*$ and $\theta_x^* = \theta_y^*$ will hold. When we substitute these two equilibrium relationships into the two equations (21.12) and (21.13), we obtain the equilibrium price $p^*$ and advertising level $\theta^*$ for each firm. (See Derivation Checkpoint: Optimal Advertising and Optimal Pricing in the Spatial Model.) These are

$$p^* = c + \sqrt{2\alpha t} \qquad\qquad (21.14)$$

and

$$\theta^* = \frac{2}{1 + \sqrt{\dfrac{2\alpha}{t}}}. \qquad\qquad (21.15)$$

Remember, though, that we assumed that some of the initial $N$ consumers in the market remain uninformed.[6] In order for this to be the case, there must be some consumers who do not receive an ad from either firm. Therefore, it must be the case that the equilibrium value of each firm's advertising effort $\theta^*$ is less than one. To guarantee that $\theta^* < 1$ we assume that the cost of advertising, as measured by the parameter $\alpha$, is not too low relative to consumers' preference for variety, as measured by $t$. Specifically we want $\alpha > t/2$ so that it is too costly for a firm to find it profitable to inform the entire consumer population about its brand.[7] When $\theta^* < 1$ we have in equilibrium a fraction $2\theta^*(1 - \theta^*)$ of consumers who know only about one brand, a fraction $\theta^{*2}$ who know about both brands, and a fraction $(1 - \theta^*)^2$ who do not know about either brand.

To make the foregoing a bit more concrete, consider a simple example in which there are $N = 1,000$ consumers, each with a reservation price of $V = 10$ and a taste parameter $t = 2$. The unit cost of production is $c = 2$, and the cost of advertising is such that $\alpha = 4$. The perfect information equilibrium or benchmark case for this example is one in which the two firms split the market with each charging a price of $c + t = 4$ by equation (21.9). How does this compare with the imperfectly informed equilibrium with advertising?

From equation (21.14), the price in the imperfectly informed equilibrium will be $p^* = 6$. From equation (21.15) the advertising effort by each firm will be $\theta^* = 2/3 = 0.67$. Note that the equilibrium price has increased from \$4 to \$6, or by a factor of 50 percent over its value in the fully informed benchmark case. Given the advertising efforts of the two firms, 22 percent $[\theta^*(1 - \theta^*)]$, or 222 of the 1,000 consumers, know about brand $x$ only. Similarly, another 22 percent know only about brand $y$. In addition, 44 percent $(\theta^*\theta^*)$, or 444, know about both brands. The remaining 12 percent $[(1 - \theta^*)(1 - \theta^*)]$ do not know about either brand.

---

6   Indeed, it is this assumption—made rather implicitly—that explains why the equilibrium price shown in equation (21.11) does not converge to the equilibrium when one lets $\alpha$ take on the value $t/2$ necessary to make $\theta$ equal 1. Having derived the equilibrium under the assumption that $\theta < 1$ and the market is imperfectly informed, we cannot now impose on that equilibrium result the contrary assumption that $\theta = 1$ and the market is perfectly informed.

7   However, we do not want the cost of advertising to be so high that firms send out so few ads that there are too few consumers who know about both brands. In such circumstances firms find it not worthwhile to compete in price to attract these consumers.

# ✔ Derivation **Checkpoint**

## Optimal Advertising and Optimal Pricing in the Spatial Model

In the Hotelling model with advertising, we must now recognize that firms are optimizing on two fronts. They must choose both a profit-maximizing price and a profit-maximizing advertising effort. In turn, this requires that we differentiate the profit function of equation (21.11) with respect to both $p_x$ and $\theta_x$ and set each derivative equal to zero. The two resulting first-order equations may be expressed as

$$\left[ \theta_x(1 - \theta_y) + \theta_x\theta_y \left( \frac{p_y + t - p_x}{2t} \right) \right] = (p_x - c)\left[ \frac{\theta_x\theta_y}{2t} \right] \text{ and}$$

$$(p_x - c)\left[ (1 - \theta_y) + \theta_y \left( \frac{p_y + t - p_x}{2t} \right) \right] = \alpha\theta_x.$$

Of course, similar necessary conditions also apply to firm Y. Multiplying through the first of these by $2t$ and simplifying yields firm X's best price response function shown in equation (21.12):

$$p_x = \frac{p_y + t + c}{2} + \left( \frac{1 - \theta_y}{\theta_y} \right) t.$$

If we now invoke the symmetry requirement that, in equilibrium, $p_x = p_y = p^*$ and $\theta_x = \theta_y = \theta^*$, this condition may be rewritten to imply that in equilibrium

$$p^* = t + c + 2\left( \frac{1 - \theta^*}{2} \right) \Rightarrow (p^* - c) = -t + \left( \frac{2}{\theta^*} \right)t,$$

while the second of the two first-order conditions implies

$$(p^* - c)\left( 1 - \frac{\theta^*}{2} \right) \Rightarrow \alpha\theta^*.$$

Substitution of the implied value for $p^* - c$ from the first condition into the second condition then yields the equilibrium advertising effort shown in equation (21.15):

$$\theta^* = \frac{2}{1 + \sqrt{\dfrac{2\alpha}{t}}}.$$

Further substitution then yields the equilibrium price shown in equation (21.14):

$$p^* = c + \sqrt{2\alpha t}.$$

These data imply that each firm sells 444 units. Each sells 222 units to the consumers that know only its brand. In addition, the two firms split the market of 444 consumers who know about both brands. At a price of $6, each firm therefore earns revenue of $2,664. At a unit cost of $2, the total production cost at each firm is $888. In addition, each firm incurs a total advertising cost of $4,000(2/3)^2/2 = $888 as well. Total cost—production plus advertising cost—is therefore $1,776. Subtracted from each firm's total revenue, this leaves each firm with a net profit of $888. Note that on a per-unit basis, each firm incurs an advertising cost of $2, which in this case is just as high as its per-unit production cost. Such costs are necessary for each firm to get its product known.

The market outcome that we have just derived yields a number of insights regarding advertising in product-differentiated markets where firms compete for consumers in price. First, note that our assumption that $\alpha > t/2$ implies that the equilibrium price will now be greater than $c + t$—the price that prevailed under the fully informed equilibrium [see equation (21.9)]. The higher price is necessary, in part, to fund the advertising that provides consumers with the information that they need in order to go shopping.

The foregoing is not to say that the higher price that now prevails only covers the cost of the advertising that now takes place. That price also reflects the advantage that each firm now has with respect to an important fraction of its customers. This advantage is that some of those customers do not know about the rival brand. As a result, those consumers are willing to pay a price for, say, brand $x$ so long as it yields any positive surplus. Had they known about the existence of brand $y$, however, they would only be willing to pay a price for brand $x$ that yielded no less a surplus than that obtained from buying this alternative good. A real-life example may be consumers who purchase a high-priced national brand of pain relief because they are unaware that a generic substitute is available.

A further insight from our analysis is that an increase in the degree of specialization in consumer tastes—an increase in $t$—causes both price and advertising to increase. That is, prices are higher and advertising expenses are larger the more the differences in product brands matter to consumers. Here is yet another case in which it is important to understand that advertising does not play a causal role in these results. Advertising is not the force that causes consumers to have specialized tastes nor is it the factor that enables firms to set high prices. Instead, it is the fact that consumers have specialized tastes to begin with that both encourages firms to advertise extensively and that permits price to be set well above costs.

The final insight of this analysis is the connection it implies between profitability and the cost of advertising. Substituting our results from equations (21.14) and (21.15) for the optimal price and advertising efforts into the profit function of equation (21.11), we find that, in equilibrium, each firm will earn a profit, $\pi^*$, equal to

$$\Pi^* = \frac{2\alpha}{\left(1 + \sqrt{2\alpha/t}\right)^2} N. \tag{21.16}$$

Inspection of equation (21.16) reveals that each firm's profit is increasing in the parameter $\alpha$, which is a measure of the cost of advertising. How is it the case that making it more difficult for firms to inform consumers about their brands could improve firm profitability? The reasoning is as follows: When $\alpha$ increases, it becomes more costly to advertise to consumers, and so firms reduce their advertising levels. As a result, consumers in the market are now less informed of alternatives and so each firm can raise the price of its brand with less fear of losing customers to its rival. The increase in the price-cost margin outweighs the increase in the overall cost of advertising.

There is a well documented "stylized fact" that in a wide cross-section of consumer good industries higher advertising expenditures are associated with higher profitability. The pioneering work in this regard is that of Comanor and Wilson (1967) and (1974). Their basic finding is that industries with high profitability are associated with high advertising-to-sales ratios, and the relationship between advertising and profitability has been found again and again both for different time periods and different countries. This model is consistent with the empirical evidence. As $\alpha$ increases both industry profitability and advertising expenditures also increase.

Another insight is that public policy that attempts to restrict advertising efforts and thereby make it more costly to reach a given number of potential consumers could actually raise the profit of the industry's firms. Perhaps this helps to explain the recent agreement of the major American tobacco companies to abide by a proposed settlement of existing litigation claims including a restriction on the firms' advertising of tobacco products. A similar outcome could occur to restrict advertising in the alcoholic beverage industry.

---

## Practice Problem 21.2

We have already mentioned the increasing use of the Internet by firms as a medium in which to advertise their products by buying "space" on a firm's home page. Suppose we now project these developments a bit into the future and consider an economy linked by an information superhighway in which the World Wide Web allows advertisers to reach hundreds of millions of potential customers. Within the model just developed, such an outcome would be reflected by a sharp fall in the parameter $\alpha$. That is, because the Web has no distribution or printing fees and because it reaches so many customers, the cost of reaching any potential consumer is sharply reduced.

a. According to the spatial competition model just developed, what effect will a sharp fall in $\alpha$ have on the fraction of potential consumers who hear a firm's message?

b. What does the model imply will be the impact of this sharp fall in $\alpha$ on the firm's price-cost margin, $p - c$? What effect will it have on firm profits? Explain.

---

## 21.3  WHAT'S IN A NAME: A BRAND NAME

Brand names such as Froot Loops or Cheerios correspond to different kinds of cereals, and consumers care about variety in the cereal market and making the right match. However, often there is more to a brand name. Brand names such as Coca-Cola in the soft drink market or Calvin Klein in the jeans market have a social or psychological edge that goes beyond our simple interpretation of matching or mapping consumers to brands. Consumers may prefer Coke to Pepsi not because of the taste but because of the brand name. Consumers may prefer to buy Calvin Klein jeans not because of the fit but because of the name. Recognizing that there is a "peer pressure" quality in brand names and their advertising points us back to the view of advertising as a persuasive message. However, such messages do not have to change consumer tastes in order to have an impact on consumer utility.

This subtle point is made particularly clearly by Becker and Murphy (1993). These authors take a different view to the persuasive role of advertising. They argue that yes, these image ads do stimulate wants but, no, such advertisements do not necessarily change consumer preferences. The reason why image advertising can affect the demand for goods *without necessarily changing the underlying preferences* of consumers is that this kind of advertising may be a complementary good to the product. That is, in the same way consumers place a greater value on lodging accommodations the better the surrounding landscape, or on pencils the greater the availability of erasers, they may also place greater value on a soft drink or an automobile or a pair of jeans the greater the advertising done by the soft drink maker, automaker, or clothing firm, respectively.

There are several ways in which advertising can be thought of as a complement to the good being promoted. One way is that some consumers may enjoy knowing that the brands of products that they buy are widely seen and recognized by lots of others on television, in the movies, and on billboards. Advertising in this case enhances the consumption value of the product by making it more prestigious and desirable because it is seen in the eyes of the consumer's friends and acquaintances.[8] This view of advertising is close in spirit to the traditional persuasive view. The difference here is that consumers are not duped into believing that advertised goods are better. Rather, the extensive advertising actually serves to make those goods better known and hence worth more to consumers who enjoy using brands that are widely known. This kind of advertising campaign is aimed at building brand value. Its goal is to make the product more desirable and to increase the willingness to pay of consumers.

At the same time, it seems clear that brand name advertising can also convey information, such as how to use the good or service more effectively. For example, the food-manufacturing giant, General Mills, operates a Web site for its brand Betty Crocker. Among other offerings, this site includes a link to "Betty's Recipes—What's on Hand?" Here, the interested browser is asked to list the ingredients that are available for that night's meal. Then, the site provides a number of "Betty's Favorite Recipes" that utilize those ingredients. The recipes include both preparation steps and nutritional information. However, when listing the ingredients necessary for each dish, the site always gives a plug for the General Mills brand of that product, for example, Gold Medal all-purpose flour.

Clearly, this kind of advertising plays an informative role. Yet the information provided is not about the product's price, quality, or retail store location. Instead, the information is of the sort that will enable the consumer to use the advertised product more effectively and, thereby, to obtain greater benefits from it. The goal of this kind of campaign is to extend the reach of the brand and to expand the market by bringing in new consumers. Alternatively, consumers would be willing to pay for this kind of information—a cookbook, a software user's guide, a car owner's manual—if such

---

8   If consumers do care about wearing the "right" clothes or eating the "right" food then Clark and Horstmann (2001) show how firms can use advertising to coordinate consumer purchases through consumer beliefs. Consumers believe that a firm that advertises more will have more purchases and so will have a more valued product. This builds on the idea that advertising is a coordinating mechanism, an idea first introduced by Bagwell and Ramey (1994).

information were not readily available. More often, however, the information is sold bundled with the good at one price. Brand-name advertising that serves a similar "how to" role may be viewed similarly. The consumer buying the product pays for both the product and the information included in the advertising. This is not so very different from the consumer who buys a software package that includes a software user's guide.

Whether advertising provides social appeal or complementary information or a bit of both, the bottom line is that consumers value the joint consumption of the product and its advertising. This approach to advertising is quite different from the approach that lies at the heart of the signaling theory of advertising discussed in the last chapter. The signaling theory of advertising is based on the premise that advertising does not itself give utility to consumers but rather it is a signal for what does give utility to consumers. The view that advertising is a complement to the good being advertised is based on the premise that advertising itself is desired by consumers.

An important advantage of the complementary approach to advertising is that it can explain why consumers who have already tried an experience good continue to respond to advertising, and why there is considerable advertising for goods that do not fit the experience good category. Moreover, the desire to use a product that is widely known and widely recognized is something that consumers care more about than firms. Viewing advertising as a way to make the product better known can also account for the observation—unexplained by the signaling approach—that advertising is much greater for experience goods sold to consumers than those sold to producers. For analytical simplicity, we first explore this approach in the context of a monopoly advertising. We then briefly outline its application in a competitive setting.

When advertising is viewed as a complement to the good being marketed firms can increase the demand for their good by increasing their advertising. Corresponding to our description above, we consider two ways that advertising, when viewed as a complementary good, can affect consumer demand. One way is by increasing the social value of brand-name appeal. This is closer in spirit to the view of the persuasive role of advertising. The second way is by conveying information on how to better use the product and this is closer to the more purely informational role of advertising.

## 21.3.1  Advertising and Building Brand Value

Consider a firm that sells a product such as a car, a new book, a film video, or a spring coat, of which each consumer typically wishes to buy only one unit. There are $N$ potential consumers of the product. Assume further that each consumer differs by how much utility he or she gets from consuming the product. Specifically, we assume that consumers can be ranked in terms of the utility each gets from consuming the good. Consumer utility ranges from a minimum value of 0 to a maximum value denoted by $\bar{V}$.[9] In the absence of advertising, the consumer least interested in the product receives a utility from consuming the product equal to 0. Such a consumer will not purchase the product unless it is given away for free. The next person obtains a utility equal to $\left(\dfrac{1}{N}\right)\bar{V}$, the third least interested consumer obtains a utility equal to $\left(\dfrac{2}{N}\right)\bar{V}$,

---

9  For example, if the good were a new cosmetic treatment and if utility were measured in dollars $\bar{V}$ could be equal to \$100, or for a new holiday package $\bar{V}$ could be \$1,000.

and so on all the way up to the most interested consumer who obtains a utility equal to $\left(\dfrac{N}{N}\right)\overline{V} = \overline{V}$ from consuming the product. We may thus think of each consumer as located along a line segment with the addresses on that line ranging from 0 to $N-1$. If we refer to consumers by their address, consumer $n$ will, in the absence of advertising, obtain a utility equal to $\left(\dfrac{n}{N-1}\right)\overline{V}$ if he or she consumes the product, where $n$ ranges from 0 to $N-1$.[10]

With advertising, however, consumer utility from consuming the product is enhanced. To be explicit, we will assume that the effect of advertising is to increase the consumer's utility multiplicatively by a factor, $v(\alpha)$, where $\alpha$ is the level of advertising services the monopoly firm employs. Hence, the utility enjoyed by consumer $n$ when consuming the good with advertising $\alpha$ is now $v(\alpha)\left(\dfrac{n}{N-1}\right)\overline{V}$. We assume that $v(0) = 1$, so that if $\alpha = 0$ and the good is not advertised at all, then each consumer $n$ merely obtains the base utility from consumption of the good. When the good is advertised and $\alpha$ is positive, then $v(\alpha)$ is greater than one and each consumer's utility from consumption is increased. Moreover, the scale factor $v(\alpha)$ increases as $\alpha$ does, or $v'(\alpha) > 0$.

Because advertising increases the overall utility derived from the consumption of the good, each consumer is willing to pay *more* for the good the *more* it is advertised. A consumer will buy the product whenever the utility level exceeds the product price; in other words, when consumer surplus is positive. Therefore, a consumer $n$ will buy the product whenever $v(\alpha)\left(\dfrac{n}{N-1}\right)\overline{V} - P \geq 0$.

We can now derive the demand curve facing the monopoly firm. Suppose that the firm decides to advertise an amount $\alpha$ and to sell the good at price $P$. How much of the good will the firm sell? To answer this question, assume that over the population of consumers, that is, over the range of addresses $n$ that run from 0 to $N-1$, there is, at these values of $\alpha$ and $P$, some consumer with address $\hat{n}$ who is just indifferent between buying and not buying. This consumer who is just indifferent is called the marginal consumer. For this consumer $\hat{n}$ it will be the case that $v(\alpha)\left(\dfrac{\hat{n}}{N-1}\right)\overline{V} = P$.

All consumers with lower addresses or lower values of $n$ will not buy the product. They do not value it highly enough. All the consumers with higher addresses or higher values of $n$ will buy the product. If we use the equality above to solve for the address of the marginal consumer, $\hat{n}$, we find that

$$\hat{n} = \frac{(N-1)P}{v(\alpha)\overline{V}}.$$  (21.17)

Recall that the minimum value of $\hat{n}$ is 0 and the maximum value is $N-1$. At a very low or zero price, $P$, or at very high levels of either $v(\alpha)$ or $\overline{V}$, all $N$ consumers

---

10 We limit *n* to range as high as *N* − 1 in the analysis because we start at 0 as the lowest valuation of the product. In order to have *N* customers with *N* separate utilities and the first being 0, we must let the addresses range from *n* = 0 to *n* = *N* − 1.

will wish to buy the good. At very high levels of $P$ or low levels of either $v(\alpha)$ or $\bar{V}$, no consumers will wish to buy the good. Accordingly, the total demand for the product when the firm advertises at level $\alpha$ and charges price $P$ is the fraction of the $N$ potential consumers whose address or $n$ value exceeds $\hat{n}$. This is given by

$$Q^D(P, \alpha) = \left[\frac{N-1-\hat{n}}{N-1}\right] N = \left[\frac{N-1-\frac{(N-1)P}{v(\alpha)\bar{V}}}{N-1}\right] N = \left[1 - \frac{P}{v(\alpha)\bar{V}}\right] N. \qquad \textbf{(21.18)}$$

The total demand for the firm's product is negatively related to the price it charges, $P$, but positively related to the extent of advertising, $\alpha$. Note that the demand function is linear in price, and can be represented in what follows more simply by the form $Q^D(P, \alpha) = a - \dfrac{b}{v(\alpha)} P$. As advertising or $\alpha$ increases, so does the factor $v(\alpha)$ and, hence, the demand curve rotates outward as shown in Figure 21-3.

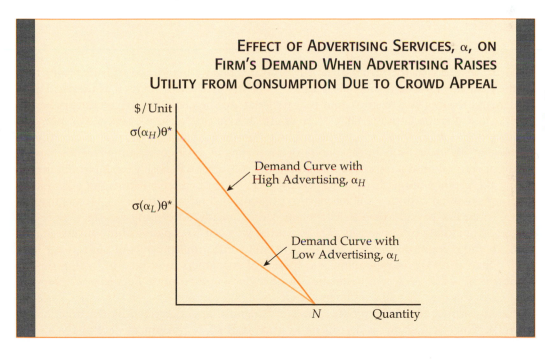

**EFFECT OF ADVERTISING SERVICES, $\alpha$, ON FIRM'S DEMAND WHEN ADVERTISING RAISES UTILITY FROM CONSUMPTION DUE TO CROWD APPEAL**

FIGURE **21-3**

As the rotation in the demand curve in Figure 21-3 shows, when advertising is increased in this model, it raises consumers' willingness to pay; that is, it raises the brand's value. It does not raise the size of the market. The rise in value is especially large for those who really like the good. These are the relatively high $V$ consumers or what economists call the inframarginal consumers. When advertising is increased, the inframarginal consumer's willingness to pay for the good goes up proportionately more than does the marginal consumer's willingness to pay.

When brand names have a social value or appeal the implicit assumption is that consumers actually enjoy watching or reading advertisements. It makes sense that they will listen to all the advertising sent out by the firm.[11] Consequently, when the firm decides to send out α advertisements, it does so knowing that all α will be heard. This assumption may be too strong for certain kinds of goods that are heavily advertised. We all know individuals who, as soon as there is a commercial break in a television program, jump up to do something else. Not everyone consumes or cares about the advertising that a firm sends out. This means that there is a "hit or miss" problem of reaching consumers with advertising and this feature is not captured well in this approach to brand names and advertising.

Suppose then that unless a firm's potential customers hear or see a commercial message they may not know that the product is available or alternatively they will not know how to use the product. However, the problem is that some consumers may not pay attention to the message when it is aired. Cellular phones are a case in point. It seems clear that many consumers are simply unaware of the easy availability of such technology or, perhaps, how to get any real use out of such devices. While this is bad enough for the uninformed consumer, it is especially disappointing to the firm who can only sell its products to consumers who know those products are there and who also understand how to work them. We now turn to an alternative view of advertising and building a brand name that captures this aspect of the firm's problem.

## 21.3.2 Advertising and Extending the Reach

Suppose now that if a firm did not advertise and build a brand name for its product then consumers would simply not know about the product or know that they had a demand for it. This scenario could be appropriate to the marketing of cellular phones or a new pharmaceutical product. The essential point is that, in the absence of information about how best to use the product, consumers may not demand any of the good at all. The informational content of advertising is, in this case, complementary to the advertised product insofar as without it, the consumer will simply refrain from buying the product altogether. We will also suppose that when a firm sends out ads, not every potential customer will receive the ad. Some will miss it altogether. Others may see it but not pay attention to its content. Consequently, advertising messages are received randomly by consumers. The issue that we want to explore is how advertising for brand recognition creates effective demand for the firm's product in this setting.[12]

Once again denote the number of potential consumers interested in buying this new product as $N$, which we assume to be a very large number. Furthermore, suppose in this case that all consumers are identical. Specifically, let each consumer, once fully informed about the product, have a demand that is described by the function $q(P)$, which we assume is decreasing in price $P$. If all $N$ consumers were in fact informed about the product, the monopolist's demand curve would be $Q(P) = Nq(P)$.

However, not all consumers may be informed. To become informed, a consumer must receive, that is, see and understand, an advertisement. Some consumers may not truly hear the advertisement's message either because it never reaches them or because, if it does, they mentally "tune it out." We model this "hit or miss" aspect of advertising by assuming that if the monopolist sends out only *one* ad to the group

---

11 On this point it is interesting to note that Becker and Murphy (1993) cite a study by several psychologists who did find that people who have recently purchased a new car were more likely to read ads for the same type of car than for other types.
12 This specification of advertising is based upon the model in Butters (1977).

of $N$ potential customers, then each such consumer has a probability $\frac{1}{N}$ of receiving it. Alternatively, each consumer has a probability of $\left(1 - \frac{1}{N}\right)$ of not receiving the one ad.

However, the monopolist can send out more than just one ad. Suppose that the monopolist sends out two ads. The probability that any one consumer receives *neither* message is $\left(1 - \frac{1}{N}\right)^2$. By extension, if the monopolist sends out $\alpha$ messages, then the probability that a consumer does *not* receive any one of these $\alpha$ advertisements is $\left(1 - \frac{1}{N}\right)^\alpha$. If $N$ is a large number, the probability that any one consumer *does not receive* an ad can be approximated by the function $e^{-\frac{\alpha}{N}}$, where $e$ is the natural logarithm base, 2.7183. That is, the probability $\left(1 - \frac{1}{N}\right)^\alpha \approx e^{-\frac{\alpha}{N}}$. Since the probabilities of all possible events must sum to 1, this in turn means that the probability that any one consumer *does receive* an ad from the monopolist is $1 - e^{-\frac{\alpha}{N}}$.

Therefore, of the $N$ potential consumers, the number of consumers the monopolist can actually expect to hear about the product when $\alpha$ ads are sent out is $\left(1 - e^{-\frac{\alpha}{N}}\right) N$. Since each of these consumers will, when informed, exhibit a demand for the product equal to $q(P)$, the monopolist's expected demand is

$$Q^D(P, \alpha) = \left(1 - e^{-\frac{\alpha}{N}}\right) Nq(P). \qquad (21.19)$$

Assuming that the individual consumer demand function $q(P)$ is linear in price, then the market demand function is also linear in price and can be more simply represented by

$$Q^D(P, \alpha) = g(\alpha)(a - bP), \text{ where } g(\alpha) = \left(1 - e^{-\frac{\alpha}{N}}\right).$$

As in the previous case, increases in advertising or $\alpha$ again shifts out the demand curve. In this case of extending brand reach, however, the rotation is as shown in Figure 21-4. Here, a rise in advertising slides the demand curve out along the horizontal axis, indicating a rise in the potential size of the market. Now it is the willingness to pay of the consumer who is on the margin of buying or not buying that increases the most, not the consumer who is inframarginal.

### 21.3.3 Brand-Name Advertising and Prices

The two cases just described are examples of the different way advertising, or a brand name, can serve as a complementary good and thereby affect the demand for

FIGURE

**21-4**

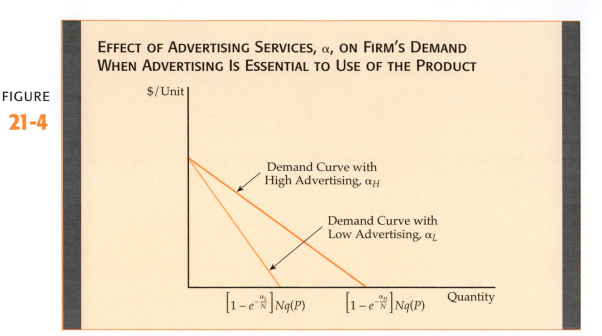

**EFFECT OF ADVERTISING SERVICES, $\alpha$, ON FIRM'S DEMAND WHEN ADVERTISING IS ESSENTIAL TO USE OF THE PRODUCT**

the advertised product. In both cases market demand is decreasing and linear in price and increasing in advertising. The way in which increases in advertising affect market demand is, however, different for the two cases. Specifically, for the social value brand name case the monopolist's demand function is represented by $Q^D(P, \alpha) = a - \dfrac{b}{v(\alpha)}\, P$, whereas for the *brand recognition* or extending reach case the monopolist's demand function is given by $Q^D(P, \alpha) = g(\alpha)(a - bP)$. The fact that increases in advertising will *at a given price* increase demand for the monopolist's product is the "good news" of advertising. The "bad news" is that advertising is costly. We will assume that every unit of advertising costs $T$ dollars.[13] We also assume that every unit of output costs $c$ dollars to produce. The task confronting the firm is to choose a level of advertising, $\alpha$, and a level of production $Q$, or price $P$, that together lead to a maximum profit.

It is interesting to compare the effect of advertising on the firm's pricing strategies in the two cases. Consider first the brand recognition case. We find it more convenient to work with the inverse demand function, which for the brand recognition case can be written as $P(Q, \alpha) = A - \left[\dfrac{B}{g(\alpha)}\right] Q$. As shown in Figure 21-4, higher advertising in the extending market reach case makes the slope of the inverse demand function less negative. The firm wants to work out the profit-maximizing quantity of output and advertising to produce. Let us first work out the profit-maximizing quantity of output to produce at a given level of advertising services, $\alpha$. Holding $\alpha$, and hence

---

13 This assumption may not always hold. Often there is considerable quantity discounting when air time, network time, or magazine space is purchased by a firm for advertising.

$g(\alpha)$, constant, the firm's marginal revenue curve is $MR = A - \left[\dfrac{2B}{g(\alpha)}\right]Q$. Equating marginal revenue to marginal production cost, $c$, then yields the optimal quantity, $Q^*$, and the corresponding optimal price, $P^*$. These are

$$Q^* = \frac{(A - c)g(\alpha)}{2B} \quad \text{and} \quad P^* = \frac{A + c}{2} \,. \qquad \textbf{(21.20)}$$

Note that for this case of expanding market reach, increases in advertising, $\alpha$, lead to a rise in the quantity sold, but not to an increase in the price.

On the other hand, for the social brand name or building value case we have the demand function $Q^D(P, \alpha) = a - \dfrac{b}{v(\alpha)}\, P$, which leads to the inverse demand function $P(Q, \alpha) = v(\alpha)[A - B]Q$. Here, profit maximization implies a very different response of output and price to advertising. The profit-maximizing quantity of output to produce at a given level of advertising services, $\alpha$, is found by equating marginal revenue equal to marginal cost. That is $MR = v(\alpha)[A - 2B]Q = c$ yields the optimal quantity, $Q^*$, and the corresponding optimal price, $P^*$. In this case, these are

$$Q^* = \frac{Av(\alpha) - c}{2Bv(\alpha)} \quad \text{and} \quad P^* = \frac{Av(\alpha) + c}{2} \,. \qquad \textbf{(21.21)}$$

In contrast to the brand recognition case, increases in advertising, $\alpha$, in the social value brand name case do lead to an increase in price. If unit cost $c$ is relatively small the effect on quantity sold of an increase in advertising in this case is relatively small. In the extreme when unit cost $c$ is equal to zero then $Q^*$ does not depend on advertising in the building brand value case. Increases in advertising lead in this case to an increase in price but no increase in quantity sold. In contrast, when $c = 0$ in the extending reach case increases in advertising lead to an increase in quantity sold but no increase in price. The two cases help us understand how advertising can have an ambiguous effect on prices depending in part on what is the value of the brand name to consumers. When the social role predominates we could expect increased advertising and increased prices, but when the informative role predominates, increased advertising should not lead to higher prices, just more output.

## Practice Problem 21.3

Suppose a firm marketing styling gel faces an inverse demand curve $P(Q, \alpha) = \alpha^{1/2}[1 - Q]$, where $Q$ is number of tubes sold per period, measured in millions, and $\alpha$ is advertising seconds on television per period. Currently the firm is advertising 100 seconds. The cost of advertising is \$10,000 per second. For simplicity suppose that the production cost of a tube of gel is constant and set to zero. There are no fixed costs.

a. Calculate the firm's profit-maximizing quantity and price. Work out the firm's profit as well.
b. Now suppose that the firm's marketing manager has struck a deal that if the firm advertises 625 seconds the cost of advertising falls to \$5,000 per second. Work out the firm's profit-maximizing strategy and profits if it increases its advertising to 625 seconds.

## 21.4 COMPLEMENTARY ADVERTISING: IMPLICATIONS FOR EFFICIENCY AND COMPETITION

A frequent complaint about network television in the United States is the abundance of commercials. Indeed, this feature is often cited as a key factor in the demand for both videocassettes and for premium cable channels, both of which permit viewing uninterrupted by commercials. Similarly, everyone has now heard of the common strategy of taping a network show and watching it later while fast-forwarding through the sales blurbs. Such anecdotes suggest that the marketplace somehow leads to too much advertising. Of course, we do need to be precise. In economics, "too much" or "too little" advertising can only be interpreted as an amount of advertising that is either greater than or less than the efficient amount, where by *efficient* we mean that amount of advertising that maximizes the sum of consumer and producer surplus.

Because we generally argue that such efficiency requires price equal to marginal cost, there at first seems to be some logic to the charge of inefficiently excessive advertising. This is because advertising is available to consumers at a zero price, which is likely less than the marginal cost of advertising. What if advertising is considered to be one of two goods which consumers wish to consume together? The relevant price in this case is the combined price of both the product and the commercial advertising it. Because the good itself is sold by a firm with monopoly power, and because the firm will maximize profit by restricting output and raising price, the combined price of the product and the commercial together may not be below its marginal cost.[14]

It turns out that when advertising is a complement to the good being advertised it is possible to show that either too much or too little advertising could result. In general, because the firm chooses the advertising level to maximize profit, the firm does not consider any additional gain in consumer surplus that results from a change in advertising and so will not be induced to produce the efficient amount of advertising. But whether the firm's choice will be too large or too small is not a priori clear. A further examination of Figures 21-3 and 21-4 suggests why this is so. The firm's choice depends on how advertising affects the willingness to pay of the marginal consumers. Consider the case when the effect of advertising is to raise the marginal consumer's willingness to pay proportionately more than the inframarginal consumer. This would be similar to the case in Figure 21-4. Alternatively, the effect of advertising could be proportionately greater for intramarginal rather than marginal consumers as is the case in Figure 21-3. These figures show that advertising works to affect consumer demand in a way similar to how changes in product quality affect consumer demand as discussed in Chapter 7. There we showed that when quality affects demand as shown in Figure 21-3, the firm will choose too low a quality. Similarly, if advertising affects demand this way, the firm will likewise choose too low a level of advertising. However, if advertising affects demand as shown in Figure 21-4, then it is possible that there may be too much advertising. The price rises as the firm advertises more and this reduces the surplus of customers who would have bought

---

14 This result is shown formally in Becker and Murphy (1993), pp. 957–58, for a more general model of advertising as a complementary good. In effect, the market for advertising is not cleared by price but, instead, rationed by the monopolist. Hence, the true marginal benefit to consumers may be either above or below the "price" for advertising that we actually observe.

the good anyway. This can make the net surplus fall even though the firm's profit rises.[15]

So far we have worked in a monopoly framework. What happens if there is competition? There are several points to consider. When the firms market a homogenous product, then advertising by any one of them increases overall market demand for the product and this benefits all the firms. In this case, a firm that incurs the cost of advertising would not appropriate the full benefit of its action. There would be a "free-rider" effect as firms that did not advertise would benefit from the increased demand caused by the one firm's advertising. Consequently, the incentive to advertise by any one firm in the market would be considerably weakened—the more so the greater the number of firms. In turn, this would lead us to predict too little advertising when there are many firms and the industry looks more or less competitive. In fact, it is precisely this problem that leads to collaborative advertising efforts such as the dairy industry's "Got Milk" campaign. If any one firm paid for such advertising, that firm would earn very little return. By arranging for many firms to sponsor such commercials jointly, the dairy industry hopes to overcome such free-rider difficulties.[16]

When the firms in the market sell differentiated as opposed to identical products matters change a good bit. If the advertisement is a complement to only the product of the firm sending out the ad, then the free-rider problem disappears and each firm appropriates the benefit from its advertising. However, because it is hard to "stand out in a crowd" we expect that this case will be more likely to hold in markets with relatively fewer firms. This suggests that we should observe a negative relationship between industry advertising expenditure and the number of firms in the industry. The fewer the number of firms, or the more concentrated the industry, the greater should be the industry advertising-to-sales ratio.

John Sutton (1991) has offered additional analysis that further supports this prediction. His work builds on the stylized fact that the greater the extent of sunk costs in the industry, the higher the equilibrium concentration tends to be.[17] Advertising may be viewed as such a sunk cost. Once the ad campaign is mounted and waged, the associated expenses can never be recovered. Hence, Sutton argues that in industries in which such product differentiation through advertising is possible, advertising expenditures will be high. Such industries will therefore be characterized by both considerable sunk cost and a high degree of concentration.

Here again, it is important to note the source of the link between concentration and market structure. If Sutton is right, this link will be observed only in those markets in which it is truly possible to differentiate one's product in the eyes of the consumer. More importantly, it is *not* the advertising that causes the concentration. It is the ability of advertising to differentiate products that leads jointly to both the large advertising expense and the concentrated industrial structure.

There is a considerable number of empirical studies linking advertising intensity to either profitability or concentration and the evidence on the relationship between

---

15 For the surplus to fall, the demand curve has to be nonlinear.

16 In early 2004 the U.S. Court of Appeals ruled that forcing dairy farmers to pay for advertising programs that promote milk is unconstitutional. Dairy Management Inc., which collects around $44 million from the "Got Milk" ads through the National Dairy Checkoff program, intends to appeal the decision. The court's ruling follows a Supreme Court decision in 2001 that said forcing farmers to pay for marketing programs was "compelled speech" and therefore unconstitutional.

17 More precisely, the higher the *minimum* concentration ratio tends to be. This relationship is developed in Chapter 4.

advertising and concentration is quite mixed. Telser (1964) was one of the first studies to look for evidence of an advertising–concentration link and he found that, if anything, higher advertising was associated with *lower* industry concentration. Many other such studies soon followed. The findings of all these studies may be closely approximated by the summary statement that about half support Telser's original finding and half support the opposite view that advertising is positively associated with concentration. Moreover, as we have repeatedly emphasized, the interpretation of any such empirical findings is far from obvious. It may well be the monopoly power associated with highly concentrated industries that generates the heavy advertising expenditures, and not the high advertising expenditures that cause concentration to be high.

In light of the mixed empirical results on advertising and concentration, the case study evidence that Sutton (1991) provides in support of his own analysis seems perhaps the most compelling. Sutton finds that in those industries in which advertising might be reasonably expected to play a significant role in distinguishing one brand from another, such as breakfast cereals and frozen food retailing, advertising expenditures and the degree of concentration are both high. Indeed, perhaps the most interesting aspect of Sutton's argument is that, all else equal, the high advertising— high concentration link will likely be strongest precisely when price competition is the most intense. This is because, beyond the large sunk cost that the heavy advertising reflects, such fierce price rivalry further limits the number of firms that can profitably enter.[18]

The famous *ReaLemon* case may be considered a good example supporting Sutton's analysis.[19] Borden's ReaLemon brand dominated the market for many years. When a rival firm, Golden Crown, entered the market with its own lemon juice product it found itself at a real disadvantage relative to ReaLemon, which had advertised heavily during the previous ten years, even though Golden Crown's product was chemically identical. Not only did Golden Crown have to sell at a 15 to 25 percent discount relative to ReaLemon's price, but substantial price competition also broke out. The result was that ReaLemon lowered its price and this in turn forced Golden Crown to do the same. Yet because of the price differential imposed on Golden Crown, it found that it could barely break even. Why? Because this was a product market in which consumers seemed particularly responsive to advertising, even though brand differences were minimal. As a result, the heavy advertising in which the makers of ReaLemon engaged gave rise to a very high concentration. Given the intense price competition that accompanied any active rivalry there was a limit to the number of firms that could sustain the sunk costs of heavy advertising in this market.

The *Clorox* bleach case may offer a further supporting example.[20] This case involved the proposed acquisition by Procter & Gamble of the Clorox bleach firm. Clorox was the dominant brand of household bleach, accounting for nearly half of industry sales and selling for a substantial premium over rival brands despite the fact that all household bleaches are chemically indistinguishable. Here again the courts found that Clorox's dominant position was due to its massive advertising. Indeed, the Supreme Court considered such advertising to be a vital part of the market for house-

---

18 Robinson and Chiang (1996) also provide evidence in support of Sutton's basic analysis.
19 *FTC v. Borden, Inc.*, 92 FTC 669, 1978. The FTC found Borden, the maker of the ReaLemon brand, guilty of monopolizing the reconstituted lemon juice market and that its successful differentiation of its product was the source of this monopoly power. The finding was later upheld by a U.S. Court of Appeals.
20 *Federal Trade Commission v. Procter & Gamble Co.*, 386 U.S. 568, 1967.

hold soaps, detergents, and cleansers. This view, therefore, suggests that this was again a market in which differentiation by advertising was feasible and, hence, that this would be a market in which the equilibrium concentration level would be quite high, exactly as it was. Moreover, it appears again to be the case that this concentration was heightened as a result of the fierce price competition in the industry. Indeed, it was the fear of such intense price competition that led Procter & Gamble to enter this market by acquiring Clorox rather than by marketing its own brand.

## 21.5  COOPERATIVE ADVERTISING

Cooperative advertising arrangements come in a variety of shapes and sizes. Up until now we have focused on advertising by manufacturers to promote their products. Nevertheless, the provision of promotional services remains one of the activities that manufacturers most commonly delegate to retailers. Moreover, in recent years, new marketing arrangements broadly categorized as cooperative advertising agreements have emerged as a common feature of such promotional contracts. In turn, these new practices have raised a number of antitrust concerns. One type of agreement commonly used in book and music retailing is a simple one in which the manufacturer helps the retailer pay for advertising space in local media and also provides in-store displays and other promotional items. A closely related set of practices used frequently in the supermarket industry is the manufacturer's payment of "slotting allowances." These include a lump-sum payment just to have one's product on the shelf. They also include (1) additional payments for display stands at the end of an aisle in which a manufacturer's product is shown at eye level; (2) so-called "pay-to-stay" fees, which are essentially a form of rent; and (3) failure fees that the manufacturer must pay when a product fails to achieve a pre-specified sales volume over, say, a six-month period.

The competitive effects of all of these arrangements are complicated. To a large extent, such agreements can be efficiency and competition enhancing. By directly involving the manufacturer in promotional activities, they may mitigate the tendency for retailers to underprovide such services.[21] In addition, slotting fees have the beneficial effect of allocating scarce shelf space to those manufacturers who value it most highly as well as providing an incentive for the expansion of the most efficient retailers over time. Further, by putting more of the risk on the manufacturer, the failure fees may help overcome the reluctance of dealers to stock new products. Yet cooperative advertising agreements also have the potential for harming competition, as illustrated by the three cases described in the following paragraphs.

Perhaps the most obvious way that a cooperative advertising arrangement can be anticompetitive is when it is used by a large manufacturer to foreclose retail outlets to a smaller rival. Suppose that a dominant manufacturer earns a profit of $10 million currently but that entry by a rival will reduce total industry profit to $8 million, half of which goes to the new entrant. The incumbent is therefore facing a reduction of its profit from $10 million to $4 million if entry occurs. As a result, it will be willing to spend up to $6 million in slotting fees to retailers in order to keep the rival off

---

21  The underprovision of retail services is discussed in Chapter 18.

the dealers' shelves. Since the most that the rival can pay is $4 million, the incumbent has a clear ability to outbid the rival and thereby to prevent entry.

The threat of foreclosure seems to lie at the heart of a recent Federal Trade Commission case against McCormick & Company, the world's largest spice company. McCormick sold a full line of prepared spices and related products such as dry seasoning mixes to supermarkets under its own name and, in different local markets, under the name of subsidiary brands. While there were other spice companies, they were all much smaller than McCormick. In fact, only one of these, Burns Philp Food, Inc., sold on a national level and actually offered a full line of spices. In the early 1990s, Burns Philp began to price its products quite aggressively and a price war erupted between the two firms.

McCormick's tactics in the price war included the offering of generous upfront fees that were essentially the equivalent of paying slotting allowances. In return, McCormick demanded that the recipient store devote the vast majority of its spice shelf space—sometimes 90 percent or more—to McCormick products alone. Because not all stores agreed to McCormick's demands or received exactly the same payments, the net payment for McCormick's products actually paid by a store was different across supermarkets. For this reason, the FTC's initial complaint was couched in terms of illegal price discrimination. However, there can be little doubt that the predatory foreclosure effect of buying up shelf space played a central role in the FTC's decision. The FTC noted that Burns Philp fared quite badly in the price war and that the loss of access to shelf space played a role in this outcome. It also noted that other competitors were now probably keenly aware of the danger of taking on McCormick. In the end, McCormick agreed to stop paying differential allowances and to charge all grocery stores the same net price. Yet while this solution addresses the price discrimination issue, the question of foreclosure and what to do about it remains. However, this issue had become rather moot in the spice market by the time of the FTC's decision. As noted, by that time Burns Philp had lost the price war.[22]

As mentioned, the FTC complaint against McCormick was largely couched in terms of illegal price discrimination that gave some grocery stores better terms than others. This is, in fact, the second way in which cooperative advertising agreements can be anticompetitive. This concern has been particularly strong in the book-selling market. Selling books is a tough business. There are over 150,000 books published each year. Even if the stock of each book is only a few thousand copies, these numbers imply a tremendous volume of books and a serious scarcity of shelf space at retail bookstores. This scarcity is obviously even more severe in the case of prime display locations at the front of the store, in the windows, and on the end of aisles. As this scarcity has intensified, shelf space and window displays have become prime real estate and publishers have paid fees ranging from $5,000 to $20,000 to have their books displayed in the window or on a popular shelf at consumer eye level.[23]

In principle, paying fees to obtain scarce shelf space is not inherently anticompetitive. However, such payments can be harmful when not all retailers are offered the same terms. This has been a persistent claim of the independent bookstores. These outlets tend to be much smaller than the large discount chains. Hence, the "rent" a publisher will pay to such dealers for their top display spots is considerably less than

---

22 See "World's Largest Manufacturer of Spice and Seasoning Products Agrees to Settle Price Discrimination Charges." FTC News Release, March 8, 2000.

23 From J. Hitt, "The Theory of Supermarkets." *The New York Times Magazine*, March 10, 1996, p. 61.

that offered to the larger chain stores. Indeed, many small independent bookstores complain that such cooperative advertising allowances are not available to them at all. When they are, these independents further claim that not only is the compensation they receive lower but that the reimbursement process is much more cumbersome. The predictable result, the independent sellers claim, is that the greater subsidization of the promotional costs at large chains allows the chains to sell their books at a lower price, thereby giving the chains an unfair advantage vis-à-vis the independent dealers. If such price discrimination occurred and if it materially weakened competition it would, of course, be a violation of the Robinson-Patman Act. The difficulty, as usual with Robinson-Patman cases, lies in distinguishing damage to competition from damage to individual competitors, that is, damage to the retail market rather than simply damage to the small booksellers.

The charges made by the booksellers were the subject of both a lengthy investigation by the FTC and a number of lawsuits filed by the American Booksellers Association (representing over 4,500 independent bookstore owners) against the major publishing houses. In the end, the FTC decided to dismiss the complaints without commenting on the legality of the practices, noting that the retailing of books was changing rapidly with the rise of e-commerce giants such as Amazon.com. The lawsuits were settled as well, typically with an agreement that each publisher make a small, lump sum payment to the independent booksellers and take some modest steps to guarantee equal access of all bookstores to cooperative advertising. These outcomes reflect the fact that while the price discrimination fear may in principle be a legitimate one, most analysts regard Robinson-Patman cases with a good bit of skepticism. Further, as the FTC noted, it became increasingly difficult to argue that competition among booksellers had been seriously threatened by the publishers' actions in light of the fierce competition provided by electronic retailers.[24]

Yet a third way that cooperative advertising can raise troublesome antitrust issues is when it is used as a means to implement what is effectively a resale price maintenance agreement. This concern is illustrated by a case in the recorded music industry. In the United States, this industry was then dominated by five major companies: Sony, TimeWarner, EMI, Bertelsman, and Universal. Together these firms accounted for about 85 percent of U.S. sales of pre-recorded music. The firms distributed their CDs and tapes through both specialized retailers such as Musicland, Tower Records, and Sam Goody, and sometimes through generalized retailers such as department stores. In the early 1990s, large discount sellers such as Best Buy Corp., Circuit City, and Wal-Mart entered the market.

In order to gain market share and establish a meaningful market presence, the discount stores entered with very low promotional CD prices. For some popular CDs, the price reductions were as much as 50 percent, resulting in retail prices of under $10. Each of the five producers responded to this fall in retail prices by adopting cooperative advertising agreements with virtually all retailers. These agreements included a minimum average price (MAP) clause. The typical arrangement called for the manufacturer to help fund the retailer's advertisements that did not mention prices below those that the manufacturer suggested. At least initially, however, the retail firm was free to run ads that mentioned lower prices so long as it did

---

24 See "FTC Dismisses Case Against Six Book Publishers." FTC New Release, September 21, 1996, http://www.ftc.gov and M. Tabour, "In Bookstore Chains, Display Space Is for Sale." *The New York Times*, January 15, 1996, p. A1.

so at its own expense. This is exactly what some retailers did, especially the discount houses. They used the cooperative advertising funds for general promotion and then used their own funds to advertise their price cuts. The result was that the price war continued.

As time passed and retail CD prices stayed low, the music producers began to receive requests for lower wholesale prices from the traditional outlets, for example, Sam Goody. These retail firms justified such requests with the claim that lower wholesale prices would enable them to confront the discount competition. Thus, from the perspective of the CD makers, the intense competition at the retail level was spilling over into competition at the wholesale level. Therefore, the five producers each revised their cooperative advertising contracts. Starting in 1995 and 1996, the agreements required that the retailer not mention a lower-than-suggested price *in any advertisement*, even those completely paid for by the retailer. Violation of this clause led to suspension of all cooperative advertising funding for 60 to 90 days. The evidence suggests that the spread of these contracts quickly led to the end of discounting and to a rise in both retail and wholesale CD prices.

In light of the foregoing, it is hard to escape the conclusion that the MAP agreements were primarily a means to implement a minimum resale price agreement. Moreover, the underlying motive does not appear to be the desire to guarantee the provision of retail services. What seems more likely based on the observed pricing behavior and company documents is that the primary purpose behind the MAP contracts was to suppress retail competition as a means to prevent the spread of such competition to the level of the five CD producers. In other words, the cooperative advertising appears really to have been a vertical arrangement designed to foster horizontal collusion. This was exactly the judgment of the FTC, which found the five music producers to be in violation of the antitrust laws and ordered a stop to the MAP agreements. The five companies quickly complied with this order but the potential for this difficulty to rise again in another context seems clear.[25]

Before ending this section, we should also note that lump sum slotting fee payments may play a similar role to the MAP agreements in weakening wholesale price competition. The basic argument here is due to Shaffer (1991). In order to pay the slotting fee, the manufacturer has to set a wholesale price above marginal cost. Therefore, at the downstream level, each retailer who signs the agreement is effectively signaling its intention to be less aggressive in its pricing because it is accepting the higher wholesale price. Even if other retailers are aggressive, the firm with the slotting fee is compensated by the lump sum payment. As a result, each retailer has an incentive to adopt the slotting fee arrangement. This is, in fact, what happens in the Nash equilibrium. In turn, the weaker retail competition and higher retail prices also spill over to higher prices at the wholesale level.

In sum, cooperative advertising and so-called slotting fees are probably, in most instances, either procompetitive or neutral. Yet as in the cases described here, there is the potential for such agreements to have anticompetitive effects. These are essentially vertical arrangements and, as we reviewed in Chapter 19, their full consequences may only be understood after careful analysis.

25 See J. R. Wilke and P. M. Reilly, "FTC Investigates Retail Pricing of CDs, Seeks Data from Recording Companies." *The Wall Street Journal*, May 7, 1997, p. B1. See also "Record Companies Settle FTC Charges of Restraining Competition in CD Music Market." FTC News Release, May 10, 2000, http://www.ftc.gov.

# SUMMARY

In this chapter, we have examined the role that advertising can play as a weapon in the arsenal of firms competing against rivals. National advertising by manufacturers can play a useful role in informing consumers of real differences in product attributes. For example, within the market for pain killers, some consumers can benefit from the anti-inflammatory effects of aspirin. Others find aspirin too abrasive to the lining of their stomachs. For these customers, knowing that aspirin alternatives, such as Tylenol with acetaminophen and Advil with ibuprofen, are available is important. In such cases, advertising improves the matching of consumers with the product types they most prefer. In markets where consumers have a strong taste for variety the matching role of advertising plays an important role affecting prices and profits.

There are also many goods such as films, clothes, cosmetics, watches, vacation packages, and hiking shoes where promotional efforts may be useful because they serve as a complement to the product being advertised. For example, one's enjoyment of a new movie may be greatly enhanced if, after viewing it, one can talk about the film with friends who will at least know a bit about the film such as the plot and the star performers. The same is true for the purchase of designer clothes. There is little status in wearing clothes designed by Calvin Smith no matter how good they are. There is considerable crowd appeal in wearing those designed by Calvin Klein. By providing such complementary services, advertising can again enhance consumer welfare.

Advertising may not be harmful and may perhaps be quite helpful in improving social welfare and economic efficiency. Yet this is not to say that advertising does not raise any public policy issues. There remains the question as to whether the market generates too little or too much advertising effort, and a case can be made for either view. In addition, the advertising agreements between manufacturers and retailers can be used to suppress both retail and wholesale price competition. All of this is a way of saying that advertising raises complicated issues that do not give rise to broad general statements. The concerns that advertising is socially excessive or anticompetitive, or possibly even both, are real and legitimate. However, what the analyses presented here suggest is that without any advertising there would likely be a different but equally real set of frustrations.

# PROBLEMS

**1.** A recent survey by an advertising agency found that many consumers thought that there were too many different brands available for sale in certain product categories. For example, 70 percent of the consumers surveyed thought that there were too many brands of dry cereal, and 60 percent thought that there were too many brands of bar soap. Explain what is meant by the phrases "too many" or "too few" from the point of view of efficiency. Explain how the market could lead to "too many" brands of a product being produced.

**2.** There are the two hair salons located on Main Street, which is one mile long. The low-cost salon, Quick-Cuts, is located at the East End of town, at the address $x = 0$. It has a constant unit cost of \$6 for a haircut. The higher cost salon, Le Coupe, is located at the West End, or $x = 1$. The unit cost of a haircut at Le Coupe is $18. There are 1,000 potential customers who live along Main Street and they are uniformly spread out along the mile. Consumers are willing to pay $50 for a haircut if it was done at their home. If a consumer has to travel to get a haircut then a travel cost of $t$ per unit mile is incurred. Suppose that $t = \$12/\text{mile}$. Each salon wants to set a price for a haircut that maximizes the salon's profit.

   **a.** What is the demand function facing Quick-Cuts? What is the demand function facing Le Coupe?

   **b.** What are the equilibrium prices set by the two salons?

   **c.** What are the market shares of the two salons at these prices?

   **d.** What happens to equilibrium prices and market shares if the travel cost $t$ increases from $12 to $20 per mile?

   **e.** What happens to equilibrium prices and market shares if the travel cost $t$ decreases from $12 to $6 per mile?

**3.** Suppose now that consumers are not perfectly informed about where the salons are and what prices are charged for a haircut.

   **a.** Which salon do you think has the greater incentive to advertise? Why?

   **b.** The incentive to advertise depends upon the cost of advertising. Let's suppose that Le Coupe is working with a more effective ad agency and so the cost of reaching consumers, as measured by the parameter $\alpha$, is lower for Le Coupe than for Quick-Cuts. In particular, suppose that the proportion of consumers along Main Street that are informed of a haircut at Quick-Cuts is $1/2$, whereas the proportion of consumers informed about Le Coupe is $3/4$. What happens to equilibrium prices?

**4.** Consider the following list of ad campaigns and evaluate them according to extending reach or building value.

   **a.** promoting quicker braking for a specific type of tire

   **b.** presentation of taste test data on french fries

   **c.** presentation of sales data on a cola product

   **d.** demonstration of a close shave by an attractive well-known athlete

   **e.** a dog taking its owner to a particular car dealership

   **f.** testimonials by adults who like a "kid's" cereal

   **g.** laundry detergent commercial showing items washed by two different brands

   **h.** liquid soap commercial showing celebrities lathering themselves

   **i.** athletic apparel commercial showing big stars being provocative

**5.** Consider again Practice Problem 21.3, only now the inverse demand curve is $P(Q, \alpha) = 1 - \alpha^{-1/2}Q$, where $Q$ is number of tubes sold per period, measured in millions, and $\alpha$ is advertising seconds on television per period. Currently the firm is advertising 100 seconds. The cost of advertising is $10,000 per second. The production cost of a tube of gel is constant and set to zero and there are no fixed costs.

   **a.** Calculate the firm's profit-maximizing quantity and price. Work out the firm's profit as well.

**b.** Now suppose that the firm's marketing manager has struck a deal that if the firm advertises 625 seconds the cost of advertising falls to $5,000 per second. Work out what the firm's profit-maximizing strategy and profits would be if it increases its advertising to 625 seconds.

**c.** Compare your answer to that for the Practice Problem.

# REFERENCES

Bagwell, K., and G. Ramey. 1994. "Coordination Economies, Advertising, and Search Behavior in Retail Markets." *American Economic Review* 84 (June): 498–517.

Becker, G., and K. Murphy. 1993. "A Simple Theory of Advertising as a Good or Bad." *Quarterly Journal of Economics* 108 (August): 941–64.

Butters, G. 1977. "Equilibrium Distribution of Sales and Advertising Prices." *Review of Economic Studies* 44 (June): 465–91.

Clark, C., and I. Horstmann. 2001. "Advertising and Coordination in Markets with Consumption Scale Effects." University of Western Ontario Working Paper.

Comanor, W. S., and T. A. Wilson. 1967. "Advertising Market Structure and Performance." *Review of Economics and Statistics* 49 (November): 423–40.

——————. 1974. *Advertising and Market Power*. Cambridge, MA: Harvard University Press.

Grossman, G. M., and C. Shapiro. 1984. "Informative Advertising with Differentiated Products." *Review of Economic Studies* 51 (February): 63–81.

Robinson, W. T., and J. Chiang. 1996. "Are Sutton's Predictions Robust? Empirical Insights into Advertising, R&D, and Concentration." *Journal of Industrial Organization* 44 (December): 389–408.

Shaffer, G. 1991. "Slotting Allowances and Resale Price Maintenance: A Comparison of Facilitating Practices." *Rand Journal of Economics* 22 (Spring): 121–35.

Sutton, J. 1991. *Sunk Costs and Market Structure*. Cambridge, MA: The MIT Press.

Telser, L. 1964. "Advertising and Competition." *Journal of Political Economy* 72 (December): 537–62.

Tirole, J. 1988. *The Theory of Industrial Organization*. Cambridge, MA: The MIT Press.

# Chapter 22

# Research and Development

The final results of the human genome project indicate that we humans are not as complicated as we thought we were. Rather than consisting of the approximately 100,000 genes that were initially predicted, it appears that we have only 30,000 genes, less than twice as many as the humble roundworm with its 19,098 genes.[1] The importance of this finding from an economic perspective lies in its implications for the development of new medical products. Genes are a crucial factor in predicting and curing many diseases. Therefore, identifying and understanding the workings of each gene could lead to the creation of a new family of custom-made drugs. The rough equation quoted by the pharmaceutical companies was "one gene, one patent, one drug."[2] If, as initially expected, there were 100,000 genes then there was potentially a vast number of revenue-generating patents. The finding that the actual number of genes is far less than 100,000 has suggested to many that genes hold many fewer of the keys to the treatment of disease. As a result, understanding genes and their functions may offer a much less lucrative source of new patentable treatments.

However, all is not necessarily lost. It is now suggested that much of human biology is determined at the protein level rather than at the DNA level, and we have nearly 250,000 different proteins in our bodies. So now we have a whole new science, proteomics—studying how genes control proteins—as a method for creating tailored drugs. Proteomics is being pursued by an increasingly wide number of companies and institutions; Harvard University, for example, has created a new Institute of Proteomics.

The race to understand the proteomic causes of diseases and to develop new drugs targeted at those diseases will not come as a surprise to anyone familiar with the popular business literature of the past twenty years. That literature has been characterized by the dominant theme that the most successful firms are those that find new ways of doing things, or that develop new products and new markets.[3] The now prevalent view is that firms become industry leaders by conducting research and development (R&D), leading to innovations in either their production technology or the products they provide. Michael Porter's *The Competitive Advantage of Nations* (1990) serves to make the point. Porter writes that any theory of competitive success

> must start from the premise that competition is dynamic and evolving. . . . Competition is a constantly changing landscape in which new products, new ways of marketing, new production processes, and whole new market segments emerge. . . . [Economic] theory must make improvement and innovation in methods and technology a central element. (p. 20)

---

1  If you are interested, the complete human genome is available as a free download from http://www.gdb.org/.
2  "Scientists, Companies Look to the Next Step After Genes." *The New York Times*, February 13, 2001.
3  This is virtually the mantra in the best-selling book by Peters and Waterman, *In Search of Excellence: Lessons from America's Best Run Companies* (1982). However, the argument is repeated frequently in other business books, including, as noted herein, Porter's (1990) encyclopedic volume.

Porter's quote could almost have been taken verbatim from Joseph Schumpeter's classic work written almost fifty years earlier. Schumpeter was both an economist and a historian. It was therefore natural that he brought a historical perspective to his study of competition and the rise and fall of corporate empires. The following dramatic passage appears in his book *Capitalism, Socialism, and Democracy*, first published in 1942.

> (I)t is not . . . [price] . . . competition which counts but competition from the new commodity, the new technology, the new source of supply, the new type of organization . . . competition which commands a decisive cost or quality advantage and which strikes not at the margins of the profits and outputs of existing firms but at their foundations and very lives. (p. 84)

Interest in the forces behind innovative activity is, if anything, even stronger today than it was when Schumpeter wrote.[4] An important issue raised by Schumpeter concerns the market environment most conducive to R&D activity. Schumpeter conjectured that R&D efforts are more likely to be undertaken by large firms than by small ones. He then speculated that monopolistic or oligopolistic firms would more aggressively pursue innovative activity than would firms with little or no market power. Accordingly, he argued that the benefits of an economy comprised largely of competitive markets populated by small firms reflected the rather modest gains of allocating resources efficiently among a *given set of goods and services produced with given technologies*. In contrast, the benefits of markets dominated by large firms, each with sizable market power, stemmed from the much larger dynamic efficiency gains of developing new products and new technologies. As Schumpeter wrote, "a shocking suspicion dawns upon us that big business may have had more to do with creating (our) standard of life than with keeping it down." (p. 88)

The validity of Schumpeter's ideas—which have come to be jointly referred to as the Schumpeterian hypothesis—is the key issue addressed in this chapter. Do larger firms do more R&D? Does a concentrated market structure provide a better environment for the development of new innovations than a competitive structure? Some evidence in favor of these suggestions comes from data produced by the U.S. Patents and Trademark Office. Table 22-1 lists the top ten companies in terms of the number of patents granted to these companies. Each of these is a fairly large company. However, great care is needed before interpreting these suggestive findings as clear evidence that Schumpeter's hypothesis is true. For example, rather than imply that large firms do more R&D, these results could imply that firms that do more R&D become large. Other interpretations—each with a different implication regarding Schumpeter's hypothesis—are also possible.

Note that the introduction of a new product by a firm undermines the marketability of existing products. Similarly, the development of a new production process requiring new equipment reduces the value of existing productive capacity. Because the process of introducing new products or processes inevitably means the destruction of

---

4   For example, see the story by C. J. Whalen, "Today's Hottest Economist Died 50 Years Ago." *Business Week*, December 11, 2000. Ever since Solow's (1956) classic work, macroeconomists studying growth have also focused intensively on technological progress and innovation as the primary source of improved living standards over time. See, for example, the books by Barro and Sala-i-Martin (1995) and Romer (1996).

TABLE
22-1

| Top Ten Companies by Patents Granted, to June 2000 | |
|---|---|
| *Company* | *Number of Patents Granted* |
| International Business Machines | 23,773 |
| Canon Kabushiki Kaisha | 19,983 |
| General Electric Company | 18,612 |
| Hitachi Ltd. | 18,024 |
| Toshiba Corporation | 17,379 |
| Mitsubishi Denki Kabushiki Kaisha | 13,745 |
| Motorola Inc. | 13,660 |
| Eastman Kodak Company | 13,152 |
| NEC Corporation | 12,903 |
| U.S. Philips Corporation | 12,307 |

**Source:** U.S. Patent and Trademark Office, Information Products Division/TAF Branch, Special Report, August 2000, Washington D.C.

old ones, Schumpeter dubbed such competition by innovation the process of "creative destruction." Since some of the products and processes that are made obsolete may well be those of the innovating firm itself we may ask our central question in a somewhat different way. In particular, we may ask why firms undermine existing activities (including their own) in this way. More generally, what are the incentives to engage in innovative activity and how do these vary with firm size and market structure?

Both the professional and the popular business literature have had much to say on the Schumpeterian hypothesis in recent years. In this chapter, we approach this topic using the tools of economic analysis and strategic interaction that we have built throughout the book. However, before we begin a more formal analysis, we need to establish some definitions or classifications to which we can easily refer.

## 22.1  A TAXONOMY OF INNOVATIONS

R&D efforts typically are classified as one of three related activities. The first is *basic research*. This includes studies that will not necessarily lead to specific applications but instead aim to improve our fundamental knowledge in a manner that may subsequently be helpful across a range of activities. The derivation and validation of the theory of laser technology is a good example. A second category is *applied research*. Such research generally involves substantial engineering input and is aimed at a more practical and specific usage than basic research. The creation of the first laser drill for dentistry would be an example of applied research. Finally, there is the *development* component of R&D. Here the goal is to move from the creation of a prototype to a product that can be used by consumers and that is capable (to some extent at least) of mass production. To continue our analogy, the transformation of the first laser drill into a small, handheld product that is affordable and usable by a large number of dentists would be an example of the development stage. For the most part, we shall be concerned with applied research rather than development, but we shall touch upon

# ✓ Reality Checkpoint

## Creative Destruction in the Pharmaceutical Industry: Will the Prozac Work If the Viagra Fails?

Perhaps no market offers better examples of Schumpeter's "process of creative destruction" or competition by means of product development than that for pharmaceuticals. Consider the market for antidepressants. For several years after its introduction in 1988 by Eli Lilly & Co., Prozac dominated this market and, in fact, it is probably the most lucrative mental health drug in history.

However, in 1992, Pfizer, Inc., introduced a rival antidepressant, Zoloft. Today, Zoloft has nearly a third of the antidepressant market, while Prozac's share has fallen to roughly 40 percent. A third antidepressant, Paxil, which is manufactured by SmithKline Beecham PLC, has also grown rapidly and now commands over 20 percent of the market. While all three drugs work by increasing the amount of serotonin in the brain, their chemical bases are slightly different as are their side effects. Prozac can occasionally cause feelings of intense anxiety and has been linked to both violent behavior and even suicide in some users. The negative publicity surrounding these effects, in part, provided the opening for Zoloft and Paxil. However, these drugs are not free from side effects. Both have been associated with digestive problems such as nausea and diarrhea and, in some cases, sexual dysfunction.

This brings us to the story of the drug to combat male impotence, Viagra. Pfizer, Inc., originally marketed the drug known as sildenafil citrate in the early 1990s as a treatment for angina. Ultimately, the drug failed in this regard but, in the process, many male users reported an increase in sexual function. In 1998 Pfizer renamed the drug Viagra and marketed it as a treatment for impotence. The result was an almost unimaginable success. Viagra sales topped $1 billion in the first year alone.

Once again, though, success breeds imitation—and improvement. By 2003, two new competitors to Viagra were approved by the Food and Drug Administration. These were Levitra (made by Bayer and GlaxoSmithKline) and Cialis (developed by a small startup firm, ICOS, and marketed by Eli Lilly). Both work in essentially the same way as Viagra. However, Levitra apparently works much faster—within 16 minutes rather than 30 minutes to an hour as may be the case with Viagra. Cialis has a serum half-life of about 17.5 hours, which means that it will be effective for nearly 36 hours. This is nine times longer than Viagra's approximate four hours of duration. The efficacy of the two new products has made them fierce competitors to Viagra. Within the first year of their introduction, Levitra and Cialis gained 15 percent and 18 percent, respectively, of the U.S. market. In countries such as Australia and France, Cialis alone reached a market share of roughly 40 percent in its first year. Potentially, the effect of such creative destruction could reach well beyond the male impotence market. The more active lifestyles that these drugs make possible may lead to a decline in the demand for antidepressants among both men and women.

**Sources:** R. Langreth, "High Anxiety: Rivals Threaten Prozac's Reign." *The Wall Street Journal*, May 9, 1996; A. Pollack, "Lilly Pays Big Fee Up Front To Share in Rival of Viagra." *The New York Times*, October 2, 1998, p. C1; and "Viagra Rival Cialis Wins Up to 40 Percent Market Share." *Reuters News Wire*, March 23, 2004.

some of the important issues that characterize the decision to move from research to development.

In considering the output of R&D, it is common to distinguish two distinct classes. *Process innovations* are discoveries of new, typically cheaper methods for producing existing goods. *Product innovations* are innovations that lead to the creation of new goods. For the most part, we shall concentrate on process innovations, but we shall also present examples showing how the analysis can be extended to product innovations.

Finally, with respect to process innovations, there is a further distinction that can be made. This is the division of innovations into *drastic* or major innovations, and *nondrastic* or minor innovations. Roughly speaking, drastic innovations are ones that reduce the firm's unit cost to such an extent that even if it charges the profit-maximizing monopoly price associated with that low cost, it will still underprice all competitors. Hence, a drastic innovation creates a monopolist who is unconstrained by any fear of entry or rival price competition—at least for some time. By contrast, a firm making a nondrastic innovation may gain some cost advantage over its rivals but not one so large that the firm can price like a monopolist without fear of competition.

The formal distinction between drastic and nondrastic innovations is illustrated in Figure 22-1. Assume that demand for a particular product is given by $P = 120 - Q$ and that before the innovation all firms could produce the product at a constant marginal cost of \$80. Assume also that the existing firms are all Bertrand competitors so that the price is \$80 and total output is 40 units.

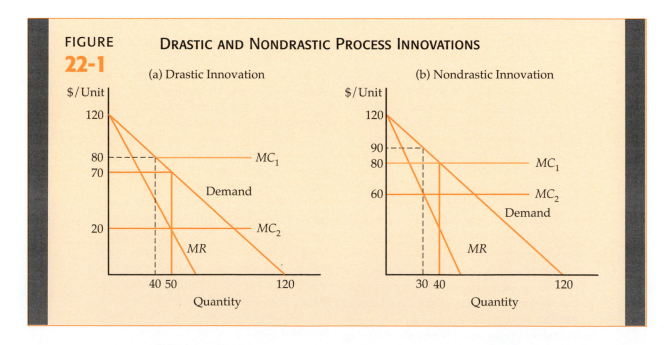

**FIGURE 22-1**

**DRASTIC AND NONDRASTIC PROCESS INNOVATIONS**

(a) Drastic Innovation

(b) Nondrastic Innovation

Now suppose that one firm gains access to a process innovation that reduces its marginal costs to \$20 as in Figure 22-1(a) and that, perhaps because of a patent, this firm is the only one able to use the new low-cost technology. If this innovator were alone in the market, it would set the monopoly price corresponding to its new, lower marginal costs of $20. Given our demand function we know that marginal revenue is $MR = 120 - 2Q$. Equating this with marginal cost of $20 gives an output of 50 units and a monopoly price of $70. Setting this monopoly price forces all the other firms out of the market. The innovation is a drastic one because the reduction in cost is so great that the innovating firm can charge the full monopoly price associated with the new low cost and still be able to undercut the marginal costs of all other firms.

Suppose by contrast that the innovation reduces marginal costs to $60 as in Figure 22-1(b). By exactly the same argument as above, the innovating firm acting as a monopolist would want to produce an output of 30 units and set a price of $90. The problem is that this will not work. The remaining firms can profitably undercut this price. The best that the innovating firm can do now is to set a price of $80 (more accurately, $79.99) and an output of 40 units. This still eliminates the other firms but only by the innovator compromising on the price that it charges. Hence, this is a nondrastic innovation.

## Practice Problem 22.1

Assume that demand in a competitive market is given by the linear function $P = 100 - 2Q$ and that current marginal cost of production is constant at $60. Now assume that there is a process innovation that reduces marginal cost to $28. Show that this is a nondrastic innovation. How much would the innovation have to lower marginal costs for it to be drastic?

## 22.2 MARKET STRUCTURE AND THE INCENTIVE TO INNOVATE

We can now begin our discussion of some of the basic questions economists have asked regarding how the incentives for making R&D expenditures are affected by market structure.[5] In order to make life a bit easier, we shall assume as in the last section that demand for a particular good is linear. Specifically, the inverse demand curve is again assumed to be given by the equation $P = 120 - Q$. We shall also assume that each producer of the good has a marginal cost of $80. Accordingly, if the market is competitive and there are many such producers, the current price is also $80.

### 22.2.1 Competition and the Replacement Effect

Suppose that a research firm that is not involved in the actual manufacture of this good discovers a new production process by undertaking research at some cost $K$. Using the notation from our previous discussion, we consider the case of a nondrastic process innovation that reduces the marginal production cost to $60. We further assume that the innovation is protected by a patent of unlimited duration that cannot be "invented around" by other potential or actual firms. What benefits does the introduction of this innovation bring, and does the market mechanism work to convey such incentives to the research firm?

---

5   This analysis owes much to Nobel Prize winner Kenneth Arrow's (1962) path-breaking work.

Let us first consider the potential gains to society as a whole that emanate from the innovation. To do this, imagine a social planner whose goal is to maximize total social surplus (producer surplus plus consumer surplus) and, moreover, who has the power to command that prices be set at whatever level requested. Such a benevolent dictator would reason as follows: With or without the innovation, optimality requires that price be set to marginal cost. The per-period value that the social planner places upon the innovation, therefore, is the increase in consumer surplus that it generates since when price equals (the constant) marginal cost there is no producer surplus. Prior to the innovation, consumer surplus at a price of $80 is, as illustrated in Figure 22-2(a), $800. After the innovation, firms in the industry will be required to set the price at the new lower marginal cost of $60, which means that consumer surplus is increased to $1,800. The increase in consumer surplus is $1,000, the lightly shaded area in Figure 22-2(a). This additional surplus will be realized not just in one period but also in all present and future periods following the innovation. Hence, using the discounting techniques discussed in Chapter 2, the total present value of the additional surplus created by the innovation is $V^p = 1,000/(1 - R)$, where $R = (1 + r)^{-1}$ and $r$ is the interest rate. The more this value exceeds the cost $K$, that is, the more it exceeds the present value of the expenses associated with discovering the process, the more desirable is the innovation.

Of course, we don't typically have a dictator and when we do his or her goal is rarely the maximization of social welfare. What we have are markets. The issue now is whether the structure of the market matters in determining the value placed on this innovation. For this purpose, first consider the incentive that the research firm has to pursue the innovation if it can auction the rights to the process to a competitive industry comprised of many firms. Prior to the innovation all firms price at marginal cost of $80 and earn zero profit. Total output each period prior to the innovation is the demand per period at price $80, which is just 40 units. What will the firm that is awarded the innovation do? Quite evidently, its best strategy is to undercut its erstwhile competitors just slightly, driving them out of the market and giving it an effective monopoly. In other words, the firm that wins the auction will set a price that is one cent less than the old competitive price, $80. At this price, the industry's total output remains identical to what it was prior to the adoption of the innovation. Consequently, the firm will earn per-period profit of $(80 - 60) \times 40 = $800. This is illustrated by the shaded rectangle in Figure 22-2(b). In other words, the present value that a competitive firm places on the innovation, and so the maximum amount it willingly bids for it, is $V^c = 800/(1 - R)$. This is less than the social value of the innovation. The reason is simple. The competitive firm only considers the profit it can earn as a result of the innovation. It ignores the additional benefit from increased consumer surplus that the innovation could bring.

Now consider the potential gain from owning the innovation that would accrue to a monopolist who faces no threat of entry. For such a firm, the gain from introducing the innovation is the additional profit it makes as a result of being able to produce at a lower marginal cost. Since the monopolist maximizes profit by setting marginal revenue equal to marginal cost, we can measure this gain by comparing the monopolist's per-period profit at its current marginal cost with its per-period profit at the lower marginal cost that the innovation permits. This is illustrated in Figure 22-2(c).

Given our demand function we know that marginal revenue is $MR = 120 - 2Q$. So, prior to the innovation, the monopolist produces an output of 20 units, sets a

## MARKET STRUCTURE AND THE DESIRE TO INNOVATE

FIGURE

**22-2**

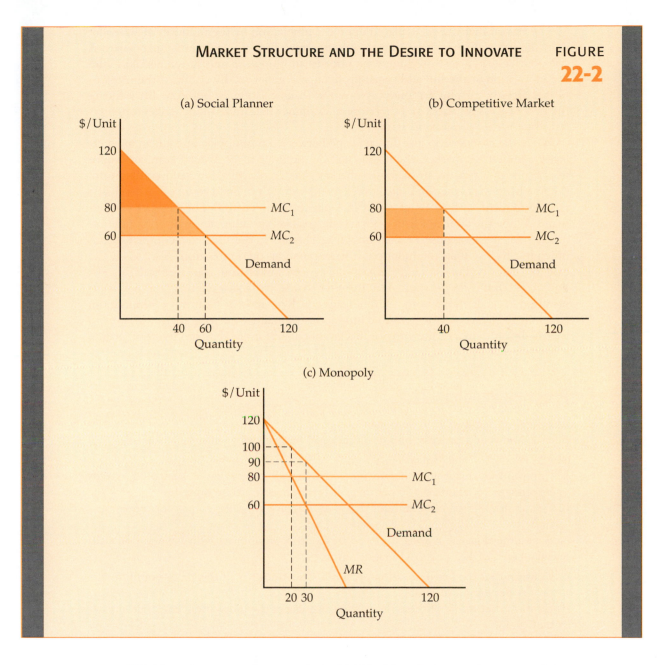

price of $100, and earns profit per period of $400. After the innovation output is increased to 30 units, price is reduced to $90, and per-period profits are $900. As a result, the per-period value placed by the monopolist on the innovation is $500—the difference between profits with and without the innovation. In turn, the total present value the monopolist places on the innovation is $V^m = 500/(1 - R)$.

From the foregoing analysis, it is obvious that $V^p > V^c > V^m$. Both the competitive firm and the monopolist undervalue the innovation relative to the social planner interested in maximizing total welfare. However, each competitive firm values the innovation more than the monopolist.

The reason that the value placed upon the innovation by the monopolist is smaller than the value of the innovation to a competitive firm is again simply explained. A competitive firm is just breaking even prior to adopting the innovation and so values the innovation at the full additional profits it will generate. By contrast, the monopolist is already earning a monopoly profit with its existing technology. Introducing the new process displaces and therefore undermines that investment. This is often referred to as the *replacement effect*.

While the comparison just drawn is one between a monopolist and a firm in a perfectly competitive market, the results will be the same if we instead compare a monopolist with a firm in an oligopoly market characterized by Bertrand competition. (Why?) Moreover, the same qualitative result will be obtained in a comparison of a monopoly firm with firms engaged in Cournot competition. The basic reason remains. While the Cournot firm enjoys some positive, pre-innovation profits, these are much smaller than those of a monopolist. Therefore, the Cournot competitor has much less to lose than the monopolist from pursuing the innovation. Also, while the case just described considered a nondrastic process innovation, the same ordering, $V^p > V^c > V^m$, holds for a drastic one. In other words, the social gain from a drastic innovation exceeds the gain to a firm engaged in Bertrand (or Cournot) competition, which in turn exceeds the gain to a monopolist. Finally, while our analysis assumes a specific linear demand, the same results are obtained for any demand function even if it is nonlinear.

## Practice Problem 22.2

Assume that demand for a homogeneous good is $P = 100 - Q$, where $P$ is measured in dollars, and that a process innovation reduces marginal costs of production from $75 to $60 per unit. Assume that the discount factor is $R = 0.9$.

a. Confirm that this is a nondrastic innovation and that marginal costs would have to be reduced to less than $50 per unit for the innovation to be drastic.

b. Calculate the maximum amount that a monopolist is willing to pay for the innovation.

Now assume that the market is served by Cournot duopolists who have an identical marginal cost of $75 prior to the innovation.

c. Confirm that the pre-innovation price is $83.33 and that at this price each firm has profits per period of $69.44.

d. Confirm that if one of these firms is granted use of the innovation, the price will fall to $78.33.

e. Show that this firm is willing to pay more for the innovation than the monopolist.

### 22.2.2  Preserving Monopoly Profit and the Efficiency Effect

The previous analysis assumed that there was only one innovator, namely, a lab outside the industry. If that laboratory company did not innovate, no one did. However, this view does not truly capture the spirit of Schumpeter's contention. Instead, Schumpeter's point is that firms typically compete by means of innovation. This means not only that firms have their own labs but that each firm is a potential innovator. As a result, even if one firm does not innovate, another might. As we are about to see, consideration of this point can reverse our previous conclusion.[6]

Suppose again that demand is described by $P = 120 - Q$, and that prior to the innovation there is an incumbent monopolist with high marginal production cost of $80 earning per-period monopoly profits of $400 at a price of $P = \$100$. The new element that we now introduce is a potential entrant along with the assumption that if entry occurs competition is Cournot. For simplicity, we will further assume that entry is only possible if the potential entrant has a lower marginal cost than does the incumbent monopolist—perhaps because the monopolist has very strong brand loyalty as a result of already being established in the market. Entry then can happen if the entrant does R&D and innovates while the monopolist does not, in which case the entrant's marginal cost falls as before to $60. Of course, as this is not a drastic innovation, such entry will not drive the monopolist out of the market altogether. Instead, the original monopolist will now compete as the high-cost firm in a duopoly. Using the techniques from Chapter 9, it is easy to verify that this yields an equilibrium in which the new entrant produces 80/3 while the initial monopolist's output falls to 20/3. The price falls to $86.67, implying a per-period profit for the new entrant of $711.11. Accordingly, the present value of the innovation to the entrant is $V^e = \$711.11/(1 - R)$.

How much is the innovation worth to the monopolist? Note that there are now two incentives for the initial monopolist to pursue the innovation. One force is the fact that such innovation allows it to lower its cost and earn higher profit as before. However, there is now a second force driving the monopolist to innovate. This is the fact that if it does not, the entrant will and the monopolist will lose its dominant position. As we have just seen, such entry lowers the monopolist's output to 20/3 and lowers the price to $86.67. In this case, the monopolist earns a post-entry profit per period of only $44.44. We may use this value as the monopolist's per period profit if it does *not* innovate. Yet if the monopolist does innovate and lowers its cost to $60, it prevents entry since, by assumption, the entrant can enter only if it has a lower cost. Thus, if the monopolist innovates, it will be alone in the market and operating with a unit cost of $60. It will therefore produce 30 units and charge a price of $90 on each unit, earning a per-period profit of $900.

Since the monopolist earns only $44.44 per period if it does not innovate but $900 per period if it does, the present value of pursuing the innovation for this firm is $V^m = (\$900 - \$44.44)/(1 - R) = (\$855.56)/(1 - R)$. Clearly this exceeds the value placed on the innovation by the entrant. Hence, the monopolist has the bigger incentive to innovate.

The foregoing result is not peculiar to the numbers we have assumed. It is in fact quite general. The best that the entrant can hope for is to change its current profit of zero to the profit earned by a duopolist with a low cost $\underline{c}$ facing a rival with high-cost $\overline{c}$, namely $\pi_e^d(\overline{c}, \underline{c})$. In contrast, the gain that the monopolist can hope for is to continue to be a monopolist but with low cost $\underline{c}$ versus being a high cost duopolist—a profit change of $\pi^m(\underline{c}) - \pi_i^d(\overline{c}, \underline{c})$. Therefore, the monopolist will always adopt the

---

6 The underlying analysis can be found in Gilbert and Newbery (1982). However, Reinganum (1983) shows that this conclusion may not hold when the timing of the successful breakthrough is uncertain. The replacement effect induces the incumbent to wait awhile and enjoy its current profit. No such effect delays the innovative activity of the potential entrant.

innovation more readily than the potential entrant if $\pi^m(\underline{c}) - \pi_i^d(\overline{c}, \underline{c}) > \pi_e^d(\overline{c}, \underline{c})$. In other words, the incumbent monopolist values the innovation more highly than the potential entrant if

$$\pi^m(\underline{c}) > \pi_i^d(\overline{c}, \underline{c}) + \pi_e^d(\overline{c}, \underline{c}). \tag{22.1}$$

Since a monopolist with the low cost $\underline{c}$ should always be able to earn at least as much total profit as would be earned by two noncooperative firms, especially when one of those firms has the high cost $\overline{c}$, the inequality in equation (22.1) should always hold. This effect is called the efficiency effect.

## 22.3 A MORE COMPLETE MODEL OF COMPETITION VIA INNOVATION

What drives the efficiency effect is the fact that the cost of non-adoption becomes higher once we recognize that it is precisely in that case that a rival may adopt. Such an increase in the cost of non-adoption makes the monopolist more willing to pay for the innovation. Clearly, this strategic interaction over potential entry by innovation seems closer to the world view Schumpeter (1942) was trying to articulate.

We can get even closer to the Schumpeterian spirit by making the decision to spend on R&D an explicit part of a firm's strategy. The simplest model in this spirit is that due to Dasgupta and Stiglitz (1980). Their model is attractive both for its key insights and because it builds on the Cournot model developed initially in Chapter 9. We present the essentials of their analysis here.

Dasgupta and Stiglitz assume an industry comprised of $n$ identical Cournot firms, each of which has to determine the level of output, $q_i$, that it will produce. Each firm must also choose the amount, $x_i$, that it will spend on R&D. The benefit of such spending is that it lowers the firm's unit cost of production, $c$. Thus each firm's unit cost is a function of the amount it spends on R&D, $c_i = c(x_i)$. However, R&D efforts are costly. Every dollar so spent—every increase in $x_i$—reduces the firm's profit from production. Total net profit for any firm, $\pi_i$, is therefore

$$\pi_i = P(Q)q_i - c(x_i)q_i - x_i. \tag{22.2}$$

Suppose that each firm spends a specific amount, $x^*$, on research. Each firm then has a unit cost of $c(x^*)$. Accordingly, if we know the value of $x^*$, we know each firm's unit cost, and we can work out the equilibrium output for each individual firm and the industry in total.[7] In particular, we know that the outcome in this symmetric, $n$-firm Cournot model results in an equilibrium price-cost margin, or Lerner Index, given by

$$\frac{[P - c(x^*)]}{P} = \frac{s_i}{\eta}. \tag{22.3}$$

---

7   If we set the derivative of equation (22.2) with respect to $q_i$ to zero, taking the production of all firms other than the $i$th, $Q_{-i}$ as given, and then solve for $q_i$, we obtain each firm's best response function.

Here, $P$ is the industry price, $s_i$ is the $i$th firm's share of industry output, $\eta$ is the elasticity of market demand, and $x^*$ is the amount that each firm spends on R&D in equilibrium. (We have dispensed with the subscript on the term $x^*$ because it is the same for each firm.) We can simplify this a bit further by recognizing that since all firms are identical, $s_i$ is just $1/n$. So, equation (22.3) can be written as

$$P\left(1 - \frac{1}{n\eta}\right) = c(x^*). \qquad (22.4)$$

Equation (22.4) does not by itself tell us the amount of R&D expenditure, $x^*$, that each firm will find optimal in the ultimate equilibrium. To determine that value we must add a second equilibrium condition indicating when a firm will know that it has spent the right amount on research activities. This is obtained by differentiating equation (22.2) with respect to the R&D expenditures, $x_i$, to give the condition

$$\frac{\partial \pi_i}{\partial x_i} = -\frac{dc(x_i)}{dx_i}\, q_i - 1 = 0, \qquad (22.5)$$

which can be simplified to the condition that in equilibrium we must have

$$-\frac{dc(x_i)}{dx_i}\, q_i = 1. \qquad (22.6)$$

What does this mean? Remember that an increase in R&D expenditures, $c(x_i)$, reduces marginal cost so that $dc(x_i)/dx_i$, the amount by which marginal cost changes as a result of an additional dollar of R&D expenditures, is negative. The left-hand side of equation (22.6) is, therefore, positive and is equal to the full marginal benefit of an extra dollar of R&D spending. The marginal cost of an extra dollar spent on R&D is simply \$1. At the equilibrium level of R&D expenditures, $x^*$, it must be the case that the marginal benefit of an extra dollar spent on R&D just equals its marginal cost.

What are the implications of the equilibrium conditions of equations (22.4) and (22.6)? The most obvious conclusion we can draw is that an increase in the number of firms in the industry will decrease the amount that each firm is willing to spend on R&D. We know from our discussion of the Cournot model that, for a given level of each firm's marginal costs, an increase in the number of firms in the industry decreases the amount that each firm will choose to produce. [This is, actually, a direct implication of equation (22.4).] But equation (22.6) makes clear that the marginal benefit of extra R&D spending is directly proportional to the volume of a firm's output. Hence, the reduction in that output that results from increasing the number of firms also reduces the marginal benefit that R&D spending yields to an individual firm. It follows that the equilibrium level of such spending per firm, $x^*$, will fall as the number of firms rises.

This does not necessarily imply, however, that the total industry spending on R&D, which is $nx^*$, will also fall. It is perfectly possible that each firm spends less on R&D but total spending increases. Dasgupta and Stiglitz show that aggregate spending on R&D may actually either increase or decrease as the number of firms in the industry increases. The key point is that for aggregate R&D spending to increase, the elasticity of market demand must be fairly large. When demand is relatively elastic, the expansion of industry output resulting from a greater number of firms will not decrease the price too much and, as a result, will not decrease the marginal revenue of equation (22.4) very much either. Since this difference between price and cost is what finances a firm's R&D expenditure, such expenditure can be expected to rise in total with the number of industry firms so long as η is relatively large. If, however, the elasticity of market demand declines as output expands (as is the case with linear demand curves), then increasing the number of firms will, beyond some point, lead to a reduction in total R&D efforts. In practice, it requires only a very small number of firms to exist before additional firms induce a decline in total R&D spending. Therefore, the Dasgupta and Stiglitz model may be taken as partial support for the Schumpeterian hypothesis that concentration fosters innovation.

It is important to recognize that the thought experiment conducted in the foregoing analysis takes the number of firms as given, and then considers how an industry's research efforts would change for different values of that fixed number of firms. There is, however, an alternative way to proceed. This second course, which is the approach chosen by Dasgupta and Stiglitz themselves, is to invoke a third equilibrium condition that, in the long run, free entry will lead to an increase in the number of firms until each firm makes zero profit. In other words, industry structure is determined endogenously by the firms' output and R&D expenditure decisions. The zero profit condition, when applied to equation (22.2), tells us that

$$P(Q^*)q^* - c(x^*)q^* - x^* = 0. \tag{22.7}$$

Aggregating this over the equilibrium number of firms in the industry, $n^*$, gives

$$P(Q^*)Q^* - c(x^*)Q^* - n^*x^* = 0, \tag{22.8}$$

which implies that $[P(Q^*) - c(x^*)]Q^* = n^*x^*$. Now since each of the $n$ firms is of the same size, each has a market share equal to $1/n$. Hence, by equation (22.3) we know that $P - c(x^*) = P/n^*\eta$. Using this substitution, the equilibrium R&D outcome derived by Dasgupta and Stiglitz then becomes

$$\frac{n^*x^*}{P(Q^*)Q^*} = \text{industry R\&D spending as a share of industry sales} = \frac{1}{n^*\eta}. \tag{22.9}$$

Comparing across industries, equation (22.9) suggests that the share of an industry's total sales revenue that will be devoted to R&D is likely to be smaller in less concentrated industries—that is, those industries with a naturally more competitive structure will do less R&D, all else equal. This may then be seen as offering fairly strong intellectual support for Schumpeter's basic claim that imperfect competition is good for technical progress.

## 22.4  EVIDENCE ON THE SCHUMPETERIAN HYPOTHESIS

From the above analysis, it would appear that the debate over the Schumpeterian hypothesis cannot be resolved by an appeal to economic theory alone. Different models yield different conclusions. Instead, we must invoke empirical evidence to push us to one side of the debate or the other. To date, a number of statistical studies relating R&D effort to firm size and industry structure have been conducted. While these

# ✓ Reality Checkpoint

## Some Little Firms That Could!

While formal evidence does not give a definitive answer as to whether an industry of large firms with market power or one comprised of many small competitors is the most conducive to innovation, there is a good bit of anecdotal evidence regarding the prowess of small firms and individual inventors in coming up with the big breakthroughs. The personal computer, for instance, was largely introduced by Apple. The light bulb and wireless telegraphy were developed by individuals, Edison in the first case and Marconi in the second. Xerox was the tiny firm Haloid when it developed the Xerographic copying method. Intel, which now controls close to 90 percent of the microprocessor market, started out as a small firm packaging transistors on a sliver of silicon. What is perhaps even more thought provoking is the fact that many large corporations initially turned their backs on those very innovations that later proved to be so successful. IBM, for instance, totally ignored the PC market at its inception. Edison himself, well after his firm had been established as the premier technical enterprise of its time, initially regarded his own invention of the motion picture as little more than a useful toy.

Today, small firms and entrepreneurs continue to be an active source of innovation and invention. For example, the two most heavily trafficked Web sites, e-Bay and Amazon, were both the creation of small independent entrepreneurs and not of existing auction houses or booksellers. Similarly, Genentech was just a tiny venture capitalist firm when it launched the biotech field of recombinant DNA. To be sure, Apple came out with the first personal digital assistant (PDA) with its Newton product. However, it was a little firm called Palm that solved the problem of making a simple connection between the PDA and the personal computer desktop, and that also made the PDA affordable just before it was bought out by U.S. Robotics.

A somewhat more recent innovation is the refrigeration idea currently being pursued by K. Gschneider, a physicist at Iowa State, and Carl Zimm, an engineer in Wisconsin. Their project uses the rare element gadolinium, which has the unusual feature that when put into a magnetic field, it heats up. When demagnetized it cools down. The two entrepreneurs have used this feature to develop a prototype refrigerator that is 50 percent more energy efficient than the most efficient conventional refrigerator and which, unlike the conventional kind, does not use any environmentally hazardous materials such as chlorofluorocarbons. Development of a commercially viable product is still some years off. Yet, if and when it happens, the gadolinium machine literally will be the coolest fridge in town!

**Source:** "The Ultimate Fridge Magnet." *Economist*, April 19–25, 1997, p. 81.

studies are far from uniform in their results, one general finding emerges. It is that R&D intensity appears to increase with increases in industrial concentration but only up to a rather modest value, after which R&D efforts appear to level off or even decline as a fraction of firm revenue.

One of the first studies exploring the link between industry structure and R&D was that of Scherer (1965). His basic finding was that while firm size and concentration are each positively associated with the intensity of R&D spending, these correlations diminish beyond a relatively low threshold. That is, once firms reach a relatively small size and/or markets reach a relatively low level of concentration, any positive effects of firm size or market concentration on innovative activity tend to vanish. Subsequent studies, including those of Levin and Reiss (1984); Levin *et al.* (1985); Lunn (1986); Scott (1990); Geroski (1990); and Blundell, Griffith, and Van Reem (1995) have tended to confirm Scherer's (1965) basic finding.[8]

In examining the influence of firm size and market structure on innovative activity, a number of important issues must be addressed. The first of these is that in comparing R&D efforts across markets, one must control for the "science-based" character of each industry. Markets in which the member firms produce goods such as chemical products or computer hardware have such a strong technical base that general advances in scientific understanding can rapidly translate into either product or process innovations. Other markets, however, such as that for haircuts or hairstyling, will have more difficulty in making use of scientific breakthroughs and therefore have less direct contact with universities and research laboratories. It turns out that measures of such technological opportunities tend to be highly correlated with the degree of industry concentration. In other words, while the simple correlation between concentration and innovation may be positive, this correlation really reflects the positive effects on innovation that come with increases in an industry's opportunity for technical advances. The more recent studies cited above demonstrate that controlling for this factor is very important.

A second factor that needs to be addressed is the distinction between R&D expenditures and true innovations. While innovative effort can be measured by the ratio of R&D spending to sales [as suggested explicitly by the work of Dasgupta and Stiglitz (1980)], such an approach really measures the inputs into the innovative process. Presumably though, what we are interested in are the outputs of that process—the true number of innovations as perhaps measured by the number of patents a firm acquires. Even though different firms do the same amount of R&D spending, the Schumpeterian hypothesis might be validated if size or concentration leads that spending to be more productive. The studies cited above do look at the patent output of firms. Here again, however, little evidence is found in support of the Schumpeterian claims. Indeed, as Cohen and Klepper (1996) note, the general finding is that large firms do proportionately somewhat more R&D than smaller firms but get fewer innovations from these efforts. A notable exception in this regard, however, is Gayle (2002), who finds that firms in concentrated industries generate many more patents when patents are not simply counted but, instead, are measured on a citation-weighted basis.[9]

Finally, a third issue with which researchers must contend is the endogeneity of market structure. Some firms, for example, Alcoa or Microsoft, came to dominate their industry on the basis of a dramatic innovation. In the case of Alcoa, it was its unique process for refining aluminum. In the case of Microsoft, it was its unique op-

---

8   See Cohen and Levin (1989) for an early summary.
9   When a patent application is filed, the applicant must cite all the prior patents related to the new process or product. It is plausible that the most important patents are those that are cited most frequently. Hence, in evaluating a firm's true innovative output, one may want to control for how often the firm's patents are cited.

erating systems for personal computers. In these and other cases, the key technology that led to the firm's dominant position was associated with a number of patents. If this experience is pervasive, a naïve researcher may find that large, dominant firms are also firms with many patents and wrongly conclude that the Schumpeterian hypothesis is validated. In these cases it is the innovative activity that leads to market power and not the other way around. Indeed, if the firms that come to dominate their markets start out as small operations and then grow on the basis of enterprise and technical breakthroughs, the implication would be quite to the contrary of Schumpeter's model.[10]

## 22.5 R&D COOPERATION BETWEEN FIRMS

Our final line of inquiry in this chapter addresses the issue of cooperation on R&D efforts between firms. Two features of the innovative process make such efforts attractive from the viewpoint of economic efficiency. First, as noted in the introduction to this chapter, modern technology is complicated and often draws on a variety of expertise and experience. Because it is doubtful that all this know-how will be possessed by the scientists and engineers in one firm, it is desirable that firms share their individual experiences, experimental results, and design solutions with each other so as to realize fully the benefits from scientific study. Second, if it only takes one firm to make an important breakthrough, then there is a potential for wasteful R&D spending as firms duplicate each other's efforts in a noncooperative R&D race.

We have explicit evidence on this score. One of the most dynamic and creative groups of firms in the U.S. economy in recent years has been the American steel minimills. These firms rely on small-scale plants using electric arc furnaces to recycle scrap steel. They are widely regarded as world leaders and have outperformed even the Japanese steel firms, once thought to be invincible. Through a series of interviews, von Hippel (1988) found that these firms regularly and routinely exchanged technical information with each other. In fact, sometimes workers of competing firms were trained (at no charge) by a rival company in the use of specific equipment. Such exchanges of information and expertise were made with the knowledge and approval of management even though they had the effect of strengthening a competitor.

To analyze the implications of research spillovers, we again make use of the Cournot duopoly model, similar to the Dasgupta and Stiglitz (1980) model except that we now explicitly permit one firm's research to benefit others.[11] We address three issues. First, how do technical spillovers affect the incentive firms have to undertake R&D? Second, what is the impact of such spillovers on the effects of R&D? Finally, what are the benefits to be gained from allowing firms to cooperate in their research, for example, by forming research joint ventures (RJVs)? Are these benefits worth the risk that cooperation in R&D might facilitate collusion between the same firms in the final product markets?

---

10 Generally, market structure and innovative activity evolve together. For example, if experience raises R&D productivity, then older firms will tend both to do more innovation because it has a higher return for them and to be more productive so that early entrants will tend to dominate an industry over time. See Klepper (2002) for an analysis along these lines.

11 The model is developed in d'Aspremont and Jacquemin (1988). A more general version of this type of investigation can be found in Kamien *et al.* (1992).

To start the analysis we will assume that we are discussing an industry in which the demand for a homogeneous good is linear and given by $P = A - BQ$. Two firms, each of which has constant marginal costs of $c$ per unit, manufacture the good. These costs can be reduced as a result of research and development activity, but there is the possibility that the knowledge developed by one firm can spill over to its rivals. This can happen, for example, because the firms fund common sources of basic research such as universities or research laboratories, because the research direction that one firm is taking becomes known to its rivals, because some of the preliminary results of research effort leak out, or because of industrial espionage.

Specifically, if firm 1 undertakes R&D at intensity $x_1$ and firm 2 undertakes R&D at intensity $x_2$, the marginal production costs of the two firms become

$$c_1 = c - x_1 - \beta x_2 \text{ and}$$
$$c_2 = c - x_2 - \beta x_1. \tag{22.10}$$

Here $0 \leq \beta \leq 1$ measures the degree to which the R&D activities of one firm spill over to the other firm.[12] If $\beta = 0$, there are no spillovers—firm 1's research effort $x_1$ yields benefits only to firm 1 itself. If $\beta = 1$, spillovers are perfect—every penny of cost reduction that $x_1$ brings to firm 1, it also yields to firm 2. For the intermediate case of $0 < \beta < 1$, spillovers are only partial—if firm 1's research lowers its own cost by one dollar per unit, it will lower firm 2's cost by some fraction of a dollar per unit.

Research is, of course, costly. Indeed, not only is it costly but we assume that R&D activity exhibits *dis*economies of scale, that is, it becomes more costly the more research the firm does. Specifically, we assume that research costs are the same for both firms and given by the research cost function

$$r(x) = \frac{x^2}{2}. \tag{22.11}$$

Thus, if the R&D intensity is $x = 10$, then the research budget $r(x) = 10^2/2 = \$50$. If the R&D intensity doubles to $x = 20$, the budgetary expense climbs to $20^2/2 = \$400$. A doubling of R&D effort therefore leads to a quadrupling of the R&D cost. This is an example of what we mean by a scale diseconomy.

### 22.5.1 Noncooperative R&D: Profit, Prices, and Social Welfare

Consider what happens when firms do not cooperate on research. For this purpose, we imagine a two-stage game. In the first stage, each firm chooses its research intensity $x_i$. In the second stage, each firm acts as a Cournot competitor in choosing its output. As usual, this game is solved backwards. From Chapter 9, we know the Cournot equilibrium for given values of $c_1$ and $c_2$, so we start by expressing this solution. The outputs for the two firms are

$$q_1^C = \frac{(A - 2c_1 + c_2)}{3B} \text{ and}$$
$$q_2^C = \frac{(A - 2c_2 + c_1)}{3B}, \tag{22.12}$$

---

12 We confine our attention to the case in which the spillovers are positive. It is possible for there to be negative spillovers. For example, firms might spread misinformation about their research or claim that they have made a breakthrough in order to discourage rivals from continuing with a particular line of research.

and their profits after paying the research costs are

$$\pi_1^C = \frac{(A - 2c_1 + c_2)^2}{9B} - \frac{x_1^2}{2} \text{ and}$$

$$\pi_2^C = \frac{(A - 2c_2 + c_1)^2}{9B} - \frac{x_2^2}{2}.$$

(22.13)

We know from equation (22.10) that $c_1 = c - x_1 - \beta x_2$ and $c_2 = c - x_2 - \beta x_1$. This allows us to express the final equilibrium outputs directly as a function of each firm's choice of R&D effort and the degree of spillover from one firm's findings to the other firm's costs. The resultant Cournot–Nash equilibrium outputs for each firm are

$$q_1^C = \frac{[A - c + x_1(2 - \beta) + x_2(2\beta - 1)]}{3B} \text{ and}$$

$$q_2^C = \frac{[A - c + x_2(2 - \beta) + x_1(2\beta - 1)]}{3B},$$

(22.14)

and their profits are

$$\pi_1^C = \frac{[A - c + x_1(2 - \beta) + x_2(2\beta - 1)]^2}{9B} - \frac{x_1^2}{2} \text{ and}$$

$$\pi_2^C = \frac{[A - c + x_2(2 - \beta) + x_1(2\beta - 1)]^2}{9B} - \frac{x_2^2}{2}.$$

(22.15)

Equation (22.14) indicates that the output of each firm is an increasing function of its own R&D expenditures, $x_i$. Such expenditures reduce a firm's costs and thereby make higher output more profitable. By contrast, the effect of the *rival's* R&D effort on a firm's production can go either way. Take firm 1. On the one hand, the R&D activity of firm 2 spills over and lowers firm 1's costs, which has an expansionary effect on firm 1's own output. On the other hand, firm 2's R&D reduces firm 2's cost. This makes firm 2 more competitive and permits it to expand its output, leaving less market available to firm 1. The net result of these two countervailing forces is ambiguous. This ambiguity is reflected in the coefficient on $x_2$ in the $q_1$ equation (and the coefficient of $x_1$ in the $q_2$ equation). In both cases, this coefficient, $2\beta - 1$, is positive only when the degree of spillover is large, that is, when $\beta > 0.5$. When spillovers are small, that is, when $\beta < 0.5$, a firm's output and profit are decreasing functions of the R&D expenditures of its rival. The same ambiguity appears in the profit equations (22.15).

We know that each firm will choose the level of research activity that maximizes its profit given the research effort of its rival. For example, every choice of effort that firm 2 makes leads firm 1 to choose its own profit-maximizing response. The same is true for firm 2 in reverse. Thus we can in principle identify the best response or *research intensity reaction function* for each firm.

This is done mathematically in the Derivation Checkpoint to confirm an intuitive result that follows from our previous discussion. When research spillovers are low, the research intensity reaction functions for the two firms are downward sloping, indicating that the research expenditures of the two firms are *strategic substitutes*—more research by one firm reduces the amount done by the other. That is, research activity by one firm substitutes for research activity by the other. The intuition is that in this case the increased research effort, say by firm 1, primarily reduces firm 1's costs and

## ✓ Derivation **Checkpoint**

### Optimal Noncooperative R&D Effort in the Presence of Spillovers

Differentiation of the profit equation (22.15) with respect to research effort at firm $i$ and setting the derivative equal to zero yields

$$\frac{\partial \pi_i^C}{\partial x_i} = \frac{2(2 - \beta)[A - c + x_i(2 - \beta) + x_j(2\beta - 1)]}{9B} - x_i = 0.$$

This result implies best response curves, $R_1$ and $R_2$, for firm 1 and firm 2 of

$$x_1 = \frac{2(2 - \beta)[A - c + x_2(2\beta - 1)]}{[9B - 2(2 - \beta)^2]} \quad \text{and}$$

$$x_2 = \frac{2(2 - \beta)[A - c + x_1(2\beta - 1)]}{[9B - 2(2 - \beta)^2]}.$$

The equilibrium must be symmetric since the two firms have identical costs in the absence of R&D and face the same demand function. Thus, in equilibrium $x_1 = x_2$. Substituting this into $R_1$, for example, and solving for $x_1$ gives the Nash equilibrium research intensity:

$$x_1^C = x_2^C = \frac{2(A - c)(2 - \beta)}{9B - 2(2 - \beta)(1 + \beta)}.$$

This is decreasing in $\beta$, implying that increased research spillovers decrease each firm's chosen research intensity. The solution for research effort, $x_i$, implies output levels and profit for each firm of

$$q_1^C = q_2^C = \frac{3(A - c)}{9B - 2(2 - \beta)(1 + \beta)};$$

$$\pi_1^C = \pi_2^C = \frac{(A - c)^2[9B - 2(2 - \beta)^2]}{[9B - 2(2 - \beta)(1 + \beta)]^2}.$$

so gives it a competitive advantage with respect to firm 2. In turn, this results in a reduction in the profitability of the rival (firm 2), which can be offset only by the rival reducing its expenditure on research.

By contrast, when spillovers are high, the research intensity reaction functions are upward sloping, meaning that the research expenditures of the two firms are *strategic complements*. When spillovers are this high, an increase in research intensity by one of the two firms induces an increase in research intensity by the other. In this case the intuition is that if firm 1 opts for a high level of R&D effort, the benefits of that activity spill over to firm 2 to such an extent that firm 2's profit also increases, providing that firm with the funds (and the desire) to increase its own R&D spending. Figure 22-3 illustrates typical research intensity reaction functions.

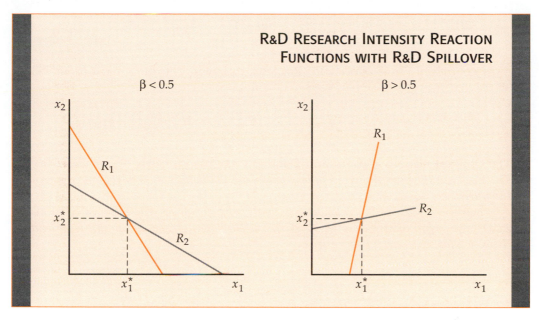

R&D RESEARCH INTENSITY REACTION FUNCTIONS WITH R&D SPILLOVER

FIGURE

22-3

However, determining whether the reaction functions slope downward or upward—whether the two firms' R&D efforts are strategic substitutes or complements—does not tell us what the equilibrium level of R&D spending is. In particular, there can be no presumption that the presence of large R&D spillovers and hence the case of strategic complements will result in a higher equilibrium level of R&D spending than the case in which such spillovers are low. The Nash equilibrium occurs at the intersection of the two response functions, and the case in which this point is farthest from the origin is far from obvious.

In order to illustrate this last point, we shall focus for the remainder of our discussion on a simplified example. The Checkpoints in this and the next section give a more general mathematical analysis. Our example has the following characteristics. Demand for the good in question is assumed to be $P = 100 - 2Q$, and each firm's marginal production cost is currently $60. The firms can choose two levels of research intensity: $x_i = 10$ or $x_i = 7.5$. Further, we assume that the degree of research spillover (which is outside the control of the two firms) takes one of two values: a low value of $\beta = 1/4$ or a high value of $\beta = 3/4$.

Consider first the low spillover case and assume that firm 2 chooses the high research intensity of $x_2 = 10$. If firm 1 also chooses high research intensity, its output and profits will be, from equations (22.14) and (22.15),

$$q_1^C = \frac{(40 + 17.5 - 5)}{6} = 8.75; \quad \pi_1^C = \frac{(40 + 17.5 - 5)^2}{18} - \frac{100}{2} = \$103.13.$$

By contrast, if it chooses the low research intensity, its output and profits will be

$$q_1^C = \frac{(40 + 13.125 - 5)}{6} = 8.02; \quad \pi_1^C = \frac{(40 + 13.125 - 5)^2}{18} - \frac{56.25}{2} = \$100.54.$$

Now assume that firm 2 chooses the low research intensity of $x_2 = 7.5$. If firm 1 chooses the high research intensity, its output and profits will be

$$q_1^C = \frac{(40 + 17.5 - 3.75)}{6} = 8.96; \quad \pi_1^C = \frac{(40 + 17.5 - 3.75)^2}{18} - \frac{100}{2} = \$110.50.$$

By contrast, if firm 1 chooses the low research intensity, its output and profit will be

$$q_1^C = \frac{(40 + 13.125 - 3.75)}{6} = 8.23; \quad \pi_1^C = \frac{(40 + 13.125 - 3.75)^2}{18} - \frac{56.25}{2} = \$107.31.$$

The same calculations apply to firm 2 and give the payoff matrix of Table 22-2(a). *The Nash equilibrium in this case of low spillovers is for both firms to adopt high research intensities.*

When the degree of R&D spillover is high, with $\beta = 0.75$, the same calculations lead to the payoff matrix of Table 22-2(b). *The Nash equilibrium in this case is for both firms to adopt low research intensities.*

**TABLE 22-2(a)**

### PAYOFF MATRIX WITH LOW R&D SPILLOVERS, $\beta = 0.25$

|  |  | Firm 1 | Firm 1 |
|---|---|---|---|
|  |  | Low Research Intensity | High Research Intensity |
| Firm 2 | Low Research Intensity | $107.31, $107.31 | $100.54, $110.50 |
| | High Research Intensity | $110.50, $100.54 | $103.13, $103.13 |

**TABLE 22-2(b)**

### PAYOFF MATRIX WITH HIGH R&D SPILLOVERS, $\beta = 0.75$

|  |  | Firm 1 | Firm 1 |
|---|---|---|---|
|  |  | Low Research Intensity | High Research Intensity |
| Firm 2 | Low Research Intensity | $128.67, $128.67 | $136.13, $125.78 |
| | High Research Intensity | $125.78, $136.13 | $133.68, $133.68 |

An increase in the degree of R&D spillover causes the two firms to reduce their research intensities. Why? Consider first the case when R&D spillovers are weak. We know that in this case the more firm 1 spends on R&D, the less firm 2 will spend because the two activities are strategic substitutes. Yet somewhat paradoxically, this gives each firm an incentive to spend aggressively on R&D so as to avoid being the loser in this war. If firm 1 spends a lot on R&D and firm 2 spends nothing, virtually all the benefits of firm 1's spending stay with firm 1. In this case, firm 2 would find itself losing significant market share and profit to a much lower-cost competitor. When each firm tries to avoid falling behind in this manner, the net result can be a substantial amount of R&D effort, both at each individual firm and in total.

Just the opposite holds in the case of large spillovers. Yes, the more firm 1 spends on R&D, the more firm 2 is induced to spend by virtue of the strategic complements setting, but this relation is a two-edged sword. Even if firm 1 spends only a little on R&D it knows that this will still induce firm 2 to do a fair bit of research activity. Moreover, this activity at firm 2 will bring substantial benefits to firm 1 by virtue of the large spillovers. In this setting, the incentive for either firm to spend much on R&D can be quite small as each firm seeks to free ride on the other's efforts.

Where graphs fail to give clear results, algebra can often save the day. That this is true is shown in the Derivation Checkpoint. We merely state the result here. The amount of research done by each firm *decreases* as $\beta$, the degree of R&D spillover, increases—the free-riding effect to which we have just referred.

### 22.5.2 Technology Cooperation

We now consider two alternative arrangements between the duopoly firms that can alter the outcome from that described in the foregoing analysis. The first possibility is that the two firms agree that while each will continue to do its own R&D, they will coordinate the extent of such research effort. Thus, the two firms now choose $x_1$ and $x_2$ to maximize their joint profit. In so doing, they continue to recognize that they will compete as Cournot firms in the product market. The other alternative is that the firms explicitly share their R&D activities by setting up a research joint venture (RJV). One way this scenario might work in practice would be for the two firms to set up a joint laboratory for experimentation and analysis with all the discoveries made at that laboratory to be made fully available to both firms.

We introduce this RJV arrangement into the model by letting the two firms choose $x_1$ and $x_2$ cooperatively but by adding the further assumption that the degree of spillover is complete, that is, $\beta = 1$. Whatever is learned in the research lab—whether discovered by a firm 1 scientist or a firm 2 scientist—reduces the cost of both firms by the same amount.

We start with the simple coordination case. What we want to do is to choose the values of $x_1$ and $x_2$ that maximize the sum of the individual profit expressions shown in equation (22.15). The mathematical solution, as in the previous section, is shown in the Derivation Checkpoint.

We shall concentrate once again on our simplified example as given by the payoff matrices of Tables 22-3(a) and (b). When the firms coordinate their research efforts they choose the combination of R&D intensities that maximizes the sum of the profits in the cells of the relevant payoff matrix. *When R&D spillovers are low, coordination leads each of the firms to choose the low R&D intensity.* Cooperation then increases

# Derivation Checkpoint

## Optimal R&D Effort with R&D Cooperation

With cooperation, each firm's optimal research intensity is the R&D effort that will maximize the sum of the two firms' profits, given that output is determined noncooperatively in the second-stage output game. From equation (22.15) we know that aggregate profit is

$$\pi_1^C + \pi_2^C = \frac{[A - c + x_1(2 - \beta) + x_2(2\beta - 1)]^2}{9B} - \frac{x_1^2}{2} + \frac{[A - c + x_2(2 - \beta) + x_1(2\beta - 1)]^2}{9B} - \frac{x_2^2}{2}.$$

Differentiating this with respect to $x_1$ gives the first-order condition

$$\frac{\partial(\pi_1^C + \pi_2^C)}{\partial x_1} = \frac{2(2 - \beta)[A - c + x_1(2 - \beta) + x_2(2\beta - 1)]}{9B} - x_1 + \frac{2(2\beta - 1)[A - c + x_2(2 - \beta) + x_1(2\beta - 1)]}{9B} = 0.$$

A similar condition applies to the second firm, but we do not need this. Rather, we can take advantage of the fact that the equilibrium for these two firms will be symmetric. Substituting $x_1 = x_2 = x^{RC}$ (where the superscript *RC* denotes "R&D cartel") and simplifying gives

$$\frac{2(1 + \beta)[A - c + x^{RC}(1 + \beta)] - 9Bx^{RC}}{9B} = 0,$$

which gives the equilibrium R&D intensity as

$$x_1^{RC} = x_2^{RC} = \frac{2(A - c)(1 + \beta)}{9B - 2(1 + \beta)^2}.$$

This is increasing in $\beta$.

The Nash equilibrium outputs and profits of the two firms when they cooperate in R&D can be identified by substituting into equations (22.14) and (22.15). After simplifying this gives

$$q_1^{RC} = q_2^{RC} = \frac{3(A - c)}{9B - 2(1 + \beta)^2} \text{ and}$$

$$\pi_1^{RC} = \pi_2^{RC} = \frac{9B(A - c)^2}{[9B - 2(1 + \beta)^2]^2}.$$

each firm's profits from \$103.13 to \$107.31. By contrast, *when the R&D spillover is high, coordination leads each firm to choose the high R&D intensity*, increasing their profits from \$128.67 to \$133.68.

What our example and the more detailed analysis of the Checkpoint show is the following. First, it is now the case that the higher the level of R&D spillover—the larger is $\beta$—the more each firm spends on research. This is because the agreement between the two firms to set their R&D efforts jointly explicitly forces each firm to internalize the external benefits that such spending has upon its rival. In turn, this eliminates the free-riding problem that characterizes R&D competition when there are spillovers. The ability to avoid this problem also means that the two firms will each enjoy a profit at least as great as that which they would have earned in the absence of such cooperation.[13]

Second, the outcome under the simple coordination plan may not necessarily be good for the consumer. In particular, consumers are hurt by the technology cooperation when $\beta < 0.5$ and the extent of spillover is small. The reason is straightforward. When $\beta$ is small, then without cooperation each firm tends to do a fair bit of research. It does so because a low value of $\beta$ means that most of the benefit from its innovative efforts will accrue to it alone and because it knows that its rival is proceeding along the same line of attack. From the viewpoint of consumers, this is great since there has been considerable cost reduction and therefore a sharp decline in the price they pay. If we now introduce a cooperative R&D agreement, the two firms realize that their best bet is to reduce R&D intensity, which otherwise simply makes competition tougher in the product market. By decreasing R&D intensity, the firms increase their profits. Unfortunately, the lower rate of innovation also implies a higher price to consumers.

By contrast, when the degree of R&D spillover is high ($\beta > 0.5$), both firms and consumers benefit from a cooperative R&D agreement. This happens because now the primary effect of the R&D cooperation is to correct a market failure. In the absence of cooperation, a large degree of spillover leads each firm to free ride on the R&D efforts of its rivals and to take no account of the beneficial effects its own R&D expenditures have on the costs and profits of other firms. The R&D cooperation internalizes these effects because it forces the cooperating firms to look at the impact their R&D expenditures have on aggregate profit rather than merely on their individual profit.

What about a research joint venture? As noted, an RJV can best be thought of as a case in which the firms take action not only to coordinate their research expenditures but also to ensure that the spillover from one firm's research success to the other firm's gain is complete, that is, so that $\beta = 1$. A little thought should convince you that an RJV will likely yield the maximum benefits to both firms and consumers. As we just saw, coordination of R&D levels benefits both producers and consumers whenever $\beta > 0.5$. Moreover, the profit outcomes in Table 22-3 indicate that if the firms could find some way of increasing the technology spillover from $\beta = 0.25$ to $\beta = 0.75$ they would both benefit at *any* research intensity. We can make this discussion even more general. The Checkpoint on R&D cooperation shows that an increase in the spillover parameter $\beta$ increases the research intensity and the profits of each firm

---

13 For $\beta = 0.5$ each firm earns exactly the same profit under uncoordinated R&D spending as each does with an R&D cartel. For all other values of $\beta$ each firm's profit is higher with the R&D cartel.

**Derivation Checkpoint**

## Optimal R&D and Output with a Research Joint Venture

The third and final case we consider is where the firms form an RJV to coordinate their research activities and ensure that these are fully shared. This case is easily dealt with. It amounts to the firms ensuring that the degree of R&D spillover is perfect, that is, that $\beta = 1$.

The optimal degree of R&D intensity, outputs, and profits are, therefore, identified by substituting $\beta = 1$ in the equations derived for R&D cooperation. Thus,

$$x_1^{RJV} = x_2^{RJV} = \frac{4(A - c)}{9B - 8} \; ;$$

$$q_1^{RJV} = q_2^{RJV} = \frac{3(A - c)}{9B - 8} \; ;$$

$$\pi_1^{RJV} = \pi_2^{RJV} = \frac{9B(A - c)^2}{(9B - 8)^2} \; .$$

An RJV in which firms coordinate their research efforts to maximize their joint profits and share the results of their R&D activities dominates the other cases we have considered in that it gives the highest per-firm profits and the lowest consumer prices.

---

*and* increases the output that each firm brings to the market. In other words, *both firms and consumers benefit* from an increase in $\beta$. The RJV takes this to its logical conclusion by ensuring that $\beta = 1$, its highest possible value.

In our example the benefits of an RJV are easily confirmed. Consider the case in which both firms choose the high degree of research intensity. Thus, with perfect R&D spillover, the profits to each firm are $(40 + 10 + 10)^2/18 - 50 = \$150$, while if each chooses the low research intensity, the profits to each firm will be $(40 + 7.5 + 7.5)^2/18 - 56.25/2 = \$139.93$. Clearly, the RJV will go for the high research intensity leading to the lowest costs. In turn, this will translate into the lowest consumer prices that these Cournot firms will offer.

The intuition behind the foregoing analysis is as follows. First, by maximizing the extent of spillovers, the RJV also maximizes the benefits of R&D. Every discovery is spread instantly to all firms in the industry. Second, despite this extensive spillover, the free-riding problem is now avoided. Because the two firms have agreed to coordinate their research effort they fully internalize the otherwise external effects of research. Thus firms will pursue extensive research, which, partly because of the extensive spillover effect of sharing, will lead to a sizable reduction in costs for every firm. In turn, this substantial cost reduction translates into an equally impressive reduction in the price to consumers.[14] The policy implication of this is obvious and important.

---

14 While we have derived this result for a duopoly, Kamien *et al.* (1992) show that it extends to an *n*-firm oligopoly.

Research joint ventures should be encouraged because they benefit both consumers and producers so long as the antitrust authorities can ensure that such cooperation on research effort will not also extend to cooperation in production and prices, that is, to a price-fixing cartel.

The potentially large benefit from technology cooperation is undoubtedly the reason that RJVs—unlike price-fixing agreements—are not treated as per se violations by the antitrust authorities. Instead, they are evaluated on a rule of reason basis. Indeed, the U.S. Congress passed legislation in 1984 to require explicitly the application of a reasonability standard in the specific case of RJVs.

## SUMMARY

Research and development is the wellspring of technical advancement. In turn, such advancement is the true source of the gain in per capita income and living standards that has characterized the developed economies for almost all of the last two centuries. It should also be clear, however, that firms will be willing to incur the heavy expenses and considerable risks associated with R&D only if they can be reasonably assured that their efforts will be rewarded. Imitation by rivals has the benefit of intensifying price competition after innovation occurs. However, it makes it less likely that the innovation will occur in the first place.

The tension between gains from competition and the gains from innovation, that is, the tension between the replacement effect and the efficiency effect is unavoidable. It therefore has led economists to consider which market environment—competitive or monopolistic—will do most to foster research and development. The Schumpeterian hypothesis is, broadly speaking, that oligopolistic market structures are best in this regard.

Both theory and empirical data give ambiguous evidence as to the market structure most conducive to R&D effort. Competitive markets can sometimes fail to be as innovative as their less competitive counterparts but a surprising number of key inventions have come from small firms. However, policy has a role to play here, too. One role for policy is to encourage cooperation in research efforts. Specifically, both antitrust and patent policy can influence the innovative climate as well as the intensity of firm competition via innovative effort. We consider patents and related policy issues in the next chapter.

## PROBLEMS

1. Assume that inverse demand is given by the linear function $P = A - BQ$ and that current marginal costs of production are $c$.

   a. By how much would an innovation have to reduce marginal cost for it to be a drastic innovation?

   b. Use your answer to derive a condition on the parameters $A$, $B$, and $c$ that determines whether a drastic innovation is feasible. (*Hint:* Costs cannot be negative.)

For Problems 2 through 5 assume the following: Inverse demand is given by $P = 240 - Q$. The discount factor is 0.9. Marginal production costs are initially $120.

2. Calculate the market equilibrium price, output, and profits (if any) on the assumption that the market is currently

   a. monopolized,

   b. a Bertrand duopoly,

   c. a Cournot duopoly.

3. Suppose that a research institute develops a new technology that reduces marginal costs to $60.

   a. Confirm that this is not a drastic innovation in either the Bertrand or Cournot cases.

   b. Calculate the new market equilibrium price, output, and profits for the monopolist and each duopolist, given that in the duopoly case the innovation is made available to only one firm.

   c. How much will the monopolist and duopolist each be willing to pay for the innovation?

4. Now assume that there is a potential entrant in the monopolized case and that the research institute is considering offering the innovation to this firm as well as to the monopolist. How does this affect the amount that the incumbent monopolist will be willing to pay for the innovation?

5. Now return to the duopoly case but assume that the research institute is considering whether it should actually sell the innovation to both firms. Will it wish to do so

   a. in the Bertrand duopoly?

   b. in the Cournot duopoly?

6. Assume that annual inverse demand for a particular product is $P = 150 - Q$. The product is offered by a pair of Bertrand competitors, each with marginal costs of $75. The discount factor is 0.9.

   a. What is the current equilibrium price and total surplus?

   Assume now that if R&D is conducted at rate $x$, it incurs one-off costs of $r(x) = 10x^2$ and reduces marginal costs to $(75 - x)$. Suppose that one firm decides to conduct R&D at rate $x = 10$. This research will be protected by a patent of $T$ years.

   b. What profit (ignoring the one-off costs of R&D) does the innovating firm make each year during the period of patent protection?

   c. What is the new equilibrium price and total surplus once patent protection expires?

   d. Use your answers to (b) and (c) to write the total net surplus from the innovation as a function of the period of patent protection. Derive (numerically) an approximation to the socially optimal period of patent protection.

   e. How are your answers to (b) and (d) affected if the innovating firm conducts research at rate $x = 15$?

   f. What research intensity will the firms choose given that the period of patent protection is set optimally in each case?

# REFERENCES

Arrow, Kenneth. 1962. "Economic Welfare and the Allocation of Resources for Inventions." In R. Nelson, ed., *The Rate and Direction of Inventive Activity: Economic and Social Factors*. National Bureau of Economic Research. Princeton: Princeton University Press.

Barro, R., and X. Sala-i-Martin. 1995. *Economic Growth*. New York: McGraw-Hill.

Blundell R., R. Griffith, and J. Van Reenen. 1995. "Dynamic Count Data Models of Technological Innovation." *The Economic Journal* 105: 333–44.

Cohen, W., and R. Levin. 1989. "Empirical Studies of Innovation and Market Structure." In R. Schmalensee and R. Willig, eds., *Handbook of Industrial Organization* Vol. 2. Amsterdam: North-Holland: 1059–98.

————, and S. Klepper. 1996. "A Reprise of Size and R and D." *Economic Journal* 106: 925–51.

Dasgupta, P., and J. Stiglitz. 1980. "Industrial Structure and the Nature of Innovative Activity." *Economic Journal* 90 (January): 266–93.

d'Aspremont, C., and A. Jacquemin. 1988. "Cooperative and Noncooperative R&D in Duopoly with Spillovers." *American Economic Review* 78 (September): 1133–7.

Gayle, P. 2002. "Market Structure and Product Innovation." Working Paper, Department of Economics, Kansas State University.

Geroski, P. 1990. "Innovation, Technology Opportunity and Market Structure." *Oxford Economic Papers* 42: 586–602.

Gilbert, R. J. and D. M. G. Newbery. 1982. "Preemptive Patenting and the Persistence of Monopoly." *American Economic Review* 72 (June): 514–27.

Kamien, M. I., E. Muller, and I. Zang. 1992. "Research Joint Ventures and R&D Cartels." *American Economic Review* 82 (December): 1293–306.

Klepper, S. 2002. "Firm Survival and the Evolution of Oligopoly." *Rand Journal of Economics* 33 (Spring): 37–61.

Levin, R., and P. Reiss. 1984. "Tests of a Schumpeterian Model of R and D and Market Structure." In Z. Griliches, ed., *R and D, Patents and Productivity*. Chicago: NBER University of Chicago Press.

Levin, R., W. Cohen, and D. C. Mowery. 1985. "R and D Appropriability, Opportunity, and Market Structure: New Evidence on Some Schumpeterian Hypotheses." *American Economic Review, Papers and Proceedings* 75 (May): 20–4.

Lunn, J. 1986. "An Empirical Analysis of Process and Product Patenting: A Simultaneous Equation Framework." *Journal of Industrial Economics* 34 (February): 319–30.

Peters, T., and P. H. Waterman. 1982. *In Search of Excellence*. New York: Harper & Row.

Porter, M. 1990. *The Competitive Advantage of Nations*. New York: The Free Press.

Reinganum, J. 1983. "Uncertain Innovation and the Persistence of Monopoly." *American Economic Review* 73 (September): 741–8.

Romer, D. 1996. *Advanced Macroeconomics*. New York: McGraw-Hill.

Scherer, F. M. 1965. "Firm Size, Market Structure, Opportunity and the Output of Patented Innovations." *American Economic Review* 55 (September): 1097–125.

Schumpeter, J. A. 1942. *Capitalism, Socialism, and Democracy*. New York: Harper.

Scott, J. T. 1990. "Purposeful Diversification of R&D and Technological Advancement." In A. Link, ed., *Advances in Applied Micro-economics*, Vol. 5. Greenwich, CT, and London: JAI Press.

Solow, R. 1956. "A Contribution to the Theory of Economic Growth." *Quarterly Journal of Economics* 70 (February): 65–94.

von Hippel, E. 1988. *The Sources of Innovation*. New York: Oxford University Press.

# Patents and Patent Policy

**Chapter** 23

In 1769, an English inventor, Richard Arkwright, patented a spinning frame that would revolutionize the production of cotton cloth. Two years later, in 1771, another invention, the spinning jenny, was introduced by Englishman James Hargreaves. With these inventions, Britain entered the Industrial Revolution. Equally important, the inventions allowed Arkwright and Hargreaves to establish a commanding position in the production of cloths and, more generally, textile products. In turn, this allowed the inventors to reap large profits and to sell at a high price in the American colonies even after these became independent states.

The British energetically protected their monopoly position. Westbound ships out of London were searched thoroughly to make sure that no passenger was a former Arkwright or Hargreaves employee or had a copy of the design plans for the Arkwright–Hargreaves machines that firms outside of Britain might copy. Such restrictions along with the high price for British textiles vexed many Americans. Consumers did not like paying the monopoly prices and firms were eager to get some version of the machines that would permit them to compete with the British producers. Indeed, some firms offered "bounties" for English apprentices who would somehow be able to obtain the necessary information. Finally, in 1789, an enterprising young Englishman and former Arkwright partner, Samuel Slater, responded to just such a bounty offer. After completely memorizing the engineering details of the Arkwright–Hargreaves machines, he disguised himself as a common laborer and set sail for America. Shortly thereafter, Slater arrived in Pawtucket, Massachusetts, and established the first of many New England textile mills, consolidating the region's manufacturing base and finally breaking the British monopoly.

The issues raised by Slater's entrepreneurship (what some might call theft) lie at the heart of this chapter. Regardless of the final verdict on the Schumpeterian hypothesis that large firms in concentrated industries do more research than small firms in competitively structured industries, there remains the question of how strongly to protect innovating firms of any type from imitative competition. On the one hand, information is a public good so that once produced, efficiency requires that access to new production techniques and new products should be unrestricted to prevent the rise of monopoly. On the other hand, if the government does not protect innovators against imitation, there may be little incentive to do the hard work that led to the invention in the first place.

The patent system was designed to create incentives for innovative activity. Patents and copyrights confer ownership to new inventions, new designs, and new creative works which, in turn, permits innovators to restrict unauthorized use of their ideas just as the British restricted the flow of information on their textile technology. The patent holder can act as a monopolist regarding its discovery and earn a monopoly profit as a result. Yet while that profit may create an incentive to undertake R&D efforts, the monopoly that generates the profit reduces the total surplus below what it could be given that the invention has occurred.

Getting this balance right is not easy. One can imagine just how much less productive the economy would be if the science behind electric lighting, the aerodynamics of airplanes, and semiconductors had never been developed. However, production also would suffer were those same technologies not now widely available to all firms. At some point, policy must shift from a stance of protecting innovators from imitation to one of permitting the use of the innovation on as wide a basis as possible. The sixty-four-million-dollar question is, exactly where does that point arise? When has protection of the innovator extended sufficiently far that we ought to start thinking about protection of consumers?

The issue as to how far patent rights should extend has two dimensions. First, what is the length of time for which any patent rights ought to extend? Second, to what range of products should the patent apply? Should the developer of a new AIDS treatment based on a special combination of protease inhibitors be protected against a rival's later development of a different AIDS treatment based on a different combination of protease inhibitors? What about a new AIDS treatment that is not based on protease inhibitors? Or what if a protease inhibitor treatment originally created as a treatment for AIDS is now applied as a treatment for multiple sclerosis? These issues—typically referred to as patent length and patent breadth—are the central questions in patent policy.

## 23.1  OPTIMAL PATENT LENGTH

Current patent law establishes a patent duration that varies from country to country. In the United Kingdom, patent protection is usually granted for fourteen years, but it can frequently be extended for a further seven years for a total of twenty-one years. Why? The reason most often advanced is that fourteen years is two times as long as a traditional craft apprenticeship. In the United States, patent protection was until recently granted for seventeen years. Again, why? One suggestion, not totally frivolous, is that when the system was taken over from the British, seventeen was seen as the obvious compromise between fourteen and twenty-one. U.S. patent law has, in fact, recently been changed to grant protection for twenty years from the date of filing the application.

Economic theory can provide some insight as to whether such durations are appropriate. The key is to find a balance between the innovator's ability to earn a return on its R&D investment and the benefits that will accrue to consumers once the patent expires and competition emerges. The basic model, which is due to Nordhaus (1969), is presented below.

Imagine a competitive industry in which each firm is pursuing a nondrastic innovation. Such innovative efforts incur costs. Each firm's unit operating cost is currently $c$. If a firm invests in R&D at some intensity $x$, it expects to reduce its unit operating costs from $c$ to $c - x$. The cost of undertaking R&D at intensity $x$ is $r(x)$. We assume that such costs rise as the level of research intensity increases and that they do so at an increasing rate. Formally, this means that $dr(x)/dx > 0$ and $d^2r(x)/dx^2 > 0$. Thus, R&D is expensive to do and exhibits decreasing returns in that a doubling of research intensity will give less than double the reduction in operating costs.

Our assumption of a competitive market implies that price equals marginal cost, which means that the initial market price is $c$ and that the output level is $Q_0^C$. This is shown in Figure 23-1. A successful innovator firm will be able either to produce at the lower unit cost of $c - x$ and drive out all its rivals by setting a price just one penny

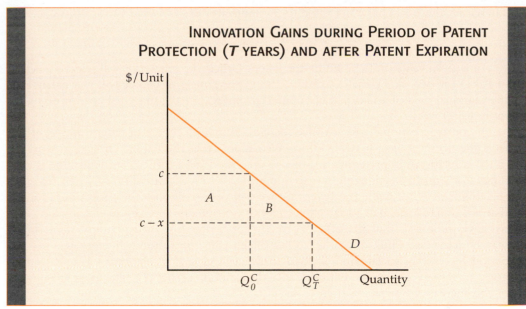

**INNOVATION GAINS DURING PERIOD OF PATENT PROTECTION ($T$ YEARS) AND AFTER PATENT EXPIRATION**

FIGURE

**23-1**

Innovator receives profit of area $A$ for the duration of the patent—$T$ years. When the patent expires, competition lowers the price to $c - x$. Consumers gain former profits $A$ and also gain area $B$ in additional consumer surplus.

less than the current price, or to license its discovery to its competitors for a fee of $c - x$ per unit produced. Either way, the current market price and volume of output remain unchanged. The innovator, however, will earn a profit equal to area $A$ in Figure 23-1. Assuming that the life of the innovator's patent is $T$ years, this profit will last for $T$ years as well.

When the patent expires, all firms will have access to the technology for free. Competition will reduce the price to $c - x$, and output will expand to $Q_T^C$. The profit that the innovator used to earn becomes consumer surplus. This is simply a transfer from a producer to consumers and so does not reflect a net gain. However, the expansion of industry output to the higher level $Q_T^C$ brings a net benefit by virtue of the additional consumer surplus this generates. This additional surplus is shown in Figure 23-1 as area $B$.

The longer the duration of the patent (the higher is $T$), the longer is the time over which the innovator earns the profit $A$ and the greater is the innovator's incentive to do costly R&D. Denote the per-period profit flow to the innovator (area $A$ in Figure 23-1) as $\pi^m(x; T)$ and the discount factor as $R$. The present value of the innovator's profit from R&D is[1]

$$V_i(x; T) = \sum_{t=0}^{T-1} R^t \pi^m(x; T) = \frac{1 - R^T}{1 - R} \pi^m(x; T). \qquad (23.1)$$

1  This result uses the following equation in calculating discounted value. Assume that a sum $A$ is to be received each period for $T$ periods, and recall from Chapter 1 that $R = (1 + r)^{-1}$ where $r$ is the interest rate. Then the discounted value of these cash flows is $S = A + RA + R^2A + R^3A + \ldots + R^{T-1}A = A(1 + R + R^2 + \ldots + R^{T-1}) = A(1 - R^T)/(1 - R)$.

Therefore, the R&D has a net value to the innovator of

$$V_i(x; T) - r(x). \qquad \textbf{(23.2)}$$

For a given value of $T$ chosen by the Patent Office, the innovator will select a level of R&D activity, $x^*(T)$, that maximizes this expression. This choice will just balance the marginal gain of additional discounted profit against the marginal cost of doing more R&D work.

Of course, a rational patent office recognizes that its choice of patent life, $T$, affects the firm's choice of R&D effort. We suppose that the Patent Office can work out this relationship precisely. In other words, the Patent Office can determine the innovator's profit-maximizing research intensity, $x^*(T)$, as a function of $T$. To make the choice of $T$ optimally the Patent Office will wish to choose the patent duration that maximizes the net social gain to both consumers and producers given, as we have indicated, that the office correctly anticipates how firms choose their research intensities. Thus, once it is freely available, the innovation will generate a per-period increase in social surplus equal to the area $A + B$ in Figure 23-1, and that goes entirely to consumers. Let us denote this amount as $cs(x; T)$. The present value of this increase in surplus is then

$$CS(x; T) = \sum_{t=T}^{\infty} R^t cs(x; T) = \frac{R^T}{1 - R} cs(x; T). \qquad \textbf{(23.3)}$$

The total net social surplus from the innovation is, therefore,

$$NS[x^*(T); T] = V_i[x^*(T); T] + CS[x^*(T); T] - r[x^*(T)], \qquad \textbf{(23.4)}$$

and the objective of the Patent Office is to choose the patent duration $T^*$ that maximizes this net surplus. This is a complicated expression but we can develop an intuitive argument to support a very important proposition, namely, that *the optimal patent duration is finite*.

To see why, note that as the Patent Office initially increases patent duration it induces greater R&D effort and, at first, a greater discounted net surplus to producers and consumers. If patent duration is zero, the returns to an innovator are also zero since the results of the innovation will be imitated immediately. Accordingly, there will be no R&D and no change in the social surplus. If we now increase the patent length to a value $T > 0$, we will induce some innovation and, thereby, some increase in the total surplus. Beyond some point, however, continued increases in $T$ will reduce net social surplus even though they lead to more R&D and therefore greater reductions in production cost. Two forces work to limit the optimal value of $T$. The first is our assumption of diminishing returns to R&D activity. Because it becomes progressively more expensive to lower production costs, it will take progressively greater increases in $T$ to achieve a given additional cost saving. The second force limiting optimal patent duration is the fact of discounting. The consumer benefits shown as area $B$ in Figure 23-1 will not be realized until after the patent expires. If the Patent Office chooses a very long duration time, $T$, the present value of those benefits will be very small indeed.

This is particularly important since it has sometimes been argued that innovation should be granted patent protection forever. Such a long patent duration puts far too

## ✓ Reality Checkpoint

### How to Agitate Your Rival and Cash in Your Chips

Our discussion of patent policy has generally assumed that the award of a patent or a copyright by the government provides certain protection against imitative products. However, such protection is far from ironclad. Firms that believe they have been the victims of patent infringement can and frequently do file suit.

One case of patent infringement involves General Electric Co. and Whirlpool Corp. A few years ago, General Electric gathered hundreds of appliance dealers from around the country at Disney World in Florida to announce what it called a "Major Laundry Breakthrough." This turned out to be the introduction of GE's new Maxus clothes washer, which used a dual-action agitator with flexible fins. While a single-action agitator simply pulls clothes in one direction, a dual-action one pushes clothes down and then forces them to turn over, providing a more thorough washing. The fins prevent tangling during this process, which again promotes cleaning action and is also easier on clothing material. There was just one small problem with the GE Maxus machine. It was an almost exact duplicate of a machine introduced by Whirlpool twenty years earlier. Moreover, while Whirlpool's U.S. patent had expired, its Canadian patent at that time was still valid. When GE began to export the Maxus to Canada, Whirlpool filed a suit claiming patent infringement. In September 1997, a judge ruled in favor of Whirlpool's claim.

Another case of interest concerns the former computer manufacturer Digital Equipment Corp. and the chip manufacturer Intel Corp. Digital had claimed that Intel's famous Pentium computer chip had only been developed by infringing on designs that Digital itself had patented in connection with its own rival Alpha chip—a chip that Digital had offered to license to Intel several years earlier. Many analysts felt that Digital's case must have had substantial merit since Digital had much to lose if it lost. Indeed, Digital was a major customer of Intel. Such speculation gained further credibility when, five months after the suit was filed, Intel settled the case out of court by agreeing to purchase all of Digital's semiconductor operations and, in addition, to pay Digital royalties for the next ten years.

**Sources:** W. Carley, "A Load Off Its Mind: Whirlpool Beats Foe in Washer Action." *The Wall Street Journal*, September 15, 1997, p. A1; L. Zuckerman, "Suit by Digital Says Intel Stole Pentium Design." *The New York Times*, May 14, 1997, p. D1; and "Intel and Digital Settle Lawsuit and Make Deal." *The New York Times*, October 28, 1997, p. D1.

heavy a value on the monopoly profits that patent protection generates and too little consideration on the additional consumer surplus that will emerge only after the patent protection has expired.[2]

---

2  The argument for an infinite patent life becomes moot if there is continual innovation that effectively limits the economic life of any one patent.

---

## Practice Problem 23.1

Let the inverse demand function for a particular product be $P = 100 - Q$, and let it be provided by a group of competitive firms, each with an identical marginal (and average) cost of $70 per unit.

a. Show that the current market output and price are, respectively, $Q = 30$ and $P = \$70$.

b. Imagine that one firm can conduct R&D at a pace $x$, at a cost of $r(x) = 15x^2$. Let the interest rate, $r$, be 10 percent so that the discount factor, $R$, is 0.9091. Show that a patent length of 25 years will induce the firm to pursue R&D at a level of approximately $x = 10$. Note that if $x = 10$, the firm's research activity will reduce the unit cost from $70 to $60.

c. Would shortening the patent duration to 20 years increase or decrease the firm's R&D effort?

d. Would shortening the duration of the patent to 20 years increase or decrease total social welfare?

---

## 23.2 THE OPTIMAL BREADTH OF PATENTS

The question of the optimal patent breadth is trickier than that of patent length, mainly because there is no universally accepted measure of breadth comparable to time as a measure of duration. Conceptually, the idea is to set a minimum amount by which a new innovation must differ from an existing process (or good) in order for the new one either to avoid infringement on an existing patent or to be itself patentable. The larger this required minimal degree of difference, the more difficult it is for other firms to "invent around" the patent and to cut into the inventor's profit. We could in principle work out an optimal patent breadth analysis just as we worked out such an analysis for the optimal patent length. But the lack of a clear method for measuring breadth makes implementing this plan very difficult. This lack of precision is reflected in the language of the Patent Office. Each application for a patent is required to specify all the "related" existing patents and to indicate not only how the patent being applied for is a discovery distinct from those already patented, but also to show that the discovery is "novel, nonobvious, useful." Such language leaves the Patent Office a lot of discretion regarding how it will rule in any particular case.

What makes the question of the optimal patent breadth even more difficult is that it cannot be divorced from the question of optimal duration. Patent policy must set both dimensions of patent protection. Typically, this amounts to choosing between a system in which patents should have a short duration but a broad coverage, the "short and fat" approach, or a long duration combined with a very narrow coverage, the "long and thin" solution. As always, these choices involve balancing the need to maintain the incentive to innovate against the need to distribute the benefits of innovation as widely as possible.

There is remarkably little agreement on the best means to achieve this balance. In some cases it has been argued that infinitely long but very narrow patents are best, while other researchers have concluded that very broad but short patents are best. Gilbert and Shapiro (1990), for example, suggest that patent breadth, even if not precisely measurable, is directly related to the flow rate of profits, $\pi$, that the patent generates during its life. They then assume that social welfare is a decreasing function of

$\pi$ and that increased patent breadth is increasingly costly in social welfare terms. If these conditions are satisfied, then the optimal patent design is to have infinitely long but very narrow patent protection. Klemperer (1990), by contrast, considers patent breadth more directly as being related to product differentiation. If we think of a Hotelling line segment of finite length, Klemperer's view is that a useful definition of patent breadth is the fraction of the line segment that is covered by the patent. He shows that there will be cases in which optimal patent design gives very narrow patent protection (cover a narrow portion of the line segment), but frequently there are cases in which protection should be broad to prevent patents from being filed on every minor differentiation. In either case, patents should only last long enough to guarantee that the sunk cost of R&D effort is just covered by the discounted present value of the additional profit generated by the patent.

Gallini (1992) makes the important point that since imitators can often get around patent protection if they spend enough money, having lengthy patents may actually depress patent-seeking and innovative activity. The reason is that when patents are short, would-be imitators are deterred because it is cheaper to wait for the patent to expire than to engage in costly efforts to imitate legally now. In contrast, if firms have to wait a long time before they can have free access to the new technology, then they have an incentive to try to copy the product now by means of a costly research effort. Thus, somewhat paradoxically, a long patent may lead to more (costly) imitation and thus more competition for the innovator than does a patent of short duration. Gallini's argument suggests that generally, patents should be short and fairly broad.

Denicolò (1996) attempts to synthesize many of the foregoing analyses in a framework that incorporates the extent of market competition. He finds that, "Loosely speaking, the less efficient is the type of competition prevailing in the product market, the more likely it is that broad and short patents are socially optimal" (p. 264). By "efficient," Denicolò means roughly the extent to which competition drives firms close to the competitive ideal. Thus, Denicolò's statement implies that markets in which firms have a greater degree of monopoly power will do best with the "short and fat" approach, while markets characterized by a good bit of competition will do best with patents that are "long and thin."

As a policy recommendation, Denicolò's recommendation has a drawback in that it seems to suggest applying different standards to different innovators depending on the structure of the innovator's basic industry. In reality, the rule of law cannot be applied so selectively without risking serious inconsistency. However, the empirical fact is that the markets in which R&D and new product development are important aspects of interfirm competition are also the markets with fairly concentrated structures (for example, the pharmaceutical market). In this light, Denicolò's reasoning gives further support to Gallini's argument and suggests that we will not go too far wrong if we adopt a one-size-fits-all policy of granting patents with "reasonable" breadth but constrained length. It is generally thought that this is a good description of the current practice in many industrialized nations.

## 23.3 PATENT RACES

The previous chapter's discussion of market structure and innovative activity was largely motivated by Schumpeter's observation that innovation is a crucial and different sort of competition from the price rivalry envisioned in basic, neoclassical economics. Quite clearly, the Schumpeter vision is one in which firms vie with each other by racing to develop new technologies or new goods and in which this sort of rivalry is potentially deadly for those who come up short. This is particularly true when innovations are eligible for patent protection. With patents, coming in first is all that matters, whether one wins by several lengths or by just a nose. The first firm to discover a treatment for male impotence or to engineer a successful system for producing "talking" pictures leaps far ahead of its rivals and stays there for some time by virtue of patent or copyright protection. In other words, patent awards have a "winner-take-all" feature so that finishing second is no better than finishing third or fourth or, for that matter, tenth.

In such a setting, innovative competition can be regarded as a race in which one player's success is the other player's serious defeat. The loser of a patent race may see years of investment and hard work wiped out overnight when the rival announces its breakthrough. We now turn to some of the issues that arise when we consider the implications of a patent system for generating a race in which finishing first is all that matters. What are the consequences of such races? Do they lead to inefficient investment in R&D? Does the innovative activity generated by the race influence market structure? These are the sorts of questions to which we now turn.

Let us consider a patent race between two firms that can choose to invest in research with a view to developing a new product. As we have just been describing, the first to make the breakthrough wins the race and files a patent giving that firm exclusive rights to its invention. This is what gives the race its winner-take-all aspect. The loser walks away empty-handed.

Because we wish to illuminate only a few key points, we will work with a simple Cournot duopoly model. Let us imagine then that two firms, BMI and ECN, are considering undertaking the R&D that is necessary to create a new product. They each estimate that if the innovation is successful they will be able to produce this new product at a marginal cost of $c$ and that demand for the new good will be $P = A - BQ$. They are also confident that the new product is a sufficiently radical departure that it will have a negligible impact on their existing business and so will not affect their existing profits—that is, there is no replacement effect.

The R&D effort by a firm requires that it establish a research division that will cost a fixed sum, $K$. This sum covers both the costs of research and of development if the research is successful and, once sunk, can never be recaptured. Given that such a division is established, the probability of a successful innovation is $\rho$. If only one firm is successful in its R&D efforts, we assume that the innovation is protected from imitation, perhaps by a patent or by some other means. If both are successful simultaneously, we assume that both firms can make the new product, in which case they will be involved in Cournot competition in selling it. To keep matters reasonably simple, we assume that both firms discount the future heavily. In particular, the interest rate $r$ is so large that the discount factor $R \approx 0$.

In order to identify the incentives each firm has to establish the research division, we need to identify their profits with and without a successful innovation. If neither firm attempts to develop the new product, neither firm will enter this new market. As a result, each will earn zero profit in this new market. Conversely, if both firms undertake R&D and are successful in making the innovation, we know that their profits, ignoring the cost of establishing the R&D division, will be the Cournot duopoly profits at marginal costs $c$:

$$\pi_b = \pi_e = \frac{(A - c)^2}{9B}.\tag{23.5}$$

If one firm, say BMI, is successful in its R&D efforts but ECN is not, then BMI will be a monopolist in the new product market getting the monopoly profits, while ECN will earn nothing from the market. In other words, the profits of the two firms in this case, again ignoring the costs of establishing the R&D division, will become

$$\pi_b = \frac{(A - c)^2}{4B}.\tag{23.6}$$

Of course, if ECN is successful but BMI is not, these profits will be reversed.

We can now calculate the expected profit for each firm depending on whether it establishes a research division. If neither firm sets up such a division, neither will innovate and each will earn zero profit in this new market. Now consider the expected profit if only one firm, say BMI, establishes an R&D division. For BMI this is made up of two components:

1. profit if the R&D division is unsuccessful, which is zero and occurs with probability $(1 - \rho)$;
2. profit if the R&D division is successful, which is the monopoly profit $(A - c)^2/4B$ and occurs with probability $\rho$.

As a result, the expected profit of BMI if it is the only firm to establish an R&D division is

$$\pi_b = \rho \frac{(A - c)^2}{4B} - K.\tag{23.7}$$

Of course, the expected profit of ECN, given that only BMI has established an R&D division, is zero. By symmetry, we reverse these payoffs to get expected profits if ECN is the only firm to establish a research division.

If both firms establish R&D divisions, the expected profit to either firm is given by

1. profit if the firm's R&D division is successful and the rival's is not, which is $(A - c)^2/4B$ and occurs with probability $\rho(1 - \rho)$;
2. profit if both R&D divisions are successful, which is $(A - c)^2/9B$ and occurs with probability $\rho^2$.

If neither firm is successful they earn nothing from the new market. This means that the expected profit of each firm, given that they both operate R&D divisions, is

$$\pi_b = \pi_e = \rho(1 - \rho) \frac{(A - c)^2}{4B} + \rho^2 \frac{(A - c)^2}{9B} - K = \frac{(A - c)^2}{36B} \rho(9 - 5\rho) - K.\tag{23.8}$$

Before we put these payoffs into a payoff matrix, we can do a bit of simplifying. The profit equations share a common expression, the monopoly profit, which we denote as $M = (A - c)^2/4B$. We can use this to define a parameter $S = K/M$, which is the share of the monopoly profits that are needed to establish the R&D division.

With the substitution of $S$ and $M$, the expected profits are summarized in the payoff matrix of Table 23-1. This matrix allows us to identify the possible Nash equilibria for this R&D game. As we shall see, these will be dependent upon the relative magnitudes of the two parameters, $S$ and $\rho$.

**PAYOFF MATRIX FOR A DUOPOLY PATENT RACE**

| | | BMI | |
|---|---|---|---|
| | | **No R&D Division** | **R&D Division** |
| **ECN** | **No R&D Division** | 0, 0 | $0, M(\rho - S)$ |
| | **R&D Division** | $M(\rho - S), 0$ | $M\left(\dfrac{\rho(9 - 5\rho)}{9} - S\right),$ $M\left(\dfrac{\rho(9 - 5\rho)}{9} - S\right)$ |

There are three possibilities that have to be considered:

1. *Neither Firm Wishes to Establish an R&D Division.* For this to be a Nash equilibrium, the payoff to BMI, for example, from not having an R&D division, given that ECN also has no R&D division, must be greater than the expected profit from investing in R&D, again given that ECN does not. In other words, BMI expects to make more profit from the strategy combination (No R&D, No R&D) than from the combination (No R&D, R&D). This requires that $M(\rho - S) < 0$, which implies that $S > \rho$; the probability of success is less than the fraction of monopoly profit required to fund the R&D. This expression is illustrated by the line $0A$ in Figure 23-2. All parameter combinations above $0A$ give the Nash equilibrium (No R&D, No R&D).

2. *Only One Firm Wishes to Establish an R&D Division.* Assume that the firm that establishes the R&D division is BMI. Then for the strategy (No R&D, R&D) to be a Nash equilibrium, two conditions must be satisfied:

    a. BMI expects its expenditure on R&D to be profitable, given that ECN is not investing in R&D—that is, BMI expects to make more profit from the strategy combination (R&D, No R&D) than from the strategy combination (No R&D, No R&D). This is just the opposite of the expression derived in part 1. It requires that $S < \rho$.

    b. ECN does not expect its expenditure on R&D to be profitable, given that BMI is investing in R&D—that is, ECN prefers the strategy combination (No R&D, R&D) to (R&D, R&D). For this to be the case, the following must be true:

$$M\left(\frac{\rho(9 - 5\rho)}{9} - S\right) < 0, \text{ which requires that } S > \frac{\rho(9 - 5\rho)}{9}.$$

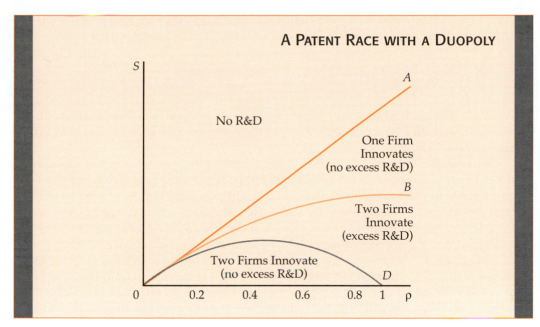

**A PATENT RACE WITH A DUOPOLY**

No R&D

One Firm
Innovates
(no excess R&D)

Two Firms
Innovate
(excess R&D)

Two Firms Innovate
(no excess R&D)

FIGURE

**23-2**

This relationship is illustrated by the curve $0B$ in Figure 23-2. All parameter combinations that lie between $0A$ and $0B$ are such that only one of the firms will establish an R&D division.

3. *Both Firms Wish to Establish an R&D Division.* For this to be a Nash equilibrium, the payoff to, for example, BMI from having an R&D division, given that ECN also has an R&D division, must be greater than the expected profit from not investing in R&D, again given that ECN does. In other words, BMI expects to make more profit from the strategy combination (R&D, R&D) than from the strategy combination (R&D, No R&D). For this to be the case we must have that

$$M\left(\frac{\rho(9-5\rho)}{9}-S\right)>0, \text{ which requires that } S<\frac{\rho(9-5\rho)}{9}.$$

Of course, exactly the same condition guarantees that ECN prefers the strategy combination (R&D, R&D) to the strategy combination (No R&D, R&D). Thus, all parameter combinations below $0B$ are such that both firms will establish an R&D division.

One question that emerges from our investigation of patent races is whether the winner-take-all feature of R&D can lead the two firms to overinvest in R&D. In this respect, you should note immediately that neither of the firms will establish an R&D division unless this division is expected to be profitable. For the strategies (R&D, No R&D), (No R&D, R&D), and (R&D, R&D) to be equilibria, they must each give positive expected profits to the two firms. This tells us that no equilibrium in which only one firm invests in R&D is characterized by "excessive" R&D in the sense that the firms would be better off without the R&D. The question that is left, therefore, is whether there is "too much" R&D when both firms establish R&D divisions. Are there situations in which the strategy combination (R&D, R&D) is a

Nash equilibrium but generates less aggregate profit than the strategy combinations (R&D, No R&D) or (No R&D, R&D)? For this to be the case it must be that

$$2M\left(\frac{\rho(9-5\rho)}{9} - S\right) < M(\rho - S), \text{ which requires that } S > \frac{\rho(9-10\rho)}{9}.$$

This is illustrated by the curve $0D$ in Figure 23-2. All parameter combinations between $0D$ and $0B$ lead to excessive R&D as the two firms race to be first to discover and introduce the new product.

Our example delineates three distinct possibilities. First, neither firm will invest in R&D unless it is expected to be profitable. Hence R&D must have a reasonably low cost relative to the monopoly profits that it might generate (low $S$), or a reasonably high probability of success. Second, for any given probability of success, a larger number of firms will establish R&D facilities when there is a lower cost of R&D relative to the profit the innovation is expected to generate. Thus, for any given probability of success, $\rho$, as $S$ is reduced, the equilibrium number of firms with R&D divisions increases from zero to one and finally to two. Third, there is an intermediate range of values for the cost of R&D in which there is excessive R&D in that both firms establish R&D divisions although this reduces their aggregate profits. In this range, the lure of profit from innovation involves the firms in a competitive R&D race that they would be better to avoid.

So far, we have only considered the gain that research brings in terms of the expected profit of the two firms. From a public policy perspective, however, increased profit is not the only potential benefit of innovation. We should also consider the gain in consumer surplus that development of this new product will generate. For example, while we have just shown that the level of R&D activity can be excessive from the viewpoint of the firms' combined profits, we have not demonstrated that this is the case when viewed with the objective of maximizing the total gain of profit plus consumer surplus. In other words, the R&D which seems excessive to the firms may still be worthwhile to society overall if the additional consumer surplus more than offsets the reduction in aggregate profit. However, as we show in Practice Problem 23.2, R&D can be excessive even when evaluated with this broader criterion. The "winner-take-all" aspect of the patent race can lead both firms to establish research divisions even when the total cost of such divisions is not justified by the sum of expected producer and consumer surplus.

Even more interesting is that we can easily show that the possibility of too little R&D—as judged from a social welfare criterion—is quite real. Consider, for example, the case in which neither firm does any R&D. As we know, this happens when $S > \rho$. Suppose that although this inequality holds, $S$ is so close to $\rho$ that one firm could almost expect to break even if it pursued the innovation (and its rival did not). In such a setting, it is apparent that if the sale of the product generates any significant consumer surplus at all, it is socially desirable that the research take place. The value of the expected consumer surplus more than provides the extra funds needed to ensure that the innovator breaks even. Yet, in the absence of some sort of government intervention, the fact that $S > \rho$ means that no such R&D efforts will occur.[3]

3   See Reinganum (1989) for a masterful survey of patent races and the timing of innovation, including the consequences for social welfare.

## Practice Problem 23.2

Consider the BMI–ECN example of a patent race. Assume that demand for the new good is $P = 100 - 2Q$, and that each firm believes that it will be able to produce this good at a unit cost of $c = \$50$. Assume further that the discount factor $R$ is so small that each firm cares only about the one-period profit it will make. (Alternatively, assume that one period is of a very long duration, say, thirty years or more.) The probability that such a lab will be successful and actually produce a discovery is $\rho = 0.8$.

a. Show that if one firm is successful in introducing the product, it will have a monopoly price of $75, sell 12.5 units, and earn monopoly profits (before paying for the research) of $M = \$312.50$. Show also that consumer surplus is $156.25.

b. Show that if each firm sets up a lab and if each lab is successful, the Cournot equilibrium output for each firm will be 8.33 units, the price will be $66.67, and each firm will earn a profit (before paying for the research) of $138.89. Confirm that consumer surplus is now $277.78.

c. Now show that the expected profit (before paying for the research) to BMI (or ECN) if it is the only firm to establish an R&D division is $250 while the expected profit to each firm if they both establish R&D divisions (again before paying for the research) is $138.89. Use these results to construct the payoff matrix for this case, now including the cost, $K$, of establishing an R&D division.

d. Show that if $K$, the cost of setting up the research lab, is such that $K > \$250$, neither firm will set up a lab, while if $K < \$138.89$, both firms will set up a lab.

e. Show that expected social surplus ignoring research costs if one firm establishes a research lab is $375, and if two research labs are established is $505.56. Hence, show that the second lab is socially desirable only if $K < \$130.56$.

We have focused on the risk that patent races may yield either too much or too little R&D investment. However, there is a further danger that patent races may involve—one that involves the choice of process or product innovation that firms involved in a patent race will make. The risk here is the distinct possibility that patent races will lead firms to pursue more risky innovations. The intuition behind this argument can be illustrated fairly simply. Suppose that firms can choose to invest either in a relatively safe R&D route that has an expected discovery time uniformly distributed between one and three years or a more risky route that has an expected time of discovery uniformly distributed between zero and four years. Both discoveries are equally costly, and both are expected to become redundant or worthless in five years' time. We will also assume that each discovery will generate the same profit of $1 million per period during the time that it is utilized and is protected from imitation by a patent.

Since the expected date of discovery is the same, namely two years for both routes, then assuming neither firm had any competition, a risk-neutral firm considering them would be indifferent between the two options, and a risk-averse firm would go for the less risky route. However, when firms are involved in a patent race, competition between the firms may lead them to choose the more variable or risky route in which success can come anytime between zero and four years.[4] The reason is that, again,

---

4  This type of case is discussed in Klette and de Meza (1986).

when innovation is protected from imitation, all that matters is winning the race. The second-place firm loses the same amount no matter how close it is behind the winner. In our example, if my rival chooses the less risky R&D route, I have an incentive to choose the more risky route, since this offers the possibility of success and a quick victory right away. Similarly, if my rival adopts the risky strategy, I can see that unless I do the same there is a real possibility that I will be left behind in the race. Of course, my rival can work out all this too. The result is that both of us choose the more risky route.

## 23.4  PATENT RACES, MONOPOLY POWER, AND "SLEEPING PATENTS"

In our discussion of patent races we typically assumed that the two contestants were on an equal footing in that both were currently in the market. However, it is important to recognize that patent policy may play a role in determining the winner of the race and, therefore, in determining what firms are producing in the first place. That is, the patent race may affect market structure itself.

The basic argument is that of Gilbert and Newbery (1982) and was outlined in Chapter 22. Whenever innovation by the monopolist can prevent the entrant from coming into the market, the monopolist has a large incentive to pursue it so as to protect its monopoly profit. In contrast, the would-be entrant can only hope to gain duopoly profit. This effect is strengthened by the patent system because it reinforces the ability of the incumbent to preclude entry. The entrant now has to "invent around" the patent.

Another way in which the patent system and innovative competition can interact to affect industrial structure is revealed in the analysis of "sleeping patents." One of the legal features of modern industry that many students at first find puzzling is the fact that very often a single firm will hold a large number of patents all related to the same process or product. (Return to Table 22-1 for some evidence on this point.) What possible reason can a firm have to establish patent rights to products and processes that it never uses, that is, what could be the rationale for a firm to create what is called a "sleeping patent"?

The motivation behind a sleeping patent is to create a buffer of protection for the monopoly profits generated by the truly valuable patent. Legal history and economic analysis have both documented that the protection granted by a single patent is often very limited. Edwin Mansfield and his associates (1981), for example, found in a study of forty-eight patented new products that 60 percent were imitated within four years after their introduction. Firms often can and do "invent around" patent protection, as we discussed earlier in the case of pharmaceuticals. Frequently, there are several technical solutions to a particular problem, such as we saw earlier in the case for the production of the whitening agent, titanium oxide (see Chapter 13). Each such alternative is a threat to the firm holding a patent on a particular process or product. Hence, by patenting as many of these alternatives as it can, a firm increases the protection it has in using whatever process it actually decides upon.

Suppose, for example, that market demand is given by $P = 100 - Q$ and that the incumbent firm has a proprietary technology with a constant marginal cost of $c_I =$ \$20. That is, the firm has a patent that protects its technology. Let us also suppose that this technology is so efficient that entry is not possible, and thus the incumbent is free to set the monopoly price and earn a monopoly profit each period of $\pi^m(c_I = 20)$. To be precise, the monopolist will sell 40 units at a price of \$60 and earn a profit of \$1,600.

Assume now that there is also an alternative technology that the monopolist has discovered, which permits production at the higher constant marginal cost of $c_E = \$30$. Clearly, the monopolist has no incentive to switch to this technology. Assume, however, that \$30 is a low enough unit cost that if any other firm could acquire this technology, it would be able to enter the industry and erode the incumbent's current monopoly. The entrant would either be the high-cost member of a Cournot duopoly or, if Bertrand competition prevailed, the entrant's cost based on using this alternative technology would at least establish a clear upper bound of \$30 on the incumbent's price—one that we know is below the incumbent's current monopoly price.

In such a setting, it is easy to see that the incumbent has an incentive to patent the higher cost technology as well as the lower cost one, even though it will never use this alternative, higher cost technology. By acquiring this patent and letting it lay dormant or sleep, the incumbent strengthens its hold on its monopoly position. The question that we need to ask is whether the incumbent's incentive to acquire the higher cost technology is so strong that it actually exceeds the incentive of the entrant to acquire the technology and enter.

The surprising answer is yes. Acquiring a patent to the high-cost technology is worth more to the incumbent monopolist than to its potential rival. This is obvious in the case of Bertrand competition. In that case, the rival's entry with a high unit cost of \$30 would provoke a price war in which the incumbent would have to lower its price from its current monopoly level to a level consistent with the marginal cost of the entrant, namely, \$30. Of course, when this happens, the entrant earns nothing. The incumbent, however, because of the lower cost, will still earn \$30 − \$20 = \$10 per unit. At this price, the incumbent will now sell \$70 units and earn a profit of \$700. This is less than what was earned previously but still better than nothing. From this it should be clear why the monopolist will place a greater value on discovering the alternative process than would the entrant. Under Bertrand competition, the entrant will never earn any money with this innovation. Hence, for the entrant, discovering the process is worthless. Yet, even though the entrant cannot make money with this higher cost process, it can put pressure on the incumbent. Specifically, discovery of the process by the entrant imposes a ceiling of \$30 on the incumbent's price. Hence, it is worth something to the monopolist to acquire the process first and thereby preclude the imposition of this price cap altogether.

The same basic result holds in a Cournot scenario. The gain to the monopolist from acquiring the second, sleeping patent on the high-cost $\bar{\bar{c}}$ process is the profit this permits it to continue earning as a monopoly firm using the low-cost technology, $\pi^m(c_I = 20) = \$1,600$, less the profit $\pi_I^d(c_I, c_E) = \pi_I^d(20, 30) = \$900$ it would earn as a duopoly firm when it has the low-cost technology and the rival has the high-cost technology. So, the total net gain to the monopolist is $\pi^m(c_I = 20) - \pi_I^d(20, 30) = \$700$. In contrast, the gain to the potential entrant is the profit it would earn as the high-cost firm in a duopoly, $\pi_E^d(c_I, c_E) = \pi_E^d(20, 30) = \$400$ less its current profit, assumed to be zero. (Note: We leave it to you to show that the Cournot equilibrium has the incumbent producing 30 units and the entrant producing 20 units implying the profit amounts we have used here.) Therefore, the entrant's net gain from developing the technology is \$400. Hence, just as in the Bertrand case, the gain to the monopolist incumbent again exceeds that to the potential entrant in a Cournot setting. The best that the entrant can hope to gain by acquiring the high-cost patent is the rather limited profit earned by a high-cost firm in a duopoly. This gain is generally much less than the loss of monopoly profit that the incumbent would suffer if such an entry occurred. So the monopoly incumbent has the greater incentive to pursue the patent the extra innovation.

The reason that the incumbent monopolist is more willing to develop the high-cost process and patent it than is a potential entrant should by now be familiar. It is because the monopolist has more at stake. If it wins the race, it gets to keep its current monopoly position. If the entrant wins the race, the best the entrant can hope for is to be the high-cost member of a duopoly. The incumbent's goal in acquiring the patent on the high-cost process is to prevent the second of these eventualities from occurring. That is, the incumbent acquires the patent on the high-cost process to make sure that nobody else will use it. Viewed in this light, acquiring "sleeping patents" amounts to broadening the patent's width.

The Reality Checkpoint on the patent for solid-state ballast to be used in fluorescent lighting is one example of the use of sleeping patents. Other examples—all instances of an incumbent attempting to inhibit rival expansion—also exist. Alcoa, for instance, achieved its dominant market position largely on the strength of Charles Martin Hall's electrolytic process for the reduction of aluminum bauxite ore. Fifteen years after it was formed, the company bought up the competing Bradley patents on an alternative reduction process—one that Alcoa never used. Similarly, DuPont's patent of the synthetic fiber nylon was accompanied by the company's filing of literally hundreds of other patents, all based on variants of the same molecule. Perhaps the best example of the use of sleeping patents comes from Hollywood. Film companies regularly buy the film rights to books, staged plays, and submitted screenplays knowing that many of these script ideas will never be turned into a final product. In part, each film company simply wants to make sure that a rival producer does not get the chance to make a film based on this material.

## 23.5 PATENT LICENSING

We have noted frequently the basic tension with which patent policy must contend. Efficiency requires that the existing stock of information should be available to all buyers at the marginal cost involved in sharing such knowledge. However, since this would imply a "price for information" of near zero, it would leave little incentive for anyone to produce new information as embodied in new goods or new technologies. Patent protection is an effort to cut a middle path between these two pressures. The firm receiving the patent is protected (to some extent) from sharing its discovery with others for free. In fact, it does not have to share it at all.

One interesting possibility that this ignores is that an innovating firm might be willing to share its technical advance with other firms for a price. When this happens, it usually results in a licensing agreement between the patent owner and the patent user. Viewed from this perspective, not sharing the patent at all can be interpreted as charging a very high (perhaps infinite) licensing fee. Actual licensing therefore reflects a movement away from such a high fee and toward a price for information that is closer to—if still some way off—the efficient charge of near zero. In this sense, the

## ✓ Reality Checkpoint

### The Light That Failed

Carlile Stevens, an inventor, and Bill Alling, his business partner, have endured a legal odyssey of longer duration than the fabled ten years' worth of wandering suffered by Ulysses. The two men met in 1969, when they both worked for Singer Corporation. Mr. Stevens was a physicist then employed at Singer on a project to make traffic lights brighter. In the course of his work, he hit upon an idea for a solid-state electronic ballast to be used in fluorescent lamps. At that time, all ballasts were magnetic ones that wore out quickly, leading the fluorescent light first to "hum" incessantly and, eventually, to fail. Mr. Stevens got together with Mr. Alling, then in Singer's marketing department. The two went out on their own and persuaded 175 investors to put up $3.6 million in seed money. By the late 1970s, they patented their product, which was shown not only to outlast the existing magnetic ballasts but also to offer a 50 to 70 percent improvement in energy efficiency—a point of particular interest in the wake of the energy shocks of the 1970s. In 1981, Universal Manufacturing Corpora-

tion, which owned one of the two major magnetic ballast manufacturers, Magnetek, approached the two about acquiring the new technology. They agreed in return for a share of the royalties that Magnetek earned through licensing the process to others. By 1984, however, Stevens and Alling realized that Magnetek had no intention of putting the new ballast on the market. Instead, Motorola—a firm that had originally approached Stevens and Alling before Magnetek—was able to invent around the patent and introduce its own solid-state ballast. Stevens and Alling filed suit arguing that Magnetek had never planned to introduce their discovery as it would undermine its own existing product. Now it looks as if Stevens' and Alling's journey may be coming to a happy end. Two juries have ruled in their favor, and they have been awarded $96 million in damages. An appeals court judge has also upheld this award. After nearly 30 years, the saga of this sleeping patent appears finally to have come to rest.

**Sources:** T. Riordan, "Patents: Two Inventors Hope They Will Finally Win Compensation for a Device That Was Squelched." *The New York Times*, July 21, 1997, p. D2; and A. Salpukas, "Award to Lighting Inventor Upheld on Appeal." *The New York Times*, September 1, 1997, p. D2.

licensing of a patent is unambiguously a good thing. The question is, does an innovating firm have a profit incentive to license its discovery?

The most obvious case in which a firm would prefer to license an innovation is if the licensee operates in a totally different market from the licensor. For example, a U.S. firm that has a patent on a particular product or process innovation may prefer to license a foreign firm to use this patent (for a fee, of course) rather than attempt to exploit the patent itself in the foreign country either by setting up a foreign subsidiary or by exporting. About the only reasons for not licensing in such circumstances are, first, that the licensor may not be able to secure a satisfactory payment for the license except after extensive bargaining. If such negotiations will be prolonged, either or both parties may decide that it is simply not worthwhile. Second, the licensor may fear that, ultimately, the foreign licensee will produce in some market where it competes directly with the licensor. Finally, there is the fear that the licensee may—by acquiring rights to use the new process or product—improve its ability to develop the next generation of this technology by itself and thereby enhance its future ability to compete.

While these fears are undoubtedly real, there are considerable offsetting benefits to licensing agreements. Licensing gains revenue for the innovator today. Because the cost of sharing the information is low, any such revenue translates into profit.

What about cases where the licensor and licensee are not separated by large geographic distance but instead are competitors in the same market? Will an innovating firm license its patented discovery for use by some or all of its rivals? The answer depends on market structure and the strength of competition in the market.

### 23.5.1  The Incentive for an Oligopolist to License a Nondrastic Innovation

Consider the toughest type of competition—Bertrand or price competition between firms making identical products. In this case, a firm that obtains a patent on a new technology that permits it to sell at a lower cost has little incentive to license the process to a competitor. Suppose, for example, that both firms are currently selling at a price equal to their (constant) marginal cost of $15 and that one firm has discovered a way to reduce this cost to $12. Without licensing its rival, the innovating firm can supply the entire market at $14.99 and drive its competitor from the market while earning a $2.99 profit on every unit sold. If it tries to sell a license to its rival, the only sensible royalty rate is $2.99 per unit. The rival firm will pay no higher royalty since then it will be unable to compete because its cost will be $12 plus the royalty, which is no better than its current cost of $15. At any lower royalty, the rival will force the innovating firm to lower its price below the current $14.99. But at a royalty of exactly $2.99, both firms will sell at $14.99 and split the market. The licensing firm loses $2.99 on those units it would have sold if it had not licensed but stayed a monopolist. It then gains the $2.99 back as a royalty payment on each of those same units now sold by its rival. In short, licensing gains the innovator nothing. Hence, the incentive to license is very small when the competition is Bertrand.[5]

By contrast, consider a market in which firms are Cournot competitors. In this case, a patent holder has a strong incentive to license, as a simple example shows. Assume that demand for the product in question is $P = 120 - Q$ and that there are three firms in the market, each with constant marginal costs of $60. We know from our earlier analysis that the Cournot equilibrium output of each firm is 15 units, total output is 45, the equilibrium price is $75, and each firm is making profits of $225.

Suppose now that one firm makes a nondrastic process innovation lowering its cost to $40 per unit, while the other two firms continue to produce at the higher value of

---

5   For the patent holder that is selling in a *differentiated products market*, the analysis is a bit more complicated. Here, each additional license has three effects. First, it adds licensing revenue. Second, it makes the market more competitive and hurts the patent holder in its product market. Third, and as a result of the second effect, each additional license sold drives down the market value of licenses in general. In other words, the demand curve for licenses will be downward sloping because the more that are sold, the more competitive is the market and therefore the less any licensee can afford to pay for a license. Because the patent holder is the monopoly supplier of such licenses, its marginal revenue curve for selling will lie below the demand curve for licenses.

$60 per unit. If the innovating firm does not license the innovation, then the Cournot–Nash equilibrium price falls to $70. The innovating firm increases its output to 30 units, while the other, high-cost firms reduce their outputs to 10 units. Profit to the innovating firm increases to $900 while profit to each of the other firms falls to $100.[6]

Now assume that the innovating firm agrees to license the innovation to its rivals at a fee of $10 per unit that each rival produces. This means that the innovator's costs are $40 per unit and the other firms' costs are $50 per unit. At the post-licensing equilibrium the innovating firm's output is 25 units while the other firms produce 15 units each so that price is $65. The profit of the innovating firm is now $25 per unit on its own sales plus $10 per unit on the sales of its two rivals, giving a total profit of $925. For each non-innovating firm, profit is $15 per unit, giving each firm profit of $225.

It would appear that licensing is, indeed, profitable. Moreover, the licensing fee of $10 that we have chosen is not even the best that the innovating firm can do.[7] We show in the Derivation Checkpoint that the innovator should actually push the license price as close as possible to the difference in costs that the innovation generates—in our example, as close as possible to $20. Suppose that the innovator charges a royalty rate of $20 per unit (more accurately, $19.99). This restores the equilibrium with the innovation but without licensing. The innovator produces 30 units and each non-innovating firm produces 10 units, giving a product price of $70. Profit of each non-innovating firm is, once again, $100 since their costs are $60 per unit. By contrast, profit of the licensing firm is $30 per unit on its own output and $20 per unit on the output of its rivals, giving the licensor a total profit of $1,300. The message then is clear. For a Cournot firm with a nondrastic innovation, licensing its discovery is very attractive.

 Derivation **Checkpoint**

### The Optimal License Fee in a Cournot Model

Suppose that the inverse demand function is $P = A - BQ$ and that the innovation results in a marginal cost of $c$. Suppose further that the innovator charges a royalty of $r$ per unit to its rivals. Assume $N$ firms in total. Then the innovator's profit is

$$\pi = \frac{[A - c + (N - 1)r]^2}{(N + 1)^2} + r(N + 1)\frac{(A - c - 2r)}{B(N + 1)}.$$

The first term in this equation is the profit from the innovator's sales. The second term is the revenue from the royalty agreement. It is clear that both terms are increasing in the royalty price $r$. Accordingly, the innovator should set as high a royalty price as is possible consistent with the non-innovating firms being willing to pay that royalty.

---

6   These numbers come from simple application of the equations for the Cournot–Nash equilibrium that we have developed in Chapter 9.
7   For details, see Katz and Shapiro (1985).

## 23.5.2 Licensing, Drastic Innovations, and Monopoly Power

What if the innovation had been drastic? Or what if the industry had been a monopoly instead of an oligopoly? Consider each question in turn. If one firm in a Cournot oligopoly patents a drastic innovation, it will not want to license its discovery. Take the simple case of a duopoly. Without licensing, the innovating firm becomes a monopoly. The innovation offers such a dramatic reduction in cost that even when it sets the monopoly price associated with that cost, it still underprices its old duopolist rival while earning considerable monopoly profit. Here, nothing can be gained by licensing. If the rival is permitted to compete, the market returns to being a duopoly except at lower cost. The most the rival would ever pay for the license is its share of the duopoly profit. Combining this with the innovator's share would yield the innovator a total profit with licensing equal to the profit earned by two duopoly firms. Yet we know that—because the firms cannot collude—this is generally a smaller amount than the innovating firm could earn as a pure monopolist without licensing. Accordingly, a Cournot firm that makes a drastic innovation will not share its discovery with rivals even for a fee. Of course, this is also true for firms engaged in Bertrand competition. In all such cases, the oligopolist that makes a truly dramatic breakthrough may be expected to emerge as a monopolist driving its former competitors from the field.

Turning next to the case of monopoly in the first place, we now have to permit the innovation to take place at an outside firm or laboratory if we are to consider any licensing. (If the monopolist makes the innovation itself, there is no other firm to which it can license!) It should be clear that in such cases—whether the innovation is drastic or nondrastic—the innovating firm will license the monopolist. Since the patent holder is not active in the market itself, the only way it can obtain any revenue from its discovery is to sell or license it to the monopolist.

The interesting point in this case is the precise form that such a licensing contract should take. Should the licensor charge a royalty of $X$ per unit? Or should it charge a fixed fee independent of output? Or should it use some combination of both? You should recognize that charging a per-unit royalty—while it has the advantage that it relates revenue directly to usage—runs into the familiar problem of double marginalization (see Chapters 17 and 18). It raises the licensed firm's marginal cost so that—after that firm adds its markup—the price to the final consumer is doubly distorted and sales volume is restricted. In this light, it should not be surprising that the innovating lab will do best by using a two-part tariff. The principal part of this scheme will be a fixed fee (per month or per year). The second part will be a small royalty per unit reflecting any per-unit cost the patent holder incurs in licensing its technology. For a transfer of pure information, this per-unit charge would be zero. But if the patent holder needs to offer services or technical advice that increases with the frequency with which the technology is used, this fee would be positive. In short, the licensing contract is much like a franchising contract. In principle, the inventor can appropriate all the increased profit that the invention brings if the contract is written correctly, that is, with a fixed fee exactly equal to that additional profit. In practice, however, the patent holder's bargaining position will usually not be strong enough to achieve this outcome. As we have already emphasized, when the manufacturer has a monopoly in the product market, the inventor needs the manufacturer just as much as the manufacturer needs the inventor.

### 23.5.3 Patent Licensing, Social Welfare, and Public Policy

The foregoing cases indicate that most of the time an innovator has an interest in licensing its discovery. This is a reassuring result because our intuition is that licensing is typically a desirable outcome. Indeed, Katz and Shapiro (1985) have provided a formal argument that social welfare is nearly always increased by licensing. Specifically, they show that licensing is socially desirable if total output increases as a result of the licensing activity. To see why, note that licensing will not take place unless it is both profitable and increases aggregate profit. The license agreement will not be signed unless the licensees see some benefit from it and will not be offered unless the licensor also sees some benefit from it. If, in addition to this mutual gain in profit, the license agreement increases total output, then the price will be lower and consumer surplus will be increased. In other words, if the license agreement increases total output, both consumers and producers gain from the agreement, and so the agreement is socially desirable. Yet even if this fails to happen—even if the industry output is unchanged—licensing is still likely to be socially beneficial since the licensing revenue at least increases producer surplus. Somebody then, either a producer or a consumer, or both, is made better off by licensing.

Moreover, licensing may have other beneficial effects. First, if a firm knows that it is going to gain profits from licensing its research findings as well as (or instead of) exploiting the research itself, this should increase the incentive to undertake research. Further, the possibility that a firm can obtain a license to use a particular innovation will reduce wasteful R&D that either duplicates existing research effort or is intended merely to invent around an existing patent.

Suppose, for instance, that the duopoly profit is (in present value terms) $5 million but that R&D expenditures of $3 million are necessary for the entrant to develop its own alternative. In the absence of any licensing, the entrant will pursue this investment since it yields a net gain of $2 million. Yet if this is the case, then the monopolist firm will know that whether it licenses or not, it will soon be a duopolist. If the monopolist firm licenses its technology to the entrant for $3 million, the entrant is just as well off and the monopolist now gets the licensing revenue. In addition, society avoids the unnecessary expenditure of $2 million that the entrant would otherwise have made. The moral of this section therefore seems quite clear. Public policy should actively encourage the licensing of innovations as much as possible.

There is, however, need for a cautionary note. We noted at the beginning of this section that licensing may involve some risks. First, consider the risks associated with licensing based upon an output-related royalty. Imagine as well that the licensing agreement holds for the outstanding duration of the patent that is being licensed since, after that, the information becomes publicly available. If the royalty rate extracts almost all of the additional profits that the licensee might expect to make, there is the risk that the licensee will take the license in order to gain experience with the technology but then actually produce very little during the period of the license agreement, which means, of course, that very little is actually paid for the license. Alternatively, if output is difficult to monitor, the licensee has the incentive to lie about how much is actually being produced. What may be necessary is that the licensor tie the license agreement to some agreed minimum level of output on the part of the licensee, but even this is not always easy to negotiate or enforce.

A further risk in licensing is that it can be difficult to write enforceable contracts that limit the ways in which licensees can use the license. Typically, the licensor will want to limit the markets into which the licensee can sell, for example, to avoid direct competition with the licensor or with other licensees. This may be possible within a particular jurisdiction such as the United States, although even here antitrust laws may prevent such market-limiting agreements. But it is almost impossible to write binding contracts that limit the international markets in which licensees can operate. In addition, access to a particular process or product technology may enhance the ability of a licensee to develop related technologies that are not covered by the patent being licensed. Once again, it is almost impossible to write enforceable contracts that protect the licensor from such imitation or at least give the licensor some return from the new technologies that licensees develop.

 # Reality Checkpoint

### Patent Policy in the Information Age:
### Getting One (click) Up (sale) on the Competition

The most valuable real estate lots bordering the information superhighway may simply be ideas about how to use this new tool in a way that increases profit. Ideas about how to do business or so-called business methods are different from the technological innovations that we have discussed elsewhere in this chapter. Yet in the information age, they may be just as valuable. A leading example in this regard is a patent issued to the online bookstore Amazon.com. Amazon customers shop the site and list the items that they wish to purchase. At the end of their visit, customers simply make one click of their mouse and their order is taken and then shipped as soon as possible. Amazon applied for and received a patent for this 1-Click feature, and touts it to all potential customers. In October 1999, the traditional "brick and mortar" bookseller Barnes & Noble introduced an Express Lane feature at its recently opened Web site. The Express Lane checkout also permitted customers to finalize their shopping with one mouse click. Amazon instantly sued, claiming that the Express Lane model was a clear infringement of its

1-Click patent. A federal appeals court then issued an injunction preventing Barnesandnoble.com from using the Express Lane feature. The firm appealed but, pending the appeal, dropped the Express Lane ordering system in favor of a two-click system called Express Checkout. In February 2001, an appeals panel lifted the injunction against Barnes & Noble until a final ruling over the validity of the patent was reached.

The 1-Click case is not unique. Consider the business method called upselling. A customer at a Burger King restaurant, for instance, might order a Whopper sandwich, an order of fries, and a small salad for a total of $7.14. When checking out, the cashier might say something like "for just 86 cents more, you can also have a soft drink that regularly sells for $1.29." If the customer agrees to this upsale, Burger King obviously receives more money (you should recognize this procedure as a quantity discount discrimination). Yet Burger King will not get to keep all the extra funds. A chunk of it will go to Walker Digital as a licensing fee because Walker (owned by Jay Walker the founder of Priceline.com) owns a patent on this process and Burger King must pay for it.

Business-method patents have become common ever since a U.S. Court of Appeals ruled in favor of Signature Financial Group's patent for an algorithm to manage mutual fund investments [*State Street Bank and Trust Co., Inc. v. Signature Financial Group, Inc.*, 149 F.3d 1368, Fed. Cir. (1998)]. Since that decision, filings for such patents have nearly tripled to between 1,000 and 2,000 a year. Such patents raise an interesting qualification to optimal patent policy. Where innovations require lots of development time and expense, can be clearly identified, and need protection

against imitation, some type of patent award is probably necessary for technical progress to occur. However, when innovations are highly incremental and build on a host of other advances so that it is hard to identify the actual breakthrough in any one application, a patent system may actually slow down the innovative progress. Many economists, like Gallini (2002) and Hall (2003), suspect that business method patents may fall in this second group. The irony is that just as the Internet and related developments are making information cheap, the rush to patent business practices may make the exploitation of that information more expensive.

---

**Sources:** S. Hansell, "Barnesandnoble Injunction Lifted." *The New York Times*, February 15, 1991, p. C1; and J. Angwin, "'Business Method' Patents, Key to Priceline, Draw Growing Protest." *The Wall Street Journal*, October 3, 2000, p. B1.

There are also public policy issues that arise in licensing and that suggest caution in favoring and promoting every licensing agreement. As we have already noted, one danger is that licensing contracts will include restrictions on price or geographic territory that create monopolies with exclusive territories that would otherwise be illegal under the antitrust laws. Matters become particularly complicated when, as so often happens, one patent leads to another, complementary development. Firm 1 creates, say, a new antibiotic that has some occasional and serious side effects. Then firm 2 develops a means to undo the side effects for firm 1's drug. The two firms may strike a deal that licenses each to produce the other's product. Yet it is easy to see that this agreement may often include terms that exclude other firms. Such dangers are recognized by U.S. policy, which tends to limit severely the ability of reciprocal licensing agreements to include exclusive provisions. Still, the example serves to make clear that the tension between promoting licensing and realizing its associated benefits, on the one hand, and the potential risk of collusion that licensing may foster, on the other, is real.

---

## Practice Problem 23.3

Two firms compete in a Cournot-type duopoly. The industry demand is given by $P = 100 - 2Q$. Each firm has a constant average and marginal cost of $60.

a. What is the current equilibrium price and quantity in the industry?

b. Suppose that one firm discovers a procedure that lowers its average and marginal cost to $50.

   1. If the innovator does not license its product but simply competes as the low-cost firm in a Cournot duopoly, what will be the innovator's profit?

2. What will be the innovator's profit if it licenses the technology to its competitor at a royalty rate of $10?

3. Suppose instead that the innovator licenses the technology for a fixed fee. What is the highest fee that the non-innovator will be willing to pay? What will the innovator's profits be if it can charge the highest possible such fee?

# SUMMARY

By giving innovators a legally enforceable means of earning a return on their discoveries, patents and copyrights provide incentives for innovative activity that might otherwise not be undertaken. Yet patents also confer monopoly power on the patent holder, with all the price distortions that such power entails. In addition, patent rules may enhance the ability of existing monopolies to maintain their current dominant position against would-be entrants. One mechanism by which this may occur is through the use of "sleeping patents" designed to buffer the invention against any and all attacks from rival innovations that might permit an entrant to "invent around" the original patent.

Licensing agreements by which firms permit the use of their patented knowledge for a fee can help ameliorate the patent tension. This is because such agreements both permit wider use of the innovation and also allow an innovator to earn a greater return on its R&D investments than otherwise would be received. However, licensing contracts can be difficult to enforce except by imposing restrictions that can be harmful to competition. There is no way to eliminate the tension between allocative efficiency and innovative activity that a patent system raises.[8]

# PROBLEMS

1. Let the inverse demand for a particular product be given by $P = 250 - Q$. The product is offered by two Cournot firms whose current marginal costs are $100. Both firms can invest a sum $K$ to establish a research facility to develop a new process with lower marginal costs. The probability of success is $\rho$.

   a. Assume that the new process is expected to have marginal costs of $70. Derive a relationship between $K$ and $\rho$ under which

   (1) neither firm establishes the research facility.

   (2) only one firm establishes a research facility.

   (3) both firms establish a research facility.

   b. Can there be "too much" R&D? Illustrate your answers in a diagram with $\rho$ on one axis and $K$ on the other.

   c. Now assume that the marginal costs of the new process are expected to be $40. How does this affect your answers to (a)?

---

8   See, however, Moser (2003) for a view that conferring monopoly power via a patent may not be terribly necessary to generate innovative activity.

2. In the text of this chapter we considered sleeping patents in the context of a process innovation. The same principles apply in the case of a product innovation. To see why, consider the following example: Assume that there are 100 aspiring Olympic swimmers whose tastes for low-water-resistance colored swimming suits are evenly distributed over the color spectrum from black to yellow. The "length" of this spectrum is normalized to be one unit. Each of these swimmers values the loss of utility from being offered swimming suits in other than their favorite color at $10 per unit of "distance." Each swimmer will buy exactly one swimming suit per period provided that the full price for the suit—the price charged by the firm plus the value of utility lost if there is a color difference between the suits on offer and the swimmer's favorite color—is less than $100 (these are very keen swimmers!). Production of low-water-resistance swimming suits is currently feasible only in black and is controlled by a monopolist who has a patent on the production of the black material. The marginal cost of making a swimming suit is $25.

   a. What is the current profit-maximizing price per suit and what are the monopolist's per-period profits?

   Now assume that research can be conducted that will allow the swimming suits also to be manufactured in yellow at the same marginal cost of $25.

   b. If the monopolist undertakes the research and introduces the new color what will be the resulting equilibrium prices of black and yellow swimming suits? What is the impact on the monopolist's per-period profit, ignoring research costs?

   c. If a new entrant undertakes the research and introduces the new color, what will be the resulting equilibrium prices of black and yellow swimming suits? What will the entrant's per-period profit be, again ignoring research costs?

   d. Confirm that the incumbent monopolist will be willing to spend more on researching the new color than the potential entrant.

   e. Assume that the research costs can be split into some amount, $R$, which is pure research cost, and another amount, $D$, which is development cost—the cost of transforming a successful innovation into a viable product. Calculate limits on $R$ and $D$ such that the monopolist will be willing to undertake the research into manufacture of yellow swimming suits and patent it but then leave the patent sleeping.

3. Consider a Cournot duopoly in which inverse demand is given by $P = 120 - Q$. Marginal cost of each firm is currently $60.

   a. What is the Cournot equilibrium quantity for each firm, product price, and profit of each firm?

   Now assume that one of the firms develops a new technology that reduces marginal cost to $30.

   b. If it keeps control of this innovation itself, what will be the new Cournot equilibrium outputs, product price, and profits of the two firms?

   c. If it licenses the innovation to its rival at some per-unit fee $r$, calculate the innovator's profit as a function of $r$. What is the profit-maximizing value of $r$ for the licensor?

   d. Assume instead that it licenses the innovation to its rival for a fixed fee of $L$. What is the maximum fee that it can charge? Will the innovator prefer to set a per-unit license fee or a fixed license fee? What kind of licensing arrangement would consumers prefer?

4. Consider the same Cournot duopoly as in problem 3, but now assume that the research has been conducted by an outside research firm. Suppose that this firm agrees to license the technology at a per-unit fee of $r$. What license fee will the research firm charge

   **a.** if it licenses to only one of the duopolists?

   **b.** if it licenses to both?

   **c.** How are your answers to (a) and (b) affected if the research firm chooses instead to charge a fixed fee of $L$ for the license?

# REFERENCES

Denicolò, V. 1996. "Patent Races and Optimal Patent Breadth and Length." *Journal of Industrial Economics* 44 (March): 249–65.

Gallini, N. 2002. "The Economics of Patents: Lessons from Recent U.S. Patent Reform." *Journal of Economic Perspectives* 16 (Spring): 131–54.

———. 1992. "Patent Policy and Costly Imitation." *Rand Journal of Economics* 23 (Spring): 52–63.

Gilbert, R. J., and D. M. G. Newbery. 1982. "Preemptive Patenting and the Persistence of Monopoly." *American Economic Review* 72 (June): 514–27.

Gilbert, R., and C. Shapiro. 1990. "Optimal Patent Length and Breadth." *Rand Journal of Economics* 21 (Spring): 106–12.

Hall, B. 2003. "Business Method Patents, Innovation, and Policy." Working Paper, Department of Economics, University of California.

Katz, M., and C. Shapiro. 1985. "On the Licensing of Innovation." *Rand Journal of Economics* 16: 504–20.

Klemperer, P. 1990. "How Broad Should the Scope of Patent Protection Be?" *Rand Journal of Economics* 21: 233–30.

Klette, T., and D. de Meza. 1986. "Is the Market Biased against R&D?" *Rand Journal of Economics* 17: 133–9.

Mansfield, E., M. Schwartz, and S. Wagner. 1981. "Imitation Costs and Patents: An Empirical Study." *The Economic Journal* 91(December): 907–18.

Moser, P. 2003. "How Do Patent Laws Influence Innovation? Evidence From Nineteenth Century World Fairs." Working Paper, MIT Sloan School of Management.

Nordhaus, W. 1969. *Invention, Growth and Welfare.* Cambridge, MA: The MIT Press.

Reinganum, J. 1989. "The Timing of Innovation: Research, Development, and Diffusion." In R. Schmalensee and R. Willig, eds., *The Handbook of Industrial Organization.* Amsterdam: North-Holland: 849–908.

# Part seven

## New Developments in Industrial Organization

# seven
# New Developments in
# Industrial Organization

In this final part we introduce two topics that do not fit easily within our earlier classifications. The first of these is the issue of network externalities. For many goods, for example, a telephone, the value of the product to any one consumer rises as additional consumers buy the product. Such network effects greatly alter both the nature of industry competition and the characteristics of the market outcome. The analysis in Chapter 24 makes clear that the introduction of network effects can have dramatic impact. Typically such effects give rise to multiple equilibria with little guarantee that the market will choose the right one. Indeed, there is a real possibility of complete market collapse in which no firm produces positive output. Moreover, because networks need to be large to be viable, such markets have a natural tendency toward either monopoly or an oligopoly with a very few firms.

In Chapter 25, we switch gears and turn to the topic of auctions. Auction markets have been around for a very long time and, partly because of this historical pedigree, are sometimes viewed as the ultimate expression of competition. Indeed, the modern use of auctions to sell such items as oil lease tracts, mineral rights, and mobile phone licenses was initially seen as the embodiment of the competitive market in action. Subsequent experience has shown, however, that certain features of auction markets may yield outcomes that lie far from the competitive ideal.

The analysis starts with a review of auction types and a derivation of the most famous result in auction theory, the Revenue Equivalence Theorem. We then turn to a consideration of common value auctions and the well-known phenomenon of the "Winner's Curse." We examine the implications of these insights for auction design with a view toward outcomes that will be efficient in that the auctioned item will go to the buyer who values the good the most and at a price that is very close to that buyer's maximum value. We also show that such designs are not always easily accomplished and that the modern history of auction markets suggests that these markets are just as subject to the problems of market power as are other industries. Few topics are better suited than that of auctions and auction markets to make clear both the value of industrial organization theory as well as its use in actual practice.

# Network Issues

# Chapter 24

Microsoft Corporation—perhaps no single firm is more closely associated with the telecommunications revolution that has swept through both businesses and households in the last part of the twentieth century than this giant of the software industry. Nor perhaps does any other company better capture the popular view of the opportunities for fame and fortune that the "new economy" presents. Starting out as a simple provider of programming language, Microsoft became the supplier of over 90 percent of the operating systems for personal computers. It holds equally commanding shares in many markets for peripheral programs, such as that for word processing (Word) and electronic spreadsheets (Excel). From a small, two-person enterprise with essentially zero net worth in 1975, the firm has grown to a firm of over 30,000 employees with a net worth of over $52 billion in 2003.

Of course, Microsoft is not the only success story of the digital economy age. Among the other Cinderella firms of recent years is eBay, the online auction company. A small startup firm started by Pierre Omidyar in 1995, eBay now has over ten million registered users and conducts over one million person-to-person auctions each day. These transactions initially involved only low-price collectibles, from Star War action figures to Japanese maple trees. However, the site now brokers trades of many everyday items including toys and games, concert tickets, and even used cars. Prior to the 1990s, direct trade in many items, especially collectibles, had been limited because of the extreme cost of matching a potential buyer with a potential seller. Omidyar was among the first to recognize the enormous potential of the Internet—which makes it easy to disseminate a vast amount of information to a large number of buyers and sellers in a very short time—to solve this problem.

Of course, neither Microsoft nor eBay are alone in their markets. There are other operating system platforms, such as Macintosh or Linux, and other online auction sites. Nevertheless, both firms have come to dominate their markets. Moreover, each of these markets shares an important feature. One reason that so many people use the Windows operating system is that they expect others will use it as well. The more people that use Windows the more software that will be written for Windows and thus the more useful Windows will be. Similarly, the more buyers that try to buy on eBay, the more sellers will want to sell there, which in turn attracts more buyers and so on.

When the value of a product to any one consumer increases as the number of other consumers using the product increases, we say that the market for that product exhibits network externalities or effects. When these effects are important, new strategic considerations come into play. In this chapter, we investigate these issues and the type of market outcomes that are likely when important network effects are present.[1]

## 24.1 MONOPOLY PROVISION OF A NETWORK SERVICE

An early but insightful analysis of network issues is that provided by Rohlfs (1974). Rohlfs' approach is quite straightforward and focuses on one primary issue, namely,

---

[1] For a formal but very readable introduction to network externalities, see Economides (1996).

the potential for multiple equilibria. For this purpose, Rohlfs assumes away any competition and concentrates on the case in which there is a monopoly provider of a network service such as a monopoly supplier of communications services. We present a simplified version of the Rohlfs model here.

Assume that the monopolist simply charges an access fee but does not impose a per-usage charge. That is, the consumer is charged a single price $p$ for "hooking up" to the network but each individual call is free, perhaps because the marginal cost of a call is zero.[2] We will also assume that there is a maximum size of the market, say one million, reflecting the maximum number of consumers who would ever willingly buy the product even if the access fee were zero. By fixing the total amount of potential customers, we can talk interchangeably about the actual number served and the fraction $f$ of the market that is served. That is, if the maximum size of the market is one million, we can characterize a market outcome in which 100,000 purchase the service either in terms of the total output of 100,000 units or the fraction $f = 0.10$ that is served. For our purposes, it is easier to work with $f$.

Consumers all agree that the service is more valuable the greater the fraction $f$ of the market that signs up for it. However, even if everyone acquires the service ($f = 1$), consumers would still vary in their valuation or willingness to pay for the service. Specifically, we denote the valuation of the $i$th consumer when $f = 1$ as $v_i$. These valuations, or $v_i$s, are assumed to be uniformly distributed between 0 and 100. For example, the one percent of consumers who most value the service (roughly about 10,000 individuals in our case) would willingly pay \$100 for it if all other consumers also acquire it. However, as the fraction of consumers who sign up declines, so does each consumer's willingness to pay. The easiest way to reflect this assumption is that the $i$th consumer's valuation of the service for any value of $f$ is given by $fv_i$. The demand by consumer $i$ for a hook up to the communications service is therefore given by

$$q_i^D = \begin{cases} 0 \text{ if } fv_i < p \\ 1 \text{ if } fv_i \geq p \end{cases}. \tag{24.1}$$

Again, it is worth pointing out that the influence of network size works here through $f$. For consumer $i$, equation (24.1) says that the consumer's willingness to pay for the service $fv_i$ increases with the fraction of potential buyers $f$ that have bought into the service. It is this interdependence between the willingness to pay and the fraction of the market served that leads to network externalities. In addition, each potential user of the network considers only the value to himself or herself of joining the network. What users do not take into account are the external benefits they create when they join the network. By joining, users will improve the usefulness of the network to all of the other users since now the network is bigger.

We can use equation (24.1) to calculate the fraction of the market that will sign on to the service at any given price $p$. As usual, we start by focusing on the marginal consumer denoted by the reservation valuation $\tilde{v}_i$. This is the consumer who is just indifferent between buying into the service network and not buying into it so that $\tilde{v}_i = p/f$. All consumers with a valuation less than $\tilde{v}_i$ will not subscribe to the service. The remainder will subscribe. Since $v_i$ is distributed uniformly between 0 and 100, the frac-

---

2    Note that this pricing policy is essentially that of a two-part tariff as described in Chapter 6.

tion of consumers with a valuation below $\tilde{v}_i$ is simply $\tilde{v}_i/100$. Hence, the fraction of consumers $f$ with valuations greater than $\tilde{v}_i$ and who therefore acquire the service is

$$f = 1 - \frac{\tilde{v}_i}{100} = 1 - \frac{p}{100f}. \qquad (24.2)$$

If we now solve for $p$ we obtain the inverse demand function confronting the monopolist expressed in terms of the fraction $f$ of the maximum potential number of customers who actually buy the service as

$$p = 100f(1 - f). \qquad (24.3)$$

This is illustrated in Figure 24-1.

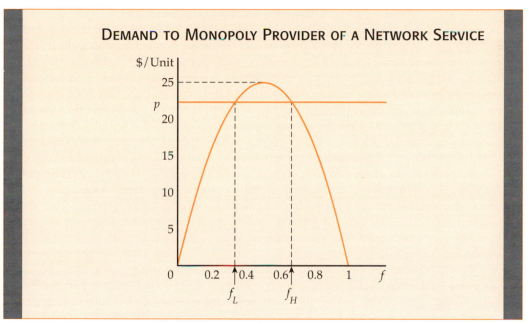

**DEMAND TO MONOPOLY PROVIDER OF A NETWORK SERVICE**

FIGURE

**24-1**

Demand for a product with network externalities. At price $p$ if fewer than $f_L$ consumers buy the service, the equilibrium will fall to $f = 0$. If more than $f_L$ consumers buy the service, the equilibrium will rise to $f_H$.

The curve shown in Figure 24-1 is interesting in a number of respects. Note first that for all prices greater than \$25, no equilibrium with a positive value of $f$ exists. If for some reason the monopolist must charge a price greater than \$25, perhaps to cover fixed costs, then the network will simply fail. This is true even though the network might be socially efficient. For example, when half the market ($f = 0.5$) or 500,000 consumers are served, we know that those who obtain the product are those

consumers with $v_i$ values in the range of \$50 to \$100. The average $v_i = \left(\dfrac{1}{50}\right) \sum\limits_{I=51}^{100} v_i$

value for this group is therefore \$75. With $f = 0.5$, the average actual willingness to pay across these consumers is accordingly $1/2 \times \$75 = \$37.50$. As long as the price is below this amount, consumers as a group gain from having the network service available. Suppose that the monopolist could in fact provide service to 500,000 customers but to do so would require that it sink development costs of $15 million, or $30 per customer. The firm would then have to charge a hook-up price of $30 just to break even.

Now, $30 is certainly less than $37.50, so such an outcome would be desirable as it would generate net positive consumer gains and no producer losses. Moreover, with an average willingness to pay of $37.50, charging a fee of $30 may also appear to be a price that the market could support. Yet as we have just stated and as Figure 24-1 illustrates, the network will not be viable at this price. Why? Because while the average consumer valuation at $f = 0.5$ is $37.50, there are some current consumers (those for whom $50 \leq v_i < \$60$) whose willingness to pay is less than $30. As the price rises toward $30, these consumers drop the service. Some (those for whom $50 \leq v_i < \$52$) drop as soon as the price rises to $26, more drop as it hits $27, and so on. The loss of these consumers, however, reduces the value of the network to those remaining. Those who were previously just willing to pay $30 when the service had 500,000 subscribers no longer will be willing to do so now that fewer people are signed on. These consumers will also cease to purchase the product, reducing still further the network's value to the now even fewer customers left behind. This process will continue until the entire market unravels and the network fails. Here one can see the externality quite explicitly. A consumer does not consider the impact that his or her choice to join or to leave the network has on the value of the network to others.

Next note that for prices less than or equal to $25, there is actually more than one equilibrium value of $f$. For instance, when $p = \$22.22$, both $f_L(p) = 1/3$ and $f_H(p) = 2/3$ are possible values for $f$. Which of these might we expect to occur? Rohlfs points out that the low-fraction equilibrium is actually unstable. Consider, for example, the effect of a small increase in the price or a small loss of customers. Starting from an equilibrium with so few subscribers, this would repeat the outcome described above. As a few consumers leave, the value of being part of the system to those remaining is reduced. Again, the eventual outcome is that all subscribers leave and the network fails. Now consider the impact of a small reduction in the price or the addition of one extra subscriber, again starting from the low-fraction equilibrium. This would increase the value of the service above the reservation price of all consumers in the interval $(0, f_H)$. It would therefore lead to the establishment of the high-fraction, or $f_H(p)$, equilibrium. These thought experiments suggest that once the fraction $f_L(p)$ of consumers subscribes to the network, it is virtually certain that the high-fraction equilibrium will be attained, since only a trivial price reduction is necessary to do so. For this reason, Rohlfs refer to this lower fraction as a "critical mass" for the network. So long as a fraction of subscribers just a bit greater than this critical mass, $f_L(p)$, can be established, the network will grow to contain the high fraction, $f_H(p)$, of the population.

An important question, therefore, is whether and how the monopolist can reach the critical mass. For as we have just seen, values of $f$ below the critical mass tend to unravel. That is, an alternative equilibrium that arises at the price of $22.22 is one in which no consumer signs up for the service at all. The reason that this can happen is fairly straightforward. At that price, no individual consumer will wish to sign up for the service unless others do. Accordingly, each consumer holds back from joining until they see some others hooking up. Hence, an outcome in which no one has joined the network can be self-sustaining.

The question as to how to get the network started and grow to a critical mass is an interesting one. One possibility is to provide the service free for a limited period of time. One way to accomplish such selling below cost is to bundle the service free with some other product. For example, access to an ATM network is bundled with banking services. Another option is to lease the equipment to potential users with a guarantee that if the service does not achieve critical mass, the lease agreement can be canceled with no penalty. A further possibility, which was employed when fax machines were first being marketed, would be to target groups of large users first. In this regard, national and multinational companies or government agencies are the obvious examples of institutions that might want to operate their own internal networks. The idea is that once the network comes into common use for internal company communications, there will be a demand for it to be extended to those with whom the company does business. Before long, this may grow into a demand by company users of the service for it to be available in their homes.

For the moment, let us assume that the monopolist does achieve the critical mass. What fee will the monopolist charge for its services and how does this compare to the social optimum? In answering this question we will again assume that the monopolist's costs are all fixed and given by $F$, so that the marginal cost of adding a further subscriber to the network is zero. Let us also assume that the maximum number of individuals who would sign up even at a zero price is $N$. (In our example above, $N$ = one million.) Then total profit to the monopolist is

$$\pi(f) = pfN - F = 100Nf^2(1 - f) - F, \text{ given that } p = 100f(1 - f). \quad \textbf{(24.4)}$$

Maximizing this with respect to $f$ indicates (see the Derivation Checkpoint) that the monopolist should choose $p$ such that $f^* = 2/3$, implying a profit-maximizing price of $p^* = \$22.22$. As just described, actually getting two-thirds of the market to sign on at a price of $22.22 may be difficult until the critical mass $f = 1/3$ is reached. Still, it is clear that this would be the monopolist's goal.

How does the combination $p = \$22.22$ and $f = 2/3$ compare with the social optimum? It should not surprise you that the profit-maximizing choice of the monopolist is to serve a smaller market than that which would maximize the total surplus. After all, monopolists achieve their profit by restricting output. The social optimum requires that the market be as large as possible at a price equal to marginal cost. In our case, this means that all $N$ consumers should be served, that is, $f = 1$.

Consider the numerical example above with $N$ = one million. At the monopolist's profit-maximizing price of $22.22, two-thirds of the market or 666,666.66 consumers are served. The monopolist therefore earns a profit of $14.81 million less fixed cost $F$. Consumer surplus may be calculated as follows. With two-thirds of the market served, all consumers with $v_i$ values in the range $33.33 \le v_i \le \$100$ hook up to the service. Hence, the average value of $v_i$ for this group is $67.67. Since $f = 2/3$, the average willingness to pay of those consumers served in this equilibrium is $0.67 \times \$67.67 \approx \$45$. Hence, with $p = \$22.22$, the average consumer earns a surplus of $22.78. Multiplying this average surplus by the 666,666.66 consumers yields a total consumer surplus of about $15,187,000. Accordingly, the monopolist's profit-maximizing price and quantity generates a total surplus of $14.81 million + $15.19 million = $30 million less the fixed cost $F$.

Now consider the social optimum in which $f = 1$. With all one million consumers receiving the service, the average value of $v_i$ (and therefore of $fv_i$) is $50. Hence, the

**Derivation Checkpoint**

### The Profit-Maximizing Network Access Price

Profit is $\pi(f) = pfN = 100Nf^2(1 - f) - F$. Differentiating with respect to $f$ gives the first-order condition

$$\frac{d\pi(f)}{df} = 100N(2f - 3f^2) = 0,$$

which implies that either $f = 0$ or $f = 2/3$. The choice of $f = 0$ generates negative profits so long as $F > 0$. The choice of $f = 2/3$ generates positive operating profits (hopefully enough to cover $F$), and so $f^* = 2/3$ is the optimal choice of $f$. From the inverse demand function, $p = 100f(1 - f)$, a value of $f$ of 2/3 implies a price of $100 \times \frac{2}{9} = \$22.22$.

---

total value of the service is $50 million. The total social surplus would then be $50 million $- F$. Clearly, this exceeds the total surplus under monopoly. Of course, just how the optimal outcome would be achieved in practice is unclear. One way is through subsidization by the government. Alternatively, it could be achieved by creating a legal monopoly and permitting it to price discriminate. A combination of these two strategies is also possible. Indeed, one can think of the postal system as a giant network served by a government monopoly that is both subsidized and that price discriminates (for example, express versus first-class mail).

## 24.2 NETWORKS, COMPETITION, AND COMPLEMENTARY SERVICES

While the Rohlfs (1974) model focuses on the provision of network services by a monopolist, it makes clear many of the major difficulties that network externalities raise when competition is considered. The market could fail altogether. Alternatively, there could be more than one equilibrium outcome and there is no guarantee that the market will choose the best one. For example, suppose that there are two firms, firm A and firm B, competing for the 1,000,000-customer market above. Suppose further that while fixed costs are zero, each firm now has a positive marginal cost of $11.11. Consumers buy the service of the network that gives them the biggest net surplus, $f_A v_i - p_A$, and $f_B v_i - p_B$, respectively. In the case of a tie, consumers are split randomly between the two services. One possible equilibrium occurs with each firm setting a price $p_A = p_B =$ marginal cost = $11.11 and two-thirds of the market being served. The firms offer identical products and, given the tie-breaking assumption, each serves half of the consumers ranging from valuations $33.33 and up. However, since each firm individually serves only one-third of the market, the valuation of the least valuable consumer in each case is $f v_i = 0.33 \times \$33.33 = \$11.11$. Neither firm has an incentive to raise its price unilaterally; this would only lose customers and make its network even less valuable to consumers. Nor does either firm have an incentive to lower its price. While this may give it an edge in attracting customers, each one served now involves a loss as the firm would be selling below cost. Hence, $p_A = p_B = \$11.11$ and two-thirds of market being served is one possible equilibrium.

However, there are two other possible outcomes. They occur when either firm A or firm B has a monopoly with respect to all consumers actually subscribing to a network at the monopoly price, while its rival has zero customers at a price equal to or greater than marginal cost. It is easy to show, for example, that with a marginal cost of $\$11.11$, the monopoly price would be $\$23.89$ and that at this price, the monopolist would serve about 60.5 percent of the market and earn a profit of $\$12.78$ on each customer. Suppose that firm A is doing precisely this. Suppose that firm B is charging a lower price but has zero consumers. Clearly, firm A has no incentive to raise or lower its price since it already has set a price that maximizes its profit. Firm B has no incentive to change its price either. Raising it surely will not help it attract any customers. Yet lowering it won't attract customers either because no one will choose a network that has no other customers regardless of the price.

A further implication of Rohlfs' analysis is that competition between two or more firms to establish the network can be particularly fierce, particularly if it is possible that only one firm or network survives. That is, the market has a "winner-take-all" feature. The winning network claims the entire (served) population and the loser gets nothing. The market is "tippy" in that once a firm starts to lose customers, the value of its product to the remaining customers falls, causing it to lose more customers, its value to fall further, and so on. In such a setting, more than market share is at stake. Survival itself is on the line. Moreover, while this "winner-take-all" feature would greatly intensify the competition by itself, coupling it with an environment in which pricing below cost may be necessary just to get any network started makes the competition truly nasty. Some economists have argued that it was precisely this dynamic that was at work in the *Microsoft versus Netscape* case and that what may look like predatory behavior when applied in other markets is really just part of the game of competition when applied in a setting of network goods.[3]

Market problems become particularly difficult when the network is a system comprised of complementary components and when we consider what happens over time. Think, for example, of the market for digital versatile disc (DVD) movies. The two components to this network are the DVD player and the movie discs themselves. This complementary relationship complicates the network effect. From the start, the socially desired outcome was that the use of DVD players and discs would become sufficiently widespread to exploit the rather sizable scale economies that characterize production, especially disc-making. The potential problem was that no firm or group of firms would be willing to sink the large up-front costs necessary to produce DVDs unless they were sure that there was going to be a substantial number of DVD players. Yet consumers were understandably reluctant at first to purchase a DVD player without any assurance that there would be a large number of films translated to DVDs. Thus, it was entirely possible that the DVD market might have failed completely

---

3   See Schmalensee (2000) for a clear statement of the view that competition in network, or (what he calls) "winner take most" markets, is likely to be extremely fierce and easily mistaken for predatory conduct when practiced by a dominant incumbent.

# Reality Checkpoint

## Testing . . . 1, 2, 3, Testing . . .

The idea of networks and common standards ought to be familiar to students around the world. This is because applications to colleges and universities, graduate schools, business schools, and law schools are competitive, and admissions committees need a common and statistically reliable standard by which to compare applicants. Similarly, students are reluctant to pay for and take an exam that few other students take.

Enter the Educational Testing Service (ETS). ETS is by far the largest testing agency in the world. In 1996 alone, it administered over 12 million tests ranging from the SAT college entrance exam to tests for licenses and certification in thirty-four professions. It also administers the test for U.S. citizenship.

The SAT illustrates the positive feedback associated with network externalities. Colleges need statistically reliable screening mechanisms. The more students who take the SAT, the more reliable the test becomes. As the SAT becomes more reliable, more colleges adopt it as a required admissions, with the result that even more students take it, and so on.

Note that there remains the danger of a bad equilibrium. The ETS exams may not do all that they are supposed to do. Many have criticized ETS exams for providing biased results because they ask questions that disadvantage those from cultures and backgrounds other than those of mainstream America. Others have criticized ETS exams as being indicative only of classroom performance and not one's innate aptitude for a particular profession. For example, the law board exams may predict how someone will do in law school but not how good a lawyer he or she will be.

Cheating is another reason that the ETS results may not measure what they claim to measure, and ETS has sometimes come under fire for not taking adequate measures against cheating. In July 1996, a scandal in Louisiana was uncovered in which scores of numerous applicants for certification as a high school administrator had to be invalidated because it was found that the exams and the correct answers had been distributed on a widespread basis prior to the test. In August 1997, federal prosecutors uncovered a nationwide operation in which hundreds of students paid as much as $9,000 for answers to graduate school and English proficiency tests. What makes ETS (which is a nonprofit organization) particularly vulnerable to these charges is that it has recently established ties with for-profit firms that teach and advise students on how to take such tests. Talk about your complementary products!

**Sources:** D. Frantz and J. Nordheimer, "Giant of Exam Business Keeps Quiet on Cheating" and "As Academic Mold Is Broken by Testing Giants, Rivals Rail." *The New York Times,* September 29, 1997, p. A1, and September 30, 1997, p. A1.

because of self-fulfilling expectations. Few or no consumers might have expected any DVD films to be made. In turn, this would not only have depressed the market for DVD players but also made it quite unlikely that firms would translate films to DVD format, thereby confirming the consumers' expectations. On the other hand, an alternative outcome was that each consumer expected others to purchase DVD players and therefore anticipated that firms would find it worthwhile to put films on DVDs. In this case, the expectation would have again been self-fulfilling as enough consumers purchased players that firms were led to produce the volume of movie discs that confirmed this optimistic expectation. As it turns out, this more hopeful outcome did materialize. Today, the DVD market is well established although more homes still have video cassette recorders (VCRs) than have DVD players. The point is simply that this good equilibrium was not guaranteed. An alternative and worse equilibrium was possible.

The DVD example also highlights another aspect of the multiple equilibria problem—namely, the possibility that the particular equilibrium realized may be one in which the market is "locked" into the wrong or inferior technology. From a durability and volume of information viewpoint, DVD technology is undoubtedly a superior and less costly way to provide movie rentals than is VHS technology, based on videocassettes and VCRs. However, because the two systems are substitutes and because VHS was the first system established, the DVD system had to attract customers away from VHS in order to gain a footing. It easily could have been the case that the number of customers so attracted was not large enough for the DVD manufacturers to exploit the available scale economies and avoid losses. To reach that volume, each potential DVD consumer needed not only to be convinced of the superiority of the DVD system but also to be sure that others shard that conviction and were willing to act on it. Again, we now know that this did happen. But had this not happened then, purely by the historical accident that the videocassette system was developed first, consumers would have remained locked into the inferior VHS system.[4]

To put it somewhat differently, network externalities are associated with "path dependence" so that which system eventually claims the market is the result of an arbitrary process, and one that may lock in a bad equilibrium for a considerable period of time. Instead of the VHS versus DVD example just given, consider a closely related one from the earlier days of home video, namely, the VHS versus Betamax versions of video cassette recorders (VCRs). Imagine that 40 percent of the population has a slight preference for VHS machines *if* the price and market share of these machines is identical to the price and market share of Betamax-based products. Similarly, the remaining 60 percent have a slight preference for Betamax. However, these slight preferences can be overcome if one firm has a much larger market share because, again, no one really wants to buy a product if it does not have a large network of users. Finally, we assume that all consumers are not initially aware of the general home video market. Instead, they learn of it over time. Each week a few more consumers randomly find out about home videos and decide to buy a VCR of either a VHS or Betamax type.

On average, we would expect each new wave of new consumers to be comprised of 60 percent of Betamax-preferring consumers and 40 percent of VHS-preferring consumers. However, it is quite possible that, selecting randomly, one could get a batch of new consumers who were comprised of 90 or even 100 percent of those who

---

4 David (1985) has argued that the standardized QWERTY keyboard used initially by typewriters and now by all PC keyboards is an example of path-dependent lock-in to an inferior technology, with the superior one being the Dvorak keyboard. While Liebowitz and Margolis (1990) cast considerable doubt on this argument, the case nevertheless makes clear that such market failure is a real possibility.

prefer VHS. Starting from a point in which each system has equal market penetration, such a random draw could easily tip the market heavily in favor of VHS. Once that happens, then even those with a slight preference for Betamax will, in subsequent rounds, choose to buy a VHS machine because that network is so much larger that many more films are going to be printed for it. Hence, the small random draw favoring VHS may tip the entire market in favor of this technology forever even though, at base, Betamax is the superior technology in that most consumers favor it over VHS when all else is equal.

Similarly, Microsoft's dominance may reflect just plain good luck as much as it does superior technology. A key development in this regard came in 1980 when IBM decided to enter the personal computer market in a major way. IBM awarded the contract for its disc operating system to Microsoft and MS-DOS was born. Many analysts think that Microsoft did not have the best product at that time. Yet having the support of IBM was clearly a major advantage in establishing a network of MS-DOS users. Note that the network effect gives Microsoft a strong defense against Linux or Apple or some other product even if it is a better operating system than Windows. Again, the lock-in effect raises the possibility that the market may adopt the inferior technology.

## 24.3  SYSTEMS COMPETITION AND THE BATTLE OVER INDUSTRY STANDARDS

Competition between systems does not always lead to one survivor. There are five major suppliers of long-distance phone service (AT&T, Verizon, SBC, MCI/World-Com, and Sprint) now active in the U.S. domestic market. There is a slightly larger number of wireless phone providers. When we allow for the co-existence of two or more firms, each operating its own network, a number of additional features enter into the analysis. In such cases, there is the important issue of compatibility. To what extent will the industry adopt a standard product design that enables consumers to "plug in" to any network? If a standard is adopted, what standard will it be? In this section, we address these and related questions using a simple illustrative model described below.

Consider the question of technology adoption. Assume that two firms have to decide on whether to stick with their individual, existing technology or switch to a new one. To be specific, suppose that the firms estimate the payoffs to their choices to be those shown in Table 24-1. The distinction between these two matrices is that in case (a) sticking with the old technology is less profitable jointly than incurring the installation costs of switching to the new technology, while in case (b) both firms switching reduces their joint profits.

The payoff received for either firm depends critically on what choice its rival makes. However, there is also a further complication, namely, the issue of compatibility. Suppose that the old technology and the new technology are incompatible in the sense that they cannot be used together. This means that if each firm makes a different choice, they do not derive any network benefits of the type we have introduced previously. By contrast, if they choose the same technologies—whether old or new—then they do enjoy network externalities. Such positive network externalities mean that the payoff to each firm if they choose the same technology is greater than if they

## EXCESS INERTIA AND EXCESS MOMENTUM WITH NETWORK EXTERNALITIES (ALL PAYOFFS IN MILLIONS OF DOLLARS)

TABLE
24-1

|  |  | Firm 1 | |
|---|---|---|---|
|  |  | Old Technology | New Technology |
| Firm 2 | Old Technology | 5, 4 | 3, 2 |
|  | New Technology | 3, 3 | 6, 7 |

*(a) The New Technology Is Pareto Superior to the Old*

A decision to stay with the old technology exhibits excess inertia.

|  |  | Firm 1 | |
|---|---|---|---|
|  |  | Old Technology | New Technology |
| Firm 2 | Old Technology | 6, 7 | 3, 2 |
|  | New Technology | 3, 3 | 5, 4 |

*(b) The Old Technology Is Pareto Superior to the New*

A decision to change to the new technology exhibits excess momentum.

choose different technologies. This is illustrated in the payoff matrices by the fact that the payoff to either firm when both firms choose the same technology, no matter which, is greater than the payoff to either firm when they choose different (incompatible) technologies.

Regardless of whether both would do best by switching to the new technology [Table 24-1(a)], or both would do best by avoiding the cost of installing the new equipment and sticking with the existing technology [Table 24-1(b)], it can be seen that there are two Nash equilibria: one in which the two firms stay with the old technology, and the other in which they both switch to the new technology. There is no simple way to choose between these two equilibrium outcomes. If the payoffs are as in Table 24-1(a) and so both switching is efficient, each firm may nevertheless choose not to switch from fear of moving alone into an incompatible technology. Farrell and Saloner (1985) refer to this as a case of excess inertia. Alternatively, with the payoffs of Table 24-1(b), we might find excess momentum with both firms making a costly switch to the new technology out of fear of being stranded alone with the old technology.

There are, of course, ways by which the firms can attempt to avoid either of these unsatisfactory outcomes. For example, the firms might be able to communicate their proposed technology choices—and they have the incentive to do so honestly since lying actually hurts both firms. Coordination may also be more likely if we extend this game to extend over many periods, since then a firm has the potential to correct a "wrong" choice, that is, one different from the choice of its rival. Nevertheless, even in these more general settings, Farrell and Saloner show that firms may in particular delay technology switching longer than they should. That is, rather than move promptly to introduce the technology soon, they may wait unduly long until a sufficiently large "bandwagon" has built up. Thus, some theater owners and film producers in the 1920s did not invest in the equipment to show or to make "talking pictures" until they were certain that the new phenomenon would catch on. As a result, the advent of "talkies" may have been suboptimally delayed.

Compatibility is clearly an important factor in technological choice. However, there is a drawback to compatibility. When each firm adopts the same technical standard, their products become very close substitutes so price competition is likely to be intense. Hence, while product differentiation by means of different technologies incurs the cost of foregoing possible network effects it has the benefit of softening price competition. Firms therefore have to make a judgment in this regard. Choosing the same technology will lead the firms into direct, intratechnology competition of the type discussed throughout the earlier chapters of this book—that is, competition on price, quality, and service. By contrast, the choice of different technologies will lead the firms into intertechnology competition.

Of course, if a firm can establish its technology as the industry standard, the rewards from this kind of competition are likely to be very large indeed. When firms choose to compete in different technologies each is likely to hope that its technology will someday win the market and become the industry standard. Think of Sony's PlayStation 2 product and rival Nintendo GameCube. These are two firms that apparently regard the advantages of compatibility to be more than offset by the disadvantages that compatibility would bring in terms of intensified price competition. As a result, the two systems are totally incompatible. Yet each hopes to win the market and to establish its technology as the standard for which all applications, that is, games, are written.

There is no a priori means of determining whether rewards will be greater under intratechnology competition "within the market" or intertechnology competition "for the market." There are, however, three main possibilities that we should consider. We illustrate these with three simple games: (1) Tweedledum and Tweedledee, (2) The Battle of the Sexes, and (3) Pesky Little Brother.[5]

### Tweedledum and Tweedledee

Assume that the payoffs for this game of technology choice are given in Table 24-2. There are two Nash equilibria in each of which the firms prefer to adopt incompatible technologies. This implies that the firms believe that network externalities are not particularly strong and that any gains from adopting a common technology will be more than offset by the fact that this will lead to particularly fierce intratechnology price competition. They also believe that a battle to establish the industry standard will not significantly delay its adoption by potential consumers and so offers large rewards.

---

5   This analysis is developed in depth in Besen and Farrell (1994). The language that follows is borrowed directly from their discussion.

TABLE
24-2

**TWEEDLEDUM AND TWEEDLEDEE**

|  |  | Firm 1 | |
|---|---|---|---|
|  |  | **Technology 1** | **Technology 2** |
| **Firm 2** | **Technology 1** | 3, 3 | 6, 7 |
|  | **Technology 2** | 8, 5 | 2, 2 |

The firms prefer to choose incompatible rather than compatible technologies and will become involved in a standards war. (All payoffs are in millions of dollars.)

With these payoffs, the firms will enter into a battle to have their choice of technology established as the standard. Firm 2 will fight to establish technology 2 and firm 1 to establish technology 1. Besen and Farrell (1994) suggest that there are four forms that this battle can take:

1. *Build on an Early Lead.* If there are any network externalities at all associated with a particular technology of the type we have discussed, there is considerable benefit to a firm that succeeds in establishing a large installed base of current users. These users will be reluctant to switch to a different technology. At the same time, the existence of such a large installed base makes the technology attractive to new users. (Just think of the choice that a new computer user has to make between buying an IBM compatible running the Windows operating system against a similar machine running OS/2 or an Apple computer with the Apple operating system.) Under this scenario, there will be intense price competition in the early stages of new technologies as each firm attempts to capture as many customers as possible. Firms will also reveal and perhaps exaggerate their sales figures in order to persuade potential buyers that a large installed base already exists.

2. *Attract Suppliers of Complements.* As we have pointed out many times, the attractiveness of a product is affected by the number of complementary products that are also available. A computer is of little use except to the most advanced users unless there is a wide range of computer software that will run on it. A Nintendo game machine becomes more attractive as Nintendo or other firms expand the number of games it can play. There is little point in owning a CD player unless recording companies offer a wide range of recordings in CD format.

   Owners of a primary technology such as IBM or Microsoft will likely encourage software developers to produce a wide range of programs that will run on their platform. Indeed, one reason that Apple lost its early lead may well have been its reluctance to have its operating system installed in clones. This restriction limited the market penetration of Apple's system and consequently reduced the incentives of software developers to produce Apple-compatible software.

3. *Product Preannouncement.* The owner of a particular technology can try to slow the growth of a rival network by regularly "preannouncing" new products in

advance of their actual introduction. This strategy is often referred to as *vapor-ware* because, in fact, the new product may not exist or be anywhere near introduction. For example, Microsoft first promised Windows 2000 in late 1997, but the operating system only arrived three years later. Similarly, when Intel was faced with increasing pressure from new rival AMD in 1999, it announced the development of a new 64-bit chip, Itanium, to be release in early 2000. The actual release was May 2001. Such product preannouncements may, of course, have been made in good faith and the subsequent delays may have been simply due to unforeseen difficulties. However, there is also the possibility that the announcements were made strategically with either the goal of attracting customers who might otherwise have purchased a rival product or of simply deterring the rival from developing that new product. Such a strategy is, of course, not without risk because it may cause the firm's current customers to delay purchasing its existing product. Still, as Haan (2003) shows, the vaporware strategy of promising new products that do not really exist may well be both an effective and commonly used method of entry deterrence.

**4.** *Price Commitments.* A contractual commitment to achieve and maintain low prices over the long term is a fourth method by which new consumers can be persuaded to adopt a particular technology. This will be especially beneficial if the firm offering the commitment knows that there are significant economies of scale or learning economies in the manufacture of the primary product. In such circumstances, building a large installed base early will generate cost reductions that will allow the firm to deliver on its low price while maintaining its profitability.

In short, when rival firms compete to establish an industry standard, a variety of strategies and outcomes emerge. Here again we find that such markets are "tippy" with multiple equilibria and in which the coexistence of incompatible products may be unstable. The tide of battle can turn rapidly and quite suddenly a dynamic can develop that leads to a single winning standard dominating the market. Moreover, there is no guarantee that the winner will offer the best technology.

### The Battle of the Sexes[6]

Rather than fight to have their own technology adopted as the industry standard, firms may agree on the adoption of a common technology. The payoff matrix in this case is as in Table 24-3. The simplest case is that illustrated in Table 24-3(a). Here, both firms are agreed that they should adopt technology 1. Accordingly, they should be able to establish this technology as a common standard by simple communication between them.

In the case of Table 24-3(b), however, there is no such agreement. The firms would prefer a common standard but they are not agreed on which of the two technologies the standard should be. Firm 1 will fight to establish technology 1 as the standard, and firm 2 will fight to establish technology 2. This is another instance in which commitment plays a crucial role. Firm 1, for example, may be able to persuade firm 2 to accept technology 1 as the standard by irrevocably committing itself to this technology. It could, for example, build an installed base rooted in technology 1. Al-

---

6   This title comes from a well-known game in which two individuals, perhaps man and wife, in choosing their entertainment for the night, agree that they would rather be together than apart, but put very different valuations on the entertainment they might share. These could be, for example, going to a ball game or to an opera.

## THE BATTLE OF THE SEXES

TABLE
24-3

|  |  | Firm 1 | |
|---|---|---|---|
|  |  | Technology 1 | Technology 2 |
| Firm 2 | Technology 1 | 10, 10 | 5, 4 |
|  | Technology 2 | 6, 5 | 8, 8 |

*(a) Agreement on Compatible Standard and Choice of Standard*

|  |  | Firm 1 | |
|---|---|---|---|
|  |  | Technology 1 | Technology 2 |
| Firm 2 | Technology 1 | 8, 12 | 5, 4 |
|  | Technology 2 | 6, 5 | 10, 7 |

*(b) Agreement to Be Compatible but Disagreement on Standard*

Firms agree that it is preferable to be compatible. In case (a) there is also agreement on the standard, but in case (b) the firms will battle over the choice of standard. (All payoffs are in millions of dollars.)

ternatively, it could invest in production capacity to build more units embodying this technology, or establish a large R&D program devoted to improving this technology. The common intent here is to broadcast the clear message that firm 1 will never give in on its demand that technology 1 be the standard because to do so would cost firm 1 too much to give in.

Other possible commitments take the form of concessions rather than threats. Thus, firm 1 could offer to license technology 1 to firm 2 for a low fee in return for firm 2 agreeing that technology 1 will be the standard. Alternatively, firm 1 can promise to develop the technology jointly, or it can suggest that the two firms develop a hybrid technology that combines the best features of each.

### Pesky Little Brother

In the "Tweedledum and Tweedledee" case, the two firms pursued intertechnology competition rather than adopt a common technology and confront each other in the market with technologically undifferentiated products. In the "Battle of the Sexes," each firm preferred competition between technically identical products, but the question of which technology was the appropriate standard remained an issue. What these two cases have in common is that there is some degree of consensus, if only on the terms on which competition between the firms will occur. If, however, there are asymmetries between the firms, it may be impossible for them to reach even this limited kind of consensus.

Assume, for example, that one of the firms, firm 2, has established a dominant position with a large installed base and a powerful reputation. It will prefer incompatibility with a small rival in order to hold its customers. The smaller rival, however, firm 1, will prefer compatibility in order to derive benefits from the network that the larger firm has established. As Besen and Farrell indicate, "The firms' problem is like the game between a big brother who wants to be left alone and a pesky little brother who wants to be with his big brother."

The payoff matrix now looks something like Table 24-4. There is no Nash equilibrium (in pure strategies) to this game if the firms make simultaneous choices—the two firms' strategic choices are inconsistent.[7] Resolution of the game then comes down again to a question of timing and commitment.

**TABLE 24-4**

### THE PESKY LITTLE BROTHER

|  |  | Firm 1 | |
|---|---|---|---|
|  |  | Technology 1 | Technology 2 |
| **Firm 2** | **Technology 1** | 12, 4 | 16, 2 |
|  | **Technology 2** | 15, 2 | 10, 5 |

There is no Nash equilibrium in simultaneous play. Firm 2, the dominant firm (or big brother), prefers that the technologies be incompatible, and firm 1 (the little brother) prefers that they be compatible. (All payoffs are in millions of dollars.)

Suppose that the dominant firm must commit to its technology choice first. This is perhaps the most plausible assumption, given that we have motivated the game by describing firm 2 as a preexisting firm with a large installed base. In this case, the smaller firm 1 may actually enjoy a second-mover advantage. If firm 2 is committed to its existing technology either because it is costly to change or because such change would lose firm 2 the guaranteed patronage it now enjoys from its customers, it may be unable to prevent firm 1 from following. In this case, firm 1's clear choice will be to establish a compatible system, precisely the outcome firm 2 had hoped to avoid.

Two tactics might be available to firm 2 that would prevent firm 1 from imitating its lead and offer firm 2 relief from its "pesky little brother." These are (a) aggressive protection of its property rights and (b) changing its technology frequently. The first tactic relates to the use of patents. If the technology the dominant firm has built up is protected by patents, then imitation may be preventable through strict enforcement of the protection such patents give and by building up a stock of sleeping patents that make it difficult for a smaller firm to invent around the current technology.

---

7   With a game of this type with a finite number of strategies, there is always a Nash equilibrium in mixed strategies in which the firms randomize their choice of technologies, but we shall not consider this equilibrium.

☑ **Reality Checkpoint**

### Circuit City's Fallen Standard

An example of a competitive battle over industry standards is the case of Circuit City Stores, Inc., with its pay-per-view digital videodisk venture. Circuit City created special video disks—called DIVXs—that required a special DVD player. The DIVX player cost about $300 more than a regular DVD player. However, the DIVX disks were programmed so that one could play them for $4 for an initial 48-hour period. Subsequent time periods cost an additional amount ranging from $1.50 to $4 until a total of about $25 was reached. At this point, the DIVX disk could be played for an unlimited amount of time. At that time, a standard DVD disk cost $15 to $30 and offers unlimited views. Circuit City had hoped to exploit what it felt was a strong consumer preference for watching the same film only one or two times. It felt that this preference was strong enough that consumers would pay more for the DIVX machine in return for lower disk prices. As it turned out, it lost this battle. In June 1999, it announced that it was ending the DIVX project. Whether this reflects a true superiority of the conventional DVD technology or only excess inertia is difficult to say.

**Source:** E. Raymond, "Circuit City Pulls the Plug On DIVX Videodisk Venture." *The Wall Street Journal*, June 17, 1999, p. C1.

Alternatively, firm 2 can try to hamper firm 1's imitation efforts by changing its technology frequently. This, of course, can be expensive and runs the risk of alienating users of the existing installed base unless they can be protected by, for example, being given favorable access to the new generation of products. The advantage to this approach is that the target at which the smaller rival is aiming is constantly shifting in ways that are difficult for the small firm to predict. If you really want to avoid your pesky little brother, don't tell him where you are going!

In short, competition over technology has a variety of implications. Often, there may be large social gains from all firms adopting a common technical approach. But the incentive for firms to differentiate their products, as well as the rivalry over which technology should become the industry standard, can frequently thwart the realization of such gains. While the gains from price competition are generally clear, the network externality effects make the gains from technology competition more ambiguous.

## 24.4 NETWORK GOODS AND PUBLIC POLICY

Our analysis of network services suggests many ways in which the market mechanism may fail to produce an efficient outcome. In some cases, a socially desirable service may fail to be provided. In other cases, multiple possible outcomes raise the possibility that the market may choose the wrong equilibrium and lock into an inferior technology. Competition may not be feasible as a workable market structure. Moreover, even where feasible, competition may not be a remedy for these failures. To the contrary, competition may intensify the rush to a particular standard or technology, which later is realized to be inferior, or to reject compatibility even when it might actually be desirable. When the market will support only one system or network, competition is likely to be intense and border on predatory conduct. An important remaining issue is the role of public policy in this area.

It is important to understand that in many respects, the problems raised by network effects are not new. The presence of dramatic scale economies and externalities has long been recognized as potential sources of market failure. Large-scale economies make marginal cost pricing unlikely because such large-scale economies means that marginal cost is below average cost over a wide range of production. Further, even when it is possible to operate at a sufficiently large size that all the scale economies are exploited, doing so will likely imply that there is room for only a few firms. Similarly, externalities always imply a divergence between private and social benefit (or cost), with the result that market outcomes based on the maximizing choices of individuals and firms are not likely to be optimal.

Saying that the problems raised by network effects are not new, however, is not the same thing as saying that they are easy. Three problems are particularly difficult in the case of network goods. The first of these is the problem of detecting or proving anticompetitive behavior. The second is the difficulty of devising an appropriate remedy once anticompetitive actions have been identified. The third is determining the proper role that the government should play in coordinating the technology choices of different firms with a view towards achieving standardization.

Consider the problem of determining anticompetitive tactics. The presence of network externalities requires that the developer of a new product such as a facsimile machine sell to a large number of consumers in order to establish any market at all. In turn, this may well mean pricing below cost, at least initially. This may result in a competitor being driven out of the business. When the winning firm later raises its price so as to earn a return on its investment, the historical record of selling below cost, eliminating a rival, and then raising price looks a lot like a case of predatory pricing. Indeed, such a record is essentially the evidence called for by Baumol (1979) to determine predation. (See Chapter 11.) Yet such a finding may simply reflect the need to price low so as to penetrate the market and the fact that the market can only support one supplier.[8]

Similarly, the developer of a platform such as Windows or PlayStation or a DVD player requires that there be a large number of applications (programs, games, or films) available at a low cost in order to gain wide acceptance of the overall system. One way to achieve this aim is to produce and market such complementary goods itself. Yet to the extent that one needs to have a Sony PlayStation machine to play a PlayStation cartridge, this arrangement resembles possibly illegal tying or an attempt at foreclosure. To take another and more pertinent example, Microsoft's Windows almost certainly gains from the availability of a compatible, low-cost Web browser. Yet to the extent that Microsoft bundles its own browser with Windows—especially at a zero price—the outcome cannot fail to raise concerns of tying with a view to driving Netscape out of the browser business.[9]

---

8   See Schmalensee (1982) on the analysis of such penetration pricing by new firms.
9   This point is made forcibly by Schmalensee (2000). See Fisher (2000) for an opposing point of view. Note that Schmalensee's argument that in some industries, for example, Web browsers, only one firm can survive is really a statement that the market is a natural monopoly of the type described in Chapter 2. The only difference here is that the scale economy lies on the demand side via the network externality.

With regard to technology adoption and product improvement, the case of Microsoft is again relevant. Sun Microsystems' Java programming language offered the possibility of greatly enhancing the functionality of Windows. However, this required that Windows be made compatible with Java. Microsoft was generally reluctant to do this at least in part because there was a widespread view that Java could provide the basis for an alternative applications platform if it ever became widely accepted. Making it compatible with Windows would have this effect. So while providing that compatibility might greatly improve the technology available for PC users, it might also provide an opportunity for entry to a new rival. Does Microsoft's reluctance in this case reflect an illegal effort to deter entry?[10]

As difficult as it is to identify anticompetitive behavior in network or systems markets, devising an appropriate remedy when such actions are discovered is perhaps even more problematic. The case of Microsoft and Sun Microsystems is instructive in this connection. Is the appropriate policy to force Microsoft to make Windows compatible with Java? Adoption of such a policy would place the government in the awkward position of pushing a particular technology. What if Java really does not offer any real improvement on the Windows product? Indeed, what if there is an alternative programming language that would offer much greater enhancement? That alternative may never break through if antitrust officials require that Windows work with Java. In other words, antitrust policy may also result in an inferior technology lock-in.[11]

This raises the general question as to the proper role for the government in coordinating the technology choices of different firms with a view towards achieving standardization. Consider the market for mobile telephone service. As a result of legislation by the European Parliament, all mobile phones in Europe adhere to the same technical standard. Consequently, a British resident traveling on the continent can use his or her mobile phone to make calls in Italy just as easily as she can at home. This is much less feasible for U.S. residents, in part because there was no centralized authority coordinating the digital standard of American mobile phone companies. Instead, the mobile phone services in the United States initially adopted four different standards and inter-service communication was impossible. On the other hand, the presence of these different standards has led to increased competition and technical development. As mobile phone companies in the United States have expanded their coverage over wider areas, the regional reach of an American consumer has become comparable to that of a European one with the American consumer enjoying the added benefit of systems competition and technical advance.

## SUMMARY

In this chapter, we have focused on the product markets exhibiting important "network externalities." In such markets, the value of the good or service to any one consumer increases as the total number of consumers using the product increases. Services with important network effects, such as telecommunications and home electronics, play an increasingly large role in modern economies.

Markets with strong network effects present special problems. Competition to establish a network service can be unusually fierce and difficult to distinguish from

---

10 Microsoft and Sun eventually did reach an agreement of sorts, but Sun was never happy with it and later the agreement was abandoned.

11 See Arthur (1989) and also Eisenach and Lenard (1999).

predation. Often, such competition will result in only one firm surviving so that the market's ultimate structure is one of monopoly. There is also a nontrivial risk that the service will be underdeveloped or not developed at all. Similarly, the course of technical development exhibits a path dependency in which the market may eventually lock into an inferior technology.

There are no easy solutions to the problems raised by network goods. On the one hand, the possibilities for anticompetitive outcomes seem sufficiently clear that such markets necessarily invite examination by the antitrust authorities. Yet it must also be acknowledged that it is not easy either to identify such actions clearly or to devise workable remedies to the market failures to which network services are prone. Such tensions have dominated the debate over policies regarding the telecommunications industry and other "new economy" markets. They will no doubt continue to dominate that debate for some time.

# PROBLEMS

1. Two banks compete for the checking and savings deposit business of a small town. Each bank has its own ATM network that works only with its own bankcards, but bank 1 has three times as many ATM machines as bank 2. Depositors value a bank's services as an increasing function of the number of machines on the network. Bank 2 approaches bank 1 and suggests that they merge their ATM networks so that depositors of either bank can use either bank's machines.

   a. Is this merger in the interest of deposit consumers in general?

   b. Do you think that bank 1 will agree with bank 2's proposal?

2. Assume that consumers contemplating buying a network service have reservation prices uniformly distributed on the interval $(0, 50)$, measured in dollars. Demand by a consumer with reservation price $w_i$ for this service is

$$q_i^D = \begin{cases} 0 \text{ if } fw_i < p \\ 1 \text{ if } fw_i \geq p \end{cases}.$$

   a. Calculate the demand function for this service.

   b. What is the critical mass if price is set at \$5?

   c. What is the profit-maximizing price for the service?

3. Many social customs exhibit network effects. To this end, consider a party given by a group of individuals at a small university. The group is called the Outcasts and has 20 members. It holds a big party on campus each year. These parties are good, but are especially good the more people there are in attendance. As a result, the number of people who actually come to the Outcasts party depends on how many people are expected to attend. The more people that are expected to attend, the more fun it will be for each attendee and, hence, the more people who actually will come. These effects are captured by the equation $A = 20 + 0.95A^e$. Here, $A$ is the number of people actually attending the party. This is equal to the 20 Outcasts members plus 0.95 times the number of partygoers $A^e$ that are expected to go.

   a. If potential party attendees are sophisticated and understand the equation describing actual party attendance, how many people are likely to attend the Outcasts party?

**b.** Suppose that each party attendee costs the Outcasts $2 in refreshments so that the Outcasts need to charge a fee $p$ for attending the party. Suppose as well that when going to the party requires paying a fee, the equation for attendance is $A = 20 + 0.95A^e - p$. What value of $p$ should the Outcasts set if they want to maximize their profit from the party? How many people will come to the party at that price?

**4.** Two firms are competing in their choice of technologies. The payoff matrix for the game between them is given by

|  |  | Firm 1 | |
|---|---|---|---|
|  |  | Technology 1 | Technology 2 |
| Firm 2 | Technology 1 | a, b | c, d |
|  | Technology 2 | e, f | g, h |

**a.** Identify constraints on the payoffs a–h such that the firms' choices reflect network externalities.

**b.** Assume that the constraints in (a) are satisfied. Identify further constraints that must be satisfied for the game between the two firms to be of the form

(1) Tweedledum and Tweedledee,

(2) The Battle of the Sexes,

(3) The Pesky Little Brother.

# REFERENCES

Arthur, W. Brian, 1989. "Competing Technologies, Increasing Returns, and Lock-in by Historical Events." *The Economic Journal* 99 (March): 116–31.

Baumol, W. 1979. "Quasi-Permanence of Price Reductions: A Policy for Prevention of Predatory Pricing." *Yale Law Journal* 89: 1–26.

Besen, S. M., and J. Farrell. 1994. "Choosing How to Compete: Strategies and Tactics in Standardization." *Journal of Economic Perspectives* 8 (Spring): 117–31.

David, P. A. 1985. "Clio and the Economics of QWERTY." *American Economic Review, Papers and Proceedings* (May): 332–37.

Economides, N. 1996. "The Economics of Networks." *International Journal of Industrial Organization* 14 (October): 673–99.

Eisenach, J. A., and T. M. Lenard. 1999. *Competition, Innovation and the Microsoft Monopoly: Antitrust in the Digital Marketplace.* Kluwer Academic Publishers.

Farrell, J., and G. Saloner. 1985. "Standardization, Compatibility and Innovation." *Rand Journal of Economics* 16 (Spring): 70–83.

Fisher, F. 2000. "The *IBM* and *Microsoft* Cases: What's the Difference?" *American Economic Review* 90 (May): 180–83.

Hahn, M. 2003. "Vaporware as a Means of Entry Deterrence." *Journal of Industrial Economics* 51(September): 345–58.

Liebowitz, S., and S. Margolis. 1990. "The Fable of the Keys." *Journal of Law and Economics* 33 (April): 1–26.

Rohlfs, J. 1974. "A Theory of Interdependent Demand for a Communications Service." *Bell Journal of Economics* 5 (Spring): 16–37.

Schmalensee, R. 2000. "Antitrust Issues in Schumpeterian Industries." *American Economic Review, Papers and Proceedings* 90(May): 192–96.

———. 1982. "Product Differentiation Advantages of Pioneering Brands." *American Economic Review* 72 (June): 349–65.

# Auctions and Auction Markets    **Chapter** 25

An interesting feature of the telecommunications revolution and the growth of e-commerce over the past fifteen years has been the explosion of auction markets. Millions of consumers all over the world now participate daily in auctions. In part, this reflects the fact that auctions are an exciting way to buy and sell. At least as important, however, has been the ability of the Internet to reduce significantly the costs of matching particular buyers and sellers. The leader in this development is eBay, which through its operations in the United States and elsewhere auctioned over $10 billion worth of goods among 30 million users who either bid, bought, or sold in 2003.[1]

Auctions, however, started long before the Internet came along. Indeed, they have existed for thousands of years. Herodotus writes of a market for auctioning wives in Babylonia in 500 BC. In A.D. 193, the Praetorian Guard auctioned the entire Roman Empire to Marcus Didius Salvius Julianus for a bid of 25,000 sesterces. Currently, the two most famous auction houses are Sotheby's (U.S.) and Christies (U.K.), each of which date back to the 1700s. These houses specialize in the sale of rare antiques and artwork, goods whose value is difficult to determine because there is a question of taste and opinion and because the value depends on market conditions that are difficult to forecast.

The sale of a good whose value is difficult to assess is exactly the kind of transaction that suits an auction because one needs a sizable number of interested buyers (or sellers) in order to get bids that reflect the spectrum of opinions as to the item's true value. Until recently, it has been feasible to incur the relatively high cost of bringing together such a critical mass of interested buyers only for auctions focused on rather specialized markets, such as art, antique furniture, and race horses. Yet as just noted, recent innovations in information technology and e-commerce have significantly lowered the cost of matching interested buyers and sellers. As a result, auctions are among the most popular sites and the fastest-growing business model on the Internet. Nor is the Internet the only place of increasing auction use. Many markets that have traditionally been regulated such as electricity and telecommunications now use auctions for trading.

Auctions bring together people with different values and different information. Whether one considers the potential buyers who go online to eBay or those who go to country auctions, the fact is that the different bidders at any auction will typically have different valuations for the goods being sold at that site. This difference may simply reflect different preferences. For example, a decorator who prefers a colonial style will value more highly a colonial-style rocking chair than an Art Deco chair. The reverse is true for the Art Deco decorator. When each participant in an auction has a different or private value for the good being auctioned we say that the auction is a private value auction. Most often individual buyers' private values for the good will be known only to themselves.

Differences in information regarding the value of the good being auctioned, rather than differences in preferences, are another source of variation among auction

---

1   See eBay's Annual Report and the *Silicon Valley Business Journal*, various issues.

participants. A common value auction is one in which the good being auctioned has one true value, but this value is not known to potential buyers. Moreover, the information that each potential buyer has for estimating the true value differs across the population of such buyers. A good example of a common value auction is the auction of rights to explore and drill for oil. In this case the bidders are oil companies who have performed tests on the oil tract and have made some estimate of the amount of oil present and then worked out a valuation for the rights to the oil tract. However, because the companies have performed the tests in different places they are likely to have different estimates and different valuations of how much the rights are worth. Yet there is just one true amount of oil present and thus only one true value of the rights to explore and drill for oil on the tract. The weekly bidding on the financial markets for U.S. Treasury securities offers another example of a common value auction.

In this chapter we will mostly consider single-unit auctions, auctions in which a single unit of some good is to be auctioned. However, in many economic markets, such as in electricity or communications, there are multiple units of the good that are being auctioned. These auctions are called multi-unit auctions.

## 25.1  A BRIEF TAXONOMY OF AUCTIONS

Before the advent of the Internet auctions often took place in a crowded room of hushed people. Those who wanted an item would raise their hands in response to the auctioneer's plea "Do I hear $5, do I hear $10 . . . ?" When the auctioneer finally cried "Going, going, gone" the auction ended and the last person to raise their hand won the good at the last price called by the auctioneer. This kind of auction is called an *ascending-bid* or *English* auction. It is probably the arrangement that the word auction first brings to mind for most people. However, the English auction is just one of a number of different auction types and not necessarily the most common. For example, rather than starting low and letting the price of the good rise with each successive bid, the auctioneer could have instead begun the auction with an extremely high price—one that exceeds anyone's reasonable valuation. The auctioneer could then reduce the price and keep on reducing it until someone in the room raises his or her hand. This type of auction in which the first one to bid wins the good is called a *descending-bid* auction. It is, in fact, how flowers have long been sold at auction in Holland and for that reason is often called a *Dutch* auction.

Bidders participating in an ascending bid auction can watch the bidding and have multiple opportunities to place a bid. In a Dutch auction, bidders observe no bids other than the winning one. Once a price is reached at which someone will buy the item, the auction ends. In this respect, the Dutch auction is strategically identical to what is called a *sealed-bid* auction. This is an auction in which the seller or auctioneer solicits a single bid in a sealed envelope from each interested buyer. The envelopes are then opened and the highest bidder wins the auction. The similarity with a Dutch auction is that no bidder can observe any other bids.

Sealed-bid auctions, however, are not all the same. In particular, such auctions are usually divided into one of two types. One of these is referred to as a *first-price* auction while the second is referred to as a *second-price* auction. In a *first-price* auction the highest bidder pays the amount bid whereas in a *second-price* auction the highest bidder pays the amount bid by the *next* highest bidder.

## Practice Problem 25.1

Show that a dominant bidding strategy in an English auction is to continue bidding as long as the price in the auction is less than your true value of the good.

## 25.2 THE REVENUE EQUIVALENCE THEOREM

There is an interesting parallel between the four auction types first recognized by Nobel Laureate William Vickrey in his classic 1961 paper. To see this, let's start by imagining that the chair of the economics department at your university decides to auction a signed copy of the textbook you are currently reading at an English auction. Let's suppose that you would be willing to pay at most $85 to win the book and that, unknown to you, this is the highest valuation of anyone in the class. Suppose further that the class is comprised of 170 students whose individual valuations may be ranked and which run from $0.50 all the way up to your value of $85, increasing by $0.50 with each student. Bidding starts at $0.50 and you and your classmates raise your hands as the chair bids up the price in one-cent increments. With this procedure, it is inevitable that the price will eventually rise to the point at which only you and one other bidder remain, namely, at the price of $84.50. At the next round, however, when the chair increases the bid to $84.51 your rival will drop out. You will then be the sole student with a hand raised. So you win the auction at a price of $84.51.

Let's now consider what the outcome would have been if instead your chair had auctioned off the textbook using a second-price sealed-bid auction. For the moment, let's assume that in this auction all the bidders write their true willingness to pay for the signed text on a piece of paper and put it in a sealed envelope. (We will show later that such a bidding strategy is in fact a dominant strategy in a second-price sealed-bid auction.) With each student bidding their true reservation price, your bid will be $85 and the next highest bid will be $84.50. You will again be the winner. However, because it is a second-price auction, you will not pay $85, but only $84.50. Note that this is very close to the $84.51 that you paid in the ascending-bid auction. In short, if bidding one's true valuation is an optimal strategy, then the English auction and the second-price sealed-bid auction yield essentially identical outcomes.

Now let's investigate whether bidding based on one's true valuation is indeed optimal. To understand why it is, note that in a second-price sealed-bid auction, the bid you submit only determines whether you win the auction. It does not affect the price that you will actually pay if you win. That price is determined by the value of the second highest bidder. Therefore, bidding less than your true value of the good will only lower your chance of winning a second-price sealed-bid auction. It does not change the price that you pay if you do win. There is then no advantage to bidding less than your true value. What about bidding more? Increasing your bid above your true willingness to pay will increase the probability that you win only in the case when there is another bidder whose valuation is higher than yours. Otherwise increasing your bid has no effect. Yet if you win in these circumstances you will end up paying the other bidder's valuation—one that is higher than your own. In other words, you will end up paying more for the good than it is worth to you. Therefore, bidding honestly is a dominant strategy in a second-price sealed-bid auction. As we have just seen, however, when everyone does this the outcome is equivalent to what occurs in an English auction.

Thus Vickrey (1961) established that if bidders pursue optimal strategies, then an English auction and a second-price sealed-bid auction yield the same outcome. This is important. For sellers who want to maximize their revenue from the auction, this fact implies that the choice between these two auction types is irrelevant. The seller will receive the same revenue either way. However, in designing an auction a seller may still wish to consider the other two remaining types, the Dutch auction and the first-price sealed-bid auction. What will happen in these two cases and how does this compare with the outcome of the English auction process? Here again, Vickrey provides the key insight.

We have already noted that the Dutch and first-price sealed-bid auctions are strategically identical. This is because they share two crucial features. One is that in each case, a bidder has no additional information about the other bidders' valuations before making a bid. Instead, the bidder must simply bid based on one's own valuation. The second feature common to these two auction types is that what one bids affects *both* one's chance of winning *and* what one pays. In both the Dutch auction and the first-price sealed-bid auction the winner pays the price that was bid to win the auction. This means that in each setting, bidders need to think strategically about what to bid.

Consider first a bidder's optimal strategy in a first-price sealed-bid auction. Suppose that there are $N$ bidders participating in the auction. Each bidder knows, of course, their own private valuation of the good being auctioned. Let us assume as well that each bidder knows the general distribution from which the other bidders' true valuations are drawn. With these assumptions, it's easy to see that no bidder has an incentive to submit a bid above their true value. If a bidder did so and then won the auction that bidder would end up paying a price greater than their true value, which means they actually lose. We can also see that the bidder who has the highest valuation of the good should, if bidding optimally, win the auction. If the highest valuation bidder did not win because the submitted bid lost to, say, the second highest bidder, then the bidder could always do better by increasing the bid slightly above the value of the bid that won and below their own.

These points suggest a possible winning strategy for any bidder. This is that you bid at least the valuation of the bidder with the next highest valuation. This ensures that you will never lose to someone with a lower valuation of the good. The only difficulty is that, by assumption, no bidder knows the next highest valuation. Each only knows one's own maximum willingness to pay. So how should a bidder proceed?

Clearly, a bidder needs to make an estimate of the next highest willingness to pay relative to his or her own. Let's consider how to do this. Suppose that the bidder knows that all of the $N$ valuations were drawn from a uniform distribution and denote the valuation by $v$. Because the bidder is particularly interested in the next highest valuation compared with his or her own the bidder will focus on the distribution of valuations between 0 and $v$. This means that the bidder acts as though each of the $N$ bidders has drawn a valuation from a uniform distribution over the interval $[0, v]$. The question then becomes what is the best guess of the next highest valuation among these remaining $N - 1$ bids? That is, what is the expected value of the second highest valuation given that the bidder's is the highest of $N$ bids? To work this out, the bidder may as well assume that the values drawn by the other bidders are equally spaced on the interval. This assumption means basically that if we were to draw many samples of $N-1$ values from the uniform distribution over $[0, v]$, then the average value of the highest draw in these samples would be $\dfrac{N-1}{N} v$, while the average value of the second highest would be $\dfrac{N-2}{N} v$, and the average value of the third highest would be $\dfrac{N-3}{N} v$, and so on. The lowest value on average would be $\dfrac{1}{N} v$.

For example, suppose that our bidder's valuation $v$ is equal to $85 and that there are 170 bidders in total participating in the auction. She can then proceed by assuming that the other bids and hers are equally spaced on the interval $[0, 85]$. The highest valuation in this interval then would be $\dfrac{169}{170} \$85 = \$84.50$, the next highest $\dfrac{168}{170} \$85 = \$84$, the next to that $\dfrac{167}{170} \$85 = \$83.50$, and so on. The bidder's optimal strategy in the first-price sealed-bid auction therefore is to write down a bid of $84.50. If she writes down more than this, she will pay more on average than is necessary. If she writes down less than this, she will on average lose the auction to someone who values the good less than she does.

The intuition of the foregoing argument is quite general. The bidder's objective is to acquire the auctioned good at the lowest possible price so long as that price does not exceed the bidder's own valuation of the object. For this reason, the bidder should condition her strategy on the assumption that her valuation is the highest because, if it is not, she will not wish to pay the price necessary to win. In turn, acting on the assumption that her valuation is the highest leads the bidder to bid the amount $\dfrac{N-1}{N} v$, which is the expected value of the second highest bidder. Recall, however, that the Dutch auction shares all the critical features of a first-price sealed-bid auction and so is strategically equivalent to that case. Such strategic equivalence implies that the optimal strategy must be the same in each case. Hence, the optimal strategy in a Dutch auction is for the bidder to raise her hand as soon as the price falls to $\dfrac{N-1}{N} v$.

In short, the first-price sealed-bid and the Dutch auctions both yield the same outcome. Note also that this in fact yields the same winning bid as that which results in the English and second-price sealed-bid auctions.

## Practice Problem 25.2

You are bidding for an original John Lennon hat in a sealed-bid first-price auction. You are one of eight bidders in this auction and the most you are willing to pay for this hat is $200. Show that your optimal strategy is to submit a bid of $175.

In short, we have uncovered a very striking result. Regardless of whether the auction is English or Dutch, or a first-price or second-price sealed-bid, the outcome is the same. The winning bid in all four cases is identical. In our example, it is consistently $84.50. This remarkable result is quite general and has been codified as auction theory's most well-known theorem, the Revenue Equivalence Theorem.[2] Informally, the Revenue Equivalence Theorem simply states that the expected revenue from an auction is the same regardless of which of the four basic types of auctions are used. A formal statement of Revenue Equivalence is as follows:

> **Revenue Equivalence Theorem (Private Values):** Assume $N$ risk-neutral bidders, each of which has a privately known valuation $v$ of a good to be sold at auction with $v$ drawn from a continuous distribution $F(v)$ that is strictly increasing over the range $[\underline{v}, \overline{v}]$. Then any auction in which the object always goes to the buyer with the highest value of $v$, and in which any bidder with a value of $\underline{v}$ enjoys an expected surplus of zero, results in exactly the same expected payment for each bidder $v$ and yields exactly the same revenue to the seller.

The Revenue Equivalence Theorem is a powerful result, in part because it implies that auction design is not really an issue. There are, however, a number of conditions necessary for the Revenue Equivalence Theorem to hold. For example, it must be the case that the auctioneer is understood by all bidders to report honestly the true value of the second highest bid in a second-price sealed-bid auction (often called a Vickrey auction in honor of his pioneering work). The problem is that the actual bids tendered are known only to the auctioneer. Consequently, the auctioneer could pretend that a bid just under the maximum winning bid was received and declare the fictitious bid to be the second highest price to be paid by the winner as a means of increasing the seller's revenue. Thus, if six bids of $40, $60, $80, $100, $120, and $140 are submitted, the auctioneer could report that the second highest bid was actually $139. The bidder offering $140 will still win but pay $19 above what should have been paid. If this is a real possibility, then bidders in a Vickrey auction will reduce their bids in order to avoid such "rip-offs."

However, Lucking-Reily (2000) demonstrates that there may be ways to overcome the fear of auctioneer cheating in a Vickrey auction. Proxy bidding, the popular method of bidding on eBay, is something of a mixture of a Vickrey and an English auction. An online bidder submits both an initial bid for the object as well as a maximum reservation bid. Then eBay raises the bid incrementally on behalf of the bidder up to the stated maximum value—a value that is kept secret from other eBay users. For example, suppose that you submit an initial bid of $20 for an out-of-print cover from a Grateful Dead album and that you simultaneously disclose to eBay that your maximum willingness to pay is $100. If the bidding stops at a price of $57, then that is the price that you will pay for the album cover. Of course, if this happens and if all bidders have, like you, submitted their true maximum willingness to pay then the reason that the bidding stops at $57 is because that is the second highest valuation among all bidders. So, once again, the winning bid will be equal to the second highest valuation. However, experience suggests that bidders do not initially put down their true maximum willingness to pay but, instead, often raise that maximum as the bids increase. In this sense, the eBay system is very much like an English auction.

Of course, it is possible that $57 was not the second highest price and that eBay is falsely claiming that value in order to claim a greater payment for itself. However, eBay makes considerable effort to persuade buyers that this is not the case. To begin

---

2   This result was first derived by Vickrey (1961) and then generalized by Myerson (1981) and Riley and Samuelson (1981).

with, eBay publishes a list of the losing bidders, their maximum bids, and their e-mail addresses after the auction closes. This permits the winning buyer to evaluate eBay's claim. In addition, eBay charges a relatively low commission from the sale of an object, roughly 5 percent or less. Such a low commission means that eBay's primary interest is to encourage trades so as to garner as wide a circle of participants as possible. This, too, reduces eBay's incentive to cheat. As noted, the great success of eBay strongly suggests that these tactics have worked and persuaded bidders to trust eBay's auctioneering. Properly designed, the Vickrey auction should be revenue equivalent to the others.

## 25.3 COMMON VALUE AUCTIONS

Suppose your university wants to sell coffee and light meals at the campus center and so decides to auction franchise rights to open a café. The auction type chosen is a first-price sealed-bid design. In this case, however, the auction is called a common value auction because the café presumably has one true value, common to all participants. However, prior to the actual operation of the café that value is not known. Instead, each firm interested in bidding for the franchise can only estimate that value based on its own market research. Each will try to determine the expected number of students, faculty, and staff that will eat there, what they will likely buy and at what price, and how much it will cost to serve them. However, it is crucial to remember that the true value of the café depends on what others are willing to pay for it. That is, this is a common value auction in which bidders start with different signals or information about the café's true worth, but eventually the market will set a price for the café rights and that price will be common to all participants, that is, it will be the price at which anyone can buy or sell the café.

The Revenue Equivalence Theorem will not hold for common value auctions, especially if players' value estimates are correlated. This is why our formal statement of the theorem contains the parenthetical phrase private values. The reason behind this non-equivalence in the case of common values is, however, quite subtle. In what follows, we try to illustrate the argument in an intuitive manner.

### 25.3.1 The "Winner's Curse"

Consider again our café example. After estimating the expected revenue and cost of operating the café, each firm interested in bidding will have an idea or estimate of what the franchise is worth and can use this estimate in submitting a bid. Of course, no two firms are likely to come up with exactly the same estimate of the café's value. Each firm is likely to survey different students or talk to different suppliers or otherwise base its estimate on information specific to that firm. Indeed, these differences in the information that each firm uses are a major source of the differences in firm estimates of the café's value and in the subsequent differences in the submitted bids.

After receiving all the tendered bids, the university will award the franchise to the highest bidder. The winner of the franchise will, of course, be the firm that made the highest bid. Yet in light of how the firms determined the amount of their bids, winning could in fact spell bad news. Because winning means that every other firm bid less for the franchise, it is quite possible that the winner overpaid for the franchise. This downside to winning is a central feature of common value auctions and is called the *winner's curse*. The curse is that the winner of a common value auction often turns out to be the loser because the winner bids too much for the good. The franchise bidders will have collected different information about its true value and the winning bidder is likely the one who has the most optimistic information, and thus made the highest estimate of the value of the franchise. The winner's information is therefore the most likely to be upwardly biased. Consequently, a bid based on that information is likely to be too high.

Bidding in a common value auction therefore requires some sophistication. Let us continue to assume that the auction is a first-price sealed-bid type. It should be clear that a bidder should not base his bid solely on the information he collected about the value of the good. He has to think about where this information came from or, alternatively, what kind of information the other bidders were likely to receive. Only by thinking this way can the bidder work out an estimate of the value of the good that will avoid the winner's curse. Suppose, for example, a bidder in our franchise auction knew that there were $N$ bidders including himself and that each bidder's estimate came from a uniform distribution whose minimum is zero and whose maximum is $U$ = \$50,000. The bidder could then work out that the mean value of this distribution is \$25,000, and that value would, in fact, be the best or unbiased guess as to what is the true value of the franchise.

The difficulty is, of course, that a bidder is unlikely to know the upper limit or most optimistic estimate of the franchise's value. The bidder only knows what estimate he received and that the true value is uniformly distributed in the interval $[0, U]$. How should he proceed?

Consider a bidder whose research leads to an estimate of \$40,000 as the true value of the café rights. However, he knows that this may well be an overestimate and he wants to avoid the winner's curse. One approach is for our bidder to assume that the estimate his research yielded is, in fact, the highest estimate obtained by any of the bidders. If so, then the bidder can use this information to work out a sensibly lower bid that should avoid the winner's curse.

What the bidder needs to do is to get a measure of the overall distribution of possible estimated values. The mean or average value of that distribution should be a good guess as to the true value of the café rights. He knows that the distribution runs from 0 to $U$. What he needs now is to get some idea of the value of $U$. Starting with the assumption that his \$40,000 is the highest of all the estimates drawn, the bidder will again assume that his and the estimates drawn by the other $N - 1$ bidders are equally spaced on the interval. Again this assumption means that if we were to draw many samples of $N$ values from the uniform distribution, then the average value of the highest draw in these samples would be $\dfrac{N-1}{N} U$, where $U$ is the upper limit of the uniform distribution. Since our bidder is assuming that his draw of \$40,000 is the highest draw, he can work out $U$ from the equation $U = \dfrac{N}{N-1} \$40,000$. Thus, if the number of bidders $N$ was 200, the estimate of $U$ would be $U = \$40,201$.

Why does the bidder assume that his own estimate is the largest? Since $U$ is not known, the bidder recognizes that there is a positive probability that others may have drawn higher estimates. However, in determining his bid, the bidder is interested in what the true value of the café rights are conditional on his winning. If that happens, then the winner can reasonably assume that his estimate was the highest. Accordingly, he will wish to work out the best bid that minimizes his winner's curse given that he actually is the winner.

Once our bidder has assigned some value to the upper limit $U$ of the distribution of estimates, he can work out his best guess regarding mean value of that distribution. Continuing with our assumption that the distribution of estimates is uniform over the interval $[0, U]$ with $U = \$40,201$, the implied mean would be \$20,100.50. Accordingly, this is our bidder's best estimate of the true value of the franchise. Note how much lower this bid is relative to the original value of \$40,000. This reduction in the estimated value of the café rights should therefore be quite effective in eliminating the winner's curse. If all the bidders in the common value auction calculate their bids in this way, each will shade his or her initial estimate in the same manner. As a result, it will still be the case that the bidder who initially drew the highest estimate will win the auction. However, he will not suffer as much from the winner's curse.

In short, the prospect of a winner's curse induces buyers in a common value auction to shade their bids below the estimate of an item's true value. The worse the winner's curse, the more such shading will occur. This is the intuition as to why, in

 **Reality Checkpoint**

### From Vickrey to eBay

Recall that as noted in the text, the Revenue Equivalence Theorem derived from Vickrey's (1961) classic work breaks down in realistic settings that include correlated information, common values, and bidder asymmetries. Once these features are present, auction design matters. In this light, we may ask about the designs actually used by auction sites. What, for example, explains eBay's use of an English or ascending auction? Recall that eBay gets its revenue from successful trades. The more trades that take place, the more it makes. Because an English auction tends to reduce the winner's curse, it tends to encourage participation by buyers. This is also good news for sellers—especially many of those who sell on eBay—because these sellers often have arcane items for which it is difficult to find any potential buyers. Of course, sellers also care about the price at which they sell. So, eBay acts to help them on this account, too. It permits sellers to set a minimum price below which the item will not be sold but does not reveal this price to bidders so that no one can simply bid the minimum plus one cent. In addition, eBay polices militantly against tactics aimed at cheating either sellers or buyers. For instance, shill bidding rings are collusive arrangements where one ring member puts in a very low bid and then one or two other members put in very high bids designed to scare off other buyers, only to retract their bids later so that their low-bidding accomplice can win the item. EBay employs over 800 monitors to detect such rings and has strict retraction rules that make this ruse difficult to use. Anyone caught in this practice is banned from eBay. Likewise, eBay allows bidders to set a maximum bid to protect them from getting lured into an artificial bidding war. Do these policies work? Judging from the volume of trade and revenue that eBay generates, one would have to say that it has solved its auction design problems quite well.

**Source:** J. Dobrzynski, "The Bidding Game, A Special Report: In Online Auction World, Hoaxes Aren't Easy to See." *The New York Times*, June 2, 2000, p. A1; and R. Konrad, "Ebay Nearly Doubles Its Quarterly Earnings." *Washington Post*, April 22, 2004, p. E5.

a formal sense, the Revenue Equivalence Theorem does not generally hold for common value auctions.[3] The reason is that different auction designs have different implications regarding the information available to bidders. In an English auction, for example, each successively higher bid indicates a lower value for the maximum winner's curse. In particular, they get increasing information about the lower bound of estimates for the café's value. In turn, this makes them more confident that the value is indeed high and so reduces the size of the winner's curse. Similarly, a second-price sealed-bid auction can also lead to higher offers because the winner only pays the second highest bid. Of course, the weaker is the winner's curse effect the more aggressive will be the bidding and the greater the seller's revenue. The conventional ranking is that revenue is greatest for an English auction, next highest for a Vickrey or second-price sealed-bid auction, and least for a first-price sealed-bid auction, which is equivalent to the case of a Dutch or descending-price auction. However, even this convention can break down when one considers slight departures from the standard common value case.[4]

---

## Practice Problem 25.3

Suppose your local town is auctioning a franchise to sell hot dogs at the July 4th celebration. You and your partner decide to bid for the franchise. Including you, there are eighty groups bidding in the auction. Your market research on expected attendance, hot dog consumption, and costs suggests that the franchise is worth $2,000. Suppose you believe that your estimate, as well as the other bidders' estimates, is generated independently from a uniform distribution that starts at zero. What is your optimal bid for the franchise assuming that the distribution of valuations is uniform? If yours is the winning bid are you cursed?

---

### 25.3.2  Almost Common Value Auctions

In our café example, we assumed that the true value was ultimately the same for everyone. The only difference among the bidders was the initial information that they had regarding precisely what that true value was. However, suppose that one of the bidders is the Starbuck's chain and that winning the franchise is more valuable to it. This may be because winning will permit Starbuck's to have a monopoly in the area, or because Starbuck's can use its experience and buying power to operate the café more efficiently than can the other bidders. Whatever the reason, we will assume that if the café is truly worth $v$ to all the other bidders, then it is worth $v + \$1,000$ to Starbuck's. For example, if the true value of the café ultimately turns out to be $25,000 for all the non-Starbuck's buyers, it is worth $26,000 to Starbuck's. In this case, the café's value is not common to all buyers. The deviation from the common value case

---

3  Strictly speaking, it is not so much the common value aspect that generates the break from revenue equivalence as it is the fact that the ascending auction reveals to the ultimate winner information regarding the signals or estimates of those bidders who drop out in a manner which lets them use that information in setting their bids, whereas it is hard to use that information in a sealed-bid process. Note also that Riley and Li (1999) show that the revenue difference between auction types may in practice be quite small, especially if the seller sets a sensible reserve price below which he or she will not sell.

4  This ranking originates from the famous paper of Milgrom and Weber (1982) on auctions with affiliated bidder values.

is, however, relatively small. For this reason, this setting is often referred to as one of an almost common value auction.

Although this auction is very similar to a common value auction, the change in the outcome can be very large. The difference once again has to do with the winner's curse. In our example, all the non-Starbuck's bidders face an exaggerated winner's curse. To beat Starbuck's in the auction requires an extra large bid, but this just exacerbates the winner's curse. That extra $1,000 that was driving Starbuck's bid will not be there for the non-Starbuck's winner who has to overbid Starbuck's. As a result of the exaggerated winner's curse, the non-Starbuck's firms will bid even more conservatively. However, this permits Starbuck's to bid more aggressively because it now faces a reduced winner's curse. Yet this makes the others bid less aggressively, and so on. The end result is that Starbuck's will always win the bidding but it will do so at a much reduced price relative to that paid in a pure common value auction because of the extra conservative bidding pursued by its rivals. Hence, another reason that revenue equivalence may break down is because different auction designs may raise or lower the ability of dominant or advantaged buyers like Starbuck's to exploit that advantage.[5]

## 25.4 AUCTION MARKETS AND INDUSTRIAL ORGANIZATION

Auction markets have become increasingly common. Firms use auctions to purchase supplies; consumers bid for a variety of products through online auction sites; and the government auctions Treasury bonds, mineral rights, and wireless spectrum licenses. In short, auction markets are common. It should come as good news, therefore, that the tools of industrial organization can yield insight into the operation of such markets. From a public policy perspective, such analysis is likely to be most useful in considering the auctions run by national and local governments. Ideally, such auctions will result in prices that are efficient in that they are close to the true market value of the item in question. However, it is also important to remember that the revenues obtained from such auctions are likely to be used by the government to reduce taxes and therefore to alleviate any tax-induced distortions. For this reason, we are particularly interested in what our analysis can suggest regarding the kinds of auction design that are most likely to yield high auction revenue for the government.

Let us start by recognizing that government-run auctions are—except in cases such as auctions of obsolete military weapons—nearly always of the common value or almost common value type. Government bonds, mineral rights, and spectrum licenses are all items whose value to any one buyer depend largely on what other buyers would willingly pay for them. This makes life more difficult because the alternative case of purely private value auctions is certainly much simpler. The Revenue Equivalence Theorem tells us that when bidders all have private values one type of auction is as good as another. Moreover, the auction outcome is efficient in that the winner will be the buyer who values the object the most and will pay a price equal to the valuation placed on the object by the buyer with the second highest valuation, that is, equal to the item's true opportunity cost as measured by the amount for which the winning bidder could sell it. Common value and almost common value

---

5   See Klemperer (1998) for an elegant presentation of this idea.

auctions are, on the other hand, different. Here, revenue equivalence does not hold, so auction design does matter. The source of revenue non-equivalence in this case can often be found in whether the auction design encourages bidders to enter the auction and in whether the design facilitates collusion among the bidders. This should hardly be surprising as entry and collusion are issues that lie at the heart of industrial organization.

We begin by observing that the winner's curse intensifies as the number of bidders who enter the auction increases. Recall our earlier café example, only now assume that the auction is a Dutch or descending-bid type. Suppose as before that you are again thinking of bidding $22,000. If there are only four other bidders and none of them have indicated their willingness to buy as the price nears this point, you might not be too worried. If there are forty other bidders, however, you might feel a good bit more hesitant. Being the high bidder out of a pool of five does not cause you to question very much your estimate of the café's value. Being the high bidder out of a pool of forty-one, though, is quite different. When there are many bidders, the odds that your high estimate of the café's value is too generous rise considerably because odds of obtaining an estimate far from above the café's true value are much higher when there are forty-one estimates than when there are five. Thus, the more bidders there are the greater is the potential winner's curse and therefore, the more each buyer shades her bids. We generally expect an increase in the number of potential buyers to raise the price of a resource whose supply is fixed. Here, however, the price-raising effect of more buyers may be more than offset by the bid-reducing effect that additional buyers have as a result of each buyer recognizing the winner's curse.[6] This suggests that one may wish to reduce the winner's curse effect by using an ascending auction.

Yet while an ascending auction may reduce the winner's curse in the case where all buyers have the same common value, the almost common value auction case is more complicated. Recall what happened when one of the bidders for our hypothetical café was Starbuck's. Because Starbuck's valued the café at slightly more than everyone else this intensifies the winner's curse for all other buyers. In turn, this induces all other bidders to shade their bids and thereby reduce the winner's curse that Starbuck's faces. Indeed, once other buyers realize Starbuck's advantage, they may drop out altogether, allowing Starbuck's to win the café rights at a very low price. This is particularly likely in an ascending auction. First, note that Starbuck's will never lose an ascending auction. If any bidder reveals that it is willing to pay $x, Starbuck's is willing to pay $x plus something. More generally, the process of an ascending auction is almost perfectly designed to reveal Starbuck's advantage. Yet if every time a buyer bids $x Starbuck's offers more, then buyers will quickly realize that Starbuck's cannot be beaten. Hence, all buyers except Starbuck's will withdraw after only a few rounds, permitting Starbuck's to win the auction at a very low price.

The foregoing example is similar to the 1995 ascending auction for mobile phone licenses in the Los Angeles area, a real-world example discussed in Klemperer (2002). Pacific Telesis, the Baby Bell that supplied fixed line telephone service, was certainly a well-known name in the area, and was widely reported to have made it clear to all potential bidders that it would bid whatever necessary to get the California market (see the Reality Checkpoint: Designing Minds). While other firms entered the auction for the Los Angeles license, the number of participants was much fewer than an-

6   See Bulow and Klemperer (2002).

ticipated and the winning bid (paid by Pacific Telephone) was much lower than had been predicted. It was $26 per head of population. By contrast, a similar auction in the Chicago area in which demand for mobile phone service was likely less than in Los Angeles resulted in a winning bid of $31 per head of population.

Another drawback to ascending auctions is that they may facilitate collusion. The repeated rounds of bidding do more than just reveal information about other buyers' estimated value. They also permit buyers to communicate and therefore to coordinate their bids. Cramton and Schwartz (2000) demonstrate this point in the context of the 1997 spectrum auctions conducted by the Federal Communications Commission (FCC). These auctions are ascending-bid multi-unit auctions. A number of licenses were simultaneously auctioned off in an English auction. Cramton and Schwartz argue that different firms seemed to be signaling in their bid the identity number of the license areas that they were most interested in acquiring by matching the last three digits of their bid with their preferred area code, for example, bidding $313,378 for license area 378. Such a bid communicates to others that the bidder

 **Reality Checkpoint**

### Designing Minds

The bidding for wireless personal communication service (PCS) licenses covering slices of the radio spectrum over geographic regions offers a good example of how difficult auction design can be. It was clear from the outset that the services provided through these licenses would compete with existing cellular operations and regular phone services. Hence, the licenses for a specific region were especially valuable to the phone companies in that same region. The Federal Communications Commission (FCC) understood this. To encourage a large number of bidders for each region and to permit bidders to react to new information, it used a multiple round approach. Bidders submitted bids for the licenses that they wanted. At the end of a round, each bid and the company who made it was reported for each license in the auction. Further rounds and bids followed until no new bid was submitted on any license. In anticipation of this process and its associated complexities, virtually all the firms involved were reported to have hired gaming experts to help devise bidding strategies.

The first auctions were held over 1994 and 1995, at which point part of the strategy of Pacific Telesis became clear. In a widely quoted interview, the firm's president stated that "If somebody takes California away from us, they'll never make any money." In retrospect, this appears to have been a somewhat successful attempt to discourage competition for the licenses that Pacific Telesis most desired, so that it could win them with a low bid.

In a later set of PCS auctions held in 1996, a possible flaw in the multiple round format was discovered. Three firms (Omnipoint, 21st Century Bidding, and Mercury) appear to have used the last three digits to signal to each other the regions they most wanted. After reading the bids in one round, the firms could drop out of the contest for each other's most preferred areas as indicated by the coded bids. This amounts to dividing the PCS market among the three companies without engaging in competitive bidding. When the Justice Department filed suit, the three firms signed a consent decree not to engage in such practices in the future and to permit their future bidding actions to be monitored. However, they did not admit any wrongdoing in the 1996 bidding.

A further problem has been recently discovered. To encourage entry by small firms, the FCC set aside some wireless airwave rights, permitting only small firms to bid for them. To make sure that many small companies joined the bidding, subsidies were offered to the winning bidder. Large firms responded to this program by making deals with some of the small firms to bankroll their bids. Thus, Alaska Native Wireless, a small new company based in Anchorage, won one of the three licenses issued for New York with a winning bid of $1.48 billion—almost all of which will be paid by its bidding partner, AT&T Wireless. Critics contend that large firms such as AT&T, Cingular, and SBC were able to win many licenses and hundreds of millions of dollars in subsidies through such partnerships.

In short, auction design is tricky business. Yet it is increasingly important. Firms and governments are using auctions more and more as a means to allocate resources and supply contracts. Auction design may be especially crucial for the former communist economies as privatization requires auctioning the assets of previously state-owned enterprises.

---

**Sources:**  L. Cauley and M. L. Carnevale, "Wireless Giants, Some Surprise Players To Seek New Generation of Licenses." *The Wall Street Journal*, October 31, 1994, p. A4; J. Simons, "Three Wireless-Communications Firms Settle Suit Involving Auction of Licenses." *The Wall Street Journal*, November 11, 1998, p. B2; S. Labaton and S. Romero, "F.C.C. Auction Hit With Claim Of Unfair Bids." *The New York Times*, February 12, 2001, p. A1.

truly wants this area and will refrain from bidding aggressively for other regions so long as other bidders do not bid aggressively for area 378.

A similar story is told in Klemperer (2002) about a 1999 spectrum auction in Germany. In that case, there were ten licenses to be auctioned and bids had to increase by a minimum of 10 percent. One bidder, Mannesmann, bid 18.18 million DM per MHz on licenses 1 to 5, and bid 20 million DM per MHz on licenses 6 to 10. Now observe that if you increase 18.18 by 10 percent the result is 20. T-Mobil, the other main bidder, later admitted that it made just such a calculation and concluded that Mannesmann's bid represented something of an offer. T-Mobil interpreted the offer as follows: It could have licenses 1 to 5 for 20 million DM per MHz (the minimum amount it would need to raise Mannesmann's bid) if it would not make any further bids for licenses 6 to 10, the other bidder in the auction. That is exactly what happened. The auction ended after just two rounds with all ten licenses going for 20 million DM per MHz—well below anyone's estimate of the true willingness to pay of either T-Mobil or Mannesmann.

The previous examples suggest that whatever advantages are associated with ascending auctions by way of limiting the winner's curse, these are more than offset by the disadvantages that such auctions have in settings of asymmetric bidding and by means of facilitating bidder collusion. Accordingly, some sort of sealed-bid auction may be best, at least in terms of raising revenue. In a sealed-bid auction firms cannot use the bidding process itself as a communication device for the purpose of coordinating bids, or similarly, an advantaged firm cannot use it to make certain it always overbids its rivals. Indeed, a sealed-bid auction tends to encourage less advantaged bidders to participate. Because each bidder submits only one offer and does so not knowing what other rival bidders will submit, the weaker bidder's bid could in fact win the auction. If the strong or advantaged bidder tries to "low ball" it could lose and, unlike the ascending auction, it then has no recourse to outbid a rival in a subsequent round. Therefore, because a weaker bidder has at least some chance to win, a sealed-bid auction encourages more entry than an ascending-bid auction and can force even advantaged firms to bid quite high to make sure that they do not lose the auction. Somewhat more broadly, while a large number of bidders can intensify the winner's curse and so lead to greatly shaded bids, some competition is nevertheless desirable. An auction with only one bidder is guaranteed to yield little revenue to the seller.

The importance of attracting entry via a sealed-bid process was potently illustrated by European mobile telephone auctions in 2000 and 2001. At that time, many governments were using auctions to allocate licenses to provide the so-called third generation (3G) of mobile telephone employing a new transmitting standard (Universal Mobile Telecommunications Service or UMTS). In the Netherlands, there were exactly five incumbent mobile telephone companies and the government chose to auction exactly five licenses using an ascending-bid auction. It is easy to see the asymmetry between the five incumbent firms and any new bidders. The five incumbents clearly valued the new licenses more than an entrant. Thus the five incumbents were advantaged. Indeed, without additional entry, the fact that there were exactly five licenses being sold—one for each incumbent—reduced the auction to one that was very much like selling just one license to just one bidder in five separate cases. Yet the use of an ascending auction discouraged such additional participation (and may have permitted coordination between the five incumbents) with the result that only one additional and not very serious bidder emerged. In the end, the auction produced revenues of only 170 euros per capita. This was less than one-fourth the 650 euros per capita earned by a similar auction in the United Kingdom held just a bit earlier and less than one-third the predictions of the Dutch government. In contrast, a year later (after the dot.com and telecommunications booms had ended), the Danish government used a sealed-bid process to allocate four licenses to four incumbents and earned twice as much revenue as expected.

To be sure, sealed-bid procedures are not without flaws. While raising revenue is one goal, putting licenses in the hands of those firms with the best business plans is another. Since, in principle, those firms with the best business plans should be those who value the licenses most highly, this means that the licenses should be awarded to those bidders with the highest values for the licenses. Yet a sealed-bid process does not achieve this efficiency criterion. Indeed, its ability to encourage entry and to generate revenue is due in part to the fact that a sealed-bid auction can end up with a low-value bidder as the winner.

In sum, auction design is important for common value auctions. Different auction types will yield different outcomes principally, in our view, because despite their appearance as the purest manifestation of the markets idealized by Adam Smith, auction markets are not immune to the problems of entry deterrence and collusion that arise elsewhere in the economy. Some auction processes exacerbate these problems. Some may encourage entry and reduce the likelihood of collusion but only by introducing other complications. Proper auction design will balance these gains and losses at the margin. Devising such designs is likely to remain an important public policy aim as auctions are increasingly used by both firms and governments. Careful application of the tools of industrial organization—both in theory and in practice—can contribute to achieving this goal.

## SUMMARY

In this chapter, we have focused on the nature and implication of strategic interaction in the context of auctions. For private value auctions in which each bidder has his or her own valuation of the auctioned commodity, the four principal auction designs—English, Dutch, first-price sealed-bid, and second-price sealed-bid—are revenue equivalent. That is, each yields the same winning bid and gives the commodity to the same winning bidder. For common and almost common value auctions, such revenue equivalence does not in general hold. In particular, for these cases, different auction designs can have very different outcomes both in terms of the revenue generated and regarding which bidder wins the auction.

Auctions have been increasingly used by governments to allocate scarce resources and license rights. Because these are common and almost common value auctions the link between auction design and auction outcomes is particularly important. In large part, the differences in outcomes across auction types is largely due to differences in how alternative auction designs work to encourage entry and limit bidder collusion. Here, both scholarly work and historical experience suggest that sealed-bid auctions are most likely to yield competitive results.

## PROBLEMS

1. Consider Practice Problem 25.2 again in which you are bidding for an original John Lennon hat in a sealed-bid first-price auction. In this case, however, let there be 20 other bidders in this auction. As before, assume that the most you would be willing to pay for this hat is $200. Show that your optimal strategy is to submit a bid of $190.

2. You are selling your house and want to get the highest price you can. What sort of auction would you prefer if:

   a. you expect there to be 25 offers?

   b. you expect the number of offers to be less than four?

   c. When more than one buyer submits a bid for the same house, most states have strict laws forbidding real estate brokers to disclose to any one buyer the bid of any other buyer. Based on your answers to (a) and (b), what do you think is the justification behind such restrictions?

3. At the time of the 2000 United Kingdom's auction of 3G telecommunication licenses, Britain had four incumbent mobile phone operators. Originally, it also planned to auction exactly four licenses. (In the end, it sold five.) Had it sold four licenses, the British planned to use a combined Anglo-Dutch approach. Under this design, the auction would proceed as an ascending auction until just five bidders were left. At that point, the auction would switch to a fourth-price sealed-bid type in which the four licenses would be allocated to the top four bidders, each paying the price offered by the lowest successful bid. Comment briefly on this model. What economic considerations do you think were behind this auction design?

# REFERENCES

Bulow, J., and P. Klemperer. 2002. "Prices and the Winner's Curse." *Rand Journal of Economics* 33: 1–21.

Cramton, P., and J. A. Schwartz. 2000. "Collusive Bidding: Lessons from FCC Spectrum Auctions." *Journal of Regulatory Economics* 17: 229–52.

Klemperer, P. D. 1998. "Auctions with Almost Common Values: The "Wallet Game" and its Applications." *European Economic Review* 42 (May): 757–69.

———. 2002. "What Really Matters in Auction Design." *Journal of Economic Perspectives* 16: 161–89.

Lucking-Reily, David. 2000. "Vickrey Auctions in Practice: From Nineteenth Century Philately to Twenty-First Century E-Commerce." *Journal of Economic Perspectives* 14: 183–92.

Milgrom, P. R., and R. J. Weber. 1982. "A Theory of Auctions and Competitive Bidding." *Econometrica* 50: 1089–1122.

Myerson, R. B. 1981. "Optimal Auction Design." *Mathematics of Operations Research* 6: 58–73.

Riley, J. G., and W. Samuelson. 1981. "Optimal Auctions." *American Economic Review* 71: 381–92.

———, and H. Li. 1999. "Auction Choice." UCLA Working Paper.

Vickrey, William. 1961. "Counterspeculation and Competitive Sealed Tenders." *Journal of Finance* 16: 8–37.

# Answers to Practice Problems

## Chapter 2

**2.1** a. Profit maximization implies $MC = 2q + 10 = P$. Hence, $q = (P - 10)/2$.

b. With 50 firms, horizontal summation of the individual marginal cost curves yields $Q^S = 50(P - 10)/2 = 25P - 250$.

c. Equilibrium: $P = \$30$ and $Q = 500$.

d. $q = (P - 10)/2 = 10$. Revenue $= Pq = \$300$. Total cost $= 100 + q^2 + 10q = \$300$. Profit $= 0$.

**2.2** a. Inverse demand curve is $P = (6,000 - 9Q)/50$. Hence, $MR = 120 - (18Q/50)$.

b. $MC = 10 + Q/25$. Equate with $MR$ to obtain $Q = 275$. At this output, $P = \$70.50$.

c. Total revenue $= \$19,387.50$. Each plant produces 5.5 units and incurs a total cost of $\$185.25$. Each plant earns a revenue of $\$387.75$. Profit at each plant is $\$202.50$. Total profit $= \$10,125$.

**2.3** a. Present value of incremental cash flows from driving out Loew $= -\$100,000 + \dfrac{R}{1-R}\$10,000 = -\$16,667$. Driving out Loew is not a good investment.

b. Present value of incremental cash flows from buying Loew $= -\$80,000 + \dfrac{R}{1-R}\$10,000 = \$3,333$. This is a good investment.

**2.4** a. Consumer surplus is the area of the triangle above the equilibrium price but below the demand curve $= (1/2)(\$120 - \$30)500 = \$22,500$. Producer surplus is the area of the triangle below the equilibrium price but above the supply curve $= (1/2)(\$30 - \$10)500 = \$5,000$. *Note:* Surplus is a marginal concept. Producer fixed cost is not considered. Total $= \$27,500$.

b. Total surplus falls by the area of the deadweight triangle. Height of the triangle is given by reduction in output, which is $500 - 275 = 225$. Marginal cost at $Q = 275$ is $\$21$. Base of the triangle is given by price less marginal cost $= \$70.50 - \$21 = \$49.50$. So, the deadweight triangle has an area equal to $(1/2)(\$49.50)225$, or by $\$5,568.75$. Thus total surplus is now $\$21,931.25$.

**2.5** a. $P = MC = \$10$, $Q = 30$.

b. Inverse demand is given by $P = 25 - Q/2$. So, $MR = 25 - Q$. Equating $MR$ and $MC (= \$10)$ yields $Q = 15$ and $P = \$17.50$.

c. $\$56.25$.

## Chapter 3

**3.1** a. $CR4^A = 70\%$; $CR4^B = 76\%$. $HHI^A = 2,698$; $HHI^B = 1,660$. Industry A has one firm that dominates the industry. Industry B has five firms that control 90 percent of the production. But these five firms may compete fiercely. The Herfindahl-Hirschman index seems to better capture the greater potential for monopoly power in Industry A.

b. With the merger of the top three firms in Industry A, the new values are $CR4^A = 80\%$; $HHI = 2,992$. Both measures rise.

**3.2** The Lerner Index is defined as $LI = (P - c)/P$. This rises as marginal cost $c$ declines. The smallest possible value for $c$ is $c = 0$, which renders a maximum Lerner Index value of $LI = P/P = 1$. Since the Lerner Index is also the inverse of the firm's demand elasticity, that is, $LI = 1/\varepsilon_D$, this implies that the firm will never produce at a point where that elasticity is less than 1.

# Chapter 4

**4.1** At $q = 11$, Average cost = \$128 and Marginal cost = \$151. $S = AC/MC =$ \$128/\$151 = 0.848 ≈ 0.85.

**4.2** a. $AC = TC/q = 50/q + 2 + 0.5q$. $AC(q = 4) = 16.5$; $AC(q = 8) = 12.25$; $AC(q = 10) = 12$; $AC(q = 12) = 12.167$; $AC(q = 15) = 12.833$.

b. $MC = \Delta TC$ per unit change. For decreases: $\Delta TC = 50 + 2q + 0.5q^2 - [50 + 2(q - 1) + 0.5(q - 1)^2] = 2 + q - 0.5$. For increases: $\Delta TC = 50 + 2(q + 1) + 0.5(q + 1)^2 - [50 + 2q + 0.5q^2] = 2 + q + 0.5$. The average of these two values is $2 + q$.

c. $S > 1$ for $q < 10$; $S = 1$ for $q = 10$; $S < 1$ for $q > 10$.

**4.3** a. For a firm producing just shirts $(q_1)$, average cost is $(2 + \sqrt{q_1})/q_1 = 2/q_1 + 1/\sqrt{q_1}$. This obviously declines as $q_1$ increases. For a firm producing just cologne $(q_2)$, average cost is $(2 + q_2^2)/q_2$. This is minimized at $q_2 = \sqrt{2}$. For all $q_2$ greater than 1.41, average cost rises. So, unless the firm is going to produce a very small amount, it will not enjoy any scale economies. By itself, this fact suggests that there is no need to operate on a large scale to be efficient and, hence, the industry can sustain many small, but nonetheless efficient, firms.

b. $S_C = 1/(3 + \sqrt{q_1} + q_2^2) > 0$ for all output combinations. The scale economies in shirts alone suggest that any firm producing shirts will wish to produce a lot of them. Yet, because of the strong scope economies between shirts and cologne, any firm producing a lot of shirts will also wish to produce a lot of cologne. Thus the cologne firms will tend to be large so that the market can only accommodate a few of them. In other words, the cologne market will likely be concentrated even though cologne firms do not enjoy any significant scale economies directly.

# Chapter 5

**5.1** a. Profit-maximizing price for common day/night pricing is $P = \$7.50$. Daytime attendance = 25; evening attendance = 65. Total daily profit = (\$7.50 – \$3.00) × 90 = \$405.

b. Daytime price = \$6.50; daytime attendance = 35. Evening price = \$8.50; evening attendance = 55. Total daily attendance is the same. Total daily profit rises to (\$6.50 – \$3.00) × 35 + (\$8.50 – \$3.00) × 55 = \$425.

**5.2** a. $P_B = \$5.5$, $Q_B = 4{,}500$ pints; $P_{NY} = \$6.00$, $Q_{NY} = 8{,}000$ pints; $P_W = \$6.50$, $Q_W = 5{,}250$ pints.

b. Boston profit = (\$5.50 – \$1.00) × 4,500 = \$20,250; New York profit = (\$6.00 – \$2.00) × 8,000 = \$32,000; Washington profit = (\$6.50 – \$3.00) × 5,250 = \$18,375.

**5.3** Without discriminatory pricing, consumer surplus for daytime consumers is (\$10.00 – \$7.50) × 25/2 = \$31.25. For evening consumers it is (\$14.00 – \$7.50) × 65/2 = \$211.25. Producer surplus is \$405. Total surplus without discriminatory pricing is \$647.50. With discriminatory pricing, consumer surplus for daytime consumers is (\$10.00 – \$6.50) × 35/2 = \$61.25. For evening consumers it is (\$14.00 – \$8.50) × 55/2 = \$151.25. Producer surplus is \$425. Total surplus with discriminatory pricing is \$637.50. Discriminatory pricing has lowered the total surplus by \$10.

# Chapter 6

**6.1** a. If $P = \$40$, then $Q = 5$. If $P = \$25$, then $Q = 10$. Hence, slope = $\Delta P/\Delta Q = -15/5 = -3$. Equation must satisfy $P =$ Intercept $- 3Q$ and pass through (5, \$40). Hence $P = 55 - 3Q$ is an approximation. $MR = 55 - 6Q$.

b. Top reservation price is \$55 (\$52 if fractional units are not counted).

c. Demand at $P = \$34 = 13$.

**6.2** a. Price per ride = $k + c$. Admission fee = area under demand curve but above $k + c$.

b. Price per ride = 0. Admission fee = entire area under demand curve.

c. Policy A recovers the per-ride cost of operating a lift but incurs the cost of ticketing. Profit is equal to the triangle below the demand curve but above the $k + c$ line. Policy B incurs no ticketing cost but does not recover the operating cost. It earns the same profit as Policy A, plus the trapezoid whose height is $k$ and whose base is $q_2$, minus the triangle of height $c$ lying above the demand curve from $q_2$ to the quantity intercept.

**6.3**  a. Assume high-demand package has 12 units. See Instructor's Manual for table.

b. Four units in low-demand package.

c. Six units in low-demand package.

d. Price of 6-unit package = $54; price of 12-unit package = $96, ratio = 1.25.

## Chapter 7

**7.1**  Locate at town center because this permits broadest market access. Demand can be approximated as $P = \$10.25 - Q/4$. Profit maximization requires $P = \$5.88$ ($\approx\$6$), $Q = 16.50$ ($\approx16$). Total profit = $64.02 ($\approx\$64$). With a mobile service, again start from center. Charge all customers $10 for smithing. Earn profit of $8 from consumer at center. Earn $7.25 from each consumer at #1 East and #1 West. Earn $6.50 from each consumer at #2 East and #2 West. Earn $5.75 from each at #3 East and #3 West. Serve all consumers in this way earning $0.25 on consumers at #10 East and #10 West. Total profit is $77.50. Employing the mobile smithy is definitely worthwhile.

**7.2**  a. The price intercept remains unchanged. The demand curve rotates out along the quantity axis.

b. If $Z = 1$, $Q = 2$ and $P = \$2$. If $Z = 2$, $Q = 4$ and $P = \$2$. If $Z = 3$, $Q = 6$ and $P = \$2$.

c. At $Z = 1$, maximum profit is $PQ - Z^2 = \$3$. At $Z = 2$, maximum profit is $PQ - Z^2 = \$4$. At $Z = 3$, maximum profit is $PQ - Z^2 = \$3$. The profit-maximizing choice is $Z = 2$.

**7.3**  a. Since both types have increasing willingness to pay as quality rises, sell maximum quality $z_1 = z_2 = 2$ to each. Price to type A consumers is $p_A = 420(2 - \underline{z}_1)$. Price to type B consumers is $p_B = \$20$.

b. From equation (7.26), $p_B = 10z_2$. From equation (7.28), $20z_1 - 10z_2 > p_A$. From equation (7.29), set quality sold to type A customers at highest possible level, that is, $z_A = 2$. Parameter $\eta$ has a negative effect on profits. So, low-quality $z_B$ needs to be set at the lowest possible value consistent with constraint reflected in previous pricing relationships [see equation (7.31)]. This implies that $z_B = 2\underline{z}_1$. Accordingly, prices are $p_A = 40 - 20\underline{z}_1$, and $p_B = 20\underline{z}_1$.

c. When $\underline{z}_1 = 0$, do not sell to low-quality types (or offer them a zero-quality good).

## Chapter 8

**8.1**  a. $P_{BASIC} = \$11$; $\pi_B = \$24$; $P_{DISNEY} = \$15$; $\pi_D = \$36$.

b. $P_{BUNDLE} = \$20$; $P_{BASIC} = \$17$; $P_{DISNEY} = \$17$. Young Adults buy the Disney Channel only. Pensioners buy the Basic Service only. All other groups buy the bundle.

c. New answers to part (a), $P_{BASIC} = \$14$; $P_{DISNEY} = \$15$. New answers to part (b), $P_{BUNDLE} = \$20$; $P_{BASIC} = \$14$; $P_{DISNEY} = \$15$. Pensioners and Hotels buy Basic Service. Students, Schools, and Young Adults buy Disney. Families may buy the bundle.

**8.2**  Let $Q$ be measured in thousands. Summing two demand curves yields combined demand of $Q = 28 - 2P$ for $P \leq 12$, and $Q = 16 - P$ for $12 < P \leq 16$. Assume firm operates where both consumers are served so that $Q = 28 - 2P$ is relevant demand. (This is easy to show.) Profit is $(P - 2)Q + 2S_L$ where $S_L$ is surplus of low-demand consumers. In turn, that surplus is given by $(12 - P)^2/2$. So, profit is $(P - 2)(28 - 2P) + (12 - P)^2$. Maximization with respect to $P$ then yields $P = \$4$. If two packages are offered, 8-shot and 14-shot, first note that low-demand consumers value 8 shots at a total of $(\$8 \times 8)/2 + \$32 = \$64$. So, set $64 as price of the 8-shot camera. High-demand consumers will earn a surplus of $32 on the 8-shot pack. They value a 14-pack camera at $126. So, price of 14-pack camera is $126 - \$32 = \$94$. If marginal cost is still $2 per exposure, profit is $(\$64 - \$16) = \$48$ on the 8-shot camera and $(\$94 - \$28) = \$66$ on 14-pack camera. Total profit if there are 1,000 of each is $114,000.

  a. If Rowling sells only the 14-shot package, it can charge $126 to each of the $N_h$ high-demand types and earn $94 $N_h$ in profit. Offering a 10-shot package allows it to earn $70 - \$20 = \$50$ from each low-demand consumer, but constrains it to lower the price of a 14-shot package to $86, from which it earns $86 - \$28 = \$58$ in profit. Total profit from this strategy is therefore $50,000 + \$58 N_h$. Profit is identical for each strategy when $50,000 + \$58 N_h = \$94 N_h$ or when $N_h = 1,389$. Once there are this many high-demand consumers, it is no longer profitable to go after the relatively few low-demand ones.

  b. From above, offering both types earns a profit of $48,000 + \$66 N_h$. Otherwise, it earns $94 N_h$ by offering just the 14-shot camera. This implies that for $N_h \geq 1,714$, only the 14-shot package will be offered.

# Chapter 9

**9.1** There is one Nash equilibrium. It is Suspense, Suspense. In each of the other three outcomes, at least one firm has an incentive to switch its strategy. Hence, in these cases, the outcome is not a pair of best responses.

**9.2** Best response: $q_1 = 22.5 - q_2/2$, and vise-versa for $q_2$. Hence, $q_1 = q_2 = 15$. $Q = 30$; $P = \$40$; and $\pi_1 = \pi_2 = \$450$.

**9.3** $Q = q_C + q_U = 1 + 2 = 3$; $P = \$60$; $\pi_C = \$20$; $\pi_U = \$80$. If $c_1 = c_2 = \$20$, then $q_1 = q_2 = 1.67$; $P = \$53.33$.

# Chapter 10

**10.1** a. Cournot equilibrium: $q_1 = q_2 = 30$; $Q = 60$; $P = \$8$; and $\pi_1 = \pi_2 = \$180$.

  b. Bertrand equilibrium: $q_1 = q_2 = 45$; $P = \$2$; and $\pi_1 = \pi_2 = 0$.

**10.2** $P_{PR} = P_{SR} = \$110$.

**10.3** a. Assume the entire market is served. Best response function for Cheap Cuts is $p_{CC} = \dfrac{p_R + c_{CC} + t}{2}$. Likewise, best response function for the Ritz is $p_R = \dfrac{p_{CC} + c_R + t}{2}$. For every $1 in one firm's unit cost the rival's optimal price rises by 50 cents.

  b. Equilibrium prices:

$$p_{CC} = t + \frac{2}{3} c_{CC} + \frac{1}{3} c_R = \$18.33;$$

$$p_r = t + \frac{1}{3} c_{CC} + \frac{2}{3} c_R = \$21.67.$$ Average price is now higher to reflect higher cost at Ritz and this softens price competition between the two firms.

# Chapter 11

**11.1** a. $q_2 = 70 - q_1/2$.

  b. $q_1 = 70$; $q_2 = 35$; $P = \$95$; profit to firm 1 (leader) = $2,450; profit to firm 2 (follower) = $1,225.

  c. $q_1 = q_2 = 46.67$; $P = \$106.67$. Profit to firm 1 = profit to firm 2 = $2,177.77. Firm 1 loses and firm 2 gains as game becomes Cournot rather than Stackelberg. Consumers enjoy more output and lower prices under Stackelberg.

**11.2** a. West End will be on its best response function, $p_{WE} = (p_{EE} + c + t)/2$. Demand for East End is $q_{EE} = (p_{WE} - p_{EE} + t)N/2t$. Substitution and profit maximization then yields $p_{EE} = c + 3t/2$ while $p_{WE} = c + 5t/4$, or $p_{EE} = \$17.50$ and $p_{WE} = \$16.25$. Because of its higher price, East End will serve only 3/8 of the 100 potential customers, or 37.5. It earns a profit of $\$7.5 \times 37.5 = \$281.25$. West End serves 62.5 customers and earns a profit of $\$6.25 \times 62.5 = \$390.63$.

b. Prices in this sequential price game are higher than they are in the simultaneous game. Prices are strategic complements. When one firm goes first it can exploit this complementarity. Sequential price setting permits the firms to coordinate prices to some extent. Note, however, that going first is a disadvantage in this game. While both firms earn more profit than when play is simultaneous, the firm setting its price second earns the most.

**11.3** a.

|  |  | Player 2 | |
| --- | --- | --- | --- |
|  |  | **Take All** | **Share** |
| **Player 1** | **Wait** | (0, 3) | (1.5, 1.5) |
|  | **Grab** | (1, 0) | |

c. Take All is a dominant strategy for Player 2. The promise to play Share is not credible. Anticipating this, Player 1 will Grab the dollar.

# Chapter 12

**12.1** a. Entrant's residual demand curve is described by $P = (100 - \bar{Q}) - q$.

b. $q^* = 30 - \bar{Q}/2$.

c. Entrant profit = $(P^* - c)q^* - 100 = [100 - \bar{Q}_L - q^* - 40]q^* - 100$. Substituting for $q^*$, entrant profit = $[30 - (\bar{Q}_L/2)]^2 - 100 = 0$ if entry is to be deterred. Incumbent should set $\bar{Q}_L = 40$. This yields a pre-entry price of $P = \$60$. The entrant's best response to $\bar{Q}_L = 40$ is $q = 10$, which would drive the price $P$ to $\$50$ and leave the entrant with zero profit.

**12.2** a. Incumbent's marginal cost for output less than $\bar{K}_1$ is 30, hence its best response function for this range of output is $q_1 = 90/2 - q_2/2 = 45 - q_2/2$. For output greater than or equal to $\bar{K}_1$, Incumbent's marginal cost is 60. Therefore, for this range of output, its best response is $q_1 = 30 - q_2/2$.

b. Entrant's marginal cost is always 60, so its best response function is always $q_2 = 30 - q_1/2$.

d. With $q_1 \leq K_1$, monopoly profit = $(P - c)q_1 - 30K_1 - \$200 = (120 - q_1 - 30)q_1 - 30K_1 - \$200 = (90 - q_1)q_1 - 30K_1 - \$200$. However, a monopoly firm will never keep capacity unused, so it will choose $K$ such that $K_1 = q_1$. Hence, profit = $[(90 - q_1)q_1 - 30q_1] - 200 = (60 - q_1)q_1 - \$200$. Maximization then yields $60 = 2q_1$ or $q_1 = 30$. Entrant's best response implies that if $q_1 = 30$, $q_2 = 15$. Total output = 45. Price = $\$75$. Incumbent profit = $\$(75 - 30)30 - \$30 \times 30 - \$200 = \$250$. Entrant's profit = $\$(75 - 60)15 - \$200 = \$25$.

e. With $K_1 = 40$, it implies that $q_1 = 40$ as well. Entrant's best response then implies that $q_2 = 30 - 40/2 = 10$. Total output is 50, so market price is $\$70$. Entrant's profit is $\$(70 - 60)q_2 - \$200 = 10 \times \$10 - \$200 = -\$100$. Entrant cannot earn positive profit, so there is no entry incentive.

f. With $K_1 = 32 =$ committed value of $q_1$, then entrant's best response is $q_2 = 16$. Total output = 48 and price is $\$72$. Entrant's profit after entry cost is $(\$72 - \$60) \times 16 = \$192$. Fixed cost is $\$200$, so net profit is $\$192 - \$200 < 0$. With $K_1 = 32 = q_1$ and no entry, $P = \$88$. Profit = $(\$88 - \$60)32 - \$200 = \$696$.

**12.3** a. The incumbent will fight if $3 > 4 - C$ or if $C > 1$.

b. For $C > 1$, the initial expenditure of $C$ implies the incumbent will always fight any entry, so entry does not occur. The incumbent therefore earns $\$(8 - C)$ by expending $C$ if $C \geq 3.5 > 1$. If $C$ is not spent, entry will occur and the incumbent earns $\$4.50$. Expenditure $C$ is only worthwhile if $\$(8 - C) > \$4.50$. If $C > 3.50$, this condition is not satisfied.

# Chapter 13

**13.1** The bank would have to ask for at least $\$137.5$ million in a good year, and $\$100$ million in a bad year. It will then earn $\$137.5$ with probability 0.4 and $\$100$ million with probability 0.6 for an average of

$115 million. No, there is no change in the incentive for predation. The bank and Newvel can still expect to make a profit by entering in the second period.

**13.2** a. $q_L = 45$, $q_f = 22.5$, $Q = 67.5$, $P = \$32.5$; $\pi_L = \$1,012.5$; $\pi_f = \$506.25$.

b. In first period, $q_L = 90$ and $\pi_L = 0$. In second period, $q_L = 45$ and $\pi_L = \$2,025$.

c. If entrant comes in, incumbent earns $1,012.50 in each period or $2,025 in total. If entrant is paid to stay out, incumbent earns $2,025 in each period or $4,050 in total less payment to entrant. So, the maximum the entrant is willing to pay is: $4,050 − $2,025, which is equal to $2,025. If entrant comes in, it earns $506.25 each period or $1,012.50 in total. Hence, $1,012.50 is the minimum amount the entrant will accept to stay out.

**13.3** The expected gain from predation (probability of failure) × $325 million must equal the cost of predation or $50 million, so lowest probability is 15.38 percent.

# Chapter 14

**14.1** Confess, Confess is the unique Nash equilibrium.

**14.2** Third-period outcome must be the one-period Nash equilibrium with both producing 40 (thousand) and earning $1.6 million each. Foreseeing the inevitability of this outcome will thwart any cooperation in periods 1 and 2. The three-period game will simply be played as three one-period games.

**14.3** The fourth period of this five-period problem is exactly analogous to the first period of the two-period problem in the text. Hence, the strategy is subgame perfect for periods four and five. It is then easy to see that no firm has an incentive to deviate from this strategy in period 3. A third-period price other than $160 will then lead to a subsequent two-period punishment at the "bad" Nash equilibrium—more harsh than the punishment for deviation in pe-

riod 4. By extension, the argument extends all the way to period 1.

**14.4** The one-period gain from cheating is $0.9 million. The loss from cheating if punishment is the "good" Nash equilibrium is $0.6 million forever. This will deter cheating if $0.9 \le \dfrac{R}{1-R} 0.6$, or $R \ge 0.6$ ($r \le 0.67$). The loss from cheating if the punishment is the "bad" Nash equilibrium is $1.7875 million forever. This will deter cheating so long as $0.9 \le \dfrac{R}{1-R} 1.7875$. In turn, this requires that $R \ge 0.336$ ($r \le 0.67$). For $0.336 < R < 0.6$, only punishment with the "bad" Nash equilibrium will deter cheating.

**14.5** When both firms produce 35 units, total output is 70 and price is $80. Each firm earns a profit of ($80 − $30)35 = $1,750. The Nash equilibrium is $q_1 = q_2 = 40$ with profit of $1,600 for each. The difference between these two profit levels is the per-period punishment for cheating that lasts forever after the cheating has been detected. If $q_2 = 35$, best response by firm 1 is to set $q_1 = 42.5$. Total output is then 77.5, implying price = $72.5. Firm 1 (the cheater) then earns a profit of $(42.5)^2 = $1,806.25. The one-period gain from cheating is therefore $1,806.25 − $1,750 = $56.25. The permanent loss is $150 per period. Cheating will be deterred so long as $56.25 \le \dfrac{R}{1-R} \$150$, or $206.25 R \ge 56.25$.

# Chapter 15

No Practice Problems in chapter.

# Chapter 16

**16.1** a. From equation (16.4) $\pi_i = \$(A - c)^2 / B(N+1)^2$, with $A = \$130$, $c = \$30$, $B = 1$, and $N = 20 \Rightarrow \pi_i = \$22.67$.

b. $M = 6$. Hence, by equation (16.7), $\pi_M^C = \pi_{nm}^C = \$100^2 / (20 - 6 + 2)^2 = \$39.06 < 6 \times \$22.67$.

c. $M = 17$. $\pi_M^C = \pi_{nm}^C = \$100^2/(20 - 17 + 2)^2 = \$400 > 17 \times \$22.67$. A merger of 17 firms is (barely) profitable. Since the profit increases monotonically in $M$, any merger with fewer firms will be unprofitable.

16.2 a. $q_1 = q_2 = (120 + 30b)/4$; $q_3 = (240 - 90b)/4$; $Q = 120 - 7.5b$, $P = 60 + 7.5b$; $\pi_1 = \pi_2 = (120 + 30b)^2/16 - 900$, positive for all values of $b \geq 1$. $\pi_3 = (240 - 90b)^2/16 - 900$. Hence, $b$ cannot exceed 1.3333, $P = \$34.76$.

b. Post-merger market is a symmetric Cournot duopoly with marginal cost = \$30 for both firms. Equilibrium has $q_1 = q_2 = 50$. $P = \$80$. Profit to nonmerged firm is \$1,600. Profit to merged firm is $\$2,500 - (1 + a)\$900$.

c. Post-merger combined profit = $\$2,500 - (1 + a)\$900 \geq (120 + 30b)^2/16 + (240 - 90b)^2/16$ = sum of pre-merger separate profit.

16.3 a. $q_i = (A - c)/B(N + 1)$, with $A = \$130$, $c = \$30$, $B = 1$, and $N = 20 \Rightarrow q_i = 4.76$. $Q = 20q_i = 95.24$.

b. From equation (16.27), $q_L = (A - c)/B(L + 1) = 100/6 = 16.67$. From equation (16.28), $q_f = (A - c)/B(L + 1)(N - L + 1) = 100/6(11) = 1.51$. $Q = 5(16.67) + 10(1.51) = 98.48$. $P = \$31.52$.

c. $q_i = 100/(15 + 1) = 6.25$. $Q = 15q_i = 93.75$.

# Chapter 17

17.1 The retailer's marginal revenue curve is $MR = 3,000 - Q$. This is the manufacturer's demand curve.

17.2 a. Profit maximization by WR implies $100 - 2Q = 5 + W_W \Rightarrow W_W = 95 - 2Q =$ WW's demand curve. Profit maximization by WW implies $95 - 4Q = 5 + W_M \Rightarrow W_M = 90 - 4Q =$ WM's demand curve. Profit maximization by WM implies $90 - 8Q = 10 \Rightarrow Q = 10$; $W_M = \$50$; $W_W = \$75$; $P = \$90$. $\pi_{WM} = \$400$; $\pi_{WW} = \$200$; $\pi_{WR} = \$150$; total profit = \$750.

b. If WM and WW merge, the demand curve then the cost of combined opera-

tion is \$15. The demand curve facing the merged firm is $W_W = 95 - 2Q$. Profit maximization implies $95 - 4Q = 15 \Rightarrow Q = 20$. The retail price to consumers falls to \$80, while the wholesale price to the retailer falls to \$55. The total producer surplus is $\pi_{WR}$ + the profit of the merged firm = \$500 + \$800 = \$1,300 > \$750. The calculations are similar for other mergers.

c. If all three firms merge, the total cost of bringing goods to the market is \$20. The merged firm faces retail demand of $P = 100 - Q$, hence, $MR = 100 - 2Q = 20$, which implies $Q = 40$ and $P = 60$. The merged firm's profit is \$1,600 > \$1,300.

17.3 a. WI derived demand is $Q = 2.075 - 3W$; where $W$ is wholesale price = \$0.396. $P_{GI} = \$0.748$. $P_{TG} = \$0.623$; Profits: $\pi_{WI} = \$0.263$; $\pi_{GI} = \$0.0635$; $\pi_{TG} = \$0.0807$.

b. Wholesale prices: Boston, $r = \$0.50$; New York, $r = \$0.375$. Retail prices: Boston, $p = \$0.80$; New York, $p = \$0.6125$. Quantity sold: Boston, $Q = 0.2$; New York, $Q = \$0.6875$. WI profit = \$0.08 + \$0.189 = \$0.269; GI profit = \$0.04; TG profit = \$0.095.

c. Assume that integration does not eliminate the retail selling costs. Merger with GI implies Boston retail price = \$0.60, Boston quantity = 0.4, integrated profit = \$0.16 + \$0.189 = \$0.349. Merger with TG implies New York retail price = \$0.475, New York quantity = 0.475, integrated profit = \$0.378 + \$0.08 = \$0.458.

d. With no price discrimination, integration increases price, reduces consumer surplus in Boston but has opposite effects in New York. With price discrimination, integration leaves Boston price and consumer surplus unchanged; reduces price and increases consumer surplus in New York.

# Chapter 18

18.1 a. Wholesale price = \$520; Retail price = \$760; $Q = 120$.

b. Tiger-el profit = $57,600; Great Toy Store profit = $28,800.

c. $Q$ = 220; retail price = $560 (includes $373.33 royalty payment). Tiger-el profit = $82,133.33; Great Toy Store profit = $32,266.67.

18.2 a. Retail service level, $s$ = 0.89; retail price, $p^M$ = $8.40; $Q \approx$ 143. Manufacturer's profit $\approx$ $143.

b. Retail service level, $s$ = 0.775; retail price, $p^M$ = $8.80; $Q$ = 93. Manufacturer's profit = $186. In both (a) and (b), the setting of a wholesale price above cost results in lower retail services, a higher retail price, and less profit to the manufacturer than occurs under integration.

18.3 a. Since cost is zero, revenue and profit maximization are identical. When demand is strong, marginal revenue is $MR^H$ = 10 – 0.02$Q$. Optimal $Q$ = 500, implying $P^H$ = $5. When demand is weak, marginal revenue is $MR^L$ = 10 – $Q$/15. Optimal $Q$ = 150, implying $P^L$ = $5.

b. Profit maximization requires selling an amount such that $MR = c = 0$. When demand is strong, all 500 units will be sold. When demand is weak, only 150 units will be sold. Expected profit is 0.5($2,500) + 0.5($750) = $1,625.

c. Once bought, the cost of acquiring the stock is sunk. Competitive retailers will sell the entire stock. If demand is strong, the quantity of 500 will sell at the market-clearing price of $5. If demand is weak, this quantity will be sold only at a price of $0.

d. Competitive retailers will expect to break even if wholesale price is $2.50. Manufacturer's profit is $1,250.

## Chapter 19

19.1 a. $n^*$ = 2.

b. $\Pi_1 = \Pi_2$ = $360.

c. $P$ = $40; $Q$ = 60.

d. Pure monopoly: $P^M$ = $62.50; $Q^M$ = 37.5.

## Chapter 20

20.1 a. $a$ = 100 implies $dP/dQ$ = –0.1; $a$ = 1,000 implies $dP/dQ$ = –0.0316.

b. 1. $MR$ = 100 – 0.04$Q$.

2. $P$ = $80; $Q$ = 1,000.

3. Price elasticity (absolute value) = 4. Elasticity of sales with respect to advertising = 1/2.

c. Dorfman-Steiner condition: $a/PQ$ = 1/8. At $a$ = 2,500, $P$ = $80; $Q$ = 10,000. $a/PQ$ = 0.03125 < 1/8. Optimal values: $a$ = 40,000; $P$ = $80; $Q$ = 4,000.

## Chapter 21

21.1 a. $P = c + t$ = $5 + $4 = $9.

b. Each firm will serve half the market. Each will earn a profit of $4$N$/2 = $2$N$.

c. 1. Original market share = 1/2; new market share = 1/2 + 1/2$t$. Market share rises by 1/2$t$ = 1/8 when $t$ = 4.

2. Original profit = $2$N$. New profit = $3$N$/2 + $3$N$/8 = $7$N$/8. Profit declines by $$N$/8.

21.2 a. As $\alpha$ falls, advertising costs decrease and $\theta$ rises. Each firm's message reaches a greater fraction of its potential customers.

b. As $\alpha$ falls, more and more customers are fully informed about the availability of substitutes. Resulting price competition leads to a decline in each firm's profit.

21.3 a. With $\alpha$ = 100, the inverse demand curve is $P$ = 10 – 10$Q$. $MR$ = 10 – 20$Q$. Profit maximization implies $Q$ = 0.5 (one half million) and $P$ = $5. Profit = $2.5 (million) – $10,000 × 100 = $1.5 million.

b. With $\alpha$ = 625, the inverse demand curve is $P$ = 25 – 25$Q$. $MR$ = 25 – 50$Q$. Profit maximization implies $Q$ = 0.5 or one half million again. $P$ = $12.5. Profit = $6.25 (million) – $5,000 × 625 = $3,125,000.

## Chapter 22

22.1 The monopoly price = $P^M = (A + c)/2$, so with $A$ = 100 and $c$ = $28, $P^M$ = $128/2 =

$64. This exceeds the initial marginal cost of $60, so the innovation does not permit any firm to price as an unconstrained monopolist. To be drastic, an innovation must yield a monopoly price $P^M = (A + c)/2$ that is less than the marginal cost with the old technology. Since again, $A = 100$, $B = 2$, and the old technology has a marginal cost of $60, the new marginal cost as a result of the innovation must be no higher than $c = $20$.

**22.2** a. Pre-innovation competitive output is $Q^C = 25$. To be drastic, the innovation must reduce marginal cost below monopoly marginal revenue at $Q = 25$ or below $50.

b. Per-period profit to monopolist with $c = $75$ is $156.25. Present value of profit stream is $1,562.50. Per-period profit to monopolist with $c = $60$ is $400. Present value of profit stream is $4,000. Value of innovation to monopolist = $4,000 − $1,562.50 = $2,437.50.

c. $q_1 = q_2 = 8.333$. $Q = 16.67$ and $P = $83.33$. $\pi_1 = \pi_2 = ($83.33 − $75)8.33 = $69.44$.

d. If firm 1 acquires the innovation: $q_1 = 18.333$; $q_2 = 3.333$. $Q = 21.67$; $P = $78.33$. Per-period profit to innovator with $c = $75 = $69.40$; present value of profit stream is $690.40. Per-period profit to innovator with $c = $60 = $336.10$; present value of profit stream is $3,361.

e. Value of innovation to duopolist = $3,361 − $690.40 = $2,670.60 > value to monopolist of $2,437.50.

# Chapter 23

**23.1** a. Competition implies $P = MC = $70$; $Q = 100 − P = 30$.

b. Per-period profit to innovator is obtained by selling original 30 units produced at unit cost $70 − x$, at price just less than $70 = $30[70 − (70 − x)] = $30x$. With $R = 0.9091$ and $T = 25$ years, net value to innovator of R&D effort less cost is $NV^m (x, T) = $30x[(1 − 0.9091^{25})/(1 − 0.9091)] − 15x^2$.

Maximization implies $dNV^m/dx = 30[(1 − 0.9091^{25})/(1 − 0.9091)] − 30x = 0$. Hence, $x \approx 10$ and innovator values innovation at $NV(25) = $1,500$.

c. If $T = 20$, $x \approx 9.37$ and per-period profit $\approx $281.1$. $NV^m (20) = $2633.91 − $1316.95 \approx $1316.96$.

d. Social welfare gain equals value of innovation to innovator plus increase in consumer surplus. At $P = c = $70$, consumer surplus is $(100 − 70)^2/2 = $450$. If $P$ falls to $60, consumer surplus is $800. At $P = c = $60.43$, consumer surplus is $775. Value of consumer surplus gained when $T = 25$ is

$$\$(800 − 450)\frac{0.9091^{25}}{(1 − 0.9091)} \approx \$355.46.$$

Value of consumer surplus gained when

$$T = 20 \text{ is } \$(775 − 450)\frac{0.9091^{20}}{(1 − 0.9091)} \approx$$

$531.56. Reduction in $T$ from 25 to 20 just barely reduces value of innovation to consumers and producer by $1,855.46 − $1,848.52, or about a $7 loss.

**23.2** a. $P^M = $(100 + 50)/2 = $75$. $Q = (100 − 75)/2 = 12.5$. $\pi^M = $(75 − 50)12.5 = $312.50$. Consumer surplus = $(100 − 75)^2/4 = $156.25$.

b. $q_1 = q_2 = (100 − 50)/6 = 8.33$. $Q = 16.67$. $P = 100 − 2Q = $66.67$. $\pi_1 = \pi_2 = 138.89$. Consumer surplus = $(100 − 66.67)^2/4 = $277.78$.

c. If only one firm does research, the expected profit is $0.8($312.50) = $250$. If both do research, the expected profit to each is $0.8(0.2)$312.50 + 0.8^2($138.89) = $138.89$. The payoff matrix is:

|  |  | BMI | |
|---|---|---|---|
|  |  | **NO R&D** | **R&D** |
| **ECN** | **NO R&D** | $0, $0 | $0, $250 − K |
|  | **R&D** | $250 − K, $0 | $138.89 − K, $138.89 − K |

d. For (no R&D, no R&D) to be a Nash equilibrium, $250 − K < 0$ or $K >$

$250. For (R&D, R&D) to be an equilibrium $138.89 − K > 0, or K < $138.89.

e. The expected social surplus with only one lab is 0.8($312.50 + $156.25) = $375. With two labs it is 2(0.8 × 0.2[$312.50 + $156.25]) + 0.8²(2 × $138.89 + $277.78) = $505.56. Two labs are optimal if $505.56 − 2K > $375 − K or K < $130.56.

**23.3** a. $P = $(100 + 120)/3 = $73.33. $q_1 = q_2$ = 6.67; $Q = 13.333$. $\pi_1 = \pi_2 = $88.89.

b. 1. The innovator's per-period profit is $\pi^I = $(100 − 100 + 60)^2 /18 = $200. Rival earns $50. Price falls to $70. Innovator produces 10 units; rival produces 5 units.

2. This arrangement restores the original equilibrium. So the innovator earns a per-period profit of $88.89 plus $10 on each unit sold or $10(13.33) = $133.33. Total profit is $222.22; greater than that without licensing.

3. Fee = $88.89 = rival's profit ($138.89) when $c_1 = c_2$ = $50 less rival's profit ($50) when $c_1$ = 60 and $c_2$ = 50. Innovator earns $88.89 + $138.89 = $227.78.

## Chapter 24

No Practice Problems in this chapter.

## Chapter 25

**25.1** A dominant strategy is one that gives you a payoff greater than any other strategy regardless of what is chosen by other players. The other strategy you could choose is to stop bidding when the price is less than your true valuation. Suppose that the auction price is $p$ and your true valuation is $V$. If $p < V$ and you stop bidding your payoff is 0, whereas if you bid $p + \varepsilon < V$ then your payoff is $V − (p + \varepsilon) > 0$. Of course if $p = V$ then you should stop bidding because $p + \varepsilon > V$ results in a payoff less than zero, which is your payoff from not bidding.

**25.2** Your best strategy here is to assume that you are the one with the highest valuation. In other words you assume that the other 7 bidders have valuations drawn from a uniform distribution over the interval [0, 200]. If we assume that these bids are evenly spaced out over the interval then the lowest would be 25(=1/8 × 200), the next 50(=2/8 × 200), the next 75, the next 100, the next 125, the next 150 and finally the highest bid from the other bidders will be 175 (=7/8 × 200). You should submit a bid of $175 to win the auction.

**25.3** You and your partner drew a value of 2,000. Other bidders are drawing other values, and you assume they are drawing from the same uniform distribution on the interval [0, $U$]. You want to know the expected value of the franchise, or $U/2$, and bid that value. By bidding the expected value and not your draw you avoid the winner's curse. To compute the mean value of the franchise you must work out the upper value of the distribution, $U$. Given that there are 8 groups drawing and you and your partner drew 2,000 your best guess is that $U = (80/79) × $2,000 = $2,025.31. Therefore, you should bid the estimated mean of the distribution, or $1,012.66.

# Glossary

## A

**Antitrust Policy:** Government policy intended to control the actions of firms in their pursuit of market power.

**Arbitrage:** Exploiting any difference in price charged to different buyers for the same item by buying where the price is low and reselling where it is high. In markets where firms attempt to price discriminate, this would involve buying and reselling among consumers to thwart such efforts at differential pricing.

**Average Cost:** The ratio of total cost to total output.

## B

**Bertrand Model:** An oligopoly model in which firms compete by choosing their prices, leaving the market to determine the amount they will sell at these prices.

**Best Response Function:** A function describing an oligopolistic firm's profit-maximizing response to any choice of action(s) by its rival(s); sometimes referred to as a *reaction function*.

**Blockaded Entry:** A situation in which entry is not feasible even if the incumbent is operating at the monopoly price and output.

## C

**Capacity Constraint:** A constraint that arises when a firm does not have enough installed capacity to serve the demand it faces at its chosen price.

**Cartel:** A national or international group of producers linked by an agreement to coordinate their actions, usually with the intention of restricting output and so increasing the firms' profits.

**Chain-Store Paradox:** A game giving the seemingly paradoxical result that a firm facing the threat of entry into a finite and known number of its markets will not attempt to deter entry into any of these markets.

**Collusion:** Agreements between firms to coordinate their actions (see *Cartel*).

**Commodity Bundling:** The practice of selling two or more products as a single package containing a specific amount of each product.

**Competitive Fringe Firms:** The set of competitive firms that constrain the ability of a dominant firm to set the monopoly price in its market.

**Complementary Goods:** Goods that consumers or firms prefer to consume jointly.

**Concentration Ratio:** The $n$-firm concentration ratio measures the percentage of a market controlled by the $n$ largest firms.

**Consumer Surplus:** For an individual consumer, the difference between the maximum amount a consumer is willing to pay for a given quantity of a good and the actual amount that the consumer is charged for that quantity. For a market, the total such surplus earned by all consumers.

**Cournot Model:** An oligopoly model in which firms compete by choosing their output levels, leaving the market to determine the market-clearing price(s) for these outputs.

**Credible Commitment:** A promise or threat to take a specific action that is rational, that is, optimal, under the conditions under which the threatened action will be taken.

## D

**Deadweight Loss:** The difference between the maximum consumer and producer surplus and the surplus realized under specified market conditions, for example, the difference between the total surplus under perfect competition and that under monopoly.

**Demand Curve:** The relationship between the price of a good and the amount of that good consumers are willing to buy.

**Dominant Firm Model:** A model in which there is a dominant firm facing a competitive fringe. The dominant firm provides price leadership by maximizing its profits, correctly anticipating the output response of the competitive fringe to any price set by the dominant firm.

**Dominant Strategy:** A strategy for a firm that outperforms any of the firm's other strategies in every possible market interaction.

**Dominated Strategy:** A strategy for a firm that is never the best or profit-maximizing strategy no matter what strategies are chosen by the firm's rivals.

**Duopoly:** A market containing two firms.

**Dynamic Game:** A game that extends over several periods.

## E

**Economic Model:** A framework that captures the essential features of the specific market and market phenomena under investigation.

**Economies of Scale:** A situation in which average cost falls as output is increased, often measured as the ratio of the elasticity of total cost with respect to total output.

**Economies of Scope:** A situation in which it is cheaper to produce a set of goods in one multiproduct firm than it is to produce it in two or more specialized firms.

**Entry Deterrence:** Actions by a firm that are intended to deter the entry of rivals to the firm's market.

**Equilibrium:** A situation in which no consumer or firm has an incentive to change its trading decisions.

## F

**First-Degree Price Discrimination:** A pricing policy that allows a firm to charge consumers their maximum willingness to pay for each unit sold.

**Flexible Manufacturing System:** A production process that can produce a wide range of product varieties at little or no cost penalty.

**Folk Theorem:** The theorem that in an infinitely repeated game any set of feasible payoffs can be supported as a subgame perfect equilibrium for that game for some discount factor sufficiently close to unity.

## G

**Game:** A setting of strategic interaction of which the elements may be described, such as the players involved in the game, the strategies they have available, the information available to the players at each point in the game, the payoffs that arise from each possible combination of strategies, and the timing of each player's moves.

**Game Theory:** A set of techniques that can be applied to study decision making by economic agents who are interdependent.

## H

**Herfindahl-Hirschman Index:** A measure of industry concentration equal to the sum of the squared market shares of all the firms in the industry.

**Horizontal Product Differentiation:** Product differentiation by means of characteristics such as color or location but not quality.

## I

**Incentive Compatibility Constraint:** The constraint that any price–quantity pair intended to attract high-demand consumers must offer them at least as great consumer surplus as they obtain from a price–quantity package aimed at low-demand consumers.

## L

**Limit Output:** The output level that is just great enough to deter the entry of a rival.

**Limit Price:** The price that is just low enough to deter entry of a potential rival.

## M

**Marginal Cost:** The change in total cost that arises from producing an additional unit of output.

**Marginal Revenue:** The change in total revenue that arises from the sale of an additional unit of output.

**Merger:** The combination of two or more firms into one.

**Monopolistic Competition:** A market in which there are many firms selling differentiated products.

**Monopoly:** A market containing only one firm.

**Mixed Bundling:** The practice of selling two or more products as a package in addition to selling them individually.

## N

**Nash Equilibrium:** An equilibrium in a noncooperative game in which each player has no incentive to change its strategy given the strategies its rivals have chosen.

**Natural Monopoly:** A market in which it is cheaper for one firm to produce the total output than for this output to be produced by two or more firms.

**Net Price:** The price of a differentiated product net of the costs of differentiation.

## O

**Oligopoly:** A market structure in which there is a relatively small number of interdependent firms.

## P

**Payoff Matrix:** A matrix detailing the payoffs to each player of a game from each strategy combination of the game, defined on the assumption that each player has a finite number of strategies.

**Perfect Competition:** A market structure in which all agents are price-takers and have no strategic power.

**Per se Rule:** A ruling that a particular set of actions violates antitrust law no matter what the proposed defense of these actions is.

**Predatory Conduct:** Actions by a single firm that are designed specifically to deter rival firms from either entering or remaining in a market.

**Predatory Pricing:** A specific form of predatory conduct that involves the deliberate practice of setting a low price to eliminate existing rival firms.

**Present Value:** The value today of a flow of future revenues and costs.

**Price Discrimination:** Selling two varieties of a product to two different buyers at different net prices, where the net price is the price paid by the buyer adjusted for the cost of product differentiation.

**Price-Fixing Agreement:** A collusive agreement between firms in a particular market to fix the price charged in that market.

**Prisoner's Dilemma Game:** A game in which the players have a mutual potential for gain that is not realized because the Nash equilibrium is determined by their conflicts of interest.

**Producer Surplus:** For an individual firm, the difference between the amount that a seller receives from the sale of a given quantity of a good and the cost of producing that quantity. For a market, the total such surplus earned by all producers.

**Product Differentiation:** Producing several varieties of a particular product, where the varieties are distinguished by characteristics such as color, location, quality, style, etc.

**Profit:** The difference between a firm's total revenue and its total cost.

**Pure Bundling:** The practice of selling two or more commodities as a package comprised of specific amounts of each but not selling them individually.

## R

**Reaction Function:** See *Best Response Function*.

**Repeated Game:** A game in which the interactions between the players are repeated over some number of periods, which may be either finite or infinite.

**Reservation Price:** The maximum price that a consumer is willing to pay for a unit of a particular commodity.

**Rule of Reason:** Testing whether particular actions breach antitrust policy by considering the reasonableness of the actions.

## S

**Second-Degree Price Discrimination:** A pricing policy employed when a firm knows that it is serving consumers of different types but is unable to distinguish the actual type of each consumer. It typically involves offering quantity discounts to high-demand consumers.

**Sequential Game:** A game in which the players choose their strategies in sequence, with the choices of earlier players being observable by later players.

**Simultaneous Game:** A game in which the players choose their strategies simultaneously.

**Stackelberg Model:** An oligopoly model in which the firms move in sequence, with the first mover usually being referred to as the market leader.

**Strategic Complements:** A situation in which rival firms' best response functions are upward sloping.

**Strategic Decision Making:** Making decisions taking account of the likely reactions of rivals who are affected by these decisions.

**Strategic Substitutes:** A situation in which rival firms' best response functions are downward sloping.

**Strategy:** A plan of action available to a player in a game-theoretic setting.

**Structure-Conduct-Performance (SCP) Paradigm:** The early paradigm in industrial organization in which it was assumed that market structure determines market conduct, which then determines the market performance or social welfare features of the equilibrium.

**Subgame:** A part of an entire game that can stand alone as a game in itself.

**Subgame Perfect:** A strategy combination is subgame perfect if the behavioral strategy it contains for each player is a best response against the behavioral strategies of the other players in every subgame.

**Sunk Cost:** An entry cost that cannot be recovered on exit from a market.

**Supply Curve:** The relationship between the price of a good and the amount of that good that firms are willing to sell.

## T

**Third-Degree Price Discrimination:** A pricing policy by which consumers of different types are charged different uniform prices.

**Tie-In Sales:** The practice of making the purchase of one good conditional upon the purchase of another, usually related or complementary good.

**Total Surplus:** The sum of consumer plus producer surplus.

**Trigger Strategy:** A strategy intended to maintain a collusive agreement, in which punishment by some subset of players is triggered by defection from the agreement of another set of players. The punishment strategy must be subgame perfect if it is to be effective and hence rational to use.

**Two-Part Pricing:** A pricing policy that consists of a fixed fee independent of the amount bought and a unit price or usage fee for each unit a consumer actually buys.

## U

**Uniform Pricing:** A pricing policy in which all units are sold at the same price.

## V

**Vertical Integration:** The merger of two or more firms operating at different stages in a production process.

**Vertical Product Differentiation:** Offering varieties of a product differentiated by quality.

# Index

## Q

## R

## S